Lecture Notes in Computer Science **13693**

More information about this series at https://link.springer.com/bookseries/558

Shai Avidan · Gabriel Brostow ·
Moustapha Cissé · Giovanni Maria Farinella ·
Tal Hassner (Eds.)

Computer Vision – ECCV 2022

17th European Conference
Tel Aviv, Israel, October 23–27, 2022
Proceedings, Part XXXIII

Editors

Shai Avidan
Tel Aviv University
Tel Aviv, Israel

Gabriel Brostow
University College London
London, UK

Moustapha Cissé
Google AI
Accra, Ghana

Giovanni Maria Farinella
University of Catania
Catania, Italy

Tal Hassner
Facebook (United States)
Menlo Park, CA, USA

ISSN 0302-9743 ISSN 1611-3349 (electronic)
Lecture Notes in Computer Science
ISBN 978-3-031-19826-7 ISBN 978-3-031-19827-4 (eBook)
https://doi.org/10.1007/978-3-031-19827-4

This Springer imprint is published by the registered company Springer Nature Switzerland AG
The registered company address is: Gewerbestrasse 11, 6330 Cham, Switzerland

Foreword

Organizing the European Conference on Computer Vision (ECCV 2022) in Tel-Aviv during a global pandemic was no easy feat. The uncertainty level was extremely high, and decisions had to be postponed to the last minute. Still, we managed to plan things just in time for ECCV 2022 to be held in person. Participation in physical events is crucial to stimulating collaborations and nurturing the culture of the Computer Vision community.

There were many people who worked hard to ensure attendees enjoyed the best science at the 16th edition of ECCV. We are grateful to the Program Chairs Gabriel Brostow and Tal Hassner, who went above and beyond to ensure the ECCV reviewing process ran smoothly. The scientific program includes dozens of workshops and tutorials in addition to the main conference and we would like to thank Leonid Karlinsky and Tomer Michaeli for their hard work. Finally, special thanks to the web chairs Lorenzo Baraldi and Kosta Derpanis, who put in extra hours to transfer information fast and efficiently to the ECCV community.

We would like to express gratitude to our generous sponsors and the Industry Chairs, Dimosthenis Karatzas and Chen Sagiv, who oversaw industry relations and proposed new ways for academia-industry collaboration and technology transfer. It's great to see so much industrial interest in what we're doing!

Authors' draft versions of the papers appeared online with open access on both the Computer Vision Foundation (CVF) and the European Computer Vision Association (ECVA) websites as with previous ECCVs. Springer, the publisher of the proceedings, has arranged for archival publication. The final version of the papers is hosted by SpringerLink, with active references and supplementary materials. It benefits all potential readers that we offer both a free and citeable version for all researchers, as well as an authoritative, citeable version for SpringerLink readers. Our thanks go to Ronan Nugent from Springer, who helped us negotiate this agreement. Last but not least, we wish to thank Eric Mortensen, our publication chair, whose expertise made the process smooth.

October 2022

Rita Cucchiara
Jiří Matas
Amnon Shashua
Lihi Zelnik-Manor

Preface

Welcome to the proceedings of the European Conference on Computer Vision (ECCV 2022). This was a hybrid edition of ECCV as we made our way out of the COVID-19 pandemic. The conference received 5804 valid paper submissions, compared to 5150 submissions to ECCV 2020 (a 12.7% increase) and 2439 in ECCV 2018. 1645 submissions were accepted for publication (28%) and, of those, 157 (2.7% overall) as orals.

846 of the submissions were desk-rejected for various reasons. Many of them because they revealed author identity, thus violating the double-blind policy. This violation came in many forms: some had author names with the title, others added acknowledgments to specific grants, yet others had links to their github account where their name was visible. Tampering with the LaTeX template was another reason for automatic desk rejection.

ECCV 2022 used the traditional CMT system to manage the entire double-blind reviewing process. Authors did not know the names of the reviewers and vice versa. Each paper received at least 3 reviews (except 6 papers that received only 2 reviews), totalling more than 15,000 reviews.

Handling the review process at this scale was a significant challenge. To ensure that each submission received as fair and high-quality reviews as possible, we recruited more than 4719 reviewers (in the end, 4719 reviewers did at least one review). Similarly we recruited more than 276 area chairs (eventually, only 276 area chairs handled a batch of papers). The area chairs were selected based on their technical expertise and reputation, largely among people who served as area chairs in previous top computer vision and machine learning conferences (ECCV, ICCV, CVPR, NeurIPS, etc.).

Reviewers were similarly invited from previous conferences, and also from the pool of authors. We also encouraged experienced area chairs to suggest additional chairs and reviewers in the initial phase of recruiting. The median reviewer load was five papers per reviewer, while the average load was about four papers, because of the emergency reviewers. The area chair load was 35 papers, on average.

Conflicts of interest between authors, area chairs, and reviewers were handled largely automatically by the CMT platform, with some manual help from the Program Chairs. Reviewers were allowed to describe themselves as senior reviewer (load of 8 papers to review) or junior reviewers (load of 4 papers). Papers were matched to area chairs based on a subject-area affinity score computed in CMT and an affinity score computed by the Toronto Paper Matching System (TPMS). TPMS is based on the paper's full text. An area chair handling each submission would bid for preferred expert reviewers, and we balanced load and prevented conflicts.

The assignment of submissions to area chairs was relatively smooth, as was the assignment of submissions to reviewers. A small percentage of reviewers were not happy with their assignments in terms of subjects and self-reported expertise. This is an area for improvement, although it's interesting that many of these cases were reviewers handpicked by AC's. We made a later round of reviewer recruiting, targeted at the list of authors of papers submitted to the conference, and had an excellent response which helped provide enough emergency reviewers. In the end, all but six papers received at least 3 reviews.

The challenges of the reviewing process are in line with past experiences at ECCV 2020. As the community grows, and the number of submissions increases, it becomes ever more challenging to recruit enough reviewers and ensure a high enough quality of reviews. Enlisting authors by default as reviewers might be one step to address this challenge.

Authors were given a week to rebut the initial reviews, and address reviewers' concerns. Each rebuttal was limited to a single pdf page with a fixed template.

The Area Chairs then led discussions with the reviewers on the merits of each submission. The goal was to reach consensus, but, ultimately, it was up to the Area Chair to make a decision. The decision was then discussed with a buddy Area Chair to make sure decisions were fair and informative. The entire process was conducted virtually with no in-person meetings taking place.

The Program Chairs were informed in cases where the Area Chairs overturned a decisive consensus reached by the reviewers, and pushed for the meta-reviews to contain details that explained the reasoning for such decisions. Obviously these were the most contentious cases, where reviewer inexperience was the most common reported factor.

Once the list of accepted papers was finalized and released, we went through the laborious process of plagiarism (including self-plagiarism) detection. A total of 4 accepted papers were rejected because of that.

Finally, we would like to thank our Technical Program Chair, Pavel Lifshits, who did tremendous work behind the scenes, and we thank the tireless CMT team.

October 2022

Gabriel Brostow
Giovanni Maria Farinella
Moustapha Cissé
Shai Avidan
Tal Hassner

Organization

General Chairs

Rita Cucchiara	University of Modena and Reggio Emilia, Italy
Jiří Matas	Czech Technical University in Prague, Czech Republic
Amnon Shashua	Hebrew University of Jerusalem, Israel
Lihi Zelnik-Manor	Technion – Israel Institute of Technology, Israel

Program Chairs

Shai Avidan	Tel-Aviv University, Israel
Gabriel Brostow	University College London, UK
Moustapha Cissé	Google AI, Ghana
Giovanni Maria Farinella	University of Catania, Italy
Tal Hassner	Facebook AI, USA

Program Technical Chair

Pavel Lifshits	Technion – Israel Institute of Technology, Israel

Workshops Chairs

Leonid Karlinsky	IBM Research, Israel
Tomer Michaeli	Technion – Israel Institute of Technology, Israel
Ko Nishino	Kyoto University, Japan

Tutorial Chairs

Thomas Pock	Graz University of Technology, Austria
Natalia Neverova	Facebook AI Research, UK

Demo Chair

Bohyung Han	Seoul National University, Korea

Social and Student Activities Chairs

Tatiana Tommasi	Italian Institute of Technology, Italy
Sagie Benaim	University of Copenhagen, Denmark

Diversity and Inclusion Chairs

Xi Yin	Facebook AI Research, USA
Bryan Russell	Adobe, USA

Communications Chairs

Lorenzo Baraldi	University of Modena and Reggio Emilia, Italy
Kosta Derpanis	York University & Samsung AI Centre Toronto, Canada

Industrial Liaison Chairs

Dimosthenis Karatzas	Universitat Autònoma de Barcelona, Spain
Chen Sagiv	SagivTech, Israel

Finance Chair

Gerard Medioni	University of Southern California & Amazon, USA

Publication Chair

Eric Mortensen	MiCROTEC, USA

Area Chairs

Lourdes Agapito	University College London, UK
Zeynep Akata	University of Tübingen, Germany
Naveed Akhtar	University of Western Australia, Australia
Karteek Alahari	Inria Grenoble Rhône-Alpes, France
Alexandre Alahi	École polytechnique fédérale de Lausanne, Switzerland
Pablo Arbelaez	Universidad de Los Andes, Columbia
Antonis A. Argyros	University of Crete & Foundation for Research and Technology-Hellas, Crete
Yuki M. Asano	University of Amsterdam, The Netherlands
Kalle Åström	Lund University, Sweden
Hadar Averbuch-Elor	Cornell University, USA

Hossein Azizpour	KTH Royal Institute of Technology, Sweden
Vineeth N. Balasubramanian	Indian Institute of Technology, Hyderabad, India
Lamberto Ballan	University of Padova, Italy
Adrien Bartoli	Université Clermont Auvergne, France
Horst Bischof	Graz University of Technology, Austria
Matthew B. Blaschko	KU Leuven, Belgium
Federica Bogo	Meta Reality Labs Research, Switzerland
Katherine Bouman	California Institute of Technology, USA
Edmond Boyer	Inria Grenoble Rhône-Alpes, France
Michael S. Brown	York University, Canada
Vittorio Caggiano	Meta AI Research, USA
Neill Campbell	University of Bath, UK
Octavia Camps	Northeastern University, USA
Duygu Ceylan	Adobe Research, USA
Ayan Chakrabarti	Google Research, USA
Tat-Jen Cham	Nanyang Technological University, Singapore
Antoni Chan	City University of Hong Kong, Hong Kong, China
Manmohan Chandraker	NEC Labs America, USA
Xinlei Chen	Facebook AI Research, USA
Xilin Chen	Institute of Computing Technology, Chinese Academy of Sciences, China
Dongdong Chen	Microsoft Cloud AI, USA
Chen Chen	University of Central Florida, USA
Ondrej Chum	Vision Recognition Group, Czech Technical University in Prague, Czech Republic
John Collomosse	Adobe Research & University of Surrey, UK
Camille Couprie	Facebook, France
David Crandall	Indiana University, USA
Daniel Cremers	Technical University of Munich, Germany
Marco Cristani	University of Verona, Italy
Canton Cristian	Facebook AI Research, USA
Dengxin Dai	ETH Zurich, Switzerland
Dima Damen	University of Bristol, UK
Kostas Daniilidis	University of Pennsylvania, USA
Trevor Darrell	University of California, Berkeley, USA
Andrew Davison	Imperial College London, UK
Tali Dekel	Weizmann Institute of Science, Israel
Alessio Del Bue	Istituto Italiano di Tecnologia, Italy
Weihong Deng	Beijing University of Posts and Telecommunications, China
Konstantinos Derpanis	Ryerson University, Canada
Carl Doersch	DeepMind, UK

Matthijs Douze	Facebook AI Research, USA
Mohamed Elhoseiny	King Abdullah University of Science and Technology, Saudi Arabia
Sergio Escalera	University of Barcelona, Spain
Yi Fang	New York University, USA
Ryan Farrell	Brigham Young University, USA
Alireza Fathi	Google, USA
Christoph Feichtenhofer	Facebook AI Research, USA
Basura Fernando	Agency for Science, Technology and Research (A*STAR), Singapore
Vittorio Ferrari	Google Research, Switzerland
Andrew W. Fitzgibbon	Graphcore, UK
David J. Fleet	University of Toronto, Canada
David Forsyth	University of Illinois at Urbana-Champaign, USA
David Fouhey	University of Michigan, USA
Katerina Fragkiadaki	Carnegie Mellon University, USA
Friedrich Fraundorfer	Graz University of Technology, Austria
Oren Freifeld	Ben-Gurion University, Israel
Thomas Funkhouser	Google Research & Princeton University, USA
Yasutaka Furukawa	Simon Fraser University, Canada
Fabio Galasso	Sapienza University of Rome, Italy
Jürgen Gall	University of Bonn, Germany
Chuang Gan	Massachusetts Institute of Technology, USA
Zhe Gan	Microsoft, USA
Animesh Garg	University of Toronto, Vector Institute, Nvidia, Canada
Efstratios Gavves	University of Amsterdam, The Netherlands
Peter Gehler	Amazon, Germany
Theo Gevers	University of Amsterdam, The Netherlands
Bernard Ghanem	King Abdullah University of Science and Technology, Saudi Arabia
Ross B. Girshick	Facebook AI Research, USA
Georgia Gkioxari	Facebook AI Research, USA
Albert Gordo	Facebook, USA
Stephen Gould	Australian National University, Australia
Venu Madhav Govindu	Indian Institute of Science, India
Kristen Grauman	Facebook AI Research & UT Austin, USA
Abhinav Gupta	Carnegie Mellon University & Facebook AI Research, USA
Mohit Gupta	University of Wisconsin-Madison, USA
Hu Han	Institute of Computing Technology, Chinese Academy of Sciences, China

Bohyung Han	Seoul National University, Korea
Tian Han	Stevens Institute of Technology, USA
Emily Hand	University of Nevada, Reno, USA
Bharath Hariharan	Cornell University, USA
Ran He	Institute of Automation, Chinese Academy of Sciences, China
Otmar Hilliges	ETH Zurich, Switzerland
Adrian Hilton	University of Surrey, UK
Minh Hoai	Stony Brook University, USA
Yedid Hoshen	Hebrew University of Jerusalem, Israel
Timothy Hospedales	University of Edinburgh, UK
Gang Hua	Wormpex AI Research, USA
Di Huang	Beihang University, China
Jing Huang	Facebook, USA
Jia-Bin Huang	Facebook, USA
Nathan Jacobs	Washington University in St. Louis, USA
C.V. Jawahar	International Institute of Information Technology, Hyderabad, India
Herve Jegou	Facebook AI Research, France
Neel Joshi	Microsoft Research, USA
Armand Joulin	Facebook AI Research, France
Frederic Jurie	University of Caen Normandie, France
Fredrik Kahl	Chalmers University of Technology, Sweden
Yannis Kalantidis	NAVER LABS Europe, France
Evangelos Kalogerakis	University of Massachusetts, Amherst, USA
Sing Bing Kang	Zillow Group, USA
Yosi Keller	Bar Ilan University, Israel
Margret Keuper	University of Mannheim, Germany
Tae-Kyun Kim	Imperial College London, UK
Benjamin Kimia	Brown University, USA
Alexander Kirillov	Facebook AI Research, USA
Kris Kitani	Carnegie Mellon University, USA
Iasonas Kokkinos	Snap Inc. & University College London, UK
Vladlen Koltun	Apple, USA
Nikos Komodakis	University of Crete, Crete
Piotr Koniusz	Australian National University, Australia
Philipp Kraehenbuehl	University of Texas at Austin, USA
Dilip Krishnan	Google, USA
Ajay Kumar	Hong Kong Polytechnic University, Hong Kong, China
Junseok Kwon	Chung-Ang University, Korea
Jean-Francois Lalonde	Université Laval, Canada

Vittorio Murino	Istituto Italiano di Tecnologia, Italy
P. J. Narayanan	International Institute of Information Technology, Hyderabad, India
Ram Nevatia	University of Southern California, USA
Natalia Neverova	Facebook AI Research, UK
Richard Newcombe	Facebook, USA
Cuong V. Nguyen	Florida International University, USA
Bingbing Ni	Shanghai Jiao Tong University, China
Juan Carlos Niebles	Salesforce & Stanford University, USA
Ko Nishino	Kyoto University, Japan
Jean-Marc Odobez	Idiap Research Institute, École polytechnique fédérale de Lausanne, Switzerland
Francesca Odone	University of Genova, Italy
Takayuki Okatani	Tohoku University & RIKEN Center for Advanced Intelligence Project, Japan
Manohar Paluri	Facebook, USA
Guan Pang	Facebook, USA
Maja Pantic	Imperial College London, UK
Sylvain Paris	Adobe Research, USA
Jaesik Park	Pohang University of Science and Technology, Korea
Hyun Soo Park	The University of Minnesota, USA
Omkar M. Parkhi	Facebook, USA
Deepak Pathak	Carnegie Mellon University, USA
Georgios Pavlakos	University of California, Berkeley, USA
Marcello Pelillo	University of Venice, Italy
Marc Pollefeys	ETH Zurich & Microsoft, Switzerland
Jean Ponce	Inria, France
Gerard Pons-Moll	University of Tübingen, Germany
Fatih Porikli	Qualcomm, USA
Victor Adrian Prisacariu	University of Oxford, UK
Petia Radeva	University of Barcelona, Spain
Ravi Ramamoorthi	University of California, San Diego, USA
Deva Ramanan	Carnegie Mellon University, USA
Vignesh Ramanathan	Facebook, USA
Nalini Ratha	State University of New York at Buffalo, USA
Tammy Riklin Raviv	Ben-Gurion University, Israel
Tobias Ritschel	University College London, UK
Emanuele Rodola	Sapienza University of Rome, Italy
Amit K. Roy-Chowdhury	University of California, Riverside, USA
Michael Rubinstein	Google, USA
Olga Russakovsky	Princeton University, USA

Mathieu Salzmann	École polytechnique fédérale de Lausanne, Switzerland
Dimitris Samaras	Stony Brook University, USA
Aswin Sankaranarayanan	Carnegie Mellon University, USA
Imari Sato	National Institute of Informatics, Japan
Yoichi Sato	University of Tokyo, Japan
Shin'ichi Satoh	National Institute of Informatics, Japan
Walter Scheirer	University of Notre Dame, USA
Bernt Schiele	Max Planck Institute for Informatics, Germany
Konrad Schindler	ETH Zurich, Switzerland
Cordelia Schmid	Inria & Google, France
Alexander Schwing	University of Illinois at Urbana-Champaign, USA
Nicu Sebe	University of Trento, Italy
Greg Shakhnarovich	Toyota Technological Institute at Chicago, USA
Eli Shechtman	Adobe Research, USA
Humphrey Shi	University of Oregon & University of Illinois at Urbana-Champaign & Picsart AI Research, USA
Jianbo Shi	University of Pennsylvania, USA
Roy Shilkrot	Massachusetts Institute of Technology, USA
Mike Zheng Shou	National University of Singapore, Singapore
Kaleem Siddiqi	McGill University, Canada
Richa Singh	Indian Institute of Technology Jodhpur, India
Greg Slabaugh	Queen Mary University of London, UK
Cees Snoek	University of Amsterdam, The Netherlands
Yale Song	Facebook AI Research, USA
Yi-Zhe Song	University of Surrey, UK
Bjorn Stenger	Rakuten Institute of Technology
Abby Stylianou	Saint Louis University, USA
Akihiro Sugimoto	National Institute of Informatics, Japan
Chen Sun	Brown University, USA
Deqing Sun	Google, USA
Kalyan Sunkavalli	Adobe Research, USA
Ying Tai	Tencent YouTu Lab, China
Ayellet Tal	Technion – Israel Institute of Technology, Israel
Ping Tan	Simon Fraser University, Canada
Siyu Tang	ETH Zurich, Switzerland
Chi-Keung Tang	Hong Kong University of Science and Technology, Hong Kong, China
Radu Timofte	University of Würzburg, Germany & ETH Zurich, Switzerland
Federico Tombari	Google, Switzerland & Technical University of Munich, Germany

James Tompkin	Brown University, USA
Lorenzo Torresani	Dartmouth College, USA
Alexander Toshev	Apple, USA
Du Tran	Facebook AI Research, USA
Anh T. Tran	VinAI, Vietnam
Zhuowen Tu	University of California, San Diego, USA
Georgios Tzimiropoulos	Queen Mary University of London, UK
Jasper Uijlings	Google Research, Switzerland
Jan C. van Gemert	Delft University of Technology, The Netherlands
Gul Varol	Ecole des Ponts ParisTech, France
Nuno Vasconcelos	University of California, San Diego, USA
Mayank Vatsa	Indian Institute of Technology Jodhpur, India
Ashok Veeraraghavan	Rice University, USA
Jakob Verbeek	Facebook AI Research, France
Carl Vondrick	Columbia University, USA
Ruiping Wang	Institute of Computing Technology, Chinese Academy of Sciences, China
Xinchao Wang	National University of Singapore, Singapore
Liwei Wang	The Chinese University of Hong Kong, Hong Kong, China
Chaohui Wang	Université Paris-Est, France
Xiaolong Wang	University of California, San Diego, USA
Christian Wolf	NAVER LABS Europe, France
Tao Xiang	University of Surrey, UK
Saining Xie	Facebook AI Research, USA
Cihang Xie	University of California, Santa Cruz, USA
Zeki Yalniz	Facebook, USA
Ming-Hsuan Yang	University of California, Merced, USA
Angela Yao	National University of Singapore, Singapore
Shaodi You	University of Amsterdam, The Netherlands
Stella X. Yu	University of California, Berkeley, USA
Junsong Yuan	State University of New York at Buffalo, USA
Stefanos Zafeiriou	Imperial College London, UK
Amir Zamir	École polytechnique fédérale de Lausanne, Switzerland
Lei Zhang	Alibaba & Hong Kong Polytechnic University, Hong Kong, China
Lei Zhang	International Digital Economy Academy (IDEA), China
Pengchuan Zhang	Meta AI, USA
Bolei Zhou	University of California, Los Angeles, USA
Yuke Zhu	University of Texas at Austin, USA

Todd Zickler Harvard University, USA
Wangmeng Zuo Harbin Institute of Technology, China

Technical Program Committee

Davide Abati
Soroush Abbasi Koohpayegani
Amos L. Abbott
Rameen Abdal
Rabab Abdelfattah
Sahar Abdelnabi
Hassan Abu Alhaija
Abulikemu Abuduweili
Ron Abutbul
Hanno Ackermann
Aikaterini Adam
Kamil Adamczewski
Ehsan Adeli
Vida Adeli
Donald Adjeroh
Arman Afrasiyabi
Akshay Agarwal
Sameer Agarwal
Abhinav Agarwalla
Vaibhav Aggarwal
Sara Aghajanzadeh
Susmit Agrawal
Antonio Agudo
Touqeer Ahmad
Sk Miraj Ahmed
Chaitanya Ahuja
Nilesh A. Ahuja
Abhishek Aich
Shubhra Aich
Noam Aigerman
Arash Akbarinia
Peri Akiva
Derya Akkaynak
Emre Aksan
Arjun R. Akula
Yuval Alaluf
Stephan Alaniz
Paul Albert
Cenek Albl
Filippo Aleotti
Konstantinos P. Alexandridis
Motasem Alfarra
Mohsen Ali
Thiemo Alldieck
Hadi Alzayer
Liang An
Shan An
Yi An
Zhulin An
Dongsheng An
Jie An
Xiang An
Saket Anand
Cosmin Ancuti
Juan Andrade-Cetto
Alexander Andreopoulos
Bjoern Andres
Jerone T. A. Andrews
Shivangi Aneja
Anelia Angelova
Dragomir Anguelov
Rushil Anirudh
Oron Anschel
Rao Muhammad Anwer
Djamila Aouada
Evlampios Apostolidis
Srikar Appalaraju
Nikita Araslanov
Andre Araujo
Eric Arazo
Dawit Mureja Argaw
Anurag Arnab
Aditya Arora
Chetan Arora
Sunpreet S. Arora
Alexey Artemov
Muhammad Asad
Kumar Ashutosh
Sinem Aslan
Vishal Asnani
Mahmoud Assran
Amir Atapour-Abarghouei
Nikos Athanasiou
Ali Athar
ShahRukh Athar
Sara Atito
Souhaib Attaiki
Matan Atzmon
Mathieu Aubry
Nicolas Audebert
Tristan T. Aumentado-Armstrong
Melinos Averkiou
Yannis Avrithis
Stephane Ayache
Mehmet Aygün
Seyed Mehdi Ayyoubzadeh
Hossein Azizpour
George Azzopardi
Mallikarjun B. R.
Yunhao Ba
Abhishek Badki
Seung-Hwan Bae
Seung-Hwan Baek
Seungryul Baek
Piyush Nitin Bagad
Shai Bagon
Gaetan Bahl
Shikhar Bahl
Sherwin Bahmani
Haoran Bai
Lei Bai
Jiawang Bai
Haoyue Bai
Jinbin Bai
Xiang Bai
Xuyang Bai

Yang Bai
Yuanchao Bai
Ziqian Bai
Sungyong Baik
Kevin Bailly
Max Bain
Federico Baldassarre
Wele Gedara Chaminda Bandara
Biplab Banerjee
Pratyay Banerjee
Sandipan Banerjee
Jihwan Bang
Antyanta Bangunharcana
Aayush Bansal
Ankan Bansal
Siddhant Bansal
Wentao Bao
Zhipeng Bao
Amir Bar
Manel Baradad Jurjo
Lorenzo Baraldi
Danny Barash
Daniel Barath
Connelly Barnes
Ioan Andrei Bârsan
Steven Basart
Dina Bashkirova
Chaim Baskin
Peyman Bateni
Anil Batra
Sebastiano Battiato
Ardhendu Behera
Harkirat Behl
Jens Behley
Vasileios Belagiannis
Boulbaba Ben Amor
Emanuel Ben Baruch
Abdessamad Ben Hamza
Gil Ben-Artzi
Assia Benbihi
Fabian Benitez-Quiroz
Guy Ben-Yosef
Philipp Benz
Alexander W. Bergman
Urs Bergmann
Jesus Bermudez-Cameo
Stefano Berretti
Gedas Bertasius
Zachary Bessinger
Petra Bevandić
Matthew Beveridge
Lucas Beyer
Yash Bhalgat
Suvaansh Bhambri
Samarth Bharadwaj
Gaurav Bharaj
Aparna Bharati
Bharat Lal Bhatnagar
Uttaran Bhattacharya
Apratim Bhattacharyya
Brojeshwar Bhowmick
Ankan Kumar Bhunia
Ayan Kumar Bhunia
Qi Bi
Sai Bi
Michael Bi Mi
Gui-Bin Bian
Jia-Wang Bian
Shaojun Bian
Pia Bideau
Mario Bijelic
Hakan Bilen
Guillaume-Alexandre Bilodeau
Alexander Binder
Tolga Birdal
Vighnesh N. Birodkar
Sandika Biswas
Andreas Blattmann
Janusz Bobulski
Giuseppe Boccignone
Vishnu Boddeti
Navaneeth Bodla
Moritz Böhle
Aleksei Bokhovkin
Sam Bond-Taylor
Vivek Boominathan
Shubhankar Borse
Mark Boss
Andrea Bottino
Adnane Boukhayma
Fadi Boutros
Nicolas C. Boutry
Richard S. Bowen
Ivaylo Boyadzhiev
Aidan Boyd
Yuri Boykov
Aljaz Bozic
Behzad Bozorgtabar
Eric Brachmann
Samarth Brahmbhatt
Gustav Bredell
Francois Bremond
Joel Brogan
Andrew Brown
Thomas Brox
Marcus A. Brubaker
Robert-Jan Bruintjes
Yuqi Bu
Anders G. Buch
Himanshu Buckchash
Mateusz Buda
Ignas Budvytis
José M. Buenaposada
Marcel C. Bühler
Tu Bui
Adrian Bulat
Hannah Bull
Evgeny Burnaev
Andrei Bursuc
Benjamin Busam
Sergey N. Buzykanov
Wonmin Byeon
Fabian Caba
Martin Cadik
Guanyu Cai
Minjie Cai
Qing Cai
Zhongang Cai
Qi Cai
Yancheng Cai
Shen Cai
Han Cai
Jiarui Cai

Bowen Cai
Mu Cai
Qin Cai
Ruojin Cai
Weidong Cai
Weiwei Cai
Yi Cai
Yujun Cai
Zhiping Cai
Akin Caliskan
Lilian Calvet
Baris Can Cam
Necati Cihan Camgoz
Tommaso Campari
Dylan Campbell
Ziang Cao
Ang Cao
Xu Cao
Zhiwen Cao
Shengcao Cao
Song Cao
Weipeng Cao
Xiangyong Cao
Xiaochun Cao
Yue Cao
Yunhao Cao
Zhangjie Cao
Jiale Cao
Yang Cao
Jiajiong Cao
Jie Cao
Jinkun Cao
Lele Cao
Yulong Cao
Zhiguo Cao
Chen Cao
Razvan Caramalau
Marlène Careil
Gustavo Carneiro
Joao Carreira
Dan Casas
Paola Cascante-Bonilla
Angela Castillo
Francisco M. Castro
Pedro Castro
Luca Cavalli
George J. Cazenavette
Oya Celiktutan
Hakan Cevikalp
Sri Harsha C. H.
Sungmin Cha
Geonho Cha
Menglei Chai
Lucy Chai
Yuning Chai
Zenghao Chai
Anirban Chakraborty
Deep Chakraborty
Rudrasis Chakraborty
Souradeep Chakraborty
Kelvin C. K. Chan
Chee Seng Chan
Paramanand Chandramouli
Arjun Chandrasekaran
Kenneth Chaney
Dongliang Chang
Huiwen Chang
Peng Chang
Xiaojun Chang
Jia-Ren Chang
Hyung Jin Chang
Hyun Sung Chang
Ju Yong Chang
Li-Jen Chang
Qi Chang
Wei-Yi Chang
Yi Chang
Nadine Chang
Hanqing Chao
Pradyumna Chari
Dibyadip Chatterjee
Chiranjoy Chattopadhyay
Siddhartha Chaudhuri
Zhengping Che
Gal Chechik
Lianggangxu Chen
Qi Alfred Chen
Brian Chen
Bor-Chun Chen
Bo-Hao Chen
Bohong Chen
Bin Chen
Ziliang Chen
Cheng Chen
Chen Chen
Chaofeng Chen
Xi Chen
Haoyu Chen
Xuanhong Chen
Wei Chen
Qiang Chen
Shi Chen
Xianyu Chen
Chang Chen
Changhuai Chen
Hao Chen
Jie Chen
Jianbo Chen
Jingjing Chen
Jun Chen
Kejiang Chen
Mingcai Chen
Nenglun Chen
Qifeng Chen
Ruoyu Chen
Shu-Yu Chen
Weidong Chen
Weijie Chen
Weikai Chen
Xiang Chen
Xiuyi Chen
Xingyu Chen
Yaofo Chen
Yueting Chen
Yu Chen
Yunjin Chen
Yuntao Chen
Yun Chen
Zhenfang Chen
Zhuangzhuang Chen
Chu-Song Chen
Xiangyu Chen
Zhuo Chen
Chaoqi Chen
Shizhe Chen

Xiaotong Chen
Xiaozhi Chen
Dian Chen
Defang Chen
Dingfan Chen
Ding-Jie Chen
Ee Heng Chen
Tao Chen
Yixin Chen
Wei-Ting Chen
Lin Chen
Guang Chen
Guangyi Chen
Guanying Chen
Guangyao Chen
Hwann-Tzong Chen
Junwen Chen
Jiacheng Chen
Jianxu Chen
Hui Chen
Kai Chen
Kan Chen
Kevin Chen
Kuan-Wen Chen
Weihua Chen
Zhang Chen
Liang-Chieh Chen
Lele Chen
Liang Chen
Fanglin Chen
Zehui Chen
Minghui Chen
Minghao Chen
Xiaokang Chen
Qian Chen
Jun-Cheng Chen
Qi Chen
Qingcai Chen
Richard J. Chen
Runnan Chen
Rui Chen
Shuo Chen
Sentao Chen
Shaoyu Chen
Shixing Chen
Shuai Chen
Shuya Chen
Sizhe Chen
Simin Chen
Shaoxiang Chen
Zitian Chen
Tianlong Chen
Tianshui Chen
Min-Hung Chen
Xiangning Chen
Xin Chen
Xinghao Chen
Xuejin Chen
Xu Chen
Xuxi Chen
Yunlu Chen
Yanbei Chen
Yuxiao Chen
Yun-Chun Chen
Yi-Ting Chen
Yi-Wen Chen
Yinbo Chen
Yiran Chen
Yuanhong Chen
Yubei Chen
Yuefeng Chen
Yuhua Chen
Yukang Chen
Zerui Chen
Zhaoyu Chen
Zhen Chen
Zhenyu Chen
Zhi Chen
Zhiwei Chen
Zhixiang Chen
Long Chen
Bowen Cheng
Jun Cheng
Yi Cheng
Jingchun Cheng
Lechao Cheng
Xi Cheng
Yuan Cheng
Ho Kei Cheng
Kevin Ho Man Cheng
Jiacheng Cheng
Kelvin B. Cheng
Li Cheng
Mengjun Cheng
Zhen Cheng
Qingrong Cheng
Tianheng Cheng
Harry Cheng
Yihua Cheng
Yu Cheng
Ziheng Cheng
Soon Yau Cheong
Anoop Cherian
Manuela Chessa
Zhixiang Chi
Naoki Chiba
Julian Chibane
Kashyap Chitta
Tai-Yin Chiu
Hsu-kuang Chiu
Wei-Chen Chiu
Sungmin Cho
Donghyeon Cho
Hyeon Cho
Yooshin Cho
Gyusang Cho
Jang Hyun Cho
Seungju Cho
Nam Ik Cho
Sunghyun Cho
Hanbyel Cho
Jaesung Choe
Jooyoung Choi
Chiho Choi
Changwoon Choi
Jongwon Choi
Myungsub Choi
Dooseop Choi
Jonghyun Choi
Jinwoo Choi
Jun Won Choi
Min-Kook Choi
Hongsuk Choi
Janghoon Choi
Yoon-Ho Choi

Yukyung Choi
Jaegul Choo
Ayush Chopra
Siddharth Choudhary
Subhabrata Choudhury
Vasileios Choutas
Ka-Ho Chow
Pinaki Nath Chowdhury
Sammy Christen
Anders Christensen
Grigorios Chrysos
Hang Chu
Wen-Hsuan Chu
Peng Chu
Qi Chu
Ruihang Chu
Wei-Ta Chu
Yung-Yu Chuang
Sanghyuk Chun
Se Young Chun
Antonio Cinà
Ramazan Gokberk Cinbis
Javier Civera
Albert Clapés
Ronald Clark
Brian S. Clipp
Felipe Codevilla
Daniel Coelho de Castro
Niv Cohen
Forrester Cole
Maxwell D. Collins
Robert T. Collins
Marc Comino Trinidad
Runmin Cong
Wenyan Cong
Maxime Cordy
Marcella Cornia
Enric Corona
Huseyin Coskun
Luca Cosmo
Dragos Costea
Davide Cozzolino
Arun C. S. Kumar
Aiyu Cui
Qiongjie Cui
Quan Cui
Shuhao Cui
Yiming Cui
Ying Cui
Zijun Cui
Jiali Cui
Jiequan Cui
Yawen Cui
Zhen Cui
Zhaopeng Cui
Jack Culpepper
Xiaodong Cun
Ross Cutler
Adam Czajka
Ali Dabouei
Konstantinos M. Dafnis
Manuel Dahnert
Tao Dai
Yuchao Dai
Bo Dai
Mengyu Dai
Hang Dai
Haixing Dai
Peng Dai
Pingyang Dai
Qi Dai
Qiyu Dai
Yutong Dai
Naser Damer
Zhiyuan Dang
Mohamed Daoudi
Ayan Das
Abir Das
Debasmit Das
Deepayan Das
Partha Das
Sagnik Das
Soumi Das
Srijan Das
Swagatam Das
Avijit Dasgupta
Jim Davis
Adrian K. Davison
Homa Davoudi
Laura Daza
Matthias De Lange
Shalini De Mello
Marco De Nadai
Christophe De Vleeschouwer
Alp Dener
Boyang Deng
Congyue Deng
Bailin Deng
Yong Deng
Ye Deng
Zhuo Deng
Zhijie Deng
Xiaoming Deng
Jiankang Deng
Jinhong Deng
Jingjing Deng
Liang-Jian Deng
Siqi Deng
Xiang Deng
Xueqing Deng
Zhongying Deng
Karan Desai
Jean-Emmanuel Deschaud
Aniket Anand Deshmukh
Neel Dey
Helisa Dhamo
Prithviraj Dhar
Amaya Dharmasiri
Yan Di
Xing Di
Ousmane A. Dia
Haiwen Diao
Xiaolei Diao
Gonçalo José Dias Pais
Abdallah Dib
Anastasios Dimou
Changxing Ding
Henghui Ding
Guodong Ding
Yaqing Ding
Shuangrui Ding
Yuhang Ding
Yikang Ding
Shouhong Ding

Haisong Ding
Hui Ding
Jiahao Ding
Jian Ding
Jian-Jiun Ding
Shuxiao Ding
Tianyu Ding
Wenhao Ding
Yuqi Ding
Yi Ding
Yuzhen Ding
Zhengming Ding
Tan Minh Dinh
Vu Dinh
Christos Diou
Mandar Dixit
Bao Gia Doan
Khoa D. Doan
Dzung Anh Doan
Debi Prosad Dogra
Nehal Doiphode
Chengdong Dong
Bowen Dong
Zhenxing Dong
Hang Dong
Xiaoyi Dong
Haoye Dong
Jiangxin Dong
Shichao Dong
Xuan Dong
Zhen Dong
Shuting Dong
Jing Dong
Li Dong
Ming Dong
Nanqing Dong
Qiulei Dong
Runpei Dong
Siyan Dong
Tian Dong
Wei Dong
Xiaomeng Dong
Xin Dong
Xingbo Dong
Yuan Dong
Samuel Dooley
Gianfranco Doretto
Michael Dorkenwald
Keval Doshi
Zhaopeng Dou
Xiaotian Dou
Hazel Doughty
Ahmad Droby
Iddo Drori
Jie Du
Yong Du
Dawei Du
Dong Du
Ruoyi Du
Yuntao Du
Xuefeng Du
Yilun Du
Yuming Du
Radhika Dua
Haodong Duan
Jiafei Duan
Kaiwen Duan
Peiqi Duan
Ye Duan
Haoran Duan
Jiali Duan
Amanda Duarte
Abhimanyu Dubey
Shiv Ram Dubey
Florian Dubost
Lukasz Dudziak
Shivam Duggal
Justin M. Dulay
Matteo Dunnhofer
Chi Nhan Duong
Thibaut Durand
Mihai Dusmanu
Ujjal Kr Dutta
Debidatta Dwibedi
Isht Dwivedi
Sai Kumar Dwivedi
Takeharu Eda
Mark Edmonds
Alexei A. Efros
Thibaud Ehret
Max Ehrlich
Mahsa Ehsanpour
Iván Eichhardt
Farshad Einabadi
Marvin Eisenberger
Hazim Kemal Ekenel
Mohamed El Banani
Ismail Elezi
Moshe Eliasof
Alaa El-Nouby
Ian Endres
Francis Engelmann
Deniz Engin
Chanho Eom
Dave Epstein
Maria C. Escobar
Victor A. Escorcia
Carlos Esteves
Sungmin Eum
Bernard J. E. Evans
Ivan Evtimov
Fevziye Irem Eyiokur Yaman
Matteo Fabbri
Sébastien Fabbro
Gabriele Facciolo
Masud Fahim
Bin Fan
Hehe Fan
Deng-Ping Fan
Aoxiang Fan
Chen-Chen Fan
Qi Fan
Zhaoxin Fan
Haoqi Fan
Heng Fan
Hongyi Fan
Linxi Fan
Baojie Fan
Jiayuan Fan
Lei Fan
Quanfu Fan
Yonghui Fan
Yingruo Fan
Zhiwen Fan

Zicong Fan
Sean Fanello
Jiansheng Fang
Chaowei Fang
Yuming Fang
Jianwu Fang
Jin Fang
Qi Fang
Shancheng Fang
Tian Fang
Xianyong Fang
Gongfan Fang
Zhen Fang
Hui Fang
Jiemin Fang
Le Fang
Pengfei Fang
Xiaolin Fang
Yuxin Fang
Zhaoyuan Fang
Ammarah Farooq
Azade Farshad
Zhengcong Fei
Michael Felsberg
Wei Feng
Chen Feng
Fan Feng
Andrew Feng
Xin Feng
Zheyun Feng
Ruicheng Feng
Mingtao Feng
Qianyu Feng
Shangbin Feng
Chun-Mei Feng
Zunlei Feng
Zhiyong Feng
Martin Fergie
Mustansar Fiaz
Marco Fiorucci
Michael Firman
Hamed Firooz
Volker Fischer
Corneliu O. Florea
Georgios Floros
Wolfgang Foerstner
Gianni Franchi
Jean-Sebastien Franco
Simone Frintrop
Anna Fruehstueck
Changhong Fu
Chaoyou Fu
Cheng-Yang Fu
Chi-Wing Fu
Deqing Fu
Huan Fu
Jun Fu
Kexue Fu
Ying Fu
Jianlong Fu
Jingjing Fu
Qichen Fu
Tsu-Jui Fu
Xueyang Fu
Yang Fu
Yanwei Fu
Yonggan Fu
Wolfgang Fuhl
Yasuhisa Fujii
Kent Fujiwara
Marco Fumero
Takuya Funatomi
Isabel Funke
Dario Fuoli
Antonino Furnari
Matheus A. Gadelha
Akshay Gadi Patil
Adrian Galdran
Guillermo Gallego
Silvano Galliani
Orazio Gallo
Leonardo Galteri
Matteo Gamba
Yiming Gan
Sujoy Ganguly
Harald Ganster
Boyan Gao
Changxin Gao
Daiheng Gao
Difei Gao
Chen Gao
Fei Gao
Lin Gao
Wei Gao
Yiming Gao
Junyu Gao
Guangyu Ryan Gao
Haichang Gao
Hongchang Gao
Jialin Gao
Jin Gao
Jun Gao
Katelyn Gao
Mingchen Gao
Mingfei Gao
Pan Gao
Shangqian Gao
Shanghua Gao
Xitong Gao
Yunhe Gao
Zhanning Gao
Elena Garces
Nuno Cruz Garcia
Noa Garcia
Guillermo Garcia-Hernando
Isha Garg
Rahul Garg
Sourav Garg
Quentin Garrido
Stefano Gasperini
Kent Gauen
Chandan Gautam
Shivam Gautam
Paul Gay
Chunjiang Ge
Shiming Ge
Wenhang Ge
Yanhao Ge
Zheng Ge
Songwei Ge
Weifeng Ge
Yixiao Ge
Yuying Ge
Shijie Geng

Zhengyang Geng
Kyle A. Genova
Georgios Georgakis
Markos Georgopoulos
Marcel Geppert
Shabnam Ghadar
Mina Ghadimi Atigh
Deepti Ghadiyaram
Maani Ghaffari Jadidi
Sedigh Ghamari
Zahra Gharaee
Michaël Gharbi
Golnaz Ghiasi
Reza Ghoddoosian
Soumya Suvra Ghosal
Adhiraj Ghosh
Arthita Ghosh
Pallabi Ghosh
Soumyadeep Ghosh
Andrew Gilbert
Igor Gilitschenski
Jhony H. Giraldo
Andreu Girbau Xalabarder
Rohit Girdhar
Sharath Girish
Xavier Giro-i-Nieto
Raja Giryes
Thomas Gittings
Nikolaos Gkanatsios
Ioannis Gkioulekas
Abhiram Gnanasambandam
Aurele T. Gnanha
Clement L. J. C. Godard
Arushi Goel
Vidit Goel
Shubham Goel
Zan Gojcic
Aaron K. Gokaslan
Tejas Gokhale
S. Alireza Golestaneh
Thiago L. Gomes
Nuno Goncalves
Boqing Gong
Chen Gong
Yuanhao Gong
Guoqiang Gong
Jingyu Gong
Rui Gong
Yu Gong
Mingming Gong
Neil Zhenqiang Gong
Xun Gong
Yunye Gong
Yihong Gong
Cristina I. González
Nithin Gopalakrishnan Nair
Gaurav Goswami
Jianping Gou
Shreyank N. Gowda
Ankit Goyal
Helmut Grabner
Patrick L. Grady
Ben Graham
Eric Granger
Douglas R. Gray
Matej Grcić
David Griffiths
Jinjin Gu
Yun Gu
Shuyang Gu
Jianyang Gu
Fuqiang Gu
Jiatao Gu
Jindong Gu
Jiaqi Gu
Jinwei Gu
Jiaxin Gu
Geonmo Gu
Xiao Gu
Xinqian Gu
Xiuye Gu
Yuming Gu
Zhangxuan Gu
Dayan Guan
Junfeng Guan
Qingji Guan
Tianrui Guan
Shanyan Guan
Denis A. Gudovskiy
Ricardo Guerrero
Pierre-Louis Guhur
Jie Gui
Liangyan Gui
Liangke Gui
Benoit Guillard
Erhan Gundogdu
Manuel Günther
Jingcai Guo
Yuanfang Guo
Junfeng Guo
Chenqi Guo
Dan Guo
Hongji Guo
Jia Guo
Jie Guo
Minghao Guo
Shi Guo
Yanhui Guo
Yangyang Guo
Yuan-Chen Guo
Yilu Guo
Yiluan Guo
Yong Guo
Guangyu Guo
Haiyun Guo
Jinyang Guo
Jianyuan Guo
Pengsheng Guo
Pengfei Guo
Shuxuan Guo
Song Guo
Tianyu Guo
Qing Guo
Qiushan Guo
Wen Guo
Xiefan Guo
Xiaohu Guo
Xiaoqing Guo
Yufei Guo
Yuhui Guo
Yuliang Guo
Yunhui Guo
Yanwen Guo

Akshita Gupta
Ankush Gupta
Kamal Gupta
Kartik Gupta
Ritwik Gupta
Rohit Gupta
Siddharth Gururani
Fredrik K. Gustafsson
Abner Guzman Rivera
Vladimir Guzov
Matthew A. Gwilliam
Jung-Woo Ha
Marc Habermann
Isma Hadji
Christian Haene
Martin Hahner
Levente Hajder
Alexandros Haliassos
Emanuela Haller
Bumsub Ham
Abdullah J. Hamdi
Shreyas Hampali
Dongyoon Han
Chunrui Han
Dong-Jun Han
Dong-Sig Han
Guangxing Han
Zhizhong Han
Ruize Han
Jiaming Han
Jin Han
Ligong Han
Xian-Hua Han
Xiaoguang Han
Yizeng Han
Zhi Han
Zhenjun Han
Zhongyi Han
Jungong Han
Junlin Han
Kai Han
Kun Han
Sungwon Han
Songfang Han
Wei Han
Xiao Han
Xintong Han
Xinzhe Han
Yahong Han
Yan Han
Zongbo Han
Nicolai Hani
Rana Hanocka
Niklas Hanselmann
Nicklas A. Hansen
Hong Hanyu
Fusheng Hao
Yanbin Hao
Shijie Hao
Udith Haputhanthri
Mehrtash Harandi
Josh Harguess
Adam Harley
David M. Hart
Atsushi Hashimoto
Ali Hassani
Mohammed Hassanin
Yana Hasson
Joakim Bruslund Haurum
Bo He
Kun He
Chen He
Xin He
Fazhi He
Gaoqi He
Hao He
Haoyu He
Jiangpeng He
Hongliang He
Qian He
Xiangteng He
Xuming He
Yannan He
Yuhang He
Yang He
Xiangyu He
Nanjun He
Pan He
Sen He
Shengfeng He
Songtao He
Tao He
Tong He
Wei He
Xuehai He
Xiaoxiao He
Ying He
Yisheng He
Ziwen He
Peter Hedman
Felix Heide
Yacov Hel-Or
Paul Henderson
Philipp Henzler
Byeongho Heo
Jae-Pil Heo
Miran Heo
Sachini A. Herath
Stephane Herbin
Pedro Hermosilla Casajus
Monica Hernandez
Charles Herrmann
Roei Herzig
Mauricio Hess-Flores
Carlos Hinojosa
Tobias Hinz
Tsubasa Hirakawa
Chih-Hui Ho
Lam Si Tung Ho
Jennifer Hobbs
Derek Hoiem
Yannick Hold-Geoffroy
Aleksander Holynski
Cheeun Hong
Fa-Ting Hong
Hanbin Hong
Guan Zhe Hong
Danfeng Hong
Lanqing Hong
Xiaopeng Hong
Xin Hong
Jie Hong
Seungbum Hong
Cheng-Yao Hong
Seunghoon Hong

Yi Hong
Yuan Hong
Yuchen Hong
Anthony Hoogs
Maxwell C. Horton
Kazuhiro Hotta
Qibin Hou
Tingbo Hou
Junhui Hou
Ji Hou
Qiqi Hou
Rui Hou
Ruibing Hou
Zhi Hou
Henry Howard-Jenkins
Lukas Hoyer
Wei-Lin Hsiao
Chiou-Ting Hsu
Anthony Hu
Brian Hu
Yusong Hu
Hexiang Hu
Haoji Hu
Di Hu
Hengtong Hu
Haigen Hu
Lianyu Hu
Hanzhe Hu
Jie Hu
Junlin Hu
Shizhe Hu
Jian Hu
Zhiming Hu
Juhua Hu
Peng Hu
Ping Hu
Ronghang Hu
MengShun Hu
Tao Hu
Vincent Tao Hu
Xiaoling Hu
Xinting Hu
Xiaolin Hu
Xuefeng Hu
Xiaowei Hu
Yang Hu
Yueyu Hu
Zeyu Hu
Zhongyun Hu
Binh-Son Hua
Guoliang Hua
Yi Hua
Linzhi Huang
Qiusheng Huang
Bo Huang
Chen Huang
Hsin-Ping Huang
Ye Huang
Shuangping Huang
Zeng Huang
Buzhen Huang
Cong Huang
Heng Huang
Hao Huang
Qidong Huang
Huaibo Huang
Chaoqin Huang
Feihu Huang
Jiahui Huang
Jingjia Huang
Kun Huang
Lei Huang
Sheng Huang
Shuaiyi Huang
Siyu Huang
Xiaoshui Huang
Xiaoyang Huang
Yan Huang
Yihao Huang
Ying Huang
Ziling Huang
Xiaoke Huang
Yifei Huang
Haiyang Huang
Zhewei Huang
Jin Huang
Haibin Huang
Jiaxing Huang
Junjie Huang
Keli Huang
Lang Huang
Lin Huang
Luojie Huang
Mingzhen Huang
Shijia Huang
Shengyu Huang
Siyuan Huang
He Huang
Xiuyu Huang
Lianghua Huang
Yue Huang
Yaping Huang
Yuge Huang
Zehao Huang
Zeyi Huang
Zhiqi Huang
Zhongzhan Huang
Zilong Huang
Ziyuan Huang
Tianrui Hui
Zhuo Hui
Le Hui
Jing Huo
Junhwa Hur
Shehzeen S. Hussain
Chuong Minh Huynh
Seunghyun Hwang
Jaehui Hwang
Jyh-Jing Hwang
Sukjun Hwang
Soonmin Hwang
Wonjun Hwang
Rakib Hyder
Sangeek Hyun
Sarah Ibrahimi
Tomoki Ichikawa
Yerlan Idelbayev
A. S. M. Iftekhar
Masaaki Iiyama
Satoshi Ikehata
Sunghoon Im
Atul N. Ingle
Eldar Insafutdinov
Yani A. Ioannou
Radu Tudor Ionescu

Umar Iqbal
Go Irie
Muhammad Zubair Irshad
Ahmet Iscen
Berivan Isik
Ashraful Islam
Md Amirul Islam
Syed Islam
Mariko Isogawa
Vamsi Krishna K. Ithapu
Boris Ivanovic
Darshan Iyer
Sarah Jabbour
Ayush Jain
Nishant Jain
Samyak Jain
Vidit Jain
Vineet Jain
Priyank Jaini
Tomas Jakab
Mohammad A. A. K. Jalwana
Muhammad Abdullah Jamal
Hadi Jamali-Rad
Stuart James
Varun Jampani
Young Kyun Jang
YeongJun Jang
Yunseok Jang
Ronnachai Jaroensri
Bhavan Jasani
Krishna Murthy Jatavallabhula
Mojan Javaheripi
Syed A. Javed
Guillaume Jeanneret
Pranav Jeevan
Herve Jegou
Rohit Jena
Tomas Jenicek
Porter Jenkins
Simon Jenni
Hae-Gon Jeon
Sangryul Jeon
Boseung Jeong
Yoonwoo Jeong
Seong-Gyun Jeong
Jisoo Jeong
Allan D. Jepson
Ankit Jha
Sumit K. Jha
I-Hong Jhuo
Ge-Peng Ji
Chaonan Ji
Deyi Ji
Jingwei Ji
Wei Ji
Zhong Ji
Jiayi Ji
Pengliang Ji
Hui Ji
Mingi Ji
Xiaopeng Ji
Yuzhu Ji
Baoxiong Jia
Songhao Jia
Dan Jia
Shan Jia
Xiaojun Jia
Xiuyi Jia
Xu Jia
Menglin Jia
Wenqi Jia
Boyuan Jiang
Wenhao Jiang
Huaizu Jiang
Hanwen Jiang
Haiyong Jiang
Hao Jiang
Huajie Jiang
Huiqin Jiang
Haojun Jiang
Haobo Jiang
Junjun Jiang
Xingyu Jiang
Yangbangyan Jiang
Yu Jiang
Jianmin Jiang
Jiaxi Jiang
Jing Jiang
Kui Jiang
Li Jiang
Liming Jiang
Chiyu Jiang
Meirui Jiang
Chen Jiang
Peng Jiang
Tai-Xiang Jiang
Wen Jiang
Xinyang Jiang
Yifan Jiang
Yuming Jiang
Yingying Jiang
Zeren Jiang
ZhengKai Jiang
Zhenyu Jiang
Shuming Jiao
Jianbo Jiao
Licheng Jiao
Dongkwon Jin
Yeying Jin
Cheng Jin
Linyi Jin
Qing Jin
Taisong Jin
Xiao Jin
Xin Jin
Sheng Jin
Kyong Hwan Jin
Ruibing Jin
SouYoung Jin
Yueming Jin
Chenchen Jing
Longlong Jing
Taotao Jing
Yongcheng Jing
Younghyun Jo
Joakim Johnander
Jeff Johnson
Michael J. Jones
R. Kenny Jones
Rico Jonschkowski
Ameya Joshi
Sunghun Joung

Felix Juefei-Xu
Claudio R. Jung
Steffen Jung
Hari Chandana K.
Rahul Vigneswaran K.
Prajwal K. R.
Abhishek Kadian
Jhony Kaesemodel Pontes
Kumara Kahatapitiya
Anmol Kalia
Sinan Kalkan
Tarun Kalluri
Jaewon Kam
Sandesh Kamath
Meina Kan
Menelaos Kanakis
Takuhiro Kaneko
Di Kang
Guoliang Kang
Hao Kang
Jaeyeon Kang
Kyoungkook Kang
Li-Wei Kang
MinGuk Kang
Suk-Ju Kang
Zhao Kang
Yash Mukund Kant
Yueying Kao
Aupendu Kar
Konstantinos Karantzalos
Sezer Karaoglu
Navid Kardan
Sanjay Kariyappa
Leonid Karlinsky
Animesh Karnewar
Shyamgopal Karthik
Hirak J. Kashyap
Marc A. Kastner
Hirokatsu Kataoka
Angelos Katharopoulos
Hiroharu Kato
Kai Katsumata
Manuel Kaufmann
Chaitanya Kaul
Prakhar Kaushik
Yuki Kawana
Lei Ke
Lipeng Ke
Tsung-Wei Ke
Wei Ke
Petr Kellnhofer
Aniruddha Kembhavi
John Kender
Corentin Kervadec
Leonid Keselman
Daniel Keysers
Nima Khademi Kalantari
Taras Khakhulin
Samir Khaki
Muhammad Haris Khan
Qadeer Khan
Salman Khan
Subash Khanal
Vaishnavi M. Khindkar
Rawal Khirodkar
Saeed Khorram
Pirazh Khorramshahi
Kourosh Khoshelham
Ansh Khurana
Benjamin Kiefer
Jae Myung Kim
Junho Kim
Boah Kim
Hyeonseong Kim
Dong-Jin Kim
Dongwan Kim
Donghyun Kim
Doyeon Kim
Yonghyun Kim
Hyung-Il Kim
Hyunwoo Kim
Hyeongwoo Kim
Hyo Jin Kim
Hyunwoo J. Kim
Taehoon Kim
Jaeha Kim
Jiwon Kim
Jung Uk Kim
Kangyeol Kim
Eunji Kim
Daeha Kim
Dongwon Kim
Kunhee Kim
Kyungmin Kim
Junsik Kim
Min H. Kim
Namil Kim
Kookhoi Kim
Sanghyun Kim
Seongyeop Kim
Seungryong Kim
Saehoon Kim
Euyoung Kim
Guisik Kim
Sungyeon Kim
Sunnie S. Y. Kim
Taehun Kim
Tae Oh Kim
Won Hwa Kim
Seungwook Kim
YoungBin Kim
Youngeun Kim
Akisato Kimura
Furkan Osman Kınlı
Zsolt Kira
Hedvig Kjellström
Florian Kleber
Jan P. Klopp
Florian Kluger
Laurent Kneip
Byungsoo Ko
Muhammed Kocabas
A. Sophia Koepke
Kevin Koeser
Nick Kolkin
Nikos Kolotouros
Wai-Kin Adams Kong
Deying Kong
Caihua Kong
Youyong Kong
Shuyu Kong
Shu Kong
Tao Kong
Yajing Kong
Yu Kong

Zishang Kong
Theodora Kontogianni
Anton S. Konushin
Julian F. P. Kooij
Bruno Korbar
Giorgos Kordopatis-Zilos
Jari Korhonen
Adam Kortylewski
Denis Korzhenkov
Divya Kothandaraman
Suraj Kothawade
Iuliia Kotseruba
Satwik Kottur
Shashank Kotyan
Alexandros Kouris
Petros Koutras
Anna Kreshuk
Ranjay Krishna
Dilip Krishnan
Andrey Kuehlkamp
Hilde Kuehne
Jason Kuen
David Kügler
Arjan Kuijper
Anna Kukleva
Sumith Kulal
Viveka Kulharia
Akshay R. Kulkarni
Nilesh Kulkarni
Dominik Kulon
Abhinav Kumar
Akash Kumar
Suryansh Kumar
B. V. K. Vijaya Kumar
Pulkit Kumar
Ratnesh Kumar
Sateesh Kumar
Satish Kumar
Vijay Kumar B. G.
Nupur Kumari
Sudhakar Kumawat
Jogendra Nath Kundu
Hsien-Kai Kuo
Meng-Yu Jennifer Kuo
Vinod Kumar Kurmi
Yusuke Kurose
Keerthy Kusumam
Alina Kuznetsova
Henry Kvinge
Ho Man Kwan
Hyeokjun Kweon
Heeseung Kwon
Gihyun Kwon
Myung-Joon Kwon
Taesung Kwon
YoungJoong Kwon
Christos Kyrkou
Jorma Laaksonen
Yann Labbe
Zorah Laehner
Florent Lafarge
Hamid Laga
Manuel Lagunas
Shenqi Lai
Jian-Huang Lai
Zihang Lai
Mohamed I. Lakhal
Mohit Lamba
Meng Lan
Loic Landrieu
Zhiqiang Lang
Natalie Lang
Dong Lao
Yizhen Lao
Yingjie Lao
Issam Hadj Laradji
Gustav Larsson
Viktor Larsson
Zakaria Laskar
Stéphane Lathuilière
Chun Pong Lau
Rynson W. H. Lau
Hei Law
Justin Lazarow
Verica Lazova
Eric-Tuan Le
Hieu Le
Trung-Nghia Le
Mathias Lechner
Byeong-Uk Lee
Chen-Yu Lee
Che-Rung Lee
Chul Lee
Hong Joo Lee
Dongsoo Lee
Jiyoung Lee
Eugene Eu Tzuan Lee
Daeun Lee
Saehyung Lee
Jewook Lee
Hyungtae Lee
Hyunmin Lee
Jungbeom Lee
Joon-Young Lee
Jong-Seok Lee
Joonseok Lee
Junha Lee
Kibok Lee
Byung-Kwan Lee
Jangwon Lee
Jinho Lee
Jongmin Lee
Seunghyun Lee
Sohyun Lee
Minsik Lee
Dogyoon Lee
Seungmin Lee
Min Jun Lee
Sangho Lee
Sangmin Lee
Seungeun Lee
Seon-Ho Lee
Sungmin Lee
Sungho Lee
Sangyoun Lee
Vincent C. S. S. Lee
Jaeseong Lee
Yong Jae Lee
Chenyang Lei
Chenyi Lei
Jiahui Lei
Xinyu Lei
Yinjie Lei
Jiaxu Leng
Luziwei Leng

Jan E. Lenssen
Vincent Lepetit
Thomas Leung
María Leyva-Vallina
Xin Li
Yikang Li
Baoxin Li
Bin Li
Bing Li
Bowen Li
Changlin Li
Chao Li
Chongyi Li
Guanyue Li
Shuai Li
Jin Li
Dingquan Li
Dongxu Li
Yiting Li
Gang Li
Dian Li
Guohao Li
Haoang Li
Haoliang Li
Haoran Li
Hengduo Li
Huafeng Li
Xiaoming Li
Hanao Li
Hongwei Li
Ziqiang Li
Jisheng Li
Jiacheng Li
Jia Li
Jiachen Li
Jiahao Li
Jianwei Li
Jiazhi Li
Jie Li
Jing Li
Jingjing Li
Jingtao Li
Jun Li
Junxuan Li
Kai Li
Kailin Li
Kenneth Li
Kun Li
Kunpeng Li
Aoxue Li
Chenglong Li
Chenglin Li
Changsheng Li
Zhichao Li
Qiang Li
Yanyu Li
Zuoyue Li
Xiang Li
Xuelong Li
Fangda Li
Ailin Li
Liang Li
Chun-Guang Li
Daiqing Li
Dong Li
Guanbin Li
Guorong Li
Haifeng Li
Jianan Li
Jianing Li
Jiaxin Li
Ke Li
Lei Li
Lincheng Li
Liulei Li
Lujun Li
Linjie Li
Lin Li
Pengyu Li
Ping Li
Qiufu Li
Qingyong Li
Rui Li
Siyuan Li
Wei Li
Wenbin Li
Xiangyang Li
Xinyu Li
Xiujun Li
Xiu Li
Xu Li
Ya-Li Li
Yao Li
Yongjie Li
Yijun Li
Yiming Li
Yuezun Li
Yu Li
Yunheng Li
Yuqi Li
Zhe Li
Zeming Li
Zhen Li
Zhengqin Li
Zhimin Li
Jiefeng Li
Jinpeng Li
Chengze Li
Jianwu Li
Lerenhan Li
Shan Li
Suichan Li
Xiangtai Li
Yanjie Li
Yandong Li
Zhuoling Li
Zhenqiang Li
Manyi Li
Maosen Li
Ji Li
Minjun Li
Mingrui Li
Mengtian Li
Junyi Li
Nianyi Li
Bo Li
Xiao Li
Peihua Li
Peike Li
Peizhao Li
Peiliang Li
Qi Li
Ren Li
Runze Li
Shile Li

Sheng Li
Shigang Li
Shiyu Li
Shuang Li
Shasha Li
Shichao Li
Tianye Li
Yuexiang Li
Wei-Hong Li
Wanhua Li
Weihao Li
Weiming Li
Weixin Li
Wenbo Li
Wenshuo Li
Weijian Li
Yunan Li
Xirong Li
Xianhang Li
Xiaoyu Li
Xueqian Li
Xuanlin Li
Xianzhi Li
Yunqiang Li
Yanjing Li
Yansheng Li
Yawei Li
Yi Li
Yong Li
Yong-Lu Li
Yuhang Li
Yu-Jhe Li
Yuxi Li
Yunsheng Li
Yanwei Li
Zechao Li
Zejian Li
Zeju Li
Zekun Li
Zhaowen Li
Zheng Li
Zhenyu Li
Zhiheng Li
Zhi Li
Zhong Li
Zhuowei Li
Zhuowan Li
Zhuohang Li
Zizhang Li
Chen Li
Yuan-Fang Li
Dongze Lian
Xiaochen Lian
Zhouhui Lian
Long Lian
Qing Lian
Jin Lianbao
Jinxiu S. Liang
Dingkang Liang
Jiahao Liang
Jianming Liang
Jingyun Liang
Kevin J. Liang
Kaizhao Liang
Chen Liang
Jie Liang
Senwei Liang
Ding Liang
Jiajun Liang
Jian Liang
Kongming Liang
Siyuan Liang
Yuanzhi Liang
Zhengfa Liang
Mingfu Liang
Xiaodan Liang
Xuefeng Liang
Yuxuan Liang
Kang Liao
Liang Liao
Hong-Yuan Mark Liao
Wentong Liao
Haofu Liao
Yue Liao
Minghui Liao
Shengcai Liao
Ting-Hsuan Liao
Xin Liao
Yinghong Liao
Teck Yian Lim
Che-Tsung Lin
Chung-Ching Lin
Chen-Hsuan Lin
Cheng Lin
Chuming Lin
Chunyu Lin
Dahua Lin
Wei Lin
Zheng Lin
Huaijia Lin
Jason Lin
Jierui Lin
Jiaying Lin
Jie Lin
Kai-En Lin
Kevin Lin
Guangfeng Lin
Jiehong Lin
Feng Lin
Hang Lin
Kwan-Yee Lin
Ke Lin
Luojun Lin
Qinghong Lin
Xiangbo Lin
Yi Lin
Zudi Lin
Shijie Lin
Yiqun Lin
Tzu-Heng Lin
Ming Lin
Shaohui Lin
SongNan Lin
Ji Lin
Tsung-Yu Lin
Xudong Lin
Yancong Lin
Yen-Chen Lin
Yiming Lin
Yuewei Lin
Zhiqiu Lin
Zinan Lin
Zhe Lin
David B. Lindell
Zhixin Ling

Zhan Ling
Alexander Liniger
Venice Erin B. Liong
Joey Litalien
Or Litany
Roee Litman
Ron Litman
Jim Little
Dor Litvak
Shaoteng Liu
Shuaicheng Liu
Andrew Liu
Xian Liu
Shaohui Liu
Bei Liu
Bo Liu
Yong Liu
Ming Liu
Yanbin Liu
Chenxi Liu
Daqi Liu
Di Liu
Difan Liu
Dong Liu
Dongfang Liu
Daizong Liu
Xiao Liu
Fangyi Liu
Fengbei Liu
Fenglin Liu
Bin Liu
Yuang Liu
Ao Liu
Hong Liu
Hongfu Liu
Huidong Liu
Ziyi Liu
Feng Liu
Hao Liu
Jie Liu
Jialun Liu
Jiang Liu
Jing Liu
Jingya Liu
Jiaming Liu
Jun Liu
Juncheng Liu
Jiawei Liu
Hongyu Liu
Chuanbin Liu
Haotian Liu
Lingqiao Liu
Chang Liu
Han Liu
Liu Liu
Min Liu
Yingqi Liu
Aishan Liu
Bingyu Liu
Benlin Liu
Boxiao Liu
Chenchen Liu
Chuanjian Liu
Daqing Liu
Huan Liu
Haozhe Liu
Jiaheng Liu
Wei Liu
Jingzhou Liu
Jiyuan Liu
Lingbo Liu
Nian Liu
Peiye Liu
Qiankun Liu
Shenglan Liu
Shilong Liu
Wen Liu
Wenyu Liu
Weifeng Liu
Wu Liu
Xiaolong Liu
Yang Liu
Yanwei Liu
Yingcheng Liu
Yongfei Liu
Yihao Liu
Yu Liu
Yunze Liu
Ze Liu
Zhenhua Liu
Zhenguang Liu
Lin Liu
Lihao Liu
Pengju Liu
Xinhai Liu
Yunfei Liu
Meng Liu
Minghua Liu
Mingyuan Liu
Miao Liu
Peirong Liu
Ping Liu
Qingjie Liu
Ruoshi Liu
Risheng Liu
Songtao Liu
Xing Liu
Shikun Liu
Shuming Liu
Sheng Liu
Songhua Liu
Tongliang Liu
Weibo Liu
Weide Liu
Weizhe Liu
Wenxi Liu
Weiyang Liu
Xin Liu
Xiaobin Liu
Xudong Liu
Xiaoyi Liu
Xihui Liu
Xinchen Liu
Xingtong Liu
Xinpeng Liu
Xinyu Liu
Xianpeng Liu
Xu Liu
Xingyu Liu
Yongtuo Liu
Yahui Liu
Yangxin Liu
Yaoyao Liu
Yaojie Liu
Yuliang Liu

Yongcheng Liu
Yuan Liu
Yufan Liu
Yu-Lun Liu
Yun Liu
Yunfan Liu
Yuanzhong Liu
Zhuoran Liu
Zhen Liu
Zheng Liu
Zhijian Liu
Zhisong Liu
Ziquan Liu
Ziyu Liu
Zhihua Liu
Zechun Liu
Zhaoyang Liu
Zhengzhe Liu
Stephan Liwicki
Shao-Yuan Lo
Sylvain Lobry
Suhas Lohit
Vishnu Suresh Lokhande
Vincenzo Lomonaco
Chengjiang Long
Guodong Long
Fuchen Long
Shangbang Long
Yang Long
Zijun Long
Vasco Lopes
Antonio M. Lopez
Roberto Javier Lopez-Sastre
Tobias Lorenz
Javier Lorenzo-Navarro
Yujing Lou
Qian Lou
Xiankai Lu
Changsheng Lu
Huimin Lu
Yongxi Lu
Hao Lu
Hong Lu
Jiasen Lu
Juwei Lu
Fan Lu
Guangming Lu
Jiwen Lu
Shun Lu
Tao Lu
Xiaonan Lu
Yang Lu
Yao Lu
Yongchun Lu
Zhiwu Lu
Cheng Lu
Liying Lu
Guo Lu
Xuequan Lu
Yanye Lu
Yantao Lu
Yuhang Lu
Fujun Luan
Jonathon Luiten
Jovita Lukasik
Alan Lukezic
Jonathan Samuel Lumentut
Mayank Lunayach
Ao Luo
Canjie Luo
Chong Luo
Xu Luo
Grace Luo
Jun Luo
Katie Z. Luo
Tao Luo
Cheng Luo
Fangzhou Luo
Gen Luo
Lei Luo
Sihui Luo
Weixin Luo
Yan Luo
Xiaoyan Luo
Yong Luo
Yadan Luo
Hao Luo
Ruotian Luo
Mi Luo
Tiange Luo
Wenjie Luo
Wenhan Luo
Xiao Luo
Zhiming Luo
Zhipeng Luo
Zhengyi Luo
Diogo C. Luvizon
Zhaoyang Lv
Gengyu Lyu
Lingjuan Lyu
Jun Lyu
Yuanyuan Lyu
Youwei Lyu
Yueming Lyu
Bingpeng Ma
Chao Ma
Chongyang Ma
Congbo Ma
Chih-Yao Ma
Fan Ma
Lin Ma
Haoyu Ma
Hengbo Ma
Jianqi Ma
Jiawei Ma
Jiayi Ma
Kede Ma
Kai Ma
Lingni Ma
Lei Ma
Xu Ma
Ning Ma
Benteng Ma
Cheng Ma
Andy J. Ma
Long Ma
Zhanyu Ma
Zhiheng Ma
Qianli Ma
Shiqiang Ma
Sizhuo Ma
Shiqing Ma
Xiaolong Ma
Xinzhu Ma

Gautam B. Machiraju
Spandan Madan
Mathew Magimai-Doss
Luca Magri
Behrooz Mahasseni
Upal Mahbub
Siddharth Mahendran
Paridhi Maheshwari
Rishabh Maheshwary
Mohammed Mahmoud
Shishira R. R. Maiya
Sylwia Majchrowska
Arjun Majumdar
Puspita Majumdar
Orchid Majumder
Sagnik Majumder
Ilya Makarov
Farkhod F. Makhmudkhujaev
Yasushi Makihara
Ankur Mali
Mateusz Malinowski
Utkarsh Mall
Srikanth Malla
Clement Mallet
Dimitrios Mallis
Yunze Man
Dipu Manandhar
Massimiliano Mancini
Murari Mandal
Raunak Manekar
Karttikeya Mangalam
Puneet Mangla
Fabian Manhardt
Sivabalan Manivasagam
Fahim Mannan
Chengzhi Mao
Hanzi Mao
Jiayuan Mao
Junhua Mao
Zhiyuan Mao
Jiageng Mao
Yunyao Mao
Zhendong Mao
Alberto Marchisio
Diego Marcos
Riccardo Marin
Aram Markosyan
Renaud Marlet
Ricardo Marques
Miquel Martí i Rabadán
Diego Martin Arroyo
Niki Martinel
Brais Martinez
Julieta Martinez
Marc Masana
Tomohiro Mashita
Timothée Masquelier
Minesh Mathew
Tetsu Matsukawa
Marwan Mattar
Bruce A. Maxwell
Christoph Mayer
Mantas Mazeika
Pratik Mazumder
Scott McCloskey
Steven McDonagh
Ishit Mehta
Jie Mei
Kangfu Mei
Jieru Mei
Xiaoguang Mei
Givi Meishvili
Luke Melas-Kyriazi
Iaroslav Melekhov
Andres Mendez-Vazquez
Heydi Mendez-Vazquez
Matias Mendieta
Ricardo A. Mendoza-León
Chenlin Meng
Depu Meng
Rang Meng
Zibo Meng
Qingjie Meng
Qier Meng
Yanda Meng
Zihang Meng
Thomas Mensink
Fabian Mentzer
Christopher Metzler
Gregory P. Meyer
Vasileios Mezaris
Liang Mi
Lu Mi
Bo Miao
Changtao Miao
Zichen Miao
Qiguang Miao
Xin Miao
Zhongqi Miao
Frank Michel
Simone Milani
Ben Mildenhall
Roy V. Miles
Juhong Min
Kyle Min
Hyun-Seok Min
Weiqing Min
Yuecong Min
Zhixiang Min
Qi Ming
David Minnen
Aymen Mir
Deepak Mishra
Anand Mishra
Shlok K. Mishra
Niluthpol Mithun
Gaurav Mittal
Trisha Mittal
Daisuke Miyazaki
Kaichun Mo
Hong Mo
Zhipeng Mo
Davide Modolo
Abduallah A. Mohamed
Mohamed Afham Mohamed Aflal
Ron Mokady
Pavlo Molchanov
Davide Moltisanti
Liliane Momeni
Gianluca Monaci
Pascal Monasse
Ajoy Mondal
Tom Monnier

Aron Monszpart
Gyeongsik Moon
Suhong Moon
Taesup Moon
Sean Moran
Daniel Moreira
Pietro Morerio
Alexandre Morgand
Lia Morra
Ali Mosleh
Inbar Mosseri
Sayed Mohammad Mostafavi Isfahani
Saman Motamed
Ramy A. Mounir
Fangzhou Mu
Jiteng Mu
Norman Mu
Yasuhiro Mukaigawa
Ryan Mukherjee
Tanmoy Mukherjee
Yusuke Mukuta
Ravi Teja Mullapudi
Lea Müller
Matthias Müller
Martin Mundt
Nils Murrugarra-Llerena
Damien Muselet
Armin Mustafa
Muhammad Ferjad Naeem
Sauradip Nag
Hajime Nagahara
Pravin Nagar
Rajendra Nagar
Naveen Shankar Nagaraja
Varun Nagaraja
Tushar Nagarajan
Seungjun Nah
Gaku Nakano
Yuta Nakashima
Giljoo Nam
Seonghyeon Nam
Liangliang Nan
Yuesong Nan
Yeshwanth Napolean
Dinesh Reddy Narapureddy
Medhini Narasimhan
Supreeth Narasimhaswamy
Sriram Narayanan
Erickson R. Nascimento
Varun Nasery
K. L. Navaneet
Pablo Navarrete Michelini
Shant Navasardyan
Shah Nawaz
Nihal Nayak
Farhood Negin
Lukáš Neumann
Alejandro Newell
Evonne Ng
Kam Woh Ng
Tony Ng
Anh Nguyen
Tuan Anh Nguyen
Cuong Cao Nguyen
Ngoc Cuong Nguyen
Thanh Nguyen
Khoi Nguyen
Phi Le Nguyen
Phong Ha Nguyen
Tam Nguyen
Truong Nguyen
Anh Tuan Nguyen
Rang Nguyen
Thao Thi Phuong Nguyen
Van Nguyen Nguyen
Zhen-Liang Ni
Yao Ni
Shijie Nie
Xuecheng Nie
Yongwei Nie
Weizhi Nie
Ying Nie
Yinyu Nie
Kshitij N. Nikhal
Simon Niklaus
Xuefei Ning
Jifeng Ning
Yotam Nitzan
Di Niu
Shuaicheng Niu
Li Niu
Wei Niu
Yulei Niu
Zhenxing Niu
Albert No
Shohei Nobuhara
Nicoletta Noceti
Junhyug Noh
Sotiris Nousias
Slawomir Nowaczyk
Ewa M. Nowara
Valsamis Ntouskos
Gilberto Ochoa-Ruiz
Ferda Ofli
Jihyong Oh
Sangyun Oh
Youngtaek Oh
Hiroki Ohashi
Takahiro Okabe
Kemal Oksuz
Fumio Okura
Daniel Olmeda Reino
Matthew Olson
Carl Olsson
Roy Or-El
Alessandro Ortis
Guillermo Ortiz-Jimenez
Magnus Oskarsson
Ahmed A. A. Osman
Martin R. Oswald
Mayu Otani
Naima Otberdout
Cheng Ouyang
Jiahong Ouyang
Wanli Ouyang
Andrew Owens
Poojan B. Oza
Mete Ozay
A. Cengiz Oztireli
Gautam Pai
Tomas Pajdla
Umapada Pal

Simone Palazzo
Luca Palmieri
Bowen Pan
Hao Pan
Lili Pan
Tai-Yu Pan
Liang Pan
Chengwei Pan
Yingwei Pan
Xuran Pan
Jinshan Pan
Xinyu Pan
Liyuan Pan
Xingang Pan
Xingjia Pan
Zhihong Pan
Zizheng Pan
Priyadarshini Panda
Rameswar Panda
Rohit Pandey
Kaiyue Pang
Bo Pang
Guansong Pang
Jiangmiao Pang
Meng Pang
Tianyu Pang
Ziqi Pang
Omiros Pantazis
Andreas Panteli
Maja Pantic
Marina Paolanti
Joao P. Papa
Samuele Papa
Mike Papadakis
Dim P. Papadopoulos
George Papandreou
Constantin Pape
Toufiq Parag
Chethan Parameshwara
Shaifali Parashar
Alejandro Pardo
Rishubh Parihar
Sarah Parisot
JaeYoo Park
Gyeong-Moon Park
Hyojin Park
Hyoungseob Park
Jongchan Park
Jae Sung Park
Kiru Park
Chunghyun Park
Kwanyong Park
Sunghyun Park
Sungrae Park
Seongsik Park
Sanghyun Park
Sungjune Park
Taesung Park
Gaurav Parmar
Paritosh Parmar
Alvaro Parra
Despoina Paschalidou
Or Patashnik
Shivansh Patel
Pushpak Pati
Prashant W. Patil
Vaishakh Patil
Suvam Patra
Jay Patravali
Badri Narayana Patro
Angshuman Paul
Sudipta Paul
Rémi Pautrat
Nick E. Pears
Adithya Pediredla
Wenjie Pei
Shmuel Peleg
Latha Pemula
Bo Peng
Houwen Peng
Yue Peng
Liangzu Peng
Baoyun Peng
Jun Peng
Pai Peng
Sida Peng
Xi Peng
Yuxin Peng
Songyou Peng
Wei Peng
Weiqi Peng
Wen-Hsiao Peng
Pramuditha Perera
Juan C. Perez
Eduardo Pérez Pellitero
Juan-Manuel Perez-Rua
Federico Pernici
Marco Pesavento
Stavros Petridis
Ilya A. Petrov
Vladan Petrovic
Mathis Petrovich
Suzanne Petryk
Hieu Pham
Quang Pham
Khoi Pham
Tung Pham
Huy Phan
Stephen Phillips
Cheng Perng Phoo
David Picard
Marco Piccirilli
Georg Pichler
A. J. Piergiovanni
Vipin Pillai
Silvia L. Pintea
Giovanni Pintore
Robinson Piramuthu
Fiora Pirri
Theodoros Pissas
Fabio Pizzati
Benjamin Planche
Bryan Plummer
Matteo Poggi
Ashwini Pokle
Georgy E. Ponimatkin
Adrian Popescu
Stefan Popov
Nikola Popović
Ronald Poppe
Angelo Porrello
Michael Potter
Charalambos Poullis
Hadi Pouransari
Omid Poursaeed

Shraman Pramanick
Mantini Pranav
Dilip K. Prasad
Meghshyam Prasad
B. H. Pawan Prasad
Shitala Prasad
Prateek Prasanna
Ekta Prashnani
Derek S. Prijatelj
Luke Y. Prince
Véronique Prinet
Victor Adrian Prisacariu
James Pritts
Thomas Probst
Sergey Prokudin
Rita Pucci
Chi-Man Pun
Matthew Purri
Haozhi Qi
Lu Qi
Lei Qi
Xianbiao Qi
Yonggang Qi
Yuankai Qi
Siyuan Qi
Guocheng Qian
Hangwei Qian
Qi Qian
Deheng Qian
Shengsheng Qian
Wen Qian
Rui Qian
Yiming Qian
Shengju Qian
Shengyi Qian
Xuelin Qian
Zhenxing Qian
Nan Qiao
Xiaotian Qiao
Jing Qin
Can Qin
Siyang Qin
Hongwei Qin
Jie Qin
Minghai Qin
Yipeng Qin
Yongqiang Qin
Wenda Qin
Xuebin Qin
Yuzhe Qin
Yao Qin
Zhenyue Qin
Zhiwu Qing
Heqian Qiu
Jiayan Qiu
Jielin Qiu
Yue Qiu
Jiaxiong Qiu
Zhongxi Qiu
Shi Qiu
Zhaofan Qiu
Zhongnan Qu
Yanyun Qu
Kha Gia Quach
Yuhui Quan
Ruijie Quan
Mike Rabbat
Rahul Shekhar Rade
Filip Radenovic
Gorjan Radevski
Bogdan Raducanu
Francesco Ragusa
Shafin Rahman
Md Mahfuzur Rahman Siddiquee
Hossein Rahmani
Kiran Raja
Sivaramakrishnan Rajaraman
Jathushan Rajasegaran
Adnan Siraj Rakin
Michaël Ramamonjisoa
Chirag A. Raman
Shanmuganathan Raman
Vignesh Ramanathan
Vasili Ramanishka
Vikram V. Ramaswamy
Merey Ramazanova
Jason Rambach
Sai Saketh Rambhatla
Clément Rambour
Ashwin Ramesh Babu
Adín Ramírez Rivera
Arianna Rampini
Haoxi Ran
Aakanksha Rana
Aayush Jung Bahadur Rana
Kanchana N. Ranasinghe
Aneesh Rangnekar
Samrudhdhi B. Rangrej
Harsh Rangwani
Viresh Ranjan
Anyi Rao
Yongming Rao
Carolina Raposo
Michalis Raptis
Amir Rasouli
Vivek Rathod
Adepu Ravi Sankar
Avinash Ravichandran
Bharadwaj Ravichandran
Dripta S. Raychaudhuri
Adria Recasens
Simon Reiß
Davis Rempe
Daxuan Ren
Jiawei Ren
Jimmy Ren
Sucheng Ren
Dayong Ren
Zhile Ren
Dongwei Ren
Qibing Ren
Pengfei Ren
Zhenwen Ren
Xuqian Ren
Yixuan Ren
Zhongzheng Ren
Ambareesh Revanur
Hamed Rezazadegan Tavakoli
Rafael S. Rezende
Wonjong Rhee
Alexander Richard

Christian Richardt
Stephan R. Richter
Benjamin Riggan
Dominik Rivoir
Mamshad Nayeem Rizve
Joshua D. Robinson
Joseph Robinson
Chris Rockwell
Ranga Rodrigo
Andres C. Rodriguez
Carlos Rodriguez-Pardo
Marcus Rohrbach
Gemma Roig
Yu Rong
David A. Ross
Mohammad Rostami
Edward Rosten
Karsten Roth
Anirban Roy
Debaditya Roy
Shuvendu Roy
Ahana Roy Choudhury
Aruni Roy Chowdhury
Denys Rozumnyi
Shulan Ruan
Wenjie Ruan
Patrick Ruhkamp
Danila Rukhovich
Anian Ruoss
Chris Russell
Dan Ruta
Dawid Damian Rymarczyk
DongHun Ryu
Hyeonggon Ryu
Kwonyoung Ryu
Balasubramanian S.
Alexandre Sablayrolles
Mohammad Sabokrou
Arka Sadhu
Aniruddha Saha
Oindrila Saha
Pritish Sahu
Aneeshan Sain
Nirat Saini
Saurabh Saini
Takeshi Saitoh
Christos Sakaridis
Fumihiko Sakaue
Dimitrios Sakkos
Ken Sakurada
Parikshit V. Sakurikar
Rohit Saluja
Nermin Samet
Leo Sampaio Ferraz Ribeiro
Jorge Sanchez
Enrique Sanchez
Shengtian Sang
Anush Sankaran
Soubhik Sanyal
Nikolaos Sarafianos
Vishwanath Saragadam
István Sárándi
Saquib Sarfraz
Mert Bulent Sariyildiz
Anindya Sarkar
Pritam Sarkar
Paul-Edouard Sarlin
Hiroshi Sasaki
Takami Sato
Torsten Sattler
Ravi Kumar Satzoda
Axel Sauer
Stefano Savian
Artem Savkin
Manolis Savva
Gerald Schaefer
Simone Schaub-Meyer
Yoni Schirris
Samuel Schulter
Katja Schwarz
Jesse Scott
Sinisa Segvic
Constantin Marc Seibold
Lorenzo Seidenari
Matan Sela
Fadime Sener
Paul Hongsuck Seo
Kwanggyoon Seo
Hongje Seong
Dario Serez
Francesco Setti
Bryan Seybold
Mohamad Shahbazi
Shima Shahfar
Xinxin Shan
Caifeng Shan
Dandan Shan
Shawn Shan
Wei Shang
Jinghuan Shang
Jiaxiang Shang
Lei Shang
Sukrit Shankar
Ken Shao
Rui Shao
Jie Shao
Mingwen Shao
Aashish Sharma
Gaurav Sharma
Vivek Sharma
Abhishek Sharma
Yoli Shavit
Shashank Shekhar
Sumit Shekhar
Zhijie Shen
Fengyi Shen
Furao Shen
Jialie Shen
Jingjing Shen
Ziyi Shen
Linlin Shen
Guangyu Shen
Biluo Shen
Falong Shen
Jiajun Shen
Qiu Shen
Qiuhong Shen
Shuai Shen
Wang Shen
Yiqing Shen
Yunhang Shen
Siqi Shen
Bin Shen
Tianwei Shen

Xi Shen
Yilin Shen
Yuming Shen
Yucong Shen
Zhiqiang Shen
Lu Sheng
Yichen Sheng
Shivanand Venkanna Sheshappanavar
Shelly Sheynin
Baifeng Shi
Ruoxi Shi
Botian Shi
Hailin Shi
Jia Shi
Jing Shi
Shaoshuai Shi
Baoguang Shi
Boxin Shi
Hengcan Shi
Tianyang Shi
Xiaodan Shi
Yongjie Shi
Zhensheng Shi
Yinghuan Shi
Weiqi Shi
Wu Shi
Xuepeng Shi
Xiaoshuang Shi
Yujiao Shi
Zenglin Shi
Zhenmei Shi
Takashi Shibata
Meng-Li Shih
Yichang Shih
Hyunjung Shim
Dongseok Shim
Soshi Shimada
Inkyu Shin
Jinwoo Shin
Seungjoo Shin
Seungjae Shin
Koichi Shinoda
Suprosanna Shit
Palaiahnakote Shivakumara
Eli Shlizerman
Gaurav Shrivastava
Xiao Shu
Xiangbo Shu
Xiujun Shu
Yang Shu
Tianmin Shu
Jun Shu
Zhixin Shu
Bing Shuai
Maria Shugrina
Ivan Shugurov
Satya Narayan Shukla
Pranjay Shyam
Jianlou Si
Yawar Siddiqui
Alberto Signoroni
Pedro Silva
Jae-Young Sim
Oriane Siméoni
Martin Simon
Andrea Simonelli
Abhishek Singh
Ashish Singh
Dinesh Singh
Gurkirt Singh
Krishna Kumar Singh
Mannat Singh
Pravendra Singh
Rajat Vikram Singh
Utkarsh Singhal
Dipika Singhania
Vasu Singla
Harsh Sinha
Sudipta Sinha
Josef Sivic
Elena Sizikova
Geri Skenderi
Ivan Skorokhodov
Dmitriy Smirnov
Cameron Y. Smith
James S. Smith
Patrick Snape
Mattia Soldan
Hyeongseok Son
Sanghyun Son
Chuanbiao Song
Chen Song
Chunfeng Song
Dan Song
Dongjin Song
Hwanjun Song
Guoxian Song
Jiaming Song
Jie Song
Liangchen Song
Ran Song
Luchuan Song
Xibin Song
Li Song
Fenglong Song
Guoli Song
Guanglu Song
Zhenbo Song
Lin Song
Xinhang Song
Yang Song
Yibing Song
Rajiv Soundararajan
Hossein Souri
Cristovao Sousa
Riccardo Spezialetti
Leonidas Spinoulas
Michael W. Spratling
Deepak Sridhar
Srinath Sridhar
Gaurang Sriramanan
Vinkle Kumar Srivastav
Themos Stafylakis
Serban Stan
Anastasis Stathopoulos
Markus Steinberger
Jan Steinbrener
Sinisa Stekovic
Alexandros Stergiou
Gleb Sterkin
Rainer Stiefelhagen
Pierre Stock

Ombretta Strafforello
Julian Straub
Yannick Strümpler
Joerg Stueckler
Hang Su
Weijie Su
Jong-Chyi Su
Bing Su
Haisheng Su
Jinming Su
Yiyang Su
Yukun Su
Yuxin Su
Zhuo Su
Zhaoqi Su
Xiu Su
Yu-Chuan Su
Zhixun Su
Arulkumar Subramaniam
Akshayvarun Subramanya
A. Subramanyam
Swathikiran Sudhakaran
Yusuke Sugano
Masanori Suganuma
Yumin Suh
Yang Sui
Baochen Sun
Cheng Sun
Long Sun
Guolei Sun
Haoliang Sun
Haomiao Sun
He Sun
Hanqing Sun
Hao Sun
Lichao Sun
Jiachen Sun
Jiaming Sun
Jian Sun
Jin Sun
Jennifer J. Sun
Tiancheng Sun
Libo Sun
Peize Sun
Qianru Sun
Shanlin Sun
Yu Sun
Zhun Sun
Che Sun
Lin Sun
Tao Sun
Yiyou Sun
Chunyi Sun
Chong Sun
Weiwei Sun
Weixuan Sun
Xiuyu Sun
Yanan Sun
Zeren Sun
Zhaodong Sun
Zhiqing Sun
Minhyuk Sung
Jinli Suo
Simon Suo
Abhijit Suprem
Anshuman Suri
Saksham Suri
Joshua M. Susskind
Roman Suvorov
Gurumurthy Swaminathan
Robin Swanson
Paul Swoboda
Tabish A. Syed
Richard Szeliski
Fariborz Taherkhani
Yu-Wing Tai
Keita Takahashi
Walter Talbott
Gary Tam
Masato Tamura
Feitong Tan
Fuwen Tan
Shuhan Tan
Andong Tan
Bin Tan
Cheng Tan
Jianchao Tan
Lei Tan
Mingxing Tan
Xin Tan
Zichang Tan
Zhentao Tan
Kenichiro Tanaka
Masayuki Tanaka
Yushun Tang
Hao Tang
Jingqun Tang
Jinhui Tang
Kaihua Tang
Luming Tang
Lv Tang
Sheyang Tang
Shitao Tang
Siliang Tang
Shixiang Tang
Yansong Tang
Keke Tang
Chang Tang
Chenwei Tang
Jie Tang
Junshu Tang
Ming Tang
Peng Tang
Xu Tang
Yao Tang
Chen Tang
Fan Tang
Haoran Tang
Shengeng Tang
Yehui Tang
Zhipeng Tang
Ugo Tanielian
Chaofan Tao
Jiale Tao
Junli Tao
Renshuai Tao
An Tao
Guanhong Tao
Zhiqiang Tao
Makarand Tapaswi
Jean-Philippe G. Tarel
Juan J. Tarrio
Enzo Tartaglione
Keisuke Tateno
Zachary Teed

Ajinkya B. Tejankar
Bugra Tekin
Purva Tendulkar
Damien Teney
Minggui Teng
Chris Tensmeyer
Andrew Beng Jin Teoh
Philipp Terhörst
Kartik Thakral
Nupur Thakur
Kevin Thandiackal
Spyridon Thermos
Diego Thomas
William Thong
Yuesong Tian
Guanzhong Tian
Lin Tian
Shiqi Tian
Kai Tian
Meng Tian
Tai-Peng Tian
Zhuotao Tian
Shangxuan Tian
Tian Tian
Yapeng Tian
Yu Tian
Yuxin Tian
Leslie Ching Ow Tiong
Praveen Tirupattur
Garvita Tiwari
George Toderici
Antoine Toisoul
Aysim Toker
Tatiana Tommasi
Zhan Tong
Alessio Tonioni
Alessandro Torcinovich
Fabio Tosi
Matteo Toso
Hugo Touvron
Quan Hung Tran
Son Tran
Hung Tran
Ngoc-Trung Tran
Vinh Tran
Phong Tran
Giovanni Trappolini
Edith Tretschk
Subarna Tripathi
Shubhendu Trivedi
Eduard Trulls
Prune Truong
Thanh-Dat Truong
Tomasz Trzcinski
Sam Tsai
Yi-Hsuan Tsai
Ethan Tseng
Yu-Chee Tseng
Shahar Tsiper
Stavros Tsogkas
Shikui Tu
Zhigang Tu
Zhengzhong Tu
Richard Tucker
Sergey Tulyakov
Cigdem Turan
Daniyar Turmukhambetov
Victor G. Turrisi da Costa
Bartlomiej Twardowski
Christopher D. Twigg
Radim Tylecek
Mostofa Rafid Uddin
Md. Zasim Uddin
Kohei Uehara
Nicolas Ugrinovic
Youngjung Uh
Norimichi Ukita
Anwaar Ulhaq
Devesh Upadhyay
Paul Upchurch
Yoshitaka Ushiku
Yuzuko Utsumi
Mikaela Angelina Uy
Mohit Vaishnav
Pratik Vaishnavi
Jeya Maria Jose Valanarasu
Matias A. Valdenegro Toro
Diego Valsesia
Wouter Van Gansbeke
Nanne van Noord
Simon Vandenhende
Farshid Varno
Cristina Vasconcelos
Francisco Vasconcelos
Alex Vasilescu
Subeesh Vasu
Arun Balajee Vasudevan
Kanav Vats
Vaibhav S. Vavilala
Sagar Vaze
Javier Vazquez-Corral
Andrea Vedaldi
Olga Veksler
Andreas Velten
Sai H. Vemprala
Raviteja Vemulapalli
Shashanka Venkataramanan
Dor Verbin
Luisa Verdoliva
Manisha Verma
Yashaswi Verma
Constantin Vertan
Eli Verwimp
Deepak Vijaykeerthy
Pablo Villanueva
Ruben Villegas
Markus Vincze
Vibhav Vineet
Minh P. Vo
Huy V. Vo
Duc Minh Vo
Tomas Vojir
Igor Vozniak
Nicholas Vretos
Vibashan VS
Tuan-Anh Vu
Thang Vu
Mårten Wadenbäck
Neal Wadhwa
Aaron T. Walsman
Steven Walton
Jin Wan
Alvin Wan
Jia Wan

Jun Wan
Xiaoyue Wan
Fang Wan
Guowei Wan
Renjie Wan
Zhiqiang Wan
Ziyu Wan
Bastian Wandt
Dongdong Wang
Limin Wang
Haiyang Wang
Xiaobing Wang
Angtian Wang
Angelina Wang
Bing Wang
Bo Wang
Boyu Wang
Binghui Wang
Chen Wang
Chien-Yi Wang
Congli Wang
Qi Wang
Chengrui Wang
Rui Wang
Yiqun Wang
Cong Wang
Wenjing Wang
Dongkai Wang
Di Wang
Xiaogang Wang
Kai Wang
Zhizhong Wang
Fangjinhua Wang
Feng Wang
Hang Wang
Gaoang Wang
Guoqing Wang
Guangcong Wang
Guangzhi Wang
Hanqing Wang
Hao Wang
Haohan Wang
Haoran Wang
Hong Wang
Haotao Wang
Hu Wang
Huan Wang
Hua Wang
Hui-Po Wang
Hengli Wang
Hanyu Wang
Hongxing Wang
Jingwen Wang
Jialiang Wang
Jian Wang
Jianyi Wang
Jiashun Wang
Jiahao Wang
Tsun-Hsuan Wang
Xiaoqian Wang
Jinqiao Wang
Jun Wang
Jianzong Wang
Kaihong Wang
Ke Wang
Lei Wang
Lingjing Wang
Linnan Wang
Lin Wang
Liansheng Wang
Mengjiao Wang
Manning Wang
Nannan Wang
Peihao Wang
Jiayun Wang
Pu Wang
Qiang Wang
Qiufeng Wang
Qilong Wang
Qiangchang Wang
Qin Wang
Qing Wang
Ruocheng Wang
Ruibin Wang
Ruisheng Wang
Ruizhe Wang
Runqi Wang
Runzhong Wang
Wenxuan Wang
Sen Wang
Shangfei Wang
Shaofei Wang
Shijie Wang
Shiqi Wang
Zhibo Wang
Song Wang
Xinjiang Wang
Tai Wang
Tao Wang
Teng Wang
Xiang Wang
Tianren Wang
Tiantian Wang
Tianyi Wang
Fengjiao Wang
Wei Wang
Miaohui Wang
Suchen Wang
Siyue Wang
Yaoming Wang
Xiao Wang
Ze Wang
Biao Wang
Chaofei Wang
Dong Wang
Gu Wang
Guangrun Wang
Guangming Wang
Guo-Hua Wang
Haoqing Wang
Hesheng Wang
Huafeng Wang
Jinghua Wang
Jingdong Wang
Jingjing Wang
Jingya Wang
Jingkang Wang
Jiakai Wang
Junke Wang
Kuo Wang
Lichen Wang
Lizhi Wang
Longguang Wang
Mang Wang
Mei Wang

Min Wang
Peng-Shuai Wang
Run Wang
Shaoru Wang
Shuhui Wang
Tan Wang
Tiancai Wang
Tianqi Wang
Wenhai Wang
Wenzhe Wang
Xiaobo Wang
Xiudong Wang
Xu Wang
Yajie Wang
Yan Wang
Yuan-Gen Wang
Yingqian Wang
Yizhi Wang
Yulin Wang
Yu Wang
Yujie Wang
Yunhe Wang
Yuxi Wang
Yaowei Wang
Yiwei Wang
Zezheng Wang
Hongzhi Wang
Zhiqiang Wang
Ziteng Wang
Ziwei Wang
Zheng Wang
Zhenyu Wang
Binglu Wang
Zhongdao Wang
Ce Wang
Weining Wang
Weiyao Wang
Wenbin Wang
Wenguan Wang
Guangting Wang
Haolin Wang
Haiyan Wang
Huiyu Wang
Naiyan Wang
Jingbo Wang
Jinpeng Wang
Jiaqi Wang
Liyuan Wang
Lizhen Wang
Ning Wang
Wenqian Wang
Sheng-Yu Wang
Weimin Wang
Xiaohan Wang
Yifan Wang
Yi Wang
Yongtao Wang
Yizhou Wang
Zhuo Wang
Zhe Wang
Xudong Wang
Xiaofang Wang
Xinggang Wang
Xiaosen Wang
Xiaosong Wang
Xiaoyang Wang
Lijun Wang
Xinlong Wang
Xuan Wang
Xue Wang
Yangang Wang
Yaohui Wang
Yu-Chiang Frank Wang
Yida Wang
Yilin Wang
Yi Ru Wang
Yali Wang
Yinglong Wang
Yufu Wang
Yujiang Wang
Yuwang Wang
Yuting Wang
Yang Wang
Yu-Xiong Wang
Yixu Wang
Ziqi Wang
Zhicheng Wang
Zeyu Wang
Zhaowen Wang
Zhenyi Wang
Zhenzhi Wang
Zhijie Wang
Zhiyong Wang
Zhongling Wang
Zhuowei Wang
Zian Wang
Zifu Wang
Zihao Wang
Zirui Wang
Ziyan Wang
Wenxiao Wang
Zhen Wang
Zhepeng Wang
Zi Wang
Zihao W. Wang
Steven L. Waslander
Olivia Watkins
Daniel Watson
Silvan Weder
Dongyoon Wee
Dongming Wei
Tianyi Wei
Jia Wei
Dong Wei
Fangyun Wei
Longhui Wei
Mingqiang Wei
Xinyue Wei
Chen Wei
Donglai Wei
Pengxu Wei
Xing Wei
Xiu-Shen Wei
Wenqi Wei
Guoqiang Wei
Wei Wei
XingKui Wei
Xian Wei
Xingxing Wei
Yake Wei
Yuxiang Wei
Yi Wei
Luca Weihs
Michael Weinmann
Martin Weinmann

Congcong Wen
Chuan Wen
Jie Wen
Sijia Wen
Song Wen
Chao Wen
Xiang Wen
Zeyi Wen
Xin Wen
Yilin Wen
Yijia Weng
Shuchen Weng
Junwu Weng
Wenming Weng
Renliang Weng
Zhenyu Weng
Xinshuo Weng
Nicholas J. Westlake
Gordon Wetzstein
Lena M. Widin Klasén
Rick Wildes
Bryan M. Williams
Williem Williem
Ole Winther
Scott Wisdom
Alex Wong
Chau-Wai Wong
Kwan-Yee K. Wong
Yongkang Wong
Scott Workman
Marcel Worring
Michael Wray
Safwan Wshah
Xiang Wu
Aming Wu
Chongruo Wu
Cho-Ying Wu
Chunpeng Wu
Chenyan Wu
Ziyi Wu
Fuxiang Wu
Gang Wu
Haiping Wu
Huisi Wu
Jane Wu
Jialian Wu
Jing Wu
Jinjian Wu
Jianlong Wu
Xian Wu
Lifang Wu
Lifan Wu
Minye Wu
Qianyi Wu
Rongliang Wu
Rui Wu
Shiqian Wu
Shuzhe Wu
Shangzhe Wu
Tsung-Han Wu
Tz-Ying Wu
Ting-Wei Wu
Jiannan Wu
Zhiliang Wu
Yu Wu
Chenyun Wu
Dayan Wu
Dongxian Wu
Fei Wu
Hefeng Wu
Jianxin Wu
Weibin Wu
Wenxuan Wu
Wenhao Wu
Xiao Wu
Yicheng Wu
Yuanwei Wu
Yu-Huan Wu
Zhenxin Wu
Zhenyu Wu
Wei Wu
Peng Wu
Xiaohe Wu
Xindi Wu
Xinxing Wu
Xinyi Wu
Xingjiao Wu
Xiongwei Wu
Yangzheng Wu
Yanzhao Wu
Yawen Wu
Yong Wu
Yi Wu
Ying Nian Wu
Zhenyao Wu
Zhonghua Wu
Zongze Wu
Zuxuan Wu
Stefanie Wuhrer
Teng Xi
Jianing Xi
Fei Xia
Haifeng Xia
Menghan Xia
Yuanqing Xia
Zhihua Xia
Xiaobo Xia
Weihao Xia
Shihong Xia
Yan Xia
Yong Xia
Zhaoyang Xia
Zhihao Xia
Chuhua Xian
Yongqin Xian
Wangmeng Xiang
Fanbo Xiang
Tiange Xiang
Tao Xiang
Liuyu Xiang
Xiaoyu Xiang
Zhiyu Xiang
Aoran Xiao
Chunxia Xiao
Fanyi Xiao
Jimin Xiao
Jun Xiao
Taihong Xiao
Anqi Xiao
Junfei Xiao
Jing Xiao
Liang Xiao
Yang Xiao
Yuting Xiao
Yijun Xiao

Yao Xiao
Zeyu Xiao
Zhisheng Xiao
Zihao Xiao
Binhui Xie
Christopher Xie
Haozhe Xie
Jin Xie
Guo-Sen Xie
Hongtao Xie
Ming-Kun Xie
Tingting Xie
Chaohao Xie
Weicheng Xie
Xudong Xie
Jiyang Xie
Xiaohua Xie
Yuan Xie
Zhenyu Xie
Ning Xie
Xianghui Xie
Xiufeng Xie
You Xie
Yutong Xie
Fuyong Xing
Yifan Xing
Zhen Xing
Yuanjun Xiong
Jinhui Xiong
Weihua Xiong
Hongkai Xiong
Zhitong Xiong
Yuanhao Xiong
Yunyang Xiong
Yuwen Xiong
Zhiwei Xiong
Yuliang Xiu
An Xu
Chang Xu
Chenliang Xu
Chengming Xu
Chenshu Xu
Xiang Xu
Huijuan Xu
Zhe Xu
Jie Xu
Jingyi Xu
Jiarui Xu
Yinghao Xu
Kele Xu
Ke Xu
Li Xu
Linchuan Xu
Linning Xu
Mengde Xu
Mengmeng Frost Xu
Min Xu
Mingye Xu
Jun Xu
Ning Xu
Peng Xu
Runsheng Xu
Sheng Xu
Wenqiang Xu
Xiaogang Xu
Renzhe Xu
Kaidi Xu
Yi Xu
Chi Xu
Qiuling Xu
Baobei Xu
Feng Xu
Haohang Xu
Haofei Xu
Lan Xu
Mingze Xu
Songcen Xu
Weipeng Xu
Wenjia Xu
Wenju Xu
Xiangyu Xu
Xin Xu
Yinshuang Xu
Yixing Xu
Yuting Xu
Yanyu Xu
Zhenbo Xu
Zhiliang Xu
Zhiyuan Xu
Xiaohao Xu
Yanwu Xu
Yan Xu
Yiran Xu
Yifan Xu
Yufei Xu
Yong Xu
Zichuan Xu
Zenglin Xu
Zexiang Xu
Zhan Xu
Zheng Xu
Zhiwei Xu
Ziyue Xu
Shiyu Xuan
Hanyu Xuan
Fei Xue
Jianru Xue
Mingfu Xue
Qinghan Xue
Tianfan Xue
Chao Xue
Chuhui Xue
Nan Xue
Zhou Xue
Xiangyang Xue
Yuan Xue
Abhay Yadav
Ravindra Yadav
Kota Yamaguchi
Toshihiko Yamasaki
Kohei Yamashita
Chaochao Yan
Feng Yan
Kun Yan
Qingsen Yan
Qixin Yan
Rui Yan
Siming Yan
Xinchen Yan
Yaping Yan
Bin Yan
Qingan Yan
Shen Yan
Shipeng Yan
Xu Yan

Yan Yan
Yichao Yan
Zhaoyi Yan
Zike Yan
Zhiqiang Yan
Hongliang Yan
Zizheng Yan
Jiewen Yang
Anqi Joyce Yang
Shan Yang
Anqi Yang
Antoine Yang
Bo Yang
Baoyao Yang
Chenhongyi Yang
Dingkang Yang
De-Nian Yang
Dong Yang
David Yang
Fan Yang
Fengyu Yang
Fengting Yang
Fei Yang
Gengshan Yang
Heng Yang
Han Yang
Huan Yang
Yibo Yang
Jiancheng Yang
Jihan Yang
Jiawei Yang
Jiayu Yang
Jie Yang
Jinfa Yang
Jingkang Yang
Jinyu Yang
Cheng-Fu Yang
Ji Yang
Jianyu Yang
Kailun Yang
Tian Yang
Luyu Yang
Liang Yang
Li Yang
Michael Ying Yang
Yang Yang
Muli Yang
Le Yang
Qiushi Yang
Ren Yang
Ruihan Yang
Shuang Yang
Siyuan Yang
Su Yang
Shiqi Yang
Taojiannan Yang
Tianyu Yang
Lei Yang
Wanzhao Yang
Shuai Yang
William Yang
Wei Yang
Xiaofeng Yang
Xiaoshan Yang
Xin Yang
Xuan Yang
Xu Yang
Xingyi Yang
Xitong Yang
Jing Yang
Yanchao Yang
Wenming Yang
Yujiu Yang
Herb Yang
Jianfei Yang
Jinhui Yang
Chuanguang Yang
Guanglei Yang
Haitao Yang
Kewei Yang
Linlin Yang
Lijin Yang
Longrong Yang
Meng Yang
MingKun Yang
Sibei Yang
Shicai Yang
Tong Yang
Wen Yang
Xi Yang
Xiaolong Yang
Xue Yang
Yubin Yang
Ze Yang
Ziyi Yang
Yi Yang
Linjie Yang
Yuzhe Yang
Yiding Yang
Zhenpei Yang
Zhaohui Yang
Zhengyuan Yang
Zhibo Yang
Zongxin Yang
Hantao Yao
Mingde Yao
Rui Yao
Taiping Yao
Ting Yao
Cong Yao
Qingsong Yao
Quanming Yao
Xu Yao
Yuan Yao
Yao Yao
Yazhou Yao
Jiawen Yao
Shunyu Yao
Pew-Thian Yap
Sudhir Yarram
Rajeev Yasarla
Peng Ye
Botao Ye
Mao Ye
Fei Ye
Hanrong Ye
Jingwen Ye
Jinwei Ye
Jiarong Ye
Mang Ye
Meng Ye
Qi Ye
Qian Ye
Qixiang Ye
Junjie Ye

Sheng Ye
Nanyang Ye
Yufei Ye
Xiaoqing Ye
Ruolin Ye
Yousef Yeganeh
Chun-Hsiao Yeh
Raymond A. Yeh
Yu-Ying Yeh
Kai Yi
Chang Yi
Renjiao Yi
Xinping Yi
Peng Yi
Alper Yilmaz
Junho Yim
Hui Yin
Bangjie Yin
Jia-Li Yin
Miao Yin
Wenzhe Yin
Xuwang Yin
Ming Yin
Yu Yin
Aoxiong Yin
Kangxue Yin
Tianwei Yin
Wei Yin
Xianghua Ying
Rio Yokota
Tatsuya Yokota
Naoto Yokoya
Ryo Yonetani
Ki Yoon Yoo
Jinsu Yoo
Sunjae Yoon
Jae Shin Yoon
Jihun Yoon
Sung-Hoon Yoon
Ryota Yoshihashi
Yusuke Yoshiyasu
Chenyu You
Haoran You
Haoxuan You
Yang You
Quanzeng You
Tackgeun You
Kaichao You
Shan You
Xinge You
Yurong You
Baosheng Yu
Bei Yu
Haichao Yu
Hao Yu
Chaohui Yu
Fisher Yu
Jin-Gang Yu
Jiyang Yu
Jason J. Yu
Jiashuo Yu
Hong-Xing Yu
Lei Yu
Mulin Yu
Ning Yu
Peilin Yu
Qi Yu
Qian Yu
Rui Yu
Shuzhi Yu
Gang Yu
Tan Yu
Weijiang Yu
Xin Yu
Bingyao Yu
Ye Yu
Hanchao Yu
Yingchen Yu
Tao Yu
Xiaotian Yu
Qing Yu
Houjian Yu
Changqian Yu
Jing Yu
Jun Yu
Shujian Yu
Xiang Yu
Zhaofei Yu
Zhenbo Yu
Yinfeng Yu
Zhuoran Yu
Zitong Yu
Bo Yuan
Jiangbo Yuan
Liangzhe Yuan
Weihao Yuan
Jianbo Yuan
Xiaoyun Yuan
Ye Yuan
Li Yuan
Geng Yuan
Jialin Yuan
Maoxun Yuan
Peng Yuan
Xin Yuan
Yuan Yuan
Yuhui Yuan
Yixuan Yuan
Zheng Yuan
Mehmet Kerim Yücel
Kaiyu Yue
Haixiao Yue
Heeseung Yun
Sangdoo Yun
Tian Yun
Mahmut Yurt
Ekim Yurtsever
Ahmet Yüzügüler
Edouard Yvinec
Eloi Zablocki
Christopher Zach
Muhammad Zaigham Zaheer
Pierluigi Zama Ramirez
Yuhang Zang
Pietro Zanuttigh
Alexey Zaytsev
Bernhard Zeisl
Haitian Zeng
Pengpeng Zeng
Jiabei Zeng
Runhao Zeng
Wei Zeng
Yawen Zeng
Yi Zeng

Yiming Zeng
Tieyong Zeng
Huanqiang Zeng
Dan Zeng
Yu Zeng
Wei Zhai
Yuanhao Zhai
Fangneng Zhan
Kun Zhan
Xiong Zhang
Jingdong Zhang
Jiangning Zhang
Zhilu Zhang
Gengwei Zhang
Dongsu Zhang
Hui Zhang
Binjie Zhang
Bo Zhang
Tianhao Zhang
Cecilia Zhang
Jing Zhang
Chaoning Zhang
Chenxu Zhang
Chi Zhang
Chris Zhang
Yabin Zhang
Zhao Zhang
Rufeng Zhang
Chaoyi Zhang
Zheng Zhang
Da Zhang
Yi Zhang
Edward Zhang
Xin Zhang
Feifei Zhang
Feilong Zhang
Yuqi Zhang
GuiXuan Zhang
Hanlin Zhang
Hanwang Zhang
Hanzhen Zhang
Haotian Zhang
He Zhang
Haokui Zhang
Hongyuan Zhang
Hengrui Zhang
Hongming Zhang
Mingfang Zhang
Jianpeng Zhang
Jiaming Zhang
Jichao Zhang
Jie Zhang
Jingfeng Zhang
Jingyi Zhang
Jinnian Zhang
David Junhao Zhang
Junjie Zhang
Junzhe Zhang
Jiawan Zhang
Jingyang Zhang
Kai Zhang
Lei Zhang
Lihua Zhang
Lu Zhang
Miao Zhang
Minjia Zhang
Mingjin Zhang
Qi Zhang
Qian Zhang
Qilong Zhang
Qiming Zhang
Qiang Zhang
Richard Zhang
Ruimao Zhang
Ruisi Zhang
Ruixin Zhang
Runze Zhang
Qilin Zhang
Shan Zhang
Shanshan Zhang
Xi Sheryl Zhang
Song-Hai Zhang
Chongyang Zhang
Kaihao Zhang
Songyang Zhang
Shu Zhang
Siwei Zhang
Shujian Zhang
Tianyun Zhang
Tong Zhang
Tao Zhang
Wenwei Zhang
Wenqiang Zhang
Wen Zhang
Xiaolin Zhang
Xingchen Zhang
Xingxuan Zhang
Xiuming Zhang
Xiaoshuai Zhang
Xuanmeng Zhang
Xuanyang Zhang
Xucong Zhang
Xingxing Zhang
Xikun Zhang
Xiaohan Zhang
Yahui Zhang
Yunhua Zhang
Yan Zhang
Yanghao Zhang
Yifei Zhang
Yifan Zhang
Yi-Fan Zhang
Yihao Zhang
Yingliang Zhang
Youshan Zhang
Yulun Zhang
Yushu Zhang
Yixiao Zhang
Yide Zhang
Zhongwen Zhang
Bowen Zhang
Chen-Lin Zhang
Zehua Zhang
Zekun Zhang
Zeyu Zhang
Xiaowei Zhang
Yifeng Zhang
Cheng Zhang
Hongguang Zhang
Yuexi Zhang
Fa Zhang
Guofeng Zhang
Hao Zhang
Haofeng Zhang
Hongwen Zhang

Hua Zhang
Jiaxin Zhang
Zhenyu Zhang
Jian Zhang
Jianfeng Zhang
Jiao Zhang
Jiakai Zhang
Lefei Zhang
Le Zhang
Mi Zhang
Min Zhang
Ning Zhang
Pan Zhang
Pu Zhang
Qing Zhang
Renrui Zhang
Shifeng Zhang
Shuo Zhang
Shaoxiong Zhang
Weizhong Zhang
Xi Zhang
Xiaomei Zhang
Xinyu Zhang
Yin Zhang
Zicheng Zhang
Zihao Zhang
Ziqi Zhang
Zhaoxiang Zhang
Zhen Zhang
Zhipeng Zhang
Zhixing Zhang
Zhizheng Zhang
Jiawei Zhang
Zhong Zhang
Pingping Zhang
Yixin Zhang
Kui Zhang
Lingzhi Zhang
Huaiwen Zhang
Quanshi Zhang
Zhoutong Zhang
Yuhang Zhang
Yuting Zhang
Zhang Zhang
Ziming Zhang
Zhizhong Zhang
Qilong Zhangli
Bingyin Zhao
Bin Zhao
Chenglong Zhao
Lei Zhao
Feng Zhao
Gangming Zhao
Haiyan Zhao
Hao Zhao
Handong Zhao
Hengshuang Zhao
Yinan Zhao
Jiaojiao Zhao
Jiaqi Zhao
Jing Zhao
Kaili Zhao
Haojie Zhao
Yucheng Zhao
Longjiao Zhao
Long Zhao
Qingsong Zhao
Qingyu Zhao
Rui Zhao
Rui-Wei Zhao
Sicheng Zhao
Shuang Zhao
Siyan Zhao
Zelin Zhao
Shiyu Zhao
Wang Zhao
Tiesong Zhao
Qian Zhao
Wangbo Zhao
Xi-Le Zhao
Xu Zhao
Yajie Zhao
Yang Zhao
Ying Zhao
Yin Zhao
Yizhou Zhao
Yunhan Zhao
Yuyang Zhao
Yue Zhao
Yuzhi Zhao
Bowen Zhao
Pu Zhao
Bingchen Zhao
Borui Zhao
Fuqiang Zhao
Hanbin Zhao
Jian Zhao
Mingyang Zhao
Na Zhao
Rongchang Zhao
Ruiqi Zhao
Shuai Zhao
Wenda Zhao
Wenliang Zhao
Xiangyun Zhao
Yifan Zhao
Yaping Zhao
Zhou Zhao
He Zhao
Jie Zhao
Xibin Zhao
Xiaoqi Zhao
Zhengyu Zhao
Jin Zhe
Chuanxia Zheng
Huan Zheng
Hao Zheng
Jia Zheng
Jian-Qing Zheng
Shuai Zheng
Meng Zheng
Mingkai Zheng
Qian Zheng
Qi Zheng
Wu Zheng
Yinqiang Zheng
Yufeng Zheng
Yutong Zheng
Yalin Zheng
Yu Zheng
Feng Zheng
Zhaoheng Zheng
Haitian Zheng
Kang Zheng
Bolun Zheng

Haiyong Zheng
Mingwu Zheng
Sipeng Zheng
Tu Zheng
Wenzhao Zheng
Xiawu Zheng
Yinglin Zheng
Zhuo Zheng
Zilong Zheng
Kecheng Zheng
Zerong Zheng
Shuaifeng Zhi
Tiancheng Zhi
Jia-Xing Zhong
Yiwu Zhong
Fangwei Zhong
Zhihang Zhong
Yaoyao Zhong
Yiran Zhong
Zhun Zhong
Zichun Zhong
Bo Zhou
Boyao Zhou
Brady Zhou
Mo Zhou
Chunluan Zhou
Dingfu Zhou
Fan Zhou
Jingkai Zhou
Honglu Zhou
Jiaming Zhou
Jiahuan Zhou
Jun Zhou
Kaiyang Zhou
Keyang Zhou
Kuangqi Zhou
Lei Zhou
Lihua Zhou
Man Zhou
Mingyi Zhou
Mingyuan Zhou
Ning Zhou
Peng Zhou
Penghao Zhou
Qianyi Zhou
Shuigeng Zhou
Shangchen Zhou
Huayi Zhou
Zhize Zhou
Sanping Zhou
Qin Zhou
Tao Zhou
Wenbo Zhou
Xiangdong Zhou
Xiao-Yun Zhou
Xiao Zhou
Yang Zhou
Yipin Zhou
Zhenyu Zhou
Hao Zhou
Chu Zhou
Daquan Zhou
Da-Wei Zhou
Hang Zhou
Kang Zhou
Qianyu Zhou
Sheng Zhou
Wenhui Zhou
Xingyi Zhou
Yan-Jie Zhou
Yiyi Zhou
Yu Zhou
Yuan Zhou
Yuqian Zhou
Yuxuan Zhou
Zixiang Zhou
Wengang Zhou
Shuchang Zhou
Tianfei Zhou
Yichao Zhou
Alex Zhu
Chenchen Zhu
Deyao Zhu
Xiatian Zhu
Guibo Zhu
Haidong Zhu
Hao Zhu
Hongzi Zhu
Rui Zhu
Jing Zhu
Jianke Zhu
Junchen Zhu
Lei Zhu
Lingyu Zhu
Luyang Zhu
Menglong Zhu
Peihao Zhu
Hui Zhu
Xiaofeng Zhu
Tyler (Lixuan) Zhu
Wentao Zhu
Xiangyu Zhu
Xinqi Zhu
Xinxin Zhu
Xinliang Zhu
Yangguang Zhu
Yichen Zhu
Yixin Zhu
Yanjun Zhu
Yousong Zhu
Yuhao Zhu
Ye Zhu
Feng Zhu
Zhen Zhu
Fangrui Zhu
Jinjing Zhu
Linchao Zhu
Pengfei Zhu
Sijie Zhu
Xiaobin Zhu
Xiaoguang Zhu
Zezhou Zhu
Zhenyao Zhu
Kai Zhu
Pengkai Zhu
Bingbing Zhuang
Chengyuan Zhuang
Liansheng Zhuang
Peiye Zhuang
Yixin Zhuang
Yihong Zhuang
Junbao Zhuo
Andrea Ziani
Bartosz Zieliński
Primo Zingaretti

Nikolaos Zioulis
Andrew Zisserman
Yael Ziv
Liu Ziyin
Xingxing Zou
Danping Zou
Qi Zou
Shihao Zou
Xueyan Zou
Yang Zou
Yuliang Zou
Zihang Zou
Chuhang Zou
Dongqing Zou
Xu Zou
Zhiming Zou
Maria A. Zuluaga
Xinxin Zuo
Zhiwen Zuo
Reyer Zwiggelaar

Contents – Part XXXIII

SimpleRecon: 3D Reconstruction Without 3D Convolutions 1
Mohamed Sayed, John Gibson, Jamie Watson, Victor Prisacariu, Michael Firman, and Clément Godard

Structure and Motion from Casual Videos 20
Zhoutong Zhang, Forrester Cole, Zhengqi Li, Michael Rubinstein, Noah Snavely, and William T. Freeman

What Matters for 3D Scene Flow Network 38
Guangming Wang, Yunzhe Hu, Zhe Liu, Yiyang Zhou, Masayoshi Tomizuka, Wei Zhan, and Hesheng Wang

Correspondence Reweighted Translation Averaging 56
Lalit Manam and Venu Madhav Govindu

Neural Strands: Learning Hair Geometry and Appearance from Multi-view Images 73
Radu Alexandru Rosu, Shunsuke Saito, Ziyan Wang, Chenglei Wu, Sven Behnke, and Giljoo Nam

GraphCSPN: Geometry-Aware Depth Completion via Dynamic GCNs 90
Xin Liu, Xiaofei Shao, Bo Wang, Yali Li, and Shengjin Wang

Objects Can Move: 3D Change Detection by Geometric Transformation Consistency 108
Aikaterini Adam, Torsten Sattler, Konstantinos Karantzalos, and Tomas Pajdla

Language-Grounded Indoor 3D Semantic Segmentation in the Wild 125
David Rozenberszki, Or Litany, and Angela Dai

Beyond Periodicity: Towards a Unifying Framework for Activations in Coordinate-MLPs 142
Sameera Ramasinghe and Simon Lucey

Deforming Radiance Fields with Cages 159
Tianhan Xu and Tatsuya Harada

FLEX: Extrinsic Parameters-free Multi-view 3D Human Motion Reconstruction 176
Brian Gordon, Sigal Raab, Guy Azov, Raja Giryes, and Daniel Cohen-Or

MODE: Multi-view Omnidirectional Depth Estimation with 360° Cameras 197
Ming Li, Xueqian Jin, Xuejiao Hu, Jingzhao Dai, Sidan Du, and Yang Li

GigaDepth: Learning Depth from Structured Light with Branching Neural Networks 214
Simon Schreiberhuber, Jean-Baptiste Weibel, Timothy Patten, and Markus Vincze

ActiveNeRF: Learning Where to See with Uncertainty Estimation 230
Xuran Pan, Zihang Lai, Shiji Song, and Gao Huang

PoserNet: Refining Relative Camera Poses Exploiting Object Detections 247
Matteo Taiana, Matteo Toso, Stuart James, and Alessio Del Bue

Gaussian Activated Neural Radiance Fields for High Fidelity Reconstruction and Pose Estimation 264
Shin-Fang Chng, Sameera Ramasinghe, Jamie Sherrah, and Simon Lucey

Unbiased Gradient Estimation for Differentiable Surface Splatting via Poisson Sampling 281
Jan U. Müller, Michael Weinmann, and Reinhard Klein

Towards Learning Neural Representations from Shadows 300
Kushagra Tiwary, Tzofi Klinghoffer, and Ramesh Raskar

Class-Incremental Novel Class Discovery 317
Subhankar Roy, Mingxuan Liu, Zhun Zhong, Nicu Sebe, and Elisa Ricci

Unknown-Oriented Learning for Open Set Domain Adaptation 334
Jie Liu, Xiaoqing Guo, and Yixuan Yuan

Prototype-Guided Continual Adaptation for Class-Incremental Unsupervised Domain Adaptation 351
Hongbin Lin, Yifan Zhang, Zhen Qiu, Shuaicheng Niu, Chuang Gan, Yanxia Liu, and Mingkui Tan

DecoupleNet: Decoupled Network for Domain Adaptive Semantic Segmentation 369
Xin Lai, Zhuotao Tian, Xiaogang Xu, Yingcong Chen, Shu Liu, Hengshuang Zhao, Liwei Wang, and Jiaya Jia

Class-Agnostic Object Counting Robust to Intraclass Diversity 388
Shenjian Gong, Shanshan Zhang, Jian Yang, Dengxin Dai, and Bernt Schiele

Burn After Reading: Online Adaptation for Cross-domain Streaming Data 404
Luyu Yang, Mingfei Gao, Zeyuan Chen, Ran Xu, Abhinav Shrivastava, and Chetan Ramaiah

Mind the Gap in Distilling StyleGANs 423
Guodong Xu, Yuenan Hou, Ziwei Liu, and Chen Change Loy

Improving Test-Time Adaptation Via Shift-Agnostic Weight Regularization and Nearest Source Prototypes 440
Sungha Choi, Seunghan Yang, Seokeon Choi, and Sungrack Yun

Learning Instance-Specific Adaptation for Cross-Domain Segmentation 459
Yuliang Zou, Zizhao Zhang, Chun-Liang Li, Han Zhang, Tomas Pfister, and Jia-Bin Huang

RegionCL: Exploring Contrastive Region Pairs for Self-supervised Representation Learning 477
Yufei Xu, Qiming Zhang, Jing Zhang, and Dacheng Tao

Long-Tailed Class Incremental Learning 495
Xialei Liu, Yu-Song Hu, Xu-Sheng Cao, Andrew D. Bagdanov, Ke Li, and Ming-Ming Cheng

DLCFT: Deep Linear Continual Fine-Tuning for General Incremental Learning 513
Hyounguk Shon, Janghyeon Lee, Seung Hwan Kim, and Junmo Kim

Adversarial Partial Domain Adaptation by Cycle Inconsistency 530
Kun-Yu Lin, Jiaming Zhou, Yukun Qiu, and Wei-Shi Zheng

Combating Label Distribution Shift for Active Domain Adaptation 549
Sehyun Hwang, Sohyun Lee, Sungyeon Kim, Jungseul Ok, and Suha Kwak

GIPSO: Geometrically Informed Propagation for Online Adaptation in 3D LiDAR Segmentation 567
Cristiano Saltori, Evgeny Krivosheev, Stéphane Lathuiliére, Nicu Sebe, Fabio Galasso, Giuseppe Fiameni, Elisa Ricci, and Fabio Poiesi

CoSMix: Compositional Semantic Mix for Domain Adaptation in 3D LiDAR Segmentation 586
Cristiano Saltori, Fabio Galasso, Giuseppe Fiameni, Nicu Sebe, Elisa Ricci, and Fabio Poiesi

A Unified Framework for Domain Adaptive Pose Estimation 603
Donghyun Kim, Kaihong Wang, Kate Saenko, Margrit Betke, and Stan Sclaroff

A Broad Study of Pre-training for Domain Generalization and Adaptation 621
Donghyun Kim, Kaihong Wang, Stan Sclaroff, and Kate Saenko

Prior Knowledge Guided Unsupervised Domain Adaptation 639
Tao Sun, Cheng Lu, and Haibin Ling

GCISG: Guided Causal Invariant Learning for Improved Syn-to-Real Generalization 656
Gilhyun Nam, Gyeongjae Choi, and Kyungmin Lee

AcroFOD: An Adaptive Method for Cross-Domain Few-Shot Object Detection 673
Yipeng Gao, Lingxiao Yang, Yunmu Huang, Song Xie, Shiyong Li, and Wei-Shi Zheng

Unsupervised Domain Adaptation for One-Stage Object Detector Using Offsets to Bounding Box 691
Jayeon Yoo, Inseop Chung, and Nojun Kwak

Visual Prompt Tuning 709
Menglin Jia, Luming Tang, Bor-Chun Chen, Claire Cardie, Serge Belongie, Bharath Hariharan, and Ser-Nam Lim

Quasi-Balanced Self-Training on Noise-Aware Synthesis of Object Point Clouds for Closing Domain Gap 728
Yongwei Chen, Zihao Wang, Longkun Zou, Ke Chen, and Kui Jia

Author Index 747

SimpleRecon: 3D Reconstruction Without 3D Convolutions

Mohamed Sayed[2(✉)], John Gibson[1], Jamie Watson[1,2], Victor Prisacariu[1,3], Michael Firman[1], and Clément Godard[4]

[1] Niantic, London, UK
{jgibson,jwatson,vprisacariu,mfirman}@nianticlabs.com
[2] UCL, London, UK
mohamed.sayed.17@ucl.ac.uk
[3] University of Oxford, Oxford, UK
[4] Google, Madison, USA
c.godard@cs.ucl.ac.uk

Abstract. Traditionally, 3D indoor scene reconstruction from posed images happens in two phases: per-image depth estimation, followed by depth merging and surface reconstruction. Recently, a family of methods have emerged that perform reconstruction directly in final 3D volumetric feature space. While these methods have shown impressive reconstruction results, they rely on expensive 3D convolutional layers, limiting their application in resource-constrained environments. In this work, we instead go back to the traditional route, and show how focusing on high quality multi-view depth prediction leads to highly accurate 3D reconstructions using simple off-the-shelf depth fusion. We propose a simple state-of-the-art multi-view depth estimator with two main contributions: 1) a carefully-designed 2D CNN which utilizes strong image priors alongside a plane-sweep feature volume and geometric losses, combined with 2) the integration of keyframe and geometric metadata into the cost volume which allows informed depth plane scoring. Our method achieves a significant lead over the current state-of-the-art for depth estimation and close or better for 3D reconstruction on ScanNet and 7-Scenes, yet still allows for online real-time low-memory reconstruction. Code, models and results are available at https://nianticlabs.github.io/simplerecon.

1 Introduction

Generating 3D reconstructions of a scene is a challenging problem in computer vision which is useful for tasks such as robotic navigation, autonomous driving, content placement for augmented reality and historical preservation [47,77]. Traditionally, such 3D reconstructions are generated from 2D depth maps obtained

M. Sayed and C. Godard—Work done while at Niantic, during Mohamed's internship.

Supplementary Information The online version contains supplementary material available at https://doi.org/10.1007/978-3-031-19827-4_1.

S. Avidan et al. (Eds.): ECCV 2022, LNCS 13693, pp. 1–19, 2022.
https://doi.org/10.1007/978-3-031-19827-4_1

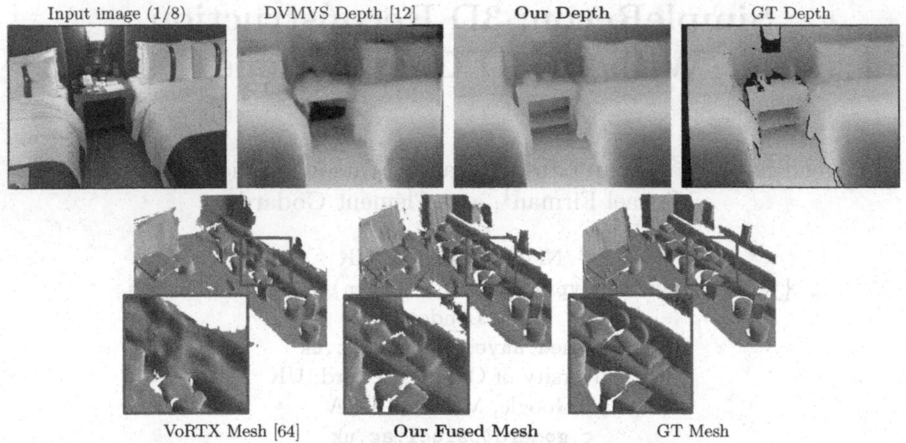

Fig. 1. Qualitative preview of our method. Our method significantly improves upon previous state-of-the-art monocular MVS methods [12] in depth prediction and matches the current volumetric state-of-the-art in full scene reconstruction [64].

using multi-view stereo (MVS) [11,56], which are then fused into a 3D representation from which a surface is extracted [31,57]. Recent advances in deep learning have enabled convolutional methods to outperform classical methods for depth prediction from multiple stereo images, spearheaded by GC-Net [32] and MVSNet [78]. Key to these methods is the use of 3D convolutions to smooth and regularize a 4D ($C \times D \times H \times W$) cost volume, which performs well in practice but is expensive in both time and memory. This could preclude their use on low power hardware e.g. smartphones, where overall compute energy and memory are limited. The same is true of recent depth estimators which use LSTMs and Gaussian processes for improved depth accuracy [12,23].

A new stream of work started by ATLAS [46] (and extended by e.g. [2,7,65]) performs the reconstruction directly in 3D space by predicting a truncated signed distance function (TSDF) from a 4D feature volume computed from the input images. Again, these works give good results but use expensive 3D convolutions.

In this paper we go *back to basics*, showing that, surprisingly, it is possible to obtain state-of-the-art depth accuracy with a simple 2D CNN augmented with a cost volume. Our method also gives competitive scores in 3D scene reconstruction using off-the-shelf TSDF fusion [47], all without expensive 3D convolutions. Key to our method is the novel incorporation of cheaply available *metadata* into the cost volume, which we show significantly improves depth and reconstruction quality. Our main contributions are: (1) The integration of keyframe and geometric metadata into the cost volume using a multi-level perceptron (MLP), which allows informed depth plane scoring, and (2) A carefully-designed 2D CNN that utilizes strong image priors alongside a plane-sweep 3D feature volume and geometric losses. We evaluate our 'back-to-basics' method against all recent published methods on the challenging ScanNetv2 [10] dataset on both depth estimation and 3D scene reconstruction (Sect. 4), and show it generalizes on 7-Scenes [18] data (Table 1) and casually captured footage (Fig. 6).

By combining our novel cost volume metadata with principled architectural decisions that result in better depth predictions, we can avoid the computational cost associated with 3D convolutions, potentially enabling use in embedded and resource-constrained environments. We have released code, models and precomputed results at https://nianticlabs.github.io/simplerecon.

2 Related Work

Our method is related to prior work in *stereo* depth estimation, *multi-view* depth estimation, and 3D reconstruction.

2.1 Depth from Calibrated Stereo Pairs

Many methods for estimating depth use calibrated stereo pairs of images in order to estimate disparity, which can be translated into depth using camera parameters and the intra-axial distance between the camera positions. Early methods compare patches [22,44,82], similar to work in optical flow estimation [16]. This laid the groundwork for GCNet [32], which built on earlier plane-sweep stereo works [8,29] to develop now-ubiquitous cost-volume-based depth estimation. The typical architecture is feature extraction from input images, then feature matching and reduction into a cost volume, followed by convolutional layers to output the final disparity. Further improvements include post-processing the cost volume [4,6,83,84] using multiscale information, carefully designed network layers that mimic classical refinement methods, and spatial pyramid pooling. The best results typically come from running 3D convolutions on a 4D ($C \times D \times H \times W$) cost volume, pioneered by Chang et al. in PSMNet [4]; this can be very computationally expensive. A more attractive option is to create a 3D cost volume ($D \times H \times W$) by reducing along the feature dimension, meaning 2D convolutions can be used for further processing [71,79]; however, this typically comes at the expense of depth quality. In this work we show how, with simple tricks and clever reduction techniques, a method with a 3D cost volume can outperform existing 4D cost volume methods for both depth estimation and 3D scene reconstruction.

2.2 Multi-view Stereo Depth

Multi-View Stereo (MVS) is a more general problem which aims to estimate depth at a *reference* viewpoint using one or more additional *source* viewpoints captured from arbitrary locations. Knowledge of camera intrinsics and extrinsics for both reference and source views are generally assumed, but can also be estimated offline using e.g. structure-from-motion [57] or on-line using inertial and camera tracking, like that provided by ARKit or ARCore.

Classical MVS methods typically use patch matching with photometric consistency to estimate a depth map followed by depth fusion and refinement [17,58]. In contrast, early learning-based methods backprojected dense image features from multiple viewpoints into 3D volumes representing the entire scene and then predicted voxel occupancy or surface probability from a fused 3D volume [27,30]. Recent methods, inspired by binocular stereo matching techniques, combine these approaches, performing epipolar-geometry-consistent matching on image pixels (e.g. in MVDepthNet [70] and DeepMVS [25]), or extracted features (e.g. in DPSNet [26] and DeepVideoMVS [12]) to produce a matching cost volume. The cost volume can optionally be reduced using a dot product [12] or mean absolute difference [48,71], and then processed using convolutional layers. Further works incorporate additional scene information to regularize the cost volume and refine the final output by using reference image features [78], by taking into account occlusions [39] and moving objects [76], or with a Gaussian process prior [23]. Others have proposed methods to combine multiple reference views, e.g. by pooling in DeepMVS [25] or averaging the feature volumes in DPSNet [26,39]. Aside from use of keyframe image values and features in a cost volume, depth-estimation approaches have used temporal information in varying ways, such as LSTMs to fuse volumes over multiple frames [12,51,68], or by a test-time optimization of reprojection error [3,5,33,42,45,61]. However, all these approaches use only the color image as inputs, discarding additional information such as viewing direction and relative pose estimation after the cost volume is computed. In this work, we extend the matching cost volume into a matching feature volume, which uses readily-available metadata to produce higher-quality depth maps.

2.3 3D Scene Reconstruction from Posed Views

Classical methods for creating dense 3D reconstructions from images typically compute dense depth per-view, such as [58], followed by a surface reconstruction such as Delaunay triangulation [34] or Poisson surface reconstruction [31]. The seminal work Kinect Fusion [47] demonstrated *real-time* 3D scene reconstruction from depth-maps using a volumetric truncated signed distance field (TSDF) representation [9], from which a mesh can be obtained using marching cubes [40]. A family of methods improved on it, allowing it to work more efficiently on larger scenes [28,49,52,73], to handle moving objects [55,59], or to perform loop closure [74], all of which solidified TSDF fusion as a key component of real-time mapping.

Recent deep learning methods forego depth estimation, instead extracting 2D image features from keyframes and backprojecting these features into 3D space to produce a 4D feature volume [63]. In ATLAS [46], 3D convolutions on such a feature volume are used to regress a TSDF for the scene, which significantly improved reconstruction quality over the then-state-of-the-art method of learning-based MVS followed by traditional TSDF fusion [47]. NeuralRecon [65] extended this to refine the TSDF in a coarse-to-fine manner using recurrent layers, while TransformerFusion [2] and VoRTX [64] further improved performance using transformers [69] to learn feature matching. Recently methods proposed combining volumetric reasoning – via a 3D encoder-decoder – with MVS reconstruction; either iteratively in the case of 3DVNet [54] or using pose-invariant 3D convolutional layers in VolumeFusion [7].

Although these methods produce high-quality reconstructions, the use of 3D convolutions, transformers, or recurrent layers makes them computationally expensive and memory-intensive. Furthermore, they predict the whole scene TSDF at once, making real-time use impossible, or rely on complex sparsification [65] or attention mechanisms [2] to allow for progressive updates. In contrast, we

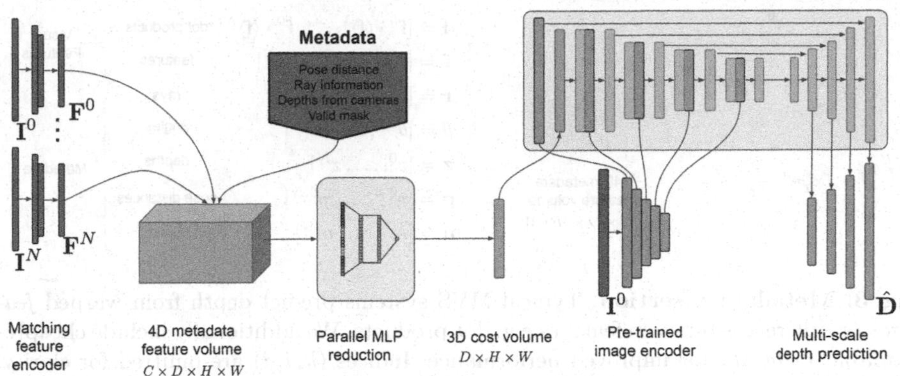

Fig. 2. Overview of our method. Our key contribution is the injection of cheaply-available *metadata* into the feature volume. Each volumetric cell is then reduced in parallel with an MLP into a feature map before input into a 2D encoder-decoder [87].

take a simpler approach: by focusing on predicting high-quality depth maps, we are able to use efficient off-the-shelf TSDF fusion methods such as Infinitam [52]. This allows our method to achieve real-time and progressive 3D reconstructions at low compute and memory footprints, with accuracy competitive with volumetric methods but without the use of 3D convolutions.

3 Method

We take as input a reference image $\mathbf{I}^0$, a set of source images $\mathbf{I}^{n\in\{1,\dots,N-1\}}$, as well as their intrinsics and relative camera poses. At training time we also assume access to a ground truth depth map $\mathbf{D}^{\text{gt}}$ aligned with each RGB image; at test time our aim is to predict dense depth maps $\hat{\mathbf{D}}$ for each reference image.

3.1 Method Overview

Our depth estimation model sits at the intersection of monocular depth estimation [13,19] and MVS via plane sweep [8]. We augment a depth prediction encoder-decoder architecture with a cost volume; see Fig. 2. Our image encoder extracts matching features from the reference and source images for input to a cost volume. The output of the cost volume is processed using a 2D convolutional encoder-decoder network, augmented with image level features extracted using a separate pretrained image encoder.

Our key insight is to inject readily available *metadata* into the cost volume alongside the typical deep image features, allowing the network access to useful information such as geometric and relative camera pose information. Figure 3 shows in detail the construction of our feature volume. By incorporating this previously unexploited information, our model is able to significantly outperform previous methods on depth prediction without the need for costly 4D cost volume reductions [32,78], complex temporal fusion [12], or Gaussian processes [23].

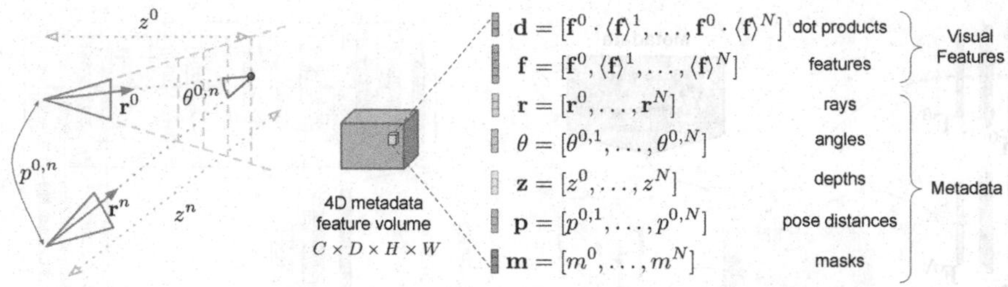

Fig. 3. Metadata insertion. Typical MVS systems predict depth from warped *features* or differences between features e.g. dot products. We additionally include cheaply-available *metadata* for improved performance. Indices (k, i, j) are omitted for clarity.

We first describe our novel metadata component and explain how it is incorporated into the network (Sect. 3.2). We then set out our network architecture and losses (Sects. 3.3 and 3.4), giving best practices for depth estimation.

3.2 Improving the Cost Volume with Metadata

In traditional stereo techniques, there exists important information which is typically ignored. In this work, we incorporate readily available *metadata* into the cost volume, allowing our network to aggregate information across views in an informed manner. This can be done both *explicitly* via appending extra feature channels and *implicitly* via enforcing specific feature ordering.

We propose injecting metadata into our network by augmenting image-level features inside the cost volume with additional metadata channels. These channels encode information about the 3D relationship between the images used to build the cost volume, allowing our network to better reason about the relative importance of each source image for estimating depth for a particular pixel.

Our cost volume is therefore a 4D tensor of dimension $C \times D \times H \times W$, where for each spatial location (k, i, j), k is the depth plane index, we have a C dimensional feature vector. This vector comprises reference image features $\mathbf{f}^0_{k,i,j}$ and a set of warped source image features $\langle \mathbf{f} \rangle^n_{k,i,j}$ for $n \in [1, N]$, where $\langle \, \rangle$ indicates that the features are perspective-warped into the reference camera frame, along with the following metadata components:

Feature dot product—The dot product between reference image features and warped source image features, i.e. $\mathbf{f}^0 \cdot \langle \mathbf{f} \rangle^n$. This is commonly used as the *only* matching affinity in the cost volume.

Ray directions $\mathbf{r}^0_{k,i,j}$ and $\mathbf{r}^n_{k,i,j} \in \mathbb{R}^3$—The normalized direction to the 3D location of a point (k, i, j) in the plane sweep from the camera origins.

Reference plane depth $z^0_{k,i,j}$—The perpendicular depth from the reference camera to the point at position k, i, j in the cost volume.

Reference frame reprojected depths $z^n_{k,i,j}$—The perpendicular depth of the 3D point at position k, i, j in the cost volume to source camera n.

Relative ray angles $\theta^{0,n}$—The angle between $\mathbf{r}^0_{k,i,j}$ and $\mathbf{r}^n_{k,i,j}$.

Relative pose distance $p^{0,n}$—A measure of the relative pose distance between the pose of the reference camera and each source frame [12]:

$$p^{0,n} = \sqrt{||\mathbf{t}^{0,n}|| + \frac{2}{3}\mathrm{tr}(\mathbb{I} - \mathbf{R}^{0,n})} \tag{1}$$

Depth validity masks $m^n_{k,i,j}$—This binary mask indicates if point (k, i, j) in the cost volume projects in front of the source camera n or not.

An overview of these features is given in Fig 3. Each resulting $\mathbf{f}_{k,i,j}$ is processed by a simple multi layer perceptron (MLP), outputting a single scalar value for each location (k, i, j). This scalar can be thought of an initial estimate of the likelihood that the depth of pixel i, j is equal to the kth depth plane.

Metadata Motivation— We argue that by appending metadata-derived features into our cost volume, the MLP can learn to correctly weigh the contribution of each source frame at each pixel location. Consider for instance the pose distance $p^{s,n}$; it is clear that for depths farther from the camera, the matching features from source frames with a greater baseline would be more informative. Similarly, ray information can be useful for reasoning about occlusions; if features from the reference frame disagree with those from a source frame but there is a large angle between camera rays, then this could be explained by an occlusion rather than incorrect depth. Depth validity masks can help the network to know whether to trust features from source camera n at (k, i, j), By allowing our network access to this kind of information, we give it the ability to conduct such geometric reasoning when aggregating information from multiple source frames.

Implicit Metadata Incorporation— In addition to explicitly providing metadata as extra features, we also propose *implicitly* encoding metadata via feature ordering. This is made possible by the inherent order dependence of MLP networks, which we exploit by choosing the ordering in which we stack our source features $\mathbf{f}^n$. We advocate ordering $\mathbf{f}^n$ by frame pose distance $p^{s,n}$, a measure shown by [12,23] to be effective for optimal keyframe selection. This ordering allows the MLP to learn a prior on pose distance and feature relevance.

Our experiments show that by including metadata in our network, both *explicitly* via extra feature channels and *implicitly* via feature ordering, we can obtain a significant boost to depth estimation accuracy, bringing with it improved 3D reconstruction quality; see Table 4. Whilst previous works have included tensors related to camera intrinsics [14] and extrinsics [86] for monocular depth estimation, we believe that our use of metadata is a novel innovation for multi-view-stereo depth estimation.

3.3 Network Architecture Design

Our network is based on a 2D convolutional encoder-decoder architecture similar to prior works such as [12,71]. When constructing such networks, we find that there are important design choices which can give significant improvements to depth prediction accuracy. We specifically aim to keep the overall architecture simple, avoiding complex structures such as LSTMs [12] or GPs [23], and making our baseline model lightweight and interpretable.

Baseline Cost Volume Fusion—While RNN-based temporal fusion methods are often used [12,65], they significantly increase the complexity of the system. We instead make our baseline cost-volume fusion as simple as possible and find that simply summing the dot-product matching costs between the reference view and each source view leads to results competitive with state-of-the-art depth estimation techniques, as shown in Table 1 with the heading "no metadata".

Image Encoder and Feature Matching Encoder—Prior depth estimation works have shown the impact of more powerful image encoders for the task of depth estimation, both in monocular [20,53,72] and multi-view estimation [71]. DeepVideoMVS [12] make use of an MnasNet [66] as their image encoder, chosen for its relatively low latency. We propose instead utilizing a still-small but more powerful EfficientNetv2 S encoder [67], the smallest of its family. While this does come with a cost of increased parameter count and 10% slower execution, it yields a sizeable improvement to depth estimation accuracy, especially for precise metrics such as Sq Rel and $\delta < 1.05$. See Table 4 for full results.

For producing matching feature maps, we use the first two blocks from ResNet18 [21] for efficiency, we experimented with FPN [37] following [12], which slightly improved accuracy at the expense of a 50% slower overall run-time.

Fuse Multi-scale Image Features into the Cost Volume Encoder—In 2D CNN based deep stereo and multi-view stereo, image features are typically combined with the output of the cost volume at a single scale [36,71].

More recently, DeepVideoMVS [12] instead proposed concatenating deep image features at *multiple* scales, adding skip connections between the image encoder and cost volume encoder at all resolutions. Whilst this has been shown to be helpful for their LSTM-based fusion network, we find that it is similarly important for our architecture.

Number of Source Images—While other methods show diminishing returns as additional source frames are added [12], our method is better able to incorporate this additional information and displays increased performance with up to 8 views. We posit that incorporating additional metadata for each frame allows the network to make a more informed decision about the relative weightings of each frame's features when inferring the final cost. In contrast, methods such as MVDepthNet [70], MVSNet [78], ManyDepth [71] and ATLAS [46] give each frame equal weight during a update, thus potentially overwhelming the most useful information with lower-quality features.

3.4 Loss

We supervise our training using a combination of geometric losses, inspired by recent MVS methods [12,13,25,78] as well as monocular depth estimation techniques [20,35,53,81]. We find that careful choice of loss function is required for best performance, and that supervising intermediate predictions at lower output scales substantially improves results.

Depth Regression Loss—We follow [13] and densely supervise predictions using log-depth, but use an absolute error on log depth for each scale s,

$$\mathcal{L}_{\text{depth}} = \frac{1}{HW} \sum_{s=1}^{4} \sum_{i,j} \frac{1}{s^2} | \uparrow_{gt} \log \hat{\mathbf{D}}^{s}_{i,j} - \log \mathbf{D}^{\text{gt}}_{i,j} |, \tag{2}$$

where we upsample each lower scale depth using nearest neighbor upsampling [12] to the highest scale we predict at with the $\uparrow_{gt}$ operator. We average this loss per pixel, per scale and per batch. Our experiments found this loss to perform better than the scale-invariant formulation of Eigen et al. [1,13], while producing much sharper depth boundaries, resulting in higher fused reconstruction quality.

Multi-scale Gradient and Normal Losses—We follow [35,53,81] and use a multi-scale gradient loss on our highest resolution network output

$$\mathcal{L}_{\text{grad}} = \frac{1}{HW} \sum_{s=1}^{4} \sum_{i,j} | \nabla \downarrow_s \hat{\mathbf{D}}_{i,j} - \nabla \downarrow_s \mathbf{D}^{\text{gt}}_{i,j} |, \tag{3}$$

where ∇ is first order spatial gradients and $\downarrow_s$ represents downsampling to scale s. Inspired by [80] we also use a simplified normal loss, where $\mathbf{N}$ is the normal map computed using the depth and intrinsics (see supp. mat. for details),

$$\mathcal{L}_{\text{normals}} = \frac{1}{2HW} \sum_{i,j} 1 - \hat{\mathbf{N}}_{i,j} \cdot \mathbf{N}_{i,j}. \tag{4}$$

Multi-view Depth Regression Loss—We use ground-truth depth maps for each source view as additional supervision by projecting predicted depth $\hat{D}$ into each source view and averaging absolute error on log depth over all valid points,

$$\mathcal{L}_{\text{mv}} = \frac{1}{NHW} \sum_{n} \sum_{i,j} | \log \hat{\mathbf{D}}^{0 \to n}_{i,j} - \log \mathbf{D}^{\text{gt}}_{n,i,j} | \tag{5}$$

where $\hat{\mathbf{D}}^{0 \to n}$ is the depth predicted for the reference image of index 0, projected into source view n. This is similar in concept to the depth regression loss above, but for simplicity is applied only on the final output scale.

Total Loss—Overall our total loss is:

$$\mathcal{L} = \mathcal{L}_{\text{depth}} + \alpha_{\text{grad}} \mathcal{L}_{\text{grad}} + \alpha_{\text{normals}} \mathcal{L}_{\text{normals}} + \alpha_{\text{mv}} \mathcal{L}_{\text{mv}}, \tag{6}$$

with $\alpha_{\text{grad}} = 1.0 = \alpha_{\text{normals}} = 1.0$, and $\alpha_{\text{mv}} = 0.2$, chosen experimentally using the validation set.

Table 1. Depth evaluation. For each metric, the best-performing method is marked in red, the second-best in orange, and the third-best in yellow. Results for previous methods were taken from [12], or evaluated for each method using their keyframes. *We boosted [12]'s scores by using three inference frames instead of two. [12] also use a custom 90/10 split; we show SimpleRecon results using this in the supplementary.

	ScanNetv2					7Scenes				
	Abs Diff↓	Abs Rel↓	Sq Rel↓	$\delta < 1.05$ ↑	$\delta < 1.25$ ↑	Abs Diff↓	Abs Rel↓	Sq Rel↓	$\delta < 1.05$ ↑	$\delta < 1.25$ ↑
DPSNet [26]	0.1552	0.0795	0.0299	49.36	93.27	0.1966	0.1147	0.0550	38.81	87.07
MVDepthNet [70]	0.1648	0.0848	0.0343	46.71	92.77	0.2009	0.1161	0.0623	38.81	87.70
DELTAS [62]	0.1497	0.0786	0.0276	48.64	93.78	0.1915	0.1140	0.0490	36.36	88.13
GPMVS [23]	0.1494	0.0757	0.0292	51.04	93.96	0.1739	0.1003	0.0462	42.71	90.32
DeepVideoMVS, fusion [12]*	0.1186	0.0583	0.0190	60.20	96.76	0.1448	0.0828	0.0335	47.96	93.79
Ours (no metadata)	0.0941	0.0467	0.0139	70.48	97.84	0.1105	0.0617	0.0175	57.30	97.02
Ours	0.0885	0.0434	0.0125	73.16	98.09	0.1045	0.0575	0.0153	59.78	97.38

3.5 Implementation Details

We implemented the method using PyTorch [15,50,75] and we use an EfficientNetV2 S backbone [67], with a decoder similar to UNet++ [87], and use the first 2 blocks of ResNet18 (R18) for matching feature extraction. Please see supplementary material for a detailed architecture description. We train with the AdamW optimizer [41] for 100k steps – approximately 9 epochs – with a weight decay of 10^{-4}, and a learning rate of 10^{-4} for 70k steps, 10^{-5} until 80k, then dropped to 10^{-6} for remainder, which takes 36 h on two 40 GB A100 GPUs. Models with the lowest validation loss are used for evaluation. We resize images to 512×384 and predict depth at half that resolution. When training, random color augmentations to brightness, contrast, saturation, and hue are applied per image using TorchVision [43] with $\delta = 0.2$ for all parameters, and horizontal flips with a probability of 50%. Keyframes are selected following DeepVideoMVS [12].

4 Experiments

We train and evaluate our method on the 3D scene reconstruction dataset ScanNetv2 [10], which comprises 1,201 training, 312 validation, and 100 testing scans of indoor scenes, all captured with a handheld RGBD sensor. We also evaluate our ScanNetv2 models without fine-tuning on 7-Scenes [60] using [12]'s test split.

4.1 Depth Estimation

In Table 1, we evaluate the depth predictions from our network using the metrics established in Eigen et al. [13]. We also introduce a tighter threshold tolerance $\delta < 1.05$ to differentiate between high quality models. We directly compare to previously published results, including DeepVideoMVS [12], on ScanNetv2 and 7-Scenes (Table 1).

We use the standard test split for ScanNetv2 and the test split defined by [12] for 7-Scenes. We compute depth metrics for every keyframe as in [12] and average across all keyframes in the test sets. Surprisingly, our model, which uses no 3D

Table 2. Mesh Evaluation. We use [2]'s evaluation. The Volumetric column designates whether a method is a volumetric 3D reconstruction method; other MVS methods that produce only depth maps were reconstructed using standard TSDF fusion.

	Volumetric	Comp↓	Acc↓	Chamfer↓	Prec↑	Recall ↑	F-Score ↑
RevisitingSI [24]	No	14.29	16.19	15.24	0.346	0.293	0.314
MVDepthNet [70]	No	12.94	8.34	10.64	0.443	0.487	0.460
GPMVS [23]	No	12.90	8.02	10.46	0.453	0.510	0.477
ESTDepth [38]	No	12.71	7.54	10.12	0.456	0.542	0.491
DPSNet [26]	No	11.94	7.58	9.77	0.474	0.519	0.492
DELTAS [62]	No	11.95	7.46	9.71	0.478	0.533	0.501
DeepVideoMVS [12]	No	10.68	6.90	8.79	0.541	0.592	0.563
COLMAP [58]	No	10.22	11.88	11.05	0.509	0.474	0.489
ATLAS [46]	Yes	7.16	7.61	7.38	0.675	0.605	0.636
NeuralRecon [65]	Yes	5.09	9.13	7.11	0.630	0.612	0.619
3DVNet [54]	Yes	7.72	6.73	7.22	0.655	0.596	0.621
TransformerFusion [2]	Yes	5.52	8.27	6.89	0.728	0.600	0.655
VoRTX [64]	Yes	4.31	7.23	5.77	0.767	0.651	0.703
Ours	No	5.53	6.09	5.81	0.686	0.658	0.671

convolutions, outperforms all baselines on depth prediction metrics. In addition, our baseline model with no metadata encoding (i.e. using only the dot product between reference and source image features) also performs well in comparison to previous methods, showing that a carefully designed and trained 2D network is sufficient for high-quality depth estimation. We show qualitative results for depth and normals in Fig. 4 and Fig. 5 respectively.

4.2 3D Reconstruction Evaluation

Our 3D reconstructions are evaluated using the standard protocol established by TransformerFusion [2]. Their evaluation uses a ground truth mesh based prediction mask to cull away parts of the prediction such that methods are not unfairly penalized for predicting potentially correct geometry that is missing in the ground truth. Scores are shown in Table 2. Our simple depth-based method outperforms state-of-the-art depth estimators for fusion by a wide margin. Although we do not perform global refinement of the resulting volume after fusion, we are still able to outperform more expensive *volumetric* methods in some metrics, showing overall competitive performance with lower complexity.

We also compute scores using the ATLAS [46] mesh evaluation protocol. However, we find this evaluation is inconsistent; comparing a ground truth mesh against itself does not result in a score of zero, nor does performance on metrics match inspection for visual quality or correlate well across methods. These scores, and more details on this discrepancy, are given in the supplementary.

4.3 3D Reconstruction Latency

For online and interactive 3D reconstruction applications, reducing the latency from sensor reading to 3D representation update is crucial. Most recent reconstruction methods use 3D CNN architectures [2,46,64,65] that require expensive

Table 3. Frame integration latencies for 3D reconstruction. We measure latency as the time to incorporate a new image measurement to a 3D representation. Note that NR reports time amortized over all keyframes. *requires sparse 3D convolutions.

	Volume update mode	Breakdown	Update latency (ms)↓	F-Score↑
ATLAS [46]	Volume 3D CNN	2D CNN (29ms) + 3D CNN (353ms)	382ms	0.636
NeuralRecon* [65]	3D Chunk Fusion + GRU	2D CNN (12ms) + GRU (78ms)	90ms	0.619
3DVNet [54]	Iterative 3D CNN	Refine Depths and Feature Cloud (23875ms)	23875ms	0.621
TransformerFusion [2]	Transformer Fusion + 3D CNN	2D CNN (131ms) + Refinement (195ms)	326ms	0.655
VoRTX [64]	Transformer Fusion + 3D CNN	2D CNN (23ms) + Refinement (4527ms)	4550ms	0.703
Ours	TSDF Fusion	2D Depth CNN (101ms) + TSDF fuse (2ms)	103ms	0.671

and often specialized hardware for sparse matrix computation. This makes them prohibitive for applications on low power devices (smartphones, IoE devices) where both compute and power are limited, or may simply not support the operations. Reconstruction methods often report amortized frame time, where the total compute time for select keyframes is averaged over all frames in a sequence. While this is a useful metric for full offline scene reconstruction performance, it is not indicative of online performance, especially when considering latency.

In Table 3 we compute the per-frame integration time given a new RGB frame. Some methods may not be designed to run on every keyframe. Notably, NeuralRecon [65] updates a chunk in world space when 9 keyframes have been received. However, for fairness across methods, we do not count the time spent waiting to satisfy a keyframe requirement and assume that the output of immediately available frames with potentially subpar pose distances is comparable to how the method was intended to perform. For methods that require a 3D CNN, we report the time for one 2D keyframe integration and a complete pass of their 3D CNN network. Although our method is slower than methods such as [65] on a per-keyframe basis, we can quickly perform updates to the reconstructed volume using online TSDF fusion methods, resulting in low update latencies.

4.4 Ablations

In order to show the importance of our best practices and novel contributions, we ablate different parts of our network and training routine. Results for depth estimation and mesh reconstruction metrics on ScanNet [10] are shown for ablations in Table 4, following the evaluation procedures in Sect. 4.

Baseline—We first show that using *no* MLP and 16 feature channels, reduced using a dot product, our performance greatly suffers. Interestingly, using 64 feature channels instead of 16 degrades accuracy while being significantly slower.

Frame Ordering—We compare two models where we shuffle the ordering of the keyframes, instead of relying on the pose distance. As we can see while both models suffer from random ordering, the full model, which has access to the pose distance as metadata, does not suffer as much.

Metadata—In this section all the models make use of the MLP cost volume reduction, but we vary the input of that MLP. We start with our baseline

Fig. 4. Depth predictions on ScanNet. Our model produces significantly sharper and more accurate depths than the baselines. See sup. mat. for additional results.

Fig. 5. Estimated Normals on ScanNet. Our model produces significantly sharper normals. We compute the estimated normals from depth, see supp. mat. for details.

model, using only the feature dot products aggregated using a sum. We then add the features, their depth and validity mask, reduced using our MLP. We keep adding more metadata until we reach our full model. Accuracy increases with the amount of information provided to the model.

Views—In addition, we show that our method can incorporate information from many source views. As we increase from 2 views to 8, our performance continues to improve. In contrast, DeepVideoMVS's performance remains relatively constant when using more than three source frames [12]. In addition, we ablate the cost volume entirely by zeroing its output (creating a monocular method), leading to greatly decreased performance, showing that a strong metric depth estimate from the cost volume is required to resolve scale ambiguity.

Table 4. Ablation Evaluation. Ablation evaluation on depth and reconstruction metrics using DVMVS keyframes for ScanNet. Scores for our full method are bolded.

	Depth evaluation					Mesh eval	
	Abs Diff↓	Sq Rel↓	RMSE↓	$\delta < 1.05$ ↑	$\delta < 1.25$ ↑	Chamfer↓	F-score↑
Ours w/ all metadata, 8 ordered frames, dot prod CV 16c, ENv2S + R18	**0.0885**	**0.0125**	**0.1468**	**73.16**	**98.09**	**5.81**	**67.1**
Ours baseline w/ dot product CV 16c	0.0941	0.0139	0.1544	70.48	97.84	6.29	64.2
Ours baseline w/ dot product CV 64c	0.0944	0.0140	0.1548	70.49	97.84	6.08	65.4
Ours w/o metadata, shuffled frames	0.0920	0.0135	0.1521	71.59	97.91	6.04	65.6
Ours w/ metadata, shuffled frames	0.0906	0.0129	0.1490	72.09	98.03	5.92	66.3
Ours baseline w/ dot product CV 16c	0.0941	0.0139	0.1544	70.48	97.84	6.29	64.2
Ours dot + feats + mask + depth	0.0904	0.0132	0.1509	72.63	98.03	5.92	66.5
Ours dot + feats + mask + depth + ray + angle	0.0896	0.0127	0.1481	72.76	98.09	5.88	66.6
Ours dot + feats + mask + depth + ray + angle + pose distance	**0.0885**	**0.0125**	**0.1468**	**73.16**	**98.09**	**5.81**	**67.1**
Ours w/ 1 frame - w/o CV	0.1742	0.0374	0.2330	40.96	90.03	9.26	47.0
Ours w/ 2 frames	0.1230	0.0198	0.1803	57.15	96.21	7.51	56.7
Ours w/ 4 frames	0.1036	0.0151	0.1611	65.62	97.60	6.57	62.3
Ours w/ metadata but w/ MnasNet at 320 × 256 (matching [12])	0.0947	0.0146	0.1587	71.24	97.68	5.92	66.3

Fig. 6. Fused meshes on unseen data. Our model generalizes on unseen environments, including outdoors, captured on smartphone. See video for live reconstruction.

5 Conclusion

We propose SimpleRecon, which produces state-of-the-art depth estimations and 3D reconstructions, all without the use of expensive 3D convolutions. Our key contribution is to inject cheaply available *metadata* into the cost volume. Our evaluation shows that metadata boosts scores, and in partnership with our set of careful architecture design choices leads to our state-of-the-art depths. Moreover, our method does not preclude the use of 3D convolutions or additional cost volume and depth refinement techniques, allowing room for further improvements when compute is less restricted. Ultimately, our back-to-basics approach shows that high-quality depths are all you need for high-quality reconstructions.

Acknowledgements. We thank Aljaž Božič [2], Jiaming Sun [65] and Arda Düzçeker [12] for quickly providing useful information to help with baselines. Mohamed is funded by a Microsoft Research PhD Scholarship (MRL 2018-085).

References

1. Bhat, S.F., Alhashim, I., Wonka, P.: AdaBins: depth estimation using adaptive bins. In: CVPR (2021)
2. Bozic, A., Palafox, P., Thies, J., Dai, A., Nießner, M.: TransformerFusion: monocular RGB scene reconstruction using transformers. In: NeurIPS (2021)
3. Casser, V., Pirk, S., Mahjourian, R., Angelova, A.: Depth prediction without the sensors: leveraging structure for unsupervised learning from monocular videos. In: AAAI (2019)
4. Chang, J.R., Chen, Y.S.: Pyramid stereo matching network. In: CVPR (2018)
5. Chen, Y., Schmid, C., Sminchisescu, C.: Self-supervised learning with geometric constraints in monocular video: Connecting flow, depth, and camera. In: ICCV (2019)
6. Cheng, X., Wang, P., Yang, R.: Learning depth with convolutional spatial propagation network. PAMI **42**, 2361–2379 (2019)
7. Choe, J., Im, S., Rameau, F., Kang, M., Kweon, I.S.: VolumeFusion: deep depth fusion for 3D scene reconstruction. In: ICCV (2021)
8. Collins, R.T.: A space-sweep approach to true multi-image matching. In: CVPR (1996)
9. Curless, B., Levoy, M.: A volumetric method for building complex models from range images. In: Proceedings of the 23rd Annual Conference on Computer Graphics and Interactive Techniques (1996)
10. Dai, A., Chang, A.X., Savva, M., Halber, M., Funkhouser, T., Nießner, M.: ScanNet: richly-annotated 3D reconstructions of indoor scenes. In: CVPR (2017)
11. Drory, A., Haubold, C., Avidan, S., Hamprecht, F.: Semi-global matching: a principled derivation in terms of message passing. In: German Conference on Pattern Recognition (2014)
12. Duzceker, A., Galliani, S., Vogel, C., Speciale, P., Dusmanu, M., Pollefeys, M.: Deepvideomvs: multi-view stereo on video with recurrent spatio-temporal fusion. In: CVPR (2021)
13. Eigen, D., Puhrsch, C., Fergus, R.: Depth map prediction from a single image using a multi-scale deep network. In: NeurIPS (2014)
14. Facil, J.M., Ummenhofer, B., Zhou, H., Montesano, L., Brox, T., Civera, J.: CAM-Convs: camera-aware multi-scale convolutions for single-view depth. In: CVPR (2019)
15. Falcon, W., et al.: Pytorch lightning. GitHub. Note: https://github.com/PyTorchLightning/pytorch-lightning (2019)
16. Fischer, P., et al.: FlowNet: learning optical flow with convolutional networks. In: ICCV (2015)
17. Furukawa, Y., Hernández, C.: Multi-view stereo: a tutorial. Found. Trends Comput. Graphics Vis. **9**, 1–148 (2015)
18. Glocker, B., Izadi, S., Shotton, J., Criminisi, A.: Real-time RGB-D camera relocalization. In: International Symposium on Mixed and Augmented Reality (ISMAR). IEEE, October 2013
19. Godard, C., Mac Aodha, O., Brostow, G.J.: Unsupervised monocular depth estimation with left-right consistency. In: CVPR (2017)
20. Godard, C., Mac Aodha, O., Firman, M., Brostow, G.J.: Digging into self-supervised monocular depth estimation. In: ICCV (2019)
21. He, K., Zhang, X., Ren, S., Sun, J.: Deep residual learning for image recognition. In: CVPR (2016)

22. Hirschmuller, H.: Stereo processing by semiglobal matching and mutual information. PAMI **30**, 328–341 (2007)
23. Hou, Y., Kannala, J., Solin, A.: Multi-view stereo by temporal nonparametric fusion. In: ICCV (2019)
24. Hu, J., Ozay, M., Zhang, Y., Okatani, T.: Revisiting single image depth estimation: toward higher resolution maps with accurate object boundaries. In: WACV (2018)
25. Huang, P.H., Matzen, K., Kopf, J., Ahuja, N., Huang, J.B.: DeepMVS: learning multi-view stereopsis. In: CVPR (2018)
26. Im, S., Jeon, H.G., Lin, S., Kweon, I.S.: DPSNet: end-to-end deep plane sweep stereo. ICLR (2019)
27. Ji, M., Gall, J., Zheng, H., Liu, Y., Fang, L.: SurfaceNet: an end-to-end 3D neural network for multiview stereopsis. In: ICCV (2017)
28. Kähler, O., Prisacariu, V., Valentin, J., Murray, D.: Hierarchical voxel block hashing for efficient integration of depth images. IEEE Robot. Autom. Lett. **1**(1), 192–197 (2015)
29. Kang, S.B., Szeliski, R., Chai, J.: Handling occlusions in dense multi-view stereo. In: CVPR (2001)
30. Kar, A., Häne, C., Malik, J.: Learning a multi-view stereo machine. In: NeurIPS (2017)
31. Kazhdan, M., Bolitho, M., Hoppe, H.: Poisson surface reconstruction. In: Eurographics. SGP 2006, Eurographics Association (2006)
32. Kendall, A., et al.: End-to-end learning of geometry and context for deep stereo regression. In: ICCV (2017)
33. Kuznietsov, Y., Proesmans, M., Van Gool, L.: CoMoDA: continuous monocular depth adaptation using past experiences. In: WACV (2021)
34. Lee, D.T., Schachter, B.J.: Two algorithms for constructing a delaunay triangulation. Int. J. Comput. Inf. Sci. **9**(3), 219–242 (1980)
35. Li, Z., Snavely, N.: MegaDepth: learning single-view depth prediction from internet photos. In: CVPR (2018)
36. Liang, Z., et al.: Learning for disparity estimation through feature constancy. In: CVPR (2018)
37. Lin, T.Y., Dollár, P., Girshick, R., He, K., Hariharan, B., Belongie, S.: Feature pyramid networks for object detection. In: Proceedings of the IEEE Conference on Computer Vision and Pattern Recognition, pp. 2117–2125 (2017)
38. Long, X., Liu, L., Li, W., Theobalt, C., Wang, W.: Multi-view depth estimation using epipolar spatio-temporal networks. In: CVPR (2021)
39. Long, X., Liu, L., Theobalt, C., Wang, W.: Occlusion-aware depth estimation with adaptive normal constraints. In: Vedaldi, A., Bischof, H., Brox, T., Frahm, J.-M. (eds.) ECCV 2020. LNCS, vol. 12354, pp. 640–657. Springer, Cham (2020). https://doi.org/10.1007/978-3-030-58545-7_37
40. Lorensen, W.E., Cline, H.E.: Marching cubes: a high resolution 3D surface construction algorithm. ACM SIGGRAPH Comput. Graphics **21**, 163–169 (1987)
41. Loshchilov, I., Hutter, F.: Decoupled weight decay regularization. arXiv preprint arXiv:1711.05101 (2017)
42. Luo, X., Huang, J.B., Szeliski, R., Matzen, K., Kopf, J.: Consistent video depth estimation. In: ACM SIGGRAPH (2020)
43. Marcel, S., Rodriguez, Y.: Torchvision the machine-vision package of torch. In: Proceedings of the 18th ACM International Conference on Multimedia, pp. 1485–1488 (2010)
44. Mayer, N., et al.: A large dataset to train convolutional networks for disparity, optical flow, and scene flow estimation. In: CVPR (2016)

45. McCraith, R., Neumann, L., Zisserman, A., Vedaldi, A.: Monocular depth estimation with self-supervised instance adaptation. arXiv:2004.05821 (2020)
46. Murez, Z., van As, T., Bartolozzi, J., Sinha, A., Badrinarayanan, V., Rabinovich, A.: Atlas: End-to-End 3D scene reconstruction from posed images. In: Vedaldi, A., Bischof, H., Brox, T., Frahm, J.-M. (eds.) ECCV 2020. LNCS, vol. 12352, pp. 414–431. Springer, Cham (2020). https://doi.org/10.1007/978-3-030-58571-6_25
47. Newcombe, R.A., Izadi, S., Hilliges, O.: KinectFusion: real-time dense surface mapping and tracking. In: UIST (2011)
48. Newcombe, R.A., Lovegrove, S.J., Davison, A.J.: DTAM: dense tracking and mapping in real-time. In: ICCV (2011)
49. Nießner, M., Zollhöfer, M., Izadi, S., Stamminger, M.: Real-time 3D reconstruction at scale using voxel hashing. ACM Trans. Graphics (ToG) **32**, 1–11 (2013)
50. Paszke, A., et al.: PyTorch: an imperative style, high-performance deep learning library. In: NeurIPS (2019)
51. Patil, V., Van Gansbeke, W., Dai, D., Van Gool, L.: Don't forget the past: recurrent depth estimation from monocular video. IEEE Robot. Autom. Lett. **5**, 6813–6820 (2020)
52. Prisacariu, V.A., et al.: Infinitam v3: a framework for large-scale 3D reconstruction with loop closure. arXiv preprint arXiv:1708.00783 (2017)
53. Ranftl, R., Lasinger, K., Hafner, D., Schindler, K., Koltun, V.: Towards robust monocular depth estimation: mixing datasets for zero-shot cross-dataset transfer. PAMI **44**, 1623–1637 (2020)
54. Rich, A., Stier, N., Sen, P., Höllerer, T.: 3dvnet: multi-view depth prediction and volumetric refinement. In: International Conference on 3D Vision (3DV) (2021)
55. Runz, M., Buffier, M., Agapito, L.: MaskFusion: real-time recognition, tracking and reconstruction of multiple moving objects. In: ISMAR (2018)
56. Scharstein, D., Szeliski, R., Zabih, R.: A taxonomy and evaluation of dense two-frame stereo correspondence algorithms. In: IEEE Workshop on Stereo and Multi-Baseline Vision (SMBV 2001) (2001)
57. Schönberger, J.L., Frahm, J.M.: Structure-from-motion revisited. In: CVPR (2016)
58. Schönberger, J.L., Zheng, E., Frahm, J.-M., Pollefeys, M.: Pixelwise view selection for unstructured multi-view stereo. In: Leibe, B., Matas, J., Sebe, N., Welling, M. (eds.) ECCV 2016. LNCS, vol. 9907, pp. 501–518. Springer, Cham (2016). https://doi.org/10.1007/978-3-319-46487-9_31
59. Scona, R., Jaimez, M., Petillot, Y.R., Fallon, M., Cremers, D.: StaticFusion: background reconstruction for dense RGB-D SLAM in dynamic environments. In: ICRA (2018)
60. Shotton, J., Glocker, B., Zach, C., Izadi, S., Criminisi, A., Fitzgibbon, A.: Scene coordinate regression forests for camera relocalization in RGB-D images. In: CVPR (2013)
61. Shu, C., Yu, K., Duan, Z., Yang, K.: Feature-metric loss for self-supervised learning of depth and egomotion. In: Vedaldi, A., Bischof, H., Brox, T., Frahm, J.-M. (eds.) ECCV 2020. LNCS, vol. 12364, pp. 572–588. Springer, Cham (2020). https://doi.org/10.1007/978-3-030-58529-7_34
62. Sinha, A., Murez, Z., Bartolozzi, J., Badrinarayanan, V., Rabinovich, A.: DELTAS: depth estimation by learning triangulation and densification of sparse points. In: Vedaldi, A., Bischof, H., Brox, T., Frahm, J.-M. (eds.) ECCV 2020. LNCS, vol. 12366, pp. 104–121. Springer, Cham (2020). https://doi.org/10.1007/978-3-030-58589-1_7
63. Sitzmann, V., Thies, J., Heide, F., Nießner, M., Wetzstein, G., Zollhöfer, M.: DeepVoxels: learning persistent 3D feature embeddings. In: CVPR (2019)

64. Stier, N., Rich, A., Sen, P., Höllerer, T.: Vortx: volumetric 3D reconstruction with transformers for voxelwise view selection and fusion. In: International Conference on 3D Vision (3DV) (2021)
65. Sun, J., Xie, Y., Chen, L., Zhou, X., Bao, H.: NeuralRecon: real-time coherent 3D reconstruction from monocular video. In: CVPR (2021)
66. Tan, M., Chen, B., Pang, R., Vasudevan, V., Sandler, M., Howard, A., Le, Q.V.: Mnasnet: platform-aware neural architecture search for mobile. In: CVPR (2019)
67. Tan, M., Le, Q.: Efficientnetv2: Smaller models and faster training. In: ICML (2021)
68. Tananaev, D., Zhou, H., Ummenhofer, B., Brox, T.: Temporally consistent depth estimation in videos with recurrent architectures. In: Leal-Taixé, L., Roth, S. (eds.) ECCV 2018. LNCS, vol. 11131, pp. 689–701. Springer, Cham (2019). https://doi.org/10.1007/978-3-030-11015-4_52
69. Vaswani, A., et al.: Attention is all you need. In: NeurIPS (2017)
70. Wang, K., Shen, S.: MVDepthNet: real-time multiview depth estimation neural network. In: 3DV (2018)
71. Watson, J., Aodha, O.M., Prisacariu, V., Brostow, G., Firman, M.: The temporal opportunist: self-supervised multi-frame monocular depth. In: CVPR (2021)
72. Watson, J., Firman, M., Brostow, G.J., Turmukhambetov, D.: Self-supervised monocular depth hints. In: ICCV (2019)
73. Whelan, T., Kaess, M., Fallon, M., Johannsson, H., Leonard, J., McDonald, J.: Kintinuous: spatially extended KinectFusion. In: RSS Workshop on RGB-D: Advanced Reasoning with Depth Camera (2012)
74. Whelan, T., Leutenegger, S., Salas-Moreno, R., Glocker, B., Davison, A.: ElasticFusion: dense SLAM without a pose graph. In: Robotics: Science and Systems (2015)
75. Wightman, R.: Pytorch image models. https://github.com/rwightman/pytorch-image-models (2019). https://doi.org/10.5281/zenodo.4414861
76. Wimbauer, F., Yang, N., von Stumberg, L., Zeller, N., Cremers, D.: MonoRec: semi-supervised dense reconstruction in dynamic environments from a single moving camera. In: CVPR (2021)
77. Yang, X., et al.: Mobile3DRecon: real-time monocular 3D reconstruction on a mobile phone. IEEE Trans. Visual. Comput. Graphics **26**, 3446–3456 (2020)
78. Yao, Y., Luo, Z., Li, S., Fang, T., Quan, L.: MVSNet: depth inference for unstructured multi-view stereo. In: Ferrari, V., Hebert, M., Sminchisescu, C., Weiss, Y. (eds.) ECCV 2018. LNCS, vol. 11212, pp. 785–801. Springer, Cham (2018). https://doi.org/10.1007/978-3-030-01237-3_47
79. Yee, K., Chakrabarti, A.: Fast deep stereo with 2D convolutional processing of cost signatures. In: WACV (2020)
80. Yin, W., Liu, Y., Shen, C., Yan, Y.: Enforcing geometric constraints of virtual normal for depth prediction. In: ICCV (2019)
81. Yin, W., et al.: Learning to recover 3D scene shape from a single image. In: CVPR (2021)
82. Žbontar, J., LeCun, Y.: Stereo matching by training a convolutional neural network to compare image patches. JMLR **17**, 2287–2318 (2016)
83. Zhang, F., Prisacariu, V., Yang, R., Torr, P.H.: GA-Net: guided aggregation net for end-to-end stereo matching. In: CVPR (2019)
84. Zhang, F., Qi, X., Yang, R., Prisacariu, V., Wah, B., Torr, P.: Domain-invariant stereo matching networks. In: Vedaldi, A., Bischof, H., Brox, T., Frahm, J.-M. (eds.) ECCV 2020. LNCS, vol. 12347, pp. 420–439. Springer, Cham (2020). https://doi.org/10.1007/978-3-030-58536-5_25

85. Zhao, W., Liu, S., Wei, Y., Guo, H., Liu, Y.J.: A confidence-based iterative solver of depths and surface normals for deep multi-view stereo. In: ICCV, pp. 6168–6177, October 2021
86. Zhao, Y., Kong, S., Fowlkes, C.: Camera pose matters: improving depth prediction by mitigating pose distribution bias. In: CVPR (2021)
87. Zhou, Z., Rahman Siddiquee, M.M., Tajbakhsh, N., Liang, J.: UNet++: a nested U-Net architecture for medical image segmentation. In: Deep Learning in Medical Image Analysis and Multimodal Learning for Clinical Decision Support (2018)

Structure and Motion from Casual Videos

Zhoutong Zhang[1,2(✉)], Forrester Cole[2], Zhengqi Li[2], Michael Rubinstein[2], Noah Snavely[2,3], and William T. Freeman[1,2]

[1] MIT CSAIL, Cambridge, USA
ztzhang@mit.edu
[2] Google Research, Cambridge, USA
[3] Cornell, Ithaca, USA

Abstract. Casual videos, such as those captured in daily life using a hand-held camera, pose problems for conventional structure-from-motion (SfM) techniques: the camera is often roughly stationary (not much parallax), and a large portion of the video may contain moving objects. Under such conditions, state-of-the-art SfM methods tend to produce erroneous results, often failing entirely. To address these issues, we propose CasualSAM, a method to estimate camera poses and dense depth maps from a monocular, casually-captured video. Like conventional SfM, our method performs a joint optimization over 3D structure and camera poses, but uses a pretrained depth prediction network to represent 3D structure rather than sparse keypoints. In contrast to previous approaches, our method does not assume motion is rigid or determined by semantic segmentation, instead optimizing for a per-pixel motion map based on reprojection error. Our method sets a new state-of-the-art for pose and depth estimation on the Sintel dataset, and produces high-quality results for the DAVIS dataset where most prior methods fail to produce usable camera poses.

Keywords: Structure from motion · Depth estimation · Casual video

1 Introduction

Structure-from-motion (SfM) and related methods for 3D reconstruction from monocular video are considered a relatively mature technology. They work quite reliably for predominantly stationary scenes involving large camera motions, such as a video of a walkthrough of a house, or a video taken from a car driving down a street. Videos taken under "casual" conditions, however, often violate these assumptions. The operator is often standing roughly stationary, capturing moving subjects such as people and pets, and the video may only be a few seconds long. Under these conditions, state-of-the-art SfM systems often fail. Worse, when SfM does fail, it tends to fail spectacularly and produce useless results (Fig. 1).

Supplementary Information The online version contains supplementary material available at https://doi.org/10.1007/978-3-031-19827-4_2.

S. Avidan et al. (Eds.): ECCV 2022, LNCS 13693, pp. 20–37, 2022.
https://doi.org/10.1007/978-3-031-19827-4_2

Fig. 1. Structure and motion for casual videos. Given a casually shot video with moving objects, our method estimates the structure and motion of the scene and the camera poses. Above: input video frame. Below: 3D reconstruction of estimated stationary points for the entire video and estimated moving points for the current frame. On these videos, the conventional SfM system COLMAP either fails to create a single camera track (top right), or produces incorrect results (bottom right). Note that COLMAP is provided GT motion masks for these examples.

In this paper, we introduce a new method for dense depth and 3D camera pose estimation designed for casual videos. Our method performs a joint optimization of cameras and 3D structure over the video, similar to methods based on bundle adjustment [1,33]. But in contrast to sparse feature matches typically used in such approaches, our method optimizes dense 3D correspondences, following recent work that fine-tunes a pre-trained depth prediction network on the input video [18,37]. While powerful, previous fine-tuning methods require known camera poses, and simply adding camera poses to the optimization produces poor results [16]. We reexamine this approach and show that with several careful modifications, camera poses and the depth network can be successfully optimized together. The pre-trained depth estimates disambiguate camera motion when parallax is small, and the fine-tuning process produces sharp, temporally-consistent depth maps, leading to previously unachievable quality on real-world videos (Fig. 1).

One key innovation is to optimize for per-pixel movement maps that effectively modulate the training loss in moving areas. Unlike masks based on semantic segmentation [6,16], the movement maps capture only the parts of the scene that are *currently* moving. These movement maps, for example, allow multi-view constraints to be enforced for stationary people and vehicles. They also help relax the multi-view constrains for moving objects that semantic segmentation may miss, such as unusual animals and moving background “stuff” (such as trees swaying in the wind).

This method, which we name CasualSAM, achieves a new state-of-the-art for simultaneous depth prediction and camera pose estimation in dynamic scenes, while remaining competitive with prior methods on traditional SfM scenarios featuring stationary scenes. Our method is simple, involving a single, joint optimization with one reprojection loss term and one depth prior loss term. And, importantly, unlike conventional SfM systems that can fail catastrophically, our method gracefully degrades in performance on especially difficult videos. We benchmark the approach on the Sintel [5] and TUM RGBD [28] datasets, and show convincing qualitative results on DAVIS [24].

2 Background

Structure from Motion and Visual SLAM. Estimating camera poses and scene structure from monocular video is a long-standing problem in computer vision and related areas. This problem is variously called structure from motion (SfM) or visual SLAM, depending on the precise inputs and constraints [8,21,26] (e.g., SLAM methods often operate in real time).

The classic approach to SfM is to compute sparse 2D correspondence across the input views, and optimize for the camera poses and sparse 3D point locations that minimize a reprojection error given these 2D observations [32]. Some visual SLAM methods instead seek to solve for dense or semi-dense depth per frame, and optimize directly based on image intensities rather than sparse correspondence [10,11,14,23]. However, SfM methods based on reprojection or photometric error fundamentally depend on a static scene assumption. For dynamic scenes, the underlying epipolar constraints break down, leading to errors or failures. In addition, these methods require parallax, and face ambiguities between rotational and translational motion in the face of small camera motion.Previous work [36] recovers sparse depth measures from accidental motion, but is limited in reconstruction quality and focuses on static scenes only When faced with videos that feature a combination of small camera motion and dynamic scene motion, classic methods often produce completely erroneous results.

A variety of methods have integrated learned components into classic SfM or SLAM methods. Previous works [20,38] explored jointly optimizing depth maps, camera poses and confidence masks for weighting the photo-metric loss during training. These methods focus on mostly static scenes, where the confidence mask is either intended for excluding out-of-view pixels, or based on a tuned prior that is sensitive for joint optimization. Notable recent examples include DROID-SLAM, which makes use of a learned bundle adjustment layer to update camera poses and dense depth maps [30], and D3VO, which leverages modules for learned prediction of depth, pose, and uncertainty within a bundle adjustment framework [35]. Like D3VO and other recent methods like CodeSLAM [3], our method leverages monocular depth prediction as a prior. However, unlike our method, these prior works tend to be designed for and evaluated on standard SLAM benchmarks (such as KITTI), that feature large camera motions and dynamic content that occupies a small fraction of the field of view (if it exists at all). We show our method, with its explicit handling of motion, leads to better performance on datasets like TUM that feature more dramatic scene motion.

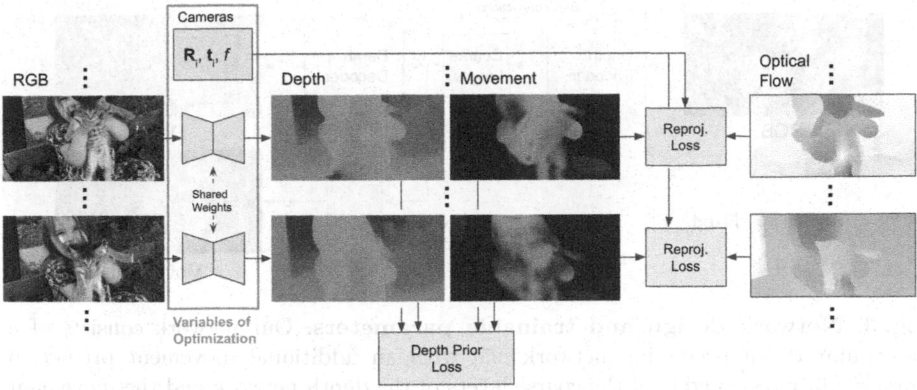

Fig. 2. System overview. Our method performs a global optimization over a video, optimizing for camera poses $\mathbf{R}_i$, $\mathbf{t}_i$, focal length f, and the weights of a monocular depth and movement prediction network. The principal loss (Reprojection Loss) compares the reprojection of the depth map with the observed optical flow, while an auxiliary loss (Depth Prior Loss) constrains the optimization to stay close to the initial depth estimates. Both losses are weighted by the estimated movement map. Only a subset of the weights of the network are optimized (see Sect. 3.2).

Some methods attempt to directly model dynamic scene motion. One class of methods, exemplified by DynamicFusion, uses explicit depth sensing (e.g., with a Kinect sensor) to reduce the ill-posedness of the problem [22]. Other *non-rigid structure from motion* methods leverage monocular video and fit a low-dimensional model to the dynamic scene [31], but have trouble scaling to arbitrary video featuring arbitrary motion. Our method works from standard RGB videos and more robustly handles scene motion.

Test-Time Refinement of Depth Estimation. Recently, methods that finetune a pretrained depth prediction network on an input video have been shown to produce high-quality, temporally-consistent depth maps [6,7,18,37]. In these methods, the optimized variables are the weights of a deep network that predicts the unknowns, rather than the unknowns themselves. A chief advantage of these methods is their ability to combine a monocular depth prior with an optimization across the entire video. These approaches can roughly be divided into methods that use a self-supervised loss to learn depth, optical flow, and camera posing [6,7], and methods that assume flow and camera poses and aim for high-quality depth map reconstruction [18,37].

Because the test-time loss is still based on triangulation, moving objects remain an issue for these methods. CVD [18] assumes a mostly stationary scene, relying on the depth prior to avoid errors due to object motion. The method of [6] segments the video and proposes separate motion models for each segment, while GLNet [7] derives motion from optical flow and estimated depth. Dynamic Video Depth [37] explicitly models scene flow with an additional neural network, but relies on accurate initial camera poses to initialize the scene flow network from

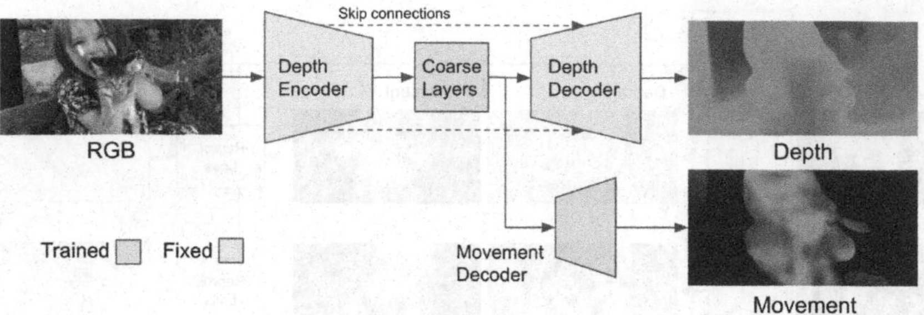

Fig. 3. Network design and trainable parameters. Our network consists of a monocular depth prediction network [25] with an additional movement prediction branch. Only the weights of the coarse layers of the depth network and the movement decoder weights are optimized. The depth prediction network is a U-net architecture with skip connections, but the movement branch is a CNN connected only to the coarse layers of the depth network.

initial depth estimates. In contrast to these approaches, we model movement as uncertainty of the reprojection accuracy. This approach is robust to camera misalignment and does not require semantic segmentation.

Most related to our work is Robust Consistent Video Depth Estimation (RCVD) [16]. Like our approach, RCVD optimizes for camera poses and depth maps in a dynamic scene using a learned depth prior, driven by observed optical flow. Unlike our method, moving objects are assumed to be masked out using semantic segmentation. Further, RCVD does not finetune the depth network, opting instead to refine depth using a spline-based warp. The reason given is that finetuning the depth network requires an alternating optimization between stochastic gradient descent for the network and global optimization for the camera poses, which is unstable. We show that this alternating optimization can be avoided by collecting a full gradient at each iteration before updating the network weights (GD vs. SGD, Sect. 3.2), and demonstrate significantly improved quality as a result (Table 1).

3 Method

Our method takes a RGB video as input and performs a joint estimation of camera poses, focal length, dense depth maps, and dense movement maps (Fig. 2). There are two key design objectives for our method: (1) robustness to camera movement featuring small translational motion and (2) robustness to significant dynamic object motion. In Sect. 3.1, we explain how our method address these two challenges. We also introduce a two-stage optimization process that aims to jointly optimize networks weights and camera poses over all input frames, similar to global bundle adjustment.

3.1 Problem Formulation

Given images of a video sequence $I_1, I_2, ..., I_n$, we aim to recover the corresponding camera rotations $\mathbf{R}_1, \mathbf{R}_2, ..., \mathbf{R}_n$, translations $\mathbf{t}_1, \mathbf{t}_2, ..., \mathbf{t}_n$, dense depth maps $D_1, D_2, ..., D_n$, and movement maps $M_1, M_2, ..., M_n$. The movement maps are not binary masks, but instead scalar fields whose magnitude correlates with object motion magnitudes. We assume a pinhole camera model whose projection center is in the middle of the image, and also aim to recover the focal length f.

Our optimization runs over a collection of pairs of frames. This collection is different between the initialization stage and the joint optimization stage. To illustrate our formulation, we start with a single pair of frames, I_i and I_j. As in geometric bundle adjustment, the major signal for driving the optimization is to make estimated depth and camera poses agree with image space pixel correspondence. In our case, the correspondence is estimated using an off-the-shelf optical flow algorithm. We denote the optical flow between I_i and I_j as $\text{flow}_{i \to j}$. If we denote camera relative transformations from I_i to I_j as $\mathbf{R}_{i \to j} = \mathbf{R}_j \mathbf{R}_i^T$ and $\mathbf{t}_{i \to j} = \mathbf{t}_j - \mathbf{t}_i$, we can write the objective as:

$$\text{Loss}_{\text{flow}}^{i \to j}(\mathbf{x}) = L(\pi(D_i(\mathbf{x})\mathbf{K}\mathbf{R}_{i \to j}\mathbf{K}^{-1}\hat{\mathbf{x}} + \mathbf{K}\mathbf{t}_{i \to j}) - \mathbf{x}, \text{flow}_{i \to j}(\mathbf{x})), \tag{1}$$

where L is some loss function, $\mathbf{x}$ is the pixel coordinate, $\hat{\mathbf{x}}$ is $\mathbf{x}$ in homogeneous coordinates, $\pi(\cdot)$ is the projection operation $(x, y, z) \to (x/z, y/z)$, and $\mathbf{K}$ is the camera intrinsics matrix derived from focal length f. Note that this formulation is equivalent to bundle adjustment using a geometric reprojection error.

However, when camera motion is dominated by rotation, as in many casual videos, Eq. 1 is less effective for optimizing D_i due to the limited parallax. This can be seen by rewriting it using disparity (1/depth) instead of depth:

$$\text{Loss}_{\text{flow}}^{i \to j}(\mathbf{x}) = L(\pi(\mathbf{K}\mathbf{R}_{i \to j}\mathbf{K}^{-1}\hat{\mathbf{x}} + \frac{1}{D_i(x)}\mathbf{K}\mathbf{t}_{i \to j}) - \mathbf{x}, \text{flow}_{i \to j}(\mathbf{x})). \tag{2}$$

When $\mathbf{t}_{i \to j}$ is small(relative to the depth D_i), the loss term's gradient w.r.t. D_i will be small due to the $\mathbf{K}\mathbf{t}_{i \to j}$ term. In such cases, another constraint is needed that keeps the depth to be consistent according to optical flow:

$$\text{Loss}_{\text{depth}}^{i \to j}(\mathbf{x}) = L(d(D_i(\mathbf{x})\mathbf{R}_{i \to j}\mathbf{K}^{-1}\hat{\mathbf{x}} + \mathbf{t}_{i \to j}), D_j(\mathbf{x} + \text{flow}_{i \to j}(\mathbf{x}))), \tag{3}$$

where $d(\cdot)$ denotes the depth of a 3D point in camera coordinates $(x, y, z) \to z$. We use both Eq. 1 and Eq. 3 for our optimization.

Note that the combination of these two objectives are found effective by CVD [18] and RCVD [16], each with their specific choice of the loss function L. For our implementation, we use L_1 for $\text{Loss}_{\text{flow}}$ and the ratio loss introduced in RCVD for $\text{Loss}_{\text{depth}}$. The ratio loss has the form:

$$L(a, b) = \left| \frac{\max(a, b)}{\min(a, b)} - 1 \right| \tag{4}$$

Handling Movement. Until now, our formulation only addresses the problem of small camera translation, and not the problem of object motion. Most SfM methods that handle scene motion do so through a required input motion mask that specifies the moving regions, since pixels that belong to moving objects are outliers in both Eq. 1 and Eq. 3, contaminating the optimization process. In many cases, semantic segmentation is used as an approximation, where objects belonging to classes that tend to move are excluded from the optimization [2,16]. As shown in Fig. 8, semantic segments can be problematic. For example, pixels corresponding to stationary people are often excluded, but they are in fact helpful for depth and camera triangulation.

Instead of semantic segmentation, we aim to estimate object movement as part of the joint optimization. We adopt the machinery of Bayesian deep learning [13] and treat movement as the *heteroscedastic aleatoric uncertainty* of the reprojection, or in other words, a spatially-varying estimate of the noise of the depth and camera predictions. Instead of a Gaussian noise model as in [13], we use a Cauchy distribution as we empirically find it more robust. Treating the movement map M_i as the γ of a zero-mean Cauchy distribution, taking the negative-log-likelihood and simplifying, the error function is:

$$\mathrm{C}(\mathbf{x}, \mathrm{Loss}) = \log(M_i(\mathbf{x}) + \frac{\mathrm{Loss}(\mathbf{x})^2}{M_i(\mathbf{x})}). \tag{5}$$

The full reprojection loss is then:

$$L_{\text{reproj}}^{i \to j} = \frac{1}{N} \sum_{\mathbf{x}} \mathrm{C}(\mathbf{x}, \mathrm{Loss}_{\text{flow}}^{i \to j}) + \mathrm{C}(\mathbf{x}, \mathrm{Loss}_{\text{depth}}^{i \to j}). \tag{6}$$

As in [13], the uncertainty M_i is learned and allows the optimization to reduce M_i where the loss can be minimized effectively, and increase M_i where it cannot. Intuitively, M_i becomes a measure of how far an outlier the optical flow at $\mathbf{x}$ is from the expected ego-flow, which is in turn an estimate of how much object movement is present.

While the above method encourages an accurate movement map M_i, by design it does not penalize inaccurate depth estimates where M_i is large. Where M_i is large and the reprojection loss is unreliable, we fall back to the depth prior. Specifically, we propose to constrain the depth estimate D to the initial depth estimate D^{init} using a movement-weighted version of the scale invariant loss [9]:

$$L_{\text{prior}}^{i} = \frac{1}{N} \sum_{\mathbf{x}} M_i(\mathbf{x}) (\log \frac{D_i(\mathbf{x})}{D_i^{\text{init}}(\mathbf{x})} + \alpha)^2, \quad \alpha = \frac{1}{N} \sum_{\mathbf{x}} \log \frac{D_i^{\text{init}}(\mathbf{x})}{D_i(\mathbf{x})} \tag{7}$$

as a depth prior loss. Finally, the total loss function we use for optimizing a pair of images is:

$$L_{\text{total}}^{i,j} = L_{\text{reproj}}^{i \to j} + \lambda L_{\text{prior}}^{i}, \tag{8}$$

where we use $\lambda = 1$ through out the experiments. To optimize over a collection of pairs, we average $L_{\text{total}}^{i,j}$ over all pairs for the total Loss L_{total}.

3.2 Two-Stage Optimization

Initialization. Since the depth maps from the depth prediction network are scale and shift invariant, we need to roughly align them before the joint optimization. Empirically, we find that calibrating only the scale is sufficient for the optimization. Specifically, for each initial depth map D_i^{init}, we assign a scale variable s_i and let $D_i = s_i D_i^{\text{init}}$ when optimizing L_{total}. During this phase, the weights of the depth network are fixed while the remaining variables are optimized.

The collection of image pairs is defined by a sliding window of 5 frames, from the beginning of the image sequence to the end. We use all pairs of frames within the sliding window, and optimize L_{total} for 600 iterations.

Full Optimization. After initialization, the camera poses are roughly aligned but not yet sufficiently accurate (Table 1). We then fix the scale factors s_i and optimize the weights of the depth network, letting $D_i = s_i \text{DepthNet}(I_i)$ while optimizing L_{total}. In contrast to the initialization stage, in this stage we optimize L_{total} over all the frames in the video, with a collection of images pairs covering the entire set of images. Empirically, we find the pair sampling strategy by CVD is simple and effective; image pair i, j is sampled if $|i - j|$ is a power of 2. Note that we compute a full gradient for each step and perform gradient descent (GD) for both network weights and camera parameters, using an adaptive first-order optimizer (Adam [15]). The per-parameter weight tuning of Adam is sufficient to deal with the widely varying gradient magnitudes between the camera parameters and network weights.

Implementation Details. We use RAFT [29] to estimate optical flow and MiDaS [25] as the depth prediction network. Since we perform a full gradient descent over all sampled pairs of frames during the full optimization, we only optimize the coarse layers (4 refinement layers) of the MiDaS decoder to make computation costs manageable. The movement maps M_i are generated by a small CNN decoder that takes as input the MiDaS encoder output (Fig. 3). The decoder is composed of 8 convolution layers with two bi-linear upsampling layers. More details of the networks can be found in the supplementary material.

The camera poses are represented with camera-to-world translations and rotations. Rotations are represented in Lie Algebra $\mathfrak{so}(3)$, and translations as 3d vectors. Focal length f is initialized as 55mm through out all the experiments.

We use a learning rate of 1e-3 for the movement map decoder, 1e-4 for the coarse layers of MiDaS network. For the full optimization, we accumulate gradients over batches of 8 pairs of frames to perform full gradient descent. We take 1800 iterations of full gradient descent for all our experiments. Since Eq. 5 is ill-defined when $M_i = 0$, we add a fixed bias of 0.5 to M_i when computing the error function.

4 Results

We evaluate CasualSAM both quantitatively and qualitatively on the MPI Sintel dataset [5], dynamic sequences from the TUM RGB-D dataset [28], and the

DAVIS video dataset [24]. We evaluate both camera pose and depth maps on Sintel, which contains fast object and camera motion with ground truth annotations. We evaluate camera pose accuracy on the TUM dynamic sequences, where motion is limited but ground truth camera poses are provided. Since no ground-truth depth or poses are available for DAVIS, we evaluate consistency between our predictions and optical flow, and show results for 3D reconstruction.

Baselines. We compare with two state-of-the-art learning-based methods: DROID-SLAM (DSLAM) [30] and Robust CVD (RCVD) [16]. DSLAM is a robust SLAM system that focuses on camera localization for almost static scenes and requires camera intrinsics as an input. RCVD is a camera localization and depth estimation system aimed at video clips. It optimizes camera focal length within its system and uses an off-the-shelf semantic segmentation as an approximation for movement masks. We also compare with COLMAP [26,27] as a non-learning based baseline to demonstrate the limitations of conventional SfM.

4.1 Camera Pose and Depth Accuracy on Sintel

Camera Pose Evaluation. We compare camera pose quality against RCVD and DSLAM. Metrics used are Absolute Translation Error(ATE), Relative Translation Error(RTE) and Relative Rotation Error(RRE). Since camera tracks in the Sintel dataset have very different lengths (from less than 1 m to larger than 100 m), simply averaging over all sequences introduces bias towards long trajectories. Therefore, before calculating the metrics, ground truth trajectories are normalized to unit length. For all methods, we align the predicted results to the normalized ground truth tracks using Umeyama [34] alignment with scale calibration. Five sequences are excluded from ATE and RTE calculation because the cameras are stationary. The overall results are reported in Table 1 and per-track statistics in Fig. 4. Our method achieves 53% smaller ATE than DSLAM given the ground truth camera intrinsics, and 46% smaller ATE than RCVD when optimizing for focal length.

Table 1. Pose and depth accuracy on Sintel. We compare camera pose accuracy on Sintel using normalized ATE and RTE (fraction of total path length) for translation, and RRE for rotation in degrees

Method	Pose Error ↓			Depth Error, Rel. L1 ↓			Avg. Depth Accuracy ↑		
	ATE	RRE	RTE	Avg.	Dynamic	Static	$\delta < 1.5$	$\delta < 1.5^2$	$\delta < 1.5^3$
DSLAM† (GT focal) [30]	0.077	1.605	0.043	–	–	–	–	–	–
Ours (GT focal)	**0.036**	**0.190**	**0.008**	0.440	1.151	0.191	0.651	0.792	0.863
RCVD‡ (Opt. focal) [16]	0.164	1.151	0.057	0.847	1.505	0.427	0.543	0.718	0.806
Ours (Init. only)	0.122	0.449	0.025	0.697	1.468	0.305	0.526	0.719	0.825
Ours (No uncertainty)	0.134	0.573	0.026	0.779	2.295	0.284	0.527	0.717	0.829
Ours (Opt. focal, full)	**0.089**	**0.410**	**0.015**	**0.484**	**1.267**	**0.227**	**0.626**	**0.775**	**0.853**

† We use the original code to run all experiments. ‡ we used the results provided by the authors.

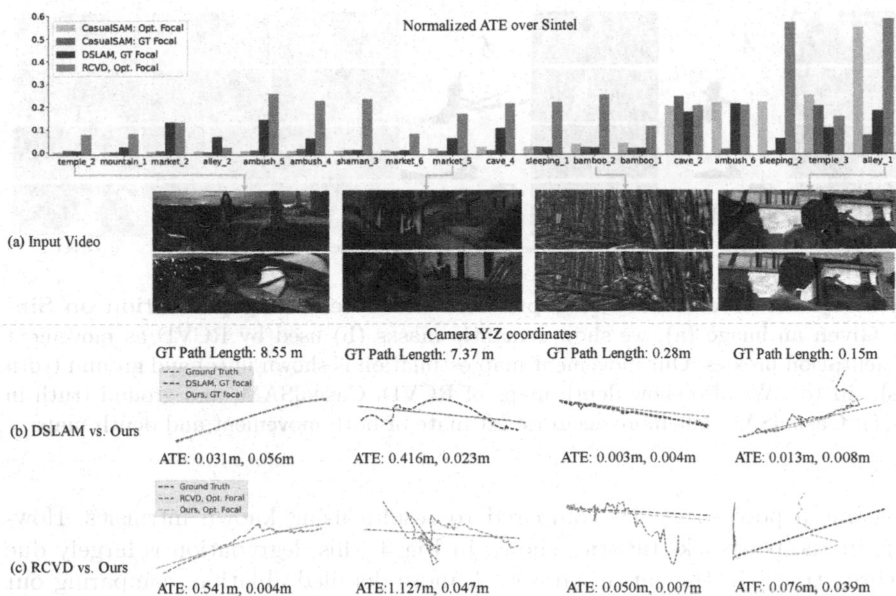

Fig. 4. Results of camera localization on Sintel. In the top row, we plot ATE results of CasualSAM, RCVD and D-SLAM over all the Sintel sequences, sorted by ATE of CasualSAM without ground truth focal length. We then select 4 sequences from low ATE to high ATE shown in (a). We plot the Y-Z coordinates of the camera locations of each method against ground truth (b-e).

Depth Map Evaluation. We evaluate the depth map quality against RCVD. Because DSLAM a slam system that focuses on camera localization, it is excluded from depth evaluation. We adopt the standard depth metrics: Absolute Relative Error and Delta accuracy measures; for Absolute Relative Error, we report results for static and dynamics regions separately, in addition to the average error. We follow the standard evaluation protocol by excluding points that are further than 80 m. Median alignment is applied for all the metric calculations. We report quantitative results in Table 1 and qualitative results in Fig. 5. Ours method produces more accurate depth maps than RCVD for dynamics and static part of the scenes, qualitatively and quantitatively.

Ablations. We perform an ablation study on the sintel dataset, quantifying the contribution of uncertainty map estimation and known intrinsics. Without uncertainty map estimation, where the reprojection and prior term are replaced with plain L1 loss, both camera pose quality and depth map quality degrades, as all the moving objects are treated as if being static. Without known intrinsics,

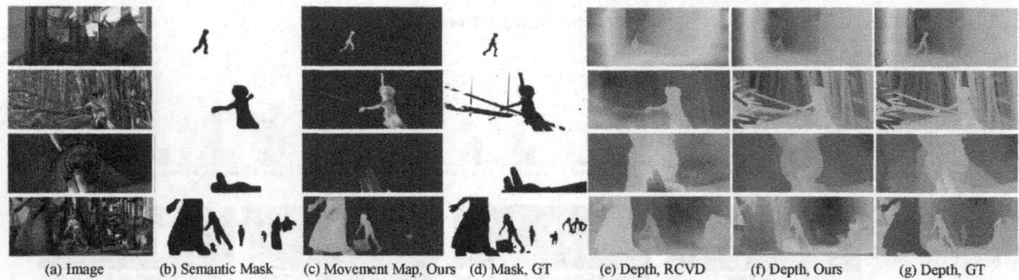

Fig. 5. Qualitative results of depth and movement map prediction on Sintel. Given an image (a), we show semantic masks (b) used by RCVD as movement segmentation proxies. Our movement map estimation is shown in (c) and ground truth masks in (d). We also show depth maps of RCVD, CasualSAM, and ground truth in (e)-(f). CasualSAM has more accurate estimate of both movement and depth maps.

the camera poses degrades compared to results using known intrinsics. However, in the per-track statistics shown in Fig. 4, this degradation is largely due to three tracks in the entire dataset. A more detailed ablation, comparing our uncertainty map estimation against previous works [20,38] can be found in the supplementary material (Table 2).

Table 2. ATE on TUM dynamic sequences. Absolute Translation Error (ATE) in meters of estimated camera poses for dynamic sequences in the TUM RGBD dataset [28]

Method	s_halfsphere	s_rpy	s_static	s_xyz	w_halfsphere	w_rpy	w_static	w_xyz
DROID-SLAM (GT focal) [30]	0.079	0.065	**0.005**	0.009	**0.023**	0.144	0.006	0.016
Ours (GT focal)	**0.045**	**0.019**	**0.005**	**0.008**	0.080	**0.032**	**0.005**	**0.012**
RCVD(Opt. K)	0.254	0.058	0.026	0.206	0.241	0.171	0.020	0.205
Ours(Opt. K)	**0.096**	**0.033**	**0.008**	**0.009**	**0.088**	**0.082**	**0.007**	**0.024**

4.2 Camera Pose Accuracy on TUM Benchmarks

We further evaluate camera pose quality of CasualSAM on the dynamic subset of the TUM benchmarks. This subset contains 8 tracks, capturing two people sitting and walking in front of an office desk. In addition to dynamic objects, this sequence is challenging due to versatile camera motions. Our method is better or on par with Droid-SLAM for 7 out 8 sequences with known intrinsics, and is better than RCVD in all sequences when intrinsics is not known.

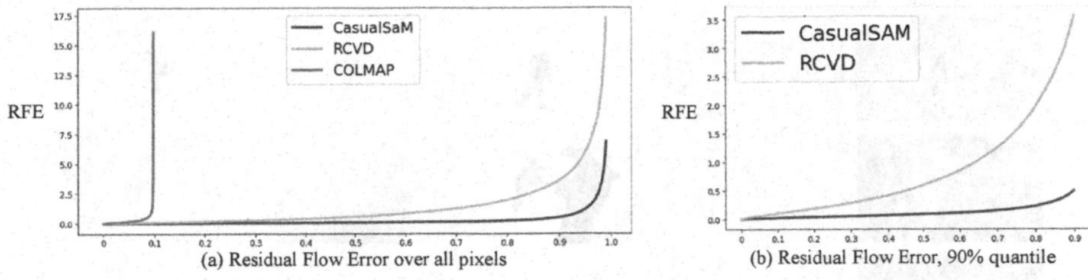

(a) Residual Flow Error over all pixels

(b) Residual Flow Error, 90% quantile

Fig. 6. Residual Flow Error Over DAVIS. (a) We show the Residual Flow Error statistics over all the valid pixels in the DAVIS dataset. Even with GT segmentation, COLMAP [27] only generates valid depth values for 10% pixels over the entire dataset. (b) 90% of the errors of CasualSAM are below 0.5 pixels.

4.3 Depth and Pose Quality on DAVIS

The DAVIS video dataset [24] is a set of 90 short videos captured with hand-held cameras and containing moving objects. Most of the videos are less than 10 s long. Though intended as a segmentation benchmark, the dataset provides an excellent range of casual videos to test our method.

Residual Flow Error. Since no ground-truth camera poses were captured, we instead evaluate how well the ego-flow induced by the camera motion and the estimated depth map agree with optical flow as measured by RAFT [29]. Since DAVIS provides segmentation masks for foreground objects, we report the differences between ego-flow and optical flow outside the mask, which is suppose to be static through out the video. We refer to this metric as Residual Flow Error(RFE). To give an accurate picture of the distribution of results, we plot the cumulative distributions of errors across all pixels of the DAVIS videos in Fig. 6. Note that the RFE of CasualSAM is 53% of RCVD and 90% of the error is less than 0.5 pixels. We show qualitative results of the RFE in Fig. 7.

We also compare with COLMAP [26,27] under RFE. COLMAP's SfM pipeline either failed or produced multiple tracks for 63 out of 90 videos, even when provided the DAVIS GT segmentation as a movement mask. For the remaining 27 sequences, we run the COLMAP's MVS pipeline for per-frame depth estimates, which provides valid depth values for only 10% of all pixels. The RFE for the majority of valid pixels is low, but still higher than the bottom 10% of pixels from our method (Fig. 6).

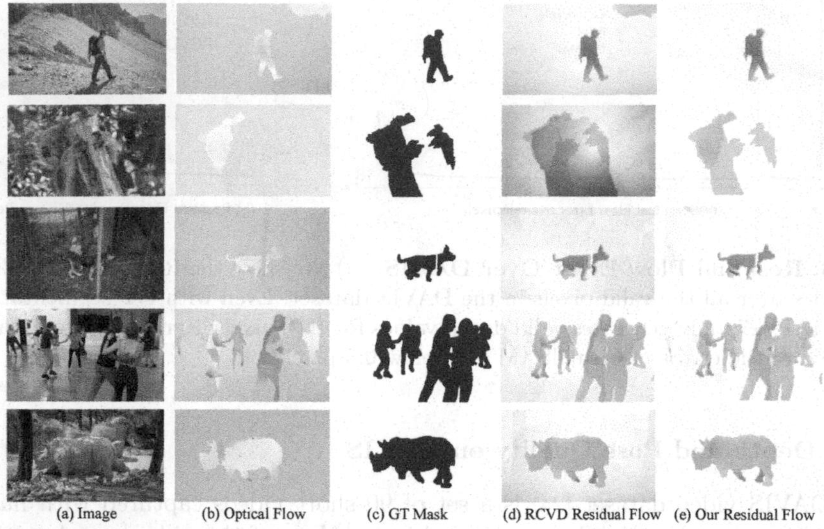

Fig. 7. Residual flow results. Given input image (a), we show its optical flow towards next frame (b) and DAVIS GT segmentation (c). Residual flow of RCVD and ours is shown in (d) and (e) respectively. GT segmentation is shown in grey and pixels outside the mask should show small errors.

Fig. 8. Learned movement map vs. alternatives. From an RGB input (a)(b), the movement prediction network produces a map of moving regions (e), blue: not moving, red: moving). We show three cases where semantic segmentation (c) is not accurate: under segmentation (top), over segmentation (middle), and segmentations (or lack thereof) of objects that are not actually moving (or moving) in the scene (bottom). (Color figure online)

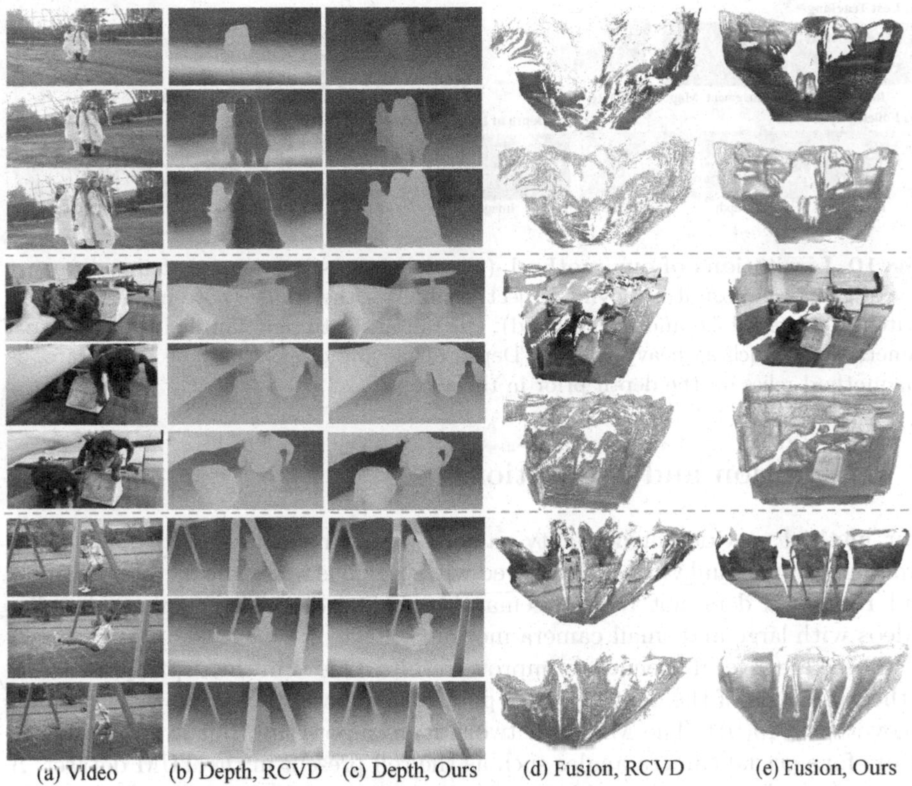

Fig. 9. Qualitative Results on Davis. (a) Input video. (b) Depth maps from Robust CVD [16]. (c) Depth maps from CasualSAM (ours). (d) KinectFusion results [12] using RCVD estimated depth maps, camera poses and motion masks (semantic segmentation). (e) KinectFusion results using our estimated depth maps, camera poses and movement maps.

Movement Mask Comparison. The movement maps M_i are more sensitive and specific than using semantic segmentation as a proxy for motion segmentation, as shown in Fig. 8. Since the semantic segmentation is ignorant of motion cues, it may exhibit different types of failures compared to ours.

Depth and Reprojection. We show qualitative results on depth and 3D reconstruction in Fig. 9. For 3D reconstruction, we use the predicted depths and camera poses as input to KinectFusion [12] to generate a mesh. To exclude moving objects from this mesh, we threshold our estimated movement map at 0.5, and use semantic segmentation for RCVD as described by the authors [16]. Our depth maps are more plausible than RCVD. Our fusion results are cleaner as well, suggesting our estimated camera poses and depth maps agree with each other better than RCVD.

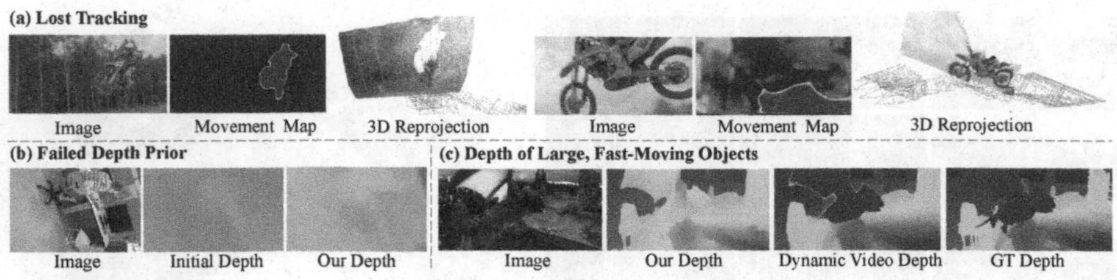

Fig. 10. Limitations of our method. (a) movement estimation may fail and camera tracking may be lost if a moving object dominates the frame (note movement map switches between bike and background). (b) Initial depth may fail due to an unusual camera angle, such as heavy roll. (c) Depth of moving objects may be inaccurate, as our method relies on the depth prior in those cases.

5 Discussion and Limitations

Our method provides high-quality camera poses and dense depth maps for a broad range of casual videos. Compared with previous work, the method is simple and robust: it does not require semantic labeling of moving regions, handles videos with large and small camera motion.

There are several avenues to improve results. One is in the depth prior itself: if the prediction of the depth CNN is particularly poor, the optimization cannot recover (Fig. 10(b)). The MiDaS network is very powerful, but is vulnerable to errors for unusual camera angles such as the roll present in the TUM dataset. A more robust depth prior would similarly make our method more robust.

Currently, the camera model is a pinhole camera with a constant focal length for the entire video. However, wide-angle, zoom, and even fisheye lenses are common in casual videos (including the DAVIS dataset; see supplemental material). While unconstrained optimization for per-frame, multi-parameter intrinsics may be unstable, recent work proposed CNNs for intrinsics prediction [4,17,19] that could optimized similarly to our depth prior.

When the camera moves very rapidly, or when a moving object covers most of the frame, our method can lose tracking (Fig. 10(a)). Improved uncertainty map estimation, possibly using semantic features, may allow the optimization maintain a consistent track across such interruptions.

Finally, our method relies on the depth prior for depth estimation in moving regions, which may be inaccurate (Fig. 10(c)). Dynamic Video Depth [37] has shown improved depth maps in moving regions by using an explicit estimate of sceneflow and using it to apply multi-view constraints to moving objects, and this approach could likely be integrated with ours.

Acknowledgements. The authors would like to thank Jian-bin Huang for providing the official results of RCVD [16].

References

1. Agarwal, S., Snavely, N., Seitz, S.M., Szeliski, R.: Bundle adjustment in the large. In: Daniilidis, K., Maragos, P., Paragios, N. (eds.) ECCV 2010. LNCS, vol. 6312, pp. 29–42. Springer, Heidelberg (2010). https://doi.org/10.1007/978-3-642-15552-9_3
2. Bescos, B., Fácil, J.M., Civera, J., Neira, J.: Dynaslam: tracking, mapping, and inpainting in dynamic scenes. IEEE Robot. Autom. Lett. **3**(4), 4076–4083 (2018)
3. Bloesch, M., Czarnowski, J., Clark, R., Leutenegger, S., Davison, A.: CodeSLAM–learning a compact, optimisable representation for dense visual SLAM. In: CVPR (2018)
4. Bogdan, O., Eckstein, V., Rameau, F., Bazin, J.C.: Deepcalib: a deep learning approach for automatic intrinsic calibration of wide field-of-view cameras. In: Proceedings of the 15th ACM SIGGRAPH European Conference on Visual Media Production (2018)
5. Butler, D.J., Wulff, J., Stanley, G.B., Black, M.J.: A naturalistic open source movie for optical flow evaluation. In: Fitzgibbon, A., Lazebnik, S., Perona, P., Sato, Y., Schmid, C. (eds.) ECCV 2012. LNCS, vol. 7577, pp. 611–625. Springer, Heidelberg (2012). https://doi.org/10.1007/978-3-642-33783-3_44
6. Casser, V.M., Pirk, S., Mahjourian, R., Angelova, A.: Depth prediction without the sensors: leveraging structure for unsupervised learning from monocular videos. In: AAAI (2019)
7. Chen, Y., Schmid, C., Sminchisescu, C.: Self-supervised learning with geometric constraints in monocular video: Connecting flow, depth, and camera. In: ICCV, pp. 7063–7072 (2019)
8. Davison, A.J., Reid, I.D., Molton, N.D., Stasse, O.: MonoSLAM: real-time single camera SLAM. TPAMI **29**(6), 1052–1067 (2007)
9. Eigen, D., Puhrsch, C., Fergus, R.: Depth map prediction from a single image using a multi-scale deep network. arXiv preprint arXiv:1406.2283 (2014)
10. Engel, J., Koltun, V., Cremers, D.: Direct sparse odometry. TPAMI **40**, 611–625 (2018)
11. Engel, J., Schöps, T., Cremers, D.: LSD-SLAM: large-scale direct monocular SLAM. In: Fleet, D., Pajdla, T., Schiele, B., Tuytelaars, T. (eds.) ECCV 2014. LNCS, vol. 8690, pp. 834–849. Springer, Cham (2014). https://doi.org/10.1007/978-3-319-10605-2_54
12. Izadi, S., et al.: Kinectfusion: real-time 3D reconstruction and interaction using a moving depth camera. In: UIST 2011 Proceedings of the 24th Annual ACM Symposium on User Interface Software and Technology, pp. 559–568. ACM, October 2011
13. Kendall, A., Gal, Y.: What uncertainties do we need in Bayesian deep learning for computer vision? In: Proceedings of the 31st International Conference on Neural Information Processing Systems. NIPS 2017, Red Hook, NY, USA, pp. 5580–5590. Curran Associates Inc. (2017)
14. Kerl, C., Sturm, J., Cremers, D.: Dense visual slam for RGB-D cameras. In: IROS (2013)
15. Kingma, D., Ba, J.: Adam: A method for stochastic optimization. In: International Conference on Learning Representations, December 2014
16. Kopf, J., Rong, X., Huang, J.B.: Robust consistent video depth estimation. In: IEEE/CVF Conference on Computer Vision and Pattern Recognition (2021)

17. Li, X., Zhang, B., Sander, P.V., Liao, J.: Blind geometric distortion correction on images through deep learning. In: Proceedings of the IEEE Conference on Computer Vision and Pattern Recognition, pp. 4855–4864 (2019)
18. Luo, X., Huang, J., Szeliski, R., Matzen, K., Kopf, J.: Consistent video depth estimation. In: ACM Transactions on Graphics (Proceedings of ACM SIGGRAPH) (2020)
19. López, M., Marí, R., Gargallo, P., Kuang, Y., Gonzalez-Jimenez, J., Haro, G.: Deep single image camera calibration with radial distortion. In: 2019 IEEE/CVF Conference on Computer Vision and Pattern Recognition (CVPR), pp. 11809–11817 (2019). https://doi.org/10.1109/CVPR.2019.01209
20. Mahjourian, R., Wicke, M., Angelova, A.: Unsupervised learning of depth and ego-motion from monocular video using 3d geometric constraints. In: Proceedings of the IEEE Conference on Computer Vision and Pattern Recognition, pp. 5667–5675 (2018)
21. Mur-Artal, R., Tardós, J.D.: ORB-SLAM2: an open-source SLAM system for monocular, stereo and RGB-D cameras. IEEE Trans. Robot. **33**(5), 1255–1262 (2017)
22. Newcombe, R.A., Fox, D., Seitz, S.M.: DynamicFusion: reconstruction and tracking of non-rigid scenes in real-time. In: CVPR (2015)
23. Newcombe, R.A., Lovegrove, S.J., Davison, A.J.: DTAM: dense tracking and mapping in real-time. In: ICCV (2011)
24. Perazzi, F., Pont-Tuset, J., McWilliams, B., Van Gool, L., Gross, M., Sorkine-Hornung, A.: A benchmark dataset and evaluation methodology for video object segmentation. In: CVPR (2016)
25. Ranftl, R., Lasinger, K., Hafner, D., Schindler, K., Koltun, V.: Towards robust monocular depth estimation: mixing datasets for zero-shot cross-dataset transfer. IEEE Trans. Pattern Anal. Mach. Intell. (TPAMI) **44**, 1623–1637 (2020)
26. Schönberger, J.L., Frahm, J.M.: Structure-from-motion revisited. In: CVPR (2016)
27. Schönberger, J.L., Zheng, E., Frahm, J.-M., Pollefeys, M.: Pixelwise view selection for unstructured multi-view stereo. In: Leibe, B., Matas, J., Sebe, N., Welling, M. (eds.) ECCV 2016. LNCS, vol. 9907, pp. 501–518. Springer, Cham (2016). https://doi.org/10.1007/978-3-319-46487-9_31
28. Sturm, J., Engelhard, N., Endres, F., Burgard, W., Cremers, D.: A benchmark for the evaluation of RGB-D slam systems. In: Proceedings of the International Conference on Intelligent Robot Systems (IROS), October 2012
29. Teed, Z., Deng, J.: RAFT: recurrent all-pairs field transforms for optical flow. In: Vedaldi, A., Bischof, H., Brox, T., Frahm, J.-M. (eds.) ECCV 2020. LNCS, vol. 12347, pp. 402–419. Springer, Cham (2020). https://doi.org/10.1007/978-3-030-58536-5_24
30. Teed, Z., Deng, J.: DROID-SLAM: deep visual SLAM for monocular, stereo, and RGB-D cameras. In: NeurIPS (2021)
31. Torresani, L., Hertzmann, A., Bregler, C.: Nonrigid structure-from-motion: estimating shape and motion with hierarchical priors. TPAMI **30**(5), 878–892 (2008)
32. Triggs, B., McLauchlan, P.F., Hartley, R.I., Fitzgibbon, A.W.: Bundle adjustment - a modern synthesis. In: Proceedings of the International Workshop on Vision Algorithms: Theory and Practice (1999)
33. Triggs, B., McLauchlan, P.F., Hartley, R.I., Fitzgibbon, A.W.: Bundle adjustment — a modern synthesis. In: Triggs, B., Zisserman, A., Szeliski, R. (eds.) IWVA 1999. LNCS, vol. 1883, pp. 298–372. Springer, Heidelberg (2000). https://doi.org/10.1007/3-540-44480-7_21

34. Umeyama, S.: Least-squares estimation of transformation parameters between two point patterns. IEEE Trans. Pattern Anal. Mach. Intell. **13**(4), 376–380 (1991). https://doi.org/10.1109/34.88573
35. Yang, N., von Stumberg, L., Wang, R., Cremers, D.: D3VO: deep depth, deep pose and deep uncertainty for monocular visual odometry. In: CVPR (2020)
36. Yu, F., Gallup, D.: 3d reconstruction from accidental motion. In: Proceedings of the IEEE Conference on Computer Vision and Pattern Recognition, pp. 3986–3993 (2014)
37. Zhang, Z., Cole, F., Tucker, R., Freeman, W.T., Dekel, T.: Consistent depth of moving objects in video. ACM Trans. Graphics (TOG) **40**(4), 1–12 (2021)
38. Zhou, T., Brown, M., Snavely, N., Lowe, D.G.: Unsupervised learning of depth and ego-motion from video. In: Proceedings of the IEEE Conference on Computer Vision and Pattern Recognition, pp. 1851–1858 (2017)

What Matters for 3D Scene Flow Network

Guangming Wang[1], Yunzhe Hu[1], Zhe Liu[2], Yiyang Zhou[3], Masayoshi Tomizuka[3], Wei Zhan[3], and Hesheng Wang[1](✉)

[1] Department of Automation, Key Laboratory of System Control and Information Processing of Ministry of Education, Key Laboratory of Marine Intelligent Equipment and System of Ministry of Education, Shanghai Jiao Tong University, Shanghai, China
{wangguangming,huyz7830,liuzhesjtu,wanghesheng}@sjtu.edu.cn

[2] MoE Key Lab of Artificial Intelligence, Shanghai Jiao Tong University, Shanghai, China

[3] Mechanical Systems Control Laboratory, University of California, Berkeley, USA
{yiyang.zhou,tomizuka,wzhan}@berkeley.edu

Abstract. 3D scene flow estimation from point clouds is a low-level 3D motion perception task in computer vision. Flow embedding is a commonly used technique in scene flow estimation, and it encodes the point motion between two consecutive frames. Thus, it is critical for the flow embeddings to capture the correct overall direction of the motion. However, previous works only search locally to determine a soft correspondence, ignoring the distant points that turn out to be the actual matching ones. In addition, the estimated correspondence is usually from the forward direction of the adjacent point clouds, and may not be consistent with the estimated correspondence acquired from the backward direction. To tackle these problems, we propose a novel all-to-all flow embedding layer with backward reliability validation during the initial scene flow estimation. Besides, we investigate and compare several design choices in key components of the 3D scene flow network, including the point similarity calculation, input elements of predictor, and predictor & refinement level design. After carefully choosing the most effective designs, we are able to present a model that achieves the state-of-the-art performance on FlyingThings3D and KITTI Scene Flow datasets. Our proposed model surpasses all existing methods by at least 38.2% on FlyingThings3D dataset and 24.7% on KITTI Scene Flow dataset for EPE3D metric. We release our codes at https://github.com/IRMVLab/3DFlow.

Keywords: 3D scene flow estimation · 3D PWC structure · All-to-all point mixture · Point clouds · 3D deep learning

1 Introduction

As a fundamental task in computer vision, scene flow estimation aims to estimate a 3D motion field consisting of point-wise or pixel-wise 3D displacement vectors between

G. Wang and Y. Hu—Contributed equally.

Supplementary Information The online version contains supplementary material available at https://doi.org/10.1007/978-3-031-19827-4_3.

S. Avidan et al. (Eds.): ECCV 2022, LNCS 13693, pp. 38–55, 2022.
https://doi.org/10.1007/978-3-031-19827-4_3

two consecutive frames of point clouds or images. It provides a low-level representation and understanding of the motion of dynamic objects in the scene. Many applications directly benefit from the techniques used in scene flow estimation, such as semantic segmentation [20], multi-object tracking [41,48], point cloud registration [19,43,45], etc. The performance of scene flow estimation algorithms on point clouds has been greatly improved since deep learning was first applied in [19]. Recent studies [4,16,17, 19,28,39,44,50] focus more on estimating scene flow in an end-to-end fashion from two consecutive frames of raw 3D point clouds. These approaches predict scene flow with only 3D coordinates of point clouds as inputs with no need for any prior knowledge of the scene structure. This paper also focuses on such a research topic.

Previous learning-based methods [19,44,50] adopt flow embedding to correlate adjacent frames of point clouds and to encode point motion. Their models then propagate the flow embedding through set upconv layers [19] or coarse-to-fine warping [44,50] to regress the scene flow. FlowNet3D [19], for example, introduces the flow embedding in a point-to-patch manner, which means that a specific point in the first point cloud PC_1 merely uses several neighbouring points in the second point cloud PC_2 to learn the correlation. PointPWC-Net [50] further improves it and proposes to learn a patch-to-patch flow embedding, which adds a second point-to-patch embedding process in PC_1 itself after the first point-to-patch embedding between two point clouds. In addition, Pyramid, Warping, and Cost volume (PWC) structure [32] is introduced to refine the scene flow for several times. HALFlow [44] also follows this PWC structure [32] but improves by introducing the attention mechanism in both embedding processes. However, during the first embedding process between two point clouds, these methods only search for K Nearest Neighbours (KNN) in PC_2 to aggregate correspondence information. Practically, K is substantially smaller than the total number of points in the second frame, making it possible for a point in PC_1 to miss the correct yet distant matching point in PC_2. Moreover, it is extremely important to obtain a reliable correlation when calculating it for the first time because it encodes the overall direction of the flow. The scene flow will be eventually misguided if this issue is ignored. To tackle this problem, we introduce a novel all-to-all flow embedding layer based on the double attentive flow embedding layer in HALFlow [44]. With all-to-all embedding, each point in PC_1 will use all points in PC_2 for correlation during the first embedding process, and each point in PC_2 can therefore obtain the correlation with all points in PC_1 too. This mechanism allows that the feature correlation of all points can be exhaustively utilized from both sides and reliable correspondence estimation can be further achieved.

This all-to-all mechanism, however, cannot guarantee that the reliable correlation is bi-directional. That is, the estimated match pair for a specific point in PC_1 in the forward direction may not be consistent with the match for the corresponding matched point in PC_2 in the backward direction. Therefore, we need another constraint on the backward match to validate its consistency with the forward pass. Mittal *et al.* [26] utilize a similar mechanism by designing a cycle-consistency loss to achieve self-supervising the scene flow estimation. However, we expect to directly incorporate this constraint of backward validation into our network to allow the network to learn this ability in forward reasoning. To this end, we propose backward reliability validation, a joint learning method of backward constraint in the all-to-all flow embedding layer.

Furthermore, there are several components of our network with alternative designs either from themselves or from other works that could affect the performance. Therefore, we conduct a series of ablation studies to compare different designs and to explore which elements are important and which designs are suitable for 3D scene flow network, including the point similarity calculation, predictor elements choice, and predictor & refinement level design. Our key contributions are as follows:

1. A novel all-to-all point mixture module with backward reliability validation is proposed for reliable correlation between point clouds. The all-to-all mechanism is adopted to capture reliable match candidates from the distance, and backward information is integrated in the inference process to validate the matching consistency.
2. Different designs and techniques of 3D scene flow network are widely compared and analyzed. *Point Similarity Calculation, Designs of Scene Flow Predictor, Input elements of Scene Flow Predictor*, and *Flow Refinement Level Design* are individually discussed and evaluated to showcase what matters in 3D scene flow network.
3. Experiments demonstrate that our model achieves state-of-the-art performance, reducing EPE3D metric by at least 38.2% on FlyingThings3D dataset [23] and 24.7% on KITTI Scene Flow dataset [25]. The effectiveness of proposed techniques and choices of network designs are demonstrated through extensive ablation studies.

2 Related Work

The concept of scene flow is first introduced by Vedula *et al.* [36] as the 3D motion field in real-world scenarios. Many previous works estimate scene flow by recovering the 3D motion from optical flow and depth information on 2D image pairs, either using RGB-stereo [7,22–24,27,35,37,38] or RGB-D [5,6,11] data. There has also been some recent works focusing on recovering scene flow from monocular camera [8,9,42,52,53]. However, since scene flow indicates the 3D motion, directly estimating scene flow from 3D data input can enable direct optimization and higher accuracy. The applications of LiDARs in recent years have created more available raw data of point cloud, and point-cloud-based scene flow estimation approaches [2,34] are rapidly emerging.

Since deep learning has shown excellent performance for raw point-cloud-based tasks [21,40,46,51] with the proposal of PointNet [29] and PointNet++ [30], many works estimate scene flow directly from raw point clouds in an end-to-end fashion. FlowNet3D [19] presents the first end-to-end scene flow estimation framework on point clouds. It uses PointNet++ [30] to extract local point features and introduces a flow embedding layer to encode the point motions. HPLFlow-Net [4] leverages the idea from Bilateral Convolutional Layers (BCL) [12,14] and proposes DownBCL, UpBCL, and CorrBCL designs to restore structural information of large-scale point clouds.

More recent works focus on improving the network performance through introducing new techniques or incorporating new components. FLOT [28] proposes to find the correspondences from an optimal transport module by graph matching. PointPWC-Net [50] follows a coarse-to-fine fashion for scene flow estimation on point clouds. It extends the important component of cost volume in optical flow network [32] and proposes a novel point-based patch-to-patch cost volume. HALFlow [44] improves the aforementioned cost volume by a novel double attentive flow embedding method that distributes more weights on task-related regions. HCRF-Flow [17] focuses on maintaining the local geometric smoothness with the help of Conditional Random Fields (CRFs) in deep neural networks and proposes a high-order CRFs module as the formulations of

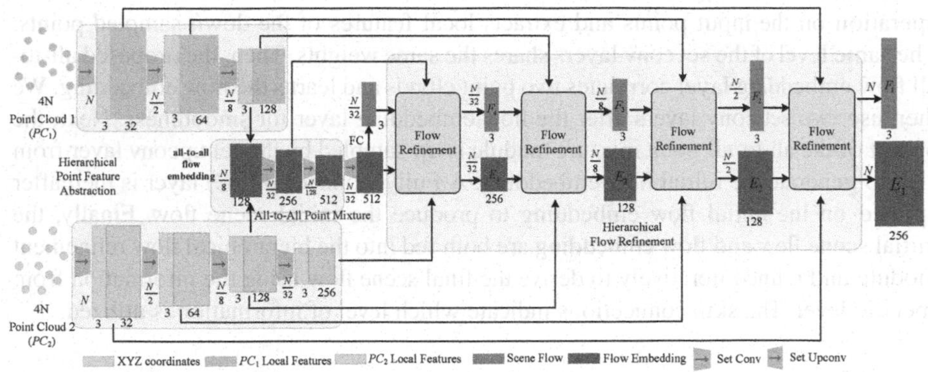

Fig. 1. The detailed architecture of our network. Three set conv layers for PC_1 and four set conv layers for PC_2 constitute the hierarchical point feature abstraction module. The all-to-all point mixture module consists of one layer of all-to-all flow embedding followed by two set conv layers. Four flow refinement layers are constructed in the hierarchical flow refinement module.

spatial smoothness and rigid motion constraints. FESTA [47] improves naive Farthest Point Sampling (FPS) by proposing a trainable Aggregate Pooling (AP) to adaptively shift points to invariant positions. Inspired by [28], FlowStep3D [16] designs a Global Correlation Unit that computes a soft correlation matrix to guide the initially estimated scene flow and adopts Gated Recurrent Unit (GRU) for local flow update. PV-RAFT [49] leverages point-based and voxel based features and presents point-voxel correlation fields to capture both local and long-range dependencies for point pairs.

In [16,50], different information is utilized for updating local scene flow but they do not show which information is more important for the input of the updating unit. In [16,49], GRU is used for iterative flow update inspired by RAFT [33] and claimed to be more effective than a fully-connected layer. Since RAFT [33] has shown a promising performance on optical flow, we also want to know whether the use of GRU will improve the performance in other scene flow network structures. In [16,28], element-wise product and cosine similarity are used to represent correlation between points while concatenation of point feature is implemented for learning correlation in [44], but none of them gives evaluation about which one is better. This paper will discuss the above issues and compare what matters for 3D scene flow network based on PWC structure.

3 3D Scene Flow Network

3.1 Network Architecture

Our proposed network, illustrated in Fig. 1, takes in two frames of point clouds with $4N$ points in each, which are PC_1 and PC_2, and estimates N points' scene flow from coarse to fine. Our network is comprised of three modules: 1) Hierarchical Point Feature Abstraction, 2) All-to-All Point Mixture, and 3) Hierarchical Flow Refinement.

The hierarchical point feature abstraction module has three set conv layers from [19] for PC_1 and four set conv layers for PC_2. Each set conv layer performs down-sampling operation on the input points and extracts local features of the down-sampled points. The same level of the set conv layers shares the same weights. Then, the proposed all-to-all flow embedding layer correlates two point clouds and learns the flow embedding. We then use two set conv layers after the flow embedding layer for smoothness. Next, the output of the all-to-all point mixture module is up-sampled by the set upconv layer from [19] to generate the initial flow embedding. A Fully-Connected (FC) layer is thereafter applied on the initial flow embedding to produce the initial scene flow. Finally, the initial scene flow and flow embedding are both fed into the hierarchical flow refinement module and refined iteratively to derive the final scene flow using the information from specific level. The skip connections indicate which level of information is utilized.

3.2 Hierarchical Point Feature Abstraction

In the hierarchical point feature abstraction module, two consecutive point clouds are down-sampled and encoded through a series of set conv layers respectively. We adopt the set conv layer in PointNet++ [30] to perform point feature abstraction.

Each set conv layer consumes n points $\{(x_i, p_i) \mid i = 1, \ldots, n\}$, where $x_i \in \mathbb{R}^3$ and $p_i \in \mathbb{R}^c$ represent 3D coordinate and the point feature. The output of each layer are n' sampled point $\{(x'_j, p'_j) \mid j = 1, \ldots, n'\}$ with $x'_j \in \mathbb{R}^3$ and $p'_j \in \mathbb{R}^{c'}$ denoting the 3D coordinate and extracted local feature. All of the output n' ($n' < n$) are sampled from the input n points using Farthest Point Sampling (FPS) [30].

For each of the n' sampled point, its K nearest neighbours $\{(x_i^k, p_i^k) \mid k = 1, \ldots, K\}$ are selected from the input n points. Then, a learnable shared Multi-Layer Perceptron (MLP) and max-pooling operation are adopted to extract the point feature p'_j of each sampled point from the K neighbouring points. The point feature p'_j is formulated as:

$$p'_j = \underset{k=1,\ldots,K}{\text{maxpool}}(\text{MLP}((x_j^k - x'_j) \oplus p_j^k)), \tag{1}$$

where $\oplus$ indicates concatenation operation. *maxpool* means max-pooling operation.

3.3 All-to-All Point Mixture

The inputs of the all-to-all embedding layer are two consecutive frames of point clouds: $PC_1 = \{(x_i, p_i) \mid i = 1, \ldots, n_1\}$ and $PC_2 = \{(y_j, q_j) \mid j = 1, \ldots, n_2\}$, sampled in the hierarchical point feature abstraction module. $x_i, y_j \in \mathbb{R}^3$ indicate 3D coordinates and $p_i, q_j \in \mathbb{R}^c$ indicate the point feature. The output of the layer will be the flow embedding $E = \{e_i \mid e_i \in \mathbb{R}^c, i = 1 \ldots, n_1\}$, which utilizes exhaustive information in two point clouds and encodes motion for points in PC_1.

Our all-to-all embedding includes a two-stage attention-based embedding process with an improved first embedding stage. For the first embedding process, we correlate points in two point clouds by incorporating the all-to-all mechanism with backward reliability validation as shown in Fig. 2. Instead of choosing only $K(K < n_2)$ nearest points, each point in PC_1 selects all n_2 points $Q_i = \{(y_i^k, q_i^k) \mid k = 1, \ldots, n_2\}$ from PC_2. In this process, all n_2 points Q_i from PC_2 are utilized to embed point motion into points in PC_1. The motion embeddings will then be updated by carefully designed

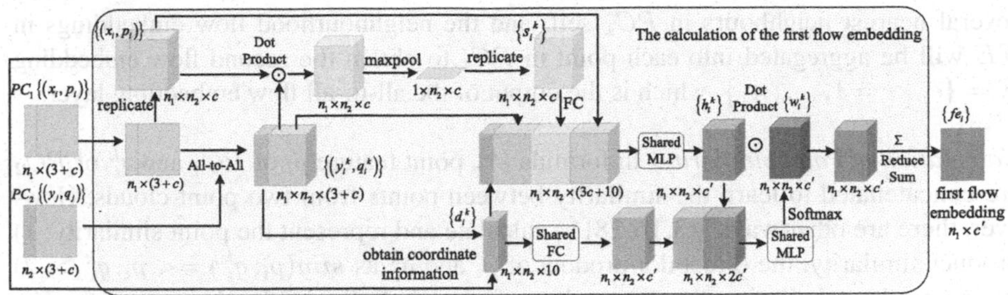

Fig. 2. The detailed calculation of the first flow embedding between PC_1 and PC_2.

attentive weighting to derive the first flow embedding $FE = \{fe_i \mid i = 1, \ldots, n_1\}$. The calculation details are elaborated as below.

A 10-dimensional vector capturing the 3D Euclidean space information is first calculated as follows:

$$d_i^k = x_i \oplus y_i^k \oplus (x_i - y_i^k) \oplus \left\| x_i - y_i^k \right\|_2, \tag{2}$$

where $\|\cdot\|_2$ indicates the L_2 norm. Then, to realize backward reliability validation, we first formulate a vector that represents a form of similarity between two point clouds by applying element-wise product of PC_1 point feature p_i and PC_2 point feature q_i^k. Max-pooling operation is then performed over n_1 candidate backward embedding features, selecting the most potential and reliable matching candidates in PC_1 for each point of PC_2. An FC layer is then adopted to encode the backward reliability information. The calculation of backward validation vector is as follows:

$$s_i^k = \text{FC}(\underset{i=1,\ldots,n_1}{\text{maxpool}}(p_i \odot q_i^k)), \tag{3}$$

where $\odot$ denotes dot product. The first flow embedding before attentive weighting is then formulated as:

$$h_i^k = \text{MLP}(d_i^k \oplus p_i \oplus q_i^k \oplus s_i^k). \tag{4}$$

Specifically, p_i and q_i^k are normalized on the feature channel before concatenation. Given the 10-dimensional vector d_i^k, the first attentive weights for soft aggregation of the queried points can be written as:

$$w_i^k = \underset{k=1,\ldots,n_2}{\text{softmax}}\,(\text{MLP}(\text{FC}(d_i^k) \oplus h_i^k)). \tag{5}$$

The first flow embedding $FE = \{fe_i \mid i = 1, \ldots, n_1\}$ corresponding to points with x_i coordinates is calculated as:

$$fe_i = \sum_{k=1}^{n_2} h_i^k \odot w_i^k. \tag{6}$$

For the second flow embedding process, we follow the same process as [44], which is an aggregation process within the PC_1 self with attention. Each point in PC_1 selects several nearest neighbours in PC_1 self, and the neighbourhood flow embeddings in FE will be aggregated into each point in PC_1 to obtain the second flow embedding $E = \{e_i \mid i = 1, \ldots, n_1\}$, which is the output of the all-to-all flow embedding layer.

Calculation of Point Similarity. In formula (4), point feature p_i of PC_1 and q_i^k of PC_2 are concatenated to learn the similarity between points from two point clouds. However, there are other ways [13,16,28] to calculate and represent the point similarity: 1) product similarity: the direct dot product of p_i and q_i^k as $sim(p_i, q_i^k) = < p_i, q_i^k >$, 2) cosine product similarity: the dot product of p_i and q_i^k divided by their respective L_2 norm as $sim(p_i, q_i^k) = < \frac{p_i}{\|p_i\|_2}, \frac{q_i^k}{\|q_i^k\|_2} >$, and 3) normalized product similarity: the dot product of p_i and q_i^k normalized by their respective mean value μ and standard deviation σ over each feature dimension as $sim(p_i, q_i^k) = < \frac{p_i - \mu_i}{\sigma_i}, \frac{q_i^k - \mu_i^k}{\sigma_i^k} >$. We intend to explore whether the concatenation of point feature is more suitable to represent similarity in our network compared with the product similarity presented above. By replacing the concatenation of feature with different forms of product of feature in formula (4), the effectiveness of our design is demonstrated in experiments.

3.4 Hierarchical Flow Refinement

The hierarchical flow refinement module consists of four flow refinement layers. The layer takes coarse sparse flow and coarse sparse flow embedding as inputs with information of PC_1 and PC_2 from the previous level while producing refined flow and refined flow embedding as outputs, as illustrated in Fig. 3. It contains four main components: 1) Set Upconv Layer, 2) Position Warping Layer, 3) Attentive Flow Re-embedding Layer, and 4) Scene Flow Predictor. For the first flow refinement layer, the set upconv layer is eliminated to keep the point number unchanged for suitable multi-scale supervision.

Set Upconv Layer. In order to up-sample the coarse sparse flow embedding, the set upconv layer in [19] is adopted here to propagate flow embedding from sparse level to dense level. The inputs of this layer are n points with coarse sparse flow embedding $\{(x_i, se_i) \mid se_i \in \mathbb{R}^{d_{sparse}}, i = 1, \ldots, n\}$ and n' ($n' > n$) points with feature $\{(x'_j, p'_j) \mid j = 1, \ldots, n'\}$ from the previous dense level. The outputs are n' points with dense flow embedding $\{(x'_j, de_j) \mid de_j \in \mathbb{R}^{d_{dense}}, j = 1, \ldots, n'\}$. Specifically, each of the n' dense points will select its KNN from the sparse n points, and the coarse sparse flow embedding will be aggregated to learn the coarse dense flow embedding by MLP.

Position Warping Layer. As a coarse-to-fine style, coarse dense flow $\{f_i^{dense} \mid i = 1, \ldots, n_1\}$ is first obtained from coarse sparse flow through Three-Nearest Neighbours (Three-NN) interpolation. Next, the coordinates of the first point cloud $PC_1 = \{(x_i, p_i) \mid i =, \ldots, n_1\}$ are updated by warping PC_1 with coarse dense flow. The warped PC_1 is signified as $PC'_1 = \{(x'_i, p_i) \mid i = 1, \ldots, n_1\}$, where $x'_i = x_i + f_i^{dense}$.

Attentive Flow Re-embedding Layer. The attentive flow embedding layer proposed in [44] is applied to derive a new flow re-embedding $\{re_i \mid re_i \in \mathbb{R}^{d_{re}}, i = 1, \ldots, = n_1\}$ between PC_1' and PC_2. Here, the flow re-embedding contains the flow encoding from each point in PC_1' toward PC_2, which is essential in the subsequent refinement.

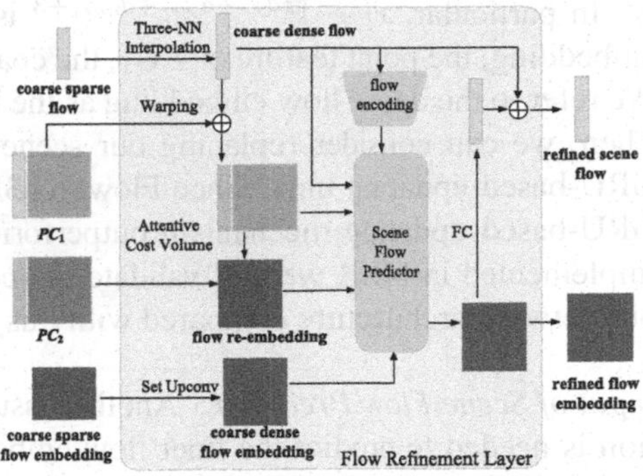

Fig. 3. The details of flow refinement layer.

Scene Flow Predictor. The scene flow predictor aims to refine coarse dense flow embedding for the input of later flow refinement layer. It takes five elements as inputs: 1) the up-sampled coarse dense flow embedding $de_i \in \mathbb{R}^{d_{dense}}$, 2) the flow re-embedding $re_i \in \mathbb{R}^{d_{re}}$, 3) the point feature of the first point cloud $p_i \in \mathbb{R}^{d_{pc_1}}$, 4) the coarse dense flow $f_i^{dense} \in \mathbb{R}^3$, and 5) the dense flow feature $f_i^{enc.} \in \mathbb{R}^{d_{enc.}}$. Specifically, the coarse dense flow is encoded by two set conv layers [19] to derive the dense flow feature $f_i^{enc.}$, but the number of points remain unchanged instead of being down-sampled. The refined dense flow embedding is formulated as:

$$de_i' = \text{MLP}(de_i \oplus re_i \oplus p_i \oplus f_i \oplus f_i^{enc.}). \tag{7}$$

Finally, we adopt a residual flow learning structure to estimate the refined scene flow. To be specific, an FC layer is first applied on the refined flow embedding to produce the residual flow f_i^{res}. Next, the refined scene flow is generated by adding f_i^{res} to f_i^{dense}. The calculation of refined scene flow is as follows:

$$f_i^{res} = \text{FC}(de_i'), \tag{8}$$

$$f_i = f_i^{dense} + f_i^{res}. \tag{9}$$

Designs of Scene Flow Predictor: The scene flow predictor corrects the coarse scene flow by regressing residual flow from the refined flow embedding. In this paper, we adopt the concatenation of all five inputs of scene flow predictor and directly feed it into shared MLP to derive the refined flow embedding. On the other hand, FlowStep3D [16] and PV-RAFT [49] propose to use a GRU-based gated activation unit on point clouds, inspired by RAFT [33], for updating a hidden state. Given a hidden state $h_{l-1} \in \mathbb{R}^c$ from previous iteration and a current iteration vector x_l, h_{l-1} is updated as follows:

$$z_l = \sigma(\text{SetConv}_\text{z}(h_{l-1} \oplus x_l)), \tag{10}$$

$$r_l = \sigma(\text{SetConv}_\text{r}(h_{l-1} \oplus x_l)), \tag{11}$$

$$\widetilde{h_l} = \tanh(\text{SetConv}_\text{h}((r_l \odot h_{l-1}) \oplus x_l)), \tag{12}$$

$$h_l = (1 - z_l) \odot h_{l-1} + z_l \odot \widetilde{h_l}, \tag{13}$$

where $\sigma(\cdot)$ represents sigmoid activation function.

In particular, $x_l \in \mathbb{R}^{d_{re}+d_{pc_1}+d_{enc.}+3}$ is defined as the concatenation of flow re-embedding, the point feature of PC_1, the coarse dense flow, and the dense flow feature. We refer to the dense flow embedding as the hidden state that will be refined iteratively. Then, we can consider replacing our scene flow predictor with this newly designed GRU-based updating unit. Since FlowStep3D [16] and PV-RAFT [49] claim that this GRU-based updating mechanism outperforms the fully-connected structure which is implemented in MLP, we will validate the performance of our scene flow predictor in our network architecture compared with this GRU-based method in the experiment.

Input of Scene Flow Predictor: Another issue we want to investigate is what information is needed to predict the finer flow embedding. i.e. what information is needed in the input of the scene flow predictor. PointPWC-Net [50] uses the flow re-embedding, the point feature of PC_1, the coarse dense flow, and the up-sampled coarse dense flow embedding as inputs. FlowStep3D [16] additionally includes the dense flow feature but do not add the up-sampled flow embedding. PV-RAFT [49], HCRF-Flow [17], and FESTA [47] all only use the flow re-embedding, the point feature of PC_1, and the coarse flow. HALFlow [44] does not add the dense flow feature. In this sense, we explore whether removing certain elements from the input will degrade the performance and the extent to which those information contributes to the performance. We consider the flow re-embedding as an indispensable element because it encodes the motion between warped PC_1 and PC_2 in the current level.

Level of Flow Refinement Layer: In [44], three flow refinement layers are applied for a more-for-less network architecture, which estimates N points' scene flow from $4N$ points of raw input. Only Three-NN interpolation is used for up-sampling in the finest level of flow estimation. Apparently, this structure does not exhaustively leverage the functionality of the whole components in the flow refinement layer. Therefore, we choose to employ an additional flow refinement layer on the finest level to estimate the final scene flow. The above consideration raises another question: Can the performance be further improved if more information from denser level is taken into account? Here we consider using raw point cloud with 4N points to estimate the 4N points' scene flow. The best choice will be demonstrated in the experiment.

4 Experiments

4.1 Datasets and Data Preprocess

Because of the inherent difficulty in acquiring large-scale ground-truth scene flow of the real world, we resort to the common synthetic FlyingThings3D dataset [23] for training and evaluation. We first train our network on FlyingThings3D dataset [23], and then directly test our trained model on real-world LiDAR scans from KITTI scene flow dataset [25] without any fine-tuning to demonstrate the generalization capability.

There are two common versions of preparing point clouds from FlyingThings3D dataset [23] and KITTI scene flow dataset [25]. The first version of data preprocessing is proposed by HPLFlowNet [4] and adopted in [4,16,17,44,50]. It does not contain occlusion for input point clouds, which means each point in PC_1 has its corresponding point in PC_2 when warped by its ground-truth scene flow. The second version is proposed by FlowNet3D [19]. This version provides occluded point clouds as inputs and masks that indicate the invalid points without corresponding ones in the adjacent frame. These masks are also used in computing training loss and evaluation metrics. To compare with all 3D scene flow estimation methods to our knowledge, we follow two versions of data preprocessing and conduct experiments on both versions of datasets. More details about datasets and preprocessing is in the supplementary material.

4.2 Training and Evaluation Details

Training Loss. We train our network in a supervised manner at different levels, similar to [32,50]. Suppose the predicted scene flow of each point at level l is $\{f_i^l \in \mathbb{R}^3 \mid i = 1, \dots, N_l\}$ and the ground-truth scene flow is $\{GT(f_i^l) \in \mathbb{R}^3 \mid i = 1, \dots, N_l\}$. Here, N_l denotes the number of points at level l. Our training loss can be therefore written as:

$$Loss = \sum_{l=1}^{4} \psi_l \frac{1}{N_l} \sum_{i=1}^{N_l} \left\| f_i^l - GT(f_i^l) \right\|_2, \tag{14}$$

where ψ_l indicates the weight at level l. We define the finest level, which is also the level with the densest points, as level $l = 1$. Specifically, our network takes in $4N = 8,912$ as inputs, $N_1 = N = 2,048$, $N_2 = N/2 = 1,024$, $N_3 = N/8 = 256$, and $N_4 = N/32 = 64$. The loss weights are $\psi_1 = 0.02$, $\psi_2 = 0.04$, $\psi_3 = 0.08$, and $\psi_4 = 0.16$.

Implementation Details. For the training and evaluation process of our network, 8,192 points are randomly sampled as inputs from the raw points clouds of two consecutive frames. Only 3D XYZ coordinates of the point clouds are fed into our network, like [4, 16, 17, 44, 50]. For fair comparison with previous methods, on FlyingThings3D prepared by [4], we first train our network on one quarter of the training set (4,910 pairs) and then fine-tune our model on the complete training set to speed up the training process. On FlyingThings3D prepared by [19], we train our model without fine-tuning.

We conduct all the experiments on a single Titan RTX GPU. Pre-training is done for 800 epochs, and fine-tuning lasts for 200 epochs after loading the pre-trained weights. Batch size is 14. Adam optimizer [15] is used in training, and $\beta_1 = 0.9$, $\beta_2 = 0.99$. The initial learning rate is 0.001 and decays for every 80 epochs exponentially with decay rate $\gamma = 0.5$. Our supplementary material provides all details of network parameters. Evaluation Metrics We adopt the same evaluation metrics used in [4, 17, 44, 50] to evaluate our model for fair comparison, including EPE3D(m), Acc3D Strict, Acc3D Relax, Outliers3D, EPE2D(px), and Acc2D. The detailed description of the metrics is shown in the supplementary material.

5 Results

5.1 Comparison with State-of-the-Art (SOTA)

Table 1 shows the quantitative comparison between previous state-of-the-arts and our approach on FlyingThings3D dataset [23] and KITTI scene flow dataset [25] prepared

Table 1. The quantitative comparison between recent state-of-the-art methods and ours on FlyingThings3D and KITTI scene flow datasets prepared by Gu *et al.* [4] without occlusion. All listed approaches are only trained on FlyingThings3D dataset. The best results are in bold. "Full" means fully-supervised training.

Evaluation Dataset	Method	Training Data	Input	Sup.	EPE3D	Acc3D Strict	Acc3D Relax	Outliers3D	EPE2D	Acc2D
FlyingThings 3D dataset [23]	FlowNet3 [10]	Quarter	RGB stereo	Full	0.4570	0.4179	0.6168	0.6050	5.1348	0.8125
	ICP [1]	No	Points	Full	0.4062	0.1614	0.3038	0.8796	23.2280	0.2913
	FlowNet3D [19]	Quarter	Points	Full	0.1136	0.4125	0.7706	0.6016	5.9740	0.5692
	SPLATFlowNet [31]	Quarter	Points	Full	0.1205	0.4197	0.7180	0.6187	6.9759	0.5512
	HPLFlowNet [4]	Quarter	Points	Full	0.0804	0.6144	0.8555	0.4287	4.6723	0.6764
	HPLFlowNet [4]	Complete	Points	Full	0.0696	—	—	—	—	—
	PointPWC-Net [50]	Complete	Points	Full	0.0588	0.7379	0.9276	0.3424	3.2390	0.7994
	HALFlow [44]	Quarter	Points	Full	0.0511	0.7808	0.9437	0.3093	2.8739	0.8056
	HALFlow [44]	Complete	Points	Full	0.0492	0.7850	0.9468	0.3083	2.7555	0.8111
	FLOT [28]	Complete	Points	Full	0.0520	0.7320	0.9270	0.3570	—	—
	HCRF-Flow [17]	Quarter	Points	Full	0.0488	0.8337	0.9507	0.2614	2.5652	0.8704
	PV-RAFT [49]	Complete	Points	Full	0.0461	0.8169	0.9574	0.2924	—	—
	FlowStep3D [16]	Complete	Points	Full	0.0455	0.8162	0.9614	0.2165	—	—
	Ours	Quarter	Points	Full	0.0317	0.9109	0.9757	0.1673	1.7436	0.9108
	Ours	Complete	Points	Full	**0.0281**	**0.9290**	**0.9817**	**0.1458**	**1.5229**	**0.9279**
KITTI dataset [25]	FlowNet3 [10]	Quarter	RGB stereo	Full	0.9111	0.2039	0.3587	0.7463	5.1023	0.7803
	ICP [1]	No	Points	Full	0.5181	0.0669	0.1667	0.8712	27.6752	0.1056
	FlowNet3D [19]	Quarter	Points	Full	0.1767	0.3738	0.6677	0.5271	7.2141	0.5093
	SPLATFlowNet [31]	Quarter	Points	Full	0.1988	0.2174	0.5391	0.6575	8.2306	0.4189
	HPLFlowNet [4]	Quarter	Points	Full	0.1169	0.4783	0.7776	0.4103	4.8055	0.5938
	HPLFlowNet [4]	Complete	Points	Full	0.1113	—	—	—	—	—
	PointPWC-Net [50]	Complete	Points	Full	0.0694	0.7281	0.8884	0.2648	3.0062	0.7673
	HALFlow [44]	Quarter	Points	Full	0.0692	0.7532	0.8943	0.2529	2.8660	0.7811
	HALFlow [44]	Complete	Points	Full	0.0622	0.7649	0.9026	0.2492	2.5140	0.8128
	FLOT [28]	Complete	Points	Full	0.0560	0.7550	0.9080	0.2420	—	—
	HCRF-Flow [17]	Quarter	Points	Full	0.0531	0.8631	0.9444	0.1797	2.0700	0.8656
	PV-RAFT [49]	Complete	Points	Full	0.0560	0.8226	0.9372	0.2163	—	—
	FlowStep3D [16]	Complete	Points	Full	0.0546	0.8051	0.9254	**0.1492**	—	—
	Ours	Quarter	Points	Full	0.0332	0.8931	0.9528	0.1690	1.2186	0.9373
	Ours	Complete	Points	Full	**0.0309**	**0.9047**	**0.9580**	0.1612	**1.1285**	**0.9451**

by [4]. It is demonstrated that our approach outperforms all other methods by a large margin for both 3D and 2D metrics on FlyingThings3D dataset [23]. Meanwhile, our method also achieves the best generalization results on KITTI scene flow [25]. Specifically, we surpasses the SOTA method, FlowStep3D [16], by 38.2% for EPE3D metric on FlyingThings3D dataset [23], and 43.4% on KITTI scene flow [25] dataset.

The recent work, FESTA [47], is only tested on the datasets prepared by [19]. To compare with all the methods to our knowledge, we also present the evaluation results on FlyingThings3D dataset [23] and KITTI scene flow dataset [25] prepared by [19] in Table 2. It can be demonstrated that our approach still outperforms previous methods substantially for all 3D metrics on both datasets. Specifically, we surpasses the SOTA method, FESTA [47], by 43.2% with respect to EPE3D metric on FlyingThings3D dataset [23], and 24.7% on KITTI scene flow [25] dataset. We believe the superior performance of our method on the datasets with occlusion partly from our backward validation, which can be aware of the occlusion in the network inference.

We also present detailed visualization of the accuracy of the estimated scene flow by our approach in Fig. 4, compared with methods in [19,44]. It can be seen that our method can better handle the structures with repetitive patterns and large motions.

Table 2. Evaluation results on FlyingThings3D and KITTI Scene Flow datasets prepared by Liu *et al.* [19] with occlusion. The best results are in bold. "Self" means self-supervised training. "Full" means fully-supervised training. All fully-supervised approaches are trained on FlyingThings3D dataset. Self-Point-Flow [18] is trained on raw LiDAR data from KITTI dataset [3].

Evaluation Dataset	Method	Input	Sup.	EPE3D	Acc3D Strict	Acc3D Relax	Outliers
FlyingThings 3D dataset [23]	FlowNet3D [19]	Points	Full	0.169	0.254	0.579	0.789
	FLOT [28]	Points	Full	0.156	0.343	0.643	0.700
	FESTA [47]	Points	Full	0.111	0.431	0.744	—
	Ours	Points	Full	**0.063**	**0.791**	**0.909**	**0.279**
	Self-Point-Flow [18]	Points	Self	0.105	0.417	0.725	0.501
KITTI dataset [25]	FlowNet3D [19]	Points	Full	0.173	0.276	0.609	0.649
	FLOT [28]	Points	Full	0.110	0.419	0.721	0.486
	FESTA [47]	Points	Full	0.097	0.449	0.833	—
	Ours	Points	Full	**0.073**	**0.819**	**0.890**	**0.261**

5.2 Ablation Study

In this section, we demonstrate the effectiveness of the proposed all-to-all point mixture module and validate our network design choices compared with other discussed alternative structures through a series of ablation studies. All methods in the ablation studies are trained on $\frac{1}{4}$ of the training set (4,910 pairs) of FlyingThings3D dataset [23] prepared by [4] and evaluated using the corresponding evaluation set.

All-to-All and Backward Information. In order to demonstrate the effectiveness of both the all-to-all mechanism and the backward validation vector, we first remove the vector that stores the backward information in the all-to-all flow embedding layer, which means s_i^k is removed from formula (4). Then, the all-to-all mechanism is removed, which means points from PC_1 will only select K nearest neighbours instead. The results in Table 3(a) show that both the all-to-all mechanism and the backward validation vector contribute to the improvement of performance. In fact, the all-to-all mechanism enables the querying point in PC_1 to expand its searching range from K nearest neighbours to all points in PC_2 to determine its most reliable matching candidate. The backward validation vector acquired based on the all-to-all mechanism brings in the information that imposes bi-directional consensus from the backward direction. Therefore, the network can be guided by this backward validation information to better learn the correct matching and estimate more accurate scene flow.

Calculation of Point Similarity. Three different forms of similarity calculation are discussed in Sect. 3.3. Since point similarity design can affect the correlation of adjacent point clouds to a large extent, we compare these product similarity methods with ours. The results in Table 3(b) demonstrate that the concatenation of point feature has the best performance than product forms of point similarity. Representing point similarity via concatenation is more suited in our network. We believe this is because the concatenation operation allows the network to fully exploit its self-learning ability.

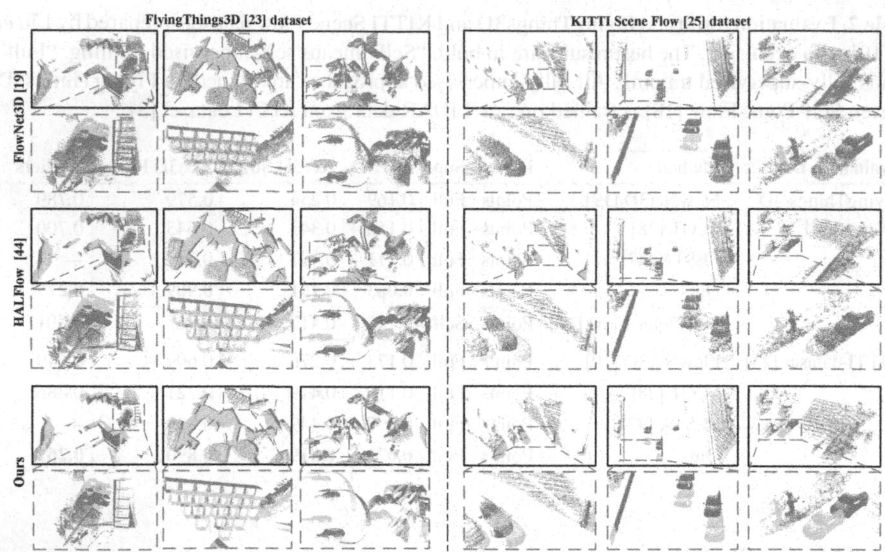

Fig. 4. The visualization results of the proposed method, compared with FlowNet3D [19] and HALFlow [44], on FlyingThings3D (left) and KITTI scene flow (right) datasets prepared by Gu *et al.* [4]. Blue points indicate PC_1. Green points indicate accurate predictions $\widehat{PC_2} = PC_1 + F$ and red points indicate inaccurate predictions (measured by Acc3D Relax).

Designs of Scene Flow Predictor. Since our scene flow predictor is only implemented with MLP, we want to know whether GRU in [16,49] can improve the performance. We consider the flow embedding as the hidden state to be updated and replace our MLP based scene flow predictor with GRU. Table 3(c) show that the performance actually degrades using GRU. For our coarse-to-fine network, GRU is less suitable for updating and refining the flow embedding. We believe this is due to the difference of the point number at different levels, which is different from FlowStep3D [16] and PV-RAFT [49].

Input of Scene Flow Predictor. As the scene flow predictor serves to refine the flow embedding for regression of more accurate scene flow, we are interested in what matters in the input information of the scene flow predictor and to what extent each of the inputs contributes to the performance. Therefore, we respectively ablate each of the five inputs except the flow re-embedding in our scene flow predictor to demonstrate their importance. Table 3(d) show that the up-sampled flow embedding is the most important element of inputs, which is intuitive because the up-sampled flow embedding is refined in the previous layer and contains abundant motion information. The removal of the coarse flow and flow feature also causes a slight decline in quantitative performance, which demonstrates that they can also provide some instructions for the improvement of the refinement.

Level of Flow Refinement Layer. In our hierarchical flow refinement module, four flow refinement layers exhaustively utilize all four levels of sampled point feature,

Table 3. The ablation study results on FlyingThings3D dataset prepared by Gu *et al.* [4]

	Method	EPE3D	Acc3D Strict	Acc3D Relax	Outliers	EPE2D	Acc2D
(a)	Ours w/o backward validation	0.0332	0.9044	0.9743	0.1766	1.8221	0.9065
	Ours w/o backward validation and all-to-all mechanism	0.0349	0.9001	0.9725	0.1798	1.9819	0.9032
	Ours (full, with backward validation and all-to-all mechanism)	**0.0317**	**0.9109**	**0.9757**	**0.1673**	**1.7436**	**0.9108**
(b)	Ours (with product similarity)	0.0356	0.8872	0.9692	0.1953	1.9872	0.8870
	Ours (with cosine product similarity)	0.0370	0.8755	0.9670	0.2142	2.0637	0.8746
	Ours (with normalized product similarity)	0.0339	0.8971	0.9724	0.1845	1.8790	0.8965
	Ours (full, with concatenated similarity)	**0.0317**	**0.9109**	**0.9757**	**0.1673**	**1.7436**	**0.9108**
(c)	Ours (replace Scene Flow Predictor with GRU)	0.0350	0.8892	0.9668	0.1827	1.9274	0.8896
	Ours (full, with Scene Flow Predictor)	**0.0317**	**0.9109**	**0.9757**	**0.1673**	**1.7436**	**0.9108**
(d)	Ours w/o features of PC_1 in Scene Flow Predictor	0.0333	0.9047	0.9743	0.1740	1.8428	0.9073
	Ours w/o up-sampled flow embedding in Scene Flow Predictor	0.0380	0.8732	0.9642	0.2099	2.0953	0.8785
	Ours w/o coarse flow in Scene Flow Predictor	0.0323	0.9076	0.9750	0.1717	1.7760	0.9083
	Ours w/o flow feature in Scene Flow Predictor	0.0327	0.9061	0.9748	0.1740	1.8063	0.9074
	Ours (full, with complete five inputs in Scene Flow Predictor)	**0.0317**	**0.9109**	**0.9757**	**0.1673**	**1.7436**	**0.9108**
(e)	Ours (with interpolation estimating 2048 points' flow)	0.0359	0.8844	0.9691	0.2004	1.9511	0.8911
	Ours (with interpolation estimating 8192 points' flow)	0.0332	0.9043	0.9739	0.1740	1.8039	0.9076
	Ours (full, with flow refinement estimating 2048 points' flow)	**0.0317**	**0.9109**	**0.9757**	**0.1673**	**1.7436**	**0.9108**

indicated by skip connection. Compared with [44], we add an additional flow refinement layer on the finest level. In order to validate its effectiveness, we remove this flow refinement layer and instead use Three-NN interpolation to obtain the final N points' scene flow from $4N$ points' inputs, as [44]. In addition, we further apply the Three-NN interpolation to obtain $4N$ points' scene flow out of $4N$ points' inputs to see whether more information from raw input will result in an improvement. It turns out in Table 3(e) that both of these designs will degrade the network performance and our four layers of flow refinement that leverage all levels' sampled point feature prove the most suitable and effective structure design for our network.

6 Conclusion

In this paper, a novel all-to-all point mixture module with backward reliability validation is proposed for reliable correlation. In addition, different designs and techniques for key components of our network are thoroughly compared. We provide a series of ablation studies to show the contributions of each element in key components and to demonstrate what matters in scene flow network. Quantitative results on FlyingThings3D [23] and KITTI scene flow dataset [25] show that our method achieves SOTA performance. Our comparison and analysis on design choices of key components and structure are expected to facilitate the design of scene flow network in future research.

Acknowledgement. This work was supported in part by the Natural Science Foundation of China under Grant 62073222, Grant U21A20480, and Grant U1913204; in part by the Science and Technology Commission of Shanghai Municipality under Grant 21511101900; and in part by the Open Research Projects of Zhejiang Laboratory under Grant 2022NB0AB01. The authors gratefully appreciate the contribution of Chaokang Jiang from China University of Mining and Technology, and Xinrui Wu from Shanghai Jiao Tong University.

References

1. Besl, P.J., McKay, N.D.: Method for registration of 3-D shapes. In: Sensor fusion IV: Control Paradigms and Data Structures, vol. 1611, pp. 586–606. SPIE (1992)
2. Dewan, A., Caselitz, T., Tipaldi, G.D., Burgard, W.: Rigid scene flow for 3D lidar scans. In: 2016 IEEE/RSJ International Conference on Intelligent Robots and Systems (IROS), pp. 1765–1770. IEEE (2016)
3. Geiger, A., Lenz, P., Stiller, C., Urtasun, R.: Vision meets robotics: the kitti dataset. Int. J. Robot. Res. **32**(11), 1231–1237 (2013)
4. Gu, X., Wang, Y., Wu, C., Lee, Y.J., Wang, P.: Hplflownet: hierarchical permutohedral lattice flownet for scene flow estimation on large-scale point clouds. In: Proceedings of the IEEE/CVF Conference on Computer Vision and Pattern Recognition, pp. 3254–3263 (2019)
5. Hadfield, S., Bowden, R.: Kinecting the dots: particle based scene flow from depth sensors. In: 2011 International Conference on Computer Vision, pp. 2290–2295. IEEE (2011)
6. Herbst, E., Ren, X., Fox, D.: RGB-D flow: Dense 3-D motion estimation using color and depth. In: 2013 IEEE International Conference on Robotics and Automation, pp. 2276–2282. IEEE (2013)
7. Huguet, F., Devernay, F.: A variational method for scene flow estimation from stereo sequences. In: 2007 IEEE 11th International Conference on Computer Vision, pp. 1–7. IEEE (2007)
8. Hur, J., Roth, S.: Self-supervised monocular scene flow estimation. In: Proceedings of the IEEE/CVF Conference on Computer Vision and Pattern Recognition, pp. 7396–7405 (2020)
9. Hur, J., Roth, S.: Self-supervised multi-frame monocular scene flow. In: Proceedings of the IEEE/CVF Conference on Computer Vision and Pattern Recognition, pp. 2684–2694 (2021)
10. Ilg, Eddy, Saikia, Tonmoy, Keuper, Margret, Brox, Thomas: Occlusions, motion and depth boundaries with a generic network for disparity, optical flow or scene flow estimation. In: Ferrari, Vittorio, Hebert, Martial, Sminchisescu, Cristian, Weiss, Yair (eds.) ECCV 2018. LNCS, vol. 11216, pp. 626–643. Springer, Cham (2018). https://doi.org/10.1007/978-3-030-01258-8_38
11. Jaimez, M., Souiai, M., Gonzalez-Jimenez, J., Cremers, D.: A primal-dual framework for real-time dense RGB-D scene flow. In: 2015 IEEE international conference on robotics and automation (ICRA), pp. 98–104. IEEE (2015)
12. Jampani, V., Kiefel, M., Gehler, P.V.: Learning sparse high dimensional filters: image filtering, dense CRFs and bilateral neural networks. In: Proceedings of the IEEE Conference on Computer Vision and Pattern Recognition, pp. 4452–4461 (2016)
13. Jonschkowski, Rico, Stone, Austin, Barron, Jonathan T.., Gordon, Ariel, Konolige, Kurt, Angelova, Anelia: What matters in unsupervised optical flow. In: Vedaldi, Andrea, Bischof, Horst, Brox, Thomas, Frahm, Jan-Michael. (eds.) ECCV 2020. LNCS, vol. 12347, pp. 557–572. Springer, Cham (2020). https://doi.org/10.1007/978-3-030-58536-5_33
14. Kiefel, M., Jampani, V., Gehler, P.: Permutohedral lattice CNNs. In: ICLR Workshop Track 2015 (2015)
15. Kingma, D.P., Ba, J.: Adam: a method for stochastic optimization. arXiv preprint arXiv:1412.6980 (2014)
16. Kittenplon, Y., Eldar, Y.C., Raviv, D.: Flowstep3D: model unrolling for self-supervised scene flow estimation. In: Proceedings of the IEEE/CVF Conference on Computer Vision and Pattern Recognition, pp. 4114–4123 (2021)
17. Li, R., Lin, G., He, T., Liu, F., Shen, C.: HCRF-flow: scene flow from point clouds with continuous high-order CRFs and position-aware flow embedding. In: Proceedings of the IEEE/CVF Conference on Computer Vision and Pattern Recognition, pp. 364–373 (2021)

18. Li, R., Lin, G., Xie, L.: Self-point-flow: Self-supervised scene flow estimation from point clouds with optimal transport and random walk. In: Proceedings of the IEEE/CVF Conference on Computer Vision and Pattern Recognition, pp. 15577–15586 (2021)
19. Liu, X., Qi, C.R., Guibas, L.J.: FlowNet3D: learning scene flow in 3D point clouds. In: Proceedings of the IEEE/CVF Conference on Computer Vision and Pattern Recognition, pp. 529–537 (2019)
20. Liu, X., Yan, M., Bohg, J.: MeteorNet: deep learning on dynamic 3D point cloud sequences. In: Proceedings of the IEEE/CVF International Conference on Computer Vision, pp. 9246–9255 (2019)
21. Liu, Z., et al.: LPD-Net: 3D point cloud learning for large-scale place recognition and environment analysis. In: Proceedings of the IEEE/CVF International Conference on Computer Vision, pp. 2831–2840 (2019)
22. Ma, W.C., Wang, S., Hu, R., Xiong, Y., Urtasun, R.: Deep rigid instance scene flow. In: Proceedings of the IEEE/CVF Conference on Computer Vision and Pattern Recognition, pp. 3614–3622 (2019)
23. Mayer, N., et al.: A large dataset to train convolutional networks for disparity, optical flow, and scene flow estimation. In: Proceedings of the IEEE Conference on Computer Vision and Pattern Recognition, pp. 4040–4048 (2016)
24. Menze, M., Geiger, A.: Object scene flow for autonomous vehicles. In: Proceedings of the IEEE Conference on Computer Vision and Pattern Recognition, pp. 3061–3070 (2015)
25. Menze, M., Heipke, C., Geiger, A.: Object scene flow. ISPRS J. Photogramm. Remote. Sens. **140**, 60–76 (2018)
26. Mittal, H., Okorn, B., Held, D.: Just go with the flow: self-supervised scene flow estimation. In: Proceedings of the IEEE/CVF conference on computer vision and pattern recognition, pp. 11177–11185 (2020)
27. Pons, J.P., Keriven, R., Faugeras, O.: Multi-view stereo reconstruction and scene flow estimation with a global image-based matching score. Int. J. Comput. Vision **72**(2), 179–193 (2007)
28. Puy, Gilles, Boulch, Alexandre, Marlet, Renaud: FLOT: scene flow on point clouds guided by optimal transport. In: Vedaldi, Andrea, Bischof, Horst, Brox, Thomas, Frahm, Jan-Michael. (eds.) ECCV 2020. LNCS, vol. 12373, pp. 527–544. Springer, Cham (2020). https://doi.org/10.1007/978-3-030-58604-1_32
29. Qi, C.R., Su, H., Mo, K., Guibas, L.J.: PointNet: deep learning on point sets for 3D classification and segmentation. In: Proceedings of the IEEE Conference on Computer Vision and Pattern Recognition, pp. 652–660 (2017)
30. Qi, C.R., Yi, L., Su, H., Guibas, L.J.: PointNet++: deep hierarchical feature learning on point sets in a metric space. In: Advances in Neural Information Processing Systems 30 (2017)
31. Su, H., et al.: SPLATNet: sparse lattice networks for point cloud processing. In: Proceedings of the IEEE Conference on Computer Vision and Pattern Recognition, pp. 2530–2539 (2018)
32. Sun, D., Yang, X., Liu, M.Y., Kautz, J.: PWC-Net: CNNs for optical flow using pyramid, warping, and cost volume. In: Proceedings of the IEEE Conference on Computer Vision and Pattern Recognition, pp. 8934–8943 (2018)
33. Teed, Zachary, Deng, Jia: RAFT: recurrent all-pairs field transforms for optical flow. In: Vedaldi, Andrea, Bischof, Horst, Brox, Thomas, Frahm, Jan-Michael. (eds.) ECCV 2020. LNCS, vol. 12347, pp. 402–419. Springer, Cham (2020). https://doi.org/10.1007/978-3-030-58536-5_24
34. Ushani, A.K., Wolcott, R.W., Walls, J.M., Eustice, R.M.: A learning approach for real-time temporal scene flow estimation from lidar data. In: 2017 IEEE International Conference on Robotics and Automation (ICRA), pp. 5666–5673. IEEE (2017)

35. Valgaerts, Levi, Bruhn, Andrés, Zimmer, Henning, Weickert, Joachim, Stoll, Carsten, Theobalt, Christian: Joint estimation of motion, structure and geometry from stereo sequences. In: Daniilidis, Kostas, Maragos, Petros, Paragios, Nikos (eds.) ECCV 2010. LNCS, vol. 6314, pp. 568–581. Springer, Heidelberg (2010). https://doi.org/10.1007/978-3-642-15561-1_41
36. Vedula, S., Baker, S., Rander, P., Collins, R., Kanade, T.: Three-dimensional scene flow. In: Proceedings of the Seventh IEEE International Conference on Computer Vision, vol. 2, pp. 722–729. IEEE (1999)
37. Vogel, C., Schindler, K., Roth, S.: Piecewise rigid scene flow. In: Proceedings of the IEEE International Conference on Computer Vision, pp. 1377–1384 (2013)
38. Vogel, C., Schindler, K., Roth, S.: 3D scene flow estimation with a piecewise rigid scene model. Int. J. Comput. Vision **115**(1), 1–28 (2015)
39. Wang, G., Jiang, C., Shen, Z., Miao, Y., Wang, H.: SFGAN: unsupervised generative adversarial learning of 3D scene flow from the 3D scene self. Advanced Intelligent Systems **4**(4), 2100197 (2022)
40. Wang, G., Liu, H., Chen, M., Yang, Y., Liu, Z., Wang, H.: Anchor-based spatio-temporal attention 3-D convolutional networks for dynamic 3-D point cloud sequences. IEEE Trans. Instrum. Meas. **70**, 1–11 (2021)
41. Wang, G., Peng, C., Zhang, J., Wang, H.: Interactive multi-scale fusion of 2D and 3D features for multi-object tracking. arXiv preprint arXiv:2203.16268 (2022)
42. Wang, G., Tian, X., Ding, R., Wang, H.: Unsupervised learning of 3D scene flow from monocular camera. In: 2021 IEEE International Conference on Robotics and Automation (ICRA), pp. 4325–4331. IEEE (2021)
43. Wang, G., Wu, X., Jiang, S., Liu, Z., Wang, H.: Efficient 3D deep lidar odometry. arXiv preprint arXiv:2111.02135 (2021)
44. Wang, G., Wu, X., Liu, Z., Wang, H.: Hierarchical attention learning of scene flow in 3D point clouds. IEEE Trans. Image Process. **30**, 5168–5181 (2021)
45. Wang, G., Wu, X., Liu, Z., Wang, H.: PWCLO-Net: deep lidar odometry in 3D point clouds using hierarchical embedding mask optimization. In: Proceedings CVPR, pp. 15910–15919 (2021)
46. Wang, G., Yang, Y., Zhang, H., Liu, Z., Wang, H.: Spherical interpolated convolutional network with distance-feature density for 3-D semantic segmentation of point clouds. IEEE Transactions on Cybernetics (2021)
47. Wang, H., Pang, J., Lodhi, M.A., Tian, Y., Tian, D.: FESTA: flow estimation via spatial-temporal attention for scene point clouds. In: Proceedings of the IEEE/CVF Conference on Computer Vision and Pattern Recognition, pp. 14173–14182 (2021)
48. Wang, S., Sun, Y., Liu, C., Liu, M.: PointTrackNet: an end-to-end network for 3-D object detection and tracking from point clouds. IEEE Robot. Autom. Lett. **5**(2), 3206–3212 (2020)
49. Wei, Y., Wang, Z., Rao, Y., Lu, J., Zhou, J.: PV-RAFT: point-voxel correlation fields for scene flow estimation of point clouds. In: Proceedings of the IEEE/CVF Conference on Computer Vision and Pattern Recognition, pp. 6954–6963 (2021)
50. Wu, Wenxuan, Wang, Zhi Yuan, Li, Zhuwen, Liu, Wei, Fuxin, Li.: PointPWC-Net: cost volume on point clouds for (self-)supervised scene flow estimation. In: Vedaldi, Andrea, Bischof, Horst, Brox, Thomas, Frahm, Jan-Michael. (eds.) ECCV 2020. LNCS, vol. 12350, pp. 88–107. Springer, Cham (2020). https://doi.org/10.1007/978-3-030-58558-7_6
51. Xia, Y., et al.: SOE-Net: a self-attention and orientation encoding network for point cloud based place recognition. In: Proceedings of the IEEE/CVF Conference on Computer Vision and Pattern Recognition, pp. 11348–11357 (2021)

52. Yang, G., Ramanan, D.: Upgrading optical flow to 3D scene flow through optical expansion. In: Proceedings of the IEEE/CVF Conference on Computer Vision and Pattern Recognition, pp. 1334–1343 (2020)
53. Yang, G., Ramanan, D.: Learning to segment rigid motions from two frames. In: Proceedings of the IEEE/CVF Conference on Computer Vision and Pattern Recognition, pp. 1266–1275 (2021)

Correspondence Reweighted Translation Averaging

Lalit Manam and Venu Madhav Govindu(✉)

Indian Institute of Science, Bengaluru 560012, India
{lalitmanam,venug}@iisc.ac.in

Abstract. Translation averaging methods use the consistency of input translation directions to solve for camera translations. However, translation directions obtained using epipolar geometry are error-prone. This paper argues that the improved accuracy of translation averaging should be leveraged to mitigate the errors in the input translation direction estimates. To this end, we introduce weights for individual correspondences which are iteratively refined to yield improved translation directions. In turn, these refined translation directions are averaged to obtain camera translations. This results in an alternating approach to translation averaging. The modularity of our framework allows us to use existing translation averaging methods and improve their results. The efficacy of the scheme is demonstrated by comparing performance with state-of-the-art methods on a number of real-world datasets. We also show that our approach yields reasonably good 3D reconstructions with straightforward triangulation, i.e. without any bundle adjustment iterations.

Keywords: Structure from motion · Translation averaging · Reweighting correspondences

1 Introduction

In Structure-from-Motion (henceforth SfM) [16], given point correspondences across many images, we solve for the corresponding camera motions and 3D scene structure. Many SfM pipelines incrementally grow the solution by adding one camera at a time [27,30,35]. While they work well, incremental methods suffer from drift and have a significant computational load owing to the repeated use of Bundle Adjustment (henceforth BA) [32]. In contrast, batch or global methods [31] determine the absolute poses of the cameras simultaneously (also known as motion averaging [14,15]). Typically one solves for rotations, followed by translations using rotation and translation averaging respectively. Subsequently, we estimate 3D structure given the camera motions, often with a final BA refinement. In this paper, we address the problem of translation averaging.

Supplementary Information The online version contains supplementary material available at https://doi.org/10.1007/978-3-031-19827-4_4.

S. Avidan et al. (Eds.): ECCV 2022, LNCS 13693, pp. 56–72, 2022.
https://doi.org/10.1007/978-3-031-19827-4_4

Using epipolar geometry, we can only recover the translation direction owing to an inherent scale ambiguity which has a number of serious implications. Firstly, it makes translation averaging a challenging problem since we need to use relative translation directions to solve for absolute camera translations. Existing methods [13,25,34,36] adopt a variety of approaches to tackle the scale estimation problem inherent to translation averaging. Secondly, in contrast to rotation averaging, determining the feasibility of solutions for a given translation averaging problem is related to the non-trivial issue of parallel rigidity [2,26]. Finally, translation directions recovered from point correspondences using epipolar geometry can be of poor quality owing to the presence of noise and outliers or when the baseline is narrow.

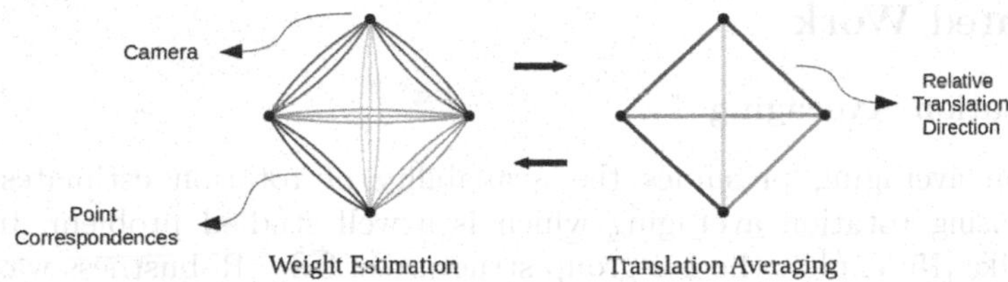

Fig. 1. Schematic diagram of our framework for a viewgraph of camera-camera relationships. Each vertex represents a camera. The multiedges on the left indicate correspondences between camera-camera pairs whereas the edges on the right indicate a relative translation estimate between camera pairs. Weight estimation for point correspondences (resulting in refined translation directions) and translation averaging are alternately carried out in our framework

All translation averaging methods solve for camera translations by exploiting consistency relationships the input translation directions should satisfy. In this paper, we argue that while this is useful, the poor quality of input translation directions obtained from epipolar geometry imposes limitations on the accuracy of translation averaging solutions. A key observation of our paper is that instead of using a single estimate of translation directions, we can refine them by introducing weights for individual correspondences. We schematically illustrate our approach in Fig. 1.

Given an initial set of translation directions, we use averaging to obtain camera translations. The translation directions obtained from translation averaging estimates are superior to the original pairwise epipolar geometry based estimates as the averaged solution is based on global consistency. Hence we can use the estimates obtained from translation averaging to refine the weights ascribed to individual point correspondences between a camera pair (shown as multiedges in Fig. 1). Subsequently, the multiedges give us an estimate of translation directions (i.e. edges in a graph) which are averaged to obtain an improved translation estimate.

We emphasize that our reweighting of individual correspondences is based on a global view of geometric consistency and not the standard approach of robustness based on a limited view of two camera epipolar geometry. Our approach is modular in nature and can use different translation averaging and weighting schemes. Thus, our method can take a translation averaging approach and improve it by refining the weighting of individual point correspondences.

The paper is organized as follows: Sect. 2 reviews existing approaches. Sect. 3 presents the formulation and details of our proposed approach. Sect. 4 presents an extensive set of experiments to demonstrate the superiority of our approach compared to the state-of-the-art methods. We provide a discussion of some aspects of our method in Sect. 5 and a brief conclusion in Sect. 6.

2 Related Work

2.1 Rotation Averaging

Translation averaging presumes the availability of rotation estimates, often obtained using rotation averaging which is a well studied problem. Intrinsic methods like [15] exploit the Lie group structure of $\mathbb{SO}_3$. Robustness was incorporated in [4,5,17]. Extrinsic methods like [6,12,22] solve for a relaxed version of the problem. Readers are referred to [10,28,29] and the references therein for recent developments.

2.2 Translation Averaging

Most translation averaging approaches are based on the structure of the essential matrix and trifocal tensor [16]. Govindu [14] proposed to minimize the cross-product between the observed directions and the estimated relative camera translations. Arie-Nachimson *et al.* [1] set up a linear system of cross product constraints based on epipolar geometry. Moulon *et al.* [24] formulated a trifocal tensor with known rotations which converted the problem to aligning triplets instead of pairs.

Jiang *et al.* [18] used camera triplets which converted pairwise constraints into constraints on a triangle. Wilson *et al.* [34] compared the observed and estimated heading directions. They added camera-to-point constraints to make the problem stable and relied on a pre-processing step to remove outliers. Tron *et al.* [33] compared squared relative displacements and used it in a distributed fashion. The Least Unsquared Deviations (LUD) method [25] proposed by Ozyesil *et al.* extended [33] by using L_1 loss for robustness and posed the problem as a convex program. Arrigoni *et al.* [3] proposed to minimize the squared error of the orthogonal projection of the estimated relative translations onto observed directions. In a similar spirit, Goldstein *et al.* [13] proposed ShapeFit/ShapeKick that minimized the orthogonal projection using ADMM but with an L_1 loss for robustness. Cui *et al.* [8] used feature tracks to construct a linear system and also solved the problem using ADMM. Cui *et al.* [7] used sin-length ratio constraints between cameras and points to estimate camera-to-camera scales and then solved a linear system. Although [7,8] used point correspondences in their method, all correspondences were treated equally. Moreover, multiple estimates of scales with different feature tracks were handled carefully to avoid the influence of outliers. Zhuang *et al.* [36] proposed a Bilinear Angle-based Translation Averaging (BATA) scheme comparing the estimated heading directions from camera translations to that of the observed directions relaxing the cost in [34].

Other related approaches include similarity averaging [9], averaging of essential and fundamental matrices [19,20] and exploiting the structure of the matrix generated from pairwise camera displacements [11].

3 Proposed Method

In this section, we define some preliminaries and develop our proposed algorithm for translation averaging. Let $\mathcal{G} = (\mathcal{V}, \mathcal{E})$ be a viewgraph, where $\mathcal{V}$ and $\mathcal{E}$ denotes the set of vertices and edges in $\mathcal{G}$ respectively. To each vertex i, we assign a 3D rotation $\mathbf{R}_i \in \mathbb{SO}(3)$ and translation $\mathbf{T}_i \in \mathbb{R}^3$ that denotes its motion with respect to a global frame of reference. Each edge $(i,j) \in \mathcal{E}$ denotes the relative rotation and translation $(\mathbf{R}_{ij}, \mathbf{T}_{ij})$ between camera vertices i and j. We note that owing to the scale ambiguity of epipolar geometry we can only recover the relative translation upto an unknown scale factor, i.e. the unit norm translation direction vectors $\mathbf{t}_{ij} \in \mathbb{S}^2$, resulting in the relationships:

$$\mathbf{R}_{ij} = \mathbf{R}_j \mathbf{R}_i^{-1},$$

$$\mathbf{t}_{ij} = \frac{\mathbf{R}_j(\mathbf{T}_i - \mathbf{T}_j)}{\|\mathbf{R}_j(\mathbf{T}_i - \mathbf{T}_j)\|_2} \tag{1}$$

$$\rightarrow \mathbf{v}_{ij} = -\mathbf{R}_j^{-1}\mathbf{t}_{ij} = \frac{\mathbf{T}_j - \mathbf{T}_i}{\|\mathbf{T}_j - \mathbf{T}_i\|_2} \tag{2}$$

where the unit vector $\mathbf{v}_{ij}$ is the translation direction represented in the global frame of reference and is defined for simplicity of notation. We assume that the rotations $\mathbf{R}_i$ for $i \in \mathcal{V}$ are either known or estimated using rotation averaging. Thus, the translation averaging problem of interest is one of recovering the absolute translations $\mathbf{T}_i$ for $i \in \mathcal{V}$ given the relative translation directions $\mathbf{t}_{ij}$ for $(i,j) \in \mathcal{E}$. For each edge $(i,j) \in \mathcal{E}$, we associate a number of point correspondences between cameras i and j. We denote these correspondences as $\{(\mathbf{p}_i^k, \mathbf{q}_j^k) | k \in \mathcal{I}_{ij}\}$ where $\mathbf{p}$ and $\mathbf{q}$ denote the homogeneous representation of correspondences in camera i and j respectively which are normalized to unit vectors, $\mathcal{I}_{ij}$ is the set of point indexes for the edge $(i,j) \in \mathcal{E}$, and k is the point index. We can now write the epipolar constraint between cameras i and j for the k-th point correspondence as

$$\left(\mathbf{q}_j^k\right)^T \left(\mathbf{t}_{ij} \times \mathbf{R}_{ij}\mathbf{p}_i^k\right) = 0 \tag{3}$$

Denoting $\tilde{\mathbf{p}}_i^k = \mathbf{R}_i^{-1}\mathbf{p}_i^k$ and $\tilde{\mathbf{q}}_j^k = \mathbf{R}_j^{-1}\mathbf{q}_j^k$, the epipolar constraint of Eq. 3 can be rewritten as

$$\begin{aligned}
&(\mathbf{q}_j^k)^T (\mathbf{t}_{ij} \times \mathbf{R}_j\mathbf{R}_i^{-1}\mathbf{p}_i^k) = 0 \\
&\Rightarrow (\mathbf{q}_j^k)^T \mathbf{R}_j (\mathbf{R}_j^{-1}\mathbf{t}_{ij} \times \mathbf{R}_i^{-1}\mathbf{p}_i^k) = 0 \qquad (4)\\
&\Rightarrow (\mathbf{R}_j^{-1}\mathbf{q}_j^k)^T (-\mathbf{v}_{ij} \times (\mathbf{R}_i^{-1}\mathbf{p}_i^k)) = 0 \\
&\Rightarrow (\mathbf{m}_{ij}^k)^T \mathbf{v}_{ij} = 0 \qquad (5)
\end{aligned}$$

where $\mathbf{m}_{ij}^k = \tilde{\mathbf{q}}_j^k \times \tilde{\mathbf{p}}_i^k$. Eq. 4 is obtained using the relationship $\mathbf{a} \times \mathbf{S}\mathbf{b} = \mathbf{S}^{-T}(\mathbf{S}^{-1}\mathbf{a} \times \mathbf{b})$ (upto scale) for any invertible matrix $\mathbf{S} \in \mathbb{R}^{3\times3}$ and $\mathbf{a}, \mathbf{b} \in \mathbb{R}^3$ (Appendix A4.2 in [16]). Collecting the relationships in Eq. 5 for all $k \in \mathcal{I}_{ij}$ we get $\mathbf{M}_{ij}\mathbf{v}_{ij} = \mathbf{0}$ where the k-th row of $\mathbf{M}_{ij}$ is $\mathbf{m}_{ij}^{kT}$. Further, to account for our confidence in each observation, we assign a scalar weight w_{ij}^k to every point correspondence $(\mathbf{p}_i^k, \mathbf{q}_j^k)$. We normalize these weights for each edge $(i,j) \in \mathcal{E}$ such that $\sum_k w_{ij}^k = 1$. We define a diagonal matrix $\mathbf{W}_{ij}$ where the k-th entry on the diagonal is w_{ij}^k. Finally, we denote the set of all the translations as $\mathbb{T} = \{\mathbf{T}_1, \cdots, \mathbf{T}_N\}$ where $N = |\mathcal{V}|$ is the number of cameras.

3.1 Our Framework for Translation Averaging

When Eq. 5 is not exactly satisfied due to noise, the least squares solution for $\mathbf{v}_{ij}$ is the smallest right singular vector of the matrix $\mathbf{M}_{ij}$. Analogously, the weighted least squares solution is the smallest right singular vector of $\mathbf{W}_{ij}\mathbf{M}_{ij}$. While this holds for a single camera pair $(i,j) \in \mathcal{E}$, in translation averaging, we seek a global solution that is most consistent with the observations on each individual edge. Thus we formulate our optimization problem as

$$\min_{\mathbb{T}} \sum_{(i,j)\in\mathcal{E}} \|\mathbf{W}_{ij}\mathbf{M}_{ij}\mathbf{v}_{ij}(\mathbb{T})\|_2^2 \qquad (6)$$

where we denote $\mathbf{v}_{ij}(\mathbb{T})$ to emphasize that it is a function of the global camera translations $\mathbb{T}$. $\mathcal{C}$ corresponds to the constraint set to fix origin and scale ambiguity in the problem. It will be immediately noted (from Eq. 2) that Eq. 6 is a highly non-linear problem and is challenging to solve for large-scale SfM datasets. When robust estimators are used, such as IRLS, the weights w_{ij}^k are iteratively updated based on a robust loss minimization. In contrast, as stated earlier, we wish to refine our weights based on the global consistency of the translation directions. In our approach, after initialization, we solve for translation directions (given translations) and then solve translation averaging (given translation directions). This is repeated till convergence. We note that our alternating approach is akin to Expectation Maximization (EM) [23] where the weights for point correspondences play the role of latent or unobserved variables. Specifically, we have the following alternating steps:

Algorithm 1: Correspondence Reweighted Translation Averaging (CReTA)

Initialize global translations $\mathbb{T}$
while *not converged* **do**
  Update weights $\forall(\mathbf{p}_i^k, \mathbf{q}_j^k)$
  Estimate $\{\mathbf{v}_{ij} | \forall(i,j) \in \mathcal{E}\}$
  Solve Translation Averaging using $\{\mathbf{v}_{ij}\}$
end

- **Weights Update:** Given the current estimate of global translations $\mathbb{T}$, for each point correspondence $(\mathbf{p}_i^k, \mathbf{q}_j^k)$, we compute the residual error using Eq. 5, i.e. $e_{ij}^k = \mathbf{m}_{ij}^{kT} \mathbf{v}_{ij}(\mathbb{T})$. We map these errors e_{ij}^k into weights w_{ij}^k using a suitable function to denote our current confidence in that correspondence.
- **Translations Update:** Given the weights defined above, the minimization problem in Eq. 6 is completely defined. Directly minimizing Eq. 6 is infeasible for large-scale datasets owing to the very large number of correspondences involved and the non-linear nature of the problem. Instead, we use a two-step procedure as follows: For each edge $(i,j) \in \mathcal{E}$, we solve for the translation direction $\mathbf{v}_{ij}$ as the null space of $\mathbf{W}_{ij}\mathbf{M}_{ij}$. As described below, we use these estimated $\mathbf{v}_{ij}$ as inputs for a translation averaging method to solve for the global translations $\mathbb{T}$. As noted in [36], this is akin to functional lifting since we solve for $\mathbf{v}_{ij}$ for all edges and then average them in terms of the smaller number of camera translations. This approach makes our optimization using point correspondence weights tractable with lower computation requirements than directly solving Eqn. 6. We also note that the modular nature of our formulation allows us to use any translation averaging scheme.

Choice of Translation Averaging Method: In an excellent discussion, [36] shows that the weakness of the LUD formulation of [25] is its use of an inequality constraint to remove scale ambiguity and prevent the collapse of camera translations to a point. They further show that this problem can be mitigated by revising the scale constraint, resulting in a Revised-LUD or RLUD method, which is shown to have a minimum identical to that of Shapefit/ShapeKick [13]. For the remainder of this paper, LUD refers to the original formulation in [25] and RLUD refers to the Revised-LUD modification given in [36]. We provide below the formulations for RLUD and BATA which we use in our experiments.

RLUD:

$$\min_{\mathbf{T}_{i,i\in\mathcal{V}}, \lambda_{ij,(i,j)\in\mathcal{E}}} \|\mathbf{T}_j - \mathbf{T}_i - \lambda_{ij}\mathbf{v}_{ij}\|_2 \tag{7}$$

$$\text{s.t.} \sum_{i\in\mathcal{V}} \mathbf{T}_i = \mathbf{0}, \sum_{(i,j)\in\mathcal{E}} \langle \mathbf{T}_j - \mathbf{T}_i, \mathbf{v}_{ij} \rangle = 1, \lambda_{ij} \geq 0, \ \forall (i,j) \in \mathcal{E}$$

BATA:

$$\min_{\mathbf{T}_i, i\in\mathcal{V}, \gamma_{ij}, (i,j)\in\mathcal{E}} \rho\left(\|\left(\mathbf{T}_j - \mathbf{T}_i\right)\gamma_{ij} - \mathbf{v}_{ij}\|_2\right) \tag{8}$$

$$\text{s.t.} \sum_{i\in\mathcal{V}} \mathbf{T}_i = \mathbf{0}, \sum_{(i,j)\in\mathcal{E}} \langle \mathbf{T}_j - \mathbf{T}_i, \mathbf{v}_{ij}\rangle = 1, \gamma_{ij} \geq 0, \ \forall (i,j) \in \mathcal{E}$$

The zero centroid and dot product constraints in Eqns. 7 and 8 remove the inherent origin and scale ambiguity. ρ denotes a robust loss function. λ_{ij} and γ_{ij} are non-negative variables that are ideally equal to baseline and inverse baseline for the edge (i, j) respectively. It can be seen that RLUD compares the relative displacements (by also computing the translation scales λ_{ij}) while BATA compares the heading directions. In other words, RLUD and BATA are representative of the two approaches feasible for translation averaging, i.e. comparing directions or comparing translation vectors.

Implementation Details: We provide a high level description of our approach in Algorithm 1. In order to remove outlier or low quality correspondences, after the initial estimate of translations, for each edge (i, j), we compute the weights for each correspondence pair and remove the bottom 25% of such correspondences. In every iteration, edges are pruned when the estimated $\mathbf{v}_{ij}$ deviates by more than 40° from the equivalent derived from the global translations estimated in the previous iteration. In the Weights Update step, we use the function $w_{ij}^k = \frac{\alpha^2}{\alpha^2 + e_{ij}^{k2}}$, with $\alpha = 0.01$. Other weighting functions are also feasible here. Estimation of $\mathbf{v}_{ij}$ involves resolving its sign ambiguity which can either be done using chirality constraint or comparing with the directions from the current estimate of global translations. The latter one is used in our implementation. In our experiments, we use RLUD and BATA for translation averaging and denote our corresponding methods as CReTA-RLUD and CReTA-BATA respectively. For CReTA-RLUD, we remove edges with negative scale factors λ_{ij} in each iteration. Algorithm 1 is run till the absolute fractional change of the translation averaging cost function is less than 10^{-5} or mean change in translations is less than 10^{-6} or the maximum number of iterations N_{max} is reached. For CReTA-RLUD and CReTA-BATA, N_{max} equals 50 and 10 respectively[1]. In addition, both RLUD and BATA are themselves iterative methods run for 20 iterations each. Finally, for BATA, we use a Cauchy loss with scale $\beta = 0.1$, as used by the authors in [36].

4 Experiments

In this section, we provide experimental comparisons of our method with state-of-the-art methods for translation averaging on synthetic and real datasets. For camera rotations, we use the rotation averaging solution obtained using the code

[1] For large datasets with number of cameras greater than 2000, N_{max} equals 30 and 5 for CReTA-RLUD and CReTA-BATA respectively.

provided by [5][2]. For all experiments, the maximal parallel rigid component of the viewgraph is extracted based on [21]. We note that although the translation directions change for each iteration in our approach, we do not recompute parallel rigidity as the maximal component does not change significantly over the iterations. We use LUD implemented in Theia [31] and BATA's code provided by the authors[3]. Our method is implemented in MATLAB. To quantitatively evaluate the performance of different schemes, the estimated camera translations are robustly aligned to the ground truth using the code provided by [34][4]. All experiments are performed on a PC with Intel Xeon Silver 4210 processor with 128 GB RAM. Finally, in each table, the best performing method for each dataset is highlighted in **bold**, μ and $\hat{\mu}$ imply mean and median errors respectively.

4.1 Synthetic Data

We carry out experiments with synthetic data to study the comparative behaviour of different methods in the presence of noise and outliers. To validate the usefulness of weighting every point correspondence based on global consistency, RLUD and BATA are compared to our methods, CReTA-RLUD and CReTA-BATA. For creating synthetic data as close to the real data as possible, we use the ground truth from two 1DSfM datasets [34], i.e. *Montreal Notre Dame* (450 nodes, 52340 edges) and *Tower of London* (467 nodes, 23777 edges). We chose these datasets as they have a similar number of cameras but a different number of edges. We refer to these synthetic datasets as MND_{syn} and TOL_{syn}. For these synthetic datasets, we create point correspondences by projecting the ground truth 3D points onto the cameras using the ground truth poses and then applying camera calibration as provided in the dataset. Only the point features within the image dimensions and with a positive depth in the camera coordinate frame are retained. For every edge, a maximum of 1000 correspondences generated in this fashion are retained. This creates a perfectly clean dataset with real-world camera motions and 3D structure. Now we perturb the image points with Gaussian noise $\mathcal{N}(0, \sigma^2)$ with $\sigma \in \{1, 3\}$ pixels. 10 instances of both datasets are generated for the two noise levels. To generate outliers, 30% of the correspondences in each edge are perturbed with Gaussian noise $\mathcal{N}(0, \sigma_o^2)$ with $\sigma_o = 10$ pixels. For every dataset, relative translations are computed in a RANSAC loop using epipolar geometry with rotations set to ground truth. This removes the effect of rotation errors from the problem. For these realizations, we extract the corresponding maximal parallel rigid graph, which are used as inputs in our experiments.

To evaluate the accuracy of camera translations, we use the normalized root mean square error (NRMSE) as in [25] and [36]. Let $\mathbf{T}_i^{gt}$ be the set of ground truth camera translations and $\mathbf{T}_i^{avg}$ estimated from different methods, then $NRMSE = \sqrt{\sum_{i \in \mathcal{V}} \|\mathbf{T}_i^{gt} - \mathbf{T}_i^{avg}\|_2^2}$. Both $\mathbf{T}_i^{avg}$ and $\mathbf{T}_i^{gt}$ are normalized such

[2] https://ee.iisc.ac.in/cvlab/research/rotaveraging/.

[3] https://bbzh.github.io/document/BATA.zip.

[4] https://github.com/wilsonkl/SfM_Init.

Table 1. Camera translation errors (in meters) for synthetic datasets. The reported values are averaged over 10 instances each (wo: with outliers)

Dataset	RLUD		BATA		CReTA-RLUD		CReTA-BATA	
	μ	$\hat{\mu}$	μ	$\hat{\mu}$	μ	$\hat{\mu}$	μ	$\hat{\mu}$
MND_{syn}, $\sigma = 1$	1.64	1.10	0.17	0.06	**0.12**	0.07	0.13	**0.05**
MND_{syn}, $\sigma = 1$, wo	1.61	1.09	0.15	**0.06**	0.14	0.08	**0.11**	**0.06**
MND_{syn}, $\sigma = 3$	1.55	1.04	0.25	0.12	**0.18**	**0.11**	0.22	0.14
MND_{syn}, $\sigma = 3$, wo	1.49	0.97	0.29	0.14	**0.19**	**0.11**	0.25	0.16
TOL_{syn}, $\sigma = 1$	12.78	2.56	2.88	1.75	7.38	**0.46**	**1.19**	0.52
TOL_{syn}, $\sigma = 1$, wo	12.36	2.13	2.56	1.56	7.51	**0.63**	**1.64**	0.92
TOL_{syn}, $\sigma = 3$	12.44	2.64	2.50	1.46	7.76	**1.00**	**2.06**	1.11
TOL_{syn}, $\sigma = 3$, wo	12.47	2.73	2.72	1.40	7.89	**0.99**	**2.52**	1.20

Table 2. Comparison of input and output relative translation directions (in degrees) on synthetic data. The reported values are averaged over 10 instances each (RMS: root mean square error; wo: with outliers)

Dataset	Input		CReTA-RLUD		CReTA-BATA	
	μ	RMS	μ	RMS	μ	RMS
MND_{syn}, $\sigma = 1$	0.33	3.80	**0.17**	**1.45**	0.23	**1.45**
MND_{syn}, $\sigma = 1$, wo	0.52	5.35	**0.18**	**1.20**	0.22	**1.20**
MND_{syn}, $\sigma = 3$	1.50	8.17	**0.72**	3.03	0.89	**3.00**
MND_{syn}, $\sigma = 3$, wo	2.00	10.34	**0.77**	3.12	0.94	**3.09**
TOL_{syn}, $\sigma = 1$	0.79	7.13	0.37	1.55	**0.30**	**1.53**
TOL_{syn}, $\sigma = 1$, wo	1.27	9.55	0.44	2.48	**0.34**	**2.46**
TOL_{syn}, $\sigma = 3$	2.74	13.56	**1.00**	3.95	**1.00**	**3.89**
TOL_{syn}, $\sigma = 3$, wo	3.60	16.15	**1.05**	3.92	1.07	**3.88**

that $\sum_{i \in \mathcal{V}} \mathbf{T}_i = 0$ and $\sum_{i \in \mathcal{V}} \|\mathbf{T}_i\|_2^2 = 1$. The evaluation is also done in terms of mean and median errors of camera translations (after aligning the solutions to ground truth) and comparing the input and output relative translations.

In Table 1, we show the translation errors for each datasets with differing scenarios ($\sigma = \{1, 3\}$, with and without outliers) averaged over 10 instances. As can be clearly seen, our CReTA methods are significantly better in accuracy compared to LUD and BATA. In Fig. 2, we show the distribution for NRMSE for different methods for the 10 instances when $\sigma = 3$ and with outliers. We show the results for only one setting of noise and outliers for visual clarity (other settings are shown in the supplementary material). The large leftward shift of the distributions for our methods clearly demonstrates a significant improvement in performance over the corresponding translation averaging methods used. Further, in Table 2, we compare the quality of input to that of output relative translations for different methods. It is seen that relative translation directions are substantially improved in our framework.

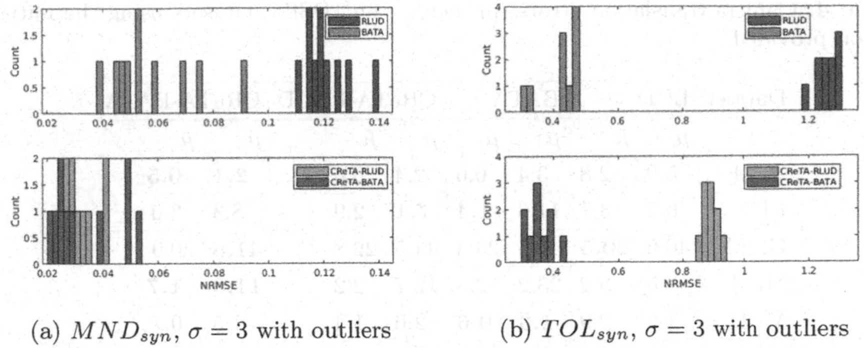

(a) MND_{syn}, $\sigma = 3$ with outliers (b) TOL_{syn}, $\sigma = 3$ with outliers

Fig. 2. Comparison of the histograms of NRMSE in 10 instances for two synthetic datasets. The leftward shift for our methods clearly indicates a significant improvement in performance

Table 3. Camera translation errors (in meters) on 1DSfM [34] datasets ($|\mathcal{V}|$: number of nodes, $|\mathcal{E}|$: number of edges)

Dataset	$\lvert\mathcal{V}\rvert$	$\lvert\mathcal{E}\rvert$	LUD [25]		ShapeFit [13]		BATA [36]		CReTA-RLUD (Ours)		CReTA-BATA (Ours)	
			μ	$\hat{\mu}$	μ	$\hat{\mu}$	μ	$\hat{\mu}$	μ	$\hat{\mu}$	μ	$\hat{\mu}$
Alamo (ALM)	586	81437	2.7	**0.5**	**0.9**	**0.5**	2.0	0.6	2.0	**0.5**	2.0	**0.5**
Ellis Island (ELS)	229	14728	6.9	3.6	12	**1.9**	6.7	3.2	**6.0**	2.9	6.2	3.3
Gendarmenkmart (GMM)	686	27145	31.2	11.3	-	-	31.3	11.4	**31.0**	11.2	31.5	**11.1**
Madrid Metropolis (MDR)	025	11995	8.4	1.9	81	6.0	6.9	**1.6**	7.6	1.7	**6.1**	**1.6**
Montreal Notre Dame (MND)	461	45737	0.9	0.5	1.7	0.8	0.8	0.5	0.9	0.5	**0.7**	**0.4**
Notre Dame (ND)	552	80647	1.2	0.3	1.5	**0.2**	**1.0**	**0.2**	2.1	1.1	**1.0**	**0.2**
NYC Library (NYC)	337	14365	2.2	0.8	162	1.4	2.1	1.7	**2.0**	**0.7**	**2.0**	**0.7**
Piazza del Popolo (PDP)	334	20974	3.8	2.8	5.9	3.6	**3.4**	**2.0**	4.5	3.4	3.8	2.5
Piccadilly (PIC)	2362	201600	**2.8**	1.3	15	1.2	3.2	**1.1**	**2.8**	**1.1**	3.0	**1.1**
Roman Forum (ROF)	1069	54207	11.9	3.3	25	4.3	8.3	2.0	13.3	3.3	**7.7**	**1.7**
Tower of London (TOL)	474	19252	14.9	3.2	164	**2.3**	9.3	3.0	13.3	3.1	**9.0**	3.0
Trafalgar (TFG)	4900	542480	8.4	5.3	-	-	7.9	4.2	8.0	4.4	**7.5**	**4.1**
Union Square (USQ)	825	19899	10.6	6.1	47	8.9	**10.2**	5.6	10.6	5.4	10.5	**4.9**
Vienna Cathedral (VNC)	826	82793	**5.1**	2.1	11	**1.9**	12.0	2.1	6.5	2.2	6.7	**1.9**
Yorkminster (YKM)	430	22692	7.6	1.8	-	-	**5.1**	**1.3**	7.0	1.6	6.0	2.0

4.2 Real World Data

In this subsection, we present results on real unordered image datasets provided by the authors of 1DSfM [34]. These datasets are pre-processed in a manner similar to that suggested in [25]: Rotation averaging is performed and inconsistent edges with an error greater than 10° are removed. Subsequently, the initial translation directions are estimated using the epipolar geometric relationship (Eq. 5) in a RANSAC loop. The results for our methods CReTA-RLUD and CReTA-BATA are shown in Table 3 along with other state-of-the-art methods. Since ShapeFit provides multiple results, the overall best results are cited. It can be seen that CReTA has the best performance or is similar in quality to the

Table 4. Camera translation errors (in meters) on 1DSfM datasets using the initialization provided

Dataset	LUD		BATA		CReTA-RLUD		CReTA-BATA	
	μ	$\hat{\mu}$	μ	$\hat{\mu}$	μ	$\hat{\mu}$	μ	$\hat{\mu}$
ALM	5.0	2.8	3.4	0.6	2.4	0.6	**2.1**	**0.5**
ELS	9.7	3.7	11.6	**1.4**	**7.1**	2.9	8.3	3.0
GMM	46.6	**20.5**	45.6	23.4	44.5	22.8	**41.8**	20.9
MDR	19.0	9.2	23.2	2.8	12.7	2.2	**11.9**	**1.7**
MND	1.6	0.9	**1.3**	**0.6**	2.6	1.4	1.5	0.7
ND	4.1	1.6	2.1	0.3	1.7	0.5	**1.1**	**0.2**
NYC	4.5	2.2	3.5	**0.7**	2.6	**0.7**	**2.3**	**0.7**
PDP	6.3	1.9	6.7	1.6	5.6	**1.2**	**5.4**	**1.2**
PIC	6.2	3.8	5.1	**1.3**	4.4	2.3	**3.4**	**1.3**
ROF	25.1	14.6	11.3	**1.6**	18.2	9.4	**9.3**	1.8
TOL	24.9	8.7	17.6	**2.0**	19.5	2.6	**16.8**	2.9
TFG	16.7	13.3	11.7	**4.4**	9.9	6.2	**9.1**	5.7
USQ	12.2	7.6	13.3	**4.8**	11.6	6.2	**10.5**	5.0
VNC	14.2	7.0	10.5	2.1	8.5	2.4	**5.8**	**1.8**
YKM	15.6	6.8	9.4	**1.3**	7.3	1.5	**5.2**	1.5

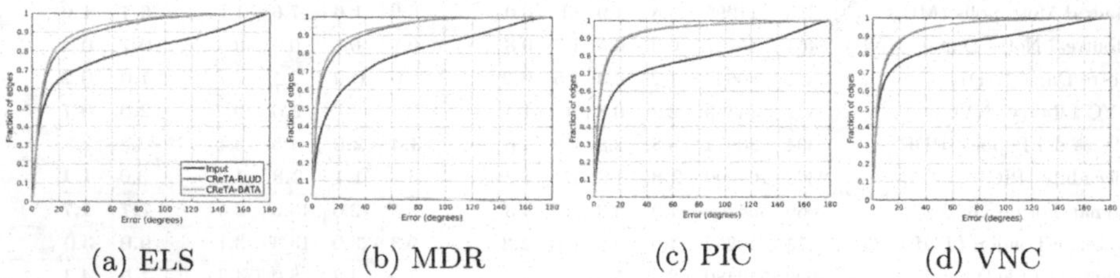

(a) ELS (b) MDR (c) PIC (d) VNC

Fig. 3. Cumulative error distributions (in degrees) for relative translation directions for inputs and CReTA estimates

best solution for most of the datasets. In particular, the improvement in mean errors is significant for many datasets when compared to the respective translation averaging scheme used, i.e. CReTA-RLUD vs. LUD and CReTA-BATA vs. BATA.

The 1DSfM datasets [34] also provide an estimate of the translation directions $\mathbf{t}_{ij}$ which are of inferior quality compared to that estimated and used in the above experiment. To assess the performance of the methods with low quality inputs, we supply the translation directions given in the 1DSfM datasets [34] to different methods and compare the camera translation accuracies in Table 4. It can be seen that even when the initial input translation directions are of inferior quality, our CReTA approach is able to obtain better accuracies with considerable improvement in the mean errors when compared to the respective translation averaging scheme used. To further illustrate the improvement obtained, in Fig. 3, we compare the cumulative error distributions of the relative translation directions obtained using CReTA and the input translation directions. As can be seen, our approaches significantly improve upon the initial directions. These results suggest that weighting point correspondences with global consistency information can improve the performance of the translation averaging methods even with low quality input translation directions.

Table 5. Reprojection errors (in pixels) and number of 3D points ($N_p \times 10^3$) reconstructed after triangulation

Dataset	LUD			BATA			CReTA-RLUD			CReTA-BATA		
	μ	$\hat{\mu}$	$\mathbf{N_p}$	μ	$\hat{\mu}$	$\mathbf{N_p}$	μ	$\hat{\mu}$	$\mathbf{N_p}$	μ	$\hat{\mu}$	$\mathbf{N_p}$
ALM	6.6	5.4	83	7.7	6.7	120	**3.0**	**1.7**	**223**	3.5	2.3	221
ELS	8.3	7.3	37	7.6	6.3	56	**4.5**	**3.2**	62	4.7	3.6	**69**
GMM	7.1	6.5	54	6.8	5.7	99	**5.1**	**3.6**	146	5.5	4.2	**159**
MDR	7.1	7.0	11	7.7	6.8	38	**4.9**	**3.5**	60	5.1	3.8	**74**
MND	8.2	7.1	87	7.3	5.9	123	**3.6**	**2.3**	178	3.8	2.5	**184**
ND	7.9	6.9	53	8.2	7.0	117	**4.8**	**3.2**	232	5.4	3.8	**240**
NYC	8.0	7.6	32	7.5	6.5	65	**3.9**	**2.5**	107	4.5	3.1	**113**
PDP	7.6	6.5	34	7.2	5.9	40	**3.8**	**2.4**	64	4.5	3.1	**65**
PIC	7.3	6.5	121	7.2	6.1	187	**5.3**	**3.7**	298	5.6	4.1	**318**
ROF	7.2	6.4	87	7.4	6.3	204	**4.5**	**3.0**	347	5.0	3.6	373
TOL	5.9	4.8	63	6.7	5.4	95	**5.1**	**3.4**	180	5.5	3.8	**189**
TFG	7.1	6.1	308	7.0	5.9	416	**4.9**	**3.3**	649	5.5	3.9	**654**
USQ	7.8	6.8	34	7.5	6.5	38	**6.3**	**4.9**	62	6.5	5.1	**66**
VNC	7.8	6.9	124	7.6	6.4	194	**4.8**	**3.3**	341	5.0	3.6	**354**
YKM	7.6	6.9	56	7.4	6.3	96	**5.1**	**3.6**	153	5.7	4.2	**171**

Impact on 3D Reconstruction: In Tables 3 and 4, we compare the quality of translation estimates based on the available pseudo ground truth. But we believe that comparing the mean and median errors for translation estimates are inadequate since, in SfM, we are also interested in estimating 3D scene structure. In order to understand this aspect of camera motion estimation, we carry out the following experiment. For all datasets used, we extract a large number of correspondences using COLMAP [27]. We use the camera motions obtained in the experiment in Table 4 and carry out triangulation using Theia [31]. This allows us to assess the quality of the different translation solutions in terms of their impact on 3D reconstruction. The reprojection errors, shown after triangulation using the different translation solutions in Table 5, are independent of the pseudo ground truth and indicate the quality of reconstruction. As can be seen, our methods yield significantly lower reprojection errors. Specifically, CReTA-RLUD has the least mean and median reprojection errors followed by CReTA-BATA. The Theia package removes triangulated points with a reprojection error larger than 15 pixels. We note that our methods yield many more triangulated points with CReTA-BATA producing the highest number of 3D points for all datasets except ALM.

In Fig. 4 we illustrate the quality of translation estimation using our reweighting scheme by visualizing the 3D reconstructions obtained. We show the reconstructions obtained by triangulation using our CReTA-RLUD solution, with additional reconstructions provided in the supplementary material. The corresponding point clouds obtained using full BA are shown for reference. As can be seen, we obtain reasonably good quality reconstructions by straightforward triangulation without having to carry out any bundle adjustment refinements. The high quality of our triangulations indicate that our translation estimates are consistent with the point correspondences.

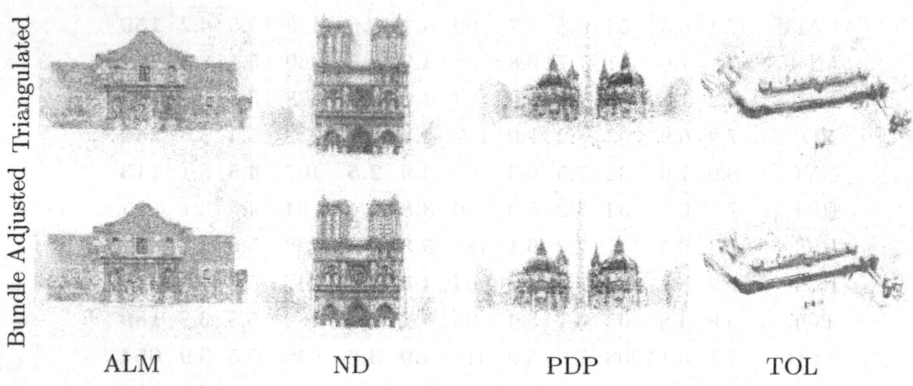

Fig. 4. Reconstructions obtained with triangulation using our CReTA-RLUD translation estimate (first row) compared to bundle adjustment (second row)

5 Discussion

As we have shown in Sect. 4, using our refined weighting of point correspondences improves the quality of the translation estimates. In this section, we briefly consider some other issues of significance.

Ablation Study: As indicated earlier, in our implementation, we remove some of the point correspondences from each edge $(i, j) \in \mathcal{E}$ after the first translation averaging estimate. This is especially useful when the input relative translations are inferior as the translation averaging steps improve the overall solution, and correspondences with low weights indicate that they are low in quality with respect to the translation averaging solution. For this study, we do not prune edges to understand the effect of removing point correspondences exclusively. Table 6 shows that removing point correspondences in the first iteration results in an improvement in our CReTA results for almost all datasets, with significant improvements for ELS, MDR, USQ and VNC datasets.

Computation Time: While RLUD and BATA are based on a single optimization, CReTA methods carry out repeated optimizations with refined input translation directions in each iteration increasing the computation load of CReTA as shown in Table 7. We believe that the additional computation time for our approach can be significantly reduced with a C++ implementation.

Limitations: Finally, we note that our improvement on translation averaging leverages the image correspondences in the dataset. We may not get as significant an improvement in performance over the translation averaging method used if there are very few point correspondences or if they have high noise and outlier ratios. Further, our method cannot be used if only the translation direction estimates are available without access to the correspondences.

Table 6. Impact of removing low quality correspondences in 1DSfM datasets after first iteration. Entries marked in **bold** shows improvement of a given method and not comparing all variants (woRC: without Removing Correspondences)

Dataset	CReTA-RLUD woRC		CReTA-RLUD		CReTA-BATA woRC		CReTA-BATA	
	μ	$\hat{\mu}$	μ	$\hat{\mu}$	μ	$\hat{\mu}$	μ	$\hat{\mu}$
ALM	**2.2**	**0.6**	**2.2**	**0.6**	**2.3**	0.7	2.4	**0.5**
ELS	28.3	3.3	**9.5**	**3.0**	21.0	3.9	**12.2**	**3.0**
GMM	45.1	21.3	**43.9**	**20.8**	**44.1**	**20.7**	**44.1**	21.3
MDR	16.4	2.7	**14.9**	**2.3**	19.8	2.8	**13.9**	**1.9**
MND	2.3	1.2	**1.9**	**1.0**	1.2	0.6	**0.8**	**0.4**
ND	1.2	0.3	**1.1**	**0.3**	1.7	0.6	**1.3**	**0.2**
NYC	4.3	1.0	**2.8**	**0.9**	3.1	0.9	**2.9**	**0.7**
PDP	6.4	**1.2**	**6.2**	1.3	6.8	1.8	**6.2**	**1.3**
PIC	**4.0**	**2.0**	**4.0**	2.3	4.2	1.5	**3.3**	**1.2**
ROF	12.1	4.0	**11.7**	**3.6**	8.6	2.0	**8.2**	**1.8**
TOL	19.6	2.8	**20.0**	**2.6**	**13.4**	3.2	14.8	**3.0**
TFG	13.6	10.0	**10.2**	**7.1**	13.7	7.8	**8.9**	**5.1**
USQ	26.3	9.1	**15.9**	**5.5**	17.9	7.3	**13.0**	**5.7**
VNC	11.4	4.0	**7.3**	**2.0**	14.0	2.7	**8.2**	**1.8**
YKM	6.7	**1.5**	**6.3**	**1.5**	12.9	**1.5**	**8.7**	**1.5**

Table 7. Computation time (in seconds) for different schemes

Dataset	RLUD	BATA	CReTA-RLUD	CReTA-BATA
ALM	42	54	225	145
ELS	6	10	33	28
GMM	14	25	84	71
MDR	7	14	45	32
MND	9	29	128	83
ND	46	56	285	188
NYC	6	14	44	31
PDP	8	16	42	43
PIC	211	249	747	521
ROF	24	52	172	128
TOL	9	19	60	43
TFG	543	862	1996	1271
USQ	8	17	63	50
VNC	54	74	283	176
YKM	11	16	74	53

6 Conclusion

This paper presents CReTA, a modular framework that iteratively refines the input translation directions by weighting individual point correspondences. The modularity of our approach allows us to use a translation averaging method and improve upon its performance. This improvement is reflected in the quality metrics for comparing translation estimates. Also of significance is the fact that our approach yields reasonably good reconstructions with triangulation when compared with BA results.

Acknowledgements. Lalit Manam is supported by a Prime Minister's Research Fellowship, Government of India. This research was supported in part by a Core Research Grant from Science and Engineering Research Board, Department of Science and Technology, Government of India.

References

1. Arie-Nachimson, M., Kovalsky, S.Z., Kemelmacher-Shlizerman, I., Singer, A., Basri, R.: Global motion estimation from point matches. In: 2012 Second International Conference on 3D Imaging, Modeling, Processing, Visualization & Transmission, pp. 81–88. IEEE (2012)
2. Arrigoni, F., Fusiello, A.: Bearing-based network localizability: a unifying view. IEEE Trans. Pattern Anal. Mach. Intell. **41**(9), 2049–2069 (2018)

3. Arrigoni, F., Rossi, B., Fusiello, A.: Robust and efficient camera motion synchronization via matrix decomposition. In: Murino, V., Puppo, E. (eds.) ICIAP 2015. LNCS, vol. 9279, pp. 444–455. Springer, Cham (2015). https://doi.org/10.1007/978-3-319-23231-7_40
4. Chatterjee, A., Govindu, V.M.: Efficient and robust large-scale rotation averaging. In: Proceedings of the IEEE International Conference on Computer Vision, pp. 521–528 (2013)
5. Chatterjee, A., Govindu, V.M.: Robust relative rotation averaging. IEEE Trans. Pattern Anal. Mach. Intell. **40**(4), 958–972 (2017)
6. Crandall, D., Owens, A., Snavely, N., Huttenlocher, D.: Discrete-continuous optimization for large-scale structure from motion. In: CVPR 2011, pp. 3001–3008. IEEE (2011)
7. Cui, H., Shen, S., Hu, Z.: Robust global translation averaging with feature tracks. In: 2016 23rd International Conference on Pattern Recognition (ICPR), pp. 3727–3732. IEEE (2016)
8. Cui, Z., Jiang, N., Tang, C., Tan, P.: Linear global translation estimation with feature tracks. In: Proceedings ECCV, vol. 3, pp. 61–75 (2014)
9. Cui, Z., Tan, P.: Global structure-from-motion by similarity averaging. In: Proceedings of the IEEE International Conference on Computer Vision, pp. 864–872 (2015)
10. Dellaert, F., Rosen, D.M., Wu, J., Mahony, R., Carlone, L.: Shonan rotation averaging: global optimality by surfing $SO(p)^n$. In: Vedaldi, A., Bischof, H., Brox, T., Frahm, J.-M. (eds.) ECCV 2020. LNCS, vol. 12351, pp. 292–308. Springer, Cham (2020). https://doi.org/10.1007/978-3-030-58539-6_18
11. Dong, Q., Gao, X., Cui, H., Hu, Z.: Robust camera translation estimation via rank enforcement. IEEE Trans. Cybern. **52**(2), 862–872 (2020)
12. Eriksson, A., Olsson, C., Kahl, F., Chin, T.: Rotation averaging and strong duality. In: 2018 IEEE/CVF Conference on Computer Vision and Pattern Recognition (CVPR), pp. 127–135 (2018)
13. Goldstein, T., Hand, P., Lee, C., Voroninski, V., Soatto, S.: Shapefit and shapekick for robust, scalable structure from motion. In: Leibe, B., Matas, J., Sebe, N., Welling, M. (eds.) ECCV 2016. LNCS, vol. 9911, pp. 289–304. Springer, Cham (2016). https://doi.org/10.1007/978-3-319-46478-7_18
14. Govindu, V.M.: Combining two-view constraints for motion estimation. In: Proceedings of the 2001 IEEE Computer Society Conference on Computer Vision and Pattern Recognition, CVPR 2001, vol. 2, pp. II-II. IEEE (2001)
15. Govindu, V.M.: Lie-algebraic averaging for globally consistent motion estimation. In: Proceedings of the 2004 IEEE Computer Society Conference on Computer Vision and Pattern Recognition, 2004. CVPR 2004, vol. 1, pp. I-I. IEEE (2004)
16. Hartley, R.I., Zisserman, A.: Multiple View Geometry in Computer Vision. Cambridge University Press, ISBN: 0521540518, second edn. (2004)
17. Hartley, R., Aftab, K., Trumpf, J.: L1 rotation averaging using the weiszfeld algorithm. In: CVPR 2011, pp. 3041–3048. IEEE (2011)
18. Jiang, N., Cui, Z., Tan, P.: A global linear method for camera pose registration. In: Proceedings of the IEEE International Conference on Computer Vision, pp. 481–488 (2013)
19. Kasten, Y., Geifman, A., Galun, M., Basri, R.: Algebraic characterization of essential matrices and their averaging in multiview settings. In: Proceedings of the IEEE/CVF International Conference on Computer Vision, pp. 5895–5903 (2019)

20. Kasten, Y., Geifman, A., Galun, M., Basri, R.: GPSfM: global projective SFM using algebraic constraints on multi-view fundamental matrices. In: Proceedings of the IEEE/CVF Conference on Computer Vision and Pattern Recognition, pp. 3264–3272 (2019)
21. Kennedy, R., Daniilidis, K., Naroditsky, O., Taylor, C.J.: Identifying maximal rigid components in bearing-based localization. In: 2012 IEEE/RSJ International Conference on Intelligent Robots and Systems, pp. 194–201. IEEE (2012)
22. Martinec, D., Pajdla, T.: Robust rotation and translation estimation in multiview reconstruction. In: 2007 IEEE Conference on Computer Vision and Pattern Recognition, pp. 1–8. IEEE (2007)
23. McLachlan, G., Krishnan, T.: The EM algorithm and extensions. Wiley, 2nd edn. (2008)
24. Moulon, P., Monasse, P., Marlet, R.: Global fusion of relative motions for robust, accurate and scalable structure from motion. In: Proceedings of the IEEE International Conference on Computer Vision, pp. 3248–3255 (2013)
25. Ozyesil, O., Singer, A.: Robust camera location estimation by convex programming. In: Proceedings of the IEEE Conference on Computer Vision and Pattern Recognition, pp. 2674–2683 (2015)
26. Ozyesil, O., Singer, A., Basri, R.: Stable camera motion estimation using convex programming. SIAM J. Imag. Sci. **8**(2), 1220–1262 (2015)
27. Schonberger, J.L., Frahm, J.M.: Structure-from-motion revisited. In: Proceedings of the IEEE conference on computer vision and pattern recognition, pp. 4104–4113 (2016)
28. Shi, Y., Lerman, G.: Message passing least squares framework and its application to rotation synchronization. In: International Conference on Machine Learning, pp. 8796–8806. PMLR (2020)
29. Sidhartha, C., Govindu, V.M.: It is all in the weights: robust rotation averaging revisited. In: 2021 International Conference on 3D Vision (3DV), pp. 1134–1143. IEEE (2021)
30. Snavely, N., Seitz, S.M., Szeliski, R.: Photo tourism: exploring photo collections in 3D. In: ACM SIGGRAPH 2006 papers, pp. 835–846 (2006)
31. Sweeney, C., Hollerer, T., Turk, M.: Theia: a fast and scalable structure-from-motion library. In: Proceedings of the 23rd ACM International Conference on Multimedia, pp. 693–696 (2015)
32. Triggs, B., McLauchlan, P.F., Hartley, R.I., Fitzgibbon, A.W.: Bundle adjustment — a modern synthesis. In: Triggs, B., Zisserman, A., Szeliski, R. (eds.) IWVA 1999. LNCS, vol. 1883, pp. 298–372. Springer, Heidelberg (2000). https://doi.org/10.1007/3-540-44480-7_21
33. Tron, R., Vidal, R.: Distributed image-based 3-D localization of camera sensor networks. In: Proceedings of the 48h IEEE Conference on Decision and Control (CDC) held jointly with 2009 28th Chinese Control Conference, pp. 901–908. IEEE (2009)
34. Wilson, K., Snavely, N.: Robust global translations with 1DSfM. In: Fleet, D., Pajdla, T., Schiele, B., Tuytelaars, T. (eds.) ECCV 2014. LNCS, vol. 8691, pp. 61–75. Springer, Cham (2014). https://doi.org/10.1007/978-3-319-10578-9_5
35. Wu, C., et al.: VisualSFM: a visual structure from motion system (2011)
36. Zhuang, B., Cheong, L.F., Lee, G.H.: Baseline desensitizing in translation averaging. In: Proceedings of the IEEE Conference on Computer Vision and Pattern Recognition, pp. 4539–4547 (2018)

Neural Strands: Learning Hair Geometry and Appearance from Multi-view Images

Radu Alexandru Rosu[1], Shunsuke Saito[3], Ziyan Wang[2,3], Chenglei Wu[3], Sven Behnke[1], and Giljoo Nam[3](✉)

[1] University of Bonn, Bonn, Germany
[2] Carnegie Mellon University, Pittsburgh, USA
[3] Reality Labs Research, Pittsburgh, USA
giljoonam@fb.com

https://radualexandru.github.io/neural_strands/

Abstract. We present Neural Strands, a novel learning framework for modeling accurate hair geometry and appearance from multi-view image inputs. The learned hair model can be rendered in real-time from any viewpoint with high-fidelity view-dependent effects. Our model achieves intuitive shape and style control unlike volumetric counterparts. To enable these properties, we propose a novel hair representation based on a neural scalp texture that encodes the geometry and appearance of individual strands at each texel location. Furthermore, we introduce a novel neural rendering framework based on rasterization of the learned hair strands. Our neural rendering is strand-accurate and anti-aliased, making the rendering view-consistent and photorealistic. Combining appearance with a multi-view geometric prior, we enable, for the first time, the joint learning of appearance and explicit hair geometry from a multi-view setup. We demonstrate the efficacy of our approach in terms of fidelity and efficiency for various hairstyles.

1 Introduction

Photorealistic rendering of digital humans plays an important role in many AR/VR applications such as virtual telepresence. In recent years, data-driven approaches have shown compelling results on geometry and appearance modeling of digital humans, especially for face [19,21,41,43] and body [2,36,46]. Hair, on the other hand, still remains a challenge due to the sheer number of thin hair strands, their complex geometric structures, and non-trivial light transport effects such as subsurface scattering and specular reflections at microscale.

R. A. Rosu—Work done during an internship at Reality Labs Research, Pittsburgh, PA, USA.

Supplementary Information The online version contains supplementary material available at https://doi.org/10.1007/978-3-031-19827-4_5.

S. Avidan et al. (Eds.): ECCV 2022, LNCS 13693, pp. 73–89, 2022.
https://doi.org/10.1007/978-3-031-19827-4_5

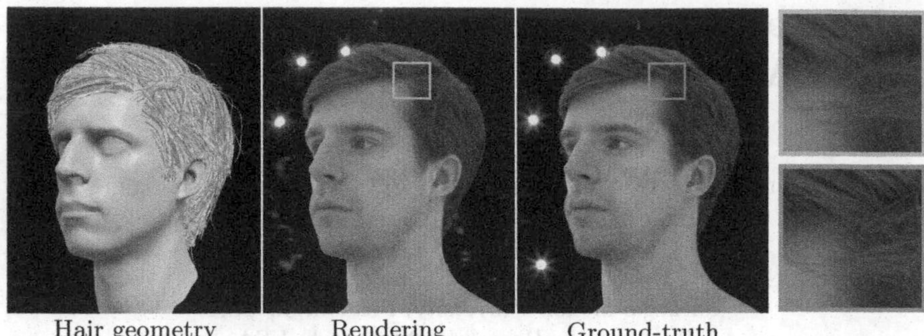

Fig. 1. Given multi-view images we recover both explicit geometry (left) and photo-realistic appearance of hair that generalizes to novel views (middle).

To enable strand-accurate hair reconstruction, a recent work [28] leveraged explicit line assumption in multi-view stereo reconstruction. However, the reconstruction does not provide complete hair strands from the root on the scalp due to heavy self-occlusions. To date, connecting line segments from the scalp to the tip of hair for a variety of hairstyles remains difficult without strong data prior.

Appearance modeling of hair is also an active research field [4,17]. Physics-based rendering approaches typically require extensive light-transport computation to represent complex appearance of 3D hair strands, hence are too slow for real-time applications. Recently, data-driven approaches [6,45] enable photorealistic rendering from geometric proxies such as orientation fields using neural rendering techniques. However, due to sub-optimal geometric quality and feature representations, these image-space neural rendering methods typically suffer from view-inconsistency and lack of fidelity. Volumetric rendering techniques [23,27], on the other hand, achieve view-consistent novel-view rendering, but geometry-driven manipulation is not possible.

In this work, we present Neural Strands, a novel learning framework for jointly modeling hair geometry and appearance, which can be readily used for real-time rendering of photorealistic hair from an arbitrary viewpoint. Our idea is to build a strong data prior using a strand-based generative model learned from synthetic data. This allows us to register complete hair strands from the partial hair reconstruction obtained by [28]. To parameterize the appearance and geometry of complete hairstyles from registration, we further present a novel hair representation called neural scalp textures, where each texel on a UV texture stores a feature vector describing both the shape and appearance of a single strand at a corresponding scalp position. With the aforementioned strand generator, the neural scalp texture is decoded into dense 3D strands, which are then rendered into RGB images by a neural renderer.

Our strand generator is a multilayer perceptron network that takes as input a strand shape feature vector and outputs the 3D shape of the strand. Inspired by neural ordinary differential equations [10], we design our strand generator to yield the first-order derivatives of a strand geometry, i.e., directional vectors

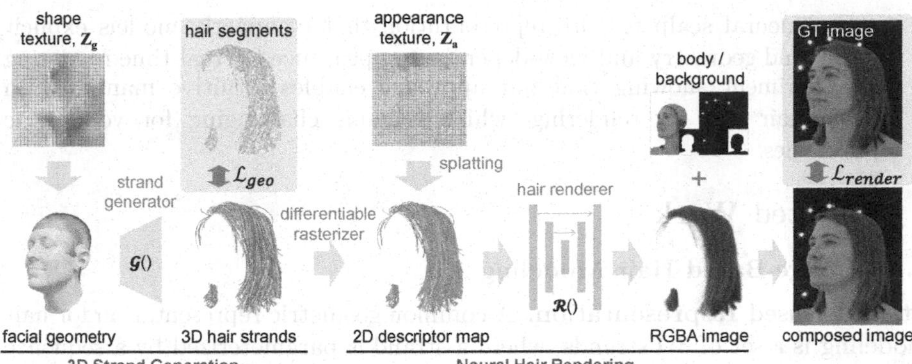

Fig. 2. System overview. A neural scalp texture describing the strand shapes is embeded onto the scalp. A strand generator decodes the shape descriptors into explicit strands. The 3D strands are then rasterized to the screen space. Finally, a hair renderer decodes the 2D descriptors into an RGBA image of the hair which is composited with the body and background. We train our system end-to-end with both a geometrical loss towards sparse line segments and a rendering loss towards the ground-truth images (Color figure online).

with magnitudes. A complete 3D strand shape can be obtained by integrating the derivatives. This formulation allows for generation of smooth strands and also enables a trade-off between compute and accuracy by changing the integration step size. To learn a generic strand generator, we pre-train the network on a wide variety of strand data, resulting in a generic strand prior for robust strand fitting to the noisy real-world scan data.

In order to render photo-realistic hair images using the generated strands, we propose a neural hair renderer. The renderer comprises two parts: a differentiable rasterizer and an image synthesizer. The rasterizer splats the appearance feature vectors onto 2D images while being differentiable w.r.t. the 3D positions of strands and the splatted features. The image synthesizer is a UNet architecture that takes as input the rasterized feature map and yields the final rendered images. We train all the components in an end-to-end manner with direct image supervision. With an explicit strand representation, our method can directly edit or control the hair for rendering, e.g. for virtual haircut or hair blowing, which differentiates our approach from the recent work on free-viewpoint volumetric rendering [22,23,27,31].

In summary, our main contributions are:

- the first joint learning framework for high-quality strand geometry and appearance from multi-view images, which can be readily used for photo-realistic real-time rendering of human hair,
- a highly expressive strand generative model, which enables strand-level hair registration from partial scan data,

- a novel neural scalp texture representation that compactly models explicit hair strand geometry and view-dependent appearance for real-time rendering
- an experiment showing that our approach enables intuitive manipulation of 3D hair and its rendering, which remains challenging for volumetric approaches.

2 Related Work

2.1 Image-Based Hair Modeling

Strand-Based Representation. A common geometric representation for hair modeling is a set of 3D strands, where a strand is parameterized by a sequence of connected 3D points. To obtain 3D hair strands, typically multi-view hair capture methods first reconstruct a low-resolution base geometry using various image-based 3D modeling techniques, and run an additional strand-fitting process to obtain dense 3D hair strands that are connected to the scalp [3,11–14,24,25]. However, these methods often lack fine details like flyaway hairs because of the low-resolution base geometry. To overcome this limitation, Nam *et al.* [28] proposed a line-based multi-view stereo (LMVS) that is tailored to hair capture tasks and directly obtains 3D line segments from images. Sun *et al.* [38] further improved LMVS and estimated the reflectance parameters of hair for photo-realistic rendering. However, the reconstructed strands from both methods [28,38] only cover the outer surface of hair and they are not connected to the scalp. Another line of research focuses on single-view hair modeling [5,7–9,47,49,50,52]. While these works show promising results from less constrained capture setups, due to the ill-posed nature, these methods do not provide metrically accurate 3D geometry of hair strands. Moreover, they are not directly applicable to novel-view synthesis in a photorealistic manner. In contrast, our approach jointly learns metrically accurate geometry and appearance from multi-view images, enabling rendering from any viewpoint.

Volumetric Representation. Volumetric representation is also used for hair modeling. Saito *et al.* [35] propose to regress 3D hair from a single image using volumetric orientation fields as an intermediate representation, which can be easily handled by 3D convolutions. However, due to the low grid resolution of voxels, fine details such as flyaway hairs are not well represented. Combined with differentiable volumetric rendering, Neural Volumes [22] and NeRF [27] enable highly expressive geometry and appearance modeling of objects from multi-view images. Mixture of volumetric primitives (MVP) addresses the performance bottleneck of volumetric representations by representing scenes as a collection of small voxels [23]. While these methods enable realistic rendering of 3D hairs, lack of geometric hair control hinders us from driving and intuitive manipulation of photorealistic hair models.

2.2 Neural Hair Rendering

Neural rendering [40] has recently gained great attention for rendering photorealistic images. Given 2D segmentation masks [39] and 2D orientation maps [15,

30, 33, 39], generative adversarial networks (GANs) are trained to create RGB hair images that match the input data. By rendering these 2D features from 3D hair strands, these approaches allow us to photorealistically render hair images as well [6, 45]. However, we observe that rendering quality of these image-based approaches is highly dependent on the conditioned 2D features, and often leads to view-inconsistent results with limited fidelity. In this work, we show that highly accurate strands with a per-strand appearance code improve view consistency and fidelity of neural hair rendering.

3 Overview

Figure 2 shows the overview of our learning framework. Neural Strands consists of three parts: neural scalp textures, strand generator, and neural hair renderer. A neural scalp texture is a 2D UV-texture that stores either the shape (shape texture, $\mathbf{Z}_g$) or the appearance (appearance texture, $\mathbf{Z}_a$) of strands. The strand generator, $\mathcal{G}()$, is a generative neural network that transforms a strand feature vector into a 3D strand geometry. Finally, the hair renderer, $\mathcal{R}()$, is a UNet-architecture that renders hair images from rasterized appearance feature maps.

The design of Neural Strands is motivated by several hair-specific attributes. First, in terms of geometry, each strand has its own attachment point in 3D scalp position. By using an explicit scalp UV-map, we can easily control or edit the geometric features of strands based on the scalp location. The shape texture $\mathbf{Z}_g$ exploits this property and enables several applications such as virtual haircut and hairstyle manipulation. Second, while hair shows extremely complex appearance in 2D images, individual strands have a smooth color variation along their strand directions. The complex hair appearance is determined by how the strands are shaped in 3D and how they are projected to each viewpoint. Therefore, we only store the low-frequency appearance information of each strand using our appearance texture $\mathbf{Z}_a$. The high-frequency appearance in 2D images can be effectively represented by our rasterizer and hair renderer. This separation of per-strand appearance modeling and rendering is one of the keys that enable our high-fidelity results. In the following sections, we explain the details of each component and how they form the final hair images (Sect. 4) and then present the training procedure of our learning framework (Sect. 5).

4 Neural Strands

4.1 Neural Scalp Textures

Neural scalp textures are our base hair representation for explicit 3D geometry and appearance of strands. Each texel in the shape texture $\mathbf{Z}_g$ stores a feature vector $\mathbf{z}_g^i \in \mathbb{R}^{D_g}$ that conveys the shape information of a single hair strand. Since the strand roots are created in 3D to ensure uniform coverage, the strands sample their corresponding $\mathbf{z}_g$ from the scalp texture using bilinear interpolation. Similarly, the appearance texture is denoted as $\mathbf{Z}_a$ and $\mathbf{z}_a^i \in \mathbb{R}^{D_a}$ stores the appearance information of the strand. For the remaining of this paper, we assume that the scalp UV-mapping is known in advance. We set the texture resolutions to 256^2 for $\mathbf{Z}_g$, 512^2 for $\mathbf{Z}_a$, and $D_g = 64$, $D_a = 16$.

4.2 Strand Generator

A single hair strand $\mathbf{S}$ is a sequence of 3D points: $\mathbf{S} = \{\mathbf{p}_k\}_{k=0}^{L}$, where L is set to 100. The full hair shape is a collection of strands $\{\mathbf{S}^j\}$, where j indexes over the strands. Our strand generator $\mathcal{G}()$ is a neural network that transforms a shape feature vector $\mathbf{z}_g$ into a full 3D strand geometry $\mathbf{S}$, i.e., $\mathcal{G}() : \mathbb{R}^{D_g} \to \mathbb{R}^{3\times L}$.

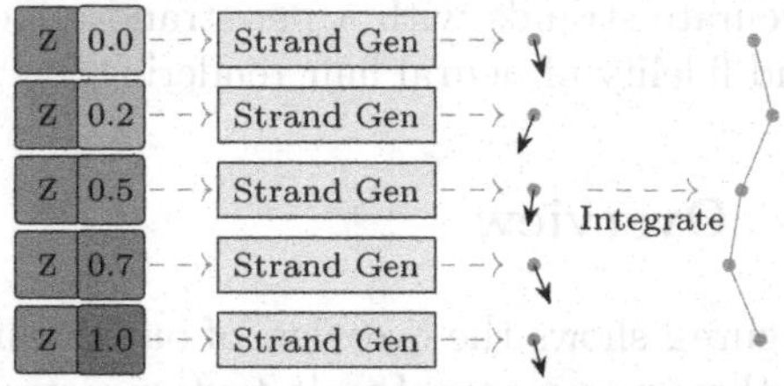

Fig. 3. The strand generator takes as input the shape descriptor z and a parameter $t \in [0, 1]$ indicating the position between root and tip. It outputs a direction vector for each section of the strand. The directions are integrated from root to tip in order to recover the explicit 3D positions of the strand nodes.

Network Architecture. Inspired by NeuralODEs [10], we model the strand generation as an integration of hair gradients along each strand. We thus design the network to output finite differences along hair growing directions, i.e., $\mathbf{d}_k = \mathbf{p}_k - \mathbf{p}_{k+1}$, instead of 3D positions $\mathbf{p}_k$.

In order to model the high-frequency geometric details, we implement our strand generator using the modulated SIREN [26]. Our strand generator has two multilayer perceptron (MLP) networks: a modulator and a synthesizer. The modulator takes as input the strand shape feature $\mathbf{z}_g$ and outputs modulation vectors that modify the amplitude, frequency, and phase shift of the sinusoidal activation functions of the synthesizer network. The SIREN [37]-based synthesizer takes as input a parameter $t \in [0, 1]$ that indicates the relative position along the strand from root (0) to tip (1). The output of the synthesizer is a 3D directional vector $\mathbf{d}_t$ with magnitude. The final positions of the strand nodes are obtained by the forward Euler method, i.e., $\mathbf{p}_k = \sum_{i=0}^{k} \mathbf{d}_i$. See Fig. 3 for illustration.

Discussion. The benefit of working in the gradient domain is that each node of the strand has only local effect. When working directly with the positions, rotating the hair along the root node modifies the positions of all the subsequent nodes of the strand since they can all be considered as a kinematic chain. However, in the gradient domain, modifying the root node direction $\mathbf{d}_0$ does not necessarily modify the rest of the directions. This independence between nodes makes the learning easier, as the network does not need to learn the kinematic dependency between hair nodes. In addition, long straight hair can be easily represented by a network which outputs mostly constant directions.

4.3 Neural Hair Renderer

Since we have an explicit hair geometry $\{\mathbf{S}^j\}$ from our strand generator, we now render the hair appearance using a differentiable rasterization-based neural renderer. We take inspiration from the Neural Point-Based Graphics (NPBG) [1] and the Deferred Neural Rendering (DNR) [42] which use a point/mesh rasterizer. Both NPBG and DNR use a geometry proxy (points or mesh) in order to carry a neural descriptor either with a texture map or at a per-point level. The neural descriptors are rasterized to a screen space and a UNet regresses the final color image.

In our case, the geometry proxy is a 3D line segment, and the neural descriptors are given by the appearance texture $\mathbf{Z}_a$. However, hair has various properties that need to be properly addressed. First, hair is not opaque and can show complex scattering effects. Second, the thin geometry also tends to create aliasing artifacts when rendered. We effectively solve these issues by using alpha blending and let the UNet renderer directly output the alpha maps for natural strand color blending.

Neural Hair Descriptor. The appearance texture $\mathbf{Z}_a$ stores the vectors $\mathbf{z}_a^i$ for each texel position i. For each strand $\mathbf{S}^j$, we bi-linearly interpolate the neighbouring four texels at the root to obtain the corresponding $\mathbf{z}_a$ for the strand. The 3D points $\{\mathbf{p}_k\}_{k=0}^{L}$ belonging to the same strand $\mathbf{S}^j$ share the same per-strand feature vector $\mathbf{z}_a$. A per-point neural descriptor is then defined as a concatenated vector of the strand feature, the point direction $\mathbf{d}$, and the t parameter:

$$\mathbf{g} = [\mathbf{z}_a, \mathbf{d}, t], \quad \mathbf{g} \in \mathbb{R}^{D_a+3+1}. \tag{1}$$

The per-point descriptors are rasterized to each viewpoint via a differentiable line rasterizer.

Differentiable Rasterization. We project the neural descriptors to screen-space by rasterizing the strand lines. However, as naïve rasterization methods are non-differentiable, we replace the hard rasterizer with soft-rasterization [20,34, 48]. We first hard-rasterize unique strand indices onto the screen using OpenGL which allow to recover for each pixel a 3D point that lies on a non-occluded strand line. The 3D point is associated with a descriptor $\tilde{\mathbf{g}}$ by linearly interpolating the descriptors from the two points that define the strand segment. At the end of this step, we obtain a point cloud of the visible points of the hair together with their neural descriptors. As a second step, we project the cloud to screen and the descriptors are bi-linearly splatted to the neighboring pixels. In the case where multiple 3D points contribute to the same pixel, the splatted descriptor at the pixel is defined as the weighted average of the contributing 3D points:

$$\mathbf{h}_u = \frac{\sum w \cdot \tilde{\mathbf{g}}}{\sum w}, \tag{2}$$

where the subscript u is the pixel index in the rasterized image space, $\mathbf{h}_u$ is the rasterized and averaged descriptor at the pixel, and w is the contribution weight of each descriptor $\tilde{\mathbf{g}}$. This soft-rasterization for hair is crucial to ensure the rendering loss to be back-propagated to the neural scalp textures $\mathbf{Z}_g$ and

$\mathbf{Z}_a$ as in Fig. 2. In order to deal with possible holes in the hair, we also splat at multiple resolutions and concatenate each resolution with the corresponding layer in the UNet, similar to the previous works [1,34].

Image Generation. The multi-resolution descriptor maps are concatenated with per-pixel viewing directions in order to model view-dependent effects and are given as input to the UNet which predicts an RGB and an opacity map for the hair. Effectively, the input to the UNet is a descriptor map of $(D_a + 3 + 1 + 3)$ channels concatenated to each downsampling stage of the network, and the output is a four-channel image of RGB and alpha.

We find that the intermediate activation maps of the UNet were aliased by the down-sampling with strided convolutions. Therefore, we replace the down-sampling and up-sampling layers of the UNet with the anti-aliased versions used in [16] and the activation function with their filtered leaky ReLU. We find this change effectively solves the aliasing issue and removes temporal flickering artifacts when rendering novel-view images.

Image Composition. In order to blend the hair with the background and body parts, we also learn a low-resolution texture for a body mesh and a background mesh represented as a sphere around the subject. The background, body, and hair are alpha-blended together in order to recover the full image. The compositing can be viewed in Fig. 2.

5 Training

Training Neural Strands is twofold. First, we pre-train the strand generator $\mathcal{G}()$ using synthetic hair models and freeze the parameters. Then, for each subject, we optimize the feature vectors of neural scalp textures $\mathbf{Z}_g$ and $\mathbf{Z}_a$, as well as the parameters of the UNet renderer $\mathcal{R}()$ using the pre-trained generator $\mathcal{G}()$.

5.1 Strand Generator

VAE Training. The role of our strand generator $\mathcal{G}()$ is to provide a strong prior of realistic hair strand shapes that can be readily used for our image-based hair modeling framework. To this end, we train it in an auto-encoder fashion with synthetic 3D curves. Concretely, we implement it as a variational autoencoder (VAE) [18] in order to obtain a smooth embedding of $\mathbf{z}_g$. The input and output of the VAE is a strand, i.e., $\{\mathbf{p}_k\}_{k=0}^{L}$.

We design a simple encoder network with a 1D CNN. Given the 3D points of a strand, the encoder outputs the parameters $\mathbf{s}_\mu$ and $\mathbf{s}_\sigma$ of the Gaussian distribution over the latent variables. During training, we sample $\mathbf{z}_g$ from this distribution using the reparameterization trick: $\mathbf{z}_g = \mathbf{s}_\mu + \epsilon \cdot \mathbf{s}_\sigma, \epsilon \sim \mathcal{N}(0, 1)$. Given the strand embedding $\mathbf{z}_g$, we decode it back to the original points using the decoder $\mathcal{G}()$ which is implemented as a modulated SIREN.

We use the L2 loss between the predicted and ground-truth 3D points. Since this loss gives little regard to high-frequency detail like curls, we add a loss on the predicted directions. The data term is defined as

$$\mathcal{L}_{data} = \sum_{i=0}^{L} \|\mathbf{p}_i - \tilde{\mathbf{p}}_i\|_2^2 + \lambda_d \left(1 - \mathbf{d}_i \cdot \tilde{\mathbf{d}}_i\right), \tag{3}$$

where $\mathbf{p}$ and $\tilde{\mathbf{p}}$ are the original and reconstructed points, and $\mathbf{d}$ and $\tilde{\mathbf{d}}$ are their directions. λ_d is set to 1×10^{-3}. We also add the Kullback–Leibler divergence term $\mathcal{L}_{KL}$ [18]. We train the VAE with the total loss:

$$\mathcal{L}_{VAE} = \mathcal{L}_{data} + \lambda_{KL}\mathcal{L}_{KL}\left(\mathcal{N}(\mathbf{s}_\mu, \mathbf{s}_\sigma) \,||\, \mathcal{N}(\mathbf{0}, \mathbf{I})\right), \tag{4}$$

where λ_{KL} is set to 1×10^{-3}. Once the VAE is trained, we discard the encoder network and only use the decoder as our pre-trained strand generator $\mathcal{G}()$.

Training Data. The dataset to train the strand generator is a set of synthetic 3D curves and each curve represents a hair strand as a sequence of 100 points. To remove the variance between the strands, we represent each one in a local coordinate system defined by the root position and the tangent-bitangent-normal (TBN) at the scalp. We also augment each strand by randomly stretching each dimension, mirroring along the tangent and bitangent vectors and rotating along the normal.

5.2 End-to-End Optimization

Data Preparation. Given multi-view images as input, we first perform multi-view stereo to obtain 3D geometry of the subject. We then fit the reconstructed face geometry to the FLAME face template [19]. This fitting process gives us a known UV-mapping for the scalp region and also effectively removes the hair geometry in the reconstructed mesh. We also perform the line-based multi-view stereo (LVMS) [28] to get partial hair strand reconstruction. Note that the partial strands only include the strands in the outer surface of hair and are not connected to the scalp. We additionally perform a diffusion algorithm based on user strokes similar to [8] in order to resolve the directional ambiguity of the line segments and obtain a consistent direction of growth.

End-to-End Training. The input to our end-to-end optimization framework are 1) multi-view images, 2) the fitted facial geometry, and 3) the partial hair strands. Given the pre-trained strand generator $\mathcal{G}$ and input data, we jointly optimize for the neural scalp textures $\mathbf{Z}_g$ and $\mathbf{Z}_a$ as well as the parameters of the UNet renderer $\mathcal{R}()$ for each captured subject.

Geometric Loss. The geometric loss encourages our strand generator $\mathcal{G}()$ to output hair strands that align with the partial hair strands from the LMVS [28]. The loss is defined as the bi-directional Chamfer of the distance and directions between the two point clouds:

$$\mathcal{L}_{geo} = \sum_{\mathbf{x} \in X} \left(\|\mathbf{x} - \mathbf{y}_\mathbf{x}\|_2 + (1 - \mathbf{d}_x \cdot \mathbf{d}_y)\right) + \sum_{\mathbf{y} \in Y} \left(\|\mathbf{x}_\mathbf{y} - \mathbf{y}\|_2 + (1 - \mathbf{d}_x \cdot \mathbf{d}_y)\right), \tag{5}$$

where X is a set of 3D points in the generated strands, Y is a set of points in the LMVS-reconstructed hair segments, and $\mathbf{y_x}$ represents the point $\mathbf{y}$ which is the closest one in Y to the point $\mathbf{x}$. Effectively, the Chamfer distance brings the closest points closer together and also aligns their directions.

While the geometric loss alone gives us plausible hair geometry, it can lead to missing or sub-optimal fitting results as the LMVS-reconstructed hair segments do not cover the entire region of the hair. Because the strands that are not reconstructed from the LMVS could still be visible from the images, there is an opportunity to supervise the strand generation with the rendering loss. We therefore also use the rendering loss to optimize for the shape texture $\mathbf{Z}_g$. This is done by back-propagating the rendering loss not only to the appearance texture $\mathbf{Z}_a$, but also to the shape texture $\mathbf{Z}_g$.

Rendering Loss. The neural renderer $\mathcal{R}()$ together with the appearance texture $\mathbf{Z}_a$ is trained using a combination of L2 and LPIPS [51] loss. The rendering loss $\mathcal{L}_{render}$ is thus defined as:

$$\mathcal{L}_{render} = \sum_{n=1}^{N} \left(\left\| I_n - \tilde{I}_n \right\|_2^2 + \lambda_L \mathcal{L}_{LPIPS}(I_n, \tilde{I}_n) \right), \tag{6}$$

where I_n and $\tilde{I}_n$ are the rendered and captured images from n-th view, and N is the number of multi-view images. We set $\lambda_L = 0.1$.

Alpha Loss. In order to also offer supervision to the predicted alpha, we rasterize the LMVS line-segments to the image. By itself, this hard LMVS mask would be inadequate to be used as alpha supervision since it enforces a strictly opaque hair. To remedy this, we dilate the mask and define a region without hair that we can claim should be empty and therefore should have an alpha of 0. After the dilation, we erode to define an interior region that we can be certain that it should be opaque. These two regions are used for supervision, while the border regions containing stray hairs are left unsupervised as we cannot reliably supervise their soft opacity. The alpha map loss $\mathcal{L}_{alpha}$ is defined as:

$$\mathcal{L}_{alpha} = \sum_{n=1}^{N} \left(\left\| A_n - \tilde{A}_n \right\|_2^2 \cdot M_n \right), \tag{7}$$

where A_n and $\tilde{A}_n$ are the reference alpha map from LMVS and the generated alpha map from n-th view, and M_n is their mask of union of the interior and exterior regions. See Fig. 4 for illustration.

Total Loss. The total loss for our end-to-end optimization is:

$$\mathcal{L}_{total} = \lambda_1 \mathcal{L}_{geo} + \lambda_2 \mathcal{L}_{render} + \lambda_3 \mathcal{L}_{alpha}, \tag{8}$$

where λ_1, λ_2, and λ_3 are set to 1, 1 $\times 10^{-3}$, and 1 $\times 10^{-3}$, respectively.

Optimization Details. Fitting the geometry of the strands based on the Chamfer loss to the line-segments is a highly ill-posed problem. To solve this, we propose two solutions: a coarse-to-fine and a root-to-tip optimization of the shape

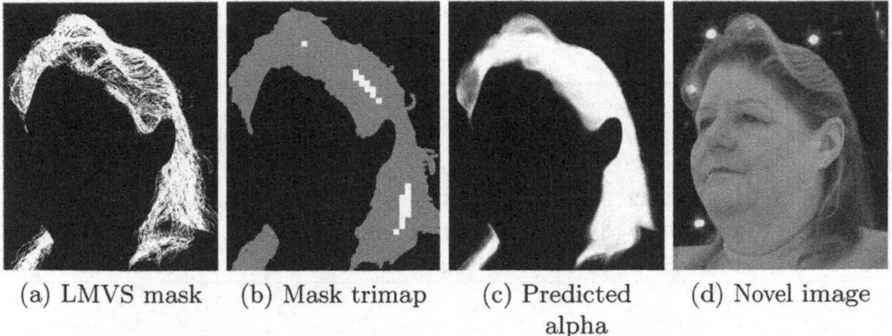

(a) LMVS mask (b) Mask trimap (c) Predicted alpha (d) Novel image

Fig. 4. Alpha prediction and blending. (a) Mask from LMVS; (b) Trimap obtained from (a); (c) Predicted alpha map; (d) Composed image using (c).

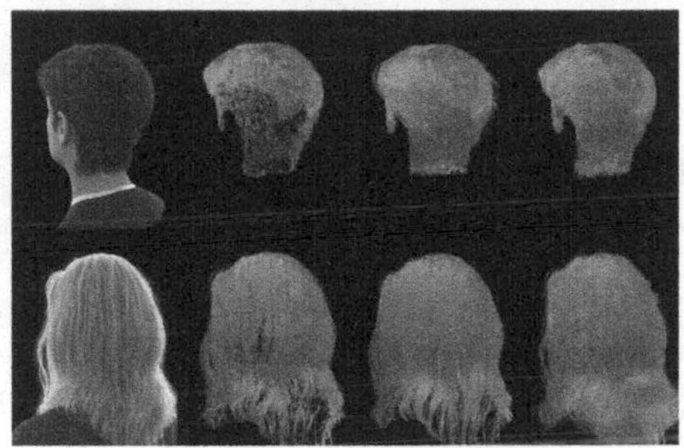

Fig. 5. Synthetic data and geometry reconstructions. From left: GT image, LMVS geometry, our geometry, GT geometry. Note that the strands from LMVS are segmented and not connected to the scalp

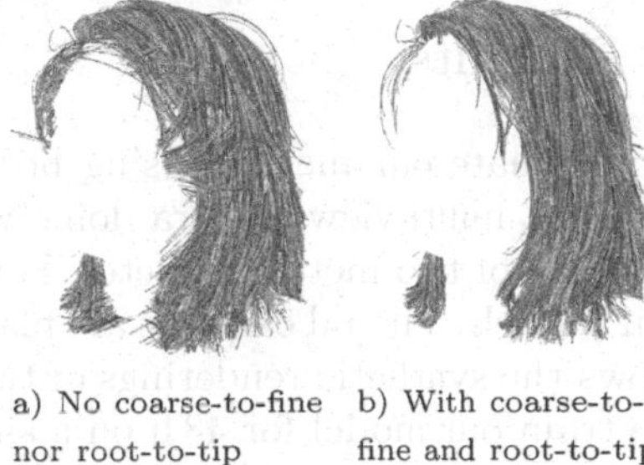

a) No coarse-to-fine nor root-to-tip b) With coarse-to-fine and root-to-tip

Fig. 6. Our coarse-to-fine and root-to-tip optimization of the shape texture helps the network converge to the correct shape

texture $\mathbf{Z}_g$. Coarse-to-fine optimization of the scalp imposes a smoothness prior on the features. We implement this by sampling from the texture map in the forward pass and blurring the gradient of the loss w.r.t to the texture $\frac{\nabla \mathcal{L}}{\nabla \mathbf{Z}_g}$ in the backward pass, so that neighboring pixels receive similar gradients. We start by blurring with a large kernel and gradually decrease it until the gradient is propagated only towards the pixels that correspond to the strand root. This optimization scheme is similar to the Laplacian Pyramid from [42]. However, instead of optimizing various textures at multiple resolutions, we optimize only one, which makes it faster for training and inference.

Root-to-tip optimization is performed by starting the training with only the roots of the strands and masking out the gradient for the rest of the strand vertices. We linearly anneal the rest of the nodes gradually during optimization. In addition, for stable training, we set λ_2 and λ_3 to 0 for the first 1,000 iterations

Table 1. Comparison between the previous work LMVS [28] and our method using synthetic dataset.

	Short hair						Long hair					
τ_p/τ_d	1 mm/10°		2 mm/20°		3 mm/30°		1 mm/10°		2 mm/20°		3 mm/30°	
Method	LMVS	Ours	LMVS	Ours	LMVS	Ours	LMVS	Ours	LMVS	Ours	LMVS	Ours
Precision	**56.91**	52.79	**93.42**	92.94	**98.85**	98.18	26.25	**32.59**	**75.13**	71.40	**93.51**	71.40
Recall	12.11	**13.78**	30.29	**48.38**	46.62	**71.51**	**16.54**	14.62	39.12	**42.06**	54.01	**62.91**
F-score	19.98	**21.85**	45.75	**63.64**	63.36	**82.75**	**20.30**	20.19	51.45	**52.94**	**68.47**	66.89

since at the beginning, the strands are far away from the correct hair region in image-space. In Fig. 6 we show the impact of our coarse-to-fine and root-to-tip optimization scheme.

6 Results

We evaluate our method using both real and synthetic data. For real images, we use a multi-view camera dome with ∼140 cameras uniformly distributed on a sphere of two meter diameter. For synthetic images, we use artist-created 3D hair models. Virtual cameras are placed to mimic the real capture setup. Figure 5 shows the synthetic renderings of two 3D models with short and long hairstyles. We train our model for 48 h on a single NVIDIA V100 GPU.

6.1 Evaluation with Synthetic Data

Since it is impossible to obtain the ground truth geometry of hair strands from real captured images, we use synthetic data for the evaluation. In Table 1, we show quantitative comparison on recovered strand geometries over the state-of-the-art hair geometry reconstruction method [28]. We follow the error metric from [28,38] and show the precision, recall, and F-scores of the reconstructed 3D point clouds over their ground truth with various threshold values. It is shown that the previous work [28] tends to have better precision (accuracy), whereas our method has better recall (completeness) and F-score values in general. This shows the effectiveness of our method to reconstruct complete hair strands that are connected to the scalp. We further emphasize that LMVS only recovers disjoint strand segments while our method recovers full strands of hair which enables further applications such as animations. Figure 5 illustrates the limitation of [28] and how Neural Strands overcomes it.

6.2 Evaluation with Real Data

We compare our method with two view-synthesis methods, NeRF [27] and MVP [23], that can model and render hair appearance from captured multi-view images. As shown in Fig. 7, our method is capable of rendering highly detailed hair textures, which is difficult to achieve with the other methods.

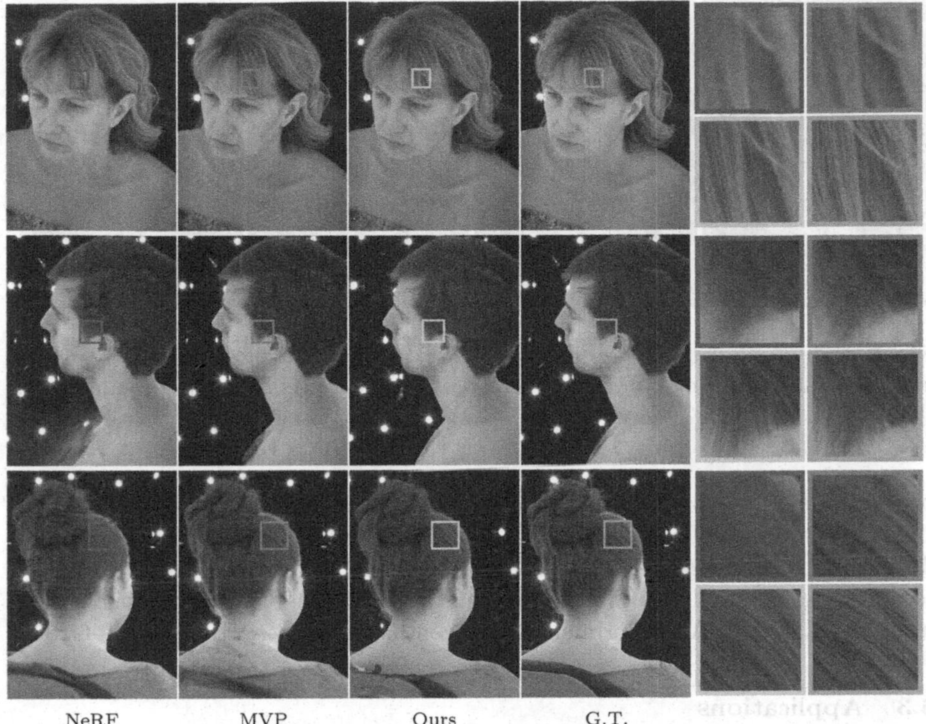

Fig. 7. We compare our method against NeRF [27] and MVP [23]. We render from novel view not seen during training. Our method can achieve higher hair detail and also recovers fine stray hairs unlike the other approaches.

Table 2. We perform better under the perceptual metric (LPIPS), indicating that ours have more realistic looking hairs

	NeRF	MVP	Ours
PSNR (↑)	31.71	**32.82**	31.30
SSIM (↑)	0.9383	**0.9599**	0.9452
LPIPS (↓)	0.1598	0.1226	**0.0811**

Table 3. Our method can render a static hair in real-time (>25 fps) and dynamic strands at interactive rates (>13 fps)

	NeRF	MVP	Ours
decode (↓)	–	**20.40**	34.54
render (↓)	–	81.60	**38.82**
total (ms) (↓)	27,910	102.00	**73.36**

Table 2 shows quantitative comparisons. We compute PSNR, SSIM [44], and LPIPS [51] for the hair region of nine novel-view images that are not used in training. The numbers show the averaged values of six subjects for each method. While our method shows the best LPIPS loss with better visual quality, PSNR and SSIM values are slightly lower than the other methods. This is also reported in previous works [29,32,51] on image quality metric; PSNR and SSIM do not

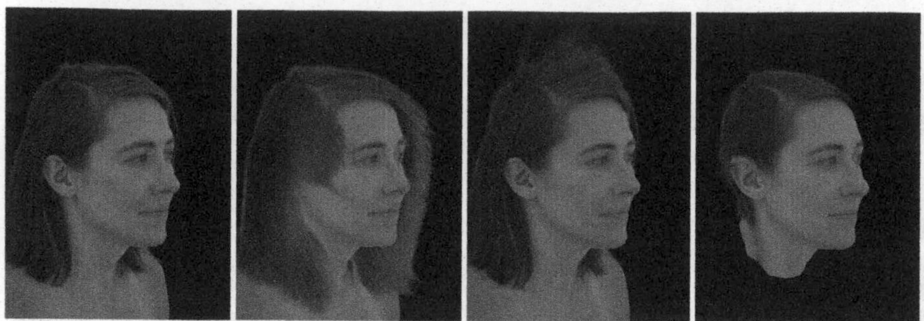

Fig. 8. Hair manipulation. Our explicit strand representation allows to directly manipulate the hair by moving it in various directions (animation) or cutting it to any length (haircut).

properly reflect the perceptual quality of reconstructed images. We also compare the rendering time of each method in Table 3. Note that we only need to run the decode step (strand generation) once, and the generated strands can be rendered to novel viewpoints in less than 40 ms, thus achieving real-time rendering of > 25 frames per second. All experiments were conducted on a NVIDIA V100 GPU.

6.3 Applications

In this section, we describe two demos that show the ability of post-capture manipulation of hair strands, which differentiates our method from other view-synthesis methods. Please see the supplemental video for better visualization.

Virtual Haircut. By having an explicit strand with the shape texture $\mathbf{Z}_g$, we can trim its length and let the neural renderer infer how the hair would look like at the new length. In Fig. 8, we show that the UNet generalizes and produces realistic appearance even for this hair configuration that was never seen during training.

Animation. The explicit hair strands can also be deformed by slightly modifying the direction between adjacent strand nodes to convey a sense of dynamics of hair blowing in the wind. In Fig. 8, we show examples of animating the hair with the appearance inferred for this novel hair configuration.

Interpretable Strand Generator. As the strands are generated from the latent space of a VAE, we can traverse this latent space to generate novel strands. In the supplemental video, we show that we can traverse each dimension of the latent space and discover interpretable controls for curliness, length, etc.

7 Limitations and Future Work

Here we discuss several exciting future research directions to overcome current limitations of our method. First, for complicated hairstyles like the hair-bun in

Fig. 7, it is challenging to infer the exact topology since most of it is occluded. Stronger priors for hairstyles learned from various subjects could help alleviate these issues. Second, although our hair model is fully editable, due to the complicated light transport, the generated appearance may not generalize to large hair movement, since lighting effects, like shadows, may be baked in the learned appearance. We will take it as future work to explore more physics-aware rendering since strand-level geometry is available from our model.

References

1. Aliev, K.-A., Sevastopolsky, A., Kolos, M., Ulyanov, D., Lempitsky, V.: Neural point-based graphics. In: Vedaldi, A., Bischof, H., Brox, T., Frahm, J.-M. (eds.) ECCV 2020. LNCS, vol. 12367, pp. 696–712. Springer, Cham (2020). https://doi.org/10.1007/978-3-030-58542-6_42
2. Bagautdinov, T., et al.: Driving-signal aware full-body avatars. ACM Trans. Graph. (TOG) **40**(4), 1–17 (2021)
3. Beeler, T., et al.: Coupled 3D reconstruction of sparse facial hair and skin. ACM Trans. Graph. (ToG) **31**(4), 117 (2012)
4. Benamira, A., Pattanaik, S.: A combined scattering and diffraction model for elliptical hair rendering. In: Computer Graphics Forum, vol. 40, pp. 163–175. Wiley Online Library (2021)
5. Chai, M., Luo, L., Sunkavalli, K., Carr, N., Hadap, S., Zhou, K.: High-quality hair modeling from a single portrait photo. ACM Trans. Graph. (TOG) **34**(6), 204 (2015)
6. Chai, M., Ren, J., Tulyakov, S.: Neural hair rendering. In: Vedaldi, A., Bischof, H., Brox, T., Frahm, J.-M. (eds.) ECCV 2020. LNCS, vol. 12363, pp. 371–388. Springer, Cham (2020). https://doi.org/10.1007/978-3-030-58523-5_22
7. Chai, M., Shao, T., Wu, H., Weng, Y., Zhou, K.: AutoHair: fully automatic hair modeling from a single image. ACM Trans. Graph. **35**(4), 1–12 (2016)
8. Chai, M., Wang, L., Weng, Y., Jin, X., Zhou, K.: Dynamic hair manipulation in images and videos. ACM Trans. Graph. (TOG) **32**(4), 75 (2013)
9. Chai, M., Wang, L., Weng, Y., Yu, Y., Guo, B., Zhou, K.: Single-view hair modeling for portrait manipulation. ACM Trans. Graph. (TOG) **31**(4), 116 (2012)
10. Chen, R.T., Rubanova, Y., Bettencourt, J., Duvenaud, D.: Neural ordinary differential equations. arXiv preprint arXiv:1806.07366 (2018)
11. Herrera, T.L., Zinke, A., Weber, A.: Lighting hair from the inside: a thermal approach to hair reconstruction. ACM Trans. Graph. (TOG) **31**(6), 146 (2012)
12. Hu, L., Bradley, D., Li, H., Beeler, T.: Simulation-ready hair capture. In: Computer Graphics Forum, vol. 36, pp. 281–294. Wiley Online Library (2017)
13. Hu, L., Ma, C., Luo, L., Li, H.: Robust hair capture using simulated examples. ACM Trans. Graph. (TOG) **33**(4), 126 (2014)
14. Hu, L., Ma, C., Luo, L., Wei, L.Y., Li, H.: Capturing braided hairstyles. ACM Trans. Graph. (TOG) **33**(6), 225 (2014)
15. Jo, Y., Park, J.: SC-FEGAN: face editing generative adversarial network with user's sketch and color. In: Proceedings of the IEEE/CVF International Conference on Computer Vision, pp. 1745–1753 (2019)
16. Karras, T., et al.: Alias-free generative adversarial networks. arXiv preprint arXiv:2106.12423 (2021)

17. Khungurn, P., Marschner, S.: Azimuthal scattering from elliptical hair fibers. ACM Trans. Graph. (TOG) **36**(2), 1–23 (2017)
18. Kingma, D.P., Welling, M.: Auto-encoding variational bayes. arXiv preprint arXiv:1312.6114 (2013)
19. Li, T., Bolkart, T., Black, M.J., Li, H., Romero, J.: Learning a model of facial shape and expression from 4D scans. ACM Trans. Graph. **36**(6), 1–194 (2017)
20. Liu, S., Li, T., Chen, W., Li, H.: Soft rasterizer: a differentiable renderer for image-based 3D reasoning. In: Proceedings of the IEEE/CVF International Conference on Computer Vision, pp. 7708–7717 (2019)
21. Lombardi, S., Saragih, J., Simon, T., Sheikh, Y.: Deep appearance models for face rendering. ACM Trans. Graph. **37**(4), 1–13 (2018). https://doi.org/10.1145/3197517.3201401
22. Lombardi, S., Simon, T., Saragih, J., Schwartz, G., Lehrmann, A., Sheikh, Y.: Neural volumes: Learning dynamic renderable volumes from images. ACM Trans. Graph. **38**(4), 1–14 (2019). https://doi.org/10.1145/3306346.3323020
23. Lombardi, S., Simon, T., Schwartz, G., Zollhoefer, M., Sheikh, Y., Saragih, J.: Mixture of volumetric primitives for efficient neural rendering. ACM Trans. Graph. **40**(4), 1–13 (2021). https://doi.org/10.1145/3450626.3459863
24. Luo, L., Li, H., Paris, S., Weise, T., Pauly, M., Rusinkiewicz, S.: Multi-view hair capture using orientation fields. In: IEEE Conference on Computer Vision and Pattern Recognition (CVPR), pp. 1490–1497 (2012). IEEE (2012)
25. Luo, L., Li, H., Rusinkiewicz, S.: Structure-aware hair capture. ACM Trans. Graph. (TOG) **32**(4), 76 (2013)
26. Mehta, I., Gharbi, M., Barnes, C., Shechtman, E., Ramamoorthi, R., Chandraker, M.: Modulated periodic activations for generalizable local functional representations. arXiv preprint arXiv:2104.03960 (2021)
27. Mildenhall, B., Srinivasan, P.P., Tancik, M., Barron, J.T., Ramamoorthi, R., Ng, R.: NeRF: representing scenes as neural radiance fields for view synthesis. In: Vedaldi, A., Bischof, H., Brox, T., Frahm, J.-M. (eds.) ECCV 2020. LNCS, vol. 12346, pp. 405–421. Springer, Cham (2020). https://doi.org/10.1007/978-3-030-58452-8_24
28. Nam, G., Wu, C., Kim, M.H., Sheikh, Y.: Strand-accurate multi-view hair capture. In: Proceedings of the IEEE/CVF Conference on Computer Vision and Pattern Recognition, pp. 155–164 (2019)
29. Nilsson, J., Akenine-Möller, T.: Understanding SSIM. CoRR abs/2006.13846 (2020)
30. Olszewski, K., et al.: Intuitive, interactive beard and hair synthesis with generative models. In: Proceedings of the IEEE/CVF Conference on Computer Vision and Pattern Recognition, pp. 7446–7456 (2020)
31. Park, K., et al.: Nerfies: deformable neural radiance fields. In: Proceedings of the IEEE/CVF International Conference on Computer Vision, pp. 5865–5874 (2021)
32. Patel, Y., Appalaraju, S., Manmatha, R.: Deep perceptual compression. CoRR abs/1907.08310 (2019). arxiv.org/abs/1907.08310
33. Qiu, H., Wang, C., Zhu, H., Zhu, X., Gu, J., Han, X.: Two-phase hair image synthesis by self-enhancing generative model. In: Computer Graphics Forum, vol. 38, pp. 403–412. Wiley Online Library (2019)
34. Rückert, D., Franke, L., Stamminger, M.: ADOP: approximate differentiable one-pixel point rendering. arXiv preprint arXiv:2110.06635 (2021)
35. Saito, S., Hu, L., Ma, C., Ibayashi, H., Luo, L., Li, H.: 3D hair synthesis using volumetric variational autoencoders. ACM Trans. Graph. (TOG) **37**(6), 1–12 (2018)

36. Saito, S., Huang, Z., Natsume, R., Morishima, S., Kanazawa, A., Li, H.: PIFu: pixel-aligned implicit function for high-resolution clothed human digitization. In: Proceedings of the IEEE/CVF International Conference on Computer Vision, pp. 2304–2314 (2019)
37. Sitzmann, V., Martel, J., Bergman, A., Lindell, D., Wetzstein, G.: Implicit neural representations with periodic activation functions. In: Advances in Neural Information Processing Systems 33 (2020)
38. Sun, T., Nam, G., Aliaga, C., Hery, C., Ramamoorthi, R.: Human hair inverse rendering using multi-view photometric data (2021)
39. Tan, Z., et al.: Michigan: multi-input-conditioned hair image generation for portrait editing. arXiv preprint arXiv:2010.16417 (2020)
40. Tewari, A., et al.: State of the art on neural rendering. Computer Graphics Forum (EG STAR 2020) (2020)
41. Tewari, A., et al.: MoFA: model-based deep convolutional face autoencoder for unsupervised monocular reconstruction. In: Proceedings of the IEEE International Conference on Computer Vision Workshops, pp. 1274–1283 (2017)
42. Thies, J., Zollhöfer, M., Nießner, M.: Deferred neural rendering: image synthesis using neural textures. ACM Trans. Graph. (TOG) **38**(4), 1–12 (2019)
43. Tran, L., Liu, X.: Nonlinear 3D face morphable model. In: Proceedings of the IEEE conference on computer vision and pattern recognition, pp. 7346–7355 (2018)
44. Wang, Z., Bovik, A.C., Sheikh, H.R., Simoncelli, E.P.: Image quality assessment: from error visibility to structural similarity. IEEE Trans. Image Process. **13**(4), 600–612 (2004). https://doi.org/10.1109/TIP.2003.819861
45. Wei, L., Hu, L., Kim, V., Yumer, E., Li, H.: Real-time hair rendering using sequential adversarial networks. In: Ferrari, V., Hebert, M., Sminchisescu, C., Weiss, Y. (eds.) ECCV 2018. LNCS, vol. 11208, pp. 105–122. Springer, Cham (2018). https://doi.org/10.1007/978-3-030-01225-0_7
46. Xiang, D., Prada, F., Wu, C., Hodgins, J.: MonoClothCap: towards temporally coherent clothing capture from monocular RGB video. In: 2020 International Conference on 3D Vision (3DV), pp. 322–332. IEEE (2020)
47. Yang, L., Shi, Z., Zheng, Y., Zhou, K.: Dynamic hair modeling from monocular videos using deep neural networks. ACM Trans. Graph. (TOG) **38**(6), 1–12 (2019)
48. Yifan, W., Serena, F., Wu, S., Öztireli, C., Sorkine-Hornung, O.: Differentiable surface splatting for point-based geometry processing. ACM Trans. Graph. (TOG) **38**(6), 1–14 (2019)
49. Zhang, M., Chai, M., Wu, H., Yang, H., Zhou, K.: A datadriven approach to four-view image-based hair modeling. ACM Trans. Graph **36**(4), 156 (2017)
50. Zhang, M., Zheng, Y.: Hair-GAN: recovering 3D hair structure from a single image using generative adversarial networks. Visual Inform. **3**(2), 102–112 (2019)
51. Zhang, R., Isola, P., Efros, A.A., Shechtman, E., Wang, O.: The unreasonable effectiveness of deep features as a perceptual metric. In: Proceedings of the IEEE conference on computer vision and pattern recognition, pp. 586–595 (2018)
52. Zhou, Y., et al.: HairNet: single-view hair reconstruction using convolutional neural networks. In: Ferrari, V., Hebert, M., Sminchisescu, C., Weiss, Y. (eds.) ECCV 2018. LNCS, vol. 11215, pp. 249–265. Springer, Cham (2018). https://doi.org/10.1007/978-3-030-01252-6_15

GraphCSPN: Geometry-Aware Depth Completion via Dynamic GCNs

Xin Liu[1], Xiaofei Shao[2], Bo Wang[2], Yali Li[1], and Shengjin Wang[1](✉)

[1] Beijing National Research Center for Information Science and Technology (BNRist), Department of Electronic Engineering, Tsinghua University, Beijing, China
xinliu20@mails.tsinghua.edu.cn, {liyali13,wgsgj}@tsinghua.edu.cn

[2] Deptrum Ltd., Shenzhen, China
{xiaofei.shao,bo.wang}@deptrum.com

Abstract. Image guided depth completion aims to recover per-pixel dense depth maps from sparse depth measurements with the help of aligned color images, which has a wide range of applications from robotics to autonomous driving. However, the 3D nature of sparse-to-dense depth completion has not been fully explored by previous methods. In this work, we propose a **Graph C**onvolution based **S**patial **P**ropagation **N**etwork (**GraphCSPN**) as a general approach for depth completion. First, unlike previous methods, we leverage convolution neural networks as well as graph neural networks in a complementary way for geometric representation learning. In addition, the proposed networks explicitly incorporate learnable geometric constraints to regularize the propagation process performed in three-dimensional space rather than in two-dimensional plane. Furthermore, we construct the graph utilizing sequences of feature patches, and update it dynamically with an edge attention module during propagation, so as to better capture both the local neighboring features and global relationships over long distance. Extensive experiments on both indoor NYU-Depth-v2 and outdoor KITTI datasets demonstrate that our method achieves the state-of-the-art performance, especially when compared in the case of using only a few propagation steps. Code and models are available at the project page. https://github.com/xinliu20/GraphCSPN_ECCV2022.

Keywords: Depth completion · Graph neural network · Spatial propagation

1 Introduction

Depth perception plays an important role in various real-world applications of computer vision, such as navigation of robotics [8,27] and autonomous vehicles [1,11], augmented reality [5,6], and 3D face recognition [16,35]. However,

---

Supplementary Information The online version contains supplementary material available at https://doi.org/10.1007/978-3-031-19827-4_6.

S. Avidan et al. (Eds.): ECCV 2022, LNCS 13693, pp. 90–107, 2022.
https://doi.org/10.1007/978-3-031-19827-4_6

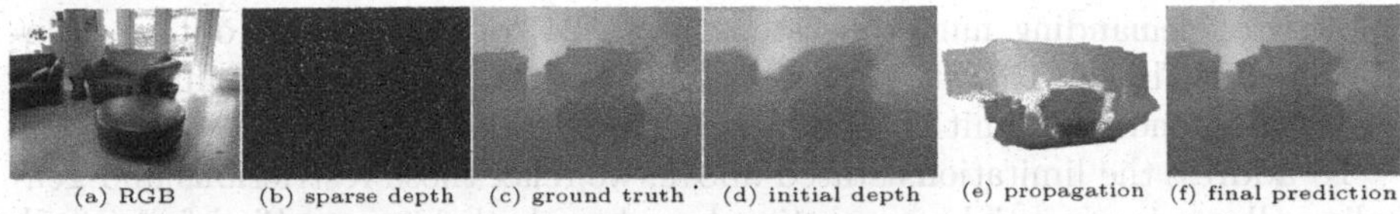

Fig. 1. Illustration of depth completion task using our framework. A backbone model receives the sparse depth map and corresponding RGB image as input and outputs an initial depth prediction. And then the initial depth is iteratively refined by our geometry-aware GraphCSPN in 3D space to produce the final depth prediction. Sparse depth map (b) has less than 1% valid values and is dilated for visualization. (Color figure online)

it is difficult to directly acquire dense depth maps using depth sensors, including LiDAR, time-of-flight or structure-light-based 3D cameras, either because of the inherent limitations of hardware or due to the interference of surrounding environment. Since depth sensors can only provide sparse depth measurements of object at distance, there has been a growing interest within both academia and industry in reconstructing depth in full resolution with the guidance of corresponding color images.

To address this challenging problem of sparse-to-dense depth completion, a wide variety of methods have been proposed. Early approaches [36,41,46] mainly focus on handcrafted features which often lead to inaccurate results and have poor generalization ability. Recent advance in deep convolutional neural networks (CNN) has demonstrated its promising performance on the task of depth completion [4,20,37]. Although CNN based methods have already achieved impressive results for depth completion, the inherent local connection property of CNN makes it difficult to work on depth map with sparse and irregular distribution, and hence fail to capture 3D geometric features. Inspired by graph neural networks (GNN) that can operate on irregular data represented by a graph, we propose a geometry-aware and dynamically constructed GNN. And it is combined with CNN in a complementary way for geometric representation learning, in order to fully explore the 3D nature of depth prediction.

Among the state-of-the-art methods for depth completion, spatial propagation [32] based models achieve better results and are more efficient and interpretable than direct depth completion models [33]. Convolutional spatial propagation network (CSPN) [4] and other methods built on it [3,37] learn the initial depth prediction and affinity matrix for neighboring pixels, and then iteratively refine the depth prediction through recurrent convolutional operations. Recently, Park *et al.* [37] propose a non-local spatial propagation network (NLSPN) which alleviates the mixed-depth problem on object boundaries. Nevertheless, there are several limitations regarding to such approaches. Firstly, the neighbors and affinity matrix are both fixed during the entire iterative propagation process, which may lead to incorrect predictions because of the propagation of errors in refinement module. In addition, the previous spatial propagation based methods perform propagation in two dimensional plane without geometric constraints, neglecting the 3D nature of depth estimation. Moreover, they suffer from the problem of demanding numerous steps (*e.g.*, 24) of iteration to obtain accurate results. The long iteration process indicates the inefficiency of information propagation and may limit their real-world applications.

To address the limitations stated above, we relax those restrictions and generalize all previous spatial propagation based methods into a unified framework leveraging graph neural networks. The motivation behind our proposed model is not only because GNN is capable of working on irregular data in 3D space, but also the message passing principle [15] of GNN is strongly in accord with the process of spatial propagation. We adopt an encoder-decoder architecture as a simple while effective multi-modality fusion strategy to learn the joint representation of RGB and depth images, which is utilized to construct the graph. Then the graph propagation is performed in 3D space under learnable geometric constraints with neighbors updated dynamically for every step. Furthermore, to facilitate the propagation process, we propose an edge attention module to aggregate information from corresponding position of neighboring patches. In summary, the main contributions of the paper are as follows:

- We propose a graph convolution based spatial propagation network for sparse-to-dense depth completion. It is a generic and propagation-efficient framework and only requires 3 or less propagation steps compared with 18 or more steps used in previous methods.
- We develop a geometry-aware and dynamically constructed graph neural network with an edge attention module. The proposed model provides new insights on how GNN can help to deal with 2D images in 3D perception related tasks.
- Extensive experiments are conducted on both indoor NYU-Depth-v2 and outdoor KITTI datasets which show that our method achieves better results than previous state-of-the-art approaches.

2 Related Work

Depth Completion. Image guided depth completion is an important subfield of depth estimation, which aims to predict dense depth maps from various input information with different modalities. However, depth estimation from only a single RGB image often leads to unreliable results due to the inherent ambiguity of depth prediction from images. To attain a robust and accurate estimation, Ma and Karaman [33] proposed a deep regression model for depth completion, which boosts the accuracy of prediction by a large margin compared to using only RGB images. To address the problems of image guided depth completion, various deep learning based methods have been proposed - *e.g.*, sparse invariant convolution [9,22,23], confidence propagation [10,18], multi-modality fusion [21, 43], utilizing Bayesian networks [39] and unsupervised learning [48], exploiting semantic segmentation [26,40] and surface normal [38,50] as auxiliary tasks.

Spatial Propagation Network. The spatial propagation network (SPN) proposed in [32] can learn semantically-aware affinity matrix for vision tasks including depth completion. The propagation of SPN is performed sequentially in a row-wise and column-wise manner with a three-way connection, which can only capture limited local features in an inefficient way. Cheng *et al.* [4] applied SPN on the task of depth completion and proposed a convolutional spatial propagation network (CSPN), which performs propagation with a manner of recurrent convolutional operation and alleviates the inefficiency problem of SPN. Later, CSPN++ [3] was proposed to learn context aware and resource aware convolutional spatial propagation networks and improves the accuracy and efficiency of depth completion. Recently, Park *et al.* [37] proposed NLSPN to learn deformable kernels for propagation which is robust to mixed-depth problem on depth boundaries. Following this family of approaches based on spatial propagation, we further propose a graph convolution based spatial propagation network (GraphCSPN) which provides a generic framework for depth completion. Unlike previous methods, GraphCSPN is constructed dynamically by learned patch-wise affinities and performs efficient propagation with geometrically relevant neighbors in three-dimensional space rather than in two-dimensional plane.

Graph Neural Network. Graph neural networks (GNNs) receive a set of nodes as input and are invariant to permutations of the node sequence. GNNs work directly on graph-based data and capture dependency of objects via message passing between nodes [15,30,52]. GNNs have been applied in various vision tasks, such as image classification [12,47], object detection [17,19] and visual question answering [34,44]. Unlike previous depth completion methods using GNNs for multi-modality fusion [51], learning dynamic kernel [49], we leverage GNNs as its message passing principle is in accord with spatial propagation. In addition, we develop a geometry-aware and dynamically constructed GCN with edge attention to aggregate and update information from neighboring nodes.

3 Method

In this section, we start by introducing the spatial propagation network (SPN) and previous methods that build on SPN. To address the limitations of those methods, we present our graph convolution based spatial propagation network and show how it extends and generalizes earlier approaches into a unified framework. Then we describe in details every component of the proposed framework, including graph construction, neighborhood estimation and graph propagation. Furthermore, a theoretical analysis of our method from the perspective of anisotropic diffusion is provided in supplementary material.

3.1 Spatial Propagation Network

In the task of sparse-to-dense depth completion, spatial propagation network [32] is designed to be a refine module working on the initial depth prediction in a recursive manner. The initial depth prediction can be the output of an encoder-decoder network or other networks utilizing more complicated multi-modality fusion strategies. After several iteration steps, the final prediction result is obtained with more detailed and accurate structure. We formulate the updating process of previous methods [3,4,32,37] in each propagation step as follows:

$$d_{p,q}^{s+1} = \mu(\mathbf{D}^s|\mathbf{A}_{p,q}, \mathcal{N}_{p,q}) = a_{p,q}^{p,q} d_{p,q}^s + \sum_{(i,j)\in\mathcal{N}_{p,q}} a_{p,q}^{i,j} d_{i,j}^s, \tag{1}$$

where s denotes the iteration step; $d_{p,q} \in \mathbf{D}$ is the depth value at coordinate (p, q) of 2D depth map; $(i, j) \in \mathcal{N}_{p,q}$ indicates the coordinate of neighbors at (p, q); and $a_{p,q}^{i,j} \in \mathbf{A}_{p,q}$ represents the affinity between the pixels at (p, q) and (i, j). During the spatial propagation, each depth value is updated by its neighbors according to the affinity matrix which defines how much information should be passed between neighboring pixels. Previous methods based on SPN construct the neighborhood through simple coordinate shift, which can be summarized as:

$$\mathcal{N}_{p,q} = \{(p+m, q+n)|(m,n) \in \Gamma(\mathbf{D}|p,q), (m,n) \neq (0,0)\}, \tag{2}$$

where (m, n) represents the coordinate shift of neighbors; and Γ denotes the estimation function of neighbors given the initial depth prediction $\mathbf{D}$ and position (p, q) as input. For local spatial propagation methods, the neighbor estimation function Γ is irrelevant to the input and falls to the fixed coordinate set, *e.g.* $\{-1, 0, 1\}$ for 3×3 kernel. The original SPN [32] performs propagation sequentially in a row-wise and column-wise manner with three-way connections which is inefficient. CSPN [4] updates the depth estimation by making use of all local neighbors simultaneously. CSPN++ [3] is able to learn square kernel of different sizes. The neighborhood estimation function of NLSPN [37] can learn non-local neighbors according to the pixel positions in 2D plane.

3.2 GraphCSPN

After closely examining the updating function and neighborhood construction function of earlier approaches, there are two major limitations that need to be addressed. Firstly, once the affinity matrix $\mathbf{A}_{p,q}$ and neighborhood matrix $\mathcal{N}_{p,q}$ is determined, they will not be changed during the entire process of spatial propagation. So there are only simple iterations and no learning process involved when propagating neighbor observations with corresponding affinities. However, the condition of pixels will be changed after each propagation step, and simple iterations with fixed affinities and neighbors fails to capture the dynamic relationships between pixels. As a result, the fixed configurations slow down the information propagation and demand a large number of iteration steps. And that's why we develop a dynamically constructed graph convolution network for propagation-efficient depth completion.

The second limitation of previous approaches is that the spatial propagation is confined in a small region and performed in two-dimensional plane without any geometric constraints. Structured kernels (*e.g.* 3×3, 5×5) used in CSPN [2] and CSPN++ [3] have a very limited receptive field for every iteration and can easily bring unrelated information into propagation from fixed neighbors, which

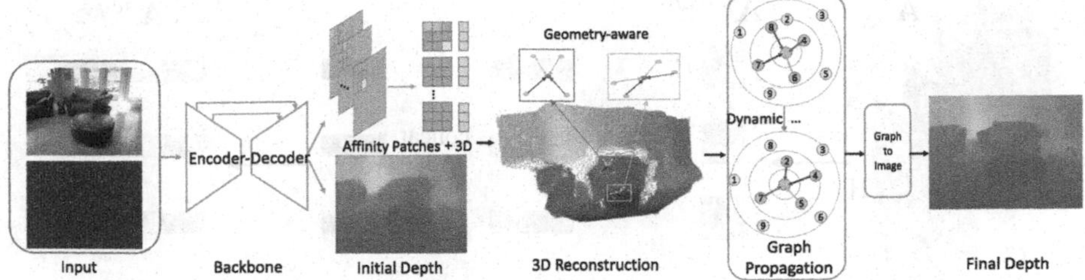

Fig. 2. Overview of the proposed network architecture (Best viewed in color). There are mainly two parts of the network. The first part utilizes an encoder-decoder to jointly learn the initial depth map and affinity matrix, which is sampled and reshaped into sequences of patches and concatenated with 3D position embeddings. The second part of our model estimates the neighbors of different patches on the basis of learned geometric constraints, and performs spatial propagation leveraging dynamic graph convolution networks with self-attention mechanism. The final depth prediction is obtained through a graph-to-image module. As can be seen in the parts of 3D reconstruction and graph propagation, the neighborhood construction in yellow is varying for different red nodes since the geometric structures surrounding red nodes are diverse in 3D space, and the graphs are also changeable because of the dynamic construction of GCN during the propagation process. Note that the different colors of the edges indicate the different attention weights between the red nodes and their yellow neighbors. (Color figure online)

may result in inaccurate predictions especially on object boundaries. Although NLSPN [37] can predict flexible neighbors, the neighbors are learned merely based on the initial depth estimation without explicit geometric constraints, thus leading to unreliable predictions. To fully explore the 3D nature of depth prediction, the model we propose is geometry-aware and capable of capturing relevant neighbors over long distance, which is critical for depth completion because of the irregular distribution of sparse depth measurements. We now explain the process of GraphCSPN in three consecutive steps: graph construction, neighborhood estimation and graph propagation.

Patch-wise Graph Construction. Graph neural networks take as input a set of node features. So the core of graph construction is to convert affinity maps $\mathbf{A} \in \mathbb{R}^{H \times W \times C}$ into a sequence of features $\mathbf{A}^{seq} \in \mathbb{R}^{N \times L}$, where (H, W) is the resolution of the affinity map, C is the number of channels, L is the length of node feature, and N is the total number of nodes. Note that the computation complexity of graph propagation increases quadratically with the number of nodes N. So we need to keep the size of graph small. To do so, we first convert $\mathbf{A}$ into a sequence of patches $\mathbf{A}^{patch} \in \mathbb{R}^{N \times P_h \times P_w}$, where (P_h, P_w) is the resolution of each affinity patch. In this way, the total number of nodes $N = (H \times W)/(P_h \times P_w)$. Otherwise, $N = H \times W$, if we use pixel-wise construction (see more discussions in supplement). For each patch $\mathbf{A}^{patch}$ with shape $P_h \times P_w$, the number of corresponding patches in $\mathbf{A}$ is C, and the pixels of each patch $\mathbf{A}^{patch}$ is from C different channels ($C = P_h \times P_w$). By our patch-wise construction, prior

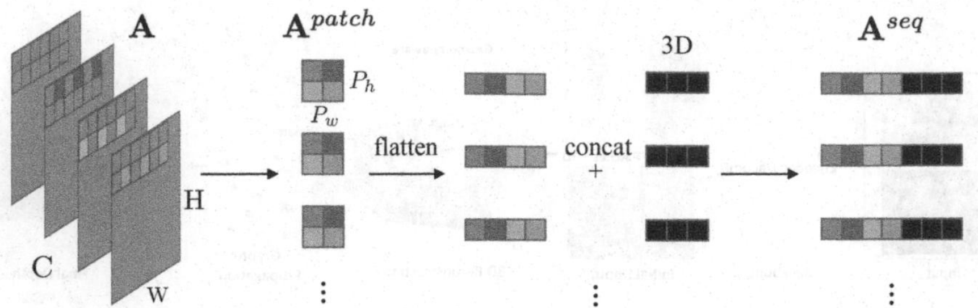

Fig. 3. Illustration of the process of graph construction (Best viewed in color). For better visibility, we set $C = 4, P_h = P_w = 2$, and use this simple example to show how to convert affinity maps into a sequence of features. (Color figure online)

knowledge about local correlations can be established. And then each patch is flattened and concatenated with 3D position as node features ($L = P_h \times P_w + 3$), so the model is also able to capture global relationships of different patches over long distance, as can be seen in the 3D reconstruction part of Fig. 2. To help for a better understanding of graph construction, we use a simple example to illustrate the above process in Fig. 3.

Geometry-Aware Neighborhood Estimation. The 3D position embedding preserves the original geometry of the local shape. To explicitly incorporate geometric constraints into the graph propagation, the 3D position embeddings are supposed to be added to patches such that the geometric information can be retained during graph propagation. To do so, we project the depth prediction after each graph propagation step into 3D space as follows:

$$\begin{bmatrix} u \\ v \\ w \\ 1 \end{bmatrix} = d \begin{bmatrix} 1/f_p & 0 & -c_p/f_p & 0 \\ 0 & 1/f_q & -c_q/f_q & 0 \\ 0 & 0 & 1 & 0 \\ 0 & 0 & 0 & 1 \end{bmatrix} \begin{bmatrix} p \\ q \\ 1 \\ 1/d \end{bmatrix}, \tag{3}$$

where (p, q) and (u, v, w) are the center coordinate of the patch in 2D plane and projected 3D space, respectively; d is the depth predictions during propagations; f_p, f_q, c_p, c_q are the camera intrinsic parameters. After obtaining the 3D position of each patch, k-nearest neighbors algorithm can be applied for neighborhood estimation in 3D space, which can be formulated as follows:

$$\mathcal{N}^G_{p,q} = \{(u, v, w)|(u, v, w) = \mathcal{K}(\mathbf{D}|p, q), (u, v, w) \in \mathbb{R}^3\}, \tag{4}$$

where $\mathcal{K}$ represents the projection and estimation function; $\mathcal{N}^G_{p,q}$ denotes the neighbors of the patch in 3D space. During the propagation process, the graph is dynamically constructed at each propagation step in line with the neighborhood estimation at that time.

Dynamic Graph Propagation. After the neighborhood for each patch is constructed, patches are represented as vertices in a graph, and edges can be established if there are connections between the vertices. Graph propagation is conducted via feature aggregation and feature update, which is as follows:

$$\mathbf{h}_{v_{s+1}} = \eta\left(\mathbf{h}_{v_s}, \rho\left(\left\{\mathbf{h}_{u_s} \mid u_s \in \mathcal{N}_{s+1}\left(v_s\right)\right\}, \mathbf{h}_{v_s}, \mathcal{W}_\rho\right), \mathcal{W}_\eta\right), \tag{5}$$

where s denotes the propagation step as before in Eq. 1; ρ and η are the feature aggregation function and update function, $\mathcal{W}_\rho$ and $\mathcal{W}_\eta$ are the learnable parameters for the two functions, respectively; $\mathbf{h}_{v_s}$ represents the features for the vertex v_s; and $\mathcal{N}_{s+1}\left(v_s\right)$ is the set of neighbors for v_s during the step $s+1$. Note that the neighborhood $\mathcal{N}_{s+1}\left(v_s\right)$ varies for different propagation steps, since the graph is dynamically constructed. To further facilitate the graph propagation process, we propose a fine-grained edge attention module as follows:

$$\mathbf{x}_i^{s+1} = \alpha_{i,i}\phi_i(\mathbf{x}_i^s) + \sum_{j \in \mathcal{N}_{s+1}(i)} \alpha_{i,j}\phi_j(\mathbf{x}_i^s || (\mathbf{x}_j^s - \mathbf{x}_i^s)), \tag{6}$$

where $\mathbf{x}_i^s$ represents the feature vector for the vertex i at propagtion step s; $||$ denotes the concatenation operation; ϕ is a neural network which is instantiated as a multi-layer perceptron (MLP) parameterized by $\mathcal{W}_\rho$. The attention is performed in a channel-wise manner and each channel denotes a different position in the original patch, and the attention coefficients $\alpha_{i,j}$ are computed as follows:

$$\alpha_{i,j} = \frac{\exp\left(\psi(\mathbf{x}_i || \mathbf{x}_j)\right)}{\sum_{k \in \mathcal{N}_{s+1}(i) \cup \{i\}} \exp\left(\psi(\mathbf{x}_i || \mathbf{x}_k)\right)}, \tag{7}$$

where ψ denotes a MLP parameterized by $\mathcal{W}_\eta$. Equation 6 details the computation process of aggregation function ρ and update function η stated in Eq. 5. ρ is instantiated as a MLP ϕ which aggregates features of vertices from their neighbors. And η works through the attention coefficient α computed by Eq. 7. By applying the proposed edge attention module, the different attention weights assigned to neighbors can effectively impede the propagation of incorrect predictions during the iterative refinement. After graph propagation, the graph-to-image module rearranges the sequences of patches to their original position in 2D image to generate the final prediction.

3.3 Overall Architecture

As can be seen in Fig. 2, the end-to-end network architecture of our model consists of two parts: an encoder-decoder backbone to learn initial depth prediction and affinity maps, and a graph convolution network for spatial propagation. Follow the common practice of previous work [3,37], we build the encoder upon residual networks and add mirror connections with the decoder to make up the lost spatial information due to the down sampling and pooling operations in the encoder. Since the input of the encoder-decoder comes from different sensing modalities, depth-wise separable convolution is utilized for the first convolution layer which performs convolution on RGB images and sparse depth map independently, followed by a pointwise convolution as a simple while effective multi-modality fusion strategy. The second part of the model is a geometry-aware graph convolution network equipped with edge attention, which is dynamically constructed for iterative refinement of depth predictions.

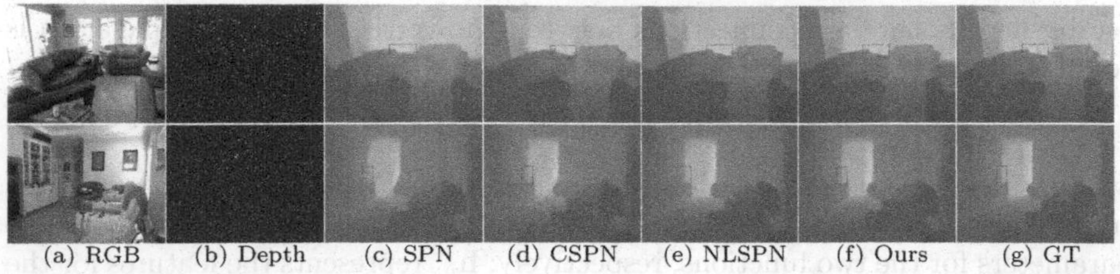

Fig. 4. Depth completion results on the NYU-Depth-v2 dataset [42]. The area inside the red bounding box reveals that our model recovers more accurate structures. (Better viewed in color and zoom in.). (Color figure online)

3.4 Loss Function

The model is trained with masked ℓ_1 loss between the ground truth depth map and predicted depth map, which is the same loss function used in previous methods [4,33,37] and defined as follows:

$$\mathcal{L}(\mathbf{D}^{gt}, \mathbf{D}^{pred}) = \frac{1}{N_v} \sum_{i,j} \mathbb{I}(d_{i,j}^{gt} > 0) \left| \; d_{i,j}^{gt} - d_{i,j}^{pred} \; \right|, \tag{8}$$

where $\mathbb{I}$ is the indication function; $d_{i,j}^{gt} \in \mathbf{D}^{gt}$ and $d_{i,j}^{pred} \in \mathbf{D}^{pred}$ represent the ground truth depth map and the depth map predicted by our model; and N_v denotes the total number of valid depth pixels. We have explored other loss functions, such as ℓ_2 loss and smooth ℓ_1 loss, and also find that the training process can be accelerated by adding extra supervision as weighted auxiliary loss to the output of each graph propagation. More details about the setting of loss functions can be found in ablation.

4 Experiments

We conduct extensive experiments and ablation studies to verify the effectiveness of our model. In this section, we first briefly introduce the datasets and evaluation metrics. Then we present qualitative and quantitative comparisons with state-of-the-arts, and ablation studies of each component of our model are also provided. Additional experiment details can be found in supplementary materials.

4.1 Datasets and Metrics

NYU-Depth-v2. The NYU-Depth-v2 dataset [42] provides RGB and depth images of 464 different indoor scenes with the Kinect sensor. We use the official split of data, where 249 scenes are used for training and the remaining 215 scenes for testing. And we sample about 50K images out of the training set and the original frames of size 640×480 are first downsampled to half and then 304×228 center-cropping is applied, as seen in previous work [7,28,33]. Following

Fig. 5. Depth completion results on the KITTI Depth Completion dataset [45]. (a) RGB, (b) Ground truth, (c) CSPN [4], (d) DepthNormal [50], (e) NLSPN [37], (f) Ours. (Better viewed in color and zoom in.). (Color figure online)

the standard setting [4,33], the official test dataset with 654 images is used for evaluating the final performance.

KITTI Dataset. KITTI dataset [13,14] is a large self-driving real-world dataset with over 90k paired RGB images and LiDAR depth measurements. We use two versions of KITTI dataset, and one is from [33], which consists of 46k images from the training sequences for training, and a random subset of 3200 images from the test sequences for evaluation. The other is KITTI Depth Completion dataset [45] which provides 86k training, 7k validation and 1k testing depth maps with corresponding raw LiDAR scans and reference images. And we evaluate and test the model on the official selected validation set and test set.

Metrics. We adopt the same metrics used in previous work [4,33,45] on NYU-Depth-v2 dataset and KITTI dataset. Given ground truth depth map $D^* = \{d^*\}$ and predicted depth map $D = \{d\}$, the metrics used in the following experiments include:

(1)RMSE: $\sqrt{\frac{1}{|D|}\sum_{d\in D}|d^* - d|^2}$;

(2)MAE: $\frac{1}{|D|}\sum_{d\in D}|d^* - d|$;

(3)iRMSE: $\sqrt{\frac{1}{|D|}\sum_{d\in D}|1/d^* - 1/d|^2}$;

(4)iMAE: $\frac{1}{|D|}\sum_{d\in D}|1/d^* - 1/d|$;

(5)REL: $\frac{1}{|D|}\sum_{d\in D}|d^* - d|/d^*$;

(6)δ_t: percentage of pixels satisfying $max(\frac{d^*}{d}, \frac{d}{d^*}) < t$, where $t \in \{1.25, 1.25^2, 1.25^3\}$.

4.2 Comparison with State-of-the-Arts

We evaluate our model on the official test split of NYU-Depth-v2 dataset and 500 depth pixels are randomly sampled from the dense depth map, as in previous works [4,33,37]. Quantitative comparison results with methods based on

Table 1. Quantitative evaluation on the NYU-Depth-v2 dataset. We highlight the best results when propagating for only 3 steps.

Methods	Iterations	RMSE ↓	REL ↓	$\delta_{1.25}$ ↑	$\delta_{1.25^2}$ ↑	$\delta_{1.25^3}$ ↑
S2D [33]	–	0.230	0.044	97.1	99.4	99.8
SPN [32]	3	0.215	0.040	94.2	97.6	98.9
	24	0.172	0.031	98.3	99.7	99.9
CSPN [4]	3	0.135	0.021	97.1	98.1	99.3
	24	0.117	0.016	99.2	99.9	100.0
CSPN++ [3]	24	0.116	–	–	–	–
NLSPN [37]	3	0.119	0.018	98.3	99.4	99.3
	18	0.092	0.012	99.6	99.9	100.0
GraphCSPN	**3**	**0.090**	**0.012**	**99.6**	**99.9**	**100.0**

Table 2. Quantitative evaluation on the KITTI dataset.

Methods	Iterations	RMSE ↓	REL ↓	$\delta_{1.25}$ ↑	$\delta_{1.25^2}$ ↑	$\delta_{1.25^3}$ ↑
S2D [33]	–	3.378	0.073	93.5	97.6	98.9
SPN [32]	3	3.302	0.069	93.7	97.6	99.0
	24	3.243	0.063	94.3	97.8	99.1
CSPN [4]	3	3.125	0.052	94.1	97.8	99.0
	24	2.977	0.044	95.7	98.0	99.1
NLSPN [37]	3	2.697	0.042	95.8	98.0	99.1
	18	2.533	0.038	96.2	98.5	99.3
GraphCSPN	**3**	**2.267**	**0.032**	**97.4**	**98.9**	**99.5**

spatial propagation networks are provided in Table 1. S2D [33] is a direct depth completion model which can only obtain blurry results. And spatial propagation networks based approaches are able to generate much more accurate and reliable results by recurrently refining the predictions. However, earlier methods have not taken the geometric constraints into account and fail to capture global relationship over long distance, thus easily leading to unreliable results on object boundaries where a holistic view is need, as can be seen in Fig. 4. Moreover, the affinity matrix and neighborhood of previous methods are fixed during propagation, and a large number of iteration steps is required because of the inefficient propagation. The results in Table 1 show that our model achieves significant improvements over previous approaches when compared using only three iteration steps.

The Table 2 shows the comparisons of evaluation results on KITTI dataset [33]. Similar to the result on NYU-Depth-v2 dataset, our model outperforms the previous methods by a large margin which reduces 0.4m in RMSE. And our model also achieves better results compared to other geometry-aware methods [25,38,50] and

Table 3. Comparison on NYU-Depth-v2 dataset with other state-of-the-arts

Method	RMSE	REL	$\delta_{1.25}$	$\delta_{1.25^2}$
DepthCoeff [25]	0.118	0.013	99.4	99.9
DeepLiDAR [38]	0.115	0.022	99.3	99.9
DepthNormal [50]	0.112	0.018	99.5	99.9
GNN [49]	0.106	0.016	99.5	99.9
FCFRNet [31]	0.106	0.015	99.5	99.9
ACMNet [51]	0.105	0.015	99.4	99.9
PRNet [29]	0.104	0.014	99.4	99.9
GuideNet [43]	0.101	0.015	99.5	99.9
TWICE [24]	0.097	0.013	99.6	99.9
GraphCSPN	**0.090**	**0.012**	**99.6**	**99.9**

Table 4. Comparison on KITTI Depth Completion test dataset

Method	RMSE	MAE	iRMSE	iMAE
CSPN [4]	1019.64	279.46	2.93	1.15
TWICE [24]	840.20	**195.58**	2.08	**0.82**
DepthNormal [50]	777.05	235.17	2.42	1.13
DeepLiDAR [38]	758.38	226.50	2.56	1.15
CSPN++ [3]	743.69	209.28	2.07	0.90
NLSPN [37]	741.68	199.59	1.99	0.84
GuideNet [43]	736.24	218.83	2.25	0.99
FCFRNet [31]	735.81	217.15	2.20	0.98
PENet [20]	**730.08**	210.55	2.17	0.94
GraphCSPN	738.41	199.31	**1.96**	0.84

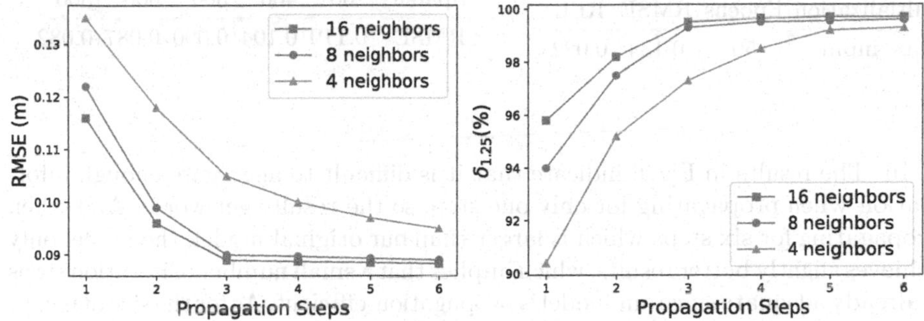

Fig. 6. Impact of number of propagation steps and neighbors on the prediction accuracy on NYU-Depth-v2 dataset.

other methods using GNNs [49,51], as can be seen in Table 3. On the challenging KITTI Depth Completion dataset [45] where the ground truth of depth map is also sparse. Our model still attains competitive results compared to other state-of-the-arts, as can be seen in Table 4. Qualitative results of the proposed method in comparison with state-of-the-arts are shown in Fig. 5. We also provide a video demo of our method using this dataset in supplement.

4.3 Ablation Studies

We conduct extensive experiments to verify the effectiveness of each proposed component. The altered components of our model include: iteration steps, the number of neighbors, the sparsity of depth samples, loss functions, the proposed edge attention and geometry-aware modules, and dynamic graph construction.

Propagation Configurations: There are two important factors in our proposed graph convolution based spatial propagation network, which are the iteration steps and the number of neighbors. To investigate the impact of those factors on final results, we set the iteration steps from 1 to 6 and the number of neighbors to 4,

Table 5. Ablation study on the choices of loss function

Loss	Epochs	RMSE	REL
ℓ_1	40	0.094	0.013
smooth ℓ_1	42	0.102	0.014
ℓ_2	46	0.104	0.015
Auxillary loss	36	0.090	0.012

Table 6. Ablation study on the configurations of graph construction

Attention	Geometry	Dynamic	RMSE	REL
	✓	✓	0.101	0.014
✓		✓	0.113	0.017
✓	✓		0.108	0.016
✓	✓	✓	0.090	0.012

Table 7. Ablation study on the initialization of graph propagation

Initialization	Epochs	RMSE	REL
Raw input	50	0.134	0.022

Table 8. Ablation study on the number of sparse depth samples

Sparsity	200	400	500	600	800
RMSE	0.119	0.104	0.090	0.087	0.082

8, 16. The results in Fig. 6 indicate that it is difficult to aggregate enough information when propagating for only one step, so the results get worse. And when propagating for six steps which is larger than our original model, the model only achieves slightly better results, which implies that a small number of iteration steps is already adequate since our model is propagation-efficient. As for the size of neighborhood, we find that a larger number of neighbors can slightly improve the results while the results degrade when there are only limited neighbors, which also takes more epochs to converge. So a combination of larger number of propagation steps and neighbors can achieves better performance which demonstrate the capacity and potential of our model, but we choose a small number instead for a balance of accuracy and efficiency. Since GNN can directly work on the irregular input data, we also try to apply the graph propagation to the raw input. The results in Table 7 show it needs more steps to converge and leads to poor performance. The learned initial depth map can be viewed as a good starting point for a fast optimization process. Moreover, the encoder-decoder architecture to generate the initial depth is an effective fusion network to learn the joint representation of multi-modality RGB and depth images. And it can work in a complementary way with GNN.

Loss Functions: Our model is driven by ℓ_1 loss. Here we use ℓ_2 loss and smooth ℓ_1 loss to study the effect of different loss functions, as they play a critical role in model training. Although it is expected that a better result in RMSE would be obtained when applying ℓ_2 loss, in experiments we do not see the expected gains and find that it takes more epochs to reach results close to ℓ_1 loss, because ℓ_2 loss is sensitive to outliers and results in very small gradients during the late stage of training. Smooth ℓ_1 loss is a compromise between ℓ_2 loss and ℓ_1 loss, but ℓ_1 loss is a more robust and suitable choice for the task of depth prediction. We also examine the impact of auxillary loss on model training and final results by adding extra supervision to the intermediate outputs of each graph propagation with weight 0.1. The results in Table 5 show that model training benefits from the auxillary loss with a faster speed of convergence, because the intermediate outputs share the same objective with the final output.

Geometry, Attention and Dynamic Construction: In this part, we verify the role of each component of our graph propagation including the geometry-aware module, edge attention, and dynamic construction. Our model explicitly incorporates geometric constraints into the process of propagation. After removing those constraints, the neighborhood estimation can only perform in the feature space of patches with no access to the knowledge of their real locations in 3D space. As a result, the performance drops by a large margin which implies the importance of 3D geometric clues in the task of depth completion. We further remove the edge attention module from our framework and use the mean aggregation function instead to verify the necessity of attention-driven aggregation. As shown in Table 6, the performance of the model without edge attention also decreases with a small degree, because the edge attention module can effectively impede the propagation of errors in refinement module. In addition, when the graph propagation is not constructed dynamically and shares the same neighborhood estimation during all the propagation steps, we can see the performance gets worse and converges at an earlier epoch. Because there is an inherent over-smoothing problem of vanilla graph convolution networks, and the dynamic construction of graph is capable of preventing such problem and helps to achieve more accurate results.

Robustness and Generalization: Following the standard procedure, our original model works on sparse depth map with 500 random samples. To evaluate the robustness of our model to different input sparsity, we test our model using sparse depth map with 200 samples which takes only 0.4% of the dense depth map. Although the performance decreases as expected, the model can still generate reasonable results and when changing the sparse input to 800 samples, the model attains a result of 0.083m evaluated by RMSE metric, which demonstrates our model is robust and generalizes well to different input sparsity. Please refer to the supplement for additional ablation studies and visualizations.

5 Conclusion

In this paper, we have proposed a graph convolution based spatial propagation network for sparse-to-dense depth completion. The proposed method generalizes previous spatial propagation based approaches into a unified framework which is geometry-aware and propagation-efficient. The graph propagation is dynamically constructed and performed with an edge attention module for feature aggregation and update. Extensive experiments demonstrate the effectiveness of the proposed method. Since our model is a generic and effective solution for 3D spatial propagation, it can be further extended to more 3D perception related tasks in the future.

Acknowledgements. This work was supported by the state key development program in 14th Five-Year under Grant Nos.2021QY1702, 2021YFF0602103, 2021YFF0602102. We also thank for the research fund under Grant No. 2019GQ G0001 from the Institute for Guo Qiang, Tsinghua University.

References

1. Bai, L., Zhao, Y., Elhousni, M., Huang, X.: DepthNet: real-time lidar point cloud depth completion for autonomous vehicles. IEEE Access **8**, 227825–227833 (2020)
2. Chen, Y., Yang, B., Liang, M., Urtasun, R.: Learning joint 2D–3D representations for depth completion. In: Proceedings of the IEEE/CVF International Conference on Computer Vision, pp. 10023–10032 (2019)
3. Cheng, X., Wang, P., Guan, C., Yang, R.: CSPN++: learning context and resource aware convolutional spatial propagation networks for depth completion. In: Proceedings of the AAAI Conference on Artificial Intelligence, pp. 10615–10622 (2020)
4. Cheng, X., Wang, P., Yang, R.: Depth estimation via affinity learned with convolutional spatial propagation network. In: Ferrari, V., Hebert, M., Sminchisescu, C., Weiss, Y. (eds.) ECCV 2018. LNCS, vol. 11220, pp. 108–125. Springer, Cham (2018). https://doi.org/10.1007/978-3-030-01270-0_7
5. Diaz, C., Walker, M., Szafir, D.A., Szafir, D.: Designing for depth perceptions in augmented reality. In: 2017 IEEE International Symposium on Mixed and Augmented Reality (ISMAR), pp. 111–122. IEEE (2017)
6. Du, R., et al.: DepthLab: real-time 3D interaction with depth maps for mobile augmented reality. In: Proceedings of the 33rd Annual ACM Symposium on User Interface Software and Technology, pp. 829–843 (2020)
7. Eigen, D., Puhrsch, C., Fergus, R.: Depth map prediction from a single image using a multi-scale deep network. arXiv preprint arXiv:1406.2283 (2014)
8. El-laithy, R.A., Huang, J., Yeh, M.: Study on the use of microsoft kinect for robotics applications. In: Proceedings of the 2012 IEEE/ION Position, Location and Navigation Symposium, pp. 1280–1288. IEEE (2012)
9. Eldesokey, A., Felsberg, M., Khan, F.S.: Propagating confidences through cnns for sparse data regression. arXiv preprint arXiv:1805.11913 (2018)
10. Eldesokey, A., Felsberg, M., Khan, F.S.: Confidence propagation through CNNs for guided sparse depth regression. IEEE Trans. Pattern Anal. Mach. Intell. **42**(10), 2423–2436 (2019)
11. Farahnakian, F., Heikkonen, J.: RGB-depth fusion framework for object detection in autonomous vehicles. In: 2020 14th International Conference on Signal Processing and Communication Systems (ICSPCS), pp. 1–6. IEEE (2020)
12. Garcia, V., Bruna, J.: Few-shot learning with graph neural networks. arXiv preprint arXiv:1711.04043 (2017)
13. Geiger, A., Lenz, P., Stiller, C., Urtasun, R.: Vision meets robotics: the kitti dataset. Int. J. Robot. Res. **32**(11), 1231–1237 (2013)
14. Geiger, A., Lenz, P., Urtasun, R.: Are we ready for autonomous driving? the kitti vision benchmark suite. In: 2012 IEEE Conference on Computer Vision and Pattern Recognition, pp. 3354–3361. IEEE (2012)
15. Gilmer, J., Schoenholz, S.S., Riley, P.F., Vinyals, O., Dahl, G.E.: Neural message passing for quantum chemistry. In: International conference on machine learning, pp. 1263–1272. PMLR (2017)

16. Gordon, G.G.: Face recognition based on depth and curvature features. In: Proceedings 1992 IEEE Computer Society Conference on Computer Vision and Pattern Recognition, pp. 808–809. IEEE Computer Society (1992)
17. Gu, J., Hu, H., Wang, L., Wei, Y., Dai, J.: Learning region features for object detection. In: Ferrari, V., Hebert, M., Sminchisescu, C., Weiss, Y. (eds.) ECCV 2018. LNCS, vol. 11216, pp. 392–406. Springer, Cham (2018). https://doi.org/10.1007/978-3-030-01258-8_24
18. Hekmatian, H., Jin, J., Al-Stouhi, S.: Conf-net: toward high-confidence dense 3D point-cloud with error-map prediction. arXiv preprint arXiv:1907.10148 (2019)
19. Hu, H., Gu, J., Zhang, Z., Dai, J., Wei, Y.: Relation networks for object detection. In: Proceedings of the IEEE Conference on Computer Vision and Pattern Recognition, pp. 3588–3597 (2018)
20. Hu, M., Wang, S., Li, B., Ning, S., Fan, L., Gong, X.: PENet: towards precise and efficient image guided depth completion. arXiv preprint arXiv:2103.00783 (2021)
21. Hu, M., Wang, S., Li, B., Ning, S., Fan, L., Gong, X.: Towards precise and efficient image guided depth completion. arXiv preprint arXiv:2103.00783 (2021)
22. Hua, J., Gong, X.: A normalized convolutional neural network for guided sparse depth upsampling. In: IJCAI, pp. 2283–2290. Stockholm, Sweden (2018)
23. Huang, Z., Fan, J., Cheng, S., Yi, S., Wang, X., Li, H.: HMS-Net: hierarchical multi-scale sparsity-invariant network for sparse depth completion. IEEE Trans. Image Process. **29**, 3429–3441 (2019)
24. Imran, S., Liu, X., Morris, D.: Depth completion with twin surface extrapolation at occlusion boundaries. In: Proceedings of the IEEE/CVF Conference on Computer Vision and Pattern Recognition, pp. 2583–2592 (2021)
25. Imran, S., Long, Y., Liu, X., Morris, D.: Depth coefficients for depth completion. In: 2019 IEEE/CVF Conference on Computer Vision and Pattern Recognition (CVPR), pp. 12438–12447. IEEE (2019)
26. Jaritz, M., De Charette, R., Wirbel, E., Perrotton, X., Nashashibi, F.: Sparse and dense data with CNNs: depth completion and semantic segmentation. In: 2018 International Conference on 3D Vision (3DV), pp. 52–60. IEEE (2018)
27. Jing, C., Potgieter, J., Noble, F., Wang, R.: A comparison and analysis of RGB-D cameras' depth performance for robotics application. In: 2017 24th International Conference on Mechatronics and Machine Vision in Practice (M2VIP), pp. 1–6. IEEE (2017)
28. Laina, I., Rupprecht, C., Belagiannis, V., Tombari, F., Navab, N.: Deeper depth prediction with fully convolutional residual networks. In: 2016 Fourth international conference on 3D vision (3DV), pp. 239–248. IEEE (2016)
29. Lee, B.U., Lee, K., Kweon, I.S.: Depth completion using plane-residual representation. In: Proceedings of the IEEE/CVF Conference on Computer Vision and Pattern Recognition, pp. 13916–13925 (2021)
30. Li, G., et al.: DeepGCNs: making GCNs go as deep as CNNs. IEEE Transactions on Pattern Analysis and Machine Intelligence (2021)
31. Liu, L., et al.: FCFR-Net: feature fusion based coarse-to-fine residual learning for depth completion. In: Proceedings of the AAAI Conference on Artificial Intelligence, pp. 2136–2144 (2021)
32. Liu, S., De Mello, S., Gu, J., Zhong, G., Yang, M.H., Kautz, J.: Learning affinity via spatial propagation networks. arXiv preprint arXiv:1710.01020 (2017)
33. Ma, F., Karaman, S.: Sparse-to-dense: depth prediction from sparse depth samples and a single image. In: 2018 IEEE International Conference on Robotics and Automation (ICRA), pp. 4796–4803. IEEE (2018)

34. Narasimhan, M., Lazebnik, S., Schwing, A.G.: Out of the box: reasoning with graph convolution nets for factual visual question answering. arXiv preprint arXiv:1811.00538 (2018)
35. Pan, G., Han, S., Wu, Z., Wang, Y.: 3D face recognition using mapped depth images. In: 2005 IEEE Computer Society Conference on Computer Vision and Pattern Recognition (CVPR2005)-Workshops, p. 175. IEEE (2005)
36. Park, J., Kim, H., Tai, Y.W., Brown, M.S., Kweon, I.S.: High-quality depth map upsampling and completion for RGB-D cameras. IEEE Trans. Image Process. **23**(12), 5559–5572 (2014)
37. Park, J., Joo, K., Hu, Z., Liu, C.K., Kweon, I.S.: Non-local spatial propagation network for depth completion. arXiv preprint arXiv:2007.10042 3(8) (2020)
38. Qiu, J., et al.: DeepLiDAR: deep surface normal guided depth prediction for outdoor scene from sparse lidar data and single color image. In: Proceedings of the IEEE/CVF Conference on Computer Vision and Pattern Recognition, pp. 3313–3322 (2019)
39. Qu, C., Liu, W., Taylor, C.J.: Bayesian deep basis fitting for depth completion with uncertainty. In: Proceedings of the IEEE/CVF International Conference on Computer Vision (ICCV), pp. 16147–16157 (2021)
40. Schneider, N., Schneider, L., Pinggera, P., Franke, U., Pollefeys, M., Stiller, C.: Semantically guided depth upsampling. In: Rosenhahn, B., Andres, B. (eds.) GCPR 2016. LNCS, vol. 9796, pp. 37–48. Springer, Cham (2016). https://doi.org/10.1007/978-3-319-45886-1_4
41. Shen, J., Cheung, S.C.S.: Layer depth denoising and completion for structured-light RGB-D cameras. In: Proceedings of the IEEE conference on computer vision and pattern recognition, pp. 1187–1194 (2013)
42. Silberman, N., Hoiem, D., Kohli, P., Fergus, R.: Indoor segmentation and support inference from RGBD images. In: Fitzgibbon, A., Lazebnik, S., Perona, P., Sato, Y., Schmid, C. (eds.) ECCV 2012. LNCS, vol. 7576, pp. 746–760. Springer, Heidelberg (2012). https://doi.org/10.1007/978-3-642-33715-4_54
43. Tang, J., Tian, F.P., Feng, W., Li, J., Tan, P.: Learning guided convolutional network for depth completion. IEEE Trans. Image Process. **30**, 1116–1129 (2020)
44. Teney, D., Liu, L., van Den Hengel, A.: Graph-structured representations for visual question answering. In: Proceedings of the IEEE conference on computer vision and pattern recognition, pp. 1–9 (2017)
45. Uhrig, J., Schneider, N., Schneider, L., Franke, U., Brox, T., Geiger, A.: Sparsity invariant cnns. In: 2017 international conference on 3D Vision (3DV), pp. 11–20. IEEE (2017)
46. Wang, L., Jin, H., Yang, R., Gong, M.: Stereoscopic inpainting: Joint color and depth completion from stereo images. In: 2008 IEEE Conference on Computer Vision and Pattern Recognition, pp. 1–8. IEEE (2008)
47. Wang, X., Ye, Y., Gupta, A.: Zero-shot recognition via semantic embeddings and knowledge graphs. In: Proceedings of the IEEE conference on computer vision and pattern recognition, pp. 6857–6866 (2018)
48. Wong, A., Soatto, S.: Unsupervised depth completion with calibrated backprojection layers. In: Proceedings of the IEEE/CVF International Conference on Computer Vision (ICCV), pp. 12747–12756 (2021)
49. Xiong, X., Xiong, H., Xian, K., Zhao, C., Cao, Z., Li, X.: Sparse-to-dense depth completion revisited: sampling strategy and graph construction. In: Vedaldi, A., Bischof, H., Brox, T., Frahm, J.-M. (eds.) ECCV 2020. LNCS, vol. 12366, pp. 682–699. Springer, Cham (2020). https://doi.org/10.1007/978-3-030-58589-1_41

50. Xu, Y., Zhu, X., Shi, J., Zhang, G., Bao, H., Li, H.: Depth completion from sparse lidar data with depth-normal constraints. In: Proceedings of the IEEE/CVF International Conference on Computer Vision, pp. 2811–2820 (2019)
51. Zhao, S., Gong, M., Fu, H., Tao, D.: Adaptive context-aware multi-modal network for depth completion. arXiv preprint arXiv:2008.10833 (2020)
52. Zhou, J., et al.: Graph neural networks: a review of methods and applications. arXiv preprint arXiv:1812.08434 (2018)

Objects Can Move: 3D Change Detection by Geometric Transformation Consistency

Aikaterini Adam[1,2(✉)], Torsten Sattler[1], Konstantinos Karantzalos[2], and Tomas Pajdla[1]

[1] Czech Institute of Informatics, Robotics and Cybernetics, CTU in Prague, Prague, Czechia
{Aikaterini.Adam,Torsten.Sattler,pajdla}@cvut.cz
[2] National Technical University of Athens, Athens, Greece
karank@scentral.ntua.gr

Abstract. AR/VR applications and robots need to know when the scene has changed. An example is when objects are moved, added, or removed from the scene. We propose a 3D object discovery method that is based only on scene changes. Our method does not need to encode any assumptions about what is an object, but rather discovers objects by exploiting their coherent move. Changes are initially detected as differences in the depth maps and segmented as objects if they undergo rigid motions. A graph cut optimization propagates the changing labels to geometrically consistent regions. Experiments show that our method achieves state-of-the-art performance on the 3RScan dataset against competitive baselines. The source code of our method can be found at https://github.com/katadam/ObjectsCanMove.

Keywords: 3D change detection · Object discovery · Graph optimization

1 Introduction

The ability to detect and interact with objects is critical to AR/VR applications and for multiple robotics tasks, such as surveillance, robotic manipulation, and maintaining order. All these tasks are operated in the same setting. Thus, the robot, or the AR/VR device stores a reference map and builds a new map upon each revisit. However, in-between the revisits, certain objects may have changed. Checking for scene consistency and detecting changes on an object-level can thus lead to 3D object discovery, without the need of labeled data.

Motivated by the above, we explore an object discovery approach, based on examining scene consistency on an object-level and without using annotated data. We are aiming at discovering entities (objects) that have changed when

Supplementary Information The online version contains supplementary material available at https://doi.org/10.1007/978-3-031-19827-4_7.

S. Avidan et al. (Eds.): ECCV 2022, LNCS 13693, pp. 108–124, 2022.
https://doi.org/10.1007/978-3-031-19827-4_7

revisiting a place. We show that it is possible to detect 3D objects purely geometrically, without a predefined notion of objects. The underlying idea is that objects, unlike the static background of a scene, can be moved. This is an intuitive definition of "objectness" that does not need any annonated data.

Segmenting dynamic objects in temporal observations is a long-standing challenge. There are two ways to apply this idea: (1) segment objects from the background by actively observing their motion, e.g., by reconstructing dynamic objects during SLAM [38], or (2) revisit the same scene after a (longer) period and detect potential objects as changes between two maps [12]. We follow the latter approach, i.e., we model the problem as a change detection task.

Detecting potential scene changes based on direct data analytics is a task attracting much attention since affordable 3D scanning technology [2,11,36] makes such data widely available. However, a straightforward approach to detecting changes between two scans based on voxel occupancy or inconsistency maps [25] would often miss changes, e.g., when an object rotates around an axis passing through the object or when it is "slid along itself". An alternative approach employs the comparison of visual features and relies on photoconsistency constraints [32]. Yet, this approach does not perform well in our setting since there can be significant illumination changes between the two maps.

To tackle the aforementioned shortcomings, we introduce a novel change detection framework, depicted in Fig. 1, that uses geometric transformation consistency towards object discovery (i.e., change detection on an object-level). 3D

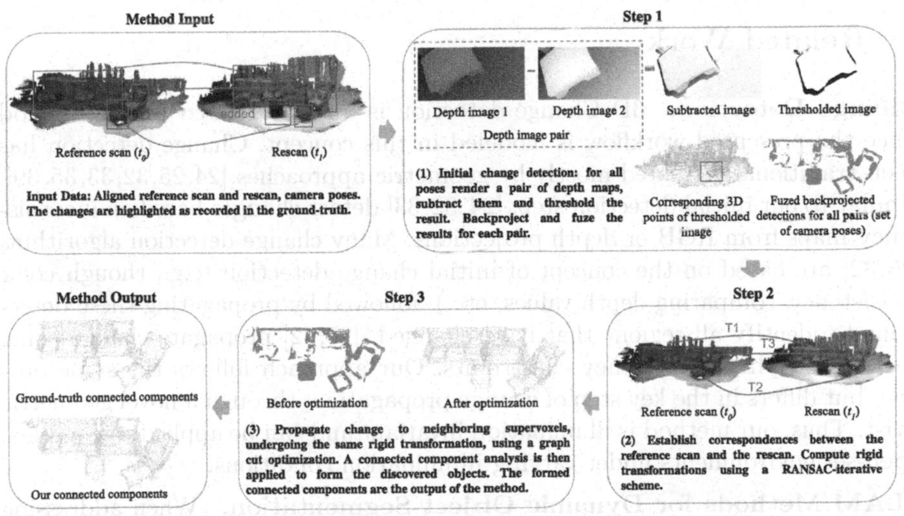

Fig. 1. Workflow of the proposed method: given two scans recording changes and the associated camera poses, we discover all objects that have been added, moved, or removed from the scene. Initial geometric changes are detected as differences in depth maps (Step 1). The dominant transformations are then computed (Step 2). The initial set of detections is incomplete and thus refined, using a graph cut-based optimization on a supervoxel representation, propagating change to all regions undergoing the same transformation (Step 3). Discovered objects are presented as the extracted connected components of the refined detections

objects are thus discovered without the need to encode what an object is. We consider a scenario where we have two 3D maps, i.e., a reference scan (recorded at time t_0) and a rescan (recorded at time t_1), of a scene, as well as the associated camera poses. Initial change detections are computed as differences in the depth maps. As shown in Figs. 1 and 2, the initial detected points mainly delineate the boundaries of the moved objects. To recover all parts, we propagate changes from regions where we can detect them to parts where no changes were seen, but which belong to the same object. Our local robust feature matching between parts of the two scans generates motion hypotheses for the scene parts, induced by the moved objects. These motions can measure consistency as scene parts that undergo the same rigid transformation.

Contributions. We introduce a novel 3D change detection framework via geometric transformation consistency. As change detection is performed on an object-level, this novel framework serves as an object discovery method in 3D scenes, without needing any strong priors or definition of what objects are. We showcase that even though we target rigid objects/changes, our method can also handle non-rigid changes, as shown in Fig. 4. The proposed method achieves state-of-the-art performance on the 3RScan dataset [36], against competitive baselines.

We evaluate our framework on the 3RScan dataset [36], initially designed for benchmarking object instance relocalization. Our evaluation shows the potential of the dataset to assess 3D change detection. We provide code to generate the ground truth annotations.

2 Related Work

Change Detection. 3D Change detection is directly related to our method since the presented workflow is modeled in this concept. Change detection has been traditionally treated mostly by geometric approaches [24,25,32,33,35,39]. Similar to our initial detection step, [24,32,33] detect changes based on inconsistency maps from RGB or depth projections. Many change detection algorithms [26,32] are based on the concept of initial change detection (e.g., though color consistency, comparing depth values, etc.), followed by propagating these detections to identify all regions that have changed. [26,32] propagate change using spatial and photoconsistency constraints. Our approach follows the same outline, but differs in the key step of change propagation, through a novel geometric twist. Thus, our method is illumination invariant and can be applied to complex, open-set environments under varying illumination conditions.

SLAM Methods for Dynamic Object Segmentation. When addressing dynamic scenes, tracking dynamic objects can be part of SLAM-based techniques. In [1], dynamic parts of the scenes are recovered and a classifier is trained on them to distinguish between static and non-static parts. Semantic SLAM for dynamic environments is presented in [7,8]. In [29], the authors first segment objects and track them separately. In a similar vein to our research, [10,14,23] aim at discovering objects through change observation on an object-level. However, these works build their methods upon a SLAM-based basis. Our method is complementary to SLAM-based techniques since these methods demand the recording of the object's actual movement in front of the camera. On the other hand, our method needs two 3D models (reference scan and rescan), and the associated camera poses, which are acquired over long time intervals. Thus, objects might have moved, appeared, or disappeared without their movement being explicitly recorded.

3D Object Discovery. Our problem can be conceived as a 3D object discovery technique when declaring as an object everything that can be moved, since movement is an inherent property of objects. Concerning unsupervised object discovery, the authors of [16] focus on identifying parts of the input mesh as candidate objects. They then classify them as an object or clutter. More similarly to our work, [20,21] extract as objects all the novel additions to the scene. Indeed, by scene comparison, they discover and label as an object anything that has been added between two scans. In contrast, our proposed method does not restrict itself only to added objects, but rather discovers all the objects that have changed (added, moved or removed).

3 Detection via Geometric Consistency

Our method aims at detecting changes on an object-level, thus leading to object discovery, without relying on annotated data. Given two 3D scans, i.e., a reference scan and a rescan, and the associated camera poses, we propose three discrete steps, as illustrated in Fig. 1: (1) initial change detection, i.e., compute the locations where a change might have occured, (2) compute dominant transformations, and (3) graph optimization to ensure geometrical transformation consistency. Differences in depth maps provide an initial but incomplete set of detections later refined using a graph cut-based optimization. The central insight is that scene parts that belong to the same object should undergo the same physical transformation, which we model through a novel geometric transformation consistency measure. A connected component analysis is then applied to form the discovered objects.

Initial changes are calculated by depth map comparison. Given a reference scan S of the scene and a rescan R aligned to each other, we render and subtract depth maps. Their subtraction records changing depth values and thus indicates changed regions. However, due to the way the objects move, it is difficult to retrieve the whole object via this single step (as illustrated in Fig. 2). To tackle this limitation, we integrate graph optimization [19], performed on supervoxels [27]. Instead of using a simple voxel representation of the scene, we firstly compute supervoxels, i.e., irregular clusters of 3D points sharing common geometrical and color characteristics. Optimizing this representation leads to more accurate results, since supervoxels separate the 3D space into elements, by clustering points with same properties. This is not the case for voxels that are created solely on spatial relations of the 3D points. Moreover, as supervoxels are irregular patches of 3D points, they can preserve objects' boundaries, contrary to the simple voxel representation.

Graph optimization aims to enforce consistency for all the regions undergoing the same rigid transformation. This will help us discover parts of the moving object that may have been missed during the initial detection step. The change is propagated to all the supervoxels undergoing the same movement. From the above, it is clear that two steps are needed before the optimization: (1) initial change detection, and (2) computation of all the dominant transformations induced by moved objects. Towards the latter goal, learned descriptors [28] are extracted for each point in the scans. We use a pre-trained model, trained on a completely different task (i.e., semantic segmentation). Matches are then computed using nearest neighbor search [15]. The resulting correspondences are used to calculate the 3D transformations.

Scan Alignment. Works and datasets [12,36] exploring changing indoor scenes demand the two scans to be registered. These datasets provide information for the alignment since registering the scans is outside the scope of their research. Similarly to these works, we use the initial alignment provided by the dataset, which was obtained via manual annotations and is imperfect. In practical applications, the alignment could be provided by re-localization to the previous scan, or by estimating the overall transformation via feature matching [3].

3.1 Initial Change Detection

The first step of our method is identifying changing regions, which we will refine via a graph optimization. Initial change detection is based on depth map comparison. We render depth maps $\mathcal{D}_{S,1,..,N}$, $\mathcal{D}_{R,1,..,N}$ from the reference scan S and the rescan R respectively, for all the viewpoints $i = 1, 2, .., N$, using the $\mathbf{P}_{1,..,N}$ projection matrices. Multiple poses cover the whole 3D scene. We use the same poses to render both the reference scan S and the rescan R, as we assume that both scans are already aligned, even if captured from different viewpoints. We render the depth images rather than simply use raw depth measurements captured by a device to ensure the best possible quality. Moreover, we use depth maps instead of directly working on the mesh, allowing us to handle occlusions and partial observations more naturally than in the 3D space. Working on depth images provides information about free space, which is not directly included in the mesh. Indeed, rendering depth allows us to know if the corresponding 3D region has been scanned or not. If one of the depth images does not contain information, we exclude this region from the initial change detection. This procedure is not straightforward in the mesh, as an intermediate step such as calculating the bounding box of the scan or computing overlapping regions would be needed to ensure that partial observations and free space is taken into consideration. Rendered maps from the reference scan and the rescan are shown in Fig. 1. Lighter regions correspond to regions that lie closer to the camera. The paired depth maps are subtracted, and the result is thresholded using [4].

The result is a binary mask, encoding information about changing regions, which are back-projected to the 3D space:

$$[X, Y, Z]^T = \mathbf{R}^T \cdot (\mathbf{K}^{-1} \cdot [x, y, 1]^T \cdot D(x, y) - \mathbf{Tr}) \ , \tag{1}$$

where $[X, Y, Z]$ stands for the world-coordinates of the 3D point, $\mathbf{R}$ for the rotation matrix, $\mathbf{K}$ for the calibration matrix and $\mathbf{Tr}$ for the translation vector, all forming the projection matrix $\mathbf{P} = \mathbf{K}[\mathbf{R}|\mathbf{Tr}]$. Vector $[x, y, 1]$ represents the pixel coordinates and $D_{1,..,N}(x, y)$ the depth value stemming from the combination of the depth of the reference scan and the depth of the rescan:

$$D(x,y)_{1,..,N} = \begin{cases} D(x,y)_{S,1,..,N} & \text{if } D(x,y)_{S,1,..,N} < D(x,y)_{R,1,..,N} \\ D(x,y)_{R,1,..,N} & \text{if } D(x,y)_{S,1,..,N} > D(x,y)_{R,1,..,N} \end{cases}. \tag{2}$$

$D(x, y)_{1,..,N}$ represents the depth value at position (x, y) for the combined masks $1, .., N$, $D(x, y)_{S,1,..,N}$ the depth value at position (x, y) for the $1, .., N$ rendered depth maps of the reference scan S and $D(x, y)_{R,1,..,N}$ the depth value of the rendered $1, .., N$ depth maps of the rescan R. This formulation always selects the closest objects to the camera. After experiments, we concluded that in 97% of examined cases, the smaller depth value corresponds to an object. In contrast, the larger depth corresponds to the static background. Figures 1 and 2 depict all the initial points labeled as changing for example scenes. Finally, as the graph optimization is applied to the supervoxel representation, the supervoxels for the scan and the rescan are extracted [27] and the number of changing points belonging to each supervoxel is computed.

3.2 Computing Dominant Transformations

As seen in Figs. 1-Before optimization, 2-Initial detected points, our initial detection step may miss changes due to occluded parts of the objects, objects partially captured in one of the scans or due to the way objects have moved. Indeed, when an object is only slightly moved or rotated, there can be regions where the depth values do not change, e.g., when a couch is only slightly shifted. As a result, the initial detections might only cover part of the object. To this end, we use a graph optimization to propagate change detection to the rest of the objects based on consistency under geometric transformations $\mathbf{T}$. We thus compute the different 3D rigid transformations $\mathbf{T}$, induced by the moving objects. Towards that, we match feature descriptors between scans.

Descriptors can be computed using hand-crafted features, such as FPFH [30] and SHOT [34], or learned features. In our case, we use features extracted from the encoder part of a pre-trained deep network. A forward-pass was deployed to densely extract descriptors from the scans, using the weights of pre-trained models on a semantic segmentation task. The models we are using are trained for a completely different task and dataset. Yet, using learned features does not affect our assertion of presenting an unsupervised method.

Correspondences were then computed over the entire scene, using the nearest neighbor search. Visualizing correspondences for the different features showed that the pre-trained Dynamic Graph CNN (DGCNN) [37] had the best preliminary results. To remove outliers from the matches, and given that we want to establish correspondences only between moving objects, we eliminate correspondences lying within a predefined distance of each other in 3D, as these points are considered part of the static background. All the valid correspondences are then employed to compute the potential transformations using RANSAC [5]. We iteratively apply RANSAC on the remaining set of matches after removing the inliers of the previous estimate and stop once less than three matches remain. Since this method will generate more transformations $\mathbf{T}$ than the real ones due to limitations in establishing correspondences, we will continue selecting the top k transformations $\mathbf{T}$, with the most inliers, to propagate change during graph optimization.

3.3 Supervoxel Graph Optimization

From the initial change detection (Sect. 3.1), we obtain an initial soft labeling L, based on the fraction of changing 3D points belonging to each supervoxel. Supervoxels with more points labeled as changing, during the initial change detection, are more likely to belong to an object. Thus, the initial labeling L determines the probability ρ of each supervoxel v_i to be labeled as changing $\rho(v_i, l_i = 1)$, or non changing $\rho(v_i, l_i = 0)$ as:

$$\rho(v_i, l_i = 1) = \begin{cases} 0.8 & \text{if changing points } \in v_i \\ 0.5 & \text{if changing points } \notin v_i \end{cases} , \tag{3}$$

$$\rho(v_i, l_i = 0) = \begin{cases} 0.2 & \text{if changing points } \in v_i \\ 0.5 & \text{if changing points } \notin v_i \end{cases} . \tag{4}$$

The weights used in Eqs. 3 and 4 were chosen based on experiments with different values on a set of scans used for tuning hyperparameters (cf. Sect. 4). From the above, it is clear that we treat supervoxels with no detected changing points as equally likely of having changed. Indeed, supervoxels without any detected changing points do not necessarily correspond to static scene parts. We thus decide whether a supervoxel belongs to a moving object or not by solving a graph optimization problem [19] that allows us to propagate changes between supervoxels, conditioned on a rigid transformation $\mathbf{T}$.

To deploy the optimization, we create an undirected graph $\mathcal{G} = (V, E)$. Each node $v \in V$ corresponds to a supervoxel in the scene. Two nodes v_i and v_j are connected through an edge $\{v_i, v_j\} \in E$ if the corresponding supervoxels are adjacent to each other. Given a rigid transformation $\mathbf{T}$ (cf. Sect. 3.2) between the rescan and the reference, our goal is to compute an optimised binary labeling $\mathcal{L}^* = \{l_i^*\}_i$. This labeling indicates for each supervoxel whether it belongs to a changing object consistent with $\mathbf{T}$ (and thus is labeled as $l_i^* = 1$) or not ($l_i^* = 0$). We compute this labeling by solving the graph optimization problem [19]:

$$L^* \in \underset{Q \in \Omega^v}{\arg\min}\{\Phi(L, Q) + \lambda \Psi(Q)\} . \tag{5}$$

Φ stands for the fidelity term (here, we use the Kullback-Leibler fidelity function [18]), Ψ for the regularizer, λ for the regularization strength, and Ω for the search space. The fidelity term $\Phi(L, Q)$ enforces the influence of the initial labeling L, i.e., it decreases when Q lies closer to L. The regularizer $\Psi(Q)$ favors geometrically smooth solutions, i.e., it enforces smoothness to all neighboring supervoxels v_i and v_j, undergoing the same transformation $\mathbf{T}$. $\Psi(Q)$is based on a Potts penalty function:

$$\Psi_{Potts}(Q) = \begin{cases} 1 & \text{if } v_i, v_j \text{ consistent under } \mathbf{T} \\ 0 & \text{otherwise} \end{cases} . \tag{6}$$

It is important to note here that the energy function from Eq. 5 is conditioned on each computed transformation $\mathbf{T}$. Thus, we iterate through the top k computed dominant transformations and we solve a series of graph cuts problems. Each iteration segments out the object undergoing the specific transformation $\mathbf{T}$. Objects added or removed, for which a transformation $\mathbf{T}$ is not established, are solely retrieved, based on the unary potentials of the optimization. The results of the iterative procedure, i.e., the set of points labeled as changing, are finally fused. A connected component analysis is finally applied to the fused results, to discover the final 3D objects. Connected component analysis is crucial to form the 3D added or removed objects that are not conditioned on a transformation, but also to overcome the problem of over-segmentation when slightly different transformations are computed for the same object. Optimization results are illustrated in Figs. 1, 2 and 3.

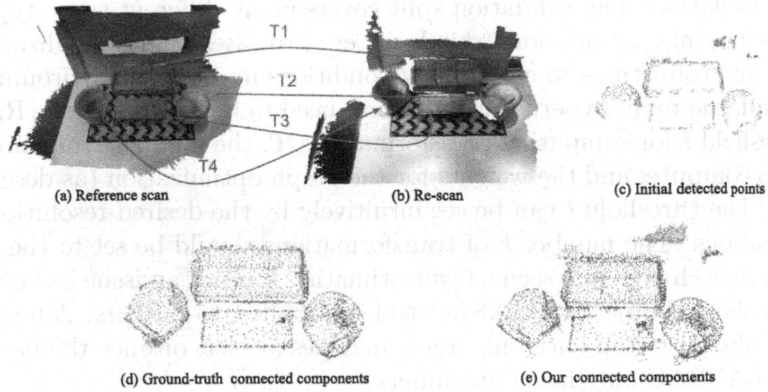

Fig. 2. Our approach: given two scans depicting a scene that has potentially changed, we discover all changes on an object-level. We initially detect potentially changed scene parts by comparing depth maps. We then propagate changes and segment out changed regions based on the principle of geometric transformation consistency. (a) Reference scan (b) Rescan (c) Initially detected areas, with false detections on the wall due to misalignments between the scans. (d) Ground truth connected components and (e) connected components detected by our approach

4 Experimental Evaluation

Datasets. To assess the performance of the proposed approach, we have conducted experiments using the 3RScan dataset [36]. The dataset comprises individual rooms, capturing natural changing indoor environments. It provides, apart from the 3D meshes of the reference scans and the rescans, a series of RGB-D images captured by a Google Tango mobile phone and information concerning objects that have changed between the scenes, along with corresponding transformations. The experiments have been conducted on the validation subset of the dataset comprising 47 different reference scans and 110 rescans. It is important to note that the 3RScan dataset was built initially for object instance relocalization tasks. Therefore, we had to generate the ground truth data for the changing objects based on the dataset's supplementary information. The code is publicly available at https://github.com/katadam/ObjectsCanMove, to enable the usage of this dataset for benchmarking indoor 3D change detection.

To the best of our knowledge, there is no other appropriatbe benchmark to assess 3D indoor change detection and 3D object discovery. Relevant works evaluate their methods on their own datasets, which are either not publicly available [10,17,21] or are very small and require manual labeling, as they do not provide appropriate annotations [1,9,23]. Please refer to the SM for specific information on discarded datasets.

Hyperparameter Tuning. Ten randomly selected scans from the training split of 3RScan were used for parameter tuning, while the validation split was used for evaluation. The validation split covers many different scene types (i.e., offices, restaurants, living rooms, kitchens, etc.) to assess the generalization performance and robustness to challenging conditions and unseen environments. In our method, the main hyperparameters that need to be tuned are: the RANSAC inlier threshold t for computing transformations $\mathbf{T}$, the number k of transformations $\mathbf{T}$ to compute, and the weights for the graph optimization (as described in Sect. 3.3). The threshold t can be set intuitively by the desired resolution of the transformations. The number k of transformations should be set to the number of objects that change in a scene. Overestimating k is not an issue as beyond the actual number of objects, RANSAC will be applied to outliers. Alternatively, one could also just stop once only a few matches are left or once the best model found by RANSAC only has a few inliers.

Baseline Methods. To compare the performance of our novel framework against a competitive set of other methods, we have searched for appropriate baselines. However, we had to discard some works treating indoor change detection and unsupervised object discovery, since they are not directly comparable to our method. More particularly, the input to our method are two scans, with changes between them but no recorded actual motion in front of the camera. As such, it is complementary to SLAM methodologies and technologies built upon SLAM systems [1,9,10,14]. Moreover, even though [12,36] deploy their methods on changing indoor scenes, they focus on instance segmentation and object instance re-localization, respectively. Thus, they cannot be evaluated against our

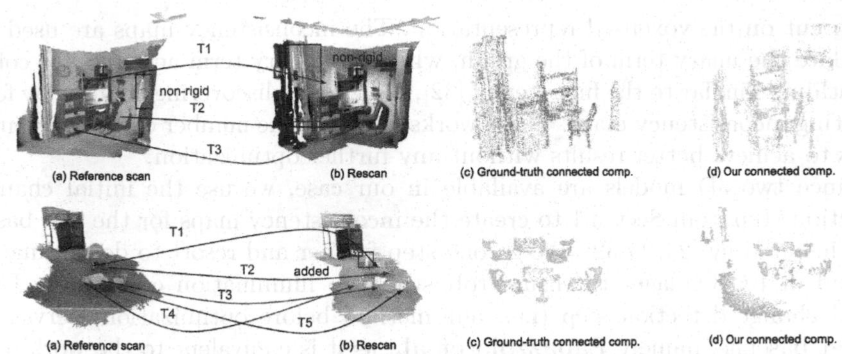

Fig. 3. Qualitative evaluation of the proposed method. Given two scans (a reference scan (a) and a rescan (b)), we perform change detection on an object-level basis, to discover 3D objects. We visualise the final results after applying connected component analysis to the ground truth (c) and to our detected changes (d)

change detection task. Approaches like [20,23] integrate semantics, contrary to our approach that discovers object-level changes without having a predefined notion of what an object is. The input of [17] is data from range sensors and a highly precise 3D map created by a 3D laser scanner, which is not the case for the 3RScan dataset. [21] aims only at discovering novel objects in the scene, while our approach retrieves all the changed objects. Towards that, we have created a sub-task of discovering only added objects and compare against [21]. Results are available in the SM. Finally, since we aim at change detection on an object-level towards unsupervised object discovery, we compared against an unsupervised 3D object discovery method [16]. [16] first discovers segments and then classifies them into objects and non-objects. However, the segments obtained via the authors' code after tuning parameter were not meaningful and we were not able to avoid a severe oversegmentation. Thus, we did not include the metrics in our experimental results. For visualizations please refer to the SM.

Our approach is mainly inspired by the change detection approach from [24, 25,32]. To the best of our knowledge, these are the most closely related baseline and one of our motivations to redefine this problem in a new framework by taking advantage of modern representations (i.e., supervoxels) and more recent graph optimization algorithms [19]. Similar to our work, [24,25,32] are also focusing on unsupervised change detection. Taking all the above into consideration, we have decided to create two main baselines inspired by these works.

In [32], change detection is based on inconsistency maps, formed by subtracting pairs of images taken at different points in time. The newly acquired image is warped into the old one, using the known 3D scene geometry and the known poses of both images with respect to the scene. Assuming similar illumination conditions, the two images should be identical if no change in the geometry has happened. In turn, changes in scene geometry will lead to inconsistent projections from one image into the other. Change detection is then optimized via a graph cut on the voxelized representation. The inconsistency maps are used to calculate the unary term of the graph, while the binary term accounts for color smoothing. Similar to the first step of [32], [24,25] are discovering changes by formulating inconsistency maps. These works augment the number of inconsistency maps to achieve better results without any further optimization.

Since two 3D models are available in our case, we use the initial change detection step from Sect. 3.1 to create the inconsistency maps for the two baselines inspired by [24,25,32]. We go one step further and resort to depth images instead of RGB images to ensure robustness to illumination conditions. This initial change detection step (i.e., our method before optimization) serves as the 1st baseline, namely **Papazzolo et al.**, as it is equivalent to the work presented in [24,25]. In these works, estimation of 3D change detection results from back-projecting inconsistencies from multiple 2D maps.

A 2nd baseline (**Taneja et al.**) is formed, following [32], where the initial change detection is optimized ensuring color consistency on a voxelized representation of the scene via a graph cut optimization (solved by max-flow algorithm [6]). The binary term of the graph is computed as described in Eq. 7:

$$\psi_{ij}(l_i, l_j) = [l_i \neq l_j] \cdot \gamma / (\sum_{I_t} ||v_t^i - v_t^j||^2 + 1), \tag{7}$$

where $||v_t^i - v_t^j||^2$ accounts for the L2-norm between RGB values of voxels v_t^i and v_t^j and γ is a regularization factor. Comparing against this baseline shows the impact of using geometric consistency for propagating change, which is the main technical contribution of this work.

Ablation Study. Three more baselines are formed in the form of an ablation study, for a better insight into the proposed method. Ablation baselines are reporting intermediate results of our framework. They also calculate the metrics when the method has access to more information, in order to test its robustness with respect to different parameters. Removing the optimization part of our method and relying only on initial change detection is equivalent to [25] and thus reported in Table 1. The first ablation baseline (**ground truth transforms.**) ensures geometric consistency using the ground truth transformations provided by the dataset instead of our computed ones. This gives an upper bound to the performance we can achieve and helps measure the impact of estimated transformation's accuracy on the overall system's efficiency.

As the 2nd ablation baseline (**RANSAC inliers**), closely related to [31], we present the metrics of the non-static points used to form the matches and compute the rigid transformations **T**. This is equivalent to only the second step of our method (Sect. 3.2), without the initial change detection and the graph optimization. Ideally, each set of inliers consistent with each RANSAC execution would form the corresponding object moved under this transformation.

Finally, as the 3rd ablation baseline (**Mask-RCNN**), we add a semantic component to the formulated algorithm, as we would like to get an idea of how well our approach performs with respect to a supervised method. Thus, we replace our novel geometric consistency-based term with a term based on

(a) Reference scan

(b) Re-scan

(c) Overlaid scans

(d) Detected changes

Fig. 4. A non-rigid change (curtain) is not recorded in the ground truth. The curtain is different between the reference (a) and rescan (b), as shown when the two scans are overlaid in (c). The detected changes are shown with red colour in (d), overlaid on the reference scan in blue (Color figure online)

Table 1. Mean IoU and mean recall for the proposed method and the published baselines

Method	IoU(%)	Recall(%)
Palazzolo et al. [25] / Ours bf optim.	54.23%	31.48%
Taneja et al. [32]	48.10%	44.50%
Our method	68.40%	76.05%

Table 2. Mean IoU and mean recall for the proposed method and the ablation study's baselines

Method	IoU(%)	Recall(%)
Our method	68.40%	76.05%
Ground truth transforms.	72.40%	93.89%
Mask-RCNN	52.96%	89.22%
RANSAC inliers	10.82%	29.50%

the instance labels of Mask-RCNN [13], propagating the change to all regions sharing the same semantic label. Mask-RCNN is a powerful method for 2D object detection. We deploy the 2D object detector, trained on the COCO dataset [22], on the RGB images of each rescan.

Experimental Results. In addition to the qualitative results presented in Figs. 1, 2, 3, we rigorously evaluate our method by using metrics that capture the success of 3D change detection and 3D object discovery. Since we are aiming at object discovery through change detection on an object-level basis, we should first evaluate the efficiency of our change detection results. Thus, we calculate the metric of recall, on a voxel basis. Recall aims to calculate how many of the ground truth changed voxels have been correctly retrieved.

Moving on to 3D object discovery, a 3D connected components analysis is applied to the change detection results. To assess the efficiency of the proposed method as an object discovery pipeline, we deploy the metric of Interestion Over Union (IoU) per discovered object, as it encapsulates both the metrics of precision and recall. To calculate this metric, the connected component analysis is also applied to the ground truth changes. For our scenario, this analysis was performed on a voxel grid of 10 cm, which could sometimes merge objects that lie together into a single component. This does not affect our metrics since the same connected component analysis is applied both to the ground truth and our solution. However, a smaller step size would lead to a more refined and detailed object discovery. The parameter can be tuned based on the size of the objects we want to discover. We consider an object as successfully discovered when the metric of IoU is more than 20%. The metrics are calculated at a voxel-level since we are interested in measuring how two objects (volumes) intersect.

Tables 1 and 2 show the mean recall over all the scans and the mean IoU of discovered objects. After close examination, it is clear that our method outperforms the most competitive baseline based on [32] by roughly 30% in terms of recall. It also improves the mean IoU by almost 20%. This shows that not only supervoxels constitute a more efficient representation compared to single voxels, when it comes to graph optimization, but also that the novel geometric transformation consistency is much more successful for propagating change, compared to photoconsistency. Moreover, evaluation metrics before and after graph optimization, demonstrate the importance of the optimization, as it improves the mean IoU by 14.17% and the mean recall by 44.57%. As explained above, the method presented in [24,25] is equivalent to the first step of our method, thus showing improved performance of our presented framework over all published baselines. Integrating a voxel graph cut optimization, propagating change to color-consistent regions [32], leads to better recall rates, but lower IoU, as change is in some cases overpropagated, resulting in low precision, an thus failure of discovering the objects, in terms of IoU.

Concerning the ablation, as denoted by the results of the MASK-RCNN baseline, adding a semantic component is not improving the overall performance. The MASK-RCNN baseline is capable of achieving a mean IoU of 52.96% and a mean recall of 89.22%. This can be attributed to noisy RGB-D images, leading to inaccurate segmentations. Indeed, background patches are falsely detected as foreground objects. Thus, change is propagated into a large percentage of the scene's background, leading to a higher recall rate, compared with a relatively low precision, and thus IoU. The solution using the ground truth transformation (baseline ground truth transforms.) is in close proximity with our method in terms of recall. Even a coarser estimation of the rigid transformation of the scene is capable of achieving close to the best possible results. However, there is still space for improvement, regarding the computation of transformations. The mean IoU of 72.40% in this baseline, is explained due to initial false detections, caused by occlusions and misalignments between scans. The experimental results indicate that the two scans need to be correctly registered to avoid false initial detections. False initial detections are merged with correctly estimated regions, reducing the IoU score. Finally, it is worth mentioning that using only non-static parts discovered by RANSAC iterations leads to results worse than our solution before graph cuts optimization. This explicitly demonstrates that the straightforward approach of feature matching and computing sets of motion-consistent points is insufficient.

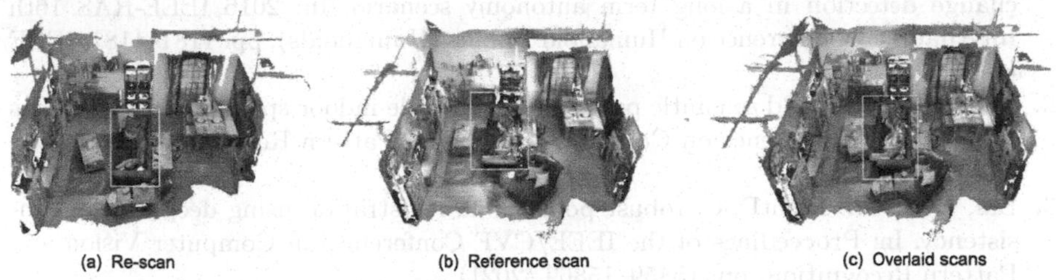

Fig. 5. A moved couch between the reference scan (a) and the rescan (b) that is not part of the ground truth annotations. Overlaid scans in (c)

Finally, 3RScan is a dataset built towards assessing object instance relocalization and not exhaustive change detection. Thus, our method uncovers changes between the scans not recorded in the ground truth. Such cases would affect the evaluation metrics, and we wanted to check their extent. We randomly selected a subset of 10 rescans and visually inspected them. In 60.00% of cases, we discovered an unrecorded change (see, for example, Fig. 5). The proposed approach has correctly detected 66,67% of these cases. Moreover, an example of a non-rigid and not recorded change is depicted in Fig. 4.

Limitations. By definition of discovering objects via change detection, we will miss objects that do not undergo a substantial enough change. Using a stricter threshold for distinguishing between inliers and outliers in the RANSAC scheme could help recover even small motions. Moreover, depth map subtraction could lead to false initial change detection when the two scans are not entirely aligned. A typical example is illustrated in the second row of Fig. 3. Parts of the floor are labeled as changing, forming a 3D object due to the scan's misalignment.

5 Conclusion

The presented method achieves state-of-the-art performance on the object discovery task, via change detection on an object-level basis, for the 3RScan dataset against a competitive set of baselines. The method shows the surprising effectiveness of using scene change for high-recall object discovery and of using motion constraints to achieve precise detections. The very general assumption that objects are connected and move in a coherent way is used to propagate initial detections. Importantly, these geometric cues can be discovered directly from unannotated data, so they do not introduce strong priors or any memorization of what objects are.

Acknowledgements. This research was supported by projects EU RDF IMPACT No. CZ.02.1.01/0.0/0.0/15_003/0000468, EU H2020 ARtwin No. 856994 and the EU Horizon 2020 project RICAIP (grant agreement No 857306).

References

1. Ambrus, R., Folkesson, J., Jensfelt, P.: Unsupervised object segmentation through change detection in a long term autonomy scenario. In: 2016 IEEE-RAS 16th International Conference on Humanoid Robots (Humanoids), pp. 1181–1187. IEEE (2016)
2. Armeni, I., et al.: 3d semantic parsing of large-scale indoor spaces. In: Proceedings of the IEEE Conference on Computer Vision and Pattern Recognition, pp. 1534–1543 (2016)
3. Bai, X., et al.: PointDSC: robust point cloud registration using deep spatial consistency. In: Proceedings of the IEEE/CVF Conference on Computer Vision and Pattern Recognition, pp. 15859–15869 (2021)
4. Barron, J.T.: A generalization of Otsu's method and minimum error thresholding. In: Vedaldi, A., Bischof, H., Brox, T., Frahm, J.-M. (eds.) ECCV 2020. LNCS, vol. 12350, pp. 455–470. Springer, Cham (2020). https://doi.org/10.1007/978-3-030-58558-7_27
5. Bolles, R.C., Fischler, M.A.: A RANSAC-based approach to model fitting and its application to finding cylinders in range data. In: IJCAI, vol. 1981, pp. 637–643. Citeseer (1981)
6. Boykov, Y., Kolmogorov, V.: An experimental comparison of min-cut/max-flow algorithms for energy minimization in vision. IEEE Trans. Pattern Anal. Mach. Intell. **26**(9), 1124–1137 (2004)
7. Brasch, N., Bozic, A., Lallemand, J., Tombari, F.: Semantic monocular slam for highly dynamic environments. In: 2018 IEEE/RSJ International Conference on Intelligent Robots and Systems (IROS), pp. 393–400. IEEE (2018)
8. Cui, L., Ma, C.: SOF-SLAM: a semantic visual slam for dynamic environments. IEEE Access **7**, 166528–166539 (2019)
9. Fehr, M., et al.: TSDF-based change detection for consistent long-term dense reconstruction and dynamic object discovery. In: 2017 IEEE International Conference on Robotics and automation (ICRA), pp. 5237–5244. IEEE (2017)
10. Finman, R., Whelan, T., Kaess, M., Leonard, J.J.: Toward lifelong object segmentation from change detection in dense RGB-D maps. In: 2013 European Conference on Mobile Robots, pp. 178–185. IEEE (2013)
11. Glocker, B., Izadi, S., Shotton, J., Criminisi, A.: Real-time RGB-D camera relocalization. In: 2013 IEEE International Symposium on Mixed and Augmented Reality (ISMAR), pp. 173–179. IEEE (2013)
12. Halber, M., Shi, Y., Xu, K., Funkhouser, T.: Rescan: inductive instance segmentation for indoor RGBD scans. In: Proceedings of the IEEE/CVF International Conference on Computer Vision, pp. 2541–2550 (2019)
13. He, K., Gkioxari, G., Dollár, P., Girshick, R.: Mask R-CNN. In: Proceedings of the IEEE International Conference on Computer Vision, pp. 2961–2969 (2017)
14. Herbst, E., Henry, P., Ren, X., Fox, D.: Toward object discovery and modeling via 3-d scene comparison. In: 2011 IEEE International Conference on Robotics and Automation, pp. 2623–2629. IEEE (2011)
15. Johnson, J., Douze, M., Jégou, H.: Billion-scale similarity search with GPUs. arXiv preprint arXiv:1702.08734 (2017)
16. Karpathy, A., Miller, S., Fei-Fei, L.: Object discovery in 3d scenes via shape analysis. In: 2013 IEEE International Conference on Robotics and Automation, pp. 2088–2095. IEEE (2013)

17. Katsura, U., Matsumoto, K., Kawamura, A., Ishigami, T., Okada, T., Kurazume, R.: Spatial change detection using normal distributions transform. ROBOMECH J. **6**(1), 1–13 (2019). https://doi.org/10.1186/s40648-019-0148-8
18. Kullback, S., Leibler, R.A.: On information and sufficiency. Ann. Math. Stat. **22**(1), 79–86 (1951)
19. Landrieu, L., Obozinski, G.: Cut pursuit: Fast algorithms to learn piecewise constant functions on general weighted graphs. SIAM J. Imag. Sci. **10**(4), 1724–1766 (2017)
20. Langer, E., Patten, T., Vincze, M.: Robust and efficient object change detection by combining global semantic information and local geometric verification. In: 2020 IEEE/RSJ International Conference on Intelligent Robots and Systems (IROS), pp. 8453–8460. IEEE (2020)
21. Langer, E., Ridder, B., Cashmore, M., Magazzeni, D., Zillich, M., Vincze, M.: On-the-fly detection of novel objects in indoor environments. In: 2017 IEEE International Conference on Robotics and Biomimetics (ROBIO), pp. 900–907. IEEE (2017)
22. Lin, T.-Y., et al.: Microsoft COCO: common objects in context. In: Fleet, D., Pajdla, T., Schiele, B., Tuytelaars, T. (eds.) ECCV 2014. LNCS, vol. 8693, pp. 740–755. Springer, Cham (2014). https://doi.org/10.1007/978-3-319-10602-1_48
23. Mason, J., Marthi, B.: An object-based semantic world model for long-term change detection and semantic querying. In: 2012 IEEE/RSJ International Conference on Intelligent Robots and Systems, pp. 3851–3858. IEEE (2012)
24. Palazzolo, E., Stachniss, C.: Change detection in 3d models based on camera images. In: 9th Workshop on Planning, Perception and Navigation for Intelligent Vehicles at the IEEE/RSJ International Conference on Intelligent Robots and Systems (IROS) (2017)
25. Palazzolo, E., Stachniss, C.: Fast image-based geometric change detection given a 3d model. In: 2018 IEEE International Conference on Robotics and Automation (ICRA), pp. 6308–6315. IEEE (2018)
26. Palma, G., Cignoni, P., Boubekeur, T., Scopigno, R.: Detection of geometric temporal changes in point clouds. In: Computer Graphics Forum, vol. 35, pp. 33–45. Wiley Online Library (2016)
27. Papon, J., Abramov, A., Schoeler, M., Worgotter, F.: Voxel cloud connectivity segmentation-supervoxels for point clouds. In: Proceedings of the IEEE Conference on Computer Vision and Pattern Recognition, pp. 2027–2034 (2013)
28. Phan, A.V., Le Nguyen, M., Nguyen, Y.L.H., Bui, L.T.: DGCNN: a convolutional neural network over large-scale labeled graphs. Neural Netw. **108**, 533–543 (2018)
29. Runz, M., Buffier, M., Agapito, L.: MaskFusion: real-time recognition, tracking and reconstruction of multiple moving objects. In: 2018 IEEE International Symposium on Mixed and Augmented Reality (ISMAR), pp. 10–20. IEEE (2018)
30. Rusu, R.B., Blodow, N., Beetz, M.: Fast point feature histograms (FPFH) for 3d registration. In: 2009 IEEE International Conference on Robotics and Automation, pp. 3212–3217. IEEE (2009)
31. Steinhauser, D., Ruepp, O., Burschka, D.: Motion segmentation and scene classification from 3d lidar data. In: 2008 IEEE Intelligent Vehicles Symposium, pp. 398–403. IEEE (2008)
32. Taneja, A., Ballan, L., Pollefeys, M.: Image based detection of geometric changes in urban environments. In: 2011 International Conference on Computer Vision, pp. 2336–2343. IEEE (2011)

33. Taneja, A., Ballan, L., Pollefeys, M.: City-scale change detection in cadastral 3d models using images. In: Proceedings of the IEEE Conference on Computer Vision and Pattern Recognition, pp. 113–120 (2013)
34. Tombari, F., Salti, S., Di Stefano, L.: Unique signatures of histograms for local surface description. In: Daniilidis, K., Maragos, P., Paragios, N. (eds.) ECCV 2010. LNCS, vol. 6313, pp. 356–369. Springer, Heidelberg (2010). https://doi.org/10.1007/978-3-642-15558-1_26
35. Ulusoy, A.O., Mundy, J.L.: Image-based 4-d reconstruction using 3-d change detection. In: Fleet, D., Pajdla, T., Schiele, B., Tuytelaars, T. (eds.) ECCV 2014. LNCS, vol. 8691, pp. 31–45. Springer, Cham (2014). https://doi.org/10.1007/978-3-319-10578-9_3
36. Wald, J., Avetisyan, A., Navab, N., Tombari, F., Nießner, M.: Rio: 3d object instance re-localization in changing indoor environments. In: Proceedings of the IEEE/CVF International Conference on Computer Vision, pp. 7658–7667 (2019)
37. Wang, Y., Sun, Y., Liu, Z., Sarma, S.E., Bronstein, M.M., Solomon, J.M.: Dynamic graph CNN for learning on point clouds. ACM Trans. Graph. (TOG) **38**(5), 1–12 (2019)
38. Wong, Y.S., Li, C., Niessner, M., Mitra, N.J.: RigidFusion: RGB-D scene reconstruction with rigidly-moving objects. Comput. Graph. Forum **40**(2), 511–522 (2021)
39. Xiao, W., Vallet, B., Paparoditis, N.: Change detection in 3d point clouds acquired by a mobile mapping system. ISPRS Ann. Photogramm. Remote Sens. Spat. Inf. Sci. **1**(2), 331–336 (2013)

Language-Grounded Indoor 3D Semantic Segmentation in the Wild

David Rozenberszki[1(✉)], Or Litany[2], and Angela Dai[1]

[1] Technical University of Munich, Munich, Germany
davidrozenberszki@gmail.com
[2] NVIDIA, Santa Clara, USA
https://rozdavid.github.io/scannet200

Abstract. Recent advances in 3D semantic segmentation with deep neural networks have shown remarkable success, with rapid performance increase on available datasets. However, current 3D semantic segmentation benchmarks contain only a small number of categories – less than 30 for ScanNet and SemanticKITTI, for instance, which are not enough to reflect the diversity of real environments (e.g., semantic image understanding covers hundreds to thousands of classes). Thus, we propose to study a larger vocabulary for 3D semantic segmentation with a new extended benchmark on ScanNet data with 200 class categories, an order of magnitude more than previously studied. This large number of class categories also induces a large natural class imbalance, both of which are challenging for existing 3D semantic segmentation methods. To learn more robust 3D features in this context, we propose a language-driven pre-training method to encourage learned 3D features that might have limited training examples to lie close to their pre-trained text embeddings. Extensive experiments show that our approach consistently outperforms state-of-the-art 3D pre-training for 3D semantic segmentation on our proposed benchmark (+9% relative mIoU), including limited-data scenarios with +25% relative mIoU using only 5% annotations.

Keywords: 3d semantic scene understanding · 3d semantic segmentation · 3d representation learning · Language + 3d vision

1 Introduction

In recent years, remarkable advances have been made in 3D semantic segmentation as a core task underlying 3D perception for myriad applications, including robotics, autonomous navigation, and mixed reality. The introduction of several large-scale real-world 3D datasets [1,4,10] has led to rapid developments in data-driven 3D deep learning techniques, with an emphasis on point- and sparse-voxel-based approaches [9,13,16,44,47] (Fig. 1). However, popular benchmarks

Supplementary Information The online version contains supplementary material available at https://doi.org/10.1007/978-3-031-19827-4_8.

S. Avidan et al. (Eds.): ECCV 2022, LNCS 13693, pp. 125–141, 2022.
https://doi.org/10.1007/978-3-031-19827-4_8

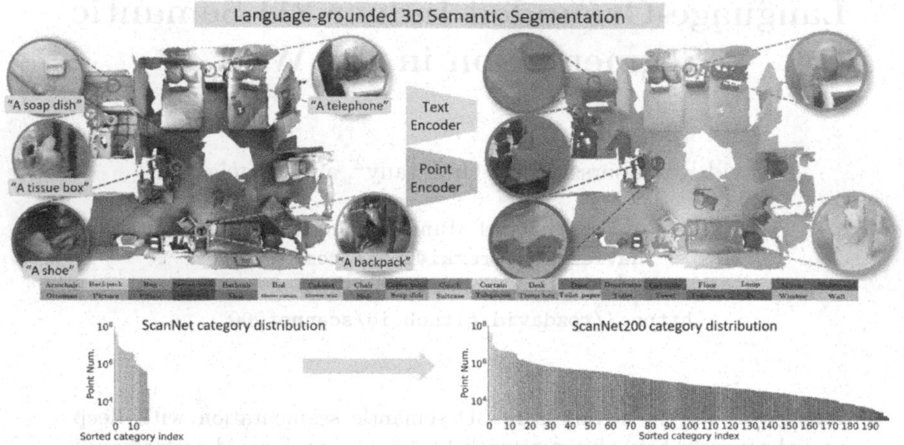

Fig. 1. We present the ScanNet200 benchmark, which studies 200-class 3D semantic segmentation - an order of magnitude more categories than previous 3D scene understanding benchmarks. To address this challenging task, we propose to guide 3D feature learning by anchoring it to the richly-structured text embedding space of CLIP for the semantic class labels. This results in improved 3D semantic segmentation across the large set of class categories.

such as ScanNet [10] or SemanticKITTI [1] focus on a limited number of class categories (20 and 28 classes, respectively), and thus these label sets do not well-represent the diversity and complexity of real scene content that would be encountered in the wild. In contrast, common image segmentation benchmarks [12,27] contain over 80 annotated class labels, with recent large-vocabulary image challenges [15] presenting over 1000 categories for recognition tasks.

Thus, we propose to address a larger-vocabulary setting for 3D semantic segmentation. In particular, we focus on the indoor domain and consider 3D scans of ScanNet [10] where a variety of different object categories are seen in the RGB-D scans despite its benchmark evaluating on only 20 classes. We present ScanNet200, a 200-class 3D semantic segmentation benchmark, considering an order of magnitude more class annotations than previously considered. This new set of classes includes both finer-grained categories of previous classes as well as a large number of previously unaddressed classes. This induces a much more challenging setting reflecting the naturally observed semantic classes already seen in the raw ScanNet RGB-D observations, where the data also reflects naturally encountered class imbalances (e.g., walls and floors are seen much more often than nightstands, which are also seen far more often than fire extinguishers). In addition considering the setting where all dense annotations are available for train scenes for the 200 classes, we also consider limited annotation scenarios with only sparse annotations per scene, given the expense of 3D data annotation.

In order to address this challenging new benchmark for 3D semantic segmentation, we explore standard techniques for data and loss balancing for the much larger number of class categories. In combination with the most effective techniques, we further observe that, unlike the limited, imbalanced geometric content, state-of-the-art language models have observed and attained rich representations of all categories, and so can induce a better structure onto learned 3D embeddings. Thus, we propose to ground 3D feature learning with strong pre-trained CLIP text features to construct a richly-structured 3D feature representation space. To this end, we formulate a language-grounded pre-training by mapping learned 3D features to pre-trained language embeddings with a contrastive loss. This enables a more robust 3D representation learning under imbalanced and limited 3D observations. Experiments on our ScanNet200 semantic segmentation as well as semantic segmentation in the limited data regime demonstrate the effectiveness of our language-grounded 3D semantic segmentation. In summary, our contributions are:

- We propose a new 200-class 3D semantic segmentation benchmark on real-world 3D ScanNet scene data, considering an order of magnitude more category annotation labels than existing 3D semantic segmentation benchmarks.
- In order to guide the construction of robust 3D semantic feature representations for this challenging task, we propose to align geometric feature extraction to the category embedding of the CLIP pretrained language model. This results in improved performance both overall and in the rarely seen, including in the limited-data regime.

2 Related Work

3D Semantic Segmentation. With the introduction of large-scale annotated real-world 3D datasets [1,4,10], 3D semantic segmentation has seen significant focus in recent years with various deep learning-based methods developed around different 3D representations. Early works tackled 3D semantic segmentation on dense volumetric grids [10,11], but were limited in cubic growth in memory and compute. The introduction of PointNet [38] presented a point-based alternative with strong memory efficiency by operating on unstructured point clouds, with various methods introducing local operators to better learn neighborhood structures [39,44,48]. Hierarchical grid structures such as octrees provided a more structured alternative for grid-based reasoning without dense memory consumption [42]. Recently, the introduction of sparse 3D convolutions [9,13] enabled significant performance improvements by leveraging a structured space representation in a sparse fashion to operate efficiently at high resolutions. In this work, we also adopt a sparse 3D convolutional backbone to explore language-guided pre-training for larger-vocabulary semantic segmentation.

3D Representation Learning. Inspired by the success of contrastive frameworks for 2D image representation learning [5,6,17,35], 3D representation learning has begun to see exploration in unsupervised contrastive pre-training. PointContrast [46] demonstrated the effectiveness of unsupervised contrastive pre-training for 3D scene understanding tasks, with various methods introducing augmentation alternatives for 3D pre-training [7,20,41,52]. Contrastive Scene Contexts [18] introduced an unsupervised contrastive pre-training in the context of data-efficient 3D scene understanding with limited reconstruction and limited annotations available. In contrast to these 3D pre-training methods, we propose a supervised multi-modal 3D representation learning guided by text encoded features to learn a more robust feature representation space covering significantly more class categories than previously studied for 3D. Inspired by the data-efficient scene understanding of [18], we additionally study a limited annotations scenario for our ScanNet200 benchmark.

Additionally, Mix3D [34] presented a data augmentation scheme to mix multiple 3D scenes together to generate semantic segmentation that is more robust against undesired context biases. Our instance-based sampling when fine-tuning the learned language-guided 3D features is inspired by the scene mixing, but operates at an instance level to help mitigate class imbalances. Previous methods have also leveraged text embeddings in 3D learning for zero-shot pointcloud segmentation [8,31] and classification [51]. More recently, CLIP [40] was shown as a powerful conditioner for generative 3D models [30,43]. We also aim to leverage powerful CLIP text embeddings for robust 3D semantic pre-training.

3D Scene Understanding Benchmarks. Recently, various large-scale real-world 3D scene understanding benchmarks have been established. Early benchmarks such as the NYUv2 dataset [33] introduced RGB-D frame-based annotations on a limited number of frames (e.g., 1449 for NYUv2). ScanNet [10] presented a much larger-scale RGB-D dataset and benchmark with 1513 densely-annotated reconstructed 3D scans. While it contains hundreds of raw annotated label data, the ScanNet benchmark evaluates only 20 class categories for its 3D scene understanding tasks. Similarly, Matterport3D [4] presents a large-scale RGB-D dataset with a 20-class semantic segmentation evaluation. Additionally, SemanticKITTI [1] established an outdoor 3D dataset and benchmark for LiDAR-based scene understanding with 28 class category annotations. We present our ScanNet200 benchmark based on ScanNet scene data with an order of magnitude more classes than previous benchmarks.

Class Imbalance. Real-world dataset annotations tend to contain natural class imbalances which can lead to skewed learning of more frequently observed class categories. Despite the lack of study on mitigating class imbalances in 3D, various methods have been presented to address them in 2D image understanding tasks.

In particular, class imbalance in image classification problems is often addressed by oversampling underrepresented categories with strong data augmentation techniques to obtain an evenly-distributed dataset. Various methods have been introduced towards data-sampling-based re-balancing, for instance random oversampling of underrepresented classes [3,45,49], sampling novel poses of known categories [29], undersampling overrepresented classes [32], frequency-based sampling [22], as well as feature-based or generative sampling [36,37,50]. Inspired by such approaches, we propose a 3D instance-based sampling to mitigate class imbalances for 3D semantic segmentation.

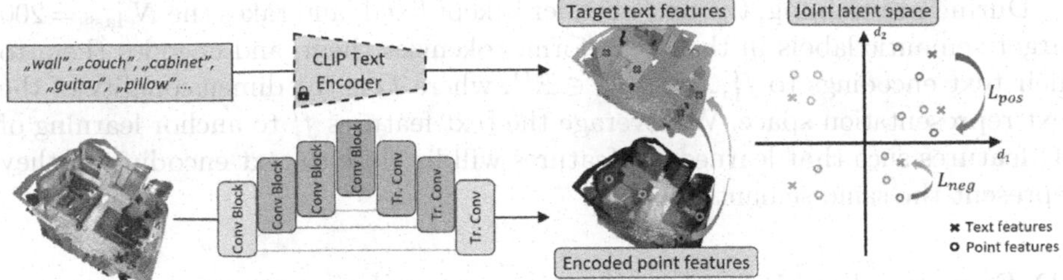

Fig. 2. During pre-training, we guide 3D feature learning by mapping learned features to text encoded anchors of the corresponding semantic labels, constructed by a constrastive loss between text and 3D. This establishes a more robust 3D feature representation space guided by the rich structure of the text embeddings.

Alternative methods have been proposed to re-balance the loss for image understanding tasks [19,25,26]. In particular, the focal loss [26] has been shown to be effective for 2D object detection and semantic segmentation by focusing the training on hard examples or to instance contours [2]. We also study the effect of focal loss balancing for the 3D semantic segmentation task.

3 Method

Our approach tackles the 200-class 3D semantic segmentation task on ScanNet [10] data, exploiting well-structured language models that have trained on rich observations across all category labels. In particular, we leverage pre-trained text embeddings from CLIP [40] as anchors to which we learn to map geometric features during the pre-training step. We then use these language-grounded features for fine-tuning downstream 3D semantic segmentation. During fine-tuning, we further address the class imbalance by instance-based augmentation as well as focal loss-based class-balancing for the downstream loss.

3.1 Language-Grounded 3D Feature Learning

As training data for language-based models are available in far greater quantities than 3D semantic annotations, we propose to ground 3D feature learning to well-structured, pre-trained text encodings. This enables a more robust construction of a learned feature space guided towards a highly-structured, rich text feature space, to support downstream 3D semantic segmentation. An overview of our language-grounded 3D pre-training is shown in Fig. 2.

Text Encoder. We leverage a pre-trained CLIP [40] to map semantic labels to text features. Note that our approach is agnostic to the specific language model used, but we found CLIP's multi-modal training is well-suited to our language-3D pre-training. We refer to the supplemental for additional analysis on alternative text embeddings.

During pre-training, the text encoder is kept fixed, and takes the $N_{\text{class}} = 200$ target semantic labels in their text form, tokenizes them, and encodes them to their text encodings to $f_1^t, ..., f_{N_{\text{class}}}^t \in \mathbb{R}^D$, where D is the dimensionality of the text representation space. We leverage the text features f_i^t to anchor learning of 3D features such that learned 3D features will lie close to text encodings if they represent the same semantic class.

3D Encoder. For 3D feature extraction, we employ a state-of-the-art sparse 3D convolutional U-Net [9]. Our 3D encoder backbone takes as input a sparse voxelized 3D scan $\mathcal{S}$, with RGB color as input features, and produces for each sparse voxel location a 3D feature $f_i^s \in \mathbb{R}^D$.

Text-supervised Contrastive Optimization. We then train the 3D feature encoder to map to the well-structured space of the text model by formulating a contrastive objective to bring together the different data modalities. For a 3D scan $\mathcal{S}$ with all N_p sparse voxel locations in the current batch, we map together 3D features f_i^s to text features $f_{h(i)}^t$ representing the semantic label text:

$$\mathcal{L}_{pos} = \sum_{i=1}^{N_p} max\left(0, 1 - \frac{f_i^s \cdot f_{h(i)}^t}{|f_i^s| \cdot |f_{h(i)}^t|} - t_{pos}\right), \tag{1}$$

where $h(i)$ is the semantic text label for location i, and t_{pos} is a threshold value for gradient clipping.

Similarly, multiple non-matching semantic text features, sampled from all text semantic labels, are pushed away from the learned features as negatives:

$$\mathcal{L}_{neg} = \sum_{i=1}^{N_p} \frac{1}{|M|} \sum_{j \in M} max\left(0, t_{neg} - 1 + \frac{f_i^s \cdot f_j^t}{|f_i^s| \cdot |f_j^t|}\right), \tag{2}$$

where $M \in N_{\text{class}}$ are a set of semantic label encodings different from i, f_j^t is the corresponding text feature, and t_{neg} is a threshold value for gradient clipping.

We found that a cosine distance between features empirically produced the best results compared to alternative distance measures such as ℓ_1, ℓ_2, or MSE. This allows for more flexibility in the feature learning by constraining only vector directions, and is similarly reflected in CLIP-driven image classification [14,24].

The final language-3D pre-training objective is then:

$$\mathcal{L} = \mathcal{L}_{pos} + \lambda \mathcal{L}_{neg} \tag{3}$$

where λ weights the effect of the multiple negatives with the positive loss. We found empirically that negative sampling was necessary for effective 3D representation learning, rather than employing positive text associations only. During optimization, multiple possible point feature trajectories are converging to the target anchors, and we encourage the solutions that maximize cluster separation at all times (see Sect. 5 for additional analysis). Additionally, as we sample

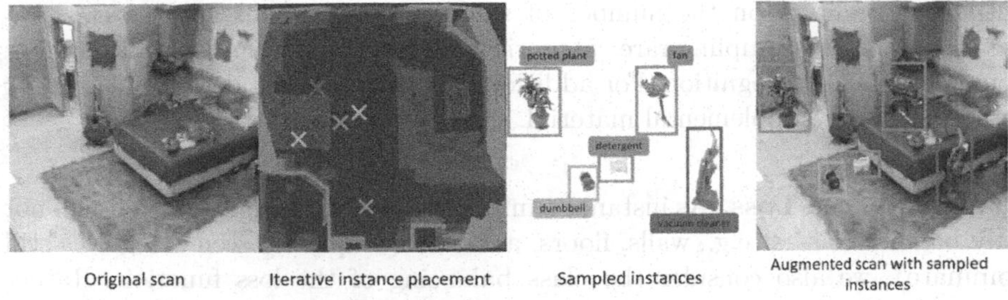

Fig. 3. Our instance sampling augments scenes during training with by placing rarely-seen class category instances into them, breaking unduly specific context dependencies that can be easily learned from only a few examples.

target feature anchors from the complete set of categories, we are able to maximize cluster separation within categories rarely appearing together in the same scenes, in contrast to unsupervised algorithms.

3.2 3D Semantic Segmentation Fine-Tuning

We use the language-grounded pre-trained 3D features for fine-tuning for 3D semantic segmentation. Here, we also directly address the inherent class imbalance due to the natural long-tail distribution of the class categories in densely-annotated 3D scenes (e.g., far more walls and floors than lamps or dumbbells). In particular, we address this through data augmentation for class balancing as well as a class-balanced loss.

Class Re-Balancing by Instance Sampling. We observe that since rare classes are not only infrequently observed but are often small objects and thus represented by smaller sets of points or voxels, they often overfit to recognizing both the surrounding context and the object. We thus propose to augment scenes by placing instances of infrequently seen class categories in them and breaking overly specific context dependencies for recognition.

An overview of our instance sampling is shown in Fig. 3. We obtain instances from ScanNet200 semantic instance annotations, and sample from instances of rare class categories from train scenes. We note here, that we relied on the available ScanNet instance annotations, but since we are augmenting long tail categories only, sparsely appearing in all scenes, the conversion from semantic to instance segmentations comes essentially free with surface label clustering. We place these sampled instances in potentially physically valid locations in a new scene. To this end, we compute a height map of the scene in which the object is to be inserted and iteratively sample instance centroid candidates where the new object can be placed. Any sampled object center where the inserted object would collide with existing objects, based on bounding box overlap, is discarded. For all accepted placements we update the height map and continue with the iterations until the condition on the number of samples is met. This enables class re-balancing by over-sampling rare categories and breaking unduly specific context dependencies for recognition. For additional implementation details please refer to Sect. 8 in our supplemental material.

Class-Balanced Loss. As instance sampling-based data augmentation will not fully balance classes (e.g., walls, floors, and other frequently seen categories still dominate), we also consider the class balancing of the loss function. Rather than a standard cross entropy loss for semantic segmentation, we adapt a focal loss [26] which was shown to be effective in mitigating class imbalance effects for 2D object detection. The focal loss applies a dynamic weighting factor based on the usefulness of a given sample to re-weight the cross entropy, focusing on difficult-to-classify examples.

In particular, the focal loss proposes a modulating factor for a cross entropy loss:

$$\mathcal{L}_{\text{focal}}(p_t) = -(1-p_t)^{\gamma} log(p_t), \tag{4}$$

where p_t is the point prediction probability for the respective target label and $\gamma \geq 0$ is focusing the modulating factor $(1-p_t)^{\gamma}$.

In practice, we did not see a direct improvement over cross entropy training by applying a focal loss directly, so we additionally re-balance the loss based on the class imbalance of the train set:

$$FL(p_t) = -\alpha(1-p_t)^{\gamma} log(p_t), \qquad \alpha_i = \frac{log(n_i)}{\sum_{j=1}^{N_{\text{class}}} log(n_j)} \tag{5}$$

By explicitly considering category imbalances, we found this to provide improved performance over both a standard focal loss or direct category-balanced cross entropy (c.f. Sect. 5 for more analysis).

3.3 Implementation Details

During pre-training, we use a sparse 3D U-Net backbone for 3D feature encoding, implemented with the MinkowskiEngine [9]. We adapt the MinkUNet34 to output feature dimension maps of size $D = 512$ to match the dimensionality of the pre-trained text encoding from CLIP [40]. For additional details on optimization please refer our supplemental at Sect. 7. We follow a two stage training with pretraining and fine-tuning for both semantic and instance segmentation, where for all comparisons we use the same 3D backbone architecture.

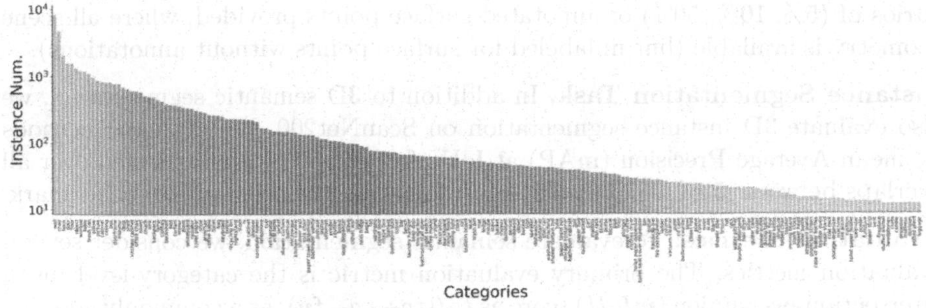

Fig. 4. Class category distribution for our ScanNet200 Benchmark showing number of instances per category; note that the frequencies are given on log-scale and ordered by number of instances per category.

4 ScanNet200 Benchmark

The ScanNet Benchmark[1] has provided an active online benchmark evaluation for 3D semantic segmentation, but only considers 20 class categories, which is insufficient to capture the diversity of many real-world environments. We thus present the ScanNet200 Benchmark for 3D semantic segmentation with 200 class categories, an order of magnitude more than previous. We follow the original train/val/test split of ScanNet [10], while training and evaluating over significantly more class categories. Figure 4 shows the class category distribution for ScanNet200 over the number of annotated instances and the number of annotated surface points per category in the train set.

To obtain the 200 class categories, we considered the raw semantic label annotations provided by ScanNet [10], which contains 607 raw categories. After merging near-duplicate labels, this resulted in 550 unique semantic classes, from which we selected the 200-most represented categories by the number of instances, forming ScanNet200. The 200-class selection enables enforcing a minimum of 10 samples from all categories.

In order to better understand performance under the natural class imbalance of the ScanNet200 benchmark, we further split the 200 categories into sets of 66, 68 and 66 categories, based on the frequency of number of labeled surface points in the train set: *head*, *common* and *tail* respectively. Evaluation over all categories as well as for the head, common, and tail splits enables a more precise understanding of segmentation performance.

Limited Annotation Task. We additionally study semantic segmentation performance on ScanNet200 in the limited annotation regime, as dense 3D annotations are expensive to acquire. In the limited annotation setting, we emulate annotations queried from annotators with a randomly sampled annotated point per object, and any additional points annotated based on farthest point sampling, similar to settings of weakly-supervised methods [28]. We consider sce-

[1] http://kaldir.vc.in.tum.de/scannet_benchmark/.

narios of (5%, 10%, 50%) of annotated surface points provided, where all scene geometry is available (but unlabeled for surface points without annotations).

Instance Segmentation Task. In addition to 3D semantic segmentation, we also evaluate 3D instance segmentation on ScanNet200. We evaluate methods by mean Average Precision (mAP) at IoU of (25%, 50%) and averaged over all overlaps between [50%, 95%] at 5% steps, following the original [10] benchmark.

Evaluation Metrics. To evaluate semantic segmentation, we consider several evaluation metrics. The primary evaluation metric is the category-level mean intersection-over-union (*mIoU*) score as $tp/(tp{+}fp{+}fn)$, as a commonly adopted segmentation measure. Additionally, we evaluate *precision* as $tp/(tp+fp)$ and *recall* as $tp/(tp+fn)$, to provide further insight towards over-prediction and under-prediction, respectively. All evaluation metrics are measured across head, common, and tail splits as well as globally across all categories, in order to consider performance for more and less frequently seen class categories.

5 Experiments

We evaluate our approach for language-grounded pre-training with state-of-the-art alternatives for 3D semantic segmentation on our ScanNet200 benchmark. For our method and all baselines, we use the same 80M parameter sparse 3D U-Net backbone implemented with MinkowskiNet [9].

Comparison to the State of the Art. We compare with a state-of-the-art pre-training approaches Contrastive Scene Contexts (CSC) [18] and Supervised Contrastive Learning (SupCon) [23], along with our instance-based data balancing and focal loss [26] training in Table 1. For CSC, we use the same pre-training experimental setup as proposed by the authors for our 3D backbone. For SupCon, we sample 5 positive and 5 negative candidates from the training scene for each source point and train it for 300 epochs with the same optimization parameters as our method. Our instance sampling, as well as focal loss, individually help

Table 1. Comparison to state of the art on ScanNet200. Our language-grounded 3D feature learning enables improved performance across frequent and infrequently seen categories in comparison with pure data augmentation or loss balancing techniques as well as state-of-the-art 3D pre-training. Our approach achieves over 5% mIoU performance over training from scratch, more than double the performance improvement of CSC [18].

	mIoU				Precision				Recall			
	Head	Common	Tail	All	Head	Common	Tail	All	Head	Common	Tail	All
Scratch	48.29	19.08	7.86	25.02	68.81	66.29	39.88	58.32	60.45	25.50	15.06	33.67
Ins. samp.	48.46	18.97	9.22	25.49	70.04	62.98	49.41	60.81	59.64	24.66	19.25	34.52
C-Focal	48.10	20.28	9.38	25.86	68.10	65.64	47.43	60.39	60.08	26.28	19.14	35.48
SupCon [23]	48.55	19.17	10.34	26.02	69.52	65.42	40.62	58.52	60.27	26.28	19.14	35.23
CSC [18]	49.43	19.52	10.28	26.41	70.00	67.75	40.78	59.51	61.01	25.75	17.62	34.79
Ours (CLIP only)	50.39	**22.84**	10.10	27.73	71.64	**69.72**	44.47	61.94	62.20	**29.37**	17.35	36.16
Ours	**51.51**	22.68	**12.41**	**28.87**	**72.72**	66.69	**58.30**	**65.90**	**62.50**	29.09	**26.61**	**39.40**

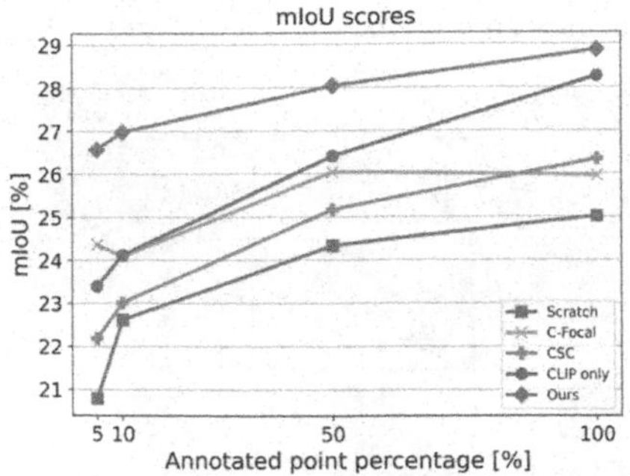

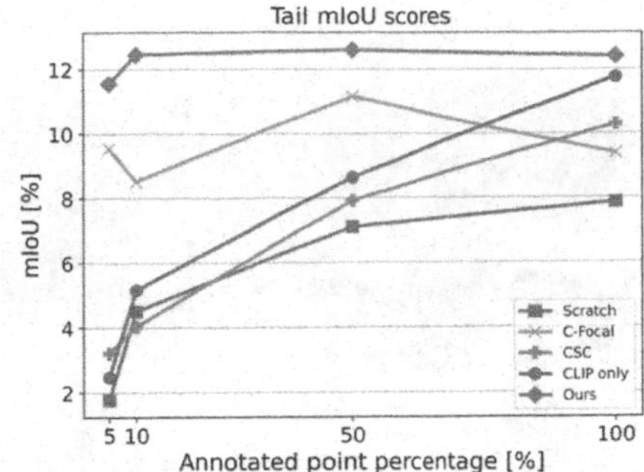

Fig. 5. 3D semantic segmentation under varying amounts of limited annotations. Even when considering only a small number of annotated surface points for our supervised language-guided 3D pre-training, our approach improves notably over the state-of-the-art 3D pre-training of CSC [18].

to improve performance, particularly for lesser-seen class categories. Additionally, all pre-training approaches improve performance over training from scratch, while our language-grounded feature learning enables more effective semantic reasoning with consistent improvements over baselines and across common and rarely seen class categories (Fig. 6).

Limited Annotation Semantic Segmentation. As data annotations remain expensive to acquire, we additionally evaluate our approach in comparison with state of the art in the limited annotation scenario of our ScanNet200 Benchmark described in Sect. 4. Figure 5 shows performance over varying amounts of labeled annotation data available (5%, 10%, 50%, 100%). Note that since our pre-training leverages text labels to guide pre-training, we only pre-train with the available annotations, whereas CSC is pre-trained with all geometric data available for the train scenes and fine-tuned with the limited annotation data. Our approach enables more robust semantic segmentation on this challenging benchmark, consistently improving and recovering the performance of training from scratch with only 5% of the annotations. Moreover, in the very low annotation regime, we see significant improvements on tail categories, with an increase of +8 mIoU from the state-of-the-art 3D pre-training of CSC with 5% of annotations available.

How Much Does a Class-Balanced Focal Loss Help? We evaluate the effect of our class-balanced focal loss [26] variant (*C-Focal*) in Table 1, which helps to improve performance over training from scratch with a standard cross entropy loss. Additionally, we see a consistent improvement with a smaller 3D backbone model in Table 3 in supplementary material, particularly for tail categories. We note that the class-balanced focal loss improves notably over both the original focal loss formulation (both using $\gamma = 2$), as well as a class-balanced cross entropy.

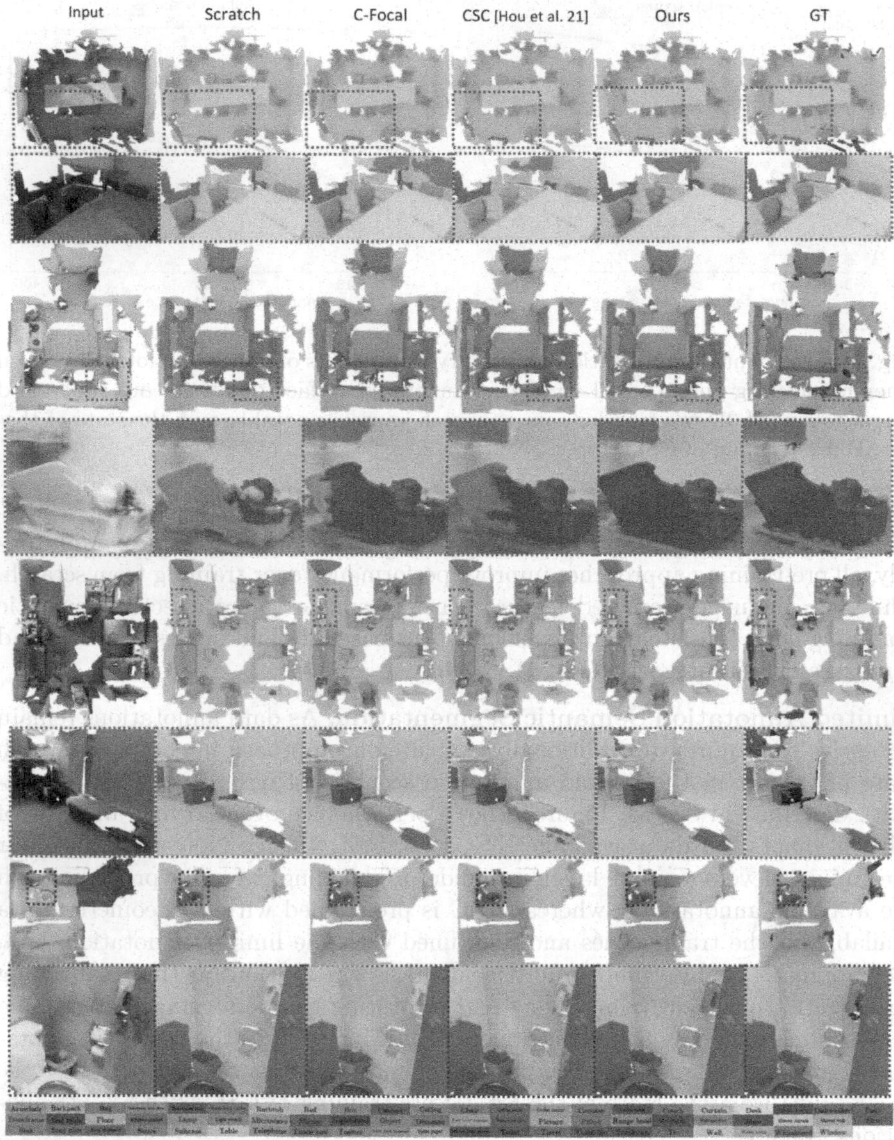

Fig. 6. Qualitative semantic segmentation results on ScanNet [10] scenes. In comparison to training from scratch, class-balance focal loss, and the 3D pre-training of CSC [18], our language-grounded 3D feature learning enables more consistent and accurate semantic segmentation, even for challenging less frequently seen class categories (e.g., *"dish rack"* in row 4, *"telephone"* in the last row).

What is the Impact of Data Balancing with Instance Sampling? We additionally evaluate the effect of applying data balancing by our instance sampling during training in Table 1 (*Ins. samp*) as well as for a smaller 3D backbone in supplemental Table 3. We find that this instance sampling consistently provides a small improvement in performance across common and rare class categories.

What is the Effect of our Language-Grounded Pre-training? Table 1 shows that our language-grounded pretraining to text-based CLIP [40] embeddings without focal loss or instance sampling already improves over all baselines. Our full approach with focal loss and instance sampling in addition to text-anchored pre-training enables consistent, effective improvement in comparison to alternative approaches.

3D Instance Segmentation Task. In addition to 3D semantic segmentation, we also analyze a 3D instance segmentation task in Table 2, showing that our approach generalizes across multiple downstream tasks with consistent performance improvement. We use the same pre-trained 3D backbones and fine-tune them for instance segmentation by predicting an offset vector for every scene point as a voting mechanism together with the semantic labels. These directional distance vectors are optimized during train time, while the clustering of the instances is calculated only at test time. For the task and clustering algorithm, we adopt the paradigms of [18,21] to our ScanNet200 benchmark. For this task, we train our models with a batch size of 8 for 300 epochs and momentum SGD optimizer with the same parameters as in the semantic segmentation experiments, except for a smaller starting learning rate of 0.02.

Table 2. 3D instance segmentation, in comparison with training from scratch and state-of-the-art 3D pre-training approach CSC [18]. Our language-grounded pre-training improves over both baselines.

	Precision	mIoU	mAP@0.5
Scratch	61.04	25.37	24.47
CSC [18]	63.13	25.92	25.24
CLIP only	64.24	27.58	**27.91**
Ours	**65.32**	**27.72**	26.09

Learned Feature Representation Space. We analyze the pre-trained representation spaces by visualizing a t-SNE projection of the learned features in Fig. 7. By anchoring 3D feature learning to a richly-structured text embedding space, we can learn a more structured 3D feature representation space.

Limitations and Future Work. We believe our language-grounded 3D feature learning provides a promising step towards more robust and general 3D scene

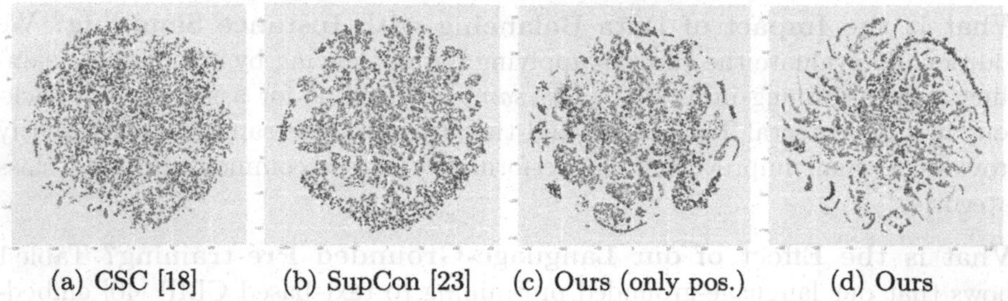

Fig. 7. We show a comparison with the representation learned by CSC [18], SupCon [23], as well as our approach when training with only positive samples. Our full language-grounded pre-training results in a more structured feature representation space with improved semantic segmentation performance.

understanding, though several important limitations remain. It is often the case that infrequently observed objects are small and their geometric resolution is limited, so while tail category performance has improved using only geometric input, there is still much room for improvement. In particular, we note that color image observations could provide significantly higher resolution signals to explore for more accurate tail category recognition. Additionally, text encodings are used to anchor learned 3D feature representations, but currently, only the semantic labels of each object are considered, whereas text caption or object attribute descriptions could potentially provide a richer signal.

6 Conclusion

We have presented ScanNet200, a new benchmark for 3D semantic segmentation with an order of magnitude more class categories, along with a new approach for language-grounded pre-training to address 3D semantic feature learning under imbalanced and limited data. Our approach demonstrates robust feature learning by anchoring learned features to richly-structured CLIP text embeddings, demonstrating consistent improvements over strong baselines on our challenging ScanNet200 Benchmark and under limited annotation scenarios. We believe that this makes an important step towards 3D semantic scene understanding in the wild, and forms a basis for future multi-modal exploration for a variety of 3D perception tasks.

Acknowledgements. This project is funded by the Bavarian State Ministry of Science and the Arts and coordinated by the Bavarian Research Institute for Digital Transformation (bidt).

References

1. Behley, J., et al.: SemanticKITTI: a dataset for Semantic Scene Understanding of LiDAR Sequences. In: Proceedings of the IEEE/CVF International Conf. on Computer Vision (ICCV) (2019)

2. Biasutti, P., Lepetit, V., Aujol, J.F., Brédif, M., Bugeau, A.: Lu-net: an efficient network for 3d lidar point cloud semantic segmentation based on end-to-end-learned 3d features and u-net. In: Proceedings of the IEEE/CVF International Conference on Computer Vision Workshops (2019)
3. Buda, M., Maki, A., Mazurowski, M.A.: A systematic study of the class imbalance problem in convolutional neural networks. Neural Netw. **106**, 249–259 (2018)
4. Chang, A., et al.: Matterport3d: learning from RGB-D data in indoor environments. arXiv preprint arXiv:1709.06158 (2017)
5. Chen, T., Kornblith, S., Norouzi, M., Hinton, G.: A simple framework for contrastive learning of visual representations. In: International Conference on Machine Learning, pp. 1597–1607. PMLR (2020)
6. Chen, X., He, K.: Exploring simple Siamese representation learning. In: Proceedings of the IEEE/CVF Conference on Computer Vision and Pattern Recognition, pp. 15750–15758 (2021)
7. Chen, Y., Nießner, M., Dai, A.: 4dcontrast: contrastive learning with dynamic correspondences for 3d scene understanding. arXiv preprint arXiv:2112.02990 (2021)
8. Cheraghian, A., Rahman, S., Chowdhury, T.F., Campbell, D., Petersson, L.: Zero-shot learning on 3d point cloud objects and beyond. CoRR abs/2104.04980 (2021). arxiv.org/abs/2104.04980
9. Choy, C., Gwak, J., Savarese, S.: 4d spatio-temporal convnets: Minkowski convolutional neural networks. In: Proceedings of the IEEE/CVF Conference on Computer Vision and Pattern Recognition, pp. 3075–3084 (2019)
10. Dai, A., Chang, A.X., Savva, M., Halber, M., Funkhouser, T., Nießner, M.: Scannet: richly-annotated 3d reconstructions of indoor scenes. In: Proceedings of Computer Vision and Pattern Recognition (CVPR), IEEE (2017)
11. Dai, A., Nießner, M.: 3DMV: joint 3d-multi-view prediction for 3d semantic scene segmentation. In: Ferrari, V., Hebert, M., Sminchisescu, C., Weiss, Y. (eds.) ECCV 2018. LNCS, vol. 11214, pp. 458–474. Springer, Cham (2018). https://doi.org/10.1007/978-3-030-01249-6_28
12. Everingham, M., Van Gool, L., Williams, C.K., Winn, J., Zisserman, A.: The pascal visual object classes (VOC) challenge. Int. J. Comput. Vision **88**(2), 303–338 (2010)
13. Graham, B., Engelcke, M., van der Maaten, L.: 3d semantic segmentation with submanifold sparse convolutional networks. In: CVPR (2018)
14. Gu, X., Lin, T.Y., Kuo, W., Cui, Y.: Zero-shot detection via vision and language knowledge distillation. arXiv e-prints, arXiv-2104 (2021)
15. Gupta, A., Dollar, P., Girshick, R.: LVIS: a dataset for large vocabulary instance segmentation. In: Proceedings of the IEEE Conference on Computer Vision and Pattern Recognition (2019)
16. Han, L., Zheng, T., Xu, L., Fang, L.: OccuSeg: occupancy-aware 3d instance segmentation. In: Proceedings of the IEEE/CVF Conference on Computer Vision and Pattern Recognition, pp. 2940–2949 (2020)
17. He, K., Fan, H., Wu, Y., Xie, S., Girshick, R.: Momentum contrast for unsupervised visual representation learning. In: Proceedings of the IEEE/CVF Conference on Computer Vision And Pattern Recognition, pp. 9729–9738 (2020)
18. Hou, J., Graham, B., Nießner, M., Xie, S.: Exploring data-efficient 3d scene understanding with contrastive scene contexts. In: Proceedings of the IEEE/CVF Conference on Computer Vision and Pattern Recognition, pp. 15587–15597 (2021)
19. Hsieh, T.I., Robb, E., Chen, H.T., Huang, J.B.: Droploss for long-tail instance segmentation. In: AAAI, vol. 3, p. 15 (2021)

20. Huang, S., Xie, Y., Zhu, S.C., Zhu, Y.: Spatio-temporal self-supervised representation learning for 3d point clouds. In: Proceedings of the IEEE/CVF International Conference on Computer Vision, pp. 6535–6545 (2021)
21. Jiang, L., Zhao, H., Shi, S., Liu, S., Fu, C.W., Jia, J.: PointGroup: dual-set point grouping for 3d instance segmentation. In: Proceedings of the IEEE Conference on Computer Vision and Pattern Recognition (CVPR) (2020)
22. Kang, B., et al.: Decoupling representation and classifier for long-tailed recognition. In: Eighth International Conference on Learning Representations (ICLR) (2020)
23. Khosla, P., et al.: Supervised contrastive learning. Adv. Neural Inf. Process. Syst. **33**, 18661–18673 (2020)
24. Li, B., Weinberger, K.Q., Belongie, S., Koltun, V., Ranftl, R.: Language-driven semantic segmentation. arXiv preprint arXiv:2201.03546 (2022)
25. Li, Y., et al.: Overcoming classifier imbalance for long-tail object detection with balanced group softmax. In: Proceedings of the IEEE/CVF Conference on Computer Vision and Pattern Recognition, pp. 10991–11000 (2020)
26. Lin, T.Y., Goyal, P., Girshick, R., He, K., Dollár, P.: Focal loss for dense object detection. In: Proceedings of the IEEE International Conference on Computer Vision, pp. 2980–2988 (2017)
27. Lin, T.-Y.: Microsoft COCO: common objects in context. In: Fleet, D., Pajdla, T., Schiele, B., Tuytelaars, T. (eds.) ECCV 2014. LNCS, vol. 8693, pp. 740–755. Springer, Cham (2014). https://doi.org/10.1007/978-3-319-10602-1_48
28. Liu, Z., Qi, X., Fu, C.W.: One thing one click: a self-training approach for weakly supervised 3d semantic segmentation. In: Proceedings of the IEEE/CVF Conference on Computer Vision and Pattern Recognition, pp. 1726–1736 (2021)
29. Manhardt, F., Kehl, W., Gaidon, A.: Roi-10d: monocular lifting of 2d detection to 6d pose and metric shape. In: Proceedings of the IEEE/CVF Conference on Computer Vision and Pattern Recognition, pp. 2069–2078 (2019)
30. Michel, O., Bar-On, R., Liu, R., Benaim, S., Hanocka, R.: Text2mesh: text-driven neural stylization for meshes. arXiv preprint arXiv:2112.03221 (2021)
31. Michele, B., Boulch, A., Puy, G., Bucher, M., Marlet, R.: Generative zero-shot learning for semantic segmentation of 3d point cloud. CoRR abs/2108.06230 (2021). arxiv.org/abs/2108.06230
32. More, A.: Survey of resampling techniques for improving classification performance in unbalanced datasets. arXiv preprint arXiv:1608.06048 (2016)
33. Silberman, N., Hoiem, D., Kohli, P., Fergus, R.: Indoor segmentation and support inference from RGBD images. In: Fitzgibbon, A., Lazebnik, S., Perona, P., Sato, Y., Schmid, C. (eds.) ECCV 2012. LNCS, vol. 7576, pp. 746–760. Springer, Heidelberg (2012). https://doi.org/10.1007/978-3-642-33715-4_54
34. Nekrasov, A., Schult, J., Litany, O., Leibe, B., Engelmann, F.: Mix3D: out-of-context data augmentation for 3D scenes. In: International Conference on 3D Vision (3DV) (2021)
35. Van den Oord, A., Li, Y., Vinyals, O.: Representation learning with contrastive predictive coding. arXiv e-prints, arXiv-1807 (2018)
36. Peng, M., et al.: Trainable undersampling for class-imbalance learning. In: AAAI (2019)
37. Perez-Ortiz, M., Tiňo, P., Mantiuk, R., Hervás-Martínez, C.: Exploiting synthetically generated data with semi-supervised learning for small and imbalanced datasets. In: Proceedings of the AAAI Conference on Artificial Intelligence, vol. 33, pp. 4715–4722 (2019)

38. Qi, C.R., Su, H., Mo, K., Guibas, L.J.: PointNet: deep learning on point sets for 3d classification and segmentation. In: Proceedings of the IEEE Conference on Computer Vision and Pattern Recognition, pp. 652–660 (2017)
39. Qi, C.R., Yi, L., Su, H., Guibas, L.J.: Pointnet++: deep hierarchical feature learning on point sets in a metric space. Adv. Neural Inf. Process. Syst. **30**, 1–10 (2017)
40. Radford, A., et al.: Learning transferable visual models from natural language supervision. In: International Conference on Machine Learning, pp. 8748–8763. PMLR (2021)
41. Rao, Y., Liu, B., Wei, Y., Lu, J., Hsieh, C.J., Zhou, J.: Randomrooms: unsupervised pre-training from synthetic shapes and randomized layouts for 3d object detection. In: Proceedings of the IEEE/CVF International Conference on Computer Vision, pp. 3283–3292 (2021)
42. Riegler, G., Osman Ulusoy, A., Geiger, A.: OctNet: Learning deep 3d representations at high resolutions. In: Proceedings of the IEEE Conference on Computer Vision and Pattern Recognition, pp. 3577–3586 (2017)
43. Sanghi, A., Chu, H., Lambourne, J.G., Wang, Y., Cheng, C., Fumero, M.: Clip-forge: towards zero-shot text-to-shape generation. CoRR abs/2110.02624 (2021). arxiv.org/abs/2110.02624
44. Thomas, H., Qi, C.R., Deschaud, J.E., Marcotegui, B., Goulette, F., Guibas, L.J.: KPConv: flexible and deformable convolution for point clouds. In: Proceedings of the IEEE/CVF International Conference on Computer Vision, pp. 6411–6420 (2019)
45. Wang, C., Ma, C., Zhu, M., Yang, X.: PointAugmenting: cross-modal augmentation for 3d object detection. In: Proceedings of the IEEE/CVF Conference on Computer Vision and Pattern Recognition, pp. 11794–11803 (2021)
46. Xie, S., Gu, J., Guo, D., Qi, C.R., Guibas, L., Litany, O.: PointContrast: unsupervised pre-training for 3D point cloud understanding. In: Vedaldi, A., Bischof, H., Brox, T., Frahm, J.-M. (eds.) ECCV 2020. LNCS, vol. 12348, pp. 574–591. Springer, Cham (2020). https://doi.org/10.1007/978-3-030-58580-8_34
47. Xu, J., Zhang, R., Dou, J., Zhu, Y., Sun, J., Pu, S.: RPVNet: a deep and efficient range-point-voxel fusion network for lidar point cloud segmentation. In: Proceedings of the IEEE/CVF International Conference on Computer Vision, pp. 16024–16033 (2021)
48. Xu, Y., Fan, T., Xu, M., Zeng, L., Qiao, Yu.: SpiderCNN: deep learning on point sets with parameterized convolutional filters. In: Ferrari, V., Hebert, M., Sminchisescu, C., Weiss, Y. (eds.) ECCV 2018. LNCS, vol. 11212, pp. 90–105. Springer, Cham (2018). https://doi.org/10.1007/978-3-030-01237-3_6
49. Yan, Y., Mao, Y., Li, B.: Second: sparsely embedded convolutional detection. Sensors **18**, 3337 (2018)
50. Yan, Y., et al.: Oversampling for imbalanced data via optimal transport. In: AAAI (2019)
51. Zhang, R., et al.: PointClip: point cloud understanding by CLIP. CoRR abs/2112.02413 (2021). arxiv.org/abs/2112.02413
52. Zhang, Z., Girdhar, R., Joulin, A., Misra, I.: Self-supervised pretraining of 3d features on any point-cloud. In: Proceedings of the IEEE/CVF International Conference on Computer Vision, pp. 10252–10263 (2021)

Beyond Periodicity: Towards a Unifying Framework for Activations in Coordinate-MLPs

Sameera Ramasinghe(✉) and Simon Lucey

Australian Institute for Machine Learning, University of Adelaide, Adelaide, Australia
{sameera.ramasinghe,simon.lucey}@adelaide.edu.au

Abstract. Coordinate-MLPs are emerging as an effective tool for modeling multidimensional continuous signals, overcoming many drawbacks associated with discrete grid-based approximations. However, coordinate-MLPs with ReLU activations, in their rudimentary form, demonstrate poor performance in representing signals with high fidelity, promoting the need for positional embedding layers. Recently, Sitzmann *et al.* [24] proposed a sinusoidal activation function that has the capacity to omit positional embedding from coordinate-MLPs while still preserving high signal fidelity. Despite its potential, ReLUs are still dominating the space of coordinate-MLPs; we speculate that this is due to the hyper-sensitivity of networks – that employ such sinusoidal activations – to the initialization schemes. In this paper, we attempt to broaden the current understanding of the effect of activations in coordinate-MLPs, and show that there exists a broader class of activations that are suitable for encoding signals. We affirm that sinusoidal activations are only a single example in this class, and propose several **non-periodic** functions that empirically demonstrate more robust performance against random initializations than sinusoids. Finally, we advocate for a shift towards coordinate-MLPs that employ these non-traditional activation functions due to their high performance and simplicity (Code available at https://github.com/samgregoost/Beyondperiodicity).

Keywords: Coordinate-networks · Implicit neural representations

1 Introduction

Despite the ubiquitous and successful usage of conventional discrete representations in machine learning (*e.g.* images, 3D meshes, and 3D point clouds etc.), coordinate MLPs are now emerging as a unique instrument that can represent multi-dimensional signals as continuously differentiable entities. Coordinate-MLPs – also known as *implicit neural representations* [24] – are fully connected networks that encode continuous signals as weights, consuming low-dimensional

Supplementary Information The online version contains supplementary material available at https://doi.org/10.1007/978-3-031-19827-4_9.

S. Avidan et al. (Eds.): ECCV 2022, LNCS 13693, pp. 142–158, 2022.
https://doi.org/10.1007/978-3-031-19827-4_9

coordinates as inputs. Such continuous representations are powerful compared to their discrete grid-based counterparts, as they can be queried up to extremely high resolutions. Furthermore, whereas the memory consumption of grid-based representations entails exponential growth rates against the dimension and the resolution of data, neural representations have displayed a much more compact relationship between the above factors. Consequently, this recent trend has influenced a proliferation of studies in vision-related research including texture generation [7,7,14,30], shape representation [1,4–6,12,15,28], and novel view synthesis [10,11,13,16,17,17,19,21,25,29,31].[1]

Notwithstanding the virtues mentioned above, coordinate MLPs, in their fundamental form, exhibit poor performance in encoding signals with high-frequency components when equipped with common activation functions such as ReLUs. An elemental reason behind this has shown to be the *spectral bias* of MLPs [2,18]. That is, the corresponding neural tangent kernel (NTK) of MLPs are prone to high-frequency fall-offs, hampering their ability to learn high-frequency functions. The prevalent work-around to this problem involves applying a *positional embedding layer* prior to the MLP, where the low-dimensional inputs are projected to a higher-dimensional space using Fourier features [27].

In contrast, Sitzmann *et al.* [24] recently portrayed that MLPs with sinusoidal activation functions are naturally suited for encoding high-frequency signals, eliminating the need for positional embedding layers. Despite its potential, much of the research that involve coordinate-MLPs still prefer positional embeddings over sinusoidal activations. We postulate that this could be for two reasons. First, Sitzmann *et al.* mainly attributed the success of sinusoidal activations to their periodicity, although the evidence for this relationship still remains scant. Consequently, this lack of understanding obfuscates some of the fundamental principles behind its effectiveness and hampers faithful usage in a wider range of applications. Second, sinusoidal activations are highly sensitive to the initialization of the MLP, showcasing significant performance drops in cases where the MLP is initialized without strictly adhering to the guidelines of Sitzmann *et al.*. The above drawbacks have heightened the need for a more rigorous analysis that facilitates more effective usage of activation functions in coordinate-MLPs.

Contributions: We offer a broader theoretical understanding of the role of activation functions within coordinate-MLPs. In particular, we show that the efficacy of a coordinate-MLP is critically bound to its Lipschitz smoothness and the singular value distribution of the hidden-layer representations, and the optimal values of these metrics depend on the characteristics of the signal that needs to be encoded. We further show that the above properties are inherently linked to each other, and by controlling one property, the other can be implicitly manipulated. We further derive formulae to connect the Lipschitz smoothness and the singular value distribution to the properties of the activation functions. The significance of this finding is two-fold: (i) providing guidelines for tuning the hyper-parameters of an activation function based on the given signal and, (ii) enabling a practitioner to theoretically predict the effect of a given activation

[1] Code available at https://github.com/samgregoost/Beyond_periodicity.

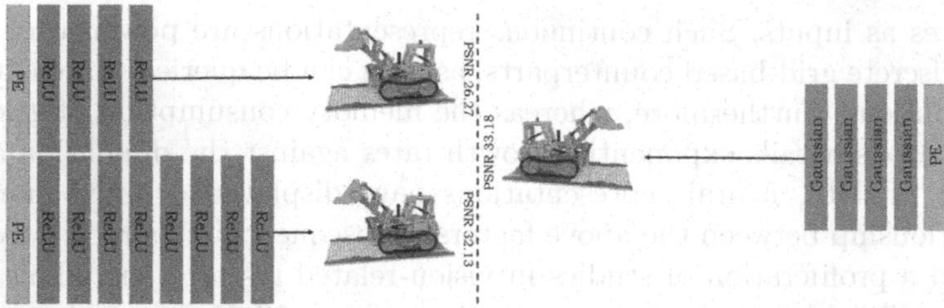

Fig. 1. ReLU vs Gaussian activations (ours). Gaussian activations achieve better results with ∼50% less parameters. These non-periodic activations also allow embedding-free architectures (see Fig. 3), and are robust to different random initializations of coordinate-MLPs than the sinusoid activations advocated in SIREN [24].

function when used in a coordinate-MLP, prior to practical implementation. We further show that sinusoidal activations are simply a single example that fulfills such constraints, and the periodicity is not a crucial factor that determine the efficacy of an activation function. Consequently, we propose a much broader class of *non-periodic* activation functions that can be used in encoding functions/signals with high fidelity, and show that their empirical properties match with theoretical predictions. We further illustrate that the newly proposed activation functions are robust to different initialization schemes, unlike sinusoidal activations. Further, picking one such proposed activation – Gaussian – as an example, we demonstrate that coordinate-MLPs with such activation functions enjoy better results, faster convergence rates, and shallower architectures in comparison to ReLU-MLPs. Finally, we show that these activations allow positional-embedding-free architectures to be used in complex tasks such as 3D view synthesis. To our knowledge, this is the first instance coordinate-MLPs have successfully been employed in such experiments in the absence of positional embeddings (Fig. 1).

2 Related Works

In recent years, there has been an increasing interest in parameterizing signals using neural networks – commonly referred to as coordinate-MLPs [26] or implicit neural functions [24] – largely owing to the seminal work by Mildenhall *et al.* [11]. The usage of coordinate-MLPs are somewhat different from conventional MLPs: i) conventional MLPs typically operate on high dimensional inputs such as images, sounds, or 3D shapes, and ii) are primarily being used for classification purposes where the decision boundaries do not have to preserve smoothness. In contrast, coordinate-MLPs are used to encode the signals as weights where the inputs are low-dimensional coordinates and the outputs have to preserve smoothness [32]. One of the most remarkable aspects of Mildenhall *et al.*'s work includes demonstrating the generalization properties of such neural signal representations, *i.e.* once trained with a handful of view points, the coordinate-MLP can reconstruct the photometric view projection from an arbitrary angle with fine-details. This ground-breaking demonstration caused a ripple of studies that include neural signal representations as the core entities across many applications including shape representation [1,4–6,12,15,28], and novel view synthesis [10,11,13,16,17,17,19,21,25,29,31]. However, for optimal performance, these coordinate-MLPs have to use positional embeddings, which allow them to encode high-frequency signal content. In contrast, Sitzmann *et al.* [24] proposed sinusoid activations that enabled coordinate-MLPs to encode signals with higher quality without positional embeddings. But, sinusoid activations have been shown to be extremely sensitive to the initialization scheme of the MLPs. A further limitation to the framework developed by Sitzmann *et al.* is its confinement to periodic activations. In contrast, our work generalizes the current understanding on the effect of activations in coordinate-MLPs and thereby propose a class of non-periodic activations that is robust under random initializations. Recently, Liang *et al.* [9] proposed a novel class of activation functions that can approximate target functions with a smaller number of parameters. However, our framework differs from theirs in two important aspects: *1)* They mix multiple activation types to expand the class of functions that can be approximated. However, NNs with *any* non-polynomial activation – thus all activations we propose – are universal approximators [8]. Thus, our setup is simpler while being more expressive. *2)* Mixing activations leads to poor controllability of memorization/generalization tradeoff, which depends on the problem domain. For instance, it is unclear how to control the coefficients of polynomials (and also other functions, when mixed together) to this end. In contrast, our framework provides a much more clear interpretation of this tradeoff, and shows compelling generalization properties in complex settings as NeRF.

3 Methodology

Notation. The set of real $n-$dimensional vectors are denoted by $\mathbb{R}^n$. The vectors are denoted by bold lower-case letters (*e.g.,* $\mathbf{x}$). The set of $m \times n$ dimensional matrices are denoted by $\mathbb{R}^{m\times n}$, and the matrices are denoted by bold upper-case letters (*e.g.,* $\mathbf{A}$). $\|\cdot\|$ denotes vector norm, $\|\cdot\|_F$ denotes the Frobenius norm, and $\|\cdot\|_o$ is the operator norm. $\mathbb{B}^n_r$ represents the $n-$ dimensional ball with radius r. Further, $g(f(\mathbf{x})) = g \circ f(x)$ where $\circ$ is the compositional operator.

3.1 Rank and Memorization

The efficacy of a coordinate-MLP largely depends on its ability to memorize training data. The objective of this section is to identify the key factors that affect memorization. To establish the foundation for our analysis, we first revisit the formulation of an MLP.

An MLP f with $k-1$ non linear hidden-layers can be described by,

$$f : \mathbf{x} \to g^k \circ \psi^{k-1} \circ g^{k-1} \circ \cdots \circ \psi^1 \circ g^1(\mathbf{x}), \tag{1}$$

where $g^i : \mathbf{x} \to \mathbf{A}^i \cdot \mathbf{x} + \mathbf{b}^i$ is an affine projection with trainable weights $\mathbf{A}^i \in \mathbb{R}^{\dim(\mathbf{x}^i) \times \dim(\mathbf{x}^{i-1})}$, $\mathbf{b}^i \in \mathbb{R}^{\dim(\mathbf{x}_i)}$ is the bias, and ψ^i is a non-linear activation function. The final layer is a linear transform such that $f : \mathbf{x} \to g^k \circ \phi(\mathbf{x})$, and ϕ is a composition of the preceding $k-1$ layers within the MLP without the final linear layer. If the number of training examples is N, we define the total (training) embedding matrix as

$$\mathbf{X} \in \mathbb{R}^{D \times N} := \left[\phi(\mathbf{x}_1)^T \phi(\mathbf{x}_2)^T \ldots \phi(\mathbf{x}_N)^T\right] \tag{2}$$

where $\{\mathbf{x}_n\}_{n=1}^N$ are the raw training inputs.

Recall that the final layer of an MLP is (typically) an affine projection without any non-linearity. Dropping the bias for simplified notation, we get,

$$\tilde{\mathbf{Y}} = \mathbf{A}^k \mathbf{X}, \tag{3}$$

where $\tilde{\mathbf{Y}} \in \mathbb{R}^{q \times N}$ are the outputs of the MLP. Suppose $\mathbf{Y} \in \mathbb{R}^{q \times N}$ are the ground truth training outputs the MLP is attempting to learn. Observe that if the MLP is perfectly memorizing the training set—if $\tilde{\mathbf{Y}} = \mathbf{Y}$—then each row of $\mathbf{Y}$ is a linear combination of the rows of $\mathbf{X}$. Assume we have no prior knowledge of $\mathbf{Y}$, that is, the rows of $\mathbf{Y}$ can be *any* arbitrary vector in $\mathbb{R}^N$. If the rows of $\mathbf{X}$ are linearly independent, they form a basis for $\mathbb{R}^N$ (assuming $D \geq N$). Therefore, if $\text{rank}(\mathbf{X}) = N$, it is guaranteed that (assuming perfect convergence) the MLP can find a weight matrix $\mathbf{A}^k$ that ensures perfect reconstruction of $\mathbf{Y}$.

One can raise the valid question: could this conclusion hold in the practical case where $D \ll N$? The answer to this question depends on the nature of the ground truth signal. Note that although the condition $\text{rank}(\mathbf{X}) = N$ is sufficient to ensure perfect memorization for *any* signal, it might not always be necessary since natural signals are typically redundant – that is of limited bandwidth. The bandwidth of a category of signals can be defined [23] as the number of linearly independent (normalized) bases required to represent them. Thus, $\text{rank}(\mathbf{X})$ can be less than N for many categories of signals whilst still enjoying perfect signal recovery by the MLP. Figure 2 is a perfect example that illustrates the above point. Note that the stable rank is a lower bound for rank [20]. Better reconstructions are shown when the stable rank is high, but the measure is bounded by the network width (D), which is lower than the number of points (N). In contrast, encoding noise signals which have limited to no redundancy – would require a larger network width – and yields poorer results with $D \ll N$ (see Appendix) as predicted. Rigorously speaking, the analysis so far only considers the penultimate layer. However, based on the gathered insights, we make the following general claim: *the potential of the hidden-layers to induce high-rank representations – that is those with very few zero singular values within* $\mathbf{X}$ *– correlates with the memorization capacity of a coordinate-MLP.*

One could also view the above result as a refashioning of the well known Nyquist-Shannon sampling theory [23] applied to-coordinate MLPs. The result is important, however, when it comes to the exposition of the rest of this paper. But, a critical component is overlooked in the above analysis. In many applications that utilize coordinate-MLPs, the ability predict values at unseen coordinates, *i.e.*, generalization, is important. For instance, in novel view synthesis of a 3D scene, the network only observes a handful of views, in which the network then has to predict the views from new angles. Therefore, the immediate question arises: *is having the ability to induce high-rank representations (i.e. very few zero singular values within* $\mathbf{X}$*) sufficient for both memorization and generalization?* In Sect. 3.2, we shall see that this is indeed not the case.

3.2 Smoothness and Generalization

To show that the rank alone is not sufficient to guarantee good generalization, we perform a simple thought experiment on 1-D input coordinates $x \in \mathbb{R}$ and single channel outputs. Let us construct a very wide layer $\phi : \mathbb{R} \rightarrow \mathbb{R}^D$ such that $D = N$, and define the layer output $\phi(x) = [e^{\frac{-(x-x_1)^2}{\sigma^2}}, \ldots, e^{\frac{-(x-x_N)^2}{\sigma^2}}]$, where $x_1, \ldots, x_N$ are the training points. With extremely small σ, $\phi(\cdot)$ is equivalent to one-hot encoding, ensuring $\text{rank}(\mathbf{X}) = N$. Then, it is guaranteed that an $\mathbf{A}$ can be found to memorize all the ground truth outputs $y_1, \ldots, y_N$. However, all the unseen points will map to $\vec{\mathbf{0}}$, and thus, the network will be obtain extremely poor generalization. In summary, having a higher rank for $\mathbf{X}$ will help in memorization, but, it will not necessarily ensure good generalization.

Moreover, strictly speaking, generalization cannot be measured independently without context. For instance, given sparse training points a neural network can, in theory, learn infinitely many functions while fitting the training points. Therefore, for good generalization, the network has to learn a function within a space restricted by certain priors and intuitions regarding the ground truth signal. The generalization then depends on the extent to which the learned function is close to these prior assumptions about the task. When no such priors are available, one intuitive solution that is widely accepted for regression (at least from an engineering perspective) is to have "smooth" interpolation between the training points [3].

In order to ensure such smooth interpolations (where second order derivatives are bounded) it is critical to preserve the smoothness across non-linear layers $\phi(\cdot)$ *locally* as $\frac{||\phi(\mathbf{x}_1)-\phi(\mathbf{x}_2)||}{||\mathbf{x}_1-\mathbf{x}_2||} = C$, where C is some constant (since the final layer is linear). Although the above condition seems overly restrictive, recall that the embeddings $\phi(\cdot)$ are learned via hidden-layers, as opposed to being analytically designed. Therefore, it is enough to reduce the search space of the parameters accordingly, as opposed to explicitly enforcing the above constraint. Thus, we can slightly relax the above equality to an inequality interms of the local Lipschitz smoothness. More precisely, in practice, it is enough to ensure

$$\|\phi(\mathbf{x}_1) - \phi(\mathbf{x}_2)\| \leq C\|\mathbf{x}_1 - \mathbf{x}_2\|, \tag{4}$$

locally, where C is a non-negative, locally varying constant that depends on the magnitude of the local first-order derivatives (*i.e.*, frequencies) of the encoded signal. That is, at intervals where encoding points exhibit large fluctuations, C needs to be higher, and vise-versa.

Thus far, we have established that the singular values of the $\mathbf{X}$ correlates with the memorization of seen coordinates and the (Lipschitz) smoothness of $\phi(\cdot)$ correlates with the generalization performance of an MLP. Thus, it is intriguing to investigate if there exists a connection between these two forces at a fundamental level, as such an analysis has the potential to provide valuable insights that enable efficient manipulation of these factors.

3.3 Singular Value Distribution as a Proxy for Smoothness

This section is devoted to exploring the interrelation between the smoothness and the singular value distribution of the hidden representations. Suppose that for coordinates $\mathbf{x}_i$ in a given small neighborhood, $\phi(\cdot)$ is Lipschitz bounded with a constant C. Then,

$$\frac{\sqrt{(\phi(\mathbf{x}_1)\phi(\mathbf{x}_1)^T - 2\phi(\mathbf{x}_1)\phi(\mathbf{x}_2)^T + \phi(\mathbf{x}_2)\phi(\mathbf{x}_2)^T)}}{\|\mathbf{x}_1 - \mathbf{x}_2\|} \leq C \tag{5}$$

With Eq. 5 in hand, let us consider two cases for $\mathbf{X}$.

Case 1. The columns of $\mathbf{X}$ are orthogonal and the singular values of $\mathbf{X}$ are identically distributed.

One can see that,

$$\frac{\sqrt{\|\phi(\mathbf{x}_i)\|^2 + \|\phi(\mathbf{x}_j)\|^2}}{\|\mathbf{x}_i - \mathbf{x}_j\|} \leq C \Rightarrow \lim_{\|\mathbf{x}_1 - \mathbf{x}_2\| \to 0} C = \infty \tag{6}$$

In other words, having (approximately) equally distributed singular values violates the Lipschitz smoothness of the network.

Case 2. The singular values of $\mathbf{X}$ are non-zero and the angle between the columns of $\mathbf{X}$ are upper-bounded by $0 < \alpha < \frac{\pi}{2}$.

Consider

$$\mathbf{x}_i^*, \mathbf{x}_j^* = \arg_{\mathbf{x}_i, \mathbf{x}_i} \Big(\frac{\|\phi(\mathbf{x}_i) - \phi(\mathbf{x}_j)\|}{\|\mathbf{x}_i - \mathbf{x}_j\|} = C \Big).$$

Then, we can define an upper bound on C as

$$C \leq \frac{\sqrt{\|\phi(\mathbf{x}_i^*)\|^2 + \|\phi(\mathbf{x}_j^*)\|^2 - 2\|\phi(\mathbf{x}_i^*)\|\|\phi(\mathbf{x}_j^*)\|\cos\alpha}}{\|\mathbf{x}_i^* - \mathbf{x}_j^*\|},$$

which can be minimized by decreasing α. Strictly speaking, C can still be considerable with a small α, if $|(\|\phi(\mathbf{x}_i^*)\| - \|\phi(\mathbf{x}_j^*)\|)|$ is large enough. However, in practice, we observe that the $\|\phi(\mathbf{x})\|$'s do not deviate from their maximum norm within the set significantly. That is, within a small sub set of $\mathbf{x}$, the vectors $\phi(\mathbf{x})$ approximately lie on a sphere (see Appendix). Therefore, we make the following claim: *the local Lipschitz constant of a network layer can be minimized by* *reducing the angles between the output vectors.* Below, we justify this claim from another perspective.

Consider a set of coordinates $\{\mathbf{x}_i\}_{i=1}^N$ and the function $\phi(\cdot)$ induced by a hidden-layer of an MLP. Let $\{\lambda\}_{i=1}^N$ be the singular values of $\mathbf{X}$ where $\mathbf{X} = [\phi(\mathbf{x}_1)^T \phi(\mathbf{x}_2)^T \dots \phi(\mathbf{x}_N)^T]$. Intuitively, if the angles α between the columns of $\mathbf{X}$ are small, most of the energy of the singular values should be concentrated on the first few components. On the other hand, if α is high, the energies should be distributed. Therefore, we advocate in this paper that the stable rank, defined as $\mathcal{S}(\mathbf{X}) = \sum_{i=1}^N \frac{\sqrt{\lambda_i}}{\max_i(\sqrt{\lambda_i})}$ [20], can be used as a useful proxy measure for the spread (angles) of the column vectors of $\mathbf{X}$, *i.e.*, $\mathcal{S}(\mathbf{X})$ is large if the spread is large, and vise-versa. We empirically demonstrate that MLPs are *not* able to obtain a high Lipschitz constant with a small $\mathcal{S}(\mathbf{X})$ (see Fig. 2 and Fig. 7). If our intuition was incorrect (*i.e.*, if the network could obtain a high Lipschitz constant with a small α by varying the norm of the layer outputs significantly), we should be able to observe high local Lipschitz constants with small $\mathcal{S}(\mathbf{X})$. Our experimental results in strongly counters this. That is, networks can *not* obtain a high Lipschitz constant if $\mathcal{S}(\mathbf{X})$ are low. In other words, coordinate-MLPs primarily try to increase the Lipschitz constant by increasing the angles between the network outputs.

Based on the gathered insights within this section, we argue that $\mathcal{S}(\mathbf{X})$ is a potentially useful proxy measure for the local Lipschitz smoothness of network layers. More precisely, if $\mathcal{S}(\mathbf{X})$ is larger, then the Lipschitz constant C tends to become larger, and vice-versa. This is a useful result, as computing the exact Lipschitz constant of an MLP is an NP-hard problem [22]. Although one can efficiently obtain upper-bounds for the Lipschitz constant, that requires calculating the gradients of the function. Instead, we can gain a rough understanding on the behavior of the Lipschitz smoothness of a particular layer by observing $\mathcal{S}$ at run-time. We should emphasize that these insights are based on intuition and empirical evaluation. A more rigorous proof on this relationship is outside the scope of this paper, but the established relationship is sufficient to allow us to make some useful architectural predictions. In Sect. 3.4, we will connect these gained insights to the *local* Lipshchitz smoothness of the signal and the properties of activation functions.

3.4 Local Lipschitz Smoothness and the Activation Function

Natural signals have varying local Lipschitz smoothness. For instance, an image may contain high variations within a particular subset of the pixels and may consist of constant pixel values within another subset. Since the final layer of an MLP is linear, the hidden non-linear layers should then have the ability to construct representations with varying local Lipschitz smoothness for better signal encoding. In this section, we show that this ability is primarily linked to the first and second-order gradients of the activation function.

In Sect. 3.3, we established that in practice, the angle between the network outputs determines the Lipschitz smoothness. It is easy to see that both the

Table 1. Comparison of existing activation functions (top block) against the proposed activation functions (bottom block). The proposed activations and the sine activations fulfill **R1** and **R2**, implying better suitability to encode high-frequency signals.

Activation (ψ)	Equation	Parameterized	ψ'	ψ''	R1	R2
ReLU	$\max(0, x)$	✗	$\begin{cases} 1, & \text{if } x > 0 \\ 0, & \text{otherwise} \end{cases}$	0	✗	✗
PReLU	$\begin{cases} x, & \text{if } x > 0 \\ ax, & \text{otherwise} \end{cases}$	✓	$\begin{cases} 1, & \text{if } x > 0 \\ a, & \text{otherwise} \end{cases}$	0	✓	✗
Sin	$\sin(ax)$	✓	$a\cos(ax)$	$-a^2\sin(ax)$	✓	✓
Tanh	$\frac{e^x-e^{-x}}{e^x+e^{-x}}$	✗	$\frac{4e^{2x}}{(e^{2x}+1)^2}$	$-\frac{8(e^{2x}-1)e^{2x}}{(e^{2x}+1)^3}$	✗	✓
Sigmoid	$\frac{1}{1+e^{-x}}$	✗	$\frac{e^x}{(e^x+1)^2}$	$-\frac{(e^x-1)e^x}{(e^x+1)^3}$	✗	✓
SiLU	$\frac{x}{1+e^{-x}}$	✗	$\frac{e^x(e^x+x+1)}{(e^x+1)^2}$	$-\frac{e^x((x-2)e^x-x-2)}{(e^x+1)^3}$	✗	✓
SoftPlus	$\frac{1}{a}\log(1+e^{ax})$	✓	$\frac{e^{cx}}{1+e^{cx}}$	$\frac{ce^{cx}}{(e^{cx}+1)^2}$	✓	✗
Gaussian	$e^{\frac{-0.5x^2}{a^2}}$	✓	$-\frac{xe^{-\frac{x^2}{2a^2}}}{a^2}$	$\frac{(x^2-a^2)e^{-\frac{x^2}{2a^2}}}{a^4}$	✓	✓
Quadratic	$\frac{1}{1+(ax)^2}$	✓	$-\frac{2a^2x}{(a^2x^2+1)^2}$	$\frac{2a^2(3a^2x^2-1)}{(a^2x^2+1)^3}$	✓	✓
Multi Quadratic	$\frac{1}{\sqrt{1+(ax)^2}}$	✓	$-\frac{a^2x}{(a^2x^2+1)^{\frac{3}{2}}}$	$\frac{2a^4x^2-a^2}{(a^2x^2+1)^{\frac{5}{2}}}$	✓	✓
Laplacian	$e^{(\frac{-\lvert x\rvert}{a})}$	✓	$\frac{xe^{\frac{\lvert x\rvert}{a}}}{a\lvert x\rvert}$	$\frac{e^{\frac{\lvert x\rvert}{a}}}{a^2}$	✓	✓
Super-Gaussian	$[e^{\frac{-0.5x^2}{a^2}}]^b$	✓	$-\frac{bxe^{-\frac{bx^2}{2a^2}}}{a^2}$	$\frac{b(bx^2-a^2)e^{-\frac{bx^2}{2a^2}}}{a^4}$	✓	✓
ExpSin	$e^{-\sin(ax)}$	✓	$ae^{\sin(ax)}\cos(ax)$	$-a^2e^{\sin(ax)}(\sin(ax)-\cos^2(ax))$	✓	✓

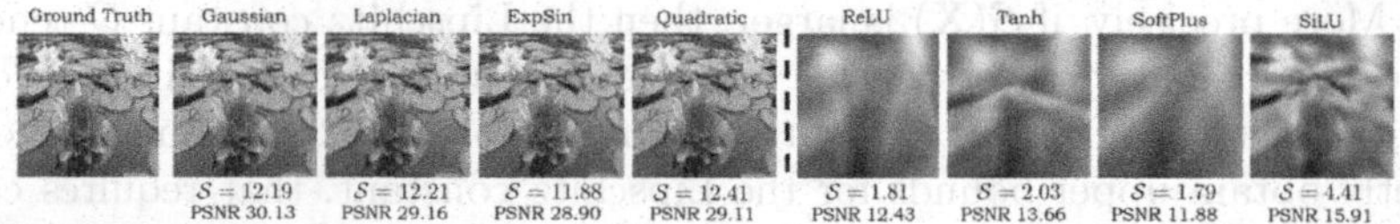

Fig. 2. Proposed activations (left block) vs. existing activations (right block) and their respective stable ranks ($\mathcal{S}$) in image encoding without positional embeddings. As predicted by Table 1, the proposed activations are better suited for encoding signals with high fidelity. As Sect. 3.2 stated, the stable ranks of the proposed activations are higher, indicating larger local Lipschitz constants which allow sharper edges.

affine transformation and the activation function contribute to the composite Lipschitz constant of a hidden layer. However, the Lipschitz constant of the affine transformation is the operator norm of its weight matrix: Let $\mathbf{x} \in \mathbb{B}^m_\delta$ with center $\mathbf{x}_0$. Then as $\lim_{\delta \to 0}$,

$$\|(\mathbf{A}\mathbf{x} + \mathbf{b}) - (\mathbf{A}\mathbf{x}_0 + \mathbf{b})\| \leq C_{\mathbf{x}_0,\delta}\|\mathbf{x} - \mathbf{x}_0\| \tag{7}$$

$$C_{\mathbf{x}_0,\delta} = \sup_{\|\mathbf{x}-\mathbf{x}_0\| \neq 0} \frac{\|\mathbf{A}(\mathbf{x} - \mathbf{x}_0)\|}{\|\mathbf{x} - \mathbf{x}_0\|}, \tag{8}$$

which is not a local property. In other words, the network can only control the Lipschitz smoothness of the network via the affine layer globally, which is not useful in encoding natural signals. Hence, we direct our attention towards the activation function. However, it is not trivial to establish the connection between the point-wise activation function $\psi : \mathbb{R} \rightarrow \mathbb{R}$ and the composite Lipschitz smoothness, given that the vector norms stays approximately the same (which is our empirical observation). Hence, we strive to obtain mathematical intuition as described next.

Consider an input vector $\mathbf{x}_0 = [x_1, \ldots, x_N]$. Further, let $\mathbf{x}_{\epsilon_1} = [x_1 + \epsilon_1, \ldots, x_N + \epsilon_1]$ and $\mathbf{x}_{\epsilon_2} = [x_1 + \epsilon_2, \ldots, x_N + \epsilon_2]$. Our intention is to obtain a measure for $\measuredangle(\mathbf{x}_0, \mathbf{x}_{\epsilon_1}) - \measuredangle(\mathbf{x}_0, \mathbf{x}_{\epsilon_2})$. Further,

$$\measuredangle(\mathbf{x}_0, \mathbf{x}_{\epsilon_1}) = \cos^{-1}\Big(\frac{\psi(\mathbf{x}_0) \cdot \psi(\mathbf{x}_{\epsilon_1})}{\|\psi(\mathbf{x}_0)\|\|\psi(\mathbf{x}_{\epsilon_1})\|}\Big).$$

Since the norms are approximately constant, we can use a proxy for $\measuredangle(\mathbf{x}_0, \mathbf{x}_{\epsilon_1}) - \measuredangle(\mathbf{x}_0, \mathbf{x}_{\epsilon_2})$ as,

$$\begin{aligned}
|\tilde{\measuredangle}(\mathbf{x}_0, \mathbf{x}_{\epsilon_1}) - \tilde{\measuredangle}(\mathbf{x}_0, \mathbf{x}_{\epsilon_2})| &= |\psi(\mathbf{x}_0) \cdot \psi(\mathbf{x}_{\epsilon_1}) - \psi(\mathbf{x}_0) \cdot \psi(\mathbf{x}_{\epsilon_2})| \\
&= |\sum_{i=i}^{N} \Big(\psi(x_i + \epsilon_1) - \psi(x_i + \epsilon_2)\Big)\psi(x_i)| \\
&\leq \sum_{i=i}^{N} |\Big(\psi(x_i + \epsilon_1) - \psi(x_i + \epsilon_2)\Big)||\psi(x_i)| \\
&\leq C_{\psi}|\epsilon_1 - \epsilon_2| \sum_{i=i}^{N} |\psi(x_i)|,
\end{aligned}$$

Fig. 3. Novel view synthesis without positional embedding (zoom in for a better view). Gaussian activations can completely omit positional embeddings while producing results with significantly better fidelity. In contrast, the performance of ReLU-MLPs severely degrade when positional embeddings are not used. We use 8-Layer MLPs for this experiment.

where C_{ψ} is the local Lipschits constant of the activation function in the corresponding interval I. We then obtain,

$$\frac{|\tilde{\measuredangle}(\mathbf{x}_0, \mathbf{x}_{\epsilon_1}) - \tilde{\measuredangle}(\mathbf{x}_0, \mathbf{x}_{\epsilon_2})|}{|\epsilon_1 - \epsilon_2|} \leq C_{\psi}|\sum_{i=i}^{N} |\psi(x_i)| \tag{9}$$

Therefore, the upper-bound on the Lipschitz constant of the angle variation in a local interval can be increased by increasing the local Lipschitz constant of the activation function. Further, by definition, the local Lipschits constant $C_\psi = \sup_{x \in I}(|\frac{d\psi}{dx}|)$. Therefore, we come to the conclusion that in order to encode signals with high frequencies (large fluctuations), one needs to use activation functions that contain first-order derivatives with large magnitudes (the converse is also true). Also, it is important to note that the magnitudes of the local variations depend on the signal. For instance, one can have an extremely smooth signal which can be encoded using activation functions with smaller magnitudes of first-order derivatives. However, the same activations would not be suitable for encoding signals with large fluctuations. Therefore, for better usability across signals with different smoothness properties, activation functions need to be parameterized where the first-order derivates can be controlled via the hyperparameters. We denote this as the requirement 1 (**R1**)

However, **R1** is not necessarily sufficient to ensure good signal fidelity when considering a particular signal with significantly varying fluctuations across different intervals. Thus, for better performance, activations should consist of varying first-order derivatives across a considerable interval, and equivalently, non-negligible second-order derivatives (to obtain varying Lipschitz smoothness). We denote this as requirement 2 (**R2**). This gives the affine transformations the ability to project the points to different regions of the activation function and achieve varying local Lipschitz smoothness.

Fig. 4. Novel view synthesis with positional embedding (zoom in for a better view). With Gaussian activations, shallow MLPs can obtain high-fidelity reconstructions. In contrast, the performance of ReLU-MLPs degrade when the depth of the MLP reduces. We use 4-layer MLPs for this comparison.

It is interesting to note that most of the commonly used activations in deep learning do not satisfy above properties. For instance, consider the ReLU activation $\psi(x) = \max(0, x)$. The derivative of the ReLU then cannot be more than 1, which hampers its ability to encode function with large local variations. Activations such as Sigmoid, Tanh, GELU also have bounded first-order gradient magnitudes within a smaller range and are not parameterized, which violates **R1**. On the other hand, PReLUs, $\psi(x) = \begin{cases} x, & \text{if } x > 0 \\ ax, & \text{otherwise} \end{cases}$, is a parameterized activation that can have extremely large derivatives by controlling the hyper-parameter a. However, this derivative is either 1 or a, which violates **R2** and hampers the network's ability to obtain varying local smoothness. In contrast, recently proposed sine activations [24] $\psi = \sin(ax)$ satisfy both **R1** and **R2**, and thus, are suitable for encoding signals. However, we show that the periodicity, as advocated in [24], is not a crucial requirement, as long as **R1** and **R2** are satisfied. Instead, we affirm that there is a much broader class of activations that can be used in coordinate-MLPs, and propose several parameterized activation functions that originate from the family of infinitely differentiable functions as examples. Table 1 compares existing and several novel activation functions that we propose, against **R1** and **R2**. Finally, it is important to note that even without the restriction that the norms of the vectors are approximately constant, the above conclusions hold (see Appendix).

Activation	Depth	PE	PSNR	SSIM
ReLU	4L	✓	27.44	0.922
Gaussian	4L	✓	**31.13**	**0.947**
ReLU	8L	✗	26.55	0.918
Gaussian	8L	✗	**31.17**	**0.949**
ReLU	8L	✓	30.91	0.941
Gaussian	8L	✓	**31.58**	**0.951**

Fig. 5. Quantitative comparison in novel view synthesis on the real synthetic dataset [11]. Gaussian activations can achieve high-fidelity reconstructions without positional embeddings. When equipped with positional embeddings, they demonstrate similar performance with $\sim 50\%$ less parameters.

Fig. 6. Qualitative comparison of convergence when MLPs are initialized without following [24] **(after 3000 epochs).** Unlike Sine activations, Gaussian activations are robust to various initialization schemes (example shown used Xavier normal initialization).

4 Experiments

4.1 Comparison of Activation Functions

We compare the capacity of a coordinate-MLP in encoding signals when equipped with different activation functions. Figure 2 illustrates an example where an image is encoded as the weights of an MLP. As shown, newly proposed Gaussian, Laplacian, ExpSin, and Quadratic activation functions are able to encode the image with significantly better fidelity with sharper gradients (high Lipschitz constants), compared to the existing activations such as ReLU, Tanh, SoftPlus, and SiLU. Also, note that the stable ranks (the energy distribution between the singular values) of the hidden representations are higher for the proposed activation functions than the rest. This matches with our theoretical predictions in Sect. 3.2

4.2 Novel View Synthesis

Without Positional Embeddings: We leverage the real synthetic dataset released by [11] to test the capacity of the Gaussian activations in encoding high-dimensional signals. Figure 3 qualitatively contrasts the performance of ReLU vs. Gaussian activations without the positional embeddings. When the positional embeddings are not used, the ReLU MLPs demonstrate poor performance in capturing high-frequency details. On the contrary, Gaussian activations can capture information with higher fidelity in the absence of positional embedding. We believe this is an interesting result that opens up the possibility of positional-embedding-free architectures.

With Positional Embeddings: Although suitably chosen activation functions can omit positional embeddings, the combination of the two can still enable shallower networks to learn high-frequency functions. Figure 4 depicts an example with 4-layer MLPs. As evident, when the network is shallower, ReLU MLPs showcase reduced quality, while the performance of Gaussian activated MLPs is on-par with deeper ReLU MLPs. This advocates that practitioners can enjoy significantly cheaper architectures when properly designed activation functions are used. Table 5 depicts the quantitative results that include above comparisons.

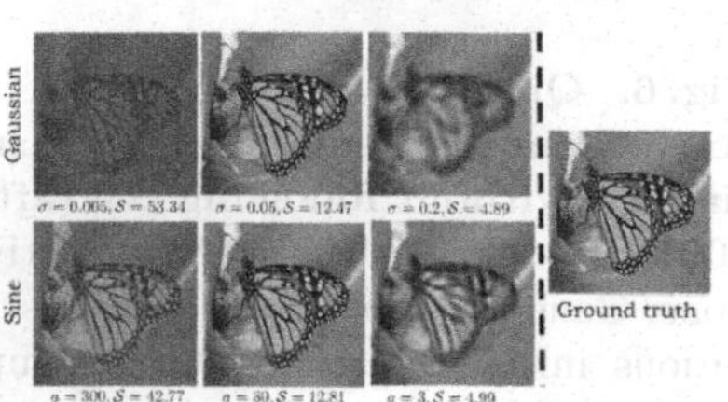

Fig. 7. Stable rank (S) vs the fidelity of reconstructions. Having an extremely high or low stable rank (or equivalently a Lipschitz constant) hampers the ability of an MLP in encoding functions with fine details (Sect. 3.2). Thus, it is important to adjust the hyper-parameters of an activation function to tune the above metrics to a suitable range.

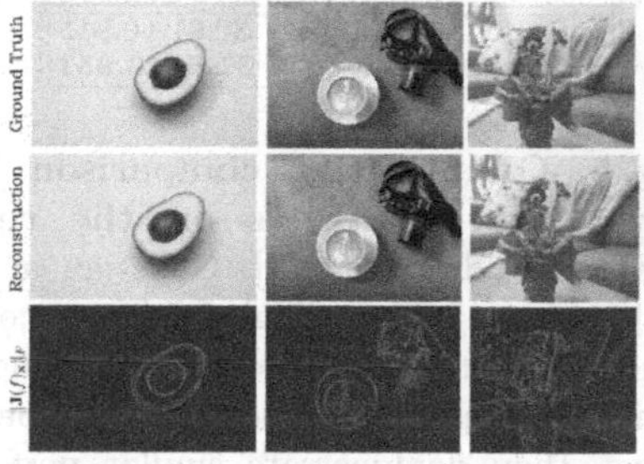

Fig. 8. Distribution of the upper-bound of the point-wise Lipschitz constant $\|\mathbf{J}(f)_\mathbf{x}\|_F$ with Gaussian reconstructions. Having an activation function with a suitable bound for the local Lipschitz constant helps the network to learn functions with properly distributed derivatives.

4.3 Convergence

Sitzmann *et al.* comprehensively demonstrated that sine activations enable MLPs to encode signals with fine details. However, a drawback entailed with the sine activations is that they are extremely sensitive to the initialization of the MLP. In comparison, the proposed non-periodic activation functions do not suffer from

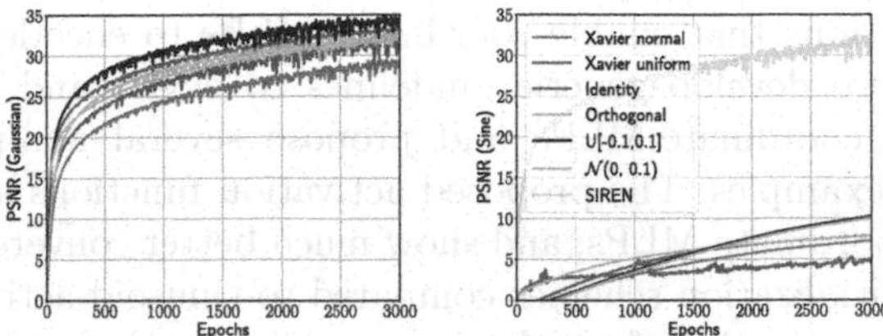

Fig. 9. Convergence rates of Gaussian and sine MLPs on natural images by [27] under different initialization schemes. Gaussian activations are significantly robust to various initialization methods compared to sine activations. Other proposed non-periodic activation functions (not shown in the figure) also demonstrate similar robustness.

such a problem. Figure 6 illustrates a qualitative example. When the initialization method of the MLP does not strictly follow the method proposed in Sitzmann *et al.*, the sine activated MLPs do not converge even after 3000 epochs. In contrast, Gaussian activations demonstrate much faster convergence. Figure 9 illustrates a quantitative comparison of convergence. We trained the networks on the natural image dataset released by [27] and the average PSNR value after each iteration is shown in Fig. 9. As clearly evident, the Gaussian activations enjoy higher robustness against the various initialization schemes of an MLP.

4.4 Local Lipschitz Smoothness

The local Lipschitz smoothness of a function converges to the Jacobian norm at the corresponding point (see Appendix). In Sect. 3.4, we showed that a good proxy measure for the Lipschitz constant is the range of the first-order derivative of the activation function. We further affirmed that the Lipschitz constant should be suitably chosen for better performance *i.e.* a too high or too low Lipschitz constant can prevent the network from properly learning a signal. Figure 7 illustrates an example that confirms this statement. When σ increases, Range$|\psi'|$ of the Gaussian activation decreases, decreasing the Lipschitz constant (see Sect. 3.4). In contrast, when a increases, the Range$|\psi'|$ of the sine activation increases, increasing the Lipschitz constant. A lower Lipschitz constant results in blurry edges as it does not allow sharp changes locally. On the other hand, an extremely large Lipschitz constant allows unwanted fluctuations. Hence, choosing the parameters to be in a suitable range is vital for better performance. Figure 8 shows the distribution of local Lipschitz constants after encoding a signal with Gaussian activations with properly chosen parameters.

5 Conclusion

We seek to extend the current understanding of activation functions that allow coordinate-MLPs to encode functions with high fidelity. We show that the previously proposed sinusoid activation [25] is a single example of a much broader class of activation functions that enable coordinate-MLPs to encode high-frequency signals. Further, we develop generic guidelines to devise and tune an activation function for coordinate-MLPs and propose several non-periodic activation functions as examples. The proposed activation functions allow positional-embedding-free coordinate-MLPs, and show much better convergence properties against various initialization schemes compared to sinusoid activations. Finally, choosing Gaussian activations from the proposed list, we demonstrate compelling results across various signal encoding tasks.

References

1. Basher, A., Sarmad, M., Boutellier, J.: LightSAL: lightweight sign agnostic learning for implicit surface representation. arXiv preprint arXiv:2103.14273 (2021)
2. Basri, R., Galun, M., Geifman, A., Jacobs, D., Kasten, Y., Kritchman, S.: Frequency bias in neural networks for input of non-uniform density. In: International Conference on Machine Learning, pp. 685–694. PMLR (2020)
3. Biship, C.M.: Pattern recognition and machine learning (information science and statistics) (2007)
4. Chen, Z., Zhang, H.: Learning implicit fields for generative shape modeling. In: Proceedings of the IEEE/CVF Conference on Computer Vision and Pattern Recognition, pp. 5939–5948 (2019)
5. Deng, B., et al.: NASA neural articulated shape approximation. In: Vedaldi, A., Bischof, H., Brox, T., Frahm, J.-M. (eds.) ECCV 2020. LNCS, vol. 12352, pp. 612–628. Springer, Cham (2020). https://doi.org/10.1007/978-3-030-58571-6_36
6. Genova, K., Cole, F., Sud, A., Sarna, A., Funkhouser, T.: Local deep implicit functions for 3D shape. In: Proceedings of the IEEE/CVF Conference on Computer Vision and Pattern Recognition, pp. 4857–4866 (2020)
7. Henzler, P., Mitra, N.J., Ritschel, T.: Learning a neural 3D texture space from 2D exemplars. In: Proceedings of the IEEE/CVF Conference on Computer Vision and Pattern Recognition, pp. 8356–8364 (2020)
8. Leshno, M., Lin, V.Y., Pinkus, A., Schocken, S.: Multilayer feedforward networks with a nonpolynomial activation function can approximate any function. Neural Netw. **6**(6), 861–867 (1993)
9. Liang, S., Lyu, L., Wang, C., Yang, H.: Reproducing activation function for deep learning. arXiv preprint arXiv:2101.04844 (2021)
10. Martin-Brualla, R., Radwan, N., Sajjadi, M.S., Barron, J.T., Dosovitskiy, A., Duckworth, D.: Nerf in the wild: neural radiance fields for unconstrained photo collections. In: Proceedings of the IEEE/CVF Conference on Computer Vision and Pattern Recognition, pp. 7210–7219 (2021)
11. Mildenhall, B., Srinivasan, P.P., Tancik, M., Barron, J.T., Ramamoorthi, R., Ng, R.: NeRF: representing scenes as neural radiance fields for view synthesis. In: Vedaldi, A., Bischof, H., Brox, T., Frahm, J.-M. (eds.) ECCV 2020. LNCS, vol. 12346, pp. 405–421. Springer, Cham (2020). https://doi.org/10.1007/978-3-030-58452-8_24
12. Mu, J., Qiu, W., Kortylewski, A., Yuille, A., Vasconcelos, N., Wang, X.: A-SDF: learning disentangled signed distance functions for articulated shape representation. arXiv preprint arXiv:2104.07645 (2021)

13. Niemeyer, M., Mescheder, L., Oechsle, M., Geiger, A.: Differentiable volumetric rendering: Learning implicit 3d representations without 3D supervision. In: Proceedings of the IEEE/CVF Conference on Computer Vision and Pattern Recognition, pp. 3504–3515 (2020)
14. Oechsle, M., Mescheder, L., Niemeyer, M., Strauss, T., Geiger, A.: Texture fields: learning texture representations in function space. In: Proceedings of the IEEE/CVF International Conference on Computer Vision, pp. 4531–4540 (2019)
15. Park, J.J., Florence, P., Straub, J., Newcombe, R., Lovegrove, S.: DeepSDF: learning continuous signed distance functions for shape representation. In: Proceedings of the IEEE/CVF Conference on Computer Vision and Pattern Recognition, pp. 165–174 (2019)
16. Park, K., et al.: Nerfies: deformable neural radiance fields. In: Proceedings of the IEEE/CVF International Conference on Computer Vision, pp. 5865–5874 (2021)
17. Pumarola, A., Corona, E., Pons-Moll, G., Moreno-Noguer, F.: D-NeRF: neural radiance fields for dynamic scenes. In: Proceedings of the IEEE/CVF Conference on Computer Vision and Pattern Recognition, pp. 10318–10327 (2021)
18. Rahaman, N., et al.: On the spectral bias of neural networks. In: International Conference on Machine Learning, pp. 5301–5310. PMLR (2019)
19. Rebain, D., Jiang, W., Yazdani, S., Li, K., Yi, K.M., Tagliasacchi, A.: DeRF: decomposed radiance fields. In: Proceedings of the IEEE/CVF Conference on Computer Vision and Pattern Recognition, pp. 14153–14161 (2021)
20. Rudelson, M., Vershynin, R.: Sampling from large matrices: an approach through geometric functional analysis. J. ACM (JACM) **54**(4), 21-es (2007)
21. Saito, S., Huang, Z., Natsume, R., Morishima, S., Kanazawa, A., Li, H.: PIFu: pixel-aligned implicit function for high-resolution clothed human digitization. In: Proceedings of the IEEE/CVF International Conference on Computer Vision, pp. 2304–2314 (2019)
22. Scaman, K., Virmaux, A.: Lipschitz regularity of deep neural networks: analysis and efficient estimation. arXiv preprint arXiv:1805.10965 (2018)
23. Shannon, C.E.: Communication in the presence of noise. Proc. IRE **37**(1), 10–21 (1949)
24. Sitzmann, V., Martel, J., Bergman, A., Lindell, D., Wetzstein, G.: Implicit neural representations with periodic activation functions. In: Advances in Neural Information Processing Systems, vol. 33 (2020)
25. Sitzmann, V., Zollhöfer, M., Wetzstein, G.: Scene representation networks: Continuous 3D-structure-aware neural scene representations. arXiv preprint arXiv:1906.01618 (2019)
26. Sun, Y., Liu, J., Xie, M., Wohlberg, B., Kamilov, U.S.: CoIL: coordinate-based internal learning for imaging inverse problems. arXiv preprint arXiv:2102.05181 (2021)
27. Tancik, M., et al.: Fourier features let networks learn high frequency functions in low dimensional domains. arXiv preprint arXiv:2006.10739 (2020)
28. Tiwari, G., Sarafianos, N., Tung, T., Pons-Moll, G.: Neural-GIF: neural generalized implicit functions for animating people in clothing. In: Proceedings of the IEEE/CVF International Conference on Computer Vision, pp. 11708–11718 (2021)
29. Wang, Z., Wu, S., Xie, W., Chen, M., Prisacariu, V.A.: Nerf-: neural radiance fields without known camera parameters. arXiv preprint arXiv:2102.07064 (2021)
30. Xiang, F., Xu, Z., Hasan, M., Hold-Geoffroy, Y., Sunkavalli, K., Su, H.: NeuTex: neural texture mapping for volumetric neural rendering. In: Proceedings of the IEEE/CVF Conference on Computer Vision and Pattern Recognition, pp. 7119–7128 (2021)

31. Yu, A., Ye, V., Tancik, M., Kanazawa, A.: pixelNeRF: neural radiance fields from one or few images. In: Proceedings of the IEEE/CVF Conference on Computer Vision and Pattern Recognition, pp. 4578–4587 (2021)
32. Zheng, J., Ramasinghe, S., Lucey, S.: Rethinking positional encoding. arXiv preprint arXiv:2107.02561 (2021)

Deforming Radiance Fields with Cages

Tianhan Xu[1] and Tatsuya Harada[1,2(✉)]

[1] The University of Tokyo, Tokyo, Japan
{tianhan.xu,harada}@mi.t.u-tokyo.ac.jp
[2] RIKEN, Tokyo, Japan

Abstract. Recent advances in radiance fields enable photorealistic rendering of static or dynamic 3D scenes, but still do not support explicit deformation that is used for scene manipulation or animation. In this paper, we propose a method that enables a new type of deformation of the radiance field: free-form radiance field deformation. We use a triangular mesh that encloses the foreground object called *cage* as an interface, and by manipulating the cage vertices, our approach enables the free-form deformation of the radiance field. The core of our approach is cage-based deformation which is commonly used in mesh deformation. We propose a novel formulation to extend it to the radiance field, which maps the position and the view direction of the sampling points from the deformed space to the canonical space, thus enabling the rendering of the deformed scene. The deformation results of the synthetic datasets and the real-world datasets demonstrate the effectiveness of our approach. Project page: https://xth430.github.io/deforming-nerf/.

Keywords: Scene representation · Radiance field · Scene manipulation · Cage-based deformation · Free-form deformation

1 Introduction

Photorealistic free-view rendering has recently received increasing attention for its various real-world applications such as virtual reality, augmented reality, games, and movies. Recently, neural scene representations [23,28,30,40] have shown better capability to capture both geometry and appearance that exceed traditional structure-from-motion [13,44] or image-based rendering [4,10]. The most representative work is Neural Radiance Field (NeRF) [28], which represents the static 3D scene as a radiance field and uses a neural network to encode the volume density and the view-dependent radiance color. With volume rendering [19], NeRF can achieve photorealistic rendering from an arbitrary viewpoint. Subsequent works extended NeRF to support modeling dynamic scenes [35,36,39,43], dark scenes [27], multi-scale rendering [1]. Manipulable or editable scene rendering is one of the directions of NeRF extensions that received attention for its numerous applications such as scene animation or new scene generation. However, the above-mentioned works focus on modeling the existing scenes and thus cannot generate scenes that are unseen during the training.

S. Avidan et al. (Eds.): ECCV 2022, LNCS 13693, pp. 159–175, 2022.
https://doi.org/10.1007/978-3-031-19827-4_10

For some specific object categories, such as the human body or articulated objects, recent studies [24,32,33,37,38,41,46] enable the generation of the unseen scene by controlling the body shape or bone pose. Besides, some works utilize the idea of compositionality to separate foreground objects in the scene during training, thus allowing the scaling or moving of objects in the scene [16,48]. However, the manipulation in these approaches only allows affine transformations of objects. Although the above methods attempted to develop for radiance field manipulation, they have a common and clear limitation: they cannot perform explicit scene manipulation with details (e.g. torsion or local scaling) for arbitrary categories of objects.

To address the above issues, we propose a new approach for manipulating the optimized radiance field. Our method allows free-form deformation of the radiance field, thus enabling explicit object-level scene deformation or animation. Our idea is an extension of cage-based deformation (CBD), which is originally proposed for mesh deformation [17,18,22]. Specifically, the deformation of a fine mesh, or the displacement of its vertices, is driven by manipulating the vertices of the coarse triangular mesh called *cage* that enclosed the fine mesh (e.g. Fig. 3(c)). Such a mesh deformation method is also known as *free-form deformation.* Extending cage-based deformation to radiance field deformation while maintaining the properties of the radiance field such as volumetric representation and view-dependent radiance is non-trivial and yet unexplored. In this paper, we derive a novel formulation for applying CBD to the radiance field that satisfies the properties of the radiance field. However, we find that simply applying the proposed formulation to achieve radiance field deformation brings a new issue: the volume rendering process of the radiance field usually requires a huge number of sampling points [28], and CBD is usually accompanied by a high-dimensional tensor computation, these facts lead to impractical deformation computation times. To address this specific issue, we also propose a discretization method specifically suitable for the radiance field that significantly reduces the computation time of CBD.

We conducted extensive experiments with various types of CBD algorithms using synthetic datasets and real-world datasets. Reasonable deformation and photorealistic rendering quality demonstrate the effectiveness of our approach.

In summary, our contributions are listed as follows:

- We proposed a new approach to explicitly manipulate the radiance fields using a coarse triangular mesh called cage, allowing free-form deformation of the scene while maintaining photorealistic rendering quality.
- We proposed a discretization method for cage coordinate computation specifically adapted for the radiance field rendering, which achieves a speedup of several orders of magnitude compared to the naive computation.
- We conducted extensive experiments to deform the radiance field and the rendering results demonstrate the soundness and effectiveness of our method.

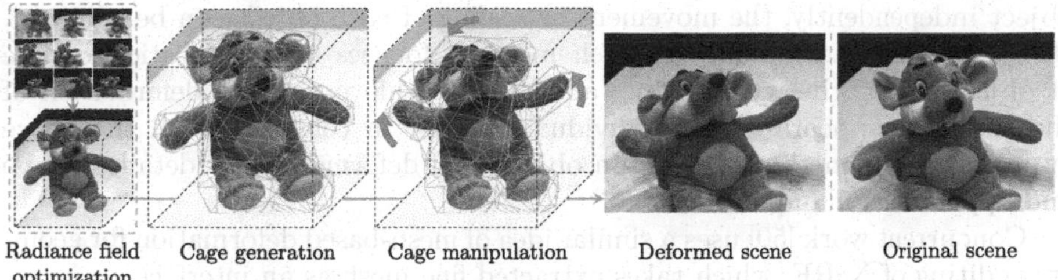

Fig. 1. An overview of our approach. Our method takes multi-view images capturing a static scene as input and uses an off-the-shelf algorithm to optimize a radiance field. Then, we automatically and/or manually generate a cage based on the optimized radiance field. By manipulating the vertices of the cage, the radiance field can be deformed accordingly. Finally, through volume rendering, the free-view rendering of the deformed scene can be achieved.

2 Related Work

Neural Scene Representation. Recently, neural scene representation, which uses a neural network to encode the 3D scenes, has received a lot of attention due to its high quality of geometry and appearance modeling compared to standard 3D representation including voxel [9,47], point clouds [6,11] or textured-mesh [20,21]. The most representative work is Neural Radiance Field (NeRF) [28], which shows that representing static scenes with volumetric density and view-dependent radiance can capture high-resolution geometry and support photorealistic novel view rendering. An obvious limitation of the original NeRF is that it can only model static scenes. Subsequent work relaxed this limitation and enabled the dynamic scene modeling by simultaneously learning the deformation fields [35,39,43] or introducing high-dimensional representation [36]. While these methods achieved the capture of dynamic scenes, none of them can generate new dynamics that are unseen in the training.

Manipulable Neural Scene Rendering. Recent work attempted to incorporate controllability into NeRF to achieve scene manipulation or new scene generation. For the specific task of human body modeling, various works proposed to combine NeRF with a parametric human model to enable human body re-posing [37,38], shape control [24] or even clothing changes [46]. For the articulated object, [33,41] proposed to build NeRF on the local coordinates of the pre-defined skeleton thus allowing the rendering of the re-posed object, and [32] proposed to learn the unknown skeleton structure along with NeRF. However, the above approaches are limited to specific categories of objects and thus cannot be generalized to the modeling and manipulating of arbitrary objects.

In addition to the above methods of using human model or skeleton to assist in modeling, another direction of manipulatable scene modeling methods utilize an idea of compositionality [12,16,34,48]. Specifically, these methods treat the 3D scene as a composition of multiple objects or backgrounds. By modeling each object independently, the movement or scaling of each object can be achieved. However, the controllability of such methods focuses on the location or size of objects w.r.t. the whole scene, and cannot achieve detailed deformation of the shape or appearance for individual objects. In contrast to all the above approaches, our method focuses on object-level deformation for detailed shape and appearance manipulation.

Concurrent work [50] uses a similar idea of mesh-based deformation for geometry editing of NeRF, which takes extracted fine mesh as an interface.

Cage-Based Deformation. Cage-based deformation (CBD) is a volumetric deformation method that is typically used for fine mesh deformation by manipulating the corresponding cage vertices. Here, *cage* denotes a watertight mesh that encloses the target fine mesh to be deformed. The core of CBD is *cage coordinates*, a generalized form of barycentric coordinates, which is used to represent the relative positions of spatial points w.r.t. the cage. The new position of a spatial point can be computed from its cage coordinates and the deformed cage. Previous works proposed several cage coordinates with different properties, including mean value coordinates (MVC) [7,18], harmonic coordinates (HC) [5,17], green coordinates (GC) [22], etc. For example, the computation of MVC and GC have closed-formulation and thus can be computed in a feed-forward manner, while HC does not have a closed-formulation and therefore its computation requires loop optimization. Specifically, the computation of HC discretizes the space into grid points and updates the HC value for each grid point by performing laplacian smoothing with certain boundary conditions. More comparisons and mathematical preliminaries can be found in [31]. In addition to the traditional CBD algorithm, recent works proposed to combine CBD with deep learning algorithm to achieve high-quality mesh deformation [14,49].

All of the above methods are focused on using CBD for mesh deformation. Our method aims to extend the CBD to the deformation of the radiance field.

3 Method

Our goal is to deform the optimized radiance field by manipulating the corresponding cage vertices, thus achieving a photorealistic rendering of the new deformed scene. An overview of our approach is shown in Fig. 1. The first step is to optimize a radiance field from the multi-view images (Sect. 3.1). Then, a cage enclosing the foreground object is generated based on the optimized radiance field (Sect. 3.2). With our proposed cage-based deformation formulation for the radiance field, the free-form deformation of the radiance field can be achieved (Sect. 3.3, Sect. 3.4).

3.1 Radiance Fields Revisited

Neural radiance field (NeRF) [28] uses a neural network to encode the 3D scene as a continuous neural representation, which receives the spatial position $\mathbf{x} \in \mathbb{R}^3$

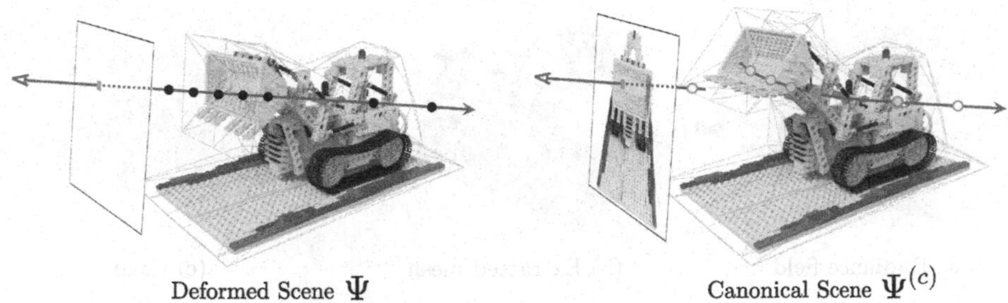

Fig. 2. Rendering process of the deformed scene. To perform volume rendering for the deformed radiance field Ψ, we map the sampling points on the ray to the canonical space through cage-based deformation and query the color and density in the canonical radiance field $\Psi^{(c)}$.

and view direction $\mathbf{d} \in \mathbb{R}^3$ as inputs and computes the RGB color $\mathbf{c} \in \mathbb{R}^3$ and density $\sigma \in \mathbb{R}$ of that point. With volume rendering, photorealistic rendering of NeRF from an arbitrary viewpoint can be achieved. Recently, some variants of radiance field representation have been proposed, for example, Plenoxels [8] use grid representation and directly optimize radiance field without using neural networks. Without loss of generality, we refer to the 3D scene representation that can be formulated as $\Psi : (\mathbf{x}, \mathbf{d}) \rightarrow (\mathbf{c}, \sigma)$ as *radiance field*.

As explored in previous studies, given a static scene, a radiance field $\Psi^{(c)}$ can be optimized from a set of multi-view images with calibrated camera parameters. Here c stands for "canonical", which denotes the original static scene, to distinguish it from the later deformed scene.

3.2 Cage Generation from Radiance Fields

In this paper, *cage* refers to a coarse 3D triangular mesh that strictly encloses the foreground object. We demonstrate a method for automatically and/or manually generating a cage from the optimized radiance field. Specifically, the first step is to convert the radiance field into a fine mesh using surface extraction methods such as marching cubes [26] (Fig. 3(b)). The second step is to create the corresponding cage for the generated mesh (Fig. 3(c)). For scenes containing only foreground objects (such as those optimized using masked images), we use [45] to compute the corresponding cage. For scenes containing backgrounds, we use Blender [3] to manually split the foreground objects from the reconstructed fine mesh and then apply [45] to compute the cage. However, some cage predictions may be inaccurate due to the complex shapes or fine details of the scenes. For these cases, we manually resolve them based on the automatically generated cage for better manipulation performance. Alternatively, if only a simple deformation (or moving, scaling) is needed, we can also use 3D software to manually build a simple cage, such as rectangle or cylinder, by referring to the extracted fine mesh.

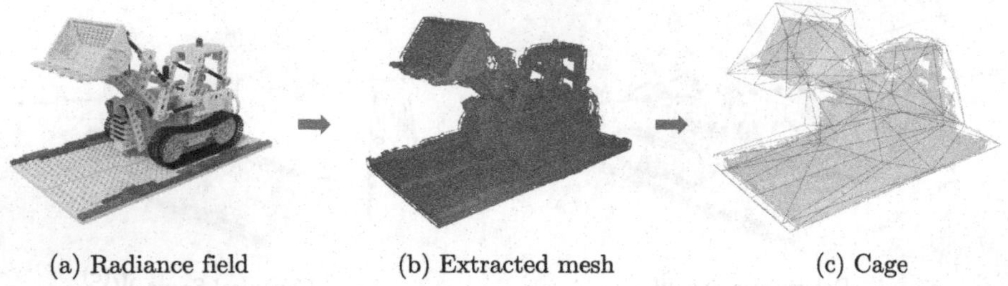

(a) Radiance field (b) Extracted mesh (c) Cage

Fig. 3. Cage generation process. After extracting a fine mesh from the optimized radiance field, a cage can be generated automatically and/or manually according to the fine mesh.

3.3 Cage-Based Deformation

Cage-based deformation (CBD) is originally proposed for deforming a fine mesh using the cage, which calculates the vertex displacement of the fine mesh caused by the cage manipulation. Specifically, given a cage $\mathcal{C}$ with vertices $\{\mathbf{v}_j\}$, points $\mathbf{x} \in \mathbb{R}^3$ inside $\mathcal{C}$ can be identified with cage coordinates $\{\omega_j\}$ which represent the relative position of $\mathbf{x}$ w.r.t. $\mathcal{C}$. Formally, the position of point $\mathbf{x}$ is weighted by the cage vertices as:

$$\mathbf{x} = \sum_j \omega_j(\mathbf{x})\mathbf{v}_j. \tag{1}$$

Consider that we manipulate the vertices of $\mathcal{C}$ and deform it to cage $\mathcal{C}'$ with vertices $\{\mathbf{v}'_j\}$. Using the calculated cage coordinate, the deformed position of $\mathbf{x}$ for the deformed cage $\mathcal{C}'$ can be calculated as:

$$\mathbf{x}' = \sum_j \omega_j(\mathbf{x})\mathbf{v}'_j. \tag{2}$$

Previous studies [17,18,22] proposed several kinds of cage coordinates and achieved promising results on the mesh deformation.

Note that although the above formulation seems simple, the actual derivation and computation of the cage coordinate $\{\omega_j\}$ is complicated and usually accompanied by a large tensor computation. For detailed computation, we recommend referring to the original papers of these cage coordinates [17,18,22].

3.4 Deforming Radiance Fields

In this section, we introduce a novel formulation that extends the application of CBD from mesh to the radiance field. Remind that our goal is to deform the optimized radiance field $\Psi^{(c)}$ for the free-view rendering of the deformed scenes. Suppose we have a cage $\mathcal{C}^{(c)}$ that accompanies $\Psi^{(c)}$ that encloses the foreground object. Consider that we manipulate the vertices of $\mathcal{C}^{(c)}$ and deform it to a new cage $\mathcal{C}$, and denote the desired radiance field after deformation as Ψ.

To achieve volume rendering of Ψ, the sampling points are required to be mapped from the deformed space to the canonical space for color and density computations, as shown in Fig. 2. To describe such deformed-to-canonical mapping, we reversely treat the cage deformation process as: the new cage $\mathcal{C}$ is deformed to the canonical cage $\mathcal{C}^{(c)}$. While contrary to the actual cage manipulation process, such a convention allows us to map the points in the deformed space back to the canonical space. Specifically, we denote the deformed-to-canonical mapping of spatial position and view direction as:

$$\phi_{\mathbf{x}} : \mathbf{x} \to \mathbf{x}^{(c)}, \quad \phi_{\mathbf{d}} : (\mathbf{x}, \mathbf{d}) \to \mathbf{d}^{(c)} \tag{3}$$

Here, $\mathbf{x}^{(c)}$ can be simply derived from Eq. (2) and $\mathbf{d}^{(c)}$ can be derived from difference approximation as $\mathbf{d}^{(c)} = \text{norm}((\phi_{\mathbf{x}}(\mathbf{x}+\Delta t\mathbf{d}) - \phi_{\mathbf{x}}(\mathbf{x}))/\Delta t)$. Δt denotes a small constant and $\text{norm}(\cdot)$ normalizes the vector length to 1. Note that the above mappings are derived from the simple CBD computation without any learnable components.

The deformed radiance field Ψ can be divided into three parts depending on the space that: (1) outside both the canonical cage and deformed cage (2) inside the canonical cages but outside the deformed cages, (3) inside the deformed cages. Specifically, it can be formulated as follows:

$$\Psi(\mathbf{x}, \mathbf{d}) = \begin{cases} \Psi^{(c)}(\mathbf{x}, \mathbf{d}), & \mathbf{x} \in \mathbb{R}^3 \setminus (\mathbb{V}^{(c)} \cup \mathbb{V}) \quad \text{(4a)} \\ (\mathbf{0}, 0), & \mathbf{x} \in \mathbb{V}^{(c)} \setminus (\mathbb{V}^{(c)} \cap \mathbb{V}) \quad \text{(4b)} \\ \Psi^{(c)}\left(\phi_{\mathbf{x}}(\mathbf{x}), \phi_{\mathbf{d}}(\mathbf{x}, \mathbf{d})\right), & \mathbf{x} \in \mathbb{V} \quad \text{(4c)} \end{cases}$$

Here, $\mathbb{V}^{(c)}, \mathbb{V} \subset \mathbb{R}^3$ denotes the space enclosed by $\mathcal{C}^{(c)}$ and $\mathcal{C}$, respectively. Equation (4a) indicates that the radiance field remains unchanged before and after deformation for the position outside the cages. For the points inside the canonical cage, we clear them, namely setting the color and density to zero, as in Eq. (4b). For the points inside the deformed cage, we map the spatial position and view direction to the canonical space through Eq. (3) and then query the color and density from $\Psi^{(c)}$, as in Eq. (4c).

4 Implementation Details

4.1 Faster Cage Coordinates Computation

Technically, the rendering of the deformed scene can be achieved by computing the deformed-to-canonical mapping in Eq. (4) for all the sampling points on all the rays. However, because of the huge number of sampling points and the fact that the computation of cage coordinates is usually accompanied by a high-dimensional tensor computation (as discussed in Sect. 3.3), the above brute-force computation is usually impractical either in terms of time or memory capacity. A rough estimation can be given as, rendering images of size (h, w) from N different viewpoints, with M points sampled on each ray, the number of points that require the cage coordinate computation is about $h \times w \times N \times M$ in order of magnitude[1]. For instance, for $M = 512$, rendering 200 images of size (800, 800) requires about $\sim 10^{10}$ orders of magnitude in the times of cage coordinates computation.

Inspired by the computation process of harmonic coordinates (HC), we propose to discretize the space into $n \times n \times n$ grid points for cage coordinates computation, even for the cage coordinates that have their closed-formulations, i.e. MVC and GC (briefly discussed in Sect. 2). At the inference time, we pre-compute the cage coordinates for each grid and use trilinear interpolation to calculate the cage coordinates for arbitrary points. We surprisingly find that such a simple discretization, however, brings great benefits for the specific nature of volume rendering of the radiance field. Note that such discretization makes the number of cage coordinates computation independent of h, w, N, M given above, that is, once the pre-computation of grid points is completed, there is no increase in the computation of cage coordinates when we want to render the scene from the additional new viewpoint or with different image resolution. The only thing to consider here is the size of n, which requires a trade-off between discretization resolution and computation speed. Here, the number of points that require cage coordinates computation is about n^3 in order of magnitude.

We practically use $n = 128$ in our experiments which gives about $\sim 10^6$ orders of magnitude in the times of computation.

4.2 Cage Refinement

The computation complexity of cage coordinates is proportional to the number of cage vertices. For fast inference, we control the hyperparameters (e.g. discrete voxel size) in cage generation algorithm [45] to ensure that the number of vertices is in the range of 30–200. For scenes with complex shapes or details, we first generate a cage with a larger number of vertices ($\sim$1000) and then manually decimate the vertices using Blender [3].

4.3 Radiance Fields Representation

We use Plenoxels [8] as radiance fields representation, which supports very fast scene optimization and rendering. Note that our method is not dependent on specific radiance field representations and thus can be directly applied to other representations such as NeRF [28] or the latest faster radiance field representations [2,29,42].

5 Experiments

In this section, we evaluate the effectiveness of our approach through a variety of scenes, including synthetic dataset and real-world dataset. We show the results of extensive ablation studies and then discuss the limitations of our approach.

[1] In fact, the actual number is smaller than this approximation since we only compute for points inside the cage.

Unless otherwise specified, the deformations of the results are performed with harmonic coordinate with discretization resolution $n = 128$. For the canonical scene optimization, we follow the default setting used in [8]. We use one Nvidia A100 GPU for all the experiments.

5.1 Datasets

NeRF and NSVF Synthetic Dataset. We use synthetic dataset in original NeRF [28] and Neural Sparse Voxel Fields (NSVF) [23] papers. These scenes contain only foreground objects, and the images are captured from multiple cameras placed on the hemisphere. We follow the train/test split as in the original papers.

DTU MVS Dataset. We use the real-world DTU MVS dataset [15], which contains a variety of static objects, and each scene uses 49 or 64 cameras to capture high-resolution images. We use all available cameras for training, and create test camera trajectories from camera interpolation for evaluation.

5.2 Results

Since our approach is the first to use a coarse cage as an interface for free-form deformation of the radiance field, there is no existing method for a direct comparison. The ground truth of the deformed scene is also not available, therefore, we show the qualitative results before and after the deformation for evaluation.

We use Blender [3] to manually deform the generated cage of the canonical scene with various types of deformations such as bending, stretching, torsion, scaling, etc. Novel view synthesis results of original/deformed scene on synthetic dataset and DTU dataset are shown in Fig. 4 and Fig. 5, respectively. As shown in the results, our proposed radiance field deformation approach enables explicit manipulation of the scene while maintaining photorealistic rendering quality. In addition to the free-form deformation of the entire object with the generated cage, our approach also allows for local manipulation of the object as in the last two figures in Fig. 5: all you need is to create a simple cage and deform it, which can be done with little effort using almost any existing 3D software.

The above features of our approach also support simple radiance field manipulation achieved by existing works [25], such as object movement, duplication, and scaling. Moreover, as shown in Fig. 6, our method also supports applications of generating continuous free-view animation from a static scene by cage interpolation.

5.3 Ablation Study

We discuss the impact of different discretization resolutions and different cage coordinates on the synthesis quality. As introduced in Sect. 2, we use three commonly used cage coordinates for comparison: mean value coordinates (MVC) [18],

Table 1. Computation time in seconds for rendering an image for three cage coordinates with different discretization resolutions. "Precise" means not using discretization, i.e., computing precise cage coordinates for all the sampling points on the rays. Here, "MVC" means mean value coordinates [18], "HC" means harmonic coordinates [17], and "GC" means green coordinates [22]. Please also refer to Sect. 5.3 and Fig. 7.

	MVC [18]	HC [17]	GC [22]
64^3	0.31	0.23	0.35
128^3	0.98	0.90	2.49
256^3	5.71	6.32	19.69
Precise	102	N/A	243

harmonic coordinates [17] and green coordinates [22]. We observed that the impact of the above two factors on the synthesis quality is subtle, we choose the synthetic "Lego" scene with relatively obvious distinction for ablation. The computation time for rendering an image and the synthesis results are shown in Table 1 and Fig. 7, respectively.

We use the same settings as assumptions in Sect. 4.1 except for the number of rendered images, i.e. $h = w = 800, M = 512, n = 128$ and $N = 1$. The cage we used for the synthetic "Lego" scene has 42 vertices.

Impact of Discretization Resolution. As shown in Table 1 and Fig. 7, although 64^3 resolution has a faster computation speed, significant artifacts can be observed in the synthesized results (e.g. blurry or fake shadow). This indicates that low discretization resolution brings a large error in the deformed-to-canonical mapping of the sampled points. For 128^3 resolution, the artifact is lightened with an acceptable computation time increase. For 256^3 resolutions, it can be seen that the improvement in synthesized quality is limited, but causes a larger increase in computation time as well as memory cost. For cage coordinates that have a closed-formulation (i.e., MVC and GC), although it is impractical due to the extremely long computation time (about 2–4 min per scene), we show the results of the precise computation of cage coordinates without using discretization as an upper limit for comparison.

Impact of Different Cage Coordinates. Comparison are also shown in Fig. 7. MVC and HC show similar synthesized quality. GC shows a more reasonable deformation for the long-striped parts in the center of the image, however, the loss of detail for small parts is also observed.

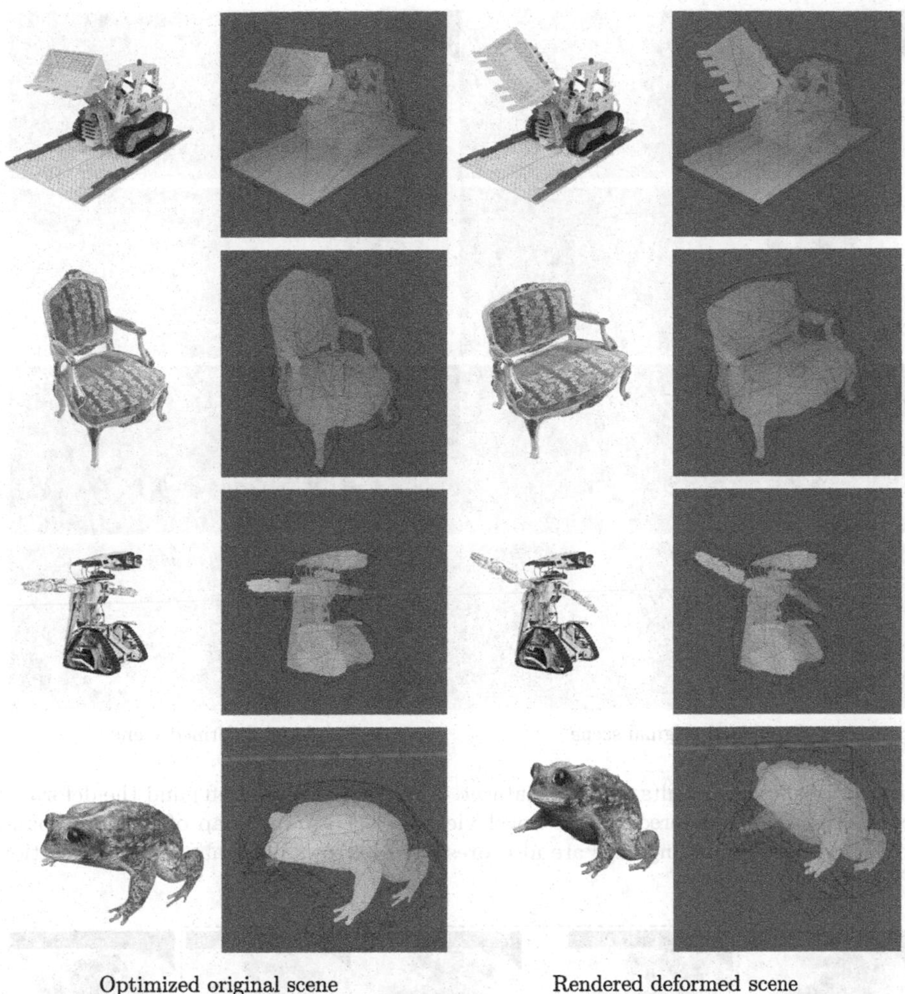

Fig. 4. Qualitative results on NeRF and NSVF synthetic dataset. The original scene (left) and the deformed scene (right) are rendered from a novel viewpoint. Disparity map and corresponding cage are also presented.

5.4 Limitations

Cage Generation. As noticed in the cage-based mesh deformation, the quality of the cage greatly affects the deformation quality. However, the method we use for cage generation shows some difficulties in representing detailed cage shapes while keeping a small number of cage vertices. For objects with difficult shapes, manual refinement of the cage comes necessary, especially for real scenes with backgrounds. We conducted an extensive survey on the automatic cage generation from 3D scenes, and to our surprise, this task seems to still be unexplored. Especially for real scenes, to the best of our knowledge, there is no effective way

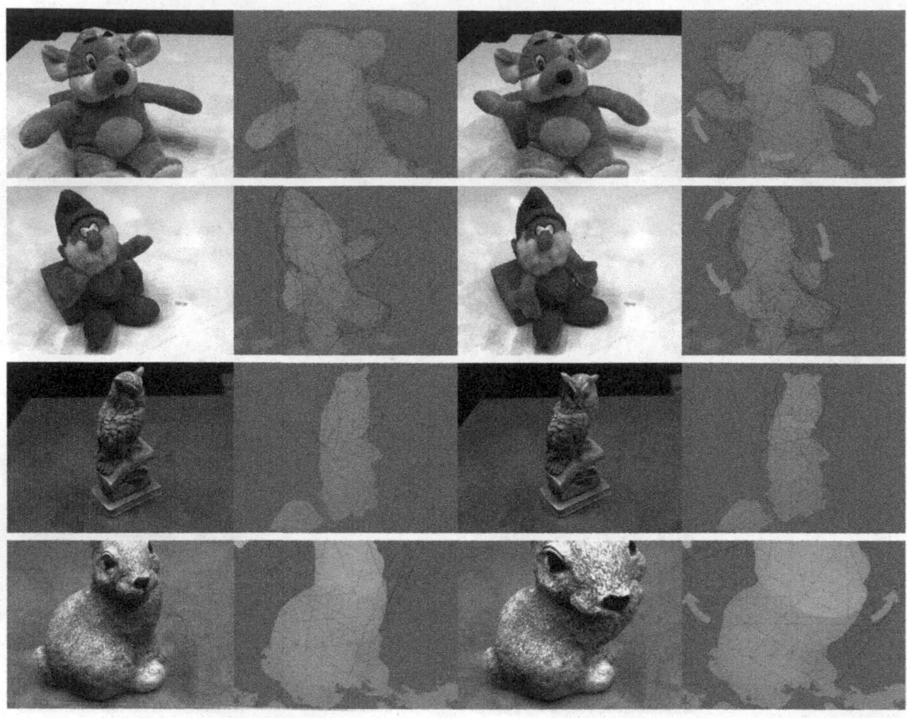

Fig. 5. Qualitative results on DTU dataset. The original scene (left) and the deformed scene (right) are rendered from a novel viewpoint. Disparity map of the foreground object and corresponding cage are also presented. Arrows illustrate the manipulation of the cage.

Fig. 6. Qualitative results of cage interpolation. Our approach can generate continuous free-view animation by interpolating the starting and ending cages.

to generate a cage automatically. We believe that the automatic generation of the cage from 3D scenes is a promising direction for future work.

Failure Cases. We report some failure cases of our approach in Fig. 8. The first typical failure case occurs when a part of the scene (usually the background) is not well modeled due to the occlusion. When deforming or moving the foreground objects so that the under-modeled part is exposed, obvious artifacts will

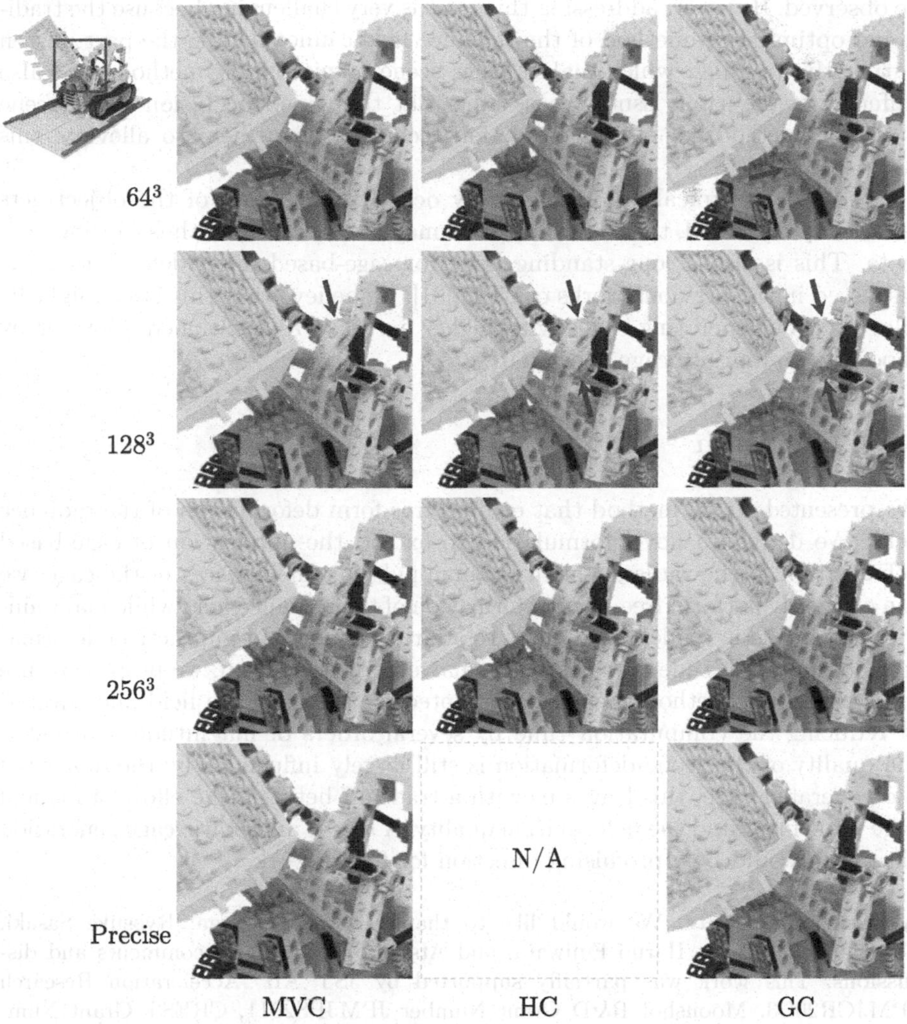

64^3

128^3

256^3

Precise

N/A

MVC HC GC

Fig. 7. Ablation on different cage coordinates and discretization resolution on synthetic "Lego" dataset. For more details please refer to Sect. 5.3 and Table 1.

Fig. 8. Failure cases. Left: moving the foreground object results in exposing the parts of the scene that are under-modeled due to occlusion. Right: drastic cage manipulation may cause the artifacts.

be observed. However, addressing this issue is very challenging because the traditional optimization method of the radiance field cannot handle the part unseen during the training, which makes other scene manipulation methods [48] also suffer from the same issue. We assume that the use of occlusion-aware scene modeling methods or scene completion techniques may help to alleviate this issue.

The second typical failure case may occur when a part of the object gets drastically deformed, the irrelevant parts may also be affected thus causing artifacts. This is also a long-standing issue for cage-based mesh deformation. As discussed in the previous works of CBD [31], we believe that this issue might be alleviated by generating cages with higher accuracy as mentioned above or by choosing appropriate cage coordinates.

6 Conclusion

We presented a new method that enables free-form deformation of the radiance field. We derived a novel formulation to extend the application of cage-based deformation to the radiance field. By manipulating the vertices of the cage, we can explicitly perform free-form deformation of the radiance field while maintaining photorealistic rendering quality. To address the issue of impractical deformation computation time that arises in a naive implementation, we propose to use a discretization method specifically adapted for the radiance field and succeed in reducing the computation time by several orders of magnitude. Currently, the quality of the scene deformation is still largely influenced by the quality of the generated cage, this leaves us with a trade-off between the effort of manual cage refinement and the deformation quality. A better automatic cage generation algorithm would be a promising direction for future work.

Acknowledgements. We would like to thank Daisuke Kasuga, Ryosuke Sasaki, Tomoyuki Takahata, Haruo Fujiwara, and Atsuhiro Noguchi for comments and discussions. This work was partially supported by JST AIP Acceleration Research JPMJCR20U3, Moonshot R&D Grant Number JPMJPS2011, CREST Grant Number JPMJCR2015, JSPS KAKENHI Grant Number JP19H01115 and Basic Research Grant (Super AI) of Institute for AI and Beyond of the University of Tokyo.

References

1. Barron, J.T., Mildenhall, B., Tancik, M., Hedman, P., Martin-Brualla, R., Srinivasan, P.P.: Mip-NeRF: a multiscale representation for anti-aliasing neural radiance fields. In: Proceedings of the IEEE/CVF International Conference on Computer Vision, pp. 5855–5864 (2021)
2. Chen, A., Xu, Z., Geiger, A., Yu, J., Su, H.: TensoRF: tensorial radiance fields. In: European Conference on Computer Vision (2022)
3. Community, B.O.: Blender - a 3D modelling and rendering package. Blender Foundation, Stichting Blender Foundation, Amsterdam (2018). http://www.blender.org

4. Davis, A., Levoy, M., Durand, F.: Unstructured light fields. In: Computer Graphics Forum, vol. 31, pp. 305–314. Wiley Online Library (2012)
5. DeRose, T., Meyer, M.: Harmonic coordinates. In: Pixar Technical Memo 06–02. Pixar Animation Studios (2006)
6. Fan, H., Su, H., Guibas, L.J.: A point set generation network for 3d object reconstruction from a single image. In: Proceedings of the IEEE Conference on Computer Vision and Pattern Recognition, pp. 605–613 (2017)
7. Floater, M.S.: Mean value coordinates. Comput. Aided Geom. Des. **20**, 19–27 (2003)
8. Fridovich-Keil, S., Yu, A., Tancik, M., Chen, Q., Recht, B., Kanazawa, A.: Plenoxels: radiance fields without neural networks. In: Proceedings of the IEEE/CVF Conference on Computer Vision and Pattern Recognition, pp. 5501–5510 (2022)
9. Girdhar, R., Fouhey, D.F., Rodriguez, M., Gupta, A.: Learning a predictable and generative vector representation for objects. In: Leibe, B., Matas, J., Sebe, N., Welling, M. (eds.) ECCV 2016. LNCS, vol. 9910, pp. 484–499. Springer, Cham (2016). https://doi.org/10.1007/978-3-319-46466-4_29
10. Gortler, S.J., Grzeszczuk, R., Szeliski, R., Cohen, M.F.: The Lumigraph. In: Proceedings of the 23rd Annual Conference on Computer Graphics and Interactive Techniques, pp. 43–54 (1996)
11. Guo, M.H., Cai, J.X., Liu, Z.N., Mu, T.J., Martin, R.R., Hu, S.M.: PCT: point cloud transformer. Comput. Vis. Media **7**, 187–199 (2021)
12. Guo, M., Fathi, A., Wu, J., Funkhouser, T.: Object-centric neural scene rendering. arXiv preprint arXiv:2012.08503 (2020)
13. Hartley, R., Zisserman, A.: Multiple View Geometry in Computer Vision. Cambridge University Press, Cambridge (2003)
14. Jakab, T., Tucker, R., Makadia, A., Wu, J., Snavely, N., Kanazawa, A.: KeypointDeformer: unsupervised 3d Keypoint discovery for shape control. In: Proceedings of the IEEE/CVF Conference on Computer Vision and Pattern Recognition, pp. 12783–12792 (2021)
15. Jensen, R., Dahl, A., Vogiatzis, G., Tola, E., Aanæs, H.: Large scale multi-view stereopsis evaluation. In: Proceedings of the IEEE Conference on Computer Vision and Pattern Recognition, pp. 406–413 (2014)
16. Jiakai, Z., et al.: Editable free-viewpoint video using a layered neural representation. In: ACM SIGGRAPH (2021)
17. Joshi, P., Meyer, M., DeRose, T., Green, B., Sanocki, T.: Harmonic coordinates for character articulation. ACM Trans. Graph. (TOG) **26**, 71-es (2007)
18. Ju, T., Schaefer, S., Warren, J.: Mean value coordinates for closed triangular meshes. In: ACM SIGGRAPH 2005 Papers, pp. 561–566 (2005)
19. Kajiya, J.T., Von Herzen, B.P.: Ray tracing volume densities. ACM SIGGRAPH Comput. Graph. **18**, 165–174 (1984)
20. Kanazawa, A., Tulsiani, S., Efros, A.A., Malik, J.: Learning category-specific mesh reconstruction from image collections. In: Ferrari, V., Hebert, M., Sminchisescu, C., Weiss, Y. (eds.) ECCV 2018. LNCS, vol. 11219, pp. 386–402. Springer, Cham (2018). https://doi.org/10.1007/978-3-030-01267-0_23
21. Kato, H., Ushiku, Y., Harada, T.: Neural 3D mesh renderer. In: Proceedings of the IEEE Conference on Computer Vision and Pattern Recognition, pp. 3907–3916 (2018)
22. Lipman, Y., Levin, D., Cohen-Or, D.: Green coordinates. ACM Trans. Graph. (TOG) **27**, 1–10 (2008)

23. Liu, L., Gu, J., Zaw Lin, K., Chua, T.S., Theobalt, C.: Neural sparse voxel fields. In: Advances in Neural Information Processing Systems, vol. 33, pp. 15651–15663 (2020)
24. Liu, L., Habermann, M., Rudnev, V., Sarkar, K., Gu, J., Theobalt, C.: Neural actor: neural free-view synthesis of human actors with pose control. ACM Trans. Graph. (ACM SIGGRAPH Asia) **40**, 1–16 (2021)
25. Liu, S., Zhang, X., Zhang, Z., Zhang, R., Zhu, J.Y., Russell, B.: Editing conditional radiance fields. In: Proceedings of the IEEE/CVF International Conference on Computer Vision, pp. 5773–5783 (2021)
26. Lorensen, W.E., Cline, H.E.: Marching cubes: a high resolution 3D surface construction algorithm. ACM SIGGRAPH Comput. Graph. **21**, 163–169 (1987)
27. Mildenhall, B., Hedman, P., Martin-Brualla, R., Srinivasan, P.P., Barron, J.T.: NeRF in the dark: high dynamic range view synthesis from noisy raw images. In: Proceedings of the IEEE/CVF Conference on Computer Vision and Pattern Recognition, pp. 16190–16199 (2022)
28. Mildenhall, B., Srinivasan, P.P., Tancik, M., Barron, J.T., Ramamoorthi, R., Ng, R.: NeRF: representing scenes as neural radiance fields for view synthesis. In: Vedaldi, A., Bischof, H., Brox, T., Frahm, J.-M. (eds.) ECCV 2020. LNCS, vol. 12346, pp. 405–421. Springer, Cham (2020). https://doi.org/10.1007/978-3-030-58452-8_24
29. Müller, T., Evans, A., Schied, C., Keller, A.: Instant neural graphics primitives with a multiresolution hash encoding. ACM Trans. Graph **41**, 1–15 (2022)
30. Niemeyer, M., Mescheder, L., Oechsle, M., Geiger, A.: Differentiable volumetric rendering: learning implicit 3D representations without 3D supervision. In: Proceedings of the IEEE/CVF Conference on Computer Vision and Pattern Recognition, pp. 3504–3515 (2020)
31. Nieto, J.R., Susín, A.: Cage based deformations: a survey. In: González Hidalgo, M., Mir Torres, A., Varona Gómez, J. (eds.) Deformation Models, vol. 7, pp. 75–99. Springer, Dordrecht (2013). https://doi.org/10.1007/978-94-007-5446-1_3
32. Noguchi, A., Iqbal, U., Tremblay, J., Harada, T., Gallo, O.: Watch it move: unsupervised discovery of 3d joints for re-posing of articulated objects. In: Proceedings of the IEEE/CVF Conference on Computer Vision and Pattern Recognition, pp. 3677–3687 (2022)
33. Noguchi, A., Sun, X., Lin, S., Harada, T.: Neural articulated radiance field. In: Proceedings of the IEEE/CVF International Conference on Computer Vision, pp. 5762–5772 (2021)
34. Ost, J., Mannan, F., Thuerey, N., Knodt, J., Heide, F.: Neural scene graphs for dynamic scenes. In: Proceedings of the IEEE/CVF Conference on Computer Vision and Pattern Recognition, pp. 2856–2865 (2021)
35. Park, K., et al.: Nerfies: deformable neural radiance fields. In: Proceedings of the IEEE/CVF International Conference on Computer Vision, pp. 5865–5874 (2021)
36. Park, K., et al.: HyperNeRF: a higher-dimensional representation for topologically varying neural radiance fields. ACM Trans. Graph **40**, 1–12 (2021)
37. Peng, S., et al.: Animatable neural radiance fields for modeling dynamic human bodies. In: Proceedings of the IEEE/CVF International Conference on Computer Vision, pp. 14314–14323 (2021)
38. Peng, S., et al.: Neural body: implicit neural representations with structured latent codes for novel view synthesis of dynamic humans. In: Proceedings of the IEEE/CVF Conference on Computer Vision and Pattern Recognition, pp. 9054–9063 (2021)

39. Pumarola, A., Corona, E., Pons-Moll, G., Moreno-Noguer, F.: D-NeRF: neural radiance fields for dynamic scenes. In: Proceedings of the IEEE/CVF Conference on Computer Vision and Pattern Recognition, pp. 10318–10327 (2021)
40. Sitzmann, V., Zollhöfer, M., Wetzstein, G.: Scene representation networks: continuous 3D-structure-aware neural scene representations. In: Advances in Neural Information Processing Systems, vol. 32 (2019)
41. Su, S.Y., Yu, F., Zollhöfer, M., Rhodin, H.: A-NeRF: articulated neural radiance fields for learning human shape, appearance, and pose. In: Advances in Neural Information Processing Systems, vol. 34, 12278–12291 (2021)
42. Sun, C., Sun, M., Chen, H.T.: Direct voxel grid optimization: super-fast convergence for radiance fields reconstruction. In: Proceedings of the IEEE/CVF Conference on Computer Vision and Pattern Recognition, pp. 5459–5469 (2022)
43. Tretschk, E., Tewari, A., Golyanik, V., Zollhöfer, M., Lassner, C., Theobalt, C.: Non-rigid neural radiance fields: reconstruction and novel view synthesis of a dynamic scene from monocular video. In: Proceedings of the IEEE/CVF International Conference on Computer Vision, pp. 12959–12970 (2021)
44. Triggs, B., McLauchlan, P.F., Hartley, R.I., Fitzgibbon, A.W.: Bundle adjustment—a modern synthesis. In: Triggs, B., Zisserman, A., Szeliski, R. (eds.) IWVA 1999. LNCS, vol. 1883, pp. 298–372. Springer, Heidelberg (2000). https://doi.org/10.1007/3-540-44480-7_21
45. Xian, C., Lin, H., Gao, S.: Automatic generation of coarse bounding cages from dense meshes. In: IEEE International Conference on Shape Modeling and Applications (2009)
46. Xu, T., Fujita, Y., Matsumoto, E.: Surface-aligned neural radiance fields for controllable 3D human synthesis. In: Proceedings of the IEEE/CVF Conference on Computer Vision and Pattern Recognition, pp. 15883–15892 (2022)
47. Yan, X., Yang, J., Yumer, E., Guo, Y., Lee, H.: Perspective transformer nets: learning single-view 3D object reconstruction without 3D supervision. In: Advances in Neural Information Processing Systems, vol. 29 (2016)
48. Yang, B., et al.: Learning object-compositional neural radiance field for editable scene rendering. In: Proceedings of the IEEE/CVF International Conference on Computer Vision, pp. 13779–13788 (2021)
49. Yifan, W., Aigerman, N., Kim, V.G., Chaudhuri, S., Sorkine-Hornung, O.: Neural cages for detail-preserving 3D deformations. In: Proceedings of the IEEE/CVF Conference on Computer Vision and Pattern Recognition, pp. 75–83 (2020)
50. Yuan, Y.J., Sun, Y.T., Lai, Y.K., Ma, Y., Jia, R., Gao, L.: NeRF-Editing: geometry editing of neural radiance fields. In: Proceedings of the IEEE/CVF Conference on Computer Vision and Pattern Recognition, pp. 18353–18364 (2022)

FLEX: Extrinsic Parameters-free Multi-view 3D Human Motion Reconstruction

Brian Gordon(✉), Sigal Raab, Guy Azov, Raja Giryes, and Daniel Cohen-Or

Tel Aviv University, Tel Aviv, Israel
{briangordon,guyazov}@mail.tau.ac.il,
{sigalraab,raja,dcor}@tauex.tau.ac.il

Abstract. The increasing availability of video recordings made by multiple cameras has offered new means for mitigating occlusion and depth ambiguities in pose and motion reconstruction methods. Yet, multi-view algorithms strongly depend on camera parameters, particularly on relative transformations between the cameras. Such a dependency becomes a hurdle once shifting to dynamic capture in uncontrolled settings. We introduce FLEX (**F**ree mu**L**ti-view r**E**constru**X**ion), an end-to-end extrinsic parameter-free multi-view model. FLEX is *extrinsic parameter-free* (dubbed *ep-free*) in the sense that it does not require extrinsic camera parameters. Our key idea is that the 3D angles between skeletal parts, as well as bone lengths, are invariant to the camera position. Hence, learning 3D rotations and bone lengths rather than locations allows for predicting common values for all camera views. Our network takes multiple video streams, learns fused deep features through a novel multi-view fusion layer, and reconstructs a single consistent skeleton with temporally coherent joint rotations. We demonstrate quantitative and qualitative results on three public data sets, and on multi-person synthetic video streams captured by dynamic cameras. We compare our model to state-of-the-art methods that are not ep-free and show that in the absence of camera parameters, we outperform them by a large margin while obtaining comparable results when camera parameters are available. Code, trained models, and other materials are available on https://briang13.github.io/FLEX.

Keywords: Motion reconstruction · Character animation · Pose estimation · Camera parameters · Deep learning

B. Gordon and S. Raab—Equal contribution.

Supplementary Information The online version contains supplementary material available at https://doi.org/10.1007/978-3-031-19827-4_11.

S. Avidan et al. (Eds.): ECCV 2022, LNCS 13693, pp. 176–196, 2022.
https://doi.org/10.1007/978-3-031-19827-4_11

1 Introduction

Human motion reconstruction is the task of associating a skeleton with temporally coherent joint locations and rotations. Acquiring accurate human motion in a controlled setting, using motion capture systems with adequate sensors is a tedious and expensive procedure that cannot be applied for capturing spontaneous activities, such as sporting events. Motion reconstruction from RGB cameras is low-cost and non-intrusive, but is an uncontrolled setup. Thus, while being simple, it has technical challenges that are worsened by occlusion and depth ambiguity. Using multiple cameras may alleviate these difficulties as different views may compensate for occlusion and be used for mutual consistency.

Fig. 1. Results on the KTH multi-view Football II dataset [33], in occluded and blurry scenes with dynamic cameras.

Fig. 2. 3D locations vary across axis systems while 3D rotation angles and bone lengths remain identical.

Recently, there has been a significant progress in using deep learning for pose and motion reconstruction [36,42,51,54,56,63,66]. Most of these methods work in a monocular setting, but a growing number of works learn a multi-view setting [19,24,29,58,60,74]. However, these approaches depend on the relative position between the cameras, derived from extrinsic camera parameters, and assume they are given. In the lack of extrinsic parameters, several works estimate them [16,37], but at the cost of innate inaccuracy of estimated values. While camera parameters are often given in multi-view datasets, they are rarely given in dynamic capture environments. We refer to cameras as *dynamic* if they occasionally move during video capture, such that their extrinsic parameters and their inter-camera relative positions are not fixed. An example of such a camera is the SkyCam [68], commonly used in sports events.

This work introduces an extrinsic parameter-free (dubbed *ep-free*) multi-view motion reconstruction method, whose setting is illustrated in the inset to the right. Our method builds upon a new conceptual observation that uses the well-known joint rotations and bone lengths, to free us from the burdening dependency on extrinsic camera parameters. Our approach relies on a key insight that joint rotations and bone lengths are identical for all views. That is, the 3D angle between skeletal parts is invariant to the camera position. We train a neural network to predict 3D joint angles and bone lengths *without* using the extrinsic camera parameters, neither in training nor in test time. Predicting motion rather than locations is not a novel idea by itself. The innovation of our work is in the way we use motion to bypass the need for camera parameters. The input from multiple cameras is integrated by a novel fusion layer that implicitly promotes joints detected by some cameras and demotes joints detected by others, hence mitigating occlusion and depth ambiguities.

Our model, named FLEX, is an end-to-end deep convolutional network. Its input is multi-view 2D joints that are either given or extracted using a 2D pose estimation technique. FLEX employs multi-view blocks with cross-view attention on top of a monocular baseline [66], and uses temporal information over a video of arbitrary length, thus obtaining temporal consistency.

We evaluate FLEX qualitatively and quantitatively using the Human3.6M [9, 28], the KTH Multi-view Football II [33] and the Ski-Pose PTZ-Camera [61] datasets. Figure 1 demonstrates qualitative results, and more are depicted in Sect. 4 and in the supplementary material. FLEX is also applied on synthetic videos. We have generated these videos using Mixamo [1] and Blender [18], to mitigate the lack of a multi-person video dataset that is captured by dynamic cameras, and created them such that they contain severe inter-person occlusions.

We compare performance with state-of-the-art methods that are not ep-free and show comparable results. To simulate an ep-free setting, we perturb ground-truth camera parameters or use works that estimate them. We show that in an ep-free setting, our model outperforms state-of-the-art by a large margin.

Our main contributions are twofold: (i) a network that reconstructs motion and pose in a multi-view setting with unknown extrinsic camera parameters, and (ii) a novel fusion layer with a multi-view convolutional layer combined with a multi-head attention mechanism over a number of views.

2 Related Work

Pose Estimation Using a Single View. Pose estimation receives significant interest in computer vision. Before the deep era, it was approached using heuristics such as physical priors [62]. The emergence of deep learning and large datasets [17, 28, 33, 49], have led to significant advances. Pose estimation methods can generally be divided into two groups. The first infers 3D locations directly from images or videos [13, 23, 39, 55, 70, 72, 83]. The second, aka *lifting*, applies two steps: (i) estimating 2D poses and (ii) lifting them to 3D space [21, 25, 42, 50, 56, 65, 69]. The first group benefits from directly using images, which are more descriptive compared to 2D joint locations. The second gains from using intermediate supervision. Recently, transformers and convolutional graph based methods were shown to improve performance [26, 40, 41, 43, 44, 53, 79].

Pose Estimation Using Multiple Views. The growing availability of synchronized video streams taken by multiple cameras has contributed to the emergence of multi-view algorithms. Such algorithms exploit the diversity in camera views to predict more accurate 3D poses. All works described below predict pose and many of them analyze each frame individually. On the other hand, our model, FLEX, reconstructs motion and exploits temporal information.

Most works in the multi-view setting rely on lifting from 2D to 3D space. Early works [4,5,7] estimate the input 2D pose from single images, while later works [10,15,16,19,24,29,30,37,58,60] obtain the 2D pose by running a CNN over 2D poses given in multiple views; resulting in an increase in 2D pose prediction accuracy. After estimating the 2D poses, most works apply heuristics such as triangulation or pictorial structure model (PSM). FLEX is one of the few works [29,74] that present an end-to-end model.

Several methods use multi-view data to improve the 2D pose estimation. Some use the camera parameters to find the matching epipolar lines such that features gathered from several cameras are aggregated [24,58]. Chen *et al.* [10] learn a geometric representation in latent space with an encoder-decoder.

Several works [16,37,73,77] use self-supervision, hence need no 3D groundtruth. Their main idea is to project the predicted 3D joints (using real or estimated camera parameters) and expect consistency with 2D input joints. Recent techniques [27,81] exploit more sensors, such as IMU, during data capturing.

Current state-of-the-art results are attained by Iskakov *et al.* [29], Tu *et al.* [74] and Reddy *et al.* [59]. They use end-to-end networks, and present a volumetric approach, where 2D features are un-projected from individual views to a common 3D space, using camera parameters. Sun *et al.* [69] show that synthetic generation of additional views helps produce more accurate lifting.

At inference time, some of the aforementioned works expect monocular inputs [10,16,24,69] and some, including FLEX, get multi-view inputs [29,58,74]. The advantage of the first is the use of monocular data that is more common, and of the second is better results on multi-view settings.

Epipolar Transformers [24] attend to spatial locations on an epipolar line in a *single* view and query it using one joint in a query view. A concurrent work, TransFusion [47], applies a transformer on inter and intra-view features.

In the absence of camera parameters, most of the methods cannot be used. Some estimate rotation assuming the translation is given [2,37] or engage an extra effort to estimate the camera parameters [11,16,71,75,77]. Such an effort is not required by FLEX as it uses no camera parameters whatsoever.

Rotation and Motion Reconstruction. Pose estimation may suffice for many applications; however, pose alone does not fully describe the motion and the rotations associated with the joints. *Rotation reconstruction* relates to the prediction of joint rotation angles, while *motion reconstruction* requires the prediction of bone lengths associated with them. Many works explore the task of *3D shape recovery* [14,22,31,32,35,36,38,45,46,80], focusing on human mesh prediction along with joint rotations. Most of them do not guarantee temporal coherence, *e.g.*, bone length may vary across time frames.

Other works [48,57] focus on motion generation. Given a series of human motions, they predict future motions, using various techniques such as temporal supervision and graph convolutional networks (GCN). Similar to us, human motion reconstruction methods [51,52,66,82] focus on the temporal coherence of the body, where the bone lengths are fixed over time and rotations are smooth.

3 Extrinsic Parameter-free Multi-view Model

The premise of our work is that 3D joint rotations and bone lengths are view-independent values. For example, the 3D angle between, say, the thigh and the shin, as well as the length of these bones, are fixed, no matter which camera transformation is used. On the other hand, joint locations differ for each camera transformation, as seen in Fig. 2. Our key idea is to directly predict joint 3D angles and bone lengths without using the extrinsic camera parameters, during both training and test time. *Extrinsic* parameters correspond to the rotation and translation (aka transformation) from 3D real world axes into 3D camera axes. A formal definition of the camera parameters can be found in see, The supplementary Material

Our method takes multi-view sequences of 2D poses and estimates the motion of the observed human. The 2D poses are either given or extracted using a prediction technique. Having multi-view data compensates for the inherent inaccuracy of 2D pose estimation algorithms. Many methods estimate view-dependent 2D joint positions and then lift them to 3D by transforming them into a shared space. Such transformations require acquaintance of the relative position (rotation and translation) between the cameras, which is derived from the extrinsic camera parameters. Our model directly predicts 3D rotations and bone lengths, which are agnostic to camera transformation. The predicted values are shared by all views, so there is no need for extrinsic parameters information.

Pose estimation methods may mitigate the lack of extrinsic parameters by estimating them [16,37]. Yet, this has two drawbacks: (i) most approaches perform the estimation in a prepossessing step that breaks the end-to-end computation, and (ii) the estimated parameters are never exact and typically lead to a performance drop, as we show in Sect. 4.

Our architecture leverages Shi *et al.* [66] and is illustrated in high-level terms in Fig. 3. FLEX is an end-to-end network that maps 2D joint positions, extracted from multiple synchronized input videos, into two separate components: (i) a sequence of 3D joint rotations, global root positions and foot contact labels (upper branch in the figure); this sequence is skeleton-independent and varies per frame; and (ii) a single, symmetric, 3D skeleton, represented by its bone lengths (lower branch in the figure). We can combine these two components into a complete description of a motion and use it for 3D animation tasks without further processing or inverse kinematics (IK).

In addition to being free of extrinsic parameters, our model does not use intrinsic parameters at all, at the cost of an up-to-scale global skeleton position. While FLEX removes the need for extrinsics, it uses the common weak perspective assumption [35] for intrinsics; in particular for mitigating the lack of focal length. Indeed, some works seek to mitigate the lack of intrinsic parameters [22,35,67] whereas this is not the focus of our work. In Sect. 4 we show that using a customary weak perspective we attain an accurate global position.

The terms *motion*, *pose*, *reconstruction* and *estimation* are used in various contexts in the literature. To avoid confusion, we define *motion* as one set of bone lengths associated with temporally coherent 3D joint rotations, and *pose* as a temporal sequence of 3D joint locations. We use the term *reconstruction* rather than *estimation*, as the latter often describes 2D spatial motion. A weakly related term, *pose tracking*, associates poses to identities in a multi-person setting.

Motion data, and in particular rotations rather than positions, are required in animation platforms and game engines. FLEX directly outputs a kinematic skeleton, which is a complete, commonly used, motion representation. On the other hand, methods that predict joint positions, rely on IK to associate a skeleton with joint rotations. IK is slow, non-unique, and prone to temporal inconsistencies and unnatural postures. Moreover, methods that only predict pose cannot guarantee the consistency of bone lengths across frames.

3.1 Architecture

We start with a high-level description of the architecture (see Fig. 3). The inputs are K synchronized video streams of T frames each. For each video stream, we obtain 2D joints, which are either the ground-truth of a dataset or the output of a 2D pose estimation algorithm. Our network is agnostic to the way those 2D joints were obtained. In addition, each estimated joint is associated with a confidence value. The confidence value plays an important role in balancing between visible and occluded joints.

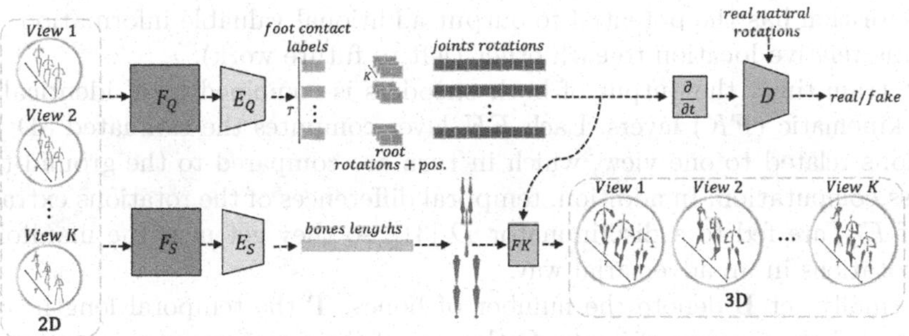

Fig. 3. FLEX takes multi-view temporal sequences of 2D poses and their confidence values. It uses two encoders, E_Q and E_S, to extracts per-frame 3D rotations and foot contact labels, per-view and per-frame 3D root transformations, and one static skeleton. A discriminator D monitors the temporal differences of rotation angles, and a forward kinematic layer, FK, combines encoders' outputs into 3D joint locations. These outputs depict *one* human, transformed into the axis systems of K cameras, to be compared with K sets of ground-truth values.

Our model takes input from all views, aggregates it, and streams it into two independent fusion layers F_S and F_Q, followed by encoders E_S and E_Q, respectively. The two fusion layers differ in some architectural details, but share the same concept. Both aggregate data of all views and frames and fuse it to exploit characteristics that recur in views and/or frames. Each fusion layer outputs view-agnostic features that represent the target human.

The fusion layers consist of two innovative elements, a multi-view convolutional layer and a *cross-view attention* mechanism, which encodes information from all views. Our use of attention is unique, as typically attention in other works is applied mostly over pixels [34] and sometimes over time [41,43,44]. Attention over views is a novel approach, which we find only in concurrent works for other tasks, assessing human shape [84] and rigid objects [78]. The fusion layers are described in detail in the supplementary material.

The encoder E_S predicts the length of each bone. As the same human is analyzed along all frames and views, the output is a single set of bone lengths.

The encoder E_Q predicts joint rotations, global root positions, and foot contact labels. Since 3D joint rotations and foot contact labels are identical to all views, E_Q predicts a single set of rotations and contact labels per frame, shared by all views. One exception is the root (pelvis) joint, whose rotation angle and position depend on the camera view and not on the human itself. Thus, for the root joint we predict the rotation angle and position for each frame and view. Root rotation and position are relative to the camera; hence visualizing the reconstructed object depicts the filmed person from the camera view, as expected. Notice that root rotation and position carry the knowledge of the relative transformation between the cameras. This insight suggests that our algorithm has the potential to output additional valuable information, *e.g.*, cameras relative location to each other (left to future work).

At train time, the output of both encoders is combined in K identical forward kinematic (FK) layers. Each FK layer computes the estimated 3D joint positions related to one view, which in turn are compared to the ground-truth for loss computation. In addition, temporal differences of the rotations extracted out of E_Q, are fed to a discriminator D [31], so they get near the manifold of true rotations in an adversarial way.

Formally, let $\mathbf{L}$ denote the number of bones, $\mathbf{T}$ the temporal length of the sequence, $\mathbf{J}$ the number of joints, $\mathbf{Q}$ the size of the rotations representation vector, and $\mathbf{K}$ the number of cameras. Let $\mathbf{P}_{s,q,r} \in \mathbb{R}^{T \times 3J \times K}$ denote K temporal sequences of 3D joint positions generated by a skeleton $\mathbf{s} \in \mathbb{R}^L$ with joint rotations $\mathbf{q} \in \mathbb{R}^{T \times Q \times (J-1)}$, and global root position and rotation $\mathbf{r} \in \mathbb{R}^{T \times (3+Q) \times K}$. Note that q is related to all joints except for the root joint. The rotation of the root joint, as well as its position, are related to r.

Our approach expects an input $\mathbf{V}_{s,q,r} \in \mathbb{R}^{T\times 3J\times K}$ denoting K temporal sequences of 2D joints and a confidence value per joint, related to a skeleton s, joint rotations q, and global root position and rotation r. Each input V is fed into our deep neural network, which in turn predicts $\tilde{\mathbf{q}} \in \mathbb{R}^{T\times Q\times (J-1)}$, that captures the dynamic, rotational information of the motion, $\tilde{\mathbf{s}} \in \mathbb{R}^{L}$, that describes a single, consistent, skeleton, $\tilde{\mathbf{r}} \in \mathbb{R}^{T\times (3+Q)\times K}$ that estimates the global position and rotation of the root along time and along views, and $\tilde{\mathbf{f}} \in \{0,1\}^{T\times 2}$ that predicts whether each of the two feet touches the ground in each frame:

$$\tilde{\mathbf{s}} = E_S(F_S(\mathbf{V}_{s,q,r})), \qquad \tilde{\mathbf{q}}, \tilde{\mathbf{r}}, \tilde{\mathbf{f}} = E_Q(F_Q(\mathbf{V}_{s,q,r})). \tag{1}$$

These attributes can be then combined via forward kinematics to estimate K global 3D pose sequences, $\tilde{\mathbf{P}}_{\tilde{s},\tilde{q},\tilde{r}} \in \mathbb{R}^{T\times 3J\times K}$, specified by joint positions:

$$\tilde{\mathbf{P}}_{\tilde{s},\tilde{q},\tilde{r}} = FK(\tilde{\mathbf{s}}, \tilde{\mathbf{q}}, \tilde{\mathbf{r}}). \tag{2}$$

We employ five loss functions. Our losses are inspired by Shi *et al.* [66] and are enhanced to encompass the multitude of views.

Joint Position Loss (the main loss). $\mathcal{L}_{\mathrm{P}}$ ensures that joints in the extracted positions are in their correct 3D positions:

$$\mathcal{L}_{\mathrm{P}} = \mathbb{E}_{\mathbf{P}_{s,q,r}\sim\mathcal{P}}\left[\|FK(\tilde{\mathbf{s}}, \tilde{\mathbf{q}}, \tilde{\mathbf{r}}_{pos_0}) - \mathbf{P}_{s,q,r_{pos_0}}\|^2\right], \tag{3}$$

where $\mathbf{P}_{s,q,r} \in \mathbb{R}^{T\times 3J\times K}$ denotes a 3D motion sequence, $\mathcal{P}$ represents the distribution of 3D motion sequences in our dataset, and $\tilde{r}_{pos_0}, r_{pos_0}$ stand for global position and rotation of the predicted and given root respectively, where the location is set to $(0,0,0)$, but the rotation is unchanged.

Skeleton Loss. $\mathcal{L}_{\mathrm{S}}$ stimulates the skeleton branch of the network, F_S and E_S, to correctly extract the skeleton $\mathbf{s}$:

$$\mathcal{L}_{\mathrm{S}} = \mathbb{E}_{\mathbf{P}_{s,q,r}\sim\mathcal{P}}\left[\|E_S(F_S(\mathbf{V}_{s,q,r})) - \mathbf{s}\|^2\right]. \tag{4}$$

Adversarial Rotation Loss. Our network learns to output rotations with natural velocity distribution using adversarial training. To achieve this, instead of focusing on rotation absolute values, like Kanazawa *et al.* [31] we focus on the temporal differences of joint rotations. We create a discriminator D_j for each joint. Note that the loss involving $D_{j\neq 0}$ takes the rotation values from $\tilde{q}$ while the loss involving D_0 takes the rotation values from $\tilde{r}$. It reads as

$$\mathcal{L}_{Q\_GAN_{j\neq 0}} = \mathbb{E}_{q\sim\mathcal{Q}}\left[\|D_j(\Delta_t q_j)\|^2\right] + \mathbb{E}_{\mathbf{P}_{s,q,r}\sim\mathcal{P}}\left[\|1 - D_j(\Delta_t E_Q(F_Q((\mathbf{V}_{s,q,r}))_{q_j}\|^2\right]$$

$$\begin{aligned}\mathcal{L}_{Q\_GAN_{j=0,k}} &= \mathbb{E}_{q\sim\mathcal{Q}}\left[\|D_j(\Delta_t q_j)\|^2\right] \\ &+ \mathbb{E}_{\mathbf{P}_{s,q,r}\sim\mathcal{P}}\left[\|1 - D_j(\Delta_t E_Q(F_Q((\mathbf{V}_{s,q,r}))_{r_{rot_k}}\|^2\right],\end{aligned} \tag{5}$$

where $\mathcal{Q}$ stands for the distribution of natural joint angles in the dataset, $E_Q(F_Q(\cdot))_{q_j}$ denotes the predicted rotations of the jth joint, $E_Q(F_Q(\cdot))_{r_{rot_k}}$ represents the predicted rotation of the pelvis joint relative to camera k, and Δ_t denotes temporal differences.

Global Root Position Loss. We estimate the depth parameter, $Z_r \in \mathbb{R}^{T \times K}$, by minimizing:

$$\mathcal{L}_{\text{R}} = \mathbb{E}_{\mathbf{P}_{s,q,r} \sim \mathcal{P}} \left[\| E_Q(F_Q(\mathbf{V}_{s,q,r}))_{r_{pos_z}} - Z_r \|^2 \right], \tag{6}$$

where Z_r is the depth of the ground-truth root, and $E_Q(F_Q(\cdot))_{r_{pos_z}}$ is the depth of the predicted root. Note that Z_r consists of values for all views and all frames.

Foot Contact Loss. We predict whether each foot contacts the ground in each frame and train the network via

$$\mathcal{L}_{\text{F}} = \mathbb{E}_{\mathbf{P}_{s,q,r} \sim \mathcal{P}} \left[\| E_Q(F_Q(\mathbf{V}_{s,q,r}))_f - \mathbf{f} \|^2 \right], \tag{7}$$

where $E_Q(F_Q((\cdot))_f$ denotes the predicted foot contact label part ($\tilde{\mathbf{f}} \in \{0,1\}^{T \times 2}$). We encourage the velocity of foot positions to be zero during contact frames, by

$$\mathcal{L}_{\text{FC}} = \mathbb{E}_{\mathbf{P}_{s,q,r} \sim \mathcal{P}} \left[\| \mathbf{f}_i \sum_j \Delta_t FK(\tilde{\mathbf{s}}, \tilde{\mathbf{q}}, \tilde{\mathbf{r}})_{f_i} \|^2 \right], \tag{8}$$

where $FK(\cdot,\cdot,\cdot)_{f_i} \in \mathbb{R}^{T \times 3}$ and $\mathbf{f}_i$ denote the positions and the contact labels of one of the feet joints ($i \in$ *left*, *right*), and $\sum_j$ sums the components for all axes.

Altogether, we obtain a total loss of:

$$\begin{aligned} \mathcal{L} = &\mathcal{L}_{\text{P}} + \lambda_{\text{S}} \mathcal{L}_{\text{S}} \lambda_{\text{Q}} \left(\sum_{j \neq 0} \mathcal{L}_{\text{Q\_GAN}_j} + \sum_{j=0,k} \mathcal{L}_{\text{Q\_GAN}_{j,k}} \right) \\ &+ \lambda_{\text{R}} \mathcal{L}_{\text{R}} + \lambda_{\text{F}} \mathcal{L}_{\text{P}_F} + \lambda_{\text{FC}} \mathcal{L}_{\text{P}_{FC}}. \end{aligned} \tag{9}$$

In most experiments we use $\lambda_{\text{S}} = 0.1$, $\lambda_{\text{Q}} = 1$, $\lambda_{\text{R}} = 1.3$, $\lambda_{\text{F}} = 0.5$ and $\lambda_{\text{FC}} = 0.5$.

In the supplementary material we provide more implementation details, such as the description of each architectural block; in particular the novel fusion layers F_S and F_Q. We discuss the advantages of early vs. middle and late fusion, and describe how we improve skeleton topology comparing to our single-view baseline. We also provide a detailed description of the datasets, a discussion of 2D pose estimators, and a description of the ground-truth we use.

Table 1. Protocol #1 MPJPE error on Human3.6M. Legend: $(*)$ is a **non** ep-free algorithm. In case parameters are not given, we imitate their computation by perturbing the GT params by an unrealistically small perturbation amount; (†) exploit temporal information; (+) extra training data. In **blue**- best result when camera parameters are not given, in **bold** - best result per method group.

Method	Dir.	Disc.	Eat	Greet	Phone	Photo	Pose	Purch.	Sit	SitD.	Smoke	Wait	WalkD.	Walk	WalkT.	Mean
Monocular methods																
Shi *et al.* [66](†)	47.3	53.1	50.3	53.9	53.5	52.8	52.0	55.4	64.2	54.8	66.8	55.0	50.3	59.1	50.3	54.6
Llopart [44](†)	42.2	44.5	42.6	43.0	46.9	53.9	42.5	41.7	55.2	62.3	44.9	42.9	45.3	31.8	31.8	44.8
Reddy *et al.* [59](†)	38.4	46.2	44.3	43.2	44.8	48.3	52.9	**36.7**	**45.3**	54.5	63.4	44.4	41.9	46.2	39.9	44.6
Li *et al.* [40](†)	39.9	43.4	40.0	40.9	46.4	50.6	42.1	39.8	55.8	61.6	44.9	43.3	44.9	29.9	30.3	43.6
Hu *et al.* [26](†)	**35.5**	41.3	**36.6**	39.1	42.4	49.0	39.9	37.0	51.9	63.3	**40.9**	**41.4**	**40.3**	**29.8**	28.9	41.1
Cheng *et al.* [13] (†)	36.2	**38.1**	42.7	**35.9**	**38.2**	**45.7**	**36.8**	42.0	45.9	**51.3**	41.8	41.5	43.8	33.1	**28.6**	**40.1**
Multi-view methods, extrinsic camera parameters are **given**																
Tome *et al.*[73] (+)	43.3	49.6	42.0	48.8	51.1	64.3	40.3	43.3	66.0	95.2	50.2	52.2	51.1	43.9	45.3	52.8
Kadkhodamohammadi and Padoy [30]	39.4	46.9	41.0	42.7	53.6	54.8	41.4	50.0	59.9	78.8	49.8	46.2	51.1	40.5	41.0	49.1
He *et al.* [24]	25.7	27.7	23.7	24.8	26.9	31.4	24.9	26.5	28.8	31.7	28.2	26.4	23.6	28.3	23.5	26.9
Qiu *et al.* [58] (+)	24.0	26.7	23.2	24.3	24.8	22.8	24.1	28.6	32.1	26.9	31.0	25.6	25.0	28.0	24.4	26.2
Ma *et al.* [47](†)	24.4	26.4	23.4	21.1	25.2	23.2	24.7	33.8	29.8	26.4	26.8	24.2	23.2	26.1	23.3	25.8
Iskakov *et al.* [29]	19.9	20.0	18.9	18.5	20.5	19.4	18.4	22.1	22.5	28.7	21.2	20.8	19.7	22.1	20.2	20.8
Reddy *et al.* [59](†)	**17.5**	**19.6**	**17.2**	**18.3**	**18.2**	**17.7**	**18.0**	**18.0**	**20.5**	**20.3**	**19.4**	**17.2**	**18.9**	**19.0**	**17.8**	**18.7**
Multi-view methods, extrinsic camera parameters are **not given**																
Chu and Pan [16](†)	49.1	63.6	48.6	56.0	57.4	69.6	50.4	62.0	75.4	77.4	57.2	53.5	57.7	37.6	38.1	56.9
Iskakov *et al.* [29]$(*)$ param. perturb by 4%	30.2	37.2	32.7	33.2	38.8	43.7	29.7	43.0	49.4	67.6	38.0	33.1	42.1	27.2	29.3	38.4
Iskakov *et al.* [29]$(*)$ param. perturb by 3%	27.6	30.3	29.0	29.4	33.1	36.5	27.4	34.8	39.1	54.0	34.4	30.7	36.2	26.2	28.4	33.1
Ours(†)	**22.0**	**23.6**	**24.9**	**26.7**	**30.6**	**35.7**	**25.1**	**32.9**	**29.5**	**32.5**	**32.6**	**26.5**	**34.7**	**26.0**	**27.7**	**30.2**

4 Experiments and Evaluation

We present quantitative results on the Human3.6M [9,28] and Ski-Pose PTZ-Camera [61] datasets. We present qualitative results on the Human3.6M, KTH Multi-view Football II [33] and Ski-Pose PTZ-Camera [61] datasets, and on synthetic videos captured by dynamic cameras. Detailed description of these datasets can be found in the supplementary material.

Quantitative Results. We show quantitative results using the Mean Per Joint Position Error (MPJPE) [9,28], and report standard protocol #1 MPJPE (that is, error relative to the pelvis), in millimeters.

Table 1 presents a quantitative comparison of the MPJPE metric on the Human3.6M [28] dataset. We present monocular methods, followed by multi-view ones that are split into ones that are acquainted with camera parameters and ones that are not. We show that in the absence of camera parameters, our model outperforms state-of-the-art methods by a large margin, and that even when camera parameters are available, FLEX is among the top methods. Note that these achievements are although FLEX aims at a slightly different task, which is motion reconstruction rather than pose estimation.

Being the only ep-free algorithm, we have no methods to compare to directly. However, algorithms can mitigate the lack of extrinsic camera parameters by estimating them. In the following comparisons, we show that when extrinsic parameters are not given, using estimated ones induces larger prediction errors, due to the innate inaccuracy of predicted values. On the other hand, FLEX is not affected by the lack of extrinsic parameters, since it does not use them whatsoever. We compare FLEX with two models:

(1) There are two methods that do not use given camera parameters [16,37]. They are not ep-free since they use estimated camera parameters, but we can still use them in settings where camera parameters are not given. Only one of them [16] publishes MPJPE protocol #1 results, and we significantly outperform it (see Table 1). This gap is mostly because of the inaccuracy of parameter prediction and partially because their model is semi-supervised.

(2) For comparing with the best available method, we have chosen the current state-of-the-art multi-view algorithm of Iskakov *et al.* [29] (TesseTrack [59] is marginally better, but it does not provide code). Since their algorithm is *not* ep-free, we imitate parameter estimation by running a controlled perturbation of the camera parameters. We re-train their method with distorted data to simulate an environment where camera distortion parameters are unknown. In addition, we perturb the extrinsic parameters by Gaussian noise with an extremely small standard deviation of 3% of each parameter's value. That is, for a parameter p, we sample $\tilde{p} \sim \mathcal{N}(p,(0.03p)^2)$ and use $\tilde{p}$ as the input extrinsic parameter. We show that increasing the standard deviation from 3% to 4% yields a significant increase in the error, reflecting the sensitivity of non ep-free methods to inaccuracy in camera parameters. To obtain an equivalent environment, we compare FLEX to the method of Iskakov *et al.* [29] after using their own 2D pose estimation. The lower part of Table 1 shows that FLEX outperforms the non ep-free state-of-the-art, even when perturbation percentage is extremely small. Their results in that lower part are grayed out, to emphasize that we simulate an unrealistic setting. Next, we show that a 3% perturbation, rather than estimation, is fairer toward the compared method, as estimation induces larger inaccuracy. We estimate the extrinsic camera parameters with two leading frameworks, COLMAP [64] and OpenCV-SFM [6], and obtain errors of 5.5% and 8.6%, respectively. The error is the mean value of $\frac{|p-\tilde{p}|}{p}$ for all extrinsic values p and their estimation $\tilde{p}$. Moreover, the estimation process involves friction: OpenCV-SFM strongly depends on an initial guess, and COLMAP requires that each pair of cameras observes partially overlapping images, a limiting factor that prevents its usage in settings where the cameras face each other.

In addition to the comprehensive comparison on the Human3.6 dataset, in Table 2 we show a quantitative comparison on the Ski-Pose PTZ-Camera [61] dataset, for methods that are trained when camera parameters are *not* given. These methods are comparable in settings that lack extrinsic parameters because they estimate them. However, since they still use (estimated) parameters, they are not ep-free. FLEX leads the table with a large gap. This gap is mostly because parameter estimation induces an inevitable inaccuracy, and partially because the compared models are self/semi-supervised.

Table 2. MPJPE on the Ski-PTZ dataset, measured for methods trained when extrinsic parameters are *not* given. (†) is self/weakly-supervised.

Method	MPJPE
CanonPose [77] (†)	128.1
Chen *et al.* [11] (†)	99.4
Ours	**65.5**

Table 3. Smoothness, measured by acceleration error (mm/s^2), on Human3.6M. ($\star$): 2D pose from [29]. ($\bullet$): ground-truth 2D poses.

Method	**Acc. Err.** ↓
VIBE [36]	18.3
MEVA [46]	15.3
HMMR [32]	9.1
TCMR [14]	5.3
Iskakov [29]	3.9
Shi [66]	3.6($\star$)/2.0($\bullet$)
FLEX	**1.6($\star$)/0.9($\bullet$)**

Table 4. Attention impact. TE: Transformer Encoder. MHA: Multi-head Attention. l: no. of stacked layers. h: no. of attention heads.

Method	MPJPE
Conv. layer	31.9
TE - $1\,l$, $64\,h$	30.9
TE - $2\,l$, $64\,h$	37.8
MHA - $128\,h$	30.5
MHA - $64\,h$	**30.2**
MHA - $32\,h$	30.6
MHA - $16\,h$	30.9

A known strength of predicting rotation angles rather than locations, is the *smoothness* of predicted motion. In Table 3 we show that FLEX's smoothness result outperforms others by a large margin. Following Kanazawa *et al.* [32], we measure smoothness using the acceleration error of each joint.

Qualitative Results. In the following figures we show rigs, that is, bone structure from reconstructed animation videos, selecting challenging scenes. Videos of the reconstructed motions are available on our project page, presenting the smoothness of motion and the naturalness of rotations. Figure 1, 4 and 5 show scenes from the KTH Multi-view Football II [33], the Human3.6M [9,28] and the Ski-Pose PTZ-Camera [61] datasets, respectively. Each row depicts three views of one time frame. To the right of each image, we place a reconstructed rig, which is sometimes zoomed in for better visualization. Notice the occluded and blurry scenes in the football Fig. (1). The KTH Football dataset is filmed using dynamic (moving) cameras, a setting where extrinsic parameters are rarely given, thus disqualifying methods that require camera parameters. Our algorithm is agnostic to the lack of camera parameters and attains good qualitative results.

In Fig. 6 we show qualitative results of FLEX, compared to current non ep-free multi-view state-of-the-art [29], and to our monocular baseline [66]. Note that the method in [29] produces unnatural poses such as a huge leg in the first row and a backward-bent elbow in the last row.

Multi-person Captured by Dynamic Cameras. We evaluate our algorithm on a setting with dynamic cameras, with multi-person scenes introducing severe inter-person occlusions. Recall that the term *dynamic* refers to moving cameras that occasionally change their location and rotation. There are several multi-view datasets. Most of them are not fully dynamic: Human3.6M [9,28], CMU Panoptic [17] and TUM Shelf & Campus [3] contain static scenes only, while Tagging [76] and Ski-Pose PTZ-Camera [61] contain rotating cameras whose locations are fixed. KTH [33] is fully dynamic, but it is too blurry and does not provide ground-truth for all subjects. Despite its limitations, we use the KTH

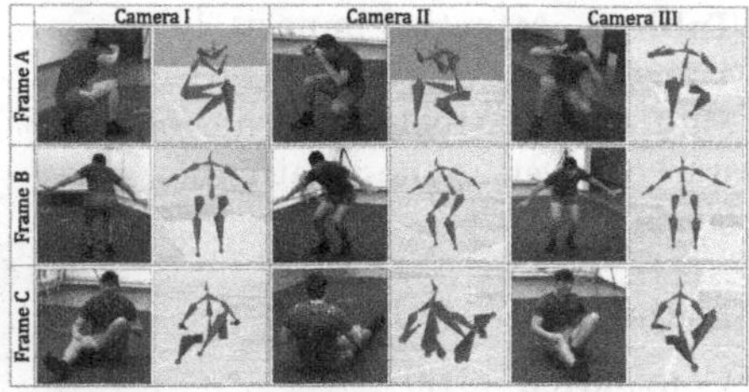

Fig. 4. Our results on videos from the Human3.6M dataset.

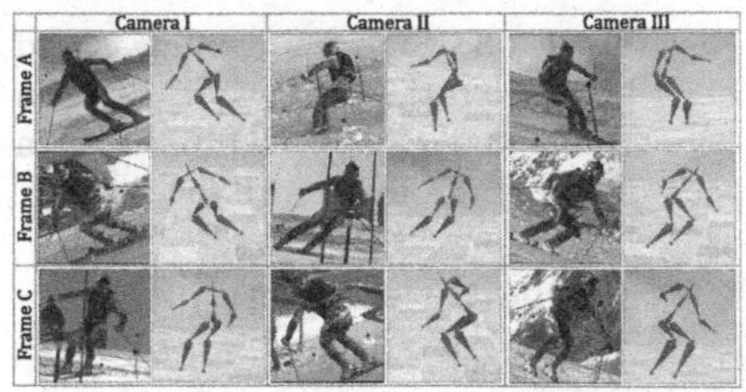

Fig. 5. Our results on videos from the Ski-Pose PTZ-Camera dataset.

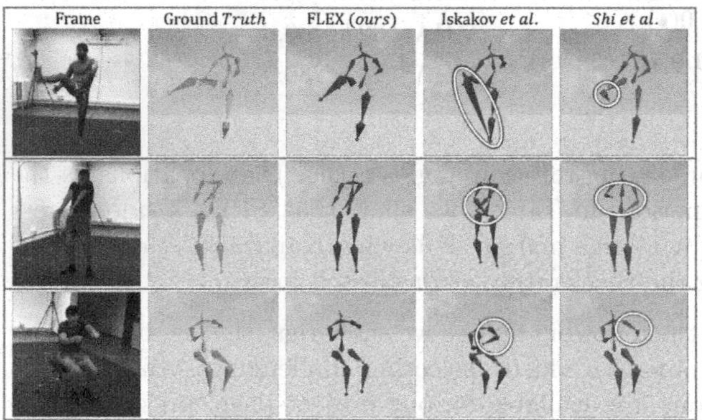

Fig. 6. Qualitative comparison of our work vs. non ep-free state-of-the-art (Iskakov *et al.* [29]) and vs. our single-view baseline (Shi *et al.* [66]).

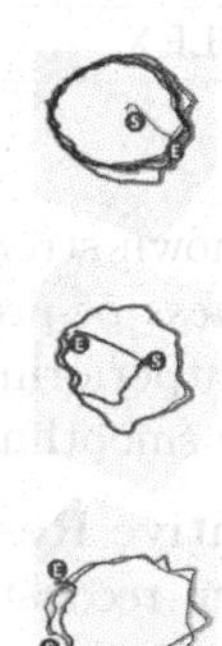

Fig. 7. Global root position. Ground-truth is in thin black.

dataset for qualitative analysis, but we cannot use it for thorough research. To mitigate the lack of a dynamic dataset, we generate synthetic videos using animated characters downloaded from Mixamo [1], an online dataset of character animation. Then, we generate video sequences of two interacting characters using Blender [18], which is a 3D creation suite. The newly created data is available on our project page. Our "synthetic studio]] is illustrated at the sup. mat., where two interacting figures are video-filmed by multiple dynamic cameras. Using Blender, we obtain a rendered video stream from the view angle of each synthetic camera. Recall that the input to our algorithm is 2D joint locations, hence it is agnostic to the video appearance, and to whether the input image is real or synthetic.

The 2D backbone we use over the rendered video sequences is Alphapose [20], a state-of-the-art multi-person 2D pose estimator. Once obtaining the 2D joint locations, we use a naïve heuristic, which is not part of the suggested algorithm, to associate each detected person with its ID: for each frame, we associate the detected 2D pose with the one that is geometrically closest to it in the previous frame. In Fig. 8 we depict qualitative results of two boxers. We emphasize several

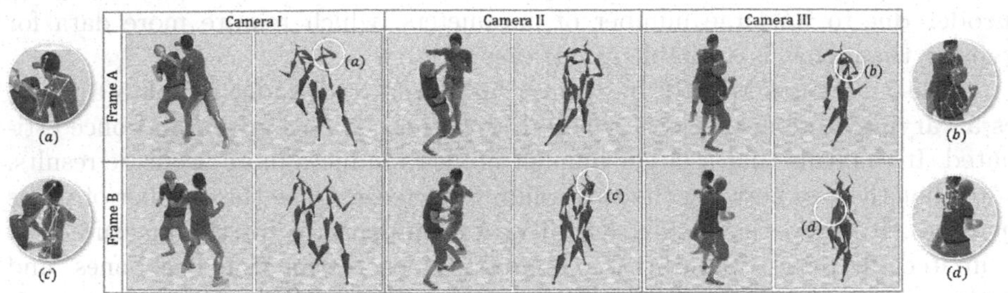

Fig. 8. Results on multi-person synthetic videos. In the zoomed-in circular images we depict 2D pose estimations, which are erroneous due to occlusion. A matching circle in the center rectangular image shows that our method reconstructs correct 3D motion although it takes inaccurate 2D joints for input.

Table 5. Ablation studies: the impact of (a) Number of views; (b) 2D backbone, and (c) Fusion method (refer to the sup. mat. for details regarding fusion).

(a)

#Views	2D backbone	
	GT	[29]
1	47.7	56.3
2	33.9	41.4
3	26.3	34.6
4	**22.9**	**30.2**

(b)

2D backbone	MPJPE
[8]	38.6
[12]	31.7
[29]	30.2
GT	**22.9**

(c)

Method	MPJPE
Averaged K views	36.4
Late fusion	31.0
FLEX	**22.9**

viewpoints where the 2D estimator attains large errors. Yet, FLEX compensates for these errors by fusing multi-view information. In the sup. mat. we show additional characters and the predicted 2D pose for all the viewpoints.

Global Position. In Fig. 7 we draw the global position of the scaled predicted root joint along time. Ground-truth is depicted using a thin black curve, and our prediction is an overlay on top of it, changing from light to dark as time progresses. The start and the end of each trajectory are signaled by the letters S and E, respectively. Depicted motions are evaluated on the test set of Human3.6M, on the motions of walking, talking on the phone, and eating. Note that our predictions almost completely overlap the ground-truth curve. Recall we use weak perspective to bypass dependency on intrinsic parameters, resulting in up-to-scale global position accuracy. Quantitatively, our MPJPE on the H36M validation set is 118 mm, outperforming Iskakov *et al.* [29] (perturbed by 3%) that attain 123 mm. The other ep-free work [16] does not solve global locations.

Ablation Study. We evaluate the impact of different settings on the performance of FLEX using various ablation tests. Table 4 compares different multi-view fusion architectures. Note that using attention rather than convolution yields a 2 mm improvement. The performance degrades with the transformer encoder due to its large number of parameters, which require more data for training than what is available in our case.

Table 5 measures MPJPE on Human3.6M in several studies. Table 5(a) studies a varying number of views, where the 2D pose is once given and once estimated. It confirms that a larger number of views induces more accurate results. Note that the gap between the two columns decreases once the number of views increases. It shows that using several views compensates for the inaccuracy of estimated 2D poses. Table 5(b) compares 2D pose estimation backbones, and justifies our use of Iskakov *et al.* [29]. Finally, in Table 5(c) we explore two variations, both with ground-truth 2D inputs. The first variation runs FLEX as a monocular method (K = 1) and averages the monocular predictions. The second changes the fusion layers, F_S and F_Q, to use late fusion instead of an early one. We conclude that the configuration used by FLEX is better than both variations.

Generalization. We exhibit generalization by training on one dataset and evaluating on a different, more challenging one. The train dataset is Human3.6M, and the evaluation ones are the KTH Football dataset, and the synthetic videos. For quantitative measurement, we train our model on two of the four cameras of the Human3.6M dataset. We test it using the other two cameras, on which the model has not been trained. We repeat this process for all possible camera pairs and obtain an average MPJPE of 148 mm. Note that this error is not large compared to the human body size, and indeed we attain pleasing visual results as shown in the inset on the right.

5 Conclusions and Limitations

We have presented FLEX, a multi-view method for motion reconstruction. It relies on a key understanding that 3D rotation angles and bone lengths are invariant to camera view, and their direct reconstruction spares the need for camera parameters. On a technical viewpoint, we presented a novel fusion layer with a multi-view convolutional layer and a multi-head attention mechanism that attends views.

One limitation of our approach is the dependency on 3D joint location ground-truth, and in particular, the requirement that it is given at the axis system of the train cameras. Another limitation is the dependency on the 2D backbone quality, and on the accuracy value associated with each joint. Lastly, being ep-free, the output 3D joint positions are only relative to the camera, lacking the transformation with respect to a global axis system.

In summary, FLEX is unique in fusing multi-view information to reconstruct motion and pose in dynamic photography environments. It is unaffected by settings in which the relative rotations between the cameras are unknown, and can maintain a high level of accuracy regardless. FLEX offers a simpler setting, where the correspondence and compatibility among the different views are rather lean, and thus more resilient to input errors and innate inaccuracies.

Acknowledgements. This research would not have been possible without the exceptional support of Mingyi Shi. We are grateful to Kfir Aberman and Yuval Alaluf for reviewing earlier versions of the manuscript, and to Yuval Alaluf and Shahaf Goren for contributing to FLEX's video clip. This work was supported in part by the Israel Science Foundation (grants no. 2366/16 and 2492/20).

References

1. Adobe Systems Inc.: Mixamo (2018). http://www.mixamo.com/
2. Bachmann, R., Spörri, J., Fua, P., Rhodin, H.: Motion capture from pan-tilt cameras with unknown orientation. In: 2019 International Conference on 3D Vision (3DV), pp. 308–317. IEEE, IEEE Computer Society, Washington, DC, USA (2019)
3. Belagiannis, V., Amin, S., Andriluka, M., Schiele, B., Navab, N., Ilic, S.: 3D pictorial structures for multiple human pose estimation. In: 2014 IEEE Conference on Computer Vision and Pattern Recognition, pp. 1669–1676 (2014). https://doi.org/10.1109/CVPR.2014.216
4. Belagiannis, V., Amin, S., Andriluka, M., Schiele, B., Navab, N., Ilic, S.: 3D pictorial structures revisited: multiple human pose estimation. IEEE Trans. Patt. Anal. Mach. Intell. **38**, 1929–1942 (2016). https://doi.org/10.1109/TPAMI.2015.2509986
5. Bergtholdt, M., Kappes, J., Schmidt, S., Schnörr, C.: A study of parts-based object class detection using complete graphs. Int. J. Comput. Vision **87**, 93–117 (2010). https://doi.org/10.1007/s11263-009-0209-1
6. Bradski, G.: The OpenCV Library. Dr. Dobb's J. Softw. Tools **120**; 122–125 (2000)
7. Burenius, M., Sullivan, J., Carlsson, S.: 3D pictorial structures for multiple view articulated pose estimation. In: Proceedings/CVPR, IEEE Computer Society Conference on Computer Vision and Pattern Recognition, pp. 3618–3625. IEEE Computer Society, Washington, DC, USA, June 2013. https://doi.org/10.1109/CVPR.2013.464
8. Cao, Z., Hidalgo, G., Simon, T., Wei, S., Sheikh, Y.: OpenPose: realtime multi-person 2D pose estimation using part affinity fields. In: Proceedings of the 2018 IEEE Conference on Computer Vision and Pattern Recognition. CVPR 2018, vol. 43, pp. 172–186. IEEE Computer Society, Washington, DC, USA (2018)
9. Ionescu, C., Fuxin Li, C.S.: Latent structured models for human pose estimation. In: International Conference on Computer Vision (2011)
10. Chen, X., Lin, K.Y., Liu, W., Qian, C., Wang, X., Lin, L.: Weakly-supervised discovery of geometry-aware representation for 3d human pose estimation. In: 2019 IEEE/CVF Conference on Computer Vision and Pattern Recognition (CVPR), pp. 10887–10896 (2019)
11. Chen, X., Wei, P., Lin, L.: Deductive learning for weakly-supervised 3D human pose estimation via uncalibrated cameras. In: Proceedings of the AAAI Conference on Artificial Intelligence, vol. 35, pp. 1089–1096 (2021)
12. Chen, Y., Wang, Z., Peng, Y., Zhang, Z., Yu, G., Sun, J.: Cascaded pyramid network for multi-person pose estimation. In: Proceedings of the IEEE Conference on Computer Vision and Pattern Recognition, pp. 7103–7112. IEEE Computer Society, Washington, DC, USA (2018)
13. Cheng, Y., Yang, B., Wang, B., Tan, R.T.: 3D human pose estimation using spatio-temporal networks with explicit occlusion training. In: Proceedings of the AAAI Conference on Artificial Intelligence, vol. 34, pp. 10631–10638 (2020)
14. Choi, H., Moon, G., Lee, K.M.: Beyond static features for temporally consistent 3d human pose and shape from a video. In: Conference on Computer Vision and Pattern Recognition (CVPR) (2021)

15. Chu, H., Lee, J.H., Lee, Y.C., Hsu, C.H., Li, J.D., Chen, C.S.: Part-aware measurement for robust multi-view multi-human 3D pose estimation and tracking. In: Proceedings of the IEEE/CVF Conference on Computer Vision and Pattern Recognition (CVPR) Workshops, pp. 1472–1481, June 2021
16. Chu, W.T., Pan, Z.W.: Semi-supervised 3d human pose estimation by jointly considering temporal and multiview information. IEEE Access **8**, 226974–226981 (2020). https://doi.org/10.1109/ACCESS.2020.3045794
17. CMU: CMU graphics lab motion capture database, May 2019. http://mocap.cs.cmu.edu/
18. Community, B.O.: Blender - a 3D Modelling and Rendering Package. Blender Foundation, Stichting Blender Foundation, Amsterdam (2018). http://www.blender.org/
19. Dong, J., Jiang, W., Huang, Q., Bao, H., Zhou, X.: Fast and robust multi-person 3D pose estimation from multiple views. In: Proceedings of the IEEE/CVF Conference on Computer Vision and Pattern Recognition, pp. 7792–7801 (2019)
20. Fang, H.S., Xie, S., Tai, Y.W., Lu, C.: RMPE: regional multi-person pose estimation. In: ICCV, pp 2334–2343. IEEE Computer Society, Washington, DC, USA (2017)
21. Fang, H.S., Xu, Y., Wang, W., Liu, X., Zhu, S.C.: Learning pose grammar to encode human body configuration for 3d pose estimation. In: Proceedings of the AAAI Conference on Artificial Intelligence, vol. 32 (2018)
22. Habermann, M., Xu, W., Zollhofer, M., Pons-Moll, G., Theobalt, C.: DeepCap: Monocular human performance capture using weak supervision. In: Proceedings of the IEEE/CVF Conference on Computer Vision and Pattern Recognition, pp. 5052–5063 (2020)
23. Habibie, I., Xu, W., Mehta, D., Pons-Moll, G., Theobalt, C.: In the wild human pose estimation using explicit 2d features and intermediate 3D representations. In: Proceedings of the IEEE/CVF Conference on Computer Vision and Pattern Recognition, pp. 10905–10914. IEEE Computer Society, Washington, DC, USA (2019)
24. He, Y., Yan, R., Fragkiadaki, K., Yu, S.I.: Epipolar transformers. In: 2020 IEEE/CVF Conference on Computer Vision and Pattern Recognition (CVPR), pp. 7776–7785 (2020)
25. Hossain, M.R.I., Little, J.J.: Exploiting temporal information for 3D human pose estimation. In: Ferrari, V., Hebert, M., Sminchisescu, C., Weiss, Y. (eds.) ECCV 2018. LNCS, vol. 11214, pp. 69–86. Springer, Cham (2018). https://doi.org/10.1007/978-3-030-01249-6_5
26. Hu, W., Zhang, C., Zhan, F., Zhang, L., Wong, T.T.: Conditional directed graph convolution for 3D Human pose estimation, In: ACM Multimedia Conference, MM 2021, pp. 602–611. Association for Computing Machinery, New York, NY, USA (2021). https://doi.org/10.1145/3474085.3475219
27. Huang, F., Zeng, A., Liu, M., Lai, Q., Xu, Q.: DeepFuse: an IMU-aware network for real-time 3d human pose estimation from multi-view image. In: 2020 IEEE Winter Conference on Applications of Computer Vision (WACV), pp. 418–427. IEEE Computer Society, Los Alamitos, CA, USA, March 2020. https://doi.org/10.1109/WACV45572.2020.9093526, https://doi.org/10.1109/WACV45572.2020.9093526
28. Ionescu, C., Papava, D., Olaru, V., Sminchisescu, C.: Human3.6m: large scale datasets and predictive methods for 3D human sensing in natural environments. IEEE Trans. Pattern Anal. Mach. Intell. **36**(7), 1325–1539 (2014)

29. Iskakov, K., Burkov, E., Lempitsky, V.S., Malkov, Y.: Learnable triangulation of human pose. In: 2019 IEEE/CVF International Conference on Computer Vision (ICCV), pp. 7717–7726 (2019)
30. Kadkhodamohammadi, A., Padoy, N.: A generalizable approach for multi-view 3D human pose regression. Mach. Vis. Appl. **32**(1), 1–14 (2021)
31. Kanazawa, A., Black, M.J., Jacobs, D.W., Malik, J.: End-to-end recovery of human shape and pose. In: Proceedings of the IEEE Conference on Computer Vision and Pattern Recognition, CVPR 2018, pp. 7122–7131. IEEE Computer Society, Washington, DC, USA (2018). https://doi.org/10.1109/CVPR.2018.00744
32. Kanazawa, A., Zhang, J.Y., Felsen, P., Malik, J.: Learning 3D human dynamics from video. In: Computer Vision and Pattern Recognition (CVPR) (2019)
33. Kazemi, V., Burenius, M., Azizpour, H., Sullivan, J.: Multi-view body part recognition with random forests. In: BMVC 2013 - Electronic Proceedings of the British Machine Vision Conference 2013. BMVA, UK (2013). https://doi.org/10.5244/C.27.48
34. Khan, S., Naseer, M., Hayat, M., Zamir, S.W., Khan, F.S., Shah, M.: Transformers in vision: a survey. ACM Comput. Surv. **54**, 1–41 (2021). https://doi.org/10.1145/3505244
35. Kissos, I., Fritz, L., Goldman, M., Meir, O., Oks, E., Kliger, M.: Beyond weak perspective for monocular 3D human pose estimation. In: Bartoli, A., Fusiello, A. (eds.) ECCV 2020. LNCS, vol. 12536, pp. 541–554. Springer, Cham (2020). https://doi.org/10.1007/978-3-030-66096-3_37
36. Kocabas, M., Athanasiou, N., Black, M.J.: VIBE: video inference for human body pose and shape estimation. In: Proceedings of the IEEE/CVF Conference on Computer Vision and Pattern Recognition, pp. 5253–5263 (2020)
37. Kocabas, M., Karagoz, S., Akbas, E.: Self-supervised learning of 3D human pose using multi-view geometry. In: 2019 IEEE/CVF Conference on Computer Vision and Pattern Recognition (CVPR), pp. 1077–1086 (2019)
38. Kolotouros, N., Pavlakos, G., Black, M.J., Daniilidis, K.: Learning to reconstruct 3D human pose and shape via model-fitting in the loop. In: Proceedings of the IEEE International Conference on Computer Vision, ICCV 2019, pp. 2252–2261. IEEE Computer Society, Washington, DC, USA (2019)
39. Li, S., Chan, A.: 3D human pose estimation from monocular images with deep convolutional neural network. Appl. Sci. **10**(15), 5186 (2014). https://doi.org/10.1007/978-3-319-16808-1_23
40. Li, W., Liu, H., Ding, R., Liu, M., Wang, P., Yang, W.: Exploiting temporal contexts with strided transformer for 3D human pose estimation. IEEE Trans. Multim, Early Access (2021)
41. Lin, K., Wang, L., Liu, Z.: End-to-end human pose and mesh reconstruction with transformers. In: Proceedings of the IEEE/CVF Conference on Computer Vision and Pattern Recognition, pp. 1954–1963 (2021)
42. Liu, D., Zhao, Z., Wang, X., Hu, Y., Zhang, L., Huang, T.: Improving 3D human pose estimation via 3D part affinity fields. In: 2019 IEEE Winter Conference on Applications of Computer Vision (WACV), pp. 1004–1013. IEEE, IEEE Computer Society, Washington, DC, USA (2019)
43. Liu, R., Shen, J., Wang, H., Chen, C., Cheung, S.c., Asari, V.: Attention mechanism exploits temporal contexts: Real-time 3D human pose reconstruction. In: Proceedings of the IEEE/CVF Conference on Computer Vision and Pattern Recognition, pp. 5064–5073. IEEE Computer Society, Washington, DC, USA (2020)
44. Llopart, A.: Liftformer: 3D human pose estimation using attention models. CoRR abs/2009.00348 (2020). 'arxiv.org/abs/2009.00348'

45. Loper, M., Mahmood, N., Romero, J., Pons-Moll, G., Black, M.J.: SMPL: a skinned multi-person linear model. ACM Trans. Graphics (Proc. SIGGRAPH Asia) **34**(6), 248:1–248:16 (2015)
46. Luo, Z., Golestaneh, S.A., Kitani, K.M.: 3D human motion estimation via motion compression and refinement. In: Proceedings of the Asian Conference on Computer Vision (ACCV), November 2020
47. Ma, H., et al.: Transfusion: cross-view fusion with transformer for 3D human pose estimation. In: British Machine Vision Conference (2021)
48. Mao, W., Liu, M., Salzmann, M., Li, H.: Learning trajectory dependencies for human motion prediction. In: Proceedings of the IEEE/CVF International Conference on Computer Vision (ICCV), October 2019
49. von Marcard, T., Henschel, R., Black, M.J., Rosenhahn, B., Pons-Moll, G.: Recovering accurate 3D human pose in the wild using IMUs and a moving camera. In: Ferrari, V., Hebert, M., Sminchisescu, C., Weiss, Y. (eds.) ECCV 2018. LNCS, vol. 11214, pp. 614–631. Springer, Cham (2018). https://doi.org/10.1007/978-3-030-01249-6_37
50. Martinez, J., Hossain, R., Romero, J., Little, J.J.: A simple yet effective baseline for 3d human pose estimation. In: Proceedings of the IEEE International Conference on Computer Vision. pp. 2640–2649 (2017)
51. Mehta, D., Sotnychenko, O., Mueller, F., Xu, W., Elgharib, M., Fua, P., Seidel, H.P., Rhodin, H., Pons-Moll, G., Theobalt, C.: XNect: real-time multi-person 3d motion capture with a single RGB camera. ACM Transactions on Graphics (TOG) **39**(4), 11–82 (2020)
52. Ohashi, T., Ikegami, Y., Yamamoto, K., Takano, W., Nakamura, Y.: Video motion capture from the part confidence maps of multi-camera images by spatiotemporal filtering using the human skeletal model. In: 2018 IEEE/RSJ International Conference on Intelligent Robots and Systems (IROS), pp. 4226–4231 October 2018. https://doi.org/10.1109/IROS.2018.8593867
53. Pavlakos, G., Malik, J., Kanazawa, A.: Human mesh recovery from multiple shots. In: Proceedings of the IEEE/CVF Conference on Computer Vision and Pattern Recognition (CVPR). pp. 1485–1495, June 2022
54. Pavlakos, G., Zhou, X., Daniilidis, K.: Ordinal depth supervision for 3D human pose estimation. In: Proceedings of the IEEE Conference on Computer Vision and Pattern Recognition, pp. 7307–7316. IEEE Computer Society, Washington, DC, USA (2018)
55. Pavlakos, G., Zhou, X., Derpanis, K.G., Daniilidis, K.: Coarse-to-fine volumetric prediction for single-image 3D human pose. In: Proceedings of the IEEE Conference on Computer Vision and Pattern Recognition, CVPR 2017, pp. 1263–1272. IEEE Computer Society, Washington, DC, USA (2017)
56. Pavllo, D., Feichtenhofer, C., Grangier, D., Auli, M.: 3D human pose estimation in video with temporal convolutions and semi-supervised training. In: Proceedings of the IEEE/CVF Conference on Computer Vision and Pattern Recognition, pp. 7753–7762 (2019)
57. Pavllo, D., Grangier, D., Auli, M.: QuaterNet: a quaternion-based recurrent model for human motion. In: British Machine Vision Conference (BMVC) (2018)
58. Qiu, H., Wang, C., Wang, J., Wang, N., Zeng, W.: Cross view fusion for 3d human pose estimation. 2019 IEEE/CVF International Conference on Computer Vision (ICCV), pp. 4341–4350 (2019)

59. Reddy, N., Guigues, L., Pischulini, L., Eledath, J., Narasimhan, S.G.: TesseTrack: end-to-end learnable multi-person articulated 3D pose tracking. In: 2021 IEEE/CVF Conference on Computer Vision and Pattern Recognition (CVPR), pp. 15185–15195 (2021)
60. Rhodin, H., et al.: Learning monocular 3D human pose estimation from multiview images. In: 2018 IEEE/CVF Conference on Computer Vision and Pattern Recognition, pp. 8437–8446 (2018)
61. Rhodin, H., et al.: Learning monocular 3D human pose estimation from multiview images. In: 2018 IEEE/CVF Conference on Computer Vision and Pattern Recognition, pp. 8437–8446 (2018)
62. Sarafianos, N., Boteanu, B., Ionescu, B., Kakadiaris, I.A.: 3D human pose estimation: a review of the literature and analysis of covariates. Comput. Vis. Image Underst. **152**(C), 1–20 (2016). https://doi.org/10.1016/j.cviu.2016.09.002
63. Sárándi, I., Linder, T., Arras, K.O., Leibe, B.: Metric-scale truncation-robust heatmaps for 3D human pose estimation. In: 2020 15th IEEE International Conference on Automatic Face and Gesture Recognition (FG 2020), pp. 407–414 (2020)
64. Schönberger, J.L., Frahm, J.M.: Structure-from-motion revisited. In: Conference on Computer Vision and Pattern Recognition (CVPR) (2016)
65. Shan, W., Lu, H., Wang, S., Zhang, X., Gao, W.: Improving robustness and accuracy via relative information encoding in 3d human pose estimation. In: Proceedings of the 29th ACM International Conference on Multimedia (2021)
66. Shi, M., et al.: MotioNet: 3D human motion reconstruction from monocular video with skeleton consistency. ACM Trans. Graph. **40**(1), 1–15 (2020)
67. Shimada, S., Golyanik, V., Xu, W., Pérez, P., Theobalt, C.: Neural monocular 3D human motion capture with physical awareness. ACM Trans. Graph. **40**(4) (2021). .https://doi.org/10.1145/3450626.3459825, https://doi.org/10.1145/3450626.3459825
68. Skycam: http://www.skycam.tv/
69. Sun, J., Wang, M., Zhao, X., Zhang, D.: Multi-view pose generator based on deep learning for monocular 3D human pose estimation. Symmetry **12**(7), 1116 (2020)
70. Sun, X., Xiao, B., Wei, F., Liang, S., Wei, Y.: Integral human pose regression. In: Proceedings of the European Conference on Computer Vision (ECCV). pp. 529–545 (2018)
71. Takahashi, K., Mikami, D., Isogawa, M., Kimata, H.: Human pose as calibration pattern: 3D human pose estimation with multiple unsynchronized and uncalibrated cameras. In: 2018 IEEE/CVF Conference on Computer Vision and Pattern Recognition Workshops (CVPRW), pp. 1856–18567 (2018). https://doi.org/10.1109/CVPRW.2018.00230
72. Tekin, B., Katircioglu, I., Salzmann, M., Lepetit, V., Fua, P.: Structured prediction of 3D human pose with deep neural networks. In: British Machine Vision Conference (BMVC) (2016)
73. Tome, D., Toso, M., Agapito, L., Russell, C.: Rethinking pose in 3D multi-stage refinement and recovery for markerless motion capture. In: 2018 International Conference on 3D Vision (3DV), pp. 474–483. IEEE, IEEE Computer Society, Washington, DC, USA (2018)
74. Tu, H., Wang, C., Zeng, W.: VoxelPose: towards multi-camera 3d human pose estimation in wild environment. In: Vedaldi, A., Bischof, H., Brox, T., Frahm, J.-M. (eds.) ECCV 2020. LNCS, vol. 12346, pp. 197–212. Springer, Cham (2020). https://doi.org/10.1007/978-3-030-58452-8_12

75. Usman, B., Tagliasacchi, A., Saenko, K., Sud, A.: MetaPose: fast 3D pose from multiple views without 3D supervision. In: Proceedings of the IEEE/CVF Conference on Computer Vision and Pattern Recognition (CVPR), pp. 6759–6770, June 2022
76. Vo, M.P., Yumer, E., Sunkavalli, K., Hadap, S., Sheikh, Y., Narasimhan, S.G.: Self-supervised multi-view person association and its applications. IEEE Trans. Pattern Anal. Mach. Intell. **43**, 2794–2808 (2021)
77. Wandt, B., Rudolph, M., Zell, P., Rhodin, H., Rosenhahn, B.: CanonPose: self-supervised monocular 3D human pose estimation in the wild. In: Computer Vision and Pattern Recognition (CVPR), June 2021
78. Wang, D., et al.: Multi-view 3d reconstruction with transformer. In: Proceeding of the IEEE International Conference on Computer Vision, ICCV2021, pp. 5722–5731 (2021)
79. Wang, J., Yan, S., Xiong, Y., Lin, D.: Motion Guided 3D pose estimation from videos. In: Vedaldi, A., Bischof, H., Brox, T., Frahm, J.-M. (eds.) ECCV 2020. LNCS, vol. 12358, pp. 764–780. Springer, Cham (2020). https://doi.org/10.1007/978-3-030-58601-0_45
80. Yoshiyasu, Y., Sagawa, R., Ayusawa, K., Murai, A.: Skeleton transformer networks: 3D human pose and skinned mesh from single RGB image. In: Jawahar, C.V., Li, H., Mori, G., Schindler, K. (eds.) ACCV 2018. LNCS, vol. 11364, pp. 485–500. Springer, Cham (2019). https://doi.org/10.1007/978-3-030-20870-7_30
81. Wang, D., et al.: Multi-view 3D reconstruction with transformer. In: Proceeding of the IEEE International Conference on Computer Vision, ICCV2021, pp. 5722–5731(2021)
82. Zhou, X., Sun, X., Zhang, W., Liang, S., Wei, Y.: Deep kinematic pose regression. In: Hua, G., Jégou, H. (eds.) ECCV 2016. LNCS, vol. 9915, pp. 186–201. Springer, Cham (2016). https://doi.org/10.1007/978-3-319-49409-8_17
83. Zhu, L., Rematas, K., Curless, B., Seitz, S.M., Kemelmacher-Shlizerman, I.: Reconstructing NBA players. In: Vedaldi, A., Bischof, H., Brox, T., Frahm, J.-M. (eds.) ECCV 2020. LNCS, vol. 12350, pp. 177–194. Springer, Cham (2020). https://doi.org/10.1007/978-3-030-58558-7_11
84. Zins, P., Xu, Y., Boyer, E., Wuhrer, S., Tung, T.: Data-driven 3D reconstruction of dressed humans from sparse views. In: 3DV (2021)

MODE: Multi-view Omnidirectional Depth Estimation with 360° Cameras

Ming Li, Xueqian Jin, Xuejiao Hu, Jingzhao Dai, Sidan Du(✉), and Yang Li(✉)

Nanjing University, Nanjing, China
{mingli,jcboxq,hxj,dg20230007}@smail.nju.edu.cn,
{coff128,yogo}@nju.edu.cn

Abstract. In this paper, we propose a two-stage omnidirectional depth estimation framework with multi-view 360° cameras. The framework first estimates the depth maps from different camera pairs via omnidirectional stereo matching and then fuses the depth maps to achieve robustness against mud spots, water drops on camera lenses, and glare caused by intense light. We adopt spherical feature learning to address the distortion of panoramas. In addition, a synthetic 360° dataset consisting of 12K road scene panoramas and 3K ground truth depth maps is presented to train and evaluate 360° depth estimation algorithms. Our dataset takes soiled camera lenses and glare into consideration, which is more consistent with the real-world environment. Experimental results show that the proposed framework generates reliable results in both synthetic and real-world environments, and it achieves state-of-the-art performance on different datasets. The code and data are available at https://github.com/nju-ee/MODE-2022.

Keywords: Omnidirectional depth estimation · Stereo matching · Spherical feature learning · 360° cameras · Multi-view

1 Introduction

Image-based depth estimation is a long-lasting and fundamental task in computer vision. Recently, omnidirectional depth estimation has attracted attention in many applications such as autonomous driving and robot navigation for its efficient perception of the 360° environment. Many algorithms have been proposed to estimate 360° depth, including monocular [14,28] and binocular [18,29] methods. However, these existing methods either extract spherical features with conventional planar convolution [14,28,29] or do not simplify the spherical epipolar constraint [18]. Apart from this, the monocular and binocular methods cannot

M. Li and X. Jin—Contributed equally to this work.

Supplementary Information The online version contains supplementary material available at https://doi.org/10.1007/978-3-031-19827-4_12.

S. Avidan et al. (Eds.): ECCV 2022, LNCS 13693, pp. 197–213, 2022.
https://doi.org/10.1007/978-3-031-19827-4_12

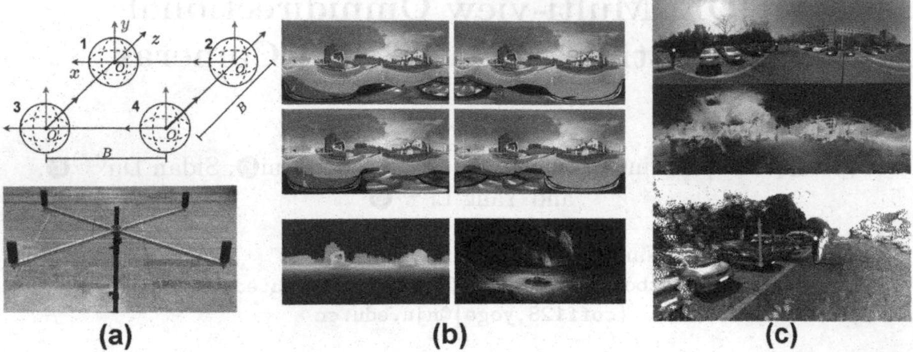

Fig. 1. Overview of the proposed multi-view omnidirectional depth estimation framework. (a) shows the multiple 360° camera rig. (b) shows the result of our method on the proposed synthetic dataset. The first two rows show the panoramas captured by the four cameras and the last row shows the predicted depth map and corresponding point cloud. (c) shows the results on the real-world environment, from top to bottom: reference panorama, predicted depth map and corresponding point cloud

obtain reliable depth maps when 360° cameras installed on vehicles are soiled by mud spots, water drops or dazzled by intense light (see Fig. 8).

Won et al. proposed multi-view methods SweepNet [30] and OmniMVS [31, 32] to estimate 360° depth maps from four fish-eye cameras. However, these methods also use planar convolution to extract spherical features, and the blind areas of fish-eye cameras introduce discontinuity in the spherical cost volume.

In this paper, we decompose the multi-view omnidirectional depth estimation into two stages. In the first stage, we choose several camera pairs from different views for omnidirectional stereo matching and obtain disparity maps. In the second stage, we convert disparity maps to aligned depth maps and fuse them to estimate the final depth map. The information fusion of different stereo pairs improves the accuracy and robustness of the final depth map. In addition, the two parts of the framework can be trained and fine-tuned independently with lower hardware demands. We use Cassini projection [2] to simplify the epipolar constraint of omnidirectional stereo matching and propose a spherical feature extraction module to overcome the distortion of panoramas[1].

Moreover, a large-scale synthetic outdoor omnidirectional dataset, Deep360, is proposed in this work. To evaluate the performance of different 360° depth estimation methods when camera lenses are soiled by mud spots, water drops or dazzled by glare, we also provide a soiled version of the dataset.

Figure 1 illustrates the overview of the proposed multi-view omnidirectional depth estimation (MODE) framework. It estimates accurate depth maps from four 360° cameras. Experimental results demonstrate that our method generates

[1] We use the terms omnidirectional, 360°, spherical and panorama interchangeably in this document.

reliable depth maps in various scenes and achieves state-of-the-art (SOTA) performance on different datasets, especially the one with soiled panoramas. This validates the robustness of our proposed framework and shows that the framework can be extended to arbitrary 360° multi-camera setups.

In summary, the main contributions of this work are as follows:

- We propose a flexible 360° depth estimation framework called MODE to obtain reliable depth maps against soiled camera lenses or glare. MODE also achieves SOTA performance.
- We introduce the spherical convolution to address panorama distortions in 360° stereo matching. We prove that using an appropriate projection to simplify the epipolar constraint is essential for this problem and introduce the Cassini projection. We adopt the training detail of removing image cropping for 360° stereo matching.
- We present a large-scale synthetic outdoor dataset, Deep360, that contains both high-quality and soiled panorama images.

2 Related Work

2.1 Deep Learning-Based Stereo Matching Methods

Deep learning methods report much improved performance in stereo matching. Zbontar and Lecun [36] propose MCCNN that extracts features by CNNs and computes disparity via conventional matching cost aggregation. GCNet [15] builds cost volume with feature maps and obtains disparity maps through 3D CNN blocks. PSMNet [4] adopts spatial pyramid pooling in feature extraction and uses the stacked hourglass architecture in regression to improve the performance. GA-Net [37] proposes the local-guided and semi-global aggregation layers to capture local and whole-image dependencies respectively. AANet [33] adopts an adaptive aggregation algorithm and replaces the costly 3D-CNN for an efficient architecture. Lipson et al. [19] proposes RAFT-Stereo which adopts multi-level GRU modules to estiamte the accurate disparity maps. CFNet [25] proposes a network based on the cascade and fused cost volume to improve the robustness in stereo matching. DispNet [20] and CRL [22] compute left-right feature correlation and then estimate disparity maps.

Multi-view stereo (MVS) has developed rapidly in recent years as well. Yao et al. [35] proposed the end-to-end MVSNet that builds cost volume by warping feature maps of different views into front-parallel planes of the reference camera to obtain depth maps. Point-MVSNet [5] adopts the feature augmented point cloud to refine the depth map iteratively. Cascade-MVS [10] and CVP-MVS [34] improve the performance with multi-scale coarse-to-fine architectures.

These stereo matching methods are designed for perspective cameras with normal field-of-view (FoV) and do not consider the property of panoramas.

2.2 Omnidirectional Depth Estimation

Recently, some learning-based algorithms have been proposed for omnidirectional depth estimation. Zioulis et al. propose two monocular networks using supervised learning [39], and adopt the extra coordinate feature in CoordNet [38] for learning context in the equirectangular projection (ERP) domain. Wang et al. [28] propose BiFuse for monocular depth estimation which combines the ERP and CubeMap projection to overcome the distortion of panoramas. Jiang et al. [14] develop BiFuse and propose UniFuse which achieves better performance via a more efficient fusion scheme. Cheng et al. [6] regard omnidirectional depth estimation as an extension of the partial depth map. Wang et al. [29] propose the 360SD-Net which estimates omnidirectional depth in the ERP domain for up-down stereo pairs. CSDNet [18] focuses on the left-right stereo and uses Mesh CNNs [13] to solve the spherical distortions. However, these methods either extract spherical features with planar convolution [14,28,29,39] or do not simplify the spherical epipolar constraint [18].

There are also some methods for obtaining omnidirectional depth maps based on multi-view fish-eye cameras. Won et al. propose SweepNet [30] which builds cost volume via spherical sweeping and estimates spherical depth by cost aggregation. They further improve the algorithm and propose the end-to-end OmniMVS [31,32] architecture to achieve better performance. However, these methods also use planar convolution to extract spherical features and the blind areas of fish-eye cameras introduce discontinuity in the spherical cost volume.

2.3 Omnidirectional Depth Datasets

Large-scale datasets with high variety are essential for training and evaluating learning-based algorithms. Recently released omnidirectional depth datasets can be divided into two categories according to the input images, one with the panoramas, and the other with the fish-eye images. These datasets are mainly collected from public available real-world and synthetic 3D datasets by repurposing them to omnidirectional by rendering.

For datasets with panoramas, Wang et al. [27] collect an indoor monocular 360° video dataset named PanoSUNCG from [26]. De La Garanderie et al. [16] provide an outdoor monocular 360° benchmark with 200 images generated from the CARLA autonomous driving simulator [8]. MP3D and SF3D [29] are indoor binocular 360° datasets collected from [1,3]. 3D60 by Zioulis et al. [38] is an indoor trinocular (central, right, up) 360° dataset collected from [1,3,11,26]. For datasets with fish-eye images, Won et al. [30–32] present three datasets: Urban, OmniHouse and OmniThings. All three datasets are virtually collected in Blender with four fish-eye cameras.

The fish-eye images need complementary information to estimate an omnidirectional depth map, which means discontinuity and requirements for camera directions. In contrast, the panoramas record all 360° information continuously without blind areas. However, as summarized above, the datasets with stereo panoramas [29,38] consist of indoor scenes only. A detailed summary of omnidirectional depth datasets can be found in Table 2.

3 Multi-view Omnidirectional Depth Estimation

3.1 Multi-view Omnidirectional Camera System

Camera System Settings. In this paper, we use the camera rig shown in Fig. 1(a) to implement the proposed framework. Four 360° cameras are arranged on a horizontal plane to form a square with side length B. The cameras are numbered from 1 to 4. Any two of the cameras can form a stereo pair, so there are 6 (C_4^2) pairs in total. We mark the different stereo pairs with the numbers of the cameras, which are 1–2, 1–3, 1–4, 2–3, 2–4 and 3–4 (i.e. 1–2 denotes the image pair of cameras 1 and 2).

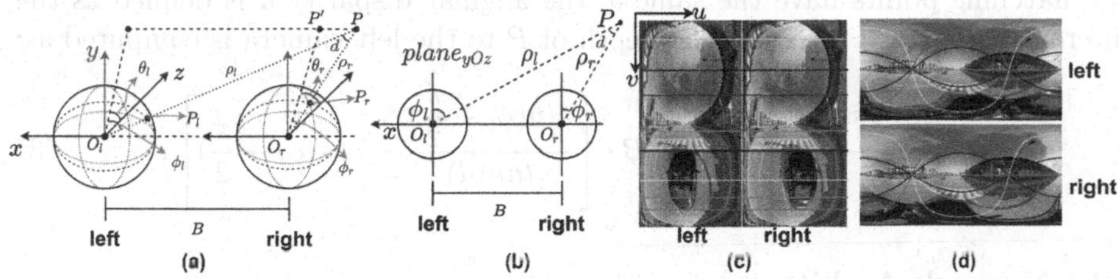

Fig. 2. Cassini projection and spherical epipolar geometry of the omnidirectional images. (a) illustrates the spherical coordinate system of omnidirectional left-right stereo cameras. (b) illustrates the angular disparity of spherical images. (c) shows the linear epipolar constraint in Cassini projection domain. The matching points are located in the same row of the left and right images. (d) shows the nonlinear epipolar constraint in ERP domain. The matching points are located on curves with the same color

Spherical Projection and Epipolar Constraint. As shown in Fig. 2(a), we define the spherical coordinate system (ρ, ϕ, θ) as follows: ρ is the distance between the camera optic center O and the point P; ϕ is the angle between line OP and the plane yOz; and θ is the angle between line OP' and positive z, where P' is the projection of P on yOz. Thus, the transformation between Cartesian coordinates and the Cassini spherical coordinates is:

$$\begin{cases} x = \rho \sin(\phi) \\ y = \rho \cos(\phi) sin(\theta), \\ z = \rho \cos(\phi) cos(\theta) \end{cases} \quad \begin{cases} \rho = \sqrt{(x^2 + y^2 + z^2)} \\ \phi = arcsin(\frac{x}{\rho}) \\ \theta = arctan(\frac{y}{z}) \end{cases} \tag{1}$$

where $\phi \in [-\frac{\pi}{2}, \frac{\pi}{2}]$, $\theta \in [-\pi, \pi]$.

As demostrated in [18], the spherical epipolar lines are projected to sinusoidal curves on the widely used ERP images (shown in Fig. 2(d)), which makes stereo matching difficult in ERP domain. While in Cassini projection [2] domain, the epipolar lines are projected to horizontal lines with the mapping function:

$$\begin{cases} u = (\phi + \frac{\pi}{2}) \cdot \frac{W}{\pi} \\ v = (\theta + \pi) \cdot \frac{H}{2\pi} \end{cases} \tag{2}$$

where (u, v) denotes the image pixel coordinates in Cassini projection and H, W denote the height and width of the image (see Fig. 2(c)). We adopt the Cassini projection in this work to achieve the linear epipolar constraint for omnidirectional stereo matching.

Figure 2(b) illustrates the angular disparity of the spherical stereo. Since the matching points have the same θ, the angular disparity d is defined as the difference of $\phi : d = \phi_l - \phi_r$. The depth of P to the left camera is computed as:

$$\rho_l = B \cdot \frac{sin(\phi_r + \frac{\pi}{2})}{sin(d)} = B \cdot \left[\frac{sin(\phi_l + \frac{\pi}{2})}{tan(d)} - cos(\phi_l + \frac{\pi}{2}) \right]. \tag{3}$$

3.2 Network Architecture

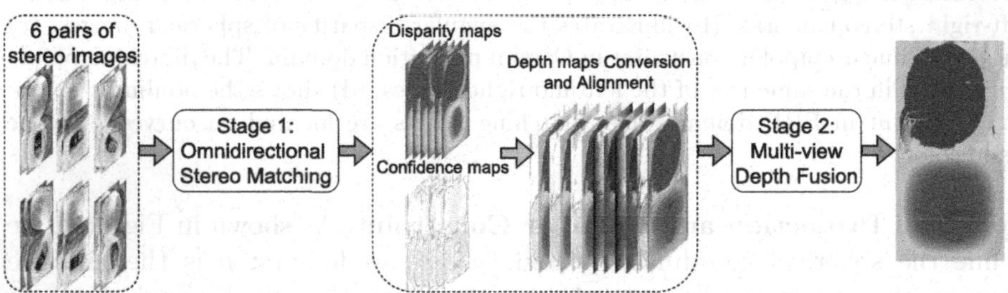

Fig. 3. The architecture of the proposed MODE

As shown in Fig. 3, the proposed MODE consists of two stages. In the first stage, six pairs of left-right panoramas are fed into the omnidirectional stereo matching network to estimate the disparity maps and confidence maps. The disparity maps from different stereo pairs are converted to depth maps and then aligned to the same viewpoint. In the second stage, we estimate the final depth map through a designed multi-view depth fusion network. The network details for the two stages are introduced in Sect. 3.3 and Sect. 3.4.

3.3 Omnidirectional Stereo Matching with Spherical Convolution

The rectified left-right panoramas follow the linear epipolar constraint in Cassini projection, but the distortion of panoramas still affects the results of stereo

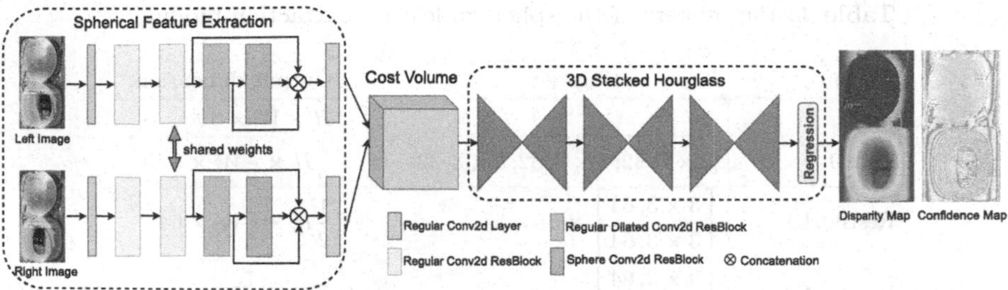

Fig. 4. The architecture of the proposed omnidirectional stereo matching network. We propose a spherical feature extraction module with spherical convolution to overcome the distortion in panoramas

matching. The regular convolution kernel suffers distortions of the 360° images near the poles. Therefore, we propose an omnidirectional stereo matching network with spherical convolution.

As shown in Fig. 4, we first build a spherical feature extraction module with spherical convolution to overcome the distortions. We follow [7] to implement the spherical convolution operator and accelerate it with CUDA. The kernel sampling pattern of the spherical convolution and the comparison with the regular convolution are shown in Fig. 5.

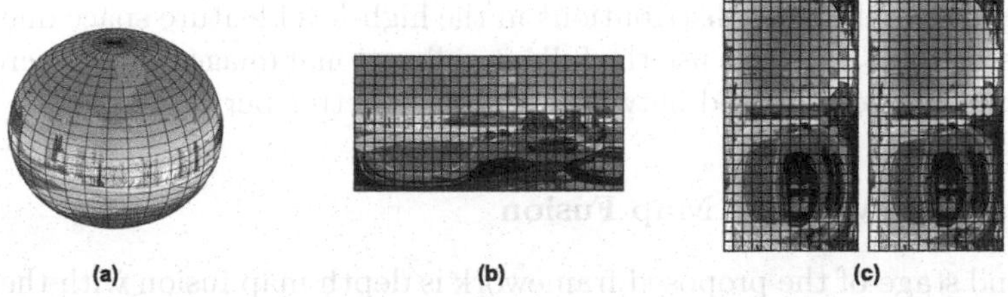

Fig. 5. The kernel sampling pattern of the sphere convolution in proposed omnidirectional stereo matching network. Red points in (a) and (b) show the sampling pattern on the sphere and the ERP image, respectively. (c) illustrates the comparison of the sphere convolution (red) and the regular convolution (yellow) on the Cassini projection image (Color figure online)

The proposed spherical feature extraction module contains four sets of residual blocks [12]. The parameters are detailed in Table 1. The dilated convolution is applied in ResBlock3 for larger receptive fields. We apply spherical convolution in the last residual block to learn the high-level semantic and context features on spherical images. We concatenate the output of ResBlock2, ResBlock3 and ResBlock4 and fuse these feature maps extracted by different kinds of convolutions through the feature fusion layers.

After spherical feature extraction, the feature maps of the stereo panoramas are shifted and concatenated to build the cost volume. Then, the omnidirectional

Table 1. Parameters of the spherical feature extraction module

Name	Layer settings	Output dimension
Input	–	$H \times W \times 3$
Conv0	$[7 \times 7, 32; 3 \times 3, 32; 3 \times 3, 32]$	$\frac{1}{2}H \times \frac{1}{2}W \times 3$
ResBlock1	$\begin{bmatrix} 3 \times 3, 64 \\ 3 \times 3, 64 \end{bmatrix} \times 3$	$\frac{1}{2}H \times \frac{1}{2}W \times 64$
ResBlock2	$\begin{bmatrix} 3 \times 3, 64 \\ 3 \times 3, 64 \end{bmatrix} \times 8$	$\frac{1}{4}H \times \frac{1}{4}W \times 64$
ResBlock3	$\begin{bmatrix} 3 \times 3, 64 \\ 3 \times 3, 64 \end{bmatrix} \times 4$, **dila** $= 2$	$\frac{1}{4}H \times \frac{1}{4}W \times 64$
ResBlock4	$\begin{bmatrix} 3 \times 3, 128 \\ 3 \times 3, 128 \end{bmatrix} \times 8$, **spherical**	$\frac{1}{4}H \times \frac{1}{4}W \times 128$
Concatenation	[ResBlock2,ResBlock3,ResBlock4]	$\frac{1}{4}H \times \frac{1}{4}W \times 256$
FeatureFusion	$[1 \times 1, 256; 3 \times 3, 128; 1 \times 1, 32]$	$\frac{1}{4}H \times \frac{1}{4}W \times 32$

disparity map is regressed through the 3D stacked hourglass as in [4]. The smooth L1 loss function is applied to train the network.

Moreover, many stereo matching algorithms [4,33] take a random crop of images as the network input. However, different crop areas on spherical projection images have different distributions in the high-level feature space due to the image distortions. Thus, we use the full omnidirectional images without cropping as the input of the proposed network to achieve better performance.

3.4 Multi-view Depth Map Fusion

The second stage of the proposed framework is depth map fusion with the incorporation of confidence maps and reference panoramas. The confidence map is used to estimate the reliability of disparity maps in many recent works. [23] reviews developments in the field of confidence estimation for stereo matching and evaluates existing confidence measures.

We first convert the omnidirectional disparity maps to depth maps according to Eq. 2 and Eq. 3. Then, all the depth maps are aligned to the same viewpoint based on the extrinsic matrix and visibility.

Considering that the stereo matching network computes each disparity value through a probability weighted sum over all disparity hypotheses, the probability distribution along the hypotheses thus reflects the quality of disparity estimation [35]. We compute the confidence for each inferred disparity value by taking a probability sum over the three nearest disparity hypotheses, which corresponds to the probability that the inferred disparity meets the 1-pixel error requirement. Then, we add the confidence map into the second stage of MODE to provide extra information for the depth map fusion since higher confidence implies higher fusion weight.

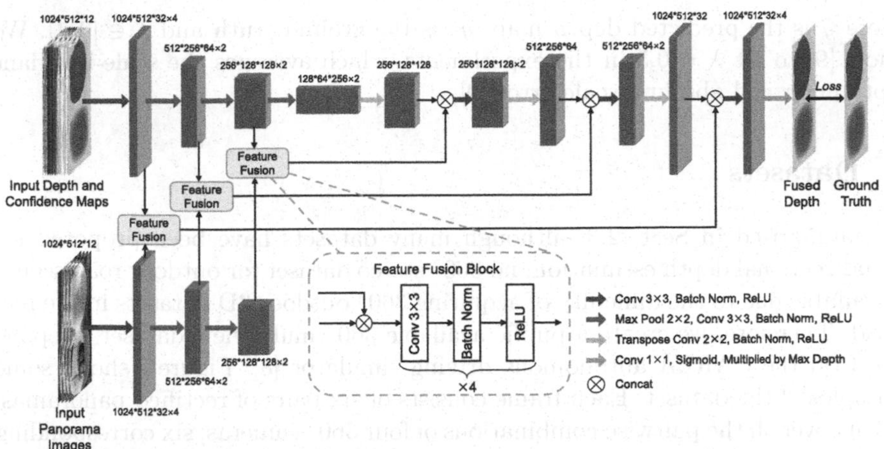

Fig. 6. The network architecture of multi-view depth map fusion. Input multi-view depth maps with confidence maps and reference panoramas are fed into two independent 2D encoder blocks. The final fused depth map output is regressed through one decoder block with skip connections between encoder and decoder blocks at each scale. '×n' denotes n times the block repeats

The architecture of the proposed depth map fusion network is illustrated in Fig. 6. In general, the network design follows the architecture of [24], which consists of an encoder-decoder path for global context extraction and skip connections between the two blocks for the transmission and localization of precise depth values. In addition to depth maps and corresponding confidence maps, we add reference panoramas to provide accurate boundary information for the fused depth map. To extract boundary features from panoramas independently, we separate the encoder block for panoramas from that for depth and confidence maps (shown at the bottom left of Fig. 6). Then, these two kinds of feature maps are fused through a designed feature fusion block at multi-scale to form a more informative feature map. The final fused depth is computed as

$$\hat{y}(\theta, \phi) = d_{max} \cdot \frac{1}{1 + e^{-\boldsymbol{D}(\theta, \phi)}}, \tag{4}$$

where d_{max} is the given maximum depth and $\boldsymbol{D}$ is the normalized depth map regressed by the decoder block.

For the loss function, we adopt the training loss developed from Scale-Invariant Error (SILog) [9] as

$$Loss(\hat{y}, y^{\star}) = \frac{1}{n} \sum_{i} d_i^2 - \frac{\lambda}{n^2} \left(\sum_{i} d_i \right)^2 \tag{5}$$

$$d_i = \log \hat{y}_i - \log y_i^{\star}, \tag{6}$$

where $\hat{y}$ is the predicted depth map, y^* is the ground truth and $\lambda \in [0, 1]$. We follow [9] to set $\lambda = 0.5$ in the experiments, which averages the scale-invariant depth error and absolute-scale error [9].

4 Datasets

As summarized in Sect. 2.3, although many datasets have been proposed for omnidirectional depth estimation, no 360° stereo dataset for outdoor road scenes is available due to the difficulty of acquiring 360° outdoor 3D datasets in the real world. Therefore, we create a public available 360° multi-view dataset Deep360 based on the CARLA autonomous driving simulator [8]. Figure 7 shows some examples of the dataset. Each frame consists of six pairs of rectified panoramas, which cover all the pairwise combinations of four 360° cameras, six corresponding disparity maps and one ground truth depth map. All these images and maps have a resolution of 1024×512.

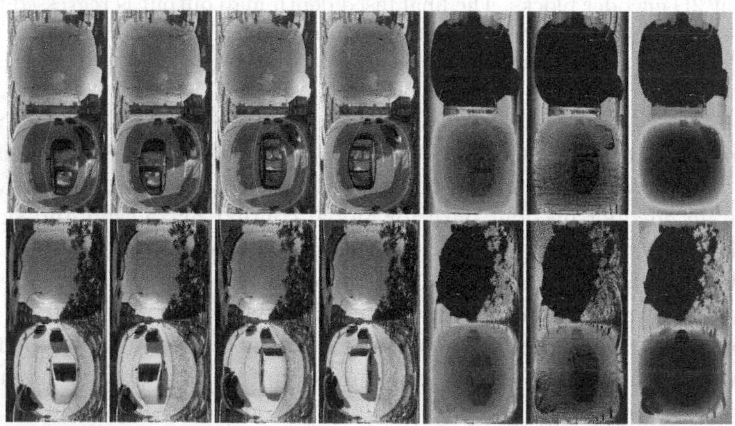

Fig. 7. Examples of the proposed Deep360 dataset. Each row shows an outdoor road scene. From left: four panoramas captured by 360° cameras, two disparity maps of 1–2 and 3–4 camera pairs, and one ground truth omnidirectional depth map

To acquire realistic 360° outdoor road scenes with high variety, we make the car with 360° cameras in CARLA drive automatically in six different towns and spawn many other random actors (pedestrian and vehicles).

We also provide a soiled version of the Deep360 dataset, which can be used to train and evaluate 360° depth estimation algorithms under the harsh circumstances in autonomous driving. The Deep360 (Soiled) dataset contains panoramas soiled or affected by three common outdoor factors: mud spots, water drops and glare. Figure 8 shows the three kinds of soiled panoramas in our dataset.

An overview of the proposed dataset and other published 360° datasets is listed in Table 2.

Fig. 8. Soiled panoramas in Deep360 (Soiled) and corresponding real-world examples. Left Four: synthetic panoramas; Right Four: real-world panoramas. Top Left: clear panoramas; Top Right: panoramas soiled by mud spots; Bottom Left: panoramas soiled by water drops; Bottom Right: panoramas dazzled by glare

Table 2. Overview of the proposed datasets and other published datasets

Dataset		SceneCategory	InputImage	#Viewpoints	# TrainingFrames	# TestFrames	# ValidationFrames
Won et al. [30–32]	Urban	Outdoor	Fish-eye	4	700	300	–
	OmniHouse	Indoor	Fish-eye	4	2048	512	–
	OmniThings	Random objects	fish-eye	4	9216	1024	–
De La Garanderie et al. [16]	–	Outdoor	panorama	1	–	200	–
Wang et al. [29]	SF3D	Indoor	Panorama	2	800	203	200
	MP3D	Indoor	Panorama	2	1602	341	431
Zioulis et al. [38]	3D60	Indoor	Panorama	3	7858	2190	1103
Ours	**Deep360**	Outdoor	Panorama	4	2100	600	300
	Deep360 (Soiled)	Outdoor	Panorama	4	2100	600	300

5 Experiments

5.1 Experimental Settings

Datasets. We train and evaluate the proposed framework on Deep360 and the widely-used 3D60 [38] because these two datasets cover the outdoor and indoor scenes. For Deep360, panoramas from all four views are used to validate the performance of MODE on a multi-view setup. For 3D60, panoramas from two of three views are used to validate the performance of MODE on a binocular setup. More training details can be found in the supplementary material.

Evaluation Metrics. For quantitative evaluation of the proposed framework, we use **MAE** (mean absolute error), **RMSE** (root mean square error), **Px1,3,5** (percentage of outliers with pixel error >1, 3, 5), **D1** [21] (percentage of outliers with pixel error >3 and >5%) to evaluate the disparity results, and use **MAE**, **RMSE**, **AbsRel** (absolute relative error), **SqRel** (square relative error), **SILog** [9] (scale-invariant logarithmic error), **δ1, 2, 3** [17] (accuracy with threshold that $\max(\frac{\hat{y}}{y^\star}, \frac{y^\star}{\hat{y}}) < 1.25, 1.25^2, 1.25^3$) to evaluate the depth results.

5.2 Experimental Results

We first evaluate the omnidirectional stereo matching network of MODE on the dataset Deep360. We compare it with the excellent stereo matching algorithms PSMNet [4] and AANet [33], and the omnidirectional algorithm 360SD-Net [29]. Because 360SD-Net is designed for up-down 360° stereo, we modified part of the model for left-right stereo matching. For PSMNet and AANet, we use the pre-trained models from the authors and follow their hyper-parameters to fine-tune on Deep360. The quantitative results in Table 3 illustrate that our stereo matching network with spherical feature learning achieves SOTA performance on 360° stereo matching.

Table 3. Quantitative results of stereo matching on the proposed Deep360 dataset. The metrics refer to disparity errors

Methods	Metrics					
	MAE(↓)	**RMSE(↓)**	**Px1(% ↓)**	**Px3(% ↓)**	**Px5(% ↓)**	**D1(% ↓)**
AANet [33]	0.5057	2.2232	7.7282	2.0914	1.1887	1.7929
360SD-Net [29]	0.4235	1.8320	6.6124	1.9080	1.0885	1.7753
PSMNet [4]	0.3501	1.8244	4.3798	1.3559	0.8398	1.2973
Ours	**0.2073**	**1.2347**	**2.6010**	**0.8767**	**0.5260**	**0.8652**

Then we evaluate the whole framework by comparing it with SOTA omnidirectional depth estimation methods. To present the performance of SOTA works on Deep360, we test different types of methods, including monocular UniFuse [14], binocular CSDNet [18], 360SD-Net [29], and multi-view OmniMVS [31]. All these models are fine-tuned with the pre-trained models from the authors. As shown in Table 4 and Fig. 9, our MODE framework performs favorably against SOTA omnidirectional depth estimation methods on different datasets, especially the one with soiled panoramas. Moreover, the consistent performance on datasets with different 360° multi-camera setups validates the extensibility of the framework. There is no result of OmniMVS on 3D60 since it can only take fish-eye images as input. We make a fish-eye version of our Deep360 dataset to implement the training and evaluation of OmniMVS. We evaluate and present the results of 360° depth estimation in ERP domain.

5.3 Ablation Studies

Table 5 shows the ablation studies of the omnidirectional stereo matching network. The results show that using panoramas without cropping and applying spherical convolution improve the performance. Table 6 illustrates the ablation studies of the depth map fusion network. The results show that the fusion stage improves the quality of depth maps. The rows of the table gradually show the improvement of adding each component into the network.

Table 4. Quantitative comparisons of omnidirectional depth estimation methods on different datasets. The metrics refer to depth errors

Datasets	Methods	Metrics							
		MAE(↓)	RMSE(↓)	AbsRel(↓)	SqRel(↓)	SILog(↓)	$\delta 1$(% ↑)	$\delta 2$(% ↑)	$\delta 3$(% ↑)
Deep360	UniFuse [14]	3.9193	28.8475	0.0546	0.3125	0.1508	96.0269	98.2679	98.9909
	CSDNet [18]	6.6548	36.5526	0.1553	1.7898	0.2475	86.0836	95.1589	97.7562
	360SD-Net [29]	11.2643	66.5789	0.0609	0.5973	0.2438	94.8594	97.2050	98.1038
	OmniMVS [31]	8.8865	59.3043	0.1073	2.9071	0.2434	94.9611	97.5495	98.2851
	MODE	**3.2483**	**24.9391**	**0.0365**	**0.0789**	**0.1104**	**97.9636**	**99.0987**	**99.4683**
Deep360(Soiled)	UniFuse [14]	5.4636	37.4313	0.1119	4.8948	0.1810	95.2379	97.8686	98.7208
	CSDNet [18]	7.5950	38.4693	0.1631	3.7148	0.2521	86.7329	95.3295	97.7513
	360SD-Net [29]	22.5495	97.3958	0.1060	1.1857	0.4465	90.5868	94.1468	95.6262
	OmniMVS [31]	9.2680	62.1838	0.1935	22.6994	0.2597	94.7009	97.3821	98.1652
	MODE	**4.4652**	**31.7124**	**0.0495**	**0.1778**	**0.1458**	**96.3504**	**98.5718**	**99.2109**
3D60 [38]	UniFuse [14]	0.1868	0.3947	0.0799	0.0246	0.1126	93.2860	98.4839	99.4828
	CSDNet [18]	0.2067	0.4225	0.0908	0.0241	0.1273	91.9537	98.3936	99.5109
	360SD-Net [29]	0.0762	0.2639	0.0300	0.0117	1.4578	97.6751	98.6603	99.0417
	MODE	**0.0713**	**0.2631**	**0.0224**	**0.0031**	**0.0512**	**99.1283**	**99.7847**	**99.9250**

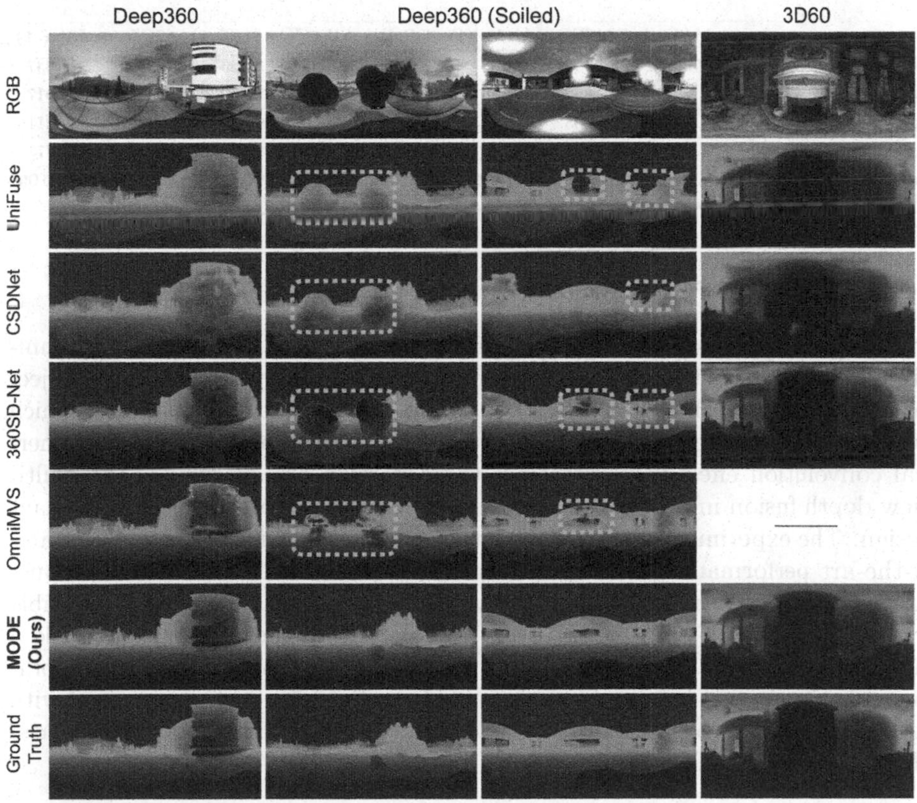

Fig. 9. Qualitative comparisons of omnidirectional depth estimation methods on different datasets. Red dotted boxes indicate the failed depth estimation caused by mud spots or glare (Color figure online)

Table 5. Ablation studies for omnidirectional stereo matching on Deep360. We compare the performance of the proposed stereo matching network with and without Input Image Cropping (**cr**) and Spherical Convolution (**SC**). The metrics refer to disparity errors

Network setting	MAE(↓)	RMSE(↓)	Px1(% ↓)	Px3(% ↓)	Px5(% ↓)	D1(% ↓)
w/ cr	0.3220	1.7425	3.9787	1.3042	0.8049	1.2588
w/o cr	0.2109	1.2408	2.6509	0.8967	0.5377	0.8846
w/o cr + SC	**0.2073**	**1.2347**	**2.6010**	**0.8767**	**0.5260**	**0.8652**

Table 6. Ablation studies for the multi-view depth map fusion network on Deep360 (Soiled). The first row shows the results without fusion(w.r.t the results of stereo matching stage). The network in the second row is the baseline in this study, which consists of stacked 2D convolution layers. Different components used by our depth map fusion network are denoted as: Encoder-Decoder and Skip Connection architecture (**En-De-SC**); incorporation of reference panoramas (**img**); incorporation of confidence maps (**conf**). The metrics refer to depth errors

Network setting	MAE(↓)	RMSE(↓)	AbsRel(↓)	SqRel(↓)	SILog(↓)	δ1(% ↑)	δ2(% ↑)	δ3(% ↑)
w/o fusion	15.2145	77.5905	0.1230	6.3135	0.5466	93.2377	96.0349	97.1837
Baseline	6.8699	50.1859	0.0586	0.8880	0.1996	95.7078	97.9644	98.6917
En-De-SC	6.2548	45.8603	0.0516	0.2702	0.1831	95.9953	98.1431	98.8211
En-De-SC+img	**4.2071**	32.0112	0.0710	0.2443	0.1554	95.1875	98.4766	99.1773
En-De-SC+img+conf	4.4652	**31.7123**	**0.0495**	**0.1778**	**0.1458**	**96.3504**	**98.5717**	**99.2109**

6 Conclusions

In this paper, we propose a two-stage framework, MODE, for multi-view omnidirectional depth estimation from 360° cameras. We adopt the Cassini projection to achieve the linear epipolar constraint of left-right 360° cameras, which improves the performance of omnidirectional stereo matching. The use of spherical convolution effectively overcomes the distortion of panoramas. The multi-view depth fusion improves the robustness of the framework through redundant design. The experimental results show that the proposed MODE achieves state-of-the-art performance on both indoor and outdoor datasets, and it is robust against soiled camera lenses and glare. Moreover, the framework is compatible with arbitrary 360° multi-camera setups. Apart from these, we also provide a large-scale synthetic road scene dataset with both high-quality and soiled panoramas. Finally, we test the proposed framework on the real-world environment with the model trained on synthetic data to validate the generalization and robustness of our framework.

Acknowledgements. We acknowledge the computational resources provided by the High-Performance Computing Center of the Collaborative Innovation Center of Advanced Microstructures, Nanjing University, and Nanjing Institute of Advanced Artificial Intelligence.

References

1. Armeni, I., Sax, S., Zamir, A., Savarese, S.: Joint 2D–3D-semantic data for indoor scene understanding. https://doi.org/10.48550/arXiv.1702.01105 (2017)
2. Cassini projection: Cassini projection – Wikipedia, the free encyclopedia (2022). https://en.wikipedia.org/wiki/Cassini_projection
3. Chang, A., et al.: Matterport3d: Learning from RGB-D data in indoor environments. In: 2017 International Conference on 3D Vision (3DV), pp. 667–676 (2017). https://doi.org/10.1109/3DV.2017.00081
4. Chang, J., Chen, Y.: Pyramid stereo matching network. In: 2018 IEEE/CVF Conference on Computer Vision and Pattern Recognition, pp. 5410–5418 (2018). https://doi.org/10.1109/CVPR.2018.00567
5. Chen, R., Han, S., Xu, J., Su, H.: Point-based multi-view stereo network. In: 2019 IEEE/CVF International Conference on Computer Vision (ICCV), pp. 1538–1547 (2019). https://doi.org/10.1109/ICCV.2019.00162
6. Cheng, X., Wang, P., Zhou, Y., Guan, C., Yang, R.: Omnidirectional depth extension networks. In: 2020 IEEE International Conference on Robotics and Automation (ICRA). pp. 589–595 (2020). https://doi.org/10.1109/ICRA40945.2020.9197123
7. Coors, B., Condurache, A.P., Geiger, A.: SphereNet: learning spherical representations for detection and classification in omnidirectional images. In: Ferrari, V., Hebert, M., Sminchisescu, C., Weiss, Y. (eds.) ECCV 2018. LNCS, vol. 11213, pp. 525–541. Springer, Cham (2018). https://doi.org/10.1007/978-3-030-01240-3_32
8. Dosovitskiy, A., Ros, G., Codevilla, F., Lopez, A., Koltun, V.: CARLA: an open urban driving simulator. In: Proceedings of the 1st Annual Conference on Robot Learning, pp. 1–16 (2017)
9. Eigen, D., Puhrsch, C., Fergus, R.: Depth map prediction from a single image using a multi-scale deep network. In: 27th Proceedings of the Conference on Advances in Neural Information Processing Systems (2014)
10. Gu, X., Fan, Z., Zhu, S., Dai, Z., Tan, F., Tan, P.: Cascade cost volume for high-resolution multi-view stereo and stereo matching. In: 2020 IEEE/CVF Conference on Computer Vision and Pattern Recognition (CVPR), pp. 2492–2501 (2020). https://doi.org/10.1109/CVPR42600.2020.00257
11. Handa, A., Pătrăucean, V., Stent, S., Cipolla, R.: SceneNet: an annotated model generator for indoor scene understanding. In: 2016 IEEE International Conference on Robotics and Automation (ICRA), pp. 5737–5743. IEEE (2016)
12. He, K., Zhang, X., Ren, S., Sun, J.: Deep residual learning for image recognition. In: 2016 IEEE Conference on Computer Vision and Pattern Recognition (CVPR), pp. 770–778 (2016). https://doi.org/10.1109/CVPR.2016.90
13. Jiang, C.M., Huang, J., Kashinath, K., Prabhat, M.P., Niessner, M.: Spherical CNNs on unstructured grids. In: International Conference on Learning Representations (2019). https://openreview.net/forum?id=Bkl-43C9FQ
14. Jiang, H., Sheng, Z., Zhu, S., Dong, Z., Huang, R.: UniFuse: unidirectional fusion for 360° panorama depth estimation. IEEE Rob. Autom. Lett. **6**(2), 1519–1526 (2021). https://doi.org/10.1109/LRA.2021.3058957
15. Kendall, A., et al.: End-to-end learning of geometry and context for deep stereo regression. In: 2017 IEEE International Conference on Computer Vision (ICCV), pp. 66–75 (2017). https://doi.org/10.1109/ICCV.2017.17

16. Payen de La Garanderie, G., Atapour Abarghouei, A., Breckon, T.P.: Eliminating the blind spot: adapting 3D object detection and monocular depth estimation to 360° panoramic imagery. In: Ferrari, V., Hebert, M., Sminchisescu, C., Weiss, Y. (eds.) ECCV 2018. LNCS, vol. 11217, pp. 812–830. Springer, Cham (2018). https://doi.org/10.1007/978-3-030-01261-8_48
17. Ladický, L., Shi, J., Pollefeys, M.: Pulling things out of perspective. In: 2014 IEEE Conference on Computer Vision and Pattern Recognition (CVPR). pp. 89–96 (2014). https://doi.org/10.1109/CVPR.2014.19
18. Li, M., Hu, X., Dai, J., Li, Y., Du, S.: Omnidirectional stereo depth estimation based on spherical deep network. Image Vis. Compu. 114, 104264 (2021).https://doi.org/10.1016/j.imavis.2021.104264, https://www.sciencedirect.com/science/article/pii/S0262885621001694
19. Lipson, L., Teed, Z., Deng, J.: Raft-stereo: Multilevel recurrent field transforms for stereo matching. In: International Conference on 3D Vision (3DV) (2021)
20. Mayer, N., et al.: A large dataset to train convolutional networks for disparity, optical flow, and scene flow estimation. In: 2016 IEEE Conference on Computer Vision and Pattern Recognition (CVPR), pp. 4040–4048 (2016). https://doi.org/10.1109/CVPR.2016.438
21. Menze, M., Heipke, C., Geiger, A.: Joint 3d estimation of vehicles and scene flow. In: ISPRS Workshop on Image Sequence Analysis (ISA) (2015)
22. Pang, J., Sun, W., Ren, J.S., Yang, C., Yan, Q.: Cascade residual learning: a two-stage convolutional neural network for stereo matching. In: 2017 IEEE International Conference on Computer Vision Workshops (ICCVW). pp. 878–886 (2017), https://doi.org/10.1109/ICCVW.2017.108
23. Poggi, M., et al.: On the confidence of stereo matching in a deep-learning era: a quantitative evaluation. IEEE Trans. Pattern Anal. Mach. Intell. pp. 1–1 (2021). https://doi.org/10.1109/TPAMI.2021.3069706
24. Ronneberger, O., Fischer, P., Brox, T.: U-Net: convolutional networks for biomedical image segmentation. In: Navab, N., Hornegger, J., Wells, W.M., Frangi, A.F. (eds.) MICCAI 2015. LNCS, vol. 9351, pp. 234–241. Springer, Cham (2015). https://doi.org/10.1007/978-3-319-24574-4_28
25. Shen, Z., Dai, Y., Rao, Z.: CfNet: cascade and fused cost volume for robust stereo matching. In: Proceedings of the IEEE/CVF Conference on Computer Vision and Pattern Recognition (CVPR), pp. 13906–13915, June 2021
26. Song, S., Yu, F., Zeng, A., Chang, A.X., Savva, M., Funkhouser, T.: Semantic scene completion from a single depth image. In: Proceedings of the IEEE Conference on Computer Vision and Pattern Recognition, pp. 1746–1754 (2017)
27. Wang, F.-E., Hu, H.-N., Cheng, H.-T., Lin, J.-T., Yang, S.-T., Shih, M.-L., Chu, H.-K., Sun, M.: Self-supervised learning of depth and camera motion from 360° Videos. In: Jawahar, C.V., Li, H., Mori, G., Schindler, K. (eds.) ACCV 2018. LNCS, vol. 11365, pp. 53–68. Springer, Cham (2019). https://doi.org/10.1007/978-3-030-20873-8_4
28. Wang, F.E., Yeh, Y.H., Sun, M., Chiu, W.C., Tsai, Y.H.: BiFuse: monocular 360 depth estimation via bi-projection fusion. In: 2020 IEEE/CVF Conference on Computer Vision and Pattern Recognition (CVPR), pp. 459–468 (2020). https://doi.org/10.1109/CVPR42600.2020.00054
29. Wang, N.H., Solarte, B., Tsai, Y.H., Chiu, W.C., Sun, M.: 360sd-net: 360° stereo depth estimation with learnable cost volume. In: 2020 IEEE International Conference on Robotics and Automation (ICRA), pp. 582–588 (2020). https://doi.org/10.1109/ICRA40945.2020.9196975

30. Won, C., Ryu, J., Lim, J.: SweepNet: wide-baseline omnidirectional depth estimation. In: 2019 International Conference on Robotics and Automation (ICRA), pp. 6073–6079 (2019). https://doi.org/10.1109/ICRA.2019.8793823
31. Won, C., Ryu, J., Lim, J.: OmniMVS: end-to-end learning for omnidirectional stereo matching. In: Proceedings of the IEEE/CVF International Conference on Computer Vision, pp. 8987–8996 (2019)
32. Won, C., Ryu, J., Lim, J.: End-to-end learning for omnidirectional stereo matching with uncertainty prior. IEEE Trans. Pattern Anal. Mach. Intell. **43**(11), 3850–3862 (2020)
33. Xu, H., Zhang, J.: AaNet: Adaptive aggregation network for efficient stereo matching. In: 2020 IEEE/CVF Conference on Computer Vision and Pattern Recognition (CVPR), pp. 1956–1965 (2020). https://doi.org/10.1109/CVPR42600.2020.00203
34. Yang, J., Mao, W., Alvarez, J., Liu, M.: Cost volume pyramid based depth inference for multi-view stereo. IEEE Trans. Pattern Anal. Mach. Intell. 44, 4748–4760 (2021). https://doi.org/10.1109/TPAMI.2021.3082562
35. Hu, Y.-T., Huang, J.-B., Schwing, A.G.: VideoMatch: matching based video object segmentation. In: Ferrari, V., Hebert, M., Sminchisescu, C., Weiss, Y. (eds.) ECCV 2018. LNCS, vol. 11212, pp. 56–73. Springer, Cham (2018). https://doi.org/10.1007/978-3-030-01237-3_4
36. Žbontar, J., LeCun, Y.: Stereo matching by training a convolutional neural network to compare image patches. J. Mach. Learn. Res. **17**(65), 1–32 (2016). http://jmlr.org/papers/v17/15-535.html
37. Zhang, F., Prisacariu, V., Yang, R., Torr, P.H.: GA-Net: guided aggregation net for end-to-end stereo matching. In: Proceedings of the IEEE Conference on Computer Vision and Pattern Recognition, pp. 185–194 (2019)
38. Zioulis, N., Karakottas, A., Zarpalas, D., Alvarez, F., Daras, P.: Spherical view synthesis for self-supervised 360° depth estimation. In: 2019 International Conference on 3D Vision (3DV), pp. 690–699 (2019). https://doi.org/10.1109/3DV.2019.00081
39. Zioulis, N., Karakottas, A., Zarpalas, D., Daras, P.: OmniDepth: dense depth estimation for indoors spherical panoramas. In: Ferrari, V., Hebert, M., Sminchisescu, C., Weiss, Y. (eds.) ECCV 2018. LNCS, vol. 11210, pp. 453–471. Springer, Cham (2018). https://doi.org/10.1007/978-3-030-01231-1_28

GigaDepth: Learning Depth from Structured Light with Branching Neural Networks

Simon Schreiberhuber[1](✉), Jean-Baptiste Weibel[1], Timothy Patten[2], and Markus Vincze[1]

[1] ACIN, TU Wien, Gusshausstrasse 27-29/E376, 1040 Vienna, Austria
{schreiberhuber,weibel,vincze}@acin.tuwien.ac.at

[2] UTS Robotics Institute, 81 Broadway, Building 11, Sydney, NSW 2007, Australia
timothy.patten@uts.edu.au

Abstract. Structured light-based depth sensors provide accurate depth information independently of the scene appearance by extracting pattern positions from the captured pixel intensities. Spatial neighborhood encoding, in particular, is a popular structured light approach for off-the-shelf hardware. However, it suffers from the distortion and fragmentation of the projected pattern by the scene's geometry in the vicinity of a pixel. This forces algorithms to find a delicate balance between depth prediction accuracy and robustness to pattern fragmentation or appearance change. While stereo matching provides more robustness at the expense of accuracy, we show that learning to regress a pixel's position within the projected pattern is not only more accurate when combined with classification but can be made equally robust. We propose to split the regression problem into smaller classification sub-problems in a coarse-to-fine manner with the use of a weight-adaptive layer that efficiently implements branching per-pixel Multilayer Perceptrons applied to features extracted by a Convolutional Neural Network. As our approach requires full supervision, we train our algorithm on a rendered dataset sufficiently close to the real-world domain. On a separately captured real-world dataset, we show that our network outperforms state-of-the-art and is significantly more robust than other regression-based approaches.

Keywords: Structured light · Depth sensing · CNN · MLP · MLP decision-tree

1 Introduction

Depth sensing is essential for safe interactions in augmented and virtual reality applications as well as mobile robotics. Structured light sensors are a particularly appealing solution for these indoor applications. These sensors predict

Supplementary Information The online version contains supplementary material available at https://doi.org/10.1007/978-3-031-19827-4_13.

S. Avidan et al. (Eds.): ECCV 2022, LNCS 13693, pp. 214–229, 2022.
https://doi.org/10.1007/978-3-031-19827-4_13

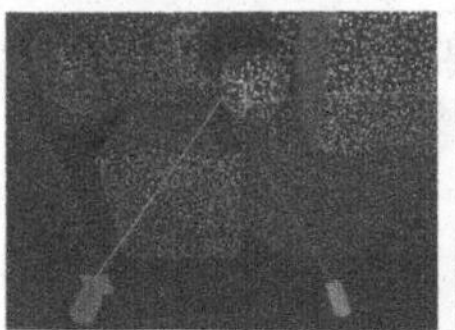
(a) Structured light

(b) Left IR image

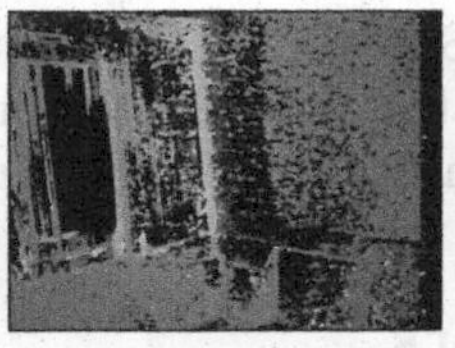
(c) Default disparity

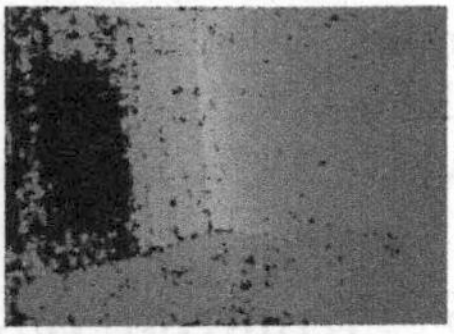
(d) Ours

Fig. 1. Triangulation driven by the principle of spatial neighbourhood encoding (a) operates on data captured by a camera (left, blue) to match the pattern projected by a projector (right, red). The pattern needs to encode the projected direction such that a small region (orange rectangle) around each captured pixel can unambiguously trace back to the pattern position along the epipolar line (transparent red). Given input images such as (b) the internal processing of the used Occipital Structure Core achieves only spotty depth estimates (c) despite using the stereo setup of the sensor. Our algorithm, GigaDepth, (d) on the other hand can derive much denser and more accurate depth due to its knowledge of the utilized pattern using only one of the cameras (b). (Color figure online)

depth from the alterations of the light patterns they project in the scene rather than the scene appearance, thus overcoming the issue of featureless areas. Spatial neighborhood encoding, which encodes the pattern position of every pixel by creating identifiable structures in the neighborhood of the pixel of interest, provides a good trade-off between accuracy, cost, and power consumption among structured light methods. The projector only needs to project a fixed sparse dot pattern once on the scene rather than encode every captured pixel separately (Fig. 1), or require multiple acquisitions like temporal multiplexing.

Such approaches are, however, very sensitive to pattern distortion, fragmentation and attenuation. In practice the correspondence problem between the captured image and the projected pattern is solved by stereo matching to a prestored reference pattern as used in the Kinect v1 or PrimeSense Carmine [16], trading in some robustness and accuracy with the simplicity of matching algorithms. More modern machine learning-based approaches spark the hope to directly, robustly and accurately decode these spatial encodings, but currently only deliver either accurate (e.g. [7]) or dense (e.g. [14,21]) depth-maps.

With GigaDepth, this work contributes a novel neural network architecture that decodes spatial neighborhood encodings even if the projected pattern is distorted, fragmented or attenuated by the scene's geometry and surface properties. By combining the strengths of Convolutional Neural Networks (CNNs) for feature encoding with those of regression trees, we are able to extract pattern positions from captured images with higher accuracy and produce much denser output. Regression trees are implemented with Multilayer Perceptrons (MLPs) in a novel weight-selective layer for which we provide an efficient CUDA implementation. Novel datasets for training and testing this approach are artificially rendered and captured with the Occipital Structure Core (Fig. 1) as well as an industrial-grade 3D Scanner for ground-truth. Our method outperforms state-of-the-art dot-pattern structured light approaches and active stereo in applications where disparity in subpixel accuracy is required.

2 Related Work

CNNs have enabled significant improvements for stereo matching [5,15,22], particularly in featureless regions, multi-view geometry [2,8,20,24] or even depth completion [11,23,25]. Their ability to extract high-level features makes them very useful in passive stereo setups, that is without a pattern projector, and even monocular setups [17] that produce depth without using any conventional principle like triangulation.

To tackle the problems unique to structured light approaches, research has taken on the problem from multiple directions. Structured light approaches depend on the specific pattern that encodes the depth information. Given hardware that is able to adjust the projected pattern on-the-fly, approaches such as [6,18] demonstrate performance improvements by selecting patterns based on an optimality criterion. Similarly, the work in [9] describes the design of Hamiltonian encodings to either improve quality or drastically reduce the amount of required images. This is a stark improvement from the beginnings of temporal multiplexing by Altschuler et al. [1] who apply binary/gray coding or the direct encoding by Carrihill et al. [3] where the position is encoded in the intensity.

On the other hand, many works improve upon the decoding step while keeping the projected pattern simple. Recent work in profilometry uses CNNs to (directly regress depth values) capture the topography of a surface from only a single exposure with one standard sinusoidal fringe pattern [13,19]. This is especially noteworthy as the employed high-frequency pattern might be well suited to resolve small details but does not feature an absolute encoding as the utilized fringes are equally spaced.

Although the use of CNNs can make encoding absolute position obsolete for some applications, optimal robustness can only be achieved with adequate encodings. Spatial neighborhood encoding like the dot-pattern often require only a small patch of pixels to regress the pattern position as shown with popular sensors as the Kinect v1, where simple block matching is executed between a captured frame and the reference pattern [16]. Learning-based methods can internalize knowledge about the pattern and the effects of the scene on its appearance to directly regress pattern positions or depth without lookups in a reference pattern. This is demonstrated in the work of Fanello et al. [7] where random forests are employed to directly regress the pattern position without a matching step by comparing intensity values in a small neighborhood around each pixel. Similarly, Riegler et al. [21] as well as Johari et al. [14] use CNNs to directly regress disparity without searching a reference pattern at run-time.

Albeit this work mainly focuses on the decoding of spatial neighborhood patterns, the sensor used is designed for active stereo and thus makes the comparison with methods like [26] possible. Zhang et al. [26] optimize a CNN based stereo algorithm [15] for active stereo and demonstrates improved performance on Intel RealSense hardware, which by default uses semi-global matching (SGM) [10].

3 Method

Precise depth estimates rely on determining pattern positions at subpixel accuracy for the entire pattern. While it is possible to solve this problem by means of a similarity search within a reference pattern, it is more suitable to use a priori knowledge about the pattern's structure to directly derive the pattern position.

Given a rectified image $I(x)$ and pattern $P(x)$ intensities along a given epipolar line, it is possible to extract the pattern position x_P, where the projected pattern $P(x_P)$ resembles the captured intensities $I(x_I)$ around pixel region x_I. The difference between these two positions (along the horizontal axis x) $d = x_P - x_I$ is called disparity and can express depth $z = {}^{fb}/_{d}$ given the baseline b and focal length f.

To estimate depth for a given pixel $I(x_I)$ both estimating the disparity d or the position x_P suffices. However, directly regressing the position x_P poses a challenge for pure CNNs as they exhibit too much noise over such a large output range. This is a motivation for [21] to limit the output range to 128 pixels and estimate disparity d instead. If, however, short-ranged depth estimates are needed, it is necessary to increase the range of disparity, which leads to the same aforementioned challenge. Another approach of splitting the range of pattern positions x_P into classes leads, together with our requirement of subpixel accuracy, to thousands of classes. While it is unmanageable to use one-hot encoded outputs as typically done in CNNs for every pixel, it is a task gracefully managed by the decision trees employed in [7].

Our approach GigaDepth thus employs a similar hierarchical principle of splitting the output range into smaller, easier to regress regions. Instead of directly deriving decisions for tree-traversal from intensity differences as in [7], we employ a CNN to extract features allowing for more robust decision functions based on MLPs. Figure 2 shows an overview of our architecture. Note that the use of Local Contrast Normalization (LCN) as shown in the figure is intended to accentuate the pattern in the captured images. While used throughout this work and, e.g. [14,21,26], we demonstrate in Sect. 4.4 that its contribution to the performance is minimal. For a deeper discussion, we refer to the mentioned works or the supplemental.

3.1 Backbone CNN

The first step in our pipeline is to condense the local image data such that the features concerning the pattern and the scene can be efficiently processed by the MLP tree. Compared to current CNNs, this backbone is implemented as a shallow CNN (Table 1a) with a receptive field of only 21 pixels, which makes the number of considered pixels similar to [7] ($(21 \cdot 2 + 1)^2 = 1849$ vs. $32^2 = 1024$ for [7]). Other networks (e.g. [17,21]) employed in similar scenarios are multiple

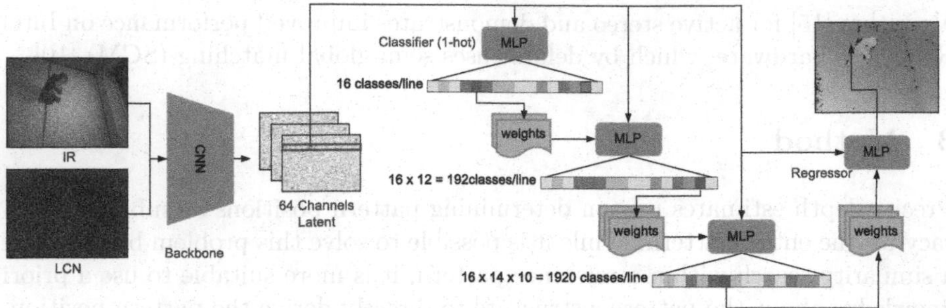

Fig. 2. The proposed network architecture: While the backbone is a relatively shallow CNN, the regressor is a hierarchy of adaptive MLPs operating on individual pixels. The stage 1 MLP features one set of weights for each line and splits it up into 16 classes. Stage 2 has 16 sets of weights for each line to classify into 12 subclasses. Stage 3 further splits these up into 10 categories. Only at the last stage one of 1920 weights/regressors is selected to perform the regression.

times deeper and use a U-shaped structure such that their receptive field spans the whole image and high-level perception of the scene can be learned. For this pattern detection task, however, we found it sufficient to only consider regions large enough to capture uniquely identifiable pattern segments and to detect cues about depth discontinuities around object boundaries.

We furthermore halve the resolution of our feature maps ($1216 \times 896 \rightarrow 608 \times 448$) by convolution with a stride of two early in the network as high-resolution depth-maps are impractical for real-time purposes.

3.2 MLP Tree

For every line of our output image we maintain one specialized tree consisting of one-hot encoding decision MLPs at each node and specialized regression MLPs at each leaf. In contrast to [7], directly comparing two intensity values for a binary decision function, the MLPs constitute much more expressive but also heavier decision functions leading to more robust performance. However, as even the minimally feasible perceptrons are relatively compute intensive, we are forced to use a much shallower tree (10–15 for [7] vs. 3) with each node splitting into more branches to reach similar width.

Each of these trees is evaluated on a per-pixel basis such that the root node would process the features of one individual pixel to split the output range $x_{P,x}$ into $c_1 = 16$ consecutive, equally spaced regions X_{i_1}. These are further split by consecutive nodes into $c_2 = 12$ regions $\mathcal{X}_{i_1,i_2}$ each. A third stage follows, splitting each of these regions into $c_3 = 10$ regions $\mathcal{X}_{i_1,i_2,i_3}$ leading to a total of $c = c_1 c_2 c_3$ classes/regions. Finally, at the leaves of this tree structure sit specialized regressors that are tuned to estimate $x_{P,x}$ in the small regions $\mathcal{X}_{i_1,i_2,i_3}$.

A few modifications are employed that deviate from this simplified description: We share the trees for two consecutive rows to reduce the overall parameter

Table 1. The compositions of our backbone CNN and MLP regression tree. CNN layers with kernel sizes k, stride s and in/output channels C_{in} and C_{out}. Each layer is combined with BatchNorm and ReLU. The classification stages of our MLP tree split the output region into ever smaller subregions until specialized MLP regressors take over. The classifiers have multiple layers with the one-hot encoded output being split in output classes c and overlap o to the neighboring group of classes

(a) CNN backbone layers

	In							Out
k	5	3	3	3	3	5	3	3
s	2	1	1	1	1	1	1	1
C_{in}	2	16	24	32	40	64	64	96
C_{out}	16	24	32	40	64	64	96	160

(b) MLP regression tree stages

stage	C_{in} [*start*, *stop*]	layers [*in*, *hidden*, c/o]
class1	[0, 64]	[64, 64, 32, 16]
class2	[16, 80]	[64, 32, $12/2$]
class3	[80, 144]	[64, 32, $10/3$]
reg(out)	[128, 160]	[32, 32, $1/1$]

count. For the same purpose, we have regressor MLPs share weights for four consecutive classes while having per-class weights for the final regression. We also allow some overlap between the classification results of the classifiers of stage 2 and 3 as the preceding classifications might be inaccurate at the boundaries between neighboring classes/regions e.g. $\mathcal{X}_{i_1}$, $\mathcal{X}_{i_1+1}$. Given e.g. $c_2 = 14$ with an overlap of $o_2 = 1$ means that the MLPs at stage 2 has 16 raw output classes with indices $i'_2 = i_2 + o_2$. In our example, raw results as $i'_2 = 0$ or $i'_2 = 15$ mean that the previous classification result will likely fall in one of the neighboring regions $\mathcal{X}'_{i'_1,0} \equiv \mathcal{X}'_{i'_1-1,14}$, $\mathcal{X}'_{i'_1,15} \equiv \mathcal{X}'_{i'_1+1,1}$. Similarly, the regressors are trained to cover for their neighbors. See Table 1b for a detailed account of the involved MLPs.

The described structure requires branching on a per-pixel basis and thus is ill-suited for an efficient implementation on the basis of high-level functionality of popular deep learning frameworks. Therefore we provide a CUDA implementation of a weight-selective layer for pytorch to keep execution time and, more importantly, the memory footprint of our architecture manageable.

3.3 Training

When traversing the MLP tree to reach a leaf, each node takes in the features extracted by the backbone to derive a decision about the path to be taken. If we only apply a loss on the regression predicted by a leaf MLP and apply backpropagation starting there, we would not be able to update the weights of the non-leaf node MLPs. The class indices i_1, i_2, i_3 stemming from these only act to select weights of the according MLPs and do not allow for the gradient to propagate back, making supervision based on principles such as, e.g. photoconsistency, a serious challenge.

We thus employ a training modality that allows full supervision for each of the trees nodes individually, shifting the focus away from elegant means of self-supervision towards the benefits of our branching architecture. We design our system around the availability of complete ground-truth data, which is provided in the form of a novel artificial dataset simulating the sensor. The classification stages of the MLP trees are supervised by class indices i_1, i_2, i_3 generated by discretizing the horizontal position of the dot-pattern into hierarchical regions $\mathcal{X}_{i_1}$, $\mathcal{X}_{i_1,i_2}$, $\mathcal{X}_{i_1,i_2,i_3}$ that are equally sized at each level. We utilize the cross entropy loss at each level of our MLP tree and apply it to the nodes that would be executed if each MLP performed perfectly. As this will not be the case in practice, we also apply the loss to MLPs that might be traversed if the preceding MLPs are off by one label (e.g. $i_1 \pm 1$). As a result, we train the overlap of class labels described in Sect. 3.2. To train the regressor MLPs at the leaves we use the L1 loss and further employ the same strategy as before to let each regressor cover for its neighbours. The gradients from both losses are propagated all the way back to the backbone CNN and used to update weights via classical Stochastic Gradient Descent. Training the whole system on our artificial dataset takes ~10 h utilizing one NVIDIA RTX 3090.

We further utilize an edge mask that marks regions around depth discontinuities to emphasise sharpness around edges by increased loss. Another mask is used to remove the loss where the training signal is too ambiguous for spatial neighborhood encodings. This mask covers pixels whose surface do not sufficiently reflect the projector's light due to albedo, distance or occlusion.

Augmentation of the data with noise and a slight vertical jitter of 4 pixels are used to introduce robustness against some of the effects of operating the sensor in real-world conditions. The impact of this measure is discussed in Sect. 4.4.

4 Experiments

Real-world applications require accurate disparity in a subpixel range as well as depth measurements that cover challenging surfaces. Similar to [21] we report the outlier ratio $o(th)$, describing the ratio between the number of pixels that feature a disparity error higher than a given threshold th and the overall number of pixels. We also present the Root Mean Square Error ($RMSE$) of the depth measurements derived by the different algorithms and our specific sensor to give a practical intuition. Pixels with a disparity error greater than one pixel are excluded. The various failure modes and outliers of the different algorithms would otherwise distort this comparison.

A thorough performance comparison to existing methods is conducted using an artificial dataset. The rendering process provides ground-truth, which we use to circumvent some of the sacrifices required by self-supervised training of baseline methods. Finally, we compare on real-world data with ground-truth captured by an industrial grade 3D scanner.

4.1 Baseline Methods

The main reference points for our method are HyperDepth [7], Connecting The Dots [21] and DepthInSpace [14], which directly regress a pixel's position within the pattern or the disparity. To contrast with these methods that need a reference image to operate, we also compare to ActiveStereoNet [26], which extends [15] by modifying the loss to emphasize the dot pattern. It is expected that the usage of the second IR camera gives ActiveStereoNet an advantage wherever the pattern is too weak and classical stereo matching can pick up scene features. Fittingly, all of these methods operate at similar execution times when tested on our RTX 2070 Max-Q with HyperDepth 20–70 ms, Connecting The Dots 40 ms, DepthInSpace 20 ms, ActiveStereoNet 45 ms and ours 60 ms.

While our rendered dataset enables training of these methods, we deviated from the original methods in a few aspects:

- **Resolution:** For the purpose of comparability, we upscale the results of algorithms operating on a lower resolution than the input resolution. The algorithms themselves operate at or close to their intended resolution.
- **Jitter:** As our sensor hardware exhibits vertical drift (Sect. 4.4) we train all approaches with the appropriately jittered inputs.
- **HyperDepth:** Unlike the original authors [7], Riegler et al. [21] published an implementation of HyperDepth that was used for their baseline comparison. We ported their implementation to CUDA for faster experiments and added k-means clustering to improve the regression accuracy at the leaf nodes. We further utilize deeper trees (16 vs. 14 levels) for improved results.
- **Connecting the Dots:** The original approach of matching with the reference pattern did not converge on our dataset. We therefore use the image captured/rendered by the right camera to have a stereo matching approach during training time. During runtime, the algorithm operates as in the original method, not utilizing the second camera. Despite these efforts, we are unable to bring Connecting The Dots to the same performance levels as on the originally intended dataset. We therefore also include a comparison of our method on the dataset presented in [21].
- **DepthInSpace:** As this method is similar to Connecting The Dots in many aspects and thus facing similar challenges during training, we adopt the same adjustments, which leads to good success. The training requires optical flow [12], such that only 241 of our captured sequences can be utilized as only those have additional captures with a disabled IR-projector. This is more than the 148 training sequences used in the original work [14] but puts it at a disadvantage to the other baseline methods trained on 967 sequences.

4.2 Dataset

The Structure Core allows us to run the algorithms of [7,14,21] and [26], thus we render a new dataset based on this sensor. The artificial data is rendered via Unity3D using the High Definition Rendering Pipeline and free assets found on the asset store. Different to [14,21], which use ShapeNet [4] objects without textures, our objects are textured with partial randomization for selected surfaces[1]. Aside from the ground-truth depth/disparity, we render stereo images as well as

[1] Randomly selected textures on planes used in walls as well as cube, sphere, cylinder and pill shapes.

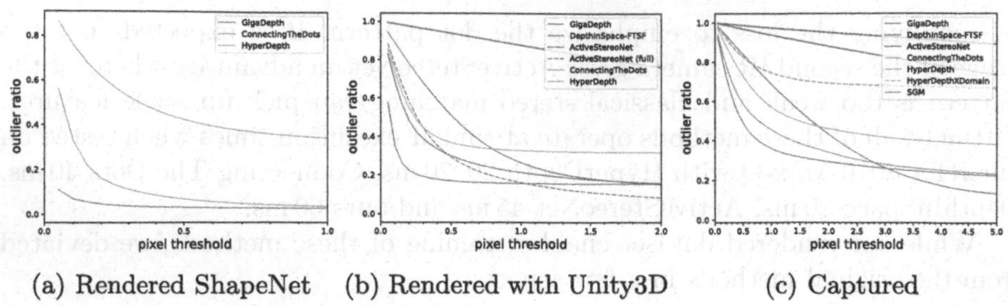

(a) Rendered ShapeNet (b) Rendered with Unity3D (c) Captured

Fig. 3. Outlier ratios over pixel thresholds on a rendered dataset by [21] (a), our dataset rendered with Unity3D (b) and our real-world captured dataset (c). Aside from HyperDepth [7] and our algorithm, experiments marked with "full" undergo fully supervised training with L1 loss.

pixel-level masks corresponding to areas where the pattern projector does not have enough influence. 15k sequences of four frames each are rendered this way. The test set features a different set of objects and textures and offers 9k frames.

To extract a texture for the pattern, we point the Structure Core as well as a RealSense sensor with disabled projector towards a wall and capture multiple IR frames. While the center of the pattern is covered by the Structure Core itself, the RealSense captures the fringes. In the next steps, center points of speckles for each IR image are extracted, manually matched between RealSense and Structure frames (three points each) and ICP aligned. Finally, a set of textures is created to vary the sharpness of speckles during rendering.

To fine-tune the baseline algorithms for the real-world domain, we capture 967 scenes with four frames each. 241 of these scenes have a second set of images with the dot-projector disabled. This is essential to train the edge detector required by Connecting The Dots [21] and precompute the optical flow required by DepthInSpace [14]. To evaluate the performance, we collect 11 scenes with ground-truth data captured by a Photoneo MotionCam-3D M in scanning mode. With an accuracy stated as $<$0.250 mm at a distance of 0.65 m this sensor is adequate for the expected accuracy of our algorithm. Translated to the Structure Core's geometry and provided the alignment between both sensors is similarly accurate, this means we can expect ground-truth disparity with an accuracy of $\sim$0.05 pixels.

4.3 Results

The experiments on rendered and real data show that we indeed have a real-time method capable of capturing dense and highly accurate disparity maps. Aside from the increased accuracy and sensitivity to comparable methods we furthermore show that our approach bridges the domain gap much more gracefully.

Rendered Data. Evaluating outlier ratios at different thresholds (Fig. 3b) and together with $RMSE$ at different distances (Figs. 4a and 4b) showcases the

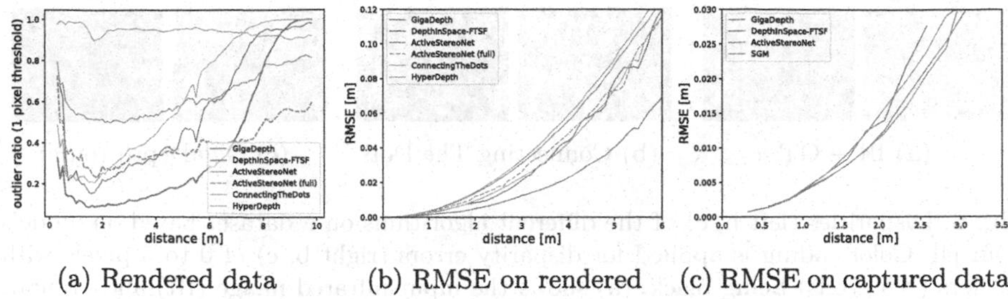

(a) Rendered data (b) RMSE on rendered (c) RMSE on captured data

Fig. 4. Outlier ratio at 1 pixel threshold (a) and RMSE of inliers (b) over distance on our rendered dataset. While the captured dataset is too small to produce a meaningful plot analog to (a) some of the algorithms produce enough inlier estimates to plot the RMSE for depth (c). Aside from HyperDepth [7] and our algorithm, experiments marked with "full" undergo fully supervised training with L1 loss.

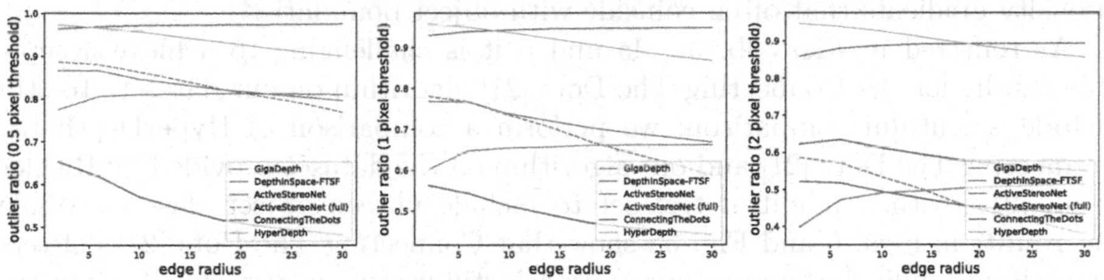

Fig. 5. Outlier ratios on regions around depth discontinuities with our rendered dataset. Evaluated for different outlier thresholds over a growing region around object edges. Note that only estimates by ActiveStereoNet [26] benefit from a proximity to the edges as they often coincide with strong intensity gradients.

accuracy as well as sensitivity of each method. To further magnify the focus on the model architectures themselves, we train versions of ActiveStereoNet [26] and Connecting The Dots [21] with full supervision by utilizing the L1 loss.

Presented in Figs. 3b, 4a and 4b as well as the qualitative results in Fig. 7, it is evident that the branching approaches of HyperDepth [7] and GigaDepth can deliver more precise results but cannot always reach the level of completeness of the CNN-based ActiveStereoNet [26] and DepthInSpace [14]. Plotting the outlier ratios with a one pixel threshold over distances in Fig. 4a we can infer that our algorithm has a higher sensitivity towards the dot-pattern than any of the baseline methods. ActiveStereoNet [26], which utilizes the second camera, performs stereo matching and therefore shows better performance at higher distances that are otherwise insufficiently lit by the projector.

To substantiate the claim about our algorithm's robustness in situations of a fragmented pattern, we evaluate its performance in regions around depth discontinuities. After extracting the depth discontinuities from the ground-truth, we increasingly dilate these edges to obtain regions of different proximity. In Fig. 5, we plot the outliers in these regions along the a range of radii around edges.

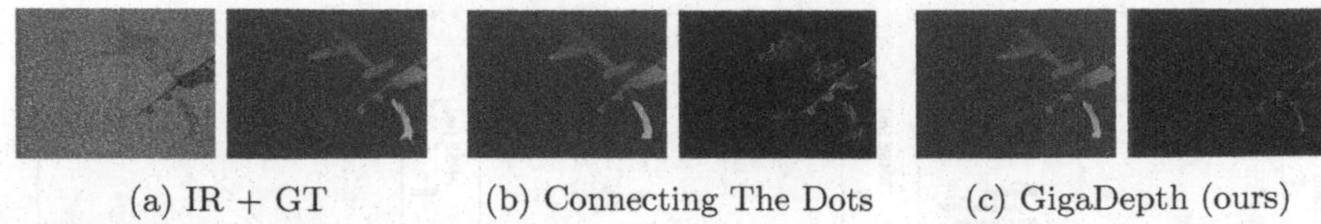

(a) IR + GT (b) Connecting The Dots (c) GigaDepth (ours)

Fig. 6. Disparities (left b, c) of the different algorithms on a dataset based on models from [4]. Color coding is applied for disparity errors (right b, c) of 0 to 5 pixels with outliers (>5 pixels) being black. (a) shows the input infrared image (IR) and ground-truth (GT).

It becomes evident that our method exceeds the remaining methods when high pixel accuracy is needed. If accuracy is not of utmost important, ActiveStereoNet [26] can achieve a lower outlier ratio as it actually benefits from the strong intensity gradients that often coincide with object boundaries.

As reflected in Figs. 3b, 3c, 4a and 5 it is challenging to achieve acceptable results for the Connecting The Dots [21] algorithm on our dataset. To still include a truthful comparison, we perform a comparison of HyperDepth [7], Connecting The Dots [21] and our algorithm on the dataset provided by Riegler et al. [21] (with a modified test set to include unseen object classes). While the results in Figs. 6 and Fig. 3a show that Connecting The Dots [21] delivers compelling subpixel accuracy, our approach still vastly outperforms it. Unfortunately, this dataset only offers a small range of distances and does not include important factors such as textures on objects, which limits its expressiveness. DepthInSpace [14], that shares many of the traits and uses a similar dataset as [21], behaves more gracefully when applied to our dataset such that we can offer a fair comparison in our more challenging scenario. We nonetheless refer to our supplementary where we offer a comparison to our method on the dataset native to [14].

Real-World Data. For our real-world evaluation, we align the data from the Photoneo MotionCam-3D M and the point clouds derived from each algorithm using ICP. Projecting the ground-truth point cloud to the respective camera frames yields the disparity maps we compare against. We plot the outlier ratios for our set of algorithms in Fig. 3c and show favorable results compared to all baselines. Only ActiveStereoNet [26] achieves superior outlier ratios above thresholds of ~3 pixels, which we attribute to this method's ability to fall back to its stereo-matching roots when the pattern is absent. Evaluating the $RMSE$ in-line with the experiment on artificial data is challenging as not all methods produce enough usable depth samples at the full range of depth. For the remaining methods (HyperDepth [7], DepthInSpace [14] and SGM [10]), we show equivalent to favorable performance. Note that basing a comparison on the depth $RMSE$ leads to a distorted view due to the influence of errors in rectification/calibration and (mis)alignment between the captured frame and ground-truth data. It is advised to focus on the pixel-metrics as they depend

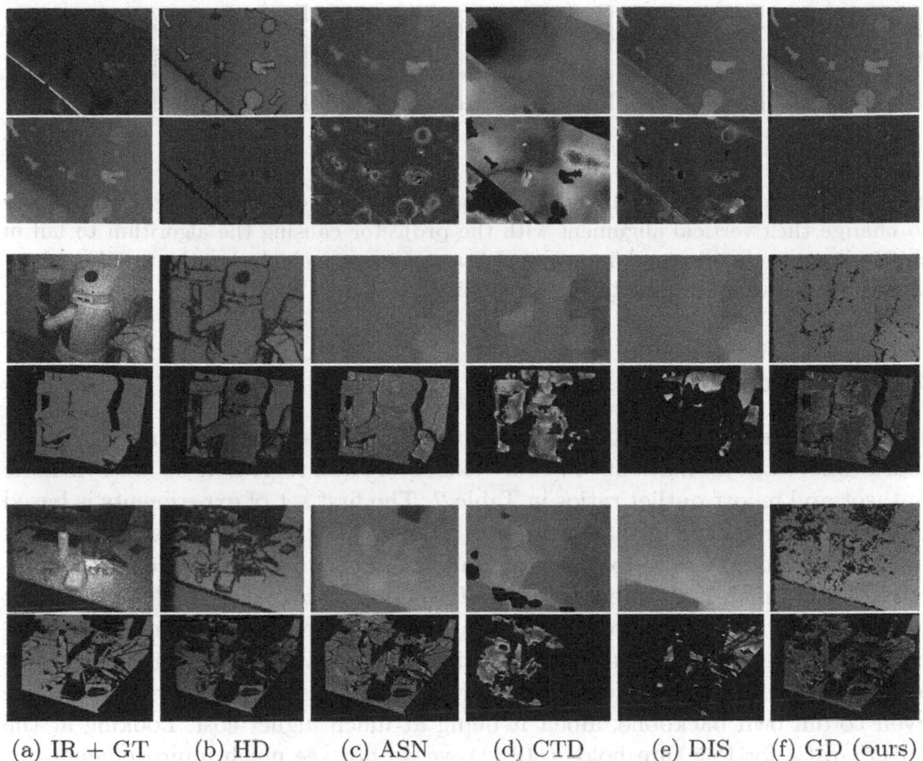

Fig. 7. Disparities (top b–f) of different algorithms applied on a scene rendered with Unity3D (rows 1, 2) or captured with the Occipital Structure Core (rows 3–6). The ground-truth (GT) is rendered or captured with the Photoneo MotionCam-3D M and compared to other algorithms. Color coding is applied for disparity errors (bottom b–f) of 0–5 pixels with outliers (>5 pixels) being black. Algorithms are: HyperDepth (b, HD), ActiveStereoNet (c, ASN), Connecting The Dots (d, CTD), DepthInSpace (e, DIS) and GigaDepth (e, GD).

less on sensor geometry and to some extent even allow for cross-sensor comparability. We also include a comparison to HyperDepth [7] when trained on artificial data (marked as XDomain) and a variant trained on SGM [10] to show a fundamental problem: While the perfect ground-truth artificial data enables the algorithm to excel for high precision tasks, this is not necessarily applicable in the real-world, leading to reduced reliability.

A qualitative assessment in Fig. 7 shows that GigaDepth delivers notably lower disparity errors compared to the baselines with measurements mostly being omitted at object fringes and pixels that are shadowed from the pattern projector. It nonetheless suffers from the domain transfer as many spots on similar surfaces, that were not a problem on artificial data, now have holes.

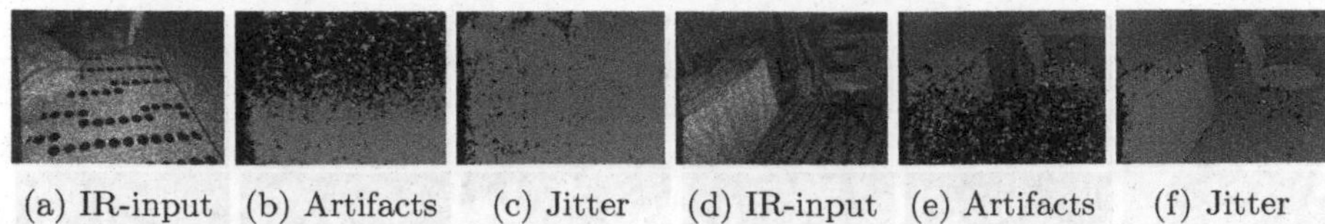

(a) IR-input (b) Artifacts (c) Jitter (d) IR-input (e) Artifacts (f) Jitter

Fig. 8. Two frames captured in the same sequence. The captured images (a, d) seem to change their vertical alignment with the projector causing the algorithm to fail in shifting regions (b, e). Applying vertical jitter of four pixels during the training phase makes the network agnostic to this variability (c, f).

4.4 Ablation

Architecture. To corroborate our choice of network architecture we benchmark different combinations of feature extractors and regressors on our synthetic dataset and report outlier ratios in Table 2. The first set of experiments is based on a relatively powerful and compute intensive UNet that takes an order of magnitude more time to execute than all the other baseline methods (1 s compared to ~50 ms). Fully supervising the UNet on our regression task without any additional network does not yield any usable behaviour. The same can be concluded when supplying output layers with per-line weights. Using the network as a backbone for our regression network, however, gives superior performance even to our own backbone, albeit it being at much higher cost. Looking at the outlier ratio for low thresholds ($o(0.1)$) we do not see much improvements but the overall amount of valid pixel ($o(1)$) seems to have increased. We can attribute this to the capacity of the network to incorporate high-level information without sacrificing the ability to encode local features.

The second set of experiments operates with the backbone we tailored for this task and aims at analysing the influence of the MLP tree structure. Varying the amount of output classes between 288 and 2688 we see the return of investment diminishing after 1280 classes. While the runtime is almost unaffected by the class count, the increasing amount of parameters is a cause for concern. Note that the parameter count would rise even more steeply if we would not be increasingly aggressive with our strategy of sharing weights between consecutive output classes in the latent regressor layers. The influence of the depth of the MLPs is shown in three variations (adding/removing one 32 channel latent layer) of the 640 class version showing diminishing returns for MLPs deeper than two layers. Finally we see in a variation (superscript ^{a}) of the 1920 class version, that the lack of the LCN input brings a slight degradation in performance.

Vertical Jitter. In Fig. 8, we explore the effect of omitting the jittering augmentation during training. It shows shifting regions of failing depth estimation even within short sequences. This is an indication that the sensor geometry and components are not entirely rigid or susceptible to temperature. Randomly shifting the training images by just a few vertical pixel robustifies the algorithm.

Table 2. Different configurations of our architecture tested on synthetic data. We test two backbones, ours as well as a full UNet network, which both dominate execution time with ∼70 ms and ∼1 s respectively (RTX 2070 Max-Q). Regressors are given as c/l with the number of classes c and MLP layers l. All networks take IR + LCN as input (superscript ^{a} omits the LCN). Note that with increasing class count, we more aggressively apply our weight sharing scheme for hidden layers of the regressor stage

B.B.	UNet			Our backbone								
Reg.	None	Lines	$1920/2$	$288/2$	$384/2$	$640/1$	$640/2$	$640/3$	$1280/2$	$1920^a/2$	$1920/2$	$2688/2$
$o(0.1)$	89.55	94.27	**34.01**	51.86	60.49	44.50	44.37	38.49	**34.91**	41.27	38.08	44.59
$o(0.5)$	54.78	72.39	**14.32**	19.88	18.64	19.05	17.53	18.11	**16.97**	17.20	17.20	17.26
$o(1)$	33.41	50.23	**12.74**	17.16	16.29	17.39	16.02	16.62	**15.72**	15.97	15.97	15.93
params	81M	105M	446M	134M	217M	131M	275M	359M	379M	388M	388M	429M

5 Conclusion

This paper introduced an algorithm that outperforms state of the art on extracting depth from structured light-based depth sensors. Benchmarks on artificial as well as real data show superior precision and sensitivity than comparable methods. It is shown that while pure CNN-based methods struggle to deliver high accuracy for these regression tasks, combining a CNN-based backbone with a regressor consisting of weight-adaptive layers can overcome this challenge. These weight-adaptive layers enable us to implement a neural decision tree with small specialized regressors at the leaf nodes. While the comparable HyperDepth [7] follows a branching approach similar to our regression stage, the decision functions on each node are comparably trivial and thus struggle to model the different influences of scene and surface compositions. The focus on dot-patterns and the strategy of keeping the receptive field small allows our large set of small neural networks to specialize on their respective regions within the pattern. Despite the necessity for accurate ground-truth to train the classification part, most easily obtained using artificial data, our approach's resilience to domain shift is demonstrated by the good performance on real-world data.

As most contemporary depth estimation algorithms cope without explicit supervision by using consistency-based loss functions, it would be most desirable to augment our approach with similar mechanisms. Generating meaningful update steps for our tree structure in a semi-supervised setting (by e.g. using principles found in reinforcement learning) would allow for easier domain adaptation.

Acknowledgements. The research leading to these results has received funding from EC Horizon 2020 for Research and Innovation under grant agreement No. 101017089, TraceBot and the Austrian Science Foundation (FWF) under grant agreement No. I3969-N30, InDex.

References

1. Altschuler, M.D., Posdamer, J.L., Frieder, G., Altschuler, B.R., Taboada, J.: The numerical stereo camera. In: Three-Dimensional Machine Perception, vol. 0283, pp. 15–24. International Society for Optics and Photonics (1981)
2. Bian, J.W., et al.: Unsupervised scale-consistent depth learning from video. Int. J. Comput. Vision **129**, 2548–2564 (2021)
3. Carrihill, B., Hummel, R.: Experiments with the intensity ratio depth sensor. Computer Vision, Graphics, and Image Processing **32**(3), 337–358 (1985)
4. Chang, A.X., et al.: ShapeNet: an information-rich 3D model repository. Tech. Rep. arXiv:1512.03012 [cs.GR], Stanford University – Princeton University – Toyota Technological Institute at Chicago (2015)
5. Chang, J.R., Chen, Y.S.: Pyramid stereo matching network. In: Proceedings of the IEEE Conference on Computer Vision and Pattern Recognition, pp. 5410–5418 (2018)
6. Chang, J.R., Chen, Y.S.: Pyramid stereo matching network. In: Proceedings of the IEEE Conference on Computer Vision and Pattern Recognition, pp. 5410–5418 (2018)
7. Fanello, S.R., et al.: HyperDepth: learning depth from structured light without matching. In: Proceedings of the IEEE Conference on Computer Vision and Pattern Recognition, pp. 5441–5450 (2016)
8. Godard, C., Aodha, O.M., Firman, M., Brostow, G.: Digging into self-supervised monocular depth estimation. In: Proceedings of the IEEE/CVF International Conference on Computer Vision, pp. 3827–3837 (2019)
9. Gupta, M., Nakhate, N.: A geometric perspective on structured light coding. In: Ferrari, V., Hebert, M., Sminchisescu, C., Weiss, Y. (eds.) ECCV 2018. LNCS, vol. 11220, pp. 90–107. Springer, Cham (2018). https://doi.org/10.1007/978-3-030-01270-0_6
10. Hirschmuller, H.: Accurate and efficient stereo processing by semi-global matching and mutual information. In: Proceedings of the IEEE Computer Society Conference on Computer Vision and Pattern Recognition, pp. 807–814 (2005)
11. Hu, M., Wang, S., Li, B., Ning, S., Fan, L., Gong, X.: PENet: towards precise and efficient image guided depth completion. In: Proceedings of the IEEE International Conference on Robotics and Automation, pp. 13656–13662 (2021)
12. Hui, T.W., Tang, X., Loy, C.C.: LiteFlowNet: a lightweight convolutional neural network for optical flow estimation. In: Proceedings of IEEE Conference on Computer Vision and Pattern Recognition, pp. 8981–8989 (2018)
13. Van der Jeught, S., Dirckx, J.J.J.: Deep neural networks for single shot structured light profilometry. Opt. Express **27**(12), 17091–17101 (2019)
14. Johari, M., Carta, C., Fleuret, F.: DepthInSpace: exploitation and fusion of multiple video frames for structured-light depth estimation. In: Proceedings of the IEEE International Conference on Computer Vision, pp. 6019–6028 (2021)
15. Khamis, S., Fanello, S., Rhemann, C., Kowdle, A., Valentin, J., Izadi, S.: StereoNet: guided hierarchical refinement for real-time edge-aware depth prediction. In: Ferrari, V., Hebert, M., Sminchisescu, C., Weiss, Y. (eds.) ECCV 2018. LNCS, vol. 11219, pp. 596–613. Springer, Cham (2018). https://doi.org/10.1007/978-3-030-01267-0_35
16. Martinez, M., Stiefelhagen, R.: Kinect unleashed: getting control over high resolution depth maps. In: Proceedings of the International Conference on Machine Vision Applications, pp. 247–240 (2013)

17. Miangoleh, S.M.H., Dille, S., Mai, L., Paris, S., Aksoy, Y.: Boosting monocular depth estimation models to high-resolution via content-adaptive multi-resolution merging. In: Proceedings of the IEEE/CVF Conference on Computer Vision and Pattern Recognition, pp. 9680–9689 (2021)
18. Mirdehghan, P., Chen, W., Kutulakos, K.N.: Optimal structured light à la carte. In: Proceedings of the IEEE Conference on Computer Vision and Pattern Recognition, pp. 6248–6257 (2018)
19. Nguyen, H., Wang, Y., Wang, Z.: Single-shot 3D shape reconstruction using structured light and deep convolutional neural networks. Sensors **20**(13), 3718 (2020)
20. Ranftl, R., Bochkovskiy, A., Koltun, V.: Vision transformers for dense prediction. In: Proceedings of the IEEE/CVF International Conference on Computer Vision, pp. 12179–12188 (2021)
21. Riegler, G., Liao, Y., Donne, S., Koltun, V., Geiger, A.: Connecting the dots: learning representations for active monocular depth estimation. In: Proceedings of the IEEE/CVF Conference on Computer Vision and Pattern Recognition, pp. 7616–7625 (2019)
22. Tankovich, V., Hane, C., Zhang, Y., Kowdle, A., Fanello, S., Bouaziz, S.: HITNet: hierarchical iterative tile refinement network for real-time stereo matching. In: Proceedings of the IEEE/CVF Conference on Computer Vision and Pattern Recognition, pp. 14362–14372 (2021)
23. Van Gansbeke, W., Neven, D., De Brabandere, B., Van Gool, L.: Sparse and noisy LiDAR completion with RGB guidance and uncertainty. In: Proceedings of the International Conference on Machine Vision Applications, pp. 1–6 (2019)
24. Watson, J., Aodha, O.M., Prisacariu, V., Brostow, G., Firman, M.: The temporal opportunist: Self-supervised multi-frame monocular depth. In: Proceedings of the IEEE/CVF Computer Vision and Pattern Recognition, pp. 1164–1174 (2021)
25. Zhang, Y., Funkhouser, T.: Deep depth completion of a single RGB-D image. In: Proceedings of the IEEE/CVF Conference on Computer Vision and Pattern Recognition, pp. 175–185 (2018)
26. Zhang, Y., et al.: ActiveStereoNet: end-to-end self-supervised learning for active stereo systems. In: Ferrari, V., Hebert, M., Sminchisescu, C., Weiss, Y. (eds.) ECCV 2018. LNCS, vol. 11212, pp. 802–819. Springer, Cham (2018). https://doi.org/10.1007/978-3-030-01237-3_48

ActiveNeRF: Learning Where to See with Uncertainty Estimation

Xuran Pan[1], Zihang Lai[2], Shiji Song[1], and Gao Huang[1(✉)]

[1] Tsinghua University, Beijing 100084, China
pxr18@mails.tsinghua.edu.cn, {shijis,gaohuang}@tsinghua.edu.cn
[2] Carnegie Mellon University, Pennsylvania 15213, USA
zihangl@andrew.cmu.edu

Abstract. Recently, Neural Radiance Fields (NeRF) has shown promising performances on reconstructing 3D scenes and synthesizing novel views from a sparse set of 2D images. Albeit effective, the performance of NeRF is highly influenced by the quality of training samples. With limited posed images from the scene, NeRF fails to generalize well to novel views and may collapse to trivial solutions in unobserved regions. This makes NeRF impractical under resource-constrained scenarios. In this paper, we present a novel learning framework, *ActiveNeRF*, aiming to model a 3D scene with a constrained input budget. Specifically, we first incorporate uncertainty estimation into a NeRF model, which ensures robustness under few observations and provides an interpretation of how NeRF understands the scene. On this basis, we propose to supplement the existing training set with newly captured samples based on an active learning scheme. By evaluating the reduction of uncertainty given new inputs, we select the samples that bring the most information gain. In this way, the quality of novel view synthesis can be improved with minimal additional resources. Extensive experiments validate the performance of our model on both realistic and synthetic scenes, especially with scarcer training data.

Keywords: Active learning · Neural radiance fields · Uncertainty estimation

1 Introduction

The task of synthesizing novel views of a scene from a sparse set of images has earned broad research interest in recent years. With the advent of neural rendering techniques, Neural Radiance Fields (NeRF) [20] shows its potential on

Z. La—Work done during an internship at Tsinghua University.

Supplementary Information The online version contains supplementary material available at https://doi.org/10.1007/978-3-031-19827-4_14.

S. Avidan et al. (Eds.): ECCV 2022, LNCS 13693, pp. 230–246, 2022.
https://doi.org/10.1007/978-3-031-19827-4_14

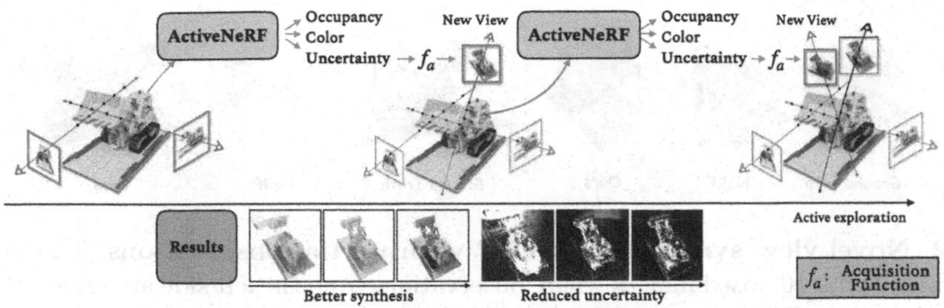

Fig. 1. ActiveNeRF: We present a flexible learning framework that *actively* expands the existing training set with newly captured samples based on an Active Learning scheme. ActiveNeRF incorporates uncertainty estimation into a NeRF model and evaluates the reduction of scene uncertainty at unobserved novel views. By selecting the view that brings the most information gain, the quality of novel view synthesis can be improved with minimal additional resources.

rendering photo-realistic images and inspires a new line of research [22,24,37]. Different from traditional Structure-from-Motion [1] or image-based rendering [28] approaches, NeRF models the emitted radiance values and volume densities in a 3D scene as a function of continuous 5D coordinates, including spatial locations x, y, z and viewing directions θ, ϕ. The learned implicit function expresses a compact representation of the scene and enables free-viewpoint synthesis through volume rendering.

Despite its success in synthesizing high-quality images, the learning scheme for a NeRF model puts forward higher demands on the training data. First, NeRF usually requires a large number of posed images and is proved to generalize poorly with limited inputs [36]. Second, it takes a whole observation in the scene to train a well-generalized NeRF. As illustrated in Fig. 2, if we remove observations of a particular part in the scene, NeRF fails to model the region and tends to collapse (*e.g.,* predicting zero density everywhere in the scene) instead of performing reasonable predictions. This poses challenges under real-world applications such as robot localization and mapping, where capturing training data can be costly, and perception of the entire scene is required [11,23,31].

In this paper, we focus on the context with constrained input image budget and attempt to address these limitations by leveraging the training data in the most efficient manner. As shown in Fig. 1, we first introduce uncertainty estimation into the NeRF framework by modeling the radiance values of each location as a Gaussian distribution. This imposes the model to provide larger variances in the unobserved region instead of collapsing to a trivial solution. On this basis, we resort to the inspiration from active learning and propose to capture the most informative inputs as supplementary to the current training data. Specifically, given a hypothetical new input, we analyze the posterior distribution of the whole scene through Bayesian estimation, and use the subtraction of the variance from prior to posterior distribution as the information gain. This finally serves as the criterion for capturing new inputs, and thus raises the quality of

Fig. 2. Novel view synthesis of NeRF with partial observations. The models are trained with 10 posed images where observations from the left side are removed from the training set. While our model can still generate reasonably good synthesis results, the original NeRF shows large errors or completely fails to generate meaningful content.

synthesized views with minimal additional resources. Extensive experiments show that NeRF with uncertainty estimation achieves better performances on novel view synthesis, especially with scarce training data. Our proposed framework based on active learning, dubbed **ActiveNeRF**, also shows superior performances on both synthetic and realistic scenes, and outperforms several heuristic baselines.

2 Related Works

2.1 Novel View Synthesis

Synthesizing novel views of a 3D scene from a sparse set of 2D images is a long-standing problem in computer vision. Earlier work, including Structure-from-Motion [1] or image-based rendering [28], mostly reconstruct a scene in sparse representations. On this basis, bundle adjustment [33] and lighting-based approaches [15] consider the light and reluctance properties to synthesize photo-realistic images. More recently, the neural rendering technique has been introduced to the scene representation task, which inspires a line of research to model the 3D scene as a continuous representation. Scene Representation Network (SRN) [30] first models the scene as a function of 3D coordinates, which are then used to predict the intersections of object surfaces and the corresponding emitted color. Following SRN, Neural Radiance Fields (NeRF) [20] considers the volume density and view-dependent emitted color in the scene and models with a simple but effective multi-layer perceptron. The outputs in each location of the scene are combined with neural rendering techniques to synthesize novel views.

Many researches follow the step of NeRF and extend the original framework from different perspectives [2,14,35]. NeRF++ [37] analyzes the modeling capacity of NeRF and proposes an inverted sphere parameterization approach to model unbounded 3D scenes. FastNeRF [9] accelerates rendering procedure in NeRF to achieve real-time view synthesis. D-NeRF [24] and other related approaches propose to model dynamic scenes with moving objects. NeRF-W [18], on the other hand, focuses on modeling the transient objects varying from different images. Several works further extend NeRF-based models to represent scenes conditioned on a scene prior, which enables NeRF to generalize to new scenes.

More related to our work, several researches have also addressed the problem of NeRF under the limited input setting. Pixel-NeRF [36] proposes to encode the image-level features into the radiance field and trains a NeRF model that can generalize across the scene. MVSNeRF [5] applies 3D CNN to reconstruct a neural encoding volume with per-voxel neural features. GRF [32] back-projects points to input images and gathers per-pixel features from each view. These approaches incorporate image features into original coordinate-based embeddings. DietNeRF [10] introduces additional semantic consistency loss with pre-trained CLIP [25] models. Compared to these works, we are the first to address the limitation of NeRF from the data perspective and effectively increase the upper bound of the model with minimum additional resources. Also, the uncertainty estimation module in our framework is orthogonal to these approaches and can serve as a plug-and-play module to further boost their performances.

2.2 Uncertainty Estimation

The computer vision community has seen the value of uncertainty estimation in various research fields. Measuring the uncertainty of a neural network can both enhance the interpretability of the model outputs and reduce the risk of making critical faults. Based on the Bayesian rule, several approaches formulate uncertainty as a probability distribution over either the model parameters or model outputs. Bayesian Neural Networks (BNN) [13,17] approaches measure the uncertainty as posterior distribution, which usually require approximate inference methods, *e.g.*, variational inference. Dropout variational inference [7,12] estimates the model uncertainty with dropout layers in the network by performing multiple inferences for the same input.

Early research has also explored the possibility of applying uncertainty estimation in the field of novel view synthesis. NeRF-W [18] introduces uncertainty to model the transient objects in the scene. Compared to our approach, the uncertainty estimation in NeRF-W focuses on the differences across the images rather than the inherent noise inside the training data. Another concurrent work S-NeRF [27] models the uncertainty of the scene with variational inference. Although the uncertainty correlates well with the predictive error, S-NeRF performs qualitatively worse (*e.g.*, it shows blurry edges in the synthesis results) than the original model. It also requires multiple identical inferences to obtain the uncertainty map. Compared to these two approaches, our simple yet effective uncertainty estimation framework strictly follows the volume rendering procedure, and shows on par or better performances over the original NeRF model under various training data settings. The proposed uncertainty modeling is also a necessary component of the full ActiveNeRF framework: the uncertainty estimation serves as the basis to evaluate the new images.

2.3 Active Learning

Active learning has been widely studied in various computer vision tasks, including image classification [6], image captioning [21], and object detection [3]. Active learning can be categorized into two classes: representativeness-based and informativeness-based approaches. Representativeness methods rely on selecting examples by increasing the diversity of the training set. Core-set technique [26] selects the samples by evaluating the Euclidean distance between candidates and labeled samples in the feature space. Also, several researches resort to the techniques in adversarial training [29] or self-supervised training [4], and select samples with an additional network, *e.g.,* a discriminator. More related to our work, informativeness methods measure the uncertainty of each data and select the most uncertain ones from an unlabelled data pool. With the uncertainty estimation approaches in the previous section, the selection criterion can be used in both Bayesian [8] and non-Bayesian [16] frameworks.

To the best of our knowledge, ActiveNeRF is the first approach to incorporating active learning scheme into the NeRF optimization pipeline. Unlike other works that focus on improving model capacities, we analyze the inherent imperfection of the training data, thereby increasing the synthesis quality of NeRF models with higher data efficiency. This is crucial for resource-constrained scenarios in real-world applications.

3 Background

In this section, we first briefly review the Neural Radiance Fields (NeRF) framework and introduce some implementation details.

NeRF models a scene as a continuous function F_θ which outputs emitted radiance value and volume density. Specifically, given a 3D position $\mathrm{x}=(x,y,z)$ in the scene and a viewing direction parameterized as a 3D Cartesian unit vector $\mathrm{d}=(d_x,d_y,d_z)$, a multi-layer perceptron model is adopted to produce the corresponding volume density σ and color $\mathrm{c}=(r,g,b)$ as follows:

$$[\sigma, f] = \mathrm{MLP}_{\theta_1}(\gamma_{\mathrm{x}}(\mathrm{x})), \quad (1)$$

$$c = \mathrm{MLP}_{\theta_2}(f, \gamma_{\mathrm{d}}(\mathrm{d})), \quad (2)$$

where $\gamma_{\mathrm{x}}(\cdot)$ and $\gamma_{\mathrm{d}}(\cdot)$ are the positional encoding functions, and f represents the intermediate feature independent from viewing direction d. An interesting observation is that the radiance color is only affected by its own 3D coordinates and the viewing direction, which makes it independent from other locations.

To achieve free view synthesis, NeRF renders the color of rays passing through the scene with the volume rendering technique. Let $\mathrm{r}(t)=\mathrm{o}+t\mathrm{d}$ be a camera ray with camera center $\mathrm{o}\in\mathcal{R}^3$ through a given pixel on the image plane, the color of the pixel can be formulated as:

$$C(\mathrm{r}) = \int_{t_n}^{t_f} T(t)\sigma(\mathrm{r}(t))\mathrm{c}(\mathrm{r}(t),\mathrm{d})ds, \quad (3)$$

where $T(t) = \exp(-\int_{t_n}^{t} \sigma(\mathrm{r}(s))ds)$ denotes the accumulated transmittance, and t_n and t_f are the near and far bounds in the scene. To make the rendering process tractable, NeRF approximates the integral based on stratified sampling, and formulates it as a linear combination of sampled points:

$$\hat{C}(\mathrm{r}) = \sum_{i=1}^{N_s} \alpha_i c(\mathrm{r}(t_i)),\ \alpha_i = \exp(-\sum_{j=1}^{i-1} \sigma_j \delta_j)(1 - \exp(-\sigma_i \delta_i)), \tag{4}$$

where $\delta_i = t_{i+1} - t_i$ is the distance between adjacent samples, and N_s denotes the number of samples. On this basis, NeRF optimizes the continuous function F_θ by minimizing the squared reconstruction errors between the ground truth from RGB images $\{\mathcal{I}_{i=1}^{N}\}$, and the rendered pixel colors.

To improve the sampling efficiency, NeRF optimizes two parallel networks simultaneously, and denote them as coarse and fine models respectively. The sampling strategy for the fine model is improved according to the result of the coarse model, where the samples are biased towards more relevant parts. In all, the optimization loss is parameterized as:

$$\sum_i \|C(\mathrm{r}_i) - \hat{C}^c(\mathrm{r}_i)\|_2^2 + \|C(\mathrm{r}_i) - \hat{C}^f(\mathrm{r}_i)\|_2^2, \tag{5}$$

where r_i is sampled ray, and $C(\mathrm{r}_i), \hat{C}^c(\mathrm{r}_i), \hat{C}^f(\mathrm{r}_i)$ correspond to the ground truth, coarse model prediction, and fine model prediction respectively.

4 NeRF with Uncertainty Estimation

In this paper, we focus on the context in some real-world applications, where the number of training data is within a limited budget. It has been proved in existing research [36] that NeRF fails to generalize well from one or few input views. If with incomplete scene observation, the original NeRF framework tends to collapse to trivial solutions by predicting the volume density as 0 for the unobserved regions.

As a remedy, we propose to model the emitted radiance value of each location in the scene as a Gaussian distribution instead of a single value. The predicted variance can serve as the reflection of the aleatoric uncertainty concerning a certain location. Through this, the model is imposed to provide larger variances in the unobserved region instead of collapsing to the trivial solution.

Specifically, we define the radiance color of a location $\mathrm{r}(t)$ follows a Gaussian distribution parameterized by mean $\bar{c}(\mathrm{r}(t))$ and variance $\bar{\beta}^2(\mathrm{r}(t))$. Following previous researches in Bayesian neural networks, we take the model output as the mean, and add an additional branch to the MLP network in Eq. (1) to model the variance as follows:

$$[\sigma, f, \beta^2(\mathrm{r}(t))] = \mathrm{MLP}_{\theta_1,\theta_3}(\gamma_\mathrm{x}(\mathrm{r}(t))), \tag{6}$$

$$\bar{c}(\mathrm{r}(t)) = \mathrm{MLP}_{\theta_2}(f, \gamma_\mathrm{d}(\mathrm{d})). \tag{7}$$

Softplus function is further adopted to produce a validate variance value:

$$\bar{\beta}^2(\mathrm{r}(t)) = \beta_0^2 + \log(1 + \exp(\beta^2(\mathrm{r}(t))), \tag{8}$$

where β_0^2 ensures a minimum variance for all the locations.

Fig. 3. Qualitative ablation on regularization term. The regularization term leads to more apparent synthesis results and greatly alleviates the blurs on the object surfaces. Quantitatively, regularization boosts performance by 1.1 PSNR on this scene

In the rendering process, the new neural radiance field with uncertainty can be similarly performed through volume rendering. As we have mentioned in Sect. 3, the design paradigm in the NeRF framework provides two valuable prerequisites. (1) The radiance color of a particular position is only affected by its own 3D coordinates, which makes the distribution of different positions independent from each other. (2) Volume rendering can be approximated as linear combination of sampled points along the ray. On this basis, if we denote the Gaussian distribution of a position at $\mathrm{r}(t)$ as $c(\mathrm{r}(t)) \sim \mathcal{N}(\bar{c}(\mathrm{r}(t)), \bar{\beta}^2(\mathrm{r}(t)))$, the rendered value along this ray naturally follows Gaussian distribution:

$$\hat{C}(\mathrm{r}) \sim \mathcal{N}(\sum_{i=1}^{N_s} \alpha_i \bar{c}(\mathrm{r}(t_i)), \sum_{i=1}^{N_s} \alpha_i^2 \bar{\beta}^2(\mathrm{r}(t_i))) \sim \mathcal{N}(\bar{C}(\mathrm{r}), \bar{\beta}^2(\mathrm{r})), \tag{9}$$

where the α_is are the same as in Eq. (4), and $\bar{C}(\mathrm{r}), \bar{\beta}^2(\mathrm{r})$ denote the mean and variance of the rendered color through the sampled ray r.

To optimize our radiance field, we first assume that each location in the scene is at most sampled once in a training batch. We believe the hypothesis is reasonable as the intersection of two rays rarely happens in a 3D scene, let alone sampling at the same position in the same batch. Therefore, the distributions of rendered rays are assumed to be independent. In this way, we can optimize the model by minimizing the negative log-likelihood of rays $\{r_{i=1}^N\}$ from a batch $\mathcal{B}$:

$$\min_\theta \; -\log p_\theta(\mathcal{B}) = -\frac{1}{N}\sum_{i=1}^{N} \log\, p_\theta(C(\mathrm{r}_i)) = \frac{1}{N}\sum_{i=1}^{N} \frac{\|C(\mathrm{r}_i) - \bar{C}(\mathrm{r}_i)\|_2^2}{2\bar{\beta}^2(\mathrm{r}_i)} + \frac{\log \bar{\beta}^2(\mathrm{r}_i)}{2}. \tag{10}$$

However, simply minimizing the above objective function leads to a sub-optimal solution where the weights α_i for different samples in a ray are driven closer. This results in an unexpectedly large fraction of non-zero density in the whole scene, causing blurs on the object's surface, as depicted in Fig. 3. There-

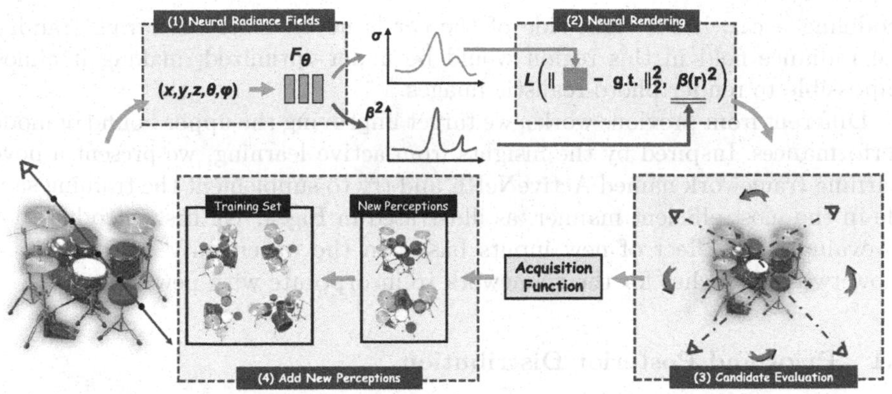

Fig. 4. The ActiveNeRF pipeline consists of 4 steps. First, the initial observation is used to train an ActiveNeRF model (Sect. 5.1). This model is then used to render novel views, from which the new viewpoint (that most reduces uncertainty) is estimated (Sect. 5.2 and 5.3). Finally, a new perception is captured and added to the training set

fore, we add an additional regularization term to force sparser volume density, and the loss function is formulated as:

$$\mathcal{L}^{uct} = \frac{1}{N}\sum_{i=1}^{N}\left(\frac{\|C(\mathrm{r}_i) - \bar{C}(\mathrm{r}_i)\|_2^2}{2\bar{\beta}^2(\mathrm{r}_i)} + \frac{\log \bar{\beta}^2(\mathrm{r}_i)}{2} + \frac{\lambda}{N_s}\sum_{j=1}^{N_s}\sigma_i(\mathrm{r}_i(t_j))\right), \tag{11}$$

where λ is a hyper-parameter that controls the regularization strength.

We follow the original NeRF framework and optimize two parallel networks. To ease the difficulty of optimization, we only adopt the uncertainty branch in the fine model and keep the coarse model the same as vanilla. The final loss function is then:

$$\mathcal{L}^{uct}(C(\mathrm{r}), \bar{C}^f(\mathrm{r})) + \frac{1}{N}\sum_{i=1}^{N}\|C(\mathrm{r}_i) - \hat{C}^c(\mathrm{r}_i)\|_2^2. \tag{12}$$

By learning a neural radiance field as Gaussian distributions, we not only produce reasonable predictions in uncertain areas but also present an interpretation of how NeRF model understands the scene. On the one hand, uncertainty can be viewed as a perception of noises, which may also reflect the degree of risk in real-world scenarios, e.g., robotic navigation. On the other hand, this can further serve as a vital criterion in the following active learning framework.

5 ActiveNeRF

Although several works have attempted to model well-generalized NeRF under a limited training budget, the upper bound of their performances is highly restricted due to the inherent blind spot in the observations. For example, when modeling a car, if the right side of the car is never observed during training, the radiance field in this region would be under-optimized, making it almost impossible to render photo-realistic images.

Different from previous works, we target improving the upper bound of model performances. Inspired by the insights from active learning, we present a novel learning framework named ActiveNeRF and try to supplement the training sample in the most efficient manner, as illustrated in Fig. 4. We first introduce how to evaluate the effect of new inputs based on the uncertainty estimation and show two approaches for the framework to incorporate with new inputs.

5.1 Prior and Posterior Distribution

Estimating the influence of new data without its actual observation is a non-trivial problem. Nevertheless, modeling the radiance field as Gaussian distribution makes the evaluation more tractable, where we can estimate the posterior distribution of the radiance field based on the Bayesian rule.

Let D_1 denote the existing training set and F_θ denote the trained NeRF model given D_1. For simplicity, we first consider the influence of a single ray r_2 from the new input D_2. Thus, for the k_{th} sampled location $\mathrm{r}_2(t_k)$, its prior distribution is formulated as:

$$P^{(\mathrm{pri})} = P(c(\mathrm{r}_2(t_k))|D_1) \sim \mathcal{N}(\bar{c}(\mathrm{r}_2(t_k)), \bar{\beta}^2(\mathrm{r}_2(t_k))). \tag{13}$$

Following the sequential Bayesian formulation, the posterior distribution can then be derived as:

$$P^{(\mathrm{post})} = P(c(\mathrm{r}_2(t_k))|D_1, \mathrm{r}_2) = \frac{p(C(\mathrm{r}_2)|c(\mathrm{r}_2(t_k)))p(c(\mathrm{r}_2(t_k))|D_1)}{\int p(C(\mathrm{r}_2)|c(\mathrm{r}_2(t_k)))p(c(\mathrm{r}_2(t_k))|D_1)dc(\mathrm{r}_2(t_k))}. \tag{14}$$

As derived in Sect. 4, rendered color of rays follows the Gaussian distribution:

$$p(C(\mathrm{r}_2)|c(\mathrm{r}_2(t_k))) \sim \mathcal{N}(\bar{C}(\mathrm{r}_2), \bar{\beta}^2(\mathrm{r}_2)) \sim \mathcal{N}(\sum_{i=1}^{N_s} \alpha_i \bar{c}(\mathrm{r}_2(t_i)), \bar{\beta}^2(\mathrm{r}_2)). \tag{15}$$

As other sampled locations in r_2 are independent with $\mathrm{r}_2(t_k)$, we can represent the unrelated part in the mean as a constant $b(t_k)$ and the distribution can be simplified as:

$$p(C(\mathrm{r}_2)|c(\mathrm{r}_2(t_k))) \sim \mathcal{N}(\alpha_k \bar{c}(\mathrm{r}_2(t_k)) + b(t_k), \bar{\beta}^2(\mathrm{r}_2)). \tag{16}$$

Finally, by substituting terms in Eq. (14) with Eq. (13) and Eq. (16), the posterior distribution is formulated as:

$$P^{(\mathrm{post})} \sim \mathcal{N}\left(\gamma \frac{C(\mathrm{r}_2) - b(t_k)}{\alpha_k} + (1-\gamma)\bar{c}(\mathrm{r}_2(t_k)), \frac{\bar{\beta}^2(\mathrm{r}_2(t_k))\bar{\beta}^2(\mathrm{r}_2)}{\alpha_k^2 \bar{\beta}^2(\mathrm{r}_2(t_k)) + \bar{\beta}^2(\mathrm{r}_2)}\right), \tag{17}$$

$$\text{with } \gamma = \frac{\alpha_k^2 \bar{\beta}^2(\mathrm{r}_2(t_k))}{\alpha_k^2 \bar{\beta}(\mathrm{r}_2(t_k)) + \bar{\beta}^2(\mathrm{r}_2)}. \tag{18}$$

Please refer to Appendix A for details.

5.2 Acquisition Function

With the posterior distribution formulated by the Bayesian rule, we quantitatively analyze the influence on the radiance field given a new input ray. As shown in Eq. (17), although the mean of the posterior distribution is unavailable due to the unknown of $C(\mathrm{r}_2)$, the variance is independent of the ground truth value and therefore can be *precisely computed* based on the current model F_θ. Additionally, it is worth noting that the variance of the posterior distribution of a newly observed location $\mathrm{r}_2(t_k)$ is consistently smaller than its prior distribution:

$$\begin{aligned}\mathrm{Var}^{(\mathrm{post})}(\mathrm{r}_2(t_k)) &= \frac{\bar{\beta}^2(\mathrm{r}_2(t_k))\bar{\beta}^2(\mathrm{r}_2)}{\alpha_k^2\bar{\beta}^2(\mathrm{r}_2(t_k)) + \bar{\beta}^2(\mathrm{r}_2)} \\ &= (\frac{1}{\bar{\beta}^2(\mathrm{r}_2(t_k))} + \frac{\alpha_k^2}{\bar{\beta}^2(\mathrm{r}_2)})^{-1} < \bar{\beta}^2(\mathrm{r}_2(t_k)) = \mathrm{Var}^{(\mathrm{pri})}(\mathrm{r}_2(t_k)).\end{aligned} \quad (19)$$

This further proves that new observations can genuinely reduce the uncertainty of the radiance field. On this basis, we consider the reduction of variance as the estimation of information gain of $\mathrm{r}_2(t_k)$ from the new ray r_2:

$$\mathrm{Var}^{(\mathrm{pri})}(\mathrm{r}_2(t_k)) - \mathrm{Var}^{(\mathrm{post})}(\mathrm{r}_2(t_k)). \quad (20)$$

For a given image with resolution H, W, we can sample $N = H \times W$ independent rays, with N_s sampled locations from each ray. Therefore, we add up the reduction of variance from all these locations and define the acquisition function as:

$$\mathcal{A}(D_2) = \sum_{\mathrm{r}_i \in D_2} \sum_{j=1}^{N_s} \left(\mathrm{Var}^{(\mathrm{pri})}(\mathrm{r}_i(t_j)) - \mathrm{Var}^{(\mathrm{post})}(\mathrm{r}_i(t_j))\right). \quad (21)$$

Similar derivation is also applicable with multiple input images, where the variance of posterior uncertainty is formulated as:

$$\mathrm{Var}^{(\mathrm{post})}(\mathrm{x}) = (\frac{1}{\bar{\beta}^2(\mathrm{x})} + \sum_i \frac{\alpha_{k_i}^2}{\bar{\beta}^2(\mathrm{r}_i(t_{k_i}))})^{-1}, \quad (22)$$

where r_i denotes ray from different images, and $\mathrm{x} = \mathrm{r}_i(t_{k_i}), \forall i$. Please refer to Appendix B for details.

In practical implementation, we first sample candidate views from a spherical space, and choose the top-k candidates that score highest in the acquisition function as the supplementary of the current training set. In this way, the captured new inputs bring the most information gain and promote the performance of the current model with the highest efficiency.

Besides, a quality-efficiency trade-off can also be achieved by evaluating new inputs with lower resolution. For example, instead of using full image size $H \times W$ as new rays, we can sample $H/r \times W/r$ rays to approximate the influence of the whole image with only $1/r^2$ time consumption.

5.3 Optimization and Inference

With the newly captured samples chosen by the acquisition function, we provide two approaches to incorporate the current NeRF model with additional inputs.

Table 1. Quantitative results in fixed training set setting: ActiveNeRF performs superior to or on par with the original NeRF in all settings. In particular, note our model performs significantly better than NeRF in low-shot settings. We report PSNR/SSIM (higher is better) and LPIPS (lower is better)

	(a) Synthetic scenes			(b) Realistic scenes		
Method	PSNR↑	SSIM↑	LPIPS↓	PSNR↑	SSIM↑	LPIPS↓
Setting I, training with all images						
SRN	22.26	0.846	0.170	22.84	0.668	0.378
LLFF	24.88	0.911	0.114	24.13	0.798	**0.212**
NeRF	**31.01**	0.947	0.081	**26.50**	0.811	0.250
IBRNet	25.62	0.939	0.110	–	–	–
MSVNeRF	27.07	0.931	0.168	–	–	–
Ours	30.45	**0.954**	**0.072**	25.96	**0.835**	**0.213**
Setting II, training with 10 images						
NeRF	28.04	0.866	0.134	23.36	0.791	0.280
DietNeRF	28.42	0.891	**0.087**	–	–	–
Ours	**28.51**	**0.932**	0.090	**23.96**	**0.803**	**0.260**
Setting III, training with 5 images						
NeRF	21.14	0.835	0.192	21.67	0.689	0.350
Ours	**23.23**	**0.866**	**0.185**	**22.03**	**0.712**	**0.292**

Bayesian Estimation. With the ground-truth value $C(\mathrm{r})$ from the new inputs, we can practically compute the posterior distribution of the locations in the scene by leveraging Eq. (17). Among these, the mean of distribution becomes the Bayesian estimation of emitted radiance value, and can be adopted in the rendering process. At inference time, we only need to substitute the prior color with the posterior Bayesian estimation:

$$\bar{c}(\mathrm{r}(t_k)) \Rightarrow \gamma \frac{C(\mathrm{r})-b(t_k)}{\alpha_k} + (1-\gamma)\bar{c}(\mathrm{r}(t_k)), \tag{23}$$

while others remain unchanged.

One of the advantages of using Bayesian estimation is that we avoid the collateral training procedure. If we consider an edge device, *e.g.*, a robot, the training-free scheme allows the agent to perform offline inference instantly, which is more friendly in resource-constrained scenarios.

Continuous Learning can also be considered if time and computation resources are not the bottlenecks. The captured inputs can be added to the training set and tune the model on the basis of the current one. We can further control the fraction of training rays from new images, forcing the model to optimize in the newly observed regions.

The two approaches can both promote the quality of the neural radiance field, and naturally achieve a trade-off between efficiency and synthesis quality.

6 Experiments

6.1 Experimental Setup

Datasets. We extensively demonstrate our approach in two benchmarks, including LLFF [19] and NeRF [20] datasets. LLFF is a real-world dataset consisting of 8 complex scenes captured with a cellphone. Each scene contains 20–62 images with 1008×756 resolution, where 1/8 images are reserved for the test. NeRF dataset contains 8 synthetic objects with complicated geometry and realistic non-Lambertian materials. Each scene has 100 views for training and 200 for the test, and all the images are at 800×800 resolution. See detailed training configurations in the Appendix.

Metrics. We report the image quality metrics PSNR and SSIM for evaluations. We also include LPIPS [38], which more accurately reflects human perception.

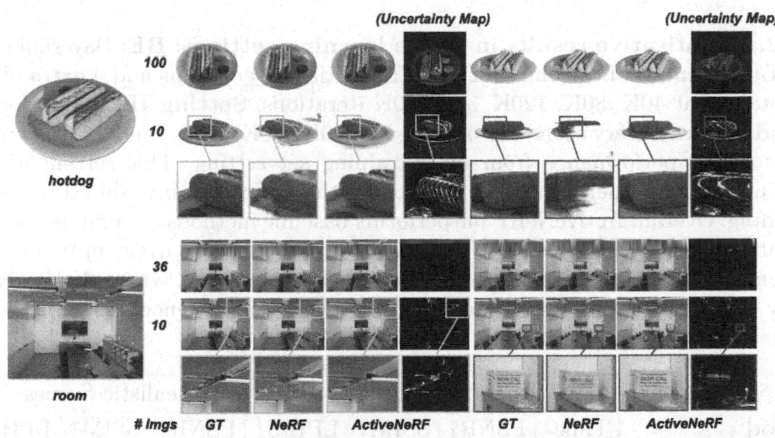

Fig. 5. Qualitative results on synthetic and realistic scenes with different fractions of training samples. Several observations can be made: First, ActiveNeRF performs significantly better than NeRF in the low-shot setting (*e.g.*, See Line. 2 and 3). Second, the uncertainty correctly reduces when more data is used (See Col. *Uncertainty Map*). Finally, ActiveNeRF and NeRF obtain similar qualitative performance when all images are used (See Line. 1 and 4), suggesting modeling uncertainty has no negative impact on the quality of view synthesis

6.2 Results

Uncertainty Estimation. We first evaluate the effectiveness of the proposed uncertainty estimation with different fractions of input samples. We compare with several competitive baselines, including Neural Radiance Fields (NeRF) [35], Local Light Field Fusion (LLFF) [19], and Scene Representation Networks

(SRN) [30]. We also compare with three competitive baselines, including IBRNet [34], MSVNeRF [5] and DietNeRF [10].

We show the performance of our proposed approach with a different number of training data over baseline approaches in Table 1. It can be seen that NeRF with uncertainty performs on par or slightly better than baseline models, showing that modeling uncertainty does not affect the quality of synthesizing novel views. When it comes to limited training samples, our model shows consistently better results. For example, in the synthetic dataset, NeRF with 10% training data fails to generalize well to some views, while our model can still provide reasonable predictions. The gap is more distinct on the perceptual loss, *e.g.*, LPIPS, showing that our model can also render high-frequency textures with limited training data. Compared to DietNeRF, our model achieves better performances on two criteria and is competitive on the third. However, ours do not require additional pretrained model (*e.g.*, CLIP for DietNeRF) and can be used in the following active learning framework. Qualitative results are shown in Fig. 5.

Table 2. Quantitative results in active learning settings: BE: Bayesian estimation; **CL:** Continuous Learning; **Setting I:** 4 initial observations and 4 extra observations obtained at 40K, 80K, 120K, and 160K iterations. **Setting II:** 2 initial observations and 2 extra observations are obtained at 40K, 80K, 120K, and 160K iterations. **NeRF†**: NeRF performance from fixed training set setting. This setting measures NeRF's upper-bound performance by removing the difficulties introduced by continuous learning. Overall, ActiveNeRF outperforms baseline methods; several metrics could even match non-CL performance. We also report the total time consumption (training + inference time) of different approaches in the **Time** column, where **ActiveNeRF-BE** only consume training time at first 40K iterations and inference time at later stages

	(a) Synthetic Scenes				(b) Realistic Scenes		
Method	Time	PSNR↑	SSIM↑	LPIPS↓	PSNR↑	SSIM↑	LPIPS↓
Setting I, 20 total observations:							
NeRF+Rand	2.0h	24.25	0.734	0.207	20.65	0.532	0.312
NeRF+FVS	2.0h	26.00	0.812	0.144	22.41	0.710	0.299
ActiveNeRF-BE	30min	25.67	0.778	0.169	21.86	0.644	0.303
ActiveNeRF-CL	2.2h	**26.24**	**0.856**	**0.124**	**23.12**	**0.765**	**0.292**
NeRF†	2.0h	28.04	0.910	0.134	23.36	0.791	0.280
Setting II, 10 total observations:							
NeRF+Rand	1.0h	18.36	0.642	0.251	18.49	0.478	0.355
NeRF+FVS	1.0h	19.24	0.735	0.227	20.02	0.633	0.344
ActiveNeRF-BE	16min	18.25	0.611	0.256	18.67	0.451	0.367
ActiveNeRF-CL	1.1h	**20.01**	**0.832**	**0.204**	**20.14**	**0.664**	**0.325**
NeRF†	1.0h	21.14	0.835	0.192	21.67	0.689	0.350

ActiveNeRF. We validate the performance of our proposed framework, ActiveNeRF, and compare it with two heuristic approaches. As an approximation, we hold out a large fraction of images in the training set and use these images as candidate samples. For baselines, we denote *NeRF+Random* as randomly capturing new images in the candidates. *NeRF+FVS (furthest view sampling)* corresponds to finding the candidates with the most distanced camera position compared with the current training set. We empirically adjust the number of the initial training set and captured samples during the training procedure.

We first show the results with continuous learning scheme, where the time and computation resources are considered sufficient. The comparison results are shown in Table 2 and Fig. 6. We can easily see that ActiveNeRF captures the most informative inputs comparing with heuristic approaches, which contributes most to synthesizing views from less observed regions. The additional training cost for ActiveNeRF is also comparably minor (2.2 h vs. 2 h).

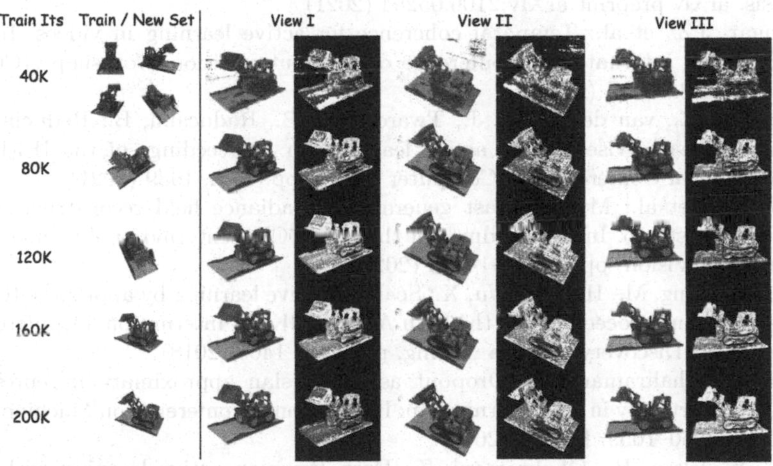

Fig. 6. Qualitative results of ActiveNeRF with four active iterations. We capture new perceptions every 40K iterations. Improved synthesis quality can be seen in unobserved regions

We further validate the model performances with Bayesian estimation. As shown in Table 2, 75% of the time consumption can be saved. Although showing inferior performance to continuous learning, the model with Bayesian estimation still synthesize reasonable images and is even competitive with heuristic approaches under continuous learning scheme.

7 Conclusion

In this paper, we present a flexible learning framework, that supplements the existing training set with newly captured samples based on an active learning scheme. We first incorporate uncertainty estimation into a NeRF model and evaluate the reduction of uncertainty in the scene given new inputs. By selecting the samples that bring the most information gain, the quality of novel view synthesis can be promoted with minimal additional resources. Also, our approach can be applied to various NeRF-extension approaches as a plug-in module, and enhance model performances in a resource-efficient manner.

Acknowledgment. This work is supported in part by National Key R&D Program of China (2021ZD0140407), the National Natural Science Foundation of China under Grants 62022048 and THU-Bosch JCML Center Beijing Academy of Artificial Intelligence.

References

1. Andrew, A.M.: Multiple view geometry in computer vision. Kybernetes (2001)
2. Arandjelović, R., Zisserman, A.: Nerf in detail: Learning to sample for view synthesis. arXiv preprint arXiv:2106.05264 (2021)
3. Bengar, J.Z., et al.: Temporal coherence for active learning in videos. In: 2019 IEEE/CVF International Conference on Computer Vision Workshop (ICCVW), pp. 914–923. IEEE (2019)
4. Bengar, J.Z., van de Weijer, J., Twardowski, B., Raducanu, B.: Reducing label effort: Self-supervised meets active learning. In: Proceedings of the IEEE/CVF International Conference on Computer Vision, pp. 1631–1639 (2021)
5. Chen, A., et al.: Mvsnerf: fast generalizable radiance field reconstruction from multi-view stereo. In: Proceedings of the IEEE/CVF International Conference on Computer Vision, pp. 14124–14133 (2021)
6. Fu, W., Wang, M., Hao, S., Wu, X.: Scalable active learning by approximated error reduction. In: Proceedings of the 24th ACM SIGKDD International Conference on Knowledge Discovery & Data Mining, pp. 1396–1405 (2018)
7. Gal, Y., Ghahramani, Z.: Dropout as a Bayesian approximation: representing model uncertainty in deep learning. In: International Conference on Machine Learning, pp. 1050–1059. PMLR (2016)
8. Gal, Y., Islam, R., Ghahramani, Z.: Deep Bayesian active learning with image data. In: International Conference on Machine Learning, pp. 1183–1192. PMLR (2017)
9. Garbin, S.J., Kowalski, M., Johnson, M., Shotton, J., Valentin, J.: FastNeRF: high-fidelity neural rendering at 200fps. arXiv preprint arXiv:2103.10380 (2021)
10. Jain, A., Tancik, M., Abbeel, P.: Putting nerf on a diet: semantically consistent few-shot view synthesis. In: Proceedings of the IEEE/CVF International Conference on Computer Vision, pp. 5885–5894 (2021)
11. Khosoussi, K., Giamou, M., Sukhatme, G.S., Huang, S., Dissanayake, G., How, J.P.: Reliable graphs for slam. Int. J. Rob. Res. **38**(2–3), 260–298 (2019)
12. Kingma, D.P., Salimans, T., Welling, M.: Variational dropout and the local reparameterization trick. Adv. Neural. Inf. Process. Syst. **28**, 2575–2583 (2015)
13. Kononenko, I.: Bayesian neural networks. Biol. Cybern. **61**(5), 361–370 (1989)
14. Kosiorek, A.R., et al.: NeRF-VAE: a geometry aware 3D scene generative model. arXiv preprint arXiv:2104.00587 (2021)
15. Levoy, M., Hanrahan, P.: Light field rendering. In: Proceedings of the 23rd Annual Conference on Computer Graphics and interactive Techniques, pp. 31–42 (1996)

16. Li, X., Guo, Y.: Adaptive active learning for image classification. In: Proceedings of the IEEE Conference on Computer Vision and Pattern Recognition, pp. 859–866 (2013)
17. MacKay, D.J.: Bayesian neural networks and density networks. Nucl. Instrum. Methods Phys. Res., Sect. A **354**(1), 73–80 (1995)
18. Martin-Brualla, R., Radwan, N., Sajjadi, M.S., Barron, J.T., Dosovitskiy, A., Duckworth, D.: Nerf in the wild: neural radiance fields for unconstrained photo collections. In: Proceedings of the IEEE/CVF Conference on Computer Vision and Pattern Recognition, pp. 7210–7219 (2021)
19. Mildenhall, B., et al.: Local light field fusion: practical view synthesis with prescriptive sampling guidelines. ACM Trans. Graph. **38**(4), 1–14 (2019)
20. Mildenhall, B., Srinivasan, P.P., Tancik, M., Barron, J.T., Ramamoorthi, R., Ng, R.: NeRF: representing scenes as neural radiance fields for view synthesis. In: Vedaldi, A., Bischof, H., Brox, T., Frahm, J.-M. (eds.) ECCV 2020. LNCS, vol. 12346, pp. 405–421. Springer, Cham (2020). https://doi.org/10.1007/978-3-030-58452-8_24
21. Miller, B., et al.: Adversarial active learning. In: Proceedings of the 2014 Workshop on Artificial Intelligent and Security Workshop, pp. 3–14 (2014)
22. Park, K., et al.: Deformable neural radiance fields. arXiv preprint arXiv:2011.12948 (2020)
23. Paull, L., Huang, G., Leonard, J.J.: A unified resource-constrained framework for graph slam. In: 2016 IEEE International Conference on Robotics and Automation (ICRA), pp. 1346–1353. IEEE (2016)
24. Pumarola, A., Corona, E., Pons-Moll, G., Moreno-Noguer, F.: D-NeRF: neural radiance fields for dynamic scenes. In: Proceedings of the IEEE/CVF Conference on Computer Vision and Pattern Recognition, pp. 10318–10327 (2021)
25. Radford, A., et al.: Learning transferable visual models from natural language supervision. In: International Conference on Machine Learning, pp. 8748–8763. PMLR (2021)
26. Sener, O., Savarese, S.: Active learning for convolutional neural networks: a core-set approach. arXiv preprint arXiv:1708.00489 (2017)
27. Shen, J., Ruiz, A., Agudo, A., Moreno-Noguer, F.: Stochastic neural radiance fields: quantifying uncertainty in implicit 3D representations. arXiv preprint arXiv:2109.02123 (2021)
28. Shum, H.Y., Chan, S.C., Kang, S.B.: Image-Based Rendering. Springer, New York (2008). https://doi.org/10.1007/978-0-387-32668-9
29. Sinha, S., Ebrahimi, S., Darrell, T.: Variational adversarial active learning. In: Proceedings of the IEEE/CVF International Conference on Computer Vision, pp. 5972–5981 (2019)
30. Sitzmann, V., Zollhöfer, M., Wetzstein, G.: Scene representation networks: continuous 3D-structure-aware neural scene representations. arXiv preprint arXiv:1906.01618 (2019)
31. Torres-González, A., Martínez-de Dios, J.R., Ollero, A.: Robot-beacon distributed range-only slam for resource-constrained operation. Sensors **17**(4), 903 (2017)
32. Trevithick, A., Yang, B.: Grf: Learning a general radiance field for 3d representation and rendering. In: Proceedings of the IEEE/CVF International Conference on Computer Vision, pp. 15182–15192 (2021)
33. Triggs, B., McLauchlan, P.F., Hartley, R.I., Fitzgibbon, A.W.: Bundle adjustment — a modern synthesis. In: Triggs, B., Zisserman, A., Szeliski, R. (eds.) IWVA 1999. LNCS, vol. 1883, pp. 298–372. Springer, Heidelberg (2000). https://doi.org/10.1007/3-540-44480-7_21

34. Wang, Q., et al.: IbrNet: learning multi-view image-based rendering. In: Proceedings of the IEEE/CVF Conference on Computer Vision and Pattern Recognition, pp. 4690–4699 (2021)
35. Wang, Z., Wu, S., Xie, W., Chen, M., Prisacariu, V.A.: NeRF-: neural radiance fields without known camera parameters. arXiv preprint arXiv:2102.07064 (2021)
36. Yu, A., Ye, V., Tancik, M., Kanazawa, A.: pixelNeRF: Neural radiance fields from one or few images. In: Proceedings of the IEEE/CVF Conference on Computer Vision and Pattern Recognition, pp. 4578–4587 (2021)
37. Zhang, K., Riegler, G., Snavely, N., Koltun, V.: NeRF++: analyzing and improving neural radiance fields. arXiv preprint arXiv:2010.07492 (2020)
38. Zhang, R., Isola, P., Efros, A.A., Shechtman, E., Wang, O.: The unreasonable effectiveness of deep features as a perceptual metric. In: Proceedings of the IEEE Conference on Computer Vision and Pattern Recognition, pp. 586–595 (2018)

PoserNet: Refining Relative Camera Poses Exploiting Object Detections

Matteo Taiana(✉), Matteo Toso, Stuart James, and Alessio Del Bue

Pattern Analysis and Computer Vision (PAVIS), Istituto Italiano di Tecnologia (IIT), Genoa, Italy
{matteo.taiana,matteo.toso,stuart.james,alessio.delbue}@iit.it

Abstract. The estimation of the camera poses associated with a set of images commonly relies on feature matches between the images. In contrast, we are the first to address this challenge by using objectness regions to guide the pose estimation problem rather than explicit semantic object detections. We propose Pose Refiner Network (PoserNet) a light-weight Graph Neural Network to refine the approximate pair-wise relative camera poses. PoserNet exploits associations between the objectness regions - concisely expressed as bounding boxes - across multiple views to globally refine sparsely connected view graphs. We evaluate on the 7-Scenes dataset across varied sizes of graphs and show how this process can be beneficial to optimisation-based Motion Averaging algorithms improving the median error on the rotation by 62° with respect to the initial estimates obtained based on bounding boxes. Code and data are available at github.com/IIT-PAVIS/PoserNet.

1 Introduction

A common problem in computer vision is the recovery of multiple camera poses in a common reference frame starting from a set of images, with applications in tasks such as Structure from Motion (SfM), Simultaneous Localisation And Mapping (SLAM) or visual odometry. Traditionally, most solutions rely on the extraction and matching of keypoint features from the images [31]. Those approaches are vulnerable to many factors, such as: changes in viewpoint, illumination, repeated patterns that can lead to mismatches; and the presence of featureless, transparent or reflective surfaces which can result in a scarcity of useful keypoints. Since all these factors commonly occur in real-world scenes, feature-based approaches often rely on extensive refinement steps of the matches, and on outlier rejection methods like RANSAC [8].

This project has received funding from the European Union's Horizon 2020 research and innovation programme under grant agreement No 870743.

Supplementary Information The online version contains supplementary material available at https://doi.org/10.1007/978-3-031-19827-4_15.

S. Avidan et al. (Eds.): ECCV 2022, LNCS 13693, pp. 247–263, 2022.
https://doi.org/10.1007/978-3-031-19827-4_15

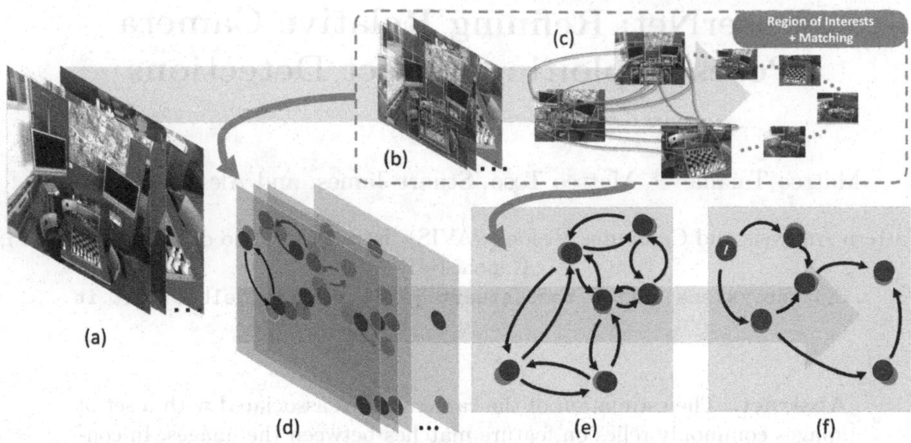

Fig. 1. (a) Our method takes a set of unordered images as input; (b) it detects ROIs; and (c) matches them between frames; (d) ROI & matches are then used to estimate an initial relative pose using 5-point algorithm; (e) the initial poses are refined exploiting the matched detections by PoserNet; and, finally, (f) the refined poses are processed by Motion Averaging to compute absolute poses.

We propose an alternative approach, instead of focusing on keypoints, we leverage on the continuous improvements in object detectors [15,27] to extract the location of potential objects in the images as the basis of our approach. This presents multiple advantages: *i)* detections matching is more reliable; *ii)* working with objects is more efficient than handling tens of thousands of keypoints; and *iii)* for many downstream applications it is convenient to reason in terms of objects present in the scene, rather than 3D points. The use of objects for camera pose estimation, *i.e.* Structure from Motion with Objects (SfMO), has been previously proposed [6,12], however, it relies on a closed-form solution based on multiple disparate views of objects and a simpler camera model that makes its application highly constrained and challenging to apply in the wild.

To overcome the limitation of SfMO and test our object-based assumptions, we propose: *i)* to extract a set of 2D bounding boxes using an objectness detector indicating the probable location of objects of interest; *ii)* to match these detections across images; *iii)* to use them to provide an initial estimate of the relative transformation between each pair of images that contain common scene elements; and *iv)* to exploit the matched detections and rough relative poses to create a view graph, which we then refine via a novel GNN-based architecture called Pose Refinement Network (PoserNet). This allows us to obtain more accurate relative camera poses, which *v)* we then use to recover absolute poses via Motion Averaging algorithms and place camera poses in a common reference frame (as seen in Fig. 1).
To summarise, the contributions of this paper are threefold:

- A GNN-based architecture, PoserNet, that exploits matched region detections to refine rough estimates of the pair-wise camera transformations, producing accurate relative poses;
- we combine the PoserNet module with two paradigms of Motion Averaging algorithms (EIG-SE3 [2] & MultiReg [36]) to estimate absolute camera poses;
- we provide experimental evidence using object detections and keypoints, comparing our method against a state-of-the-art methods for small view-graphs on 7-Scenes.

2 Related Work

Recovering camera poses from a sparse set of images is a well studied problem, especially in the context of SfM, and there are extensive reviews on the topic (see Bianco *et al.* [3]). Similarly, many works discussed in this paper, and our PoserNet model, are based on Graph Neural Networks (GNN). These have recently received a lot of attention, due to their successful applications in many domains, and we point to Wu *et al.* [32] and Zhou *et al.* [37] for an extensive review of GNNs. In this section, we will instead discuss: methods for relative camera pose estimation (Sect. 2.1), as these are the approaches PoserNet aims to improve on; Motion Averaging works (Sect. 2.2), which allow us to evaluate the effects of PoserNet pose refinements; and object-based approaches in 3D Computer Vision (Sect. 2.3), as PoserNet takes as inputs matched object detections.

2.1 Relative Pose Estimation

The most common approach to relative pose estimation is to extract a large number of keypoints, matched across the images, and to apply geometrical methods like Hartley's normalised eight-point algorithm [14], Nistér's five-point algorithm [25] or its simplified implementation introduced by Li and Hartley [17]. This problem is hard in real scenarios, since pixel locations and camera extrinsics can assume a wide range of values, and keypoint matches are noisy and unreliable in many practical application. For this reason, such geometrical methods are typically paired with tools like RANSAC to reduce the impact of outliers. The advancement of deep learning allowed approaching relative pose estimation as a learning problem: Li *et al.* [18] directly trained a deep network to predict the relative pose and orientation between two images, in the context of image relocalisation. Moran *et al.* [21] directly recovered global camera poses from feature matches and a sparse scene reconstruction, minimizing an unsupervised reprojection loss exploiting one encoder equivariant to feature permutations. Cai *et al.* [4] proposed an encoders-based network, with dense correlation volume representation, trained to estimate the relative pose from image pairs via cues like light source directions, vanishing points, and scene symmetries. Alternatively, Neural Radiance Fields for View Synthesis (NeRF) [20] was re-framed by Yen-Chen *et al.* [35] and used for camera pose estimation. Yan *et al.* [33], used a GNN to frame the problem of image retrieval for camera relocalisation as a node binary classification in a subgraph.

Unlike these methods, we suggest that the relative poses estimated via geometrical approaches - which are typically computationally efficient and do not require training - can provide competitive performance, if properly refined. We exemplify this by showing how even rough estimates obtained by applying a standard geometrical method to a small number of loosely matched points (the centres of matched detections) can be refined by our PoserNet.

2.2 Motion Averaging

Given a set of relative poses, there are different approaches to reconstruct absolute poses in a common reference frame (*i.e.* the Motion Averaging or synchronisation problem). Classically, this is done via optimisation algorithms, like the ones of standard global SfM [22], or of Arrigoni *et al.* [2], who proposed a closed-form solution based on spectral decomposition, using an iteratively reweighted Least Squares scheme to reduce the impact of outliers. Recently, Arrigoni *et al.* [1] showed how cycle consistency allows establishing whether a view graph is solvable or not. Lee and Civera [16] proposed a rotation-only Bundle Adjustment (BA) framework, decoupling rotation estimation from translation and scene reconstruction, and Chen *et al.* [5] combined a global optimiser with fast view graph filtering and a local optimiser, improving on the traditional BA loss.

Also in the case of Motion Averaging, there has been a proliferation of deep models, such as NeuRoRA [26], which employed two GNNs to clean the relative camera poses before computing absolute poses. Yang *et al.* [34] introduced an end-to-end neural network for multiple rotation averaging and optimisation. Its view-graph is refined by fusing image context and features to predict outlier rotations, and initialising the rotation averaging process through a differentiable module, that allows outlier refinement at test time. Similarly, Yew and Lee [36] used a GNN to learn transformation synchronisation, but use an iterative approach in the tangent space where each step consists of a single weight-shared message passing layer that refines the absolute poses.

We test the effects of relative pose refinement via PoserNet on one optimisation-based [2] and one deep model [36], as both cases present interesting advantages. Classical methods do not require training, and therefore generalise better to different use cases, and are typically efficient, easy to deploy and well-studied; on the other hand, successfully combining PoserNet with a deep learning method would allow merging them in an end-to-end pipeline. While PoserNet shares some similarities with methods like [26], we focus on refining the relative poses before the Motion Averaging task, providing better inputs. Moreover, our method reasons about all relative poses of the graph while also exploiting bounding box information usually not used by models like [26] (*e.g.* the location of the object detections).

2.3 Object-Based Computer Vision

One of our key insight is the use of object locations instead of generic keypoints, as initial step of the camera pose reconstruction process. Other works have already suggested reasoning about the world in terms of object detections: Rubino *et al.* [28] proposed a closed-form solution for estimating the 3D occupancy of an object, from multiview 2D object detections, and Gaudilliere *et al.* [9] used a similar representation to show how, in a scene represented as a collection of ellipsoids, a single ellipse-ellipsoid match and an approximate orientation from IMUs or vanishing point algorithms is enough to recover the camera location. They later [10] showed how, given two ellipse-ellipsoid correspondences, the camera rotation is recovered via an optimisation problem over the three Euler angles. The problem can then be further simplified [11], reducing it to an optimisation over a single angle by introducing constraints satisfied in many real world applications, *i.e.* that the images have null azimuth angle, and that the segment connecting the centres of the ellipsoids projects on the one connecting the centres of the detected ellipses.

In the context of object-level SLAM, notable contributions include Fusion++ [19], which combines Microsoft Fusion's [23] TSDF and instance segmentation for indoor scene understanding; or SLAM++ [29], which implements real-time object detection, tracking and mapping in a dense RGB-D framework, but requires a database of well defined 3D models of the objects; or QuadricSLAM [24], which uses noisy odometry and object detections (as bounding boxes) to simultaneously estimate camera poses and objects locations, expressed as ellipsoids.

Unlike the aforementioned methods, we do not use a specific parameterisation of the objects shape (*e.g.* ellipsoid), and only rely on the approximate location of generic ROIs. Moreover, our method can be seen as complementary to theirs, as in principle we could take the bounding boxes associated with our ROIs, and the camera poses produced by combining PoserNet with a Motion Averaging approach, and use one of the approaches to localise the scene elements in 3D. Regarding SLAM methods, a direct comparison is not possible, as our approach is aimed at scenes with large camera baseline displacement and sparsely connected view-graphs, with minimal overlapping views.

3 Methodology

Our approach takes as input an unordered set of images $\{I_i\}$, $i \in [1, ..., N]$ and their respective camera matrix intrinsics (K_i). We then aim to reconstruct the extrinsics $M_i = [R_i|t_i]$, with rotation $R_i \in SO(3)$ *i.e.* Special Orthogonal Group, and translation $t_i \in \mathbb{R}^3$ that map from the world reference frame to the camera reference frame (as shown in Fig. 1). Firstly we detect ROIs within I_i, then we perform matching between ROIs and in turn solve for an initial estimate of the pairwise problem (Sect. 3.1). The ROIs represented as bounding boxes (BB) and the initial estimates are then passed to our PoserNet module to refine the relative poses (Sect. 3.2). Finally, the refined relative poses are processed by a rotation averaging method, which computes the absolute poses estimates of the cameras (Sect. 3.3).

3.1 Objectness, Matching and Initial Poses

For each image, we compute a set of bounding boxes $bb_{i,a}$, $a \in [1, ..., 50]$ which represent the top most confident ROIs candidates for objects. We opt for ROIs instead of the explicit object detections, as we make no assumption on semantic classes and they provide bounding boxes even in scenes with few objects. We use the *objectness*-based detector, Object Localisation Network (OLN) [15]. OLN is a generalisation of common detectors, substituting the classification layer (object semantic class) with a localisation confidence and trained in a weakly supervised manner relying on intersection over union and centreness.

Once we have a set of bounding boxes for each image, we then match them to obtain tracks of detections across the multi-view images. The matching of bounding boxes, or their image patches, between images is in a non-trivial problem, therefore we treat it as a black-box task. For simplicity, we solve the matching problem by applying the pre-trained SuperGlue model [30], which can be replaced by any matching approach. From the matches we construct a view graph, two images are considered connected if they share at least five matched ROIs. In addition, only images that are connected to at least another image are used in the graph, and the graph is built so that its connections form a chain that passes through all N images. This is necessary to ensure that the set of images and their matches constitute a solvable problem, in which no image view is completely disconnected from the others.

For each connected pair of images I_i, I_j, we estimate the relative transformation mapping from one image to the other, *i.e.* $\hat{R}_{i,j}$ and translation $\hat{t}_{i,j}$ that satisfy: $\hat{R}_{i,j} = R_j R_i^T$ and $\hat{t}_{i,j} = t_j - R_j^T t_i$. We compute the relative transformation using the 5-point algorithm and RANSAC. We experiment using both BB centres, which are sensitive to the quality of the BB detection, and SuperGlue keypoint matches within the region, which are sensitive to mismatches.

3.2 PoserNet: Graph-Based Relative Camera Pose Refinement

We define the PoserNet Graph Neural Network (GNN) as a special case of a multi-layer GNN, with shared edges representing the relative transformations and a partly shared node encoding. Therefore, we first review a general formulation of GNNs and then we describe our directed GNN with matched detections.

General Graph Neural Networks: The standard GNN formulation employs a graph $\mathcal{G} = \langle N, E \rangle$, representing a structure of nodes $N = \{N_1 \dots N_p\}$ and edges $E = \{E_1 \dots E_q\}$. Each N_i or E_i has an embedding (h_i^N, h_i^E) representing its latent information, which can be initialised based on *a priori* information (*e.g.* relative poses). The representations are then updated independently via a combination of message passing, nonlinear update functions ($\Psi^N(\cdot)$ and $\Psi^E(\cdot)$) and aggregation functions. Each update constitutes a step (k) of the graph. The message m^N between nodes from j to i, for step (k), is defined as:

$$m_{i,j,k}^N = \Psi^N(h_{i,k}^N, h_{j,k}^N, h_{i,j,k}^E). \tag{1}$$

To update N_i, a message is computed for all its neighbouring nodes $j \in \mathcal{N}_i$. Finally, the aggregation function averages the incoming messages to produce the latent information for node i for the $(k+1)^{th}$ iteration:

$$h_{i,k+1}^N \leftarrow \frac{1}{|\mathcal{N}_i|} \sum_{j \in \mathcal{N}_i} m_{i,j,k}^N. \quad (2)$$

Edges are updated in a similar fashion by applying a nonlinear transformation ($\Psi^E(\cdot)$) to information from the neighbour nodes and from their current latent space, *i.e.* $h_{i,j,k+1}^E \leftarrow m_{i,j,k}^E = \Psi^E(h_{i,k}^N, h_{j,k}^N, h_{i,j,k}^E)$. The formulation can be generalised to multi-layer graphs simply by connecting nodes across layers and having a custom (or repeating) $\mathcal{G}$ topography for each layer.

PoserNet: The Pose Refinement network (PoserNet) takes as input a graph which contains the noisy relative camera poses obtained via pairwise geometry estimation (Sect. 3.1) to initialise its edges, and it outputs a graph with the same topology, but having refined estimates for the same relative poses. Therefore, PoserNet is a special case of the multi-layer GNN paradigm. At its simplest, it works on a graph representing an enriched version of the view graph of a scene, however, across layers of matched detections $l = \{l_1 \dots l_r\}$, with a shared node encoding (h^N), and with a shared edge representation (h^E). See Fig. 2 for a graphical representation of the structure of such a graph.

Specifically, PoserNet works on a graph in which nodes (N_i) represent camera poses, while directed edges ($E_{i,j}$) represent pairwise relative camera poses. Each node is associated with one of the input images, I_i. It contains the corresponding intrinsic camera parameters and it is associated with the list of bounding boxes detected on that image, arranged as layers. The embedding for a detection consists of the normalised information on the BB location, height, and width: $bb_{i,l} \in \mathbb{R}^4$. Detections from different nodes are connected pairwise when matched (*i.e.* they represent the same object in multi-view), where matched detections are represented as logical layers in the graph. Edge $E_{i,j}$ exists in the graph only if nodes N_i and N_j have at least one detection in common. For the message passing, the Ψ functions are implemented as a multi-layer perception (MLP).

Edge Representation and Update: The relative camera transformations are encoded in the edges as a translation vector plus a quaternion: $h_{i,j}^E \in \mathbb{R}^7$. We encode the transformation induced by traversing the edge in one, specified, direction, and we enforce that the transformation observed by traversing the edge in the opposite direction is the inverse of that transformation. Updating the edge representation requires creating one message per active layer ($l \in \mathcal{N}_l$), based on a pair of matched detections at its sides. Thus, for PoserNet the message is enriched in contrast to traditional GNNs, as it takes as additional input the representations of a pair of detections. A message is defined as:

$$m_{i,j,k,l}^E = \Psi^E(h_{i,k}^N, h_{j,k}^N, h_{i,j,k}^E, bb_{i,l}, bb_{j,l}), \quad (3)$$

and the updated representation for the edge is computed as the average of the messages for all layers: $h_{i,j,k+1}^E \leftarrow \frac{1}{|\mathcal{N}_l|} \sum_{l \in \mathcal{N}_l} m_{i,j,k,l}^E$.

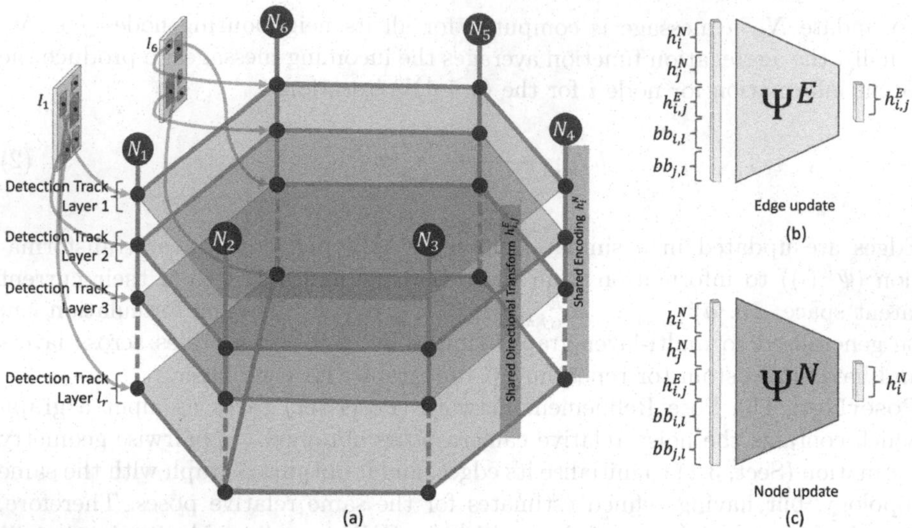

Fig. 2. (a) The structure of graphs processed by PoserNet. Each image I_i is associated with a node N_i where the corresponding edges are relative transformations. Each set of corresponding detections (orange lines) between nodes refers to a layer of the graph for message passing (Detection track). (b) Nodes and (c) edges are updated by passing through $\Psi(\cdot)$ the node and edge information and respective bounding boxes (bb) for a given layer. (Color figure online)

Node Representation and Update: The information contained in each node consists of image height and width, the camera focal length and the first coefficient of radial distortion, all normalised: $h_i^n \in \mathbb{R}^4$. For updating the latent representation of a node in PoserNet, each of its neighbours can send not just one, but a set of messages, each of which corresponds to a layer with a matched pair of detections. A message is defined as:

$$m^N_{i,j,k,l} = \Psi^N(h^N_{i,k}, h^N_{j,k}, h^E_{i,j,k}, bb_{i,l}, bb_{j,l}), \tag{4}$$

and the updated representation for the node is computed as the average of the messages from all of its neighbours ($j \in \mathcal{N}_i$), for all layers ($l \in \mathcal{N}_l$):

$$h^N_{i,j,k+1} \leftarrow \frac{1}{|\mathcal{N}_j|} \sum_{j \in \mathcal{N}_j} \frac{1}{|\mathcal{N}_l|} \sum_{l \in \mathcal{N}_l} m^N_{i,j,k,l}. \tag{5}$$

This message-passing and data processing scheme is repeated a fixed number of times (one of the hyperparameters of GNNs), and it finally produces the output edge embeddings which represent the refined estimates for inter-camera pose transformations. During this process, the embedding on the nodes and edges are updated, but the information relative to bounding boxes is kept constant.

Loss Function: PoserNet is trained using graphs for which the relative transformations between camera poses are known. The loss function comprises four components: the first and second component drive the network to produce accurate estimates for the relative poses:

$$\mathcal{L}_{orient} = \angle(q^*_{GT} \circ q_{est}), \tag{6}$$

$$\mathcal{L}_{tr\_dir} = \angle(tr_{GT}, tr_{est}). \tag{7}$$

The orientation loss, $\mathcal{L}_{orient}$, encodes the angle between ($\angle$) the ground-truth and the estimated quaternion, where $\circ$ represents quaternion composition, and q^*_{GT} is the conjugate of the ground-truth quaternion. The translation direction loss, $\mathcal{L}_{tr\_dir}$, encodes the angle between ground-truth (tr_{GT}) and estimated translation vectors. The remaining two components are the quaternion normalisation loss, $\mathcal{L}_{q||}$, and the translation normalisation loss, $\mathcal{L}_{tr||}$. They push the network towards producing unit norm outputs:

$$\mathcal{L}_{q||} = |\|q_{est}\| - 1|, \tag{8}$$

$$\mathcal{L}_{tr||} = |\|tr_{est}\| - 1|. \tag{9}$$

The total loss function of PoserNet is defined as:

$$\mathcal{L}_{PoserNet} = \mathcal{L}_{orient} + \mathcal{L}_{tr\_dir} + \alpha(\mathcal{L}_{q||} + \mathcal{L}_{tr||}), \tag{10}$$

where α is a coefficient used to tune the strength of the contribution of the different components of the loss.

3.3 Absolute Pose Estimation

The relative poses refined by PoserNet can be used to compute absolute camera poses; for this, we look at State-of-the-Art methods for two common approaches: optimisation and deep learning. With the former, we want to show how modern convolution techniques can improve "classical" approaches, while combining PoserNet with a deep-learning model could lead to an end-to-end pipeline.

EIG-SE3 [2]: This method solves the Motion Averaging problem in closed-form using spectral decomposition. Given a fully connected graph with n nodes, and accurate estimates of the relative and absolute transformations between the cameras expressed as:

$$M_{i,j} = \begin{pmatrix} R_{i,j} & t_{i,j} \\ 0 & 1 \end{pmatrix}, M_i = \begin{pmatrix} R_i & t_i \\ 0 & 1 \end{pmatrix}, \tag{11}$$

with $M_{i,j} \in SE(3)$, $SE(3)$ the Special Euclidean Group (3), the absolute camera poses $M_i \in SE(3)$, with $M_{i,j} = M_i M_j^{-1}$, can be recovered solving the problem $\mathbf{XM} = n\mathbf{M}$, where $\mathbf{M}$ is the $4n \times 4$ matrix obtained concatenating all matrices M_i and $\mathbf{X}$ is a block matrix with block $i, j = M_{i,j}$.

If the relative transformations are exact, this problem can be solved in closed form in two steps: *i)* the columns of M are four eigenvectors of $\mathbf{X}$ associated with the eigenvalue n, found as the 4-dimensional basis of the null-space of

$L = (n\mathbf{I}_{4n} - \mathbf{X})$; *ii)* the basis found at the previous point is not guaranteed to be composed of Euclidean motions, *i.e.* it is not guaranteed that each 4×4 block belongs to SE(3). This is addressed by extracting every fourth row of M and finding the change of basis that maps them to $[0, 0, 0, 1]$.

In the original work, the authors show how this approach can be generalised to problems with noisy relative transformation, by solving the Least Squares problem $\min_{M \in SE(3)} ||LM||_F^2$. They also extend the approach to work on graphs that are not fully connected - *i.e.* some of the off-diagonal blocks of $\mathbf{X}$ are zero - and show how the optimisation problem can be included in an iteratively reweighted Least Squares scheme to reduce the impact of outliers, which are a common occurrence in most camera pose estimation applications. See [2] for a full description of the optimisation algorithm.

MultiReg: computes incremental pose updates within tangent space to ensure that poses remain on the SO(3) or SE(3) manifold. Like PoserNet, a GNN is used where, however, nodes represent camera poses and the edges represent transformations, $\mathcal{G}_a = \langle N_a, E_a \rangle$. In addition, only the absolute pose and a latent representation is updated on a node, with no edge update. To achieve this each increment ϵ_i is computed from the pose residuals $\Gamma_{i,j} = T_i T_j^{-1} \hat{T}_{i,j}^{-1}$ based on the current absolute pose and the latent encoding (h^N) stored in the node. Therefore each update is equivalent to:

$$\left(\epsilon_i, \Delta h_i^N\right) \leftarrow \Psi^N(h_i^N, u, \Psi^E(h_i^N, h_j^N \Gamma_{i,j})), \tag{12}$$

where Ψ^N and Ψ^E are MLPs and u is a global encoding from average pooling of f over the graph. The transform update is therefore $T_i \leftarrow \exp(\hat{\epsilon}_i) T_i$ which corresponds to addition in Euclidean space for Lie Groups. Finally, similar to pair-wise we compute the loss based on the decomposed rotation and translation.

$$\mathcal{L}_{abs} = \frac{1}{|\epsilon^c|} \sum_{(i,j) \in \epsilon^c} \left(\left| R_{i,j} - R_{i,j}^{GT} \right| + \lambda_t \left| t_{i,j} - t_{i,j}^{GT} \right| \right). \tag{13}$$

4 Experiments

In this section, we provide an evaluation of the proposed PoserNet model. We validate our choice of PoserNet structure (*i.e.* depth, choice of training data), and show how PoserNet can improve the accuracy of relative pose estimation. We then investigate the effects of this refinement on Motion Averaging. As an implementation detail, PoserNet partially relies on PyTorch Geometric (PyG) [7].

For each experiment we report separately the error on the camera rotation and the translation error; the former is expressed in degrees, while the translation is reported in meters for absolute poses and in degrees for relative poses. This is due to the fact that relative poses are defined up to a scale, and we therefore report the angular distance between the ground-truth and the estimated translation unit vector. These results are expressed in form of the median error η (the smaller the better) and as the percentage of testing graphs with and

Table 1. Composition of the small and large graph datasets used to validate the proposed method. The different graph-building strategies result in large graphs which have a higher (18-fold higher) connectivity than the small graphs.

Dataset part	Graphs	Nodes	Edges	Nodes/graph	Edges/graph	Edges/node
Small graphs, train	14000	112000	215790	8	15.4	1.9
Small graphs, test	7000	56000	110367	8	15.8	2.0
Large graphs, train	5	625	22674	125	4534.8	36.3
Large graphs, test	5	625	22606	125	4521.2	36.2

average error smaller than predefined thresholds (the higher the better). Such thresholds are 3, 5, 10, 30 and 45 degrees for the angular metrics, and 0.05, 0.1, 0.25, 0.5 and 0.75 for errors expressed in meters. For all experiments that required training network, we trained three separate models and report their average performance, with their standard deviation.

4.1 Dataset

For our experiments, we use graphs built from the 7-Scenes [13]: this is a collection of $41k$ images acquired in seven small-sized indoor environments with a Microsoft Kinect. The RGB-D information has been used to compute accurate ground-truth camera poses. For each scene, several sequences were recorded by different users, and they are split into distinct training and testing sequence sets. Starting from 7-Scenes data, we created two datasets comprising graphs of different sizes: a small graphs dataset and a larger graph dataset. In each case, we followed the split between training and test data or the original work.

Small Graphs Dataset: It contains 8-node graphs. For each scene we created $2k$ graphs from the training sequences, and $1k$ from the test ones. Each graph was created by randomly selecting eight images that satisfy the connectivity constraints outlined in Sect. 3.1. We thus ensure that all graph nodes are connected, while not requiring the graph to be fully connected.

Large Graphs Dataset: The graphs are generated sampling, for each scene, 125 frames from the aggregated training or testing sequences. In this case, we do not explicitly enforce a connectivity constraint, because the limited size of the scenes and the large number of nodes guarantee a large number of connected edges. We extracted only one training and one testing graphs from the first five scenes, due to the difficulty in identifying large graphs.

4.2 PoserNet Refining Relative Poses

We present an analysis designed to assess the effectiveness of PoserNet in refining relative camera poses. We first show how PoserNet successfully improves relative poses provided by different initialisation algorithms, and secondly how PoserNet generalises well to graphs of different sizes. In Supplementary Material we discuss the impact of choosing different depths for PoserNet's GNN, we identify a depth of 2 as the best and we use it throughout the remaining experiments.

Refining Relative Poses from Different Initialisation Modes: We assessed the effectiveness of PoserNet in refining the relative pose estimates initialised from bounding box centres (BB) and keypoints (KP), as discussed in Sect. 3.1. We evaluate the PoserNet model on the small graphs dataset as shown in Table 2. In both cases we see a significant performance gain, with median rotation error reduction of over 76° and 28° for the BB and KP cases respectively, and an improvement of over 42° and 72° for the translation median angular error. This confirms PoserNet's effectiveness at refining relative poses generated by different algorithms, with different levels of noise.

Dealing with Graphs of Different Sizes: We explore the impact of using the large and small graphs to train and test PoserNet. The results are summarised in Table 3. For each test set, we provide the baseline errors of the unrefined graphs, and the performances of models trained on either the large graph or small graph dataset. From the results, we make three observations. First, we verify that PoserNet is effective at refining relative poses: models trained on either small or large graphs and tested on the corresponding test set achieve a significant accuracy improvement over the baseline. Second, we see that PoserNet has good generalisation capabilities: the pose refinement performance generalises quite well when training on one dataset, *e.g.* small graphs, and testing on large graphs. Finally, we observe that models trained on small graphs perform better, while testing on large graphs leads to more accurate estimates.

Generalisation to Unseen Graphs: To test the ability of our method to generalise to novel scenes, we evaluate PoserNet's performance on relative pose refinement for 8-node graphs using a leave-one-out scheme. This is done evaluating on each of the seven scenes of the dataset a model trained only on the other six scenes. The results of this test, reported in the Supplementary Material, show median orientation and translation orientation errors of 8.04° and 19.75° respectively, comparable with the performance on the full dataset (7.31° and 14.54°).

4.3 Absolute Pose Estimates

The last experiments show the impact of PoserNet on the motion averaging task (*i.e.* extract absolute camera poses from the relative ones). We consider two possible approaches: a modern, graph-network based model (MultiReg); and an optimisation-based algorithm (EIG-SE3). Results for both Motion Averaging approaches are reported in Table 4, using the same notation of previous experiments. However, since the Motion Averaging process reintroduces the scale of the translation vector, the error on the translations is reported as the Euclidean distance between the ground-truth and estimated vectors, expressed in meters.

Table 2. PoserNet performances in refining relative pose computed from the centres of matched bounding boxes (BB) or from a standard keypoints approach (KP). For both cases, the initial orientation and translation direction error are improved by PoserNet processing.

Input		Orientation error (deg)						Translation direction error (deg)					
		3	5	10	30	45	η	3	5	10	30	45	η
BB	Initial	0.00	0.00	0.00	0.16	1.44	96.48	0.00	0.00	0.00	0.00	0.00	89.30
	PoserNet	0.00 ±0.00	0.00 ±0.00	0.74 ±0.14	88.18 ±0.28	99.02 ±0.02	20.39 ±0.20	0.00 ±0.00	0.00 ±0.00	0.00 ±0.00	7.92 ±0.25	45.63 ±0.43	46.60 ±0.14
KP	Initial	0.74	4.01	11.16	41.46	62.53	36.26	0.00	0.03	0.10	1.37	5.49	87.23
	PoserNet	1.13 ±0.11	17.24 ±0.86	78.19 ±1.36	98.78 ±0.02	99.86 ±0.01	7.31 ±0.11	0.01 ±0.01	1.42 ±0.28	27.67 ±0.70	80.07 ±0.31	90.01 ±0.68	14.54 ±0.14

Table 3. PoserNet performances when trained and evaluated on small (Small) or large (Large) graphs. While versions of PoserNet trained on either largely outperform the baseline error (Raw), models trained on small give the best performances on both testing datasets. (Highlighted in bold).

Train	Test	Orientation error (deg)						Translation direction error (deg)					
		3	5	10	30	45	η	3	5	10	30	45	η
Raw	Small	0.74	4.01	11.16	41.46	62.53	36.26	0.00	0.03	0.10	1.37	5.49	87.23
Small	Small	1.13 ±0.11	17.24 ±0.86	78.19 ±1.36	98.78 ±0.02	99.86 ±0.01	**7.31** ±0.11	0.01 ±0.01	1.42 ±0.28	27.67 ±0.70	80.07 ±0.31	90.01 ±0.68	**14.54** ±0.14
Large	Small	0.00 ±0.00	0.04 ±0.03	13.26 ±5.55	96.98 ±0.37	99.61 ±0.09	13.97 ±0.94	0.00 ±0.00	0.00 ±0.00	0.11 ±0.10	57.19 ±5.72	81.26 ±1.16	27.56 ±2.02
Raw	Large	0.00	0.00	0.00	20.00	60.00	37.70	0.00	0.00	0.00	0.00	0.00	79.60
Small	Large	0.00 ±0.00	0.00 ±0.00	80.0 ±0.00	100.00 ±0.00	100.00 ±0.00	**6.85** ±0.11	0.00 ±0.00	0.00 ±0.00	20.00 ±0.00	100.00 ±0.00	100.00 ±0.00	**12.62** ±0.48
Large	Large	0.00 ±0.00	0.00 ±0.00	13.33 ±9.43	100.00 ±0.00	100.00 ±0.00	12.11 ±1.10	0.00 ±0.00	0.00 ±0.00	0.00 ±0.00	100.00 ±0.00	100.00 ±0.00	21.58 ±1.36

Table 4. Motion averaging performances on the 7-Scenes dataset using the Multi-Reg and EIG-SE3 algorithms. We report results for different initialisation methods: bounding box centres (BB) and keypoints (KP).

Model	Init	Orientation error (deg)						Translation error (meters)					
		3	5	10	30	45	η	0.05	0.1	0.25	0.5	0.75	η
MultiReg	BB	0.60 ±0.00	2.10 ±0.00	8,10 ±0.10	47.60 ±0.53	69.13 ±0.47	31.37 ±0.30	0.50 ±0.00	1.47 ±0.06	6.93 ±0.12	23.03 ±0.70	40.80 ±0.85	0.89 ±0.01
	KP	10.23 ±0.12	24.23 ±0.25	39.7 ±0.40	67.97 ±0.06	79.90 ±0.00	**15.69** ±0.08	1.00 ±0.00	3.77 ±0.06	17.77 ±0.12	40.30 ±0.17	57.23 ±0.06	**0.64** ±0.01
MultiReg + PoserNet	BB	0.50 ±0.00	1.60 ±0.00	6.10 ±0.10	41.03 ±0.42	62.50 ±0.14	35.60 ±0.33	0.60 ±0.00	1.50 ±0.00	6.53 ±0.06	21.60 ±0.00	39.33 ±0.06	0.91 ±0.00
	KP	0.50 ±0.00	1.63 ±0.06	6.20 ±0.10	40.90 ±0.44	62.60 ±0.53	35.73 ±0.37	0.60 ±0.00	1.50 ±0.00	6.40 ±0.10	21.43 ±0.12	39.23 ±0.12	0.91 ±0.00
EIG-SE3	BB	0.00	0.00	0.09	2.46	7.84	78.46	0.00	0.00	0.00	0.57	13.47	0.65
	KP	11.99	23.87	34.49	57.59	62.09	25.37	0.00	0.06	2.63	31.39	74.40	0.61
EIG-SE3 + PoserNet	BB	0.00	0.09	10.36	88.00	94.06	15.80	0.00	0.00	7.54	46.80	83.23	0.52
	KP	15.56	48.36	82.14	93.14	5.69	**5.10**	0.04	1.94	34.51	76.43	94.49	**0.32**

Motion Averaging via MultiReg: In the case of MultiReg, the refinement of the relative poses via PoserNet does not improve the performance, leading instead to larger errors. Specifically, refining the poses makes the orientation and translation errors respectively 4.2° and 0.02 m worse in the case of BB initialisation, and 20° and 0.27 m worse in the case of KP initialisation.

While this performance is disappointing, it is not completely unexpected. Firstly, the original MultiReg model was tested on large, very connected graphs, which means its structure and parameters might not be well-suited for our small graph dataset. On the other hand, the MultiReg model is too complex to be trained only on our limited large graph dataset. Moreover, [36] discarded as outliers all edges initialised with a rotation error larger than 15° and a translation error of more than 15 cm, which makes our initial error condition very challenging in comparison.

Motion Averaging via EIG-SE3: Finally, we show the performance gain obtained by combining PoserNet with a closed-form approach to solve Motion Averaging, the EIG-SE3. Unlike MultiReg, this approach does not require training, making it easier to deploy and more general. Given the deterministic nature of this model, we report results of only one evaluation run.

Results of this experiment are reported in the bottom two rows of Table 4; in this case, PoserNet results in improvement over the baseline error for both the BB and KP initialisation modes. In the BB case, the median error on the rotation improves by 62°, and in the KP case the orientation error is reduced by 20°. Performance on the translation are also clearly noticeable, with an improvement of 0.13 m and 0.29 m for the BB and KP initialisation respectively.

5 Conclusions

We have proposed the novel PoserNet module for relative pose refinement driven by matched detections, based on ROIs generated from objectness-based detectors. We have shown that such ROIs are sufficient to recover accurate camera poses, with a large improvement with respect to the initial pair-wise estimates. In addition, we have shown how PoserNet can improve the outcome of the optimisation-based Motion Averaging EIG-SE3. The proposed model is a relatively simple and fast network relying on sparse object detections (in contrast to keypoints) and relatively lightweight bounding box representation. Therefore, the combination with a 'classical' geometric approach, such as EIG-SE3, yields increased performance compared to the more complex state-of-the-art networks like MultiReg. While the lack of improvement in combination with MultiReg highlights a challenge of deep learning methods being able to generalise to other scenarios outside of their initial design. We point to this limitation as a direction for future work, which could result in a generalised Motion Averaging method as flexible as optimisation methods and able to incorporate specific elements such as PoserNet for task or domain-specific improvement.

References

1. Arrigoni, F., Fusiello, A., Ricci, E., Pajdla, T.: Viewing graph solvability via cycle consistency. In: Proceedings of the IEEE/CVF International Conference on Computer Vision (ICCV), pp. 5540–5549, October 2021
2. Arrigoni, F., Rossi, B., Fusiello, A.: Spectral synchronization of multiple views in SE(3). SIAM J. Imag. Sci. **9**(4), 1963–1990 (2016)
3. Bianco, S., Ciocca, G., Marelli, D.: Evaluating the performance of structure from motion pipelines. J. Imaging **4**(8), 98 (2018)
4. Cai, R., Hariharan, B., Snavely, N., Averbuch-Elor, H.: Extreme rotation estimation using dense correlation volumes. In: IEEE/CVF Conference on Computer Vision and Pattern Recognition (CVPR) (2021)
5. Chen, Y., Zhao, J., Kneip, L.: Hybrid rotation averaging: a fast and robust rotation averaging approach. In: 2021 IEEE/CVF Conference on Computer Vision and Pattern Recognition (CVPR), pp. 10353–10362 (2021)
6. Crocco, M., Rubino, C., Del Bue, A.: Structure from motion with objects. In: Proceedings of the IEEE Conference on Computer Vision and Pattern Recognition, pp. 4141–4149 (2016)
7. Fey, M., Lenssen, J.E.: Fast graph representation learning with PyTorch Geometric. In: ICLR Workshop on Representation Learning on Graphs and Manifolds (2019)
8. Fischler, M.A., Bolles, R.C.: Random sample consensus: a paradigm for model fitting with applications to image analysis and automated cartography. Commun. ACM **24**(6), 381–395 (1981)
9. Gaudilliere, V., Simon, G., Berger, M.: Camera relocalization with ellipsoidal abstraction of objects. In: 2019 IEEE International Symposium on Mixed and Augmented Reality (ISMAR), Los Alamitos, CA, USA, October 2019. IEEE Computer Society (2019)
10. Gaudillière, V., Simon, G., Berger, M.-O.: Camera pose estimation with semantic 3d model. In: 2019 IEEE/RSJ International Conference on Intelligent Robots and Systems (IROS), pp. 4569–4576 (2019)
11. Gaudillière, V., Simon, G., Berger, M.-O.: Perspective-2-ellipsoid: bridging the gap between object detections and 6-DoF camera pose. IEEE Robot. Autom. Lett. **5**(4), 5189–5196 (2020)
12. Gay, P., Rubino, C., Bansal, V., Del Bue, A.: Probabilistic structure from motion with objects (PSfMO). In: Proceedings of the IEEE International Conference on Computer Vision, pp. 3075–3084 (2017)
13. Glocker, B., Izadi, S., Shotton, J., Criminisi, A.: Real-time RGB-D camera relocalization. In: International Symposium on Mixed and Augmented Reality (ISMAR). IEEE, October 2013
14. Hartley, R.I.: In defense of the eight-point algorithm. IEEE Trans. Pattern Anal. Mach. Intell. **19**(6), 580–593 (1997)
15. Kim, D., Lin, T.-Y., Angelova, A., Kweon, I.S., Kuo, W.: Learning open-world object proposals without learning to classify. IEEE Robot. Autom. Lett. (RA-L) **7**, 5453–5460 (2022)
16. Lee, S.H., Civera, J.: Rotation-only bundle adjustment. In: Proceedings of the IEEE/CVF Conference on Computer Vision and Pattern Recognition (CVPR), June 2021
17. Li, H., Hartley, R.: Five-point motion estimation made easy. In: Proceedings of the 18th International Conference on Pattern Recognition, ICPR 2006, USA, vol. 01, pp. 630–633. IEEE Computer Society (2006)

18. Li, Q., et al.: Relative geometry-aware Siamese neural network for 6DoF camera relocalization. Neurocomputing **426**, 134–146 (2021)
19. McCormac, J., Clark, R., Bloesch, M., Davison, A.J., Leutenegger, S.: Fusion++: volumetric object-level slam (2018)
20. Mildenhall, B., Srinivasan, P.P., Tancik, M., Barron, J.T., Ramamoorthi, R., Ng, R.: NeRF: representing scenes as neural radiance fields for view synthesis. In: Vedaldi, A., Bischof, H., Brox, T., Frahm, J.-M. (eds.) ECCV 2020. LNCS, vol. 12346, pp. 405–421. Springer, Cham (2020). https://doi.org/10.1007/978-3-030-58452-8_24
21. Moran, D., Koslowsky, H., Kasten, Y., Maron H., Galun, M., Basri, R.: Deep permutation equivariant structure from motion (2021)
22. Moulon, P., Monasse, P., Perrot, R., Marlet, R.: OpenMVG: open multiple view geometry. In: Kerautret, B., Colom, M., Monasse, P. (eds.) RRPR 2016. LNCS, vol. 10214, pp. 60–74. Springer, Cham (2017). https://doi.org/10.1007/978-3-319-56414-2_5
23. Newcombe, R.A., et al.: KinectFusion: real-time dense surface mapping and tracking. In: 2011 IEEE International Symposium on Mixed and Augmented Reality (ISMAR) (2011)
24. Nicholson, L., Milford, M., Sunderhauf, N.: QuadricSLAM: dual quadrics from object detections as landmarks in object-oriented slam. IEEE Robot. Autom. Lett. **4**, 1–8 (2018)
25. Nistér, D.: An efficient solution to the five-point relative pose problem. IEEE Trans. Pattern Anal. Mach. Intell. **26**(6), 756–770 (2004)
26. Purkait, P., Chin, T.-J., Reid, I.: NeuRoRA: neural robust rotation averaging. In: Vedaldi, A., Bischof, H., Brox, T., Frahm, J.-M. (eds.) ECCV 2020. LNCS, vol. 12369, pp. 137–154. Springer, Cham (2020). https://doi.org/10.1007/978-3-030-58586-0_9
27. Ren, S., He, K., Girshick, R., Sun, J.: Faster R-CNN: towards real-time object detection with region proposal networks. In: Advances in Neural Information Processing Systems (NIPS) (2015)
28. Rubino, C., Crocco, M., Del Bue, A.: 3d object localization from multi-view image detections. IEEE Trans. Pattern Anal. Mach. Intell. (TPAMI) **40**, 1281–1294 (2017)
29. Salas-Moreno, R.F., Newcombe, R.A., Strasdat, H., Kelly, P.H.J., Davison, A.J.: Slam++: simultaneous localisation and mapping at the level of objects. In: Conference on Computer Vision and Pattern Recognition (CVPR) (2013)
30. Sarlin, P.-E., DeTone, D., Malisiewicz, T., Rabinovich, A.: SuperGlue: learning feature matching with graph neural networks. In: CVPR (2020)
31. Schönberger, J.L., Frahm., J.-M.: Structure-from-motion revisited. In: Conference on Computer Vision and Pattern Recognition (CVPR) (2016)
32. Wu, Z., Pan, S., Chen, F., Long, G., Zhang, C., Yu, P.S.: A comprehensive survey on graph neural networks. IEEE Trans. Neural Netw. Learn. Syst. **32**, 4–24 (2021)
33. Yan, S., Pen, Y., Lai, S., Liu, Y., Zhang, M.: Image retrieval for structure-from-motion via graph convolutional network. CoRR, abs/2009.08049 (2020)
34. Yang, L., Li, H., Rahim, J.A., Cui, Z., Tan, P.: End-to-end rotation averaging with multi-source propagation. In: Proceedings of the IEEE/CVF Conference on Computer Vision and Pattern Recognition (CVPR), pp. 11774–11783, June 2021
35. Yen-Chen, L., Florence, P., Barron, J.T., Rodriguez, A., Isola, P., Lin, T.-Y.: iNeRF: inverting neural radiance fields for pose estimation. In: IEEE/RSJ International Conference on Intelligent Robots and Systems (IROS) (2021)

36. Yew, Z.J., Lee, G.H.: Learning iterative robust transformation synchronization. In: International Conference on 3D Vision (3DV) (2021)
37. Zhou, J., et al.: Graph neural networks: a review of methods and applications. AI Open **1**, 57–81 (2020)

Gaussian Activated Neural Radiance Fields for High Fidelity Reconstruction and Pose Estimation

Shin-Fang Chng(✉), Sameera Ramasinghe, Jamie Sherrah, and Simon Lucey

Australian Institute for Machine Learning, University of Adelaide, Adelaide, Australia
{shinfang.chng,sameera.ramasinghe,jamie.sherrah,
simon.lucey}@adelaide.edu.au

Abstract. Despite Neural Radiance Fields (NeRF) showing compelling results in photorealistic novel views synthesis of real-world scenes, most existing approaches require accurate prior camera poses. Although approaches for jointly recovering the radiance field and camera pose exist, they rely on a cumbersome coarse-to-fine auxiliary positional embedding to ensure good performance. We present Gaussian Activated Neural Radiance Fields (GARF), a new positional embedding-free neural radiance field architecture – employing Gaussian activations – that is competitive with the current state-of-the-art in terms of high fidelity reconstruction and pose estimation.

Keywords: Neural scene representation · Joint scene reconstruction and pose estimation · Coordinate network · View synthesis · 3D deep learning

1 Introduction

Recent work by Lin *et al.* [12] – Bundle Adjusted Neural Radiance Fields (BARF) – revealed that an architecturally-modified Neural Radiance Field (NeRF) [18] could effectively solve the joint task of scene reconstruction and pose optimization. One crucial insight from this work is that the error backpropagation to the pose parameters in traditional NeRF is hampered by large gradients due to the high-frequency components in the positional embedding. To ameliorate this effect, the authors proposed a coarse-to-fine scheduler to gradually enable the frequency support of the positional embedding layer throughout the joint optimisation. Although achieving impressive results, this workaround requires careful tuning of the frequency scheduling process through a cumbersome *multi-dimensional* parameter sweep. In this paper we investigate if this coarse-to-fine strategy can be bypassed through other means; simplifying the approach and potentially opening up new avenues for improvement.

Supplementary Information The online version contains supplementary material available at https://doi.org/10.1007/978-3-031-19827-4_16.

S. Avidan et al. (Eds.): ECCV 2022, LNCS 13693, pp. 264–280, 2022.
https://doi.org/10.1007/978-3-031-19827-4_16

NeRF is probably the most popular application of coordinate multi-layer perceptrons (MLPs). NeRF maps an input 5D coordinate (3D position and 2D viewing direction) to the scene properties (view-dependent emitted radiance and volume density) of the corresponding location. A crucial ingredient of most coordinate MLPs is positional encoding. Traditional MLPs suffer from *spectral-bias* – *i.e.*, they are biased towards learning low-frequency functions – when used for signal reconstruction [22]. Thus, MLPs, in their rudimentary form, are not ideal for encoding natural signals with fine detail, which entails modeling large fluctuations [23]. To circumvent this issue, NeRF architecturally modifies the MLPs by projecting the low-dimensional coordinate inputs to a higher dimensional space using a positional embedding layer, which allows NeRF to learn high-frequency components of the target function rapidly [18,35].

Recently, there has been an increasing advocacy towards self-contained coordinate networks. By replacing conventional activations (ReLU) with periodic activations, Sitzmann *et al.* [30] demonstrated that sine enables a MLP to learn high frequency functions without any type of positional embedding. However, sine-MLPs have been found experimentally to be sensitive to weight initialization [24,30]. While Sitzmann *et al.* [30] proposed an initialization scheme that aids sine-MLPs to achieve faster convergence when solving for signal reconstruction, their deployment within NeRF has been limited, with most of the community still opting for positional embedding with conventional activations.

Contributions: In this paper, we draw inspiration from a recent work [24] which has advocated for a broader class of effective activation functions – beyond sine that can also circumvent the need for positional encoding. Of particular note in this regard are Gaussian activations. To our knowledge, their use in simultaneous neural reconstruction and pose estimation has not been previously explored. We show that Gaussian activations can preserve the first-order gradients of the target function better than conventional activations enhanced with positional embedding layers. When applied to BARF – that is simultaneously solving for pose and radiance field reconstruction – sine-MLPs are quite susceptible to local minima (even with good initialization), but our proposed Gaussian Activated Neural Radiance Fields (GARF) exhibit robust state-of-the-art performance.

In summary, we present the following contributions:

- We present GARF, a self-contained approach for reconstructing neural radiance field from imperfect camera poses without cumbersome hyper-parameter tuning and model initialisation.
- We establish theoretical insights of the effect of Gaussian activation in the joint optimisation problem of neural radiance field and camera poses, supported by an extensive empirical results.

We demonstrate that our proposed GARF can successfully recover scene representations from unknown camera poses, even on challenging scenes with low-textured regions, paving the way for unlocking NeRF for real-world applications.

2 Related Work

2.1 Neural Scene Representations

Recent works have demonstrated the potential of multi-layer perceptrons or also known as MLPs as *continuous* and *memory efficient* representation for 3D geometry, including shapes [4,5], objects [1,16,20] or scenes [8,30,31]. Using 3D data such as point clouds as supervision, these approaches typically optimise signed distance functions [8,20] or binary occupancy fields [4,16]. To alleviate the dependency of 3D training data, several methods formulate differentiable rendering functions which enables the networks to be optimised using multiview 2D images [18,19,31,36]. Of particular interest is NeRF [18], which models the continuous radiance field of a scene using a coordinate-MLP in a volume rendering framework by minimising the photometric errors. Due to its simplicity and unprecedented high fidelity novel view synthesis, NeRF has attracted wide attention across the vision community [2,14,21,34,37,44]. Numerous extensions have been made on many fronts, e.g., faster training and inference [2,13,27,43], deformable fields [21], dynamic scene modeling [3,11,40], generalisation [29,38] and pose estimation [7,12,15,32,33,39,42].

2.2 Positional Embedding for Pose Estimation

Positional embedding is an integral component of MLPs [25,35,46] which enable them to learn high frequency functions in a low dimensional domain. One of the earliest roots of this approach can be traced to the work by Rahimi *et al.* [23], who discovered that random Fourier Features can be used to approximate an arbitrary stationary kernel function. Leveraging such an insight, Mildenhall et al. [18,35] recently demonstrated that encoding input coordinates with sinusoids allows MLPs to represent higher frequency content, which enables a high-fidelity neural scene reconstruction in novel view synthesis.

Despite the ability of positional embedding in enabling MLPs to represent high frequency components, it is critical to choose the right frequency scale which often involves a cumbersome parameter tuning. If the bandwidth of the signal is increased excessively, a coordinate-MLP tends to produce noisy signal interpolations [6,26,35].

More recently, there has been an increasing interest in using coordinate-MLPs to tackle the joint problem of neural scene reconstruction and pose optimization [7,12,15,32,33,39,42,47]. Remarkably, Lin *et al.* [12] demonstrated that coordinate-MLPs entail an unanticipated drawback in camera registration – *i.e.*, large gradients due to the high frequency components in the positional encoding function could hamper the error backpropagation to the pose parameters. Based on this observation, they proposed a work-around to anneal each component of the frequency function in a coarse-to-fine manner. By enabling a smoother trajectory for the optimisation problem, they show that such a strategy can lead to better pose estimation, compared to *full* positional encoding. Unlike BARF, we take a different stance – is there a *self-contained* architecture which can tackle the pose estimation problem optimally and simultaneously attain a high fidelity neural scene reconstruction without a positional embedding?

2.3 Embedding-Free Coordinate-Networks

Sitzmann *et al.* [30] alternatively proposed sinusoidal activation functions which enable coordinate MLPs to encode high frequency functions without a positional embedding layer. Despite its potential, networks that employ sinusoidal activations are hyper-sensitive to the initialisation scheme [24,26,30]. Taking a step further, Ramasinghe *et al.* [24], recently broadened the understanding of the effect of different activations in MLPs. They proposed a class of novel *non-periodic* activations that can enjoy more robust performance against random initialisation than sinuosoids. Our work significantly differs from the above-mentioned works. While we also advocate for a simple and robust embedding-free coordinate network, our work focuses on the joint problem of high fidelity neural scene reconstruction and pose estimation.

3 Method

In this section, we will provide an exposition of our problem formulation and different classes of coordinate networks, characterising the relative merits of each class for joint optimisation of neural scene reconstruction and pose estimation.

3.1 Formulation

We first present the formulation of recovering the 3D neural radiance field from NeRF [18] jointly with camera poses. We denote T as the camera pose transformations, and F as the network in NeRF, respectively. NeRF encodes the volumetric field of a 3D scene using a coordinate-network as $F : \mathbb{R}^3 \rightarrow \mathbb{R}^4$, which maps each input 3D coordinate $\mathbf{x} \in \mathbb{R}^3$ to its corresponding volume density $\sigma \in \mathbb{R}$ and directional emitted colour $\mathbf{c} \in \mathbb{R}^3$, i.e., $F(\mathbf{x}; \mathbf{\Theta}) = [\mathbf{c}, \sigma]$, where $\mathbf{\Theta}$ is the network weights[1].

Let $\mathbf{u} \in \mathbb{R}^2$ be the pixel coordinates, $\mathcal{I} : \mathbb{R}^2 \rightarrow \mathbb{R}^3$ be the imaging function. Given a set of images $\{\mathcal{I}_i\}_{i=1}^M$, we aim to solve for a volumetric radiance field $\mathbf{\Theta}$ of a 3D scene and the camera poses $\{\mathbf{p}_i\}_{i=1}^M$ by minimizing the photometric loss

$$\min_{\{\mathbf{p}_i\}_{i=1}^M \in \mathfrak{se}(3), \mathbf{\Theta}} \sum_{i=1}^{M} \sum_{\mathbf{u} \in \mathbb{R}^2} \|\hat{\mathcal{I}}(\mathbf{u}; \mathbf{p}_i, \mathbf{\Theta}) - \mathcal{I}_i(\mathbf{u})\|_2^2. \tag{1}$$

First, we assume the rendering operation of NeRF in the camera coordinate system. Expressing the pixel coordinate in its homogeneous coordinate as $\tilde{\mathbf{u}}$, we can define a 3D point $\mathbf{x}_i$ along a camera ray sampled at depth t_i as $\mathbf{x}_i = t_i \tilde{\mathbf{u}}$.

[1] f is also conditioned on viewing direction for modeling view-dependent effect, for which we omit here in the derivation for simplicity.

The estimated RGB colour of $\hat{\mathcal{I}}$ at pixel coordinate $\mathbf{u}$ is then computed by aggregating the predicted $\mathbf{c}$ and σ as

$$\hat{\mathcal{I}}(\mathbf{u}) = \int_{t_n}^{t_f} T(\mathbf{u}, t)\sigma(t\tilde{\mathbf{u}})\mathbf{c}(t\tilde{\mathbf{u}})dt \tag{2}$$

where $T(\mathbf{u}, t) = \exp(-\int_{t_n}^{t} \sigma(t'\tilde{\mathbf{u}}))dt'$, and t_n and t_f are the bounds of the depth range of interest; see [10] for more details of volume rendering operation. In practice, the integral is commonly approximated using quadrature [18] which evaluates the network F at a discrete set of N points through stratified sampling [18] at depth $\{t_1, ..., t_N\}$. Therefore, this entails N querying of the network F, whose output $\{\mathbf{y}_i\}_{i=1}^{N}$ are composited through volume rendering. Denoting the ray compositing function as $G : \mathbb{R}^{4N} \rightarrow \mathbb{R}^3$, we can rewrite $\tilde{\mathcal{I}}(\mathbf{u})$ as $\tilde{\mathcal{I}}(\mathbf{u}) = G(\mathbf{y}_1, ..., \mathbf{y}_N)$. Given a camera pose $\mathbf{p}$, we can transform a 3D point $\mathbf{x}$ in the camera coordinate system to the world coordinate system through a 3D rigid transformation $\mathcal{T}$ to obtain the synthesized image as

$$\hat{\mathcal{I}}(\mathbf{u}; \mathbf{p}) = G\bigg(\{F(\mathcal{T}(t_i\tilde{\mathbf{u}}; \mathbf{p}); \mathbf{\Theta})\}_{i=1}^{N}\bigg). \tag{3}$$

We solve the optimization problem (1) using gradient descent. Next, we will give a brief exposition of coordinate-networks and compare them.

3.2 Coordinate-Networks

Coordinate-networks are a special class of MLPs that are used to encode signals as trainable weights. An MLP with L layers can be formulated as

$$F(\mathbf{x}) = (g^{[L]} \circ \Phi^{[L-1]} \circ g^{[L-1]} \circ \ldots \Phi^{[1]} \circ g^1)(\mathbf{x}^1) + \mathbf{b}^{[L]}, \tag{4}$$

where $g^{[l]} = \mathbf{W}^{[l]}\mathbf{x}^{[l]} + \mathbf{b}^{[l]}$, $\mathbf{W}^{[l]}$ are trainable weights at the lth layer, $\mathbf{b}^{[l]}$ is the bias, and $\Phi^{[l]}(\cdot)$ is a non linear function. With this definition in hand, we briefly discuss several types of coordinate-networks below.

ReLU-MLPs: employ the ReLU activation function $\Phi(x) = max(0, x)$. Despite being a universal approximator in theory, ReLU-MLPs are biased towards learning low-frequency functions [22,41], making them sub-optimal candidates for encoding natural signals with high fidelity. To circumvent this issue, various methods have been proposed in the literature, which we shall discuss next.

PE-MLPs: are the most widely adapted class of coordinate-networks and were popularized by the seminal work of [18] through the use of positional embedding (PE). In PE-MLPs, the low-dimensional input coordinates are projected to a higher-dimensional hypersphere via a positional embedding layer $\gamma(\mathbf{x}) \in \mathbb{R}^3 \rightarrow \mathbb{R}^{3+6D}$, which takes the form

$$\gamma(\mathbf{x}) = \big[\mathbf{x}, [\sin(2\pi\mathbf{x}), \cos(2\pi\mathbf{x})], ..., [\sin(2^{D-1}\pi\mathbf{x}), \cos(2^{D-1}\pi\mathbf{x})]\big], \tag{5}$$

where D is a hyper-parameter that controls the total number of frequency bands. After computing (5), the embedded 3D input points are then passed through a conventional ReLU-MLPs to obtain $F(\gamma(\mathbf{x}); \mathbf{\Theta})$.

Sine-MLPs: are a coordinate-network without a positional embedding proposed by [30]. In sine-MLPs, the activation function is a sinusoid of the form

$$\mathbf{x}^{[l]} \mapsto \Phi^{[l]}(\mathbf{x}^{[l]}) = \sin(2\pi\omega_o \mathbf{x}^{[l]}), \tag{6}$$

where w_0 is a hyperparameter. A larger w_0 increases the bandwidth of the network, allowing it to encode increasingly higher frequency functions.

Gaussian-MLPs: are a recent class of positional-embedding less coordinate-networks [24], where the activation function is defined as

$$\mathbf{x}^{[l]} \mapsto \Phi^{[l]}(\mathbf{x}^{[l]}) = \exp(\frac{-\mathbf{x}^{[l]^2}}{2\sigma^2}), \tag{7}$$

where σ is a hyperparameter that can be used to tune the bandwidth of the network: a larger σ corresponds to a lower bandwidth, and vise-versa.

3.3 GARF for Reconstruction and Pose Estimation

In this paper, we advocate the use of Gaussian-MLPs for jointly solving pose estimation and scene reconstruction, and show substantial empirical evidences that they yield better accuracy and easier optimization over the other choices. We speculate the reason for this superior performance as follows. The pose parameters are optimized using the gradients flow through the network. Hence, the ability to accurately represent the first-order derivatives of the encoded signal plays a key role in optimizing pose parameters. However, Sitzmann *et al.* [30] showed that PE-MLPs are incapable of accurately model first-order derivatives of the target signal, resulting in noisy artifacts. This impacts the Fourier spectrum of the network function, which is implicitly related to the derivatives. As shown in [26], the Fourier transform $f(\mathbf{b}k)$ of a shallow Gaussian-MLP is

$$f(\mathbf{b}k) = \sum_{i=1}^{m} w_i^{(2)} \frac{(2\pi)^{\frac{n+1}{2}}\sigma}{|\mathbf{b}w_i^{(1)}|} e^{-\left(\sqrt{2}\pi \frac{\mathbf{b}w_i^{(1)}}{|\mathbf{b}w_i^{(1)}|^2} \cdot \mathbf{b}k\sigma\right)^2} \delta_{\mathbf{b}w_i^{(1)}}(\mathbf{b}k), \tag{8}$$

where $\mathbf{b}k$ is the frequency index, $\delta_{\mathbf{b}w}(\mathbf{b}k)$ is the Dirac delta distribution which concentrates along the line spanned by $\mathbf{b}w$, and $\mathbf{b}w^{(i)}$ are the weight vectors corresponding to the ith layer. Note that (8) is a smooth distribution, which is parameterized by σ and $\mathbf{b}w^{(i)}$'s. In other words, for a suitably chosen σ, the bandwidth of the network can be increased in a continuous manner by appropriately learning the weights. Moreover, as σ is a continuous parameter, it provides MLPs with the ability to smoothly manipulate the spectrum of the network.

Fig. 1. A 2D planar image alignment instance for (10). *Left*: Input image patches with $N = 6$. *Right*: The initial poses (represented as black box) are initialised as identity.

In contrast, [45] demonstrated that spectrum of a PE-MLP tends to consist of discrete spikes, where the spikes are placed on the integer harmonics of the positional embedding frequencies. Approximating the ReLU function via a polynomial in the form $\rho(x) = \sum_{i=1}^{K} \alpha_i x^i$, where α_i are constants, they showed that the spectrum is concentrated on the frequency set

$$\left\{ \sum_{d=1}^{D} s_d 2^d \pi | s_d \in \mathbb{Z} \wedge \sum_{d=1}^{D} |s_d| < K \right\}. \tag{9}$$

Recall that in order to increase the frequency support of the positional embedding layer, one needs to increase D. It is evident that increasing D even by one adds many harmonic spikes on the spectrum at the high-frequency end, irrespective of the network weights. Therefore, it is not possible to manipulate the spectrum of the PE-MLP continuously under a controlled setting. This can result in unnecessary high-frequency components that lead to unwanted artifacts.

On the other hand, sine-MLPs are able to construct rich spectra and represent first-order derivatives accurately [30]. However, sine-MLPs are extremely sensitive to initialization. Sitzmann *et al.* [30] proposed an initialization scheme for sine-MLPs in signal reconstruction, under which they show strong convergence properties. However, we empirically demonstrate that when jointly optimizing for the pose parameters and scene reconstruction, the above initialization yields sub-par performance, making sine-MLPs highly likely to get trapped in local minima. We also show that, in comparison, Gaussian-MLPs exhibit far superior convergence properties, indicating that they entail a simpler loss landscape.

4 Experiments

This section validates and analyses the effectiveness of our proposed GARF with other coordinate networks. We first unfold the analysis on a 2D planar image alignment problem, and demonstrate extensive results on learning NeRF from unknown camera poses.

4.1 2D Planar Image Alignment

To develop intuition, we first consider the case of 2D planar image alignment problem. More specifically, let $\mathbf{u} \in \mathbb{R}^2$ be the 2D pixel coordinates and $\mathcal{I} : \mathbb{R}^2 \rightarrow \mathbb{R}^3$, we aim to optimize a neural image representation parameterised as the weights of coordinate network F while also solving for warp parameters as

$$\min_{\{\mathbf{p}_i\}_{i=1}^N \in \mathfrak{sl}(3), \mathbf{\Theta}} \sum_{i=1}^{N} \sum_{\mathbf{u} \in \mathbb{R}^2} \| F(\mathcal{W}(\mathbf{u}; \mathbf{p}_i); \mathbf{\Theta}) - \mathcal{I}_i(\mathbf{u}) \|_2^2, \tag{10}$$

where $\mathcal{W} : \mathbb{R}^2 \rightarrow \mathbb{R}^2$ denotes the warp function parameterised as $\mathbf{p} \in \mathfrak{sl}(3)$. Given $N = 6$ patches from the image $\mathcal{I}$ generated with random homography perturbations, we aim to jointly estimate the *unknown* homography warp parameters $\mathbf{p}_i$ and network weights $\mathbf{\Theta}$. We fix the gauge freedom by anchoring the first patch as identity; see Fig. 1 for an example.

Fig. 2. Qualitative and quantitative results of the 2D planar image alignment problem. *Left*: Visualisation of the estimated poses with the $\mathfrak{sl}(3)$ error. *Center*: Reconstruction of each warped patches. *Right*: Final image reconstruction with the patch PSNR.

Experimental Settings. We compare our proposed GARF with the following networks: PE-MLP with a coarse-to-fine embedding annealer (BARF) [12] and sine-MLP (SIREN) [30]. We use a 5-layer MLP with 256 hidden units for all networks. We use the Adam optimizer to optimize both the network weights $\mathbf{\Theta}$ and the warp parameters $\mathbf{p}$. We use a learning rate that begins at 1×10^{-3} for $\mathbf{\Theta}$, and 3×10^{-3} for $\mathbf{p}$, with both decaying exponentially to 1×10^{-4} for GARF and BARF. For SIREN, we use a learning rate of 1×10^{-4} for both $\mathbf{\Theta}$ and $\mathbf{p}$ decaying exponentially to 1×10^{-5}. For BARF, we use $D = 8$ frequency bands Eq. (5), which is linearly annealed over 12K iterations. At each optimization step, we randomly sample 15% of the pixel coordinates for each patch.

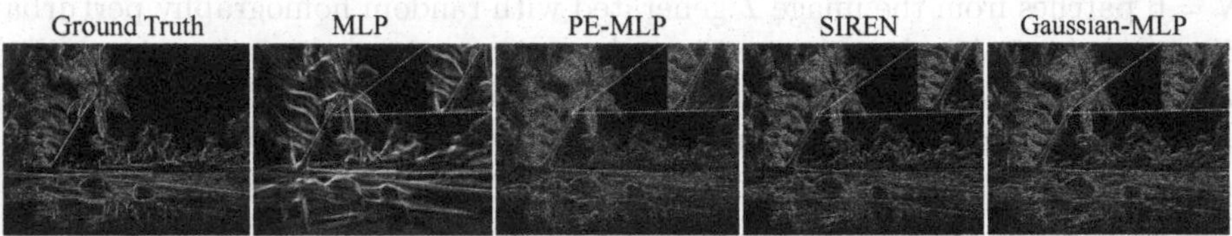

Fig. 3. Comparison of the first-order derivatives of encoded signal ∇F on solving an image reconstruction problem (Best viewed in electronic version). The first-order derivative of each function is computed using network's output with respect to the coordinates. Note that *only* the groundtruth derivative is computed using Sobel Filter.

Initialisation. For BARF and SIREN, we use the initialisation scheme proposed in the original paper [12,18,30], whereas for our proposed GARF we simply use randomly initialised weights. We initialise the warp parameters $\{\mathbf{p}_i\}_{i=1}^{N}$ as identity for all models; see Fig. 1.

Results. We demonstrate the quantitative and qualitative registration results in Fig. 2. As GARF is able to correctly estimate the warp parameters of all patches, GARF can reconstruct the image with high fidelity. On the other hand, BARF and SIREN struggle with the image reconstruction due to misalignment. It is important to note that the Gaussian-MLP initialisation protocol put the proposed method at a disadvantage. This further demonstrates the robustness of Gaussian-MLP towards initialisation.

First-Order Derivatives Analysis. For completeness, we first inspect the first-order derivations of each coordinate network when solving for an image reconstruction task as $\min_{\mathbf{\Theta}} \sum_{\mathbf{u} \in \mathbb{R}^2} \|F(\mathbf{u}; \mathbf{\Theta}) - \mathcal{I}(\mathbf{u})\|_2^2$; note that we use the same notations as in (10). As discussed in Sect. 3.3, the ability to accurately represent the first-order derivatives of the encoded signal plays a crucial role in optimizing pose parameters. Figure 3 reinforces that the first-order derivative of the encoded signal of PE-MLP has a lot of noise artifacts – results in poor error backpropagation to pose parameters. Although a properly-initialised SIREN is capable of representing the derivatives of the signal when solving for signal reconstruction, the initialisation strategy of sine-activation is sub-optimal when jointly optimizing for neural image reconstruction and warp. As a result, the resulting function derivative is no longer well-defined; see Fig. 4. In contrast, GARF exhibit far superior convergence properties, albeit the model weights are initialised randomly.

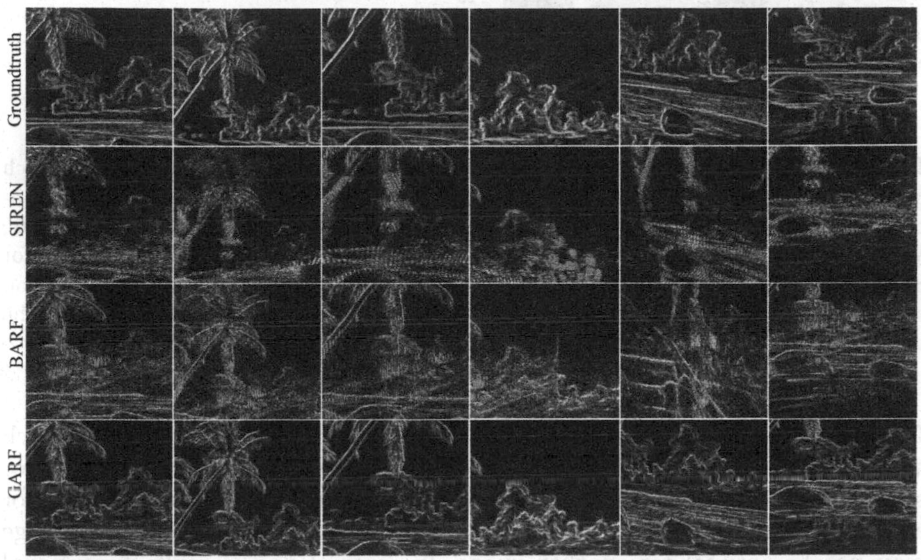

Fig. 4. Comparison of the first-order derivatives of encoded signal ∇F. The first-order derivative of each function is computed using network's output with respect to the coordinates. Note that *only* the groundtruth derivative is computed using Sobel Filter.

Robustness of Initialisation Scheme. Additionally, we run an experiment to investigate the sensitivity of SIREN and GARF to initialisation. We denote $\mathbf{\Theta}^*$ as the optimal model weights, which is obtained by solving (10) for a neural image representation by fixing the warp parameters, and $\bar{\mathbf{\Theta}}$ as the randomly initialised model weights, *i.e.*, weights are initialised using PyTorch default initialisation. Our goal is to solve the joint optimisation problem (10) by initialising $\mathbf{\Theta}$ with different scaled model weights, *i.e.*, $\alpha\bar{\mathbf{\Theta}} + (1-\alpha)\mathbf{\Theta}^*$ by linearly adjusting α. As shown in Fig. 5, GARF (*green curve*) is marginally affected by the initialisation, while SIREN (*blue curve*) fails drastically (starting from $\alpha = 0.3$). When SIREN is initialised carefully using the initialisation scheme proposed by Sitzmann *et al.* [30] (*red curve*), its performance decreases as α gradually increases, *i.e.*, as the perturbation to the optimal model weights increases. Note that the variance of performance in the GARF is much smaller compared to SIREN.

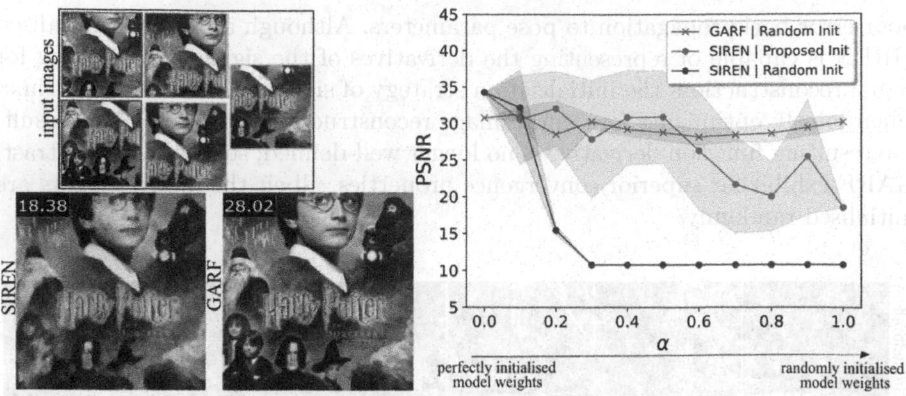

Fig. 5. *Left*: Input images and the image reconstruction for SIREN and GARF, which correspond to the *red* and *green* curve, respectively. *Right*: Robustness of the initialisation at different α. When $\alpha = 0$, all the networks are initialised with *optimal* weights; When $\alpha = 1$, all the networks are initialised with *random* weights. Note that for SIREN, we also investigate the case when SIREN strictly adheres to the initialisation scheme proposed by Sitzmann *et al.* [30] (*red*). The shaded regions correspond to the two standard deviations over 10 runs. (Color figure online)

Generalisation of Coarse-to-Fine Scheduling. We exhaustively search through the log-space for the optimal coarse-to-fine schedulers for BARF; see supp. material for more details. The optimal coarse-to-fine hyper-parameters for each image are data-dependent, *i.e.*, the hyperparameters tuned for one image may not be optimal for another image. In contrast to the multi-dimensional scheduler, Gaussian activation involves one-dimensional search space (7).

4.2 3D NeRF: Real World Scenes

This section investigates the task of jointly learning neural 3D representations with NeRF [18] on real world scenes where the camera poses are *unknown*. We evaluate all the methods on the standard benchmark LLFF dataset [17], which consists of 8 real world forward-facing scenes captured by hand-held cameras.

Experimental Settings. We compare our proposed GARF with BARF and reference NeRF (ref-NeRF). As we empirically observe that PE-MLP with scheduler (BARF) achieves better performance compared to PE-MLP [39] in the joint optimisation of neural radiance field and camera poses, we opted not to include the comparisons with PE-MLP here; see [12] or supp. for comparisons with PE-MLP. We parameterise the camera poses with the $\mathfrak{se}(3)$ Lie algebra and initialise them as *identity* for GARF and BARF. We assume known intrinsics.

4.3 Implementation Details

We implement our framework following the settings from [12,18] with some modifications. For simplicity, we train a 8-layer MLP with 256 hidden units in each layer and *without hierarchical sampling.* We resize the images to 480×640 pixels and randomly sample 2048 pixel rays every iteration, each sampled at $N = 128$ coordinates. We use the Adam optimizer [9] and train all models for 200K iterations, with a learning rate that begins at 1×10^{-4} decaying exponentially to 5×10^{-5}, and 3×10^{-3} for the poses $\mathbf{p}$ decaying to 1×10^{-5}. We use the default coarse-to-fine scheduling for BARF [12]. We use the same network size and sampling strategy for all the methods throughout our evaluation. Note that for BARF and ref-NeRF, we use the implementation from BARF; all the hyperparameters are configured as per proposed in the paper.

Evaluation Details. We evaluate the performance of each method in terms of pose accuracy for registration and view synthesis quality for the scene reconstruction. Following [12,39], we evaluate the pose error by aligning optimized poses to groundtruth via Proscustes analysis which computes the similarity transformation Sim(3) between them. Note that as the "groundtruth" camera poses provided in LLFF real-world scenes are the estimations from Colmap [28], the pose accuracy is only an indicator how well the estimations agree with the classical method. We report the mean rotation and translation errors for pose, as well as PSNR, SSIM and LPIPS [18] for view synthesis in Table 1.

Table 1. Quantitative comparison of GARF (Ours), BARF [12] and ref-NeRF on real-world scenes [17] given *unknown* camera poses.

Scene	Pose accuracy				View synthesis								
	Rotation (°)		Translation (10^{-2})		PSNR ↑ (dB)			SSIM ↑			LPIPS ↓		
	[12]	Ours	[12]	Ours	[12]	Ours	ref-NeRF	[12]	Ours	ref-NeRF	[12]	Ours	ref-NeRF
flower	0.47	**0.46**	0.25	**0.22**	23.58	**26.40**	23.20	0.67	**0.79**	0.66	0.27	**0.11**	0.27
fern	**0.16**	0.47	**0.20**	0.25	23.53	**24.51**	23.10	0.69	**0.74**	0.71	0.34	**0.29**	**0.29**
leaves	1.00	**0.13**	0.30	**0.23**	18.15	**19.72**	14.42	0.48	**0.61**	0.24	0.40	**0.27**	0.58
horns	0.80	**0.03**	**0.17**	0.21	**23.03**	22.54	19.93	**0.73**	0.69	0.59	**0.29**	0.33	0.45
trex	**0.42**	0.66	**0.36**	0.48	22.63	**22.86**	21.42	0.75	**0.80**	0.69	0.24	**0.19**	0.32
orchids	0.71	**0.43**	0.42	**0.41**	19.14	**19.37**	16.54	0.55	**0.57**	0.46	0.33	**0.26**	0.37
fortress	0.17	**0.03**	0.32	**0.27**	28.48	**29.09**	25.62	0.80	**0.82**	0.78	0.16	**0.15**	0.19
room	**0.27**	0.42	**0.20**	0.32	31.43	**31.90**	31.65	0.93	**0.94**	0.94	0.11	0.13	**0.09**

Results. Table 1 quantitatively contrasts the performance of GARF, BARF and ref-NeRF. As evident, Gaussian activations enable GARF to recover camera poses which matches the camera poses from off-the-shelf SfM methods. Moreover, Gaussian activations can successfully recover the 3D scene representation with higher fidelity in the absence of positional embedding, compared to BARF and ref-NeRF; see the qualitative results in Fig. 6.

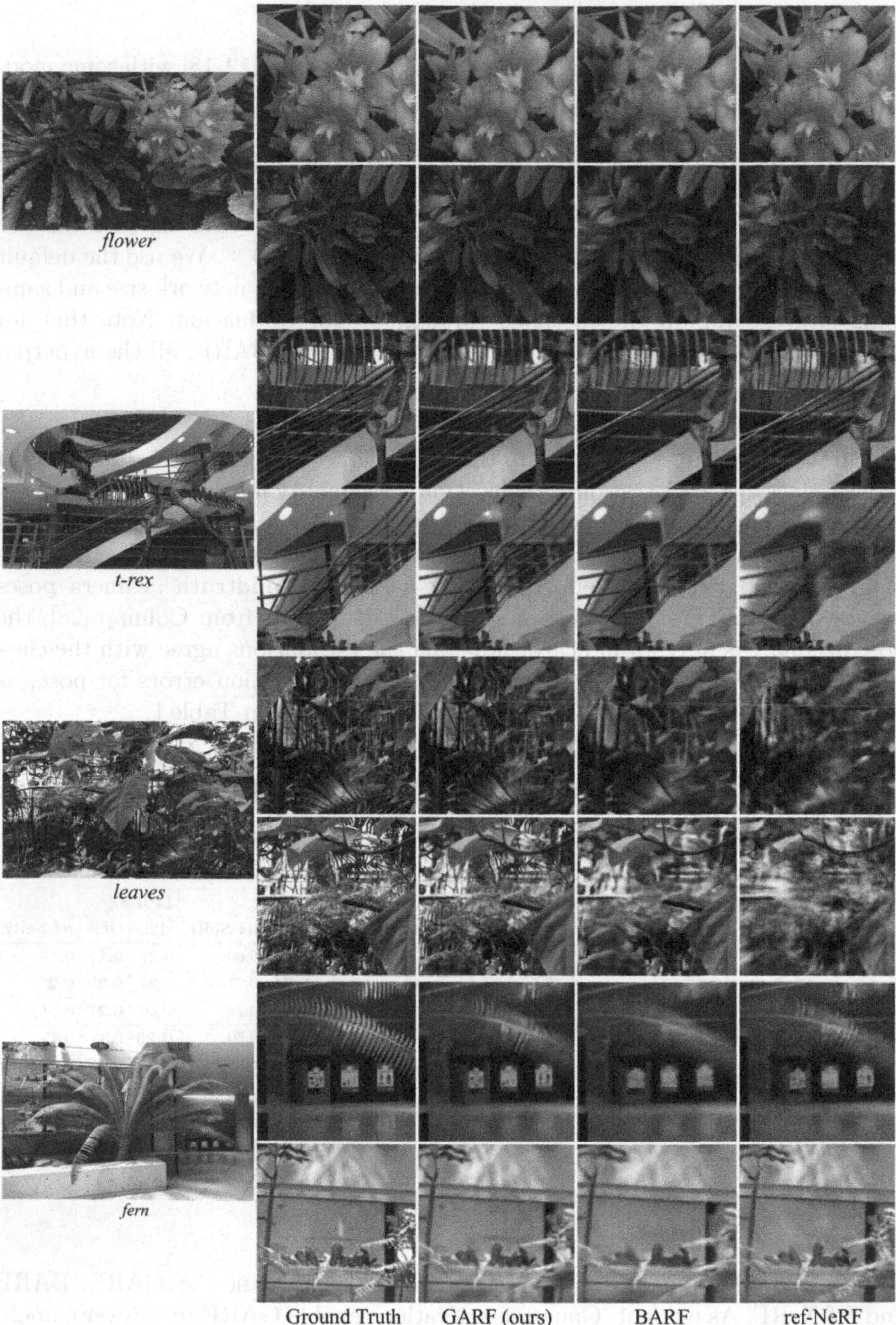

Fig. 6. Qualitative results on test-views of real world scenes [17]. While BARF and GARF can jointly optimize pose and the scene representation, GARF produces results with higher fidelity.

4.4 Real-World Demo

To showcase the practicability of GARF, we take one step further to test it on images of low-textured scene captured using an iPhone. Figure 7 remarkably demonstrate the potential of GARF on a scene with a lot of low-textured region while ref-NeRF exhibits artifacts on the novel view due to existence of outliers in front-end of SfM pipeline, which results in unreliable camera pose estimations; see supp. for more results.

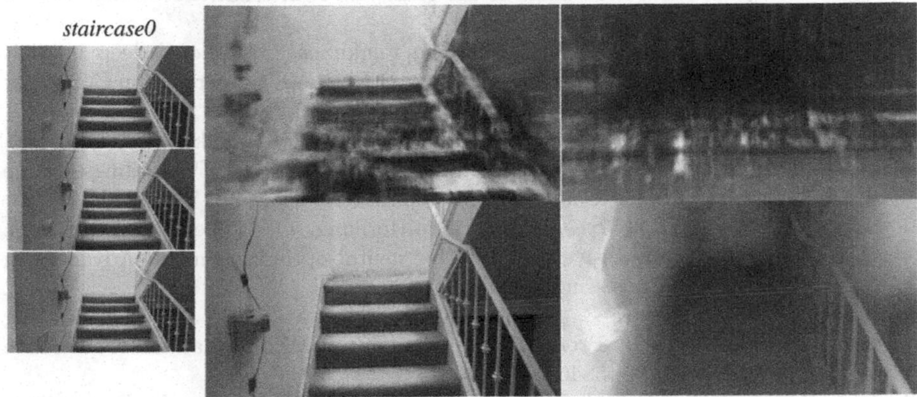

Fig. 7. Novel view synthesis result on a low-textured scene captured using iPhone. *Left banner*: Training images. *Top row*: Rendered image and depth using ref-NeRF. *Bottom row*: Rendered image and depth using GARF.

5 Conclusions

We present GARF, a new positional embedding-free architecture for the simultaneous neural radiance fields reconstruction and pose estimation problem without cumbersome hyperparameter and model initialisation. By establishing theoretical intuition, we demonstrate that the ability of the model to preserve the first-order gradients of the target function plays an imperative role in the joint optimization problem. Experimental results reinforced our theoretical intuition and demonstrated the superiority of GARF, even on challenging scenes with low textured region.

Despite the encouraging results, as with NeRF and its variants, GARF requires lengthy training time. Nevertheless, many of the current advances in NeRF could potentially be applied to speed up the training of GARF. We believe that there is still much more progress to be made in enabling GARF for real-time SLAM applications.

Acknowledgment. We thank Chen-Hsuan Lin, Huangying Zhan, and Tong He for fruitful discussions.

References

1. Chabra, R., et al.: Deep local shapes: learning local SDF priors for detailed 3D reconstruction. In: Vedaldi, A., Bischof, H., Brox, T., Frahm, J.-M. (eds.) ECCV 2020. LNCS, vol. 12374, pp. 608–625. Springer, Cham (2020). https://doi.org/10.1007/978-3-030-58526-6_36
2. Deng, K., Liu, A., Zhu, J.Y., Ramanan, D.: Depth-supervised NeRF: fewer views and faster training for free. arXiv preprint arXiv:2107.02791 (2021)
3. Gao, C., Saraf, A., Kopf, J., Huang, J.B.: Dynamic view synthesis from dynamic monocular video. In: Proceedings of the IEEE/CVF International Conference on Computer Vision, pp. 5712–5721 (2021)
4. Genova, K., Cole, F., Sud, A., Sarna, A., Funkhouser, T.: Local deep implicit functions for 3d shape. In: Proceedings of the IEEE/CVF Conference on Computer Vision and Pattern Recognition, pp. 4857–4866 (2020)
5. Genova, K., Cole, F., Vlasic, D., Sarna, A., Freeman, W.T., Funkhouser, T.: Learning shape templates with structured implicit functions. In: Proceedings of the IEEE/CVF International Conference on Computer Vision, pp. 7154–7164 (2019)
6. Hertz, A., Perel, O., Giryes, R., Sorkine-Hornung, O., Cohen-Or, D.: SAPE: spatially-adaptive progressive encoding for neural optimization. In: Advances in Neural Information Processing Systems 34 (2021)
7. Jeong, Y., Ahn, S., Choy, C., Anandkumar, A., Cho, M., Park, J.: Self-calibrating neural radiance fields. In: Proceedings of the IEEE/CVF International Conference on Computer Vision, pp. 5846–5854 (2021)
8. Jiang, C., et al.: Local implicit grid representations for 3d scenes. In: Proceedings of the IEEE/CVF Conference on Computer Vision and Pattern Recognition, pp. 6001–6010 (2020)
9. Kingma, D.P., Ba, J.: Adam: a method for stochastic optimization. arXiv preprint arXiv:1412.6980 (2014)
10. Levoy, M.: Efficient ray tracing of volume data. ACM Trans. Graph. (TOG) **9**(3), 245–261 (1990)
11. Li, Z., Niklaus, S., Snavely, N., Wang, O.: Neural scene flow fields for space-time view synthesis of dynamic scenes. In: Proceedings of the IEEE/CVF Conference on Computer Vision and Pattern Recognition, pp. 6498–6508 (2021)
12. Lin, C.H., Ma, W.C., Torralba, A., Lucey, S.: BARF: bundle-adjusting neural radiance fields. In: Proceedings of the IEEE/CVF International Conference on Computer Vision, pp. 5741–5751 (2021)
13. Lindell, D.B., Martel, J.N., Wetzstein, G.: AutoInt: automatic integration for fast neural volume rendering. In: Proceedings of the IEEE/CVF Conference on Computer Vision and Pattern Recognition, pp. 14556–14565 (2021)
14. Martin-Brualla, R., Radwan, N., Sajjadi, M.S., Barron, J.T., Dosovitskiy, A., Duckworth, D.: NeRF in the wild: neural radiance fields for unconstrained photo collections. In: Proceedings of the IEEE/CVF Conference on Computer Vision and Pattern Recognition, pp. 7210–7219 (2021)
15. Meng, Q., et al.: GNeRF: GAN-based neural radiance field without posed camera. In: Proceedings of the IEEE/CVF International Conference on Computer Vision, pp. 6351–6361 (2021)
16. Mescheder, L., Oechsle, M., Niemeyer, M., Nowozin, S., Geiger, A.: Occupancy networks: learning 3d reconstruction in function space. In: Proceedings of the IEEE/CVF Conference on Computer Vision and Pattern Recognition, pp. 4460–4470 (2019)

17. Mildenhall, B., et al.: Local light field fusion: practical view synthesis with prescriptive sampling guidelines. ACM Trans. Graph. (TOG) **38**(4), 1–14 (2019)
18. Mildenhall, B., Srinivasan, P.P., Tancik, M., Barron, J.T., Ramamoorthi, R., Ng, R.: NeRF: representing scenes as neural radiance fields for view synthesis. In: Vedaldi, A., Bischof, H., Brox, T., Frahm, J.-M. (eds.) ECCV 2020. LNCS, vol. 12346, pp. 405–421. Springer, Cham (2020). https://doi.org/10.1007/978-3-030-58452-8_24
19. Niemeyer, M., Mescheder, L., Oechsle, M., Geiger, A.: Differentiable volumetric rendering: learning implicit 3d representations without 3d supervision. In: Proceedings of the IEEE/CVF Conference on Computer Vision and Pattern Recognition, pp. 3504–3515 (2020)
20. Park, J.J., Florence, P., Straub, J., Newcombe, R., Lovegrove, S.: DeepSDF: learning continuous signed distance functions for shape representation. In: Proceedings of the IEEE/CVF Conference on Computer Vision and Pattern Recognition, pp. 165–174 (2019)
21. Park, K., et al.: Nerfies: deformable neural radiance fields. In: Proceedings of the IEEE/CVF International Conference on Computer Vision, pp. 5865–5874 (2021)
22. Rahaman, N., et al.: On the spectral bias of neural networks. In: International Conference on Machine Learning, pp. 5301–5310. PMLR (2019)
23. Rahimi, A., Recht, B.: Random features for large-scale kernel machines. In: Advances in Neural Information Processing Systems 20 (2007)
24. Ramasinghe, S., Lucey, S.: Beyond periodicity: towards a unifying framework for activations in coordinate-MLPs. arXiv preprint arXiv:2111.15135 (2021)
25. Ramasinghe, S., Lucey, S.: Learning positional embeddings for coordinate-MLPs. arXiv preprint arXiv:2112.11577 (2021)
26. Ramasinghe, S., MacDonald, L., Lucey, S.: On regularizing coordinate-MLPs arXiv preprint arXiv:2202.00790 (2022)
27. Reiser, C., Peng, S., Liao, Y., Geiger, A.: KiloNeRF: speeding up neural radiance fields with thousands of tiny MLPs. In: Proceedings of the IEEE/CVF International Conference on Computer Vision, pp. 14335–14345 (2021)
28. Schonberger, J.L., Frahm, J.M.: Structure-from-motion revisited. In: Proceedings of the IEEE Conference on Computer Vision and Pattern Recognition, pp. 4104–4113 (2016)
29. Schwarz, K., Liao, Y., Niemeyer, M., Geiger, A.: GRAF: generative radiance fields for 3d-aware image synthesis. Adv. Neural. Inf. Process. Syst. **33**, 20154–20166 (2020)
30. Sitzmann, V., Martel, J., Bergman, A., Lindell, D., Wetzstein, G.: Implicit neural representations with periodic activation functions. Adv. Neural. Inf. Process. Syst. **33**, 7462–7473 (2020)
31. Sitzmann, V., Zollhöfer, M., Wetzstein, G.: Scene representation networks: continuous 3d-structure-aware neural scene representations. In: Advances in Neural Information Processing Systems 32 (2019)
32. Su, S.Y., Yu, F., Zollhoefer, M., Rhodin, H.: A-NeRF: surface-free human 3d pose refinement via neural rendering. arXiv preprint arXiv:2102.06199 (2021)
33. Sucar, E., Liu, S., Ortiz, J., Davison, A.J.: iMAP: implicit mapping and positioning in real-time. In: Proceedings of the IEEE/CVF International Conference on Computer Vision, pp. 6229–6238 (2021)
34. Tancik, M., et al.: Block-NeRF: scalable large scene neural view synthesis. arXiv preprint arXiv:2202.05263 (2022)
35. Tancik, M., et al.: Fourier features let networks learn high frequency functions in low dimensional domains. Adv. Neural. Inf. Process. Syst. **33**, 7537–7547 (2020)

36. Tewari, A., et al.: Advances in neural rendering. arXiv preprint arXiv:2111.05849 (2021)
37. Turki, H., Ramanan, D., Satyanarayanan, M.: Mega-NeRF: scalable construction of large-scale NeRFs for virtual fly-throughs. arXiv preprint arXiv:2112.10703 (2021)
38. Wang, Q., et al.: IBRNet: learning multi-view image-based rendering. In: Proceedings of the IEEE/CVF Conference on Computer Vision and Pattern Recognition, pp. 4690–4699 (2021)
39. Wang, Z., Wu, S., Xie, W., Chen, M., Prisacariu, V.A.: NeRF: neural radiance fields without known camera parameters. arXiv preprint arXiv:2102.07064 (2021)
40. Xian, W., Huang, J.B., Kopf, J., Kim, C.: Space-time neural irradiance fields for free-viewpoint video. In: Proceedings of the IEEE/CVF Conference on Computer Vision and Pattern Recognition, pp. 9421–9431 (2021)
41. Xu, Z.-Q.J., Zhang, Y., Xiao, Y.: Training behavior of deep neural network in frequency domain. In: Gedeon, T., Wong, K.W., Lee, M. (eds.) ICONIP 2019. LNCS, vol. 11953, pp. 264–274. Springer, Cham (2019). https://doi.org/10.1007/978-3-030-36708-4_22
42. Yen-Chen, L., Florence, P., Barron, J.T., Rodriguez, A., Isola, P., Lin, T.Y.: INeRF: inverting neural radiance fields for pose estimation. In: 2021 IEEE/RSJ International Conference on Intelligent Robots and Systems (IROS), pp. 1323–1330. IEEE (2021)
43. Yu, A., Li, R., Tancik, M., Li, H., Ng, R., Kanazawa, A.: PlenOctrees for real-time rendering of neural radiance fields. In: Proceedings of the IEEE/CVF International Conference on Computer Vision, pp. 5752–5761 (2021)
44. Yu, A., Ye, V., Tancik, M., Kanazawa, A.: pixelNeRF: neural radiance fields from one or few images. In: Proceedings of the IEEE/CVF Conference on Computer Vision and Pattern Recognition, pp. 4578–4587 (2021)
45. Yüce, G., Ortiz-Jiménez, G., Besbinar, B., Frossard, P.: A structured dictionary perspective on implicit neural representations. arXiv preprint arXiv:2112.01917 (2021)
46. Zheng, J., Ramasinghe, S., Lucey, S.: Rethinking positional encoding. arXiv preprint arXiv:2107.02561 (2021)
47. Zhu, Z., et al.: NICE-SLAM: neural implicit scalable encoding for SLAM. arXiv preprint arXiv:2112.12130 (2021)

Unbiased Gradient Estimation for Differentiable Surface Splatting via Poisson Sampling

Jan U. Müller[1(✉)], Michael Weinmann[2], and Reinhard Klein[1]

[1] Institute of Computer Science, University of Bonn, Bonn, Germany
muellerj@cs.uni-bonn.de

[2] Department of Intelligent Systems, Delft University of Technology, Delft, Netherlands

Abstract. We propose an efficient and GPU-accelerated sampling framework which enables unbiased gradient approximation for differentiable point cloud rendering based on surface splatting. Our framework models the contribution of a point to the rendered image as a probability distribution. We derive an unbiased approximative gradient for the rendering function within this model. To efficiently evaluate the proposed sample estimate, we introduce a tree-based data-structure which employs multipole methods to draw samples in near linear time. Our gradient estimator allows us to avoid regularization required by previous methods, leading to a more faithful shape recovery from images. Furthermore, we validate that these improvements are applicable to real-world applications by refining the camera poses and point cloud obtained from a real-time SLAM system. Finally, employing our framework in a neural rendering setting optimizes both the point cloud and network parameters, highlighting the framework's ability to enhance data driven approaches.

Keywords: Differentiable rendering · Point cloud · Multipole method · Shape recovery · Scene reconstruction

1 Introduction

Inverse rendering, i.e. the inference of scene parameters such as scene geometry, reflectance or illumination as well as imaging parameters based on observations [4], has become a central problem in Computer Vision and Graphics. A wide range of applications utilize inverse rendering; including reflectance estimation [47], object reconstruction, face remapping, body pose estimation and teeth modeling [23]. Additionally, inverse rendering can improve scene understanding

Supplementary Information The online version contains supplementary material available at https://doi.org/10.1007/978-3-031-19827-4_17.

S. Avidan et al. (Eds.): ECCV 2022, LNCS 13693, pp. 281–299, 2022.
https://doi.org/10.1007/978-3-031-19827-4_17

in robotics [57] and can be applied to a variety of problems in Geodesy [12]. A current approach that receives a lot of attention from the research community is differentiable rendering. It describes rendering methods that provide a gradient of a rendering function with respect to scene and imaging parameters, which promises a general purpose solution to the inverse rendering problem. Intuitively, the gradient conveys information about how parameters have to be changed to match a reference observation. The potential of this approach has led to the development of a variety of differentiable rendering algorithms, categorized by rendering technique or geometry representation: differentiable light transport [40,44,49], implicit neural representations [41], voxel-based [20,37,69], mesh-based [30,36,39] and point-based representations [31,61,66]. Differentiable light transport uses Monte-Carlo sampling which makes the approach computationally expensive. Recent advances made NeRF approaches real-time capable [42], however, these techniques are view synthesis methods and currently do not focus on generalization between scenes. Voxel-based methods can be combined with 3D-CNNs to augment data-driven approaches [17,20,37,60], however, voxel methods are memory constrained which prevents accurate representation of fine geometric details. Differentiable rendering of mesh representations [25,30,36,39] is more scalable but is constrained by the discrete topology of meshes which requires a work-around to allows for strong shape deformations.

Our approach relies on point-based representations, which do not require the initialization to approximate the final topology and are memory efficient compared to voxel-based representations. The method interprets a Gaussian kernel in a point's tangent space, which was introduced in surface splatting [16,77], as a probability density of the points' influence on the overall image. Our method does not require a truncation of the kernels to allow for efficient rendering but instead adapts the concept of importance sampling to point cloud rendering. Without a truncation step there are fewer discontinuities in our rendering pipeline. Importantly, our stochastic interpretation allows to derive an unbiased gradient estimator which is not limited to a local region around each point but approximates the gradient over the complete image space. This allows our method to over-

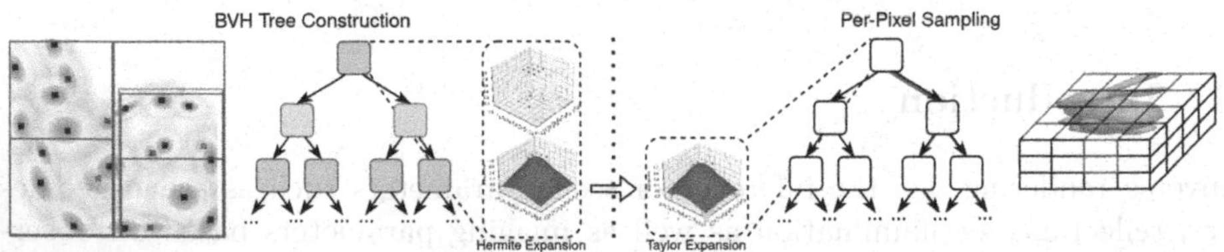

Fig. 1. Illustration of our proposed algorithm to draw per-pixel samples while still scaling linear with respect to image and point cloud size. The construction steps builds a BVH tree and computes Hermite coefficients on the GPU. Afterwards the tree is traversed for each pixel in parallel and the Hermite coefficients are used to identify points with a high contributions to the pixels. Hermite coefficients might be converted into Taylor expansions to improve performance.

come the major challenge of defining an useful surrogate gradient which often requires additional regularization. Previous methods only accumulate local gradients around a surfel [31,61] or rely on a finite-differences surrogate gradient [66]. To efficiently evaluate our sample estimate, we augment a radix-tree [22] to provide an approximation of cumulative inclusion probabilities via Hermite expansions. This yields a space partitioning scheme that is used to draw samples for each pixel while scaling linearly with instance size. An overview of this framework is presented in Fig. 1. Furthermore, it is designed with the constraint of shared-memory multiprocessors in mind, consequently maps well to GPUs and is publicly available[1]. Our overall contributions can be summarized as:

- We introduce a stochastic interpretation of surface splatting that abstains from kernel truncation and the resulting discontinuity. This interpretation allows us to derive an unbiased estimator for the sampling based renderer without relying on surrogates such as finite-differences [66] or sub-gradients [61].
- The proposed sampling algorithm used to generate the necessary samples per pixel scales near linearly with respect to the image size and number of points. By design, it allows parallelization of data processing and maps well to the constraints of shared memory multiprocessors, which allows for a GPU-accelerated implementation.
- We demonstrate that our approach yields a differentiable renderer that does not require regularization and improves the fidelity of shape reconstructions over current point-based differentiable rendering methods. We further demonstrate the framework's flexibility by exploring its use to improve scene reconstruction and train it in conjunction with a neural network.

2 Related Works

In this section, we briefly review work on the topics of differentiable rendering and discrete Gaussian transform approximation.

Differentiable Rendering. A large body of work exists which proposes applica-tion-specific methods that can be classified as differentiable rendering [1,21,27,53,63,71,74]. However, these methods use domain-specific knowledge whereas our approach is not limited to a specific application. Another parallel research direction is differentiable simulation of light transport via computationally expensive Monte-Carlo estimation to render images and propagate the gradients [43,44]. Recently, this method has been extended to also provide a gradient for any scene parameter including geometry and camera parameters [3,40,72,73]. In this work, we focus on fast shape recovery from RGB images and integration into deep neural networks, instead of using more computationally expensive differentiable light transport techniques. In the remainder of this paragraph, we focus on related work that is comparable to our method.

[1] https://github.com/muellerju/unbiased-differentiable-splatting.

Voxel, Signed Distance (SDF) and Implicit Representations. Early approaches use a differentiable projection to obtain a silhouette from a voxel grid [64,75,76]. Recent approaches use differentiable ray marching through a density voxel field [64,75,76] or sphere tracing in an opaque voxel field [20]. However, voxel-based representations require large amounts of memory in order to represent fine geometric details. Deformations of the voxel-grid have been explored to address this drawback [8,37,38]. "Neural Radiance Field" (NeRF) [41] has been demonstrated to reproduce finer details with a smaller memory footprint and has been improved by increasing inference performance [13,51,69], making it real-time capable [42,70] or enabling scene relighting [7,58]. Point-based representations are more memory efficient than dense voxel-grids and scale to larger scenes without workarounds. Furthermore, our point based method can be incorporated into deep neural networks as opposed to real-time "NeRF" approaches for which the integration into neural networks appears to be non-trivial since they are designed for novel view synthesis of individual scenes. In addition, our rendering pipeline does not entangle geometry and reflectance representations which significantly simplifies scene relighting.

Mesh-Based Representations. Mesh-based representations have non-continuous boundaries that can be circumvented with surrogate gradients [25,39] which require regularization to avoid object shrinkage [24]. The "Soft Rasterizer" [36] proposes a probabilistic approximation of the rendering pipeline and has been improved to enable optimization of diffuse shading [10,48] and to increase performance [49]. Recently, flexible mesh-based differentiable rendering frameworks have been introduced [50] which includes hardware accelerated deferred rendering [30]. However, mesh-based differentiable renderers have been demonstrated to be unable to perform complex deformations [66]. This is an inherent problem of their discrete topology, which does not exist in an unstructured point cloud. Similar to the "Soft Rasterizer" [36], our proposed method uses a probabilistic interpretation to mitigate discontinuities. However, the our sampling method avoids the quadratic scaling of the "Soft Rasterizer" and has a lower variance than mesh rendering which uses uniform sampling [52]. Our implementation does not utilize any graphics hardware specific instructions, which allows it to be run on any general purpose computing hardware.

Point-Based Representations. Several point-based methods have been proposed which do not present a general purpose renderer [18,34,54]. Smoothed boundary approaches similar to the "Soft Rasterizer" [36] have only been demonstrated to render low resolution patches [33] or truncate the smoothed boundary to render full images but use a sub-gradient approximation at the boundary [61]. "Pulsar" [31] associates a sphere with each point similar to [33] but proposes a more efficient acceleration structure. In contrast to these surfel methods, our method also takes the surface normal into consideration which allows for a more accurate representation of a surface given the same number of points. "Differentiable surface splatting" (DSS) [66] adapts surface splatting [77] into a general differentiable renderer by introducing a surrogate gradient. In our evaluation, we will highlight that our stochastic framework yields a more faithful shape recovery compare to previous methods. Additionally, our unbiased estimator avoids the use of expensive finite-differences surrogate gradients [66] which enables its application to room-scale scenes. Several works combine point-rendering with neural rendering [2,29,55]; either by rendering pixel-sized points [2,55] or by utilizing DSS in "Point-based neural graphics" [29]. Pixel-sized methods render sparse images at multiple resolutions and require a rendering network to perform hole-filling. This necessitates a per-scene training of the rendering network whereas our method allows for direct optimization of large-scale scenes. Since we improve upon results obtained with DSS and demonstrate that our method can be used in conjunction with a neural rendering network, our framework should be a drop-in replacement into the "Point-based neural graphics" pipeline.

Discrete Gaussian Transform Approximation. The discrete Gaussian Transform (DGT) is a finite mixture of Gaussians (whereas a Gaussian mixture model is a convex combination). "Fast Gaussian Transform" [15] proposes a "fast multipole method" (FMM) based on Hermite and Taylor expansions and a spatial grid to approximate the DGT for large numbers of source and target points in linear time. Subsequent works proposed improvements to the spatial data-structure [14,32,65] and generalize to larger classes of kernel functions [11,56]. In particular, [32] proposes the use of a dual kD-tree and a coupled traversal of both trees to evaluate the DGT. More recently, task-based threading models have been proposed to improve throughput on CPUs [68] and shared memory architectures [35,62]. Our algorithm builds on previous ideas [15,32], however, we adapt these concepts to not only provide an approximation of DGT at the root node but potentially at every node in the source tree. Furthermore, we employ domain-specific knowledge by replacing the target-tree with a grid structure, since the pixels are uniformly distributed. Lastly, we use a BVH-tree that can be efficiently constructed on the GPU [22] to store source points, which is in contrast to previous techniques [35,62] that only accelerate the traversal with GPUs.

3 Statistical Splatting with Unbiased Gradient Estimator

In our rendering algorithm we avoid the additional discontinuity that comes with truncating the Gaussian kernel introduced in "surface splatting" [77]. This removes the bias that leads to shrinkage in previous "DSS" [66]. However, a naive evaluation of the complete Gaussian kernel scales quadratic (i.e. number of pixels times number of points); to obtain an efficient renderer we approximate pixel and gradient values using unbiased sample estimates. "Surface splatting" is a resampling framework for aliasing-free point cloud rendering that associates each point with a resampling kernel $\rho_k(x)$. This kernel is approximated by projecting a Gaussian basis function from a point's tangent plane into screen-space. Let $\mathcal{N}_x$ be the set of points that describe the surface at a pixel x and f_k an attribute value for each point k (e.g. albedo color). Surface splatting computes the pixel value $f_c(x)$ at position x as the weighted sum of pixel contributions:

$$f_c(x) := \sum_{k \in N_x} f_k \rho_k(x) \text{ with } \rho_k(x) := \frac{1}{|J_k^{-1}|} G_{J_k V_k J_k^T + I}(x - m(u_k)) \tag{1}$$

where $m(u_k)$ is the projection of the point position u_k into screen space, J_k^{-1} is the Jacobian of the camera transformation and perspective projection, V_k is a diagonal matrix to control the splat sizes and $G_A(x)$ is the multivariate Gaussian density function with covariance matrix A. For more details, we refer to Zwicker et al. [77]. Previous methods [77,78] truncate the Gaussian kernel $\rho_k(x)$ to obtain an elliptical splat. Limiting the Gaussian kernel to have a local support decreases the algorithm's runtime but requires a finite-differences approach [66] to compute a gradient. In the following, we detail a stochastic framework used in the forward and backward pass as well as an algorithm to efficiently evaluate this framework.

Forward Pass. First, we identify a set of candidate points which could have an effect on the pixel's filtered attribute value without taking occlusion into consideration. We propose to draw this set of points $\tilde{\mathcal{N}}_x$ for each pixel x by sampling without replacement (SWOR) such that the inclusion probability of point k at pixel x is proportional to its influence on the pixel: $\tilde{p}_k(x) \sim f_k \rho_k(c)$. Afterwards, our method evaluates the contributions of the sampled points $\tilde{\mathcal{N}}_x$ at pixel x according to Eq. 1 and resolves the occlusion in a depth filtering step to determine the set of visible points $\mathcal{N}_x$. Our algorithm uses an alpha-blending method, which was originally introduce by Zwicker et al. [78], to perform the depth-filtering. The alpha-based methods sorts the points in $\tilde{\mathcal{N}}_x$ by descending distance from the camera and accumulates the contributions of a point such that its contribution is at most one minus all previous contributions. Wiles et al. [61] have demonstrated that alpha-blending yields an improved gradient propagation compared to the z-Buffer approximation in DSS [66].

Backward Pass. Second, our novel backward pass utilizes of an unbiased estimator to compute the gradient using the samples computed during the forward pass as follows: Let $\mathcal{L}$ be a differentiable image loss function. The derivative of a point parameter ω_k (e.g. position or normal) can be computed by accumulating its derivative over the complete image

$$\frac{\partial \mathcal{L}}{\partial \omega_k} = \sum_x \frac{\partial \mathcal{L}}{\partial f_c(x)} \frac{\partial f_c(x)}{\partial \omega_k}. \tag{2}$$

However, at pixel x we only consider the points in $\tilde{\mathcal{N}}_x$ which have been drawn by SWOR such that $P(k \in \tilde{\mathcal{N}}_x) = \tilde{p}_k(x)$. To obtain an unbiased estimator for Eq. 2, we make the following observations: First, the set of pixels $\mathcal{N}_k := \{x \mid k \in \tilde{\mathcal{N}}_x\}$ that are influenced by point k contains no duplicates, since $\tilde{\mathcal{N}}_x$ was drawn with SWOR and does not have any duplicates. Second, the probability that a pixel is included in $\mathcal{N}_k$ is equal to $P(k \in \tilde{\mathcal{N}}_x)$ by construction. Finally, note that the size of the set $\mathcal{N}_k$ is a random variable. This allows us to use a modified Horvitz-Thompson estimator [9] to approximate the derivative in Eq. 2 as

Algorithm 1: Our adaption of the Sequential Poisson sampling algorithm to generate a sample for each pixel in parallel.

for all all pixels x in parallel **do**
  Let S_x be an empty list of size s to store sampled indices.
  Initialize $\xi = \infty$ the upper bound of transformed random numbers.
  while $\epsilon \leq \xi \cdot c_{x,r} \cdot \sigma_r(x)$ **do**
    Let n be the root of the tree T with point indices $I_n \subseteq [1:N]$.
    while $|I_n| > m$ **do**
      Let n_l, n_r be the left and right child node of n.
      Set $n \leftarrow n_l$ if $c_{x,n_l}\sigma_{n_l}(x) > c_{x,n_r}\sigma_{n_r}(x)$ else set $n \leftarrow n_r$.
    Compute and sort ξ_k in ascending order for all $k \in I_n$.
    Merge I_n with S_x to obtain a SPS sample.
    Set $\xi \leftarrow \max_{k \in S_x} \xi_k$.
    Initialize the path probability $\beta = 1$.
    while n is not the root **do**
      Update the capacity $c_{x,n} \leftarrow \max\{0, c_{x,n} - \beta\}$.
      Let n' be the node which shares a parent with the node n.
      Set $\beta \leftarrow \beta \cdot \frac{\sigma_n(x)}{\sigma_n(x)+\sigma_{n'}(x)}$ and $n \leftarrow \text{parent}(n)$.

$$\frac{\partial \mathcal{L}}{\partial \omega_k} \approx \frac{1}{|\mathcal{N}_k|} \sum_{x \in \mathcal{N}_k} \frac{1}{\tilde{p}_k(x)} \frac{\partial \mathcal{L}}{\partial f_c(x)} \frac{\partial f_c(x)}{\partial \omega_k} \tag{3}$$

if $|\mathcal{N}_k| > 0$ and $\partial \mathcal{L}/\partial \omega_k = 0$ otherwise. Note that the inclusion probability is not strictly proportional-to-size, since $\tilde{p}_k$ is not scaled according to the loss derivative $\partial \mathcal{L}/\partial \omega_k$. However, the gradient is dominated by the exponential decay of the Gaussian kernel $\rho_k(x)$ that outweighs the unaccounted scaling term even for pixels close to a point.

3.1 Efficient Pixel-Wise Sampling

In order to evaluate our sampling-based splatting framework efficiently we introduce a tree-based sampling algorithm that serves two purposes: First, the algorithm allows to approximate the total contribution $f_c(x)$ of all points at each pixel x (i.e. $\mathcal{N}_x = [1:N]$) which allows for proportional-to-size sampling in the forward step. Second, it allows us to draw the set $\tilde{\mathcal{N}}_x$ for each pixel and provide the inclusion probabilities of points within the samples.

In order to achieve these objectives, our algorithm utilizes a fast multipole method (FMM) [15,32] which was originally introduced for N-body simulations to approximate a sum of Gaussians (DGT) at multiple points in linear instead of quadratic time. The idea of FMM is that a DGT of nearby points can be approximated with a truncated Hermite expansion which provides a global approximation. This Hermite expansion can be converted into a truncated Taylor expansion, which approximates the DGT only locally but is more efficient to evaluate for multiple points:

$$f_c(x) \approx \underbrace{\sum_{0 \le \alpha \le n} A_\alpha h_\alpha \left(\frac{x - x_H}{\sqrt{2h^2}} \right)}_{\text{truncated Hermite expansion}} \text{ and } f_c(x) \approx \underbrace{\sum_{0 \le \beta \le n} B_\beta \left(\frac{x - x_T}{\sqrt{2h^2}} \right)^\beta}_{\text{truncated Taylor expansion}}$$

where $h_\alpha = e^{-t^2} H_\alpha(t)$ is a Hermite function of the Hermite polynomial H_α, A_α are the coefficients of a truncated Hermite expansion at point X_H which can be converted into coefficients B_β of a truncated Taylor expansion at point X_T and h is the Gaussian's bandwidth parameter. For details on computing and converting the coefficients we refer to *Lee et al.* [32]. Since FMM assumes isotropic Gaussians with bandwidth h, we derive a best fit bandwidth for the multivariate Gaussians. For further details on this step we refer to the supplemental.

Tree Construction. For each batch of points, we construct a bounding-volume-hierarchy (BVH) tree using a radix-sort based algorithm [22]. The algorithm enables the BVH-tree construction in near linear time on the GPU. We extend the last step of the construction in this algorithm which propagates the

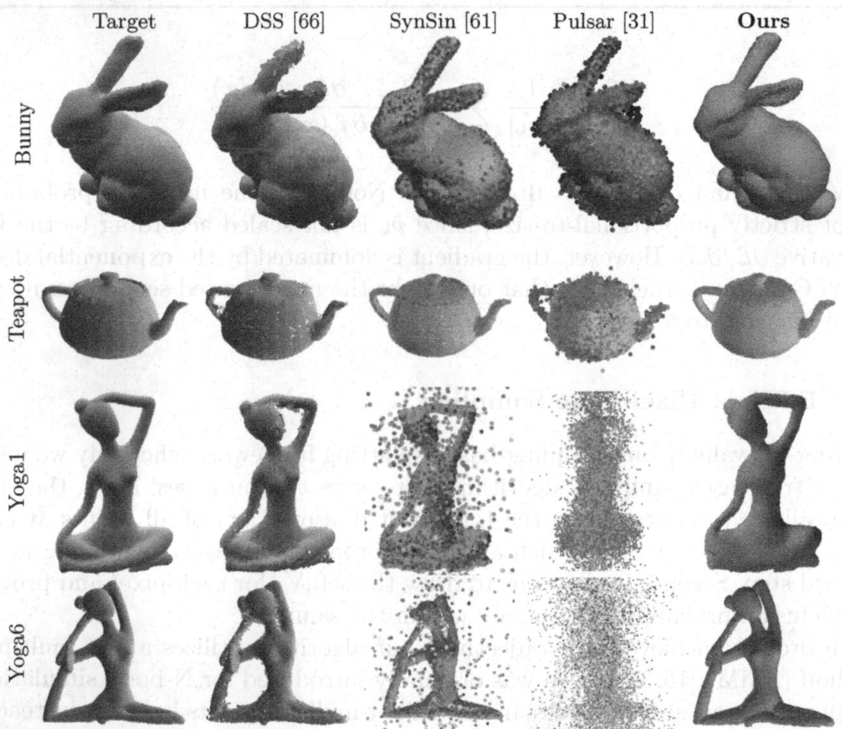

Fig. 2. Shape reconstruction from images using the proposed method compared to results obtained using previous methods. Our method exhibits fewer outliers, more accurate normal directions and an improved reconstruction of extremities. Images were rendered after converged optimization based on the lighting conditions used in Yifan et al. [66], which was not provided but manually recreated.

bounding-boxes (BB) from leafs to the root, to also compute an Hermite expansion for each node within the tree: If the nodes' BB has a side length smaller than 2 h a Hermit expansion can be computed. The expansion point X_H is chosen to be the average of the child nodes' expansion points and the Hermite degree is increased until the approximation error is smaller than a user-defined threshold ϵ. Finally, the Hermite coefficients of the children are shifted and accumulated at the new expansion point. Otherwise, the BB side length is greater or equal to 2 h and the node is marked to have no valid Hermite expansion. The shift operation between nodes, bound for the approximation error have been established by Lee et al. [32] for the use in dual-trees. In contrast to this method, our algorithm computes the Hermite coefficients during the tree construction in parallel whereas Lee et al. [32] only compute the coefficients during sequential depth first traversal.

Sampling. Poisson sampling performs sampling without replacement and by design provides an element's inclusion probability. Therefore it satisfies the requirements introduced by our gradient estimator in Eq. 3, but its sample size is a random variable which is not well-suited for regular shaped tensor objects used in deep-learning frameworks. Instead we generate the samples by adapting sequential Poisson sampling (SPS), which returns a fixed size sample with user specified size m and has been demonstrated empirically to approximate proportional-to-size sampling without replacement [45]. SPS computes a transformed random number $\xi_{x,k} = u_{x,k}/\tilde{p}_k(x)$ where $u_{x,k}$ is a uniform sample between $[0, 1]$ and returns the indices which have the m smallest transformed random numbers. However, drawing a SPS sample for each pixel with this naive algorithm has at least quadratic runtime.

Our algorithm returns a sample and its inclusion probability for each pixel, which has size m and is with probability $1 - \epsilon$ a SPS sample. The algorithm searches for nodes in the tree which have a high likelihood to include points that are contained in a SPS sample and merges them with the current sample. It terminates if the likelihood of all remaining points to be in a SPS sample is smaller than a user-defined threshold ϵ. The search traverses the tree from the root to leaf by choosing the node n with the largest cumulative probability $\sigma_n(x) = \sum_{i \in I_n} f_k \rho_k(x)$ where I_n are the indices of points contained in node n. We describe the evaluation of $\sigma_n(x)$ in the next paragraph. Duplicate samples are avoided by reducing the capacity $c_{x,n}$ along the path. Our parallel SPS procedure is described in detail in Algorithm 1. The runtime of our algorithm is a random variable. Our algorithm scales linearly in an average case, since the expected likelihood for a point to be included in the SPS drops exponentially with distance to a pixel. For a detailed analysis we refer to the supplemental.

Approximating Cumulative Inclusion Probabilities. Our implementation of Algorithm 1 maps each pixel to a thread on the GPU. We choose this mapping such that a thread-block processes a rectangular block of pixels whose size is chosen to maximize processor occupancy. We utilize this spatial relationship

Table 1. Quantitative comparison between the reconstructed and ground-truth pointsets using the Hausdorff (HD) and Chamfer (CD) distance. Our method with non-visible point repositioning outperforms previous methods significantly. The values are an average of 10 runs with a maximum std. deviation of at most 0.0121. Further details are provided in the supplemental.

Dataset	Bunny		Teapot		Yoga1		Yoga6	
	HD ↓	CD ↓	HD ↓	CD ↓	HD ↓	CD ↓	HD ↓	CD ↓
DSS [66]	7.73	1.817	12.766	1.586	14.039	6.351	12.631	3.84
SynSin [61]	75.806	4.074	13.019	4.771	7375.3279	572.224	7861.088	344.151
Pulsar [31]	4.463	1.371	17.036	15.478	25241.71	7746.145	43641.085	12621.735
Ours	**0.442**	**0.125**	**0.453**	**0.289**	**3.355**	**1.385**	**1.551**	**0.517**

by pre-computing Taylor expansions for nodes that are close to the root. In a pre-processing sub-routine to Algorithm 1 the first k' threads within a block compute a Taylor expansion for the first k' nodes in level order and store them in shared memory. The number of pre-computed Taylor coefficients depends on the available shared memory. This accelerates the evaluation of the CDF $\sigma_n(x)$ for frequently visited nodes during the execution of Algorithm 1. After the pre-processing step Algorithm 1 is executed and uses the following heuristic to select between the evaluation techniques:

- The thread searches via linear probing for Taylor coefficients of node n in shared memory. If a local expansions exists, it is used to evaluate $\sigma_n(x)$.
- Otherwise, if node n has a valid Hermite expansion, its Hermite coefficients are used to evaluate the CDF.
- If the node has neither expansion, the algorithm traverses the sub-tree and evaluates the Hermite expansions of the nodes' children to compute the CDF.

Implementation. Our framework is implemented as two CUDA extensions for "PyTorch" [46] where each extension combines multiple kernels. An implementation as a custom "PyTorch" extension provides flexibility when exploring the choice of optimizer, learning rate schedule or loss function. It further allows our method to be easily combined with existing neural network building blocks. The majority of the extensions are written as native CUDA kernels in CUDA-C and use the "PyTorch" C++ wrapper to provide memory management as well as a Python wrapper; only the construction of the tree is implemented using the "Thrust" library [5]. We keep track of the capacity values for each pixel and node combination required in Algorithm 1 by using a hash map. This map can be substantially smaller than the number of pixels times the number of points since the algorithm only needs to store the capacity of visited nodes. Additional details regarding our implementation are provided in the supplementary.

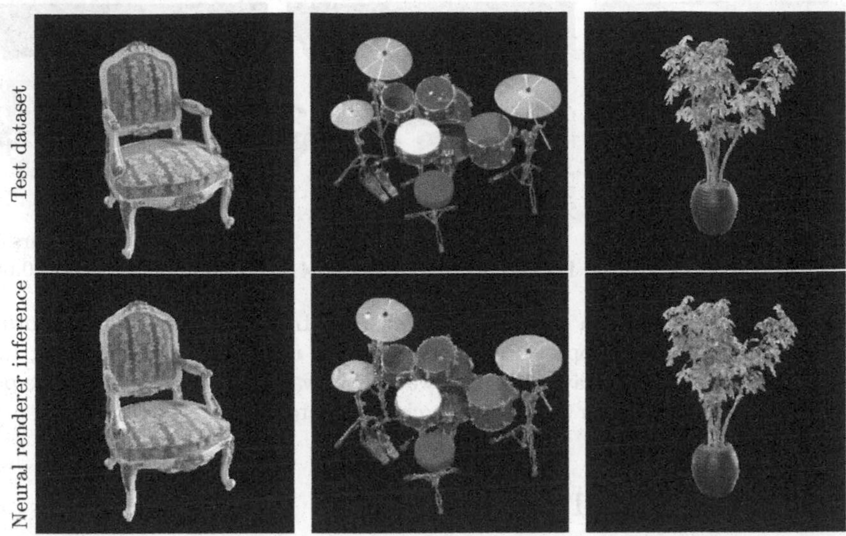

Fig. 3. Comparison between test images in the dataset by Mildenhall et al. [41] and the inference from the neural renderer which uses our method as an intermediate layer. The dataset was scaled to 256 × 256 pixels due to limited hardware.

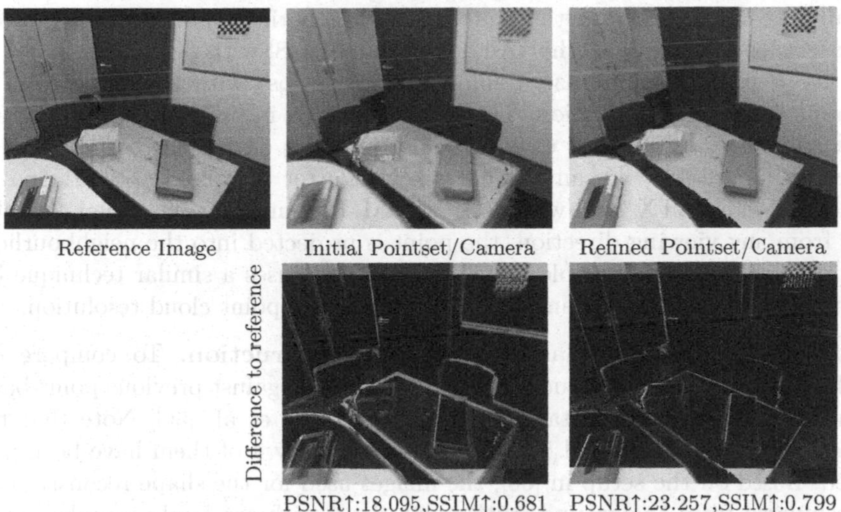

Fig. 4. Comparison between the reference image by Bode et al. [6], a rendered image from the initial SLAM reconstruction and a rendered image after refining the scene using our method. The masked areas in the reference image are a result of calibration and are not considered in the loss, PSNR or SSIM. The pixel-wise difference between the reference image and the rendered images is also depicted (darker values correspond to a smaller error). These highlight an improved alignment of the geometry with the reference image, the removal of outliers and the restoration of sharper textures after the refinement.

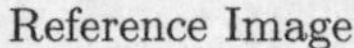

Reference Image | Refinement using DSS PSNR↑:15.412,SSIM↑:0.541 | Refinement using Ours PSNR↑:19.282,SSIM↑:0.683

Fig. 5. Comparison between the refinement of the SLAM reconstruction performed using either DSS or our proposed method. DSS [66] requires a downsampling by a factor of 10 to be run on the available hardware; DSS was also unable to align the pose correctly (compare the upper corner of the checkerboard).

4 Applications and Results

We provide a qualitative and quantitative comparison between our method and previous differentiable point renderer in Fig. 2 and Table 1. Furthermore, we demonstrate that our method can be applied to room-scale scenes with moderate hardware requirements (Fig. 4) whereas DSS is unable to do so (Fig. 5). Finally, we integrate our method into a neural rendering pipeline (Fig. 3). Unless otherwise specified we use the "Adam" optimizer [28] with decay-rates $\beta_1 = 0.9$ and $\beta_2 = 0.999$ to minimize a simple L_1-image loss with a batch size of 12 without further regularization. The learning rate is initially set to be 0.01 and reduced 5 times by a factor of 2 at regular intervals during the 300 epochs. All experiments use $m = 40$ samples per pixel, an error threshold $\epsilon = 0.01$ and are run on a Nvidia GTX 1080 with 8GB VRAM. If points have no visual contribution from any viewing direction, the point is projected into the neighbourhood of a randomly selected visible point. "Pulsar" [31] uses a similar technique but prunes non-contributing points which decreases the point cloud resolution.

Comparison - Image-Based Shape Reconstruction. To compare our method's ability to reconstruct shapes from images against previous point-based approaches, we use the dataset published in Yifan et al. [66]. Note that this dataset originally contained 5 objects, however, only 4 of them have been published. Based on the setup in [66], the images used for the shape reconstruction are rendered from the ground-truth point cloud with randomly sampled poses. For DSS [66] we compare against the results obtained using its published implementation [67]. For "SynSin" [61] and "Pulsar" [31] we use the implementations provided in [50] and apply them using our setup described in the previous paragraph.

The results in Fig. 2 demonstrate that the proposed method is able to successfully reconstruct all objects. When comparing the results to reconstruction obtained with DSS, SynSin or Pulsar, it is apparent that the results obtained with our approach exhibit fewer outliers, holes in the surface and reconstructs smaller details more faithfully. The distances between the reconstructed and ground-truth point clouds reported in Table 1 emphasize that the improved reconstruction accuracy is not limited to the viewing direction in Fig. 2. The proposed method achieves distances that are smaller by a factor of at least 2.9 and 2.8 for the Hausdorff and Chamfer distance when compared to previous methods and indicates more faithfully recovered shapes. For a additional comparisons and the runtime we refer to the supplementary.

Application - Room-Scale Scene Refinement. To demonstrate that our meth-od scales well to room-scale scenes, we utilize sequence RGB-D datasets by Steinbrucker et al. [59] and Bode et al. [6]. The latter registers RGB and depth measurements by masking RGB pixels which have no corresponding depth values. For the refinement we use point-based SLAM [26] to obtain an initial estimate for the point cloud and camera poses and optimize geometry, shading and camera parameters to improve the alignment between RGB images and observations using our method. Further details on this setup and results are provided in the supplementary. After the refinement, the SSIM improves by 17.33% compared to a frame rendered directly after SLAM reconstruction. The improvements exemplified in Fig. 4 are a result of an improved pose alignment between frames and an improvement of shading and geometry. We would like to highlight the improved alignment of the table edge and the checkerboard pattern as a result of improved camera poses, which allows for sharper texture details. Furthermore, outliers near the table and chair were removed in the refinement using our method. In addition to the improvements of the camera poses, albedo values, and spherical harmonics coefficients, improvements to the geometry can be observed which contribute to the lower error. In contrast to "Adop" [55], which demonstrate a similar application, our method does not require training a network and avoids this overhead. We conduct the same experiments using DSS [66]. However, we found that DSS requires to downscale the point cloud by a factor of 10 to avoid out-of-memory exceptions on the used hardware. Figure 5 demonstrates that our method allows the refinement of room-scales scenes with higher fidelity compared to DSS on the same hardware.

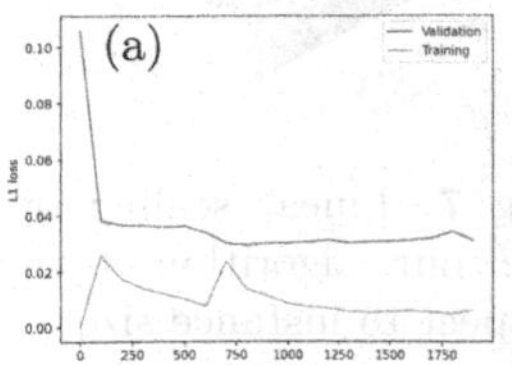

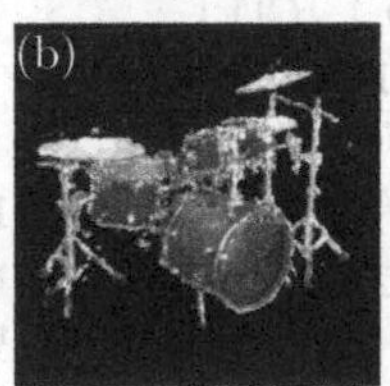

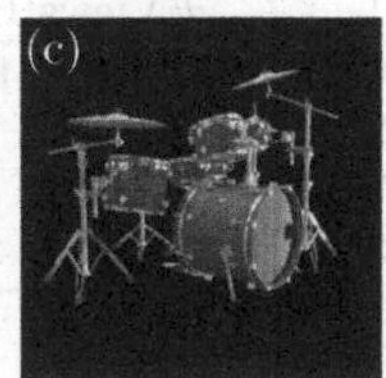

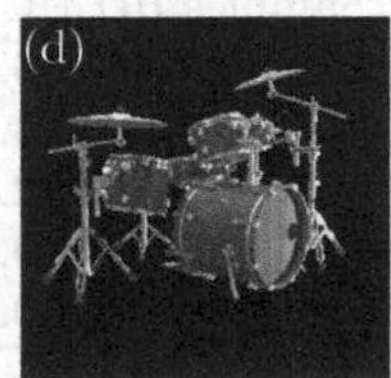

Fig. 6. The neural rendering framework suffers from overfitting, as indicated by the discrepancy between the training and validation loss curve (a). The neural renderer fails to reproduce certain test views (b) but is able to accurately reproduce its nearest training view; compare (c) and (d).

Application - Neural Rendering. To demonstrate the flexibility of our framework beyond shape reconstruction/refinement, we combine it with a neural shading network and train the model on the synthetic dataset by Mildenhall et al. [41]. The design of the neural shading pipeline follows an approach similar to Lassner and Zollhöfer [31]: The shading network is a U-Net generator and the model is trained to minimize an image loss and adversarial loss based on a Patch-GAN discriminator which we adapted from Isola et al. [19]. A detailed description of the initialization, architecture and all parameters is provided in the supplemental. Figure 3 depicts the results obtained by evaluating the trained model on the test split of the dataset. The neural shading network allows the model to render fine details for which the point cloud resolution would not suffice. However, the failure case in Fig. 6 indicates that the neural shading model does not generalize equally well to every camera pose. Lassner and Zollhöfer [31] report a similar problem when demonstrating "Pulsar" as part of their neural rendering model. This suggests that overfitting is not a problem of our renderer but a limitation of neural shading models.

Scaling and Ablation. To study the effect of the user-defined parameters on the shape recovery results, we use the results on the bunny dataset as a baseline. We report the effect of the per-pixel sample size m in Table 2 and the algorithm's robustness with respect to the number of viewing direction in Table 3. While increasing the sample size improves the reconstruction, a sample size beyond 40 is not possible in our implementation since it is constraint by the amount of shared memory. We found that increasing the number of views beyond 100 does result in significant improvements on this scene. We further demonstrate that Algorithm 1 scales linearly with respect to the number of points and pixels in Fig. 7. We provide a more detailed study of the runtime in the supplementary.

Table 2. Influence of the number of samples on Hausdorff and Chamfer distance.

#Samples	HD ↓	CD ↓
1	8.287	6.766
3	8.87	3.532
5	8.189	2.717
20	1.07	0.105
40	0.442	0.125

Table 3. Influence of the number of views on Hausdorff and Chamfer distance.

#Views	HD ↓	CD ↓
16	49.159	20.138
64	1.097	0.156
124	0.442	0.125
300	0.409	0.13

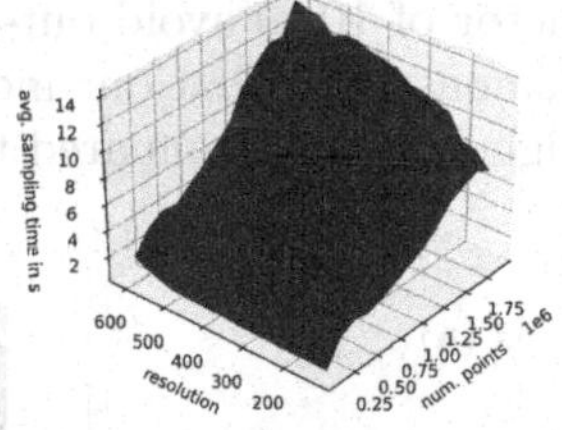

Fig. 7. Linear scaling of the our algorithm with respect to instance size.

5 Conclusion

Our stochastic framework for differentiable point-rendering addresses the inherent bias or locality in the gradient computation of previous methods by deriving an unbiased gradient estimator. To evaluate this estimator we introduce a near linear-time algorithm to perform efficient sampling in image space. We empirically verified that our proposed method enables more faithful image-based object reconstruction without relying on regularization. Furthermore, we demonstrated the scalability and flexibility of our approach by its application for room-scale scene refinement and integrating it into a neural rendering pipeline.

Future Work. Although the current implementation of the sampling algorithm is hardware-agnostic, we anticipate that the integration into a hardware-accelerated rendering pipeline may be beneficial. This is in light of recent developments in neural implicit representations [42], which have significantly improved their efficiency. We believe that reducing the hardware requirements makes methods more accessible and can yield more energy-efficient models.

Acknowledgments. This work was partially funded by the DFG (German Research Foundation) KL 1142/11-2 (FOR 2535 Anticipating Human Behavior).

References

1. Aberman, K., Shi, M., Liao, J., Lischinski, D., Chen, B., Cohen-Or, D.: Deep video-based performance cloning. In: Computer Graphics Forum, vol. 38, pp. 219–233. Wiley Online Library (2019)
2. Aliev, K.-A., Sevastopolsky, A., Kolos, M., Ulyanov, D., Lempitsky, V.: Neural point-based graphics. In: Vedaldi, A., Bischof, H., Brox, T., Frahm, J.-M. (eds.) ECCV 2020. LNCS, vol. 12367, pp. 696–712. Springer, Cham (2020). https://doi.org/10.1007/978-3-030-58542-6_42
3. Bangaru, S.P., Li, T.M., Durand, F.: Unbiased warped-area sampling for differentiable rendering. ACM Trans.Graphics (TOG) **39**(6), 1–18 (2020)
4. Beigpour, S., Kolb, A., Kunz, S.: A comprehensive multi-illuminant dataset for benchmarking of intrinsic image algorithms. In: Proc. IEEE International Conference on Computer Vision (ICCV), pp. 172–180 (12 2015)
5. Bell, N., Hoberock, J.: Thrust: A productivity-oriented library for cuda. In: GPU computing gems Jade edition, pp. 359–371. Elsevier (2012)
6. Bode, L., Merzbach, S., Stotko, P., Weinmann, M., Klein, R.: Real-time multi-material reflectance reconstruction for large-scale scenes under uncontrolled illumination from rgb-d image sequences. In: 2019 International Conference on 3D Vision (3DV), pp. 709–718. IEEE (2019)
7. Boss, M., Braun, R., Jampani, V., Barron, J.T., Liu, C., Lensch, H.: Nerd: Neural reflectance decomposition from image collections. In: Proceedings of the IEEE/CVF International Conference on Computer Vision, pp. 12684–12694 (2021)
8. Bozic, A., Zollhofer, M., Theobalt, C., Nießner, M.: Deepdeform: Learning non-rigid rgb-d reconstruction with semi-supervised data. In: Proceedings of the IEEE/CVF Conference on Computer Vision and Pattern Recognition, pp. 7002–7012 (2020)
9. Brewer, K.R., Early, L., Joyce, S.: Selecting several samples from a single population. Australian J. Stat. **14**(3), 231–239 (1972)
10. Wengzheng, C., et al.: Learning to predict 3d objects with an interpolation-based differentiable renderer. Adv. Neural. Inf. Process. Syst. **32**, 9609–9619 (2019)

11. Curtin, R., March, W., Ram, P., Anderson, D., Gray, A., Isbell, C.: Tree-independent dual-tree algorithms. In: International Conference on Machine Learning, pp. 1435–1443. PMLR (2013)
12. Dave, C.P., Joshi, R., Srivastava, S.: A survey on geometric correction of satellite imagery. Int. J. Comput. Appl. **116**(12), 24–27 (2015)
13. Garbin, S.J., Kowalski, M., Johnson, M., Shotton, J., Valentin, J.: Fastnerf: High-fidelity neural rendering at 200fps. In: Proceedings of the IEEE/CVF International Conference on Computer Vision, pp. 14346–14355 (2021)
14. Greengard, L., Huang, J., Rokhlin, V., Wandzura, S.: Accelerating fast multipole methods for the helmholtz equation at low frequencies. IEEE Comput. Sci. Eng. **5**(3), 32–38 (1998)
15. Greengard, L., Strain, J.: The fast gauss transform. SIAM J. Sci. Stat. Comput. **12**(1), 79–94 (1991)
16. Heckbert, P.S.: Fundamentals of texture mapping and image warping (1989)
17. Henzler, P., Mitra, N.J., Ritschel, T.: Escaping plato's cave: 3d shape from adversarial rendering. In: Proceedings of the IEEE/CVF International Conference on Computer Vision, pp. 9984–9993 (2019)
18. Insafutdinov, E., Dosovitskiy, A.: Unsupervised learning of shape and pose with differentiable point clouds. arXiv preprint arXiv:1810.09381 (2018)
19. Isola, P., Zhu, J.Y., Zhou, T., Efros, A.A.: Image-to-image translation with conditional adversarial networks. In: Proceedings of the IEEE Conference on Computer Vision and Pattern Recognition, pp. 1125–1134 (2017)
20. Jiang, Y., Ji, D., Han, Z., Zwicker, M.: Sdfdiff: Differentiable rendering of signed distance fields for 3d shape optimization. In: Proceedings of the IEEE/CVF Conference on Computer Vision and Pattern Recognition, pp. 1251–1261 (2020)
21. Kappel, M., et al.: High-fidelity neural human motion transfer from monocular video. In: Proceedings of the IEEE/CVF Conference on Computer Vision and Pattern Recognition, pp. 1541–1550 (2021)
22. Karras, T.: Maximizing parallelism in the construction of bvhs, octrees, and k-d trees. In: Proceedings of the Fourth ACM SIGGRAPH/Eurographics conference on High-Performance Graphics, pp. 33–37 (2012)
23. Kato, H., Beker, D., Morariu, M., Ando, T., Matsuoka, T., Kehl, W., Gaidon, A.: Differentiable rendering: A survey. arXiv preprint arXiv:2006.12057 (2020)
24. Kato, H., Harada, T.: Learning view priors for single-view 3d reconstruction. In: Proceedings of the IEEE/CVF Conference on Computer Vision and Pattern Recognition, pp. 9778–9787 (2019)
25. Kato, H., Ushiku, Y., Harada, T.: Neural 3d mesh renderer. In: Proceedings of the IEEE conference on computer vision and pattern recognition, pp. 3907–3916 (2018)
26. Keller, M., Lefloch, D., Lambers, M., Izadi, S., Weyrich, T., Kolb, A.: Real-time 3d reconstruction in dynamic scenes using point-based fusion. In: 2013 International Conference on 3D Vision-3DV 2013, pp. 1–8. IEEE (2013)
27. Kim, H., et al.: Deep video portraits. ACM Trans. Graphics (TOG) **37**(4), 1–14 (2018)
28. Kingma, D.P., Ba, J.: Adam: A method for stochastic optimization. arXiv preprint arXiv:1412.6980 (2014)
29. Kopanas, G., Philip, J., Leimkühler, T., Drettakis, G.: Point-based neural rendering with per-view optimization. In: Computer Graphics Forum. vol. 40, pp. 29–43. Wiley Online Library (2021)

30. Laine, S., Hellsten, J., Karras, T., Seol, Y., Lehtinen, J., Aila, T.: Modular primitives for high-performance differentiable rendering. ACM Trans. Graphics (TOG) **39**(6), 1–14 (2020)
31. Lassner, C., Zollhofer, M.: Pulsar: Efficient sphere-based neural rendering. In: Proceedings of the IEEE/CVF Conference on Computer Vision and Pattern Recognition, pp. 1440–1449 (2021)
32. Lee, D., Moore, A.W., Gray, A.G.: Dual-tree fast gauss transforms. In: Advances in Neural Information Processing Systems, pp. 747–754 (2006)
33. Li, L., Zhu, S., Fu, H., Tan, P., Tai, C.L.: End-to-end learning local multi-view descriptors for 3d point clouds. In: Proceedings of the IEEE/CVF Conference on Computer Vision and Pattern Recognition, pp. 1919–1928 (2020)
34. Lin, C.H., Kong, C., Lucey, S.: Learning efficient point cloud generation for dense 3d object reconstruction. In: proceedings of the AAAI Conference on Artificial Intelligence, vol. 32 (2018)
35. Lingg, M.P., Hughey, S.M., Dikbayir, D., Shanker, B., Aktulga, H.M.: Exploring task parallelism for the multilevel fast multipole algorithm. In: 2020 IEEE 27th International Conference on High Performance Computing, Data, and Analytics (HiPC), pp. 41–50. IEEE (2020)
36. Liu, S., Li, T., Chen, W., Li, H.: Soft rasterizer: A differentiable renderer for image-based 3d reasoning. In: Proceedings of the IEEE/CVF International Conference on Computer Vision, pp. 7708–7717 (2019)
37. Lombardi, S., Simon, T., Saragih, J., Schwartz, G., Lehrmann, A., Sheikh, Y.: Neural volumes: Learning dynamic renderable volumes from images. arXiv preprint arXiv:1906.07751 (2019)
38. Lombardi, S., Simon, T., Schwartz, G., Zollhoefer, M., Sheikh, Y., Saragih, J.: Mixture of volumetric primitives for efficient neural rendering. arXiv preprint arXiv:2103.01954 (2021)
39. Loper, M.M., Black, M.J.: OpenDR: an approximate differentiable renderer. In: Fleet, D., Pajdla, T., Schiele, B., Tuytelaars, T. (eds.) ECCV 2014. LNCS, vol. 8695, pp. 154–169. Springer, Cham (2014). https://doi.org/10.1007/978-3-319-10584-0_11
40. Luan, F., Zhao, S., Bala, K., Dong, Z.: Unified shape and svbrdf recovery using differentiable monte carlo rendering. arXiv preprint arXiv:2103.15208 (2021)
41. Mildenhall, B., Srinivasan, P.P., Tancik, M., Barron, J.T., Ramamoorthi, R., Ng, R.: NeRF: representing scenes as neural radiance fields for view synthesis. In: Vedaldi, A., Bischof, H., Brox, T., Frahm, J.-M. (eds.) ECCV 2020. LNCS, vol. 12346, pp. 405–421. Springer, Cham (2020). https://doi.org/10.1007/978-3-030-58452-8_24
42. Müller, T., Evans, A., Schied, C., Keller, A.: Instant neural graphics primitives with a multiresolution hash encoding. arXiv preprint arXiv:2201.05989 (2022)
43. Nimier-David, M., Speierer, S., Ruiz, B., Jakob, W.: Radiative backpropagation: an adjoint method for lightning-fast differentiable rendering. ACM Transactions on Graphics (TOG) **39**(4), 146–1 (2020)
44. Nimier-David, M., Vicini, D., Zeltner, T., Jakob, W.: Mitsuba 2: A retargetable forward and inverse renderer. ACM Trans. Graph. (TOG) **38**(6), 1–17 (2019)
45. Ohlsson, E.: Sequential poisson sampling. J. Official Stat. **14**(2), 149 (1998)
46. Paszke, A., et al.: Pytorch: an imperative style, high-performance deep learning library. Adv. Neural. Inf. Process. Syst. **32**, 8026–8037 (2019)
47. Patow, G., Pueyo, X.: A survey of inverse rendering problems. In: Computer graphics forum. vol. 22, pp. 663–687. Wiley Online Library (2003)

48. Petersen, F., Bermano, A.H., Deussen, O., Cohen-Or, D.: Pix2vex: Image-to-geometry reconstruction using a smooth differentiable renderer. arXiv preprint arXiv:1903.11149 (2019)
49. Poursaeed, O., Fisher, M., Aigerman, N., Kim, V.G.: Coupling explicit and implicit surface representations for generative 3D modeling. In: Vedaldi, A., Bischof, H., Brox, T., Frahm, J.-M. (eds.) ECCV 2020. LNCS, vol. 12355, pp. 667–683. Springer, Cham (2020). https://doi.org/10.1007/978-3-030-58607-2_39
50. Ravi, N., Reizenstein, J., Novotny, D., Gordon, T., Lo, W.Y., Johnson, J., Gkioxari, G.: Accelerating 3d deep learning with pytorch3d. arXiv preprint arXiv:2007.08501 (2020)
51. Reiser, C., Peng, S., Liao, Y., Geiger, A.: Kilonerf: Speeding up neural radiance fields with thousands of tiny mlps. In: Proceedings of the IEEE/CVF International Conference on Computer Vision, pp. 14335–14345 (2021)
52. Rhodin, H., Robertini, N., Richardt, C., Seidel, H.P., Theobalt, C.: A versatile scene model with differentiable visibility applied to generative pose estimation. In: Proceedings of the IEEE International Conference on Computer Vision, pp. 765–773 (2015)
53. Rossler, A., Cozzolino, D., Verdoliva, L., Riess, C., Thies, J., Nießner, M.: Faceforensics++: Learning to detect manipulated facial images. In: Proceedings of the IEEE/CVF International Conference on Computer Vision. pp. 1–11 (2019)
54. Roveri, R., Rahmann, L., Oztireli, C., Gross, M.: A network architecture for point cloud classification via automatic depth images generation. In: Proceedings of the IEEE Conference on Computer Vision and Pattern Recognition, pp. 4176–4184 (2018)
55. Rückert, D., Franke, L., Stamminger, M.: Adop: Approximate differentiable one-pixel point rendering. arXiv preprint arXiv:2110.06635 (2021)
56. Ryan, J.P., Ament, S., Gomes, C.P., Damle, A.: The fast kernel transform. arXiv preprint arXiv:2106.04487 (2021)
57. Sengupta, S.: Constraints and Priors for Inverse Rendering from Limited Observations. Ph.D. thesis, University of Maryland, College Park (2019)
58. Srinivasan, P.P., Deng, B., Zhang, X., Tancik, M., Mildenhall, B., Barron, J.T.: Nerv: Neural reflectance and visibility fields for relighting and view synthesis. In: Proceedings of the IEEE/CVF Conference on Computer Vision and Pattern Recognition, pp. 7495–7504 (2021)
59. Steinbrücker, F., Sturm, J., Cremers, D.: Real-time visual odometry from dense rgb-d images. In: 2011 IEEE international conference on computer vision workshops (ICCV Workshops), pp. 719–722. IEEE (2011)
60. Tulsiani, S., Zhou, T., Efros, A.A., Malik, J.: Multi-view supervision for single-view reconstruction via differentiable ray consistency. In: Proceedings of the IEEE Conference on Computer Vision and Pattern Recognition, pp. 2626–2634 (2017)
61. Wiles, O., Gkioxari, G., Szeliski, R., Johnson, J.: Synsin: End-to-end view synthesis from a single image. In: Proceedings of the IEEE/CVF Conference on Computer Vision and Pattern Recognition, pp. 7467–7477 (2020)
62. Wilson, L., Vaughn, N., Krasny, R.: A gpu-accelerated fast multipole method based on barycentric lagrange interpolation and dual tree traversal. Comput. Phys. Commun. **265**, 108017 (2021)
63. Xian, W., Huang, J.B., Kopf, J., Kim, C.: Space-time neural irradiance fields for free-viewpoint video. In: Proceedings of the IEEE/CVF Conference on Computer Vision and Pattern Recognition, pp. 9421–9431 (2021)

64. Yan, X., Yang, J., Yumer, E., Guo, Y., Lee, H.: Perspective transformer nets: Learning single-view 3d object reconstruction without 3d supervision. arXiv preprint arXiv:1612.00814 (2016)
65. Yang, C., Duraiswami, R., Gumerov, N.A., Davis, L.: Improved fast gauss transform and efficient kernel density estimation. In: Computer Vision, IEEE International Conference on, vol. 2, pp. 464–464. IEEE Computer Society (2003)
66. Yifan, W., Serena, F., Wu, S., Öztireli, C., Sorkine-Hornung, O.: Differentiable surface splatting for point-based geometry processing. ACM Trans. Graph. (TOG) **38**(6), 1–14 (2019)
67. Yifan, W., Serena, F., Wu, S., Öztireli, C., Sorkine-Hornung, O.: Github - yifita/dss: Differentiable surface splatting (2019). https://github.com/yifita/DSS/tree/44732f9b771ca7e5ee4cfebeaf8528be1d097e3e
68. Yokota, R.: An fmm based on dual tree traversal for many-core architectures. J. Algorith. Comput. Technol. **7**(3), 301–324 (2013)
69. Yu, A., Fridovich-Keil, S., Tancik, M., Chen, Q., Recht, B., Kanazawa, A.: Plenoxels: Radiance fields without neural networks. arXiv preprint arXiv:2112.05131 (2021)
70. Yu, A., Li, R., Tancik, M., Li, H., Ng, R., Kanazawa, A.: Plenoctrees for real-time rendering of neural radiance fields. arXiv preprint arXiv:2103.14024 (2021)
71. Zakharov, E., Shysheya, A., Burkov, E., Lempitsky, V.: Few-shot adversarial learning of realistic neural talking head models. In: Proceedings of the IEEE/CVF International Conference on Computer Vision, pp. 9459–9468 (2019)
72. Zeltner, T., Speierer, S., Georgiev, I., Jakob, W.: Monte carlo estimators for differential light transport. ACM Trans. Graph. (TOG) **40**(4), 1–16 (2021)
73. Zhang, C., Miller, B., Yan, K., Gkioulekas, I., Zhao, S.: Path-space differentiable rendering. ACM Trans. Graph. **39**(4) (2020)
74. Zhou, H., Sun, Y., Wu, W., Loy, C.C., Wang, X., Liu, Z.: Pose-controllable talking face generation by implicitly modularized audio-visual representation. In: Proceedings of the IEEE/CVF Conference on Computer Vision and Pattern Recognition, pp. 4176–4186 (2021)
75. Zhu, J.Y., Zhang, Z., Zhang, C., Wu, J., Torralba, A., Tenenbaum, J.B., Freeman, W.T.: Visual object networks: Image generation with disentangled 3d representation. arXiv preprint arXiv:1812.02725 (2018)
76. Zhu, R., Kiani Galoogahi, H., Wang, C., Lucey, S.: Rethinking reprojection: Closing the loop for pose-aware shape reconstruction from a single image. In: Proceedings of the IEEE International Conference on Computer Vision, pp. 57–65 (2017)
77. Zwicker, M., Pfister, H., Van Baar, J., Gross, M.: Surface splatting. In: Proceedings of the 28th Annual Conference on Computer Graphics and Interactive Techniques, pp. 371–378 (2001)
78. Zwicker, M., Pfister, H., Van Baar, J., Gross, M.: Ewa splatting. IEEE Trans. Visual Comput. Graphics **8**(3), 223–238 (2002)

Towards Learning Neural Representations from Shadows

Kushagra Tiwary[(✉)], Tzofi Klinghoffer, and Ramesh Raskar

Massachusetts Institute of Technology, Cambridge, USA
{ktiwary,tzofi,raskar}@mit.edu

Abstract. We present a method that learns neural shadow fields, which are neural scene representations that are *only* learnt from the shadows present in the scene. While traditional shape-from-shadow (SfS) algorithms reconstruct geometry from shadows, they assume a fixed scanning setup and fail to generalize to complex scenes. Neural rendering algorithms, on the other hand, rely on photometric consistency between RGB images, but largely ignore physical cues such as shadows, which have been shown to provide valuable information about the scene. We observe that shadows are a powerful cue that can constrain neural scene representations to *learn* SfS, and even outperform NeRF to reconstruct otherwise hidden geometry. We propose a graphics-inspired differentiable approach to render accurate shadows with volumetric rendering, predicting a shadow map that can be compared to the ground truth shadow. Even with just binary shadow maps, we show that neural rendering can localize the object and estimate coarse geometry. Our approach reveals that sparse cues in images can be used to estimate geometry using differentiable volumetric rendering. Moreover, our framework is highly generalizable and can work alongside existing 3D reconstruction techniques that otherwise only use photometric consistency. Code is available here.

Keywords: Scene representations · Differentiable rendering · 3D scene reconstruction · Shape-from-shadows · Volume rendering

1 Introduction

Recovering 3D geometry from 2D images remains an extremely important, yet unsolved problem in computer vision and inverse graphics. Considerable progress has been made in the field when assumptions are made, such as bounded scenes, diffuse surfaces, and specific materials. However, reconstruction algorithms still

K. Tiwary and T. Klinghoffer—Equal contribution.

Supplementary Information The online version contains supplementary material available at https://doi.org/10.1007/978-3-031-19827-4_18.

S. Avidan et al. (Eds.): ECCV 2022, LNCS 13693, pp. 300–316, 2022.
https://doi.org/10.1007/978-3-031-19827-4_18

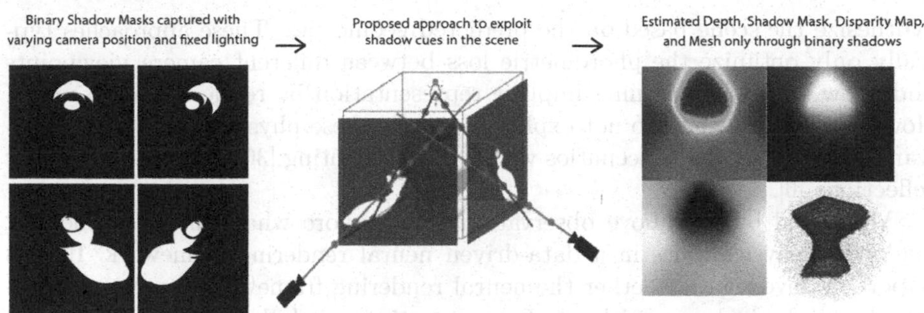

Fig. 1. Exploiting physical cues in neural rendering. Our approach takes sparse binary shadow masks captured with varying camera positions under fixed lighting and uses our proposed differentiable shadow rendering model to estimate shadow maps, thereby learning neural scene representations. We can visualize the learned implicit representations by rendering estimated depth maps and estimated shadow maps from novel views. We also run marching cubes [15] on our learned representations to get explicit meshes for a quantitative analysis.

remain largely susceptible to real world effects, such as specularity, shadows, and occlusions [35]. This susceptibility is largely due the variation in different materials and textures, and a non-unique mapping from 3D geometries to 2D images. Even though these effects cause issues for many methods, they also provide valuable information about the scene and geometry of the object. For example, cues like self-shadows provide vital information about an object's concavities, while shadows cast on the ground plane provide information about its geometry. Moreover, shadows are independent of textures and surface reflectance models and are a strong cue in overhead imagery where vertical surfaces, like facades, are sampled poorly, whereas oblique lighting can expose this geometry. Exploiting, instead of ignoring these cues, can make algorithms robust and the fundamental problem of 3D reconstruction less ill-posed.

Previous works in recovering 3D shape of objects by exploiting physical cues has relied on constructing inverse models to explicitly handle and exploit cues such as shadows, shading, motion, or polarization [2,41,42]. These approaches are physically anchored as they use properties of light or surface reflectance models to exploit cues and only need up to a single image to reconstruct simple objects. Albeit successful under strict assumptions about lighting, camera, and the object, these models typically cannot handle complex scenes and do not translate well into real-world scenarios as creating inverse models to capture complex physical phenomenon soon becomes intractable and hard to optimize (Fig. 1).

To combat the problem of real world variability, modern methods such as [13,17,22,29,32,38] have largely been data-driven by directly learning 3D representations on real-world scenes based on photometric consistency. Such methods employ an *analysis-by-synthesis* approach to solve the problem by using machine learning to search the space of possible 3D geometries and an inverse model to synthesize the scene based on the predicted geometries. These approaches typically only optimize the photometric loss between different camera viewpoints and show success in learning implicit representation by rendering novel views. However, because they do not explicitly handle these physical cues in their forward model, they fail in scenarios with complex lighting [30], specularity [40], or reflections [6].

Motivated by the above observations, we explore what can be learned by exploiting physical cues in a data-driven neural rendering framework. In this paper, we investigate whether the neural rendering framework can learn geometry from physical cues without the assumptions made by the aforementioned methods. We study the use of shadows cast by objects onto themselves and nearby surfaces as the only source of information for 3D reconstruction. While modern approaches for 3D reconstruction ignore such cues, we aim to exploit them. Our unsupervised approach uses *only* shadows to reconstruct the scene by leveraging recent advances in volumetric rendering and machine learning, and therefore proposes a physically anchored data-driven framework to the problem of shape from shadows. Moreover, unlike previous work in shape from shadows, we present a novel method that uses differentiable rendering in the loop to iteratively reconstruct the object based on a loss function instead of iteratively refining the object through explicit carving. Specifically, we use an efficient shadow rendering technique called shadow mapping as the forward model and make it differentiable so that it can be used as an inverse model to iteratively reconstruct the object. Our work also reveals that from limited cues the differentiable volumetric rendering component can *quickly converge to localize and reconstruct a coarse estimate of the object when such cues are explicitly modeled by a forward model.* Our work also suggests that neural rendering can exploit shadows to recover hidden geometry, which otherwise may not be discovered by photometric cues (Fig. 2).

1.1 Contributions

Our contributions in this paper are the following:

- A framework that directly exploits physical cues like shadows in neural renderers to recover scene geometry.
- A novel technique that integrates volumetric rendering with a graphics-inspired forward model to render shadows in an end-to-end differentiable manner.
- Results showing that our framework can learn coarse scene representations from just shadows masks. We evaluate the learned representations qualitatively and quantitatively against vanilla neural rendering approaches. To the best of our knowledge, we are the first to show that it is possible to learn neural scene representations from binary shadow masks.

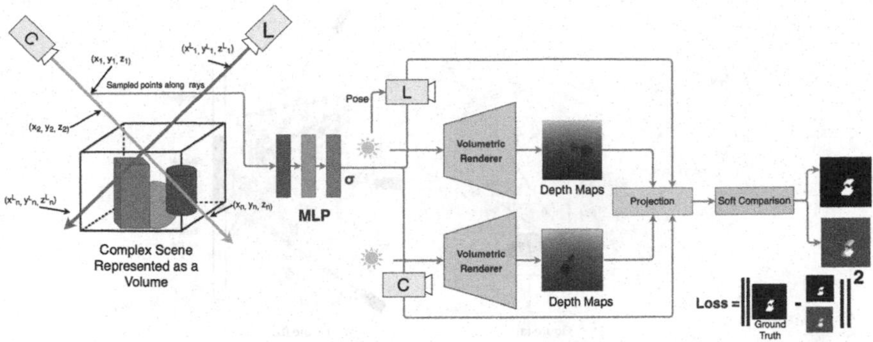

Fig. 2. Overview of the proposed pipeline We train a neural network to predict opacity at points along the camera and light rays. The opacities are used by the volumetric renderer to output the ray-termination distance which we use to estimate the *z-buffer* from the camera and the light perspective, the latter also known as the shadow map. The estimated *z-buffer* is fed into a **Projection** step that projects the camera pixels and their associated depths into the light's reference frame. The shadow map is indexed to obtain the corresponding depth values at these new points. The projected depths and indexed depths go through a **Soft Comparison** step which outputs predicted cast shadows in the scene from the camera's perspective. A loss is computed on the *predicted* and the *ground-truth* shadow mask.

2 Related Work

Shape from Shadows. Shadowgram imaging deals with estimating the shape of an object through a sequence of shadow masks captured with light sources at various locations. These methods typically assume a controlled and fixed object scanning setup [27,37]. Martin & Aggarwal [16] introduced a volumetric space carving approach to SfS which outputs a visual hull around the object by carving out voxels lying outside the visual cone. Other work takes a more probabilistic approach to the shape-from-silhouettes problem to make the algorithm more robust to errors [9]. However, interpreting shadows as silhouettes means that self-shadows are not handled, thus motivating Savarese et al. [27] to propose a method to "carve" out objects based on self-shadows to create more complete reconstructions.

In contrast, our work takes a differentiable approach to solving the problem through learning. Instead of an explicit carving of voxels we first construct a differentiable forward model that casts shadows based on some geometry. Then, we let the machine learning component predict geometry, which is synthesized by the renderer to cast shadows. Finally, we optimize this setup based on a mean square error between predicted and ground truth shadow masks.

Neural Rendering. Broadly speaking, a neural rendering framework is composed of a differentiable renderer, which can render the scene based on input parameters and is able to differentiate the scene w.r.t. those input parameters. While there are many formulations of differentiable renderers [8,10,14,21] that can synthesize scenes, state-of-art approaches have shown tremendous

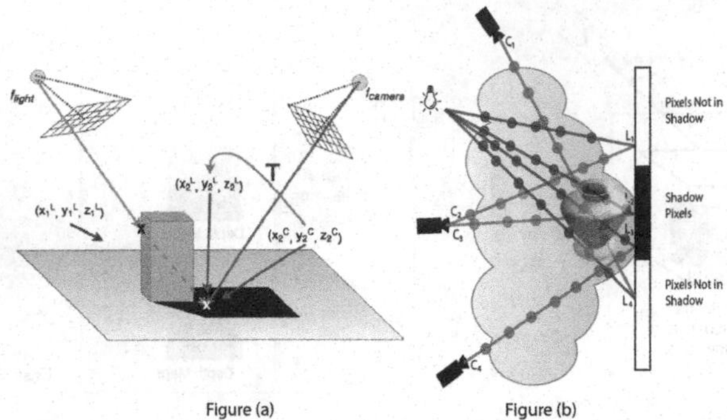

Fig. 3. Figure **(a)**: A point $\mathbf{x} \in \mathbb{R}^3$ in the scene is defined to be in shadow if no direct path exists from the point $\mathbf{x}$ to the light source, implying that there **must** be an occluding surface between $\mathbf{x}$ and the light source. We differentiably render the scene's depth from the camera and the light's perspective at each pixel and then project the camera pixel and its depth into the light's frame of reference. We then index the light's depth map, or z-buffer, to get z_1^L. We note that z_1^L is less than z_2^L, i.e. there must be an occluding surface as a ray projected from the light's perspective terminates early. This implies that this point is in shadow. Figure **(b)** shows a 2D slice of our approach and represents a volume (cloud) with the shadow mask unraveled. The network learns an opacity per point (dots) via the shadow mapping objective which penalizes predicted geometries that don't cast perfect ground truth shadows. Through this, the networks learns 3D geometry that is consistent across all shadows maps for all cameras given a particular light source.

success by relying on differentiable volumetric rendering [20]. Volumetric rendering approaches can realistically render complex scenes and are gradient-friendly. Thus, typical approaches train a neural network to encode the scene and optimize it for photometric consistency between input 2D images from different viewpoints [17–19, 29]. Recent methods such as [3, 6, 30, 34] explicitly account for specularity, reflections and other such phenomenon, however, the goal of these works are to improve novel view synthesis. Thus, these methods still rely on learning the scene using photometric information.

In contrast, our work deals with 3D reconstruction, not novel view synthesis, and explores what can be learned by relying on shadow cues in the scene. Our framework only operates in the shadow input and output space to infer a 3D representation of the scene. In addition, similar to [26, 39], our work also reveals that differentiable volumetric rendering is a powerful component that can learn the scene by only relying on sparse physical cues. While volumetric approaches rely on a photometric cues, differentiable rasterization [8, 12] has been shown to reconstruct 3D mesh using single low dimensional images of ShapeNet objects [4] by only using silhouettes. However, these methods fail to show success on high dimensional images, while our approach can scale up to higher dimensional images. Concurrent work by Liu *et al.* [11] also leverages shadows to perform 3D reconstruction, but integrates learned object priors, whereas we solely rely on binary shadow masks and use volumetric rendering.

Shadows in Graphics. Graphics deals with the forward model and shadow mapping [36] is one of the most efficient techniques to render shadows in a scene given the scene's geometry, camera viewpoint and light position. While differentiability is not important for graphics, we make the shadow mapping framework differentiable to work with modern 3D reconstruction algorithms. We describe the algorithm and our implementation in Sect. 3.

3 Neural Representations from Shadows

Our goal is to recover the scene through shadows cast on the other objects or onto itself. Our method recovers shadows in an image by applying a threshold on that image thereby making no distinction between types of shadows. We show how we model the shape-from-shadows problem using differentiable rendering and implicit representations in Sect. 3.1 and our graphics-inspired differentiable forward model in Sect. 3.2. In Sect. 3.3, we discuss our additional techniques that we use to enable optimization on binary shadow masks.

3.1 Scenes as Neural Shadow Fields

Implicit Scene Representations. Similar to Mildenhall *et al.* [17], we represent a continuous scene by parametrizing it using a learnable function f_θ. However, our approach does not include any photometric component, therefore we represent the scene as a 3D function with input $\mathbf{x} = (x, y, z)$ and a volumetric density σ as output.

$$\begin{gathered}\gamma(\mathbf{x}) = \left(\sin(2^0\pi\mathbf{x}), \cos(2^1\pi\mathbf{x}), ..., \sin(2^L - 1\pi\mathbf{x}), \cos(2^L - 1\pi\mathbf{x}) \right) \\ f_\theta : \mathbb{R}^L \to \mathbb{R}^+; (\gamma(\mathbf{x})) \mapsto (\sigma)\end{gathered} \tag{1}$$

We use a positional-encoded 3D point $\gamma(\mathbf{x})$, $\{\gamma(\mathbf{x}) \in \mathbb{R}^L, \mathbf{x} \in \mathbb{R}^3\}$ as input, which maps to an associated volumetric density $\sigma \in \mathbb{R}^+$ [17,31]. In contrast, f does not encode view dependant color and is independent to viewing direction.

Volumetric Renderer. We define a volumetric renderer $\mathbf{R}_{\text{vol}}$ that takes N opacities $\{\sigma\}_{i=1}^N$ at N discretely sampled points $\{\mathbf{x}\}_{i=1}^N$ along a ray $\mathbf{r}$.

$$\mathbf{R}_{\text{vol}} : \left[\mathbb{R}^+\right]_{i=1}^N \to \left[\mathbb{R}^+\right]_{i=1}^N; (\{\sigma\}_{i=1}^N) \mapsto (\mathbf{d}) \tag{2}$$

Since we only have binary shadows as input, we modify the renderer to output the ray termination distance, $\mathbf{d}$, instead of the radiance at that ray. $\mathbf{R}_{\text{vol}}$ is not a trainable component, but the ray termination distance, $\mathbf{d}$, is differentiable w.r.t. the input opacities. The estimated ray-termination distance, range, is computed as follows:

$$\hat{\mathbf{D}}(\mathbf{r}) = \sum_{i=1}^N T_i \alpha_i t_i; T_i = \prod_{j=1}^{i-1} (1 - \alpha_j); \alpha_i = \left(1 - e^{-\sigma_i \delta_i}\right) \tag{3}$$

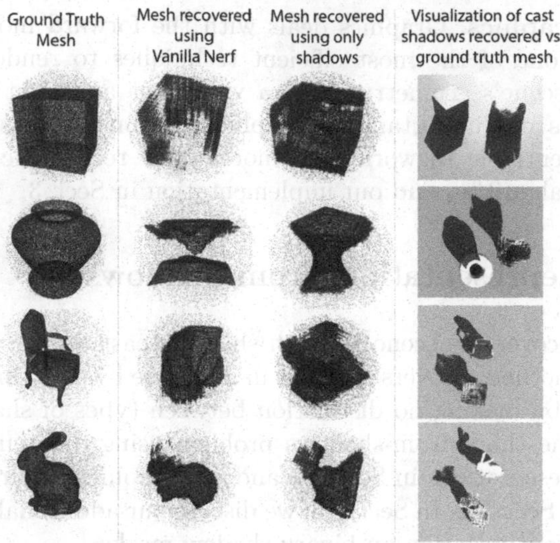

Fig. 4. Qualitative Results. We observe that for overhead views of the scene where the vertical surface of the vase is sampled poorly in the RGB space, vanilla NeRF fails to exploit geometry cues hidden in cast shadows compared to our approach. Our method doesn't impose any object priors therefore it infers a geometry that will minimize the difference between the predicted and true shadow. Column 4 illustrates that rendered shadows are very similar, indicating that the differentiable rendering framework can indeed learn geometry from sparse shadow cues. Some parts of the objects such as the upper face of cuboid are never in shadow, therefore our approach yields no reconstruction for those surfaces, further showing that the geometry is indeed *only* learnt from cast shadows. We extract the mesh from the volume using marching cubes and visualize it here using a point-cloud SDF representation.

We sample $\mathbf{r}(t)$ at points $\{t_0, ..., t_N\}$ and evaluate the function $\mathbf{r}(t) = \mathbf{o} + t\mathbf{d}$ to get sampled points $\{x_0, ..., x_N\}$ in the scene. T_i is defined as the cumulative transmittance from t_0 until t_i and $\delta_i = t_{i+1} - t_i$ which is the distance between two samples. σ_i is the estimated opacity at point i by a learned function f_θ. Intuitively, the renderer gives us the ray termination distance for each ray shooting through a pixel.

3.2 Differentiable Shadow Mapping

We define any point $\mathbf{x} \in \mathbb{R}^3$ in the scene to be in shadow if no direct path exists from point $\mathbf{x}$ to the light source $\mathbf{L}$. This logic implies that there **must** be some object or an occluding surface between the point $\mathbf{x}$ and $\mathbf{L}$ that occludes the light ray from reaching point $\mathbf{x}$. In graphics, shadow mapping [36] uses this observation to construct a forward model to render efficient and accurate shadows in the scene based on known light and camera sources. Our approach makes this efficient shadow rendering forward model differentiable so that it can be used as an inverse model. We then pose the problem of shape from shadows and use our proposed inverse model to estimate the 3D geometry of the scene.

Estimated z-Buffer. We first evaluate the renderer from the camera's perspective to get the estimated ray termination distance, or range map, $\hat{\mathbf{D}}_{cam}$ for all rays coming out of the binary shadow map. However, shadow mapping requires the depth perpendicular to the image plane, i.e. along the z axis of the camera's local coordinate system. This depth is equivalent to a *z-buffer* in graphics and we refer to this value as the *depth* at that pixel. We define a function g to estimate the *z-buffer* $\hat{\mathbf{Z}}$ from the range map $\hat{\mathbf{D}}$.

$$\hat{\mathbf{z}}_{u,v} = g(\mathbf{d}_{u,v}) = \frac{\mathbf{d}_{u,v}}{||(u,v,1)\cdot\mathcal{E}||_2} \tag{4}$$

The function takes a ray shooting from a pixel (u, v) and a predicted range, $\hat{\mathbf{D}}^{u,v}_{cam}$ as input. $\mathcal{E}$ is the rotational component of the camera's extrinsic matrix, $\mathbf{d}_{u,v}$ is the ray termination distance from camera's focal point, and $\hat{\mathbf{z}}_{u,v}$ is the depth along the z-axis from the pixel (u, v). We also compute the estimated z-buffer from the light's perspective, which we refer to as the estimated *shadow map.*

Projection. With the estimated depths at each pixel from the camera and the light source, we now need to estimate which camera pixels are in shadow given the particular light source. As illustrated in Fig. 3, we do this by projecting all pixels and their associated depths visible by the camera into the light's frame of reference. We then use this projected coordinate to index the shadow map to get the depth to that point from the light's perspective. We formally write this as follows:

$$\begin{aligned}(U^l_{cam}, V^l_{cam}, \hat{\mathbf{Z}}^l{}_{cam}) &= (U_{cam}, V_{cam}, \hat{\mathbf{Z}}_{cam}) \cdot P_{light\_from\_cam} \\ \hat{\mathbf{Z}}^{U^l_c, V^l_c}_{light} &= \hat{\mathbf{Z}}_{light}\left[U^l_{cam}, V^l_{cam}\right]\end{aligned} \tag{5}$$

Here, $\hat{\mathbf{Z}}_{cam} \in \mathbb{R}^{H\times W}$ is the estimated z-buffer from the camera's perspective at pixels $\{U_{cam}, V_{cam}\} \in \mathbb{R}^{H\times W}$. $P_{light\_from\_cam}$ is the projection matrix to the light's reference frame from the camera's. We denote $(U^l_{cam}, V^l_{cam}, \hat{\mathbf{Z}}^l{}_{cam})$ as the pixels and depth in camera's frame (subscript) projected into the light's frame, denoted by the superscript l. We index the shadow map, $\hat{\mathbf{Z}}_{light} \in \mathbb{R}^{H\times W}$, at the projected camera pixels to retrieve the depth of the projected camera pixels from the light source. This is denoted as $\hat{\mathbf{Z}}^{U^l_c, V^l_c}_{light}$ which is the shadow map indexed at pixel locations U^l_c, V^l_c. In practice, not all pixels will project within the shadow map's height and width constraints specified at the start of training. In graphics, these pixels are usually ignored, however, we clamp all our projections to lie within the height and width bounds to maintain differentiability.

Soft Comparison. Once we have the depths to the projected camera pixels and the depths from the light source to those pixels in the same reference frame, we can then compare them to discover if the camera pixel is in shadow. As illustrated by Fig. 3, if the depth from the light source to a point is less than the depth from the camera projected into the light's frame, it means that the light ray must have intersected an object before reaching that point. Thus, that point must be in shadow. Based on this logic, we formulate a soft comparison, which compares different depths to output the predicted binary shadow mask as follows:

$$\begin{aligned} \Delta\hat{Z}_{light} &= \left(\hat{\mathbf{Z}}^{l}{}_{cam} - \hat{\mathbf{Z}}_{light}^{U_c^l, V_c^l}\right) \\ \hat{\mathbf{M}}_{binary} &= \mathbf{max}\left(\frac{\Delta\hat{Z}_{light}}{\beta}, \epsilon\right) \end{aligned} \tag{6}$$

We denote $\hat{\mathbf{M}} \in \mathbb{R}^{H \times W}$ as the output of the entire pipeline: predicted shadow masks. The input to our soft comparison is the projected camera z-buffer into the light's frame, $\hat{\mathbf{Z}}^{l}{}_{cam}$, and the shadow map indexed at the projected points $\hat{\mathbf{Z}}_{light}^{U_c^l, V_c^l}$ from the **Projection** step. β is a scaling hyper-parameter used to enlarge or decrease the difference, and ϵ is a threshold. We also formulate a "smoother" version of the predicted shadows:

$$\hat{\mathbf{M}}_{smooth} = \mathbf{S}\Big(\mathbf{normalize}\big(\Delta\hat{Z}_{light}, \mu_{min}, \mu_{max}\big)\Big) \tag{7}$$

Here, μ_{min}, μ_{max} are used to control the normalization function and $\mathbf{S}$ is the sigmoid function.

3.3 Optimization

To enable convergence, we smooth the binary ground truth shadow masks $\mathbf{M}$ to better guide the framework in predicting accurate shadow masks.

Distance Transform. Binary images contain limited information for differentiation as the gradient is zero everywhere except for the edges where it is one. To encourage our model to estimate better shadow masks, thereby learning a better 3D model, we use a distance transform on the ground truth shadow masks. Specifically, we scale pixel intensities of a binary shadow mask by their distance to the nearest shadow edge. We modify the weighted distance transform in [25] for our approach. The transformed binary shadow mask, $w(\mathbf{M}, \sigma) = \mathbf{M}_w$ is computed as follows:

$$w(\mathbf{M}, \sigma) = \mathbf{M} + \left(w_c(\mathbf{M}) + w_0 \cdot \exp\Big(-\frac{(d_1(\mathbf{M}) + d_2(\mathbf{M}))^2}{2\sigma^2}\Big)\right) \tag{8}$$

Here, $\mathbf{M}$ is the ground truth binary shadow mask computed after applying a fixed threshold on binary images. w_c is weight map to balance class frequencies, w_0 and σ are hyper parameters. d_1 and d_2 are distances to the nearest and second nearest cell, respectively. We note from our experiments that this particular distance transform yields the most consistent convergence compared to other distance transforms, such as blurring.

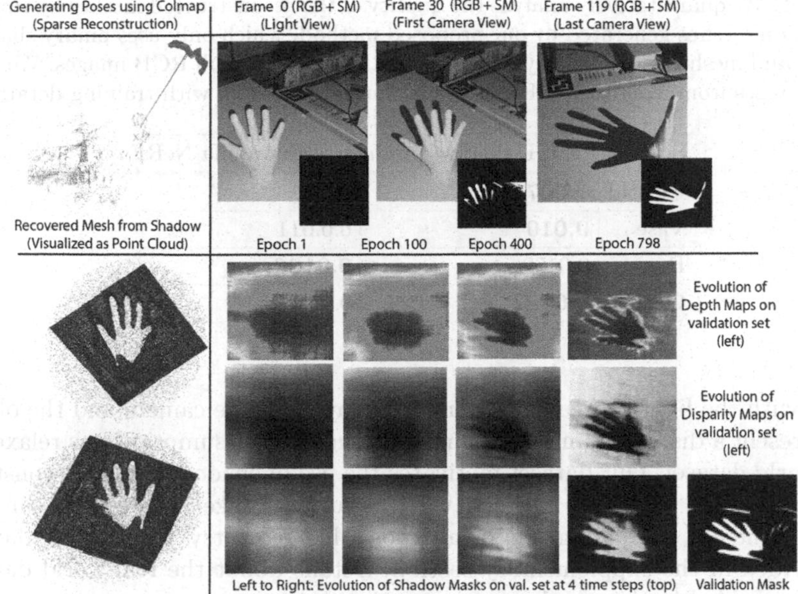

Fig. 5. Real-World Experimentation: We use the *exact same pipeline and training scheme to reconstruct a 3D mesh from real-world data.* We take a video on the iPhone to generate poses for light and camera using COLMAP [28] (video link) and extract shadows using an intensity threshold. We show that our method can reconstruct a finer mesh of the hand from the real-world images. We highlight that our method can more easily generalize from sim2real in comparison to photometric approaches since we learn from only shadow masks, which are invariant to many real-world effects, such as texture.

Shadow Mapping Loss. We optimize our entire framework on binary shadow masks and train the MLP on the following loss:

$$\mathcal{L}_{sm} = ||w(\mathbf{M}, \sigma) - \hat{\mathbf{M}}||^2 \tag{9}$$

Here, $w(\mathbf{M}, \sigma)$ is the σ weighted ground truth shadow mask, and $\hat{\mathbf{M}}$ is the predicted shadow mask from Eq. (7).

4 Implementation

4.1 Dataset

We create a dataset of objects, including a cuboid, vase, chair and bunny in blender and render images of size 800 × 800. Although our approach does not have any constraints on the number or positions of light and camera, we fix one light source and randomly sample 200 camera positions on along the upper half of a sphere around the object. In simulation, we only consider top down/satellite

Table 1. We quantitatively analyze the quality of the reconstructed meshes by running ICP [1] on meshes generated by our proposed method, which only uses binary shadows masks, and meshes generated by a vanilla NeRF trained on full RGB images. We show RGB images from Vanilla NeRF in the supplementary along with training details.

Scene	RMSE shadow mesh	RMSE vanilla NeRF
Cuboid	**0.0078**	0.097
Vase	**0.010**	0.0.011
Bunny	0.0109	**0.0106**
Chair	**0.0092**	0.0096

views with the light source being very far away from the camera and the object to represent a distant "sun-like" source although this assumption was relaxed in real world dataset. Our dataset motivates the use of shadows for 3D reconstruction because in overhead imagery, vertical surfaces, like facades, are sampled poorly, whereas oblique lighting can expose this geometry. Link to the dataset is provided in the supplementary section. Details about the real world dataset is also provided in the supplementary section.

4.2 Training Details

We use a faster implementation of NeRF [17] from [24], which uses PyTorch Lightning as its backend [5,23]. We down sample all images from 800×800 to 64×64 to fit on one RTX-3080 GPU. We use the same positional encoding scheme, $\gamma(x)$ and the MLP configuration f_θ used in [17]. For camera projections, we write a custom *Planar Projection Camera* class that encapsulates the projections and readily works with OpenGL and blender cameras. We gradually decreases the σ (Eq. 8) from $\{150, 100, 50\}$ during training to encourage the network to learn coarse to fine geometry. We also train a Vanilla NeRF model on RGB images of the same scene on resolution 64×64. To reconstruct the meshes, we run marching cubes on the learned implicit representations. More information on the exact training details is given in the supplementary section, including details about our more efficient differentiable shadow mapping implementation, which decreases the training time by half.

5 Results

Evaluation Details. We evaluate the performance of our method using root mean square error (RMSE) between the predicted point cloud and the ground truth point cloud, acquired with the iterative closest point (ICP) [1] algorithm, as reported in Table 1. In addition, we assess the visual quality of the predicted depth and shadow masks, and surface mesh, as shown in Figs. 4 and 6. The thresholds used to get the mesh from a volumetric representation are given in supplementary material.

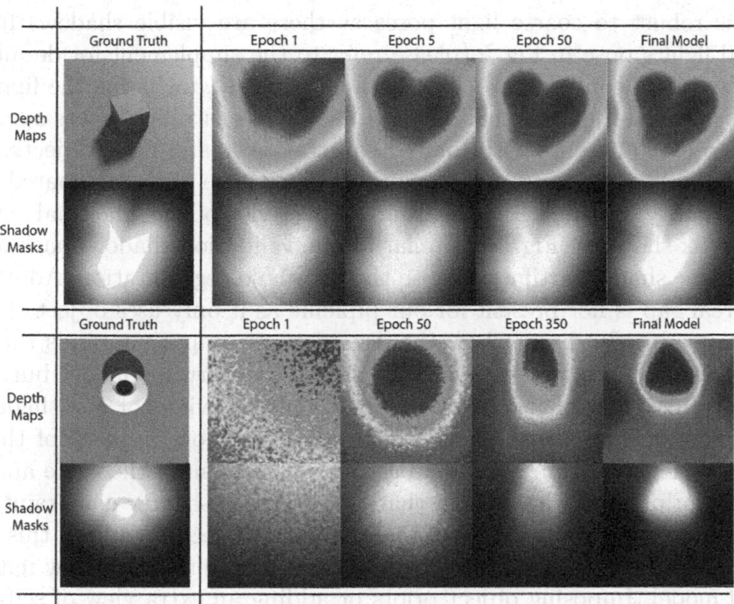

Fig. 6. Evolution of depth maps during training through a novel camera viewpoint. We visualize how the proposed forward model and differentiable rendering framework quickly converges to localize the object based on sparse shadow cues present and then slowly refines the coarse estimate on novel camera viewpoints. We believe that these results reveal that the differentiable volumetric rendering is a powerful framework that can rely on exploiting such physical cues to infer scene information.

Simulated 3D Reconstruction Results. We show the learned scene representations qualitatively by converting them to explicit meshes and rendering them using a signed distance function (SDF). Figure 4 shows the estimated meshes from our method on four object types. We compare our meshes to meshes generated by running vanilla NeRF on RGB images, and the ground truth by running marching cubes on the volume. Our datasets are rendered with overhead camera viewpoints, which enables shadows to be exploited. Given the binary and sparse nature of shadow masks in terms of their information content, we observe that our forward model coupled with the differentiable rendering framework converges to good coarse estimates of object geometry. Moreover, in the case of vases, the mesh reconstruction benefits from exploiting shadows as the algorithm can use *hidden* cues present in the scene, such as the curvature of the vase, which are only partially visible when relying on photometric cues. We also show predicted depth maps and shadow masks on novel camera viewpoints not used during training in the supplementary materials.

Real-World Reconstruction Results. We show our method's ability to converge to a fine mesh on real-world data of a hand in Fig. 5. Information on data acquisition is provided in the supplementary materials. We first note that our method is robust to coarse light poses as there are visible shadows from the estimated light's pose in Fig. 5 (please refer to the supplement for details). Our method is able to converge to a fine mesh of the hand, including the fingers and the space between them. We use only 74 shadow masks which makes our method versatile to environments with limited camera views and rarer objects, and no object priors. Moreover, we also show the convergence of the estimated shadow masks, disparity and depth maps from a novel viewpoint. The final estimated shadow mask shown in Fig. 5 is similar to the validation shadow mask and also contains some shadow artifacts due to the threshold segmentation. Additionally, the sim2real gap is not present for our pipleine as it only uses object shadows.

Lastly, we briefly discuss how the data-driven components finds the easiest solution that is consistent with our physics-driven forward model but not the actual world. We note that our training data only has views of cast shadows and does not contain any self-shadows which are present on the back of the hand. This causes the algorithm to instead estimate the mesh of the table and create a hollow imprint of the hand such that the specified shadow constraint is met. We note that a stand-alone mesh of the hand can be recovered from this imprint and that the recovered mesh is a possible solution given the shadow masks and proposed model. Imposing object priors or adding an extra view of self-shadow to the training set could result in a stand-alone mesh.

Novel Viewpoint Rendering. We observe predicted depth and shadow masks rendered from novel viewpoints in Fig. 6. The depth maps converge quite quickly to localize the object even when optimizing on the sparse physical cue of shadows. We posit that this convergence shows how powerful differentiable rendering is for exploiting physical cues to enable better 3D reconstruction. The depth maps converge slowly and we nudge the convergence by gradually decreasing the sigma values for the distance transform. The use of the distance transform leads to blurrier boundaries, however, the rendered mesh shows that a reasonably coarse 3D estimate is captured.

Quantitative Analysis. We also run our datasets on a vanilla NeRF [17] implementation [24]. At lower resolutions and overhead viewpoints, we see that the NeRF approach fails to provide a reasonable fine mesh. We believe this failure is due to the down-sampling of images to 64×64, which may also be a reason as to why our meshes fail to capture fine details. We run ICP [1] on the generated points cloud and show on-par results to the NeRF approach. Our goal, however, is not to outperform NeRF but to show the effectiveness of differentiable rendering framework in exploiting physical cues instead of ignoring them. The main takeaway from Table 1 is that differentiable volumetric renderers do not need to rely on 8 bit RGB information to reconstruct accurate meshes, but can also leverage other sources of information in the image in addition to relying on photometric cues.

Limitations. In cases such as the cuboid and the vase, we observe that the renderer converges to a predicted mesh that minimizes the shadow masks and the predicted shape even though it is typically a coarse estimate that envelopes the entirety of the object. This means that we see artifacts such as the pointed curve in the vase mesh, or the curvature of the bunny. Since our algorithm only has geometry information where the binary shadow mask is true, areas that are never in shadow have no surface, which leads to incomplete meshes. Imposing a prior can be a solution to this problem. Moreover, our method also assumes known lighting position, which may not always be available.

6 Discussion

Exploiting Physical Cues. One of the major goals of our work is to propose a framework within neural rendering that can readily exploit and learn from, instead of ignore, sparse physical cues, such as shadows. We believe that Fig. 5 shows that sparse physical cues like shadows, actually encode a lot of *hidden* information about the scene and can indeed be exploited. By constructing explicit differentiable forward models and leveraging gradient-friendly volumetric rendering, we can exploit these cues in conjunction with relying on photometric consistency between images.

Differentiable Shadow Rendering. In rasterization, shadow computation is done through shadow mapping as it is well suited and efficient. However, shadow computation in ray tracing are expensive as every ray needs to compute a path to the light source. Therefore, many ray tracing approaches also use shadow mapping to compute shadows efficiently. We use shadow mapping in our neural rendering approach as well. Our approach is similar to the shadow mapping in graphics as it assumes a binary label on shadows and does not consider soft shadows or ambient lighting. However, we invert shadow mapping and exploit it to do 3D reconstruction, not to render photorealistic images. Moreover, our approach is readily extendable to varying light and camera sources.

6.1 Future Work

We observe that volumetric rendering can converge onto coarse estimates of the object geometry by only relying on shadows, and can be extended to problems such as non-line-of-sight imaging (NLOS) [33] and imaging behind occluders [7]. As shadows themselves are never the only cue present to reconstruct the scene, our work can also be easily integrated with existing NeRF approaches that rely only on photometric cues as our shadow loss 7 can be used as a regularizer or an auxiliary loss, especially as shadows are invariant to viewpoint changes, surface reflectance properties, or texture changes.

6.2 Conclusions

We show that modern neural rendering techniques can learn neural scene representations (neural shadow fields) and encode 3D geometry just from binary shadow masks. We are motivated by traditional shape-from-X algorithms that typically construct physics-driven inverse models that can exploit cues for 3D reconstruction. We observe that data-driven neural rendering frameworks ignore cues such as shadows, relying on photometric cues instead. We thus propose a graphics-inspired differentiable shadow rendering component that leverages a volumetric renderer to encode a scene solely from its shadows.

Acknowledgement. This research was supported by the SMART Contract IARPA Grant #2021-20111000004. We would also like to thank Systems & Technology Research (STR). In addition, the authors would also like to thank Professor Voicu Popescu (Purdue University) for being so generous with his time and the valuable discussions that came from our meetings.

References

1. Besl, P., McKay, N.D.: A method for registration of 3-d shapes. IEEE Trans. Pattern Anal. Mach. Intell. **14**(2), 239–256 (1992). https://doi.org/10.1109/34.121791
2. Bobrow, D.G.: Comment on "Numerical shape from shading and occluding boundaries", pp. 89–94. The MIT Press (1994)
3. Boss, M., Braun, R., Jampani, V., Barron, J.T., Liu, C., Lensch, H.P.: Nerd: neural reflectance decomposition from image collections. In: IEEE International Conference on Computer Vision (ICCV) (2021)
4. Chang, A.X., et al.: ShapeNet: an Information-Rich 3D Model Repository. Technical report arXiv:1512.03012 [cs.GR], Stanford University – Princeton University – Toyota Technological Institute at Chicago (2015)
5. Falcon, W., et al.: Pytorch lightning. GitHub. Note (2019): https://github.com/PyTorchLightning/pytorch-lightning 3
6. Guo, Y., Kang, D., Bao, L., He, Y., Zhang, S.: Nerfren: neural radiance fields with reflections. CoRR abs/2111.15234 (2021). https://arxiv.org/abs/2111.15234
7. Henley, C., Maeda, T., Swedish, T., Raskar, R.: Imaging behind occluders using two-bounce light. In: Vedaldi, A., Bischof, H., Brox, T., Frahm, J.-M. (eds.) ECCV 2020. LNCS, vol. 12374, pp. 573–588. Springer, Cham (2020). https://doi.org/10.1007/978-3-030-58526-6_34
8. Kato, H., Ushiku, Y., Harada, T.: Neural 3d mesh renderer. In: The IEEE Conference on Computer Vision and Pattern Recognition (CVPR) (2018)
9. Landabaso, J.L., Pardàs, M., Casas, J.R.: Shape from inconsistent silhouette. Comput. Vis. Image Underst. **112**, 210–224 (2008)
10. Li, T.M., Aittala, M., Durand, F., Lehtinen, J.: Differentiable monte carlo ray tracing through edge sampling. ACM Trans. Graph. (Proc. SIGGRAPH Asia) **37**(6), 222:1–222:11 (2018)
11. Liu, R., Menon, S., Mao, C., Park, D., Stent, S., Vondrick, C.: Shadows shed light on 3d objects. arXiv e-prints pp. arXiv-2206 (2022)
12. Liu, S., Li, T., Chen, W., Li, H.: Soft rasterizer: a differentiable renderer for image-based 3d reasoning. In: Proceedings of the IEEE/CVF International Conference on Computer Vision, pp. 7708–7717 (2019)
13. Lombardi, S., Simon, T., Saragih, J., Schwartz, G., Lehrmann, A., Sheikh, Y.: Neural volumes: learning dynamic renderable volumes from images. ACM Trans. Graph. **38**(4), 65:1–65:14 (2019)

14. Loper, M.M., Black, M.J.: OpenDR: an approximate differentiable renderer. In: Fleet, D., Pajdla, T., Schiele, B., Tuytelaars, T. (eds.) ECCV 2014. LNCS, vol. 8695, pp. 154–169. Springer, Cham (2014). https://doi.org/10.1007/978-3-319-10584-0_11
15. Lorensen, W.E., Cline, H.E.: Marching cubes: a high resolution 3d surface construction algorithm. ACM Siggraph Comput. Graph. **21**(4), 163–169 (1987)
16. Martin, W.N., Aggarwal, J.K.: Volumetric descriptions of objects from multiple views. IEEE Trans. Pattern Anal. Mach. Intell. **PAMI-5**(2), 150–158 (1983). https://doi.org/10.1109/TPAMI.1983.4767367
17. Mildenhall, B., Srinivasan, P.P., Tancik, M., Barron, J.T., Ramamoorthi, R., Ng, R.: NeRF: representing scenes as neural radiance fields for view synthesis. In: Vedaldi, A., Bischof, H., Brox, T., Frahm, J.-M. (eds.) ECCV 2020. LNCS, vol. 12346, pp. 405–421. Springer, Cham (2020). https://doi.org/10.1007/978-3-030-58452-8_24
18. Niemeyer, M., Geiger, A.: GIRAFFE: representing scenes as compositional generative neural feature fields (2020). https://arxiv.org/abs/2011.12100
19. Niemeyer, M., Mescheder, L., Oechsle, M., Geiger, A.: Differentiable volumetric rendering: Learning implicit 3D representations without 3D supervision. In: Proceedings of the IEEE/CVF Conference on Computer Vision and Pattern Recognition (CVPR) (2019)
20. Niemeyer, M., Mescheder, L., Oechsle, M., Geiger, A.: Differentiable volumetric rendering: Learning implicit 3d representations without 3d supervision. In: Proceedings of IEEE Conference on Computer Vision and Pattern Recognition (CVPR) (2020)
21. Nimier-David, M., Vicini, D., Zeltner, T., Jakob, W.: Mitsuba 2: a retargetable forward and inverse renderer. ACM Trans. Graph. (TOG) **38**(6), 1–17 (2019)
22. Park, J.J., Florence, P., Straub, J., Newcombe, R., Lovegrove, S.: DeepSDF: Learning continuous signed distance functions for shape representation. In: Proceedings of the IEEE/CVF Conference on Computer Vision and Pattern Recognition (CVPR), pp. 165–174 (2019)
23. Paszke, A., et al.: Pytorch: an imperative style, high-performance deep learning library. In: Wallach, H., Larochelle, H., Beygelzimer, A., d'Alché-Buc, F., Fox, E., Garnett, R. (eds.) Adv. Neural Inf. Process. Syst. **32**, pp. 8024–8035. Curran Associates, Inc. (2019). https://papers.neurips.cc/paper/9015-pytorch-an-imperative-style-high-performance-deep-learning-library.pdf
24. Quei-An, C.: Nerf_pl: a pytorch-lightning implementation of nerf (2020). https://github.com/kwea123/nerf_pl/
25. Ronneberger, O., Fischer, P., Brox, T.: U-net: convolutional networks for biomedical image segmentation (2015)
26. Fridovich-Keil, S., Yu, A., Tancik, M., Chen, Q., Recht, B., Kanazawa, A.: Plenoxels: radiance fields without neural networks. In: CVPR (2022)
27. Savarese, S., Rushmeier, H., Bernardini, F., Perona, P.: Shadow carving. In: Proceedings Eighth IEEE International Conference on Computer Vision. ICCV 2001, vol. 1, pp. 190–197. IEEE (2001)
28. Schönberger, J.L., Frahm, J.-M.: Structure-from-Motion Revisited. In: Conference on Computer Vision and Pattern Recognition (CVPR) (2016)
29. Sitzmann, V., Thies, J., Heide, F., Nießner, M., Wetzstein, G., Zollhofer, M.: Deepvoxels: learning persistent 3d feature embeddings. In: Proceedings of the IEEE/CVF Conference on Computer Vision and Pattern Recognition, pp. 2437–2446 (2019)

30. Srinivasan, P.P., Deng, B., Zhang, X., Tancik, M., Mildenhall, B., Barron, J.T.: Nerv: neural reflectance and visibility fields for relighting and view synthesis (2020)
31. Tancik, M., et al.: Fourier features let networks learn high frequency functions in low dimensional domains (2020)
32. Tulsiani, S., Efros, A.A., Malik, J.: Multi-view consistency as supervisory signal for learning shape and pose prediction. In: Computer Vision and Pattern Regognition (CVPR) (2018)
33. Velten, A., Willwacher, T., Gupta, O., Veeraraghavan, A., Bawendi, M.G., Raskar, R.: Recovering threedimensional shape around a corner using ultrafast time-of-flight imaging. Nature, p. 745 (2012)
34. Verbin, D., Hedman, P., Mildenhall, B., Zickler, T., Barron, J.T., Srinivasan, P.P.: Ref-NeRF: structured view-dependent appearance for neural radiance fields. arXiv (2021)
35. Vogel, O., Valgaerts, L., Breuß, M., Weickert, J.: Making shape from shading work for real-world images. In: Denzler, J., Notni, G., Süße, H. (eds.) DAGM 2009. LNCS, vol. 5748, pp. 191–200. Springer, Heidelberg (2009). https://doi.org/10.1007/978-3-642-03798-6_20
36. Williams, L.: Casting curved shadows on curved surfaces. In: Proceedings of the 5th Annual Conference on Computer Graphics and Interactive Techniques, pp. 270–274 (1978)
37. Yamazaki, S., Srinivasa Narasimhan, G., Baker, S., Kanade, T.: The theory and practice of coplanar shadowgram imaging for acquiring visual hulls of intricate objects. Int. J. Comput. Vis. **81**, March 2009. https://doi.org/10.1007/s11263-008-0170-4
38. Ye, Y., Tulsiani, S., Gupta, A.: Shelf-supervised mesh prediction in the wild. In: Computer Vision and Pattern Recognition (CVPR) (2021)
39. Yu, A., Li, R., Tancik, M., Li, H., Ng, R., Kanazawa, A.: PlenOctrees for real-time rendering of neural radiance fields. In: ICCV (2021)
40. Zhang, J.Y., Yang, G., Tulsiani, S., Ramanan, D.: NeRS: neural reflectance surfaces for sparse-view 3d reconstruction in the wild. In: Conference on Neural Information Processing Systems (2021)
41. Zhang, R., Tsai, P.S., Cryer, J., Shah, M.: Shape-from-shading: a survey. IEEE Trans. Pattern Anal. Mach. Intell. **21**(8), 690–706 (1999). https://doi.org/10.1109/34.784284
42. Zheng, Q., Chellappa, R.: Estimation of illuminant direction, albedo, and shape from shading. IEEE Trans. Pattern Anal. Mach. Intell. **13**(7), 680–702 (1991). https://doi.org/10.1109/34.85658

Class-Incremental Novel Class Discovery

Subhankar Roy[1,2], Mingxuan Liu[1], Zhun Zhong[1(✉)], Nicu Sebe[1], and Elisa Ricci[1,2]

[1] University of Trento, Trento, Italy
{subhankar.roy,mingxuan.liu,zhun.zhong,niculae.sebe,e.ricci}@unitn.it
[2] Fondazione Bruno Kessler, Trento, Italy

Abstract. We study the new task of class-incremental Novel Class Discovery (class-iNCD), which refers to the problem of discovering novel categories in an unlabelled data set by leveraging a pre-trained model that has been trained on a labelled data set containing disjoint yet related categories. Apart from discovering novel classes, we also aim at preserving the ability of the model to recognize previously seen base categories. Inspired by rehearsal-based incremental learning methods, in this paper we propose a novel approach for class-iNCD which prevents forgetting of past information about the base classes by jointly exploiting base class feature prototypes and feature-level knowledge distillation. We also propose a self-training clustering strategy that simultaneously clusters novel categories and trains a joint classifier for both the base and novel classes. This makes our method able to operate in a class-incremental setting. Our experiments, conducted on three common benchmarks, demonstrate that our method significantly outperforms state-of-the-art approaches. Code is available at https://github.com/OatmealLiu/class-iNCD.

Keywords: Novel class discovery · Class-incremental learning

1 Introduction

Humans are bestowed with the excellent cognitive skills to learn continually over their lifetime [12], and in most cases without the need of explicit supervision [1]. Thus, it has been a long-standing goal of the machine learning research community to build Artificial Intelligence (AI) systems that can mimic this human-level performance. In an attempt to realize this, much effort has been dedicated to learn deep learning models from large reservoirs of both labelled [10,17,24] and unlabelled data [3,4]. Aside from being effective learners, by imitating human learning mechanisms, neural networks should also be flexible to absorb novel concepts (or *classes*) after having learned some patterns with the past data. The

S. Roy and M. Liu—Contributed equally.

Supplementary Information The online version contains supplementary material available at https://doi.org/10.1007/978-3-031-19827-4_19.

S. Avidan et al. (Eds.): ECCV 2022, LNCS 13693, pp. 317–333, 2022.
https://doi.org/10.1007/978-3-031-19827-4_19

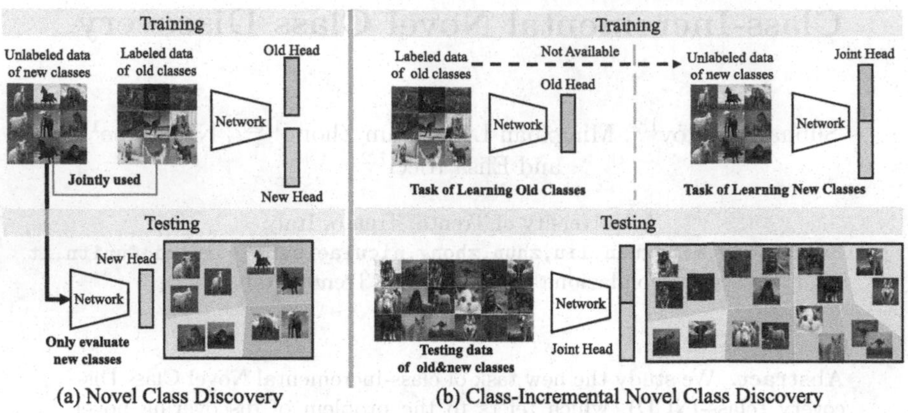

Fig. 1. Comparison between the settings (a) Novel Class Discovery (NCD) which solely concerns the performance of novel classes, and (b) the proposed class-incremental NCD (class-iNCD) measures performance of all the classes seen so far with a single classifier.

task of automatically discovering novel (or *new*) classes in an unsupervised fashion while leveraging some previously learned knowledge is referred to as *novel class discovery* (NCD) [11,15,16,37,38] (see Fig. 1(a)). NCD has gained significant attention in the recent times due to its practicality of efficiently learning novel classes without relying on large quantities of unlabelled data [15].

Most of the proposed NCD solutions rely on stage-wise [16,19,20] or joint [11,15,37] learning schemes on the labelled and the unlabelled data, with the assumption that structures discovered on the labelled images could be leveraged as a proxy supervision on the unlabelled images. It has been shown that NCD benefits more when the model is trained jointly on the labelled data while using a clustering objective on the unlabelled data [11,15,37,38]. However, access to the labelled data after the pre-training stage can not always be guaranteed in real-world applications due to privacy or storage issues. This calls for a more pragmatic NCD setting where the labelled images would be discarded and only the pre-trained model could be transferred for learning the novel classes. Being meaningful, such *source-free* model adaptation has been explored in the related areas of domain adaptation [28,36]. Although seems more practical, such a training scheme would gradually cause the network to erase all the previously learned information about the old (or *base*) classes. This drop in the base class performance when the labelled data set becomes unavailable is primarily attributed to the phenomenon of *catastrophic forgetting* [8] in neural networks. In most of the aforementioned NCD methods the performance on the novel classes are only deemed important, without any consideration for preserving the performance on the base classes. We believe that such a setting is of little practical significance in the real world because the adapted model becomes unusable on the base classes and retraining is infeasible.

Given the inherent drawbacks of the existing NCD setting, we argue that an ideal NCD method should aim to learn novel classes without the explicit presence of the labelled data and at the same time preserve the performance on the base classes. This new setting is referred to as *task-incremental* NCD (iNCD), and indeed has been very recently studied in [29]. In details, ResTune [29] uses knowledge distillation [27] on the network logits to prevent forgetting on the base classes and a clustering objective [33] with task specific network weights for the novel classes. As opposed to the ResTune [29], which facilitates iNCD by solely improving the ability of the network to learn novel classes, we additionally improve the incremental learning aspect in iNCD as well. Specifically, inspired by the rehearsal-based incremental learning methods [2,7,31] which are known to be effective, we propose to store the base class feature *prototypes* from the previous task as exemplars, instead of raw images. Features derived from the stored prototypes are then *replayed* to prevent forgetting old information on the base classes in addition to feature-level knowledge distillation. On the other hand, to facilitate learning of novel classes, we dedicate a task specific classifier that is optimized with robust rank statistics [15]. Disadvantageously, the introduction of task specific classifier leads to the dependence on the task-id of an input sample during inference. To overcome reliance on task-id, we propose to maintain a joint classifier for both the base and novel classes, which is trained with the pseudo-labels generated by the task specific one. We call this setting as *class-incremental* NCD (class-iNCD) as it does not allow the task-id information to be used during inference. The high level overview of the new class-iNCD setting is shown in the Fig. 1(b). As our proposed method amalgamates **F**eature **R**eplay and Distillati**o**n with **S**elf-**T**raining we name it FRoST. In summary, the contributions of this work are three-fold:

- We propose a novel framework, FRoST, that can tackle the newly introduced and relevant task of class-incremental novel class discovery (class-iNCD).
- Our FRoST is equipped with prototypes for feature-replay and employs feature-level knowledge distillation to prevent forgetting. Moreover, it uses pseudo-labels from the task specific head to efficiently learn novel classes without interference, enabling us to achieve a task-agnostic classifier.
- We run extensive experiments on three common benchmarks to prove the effectiveness of our method. FRoST also obtains state-of-the-art performance when compared with the existing baselines. Additionally, we run experiments on a sequence of tasks of unlabelled sets and verify its generality.

2 Related Works

Novel Class Discovery (NCD) deals with the task of learning to discover new semantic classes in an unlabelled data set by utilizing the knowledge acquired from another labelled data set [16,35]. It is assumed that the classes in the labelled and unlabelled set are disjoint. So far, several NCD methods have been proposed and they can be broadly classified into two broad sub-categories. The first category of NCD methods use a stage-wise training scheme where the model is first pre-trained on the labelled set, followed by fine-tuning on the unlabelled data using an unsupervised clustering loss [16,19,20,29]. Barring [29], none of the above methods consider to tackle the forgetting issue, and as a result the model loses the ability to classify the base classes. The second category comprise of NCD methods that assume both the labelled and unlabelled data are available simultaneously, which are then trained jointly [11,15,21,37,38]. As demonstrated in [29], the NCD methods which rely on joint training always outperform the stage-wise NCD methods. However, the latter family of NCD methods rely on the availability of labelled data, which is often not permitted due to privacy reasons. This makes stage-wise training scheme favourable to tackle class-iNCD, but it lacks the capability to prevent forgetting. Similar to the ResTune [29], we also build our framework that can be trained in a stage-wise manner and also be able to maintain performance on the base classes. Different from the ResTune we use the predictions of the novel class classifier as pseudo-labels (PL) to train a single joint classifier that can classify both base and novel classes.

Incremental Learning (IL) is a learning paradigm where a model is trained on a sequence of tasks such that data from only the current task is available for training, while the model is evaluated on all the observed tasks. The IL methods are designed so as to prevent catastrophic forgetting [13] of the model on the old tasks and at the same time flexible enough to learn on new tasks [6]. Most early IL methods addressed the *task-incremental learning* setting (task-IL), where the model has access to a task-id for choosing the task-specific classifier during the testing phase. Given the practical limitations of knowing the task-id during inference, more recent IL methods have started to address the *class-incremental learning* (class-IL) setting, where the task-id is not available during inference. This makes class-IL setting practical and at the same time more challenging than the task-IL setting. Our FRoST also operates in the class-IL setting, which we call as class-iNCD. Existing IL methods can be subdivided into three broad categories: *regularization-based* methods [9,22,27,34], *exemplar-based* methods [2,5,7,31] and methods focused on *task-recency bias* problem [32]. We refer the readers to the survey in [30] for an exhaustive list of class-IL methods. In our FRoST we propose to use a combination of knowledge distillation [27] at intermediate feature-level and storage of base class feature prototypes as exemplars to prevent forgetting in feature extractor and classifier, respectively. We discuss later in Sect. 3 why this choice is suitable for the class-iNCD setting.

3 Method

In this section we describe our FRoST for the task of class-iNCD. Before delving into the detail we lay down some preliminaries related to our method.

Problem Definition and Notation. In the setting of class-incremental novel class discovery (class-iNCD) we are initially given $n^{[\mathrm{L}]}$ instances of a labelled data set $\mathcal{D}^{[\mathrm{L}]} = \{(\mathbf{x}_i^{[\mathrm{L}]}, \mathbf{y}_i^{[\mathrm{L}]})\}_{i=1}^{n^{[\mathrm{L}]}}$ belonging to the supervised task $\mathcal{T}^{[\mathrm{L}]}$, where

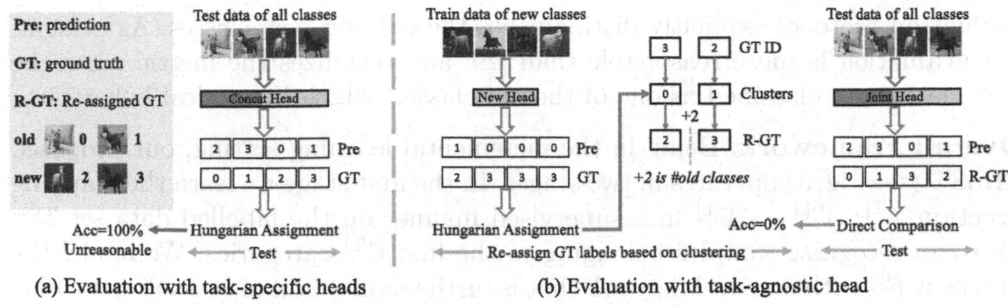

Fig. 2. Evaluation protocol comparison (a) evaluation with task-specific heads in iNCD [29] and (b) evaluation with task-agnostic head in our class-iNCD.

$\mathbf{x}^{[\text{L}]} \in \mathcal{X}^{[\text{L}]}$ represents the input images and $\mathbf{y}^{[\text{L}]} \in \mathcal{Y}^{[\text{L}]}$ as $|\mathcal{C}^{[\text{L}]}|$-dimensional one-hot labels. Once standard supervised training is finished on the task $\mathcal{T}^{[\text{L}]}$, the data set $\mathcal{D}^{[\text{L}]}$ is discarded and we are presented with $n^{[\text{U}]}$ instances from a new task $\mathcal{T}^{[\text{U}]}$. The task $\mathcal{T}^{[\text{U}]}$ has an unlabelled data set $\mathcal{D}^{[\text{U}]} = \{\mathbf{x}_j^{[\text{U}]}\}_{j=i}^{n^{[\text{U}]}}$ where $\mathbf{x}^{[\text{U}]} \in \mathcal{X}^{[\text{U}]}$ are the unlabelled images containing $\mathcal{C}^{[\text{U}]}$ classes. As in any NCD setting [16], it is assumed that the labels in $\mathcal{Y}^{[\text{L}]}$ and $\mathcal{Y}^{[\text{U}]}$ are disjoint, *i.e.*, $\mathcal{Y}^{[\text{L}]} \cap \mathcal{Y}^{[\text{U}]} = \emptyset$. The goal of class-iNCD is to cluster the images in $\mathcal{D}^{[\text{U}]}$ by just leveraging the learnt information contained in the mapping function $f^{[\text{L}]} \colon \mathcal{X}^{[\text{L}]} \to \mathcal{Y}^{[\text{L}]}$, while still behaving well on the previous task $\mathcal{T}^{[\text{L}]}$. In other words, we are interested in learning a single mapping function $f \colon \mathcal{X} \to \mathcal{Y}^{[\text{L}]} \cup \mathcal{Y}^{[\text{U}]}$ that can be used to infer the label of any test image $\mathbf{x} \in \{\mathcal{X}^{[\text{L}]} \cup \mathcal{X}^{[\text{U}]}\}$. This is in sharp contrast to the existing NCD methods where the performance on $\mathcal{T}^{[\text{L}]}$ is not of interest.

Evaluation Protocol. In the NCD methods [11,37], task-specific heads are trained for old and new classes[1], respectively. This poses a limitation, as they can only operate in task-specific NCD setting. To address this problem, ResTune [29] uses the concatenation of old and new heads during inference. The class-incremental performance is estimated with the Hungarian Assignment (HA) [25] by regarding this problem as a clustering task. However, this evaluation protocol is indeed improper in class-iNCD, since it does not explicitly distinguish the old and new classes. As shown in the Fig. 2(a), the classifier recognizes the samples of old classes as novel classes (and vice versa), and yet the accuracy obtained by HA is still 100%, making the evaluation in [29] unfair.

In this work, we learn a task-agnostic head (or *joint* head) and propose a new evaluation protocol for class-iNCD (see Fig. 2(b)). In details, we first use the *new head* to estimate the predictions of unlabeled data from the new classes. We utilize the HA [25] to re-assign ground-truth IDs based on the predictions and ground-truth labels for the new classes only. The joint (task-agnostic) classifier is used to evaluate the new classes test samples by directly comparing the predictions with these re-assigned ground-truth labels. Whereas for the old classes test data, we evaluate using the old classes ground truth. As shown in Fig. 2(b), our

[1] When referring to classes, we regard old & base; and, new & novel interchangeably.

evaluation protocol explicitly distinguishes the old and new classes. As evident, our evaluation is more reasonable than [29] and penalizes the metric when the new classes are classified as one of the old classes, which is an ideal behaviour.

Overall Framework. Being in the incremental learning setting, our proposed FRoST (see Fig. 3) operates in two stages. In the first stage we learn the mapping function $f^{[L]}: \mathcal{X}^{[L]} \rightarrow \mathcal{Y}^{[L]}$ in a supervised manner on the labelled data set $\mathcal{D}^{[L]}$ that can recognize samples belonging to the first $\mathcal{C}^{[L]}$ categories. We model the function $f^{[L]}$ with a neural network that is further composed of two sub-networks: feature extractor $g(\cdot)$ and a linear classifier $h^{[L]}(\cdot)$ that outputs $\mathcal{C}^{[L]}$ logits, such that $f^{[L]} = h^{[L]} \circ g$. The feature extractor g and classifier $h^{[L]}$ are parameterized by θ_g and $\theta_{h^{[L]}}$, respectively. Before we move to the second stage, we compute per-class intermediate feature prototypes $\boldsymbol{\mu}_c$ from the intermediate features $\mathbf{z}^{[L]} = g(\mathbf{x}^{[L]})$, belonging to each class c. Additionally, we also compute and store the variance of the features of class c as $\boldsymbol{v}_c{}^2$.

In the second stage, the $\mathcal{D}^{[L]}$ is discarded and the novel classes are learned on $\mathcal{D}^{[U]}$ by reusing the transferred network weights $f^{[L]}$. Since our goal is to learn an unique classifier that can accommodate $\mathcal{C}^{[A]} = \mathcal{C}^{[L]} + \mathcal{C}^{[U]}$ classes, we extend the classifier $h^{[L]}$ to $h^{[A]}$ in order to incorporate the $\mathcal{C}^{[U]}$ novel classes. Besides $h^{[A]}$, we instantiate a new task-specific classifier $h^{[U]}$ for $\mathcal{T}^{[U]}$ that is trained on $\mathcal{D}^{[U]}$ to exclusively classify the novel classes. The classifiers $h^{[A]}$ and $h^{[U]}$ are parameterized by $\theta_{h^{[U]}}$ and $\theta_{h^{[A]}}$, respectively. In details, the network $f^{[U]} = h^{[U]} \circ g$ is trained using the clustering objective in [15] that leverages previously learned information to provide supervision using the robust rank statistics. With the goal of learning a joint classifier $h^{[A]}$, we obtain pseudo-label for $\mathbf{x}^{[U]}$ from $h^{[U]}$ and distill it to the newly extended part of $h^{[A]}$, which handles the novel classes. On the other hand, to mitigate forgetting on the base classes of $\mathcal{T}^{[L]}$ we employ two strategies: *feature-level* knowledge distillation [18,27] on g that ensures the feature encoding for the old task $\mathcal{T}^{[L]}$ does not drift too far while learning on $\mathcal{T}^{[U]}$; and *generative feature-replay* drawn from a Gaussian distribution $\mathcal{N}(\boldsymbol{\mu}_c, \boldsymbol{v}_c{}^2)$ is used to preserve performance of the top part of the $h^{[A]}$, which is responsible for classifying the base classes. During inference the classifier $h^{[A]}$ is used.

3.1 Preliminaries

Supervised Training. In the first stage of the class-iNCD task we have at disposal the labelled images from $\mathcal{D}^{[L]}$. This stage consists in learning a supervised model $f^{[L]}$ that can classify the base classes drawn from the task $\mathcal{T}^{[L]}$. We aim to learn the parameters $(\{\theta_g, \theta_{h^{[L]}}\})$ of the model $f^{[L]} = h^{[L]} \circ g$ by using a supervised *cross-entropy* loss:

$$\mathcal{L}_{\text{ce}} = -\mathbb{E}_{p(\mathbf{x}^{[L]},\mathbf{y}^{[L]})} \frac{1}{C^{[L]}} \sum_{k=1}^{C^{[L]}} y_k^{[L]} \log \sigma_k(h^{[L]}(g(\mathbf{x}^{[L]}))), \tag{1}$$

where $\sigma_k(\mathbf{l}) = {}^{\exp(l_k)}/{}_{\sum_j \exp(l_j)}$ represents the likelihood corresponding to the kth output from the model and $C^{[L]}$ is the number of classes in the task $\mathcal{T}^{[L]}$.

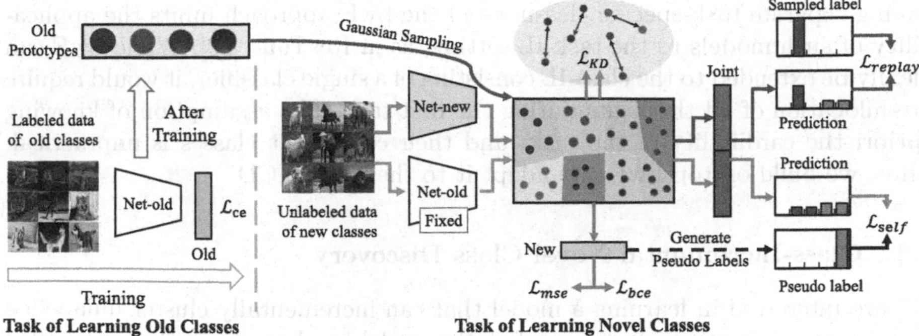

Fig. 3. An overview of the proposed FroST. **Left**: a base model is learned supervisedly ($\mathcal{L}_{\text{ce}}$) on the old classes. Old class-prototypes and variances are stored. **Right**: the new classes are learned with a clustering objective ($\mathcal{L}_{\text{bce}}$). Forgetting on old classes is prevented by using feature-distillation ($\mathcal{L}_{\text{KD}}$) and feature-replay ($\mathcal{L}_{\text{replay}}$) with the class-prototypes. A joint classifier is learned by self-training ($\mathcal{L}_{\text{self}}$) with pseudo-labels.

Knowledge Distillation to Prevent Forgetting. Having learned an optimal model on a given task, the main challenge in IL is to learn new tasks without forgetting the past information. A very popular regularization-based approach to overcome forgetting on previously learned tasks is by using *knowledge distillation* (KD) [18]. Concretely, based on KD, *Learning without Forgetting* (LwF) [27] is an effective method commonly used in IL. It consists in penalizing the network if the representation of data from previous tasks drifts too far while learning on a new task. Assuming a simplified task-IL learning scenario containing just two tasks: $\mathcal{T}^{[\text{old}]}$ and $\mathcal{T}^{[\text{new}]}$, where a model $f^{[\text{old}]} = h^{[\text{old}]} \circ g$ has already been trained using the objective in Eq. (1) and a new task $\mathcal{T}^{[\text{new}]}$ has been presented to the learning algorithm. The goal of LwF is to prevent forgetting on $\mathcal{T}^{[\text{old}]}$ while learning on $\mathcal{T}^{[\text{new}]}$. LwF keeps a copy of the old model $f^{[\text{old}]} = h^{[\text{old}]} \circ g^{[\text{old}]}$ and simultaneously creates a new instance $f^{[\text{new}]} = h^{[\text{new}]} \circ g^{[\text{new}]}$ (with $g^{[\text{new}]} = \text{g}^{[\text{old}]}$) for learning on $\mathcal{T}^{[\text{new}]}$. The $f^{[\text{new}]}$ differs from $f^{[\text{old}]}$ in the final classification head where the task-specific classifier $h^{[\text{new}]}$ exclusively handles the class assignment for the new classes in $\mathcal{T}^{[\text{new}]}$. Given a sample $\mathbf{x}^{[\text{new}]}$ from the new task $\mathcal{T}^{[\text{new}]}$, LwF aims to match the pre-recorded logits $\mathbf{a}^{[\text{old}]} = h^{[\text{old}]}(g^{[\text{old}]}(\mathbf{x}^{[\text{new}]}))$ from the frozen $f^{[\text{old}]}$ with the old task logits $\hat{\mathbf{a}}^{[\text{old}]} = h^{[\text{old}]}(g^{[\text{new}]}(\mathbf{x}^{[\text{new}]}))$. Essentially, this prevents $g^{[\text{new}]}$ to produce feature encoding that is too different from that of $g^{[\text{old}]}$, since the success for the old task heavily depends on it. Formally, the LwF loss at logits-level is given as:

$$\mathcal{L}_{\text{KD}}^{\text{logits}} = -\mathbb{E}_{p(\mathbf{x}^{[\text{new}]})} \frac{1}{K^{[\text{old}]}} \sum_{k=1}^{K^{[\text{old}]}} \pi_k(h^{[\text{old}]}(g^{[\text{old}]}(\mathbf{x}^{[\text{new}]}))) \log \pi_k(h^{[\text{old}]}(g^{[\text{new}]}(\mathbf{x}^{[\text{new}]}))), \quad (2)$$

where $\pi_k(\mathbf{a}) = {}^{\exp(a_k/\tau)}/_{\sum_j \exp(a_j/\tau)}$ is the temperature controlled likelihood of the model with τ being the temperature. The parameters ($\{\theta_{g^{[\text{new}]}}, \theta_{h^{[\text{old}]}}\}$) corresponding to $g^{[\text{new}]}$ and $h^{[\text{old}]}$ are updated with Eq. (2). However, the need of having separate task-specific classifiers in the LwF approach limits the applicability of such models to the task-IL setting, as in ResTune [29]. While LwF can ideally be extended to the class-IL consisting of a single classifier, it would require pre-allocation of all the logits during the first task. The assumption of knowing apriori the cardinality of the tasks and their contituent classes is impractical. Thus, we build on top LwF and adapt it to the class-iNCD.

3.2 Class-Incremental Novel Class Discovery

We are interested in learning a model that can incrementally cluster unlabelled images into a set of novel classes, after the model has been trained on a labelled set of images. Besides good performance on the novel classes we also desire to preserve the performance on the previously seen classes, without having access to or storing images from the previous tasks. Most importantly, at any point of time during the training sessions, we maintain a single classification head for all the classes seen so far. To address the challenging task of class-iNCD we propose to tackle it from two different axes. The first axis is concerned with learning discriminative features on the unlabelled data set $\mathcal{D}^{[\mathtt{U}]}$ by using a clustering objective. Although the model gets better at classifying the novel classes, it's performance gradually deteriorates on the base classes due to forgetting [8]. To overcome this issue, the second axis deals with preventing forgetting on all base classes by using the images only from the new task, combined with a feature-replay strategy. We elaborate them below.

Self-training for Novel Class Discovery. When presented with an unlabelled data set $\mathcal{D}^{[\mathtt{U}]}$, the discovery step in class-iNCD involves learning the weights of the network $f^{[\mathtt{U}]} = h^{[\mathtt{U}]} \circ g$. While the newly initialized classifier $h^{[\mathtt{U}]}$ yet lacks the capability to classify images into novel categories, the feature extractor g on the other hand has already been trained on a related labelled data set $\mathcal{D}^{[\mathtt{L}]}$ and has a notion of what constitutes a semantic concept in an image. Adopting this ideology from the NCD method AutoNovel [15], the pairwise similarity between a pair of unlabelled images $(\mathbf{x}_i^{[\mathtt{U}]}, \mathbf{x}_j^{[\mathtt{U}]})$ is inferred and provided as a weak form of supervision in the discovery step. The feature descriptors $\mathbf{z}_i^{[\mathtt{U}]} = g(\mathbf{x}_i^{[\mathtt{U}]})$ and $\mathbf{z}_j^{[\mathtt{U}]} = g(\mathbf{x}_j^{[\mathtt{U}]})$ corresponding to the pair $(\mathbf{x}_i^{[\mathtt{U}]}, \mathbf{x}_j^{[\mathtt{U}]})$ are then compared using the robust rank statistics. If the top-k ranked dimensions of the feature descriptor pair $(\mathbf{z}_i^{[\mathtt{U}]}, \mathbf{z}_j^{[\mathtt{U}]})$ are found the same then $(\mathbf{x}_i^{[\mathtt{U}]}, \mathbf{x}_j^{[\mathtt{U}]})$ can be considered to belong to the same class. The pairwise pseudo-label is formulated as:

$$\tilde{y}_{ij}^{[\mathtt{U}]} = \mathbb{1}\{\text{top}_k(\mathbf{z}_i^{[\mathtt{U}]}) = \text{top}_k(\mathbf{z}_j^{[\mathtt{U}]})\}, \tag{3}$$

where $\text{top}_k : \mathbf{z}^{[\mathtt{U}]} \rightarrow \mathcal{S}\{(1, \dots, k)\} \subset \mathcal{P}\{(1, \dots, |\mathbf{z}^{[\mathtt{U}]}|)\}$ denotes the subset of top-k most activated feature indices in $\mathbf{z}^{[\mathtt{U}]}$. This pairwise pseudo-label is then used to train the classifier $h^{[\mathtt{U}]}$ for the novel classes. In detail, the dot-product of the classifier's predictions $p_{ij} = \sigma(\langle h^{[\mathtt{U}]}(g(\mathbf{x}_i^{[\mathtt{U}]})), h^{[\mathtt{U}]}(g(\mathbf{x}_j^{[\mathtt{U}]}))\rangle)$ can be interpreted as a similarity between $\mathbf{x}_i^{[\mathtt{U}]}$ and $\mathbf{x}_j^{[\mathtt{U}]}$, where $\sigma(\cdot)$ is a logistic function. Thus, the pairwise pseudo-label $\tilde{y}_{ij}^{[U]}$ computed in Eq. (3) is used to enforce this association between $\mathbf{x}_i^{[U]}$ and $\mathbf{x}_j^{[U]}$. The parameters $(\{\theta_g, \theta_{h^{[U]}}\})$ are trained with a *binary cross-entropy* loss as:

$$\mathcal{L}_{\text{bce}} = -\mathbb{E}_{p(\mathbf{z}^{[U]})}\tilde{y}_{ij}^{[U]} \log(p_{ij}) + (1 - \tilde{y}_{ij}^{[U]}) \log(1 - p_{ij}). \tag{4}$$

While the objective in Eq. (4) learns a classifier for the novel classes, such training scheme makes the inference step dependent on task-id like ResTune. In order to make our model suitable for class-iNCD we resort to self-training with the help of pseudo-labels that are computed from $f^{[U]}$ to train the joint classifier $h^{[A]}$. In details, given the goal of learning the model $f^{[A]} = h^{[A]} \circ g$, we use $h^{[U]}$ to compute the pseudo-label $\hat{y}^{[U]}$ for an unlabelled image $\mathbf{x}^{[U]}$. The $\hat{y}^{[U]}$ is then used to supervise the training of $h^{[A]}$. The self-training loss is described as:

$$\mathcal{L}_{\text{self}} = -\mathbb{E}_{(\mathbf{x}^{[U]}, \hat{\mathbf{y}}^{[U]})} \frac{1}{|C^{[A]}|} \sum_{k=1}^{|C^{[A]}|} \hat{y}_k^{[U]} \log \sigma_k(h^{[A]}(g(\mathbf{x}^{[U]}))), \tag{5}$$

where

$$\hat{y}^{[U]} = C^{[L]} + \arg\max_{k \in C^{[U]}} h^{[U]}(g(\mathbf{x}^{[U]})). \tag{6}$$

Since the pairwise pseudo-labels in Eq. (3) can be noisy, it can lead to a poorly trained $h^{[U]}$. As a consequence, the noisy pseudo-labels $\hat{y}^{[U]}$ from $h^{[U]}$ can have an adverse impact on the training of the joint classifier $h^{[A]}$. To minimize the cascading error propagation we also enforce consistency between two correlated views for an unlabelled image $\mathbf{x}^{[U]}$. Specifically, using stochastic data augmentation on $\mathbf{x}^{[U]}$ we generate a correlated view $\bar{\mathbf{x}}^{[U]}$ and optimize $(\{\theta_g, \theta_{h^{[U]}}\})$ with a *mean-squared error* loss as:

$$\mathcal{L}_{\text{mse}} = \mathbb{E}_{p(\mathbf{x}^{[U]}, \bar{\mathbf{x}}^{[U]})} \frac{1}{|C^{[U]}|} \sum_{k=1}^{|C^{[U]}|} \Big(\sigma_k\big(h^{[U]}(g(\mathbf{x}^{[U]}))\big) - \sigma_k\big(h^{[U]}(g(\bar{\mathbf{x}}^{[U]}))\big)\Big)^2. \tag{7}$$

Finally, the overall loss for discovering novel classes and having a single classifier for all the classes seen so far can be written as:

$$\mathcal{L}_{\text{novel}} = \mathcal{L}_{\text{bce}} + \omega_{\text{self}}(t)\mathcal{L}_{\text{self}} + \omega_{\text{mse}}(t)\mathcal{L}_{\text{mse}}, \tag{8}$$

where $\omega_{\text{self}}(t)$ and $\omega_{\text{mse}}(t)$ are ramp-up functions to ensure stability in learning.

Feature Replay and Distillation for Class-Incremental Learning. While the proposed self-training assists the model $f^{[A]}$ in discovering the novel classes, it simultaneously loses the ability to predict the old classes in $\mathcal{T}^{[U]}$. To mitigate the forgetting we propose feature replay and feature distillation. To recall, at the end supervised training on $\mathcal{T}^{[L]}$ and before discarding $\mathcal{D}^{[L]}$ we compute the class prototype $\boldsymbol{\mu}_c^{[L]}$ and variance $\boldsymbol{v}_c^{[L]^2}$ for each base class as:

$$\boldsymbol{\mu}_c^{[L]} = \frac{1}{n_c^{[L]}} \sum_{i=1}^{n_c^{[L]}} g(\mathbf{x}_i^{[L]}), \qquad \boldsymbol{v}_c^{[L]^2} = \frac{1}{n_c^{[L]}} \sum_{i=1}^{n_c^{[L]}} (g(\mathbf{x}_i^{[L]}) - \boldsymbol{\mu}_c^{[L]})^2, \tag{9}$$

where $n_c^{[\text{L}]}$ denotes the number of samples belonging to class c in $\mathcal{D}^{[\text{L}]}$. While learning on the new task $\mathcal{T}^{[\text{U}]}$; the weights of the joint classifier $h^{[\text{A}]}$, corresponding to the base classes $C^{[\text{L}]}$, are trained by replaying features from the class-specific Gaussian distribution $\mathcal{N}(\boldsymbol{\mu}_c^{[\text{L}]}, \boldsymbol{v}_c^{[\text{L}]^2})$ of $\mathcal{T}^{[\text{L}]}$. The feature-replay loss is given as:

$$\mathcal{L}_{\text{replay}} = -\mathbb{E}_{c \sim C^{[\text{L}]}} \mathbb{E}_{(\mathbf{z}^{[\text{L}]}, \mathbf{y}_c^{[\text{L}]}) \sim \mathcal{N}(\boldsymbol{\mu}_c, \boldsymbol{v}_c{}^2)} \sum_{k=1}^{|C^{[\text{A}]}|} y_{kc}^{[\text{L}]} \log \sigma_k(h^{[\text{A}]}(\mathbf{z}^{[\text{L}]})). \quad (10)$$

As the feature extractor g also gets updated during the optimization of Eq. (8), this will make the prototypes outdated. To keep the feature replay useful we add an extra regularization on g with the help of feature distillation, which is given as:

$$\mathcal{L}_{\text{KD}}^{\text{feat}} = -\mathbb{E}_{p(\mathbf{x}^{[\text{U}]})} \left|\left| g^{[\text{L}]}(\mathbf{x}^{[\text{U}]}) - g(\mathbf{x}^{[\text{U}]}) \right|\right|_2, \quad (11)$$

where $g^{[\text{L}]}$ is the feature extractor from the previous task and is kept frozen.

Conventionally, in supervised class-IL or task-IL, regularization with the LwF loss in the logits space while learning supervisedly on a new task is usually effective in preventing forgetting. Contrarily in class-iNCD, as the novel classes need to be learned without explicit supervision, it makes the optimization of NCD part interfere with that of forgetting. This motivates us to decouple the objective for *not-forgetting* into $\mathcal{L}_{\text{replay}}$ and $\mathcal{L}_{\text{KD}}^{\text{feat}}$. We show later in Sect. 4 with adequate experiments the disadvantages of using LwF on the logits of the network. The overall objective for not-forgetting past information is given as:

$$\mathcal{L}_{\text{past}} = \mathcal{L}_{\text{replay}} + \lambda \mathcal{L}_{\text{KD}}^{\text{feat}}, \quad (12)$$

where λ is used to weight the feature distillation loss.

Overall Training. Finally, our FRoST is optimized with the following objective:

$$\mathcal{L}_{\text{FRoST}} = \mathcal{L}_{\text{novel}} + \mathcal{L}_{\text{past}}. \quad (13)$$

4 Experiments

4.1 Experimental Setup

Datasets. We have used three data sets to conduct experiments for class-iNCD: CIFAR-10 [23], CIFAR-100 [23] and Tiny-ImageNet [26]. We split the data sets into the old and new classes following the existing NCD and iNCD works [15, 29, 37]. The splits are reported in the supplementary material.

Evaluation Metrics. We used our new evaluation protocol (Sect. 3) to evaluate the performance on the test data for all the classes. We report three classification accuracies, denoted as **Old**, **New** and **All**. They represent the accuracy obtained from the joint classifier head on the samples of the old, new and old+new classes, respectively. Refer to the supplementary material for details.

Implementation Details. We used ResNet-18 [17] as the backbone in all the experiments. We have adopted most of the hyperparameters from AutoNovel [15]. We introduce only one additional hyperparemeter λ, which is set to 10. Rest of the implementation details can be found in the supplementary material.

4.2 Ablation Studies

Effectiveness of Feature Replay and Distillation. In Table 1 we measure the impact of the components proposed for not forgetting: feature distillation (FD), and feature replay (FR). The FRoST without FD and FR results in complete forgetting of the old classes. This is not surprising because without FD the feature extractor has moved far away from the original configuration. Moreover, as the joint classifier weights corresponding to the new classes are only optimized during the NCD stage (due to the disabled loss Eq. (10)), it leads to what is called the task-recency bias, resulting in higher norms for the new classes weights (see Fig. 4). In other words, for any old test sample, the classifier is highly biased to predict the new classes, leading to complete misclassification of old classes. Similar effect is observed when FD is enabled but FR is disabled.

Table 1. Ablation study of the proposed feature distillation (FD), feature replay (FR) and self-training (ST) that form our FRoST for the class-iNCD.

Methods	CIFAR-10			CIFAR-100			Tiny-ImageNet			Average		
	Old	New	All	Old	New	All	Old	New	All	Old	New	All
FRoST (Ours)	77.4	49.5	**63.5**	62.5	45.8	**59.2**	54.4	33.9	**52.4**	64.8	43.1	**58.3**
w/o FD & FR	0.0	36.4	18.2	0.0	33.1	6.6	0.0	37.2	3.7	0.0	35.6	9.5
w/o FD	0.0	39.4	19.7	0.0	33.1	6.6	0.0	34.3	3.4	0.0	35.6	9.9
w/o FR	0.0	**73.3**	36.6	0.0	**57.8**	11.6	0.0	**40.9**	4.1	0.0	**57.3**	17.4
w/o ST	**91.7**	0.0	45.8	**69.2**	0.0	55.4	**57.5**	0.0	51.7	**72.8**	0.0	51.0
w/o FD & FR & ST	16.6	0.0	8.3	2.7	0.0	2.1	2.0	0.0	1.8	7.1	0.0	4.1

Effectiveness of Self-training. In the bottom half of Table 1 we show the impact of the absence of self-training (ST) on the performance. The FRoST w/o ST causes no interference in the optimization from the new classes and the joint classifier is able to preserve the performance on old classes. This highlights the truly complex nature of balancing the performance of both old and new classes in the class-iNCD setting. This phenomenon is visualized in Fig. 4 through the norms of the weights of the joint classifier where exists large discrepancies between the old versus new classes. Similar conclusions can also be drawn by observing the confusion matrix reported in Fig. 5. Furthermore, when we drop FD and FR along with ST, we notice a further degradation of the performance of old classes, demonstrating the positive impact of FR and FD in not forgetting.

Comparison of Our Feature Replay and Distillation with LwF. Here we empirically demonstrate the need of decoupling the LwF objective into FR

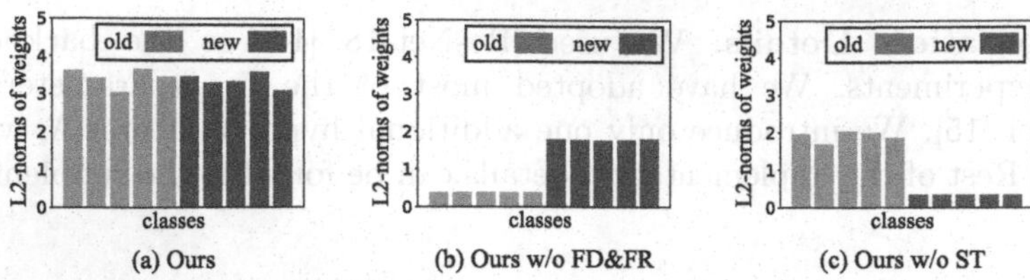

Fig. 4. Comparison of L2 norms of the classifier weights. Our full method has balanced L2-norms leading to a better balance in classification for old and new classes.

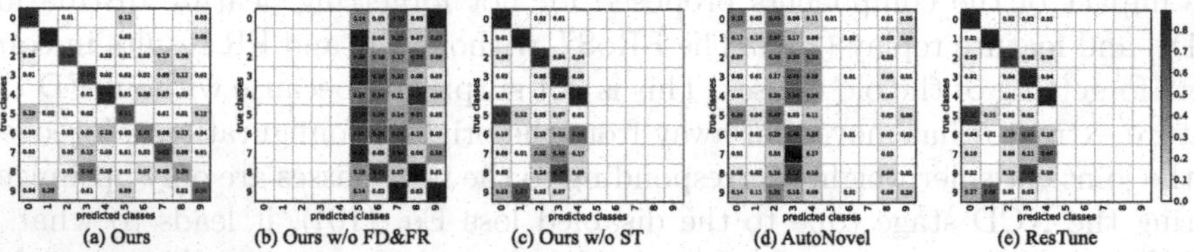

Fig. 5. Comparisons of confusion matrix of different methods. Note that, the label IDs of novel classes are re-assigned by our evaluation protocol.

and FD when it comes to learning a joint classifier for the class-iNCD. As a control experiment, we use the original formulation of LwF (as in Eq. (2)) as a drop-in replacement for our FR and FD. We optimize with the original LwF loss, applied both at the softmax and pre-softmax outputs, and found that compared to FRoST the performance on the new classes improves but at the cost of a large drop in the old classes performance. We conjecture that since the weights for the new classes are randomly initialized in $h^{[\mathtt{A}]}$ at the start of the NCD stage, the joint classifier as a whole learns at a different rate than the feature extractor g, which is already pre-trained on the old classes. As the LwF loss optimizes both the g and $h^{[\mathtt{A}]}$, it causes slow-fast learning interference from the new classes. This is evident from better new classes performance *w.r.t* FRoST. As shown in Table 2, indeed adding FR to LwF improves the performance on the old classes (*e.g.*, 6.8% vs 49.9% for Tiny-ImageNet). This again proves the effectiveness of FR and the need of decoupled *not-forgetting* objective in the class-iNCD.

Table 2. Ablation study comparing FRoST with LwF (logits-KD).

IL Methods	CIFAR-10			CIFAR-100			Tiny-ImageNet			Average		
	Old	New	All	Old	New	All	Old	New	All	Old	New	All
FRoST (Ours)	**77.4**	49.5	**63.5**	**62.5**	45.8	**59.2**	**54.4**	33.9	**52.4**	**64.8**	43.1	**58.3**
LwF (softmax)	13.6	63.2	38.4	7.4	**63.5**	18.6	2.1	**42.8**	6.2	7.7	56.5	21.1
LwF (softmax) + FR	21.4	61.1	41.3	33.3	61.2	38.9	35.3	33.1	35.0	30.0	51.8	38.4
LwF (pre-softmax)	19.4	76.3	47.9	13.6	61.4	23.2	6.8	38.7	10.0	13.3	**58.8**	27.0
LwF (pre-softmax) + FR	24.8	**77.5**	51.1	49.3	58.3	51.1	49.9	26.8	47.6	41.3	54.2	49.9

Table 3. Ablation study on having a single and separated heads for old and new classes. Joint: class-agnostic head; Novel: new classes classifier head.

Classifier Head	CIFAR-10			CIFAR-100			Tiny-ImageNet			Average		
	Old	New	All	Old	New	All	Old	New	All	Old	New	All
Joint + Novel (Ours)	77.4	**49.5**	**63.5**	62.5	45.8	59.2	54.4	**33.9**	**52.4**	64.8	**43.1**	**58.3**
Joint	81.3	41.5	61.4	64.5	**46.3**	**60.9**	56.8	8.4	52.0	67.5	32.1	58.1
Joint w/o ST	91.7	0.0	45.8	68.6	29.4	60.7	57.5	0.1	51.7	**72.6**	9.9	52.8
Novel w/o ST	**92.0**	0.0	46.0	**67.9**	32.1	60.7	**57.9**	0.0	52.1	**72.6**	10.7	52.9

Table 4. Comparison with state-of-the-art methods in class-iNCD.

Methods	CIFAR-10			CIFAR-100			Tiny-ImageNet			Average		
	Old	New	All	Old	New	All	Old	New	All	Old	New	All
AutoNovel [15]	27.5	3.5	15.5	2.6	15.2	5.1	2.0	26.4	4.5	10.7	15.0	8.4
ResTune [29]	91.7	0.0	45.9	**73.8**	0.0	59.0	44.3	0.0	39.9	**69.9**	0.0	48.3
NCL [37]	**92.0**	1.1	46.5	73.6	10.1	**60.9**	0.8	6.5	1.4	55.5	5.9	36.3
DTC [14]	64.0	0.0	32.0	55.9	0.0	44.7	35.5	0.0	32.0	51.8	0.0	36.2
FRoST	77.5	**49.5**	**63.4**	64.6	**45.8**	59.2	**54.5**	**33.7**	**52.3**	65.5	**39.8**	**54.9**

Effect of Using Joint and Novel Classifiers. Here we elaborate on the choice of using the joint $h^{[A]}$ and novel $h^{[U]}$ classification heads in FRoST to address class-iNCD. We report the `Joint` baseline in Table 3, where we discard the novel classifier head and solely use the joint classifier for learning the new classes and the old classes. We find that this approach causes hindrance in learning the new classes for CIFAR10 and Tiny-ImagenNet data sets because two parts of the same classifier are subject to gradients of different magnitudes, highlighting the need to decouple the learning of two tasks. In the next ablation, we also disable the ST with pseudo-labels that are generated by joint itself and we find that it destabilizes the performance on the new classes. Finally, we construct an ablation where we do not extend $h^{[L]}$ to $h^{[A]}$, but instead use $h^{[L]}$ in conjunction with $h^{[U]}$ and is denoted with `Novel w/o ST`. We observe that this behaves similarly with the previous ablation analysis of `FRoST w/o ST` in Table 1. Thus, we conclude that having joint and novel heads trained with ST is crucial in class-iNCD.

4.3 Comparison with State-of-the-Art Methods

We compare our FRoST with the state-of-the-art NCD methods under the newly proposed class-iNCD setting. We also compare with ResTune [29] which is a recently proposed method for iNCD. As none of these existing methods have been evaluated in the class-iNCD setting, we re-run the baselines and simply modify the evaluation protocol which is described in Sect. 3. We report the results of the NCD [15,16,37], iNCD [29] baselines and FRoST in the Table 4. As can be observed, under the class-iNCD all the NCD [15,16,37] fail to obtain a good balance on the old and new classes. Interestingly, while none of these NCD methods use any explicit objectives to prevent forgetting, they tend to predict well the old classes (see column **Old** in Table 4) and poor performance on new classes (see column **New** in Table 4). When visualizing the confusion matrix in Fig. 5 we found that most of the test samples get classified as old classes due to the old classes classifier having higher norms. As a consequence, this gives the impression that the baselines methods are able to retain performance on old classes. Second, for the above methods, although the new classes performance obtained with the joint head appears to be low, the actual performance of their novel head in the task-aware evaluation is indeed high. We report the breakdown of the novel classes performance in Table 5 where, for instance, the column **New-1-N** denotes the task-aware clustering performance of the novel head on the new classes. As can be observed, the new classes classifier of the NCD baselines can indeed learn on the new classes (*e.g.*, 34.2% in NCL vs 32.4% in FRoST).

ResTune, although designed specifically for the iNCD setting, exhibits similar counter-intuitive behaviour with the performance on the old classes dominating the new classes. To investigate this pathology, we inspect into the confusion matrix in Fig. 5(e) and find that all the samples get predicted to the first five old classes for CIFAR10. In other words, the overall performance reported in ResTune [29] is actually dominated by the old classes performance. We report confusion matrices on bigger data sets in the supplementary material. This shows that the existing evaluation method for iNCD is flawed and our proposed class-iNCD is indeed more meaningful that properly evaluates the effectiveness of a learning algorithm. Contrarily our proposed FRoST consistently achieves a good balance in performance in all the tested data sets. This also demonstrates the validity of the components in our proposed FRoST. We present a detailed comparison analysis between ResTune and FRoST in the supplementary material.

Table 5. Comparison with the state-of-the-art methods in the two-step class-iNCD setting where new classes arrive in two episodes, instead of one. New-1-J: new classes performance from joint head at first step, New-1-N: new classes performance from novel head at first step, etc.

Methods	Tiny-ImageNet									
	First Step (180-10)				Second Step (180-10-10)					
	Old	New-1-J	New-1-N	All	Old	New-1-J	New-2-J	New-1-N	New-2-N	All
ResTune [29]	39.7	0.0	38.0	37.6	34.9	0.0	0.0	25.4	42.8	31.4
DTC [14]	38.9	0.0	**43.8**	36.9	33.4	0.0	0.0	28.0	**59.4**	30.1
NCL [37]	5.6	0.0	34.2	5.3	1.4	0.0	2.6	21.6	41.6	1.4
FRoST	**55.2**	**27.6**	32.0	**53.8**	**42.5**	**34.8**	**31.2**	**31.2**	46.8	**41.6**

Two-Step Class-iNCD. As done in the class-IL literature [30], we also run experiments on a sequence of novel tasks, which we call as two-step class-iNCD, where 20 novel classes in Tiny-ImageNet are added in two steps, each step dealing with 10 novel classes. We compare our FRoST with the baseline methods in

Table 5 where we show not only the joint classifier head performance (*e.g.*, **New-1-J**), but also from the novel classifier head (*e.g.*, **New-1-N** and **New-2-N**) at each step. As can be seen, for the baseline methods the novel classifier heads can satisfactorily discover the new classes at each step, but when evaluated with the joint head biases the predictions to the old classes. Unlike the baselines, FRoST does not suffer from this issue and leads to more balanced predictions.

5 Conclusion

In this work we addressed the novel problem of class-incremental NCD. This task differs from the traditional NCD since we are not only interested in discovering novel classes but also aim to prevent forgetting on the old classes. To prevent this forgetting phenomenon we proposed feature replay and feature-level distillation that is well suited for the class-iNCD. Moreover, to make inference task-agnostic, we propose to maintain a joint classifier that can classify any of the previously seen classes. We train this joint classifier using the pseudo-labels generated by the novel classifier head that is trained with a clustering loss. We compared our method to many relevant works and obtained superior performance on various benchmarks. Given the practical nature of class-iNCD and encouraging results with our FRoST, we believe this work will stimulate further research.

Acknowledgement. We thank the funding agencies: EU H2020 projects SPRING (No. 871245) and AI4 Media (No. 951911); and the EUREGIO project OLIVER.

References

1. Anderson, B.L.: Can computational goals inform theories of vision? Topics in Cognitive Science (2015)
2. Buzzega, P., Boschini, M., Porrello, A., Abati, D., Calderara, S.: Dark experience for general continual learning: a strong, simple baseline. In: NeurIPS (2020)
3. Caron, M., Misra, I., Mairal, J., Goyal, P., Bojanowski, P., Joulin, A.: Unsupervised learning of visual features by contrasting cluster assignments. In: NeurIPS (2020)
4. Caron, M., et al.: Emerging properties in self-supervised vision transformers. In: ICCV (2021)
5. Castro, F.M., Marín-Jiménez, M.J., Guil, N., Schmid, C., Alahari, K.: End-to-end incremental learning. In: Ferrari, V., Hebert, M., Sminchisescu, C., Weiss, Y. (eds.) ECCV 2018. LNCS, vol. 11216, pp. 241–257. Springer, Cham (2018). https://doi.org/10.1007/978-3-030-01258-8_15
6. Chaudhry, A., Dokania, P.K., Ajanthan, T., Torr, P.H.S.: Riemannian walk for incremental learning: understanding forgetting and intransigence. In: Ferrari, V., Hebert, M., Sminchisescu, C., Weiss, Y. (eds.) ECCV 2018. LNCS, vol. 11215, pp. 556–572. Springer, Cham (2018). https://doi.org/10.1007/978-3-030-01252-6_33
7. Chaudhry, A., et al.: Continual learning with tiny episodic memories. In: ICML (2019)
8. Delange, M., Aljundi, R., Masana, M., Parisot, S., Jia, X., Leonardis, A., Slabaugh, G., Tuytelaars, T.: A continual learning survey: Defying forgetting in classification tasks. TPAMI (2021)

9. Dhar, P., Singh, R.V., Peng, K.C., Wu, Z., Chellappa, R.: Learning without memorizing. In: CVPR (2019)
10. Dosovitskiy, A., et al.: An image is worth 16 × 16 words: transformers for image recognition at scale. In: ICLR (2021)
11. Fini, E., Sangineto, E., Lathuilière, S., Zhong, Z., Nabi, M., Ricci, E.: A unified objective for novel class discovery. In: ICCV (2021)
12. French, R.M.: Catastrophic forgetting in connectionist networks. Trends in cognitive sciences (1999)
13. Goodfellow, I.J., Mirza, M., Xiao, D., Courville, A., Bengio, Y.: An empirical investigation of catastrophic forgetting in gradient-based neural networks. In: ICLR (2014)
14. Han, K., Vedaldi, A., Zisserman, A.: Learning to discover novel visual categories via deep transfer clustering. In: ICCV (2019)
15. Han, K., Rebuffi, S.A., Ehrhardt, S., Vedaldi, A., Zisserman, A.: Automatically discovering and learning new visual categories with ranking statistics. In: ICLR (2020)
16. Han, K., Vedaldi, A., Zisserman, A.: Learning to discover novel visual categories via deep transfer clustering. In: ICCV (2019)
17. He, K., Zhang, X., Ren, S., Sun, J.: Deep residual learning for image recognition. In: CVPR (2016)
18. Hinton, G., Vinyals, O., Dean, J., et al.: Distilling the knowledge in a neural network. In: NeurIPS Workshop (2014)
19. Hsu, Y.C., Lv, Z., Kira, Z.: Learning to cluster in order to transfer across domains and tasks. In: ICLR (2018)
20. Hsu, Y.C., Lv, Z., Schlosser, J., Odom, P., Kira, Z.: Multi-class classification without multi-class labels. In: ICLR (2019)
21. Jia, X., Han, K., Zhu, Y., Green, B.: Joint representation learning and novel category discovery on single-and multi-modal data. In: ICCV (2021)
22. Kirkpatrick, J., et al.: Overcoming catastrophic forgetting in neural networks. In: NAS (2017)
23. Krizhevsky, A., Hinton, G., et al.: Learning multiple layers of features from tiny images. University of Tronto (2009)
24. Krizhevsky, A., Sutskever, I., Hinton, G.E.: Imagenet classification with deep convolutional neural networks. In: NeurIPS (2012)
25. Kuhn, H.W.: The hungarian method for the assignment problem. Naval research logistics quarterly (1955)
26. Le, Y., Yang, X.: Tiny imagenet visual recognition challenge. CS 231N (2015)
27. Li, Z., Hoiem, D.: Learning without forgetting. TPAMI (2017)
28. Liang, J., Hu, D., Feng, J.: Do we really need to access the source data? source hypothesis transfer for unsupervised domain adaptation. In: ICML (2020)
29. Liu, Y., Tuytelaars, T.: Residual tuning: Toward novel category discovery without labels. TNNLS (2022)
30. Masana, M., Liu, X., Twardowski, B., Menta, M., Bagdanov, A.D., van de Weijer, J.: Class-incremental learning: survey and performance evaluation on image classification. arXiv preprint arXiv:2010.15277 (2020)
31. Rebuffi, S.A., Kolesnikov, A., Sperl, G., Lampert, C.H.: icarl: Incremental classifier and representation learning. In: CVPR (2017)
32. Wu, Y., Chen, Y., Wang, L., Ye, Y., Liu, Z., Guo, Y., Fu, Y.: Large scale incremental learning. In: CVPR (2019)
33. Xie, J., Girshick, R., Farhadi, A.: Unsupervised deep embedding for clustering analysis. In: ICML (2016)

34. Zenke, F., Poole, B., Ganguli, S.: Continual learning through synaptic intelligence. In: ICML (2017)
35. Zhao, Y., Zhong, Z., Sebe, N., Lee, G.H.: Novel class discovery in semantic segmentation. In: CVPR (2022)
36. Zheng, Z., Yang, Y.: Rectifying pseudo label learning via uncertainty estimation for domain adaptive semantic segmentation. IJCV (2021)
37. Zhong, Z., Fini, E., Roy, S., Luo, Z., Ricci, E., Sebe, N.: Neighborhood contrastive learning for novel class discovery. In: CVPR (2021)
38. Zhong, Z., Zhu, L., Luo, Z., Li, S., Yang, Y., Sebe, N.: Openmix: reviving known knowledge for discovering novel visual categories in an open world. In: CVPR (2021)

Unknown-Oriented Learning for Open Set Domain Adaptation

Jie Liu, Xiaoqing Guo, and Yixuan Yuan(✉)

City University of Hong Kong, Hong Kong, China
{jliu.ee,xqguo.ee}@my.cityu.edu.hk, yxyuan.ee@cityu.edu.hk

Abstract. Open set domain adaptation (OSDA) aims to tackle the distribution shift of partially shared categories between the source and target domains, meanwhile identifying target samples non-appeared in source domain. The key issue behind this problem is to classify these various unseen samples as unknown category with the absent of relevant knowledge from the source domain. Though impressing performance, existing works neglect the complex semantic information and huge intra-category variation of unknown category, incapable of representing the complicated distribution. To overcome this, we propose a novel Unknown-Oriented Learning (UOL) framework for OSDA, and it is composed of three stages: true unknown excavation, false unknown suppression and known alignment. Specifically, to excavate the diverse semantic information in unknown category, the multi-unknown detector (MUD) equipped with weight discrepancy constraint is proposed in true unknown excavation. During false unknown suppression, Source-to-Target grAdient Graph (S2TAG) is constructed to select reliable target samples with the proposed super confidence criteria. Then, Target-to-Target grAdient Graph (T2TAG) exploits the geometric structure in gradient manifold to obtain confident pseudo labels for target data. At the last stage, known alignment, the known samples in the target domain are aligned with the source domain to alleviate the domain gap. Extensive experiments demonstrate the superiority of our method compared with state-of-the-art methods on three benchmarks.

Keywords: Domain adaptation · Open set · Graph

1 Introduction

Deep learning has made spectacular progress in diverse application such as face recognition [24], medical image understanding [3,11] and autonomous driving

This work was supported by Hong Kong Research Grants Council (RGC) General Research Fund 11211221 (CityU 9043152), and Hong Kong Research Grants Council (RGC) Early Career Scheme grant 21207420 (CityU 9048179).

Supplementary Information The online version contains supplementary material available at https://doi.org/10.1007/978-3-031-19827-4_20.

S. Avidan et al. (Eds.): ECCV 2022, LNCS 13693, pp. 334–350, 2022.
https://doi.org/10.1007/978-3-031-19827-4_20

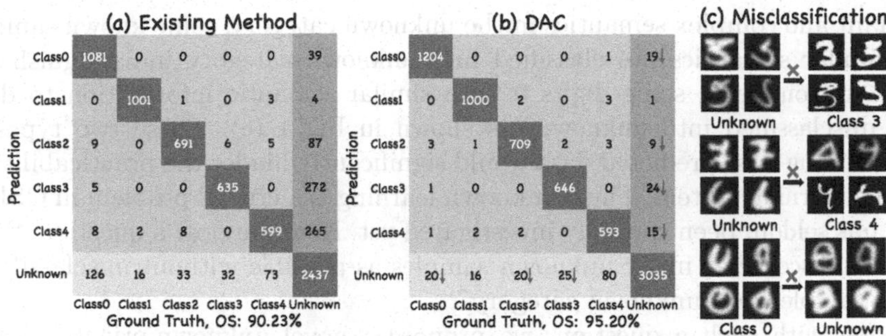

Fig. 1. The digital recognition confusion matrix of (a) existing method [23] and (b) our method. (c) Misclassification Example. (Color figure online)

[4,46]. These models are commonly trained under the supervised learning with assumption that the training and test data come from the same distribution. However, this assumption, in practice, can be easily violated due to the change of environment or data acquisition device, leading to degraded performance in other domains. Unsupervised Domain Adaptation (UDA) techniques are proposed to alleviate this degeneration problem via narrowing down the domain gap. The main paradigm in UDA minimizes discrepancy metrics to reduce the distribution divergence [16,22,27], and the other paradigm leverages the adversarial learning to learn domain-invariant feature representations [20,21,45].

The aforementioned UDA algorithms work competently under the closed set regime, a.k.a. closed set domain adaptation (CSDA), where the label space shares in two domains ($\mathcal{C}_s = \mathcal{C}_t$). However, the target domain always contains unknown category (unseen in the source domain) in real-world scenarios, severely restricting the applicability of CSDA models. For example, a medical diagnosis intelligent system should recognize data as unknown when data belonging to an unseen category is accidentally inputted. The corresponding decision process should be transferred to the surgeon for safety diagnosis. Therefore, a more realistic setting, Open Set Domain Adaptation (OSDA) [34,37], is recently studied, wherein the target domain contains irrelevant categories not presented in the source domain ($\mathcal{C}_s \subset \mathcal{C}_t$) [37]. Compared with CSDA, the goal of OSDA is not only to adapt the model from source to target domain for precise predictions within known categories, but also to reject unseen samples as unknown category.

To distinguish unknown samples from known ones, existing OSDA methods employ an additional logit to indicate the unknown [1,8,23,34,37]. However, the unknown category, containing a set of unseen classes, possesses complex visual semantics and huge intra-category variation. For example, digits 0 to 4 are known categories and 5 to 9 are unseen classes in digital recognition task. This phenomenon make the single classifier weight incapable of representing the dispersed distribution of unknown category, leading to misclassification of unknown samples into known categories and high false positive rate for known categories, as shown in the blue region of Fig. 1 (a). In addition, since there are abundant and complex semantics in the unknown category, some known samples with similar semantics are classified into unknown category indistinguishably (yellow region), e.g., some digits 0 with similar semantic information to digit 8 are misclassified into unknown, as shown in Fig. 1 (c). These two types of overwhelming false predicted data would significantly hinder the practicability of machine learning system. Thus, unknown learning is a crucial problem in OSDA, but it has seldom been specially investigated yet. Here, we post a question: 'How could we discover as many unknown samples as possible without misclassifying known samples into unknown category?'

Along with such a question, we propose a novel unknown-oriented learning (**UOL**) framework to solve OSDA, including *true unknown excavation*, *false unknown suppression* and *known alignment* three stages. To handle the complex visual semantics and huge intra-category variation, we propose the Multi-Unknown Detector (MUD) with a weight discrepancy constraint to detect the unseen samples scattered around the feature space and represent the dispersed distribution of unknown category in *true unknown excavation*. The weight discrepancy constraint enables the MUD to capture diverse semantic information of unknown category and excavate as many unknown samples as possible, which reduces the false positive rate for known category. Considering that the gradient of model parameters contains recognition-relevant information [30] and directional information [18], we advance two gradient graphs named Source-to-Target grAdient Graph (S2TAG) and Target-to-Target grAdient Graph (T2TAG) in *false unknown suppression* to fully delve into the knowledge of known samples in gradient space. Through exploiting the intrinsic relationship among samples in gradient space, we rectify the false unknown samples in the first stage and enhance the performance of known categories. Specifically, the S2TAG bridges the source domain with target domain, and selects confident target samples with the proposed super confidence criteria. Then, the T2TAG is devised to propagate the confidence of these target samples in the gradient manifold and obtain pseudo labels through solving a defined energy function. After distinguishing unknown samples, the scenario of OSDA is simplified as the CSDA problem. The *known alignment* stage is proceeded to alleviate the domain gap between the shared categories. In summary, our major contributions are summarized as follows:

- To explicitly learn the unknown category, a novel framework **UOL** is designed to conquer the OSDA problem with three stages, *true unknown excavation*, *false unknown suppression* and *known alignment*.
- In *true unknown excavation*, multi-unknown detector equipped with weight discrepancy constraint is proposed to explore the diverse semantic information of unknown. In *false unknown suppression*, two gradient graphs are constructed to obtain confident pseudo labels by exploiting the essential geometric structure of data.
- Extensive experiments are carried out on two standard OSDA benchmarks and one newly built medical diagnosis benchmark. The results demonstrate the superiority compared with other SOTA methods. Moreover, ablation studies validate the impact and effectiveness of the proposed **UOL** framework.

2 Related Work

2.1 Closed Set Domain Adaptation (CSDA)

CSDA is intended to alleviate the performance degradation caused by domain discrepancy. Existing methods could be mainly categorized into two streams: adversarial learning based methods [5,10,41,45] and discrepancy metric based methods [16,22,38]. The first stream trains a domain discriminator to distinguish the source and target domains, and encourages feature extractor to learn domain-invariant feature via fooling the discriminator. Ganin et al. [10] advance a pioneering work, where a gradient reversal layer is proposed to connect the feature extractor and domain classifier. Subsequently, many adversarial based methods [5,36,39,41,42] are well designed. The second stream explicitly measures the domain gap by discrepancy metrics and narrows down the domain gap via minimizing the metrics [22,26,38,44]. For instance, Long et al. [25] minimize the multi-kernel maximum mean discrepancy between two domains. Zhu et al. [27] propose the joint maximum mean discrepancy among multiple layers. While in real-world applications, open set is a more common scenario. But these CSDA methods fail in solving the problem of open set domain adaptation since they are incapable of rejecting unknown samples and the alignment of shared known distributions will be destructed.

2.2 Open Set Domain Adaptation (OSDA)

The purpose of open set domain adaptation is to reject unknown samples in target domain and align distributions of known categories between two domains, with the absent target annotations. Saito et al. [37] raise the realistic OSDA setting where unknown samples are only existing in the target domain. They train a classifier to build a boundary between source and target samples and train a generator to make target samples far from the boundary, so that unknown samples would be rejected and known distributions are aligned. In addition, Liu et al. [23] adopt a coarse-to-fine weighting mechanism to separate the target into known and unknown. Recently, subsequent works [1,8,14,28,33,35,43] introduce various techniques to generate more discriminative features in the target domain and benefit the OSDA problem. Feng et al. [8] emphasize the semantic structure of open set data via contrastive mapping. Pan et al. [33] employ the self-ensemble framework with category-agnostic clustering in the target domain and exploit the underlying structure of each cluster to learn more discriminative target information. Xu et al. [43] couple all data optimally and propose a prototypical loss to achieve intra-class compactness and inter-class separability. Luo et al. [28] utilize graph convolution to propagate the category information and achieve a tighter upper bound of the target error. Bucci et al. [1] use the inherent properties of self-supervision to achieve a more robustness recognition. Jing et al. [14] project the feature to a hyper-spherical latent space and constrain the centroid deviation angle to align the distribution.

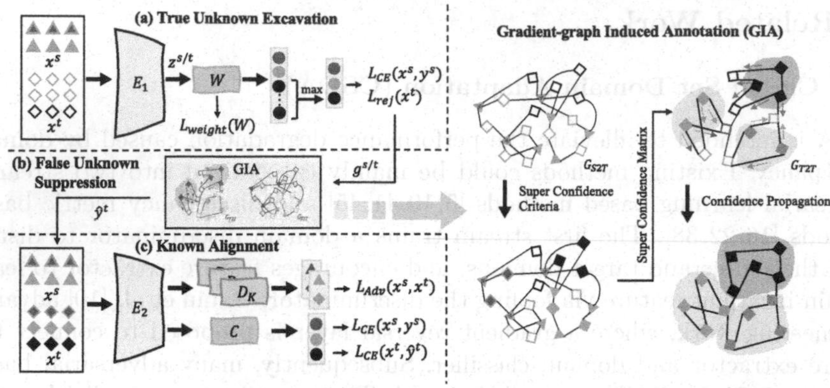

Fig. 2. Overview of the proposed framework, UOL, which includes three stages, i.e. (a) *True Unknown Excavation*, (b) *False Unknown Suppression* and (c) *Known Alignment.* In (a), source data $\boldsymbol{x}^s$ and target data $\boldsymbol{x}^t$ are fed into backbone E_1 to extract feature $\boldsymbol{z}$. Then, the multi-unknown detector W distinguishes the samples from diverse unseen categories and initially aligns the distribution of known categories. In (b), the gradients $\hat{g}^{s/t}$ derived from back-propagation are utilized to generate pseudo labels $\hat{y}^t$ through GIA, where S2TAG G_{S2T} is built to produce super confidence matrix and T2TAG G_{T2T} is built to propagate confidence in target domain. In (c), category-level discriminators $\{D_i\}_{i=1}^K$ align the feature distributions in category level, and extended classifier recognizes data into $K+1$ categories.

However, the complicated unknown category distribution makes it hard to reject the unseen samples completely, which negatively influences the distribution alignment of known categories. Differently, we introduce multi-unknown detector with the help of discrepancy constraint to explore the diverse semantic information for unknown category. In addition, two graph structures are advanced to rectify the false prediction, so as to avoid the deconstruction from unknown samples.

3 Unknown-Oriented Learning

In OSDA, we have a source domain $\mathcal{D}^s = (\boldsymbol{x}_i^s, y_i^s)_{i=1}^{n_s}$ of n_s labeled samples associated with $\mathcal{C}_s$ label space and a target domain $\mathcal{D}^t = (\boldsymbol{x}_i^t)_{i=1}^{n_t}$ of n_t unlabeled target samples associated with $\mathcal{C}_t$ label space. The source label space $\mathcal{C}_s$ is a subset of target label space $\mathcal{C}_t$, i.e. $\mathcal{C}_s \subset \mathcal{C}_t$, while target label space further includes a set of additional categories $\mathcal{C}_{unk}$, i.e. $\mathcal{C}_t = \mathcal{C}_s \cup \mathcal{C}_{unk}$. These unseen categories should be recognized as 'unknown' category in OSDA. Assuming the source and target domains are drawn from the distributions p and q respectively, where $p \neq q$, we further observe that probability distributions of shared categories are different, i.e. $p \neq q_{\mathcal{C}_s}$, due to the domain gap. In summary, we face a label space shift problem $\mathcal{C}_s \neq \mathcal{C}_t$ and a distribution shift problem $p \neq q_{\mathcal{C}_s}$ in OSDA. Thus, this study aims to reject unseen samples as unknown category for the label space shift problem and to alleviate the domain gap of remaining samples for the distribution shift problem.

To ensure the distribution alignment among shared categories instead of mixing with unknown categories, we reject unseen data first (*true unknown excavation* and *false unknown suppression*) and then align distributions of the remaining data in category level (*known alignment*). The whole Unknown-Oriented Learning (**UOL**) framework is shown in Fig. 2. For the *true unknown excavation* stage, data in both domains are fed into feature extractor E_1. Then, a multi-unknown detector W equipped with weight discrepancy constraint L_{weight} is advanced to represent diverse distributions of unseen data and reject these data as unknown category. After that, data gradients are back-propagated and two gradient graphs G_{S2T}, G_{T2T} are built in the *false unknown suppression* stage. Pseudo labels $\hat{Y}_T$ could be obtained through propagating the confidence and rectifying false unknown data. At last, we can align distributions of shared known categories via category-level discriminator $\{D_i\}_{i=1}^{K}$ and train an extended classifier C to recognize target data.

3.1 True Unknown Excavation

In OSDA, a set of unseen samples are holistically represented by a single unknown category. These unseen samples with various visual characteristics are generally scattered into several clusters in the embedding space, and the corresponding distribution is complicated [1,23]. Hence, we propose multi-unknown detector (MUD) to explore diverse semantic information of unknown category and excavate more unseen samples. Specifically, the proposed MUD composes of $K+N$ weights $\boldsymbol{w}$, i.e. $W = [\boldsymbol{w}_1, ..., \boldsymbol{w}_K, \boldsymbol{w}_{K+1}, ..., \boldsymbol{w}_{K+N}]$, where $\boldsymbol{w} \in \mathcal{R}^{d\times 1}$, K denotes the number of known categories and N indicates the number of additional weights. After obtaining the feature embedding from feature extractor, $\boldsymbol{z} = E_1(\boldsymbol{x}) \in \mathcal{R}^{d\times 1}$, MUD outputs a $K+N$ dimensional logits vector for each sample with the kth output logit $\boldsymbol{w}_k^\top \boldsymbol{z}$. Then, the maximum of last N logits is selected to represent the unknown and the softmax is applied to the $K+1$ dimensional logits vector to produce the posterior probability, $\boldsymbol{p} = softmax[\boldsymbol{w}_1^\top \boldsymbol{z}, ..., \boldsymbol{w}_K^\top \boldsymbol{z}, \max_{k=K+1,...,K+N} \boldsymbol{w}_k^\top \boldsymbol{z}]$. In order to identify intrinsic characteristics on unseen categories, weights in W are supposed to have diverse parameters. Therefore, the weight discrepancy constraint is advanced to enforce the divergence of weights via minimizing their cosine similarity,

$$L_{weight}(W) = \sum_{i=1} \sum_{j=1, j\neq i} \frac{\boldsymbol{w}_i \cdot \boldsymbol{w}_j}{||\boldsymbol{w}_i|| ||\boldsymbol{w}_j||}. \tag{1}$$

with this constraint, the introduced weights N for unknown categories will be mutually discrepant, thereby representing various semantics and learning diverse

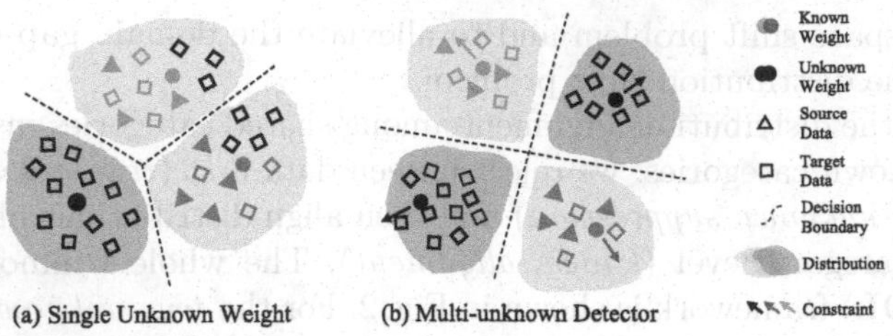

Fig. 3. Comparison between (a) single unknown weight and (b) multi-unknown detector.

knowledge for unseen categories. To recognize unknown samples in the target domain, an adversarial loss [37] is employed,

$$L_{rej}(x^t) = -\epsilon \log(\boldsymbol{p}_{K+1}(\boldsymbol{x}^t)) - (1-\epsilon)\log(1-\boldsymbol{p}_{K+1}(\boldsymbol{x}^t)), \tag{2}$$

where ϵ is a pre-defined parameter to balance the adversarial learning, and $\boldsymbol{p}_{K+1}(\cdot)$ indicates the unknown probability. With gradient reverse [9], this adversarial loss will encourage the unknown probability far away from ϵ, i.e., enhancing it to 1 or suppressing it to 0, and recognize the unknown samples. Moreover, the source knowledge is also utilized to help recognize unknown samples through cross-entropy loss,

$$L_{CE}(x^s, y^s) = -\log(\boldsymbol{p}_{y^s}(\boldsymbol{x}^s)). \tag{3}$$

To update parameters of feature extractor E_1 and MUD W simultaneously, the gradient reverse layer [9] is introduced to flip the sign of L_{rej}. The object can be formulated as

$$\begin{aligned} E_1^* &= \arg\min_{E_1} L_{CE}(\boldsymbol{x}^s, y^s) - L_{rej}(\boldsymbol{x}^t), \\ W^* &= \arg\min_{W} L_{CE}(\boldsymbol{x}^s, y^s) + L_{rej}(\boldsymbol{x}^t) + \mu L_{weight}(W). \end{aligned} \tag{4}$$

As shown in Fig. 3, comparing with traditional methods employing a single additional logit of linear classifier to represent the unknown category [1,8,23,37], the proposed MUD and weight discrepancy constraint excavate more unknown samples with various semantic information and achieve inter-class separability.

3.2 False Unknown Suppression

The overwhelming semantic information in unknown category will cause some known samples with similar information to be classified into unknown category. To rectify these false unknown samples, we propose the gradient-graph induced annotation (GIA) module to take advantage of gradient information and build a dense graph structure in sample level to enhance the relationship among known samples, as shown in Fig. 2 (b). To be specific, in the Source-to-Target grAdient Graph (S2TAG), the target samples with high confidence are selected as super confident samples with corresponding pseudo labels. Then, based on the smoothness assumption [13,48], the intrinsic relationship among target samples in gradient manifold is exploited to propagate the confidence of super confident samples via Target-to-Target grAdient Graph (T2TAG). Finally, we acquire refined pseudo labels $\hat{Y}_T$ for the *known alignment* in Sect. 3.3.

Since gradient can reserve the learned knowledge of unseen categories in *True Unknown Excavation* and incorporate information beneficial to recognition, we utilize the gradient via back-propagation to characterize data, i.e. $\hat{\boldsymbol{g}}^s = \mathrm{Vec}(\frac{\partial}{\partial W} L_{CE}(\boldsymbol{x}^s, y^s))$, $\hat{\boldsymbol{g}}^t = \mathrm{Vec}(\frac{\partial}{\partial W} L_{CE}(\boldsymbol{x}^t, \arg\max_i \boldsymbol{p}_i))$, where $\mathrm{Vec}(\cdot)$ represents the vectorization. Notably, we only make use of gradient features from the classifier W. Considering the gradient vector with high-dimensional cost high storage and computational resource, kernel-PCA [29,32] is utilized to determine the low-dimensional gradient manifold and reduce the resource consumption. After applying k-PCA, we obtain vectors $\boldsymbol{g}^{s/t} \in \mathcal{R}^M$ representing the coordinate, w.r.t. the M principal components in a reproducing kernel Hilbert space, for each sample in the gradient manifold.

S2TAG. To select the target sample with high confidence, we build a bipartite graph $G_{S2T} = \langle V_{S2T}, \mathcal{E}_{S2T} \rangle$ and model the relationship between source and target domains. V_{S2T} includes all samples in source and target domains. The weighted edge matrix encodes the non-negative pairwise similarity between target sample and k-nearest neighbors in source domain, $[\mathcal{E}_{S2T}]_{ij} = [{\boldsymbol{g}_i^t}^\top \boldsymbol{g}_j^s]_+$, when $\boldsymbol{g}_j^s \in \mathbf{NN}_k(\boldsymbol{g}_i^t)$, otherwise, $[\mathcal{E}_{S2T}]_{ij} = 0$.

Then, we select super confident samples in the target domain via super confidence criteria. For known samples, they are supposed to be similar with source samples of the same category. Their k-neighbors should belong to the same category and the average similarity is large. As for unseen samples, they do not belong to any categories in the source domain. Their k-neighbors should distribute in different categories and the average similarity is small. Based on these two criteria, the super confidence matrix $\widetilde{C} \in \mathcal{R}^{n_t \times (K+1)}$ is generated with elements

$$\widetilde{C}_{ij}^T = \begin{cases} \boldsymbol{m}_i, \text{ if } \boldsymbol{m}_i > \alpha \wedge |N_i| = 1 \wedge j = N_i[0] \\ 1 - \boldsymbol{m}_i, \text{ if } \boldsymbol{m}_i < 1 - \alpha \wedge |N_i| > 1 \wedge j = K+1 \\ 0, \text{ otherwise,} \end{cases} \tag{5}$$

where $\boldsymbol{m}$ indicates the average similarity vector for target sample, i.e. $\boldsymbol{m}_i = mean([\mathcal{E}_{S2T}]_{ij})$ when $\boldsymbol{g}_j^s \in \mathbf{NN}_k(\boldsymbol{g}_i^t)$, α denotes the threshold to identify the super confident samples, N_i represents the label set of k-neighbors of each target sample i, and $|\cdot|$ is the cardinality of a set. To this end, the generated confidence matrix encodes the confidence of selected confident samples with super confidence criteria. Moreover, We also generate the corresponding super confident index $\boldsymbol{s} \in \mathcal{R}^{n_t}$, where 1 indicates the selected sample and vice versa. Through the proposed S2TAG, confident samples in target domain are selected for subsequent propagation.

T2TAG. With selected confident target domain samples, we exploit the intrinsic relationship among target samples in gradient manifold to construct an undirected graph $G_{T2T} = \langle V_{T2T}, \mathcal{A}_{T2T} \rangle$, thereby propagating the confidence information within the target domain and obtaining the robust pseudo labels. The set of vertices V_{T2T} is composed of all target samples. The data relation in the gradient manifold is encoded using the adjacent matrix $\mathcal{A}_{T2T}$, and each element is calculated via $[\mathcal{A}_{T2T}]_{ij} = [\boldsymbol{g}_i^{t\top} \boldsymbol{g}_j^t]_+$, when $\boldsymbol{g}_j^t \in \mathbf{NN}_k(\boldsymbol{g}_i^t) \wedge j \neq i$, otherwise $[\mathcal{A}_{T2T}]_{ij} = 0$. To ensure the adjacent matrix $\mathcal{A}_{T2T}$ of an undirected graph is symmetric nonnegative with zero diagonal, we have $\mathcal{A}_{T2T} := \mathcal{A}_{T2T} + \mathcal{A}_{T2T}^\top$. Then, the adjacent matrix is normalized symmetrically as $\mathcal{W} = D^{-1/2}\mathcal{A}_{T2T}D^{-1/2}$, where $D = diag(\mathcal{A}_{T2T}\mathbf{1}_n)$ and $\mathbf{1}_n$ is the all-ones n-vector.

Based on the normalized adjacency matrix $\mathcal{W}$, we propagate the confidence in matrix $\widetilde{C}$ to obtain the confidence matrix for the whole target dataset $\hat{C}$. With the prior that adjacent samples are supposed to possess comparable confidence [13,48], an energy function is advanced to measure the propagation result:

$$\mathcal{Q}(\hat{C}) = \mathbf{Tr}(\hat{C}^T(I - \mathcal{W})\hat{C}) + \lambda||S\hat{C} - S\widetilde{C}||_F^2, \tag{6}$$

where $\mathbf{Tr}(\cdot)$ denotes the trace of a squared matrix, $||\cdot||_F$ represents the Frobenius norm of matrix, and $S = \text{diag}(\boldsymbol{s})$. The first term of this energy function describes the smoothness based on the relationship in the manifold, and the second term maintains the corresponding value in the super confident matrix. Through minimizing the energy function, we could obtain the optimal confidence matrix encoding the refined pseudo label for the whole target dataset.

Since this energy function is convex, the global optimal propagation result can be derived when the derivative of energy function is 0, i.e. $\frac{\partial \mathcal{Q}(\hat{C})}{\partial \hat{Y}}|_{\hat{C}=\hat{C}^*} = 0$. Thus, the optimal equation is $(I - \mathcal{W} + \lambda S)\hat{C}^* = \lambda S\widetilde{C}$. Considering the computational inefficiency of large matrix inversion and the positive definiteness of matrix $(I - \mathcal{W} + \lambda S)$, the conjugate gradient method [2,13] is applied to solve this linear equation. After propagating, we obtain the pseudo labels with matrix $\hat{C}^*$ to guide the known alignment training, $\hat{Y}_T = \{\hat{y}_i^t | \hat{y}_i^t = \arg\max_j \hat{C}_{ij}^*\}$.

3.3 Known Alignment

After recognizing unknown samples, the OSDA problem turns into CSDA problem. The source and target domains can be aligned in shared label space $\mathcal{C}_s$ without deconstruction from unseen categories. Inspired by previous works [7,40], the network in this stage is composed of an encoder E_2, category-level discriminator and extended classifier C. The category-level discriminator have K sub-discriminators $\{D_i\}_{i=1}^K$, each of which aligns the distribution for specific category via a category-level adversarial loss:

$$\begin{aligned} L_{adv}(x^s, x^t) = &\sum_{i=1}^{K} \mathbb{I}_{i=y^s} \log[D_i(E_2(x^s))] \\ &+ \sum_{i=1}^{K} \mathbb{I}_{i=\hat{y}^t} \log[1 - D_i(E_2(x^t))]. \end{aligned} \tag{7}$$

Moreover, both source and target data are utilized to train the extended classifier via cross entropy, $L_{CE}(x^s, y^s)$ and $L_{CE}(x^t, \hat{y}^t)$ as Eq. 3. During the inference, only encoder E_2 and extended classifier C need to be reserved. The prediction can be obtained through $C(E_2(x^t))$.

4 Experiments

4.1 Experimental Details

Datasets and Baselines. *Digital Recognition* is a popular benchmark for OSDA with three datasets, i.e. MNIST [19], USPS [12], SVHN [31]. Each dataset contains 10 digitals from 0 to 9. Following the previous work [37], three adaptation tasks is constructed, i.e. SVHN→MNIST, MNIST→USPS and USPS→MNIST.

Office-Home is a challenge domain adaptation benchmark consisting of 15500 images from 65 categories of everyday objects in four domains, i.e. Art (**Ar**), Clipart (**Cp**), Product (**Pr**), and Real-World (**Rw**). We follow the same split set in previous work [23].

Endo-c2k is a new medical diagnosis benchmark related to endoscopy. The source domain is CAD-CAP WCE dataset [6] including 1800 images. The target domain is KID WCE dataset [17] including 2371 images. Three common categories are shared in two domains (normal, inflammatory and vascular), and two categories are exclusive in target domain (polyp and ampulla vater).

We compared the proposed UOL against other state-of-the-art OSDA methods including ATI-λ [17], OSBP [37], AoD [8], STA [23], JPOT [43], ROS [1] and ϵ-OSD [47]

Implementation. For *Digital Recognition*, we use LeNet as backbone. For the other two benchmark, we use the pre-trained ResNet-50 on ImageNet as the backbone. Multi-unknown detector W, extended classifier C and category-level discriminator $\{D_i\}_{i=1}^K$ are fully connected neural networks, and the output dimension of W, C and $\{D_i\}_{i=1}^K$ are $K+N$, $K+1$ and 1. They are randomly initialized. The additional weights number N is set as 5 for *digital recognition*, 10 for *Office-Home*, 2 for *Endo-c2k*. The hyper-parameters are tuned in Office-Home $Ar \rightarrow Cp$ task and fixed for all other OfficeHome tasks, $\mu = 10^{-3}$, $\alpha = 0.9$, $\lambda = 0.95$. As for the graph part, k-nearest neighbors search is accelerated by Faiss [15], and k is set as 20. Radial basis function is employed for kernel-PCA. We employ SGD optimizer with 0.9 momentum and 10^{-4} decay weight to optimize the network. The learning rate is set as 10^{-3} initially and decreases according to the cosine annealing policy. All experiments are done in GTX 2080Ti GPU. We run each setting 3 times and report the average results.

Evaluation Metrics. Four widely used metrics [1,37] are employed to measure the performance of all methods, i.e. **OS**: normalized accuracy for all classes, **OS***: normalized accuracy for the known classes only, **Unk:** the accuracy of unknown samples and **HOS**: the harmonic mean of *OS** and *UNK*. Among all metrics, *HOS* evaluates the performance of OSDA methods more comprehensively. The *HOS* will be high only if the algorithm achieves high performance on both known and unknown category.

Table 1. Classification accuracy (%) on *Digital Recognition* for OSDA. The best and second best results are highlighted by bold and underline separately.

Method	MNIST→USPS				USPS→MNIST				SVHN→MNIST				Average			
	OS	OS*	Unk	HOS	OS	OS*	Unk	HOS	OS	OS*	Unk	HOS	OS	OS*	Unk	HOS
ATI-λ [34]	86.8	89.6	73.0	80.4	82.4	81.5	86.7	84.0	67.6	66.5	73.0	69.6	78.9	79.2	77.6	78.0
OSBP [37]	92.1	94.9	78.0	85.6	92.3	91.2	97.6	94.3	63.0	59.1	82.3	68.8	82.4	81.7	85.9	82.9
STA [23]	93.0	94.9	83.5	88.8	92.2	91.3	96.5	93.8	76.9	75.4	84.4	79.6	87.3	87.2	88.1	87.4
AoD [8]	91.3	92.0	87.8	89.9	93.1	95.2	91.7	93.4	68.6	65.5	84.3	73.7	84.3	84.2	87.9	85.7
JPOT [43]	92.9	92.1	96.9	93.3	92.4	91.2	**98.4**	94.2	79.2	75.3	86.7	79.9	88.2	85.4	**94.0**	88.9
UOL	**95.6**	**95.1**	**97.8**	**96.5**	**96.9**	**96.9**	96.7	**96.8**	**82.4**	**84.1**	**88.2**	**86.1**	**92.1**	**91.6**	93.5	**93.1**

Table 2. Recognition accuracy (%) on 12 pairs of source and target domains from *Office-Hone* benchmark including four domains, i.e. Art (Ar), Clipart (Cp), Product (Pr), and Real-World (Rw). The best and second best results are highlighted by bold and underline separately.

Setting	OSBP [37]				AoD [8]				STA [23]				ROS [1]				ϵ-OSD [47]				UOL			
	OS	OS*	Unk	HOS	OS	OS*	Unk	HOS	OS	OS*	Unk	HOS	OS	OS*	Unk	HOS	OS	OS*	Unk	HOS	OS	OS*	Unk	HOS
Ar→Cp	50.6	50.2	61.1	55.1	58.9	59.9	33.9	43.3	46.6	45.9	64.1	53.5	51.5	50.6	**74.1**	60.1	**61.6**	**62.8**	31.6	42.0	58.9	58.3	73.8	**65.2**
Ar→Pr	71.3	71.8	59.8	65.3	73.4	74.4	48.4	58.6	67.0	67.2	62.0	64.5	68.5	68.4	70.3	69.3	76.6	78.3	34.1	47.5	**78.3**	**78.5**	**72.8**	**75.6**
Ar→Rw	78.8	79.3	67.5	72.9	79.2	80.2	54.2	64.7	76.2	76.7	63.7	69.6	75.9	75.8	77.2	76.5	83.2	85.0	38.2	52.7	**89.2**	**89.4**	**83.7**	**86.4**
Cp→Ar	59.8	59.4	70.3	64.4	60.6	61.5	38.1	47.1	50.2	49.3	72.7	58.8	54.1	53.6	65.5	58.9	**62.2**	**62.8**	47.2	53.9	59.6	58.8	**78.9**	**67.4**
Cp→Pr	66.8	67.0	62.7	64.8	67.5	68.4	45.0	54.3	57.7	57.6	60.2	58.9	60.3	59.8	**71.6**	65.2	71.0	**72.2**	41.0	52.3	**71.7**	71.8	68.2	**69.9**
Cp→Rw	71.9	72.0	69.2	70.6	74.8	75.8	49.8	60.1	64.9	65.2	57.4	61.1	65.6	65.3	72.2	68.6	**77.7**	**79.0**	45.2	57.5	76.0	76.0	**74.1**	**75.1**
Pr→Ar	59.4	59.1	68.1	63.3	63.8	64.7	41.3	50.4	49.5	48.4	77.0	59.4	57.6	57.3	64.3	60.6	**64.6**	**65.4**	44.6	53.0	**64.6**	64.2	**74.3**	**68.9**
Pr→Cp	45.3	44.5	66.3	53.3	58.1	59.0	35.6	44.4	42.9	40.8	**95.4**	57.2	47.5	46.5	71.2	56.3	**60.0**	**60.8**	40.0	48.3	56.6	55.6	81.2	**66.0**
Pr→Rw	76.0	76.2	71.7	73.9	77.7	78.7	52.7	63.1	76.6	77.3	59.1	67.0	71.1	70.8	78.4	74.4	81.5	82.9	46.5	59.6	**85.1**	**85.2**	**83.2**	**84.2**
Rw→Ar	66.1	66.1	67.3	66.7	67.3	68.2	44.8	54.1	68.7	68.6	71.2	69.9	67.1	67.0	70.8	68.8	70.6	71.6	45.6	55.7	**75.2**	**75.0**	**79.2**	**77.1**
Rw→Cp	48.6	48.0	63.0	54.5	55.8	56.7	33.3	42.0	46.0	45.4	61.0	52.1	52.3	51.5	**73.0**	60.4	58.8	59.6	38.8	47.0	**63.4**	**63.0**	**73.0**	**67.7**
Rw→Pr	76.0	76.3	68.6	72.2	77.7	78.6	55.2	64.9	73.9	74.5	58.9	65.8	72.3	72.0	80.0	75.7	81.3	82.8	43.8	57.3	**85.5**	**85.3**	**89.3**	**87.2**
Average	64.2	64.2	66.3	65.2	67.9	68.8	45.4	54.7	60.0	59.8	65.0	62.3	62.0	61.6	72.4	66.2	70.8	**71.9**	43.3	54.0	**72.0**	71.8	**77.6**	**74.2**

4.2 Results for Benchmarks

Digital Recognition. Experiments are conducted in the digital recognition benchmark. As shown in Table 1, UOL overpasses state-of-the-art methods [34], [37], [23], [8], [43] with 15.1%, 10.2%, 5.7%, 7.4% and 4.2% increments in average *HOS*. These encouraging results demonstrate that the proposed UOL can recognize unknown samples better while achieving high performance in classifying known samples.

Office-Home. We further illustrate the experimental results on all 12 tasks of this benchmark in Table 2. Due to the high openness [1,23] and large domain gap, we can observe that previous methods achieve poor performance either in unknown recognition or in known classification. For example, ϵ-OSD [47] only achieves 43.3% unknown category accuracy despite high performance for known classes, leading to an unsatisfactory *HOS* score. On the contrary, UOL achieves competitive result for known categories with 71.8% average *OS** and also superior accuracy 77.6% for unknown samples, which demonstrates the better unknown recognition ability of UOL than ϵ-OSD [47]. Moreover, UOL surpasses all other OSDA methods with *HOS* metric by a large gap in 12 tasks and possesses superior capability with increments of 26.6%, 19.5%, 11.9%, 8.0% and

Table 3. Classification accuracy (%) on *Endo-c2k*.

Method	Norm.	Vasc.	Infl.	Unk	OS	OS*	HOS
Source Only	31.9	53.1	31.3	0.0	29.1	38.8	0.0
OSBP [37]	22.8	56.8	63.0	14.3	39.2	47.5	22.0
STA [23]	28.8	42.6	34.8	25.4	32.9	35.4	29.6
AoD [8]	20.8	55.8	**65.6**	22.2	41.1	47.4	30.2
ROS [1]	32.4	59.1	49.3	23.8	41.2	46.9	31.6
UOL	**38.3**	**59.4**	56.0	**30.2**	**46.0**	**51.2**	**38.0**

Table 4. Ablation performance on the $Ar \rightarrow Cp$ task.

MUD	WDC	GIA			OS	OS*	Unk	HOS
		Graph	Grad.	k-PCA				
					53.1	53.3	48.1	50.6
✓					52.9	52.8	54.3	53.5
✓	✓				54.8	54.2	68.8	60.6
✓	✓	✓			56.8	56.3	69.1	62.0
✓	✓	✓	✓		57.7	57.1	73.1	64.1
✓	✓	✓	✓	✓	58.9	58.3	73.8	65.2

20.2% average *HOS* comparing with state-of-the-art methods [37], [8], [23], [1], [47], which reveal that the proposed UOL is robust to the severe domain gap and high openness.

Endo-c2k. Table 3 shows the OSDA results in Endo-c2k benchmark. We firstly evaluate the performance in 'source only' setting where only source samples are utilized to train the network, which can be regarded as a lower bound. From the results, we observe that the proposed UOL outperforms all other methods [37], [23], [8], [1] in term of unknown samples recognition with a large gap, i.e. 15.9%, 4.8%, 8.0% and 6.4%. This significant improvement comes from the additional weights representing the unknown category in MUD. Furthermore, the normal category accuracy for OSBP [37], STA [23] and AoD [8] is lower than that for 'source only' while that for UOL is not. This shows that UOL can avoid the deconstruction of shared known distributions during alignment.

4.3 Ablation Study

Effectiveness for Multi-unknown Detector and Weight Discrepancy Constraint. To evaluate the contribution of proposed multi-unknown detector and weight discrepancy constraint, qualitative and quantitative ablation results are shown in Fig. 4 and Table 4, respectively. The additional weight number N is set as 1 in the first row and set as 5 for the second row in Fig. 4. We observe that the distribution of unknown samples often overlap with distributions of known categories for three scenarios in the first row, due to the discrepant visual information inner unknown category. In the second row, the unknown samples are grouped into several clusters with the guidance of multi-unknown weights, and intra-class compactness and inter-class separability is achieved with the help of weight discrepancy constraint. Moreover, comparing the 3rd row and 2nd row with the 1st row in Table 4, the unknown recognition performance increase with 6.2% and 20.7% *Unk*, which verifies that multi-unknown detector (MUD) equipped with weight discrepancy constraint (WDC) can help recognize the unknown samples.

Effectiveness for GIA. We ablate two graph structures, gradient and k-PCA successively to validate the effectiveness of each component in Gradient-graph Induced Annotation. Comparing the three confusion matrices in Fig. 5, lots of

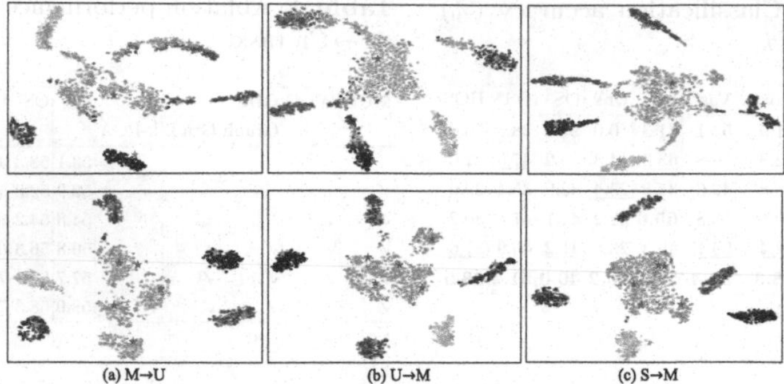

Fig. 4. T-SNE visualization of the target features for the digital recognition benchmark including MNIST (M), USPS (U) and SVHN (S). Gray points indicate the unknown features and points with other colors indicate known features. Red stars represent the classifier weights of unknown category and Blue stars represent the weights of known categories. (Color figure online)

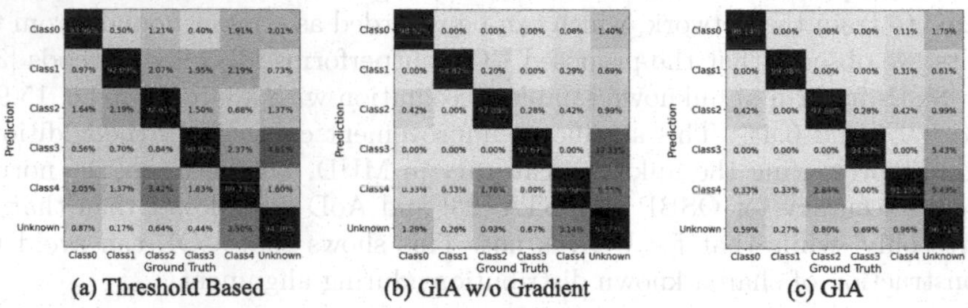

Fig. 5. Confusion matrices of pseudo labels in MNIST→USPS task for (a) threshold base method, (b) GIA without gradient and (c) GIA.

off-diagonal elements are non-zero in the 1st matrix, while most of these are zero in the 2nd and 3rd matrices. This indicates two proposed graph structures could fully utilize the intrinsic relationship of data and suppress noisy pseudo labels. Moreover, the false unknown samples in the 3rd confusion matrix are less than those in 2nd one, which certifies that gradient manifold incorporates the information beneficial to recognition. As for the numerical results in Table 4, it is reported that the unknown accuracy is promoted by 4.0% comparing the 5th row with 4th row, which indicates that gradient can reserve the learned knowledge of unseen categories in the *true unknown excavation*. Comparing the 6th row with the 5th row, the HOS score increases by 1.1% , which validates that k-PCA can learn a appropriate low-dimensional gradient to represent the intrinsic relationship.

Robustness to openness and sensitivity to additional weights number *N*. In Fig. 6 (a), the relationship between openness and additional weights number N is further discussed. The openness is defined as the $\mathbb{O} = 1 - \frac{|\mathcal{C}_s|}{|\mathcal{C}_t|}$, where

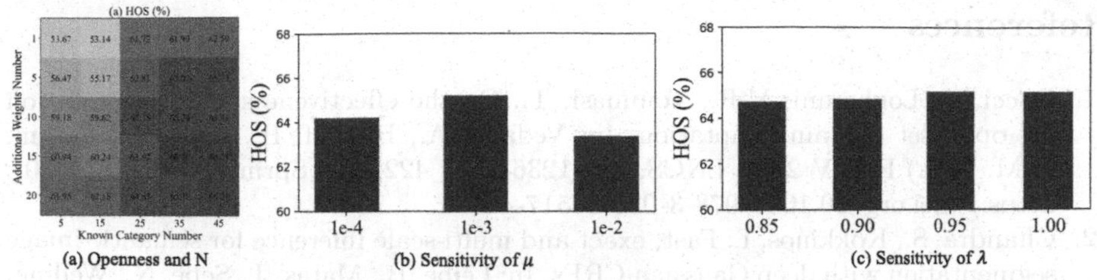

(a) Openness and N (b) Sensitivity of μ (c) Sensitivity of λ

Fig. 6. (a) Ablation study for openness and additional weights number N, (b) Sensitivity analysis of μ and (c) Sensitivity analysis of λ. All experiments are conducted on the $Ar \rightarrow Cp$ task.

$|\mathcal{C}_s|$ and $|\mathcal{C}_t|$ is the category number is source and target domain. We investigate this setting using $Ar \rightarrow Cp$ task with increasing openness, i.e. 45 known classes $\mathbb{O} = 0.38$, 35 known classes $\mathbb{O} = 0.46$, 25 known classes $\mathbb{O} = 0.62$, 15 known classes $\mathbb{O} = 0.77$ and 5 known classes $\mathbb{O} = 0.92$. For each setting, we conduct experiments with 1, 5, 10, 15 and 20 additional weights number separately. Experimental results represent that UOL framework achieves satisfactory performance in each openness setting with 61.95%, 62.18%, 65.18%, 66.24% and 66.28% *HOS*, which demonstrates that the proposed method maintains a consistent performance for various openness. Moreover, we observe that *HOS* scores are stable when the additional weights number is within the interval of [10, 20] in each openness setting. This indicates the results are not sensitive to the additional weight number N within a certain range of [10, 20].

Sensitivity to Coefficients μ and λ. We show the sensitivity analysis for weight discrepancy constraint coefficient μ and super confident matrix coefficient λ in Fig. 6 (b) and (c). We vary the value of μ from $1e-4$ to $1e-2$ and the value of λ from 0.85 to 1.00. The results show that the scores are stable to these two coefficients within a range. Limited by space, more experiments and implementation details can be found in supplementary material.

5 Conclusion

This paper presents a novel framework **UOL** for open set domain adaptation with a focus on unknown discovery. We propose the multi-unknown detector equipped with weight discrepancy constraint to excavate the diverse unknown knowledge. Meanwhile, gradient-graph induced annotation module is advanced to exploit the intrinsic relationship in gradient manifold and rectify the false unknown samples. After unknown discovery, the remaining samples are aligned in category level. Extensive experiments show that the proposed framework **UOL** performs consistently well on three benchmarks with diverse openness and domain discrepancy. In future, we plan to introduce other prior knowledge such as visual-linguistic embedding to the unknown category.

References

1. Bucci, S., Loghmani, M.R., Tommasi, T.: On the effectiveness of image rotation for open set domain adaptation. In: Vedaldi, A., Bischof, H., Brox, T., Frahm, J.-M. (eds.) ECCV 2020. LNCS, vol. 12361, pp. 422–438. Springer, Cham (2020). https://doi.org/10.1007/978-3-030-58517-4_25
2. Chandra, S., Kokkinos, I.: Fast, exact and multi-scale inference for semantic image segmentation with deep Gaussian CRFs. In: Leibe, B., Matas, J., Sebe, N., Welling, M. (eds.) ECCV 2016. LNCS, vol. 9911, pp. 402–418. Springer, Cham (2016). https://doi.org/10.1007/978-3-319-46478-7_25
3. Chen, Z., Guo, X., Woo, P.Y., Yuan, Y.: Super-resolution enhanced medical image diagnosis with sample affinity interaction. IEEE Trans. Med. Imaging **40**(5), 1377–1389 (2021)
4. Choi, S., Kim, J.T., Choo, J.: Cars can't fly up in the sky: improving urban-scene segmentation via height-driven attention networks. In: CVPR, pp. 9373–9383 (2020)
5. Cui, S., Wang, S., Zhuo, J., Su, C., Huang, Q., Tian, Q.: Gradually vanishing bridge for adversarial domain adaptation. In: CVPR, pp. 12455–12464 (2020)
6. Dray, X., et al.: Cad-cap: une base de données française à vocation internationale, pour le développement et la validation d'outils de diagnostic assisté par ordinateur en vidéocapsule endoscopique du grêle. Endoscopy **50**(03), 000441 (2018)
7. Du, L., et al.: SSF-DAN: separated semantic feature based domain adaptation network for semantic segmentation. In: CVPR, pp. 982–991 (2019)
8. Feng, Q., Kang, G., Fan, H., Yang, Y.: Attract or distract: exploit the margin of open set. In: ICCV, pp. 7990–7999 (2019)
9. Ganin, Y., Lempitsky, V.: Unsupervised domain adaptation by backpropagation. In: ICML, pp. 1180–1189. PMLR (2015)
10. Ganin, Y., et al.: Domain-adversarial training of neural networks. J. Mach. Learn. Res. **17**(1), 2030–2096 (2016)
11. Guo, X., Yang, C., Liu, Y., Yuan, Y.: Learn to threshold: thresholdnet with confidence-guided manifold mixup for polyp segmentation. IEEE Trans. Med. Imaging **40**(4), 1134–1146 (2020)
12. Hull, J.J.: A database for handwritten text recognition research. IEEE TPAMI **16**(5), 550–554 (1994)
13. Iscen, A., Tolias, G., Avrithis, Y., Furon, T., Chum, O.: Efficient diffusion on region manifolds: Recovering small objects with compact CNN representations. In: CVPR, pp. 2077–2086 (2017)
14. Jing, M., Li, J., Zhu, L., Ding, Z., Lu, K., Yang, Y.: Balanced open set domain adaptation via centroid alignment. In: AAAI, vol. 35, pp. 8013–8020 (2021)
15. Johnson, J., Douze, M., Jégou, H.: Billion-scale similarity search with GPUs. IEEE Trans, Big Data. **7**, 535–543 (2019)
16. Kang, G., Jiang, L., Yang, Y., Hauptmann, A.G.: Contrastive adaptation network for unsupervised domain adaptation. In: CVPR, pp. 4893–4902 (2019)
17. Koulaouzidis, A., et al.: Kid project: an internet-based digital video atlas of capsule endoscopy for research purposes. Endosc. Int. Open **5**(06), E477–E483 (2017)
18. Kwon, G., Prabhushankar, M., Temel, D., AlRegib, G.: Backpropagated gradient representations for anomaly detection. In: Vedaldi, A., Bischof, H., Brox, T., Frahm, J.-M. (eds.) ECCV 2020. LNCS, vol. 12366, pp. 206–226. Springer, Cham (2020). https://doi.org/10.1007/978-3-030-58589-1_13

19. LeCun, Y., Bottou, L., Bengio, Y., Haffner, P.: Gradient-based learning applied to document recognition. Proc. IEEE **86**(11), 2278–2324 (1998)
20. Lee, C.Y., Batra, T., Baig, M.H., Ulbricht, D.: Sliced Wasserstein discrepancy for unsupervised domain adaptation. In: CVPR, pp. 10285–10295 (2019)
21. Li, J., Chen, E., Ding, Z., Zhu, L., Lu, K., Huang, Z.: Cycle-consistent conditional adversarial transfer networks. In: ACM MM, pp. 747–755 (2019)
22. Li, J., Chen, E., Ding, Z., Zhu, L., Lu, K., Shen, H.T.: Maximum density divergence for domain adaptation. IEEE Trans. Pattern Anal. Mach. Intell. **43**, 3918–3930 (2020)
23. Liu, H., Cao, Z., Long, M., Wang, J., Yang, Q.: Separate to adapt: open set domain adaptation via progressive separation. In: CVPR, pp. 2927–2936 (2019)
24. Liu, W., Wen, Y., Yu, Z., Li, M., Raj, B., Song, L.: SphereFace: deep hypersphere embedding for face recognition. In: CVPR, pp. 212–220 (2017)
25. Long, M., Cao, Y., Wang, J., Jordan, M.: Learning transferable features with deep adaptation networks. In: ICML, pp. 97–105. PMLR (2015)
26. Long, M., Zhu, H., Wang, J., Jordan, M.I.: Unsupervised domain adaptation with residual transfer networks. In: NIPS (2016)
27. Long, M., Zhu, H., Wang, J., Jordan, M.I.: Deep transfer learning with joint adaptation networks. In: ICML, pp. 2208–2217. PMLR (2017)
28. Luo, Y., Wang, Z., Huang, Z., Baktashmotlagh, M.: Progressive graph learning for open-set domain adaptation. In: ICML, pp. 6468–6478. PMLR (2020)
29. Merrill, N., Olson, C.C.: Unsupervised ensemble-kernel principal component analysis for hyperspectral anomaly detection. In: CVPR, pp. 112–113 (2020)
30. Mu, F., Liang, Y., Li, Y.: Gradients as features for deep representation learning. In: ICLR (2020). https://openreview.net/forum?id=BkeoaeHKDS
31. Netzer, Y., Wang, T., Coates, A., Bissacco, A., Wu, B., Ng, A.Y.: Reading digits in natural images with unsupervised feature learning (2011)
32. O'Reilly, C., Moessner, K., Nati, M.: Univariate and multivariate time series manifold learning. Knowl. Based Syst. **133**, 1–16 (2017)
33. Pan, Y., Yao, T., Li, Y., Ngo, C.W., Mei, T.: Exploring category-agnostic clusters for open-set domain adaptation. In: CVPR, pp. 13867–13875 (2020)
34. Panareda Busto, P., Gall, J.: Open set domain adaptation. In: ICCV, pp. 754–763 (2017)
35. Saito, K., Saenko, K.: Ovanet: One-vs-all network for universal domain adaptation. In: ICCV, pp. 9000–9009 (2021)
36. Saito, K., Watanabe, K., Ushiku, Y., Harada, T.: Maximum classifier discrepancy for unsupervised domain adaptation. In: CVPR, pp. 3723–3732 (2018)
37. Saito, K., Yamamoto, S., Ushiku, Y., Harada, T.: Open set domain adaptation by backpropagation. In: Ferrari, V., Hebert, M., Sminchisescu, C., Weiss, Y. (eds.) ECCV 2018. LNCS, vol. 11209, pp. 156–171. Springer, Cham (2018). https://doi.org/10.1007/978-3-030-01228-1_10
38. Tang, H., Chen, K., Jia, K.: Unsupervised domain adaptation via structurally regularized deep clustering. In: CVPR, pp. 8725–8735 (2020)
39. Tzeng, E., Hoffman, J., Saenko, K., Darrell, T.: Adversarial discriminative domain adaptation. In: CVPR, pp. 7167–7176 (2017)
40. VS, V., Gupta, V., Oza, P., Sindagi, V.A., Patel, V.M.: Mega-CDA: memory guided attention for category-aware unsupervised domain adaptive object detection. In: CVPR, pp. 4516–4526 (2021)
41. Wang, X., Li, L., Ye, W., Long, M., Wang, J.: Transferable attention for domain adaptation. In: AAAI, vol. 33, pp. 5345–5352 (2019)

42. Xie, S., Zheng, Z., Chen, L., Chen, C.: Learning semantic representations for unsupervised domain adaptation. In: ICML, pp. 5423–5432. PMLR (2018)
43. Xu, R., et al.: Joint partial optimal transport for open set domain adaptation. In: IJCAI, pp. 2540–2546 (2020)
44. Zellinger, W., Grubinger, T., Lughofer, E., Natschläger, T., Saminger-Platz, S.: Central moment discrepancy (CMD) for domain-invariant representation learning. arXiv preprint arXiv:1702.08811 (2017)
45. Zhang, Y., Tang, H., Jia, K., Tan, M.: Domain-symmetric networks for adversarial domain adaptation. In: CVPR, pp. 5031–5040 (2019)
46. Zheng, S., et al.: Rethinking semantic segmentation from a sequence-to-sequence perspective with transformers. In: CVPR, pp. 6881–6890 (2021)
47. Zhong, L., Fang, Z., Liu, F., Yuan, B., Zhang, G., Lu, J.: Bridging the theoretical bound and deep algorithms for open set domain adaptation. IEEE Trans. Neural Netw. Learn. (2021)
48. Zhou, D., Bousquet, O., Lal, T.N., Weston, J., Schölkopf, B.: Learning with local and global consistency. In: NeurIPS, pp. 321–328 (2004)

Prototype-Guided Continual Adaptation for Class-Incremental Unsupervised Domain Adaptation

Hongbin Lin[1,3], Yifan Zhang[2], Zhen Qiu[1], Shuaicheng Niu[1], Chuang Gan[4], Yanxia Liu[1(✉)], and Mingkui Tan[1,5(✉)]

[1] South China University of Technology, Guangzhou, China
{sehongbinlin,seqiuzhen,sensc}@mail.scut.edu.cn
{cslyx,mingkuitan}@scut.edu.cn
[2] National University of Singapore, Singapore, Singapore
yifan.zhang@u.nus.edu
[3] Information Technology R&D Innovation Center of Peking University, Beijing, China
[4] MIT-IBM Watson AI Lab, Cambridge, USA
[5] Key Laboratory of Big Data and Intelligent Robot, Ministry of Education, Guangzhou, China

Abstract. This paper studies a new, practical but challenging problem, called *Class-Incremental Unsupervised Domain Adaptation* (CI-UDA), where the labeled source domain contains all classes, but the classes in the unlabeled target domain increase sequentially. This problem is challenging due to two difficulties. First, source and target label sets are inconsistent at each time step, which makes it difficult to conduct accurate domain alignment. Second, previous target classes are unavailable in the current step, resulting in the forgetting of previous knowledge. To address this problem, we propose a novel *Prototype-guided Continual Adaptation* (ProCA) method, consisting of two solution strategies. 1) Label prototype identification: we identify target label prototypes by detecting shared classes with cumulative prediction probabilities of target samples. 2) Prototype-based alignment and replay: based on the identified label prototypes, we align both domains and enforce the model to retain previous knowledge. With these two strategies, ProCA is able to adapt the source model to a class-incremental unlabeled target domain effectively. Extensive experiments demonstrate the effectiveness and superiority of ProCA in resolving CI-UDA. The @scut.edu.cnsource code is available at https://github.com/Hongbin98/ProCA.git.

Keywords: Domain adaptation · Class-incremental learning

H. Lin , Y. Zhang and Z. Qiu—Authors contributed equally.

Supplementary Information The online version contains supplementary material available at https://doi.org/10.1007/978-3-031-19827-4_21.

S. Avidan et al. (Eds.): ECCV 2022, LNCS 13693, pp. 351–368, 2022.
https://doi.org/10.1007/978-3-031-19827-4_21

1 Introduction

Unsupervised domain adaptation (UDA) seeks to improve the performance on an unlabeled target domain by leveraging a label-rich source domain via knowledge transfer [5,6,8,12,15,31,47,55]. The key challenge of UDA is the distributional shift between the source and target domains [32,38,51,54,56]. To deal with this, existing UDA methods conduct domain alignment either by domain-invariant feature learning [8,52] or by image transformation [12,37].

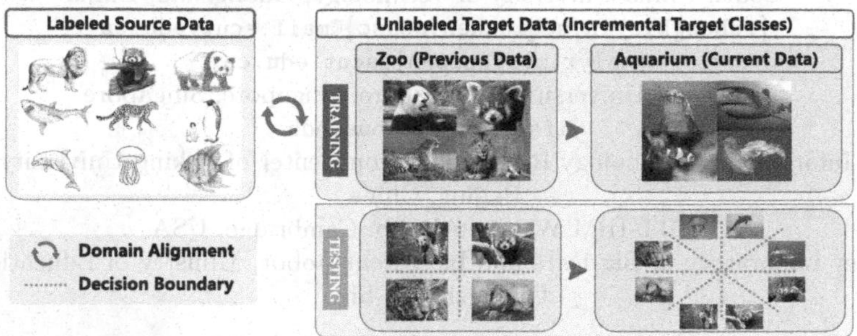

Fig. 1. An illustration of Class-incremental Unsupervised Domain Adaptation (CI-UDA), where labeled source data are accessible all the time, while unlabeled target data come online class-incrementally. When new target classes arrive, CI-UDA seeks to align the new target data to the source domain and retain the knowledge of previous target data since previous target data are unavailable.

Most existing UDA methods assume the availability of all target data in advance. However, in practice, target data often come in a streaming manner with different categories [19,28,46]. For example, a practical scenario is to transfer the knowledge of sketch images for real-world animal recognition as shown in Fig. 1, where plenty of labeled sketches are easily collected in advanced but unlabeled real-world images come incrementally (*e.g.,* the images of the land animals in the zoo come first, followed by the sea animals in the aquarium). In such a scenario, it is more appropriate to adapt the source model with the target images observed so far (from partial animal classes) instead of waiting for the images of all animals to be available, which can be more memory-efficient and time-efficient. That is, the model needs to be first adapted with the target images from land animals, and then with the images from sea animals. Note that when adapting the source model with sea animals, the previous samples of land animals are unavailable for saving the data storage cost. In this scenario, existing UDA methods that assume all target classes to be available in advance tend to fail. To address this, we explore a new and practical task, called *Class-Incremental Unsupervised Domain Adaptation* (CI-UDA), where the labeled source samples are available all the time, but the unlabeled target samples come incrementally and only partial target classes are available at a time.

CI-UDA has two characteristics: 1) the target categories at the current time step are never seen before and only occupy a subspace of the source label space; 2) the target samples of previously seen categories will be unavailable for later adaptation. As a result, besides the common challenge of domain shifts in UDA [8,40], CI-UDA poses two new challenges. The first is how to detect the shared classes between source and target domains in each time step. Since only a portion of target data is available at each time step, the label space of the target domain *is inconsistent with and is partial of* the source label space at each step, which makes domain alignment difficult. The second is how to alleviate catastrophic forgetting [43] of the old-class knowledge when learning new target classes. Since previous target samples are unavailable, later adaptation with new target classes results in knowledge forgetting of previous classes.

In CI-UDA, the key is to continually conduct domain adaptation in the absence of previous target samples. To deal with knowledge forgetting, a recent work [33] has shown that storing image prototypes for previous classes helps to retain knowledge. In addition, feature prototypes can also be used for domain alignment [29]. In other words, label prototypes open an opportunity for handling all challenges, simultaneously. However, a simple combination of existing methods [29,32,33] is not feasible for CI-UDA, since obtaining image prototypes for knowledge retaining [33] requires data labels but the target domain in CI-UDA is totally unlabeled. Moreover, feature prototypes [29,32] cannot update the feature extractor, so simply detecting them is unable to overcome the knowledge forgetting issue of the feature extractor in CI-UDA.

To better handle CI-UDA, we develop a new Prototype-guided Continual Adaptation (ProCA) method. To be specific, ProCA presents two solution strategies: 1) a label prototype identification strategy: we identify target label prototypes by detecting the shared class between source and target domains. Note that identifying label prototypes is challenging due to the inconsistent class space between the source and target domains. Therefore, detecting the shared classes is important, but is unfortunately difficult due to the absence of target labels. To overcome this, we dig into the difference between the shared classes and source private classes, and empirically observe (c.f. Fig. 3) that the cumulative probabilities of the shared classes are often higher than those of source private classes. Following this finding, we exploit the cumulative probabilities of target samples to detect the shared classes, and use the detected shared classes to identify target label prototypes. 2) a prototype-based alignment and replay strategy: based on the identified label prototypes, we conduct domain adaptation by aligning each target label prototype to the source center with the same class, and overcome catastrophic forgetting by enforcing the model to retain knowledge carried by the label prototypes learned from previous categories.

Extensive experiments on three benchmark datasets (*i.e.*, Office-31-CI, Office-Home-CI and ImageNet-Caltech-CI) demonstrate that ProCA is capable of handling CI-UDA. Moreover, we empirically show that ProCA can be used to improve existing partial UDA methods for tackling CI-UDA, which verifies the applicability of our method.

We summarize the main contributions of this paper as follows:

- We study a new yet difficult problem, called Class-incremental Unsupervised Domain Adaptation (CI-UDA), where unlabeled target samples come incrementally and only partial target classes are available at a time. Compared to vanilla UDA, CI-UDA does not assume all target data to be known in advance, and thus opens the opportunity for tackling more practical UDA scenarios in the wild.
- We propose a novel ProCA to handle CI-UDA. By innovatively identifying target label prototypes, ProCA is able to alleviate both domain discrepancies via prototype-based alignment and catastrophic forgetting via prototype-based knowledge replay. Moreover, ProCA can be applied to enhance existing partial domain adaptation methods to overcome CI-UDA.

2 Related Work

We first review the literature of unsupervised domain adaptation, including closed-set unsupervised domain adaptation, partial domain adaptation and continual domain adaptation. After that, we discuss a more relevant task, *i.e.*, class-incremental domain adaptation. Due to the page limit, we provide the literature of universal domain adaptation [49] and the difference between our ProCA and existing methods [1–3,29,32,33,43] in the supplementary (see Appendix A).

2.1 Unsupervised Domain Adaptation

Closed-set Unsupervised Domain Adaptation (UDA). The goal of UDA [7,21,26,27,48,52] is to improve the model performance on the unlabeled target domain based on a label-rich relevant source domain. In this field, the most common task is closed-set UDA [30] which assumes that source and target domains share the same set of classes. Existing UDA methods have shown great progress in alleviating domain shifts by matching high-order moments of distributions [4,16,41], by learning domain-invariant features in an adversarial manner [8,13,36,52], or by image transformation via generative adversarial models [12,37,44]. Recently, OP-GAN [45] combines UDA with self-supervised learning, involving a self-supervised module to enforce the image content consistency.

Partial Domain Adaptation (PDA). Compared to closed-set UDA, PDA [1] assumes that the target label set is a subset of the source label set instead of restricting the same label set. In general, PDA aims to transfer a deep model trained from a big labeled source domain to a small unlabeled target domain. To handle the inconsistent label space, most existing methods assign class-level [1] or instance-level [2] transferability weights for source samples. To reduce negative transfer caused by source private classes, BA^3US [24] augments the target domain to conduct balanced adversarial alignment, while DPDAN [14] aligns the positive part of the source domain to the target domain by decomposing the source domain distribution into two parts.

Continual Domain Adaptation (CDA). Different from the above tasks, CDA [39] assumes that more than one unlabeled target domains come sequentially, and seeks to incrementally adapt the model to each new incoming domain without forgetting knowledge on previous domains. To this end, Dlow [9] bridges source and multiple target domains by generating a continuous flow of intermediate states, while VDFR [20] proposes to replay variational domain-agnostic features to tackle the domain shift and task shift. Recently, GRCL [39] regularizes the gradient of losses to learn discriminative features and preserve the previous knowledge, respectively.

Overall, the above methods are inapplicable in CI-UDA due to two aspects. On the one hand, closed-set UDA and PDA methods rely on the assumption that all target data are available in advance. In other words, these methods take no consideration of retaining previous knowledge. On the other hand, CDA assumes that the label set of each target domain is the same as the source label set, ignoring domain-shared classes detection. As a result, they tend to fail in handling the challenging CI-UDA.

2.2 Class-incremental Domain Adaptation

Class-incremental Domain Adaptation is related to class-incremental learning (CIL) that learns a model continuously from a data stream, where the classes increase gradually and only new classes are available at each time. CIL requires the model to classify the samples of all classes observed so far. To overcome the issue of catastrophic forgetting, existing CIL methods retain the knowledge of previous classes either by storing or generating data from previous classes [3,33,43], or by preserving the relevant model weights of the previous classes [18,25,50].

Recently, researchers extend CIL to domain adaptation and study a new task, called class-incremental domain adaptation [19,46]. Specifically, this task seeks to alleviate the domain shift between domains and incrementally learn the private classes in the target domain. To this end, with *partial labeled target private samples*, CIDA [19] generates class-specific prototypes and learns a target-specific latent space to obtain centroids under the source-free domain adaptation scenario, and CBSC [46] utilizes supervised contrastive learning for novel class adaptation and domain-invariant feature extraction.

The above class-incremental domain adaptation is different from CI-UDA in two aspects. 1) Goal: class-incremental domain adaptation seeks to handle the issue of learning new target private classes incrementally, while CI-UDA seeks to handle the issue of domain adaptation with a class-incremental target domain that has no target private class. 2) Target Labels: class-incremental domain adaptation requires one-shot or few-shot labeled target samples as a prerequisite, while CI-UDA assumes a totally unlabeled target domain. Thus, directly applying existing methods to solve CI-UDA is unfeasible. In contrast, ProCA conducts unsupervised domain alignment and knowledge replay by identifying target label prototypes, thus providing the first feasible solution to CI-UDA.

3 Problem Definition

Notation. Let $\mathcal{D}_s$=$\{(\mathbf{x}_j^s, y_j^s)|\ y_j^s \in \mathcal{C}_s\}_{j=1}^{n_s}$ denotes the source domain, where n_s is the number of source data pairs $(\mathbf{x}^s, y^s)$ and $\mathcal{C}_s$ denotes the source label set with the class number $|\mathcal{C}_s| = K$. Moreover, we denote the unlabeled target domain as $\mathcal{D}_t$=$\{\mathbf{x}_i\}_{i=1}^{n_t}$ with n_t target samples. $\mathcal{C}_t$ denotes the target label set.

Class-Incremental Unsupervised Domain Adaptation. Unsupervised domain adaptation (UDA) aims to transfer knowledge from a label-rich source domain $\mathcal{D}_s$ to an unlabeled target domain $\mathcal{D}_t$. The key to resolving UDA is to conduct domain alignment for mitigating domain shift. Existing UDA methods generally assume that all target samples are accessible in advance and have a fixed label space that is the same to the source domain (*i.e.*, $\mathcal{C}_t = \mathcal{C}_s$). However, in real-world applications, target samples often come in a streaming manner, and meanwhile, the number of target categories may increase sequentially. To address this, we seek to explore a more practical task, namely Class-Incremental Unsupervised Domain Adaptation (CI-UDA), where labeled source samples are available all the time, but unlabeled target samples come incrementally and only partial target classes are available at a time. Here, we reuse $\mathcal{D}_t$ to denote the unlabeled target domain at the current time. Note that the label set of the target data in each time step is a subset of that of the source domain, *i.e.*, $\mathcal{C}_t \subset \mathcal{C}_s$.

Besides the domain shift that all UDA methods resolve, CI-UDA poses two new challenges: 1) how to identify the shared classes between two domains in each time step; 2) how to alleviate knowledge forgetting of old classes when learning new target classes. Due to the integration of these challenges, existing UDA methods [8,12,21,31,40,48] are incapable of handling CI-UDA. Therefore, how to handle this practical yet difficult task remains an open question.

4 Prototype-guided Continual Adaptation

Previous studies have shown that label prototypes are effective in independently handling either UDA [13,29,32] or class-incremental learning [3,33,43] tasks. Although these methods cannot be directly used to handle CI-UDA, they inspire us to explore a unified prototype-based method to handle all challenges in CI-UDA, simultaneously. This idea, however, is non-trivial to explore in practice. Since the source and target domains have different label spaces at different time steps, it is difficult to identify target label prototypes. To address these challenges, we propose a novel Prototype-guided Continual Adaptation (ProCA) method.

Method Overview. We summarize the overall training scheme of ProCA in Fig. 2. ProCA consists of two solution strategies, that are, 1) label prototype identification and 2) prototype-based alignment and replay. We first briefly introduce the two strategies below.

First, we develop a label prototype identification strategy (c.f. Sect. 4.1) to identify target label prototypes at each time step under inconsistent label spaces

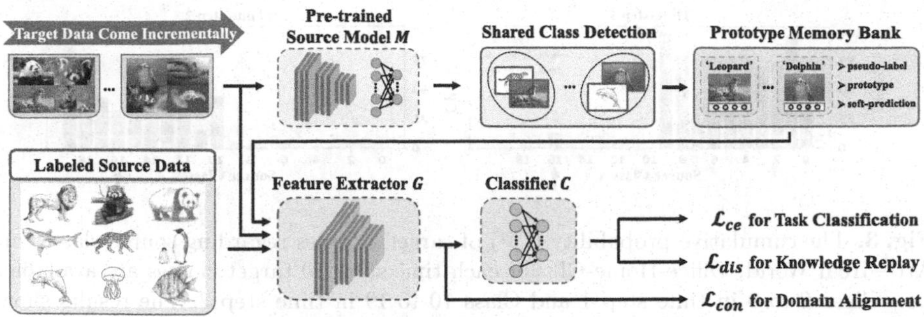

Fig. 2. An overview of Prototype-guided Continual Adaptation, ProCA consists of two strategies: 1) Label prototype identification: by detecting the shared classes between source and target domains at each time step, we identify target label prototypes for each class and record them in a memory bank. 2) Prototype-based alignment and replay: we align each target label prototype to the corresponding source center for training a domain-invariant feature extractor via $\mathcal{L}_{con}$; meanwhile, we use the saved label prototypes to enforce the model to retain knowledge learned from previous classes via $\mathcal{L}_{dis}$. Moreover, we use the cross-entropy $\mathcal{L}_{ce}$ for task classification based on the labeled source samples and pseudo-labeled target samples.

between source and target domains. To this end, we firstly propose a shared class detection method to distinguish the domain-shared classes from the source private classes. Based on the detected shared label set and the target pseudo labels generated by clustering, we identify target label prototypes for each shared class and construct an adaptive memory bank $\mathcal{P}$ to record them.

Second, based on the identified label prototypes, we propose a prototype-based alignment and replay strategy (c.f. Sect. 4.2) to align each image prototype to the corresponding source center and enforce the model to retain knowledge learned on previous classes. Specifically, we conduct prototype-based alignment by training the feature extractor G to learn domain-invariant features through a supervised contrastive loss $\mathcal{L}_{con}$. Meanwhile, we impose a knowledge distillation loss $\mathcal{L}_{dis}$ for prototype-based knowledge replay. Moreover, based on the pseudo-labeled target data and labeled source data, we train the whole model $\{G, C\}$ via the standard cross-entropy loss $\mathcal{L}_{ce}$.

Overall, the training objective of ProCA is as follows:

$$\min_{\{\theta_g, \theta_c\}} \mathcal{L}_{ce}(\theta_g, \theta_c) + \lambda \mathcal{L}_{con}(\theta_g) + \eta \mathcal{L}_{dis}(\theta_g, \theta_c), \tag{1}$$

where θ_g and θ_c denote the parameters of the feature extractor G and the classifier C, respectively. Moreover, λ and η are trade-off parameters.

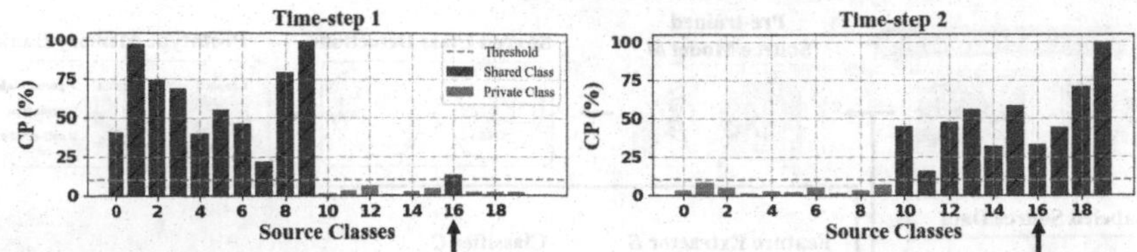

Fig. 3. The cumulative probability (CP) of target samples regarding source classes on Art→Real World, Office-Home-CI. For each time step, 10 target classes are available, *i.e.*, Class 0 to 9 in time step 1 and Class 10 to 19 in time step 2. The results show that the CP values of the shared classes are often higher than those of source private classes. Moreover, during training, since the CP of the 16-th class in time step 2 is higher than that in time step 1, we update the corresponding target class prototypes.

4.1 Label Prototype Identification

The key step in our proposed ProCA is to identify target label prototypes, which is non-trivial in the setting of CI-UDA. To this end, we propose a label prototype identification strategy that consists of four components: 1) shared class detection; 2) pseudo label generation for target data; 3) prototype memory bank construction and 4) prototype memory bank updating.

Shared Class Detection. When new unlabeled target samples arrive, it is difficult to detect the shared classes between the source and target domains since the target samples are unlabeled. To resolve this, we dig into the difference of the pre-trained source model in predicting the shared classes and the source private classes. As shown in Fig. 3, we find that the cumulative prediction probabilities of the target samples regarding the shared classes are higher than those regarding source private classes. Following this, we propose to detect the shared classes based on the cumulative probabilities of target samples. Specifically, as shown in Fig. 4, we exploit the source pre-trained model M to infer all target samples in each time step and obtain the cumulative probability of each class k by:

$$u_k = \sum_{i=1}^{n_t} C_k(G(\mathbf{x}_i)), \tag{2}$$

where $C_k(\cdot)$ denotes the k-th element in the softmax output prediction and n_t denotes the number of target samples at the current time. To enhance the generalization, we normalize the cumulative probability u_k to $[0, 1]$ by $u_k = \frac{u_k - min(\mathbf{u})}{max(\mathbf{u}) - min(\mathbf{u})}$, where $\mathbf{u}=[u_0, u_1, ..., u_K]$ is the probability vector in terms of all K classes.

Based on the cumulative probability u_k and a pre-defined threshold α, the judgement of the class k is made by: if $u_k \geq \alpha$, class k is a shared class; otherwise, class k is a source private class.

Pseudo Label Generation for Target Data. Based on the identified shared classes, we next generate pseudo labels for unlabeled target samples with a self-supervised pseudo-labeling strategy [23]. To be specific, let $\mathbf{q}_i = G(\mathbf{x}_i)$ be the extracted feature w.r.t. $\mathbf{x}_i$ and let $\hat{y}_i^k = C_k(\mathbf{q}_i)$ be the predicted probability of the classifier regarding class k, we first attain the initial centroid for each class k in the shared label set by:

$$\mathbf{c}_k = \frac{\sum_{i=1}^{n_t} \hat{y}_i^k \mathbf{q}_i}{\sum_{i=1}^{n_t} \hat{y}_i^k}. \tag{3}$$

Such an initialization is able to characterize well the distribution of different categories [23]. Based on these centroids, the pseudo label of the i-th target data is obtained via a nearest centroid approach:

$$\bar{y}_i = \arg\max_k \phi(\mathbf{q}_i, \mathbf{c}_k), \tag{4}$$

where $\phi(\cdot,\cdot)$ denotes the cosine similarity, and the pseudo label $\bar{y}_i \in \mathbb{R}^1$ is a scalar. During pseudo label generation, we update the centroid of each class by $\mathbf{c}_k = \frac{\sum_{i=1}^{n_t} \mathbb{I}(\bar{y}_i=k)\mathbf{q}_i}{\sum_{i=1}^{n_t} \mathbb{I}(\bar{y}_i=k)}$ and then update pseudo labels based on Eq. (4) one more time, where $\mathbb{I}(\cdot)$ is the indicator function. Note that we only compute the class centroids for the shared classes.

Prototype Memory Bank Construction. Based on the detected shared label set and the generated target pseudo labels, we then identify target label prototypes for each shared class. Specifically, we maintain a memory bank $\mathcal{P} = \{(\mathbf{p}_i, \mathbf{h}_i, \bar{y}_i)\}_{i=1}^N$ to record prototypes for all detected shared classes, where $\mathbf{p}_i$, $\mathbf{h}_i$, $\bar{y}_i$ and N denote the image prototype, the predicted soft label, the predicted hard pseudo label and the number of prototypes, respectively. Moreover, we denote all seen target label set as $\mathcal{C}_{at}$ and save M image prototypes for each class in the memory bank, *i.e.*, $N = |\mathcal{C}_{at}|M$. During the training process, when a new pseudo-labeled target class comes, we expand the memory bank by adding the corresponding target prototypes. Formally, for the k-th class, we denote the pseudo-labeled target domain as $\mathcal{D}_t^k = \{\mathbf{x}_i^k\}_{i=1}^{n_k}$ and attain its feature center by $\mathbf{f}_t^k = \frac{1}{n_k}\sum_{i=1}^{n_k} G(\mathbf{x}_i^k)$. Inspired by iCaRL [33], we select the image prototype for the k-th class via a nearest neighbor approach based on the target feature center:

$$\mathbf{p}_m^k = \arg\min_{\mathbf{x}^k \in \mathcal{D}_t^k} \left\| \mathbf{f}_t^k - \frac{1}{m}[G(\mathbf{x}^k) + \sum_{i=1}^{m-1} G(\mathbf{p}_i^k)] \right\|_2, \tag{5}$$

where m is the iterative index range from 1 to M. Note that we iterate Eq. (5) for M times to obtain M prototypes.

Prototype Memory Bank Updating. During the shared class detection process, false shared classes may exist, disturbing pseudo label generation for target data. In this sense, the image prototypes of these classes need to be updated. To this end, we devise an updating strategy based on the cumulative probability u_k. Specifically, for a target class k existing in the memory bank, we update its prototypes when a higher u_k occurs. For example, in Fig. 3, when the cumulative probability of the 16-th class in the time step 2 is higher than that in the time step 1, the image prototypes of the 16-th class would be updated via Eq. (5).

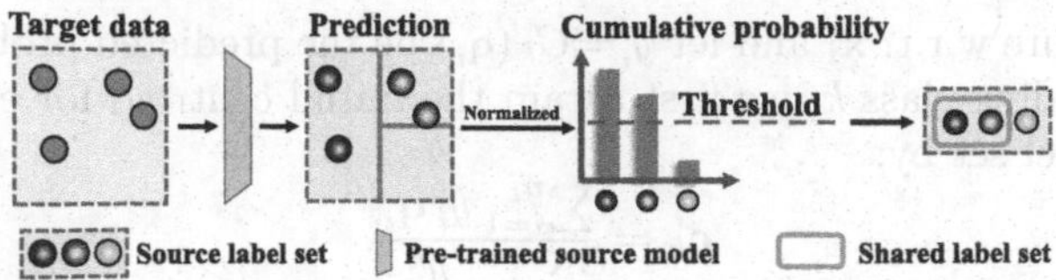

Fig. 4. The process of shared class identification. We first compute the cumulative probabilities by summing the output predictions of the pre-trained source model regarding all target samples. Then, we rescale the cumulative probabilities to $[0, 1]$ by min-max normalization. Based on the normalized probabilities, we judge the shared classes through thresholding.

Algorithm 1. Training paradigm of ProCA

```
Require: Unlabeled target data D_t={x_i}_{i=1}^{n_t} at the current time; Pre-trained source model {G, C};
    Prototype memory bank P; Training epoch E; Parameters η, λ, α, T.
Detect shared classes based on Eq. (2);
Obtain target pseudo labels based on Eq. (4);
for e = 1 → E do
    Update target label prototypes based on Eq. (5);
    Extract target data features G(x) based on G;
    Obtain target predictions C(G(x)) based on C;
    Compute L_con, L_dis based on Eqs. (7) and (8);
    Update G and C by optimizing Eq. (1)
end for
return G and C.
```

4.2 Prototype-Based Alignment and Replay

Based on target label prototypes, we develop a new prototype-based alignment and replay strategy to handle the issues of domain shifts and catastrophic forgetting below.

Prototype-Based Domain Alignment. Based on the target label prototypes, we are able to conduct class-wise alignment to explicitly mitigate domain shifts. To this end, we propose to align each pseudo-labeled prototype to the source center of the corresponding class. To be specific, for the k-th class, we first attain source feature center $\mathbf{f}_s^k$ by:

$$\mathbf{f}_s^k = \frac{\sum_{j=1}^{n_s} \mathbb{I}(y_j^s = k) G(\mathbf{x}_j^s)}{\sum_{j=1}^{n_s} \mathbb{I}(y_j^s = k)}. \tag{6}$$

Then for any image prototype $\mathbf{p}_i$ as an anchor, we conduct prototype alignment via the contrastive loss [17,53]:

$$\mathcal{L}_{con} = -\log \frac{\exp(\mathbf{v}_i^\top \mathbf{f}_s^{\bar{y}_i}/\tau)}{\exp(\mathbf{v}_i^\top \mathbf{f}_s^{\bar{y}_i}/\tau) + \sum_{j=1, j\neq \bar{y}_i}^{K-1} \exp(\mathbf{v}_i^\top \mathbf{f}_s^{j}/\tau)}, \tag{7}$$

where $\mathbf{v}_i = G(\mathbf{p}_i)$ denotes the extracted feature of the image prototype $\mathbf{p}_i$ with $\bar{y}_i$ as its pseudo label and τ denotes a temperature factor. This loss enables the feature extractor G to learn domain-invariant features, which helps to alleviate domain discrepancies.

Prototype-Based Knowledge Replay. Since target samples of previous classes are unavailable, the model suffers from catastrophic forgetting [43] during CI-UDA. To overcome this, based on the identified prototypes with soft labels, we adopt knowledge distillation [22] to enforce the model to retain the knowledge acquired from previous classes:

$$\mathcal{L}_{dis} = -\frac{1}{N}\sum_{i=1}^{N} \mathbf{h}_i^\top \log C(G(\mathbf{p}_i)), \tag{8}$$

where N denotes the number of prototypes.

At last, we summarize the pseudo-code of ProCA in Algorithm 1, while the pseudo-code of the prototype identification scheme is put in Appendix B.

5 Experiments

5.1 Experimental Setup

To verify the effectiveness of the proposed method, we conduct empirical studies based on the following experimental settings.

Datasets. We construct three dataset variants to simulate class-incremental scenarios, based on benchmark UDA datasets, *i.e.*, Office-31 [35], Office-Home [42], and ImageNet-Caltech [10,34]. 1) ***Office-31-CI*** consists of three distinct domains, *i.e.*, Amazon (A), Webcam (W) and DSLR (D). Three domains share 31 categories. We divide each domain into three disjoint subsets with each containing 10 categories in alphabetic order. 2) ***Office-Home-CI*** contains four distinct domains, *i.e.*, Artistic images (Ar), Clip Art (Cl), Product images (Pr) and Real-world images (Rw), each with 65 categories. For each domain, we build six disjoint subsets with 10 categories in random order. 3) ***ImageNet-Caltech-CI*** includes ImageNet-1K [34] and Caltech-256 [10]. Based on the shared 84 classes, we form two tasks: ImageNet (1000) → Caltech (84) and Caltech (256) → ImageNet (84). For target domains, we build eight disjoint subsets with each containing 10 categories. More details of data construction are in Appendix C.

Implementation Details. We implement our method in PyTorch and report the mean ± stdev result over 3 different runs. ResNet-50 [11], pre-trained on ImageNet, is used as the network backbone. In ProCA, we train the model using the SGD optimizer with a learning rate of 0.001. In addition, the training epochs are set to 10 for Office-31-CI, 30 for Office-Home-CI, and 15 for ImageNet-Caltech-CI, respectively. For hyper-parameter, we set λ, η, α and M to 0.1, 1, 0.15 and 10. More training details of ProCA are in Appendix D.

Compared methods. We compare ProCA with four categories of baselines: (1) source-only: ResNet-50 [11]; (2) unsupervised domain adaptation: DANN [8]; (3) partial domain adaptation: PADA [1], ETN [2], BA^{3}US [24]; (4) class-incremental domain adaptation: CIDA [19].

Table 1. Final Accuracy (%) on **Office-Home-CI**. DA and CI indicate domain adaptation and class-incremental learning.

Method	DA	CI	Ar→Cl	Ar→Pr	Ar→Rw	Cl→Ar	Cl→Pr	Cl→Rw	Pr→Ar	Pr→Cl	Pr→Rw	Rw→Ar	Rw→Cl	Rw→Pr	Avg.
ResNet-50	✗	✗	47.6	65.2	72.7	54.7	62.8	66.1	52.4	44.7	74.0	66.2	47.4	77.4	60.9
DANN [8]	✓	✗	33.1	40.0	45.8	36.8	36.6	44.1	32.0	29.8	49.8	42.4	40.2	55.2	40.5
PADA [1]	✓	✗	24.8	41.4	55.1	18.3	35.0	36.3	25.9	26.2	53.7	46.8	31.4	50.0	37.1
ETN [2]	✓	✗	42.4	2.8	7.4	4.3	60.3	6.3	50.7	33.8	70.8	3.7	43.5	75.1	33.4
BA^{3}US [24]	✓	✗	33.7	39.7	63.2	36.6	39.1	53.7	36.5	24.9	53.4	52.2	35.9	65.9	44.6
CIDA [19]	✓	✓	32.2	45.9	49.1	36.5	48.6	46.6	51.6	33.5	59.0	64.0	38.0	65.1	47.5
ProCA (ours)	✓	✓	**51.9**$_{\pm 0.4}$	**75.2**$_{\pm 0.2}$	**86.1**$_{\pm 0.3}$	**60.8**$_{\pm 0.1}$	**69.7**$_{\pm 0.1}$	**74.7**$_{\pm 0.7}$	**60.1**$_{\pm 0.2}$	**51.0**$_{\pm 0.2}$	**84.2**$_{\pm 0.4}$	**75.8**$_{\pm 0.2}$	**51.2**$_{\pm 0.5}$	**86.4**$_{\pm 0.1}$	**68.9**$_{\pm 0.1}$

Table 2. Final Accuracy (%) on **Office-31-CI** and **ImageNet-Caltech-CI**. DA and CI indicate adaptation and class-incremental learning.

Method	DA	CI	Office-31-CI							ImageNet-Caltech-CI		
			A→D	A→W	D→A	D→W	W→A	W→D	Avg.	C→I	I→C	Avg.
ResNet-50	✗	✗	74.1	74.4	58.5	96.9	61.2	99.6	77.5	72.3	70.7	71.5
DANN [8]	✓	✗	74.9	72.5	55.7	96.6	51.4	97.7	74.8	58.8	31.4	45.1
PADA [1]	✓	✗	56.9	61.5	12.5	82.4	46.7	84.3	57.4	37.3	45.9	41.6
ETN [2]	✓	✗	21.3	82.2	61.7	94.3	**64.1**	**100.0**	70.6	1.4	3.1	2.3
BA^{3}US [24]	✓	✗	74.1	73.3	63.3	94.8	64.0	**100.0**	78.3	60.8	45.0	52.9
CIDA [19]	✓	✓	70.4	64.5	48.1	95.1	52.7	98.8	71.6	69.3	49.2	59.2
ProCA (ours)	✓	✓	**81.8**$_{\pm 0.6}$	**82.5**$_{\pm 0.4}$	**65.2**$_{\pm 0.3}$	**99.1**$_{\pm 0.1}$	**64.1**$_{\pm 0.2}$	99.6$_{\pm 0.2}$	**82.1**$_{\pm 0.3}$	**82.9**$_{\pm 0.2}$	**83.1**$_{\pm 0.3}$	**83.0**$_{\pm 0.1}$

Evaluation Protocols. To fully evaluate the proposed method, we report three kinds of accuracy measures. 1) ***Final Accuracy***: the classification accuracy in the final time step of CI-UDA. 2) ***Step-level Accuracy***: the accuracy in each time step to evaluate the ability of sequentially learning. 3) ***Final S-1 Accuracy***: the average accuracy of step-1 classes in the final time step to evaluate the ability to handle catastrophic forgetting.

5.2 Comparisons with Previous Methods

We first compare our ProCA with previous methods in terms of Final Accuracy. The results are reported in Tables 1 and 2, which give the following observations. 1) ProCA outperforms all compared methods by a large margin in terms of the averaged Final Accuracy. To be specific, ProCA achieves the best or comparable performance on all transfer tasks (*e.g.,* Ar→Cl on Office-Home-CI), which demonstrates the effectiveness of our method. 2) Compared with PDA methods, *i.e.,* PADA [1], ETN [2] and BA^{3}US [24], the superior performance of our method shows that retaining knowledge learned from previous categories is important for handling CI-UDA. 3) Since CIDA [19] also designs a regularization term to prevent catastrophic forgetting, it performs better than PDA methods in CI-UDA. However, CIDA ignores the source private classes in CI-UDA, which may result in negative transfer, and thus cannot handle CI-UDA very well. 4) Domain adaptation methods even perform worse than ResNet-50, which implies that only conducting alignment may make the model biased towards the target categories at the current step and forget the knowledge of previous categories.

Table 3. Step-level Accuracy (%) on **Office-31-CI** and **Office-Home-CI**. DA and CI indicate adaptation and class-incremental learning.

Method	DA	CI	Office-31-CI				Office-Home-CI						
			Step 1	Step 2	Step 3	Avg.	Step 1	Step 2	Step 3	Step 4	Step 5	Step 6	Avg.
ResNet-50 [11]	✗	✗	85.7	81.8	77.5	81.6	61.2	61.7	61.2	62.0	62.3	62.4	61.8
DANN [8]	✓	✗	82.4	79.6	74.8	78.9	42.7	40.5	41.1	41.1	39.8	40.5	40.9
PADA [1]	✓	✗	87.5	69.9	57.4	71.6	63.0	49.3	40.4	37.7	37.4	37.1	44.2
ETN [2]	✓	✗	**92.0**	82.7	70.6	81.8	62.7	62.0	59.2	58.7	49.0	33.4	54.2
BA^{3}US [24]	✓	✗	90.7	**85.9**	78.3	85.0	66.6	60.4	53.6	49.1	46.0	44.6	53.4
CIDA [19]	✓	✓	85.5	79.1	71.6	78.7	57.9	53.6	51.8	50.1	49.6	47.5	51.8
ProCA (ours)	✓	✓	91.3	**85.9**	**82.1**	**86.3**	**70.2**	**70.1**	**68.2**	**68.5**	**68.7**	**68.9**	**86.0**

We also report the Step-level Accuracy of all methods in Tables 3. If only considering the time step 1, CI-UDA degenerates to a standard PDA problem. In this case, previous PDA methods (*i.e.*, PADA [1], ETN [2] and BA^{3}US [24]) perform well. However, when learning new target samples at a new time step, these methods suffer from severe performance degradation while our ProCA maintains a relatively stable yet promising performance. To investigate the reason, we show the accuracy drop in percentage of these step-1 classes between the time step 1 and each time step. As shown in Fig. 5, when learning new target categories, the absence of target samples from previous categories causes state-of-the-art PDA methods to forget previous knowledge, leading to a severe accuracy drop of step-1 classes. In contrast, ProCA handles catastrophic forgetting effectively and shows a promising result in terms of Step-level Accuracy. Due to the page limitation, we put more detailed results of *each subtask* in the three datasets in terms of the Step-level Accuracy and the Final S-1 Accuracy in Appendix H.

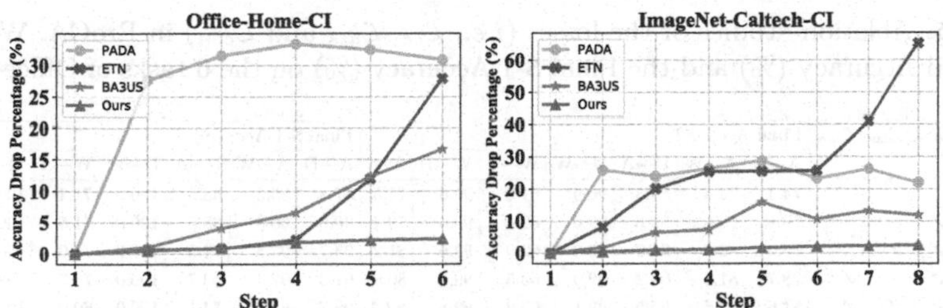

Fig. 5. Accuracy drop in percentage of different methods on **Office-Home-CI** and **ImageNet-Caltech-CI**. The accuracy drop means the accuracy difference of the step-1 classes between the time step 1 and the following each time step. The results show that our method has a significantly smaller accuracy drop in percentage than the compared methods, which shows that our method is skilled at alleviating catastrophic forgetting.

Table 4. Comparisons of the existing partial domain adaptation methods with and without our label prototype identification strategy on **Office-31-CI**. We show the final accuracy (%) and final S-1 accuracy (%) of two partial domain adaptation methods.

Method	Prototypes	Metric	A→D	A→W	D→A	D→W	W→A	W→D	Avg.
PADA	✗	Final Acc. (%)	56.9	61.5	12.5	82.4	46.7	84.3	57.4
	✓		70.8	76.2	40.9	94.6	55.6	99.8	73.0
	✗	Final S-1 Acc. (%)	35.2	49.9	17.2	74.8	39.9	72.8	48.3
	✓		79.5	80.9	62.6	96.6	62.5	100.0	80.4
BA^{3}US	✗	Final Acc. (%)	74.1	73.3	63.3	94.8	64.0	100.0	78.3
	✓		75.4	77.4	64.2	100.0	65.5	100.0	80.4
	✗	Final S-1 Acc. (%)	89.7	89.0	76.7	100.0	77.3	99.8	88.7
	✓		92.4	90.9	78.6	100.0	77.3	100.0	89.8
ProCA (ours)	✓	Final Acc. (%)	81.6	82.6	65.5	99.1	63.9	99.8	82.1
	✓	Final S-1 Acc. (%)	96.7	94.2	74.1	100.0	80.0	100.0	90.8

5.3 Application to Enhancing Partial Domain Adaptation

In this section, we seek to determine whether ProCA can be used to enhance existing PDA methods, which cannot overcome catastrophic forgetting of previously seen categories in CI-UDA. To this end, we apply ProCA to improve classic PDA methods (*i.e.*, PADA [1] and BA^{3}US [24]) by integrating them with our label prototype identification strategy. As shown in Table 4, combining with ProCA significantly increases the performance of PDA methods, which demonstrates the applicability of our method to boost existing PDA methods for handling CI-UDA. Such an observation can also be supported by the results of applying ProCA to improve ETN [2], as shown in Appendix E.

Table 5. Ablation studies of the losses (*i.e.*, $\mathcal{L}_{ce}$, $\mathcal{L}_{dis}$ and $\mathcal{L}_{con}$) in ProCA. We show the Final Accuracy (%) and the Final S-1 Accuracy (%) on the 6 tasks of Office-31-CI.

Backbone	$\mathcal{L}_{ce}$	$\mathcal{L}_{dis}$	$\mathcal{L}_{con}$	Final Acc. (%)							Final S-1 Acc. (%)						
				A→D	A→W	D→A	D→W	W→A	W→D	Avg.	A→D	A→W	D→A	D→W	W→A	W→D	Avg.
✓				74.1	74.4	58.5	96.9	61.2	99.6	77.5	87.8	85.3	68.5	100.0	71.4	100.0	85.5
✓	✓			76.8	78.8	59.6	99.0	62.4	99.6	79.4	90.0	90.8	68.6	100.0	71.5	100.0	86.8
✓	✓	✓		79.9	82.0	64.0	99.0	62.9	99.6	81.2	93.7	93.8	71.5	100.0	75.0	100.0	89.0
✓	✓		✓	78.7	81.5	63.2	99.0	63.5	99.0	80.8	91.3	92.4	69.7	100.0	76.7	98.0	88.0
✓	✓	✓	✓	81.6	82.6	65.5	99.1	63.9	99.8	**82.1**	96.7	94.2	74.1	100.0	80.0	100.0	**90.8**

5.4 Ablation Studies

To examine the effectiveness of the losses in ProCA, we show the quantitative results of the models optimized by different losses. As shown in Table 5, introducing $\mathcal{L}_{dis}$ or $\mathcal{L}_{con}$ enhances the model performance compared to optimizing the model with $\mathcal{L}_{ce}$ only. On the one hand, such a result verifies that prototype-based knowledge replay is able to alleviate catastrophic forgetting, resulting in promoting Final S-1 Accuracy. On the other hand, it also verifies that prototype-based domain alignment is able to mitigate domain shifts, resulting in promoting Final Accuracy. When combining the losses (*i.e.*, $\mathcal{L}_{ce}$, $\mathcal{L}_{dis}$, $\mathcal{L}_{con}$) together, we obtain the best performance.

In addition, we investigate the influences of hyper-parameters. The results in Appendix F show that ProCA is non-sensitive to λ and η, and the best performance of ProCA can be usually achieved by setting $\lambda = 0.1$ and $\eta = 1$. Moreover, we recommend setting $\alpha = 0.15$ since a high threshold helps to filter domain-shared classes out. Furthermore, we also investigate the influence of the number of prototypes and incremental classes in Appendix F, and evaluate the effectiveness of our shared class detection strategy in Appendix G.

6 Conclusions

In this paper, we have explored a practical transfer learning task, namely class-incremental unsupervised domain adaptation. To solve this challenging task, we have proposed a novel Prototype-guided Continual Adaptation (ProCA) method, which presents two solution strategies. 1) Label prototype identification: we identify target label prototypes with the help of a new shared class detection strategy. 2) Prototype-based alignment and replay: based on the identified label prototypes, we resolve the domain discrepancies and catastrophic forgetting via prototype-guided contrastive alignment and knowledge replay, respectively. Extensive experiments on three benchmark datasets , *i.e.*, Office-31-CI, Office-Home-CI and ImageNet-Caltech-CI, have demonstrated the effectiveness of ProCA in handling class-incremental unsupervised domain adaptation.

Acknowledgements. This work was partially supported by National Key R&D Program of China (No.2020AAA0106900), National Natural Science Foundation of China (NSFC) 62072190, Program for Guangdong Introducing Innovative and Enterpreneurial Teams 2017ZT07X183.

References

1. Cao, Z., Ma, L., Long, M., Wang, J.: Partial adversarial domain adaptation. In: Ferrari, V., Hebert, M., Sminchisescu, C., Weiss, Y. (eds.) ECCV 2018. LNCS, vol. 11212, pp. 139–155. Springer, Cham (2018). https://doi.org/10.1007/978-3-030-01237-3_9
2. Cao, Z., et al.: Learning to transfer examples for partial domain adaptation. In: CVPR, pp. 2985–2994 (2019)
3. Castro, F.M., Marín-Jiménez, M.J., Guil, N., Schmid, C., Alahari, K.: End-to-end incremental learning. In: Ferrari, V., Hebert, M., Sminchisescu, C., Weiss, Y. (eds.) ECCV 2018. LNCS, vol. 11216, pp. 241–257. Springer, Cham (2018). https://doi.org/10.1007/978-3-030-01258-8_15

4. Chen, C., et al.: HOMM: Higher-order moment matching for unsupervised domain adaptation. In: AAAI, pp. 3422–3429 (2020)
5. Chen, S., Harandi, M., Jin, X., Yang, X.: Domain adaptation by joint distribution invariant projections. IEEE Trans. Image Process. **29**, 8264–8277 (2020)
6. Chen, Y., et al.: Domain adaptive faster R-CNN for object detection in the wild. In: CVPR, pp. 3339–3348 (2018)
7. Du, Z., Li, J., Su, H., Zhu, L., Lu, K.: Cross-domain gradient discrepancy minimization for unsupervised domain adaptation. In: CVPR, pp. 3937–3946 (2021)
8. Ganin, Y., Lempitsky, V.: Unsupervised domain adaptation by backpropagation. In: ICML (2015)
9. Gong, R., et al.: DLOW: domain flow for adaptation and generalization. In: CVPR, pp. 2477–2486 (2019)
10. Griffin, G., Holub, A., Perona, P.: Caltech-256 object category dataset (2007)
11. He, K., et al.: Deep residual learning for image recognition. In: CVPR (2016)
12. Hoffman, J., et al.: CYCADA: cycle-consistent adversarial domain adaptation. In: ICML (2018)
13. Hu, D., Liang, J., Hou, Q., Yan, H., Chen, Y.: Adversarial domain adaptation with prototype-based normalized output conditioner. IEEE Trans. Image Process. **30**, 9359–9371 (2021)
14. Hu, J., et al.: Discriminative partial domain adversarial network. In: Vedaldi, A., Bischof, H., Brox, T., Frahm, J.-M. (eds.) ECCV 2020. LNCS, vol. 12372, pp. 632–648. Springer, Cham (2020). https://doi.org/10.1007/978-3-030-58583-9_38
15. Inoue, N., et al.: Cross-domain weakly-supervised object detection through progressive domain adaptation. In: CVPR, pp. 5001–5009 (2018)
16. Kang, G., et al.: Contrastive adaptation network for unsupervised domain adaptation. In: CVPR, pp. 4893–4902 (2019)
17. Khosla, P., et al.: Supervised contrastive learning. In: NeurIPS (2020)
18. Kirkpatrick, J., Pascanu, R., Rabinowitz, N., et al.: Overcoming catastrophic forgetting in neural networks. Proc. Natl. Acad. Sci. **114**(13), 3521–3526 (2017)
19. Kundu, J.N., Venkatesh, R.M., Venkat, N., Revanur, A., Babu, R.V.: Class-incremental domain adaptation. In: Vedaldi, A., Bischof, H., Brox, T., Frahm, J.-M. (eds.) ECCV 2020. LNCS, vol. 12358, pp. 53–69. Springer, Cham (2020). https://doi.org/10.1007/978-3-030-58601-0_4
20. Lao, Q., et al.: Continuous domain adaptation with variational domain-agnostic feature replay. ArXiv (2020)
21. Li, C., Lee, G.H.: From synthetic to real: Unsupervised domain adaptation for animal pose estimation. In: CVPR. pp. 1482–1491 (2021)
22. Li, Z., Hoiem, D.: Learning without forgetting. IEEE Trans. Pattern Anal. Mach. Intell. **40**, 2935–2947 (2018)
23. Liang, J., Hu, D., Feng, J.: Do we really need to access the source data? Source hypothesis transfer for unsupervised domain adaptation. In: ICML (2020)
24. Liang, J., Wang, Y., Hu, D., He, R., Feng, J.: A balanced and uncertainty-aware approach for partial domain adaptation. In: Vedaldi, A., Bischof, H., Brox, T., Frahm, J.-M. (eds.) ECCV 2020. LNCS, vol. 12356, pp. 123–140. Springer, Cham (2020). https://doi.org/10.1007/978-3-030-58621-8_8
25. Liu, X., et al.: Rotate your networks: better weight consolidation and less catastrophic forgetting. In: International Conference on Pattern Recognition, pp. 2262–2268 (2018)
26. Melas-Kyriazi, L., Manrai, A.K.: PixMatch: unsupervised domain adaptation via pixelwise consistency training. In: CVPR, pp. 12435–12445 (2021)

27. Na, J., Jung, H., Chang, H.J., Hwang, W.: FixBi: bridging domain spaces for unsupervised domain adaptation. In: CVPR, pp. 1094–1103 (2021)
28. Niu, S., et al.: Efficient test-time model adaptation without forgetting. In: ICML (2022)
29. Pan, Y., et al.: Transferrable prototypical networks for unsupervised domain adaptation. In: CVPR (2019)
30. Panareda Busto, P., Gall, J.: Open set domain adaptation. In: ICCV, pp. 754–763 (2017)
31. Pei, Z., et al.: Multi-adversarial domain adaptation. In: AAAI (2018)
32. Qiu, Z., et al.: Source-free domain adaptation via avatar prototype generation and adaptation. In: IJCAI (2021)
33. Rebuffi, S.A., et al.: ICARL: incremental classifier and representation learning. In: CVPR, pp. 5533–5542 (2017)
34. Russakovsky, O., Deng, J., Su, H., et al.: Imagenet large scale visual recognition challenge. IJCV **115**(3), 211–252 (2015)
35. Saenko, K., Kulis, B., Fritz, M., Darrell, T.: Adapting visual category models to new domains. In: Daniilidis, K., Maragos, P., Paragios, N. (eds.) ECCV 2010. LNCS, vol. 6314, pp. 213–226. Springer, Heidelberg (2010). https://doi.org/10.1007/978-3-642-15561-1_16
36. Saito, K., et al.: Maximum classifier discrepancy for unsupervised domain adaptation. In: CVPR, pp. 3723–3732 (2018)
37. Sankaranarayanan, S., et al.: Generate to adapt: aligning domains using generative adversarial networks. In: CVPR (2018)
38. Tang, H., Chen, K., Jia, K.: Unsupervised domain adaptation via structurally regularized deep clustering. In: CVPR (2020)
39. Tang, S., et al.: Gradient regularized contrastive learning for continual domain adaptation. In: AAAI, pp. 2–13 (2021)
40. Tzeng, E., et al.: Adversarial discriminative domain adaptation. In: CVPR, pp. 2962–2971 (2017)
41. Tzeng, E., et al.: Deep domain confusion: Maximizing for domain invariance. ArXiv (2014)
42. Venkateswara, H., et al.: Deep hashing network for unsupervised domain adaptation. In: CVPR (2017)
43. Wu, Y., et al.: Large scale incremental learning. In: CVPR, pp. 374–382 (2019)
44. Xia, H., Ding, Z.: HGNet: hybrid generative network for zero-shot domain adaptation. In: Vedaldi, A., Bischof, H., Brox, T., Frahm, J.-M. (eds.) ECCV 2020. LNCS, vol. 12372, pp. 55–70. Springer, Cham (2020). https://doi.org/10.1007/978-3-030-58583-9_4
45. Xie, X., Chen, J., Li, Y., Shen, L., Ma, K., Zheng, Y.: Self-supervised CycleGAN for object-preserving image-to-image domain adaptation. In: Vedaldi, A., Bischof, H., Brox, T., Frahm, J.-M. (eds.) ECCV 2020. LNCS, vol. 12365, pp. 498–513. Springer, Cham (2020). https://doi.org/10.1007/978-3-030-58565-5_30
46. Xu, M., Islam, M., Lim, C.M., Ren, H.: Class-incremental domain adaptation with smoothing and calibration for surgical report generation. In: de Bruijne, M., et al. (eds.) MICCAI 2021. LNCS, vol. 12904, pp. 269–278. Springer, Cham (2021). https://doi.org/10.1007/978-3-030-87202-1_26
47. Yang, J., et al.: St3d: self-training for unsupervised domain adaptation on 3d object detection. In: CVPR, pp. 10363–10373 (2021)
48. Yang, J., et al.: St3d: self-training for unsupervised domain adaptation on 3d object detection. In: CVPR, pp. 10368–10378 (2021)

49. You, K., et al.: Universal domain adaptation. In: CVPR, pp. 2720–2729 (2019)
50. Zenke, F., Poole, B., Ganguli, S.: Continual learning through synaptic intelligence. In: ICML, pp. 3987–3995 (2017)
51. Zhang, Y., David, P., Gong, B.: Curriculum domain adaptation for semantic segmentation of urban scenes. In: ICCV, pp. 2039–2049 (2017)
52. Zhang, Y., et al.: From whole slide imaging to microscopy: deep microscopy adaptation network for histopathology cancer image classification. In: Shen, D., et al. (eds.) MICCAI 2019. LNCS, vol. 11764, pp. 360–368. Springer, Cham (2019). https://doi.org/10.1007/978-3-030-32239-7_40
53. Zhang, Y., et al.: Unleashing the power of contrastive self-supervised visual models via contrast-regularized fine-tuning. In: NeurIPS (2021)
54. Zhang, Y., Kang, B., Hooi, B., Yan, S., Feng, J.: Deep long-tailed learning: a survey. Arxiv (2021)
55. Zhang, Y., et al.: Collaborative unsupervised domain adaptation for medical image diagnosis. IEEE Trans. Image Process. **29**, 7834–7844 (2020)
56. Zou, Y., Yu, Z., Vijaya Kumar, B.V.K., Wang, J.: Unsupervised domain adaptation for semantic segmentation via class-balanced self-training. In: Ferrari, V., Hebert, M., Sminchisescu, C., Weiss, Y. (eds.) ECCV 2018. LNCS, vol. 11207, pp. 297–313. Springer, Cham (2018). https://doi.org/10.1007/978-3-030-01219-9_18

DecoupleNet: Decoupled Network for Domain Adaptive Semantic Segmentation

Xin Lai[1], Zhuotao Tian[1], Xiaogang Xu[1], Yingcong Chen[3,4,5](✉), Shu Liu[2], Hengshuang Zhao[6,7], Liwei Wang[1], and Jiaya Jia[1,2]

[1] CUHK, Ma Liu Shui, Hong Kong
[2] SmartMore, Shenzhen, China
[3] HKUST(GZ), Guangzhou, China
[4] HKUST, Clear Water Bay, Hong Kong
[5] HKUST(GZ)-SmartMore Joint Lab, Clear Water Bay, Hong Kong
yingcongchen@ust.hk
[6] HKU, Pok Fu Lam, Hong Kong
[7] MIT, Cambridge, USA

Abstract. Unsupervised domain adaptation in semantic segmentation alleviates the reliance on expensive pixel-wise annotation. It uses a labeled source domain dataset as well as unlabeled target domain images to learn a segmentation network. In this paper, we observe two main issues of existing domain-invariant learning framework. (1) Being distracted by the feature distribution alignment, the network cannot focus on the segmentation task. (2) Fitting source domain data well would compromise the target domain performance. To address these issues, we propose DecoupleNet to alleviate source domain overfitting and let the final model focus more on the segmentation task. Also, we put forward Self-Discrimination (SD) and introduce an auxiliary classifier to learn more discriminative target domain features with pseudo labels. Finally, we propose Online Enhanced Self-Training (OEST) to contextually enhance the quality of pseudo labels in an online manner. Experiments show our method outperforms existing state-of-the-art methods. Extensive ablation studies verify the effectiveness of each component. Code is available at https://github.com/dvlab-research/DecoupleNet.

Keywords: Unsupervised domain adaptation · Semantic segmentation

1 Introduction

Semantic segmentation has made tremendous progress in recent years and it has benefited plenty of applications. Its performance highly relies on pixel-wise

Supplementary Information The online version contains supplementary material available at https://doi.org/10.1007/978-3-031-19827-4_22.

S. Avidan et al. (Eds.): ECCV 2022, LNCS 13693, pp. 369–387, 2022.
https://doi.org/10.1007/978-3-031-19827-4_22

annotation. In this paper, we alleviate data-reliance and focus on unsupervised domain adaptation (UDA). We learn a segmentation network with a labeled source-domain dataset (usually a physically synthetic dataset) and an unlabeled target domain dataset.

Due to "domain shift" [13,62] between the source and target domains, directly adopting the model trained on the source domain causes performance degradation on the target one. To minimize domain shift, domain-invariant learning [14,46,64,65,69,70] aligns distributions of source and target features. Specifically, the features or predictions from different domains are aligned with a discriminator by adversarial learning, as shown in Fig. 1(a). The discriminator learns to distinguish between source and target features, while the segmentation network learns to generate features that can fool the discriminator.

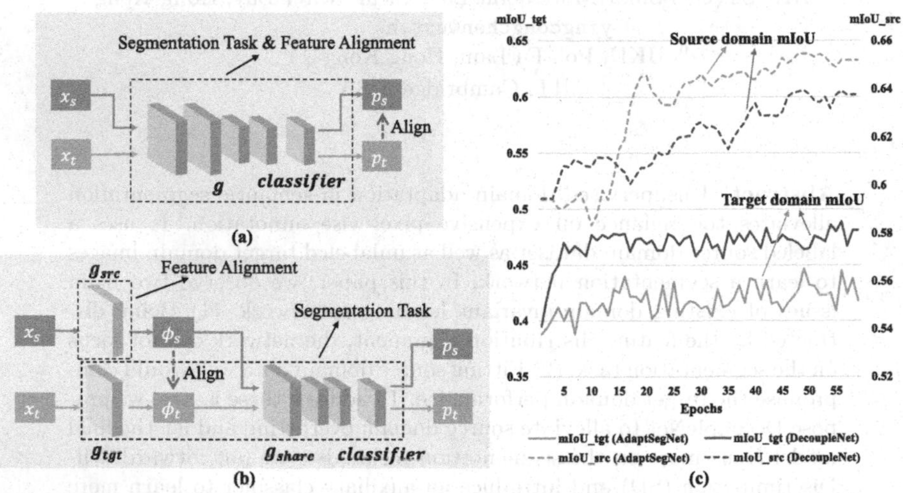

Fig. 1. (a) Domain-invariant learning. (b) Our proposed DecoupleNet. The original encoder g is split into g_{tgt} and g_{share}. Also, g_{src} and g_{tgt} share the same architecture but not the parameters. The source-domain shallow features ϕ_s are aligned towards ϕ_t with an adversarial loss. During inference, $g = g_{share} \circ g_{tgt}$ is used, and g_{src} is simply discarded. (c) Plot of the validation mIoU on source domain data (mIoU_src) by the dashed line and on target domain data (mIoU_tgt) by the solid line. We compare our DecoupleNet (blue line) with a representative domain-invariant learning method, i.e., AdaptSegNet [64] (orange line) (Color figure online)

Domain-invariant learning alleviates domain shift. However, we still observe the following two problems.

(1) *Tasks entanglement.* The feature distribution alignment and the segmentation task are conducted simultaneously in a single network, as shown in Fig. 1(a). Being distracted by feature distribution alignment, the network cannot focus on semantic segmentation, leading to inferior performance.

(2) *Source domain overfitting.* Since the training objective involves cross-entropy loss that minimizes errors on the source domain data, the trained model would fit the source domain data well, as shown in Fig. 1(c). However, in UDA, we only care about the performance on the target domain, regardless of how it performs on the source domain. Moreover, as we will discuss in Sect. 3.2, fitting the source domain very well would contrarily compromise the target domain performance.

Based on these two observations, we design DecoupleNet to decouple feature distribution alignment and the segmentation task. As shown in Fig. 1(b), we introduce a copy of shallow encoder layers for the source domain, i.e., $\boldsymbol{g}_{src}$, during training. Our goal is to let $\boldsymbol{g}_{src}$ conduct feature distribution alignment, such that the final model $\boldsymbol{g} = \boldsymbol{g}_{share} \circ \boldsymbol{g}_{tgt}$ focuses more on the downstream segmentation task. Also, it is notable that $\boldsymbol{g}_{src}$ is simply discarded during inference, and it only incurs negligible computational costs during training as shown in the supplementary material.

With our new design, the issue of *tasks entanglement* can be addressed, as shown in Fig. 1(b). Moreover, during training, we only require the model $\boldsymbol{g}_{share} \circ \boldsymbol{g}_{src}$ to fit well on the source domain, but never require the final model $\boldsymbol{g} = \boldsymbol{g}_{share} \circ \boldsymbol{g}_{tgt}$ to do so. Thus, the final model avoids overfitting in the source domain. As shown in Fig. 1(c), compared to the domain-invariant method (AdaptSegNet [64]), DecoupleNet alleviates the *source domain overfitting* problem, and boosts the target domain performance.

In addition, in order to learn more discriminative features for the target domain, we propose the Self-Discrimination (SD) technique by virtue of pseudo labels. Unlike most self-training-based methods [29,51,59,70,77,83,90], SD does not need another training phase to re-train the whole network from scratch. Instead, pseudo labels are generated at each training iteration and can be employed as an additional supervision in an online manner. Given the fact that directly adopting the noisy pseudo labels to supervise itself could corrupt the existing classifier, we introduce an auxiliary classifier during training to prevent contamination.

Finally, we propose Online Enhanced Self-Training (OEST) to further boost the performance by extending DecoupleNet to a multi-stage training paradigm. Most existing self-training-based methods [29,51,59,70,77,90] directly use the generated pseudo labels without updating them in the re-training process. Contrarily, at each training iteration, OEST updates the pseudo labels by fusing current contextually enhanced predictions, which effectively improves the quality of pseudo labels.

In summary, our contribution is threefold.

- We propose DecoupleNet to decouple feature distribution alignment and semantic segmentation. This lets the network avoid tasks entanglement and focus more on the segmentation task.
- To learn more discriminative features, we put forward Self-Discrimination by introducing an auxiliary classifier. Moreover, we propose Online Enhanced Self-Training to contextually enhance the quality of pseudo labels.

– Experiments show that our approach outperforms existing state-of-the-art methods by a large margin. Also, extensive ablation studies verify the effectiveness of each component in our method.

2 Related Work

Semantic Segmentation. Semantic segmentation aims to assign a class label to every pixel in an image. FCN [58] is a classic semantic segmentation network, which introduces a fully-convolutional network. Considering that the final output size of FCN is smaller than the input, methods based on encoder-decoder structures [2,52,56] are proposed to refine the output. Though the high-level feature has already encoded the semantic information, it cannot well capture the long-range relationship. Dilated convolution [5,81], global pooling [38], pyramid pooling [79,86,87] and attention mechanism [15,26,88,89] are used to better incorporate the context. Despite the success, all the models need annotations to accomplish training, which costs much human effort.

Unsupervised Domain Adaptation. Unsupervised dmain adaptation [19] intends to alleviate the data-reliance with a labeled dataset from a different domain. Distance-based methods [33,41–44,61,67,72] minimize the distribution distance such as MMD [67] between the source and target domain. With the development of Generative Adversarial Network (GAN) [18], adversarial learning methods [1,3,9,12,16,24,28,30,36,37,40,47,66,68,74,75,85] get popular to align the marginal or conditional feature distributions between the source and target domains. Also, methods of [11,54] factorize the feature into domain-specific and domain-agnostic features.

UDA in Semantic Segmentation. AdaptSegNet [64] employs adversarial learning to align predictions between the source and target domain in the output space and method of [45] makes further improvement. Patch-level information is used in [65] to improve the performance and contextual relationship is considered in [25,27] explicitly. In [53,71,84], feature distance is directly minimized. In [31,32,39,60,63,69,76,78,82], semi-supervised learning methods, such as entropy minimization, adding perturbation, contrastive learning and randomly dropout, further boost performance. Methods of [14,46,70] align class-conditioned feature distribution. Those of [34,48,50,73] provide distinct processing for features from different domains on some modules. On the other hand, image-to-image translation methods were considered in [8,17,23,35,77,80]. Recently, self-training-based methods [20,21,29,51,59,70,77,83,90] re-train the network with the pseudo labels generated from the initial network, yielding considerable improvement.

3 Our Method

In this section, we first introduce the preliminary in Sect. 3.1. Then, the key observations are presented as our motivation in Sect. 3.2. Afterwards, DecoupleNet, SD and OEST are elaborated in Sects. 3.3, 3.4 and 3.5, respectively.

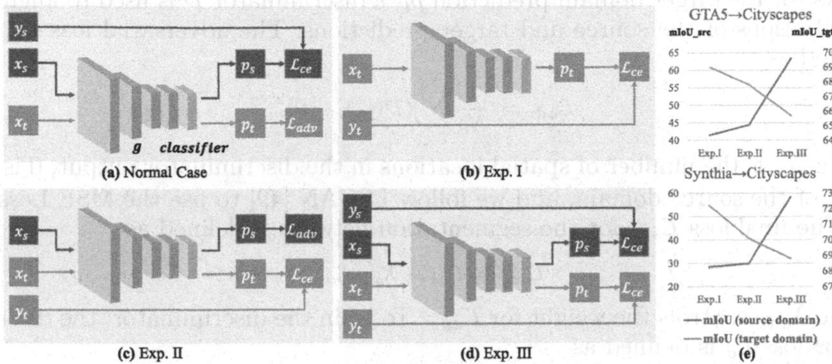

Fig. 2. (a) A representative domain-invariant method, AdaptSegNet [64]. The normal case: the ground-truth labels for the target domain are not available. The brown and green lines represent the source and target domain branches, respectively. (b) Exp. I: training by target domain images and their ground-truth labels with CE loss. (c) Exp. II: training by source domain images with the adversarial loss, as well as the target domain images and labels with CE loss. The discriminator is not shown in the figure. (d) Exp. III: training by both source and target domains images and labels with two CE losses. Note that unlike the normal case in (a), we use target domain ground-truth labels in the toy experiments to support our idea only rather than give a complete solution. (e) Evaluation results of two benchmarks on both source (blue line) and target (orange line) domain validation sets (best viewed in color) (Color figure online)

3.1 Preliminary

Problem Definition. We define the source domain images $\mathcal{X}_s$ along with ground-truth labels $\mathcal{Y}_s$, and the unlabeled target domain images $\mathcal{X}_t$. Our goal is to train a segmentation model $\mathcal{G}$ that performs well on the target domain.

A representative domain-invariant solution [64] is shown in Fig. 2(a). The source and target domain images (x_s, x_t) pass forward the segmentation network $\mathcal{G}$, which is typically composed of an encoder $\boldsymbol{g}$ and a classifier $\mathcal{C}$, to obtain the predictions (p_s, p_t), respectively. It is written as

$$p_s = \mathcal{C}(g(x_s)), \quad p_t = \mathcal{C}(g(x_t)). \tag{1}$$

For the source domain prediction p_s, the cross-entropy loss is employed with its ground-truth label y_s as

$$\mathcal{L}_{ce} = -\frac{1}{N}\sum_{i=1}^{N}\sum_{c=1}^{C}\mathbf{1}\{y_{s,i}=c\}\log p_{s,i,c}, \tag{2}$$

where N is the number of spatial locations in the source prediction map p_s, C is the number of classes, $y_{s,i}$ represents the class label at the i-th location, and $p_{s,i,c}$ represents the source prediction score of the c-th class at the i-th location.

As for the target domain prediction p_t, a discriminator $\mathcal{D}$ is used to align the distributions of the source and target predictions. The adversarial loss $\mathcal{L}_{adv}$ is defined as

$$\mathcal{L}_{adv} = \frac{1}{N_d}\sum_{i=1}^{N_d}(\mathcal{D}(p_t)_i - 0)^2, \tag{3}$$

where N_d is the number of spatial locations in the discriminator output, 0 is the label of the source domain, and we follow LSGAN [49] to use the MSE Loss.

The final loss $\mathcal{L}_{seg}$ for the segmentation network is defined as

$$\mathcal{L}_{seg} = \mathcal{L}_{ce} + \lambda_{adv}\mathcal{L}_{adv}, \tag{4}$$

where λ_{adv} controls the weight for $\mathcal{L}_{adv}$. To train the discriminator, the discriminator loss $\mathcal{L}_d$ is defined as

$$\mathcal{L}_d = \frac{1}{N_d}\sum_{i=1}^{N_d}(\mathcal{D}(p_s)_i - 0)^2 + \frac{1}{N_d}\sum_{i=1}^{N_d}(\mathcal{D}(p_t)_i - 1)^2, \tag{5}$$

where the labels of source and target domain are 0 and 1, respectively. Training alternates between updating the segmentation network with $\mathcal{L}_{seg}$ and the discriminator with $\mathcal{L}_d$.

3.2 Motivation

The method above aligns the distributions of source and target domain features for domain-invariant learning. However, as shown in Fig. 2(a), since the learning objective involves $\mathcal{L}_{ce}$ during training, the trained network has to fit the source domain data very well. The source domain overfitting issue potentially impairs the segmentation performance on the target domain.

We conduct three experiments to verify this fact, and show them in Fig. 2(b)–(d). Unlike the normal case (Fig. 2(a)), we use the target domain ground-truth labels in the toy experiments only to support our idea rather than give a solution. As shown in Fig. 2(e), from Exp. I to II, we apply an extra adversarial loss, so the model performs slightly better on the source domain data. Further, from Exp. II to III, we apply a stronger CE loss on the source domain, so it performs very well on the source domain. However, the results in Fig. 2(e) reveal the fact that the better the model fits on the source domain data, the worse it performs on the target domain. This exactly supports our idea, i.e., overfitting the source domain data actually impairs the final performance on the target domain.

Motivated by the observations, we propose a new framework to decouple the feature distribution alignment from the segmentation task. It alleviates the issue of source domain overfitting, and enables the final model to focus more on target-domain semantic segmentation.

3.3 DecoupleNet

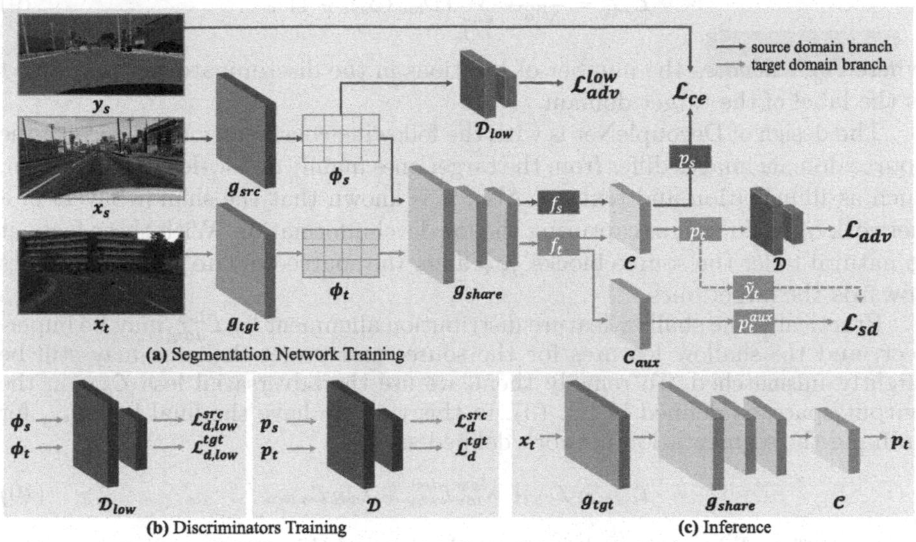

Fig. 3. Framework of DecoupleNet. (a) Segmentation network training. The brown line represents the source branch, while the green line denotes the target branch. Note that the dashed line means stopping gradients. (b) Discriminators training. (c) Inference pipeline. Best viewed in color (Color figure online)

The framework of DecoupleNet is shown in Fig. 3. We first split the feature encoder $\boldsymbol{g}$ into two parts, i.e., $\boldsymbol{g}_{tgt}$ and $\boldsymbol{g}_{share}$. Besides, we maintain another module $\boldsymbol{g}_{src}$, which shares the same architecture with $\boldsymbol{g}_{tgt}$. The source and target domain images (x_s, x_t) are fed into the source blocks $\boldsymbol{g}_{src}$ and target blocks $\boldsymbol{g}_{tgt}$ to yield the shallow features (ϕ_s, ϕ_t), respectively. They further pass through the shared blocks $\boldsymbol{g}_{share}$ to get the features (f_s, f_t). Afterwards, they are passed into the classifier $\mathcal{C}$ to obtain the predictions (p_s, p_t). Initially, we have

$$\phi_s = \boldsymbol{g}_{src}(x_s), \quad f_s = \boldsymbol{g}_{shared}(\phi_s), \quad p_s = \mathcal{C}(f_s), \tag{6}$$

$$\phi_t = \boldsymbol{g}_{tgt}(x_t), \quad f_t = \boldsymbol{g}_{shared}(\phi_t), \quad p_t = \mathcal{C}(f_t). \tag{7}$$

Then, we adopt cross-entropy loss $\mathcal{L}_{ce}$ for the labeled source domain data as

$$\mathcal{L}_{ce} = -\frac{1}{N}\sum_{i=1}^{N}\sum_{c=1}^{C} \mathbf{1}\{y_{s,i} = c\} \log p_{s,i,c}. \tag{8}$$

Besides, we require the distribution of the source-domain shallow features ϕ_s to align towards that of the target domain, i.e., ϕ_t, since our goal is to let the source blocks $\boldsymbol{g}_{src}$ bear the responsibility of feature distribution alignment.

Specifically, adversarial learning is adopted for the shallow feature alignment with an additional discriminator $\mathcal{D}_{low}$ and an adversarial loss $\mathcal{L}_{adv}^{low}$ as

$$\mathcal{L}_{adv}^{low} = \frac{1}{N_d^{low}} \sum_{i=1}^{N_d^{low}} (\mathcal{D}_{low}(\phi_s)_i - 1)^2, \tag{9}$$

where N_d^{low} denotes the number of locations in the discriminator output, and 1 is the label of the target domain.

The design of DecoupleNet is with the following considerations. Basically, the source domain images differ from the target ones mainly on low-level information, such as illumination and texture. Also, it is known that the shallow layers in a network often do well in capturing the low-level information. With these facts, it is natural to let the source blocks g_{src} align the source-domain shallow features towards the target ones.

Practically, the shallow feature distribution alignment by $\mathcal{L}_{adv}^{low}$ may be imperfect, and the shallow features for the source and target domains may still be slightly mismatched. To remedy them, we use the adversarial loss $\mathcal{L}_{adv}$ in the output space, as defined in Eq. (3). In this way, we have the final loss $\mathcal{L}_{seg}$ for training the segmentation network defined as

$$\mathcal{L}_{seg} = \mathcal{L}_{ce} + \lambda_{adv}^{low}\mathcal{L}_{adv}^{low} + \lambda_{adv}\mathcal{L}_{adv}, \tag{10}$$

where λ_{adv}^{low} and λ_{adv} control the contributions of the corresponding loss. It is notable that the incorporation of $\mathcal{L}_{adv}$ only brings minor improvement (+0.3% mIoU), as shown in Exp. 5 and 6 of Table 3. This shows the feature alignment is mainly attributed to $\mathcal{L}_{adv}^{low}$. The $\mathcal{L}_{adv}$ only serves as a complement.

To train the discriminators, as shown in Fig. 3(b), we follow previous work [64] to yield the discriminator loss as

$$\mathcal{L}_d^{low} = \frac{1}{N_d^{low}} \sum_{i=1}^{N_d^{low}} (\mathcal{D}_{low}(\phi_s)_i - 0)^2 + \frac{1}{N_d^{low}} \sum_{i=1}^{N_d^{low}} (\mathcal{D}_{low}(\phi_t)_i - 1)^2, \tag{11}$$

$$\mathcal{L}_d = \frac{1}{N_d} \sum_{i=1}^{N_d} (\mathcal{D}(p_s)_i - 0)^2 + \frac{1}{N_d} \sum_{i=1}^{N_d} (\mathcal{D}(p_t)_i - 1)^2. \tag{12}$$

During inference, as shown in Fig. 3(c), we adopt $\mathcal{F} = \mathcal{C} \circ g_{share} \circ g_{tgt}$ as the final model. All other modules are simply discarded. Note that we do not introduce extra parameters during inference.

Advantage of DecouleNet. First, the source blocks $\boldsymbol{g}_{src}$ now bear the responsibility of feature distribution alignment. Being less distracted by feature alignment, the final model (i.e., $\boldsymbol{g}_{share} \circ \boldsymbol{g}_{tgt}$) focuses more on the segmentation task. Second, though the source domain branch $\boldsymbol{g}_{share} \circ \boldsymbol{g}_{src}$ needs to directly fit the source domain data with $\mathcal{L}_{ce}$, the final model $\boldsymbol{g} = \boldsymbol{g}_{share} \circ \boldsymbol{g}_{tgt}$ is never required to perform well on the source domain during training. This alleviates the source domain overfitting problem and facilitates performance boosting on the target domain, as shown in Fig. 1(c).

3.4 Self-discrimination

Despite the effectiveness of DecoupleNet, the target blocks $\boldsymbol{g}_{tgt}$ is updated only according to $\mathcal{L}_{adv}$, which may not be strong enough to learn optimal parameters for $\boldsymbol{g}^{tgt}$. Also, without a proper learning objective for the target domain, the features f_t may not be discriminative enough. To address them, we propose Self-Discrimination (SD) to provide more supervision on the target domain branch.

As shown in Fig. 3(a), we introduce an auxiliary classifier $\mathcal{C}_{aux}$, which shares the same architecture with the main classifier $\mathcal{C}$. As the target domain feature f_t passes the classifier $\mathcal{C}$ to yield p_t, we also forward f_t into the auxiliary classifier $\mathcal{C}^{aux}$ to get the auxiliary prediction p_t^{aux}. Meanwhile, we calculate the pseudo label $\tilde{y}_t$ according to the main prediction p_t. Similar to [90], we adopt class-wise thresholds $\boldsymbol{\tau}$ to ignore uncertain pixels in the pseudo labels and maintain class balancing as well. Finally, we yield the self-discrimination loss $\mathcal{L}_{sd}$ as

$$p_t^{aux} = \mathcal{C}_{aux}(f_t), \quad \hat{y}_{t,i} = \operatorname*{argmax}_{c=1}^{C} p_{t,i,c}, \quad \tilde{y}_{t,i} = \begin{cases} \hat{y}_{t,i} & p_{t,i,c=\hat{y}_{t,i}} \geq \boldsymbol{\tau}_{c=\hat{y}_{t,i}} \\ -1(ignored) & otherwise \end{cases},$$

$$\mathcal{L}_{sd} = -\frac{1}{N_t}\sum_{i=1}^{N_t}\sum_{c=1}^{C} \mathbf{1}\{\tilde{y}_{t,i} = c\} \log p_{t,i,c}^{aux}, \tag{13}$$

where C is the number of classes, N_t is the number of spatial locations in the auxiliary prediction map p_t^{aux}, $\boldsymbol{\tau}_c$ is the threshold for the c-th class, $p_{t,i,c}$ and $p_{t,i,c}^{aux}$ are the main and auxiliary prediction scores of the c-th class for the feature at the i-th location, respectively, and $\tilde{y}_{t,i}$ is the pseudo label for the i-th location in the prediction map p_t.

It is notable that the class-wise thresholds $\boldsymbol{\tau}$ are initialized to zero when starting training. It is updated with the current predictions p_t at each iteration. The implementation details are given in the supplementary material.

Basically, $\mathcal{L}_{sd}$ is a cross-entropy loss applied to $p_{t,i,c}^{aux}$. It has a nice property that can adaptively scale the gradients with the current prediction error. Hence, it is capable of yielding more discriminative target features f_t. To verify the effectiveness, we compare the t-SNE visualizations with and without SD in the supplementary material. During inference, we only use the main classifier, and the auxiliary classifier is simply discarded.

Remarkably, the accuracy of the pseudo labels is more than 80%, and continues to increase during training, as shown in Fig. 4. Therefore, although there might be wrong supervision from pseudo labels, the benefits brought by SD still outweigh the risks.

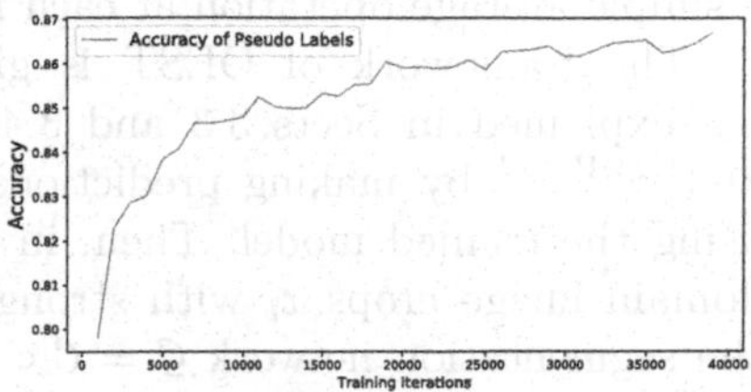

Fig. 4. Accuracy of pseudo labels during training

Finally, we incorporate $\mathcal{L}_{sd}$ into the final segmentation loss $\mathcal{L}_{seg}$ as

$$\mathcal{L}_{seg} = \mathcal{L}_{ce} + \lambda_{adv}^{low}\mathcal{L}_{adv}^{low} + \lambda_{adv}\mathcal{L}_{adv} + \lambda_{sd}\mathcal{L}_{sd}.$$

The Auxiliary Classifier. The auxiliary classifier plays an important role in SD. If we directly apply the self-discrimination loss $\mathcal{L}_{sd}$ on the main prediction p_t without the auxiliary classifier, the noisy pseudo labels may corrupt the normal training of the main classifier with $\mathcal{L}_{ce}$ and cause large performance degradation, as shown in Exp. 1 and 2 of Table 6. In contrast, introducing an auxiliary classifier avoids the side effect on the main classifier.

3.5 Online Enhanced Self-training

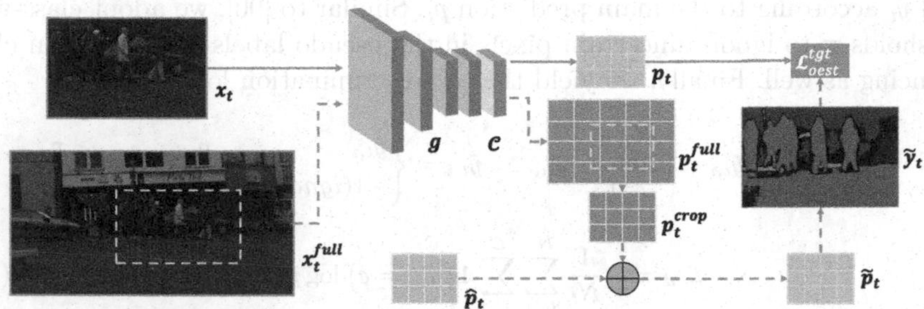

Fig. 5. Framework of online enhanced self-training. dashed line: stopping gradients

To further boost performance, we extend DecoupleNet from a single stage to a multi-stage self-training paradigm. Most existing self-training-based methods [29,51,59,70,77,83,90] generate pseudo labels in the re-labeling phase and directly use them to provide supervision without further update in the re-training phase. Generally, the predictions get more accurate during the re-training process. Fixing the generated pseudo labels may lead to inferior performance. ProDA [83] uses prototypes to denoise the pseudo labels. But it requires to maintain an extra momentum encoder and needs to update the prototypes at each iteration. In contrast, we propose a simple yet effective method, i.e., Online Enhanced Self-Training (OEST), to contextually enhance the pseudo labels via a simple average operation at each iteration.

The framework of OEST is given in Fig. 5. After the first-stage training explained in Sects. 3.3 and 3.4, we generate the pseudo soft labels $\hat{p}_t \in [0,1]^{H\times W\times C}$ by making predictions on each target domain training image x_t using the trained model. Then, in the re-training process, we pass the target domain image crops x_t with strong data augmentation (e.g., color jitter) into the segmentation network $\mathcal{G} = \mathcal{C} \circ \boldsymbol{g}$ to yield their predictions p_t. In addition, we forward their corresponding full images x_t^{full} with weak data augmentation (e.g., random horizontal flip) to obtain the full predictions p_t^{full} as

$$p_t = softmax(\mathcal{G}(x_t)), \quad p_t^{full} = softmax(\mathcal{G}(x_t^{full})). \tag{14}$$

Table 1. Results on GTA5→Cityscapes with ResNet101 and DeepLabv2. ST: self-training

Method	ST	road	sw.	build	wall	fence	pole	light	sign	veg.	terrain	sky	person	rider	car	truck	bus	train	moto.	bicycle	mIoU
SourceOnly		27.0	20.6	53.9	20.8	19.4	35.3	40.7	23.0	84.6	30.1	73.5	63.9	31.4	65.7	10.5	26.3	2.1	34.1	21.8	36.0
AdaptSeg [64]		86.5	36.0	79.9	23.4	23.3	23.9	35.2	14.8	83.4	33.3	75.6	58.5	27.6	73.7	32.5	35.4	3.9	30.1	28.1	42.4
AdaptSeg*(LS)*		**91.4**	**48.4**	81.2	27.4	21.2	31.2	35.3	16.1	84.1	32.5	78.2	57.7	28.2	85.9	33.8	43.5	0.2	23.9	16.9	44.1
CLAN [46]		87.0	27.1	79.6	27.3	23.3	28.3	35.5	24.2	83.6	27.4	74.2	58.6	28.0	76.2	33.1	36.7	6.7	31.9	31.4	43.2
AdvEnt [69]		89.4	33.1	81.0	26.6	26.8	27.2	33.5	24.7	83.9	**36.7**	78.8	58.7	30.5	84.8	**38.5**	**44.5**	1.7	31.6	32.4	45.5
FADA [70]		88.5	39.7	**83.6**	**37.9**	24.7	27.5	34.1	21.3	83.3	32.9	**83.4**	58.0	33.5	84.7	37.9	39.8	25.2	30.8	27.6	47.1
Ours		87.5	37.6	83.2	31.6	**28.3**	**38.6**	**44.3**	**24.9**	**85.1**	31.0	76.0	**68.1**	**36.9**	**86.4**	28.4	39.0	**25.5**	**42.8**	**36.1**	**49.0**
CBST [90]	✓	91.8	53.5	80.5	32.7	21.0	34.0	28.9	20.4	83.9	34.2	80.9	53.1	24.0	82.7	30.3	35.9	16.0	25.9	42.8	45.9
AdaptPatch [65]	✓	92.3	51.9	82.1	29.2	25.1	24.5	33.8	33.0	82.4	32.8	82.2	58.6	27.2	84.3	33.4	46.3	2.2	29.5	32.3	46.5
Label-Driven [77]	✓	90.8	41.4	84.7	35.1	27.5	31.2	38.0	32.8	85.6	42.1	84.9	59.6	34.4	85.0	**42.8**	52.7	3.4	30.9	38.1	49.5
FADA [70]	✓	91.0	50.6	86.0	**43.4**	29.8	36.8	43.4	25.0	86.8	38.3	87.4	64.0	38.0	85.2	31.6	46.1	6.5	25.4	37.1	50.1
Kim et al. [29]	✓	92.9	55.0	85.3	34.2	31.1	34.9	40.7	34.0	85.2	40.1	87.1	61.0	31.1	82.5	32.3	42.9	0.3	36.4	46.1	50.2
FDA-MBT [80]	✓	92.5	53.3	82.4	26.5	27.6	36.4	40.6	38.9	82.3	39.8	78.0	62.6	34.4	84.9	34.1	53.1	16.9	27.7	46.4	50.5
TPLD [59]	✓	**94.2**	**60.5**	82.8	36.6	16.6	39.3	29.0	25.5	85.6	**44.9**	84.4	60.6	27.4	84.1	37.0	47.0	31.2	36.1	50.3	51.2
IAST [51]	✓	94.1	58.8	85.4	39.7	29.2	25.1	43.1	34.2	84.8	34.6	88.7	62.7	30.3	87.6	42.3	50.3	24.7	35.2	40.2	52.2
MetaCorrection [21]	✓	92.8	58.1	86.2	39.7	33.1	36.3	42.0	38.6	85.5	37.8	87.6	62.8	31.7	84.8	35.7	50.3	2.0	36.8	48.0	52.1
DPL [8]	✓	92.8	54.4	86.2	41.6	32.7	36.4	49.0	34.0	85.8	41.3	86.0	63.2	34.2	87.2	39.3	44.5	18.7	42.6	43.1	53.3
ProDA [83]	✓	91.5	52.3	82.9	41.8	35.7	40.3	44.3	**43.2**	87.1	43.4	79.6	66.6	31.6	86.9	40.1	53.0	0.0	45.7	53.2	53.6
Ours+ST	✓	88.5	47.8	**87.4**	38.3	**36.9**	**44.9**	**53.8**	39.6	**88.0**	38.7	**88.8**	**70.4**	**39.4**	**87.8**	31.4	**55.0**	**37.4**	**47.1**	**55.9**	**56.7**
ProDA *(w/ SimCLR)*	✓	**87.8**	**56.0**	79.7	**46.3**	**44.8**	45.6	53.5	**53.5**	88.6	**45.2**	82.1	70.7	39.2	**88.8**	**45.5**	**59.4**	1.0	48.9	56.4	57.5
Ours *(w/ SimCLR)*	✓	87.6	49.3	**87.2**	42.5	41.6	**46.6**	**57.4**	44.0	**89.0**	43.9	**90.6**	**73.0**	**43.8**	88.1	32.9	53.7	**44.3**	**49.8**	**57.2**	**59.1**

Afterwards, we crop p_t^{crop} from p_t^{full} in the same way as cropping x_t from x_t^{full}, and enhance the original pseudo soft labels $\hat{p}_t$ with p_t^{crop} via a simple average operation to yield $\tilde{p}_t$. It follows by ignoring uncertain pixels with class-wise thresholds $\boldsymbol{\tau}^{st}$ as in [90] to obtain the updated pseudo labels $\tilde{y}_t$ as

$$\tilde{p}_t = \frac{1}{2}(\hat{p}_t + p_t^{crop}), \quad \hat{y}_{t,i} = \operatorname*{argmax}_{c=1}^{C} \tilde{p}_{t,i,c}, \quad \tilde{y}_{t,i} = \begin{cases} \hat{y}_{t,i} & \tilde{p}_{t,i,c=\hat{y}_{t,i}} \geq \boldsymbol{\tau}^{st}_{c=\hat{y}_{t,i}} \\ -1(ignored) & otherwise \end{cases}.$$

Since p_t^{crop} is aware of the contexts in the full image, the quality of the original pseudo labels can be contextually enhanced via simple fusion. Finally, we yield the self-training loss $\mathcal{L}_{oest}^{tgt}$ on p_t with $\tilde{y}_t$, and add it to the source domain CE loss $\mathcal{L}_{ce}^{src}$ to obtain the final loss $\mathcal{L}$ as

$$\mathcal{L}_{oest}^{tgt} = -\frac{1}{N_t}\sum_{i=1}^{N_t}\sum_{c=1}^{C} \mathbf{1}\{\tilde{y}_{t,i} = c\} \log p_{t,i,c}, \quad \mathcal{L} = \mathcal{L}_{ce}^{src} + \mathcal{L}_{oest}^{tgt}. \tag{15}$$

4 Experiment

4.1 Implementation Details

Experimental Setting. Following previous work [14,45,46,64,65,69,70], we use the ResNet-101 [22] and DeepLabv2 [4] as our base model. To split the feature encoder, we take {layer0, layer1} as the target blocks $\boldsymbol{g}_{tgt}$ and the rest as the shared blocks $\boldsymbol{g}_{share}$ for GTA5 dataset, while {layer0, layer1, layer2} as $\boldsymbol{g}_{tgt}$ and the rest as $\boldsymbol{g}_{share}$ for Synthia dataset. Note that layer0 refers to {conv1, bn1, relu, maxpool}. More details are given in the supplementary material.

Datasets. Following most previous work, evaluation is performed on GTA5 → Cityscapes, Synthia → Cityscapes and Cityscapes → Cross-City. The details of the datasets [7,10,55,57] are given in the supplementary material.

4.2 Results

The comparison with existing state-of-the-art methods is given in Tables 1 and 2. Clearly, our method outperforms others by a large margin. Previous methods [64,65,69,70] neglect the adverse effect brought by entanglement of feature distribution alignment and the segmentation task. Contrarily, DecoupleNet decouples these two tasks, and boosts the performance.

Table 2. Results on Synthia→Cityscapes with ResNet101 and DeepLabv2. ST: self-training. mIoU$^+$: mIoU of 13 classes

Method	ST	road	sw.	build	wall	fence	pole	light	sign	veg.	sky	person	rider	car	bus	moto.	bicycle	mIoU	mIoU$^+$
SourceOnly		59.9	24.7	57.7	6.3	0.0	32.5	**29.7**	15.0	72.8	70.8	59.2	17.7	73.0	23.0	11.6	22.6	36.0	41.4
AdaptSeg [64]		79.2	37.2	78.8	10.5	0.3	25.1	9.9	10.5	78.2	80.5	53.5	19.6	67.0	29.5	21.6	31.3	39.5	45.9
AdaptSeg*(LS)*		84.0	40.5	79.3	10.4	0.2	22.7	6.5	8.0	78.3	82.7	56.3	22.4	74.0	33.2	18.9	**34.9**	40.8	47.6
CLAN [46]		81.3	37.0	**80.1**	–	–	–	16.1	13.7	78.2	81.5	53.4	21.2	73.0	32.9	22.6	30.7	-	47.8
AdvEnt [69]		**85.6**	**42.2**	79.7	8.7	**0.4**	25.9	5.4	8.1	80.4	**84.1**	57.9	23.8	73.3	**36.4**	14.2	33.0	41.2	48.0
Ours		77.9	38.9	74.4	**11.9**	0.2	**33.3**	26.5	**17.1**	**83.6**	80.0	**60.7**	**26.5**	**79.9**	26.4	**25.5**	33.5	**43.5**	**50.1**
CBST [90]	✓	68.0	29.9	76.3	10.8	1.4	33.9	22.8	29.5	77.6	78.3	60.6	28.3	81.6	23.5	18.8	39.8	42.6	48.9
AdaptPatch [65]	✓	82.4	38.0	78.6	8.7	0.6	26.0	3.9	11.1	75.5	84.6	53.5	21.6	71.4	32.6	19.3	31.7	40.0	46.5
FADA [70]	✓	84.5	40.1	83.1	4.8	0.0	34.3	20.1	27.2	84.8	84.0	53.5	22.6	85.4	43.7	26.8	27.8	45.2	52.5
Label-Driven [77]	✓	85.1	44.5	81.0	-	-	-	16.4	15.2	80.1	84.8	59.4	31.9	73.2	41.0	32.6	44.7	-	53.1
Kim et al. [29]	✓	79.3	35.0	73.2	-	-	-	19.9	24.0	61.7	82.6	61.4	31.1	83.9	40.8	38.4	51.1	-	52.5
FDA-MBT [80]	✓	79.3	35.0	73.2	-	-	-	19.9	24.0	61.7	82.6	61.4	31.1	83.9	40.8	38.4	51.1	-	52.5
TPLD [59]	✓	80.9	44.3	82.2	19.9	0.3	40.6	20.5	30.1	77.2	80.9	60.6	25.5	84.8	41.1	24.7	43.7	47.3	53.5
MetaCorrection [21]	✓	**92.6**	**52.7**	81.3	8.9	2.4	28.1	13.0	7.3	83.5	85.0	60.1	19.7	84.8	37.2	21.5	43.9	45.1	52.5
DPL [8]	✓	87.5	45.7	82.8	13.3	0.6	33.2	22.0	20.1	83.1	86.0	56.6	21.9	83.1	40.3	29.8	45.7	47.0	54.2
IAST [51]	✓	81.9	41.5	**83.3**	17.7	**4.6**	32.3	30.9	28.8	83.4	85.0	65.5	30.8	86.5	38.2	33.1	52.7	49.8	57.0
ProDA [83]	✓	87.3	44.2	**83.3**	26.6	0.3	41.8	43.8	**33.1**	86.7	82.4	69.1	25.7	88.0	50.3	31.1	43.8	52.3	59.1
Ours+ST	✓	78.7	47.4	75.7	**27.8**	1.0	**43.3**	**49.1**	32.6	**87.8**	**87.3**	**69.3**	**34.4**	**88.5**	**55.0**	**44.8**	**58.5**	**55.1**	**62.2**
ProDA *(w/ SimCLR)*	✓	**87.8**	45.7	**84.6**	**37.1**	0.6	44.0	**54.6**	37.0	**88.1**	84.4	**74.2**	24.3	88.2	51.1	40.5	45.6	55.5	62.0
Ours *(w/ SimCLR)*	✓	77.8	**48.6**	75.6	32.0	**1.9**	**44.4**	52.9	**38.5**	87.8	**88.1**	71.1	**34.3**	**88.7**	**58.8**	**50.2**	**61.4**	**57.0**	**64.1**

Further, equipped with OEST, our method demonstrates stronger performance. It is also notable that our method even surpasses ProDA [83] by 3.1 points on GTA5→Cityscapes and 2.8 points on Synthia→Cityscapes, achieving a new state-of-the-art result. It is notable that following ProDA to distill the SimCLR [6] initialized student, our method still outperforms ProDA on both benchmarks. On Cityscapes → Cross-City, our method also manifests competitive results given in the supplementary material.

4.3 Ablation Study

DecoupleNet. Comparing Exp. 2 and 4 in Table 3 reveals that DecoupleNet outperforms the domain-invariant method (AdaptSegNet [64]) by 3.0% mIoU,

Table 3. Ablation study for DecoupleNet and SD. Decouple: decoupled network architecture. SD: Self-discrimination

ID	Method	Decouple	$\mathcal{L}_{ce}$	$\mathcal{L}_{adv}$	$\mathcal{L}_{adv}^{low}$	$\mathcal{L}_{sd}$	mIoU
1	SourceOnly		✓				36.0
2	AdaptSegNet		✓	✓			44.1
3	AdaptSegNet + SD		✓	✓		✓	46.0
4	DecoupleNet	✓	✓	✓	✓		47.1
5	DecoupleNet + SD (*w/o* $\mathcal{L}_{adv}^{low}$)	✓	✓	✓		✓	46.8
6	DecoupleNet + SD (*w/o* $\mathcal{L}_{adv}$)	✓	✓		✓	✓	48.7
7	DecoupleNet + SD	✓	✓	✓	✓	✓	**49.0**
8	DecoupleNet (*w/o* $\mathcal{L}_{adv}^{low}$)	✓	✓	✓			44.7

Table 4. Ablation study for the decoupled layers, i.e., the architecture of $\boldsymbol{g}_{src}$ or $\boldsymbol{g}_{tgt}$. Note that ResNet has 5 layers in total, and layer0 refers to the stem layer, i.e., {conv1, bn1, relu, maxpool}

Decoupled layers	{layer0}	{layer0,1}	{layer0,1,2}
mIoU (%)	47.7	**49.0**	47.9

which reveals the effectiveness of DecoupleNet. Note that except the decoupled architecture and $\mathcal{L}_{adv}^{low}$, Exp. 2 and 4 are kept all the same for fair comparison.

Notably, we emphasize that $\mathcal{L}_{adv}$ brings only slight improvement (+0.3% mIoU) by comparing Exp. 6 and 7 in Table 3. On the other hand, $\mathcal{L}_{adv}^{low}$ brings large performance boost (+2.2% mIoU), in the comparison between Exp. 5 and 7. This shows that the huge performance boost by DecoupleNet mainly comes from the decoupled network architecture and $\mathcal{L}_{adv}^{low}$, rather than $\mathcal{L}_{adv}$. $\mathcal{L}_{adv}$ only serves as a complement for the imperfect alignment by $\mathcal{L}_{adv}^{low}$. This demonstrates the effectiveness of DecoupleNet from another perspective.

Besides, we investigate the effect of decoupled layers (i.e., the architecture of $\boldsymbol{g}_{src}$ or $\boldsymbol{g}_{tgt}$) in Table 4. Making it too shallow leads to insufficient capability for feature alignment, while making it too deep may interfere segmentation.

Table 5. Ablation study for the alignment direction between ϕ_s and ϕ_t. $\phi_s \to \phi_t$: applying $\mathcal{L}_{adv}^{low}$ on ϕ_s. $\phi_t \to \phi_s$: applying $\mathcal{L}_{adv}^{low}$ on ϕ_t. No alignment: $\lambda_{adv}^{low} = 0$

Alignment direction	$\phi_s \to \phi_t$	$\phi_t \to \phi_s$	No alignment
mIoU (%)	**49.0**	47.3	46.8

Also, we highlight the importance of the alignment direction of ϕ_s and ϕ_t in Table 5. $\phi_s \to \phi_t$ performs the best. We explain that this prevents the segmentation network $\boldsymbol{g} = \boldsymbol{g}_{share} \circ \boldsymbol{g}_{tgt}$ from being distracted by feature alignment.

Self-discrimination. By comparing Exp. 4 and 7 in Table 3, we observe a performance boost of 1.9% mIoU brought by SD, which clearly demonstrates its effectiveness. Also, it is notable that when we directly apply SD on the domain-invaraint method (i.e., AdaptSegNet [64]), the performance still continues to improve by a large margin, through the comparison between Exp. 2 and 3 in Table 3. It shows that SD is not limited to DecoupleNet and can serve as a plugin to existing methods by providing an additional supervision.

In addition, we show the t-SNE visualizations of the target domain features f_t with and without SD in the supplementary material. It reveals the fact that the model tends to learn more discriminative target domain features with SD.

Moreover, to show the necessity of the auxiliary classifier, we make comparison in Table 6. For the model w/o auxiliary classifier (Exp. 2), we directly apply $\mathcal{L}_{sd}$ on the main predictions p_t, which leads to large degradation (–3.0% mIoU) compared to Exp. 1. We conjecture that the supervision signal from the noisy pseudo labels may interfere the normal training of the main classifier with source domain ground-truth labels. Further, Exp. 1 and 3 in Table 6 show the effectiveness of the class-wise thresholds, since it alleviates the class-imbalance issue on pseudo labels.

Table 6. Ablation study for class-wise thresholds and the auxiliary classifier. class-balance: class-wise thresholds. aux: auxiliary classifier

ID	Class-balance	Aux	mIoU	Δ
1	✓	✓	49.0	0.0
2	✓		46.0	–3.0
3		✓	48.4	–0.6

Table 7. Ablation study for OEST. Avg *(full)*: average pseudo soft labels and predictions from full images. avg *(crop)*: average pseudo soft labels and predictions from crops. Fix: use fixed pseudo soft labels only. Pred only: use predictions only

Fusion method	avg *(full)*	avg *(crop)*	fix	pred only
mIoU (%)	**56.7**	55.2	55.6	25.8

Online Enhanced Self-training. As shown in Table 7, we compare the models with various fusion methods. The comparison between 'avg *(full)*' and 'avg *(crop)*' show the effectiveness of contextual enhancement via full predictions. Moreover, 'fix' is inferior to 'avg *(full)*' by 1.1% mIoU, which shows that online updating pseudo labels with current predictions indeed improves the quality of pseudo labels and brings performance boost. As for 'pred only', it totally corrupts the training potentially due to the instability of the online prediction.

5 Conclusion

We have observed two issues of existing domain-invariant learning methods – *tasks entanglement* and *source domain overfitting*. We propose DecoupleNet to enable the final model to focus more on the segmentation task. Moreover, Self-Discrimination is put forward to learn more discriminative target features. Finally, we design OEST to contextually enhance the pseudo labels.

References

1. Nie, Z., Lin, Y., Yan, M., Cao, Y., Ning, S.: An adversarial training method for improving model robustness in unsupervised domain adaptation. In: Qiu, H., Zhang, C., Fei, Z., Qiu, M., Kung, S.-Y. (eds.) KSEM 2021. LNCS (LNAI), vol. 12817, pp. 3–13. Springer, Cham (2021). https://doi.org/10.1007/978-3-030-82153-1_1
2. Badrinarayanan, V., Kendall, A., Cipolla, R.: SegNet: a deep convolutional encoder-decoder architecture for image segmentation. Trans. Pattern Aanal. Mach. Intell. (2017)
3. Chen, C., et al.: Progressive feature alignment for unsupervised domain adaptation. In: CVPR (2019)
4. Chen, L.C., Papandreou, G., Kokkinos, I., Murphy, K., Yuille, A.: LDeepLab: semantic image segmentation with deep convolutional nets, atrous convolution, and fully connected CRFs. Trans. Pattern Anal. Mach. Intell. (2017)
5. Chen, L.C., Papandreou, G., Kokkinos, I., Murphy, K., Yuille, A.: LDeepLab: semantic image segmentation with deep convolutional nets, atrous convolution, and fully connected CRFs. Trans. Pattern Anal. Mach. Intell. (2018)
6. Chen, T., Kornblith, S., Norouzi, M., Hinton, G.E.: A simple framework for contrastive learning of visual representations. In: ICML(2020)
7. Chen, Y.H., Chen, W.Y., Chen, Y.T., Tsai, B.C., Frank Wang, Y.C., Sun, M.: No more discrimination: Cross city adaptation of road scene segmenters. In: ICCV (2017)
8. Cheng, Y., Wei, F., Bao, J., Chen, D., Wen, F., Zhang, W.: Dual path learning for domain adaptation of semantic segmentation. In: ICCV (2021)
9. Cicek, S., Soatto, S.: Unsupervised domain adaptation via regularized conditional alignment. In: ICCV (2019)
10. Cordts, M., et al.: The cityscapes dataset for semantic urban scene understanding. In: CVPR (2016)
11. Cui, S., Wang, S., Zhuo, J, Su, C., Huang, Q., Tian, Q.: Gradually vanishing bridge for adversarial domain adaptation. In: CVPR (2020)
12. Deng, Z., Luo, Y., Zhu, J.: Cluster alignment with a teacher for unsupervised domain adaptation. In: ICCV (2019)
13. Donahue, J., et al.: DeCAF: a deep convolutional activation feature for generic visual recognition. In: ICML (2014)
14. Du, L., et al.: SSF-DAN: separated semantic feature based domain adaptation network for semantic segmentation. In: ICCV (2019)
15. Fu, J., et al.: Dual attention network for scene segmentation. In: CVPR (2019)
16. Ganin, Y., Lempitsky, V.: Unsupervised domain adaptation by backpropagation. In: ICML (2015)
17. Gong, R., Li, W., Chen, Y., Gool, L.V.: Dlow: domain flow for adaptation and generalization. In: CVPR (2019)
18. Goodfellow, I.J., et al.: Generative adversarial networks. arXiv:1406.2661 (2014)
19. Gopalan, R., Li, R., Chellappa, R.: Domain adaptation for object recognition: an unsupervised approach. In: ICCV (2011)

20. Guizilini, V., Li, J., Ambrus, R., Gaidon, A.: Geometric unsupervised domain adaptation for semantic segmentation. In: ICCV (2021)
21. Guo, X., Yang, C., Li, B., Yuan, Y.: MetaCorrection: domain-aware meta loss correction for unsupervised domain adaptation in semantic segmentation. In: CVPR (2021)
22. He, K., Zhang, X., Ren, S., Sun, J.: Deep residual learning for image recognition. In: CVPR (2016)
23. Hoffman, J., et al.: CYCADA: cycle-consistent adversarial domain adaptation. In: ICML (2018)
24. Hong, W., Wang, Z., Yang, M., Yuan, J.: Conditional generative adversarial network for structured domain adaptation. In: CVPR (2018)
25. Huang, J., Lu, S., Guan, D., Zhang, X.: Contextual-relation consistent domain adaptation for semantic segmentation. In: Vedaldi, A., Bischof, H., Brox, T., Frahm, J.-M. (eds.) ECCV 2020. LNCS, vol. 12360, pp. 705–722. Springer, Cham (2020). https://doi.org/10.1007/978-3-030-58555-6_42
26. Huang, Z., Wang, X., Huang, L., Huang, C., Wei, Y., Liu, W.: CCNet: crisis-cross attention for semantic segmentation. In: ICCV (2019)
27. Kang, G., Wei, Y., Yang, Y., Zhuang, Y., Hauptmann, A.: Pixel-level cycle association: A new perspective for domain adaptive semantic segmentation. In: NeurIPS (2020)
28. Kang, G., Zheng, L., Yan, Y., Yang, Y.: Deep adversarial attention alignment for unsupervised domain adaptation: the benefit of target expectation maximization. In: Ferrari, V., Hebert, M., Sminchisescu, C., Weiss, Y. (eds.) ECCV 2018. LNCS, vol. 11215, pp. 420–436. Springer, Cham (2018). https://doi.org/10.1007/978-3-030-01252-6_25
29. Kim, M., Byun, H.: Learning texture invariant representation for domain adaptation of semantic segmentation. In: CVPR (2020)
30. Kurmi, V.K., Kumar, S., Namboodiri, V.P.: Attending to discriminative certainty for domain adaptation. In: CVPR (2019)
31. Lai, X., et al.: Semi-supervised semantic segmentation with directional context-aware consistency. In: CVPR (2021)
32. Lee, S., Kim, D., Kim, N., Jeong, S.G.: Drop to adapt: Learning discriminative features for unsupervised domain adaptation. In: ICCV (2019)
33. Li, S., et al.: Semantic concentration for domain adaptation. In: ICCV (2021)
34. Li, Y., Wang, N., Shi, J., Liu, J., Hou, X.: Revisiting batch normalization for practical domain adaptation. arXiv:1603.04779 (2016)
35. Li, Y., Yuan, L., Vasconcelos, N.: Bidirectional learning for domain adaptation of semantic segmentation. In: CVPR (2019)
36. Liu, H., Long, M., Wang, J., Jordan, M.: Transferable adversarial training: a general approach to adapting deep classifiers. In: ICML (2019)
37. Liu, M.Y., Tuzel, O.: Coupled generative adversarial networks. arXiv:1606.07536 (2016)
38. Liu, W., Rabinovich, A., Berg, A.C.: ParseNet: looking wider to see better. arXiv (2015)
39. Liu, W., Ferstl, D., Schulter, S., Zebedin, L., Fua, P., Leistner, C.: Domain adaptation for semantic segmentation via patch-wise contrastive learning. arXiv:2104.11056 (2021)
40. Liu, X., et al.: Adversarial unsupervised domain adaptation with conditional and label shift: Infer, align and iterate. In: ICCV (2021)
41. Liu, X., Li, S., Ge, Y., Ye, P., You, J., Lu, J.: Recursively conditional gaussian for ordinal unsupervised domain adaptation. In: ICCV (2021)

42. Long, M., Cao, Y., Wang, J., Jordan, M.: Learning transferable features with deep adaptation networks. In: ICML (2015)
43. Long, M., Zhu, H., Wang, J., Jordan, M.I.: Unsupervised domain adaptation with residual transfer networks. arXiv:1602.04433 (2016)
44. Long, M., Zhu, H., Wang, J., Jordan, M.I.: Deep transfer learning with joint adaptation networks. In: ICML (2017)
45. Luo, Y., Liu, P., Guan, T., Yu, J., Yang, Y.: Significance-aware information bottleneck for domain adaptive semantic segmentation. In: ICCV (2019)
46. Luo, Y., Zheng, L., Guan, T., Yu, J., Yang, Y.: Taking a closer look at domain shift: Category-level adversaries for semantics consistent domain adaptation. In: CVPR (2019)
47. Ma, X., Zhang, T., Xu, C.: GCAN: graph convolutional adversarial network for unsupervised domain adaptation. In: CVPR (2019)
48. Mancini, M., Porzi, L., Bulo, S.R., Caputo, B., Ricci, E.: Boosting domain adaptation by discovering latent domains. In: CVPR (2018)
49. Mao, X., Li, Q., Xie, H., Lau, R.Y.K., Wang, Z., Smolley, S.P.: Least squares generative adversarial networks. In: ICCV (2017)
50. Maria Carlucci, F., Porzi, L., Caputo, B., Ricci, E., Rota Bulo, S.: Autodial: Automatic domain alignment layers. In: ICCV (2017)
51. Mei, K., Zhu, C., Zou, J., Zhang, S.: Instance adaptive self-training for unsupervised domain adaptation. In: Vedaldi, A., Bischof, H., Brox, T., Frahm, J.-M. (eds.) ECCV 2020. LNCS, vol. 12371, pp. 415–430. Springer, Cham (2020). https://doi.org/10.1007/978-3-030-58574-7_25
52. Noh, H., Hong, S., Han, B.: Learning deconvolution network for semantic segmentation. In: ICCV (2015)
53. Pandey, P., Tyagi, A.K., Ambekar, S., Prathosh, A.P.: Unsupervised domain adaptation for semantic segmentation of NIR images through generative latent search. In: Vedaldi, A., Bischof, H., Brox, T., Frahm, J.-M. (eds.) ECCV 2020. LNCS, vol. 12351, pp. 413–429. Springer, Cham (2020). https://doi.org/10.1007/978-3-030-58539-6_25
54. Peng, X., Li, Y., Saenko, K.: Domain2Vec: domain embedding for unsupervised domain adaptation. arXiv:2007.09257 (2020)
55. Richter, S.R., Vineet, V., Roth, S., Koltun, V.: Playing for data: ground truth from computer games. In: ECCV (2016)
56. Ronneberger, O., Fischer, P., Brox, T.: U-Net: convolutional networks for biomedical image segmentation. In: Navab, N., Hornegger, J., Wells, W.M., Frangi, A.F. (eds.) MICCAI 2015. LNCS, vol. 9351, pp. 234–241. Springer, Cham (2015). https://doi.org/10.1007/978-3-319-24574-4_28
57. Ros, G., Sellart, L., Materzynska, J., Vazquez, D., Lopez, A.M.: The SYNTHIA dataset: a large collection of synthetic images for semantic segmentation of urban scenes. In: CVPR (2016)
58. Shelhamer, E., Long, J., Darrell, T.: Fully convolutional networks for semantic segmentation. Trans. Pattern Anal. Mach. Intell. (2017)
59. Shin, I., Woo, S., Pan, F., Kweon, I.S.: Two-phase pseudo label densification for self-training based domain adaptation. In: Vedaldi, A., Bischof, H., Brox, T., Frahm, J.-M. (eds.) ECCV 2020. LNCS, vol. 12358, pp. 532–548. Springer, Cham (2020). https://doi.org/10.1007/978-3-030-58601-0_32
60. Sohn, K., Fixmatch: Simplifying semi-supervised learning with consistency and confidence. In: NeurIPS (2020)

61. Sun, B., Saenko, K.: Deep CORAL: correlation alignment for deep domain adaptation. In: Hua, G., Jégou, H. (eds.) ECCV 2016. LNCS, vol. 9915, pp. 443–450. Springer, Cham (2016). https://doi.org/10.1007/978-3-319-49409-8_35
62. Torralba, A., Efros, A.A.: Unbiased look at dataset bias. In: CVPR (2011)
63. Truong, T.D., Duong, C.N., Le, N., Phung, S.L., Rainwater, C., Luu, K.: BiMaL: Bijective maximum likelihood approach to domain adaptation in semantic scene segmentation. In: ICCV (2021)
64. Tsai, Y.H., Hung, W.C., Schulter, S., Sohn, K., Yang, M.H., Chandraker, M.: Learning to adapt structured output space for semantic segmentation. In: CVPR (2018)
65. Tsai, Y.H., Sohn, K., Schulter, S., Chandraker, M.: Domain adaptation for structured output via discriminative patch representations. In: ICCV (2019)
66. Tzeng, E., Hoffman, J., Saenko, K., Darrell, T.: Adversarial discriminative domain adaptation. In: CVPR (2017)
67. Tzeng, E., Hoffman, J., Zhang, N., Saenko, K., Darrell, T.: Deep domain confusion: Maximizing for domain invariance. arXiv:1412.3474 (2014)
68. Volpi, R., Morerio, P., Savarese, S., Murino, V.: Adversarial feature augmentation for unsupervised domain adaptation. In: CVPR (2018)
69. Vu, T.H., Jain, H., Bucher, M., Cord, M., Pérez, P.: Advent: adversarial entropy minimization for domain adaptation in semantic segmentation. In: CVPR (2019)
70. Wang, H., Shen, T., Zhang, W., Duan, L.-Y., Mei, T.: Classes matter: a fine-grained adversarial approach to cross-domain semantic segmentation. In: Vedaldi, A., Bischof, H., Brox, T., Frahm, J.-M. (eds.) ECCV 2020. LNCS, vol. 12359, pp. 642–659. Springer, Cham (2020). https://doi.org/10.1007/978-3-030-58568-6_38
71. Wang, Q., Dai, D., Hoyer, L., Van Gool, L., Fink, O.: Domain adaptive semantic segmentation with self-supervised depth estimation. In: ICCV (2021)
72. Wei, G., Lan, C., Zeng, W., Chen, Z.: MetaAlign: coordinating domain alignment and classification for unsupervised domain adaptation. In: CVPR (2021)
73. Woong-Gi, C., Tackgeun, Y., Seonguk, S., Suha, K., Bohyung, H.: Domain-specific batch normalization for unsupervised domain adaptation. In: CVPR (2019)
74. Xie, S., Zheng, Z., Chen, L., Chen, C.: Learning semantic representations for unsupervised domain adaptation. In: ICML (2018)
75. Xu, M., Zhang, J., Ni, B., Li, T., Wang, C., Tian, Q., Zhang, W.: Adversarial domain adaptation with domain mixup. In: AAAI (2020)
76. Yang, J., et al.: An adversarial perturbation oriented domain adaptation approach for semantic segmentation. In: AAAI (2020)
77. Yang, J., An, W., Wang, S., Zhu, X., Yan, C., Huang, J.: Label-driven reconstruction for domain adaptation in semantic segmentation. In: Vedaldi, A., Bischof, H., Brox, T., Frahm, J.-M. (eds.) ECCV 2020. LNCS, vol. 12372, pp. 480–498. Springer, Cham (2020). https://doi.org/10.1007/978-3-030-58583-9_29
78. Yang, J., et al.: Exploring robustness of unsupervised domain adaptation in semantic segmentation. In: ICCV (2021)
79. Yang, M., Yu, K., Zhang, C., Li, Z., Yang, K.: DenseASPP for semantic segmentation in street scenes. In: CVPR (2018)
80. Yang, Y., Soatto, S.: FDA: Fourier domain adaptation for semantic segmentation. In: CVPR (2020)
81. Yu, F., Koltun, V.: Multi-scale context aggregation by dilated convolutions. In: ICLR (2016)
82. Zhang, F., Koltun, V., Torr, P., Ranftl, R., Richter, S.R.: Unsupervised contrastive domain adaptation for semantic segmentation. arXiv:2204.08399 (2022)

83. Zhang, P., Zhang, B., Zhang, T., Chen, D., Wang, Y., Wen, F.: Prototypical pseudo label denoising and target structure learning for domain adaptive semantic segmentation. In: CVPR (2021)
84. Zhang, Q., Zhang, J., Liu, W., Tao, D.: Category anchor-guided unsupervised domain adaptation for semantic segmentation. In: NeurIPS (2019)
85. Zhang, Y., Tang, H., Jia, K., Tan, M.: Domain-symmetric networks for adversarial domain adaptation. In: CVPR (2019)
86. Zhao, H., Qi, X., Shen, X., Shi, J., Jia, J.: ICNet for real-time semantic segmentation on high-resolution images. In: Ferrari, V., Hebert, M., Sminchisescu, C., Weiss, Y. (eds.) ECCV 2018. LNCS, vol. 11207, pp. 418–434. Springer, Cham (2018). https://doi.org/10.1007/978-3-030-01219-9_25
87. Zhao, H., Shi, J., Qi, X., Wang, X., Jia, J.: Pyramid scene parsing network. In: CVPR (2017)
88. Zhao, H., Zhang, Y., Liu, S., Shi, J., Loy, C.C., Lin, D., Jia, J.: PSANet: point-wise spatial attention network for scene parsing. In: Ferrari, V., Hebert, M., Sminchisescu, C., Weiss, Y. (eds.) ECCV 2018. LNCS, vol. 11213, pp. 270–286. Springer, Cham (2018). https://doi.org/10.1007/978-3-030-01240-3_17
89. Zhu, Z., Xu, M., Bai, S., Huang, T., Bai, X.: Asymmetric non-local neural networks for semantic segmentation. In: ICCV (2019)
90. Zou, Y., Yu, Z., Vijaya Kumar, B.V.K., Wang, J.: Unsupervised domain adaptation for semantic segmentation via class-balanced self-training. In: Ferrari, V., Hebert, M., Sminchisescu, C., Weiss, Y. (eds.) ECCV 2018. LNCS, vol. 11207, pp. 297–313. Springer, Cham (2018). https://doi.org/10.1007/978-3-030-01219-9_18

Class-Agnostic Object Counting Robust to Intraclass Diversity

Shenjian Gong[1], Shanshan Zhang[1(✉)], Jian Yang[1], Dengxin Dai[2], and Bernt Schiele[2]

[1] PCA Lab, Key Lab of Intelligent Perception and Systems for High-Dimensional Information of Ministry of Education, and Jiangsu Key Lab of Image and Video Understanding for Social Security, School of Computer Science and Engineering, Nanjing University of Science and Technology, Nanjing, China
{shenjiangong,shanshan.zhang,csjyang}@njust.edu.cn

[2] MPI Informatics, Saarbrcken, Germany
{ddai,schiele}@mpi-inf.mpg.de

Abstract. Most previous works on object counting are limited to pre-defined categories. In this paper, we focus on class-agnostic counting, i.e., counting object instances in an image by simply specifying a few exemplar boxes of interest. We start with an analysis on intraclass diversity and point out three factors: color, shape and scale diversity seriously hurts counting performance. Motivated by this analysis, we propose a new counter robust to high intraclass diversity, for which we propose two effective modules: Exemplar Feature Augmentation (EFA) and Edge Matching (EM). Aiming to handle diversity from all aspects, EFA generates a large variety of exemplars in the feature space based on the provided exemplars. Additionally, the edge matching branch focuses on the more reliable cue of shape, making our counter more robust to color variations. Experimental results on standard benchmarks show that our Robust Class-Agnostic Counter (RCAC) achieves state-of-the-art performance. The code is publicly available at https://github.com/Yankeegsj/RCAC.

Keywords: Object counting · Few-shot learning

1 Introduction

Object counting, i.e., estimating the number of object instances of a certain category in a given image, has a wide range of applications such as video surveillance and agriculture. However, most methods in previous works can only count pre-defined categories, such as people [13,16], animals [3], plants [18,22] and cars [17]. For most existing works, each model is typically trained for one category with a large amount of labeled data. They have two notable limitations. On one hand, we need to train multiple models if we are required to count objects of various categories, which is computationally expensive and inconvenient. On the other hand, such models cannot be adapted to unseen categories at test time. But in practice, it is desirable to develop counting methods that are

Supplementary Information The online version contains supplementary material available at https://doi.org/10.1007/978-3-031-19827-4_23.

S. Avidan et al. (Eds.): ECCV 2022, LNCS 13693, pp. 388–403, 2022.
https://doi.org/10.1007/978-3-031-19827-4_23

more general and flexible, which are extendable to any arbitrary new category at test time.

To this end, class-agnostic object counting is more suited for real applications and has been investigated recently. Interactive Object Counting (IOC) [2] addresses the counting task with human interaction. The user is asked to annotate a small number of objects with dots and the algorithm learns a codebook and partitions all pixels into object and background groups. This process is repeated until the results are satisfactory. In contrast, some more recent works [15,19] formulate counting as a matching problem, turning out to be more effective and efficient. Generic Matching Network (GMN) [15] learns the matching function from concatenation of query image and exemplar box features to a similarity heatmap. When adapting the model to a novel category, only a fraction of parameters need to be optimized. Few-shot adaptation & matching Network (FamNet) [19] computes the correlation maps between exemplar box and image features and then predicts the density map.

However, the current best performance is still far from satisfactory. For example, the average ground truth count on the FSC-147 validation set is 63.54, while the mean average error (MAE) of the current top method FamNet [19] is as high as 24. In order to understand the limitations of current methods, we analyze failure cases and find that objects of interest in the same image may differ in color, shape and scale, which largely hinders counting performance. A detailed analysis can be found in Sect. 3. It has been shown by FamNet [19] that it is helpful to provide more diverse exemplar boxes. Yet the exemplar boxes are provided by annotators subjectively and thus the diversity cannot be guaranteed; also, the number of provided exemplar boxes is limited, potentially not covering all instances. To address this problem, in this paper, we aim to develop a new counting method, which is more robust to intraclass diversity. Specifically, we propose two effective modules. One the one hand, we apply exemplar augmentation in the feature space to handle high diversity in various aspects. One the other hand, we introduce an additional matching branch that uses edge features to deal with diversity in color.

To summarize, the main contributions of our work are as follows: (1) We analyze the top-performing class-agnostic counting method FamNet [19], showing that intra-class diversity is a key factor decreasing counting performance, and point out the diversity comes from three aspects: color, shape and scale. (2) Two modules are proposed to overcome the high diversity challenge. The exemplar feature augmentation module increases the exemplar diversity so as to achieve more effective matching with a wide range of instances. Moreover, the additional matching branch using edge features focuses on the more reliable cue of shape, down-weighing some less reliable cues, including background and object colors. (3) Experimental results on two related datasets show that our method achieves state-of-the-art results for class-agnostic counting, outperforming previous methods by a large margin; also, since no test time adaptation is employed, our method is more convenient to apply.

2 Related Work

In this section, we first briefly review recent works on class-aware object counting and then focus on class-agnostic object counting methods.

Class-Aware Object Counting. Most object counting methods are limited to predefined categories, e.g., people, animals and cars. Generally, they can be divided into two groups. One of them is detection based counting [4,9,12]. Each of them applies an object detector on the given image, and then counts the number of bounding boxes. However, it is hard to choose a proper threshold for the detection confidence to select out reasonable boxes; and object detectors usually perform poorly at crowds. The other group is regression based counting [5,6,13,16,19,22]. These methods estimate a density map for each image, and counting is achieved by summing up the pixel values. For both kinds of methods, box or point annotations for all persons are required at training time, which are rather expensive. Class-aware object counters perform well on trained categories but they cannot be adapted to a new category at test time. Also, it is expensive to obtain rich training annotations.

Class-Agnostic Object Counting. Similar to class-aware object counting, a straightforward way for class-agnostic object counting is to apply a few-shot object detector [7,10,11] on the given image. But the major disadvantage is that it is tricky to choose a proper detection score threshold for counting; also, the detectors usually fail at crowded scenes. In contrast, regression based methods are cleaner and expected to achieve higher performance.

Some early regression based works perform pixel-wise classification. For example, IOC [2] learns a codebook from a few dot annotations marked by the user, so as to distinguish object and background pixels. Few-Shot Sequential Approach (FSSA) [24] uses the extracted prototype features to classify each pixel as one of the object classes present in the support set or as background. More recently, counting is formulated as a matching problem, which becomes more effective and efficient. GMN [15] proposed a class-agnostic counting approach consisting of three modules, namely embedding module, matching module and adaptation module. The exemplar box and query image features extracted from the embedding module are concatenated and fed to the matching module to predict a similarity heatmap. The adaption module is used to adapt to a new domain and is the only module needs to be updated for adaptation. FamNet [19] and Class-agnostic Few-shot Object Counting Network (CFOCNet) [25] are most related to our work. They both take correlation matching maps between the exemplar box and query images and then predict the density maps based on them. FamNet performs additional fine-tuning at test time. Model Agnostic Meta Learning (MAML) [8] based few-shot approaches also fine-tune some parameters to make the model better adapt to novel classes. In this paper, we also employ correlation maps for matching. The major difference is that, we propose new modules against high diversity aiming for more effective matching.

3 Analysing Intraclass Diversity for Counting

In this section, we aim to analyse the impact of intraclass diversity on counting performance.

We choose the method of FamNet* as our baseline, which is a simpler version of FamNet [19] without test-time adaptation. It has been shown [19] that test-time adaptation only brings minimal improvements and thus we do not consider it here.

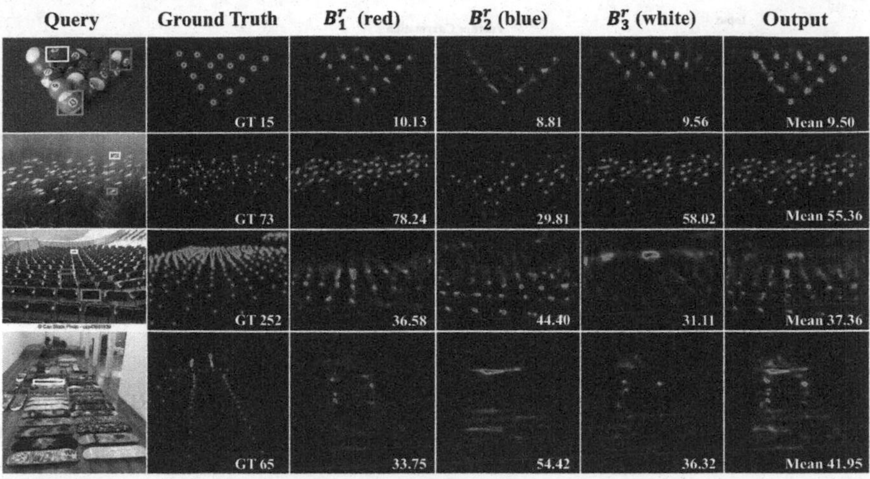

Fig. 1. Some Failure cases of FamNet* [19] from the FSC-147 dataset. At each row, from left to right, We show each query image, its ground truth density map, estimated density map given each exemplar box and the final average density map. $B^{r,1}$, $B^{r,2}$, $B^{r,3}$ are shown in red, blue and white bounding boxes respectively. The numbers indicate the ground truth counting number or estimated counting results. Colorful for better visualization.

The pipeline of FamNet* is as follows (shown as the black arrows in Fig. 2): the query image is fed to the backbone network (ResNet-50) for feature extraction, which is trained on ImageNet and not updated during training; multi-scale features for each exemplar box are obtained by performing ROI pooling on the feature maps from the third and fourth ResNet-50 blocks; the query image features also come from the third and fourth blocks; correlation maps are calculated by taking each exemplar box feature as a convolution kernel, which is applied to the query image feature maps; the density map is then predicted by a shallow subnet consisting of 5 conv layers using the correlation matching maps as input.

We start with analyzing failure cases for the FamNet* we trained on the FSC-147. We pick those samples with relative errors higher than 20% and do visual inspection. The relative error is calculated as absolute prediction error divided by the ground truth count. By observing the above samples, we find three typical factors that affect the performance: high diversity w.r.t. color, scale and shape. In Fig. 1 we show some failure cases from the FSC-147 dataset. Each image is provided with three exemplar boxes (B_1^r, B_2^r, B_3^r), each generates a density map and the final output density map is obtained by averaging the above three. The counting number (shown at the right bottom) of each density map is calculated by summing up all pixel values on it.

The color diversity comes from two aspects: the foreground objects and the background. For the query image in row 1, there is a high color difference among the object instances. Although the provided three exemplar boxes are of different colors, they still fail to cover all colors of different objects. Similarly, in row 2, we can also see color

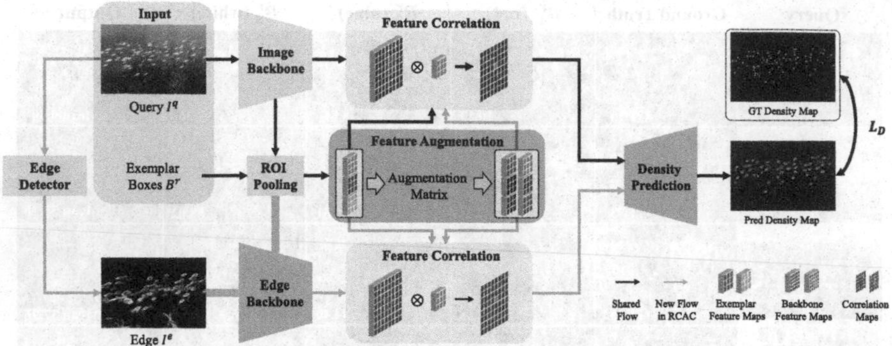

Fig. 2. Pipeline of our proposed method – Robust Class-Agnostic Counter (RCAC). Given an input query image I_q along with several exemplar boxes B^r, we first apply an edge detector to obtain a gray-scale edge image, and then we have a two-stream scheme using the RGB and edge images for matching in parallel. Specifically, the RGB and edge images are fed into separate backbone networks for feature extraction; exemplar box features are cropped from the full feature maps via ROI pooling, which are augmented via our proposed feature augmentation module; after that, feature correlation layer takes feature maps of each exemplar feature as convolution kernel to calculate the correlation map on the full feature maps; correlation maps come from the same exemplar goes through the density prediction module to generate one density map, and the final predicted density map is obtained by averaging all the density maps. Need to note that only the edge backbone and density prediction module represented with blue trapezoid are optimized during training. The black arrows indicate the shared flows between ours and the baseline method.

difference inside object boxes. The fishes are all white but their background regions differ in color. The high diversity w.r.t. color results in large counting errors.

For the query image in row 3, the chairs distribute from the near to the distant, showing large variance in scale. Although the provided three exemplar boxes are of different scales, they are not able to cover the full scale range of all instances. This challenging scenario makes the predicted counting number (37.36) become much lower than the ground truth (252).

For the query image in row 4, the skateboards show different shapes caused by different orientations. We can see many of them are put horizontally, but some are put vertically, e.g. those ones close to the blue box. Also, they are of different scales from the near to the distant. Moreover, the color varies a lot across different instances. This example is representative that different factors may happen at the same time, leading to very challenging scenarios.

We further provide some quantitative analysis regarding the impact of diversity. First, from the full validation set we select three subsets with high diversity w.r.t. color, scale and shape respectively in the following way. For each image, we compute the variance values w.r.t. color (represented by hue), scale (represented by area) and shape (represented by aspect ratio) based on the provided exemplar boxes. Then we select top hundreds of images with highest scale variance as the scale diversity subset, similar for color and shape. A comparison of results of FamNet* on the full validation set and three diverse subsets is shown in Table 1. We can find that compared to the full validation set, diversity w.r.t. color, scale and shape all bring a significant performance drop. Especially for the subsets with high color and scale diversity, the performance drops by –20 pp w.r.t. MAE.

The above analysis indicates that counting performance is highly affected by the diversity of object instances. Therefore, we are aiming to develop a new counting method robust to high intraclass diversity. Qualitative results of our method on high intraclass diversity images is shown in Fig. 4.

4 Our Robust Class-Agnostic Counter

In this section, we first introduce the setting of few-shot counting. After that, we provide the pipeline of our method, followed by detailed description of two new modules: exemplar feature augmentation and edge matching.

4.1 Problem Formulation

We follow the few-shot setting from our baseline method FamNet* [19]: given a query image ($I^q \in \mathbb{R}^{3\times H\times W}$) and K exemplar bounding boxes ($B^r \in \mathbb{R}^{K\times 4}$) that locate the reference instances belonging to the same category, the task is to predict the density map $\widetilde{Y}$ of the query image and the counting number is calculated by summing up all pixel values of $\widetilde{Y}$.

4.2 Pipeline

The overall pipeline is depicted in Fig. 2. We have a two-stream feature extraction, obtaining feature maps for each input RGB query image and its gray-scale edge image. For each stream, the exemplar features are cropped from the full feature maps via ROI pooling and then augmented via our proposed exemplar feature augmentation module. After that, correlation maps are calculated by taking each exemplar box features as a convolution kernel, which is applied to the entire query image feature maps. Then the correlation maps generated by the same exemplar box from two streams are concatenated and sent to the density prediction module, which outputs one density map for each exemplar. The final density map is obtained by averaging all density maps and the counting number is calculated by summing up all pixel values.

Feature Extraction. For the RGB image (I^q) stream, we use the ImageNet pre-trained ResNet-50 backbone, obtaining the query feature maps F^q. Please note we take the output of two layers as feature maps (3rd and 4th blocks of ResNet-50), denoted as F_i^q, $i \in \{1, 2\}$, and the network is frozen during training. For the edge image (I^e) stream, we use a light version of VGG net, which is initialized randomly and optimized during training.

ROI Pooling. This operation (ROI) crops the exemplar feature maps based on exemplar boxes B^r. The feature maps of the k-th exemplar box B_k^r are obtained as follows:

$$F_{k,i}^{q,r} = ROI(F_i^q, B_k^r), \; i \in \{1, 2\} . \tag{1}$$

Each exemplar feature map is first resized to the same size based on the maximal exemplar box. And then we resize each exemplar feature map by 0.9 and 1.1 to obtain multi-scale features, following FamNet*. In this way, we obtain multi-level and multi-scale feature maps for each exemplar:

$$
\begin{aligned}
F_{k,i,s}^{q,r} &= Resize(F_{k,i}^{q,r}, s), \\
i \in \{1,2\}&, \ s \in \{0.9, 1.0, 1.1\}.
\end{aligned} \tag{2}
$$

Feature Correlation. The correlation maps $M = \{M_1^q, M_2^q, ...M_K^q\}$ are obtained by convolving the query image and each exemplar box and are used for density prediction. The process is denoted as:

$$
\begin{aligned}
M_{k,i,s}^{q} &= Conv(F_i^q, kernel), kernel = F_{k,i,s}^{r}, \\
i \in \{1,2\}&, \ s \in \{0.9, 1.0, 1.1\},
\end{aligned} \tag{3}
$$

where $Conv$ denotes the convolution operation that correlate the exemplar features with the query features to obtain multiple correlation maps. After convolution, for each exemplar, we append the obtained 6 correlation maps (2 × 3: two-level (output of 3rd and 4th blocks of ResNet-50) and three-scale (0.9, 1.0, 1.1) features) to M_k^q for density prediction.

Density Prediction. For the k-th exemplar, given M_k^q from the previous step, the density prediction module ($\mathcal{D}$) predicts a relevant density map. The final density map is obtained by averaging K density maps.

$$
\widetilde{Y} = Mean(\mathcal{D}(M_1^q), \mathcal{D}(M_2^q), ..., \mathcal{D}(M_K^q)) \tag{4}
$$

Optimization. Our objective is to minimize the difference between Y and $\widetilde{Y}$:

$$
L_D = \sum \left\| Y - \widetilde{Y} \right\|^2 . \tag{5}
$$

4.3 Exemplar Feature Augmentation (EFA)

To obtain more exemplars for robust prediction, we propose to apply exemplar feature augmentation to generate other latent exemplar features. To be specific, given $B^r \in \mathbb{R}^{K\times 4}$, we compute a weighted sum of these K features with a weight vector $\boldsymbol{\alpha} = (\alpha_1, \alpha_2, ..., \alpha_K)$, $\sum_{i=1}^{K} \alpha_i = 1$. Besides the original K exemplar features, we generate additional N augmented features using an augmentation matrix $\nu \in \mathbb{R}^{N\times K}$, consisting of N different weight vectors. The nth augmentation feature is denoted as:

$$
\begin{aligned}
F_{K+n,i}^{q,r} &= \sum_k \nu(n,k) F_{k,i}^{q,r} . \\
i \in \{1,2\}, k \in \{1,2,...,K\}&, n \in \{1,2,...,N\} .
\end{aligned} \tag{6}
$$

For instance, when the weight vector is equal to $(1, 0, ..., 0)$, the augmented feature is the same as $F_{1,i}^{q,r}$. Please note that we sample $\boldsymbol{\alpha}$ with a multinomial dirichlet distribution.

In this way, we obtain a larger set of density maps, and the final density map can be formulated as:

$$\widetilde{Y} = Mean(\mathcal{D}(M_1^q), \mathcal{D}(M_2^q), ..., \mathcal{D}(M_{K+N}^q)). \tag{7}$$

Imagine that we want to count objects of various colors, but only three samples are given. EFA is like creating new samples of different colors in the feature space via combining the provided exemplars. In this way, objects with various colors can be better matched; and similarly, the intraclass diversity w.r.t. shape and scale can be also handled.

Dirichlet Distribution. In machine learning, one common distribution called Beta distribution is denoted as:

$$Beta(\alpha \mid \theta_1, \theta_2) = \frac{\Gamma(\theta_1)\Gamma(\theta_2)}{\Gamma(\theta_1 + \theta_2)} \alpha^{\theta_1 - 1}(1-\alpha)^{\theta_2 - 1}, \tag{8}$$

where Γ represents Gamma function. Dirichlet distribution generalizes the Beta distribution to a multinomial distribution. It is expressed as:

$$\begin{aligned} &Dirichlet(\{\alpha_1,\alpha_2,...,\alpha_K\} \mid \{\theta_1, \theta_2, ..., \theta_K\}) \\ &= \frac{\prod_{i=1}^{K} \Gamma(\theta_i)}{\Gamma(\sum_{i=1}^{K} \theta_i)} \prod_{i=1}^{K} \alpha_i^{\theta_i - 1}, \end{aligned} \tag{9}$$

where $\sum_{i=1}^{K} \alpha_i = 1$ and $\alpha_i \geq 0$. We choose the multinomial Dirichelet distribution as it meets the following requirements: (1) The sum of all weights equals to 1, so that the value level of the augmented features and the original features remain unchanged. (2) The number of exemplars can vary. (3) The diversity of sampled weights is high. Fig. 3 shows the sampling probability of dirichlet distribution with different θ. First of all, we treat K exemplars equally, therefore, the parameters of the distribution satisfy the condition that θ_i are equal. In addition, the original sample occupies three vertices of the triangle shown in Fig. 3. Expect not to generate features similar to the original, we adopt the sampling distribution with the maximum sampling probability for the average fusion of the K exemplars. Meanwhile, in order to make the sampling area large, the center sampling probability should not be too large. Based on the above considerations, we adopt the dirichlet distribution with $\theta_i = 2$.

4.4 Edge Matching (EM)

Different object instances may differ in color, while shape is a more reliable cue across instances, leading to more robust counting. On the other hand, edge is a kind of class-agnostic knowledge, which will not bring category bias. To allow our model more focus on the shape cue, we introduce an additional stream for matching, where edge features are used instead of RGB features.

The gray-scale edge image we use in this paper is generated by the RCF model [14] trained on the BSDS500 dataset [1]. We obtain one edge image for each RGB image. For instance, in Fig. 2, I^e is predicted from I^q with the trained RCF model.

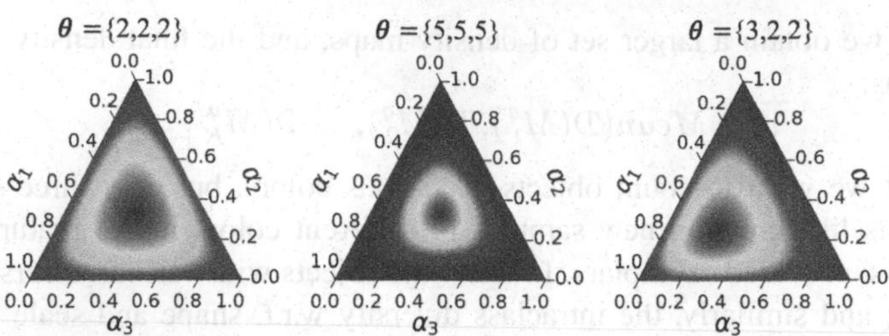

Fig. 3. Dirichlet sampling distributions with different configuration parameters.

The structure of the edge stream is the same as the RGB stream. The only difference is that we use a shallower network for edge feature extraction. Since the gray-scale edge image is much lighter than the RGB image, we employ a VGG-like net [23] with a smaller number of channels as the edge backbone, and update it during training.

In the same way as depicted in Sect. 4.2, for the k-th exemplar, we get 6 edge correlation maps and append them to M_k^e for the edge branch. Finally, the density prediction module takes M_k^q and M_k^e as input and then predicts the corresponding density map. The final density map can be computed as:

$$\widetilde{Y} = Mean(\mathcal{D}(M_1^q, M_1^e), ..., \mathcal{D}(M_K^q, M_K^e)) \tag{10}$$

5 Experiments

In this section, we first describe the datasets and evaluation metrics we use, followed by implementation details; then we show our experimental results with comparisons to the state-of-the-art; finally, we perform ablation studies.

5.1 Datasets

FSC-147 [19] is a recently proposed dataset for class-agnostic counting. It consists of 6135 images with 147 object categories, from animals and plants to vehicles and toys. The number of counted objects in a single picture varies greatly, ranging from 7 to 3731, and the average number is 56. Approximate center of each object instance is annotated with a dot to generate the ground truth density map. On each image, three object instances with bounding boxes are selected as exemplars. The training, validation and test sets consist of 3659 images (89 categories), 1286 images (29 categories), and 1190 images (29 categories), respectively.

CARPK [9] is a car counting dataset which contains 459 images collected from different parking lots taken by drone cameras. There are nearly 90,000 cars in total and each instance is annotated with one bounding box. We use the center points of bounding boxes to get density maps. Moreover, same with [19], a set of 12 bounding boxes from the training set are sampled randomly as exemplars used for all the training and test images.

5.2 Evaluation Metrics

Following previous works [15,19], we adopt Mean Absolute Error (MAE) and Root Mean Squared Error (RMSE) as evaluation metrics. They are formulated as follows:

$$MAE = \frac{1}{N}\sum_{i=1}^{N}\left|\sum Y_i - \sum \widetilde{Y}_i\right|, \tag{11}$$

$$RMSE = \sqrt{\frac{1}{N}\sum_{i=1}^{N}\left|\sum Y_i - \sum \widetilde{Y}_i\right|^2}, \tag{12}$$

where N is the number of test images; $\sum Y_i$, $\sum \widetilde{Y}_i$ represent ground truth and predicted counts.

5.3 Implementation Details

The architectures of RGB image backbone (ResNet-50) and the density prediction module are the same as [19]. For the edge backbone, we use the block of a Conv2d layer (with a 3×3 kernel) in VGG [23] as the basic unit. The number of channels of Conv2d layers are: [16, 16 (s = 2), 32, 32 (s = 2), 64, 64, 64 (s = 2), 128, 128, 128, 128 (s = 2), 128, 128], where 's' denotes the stride of each unit with 1 for default. In fact, our VGG-like network is quite light, even lighter than Resnet18. The numbers of parameters of our VGG-like net and Resnet18 are 0.92M and 2.78M respectively. Following [19], we generate the ground truth density maps using an Adaptive Gaussian kernel. No data augmentation is applied in all experiments. For FSC-147, we set $K = 3$, and we generate $N = 7$ augmentation features. For CARPK, there are totally 12 exemplars, but at each iteration we randomly take $K = 5$ and generate $N = 25$ augmentation features for matching. We train the network with Adam optimizer, and the learning rate is set to 10^{-5} and our model converges at 500 th epoch. All experiments are conducted on a single NVIDIA RTX 2080TI GPU with 11 GB of VRAM and our code is implemented with Pytorch.

5.4 Comparisons with State-of-the-Art Methods

FSC-147 Dataset. As shown in Table 2, we compare our method with previous published class-agnostic counting methods on the FSC-147 dataset.

Table 1. Comparison on high-diversity subsets (w.r.t. MAE).

Subset	FamNet*	EFA	Δ	EM	Δ
Full val set	24.32	23.08	1.24	23.29	1.03
Color diversity	42.32	38.43	3.89	35.84	6.84
Scale diversity	42.65	38.95	3.70	39.09	3.56
Shape diversity	29.68	27.82	1.86	28.07	1.61

From the results in Table 2, we have the following observations. (1) Generally, regression based counting methods (GMN [15], MAML [8], FamNet [19] and Ours) perform better than detection based approaches (FR [11], FSOD [7]). (2) Our method outperforms the baseline method FamNet [19] by a large margin. In particular, on the validation set, the gain is 3.21 pp w.r.t. MAE; on the test set, the improvement is as large as 17.68 pp. These improvements demonstrate the effects of our proposed two new modules. (3) Our method surpasses all existing methods, defining a new state-of-the-art on the FSC-147 dataset.

Table 2. Comparison of our method and previous methods on the FSC-147 dataset.

Method	Val set		Test set	
	MAE	RMSE	MAE	RMSE
Mean	53.38	124.53	47.55	147.67
Median	48.68	129.70	47.73	152.46
FR [11]	45.45	112.53	41.64	141.04
FSOD [7]	36.36	115.00	32.53	140.65
Pre-trained GMN [15]	60.56	137.78	62.69	159.67
GMN [15]	29.66	89.81	26.52	124.57
MAML [8]	25.54	79.44	24.90	112.68
CFOCNet [25]	27.82	71.99	28.60	123.96
FamNet [19]	23.75	69.07	22.08	99.54
RCAC (Ours)	**20.54**	**60.78**	**20.21**	**81.86**

We further observe the improvements of our method to the baseline on high diversity images. We show the effects of two modules on high-diversity subsets from the comparison in Table 1. As stated in our abstract and introduction, EFA handles all kinds of diversity, while EM focuses on handling color diversity, indicating that our method is more robust to high intraclass diversity.

Additionally, Fig. 4 shows some qualitative results on the FSC-147 dataset. In row 1, our method obtains stronger responses and a more accurate count number at the scenario of high shape diversity led by severe occlusion. In row 2, our method produces cleaner density maps with less noises at the background regions than the baseline by handling color diversity. Inside each exemplar box, the background colors are dominant, resulting in noisy responses at background regions on the baseline density map. In row 3, our method produces more balanced density maps across different scales than the baseline by handling scale diversity. In row 4, our method produces more uniform density maps across different foreground color diversity.

CARPK Dataset. Similar to [19], we further verify our method on the CARPK dataset, due to the lack of class-agnostic counting datasets. The experiments are implemented under the same few-shot setting. Since there is only one category for CARPK, it is considered rather a simple version of class-agnostic object counting. The results are shown in Table 3. Our model outperforms all previous approaches except GMN, which

Table 3. Comparison of car counting performance on the CARPK dataset. *GMN uses extra images of cars from the ILSVRC video dataset for training. "Fine-tuned" denotes whether the models are further fine-tuned on CARPK.

Method	Fine-tuned	MAE	RMSE
YOLO [9,20]	✓	48.89	57.55
Faster RCNN [9,21]	✓	47.45	57.39
One-look regression [9,17]	✓	59.46	66.84
Faster RCNN (RPN-small) [9,21]	✓	24.32	37.62
Spatially regularized RPN [9]	✓	23.80	36.79
GMN* [15]	✓	7.48	9.90
FamNet [19]	✓	18.19	33.66
RCAC (Ours)	✓	**13.62**	**19.08**
FamNet [19]	×	28.84	44.47
RCAC (Ours)	×	**17.98**	**24.21**

uses external training images of cars from the ILSVRC video dataset. It is notable that our approach improves over FamNet by 4.57 pp w.r.t MAE and 14.58 pp w.r.t RMSE. These results indicate that our method generalizes well to different datasets.

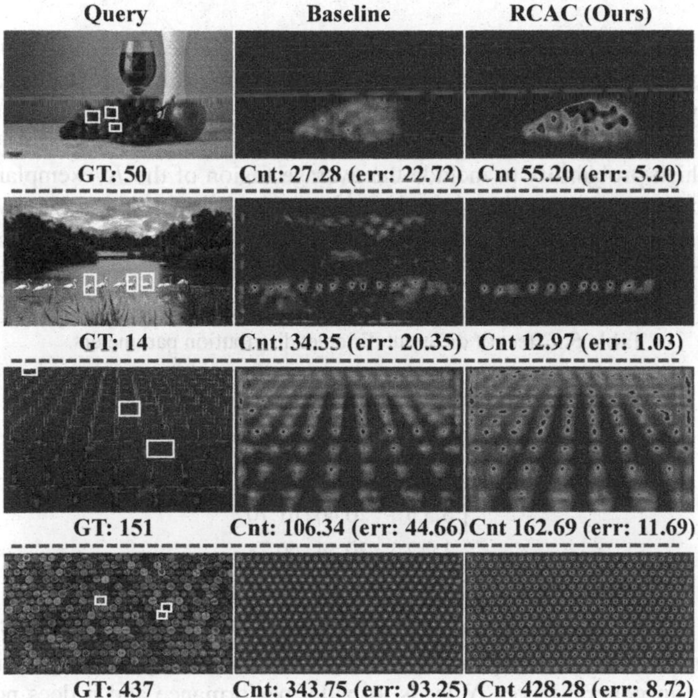

Fig. 4. Qualitative results of different methods on high intraclass diversity images from FSC-147. Zoom in and colorful for better visualization. (Color figure online)

5.5 Ablation Studies

In the following, we conduct some ablation studies to analyze our proposed exemplar feature augmentation and edge matching modules. All experiments are conducted on the validation set of FSC-147.

Effects of Two New Modules. As shown in Table 4, the performance is improved by 1.24 pp w.r.t MAE (from 24.32 to 23.08) when exemplar feature augmentation is employed. On the other hand, we also observe a remarkable improvement of 1.03 pp w.r.t MAE (from 24.32 to 23.29) from edge matching. Moreover, we obtain a total gain of 3.78 pp w.r.t MAE by adding both modules. These results indicate the effects of two proposed modules.

Table 4. Effects of two proposed components.

Exemplar feature augmentation	Edge matching	MAE	RMSE
×	×	24.32	70.94
✓	×	23.08	67.23
×	✓	23.29	63.35
✓	✓	20.54	60.78

Impact of Dirichlet Distribution Parameter θ**.** From Table 5, we can see our method obtains consistent improvements to the baseline by using exemplar feature augmentation no matter which sampling parameter we choose. By analyzing Fig. 3 and Table 5 simultaneously, we find it works better to set θ_i evenly ({2,2,2} vs. {3,2,2}) such that we have a high probability to include the average fusion of the K exemplars. Also, it helps to have a larger sampling area ({2,2,2} vs. {5,5,5} such that more diverse combinations can be generated. Finally we set θ to {2,2,2} for all our experiments as it performs the best.

Table 5. Effect of different dirichlet distribution parameters.

θ	MAE	RMSE
–	23.29	63.35
{ 3,2,2 }	21.44	63.40
{ 5,5,5 }	20.46	61.70
{ 2,2,2 }	20.54	60.78

Impact of Feature Augmentation Quantity. We analyze how the value of N affects the performance of our exemplar feature augmentation strategy. As shown in Table 6, we find that in general larger N leads to better performance and it does not seem to saturate at $N = 7$. Due to the limited memory of our NVIDIA RTX 2080TI GPU, we select $N = 7$ for our experiments. But we expect to achieve better performance with a large value.

Table 6. Impact of different values for augmentation quantity N.

Augmentation quantity N	MAE	RMSE
0	23.29	63.35
1	22.19	62.99
3	21.21	62.07
5	21.14	62.92
7	20.54	60.78

Inference Time Analysis. To verify the efficiency of our RCAC, we compare the inference time of our RCAC with FamNet* and FamNet in Table 7. We can see our RCAC runs slightly slower than our baseline FamNet* (75 ms vs. 47 ms) due to additional computations for edge detection. In order to accelerate our RCAC, we replace RCF with Sobel operators, which reduces the inference time at a cost of small performance drop. Please note our RCAC (w/ Sobel) still outperforms FamNet* by –2pp at a similar speed; and compared to previous top method FamNet, our RCAC (w/ RCF) not only obtains better performance (by –3pp), but also runs much faster (75 ms vs. 3,900 ms).

Table 7. Inference time analysis. "T" represents the inference time.

Method	$K = 3, N = 0$	
	MAE	T (ms)
FamNet†	24.32	47
FamNet	23.75	3,900
RCAC (w/ Sobel)	22.41	59
RCAC (w/ RCF)	20.94	75

In the supplementary material, we provide more ablation studies on the impact of the effect of using edge images at the 2nd branch, effect of number of exemplars, qualitative results of augmented exemplars and application of EFA in another task.

6 Conclusion

In this paper, we analyze failure cases of previous top-performing class-agnostic object counter and find high intraclass diversity in the query image has an adverse effect on counting performance. To solve this problem, we propose two novel modules: exemplar feature augmentation and edge matching. They make our counter robust to high intraclass diversity. Extensive experiments have demonstrated the effectiveness and robustness of our method.

Acknowledgements. This work was supported in part by the National Natural Science Foundation of China (Grant No. 62172225), Fundamental Research Funds for the Central Universities (No. 30920032201) and the "111" Program B13022.

References

1. Arbelaez, P., Maire, M., Fowlkes, C., Malik, J.: Contour detection and hierarchical image segmentation. PAMI **33**(5), 898–916 (2010)
2. Arteta, C., Lempitsky, V., Noble, J.A., Zisserman, A.: Interactive object counting. In: Fleet, D., Pajdla, T., Schiele, B., Tuytelaars, T. (eds.) ECCV 2014. LNCS, vol. 8691, pp. 504–518. Springer, Cham (2014). https://doi.org/10.1007/978-3-319-10578-9_33
3. Arteta, C., Lempitsky, V., Zisserman, A.: Counting in the wild. In: Leibe, B., Matas, J., Sebe, N., Welling, M. (eds.) ECCV 2016. LNCS, vol. 9911, pp. 483–498. Springer, Cham (2016). https://doi.org/10.1007/978-3-319-46478-7_30
4. Chattopadhyay, P., Vedantam, R., Selvaraju, R.R., Batra, D., Parikh, D.: Counting everyday objects in everyday scenes. In: CVPR, pp. 1135–1144 (2017)
5. Cholakkal, H., Sun, G., Khan, F.S., Shao, L.: Object counting and instance segmentation with image-level supervision. In: CVPR, pp. 12397–12405 (2019)
6. Cholakkal, H., Sun, G., Khan, S., Khan, F.S., Shao, L., Van Gool, L.: Towards partial supervision for generic object counting in natural scenes. PAMI (2020)
7. Fan, Q., Zhuo, W., Tang, C.K., Tai, Y.W.: Few-shot object detection with attention-RPN and multi-relation detector. In: CVPR, pp. 4013–4022 (2020)
8. Finn, C., Abbeel, P., Levine, S.: Model-agnostic meta-learning for fast adaptation of deep networks. In: ICML, pp. 1126–1135 (2017)
9. Hsieh, M.R., Lin, Y.L., Hsu, W.H.: Drone-based object counting by spatially regularized regional proposal network. In: ICCV, pp. 4145–4153 (2017)
10. Hsieh, T.I., Lo, Y.C., Chen, H.T., Liu, T.L.: One-shot object detection with co-attention and co-excitation. In: NIPS, pp. 2725–2734 (2019)
11. Kang, B., Liu, Z., Wang, X., Yu, F., Feng, J., Darrell, T.: Few-shot object detection via feature reweighting. In: ICCV, pp. 8420–8429 (2019)
12. Laradji, I.H., Rostamzadeh, N., Pinheiro, P.O., Vazquez, D., Schmidt, M.: Where are the blobs: counting by localization with point supervision. In: ECCV, pp. 547–562 (2018)
13. Liu, Y., Wen, Q., Chen, H., Liu, W., Qin, J., Han, G., He, S.: Crowd counting via cross-stage refinement networks. IEEE TIP **29**, 6800–6812 (2020)
14. Liu, Y., Cheng, M.M., Hu, X., Bian, J.W., Zhang, L., Bai, X., Tang, J.: Richer convolutional features for edge detection. PAMI **41**(8), 1939–1946 (2019)
15. Lu, E., Xie, W., Zisserman, A.: Class-agnostic counting. In: Jawahar, C.V., Li, H., Mori, G., Schindler, K. (eds.) ACCV 2018. LNCS, vol. 11363, pp. 669–684. Springer, Cham (2019). https://doi.org/10.1007/978-3-030-20893-6_42
16. Mo, H., Ren, W., Xiong, Y., Pan, X., Zhou, Z., Cao, X., Wu, W.: Background noise filtering and distribution dividing for crowd counting. IEEE TIP **29**, 8199–8212 (2020)
17. Mundhenk, T.N., Konjevod, G., Sakla, W.A., Boakye, K.: A large contextual dataset for classification, detection and counting of cars with deep learning. In: Leibe, B., Matas, J., Sebe, N., Welling, M. (eds.) ECCV 2016. LNCS, vol. 9907, pp. 785–800. Springer, Cham (2016). https://doi.org/10.1007/978-3-319-46487-9_48
18. Rahnemoonfar, M., Sheppard, C.: Deep count: fruit counting based on deep simulated learning. Sensors **17**(4), 905 (2017)
19. Ranjan, V., Sharma, U., Nguyen, T., Hoai, M.: Learning to count everything. In: CVPR, pp. 3394–3403 (2021)
20. Redmon, J., Divvala, S., Girshick, R., Farhadi, A.: You only look once: unified, real-time object detection. In: CVPR, pp. 779–788 (2016)
21. Ren, S., He, K., Girshick, R., Sun, J.: Faster r-CNN: towards real-time object detection with region proposal networks. NIPS **28**, 91–99 (2015)

22. Ribera, J., Guera, D., Chen, Y., Delp, E.J.: Locating objects without bounding boxes. In: CVPR, pp. 6479–6489 (2019)
23. Simonyan, K., Zisserman, A.: Very deep convolutional networks for large-scale image recognition. arXiv preprint arXiv:1409.1556 (2014)
24. Sokhandan, N., Kamousi, P., Posada, A., Alese, E., Rostamzadeh, N.: A few-shot sequential approach for object counting. arXiv preprint arXiv:2007.01899 (2020)
25. Yang, S.D., Su, H.T., Hsu, W.H., Chen, W.C.: Class-agnostic few-shot object counting. In: WACV, pp. 870–878 (2021)

Burn After Reading: Online Adaptation for Cross-domain Streaming Data

Luyu Yang[1(✉)], Mingfei Gao[2], Zeyuan Chen[2], Ran Xu[2], Abhinav Shrivastava[1], and Chetan Ramaiah[3]

[1] University of Maryland, College Park, USA
{loyo,abhinav}@cs.umd.edu
[2] Salesforce Research, Palo Alto, USA
{mingfei.gao,zeyuan.chen,ran.xu}@salesforce.com
[3] Google, Menlo Park, USA
cramaiah@google.com

Abstract. In the context of online privacy, many methods propose complex security preserving measures to protect sensitive data. In this paper we note that: not storing any sensitive data is the best form of security. We propose an online framework called "Burn After Reading", *i.e.* each online sample is permanently deleted after it is processed. Our framework utilizes the labels from the public data and predicts on the unlabeled sensitive private data. To tackle the inevitable distribution shift from the public data to the private data, we propose a novel unsupervised domain adaptation algorithm that aims at the fundamental challenge of this online setting–the lack of diverse source-target data pairs. We design a **Cross-Domain Bootstrapping** approach, named **CroDoBo**, to increase the combined data diversity across domains. To fully exploit the valuable discrepancies among the diverse combinations, we employ the training strategy of multiple learners with co-supervision. CroDoBo achieves state-of-the-art online performance on four domain adaptation benchmarks. *Code is available here*.

Keywords: Domain adaptation · Online learning · Privacy preserving

1 Introduction

With the onslaught of the pandemic, the internet has become an even more ubiquitous presence in all of our lives. Living in an enormous web connecting us to each other, we now face a new reality: it is very hard to escape one's past on the Internet since every photo, status update, and tweet lives forever in the cloud [13,54]. Moreover, recommender systems that actively explore the

C. Ramaiah—Work was done at Salesforce.

Supplementary Information The online version contains supplementary material available at https://doi.org/10.1007/978-3-031-19827-4_24.

S. Avidan et al. (Eds.): ECCV 2022, LNCS 13693, pp. 404–422, 2022.
https://doi.org/10.1007/978-3-031-19827-4_24

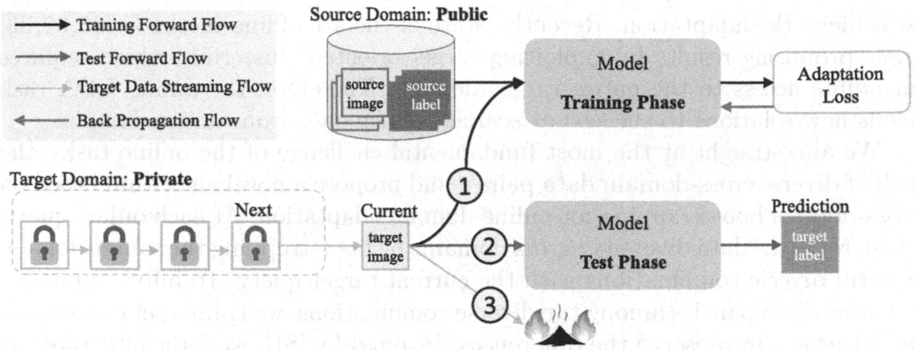

Fig. 1. The data-flow of the proposed **Burn After Reading** framework at one iteration. The iteration contains a training and a test phase. In training phase, the model takes labeled data from the public source domain, and the current unlabeled target data from the private target domain. The model updates based on the adaptation loss and then moves to test phase. After prediction, the current target data is permanently **deleted** from the target domain. Each target data is (1) trained (2) tested (3) deleted. *Best viewed in color.*

user data [16,82] for data-driven algorithms have brought controversy that the right to privacy is more important than the convenience. Fortunately, we have *the Right to Be Forgotten* (RTBF), which gives individuals the right to ask organizations to delete their personal data. Recently, many solutions [83,88] have been proposed that try to preserve privacy in the context of deep learning, mostly focused on the Federated Learning [24,75]. Federated Learning allows asynchronous update of multiple nodes, in which sensitive data is stored only on a few specific nodes. However, recent studies [23,79,87] show that private training data can be leaked through the gradients sharing mechanism deployed in distributed models. In this paper, we argue that: *not storing any sensitive data is the best form of security.*

The best form of security requires us to delete the user data after use, which necessitates an online framework. However, existing online learning frameworks [34,56] cannot meet this need without addressing the distribution shift from public data, *i.e.* source domain, to the private user data, *i.e.* target domain. Therefore, in this paper we propose an online domain adaptation framework in which the target domain streaming data is deleted immediately after adapted. We name the framework "Burn After Reading", as illustrated in Fig. 1. The task that is seemingly an extended setting of unsupervised domain adaptation (UDA), however, cannot simply be solved by the online implementation of the offline UDA methods. We explain the reason with a comprehensive analysis of the existing domain adaptation methods. To begin with, existing offline UDA methods rely heavily on the rich combinations of cross-domain mini-batches that gradually adjust the model for adaptation [29,48,59,62,67,70,73,76,77,80,85], which the online streaming setting cannot afford to provide. In particular, many domain adversarial-based methods [3,19,27,72] depend on a slowly annealing adversarial mechanism that requires discriminating large number of source-target pairs to achieve the adaptation. Recently, state-of-the-art offline methods [25,32,33] show promising results by exploiting target-oriented clustering, which requires an offline access to the entire target domain. Therefore, the online UDA task needs new solutions to succeed at scarcity of the data from target domain.

We aim straight at the most fundamental challenge of the online task—the lack of diverse cross-domain data pairs—and propose a novel algorithm based on cross-domain bootstrapping for online domain adaptation. At each online query, we increase the data diversity across domains by bootstrapping the source domain to form diverse combinations with the current target query. To fully exploit the valuable discrepancies among the diverse combinations, we train a set of independent learners to preserve the differences. Inspired by [81], we later integrate the knowledge of learners by exchanging their predicted pseudo-labels on the current target query to co-supervise the learning on the target domain, but without sharing the weights to maintain the learners' divergence. We obtain more accurate prediction on the current target query by an average ensemble of the diverse expertise of all the learners. We call it **CroDoBo**: **Cro**ss-**Do**main **Bo**otstrapping for online domain adaptation, an overview of CroDoBo pipeline is shown in Fig. 3.

We conduct extensive evaluations on our method, including the classic UDA benchmark *VisDA-C* [49], a practical medical imaging benchmark *COVID-DA* [84] and the large-scale distribution shift benchmark *WILDS* [26] subset *Camelyon*. Moreover, we propose a new adaptation scenario in this paper from *Fashion-MNIST* [78] to *DeepFashion* [35]. On all the benchmarks, our method outperforms the state-of-the-art UDA methods that are eligible for the online setting. Further, without the reuse of any target sample, our method achieves comparable performance to the offline setting. We summarize the contributions as follows.

- To our best knowledge, we are the first to propose an online domain adaptation framework to implement *the right to be forgotten*.
- We study the fundamental drawback of the online setting compared to offline–the lack of data diversity, and designed a novel online domain adaptation method that improves, and exploits the data diversity.
- Our proposed algorithm achieves new state-of-the-art online results on four challenging benchmarks.
- Although designed for online setting, our method yields comparable performance to the offline setting, suggesting that it is a superior choice even just for time efficiency.

2 Related Work

The Right to Be Forgotten [13,15,46,69], also referred to as *right to vanish*, *right to erasure* and *courtesy vanishing*, is the right given to each individual to ask organizations to delete their personal data. RTBF is part of the General Data Protection Regulation (GDPR). As a legal document, the GDPR outlines the specific circumstances under which the right applies in *Article 17* GDPR[1]. The first item

[1] Article 17 GDPR - Right to be forgotten https://gdpr.eu/article-17-right-to-be-forgotten/.

is: *The personal data is no longer necessary for the purpose an organization originally collected or processed it.* Yet, the exercise of this right has become a thorny issue in applications. Politou *et al.* [50] discussed that the technical challenges of aligning modern systems and processes with the GDPR provisions are numerous and in most cases insurmountable. In the context of machine learning, Villaronga *et al.* [69] addressed that the core issue of the AI and Right to Be Forgotten problem is the dearth of interdisciplinary scholarship supporting privacy law and regulation. Graves *et al.* [15] proposed three defense mechanisms against a general threat model to enable deep neural networks to forget sensitive data while maintaining model efficacy. In this paper, we focus on how to obtain model efficacy while erasing data online to protect the user's right to be forgotten.

Online Adaptation to Shifting Domains was first investigated in Signal Processing [9] and later studied in Natural Language Processing [8] and Vision tasks [6,22,40,42,52]. Jain *et al.* [22] assumed the original classifier output a continuous number of which a threshold gives the class, and reclassify points near the original boundary using a Gaussian process regression scheme. The procedure is presented as a Viola-Jones cascade of classifiers. Moon *et al.* [42] proposed a four-stage method by assuming a transformation matrix between the source subspace and the mean-target subspace embedded in the Grassmann manifold. The method is designed for handcrafted features. In the context of deep neural network, one transformation matrix might not be sufficient to describe the correlation between source and target deep representations [44]. Taufique *et al.* [66] approached the task by selectively mixing the online target samples with those that were saved in a buffer. Since in [66] the approach relies on saved target samples, it is not applicable to the "Burn After Reading" framework.

Active Domain Adaptation [4,39,51,53] also benefits the online learning of shifting domains. But it has a different setting: the target domain can actively acquire labeled data online. Rai *et al.* [53] presented an algorithm that harnessed the source domain data to learn a initializer hypothesis, which is later used for active learning on the target domain. Ma *et al.* [39] allowed a small budget of target data for the categories that appeared only in target domain and presented an algorithm that jointly trains two sub-networks of different learning strategies. Chen *et al.* [4] proposed an algorithm that can adaptively deal with interleaving spans of inputs from different domains by a tight trade-off that depends on the duration and dimensionality of the hidden domains. The active acquisition of target labels is not feasible for the unsupervised domain adaptation, thus is beyond the scope of this paper.

Test-Time Domain Adaptation [65,68,71] is another related task. Similar to the "burn after reading", test-time DA also aims at a fast adaptation to the target samples. Differently, test-time DA is motivated by the unavailability of the source domain [71], which is a variant of source-free domain adaptation [32]. Thus, it is based on a continual setting. Meanwhile, test-time domain adaptation does not require target samples being deleted after training, although Wang *et al.* [71] and Sun *et al.* [65] both discussed the extension to an online setting in the experiments. Without the access to source samples, Varsavsky *et al.* [68] leverages a combination of adversarial learning and consistency under augmentation. Sun *et al.* [65] exploits the self-supervision with auxiliary rotation prediction. In this paper, we compare with test-time DA with a devised continual version of our method in the supplementary.

Ensemble Methods for Online Learning [1,41] such as bagging and boosting have shown advantages handling *concept drift* [38] and class imbalance, which are common challenges in the online learning task. MinKu *et al.* [41] addressed the importance of ensemble diversity to improve accuracy in changing environments and proposed the measurement of ensemble diversity. Han *et al.* [17] proposed a regularization for online tracking with a subset of branches in the neural network that are randomly selected. Although online learning and online domain adaptation share similar streaming form of data input, the two tasks face fundamentally different challenges. For online learning, the challenge is to select the most trustworthy supervisions from the streaming data by differentiating the informative vs. misleading data points, also known as the *stability-plasticity dilemma* [21]. However, for online domain adaptation (our task), the streaming data of target domain naturally comes unlabeled, and the challenge is the scarcity of supervision. Thus the goal is how to maximize the utilization of the supervision from a different but related labeled source domain.

3 Approach

In this section, we introduce the proposed method for "Burn After Reading" framework, in which the samples from the public source domain are fully accessible, while only one/a batch of the target samples is available at each iteration. The model "reads" the current target data, updates, then predicts, after which the target data is deleted permanently from the target domain. In Sect. 3.1 we describe the difference between online and the offline setting. In Sect. 3.2, we first introduce the cross-domain bootstrapping strategy and the theoretical insights behind. Then we describe the details of the co-supervision.

3.1 Offline vs. Online

Given the labeled source data $D_{\mathcal{S}} = \{(s_i, y_i)\}_{i=1}^{N_S}$ drawn from the source distribution $p_s(x, y)$, and the unlabeled target data $D_{\mathcal{T}} = \{t_i\}_{i=1}^{N_T}$ drawn from the target distribution $p_t(x, y)$, where N_S and N_T represent the number of source and target samples, both offline and online adaptation aim at learning a classifier that make accurate predictions on $D_{\mathcal{T}}$. The *offline adaptation* assumes access to every data point in both $D_{\mathcal{S}}$ and $D_{\mathcal{T}}$, synchronous [12,59,62,67] or domain-wise asynchronous [32]. The inference on $D_{\mathcal{T}}$ happens after the model is trained on both $D_{\mathcal{S}}$ and $D_{\mathcal{T}}$ entirely. Differently for *online adaptation*, we assume the access to the entire $D_{\mathcal{S}}$, while the data from $D_{\mathcal{T}}$ arrives in a streaming data of random mini-batches $\{T_j = \{t_b\}_{b=1}^{B}\}_{j=1}^{M_T}$. B is the batch size and M_T is the total number of target batches. Each mini-batch T is first adapted, tested and then erased from $D_{\mathcal{T}}$ without replacement, as shown in Figs. 1 and 3. We refer each online batch of target data as a target *query*.

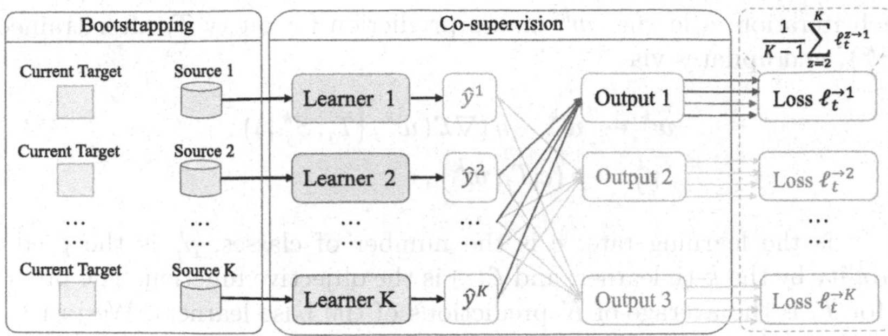

Fig. 2. Illustration of computing co-supervision loss ($\ell_t^{z\to k}$ in Eq. 4), taking $\ell_t^{\to 1}$ for example. The co-supervision for learner 1 is from the *other* $K-1$ learners. The current target data is repeatedly paired with each bootstrapped source data to improve data diversity. Each learner takes a unique data combination and generates pseudo-label $\hat{y}^k$ of the current target data. Then $\ell_t^{\to 1}$ receives co-supervision averagely from the pseudo-labels $\{\hat{y}^2, \hat{y}^3, ..., \hat{y}^K\}$.

The fundamental challenge of our online task is the limited access to the training data at each inference query, compared to the offline task. For generality, we can assume there are 10^3 source and target batches, respectively. In an offline setting, the model is tested after training on at most 10^6 combinations of source-target data pairs, while in an online setting, an one-stream model can see at most $10^3 + 500$ combinations at the 500-th query. Undoubtedly, the online adaptation faces a significantly compromised data diversity. The training process of our task suffers from two major drawbacks: (I) The model is prone to underfitting on target domain due to the lack of seen target samples, especially at the early stage of training. (II) Due to the deletion of previous data, the model lacks the diverse combinations of source-target data pairs that enable the deep network to find the optimal cross-domain classifier [30].

The goal of the proposed method is to minimize the two drawbacks of the online setting. We first propose to increase the data diversity by cross-domain bootstrapping, and we preserve the discrepancy in independently trained learners. Then we fully exploit the valuable discrepancies of these learners by exchanging their expertise on the current target query to co-supervise each other.

3.2 Proposed Method

Cross-domain Bootstrapping for Data Diversity The diversity of cross-domain data pairs is crucial for most prior offline methods [12,48,59] to succeed. Since the target samples cannot be reused in the online setting, we propose to increase the data diversity across domains by bootstrapping the source domain to form diverse combinations with the current target domain query, as shown in Fig. 2. Specifically, for each target query T_j, we randomly select a set of K mini-batches $\{S_j^k = \{(s_b)_{b=1}^B\}\}_{k=1}^K$ of the same size from the source domain with replacement. Correspondingly, we define a set of K base learners $\{\boldsymbol{w}^k\}_{k=1}^K$.

At each iteration, a learner $\boldsymbol{w}^k$ makes prediction for query T_j after trained on $\{T_j, S_j^k\}$, and updates via

$$\begin{aligned} \boldsymbol{w}^k &\leftarrow \boldsymbol{w}^k - \eta\left(\nabla\mathcal{L}(\boldsymbol{w}^k, \{T_j, S_j^k\})\right), \\ p_j^k &= p\left(c|T_j; \boldsymbol{w}^k\right), \end{aligned} \tag{1}$$

where η is the learning rate, c is the number of classes, p_j^k is the predicted probability by the k-th learner, and $\mathcal{L}(,)$ is the objective function. The predicted class for T_j is the average of K predictions of the base learners. We justify our design choice from the perspective of uncertainty estimation in the following discussion.

Theoretical Insights. As mentioned in Sect, 3.1, we aim at the best estimation of the current target query. We first consider a single learner situation. At the j-th query, the learner faces a fundamental trade-off: by minimizing the uncertainty of the j-th query, the learner can attain the best current estimation. Yet the risk of fully exploring the uncertainty is to spoil the existing knowledge from the previous j-1 target domain queries. However, if we don't treat the uncertainty, the single observation on j-th query is less informative for current query estimation. Confronting the dilemma, we should not ignore that the uncertainty captures the variability of a learner's posterior belief which *can* be resolved through statistical analysis of the appropriate data [45]. This gives us hope for a more accurate model via uncertainty estimation. One popular suggestion for resolving uncertainty is to use *Dropout* [10,11,58] sampling, where individual neurons are independently set to zero with a probability. As a sampling method on the neurons, *Dropout* works in a similar form of *bagging* [60,74] of multiple decision trees. It might equally reduce the overall noise of the network regardless of domain shift but it does not address the problem of our task, which is the lack of diverse cross-domain combinations.

Alternatively, we employ another pragmatic approach *Bootstrap* for uncertainty estimation on the target domain that offsets the source dominance. With the scarcity of target samples, we propose to bootstrap source-target data pairs for a more balanced cross-domain simulation. At high-level, the bootstrap simulates multiple realizations of a specific target query given the diversity of source samples. Specifically, the bootstrapped source approximate a distribution over the current query T_j via the bootstrap.

The bootstrapping brings multi-view observations on a single target query by two means. First, given K sampling subsets from $D_{\mathcal{S}}$, let $\mathcal{F}$ be the ideal estimate of T_j, $\hat{\mathcal{F}}$ be the practical estimate of the dataset, and $\hat{\mathcal{F}}^*$ be the estimate from a bootstrapped source paired with the target query, $\hat{\mathcal{F}}^* = K^{-1}\sum_{k=1}^{K}\hat{\mathcal{F}}_k^*$ will be the average of the multi-view K estimates. Second, besides the learnable parameters, the *Batch-Normalization* layers of K learners generate result in a set of different means and variances $\{\mu_k, \sigma_k\}_{k=1}^K$ that serve as K different initializations that affects the learning of $\hat{\mathcal{F}}^*$.

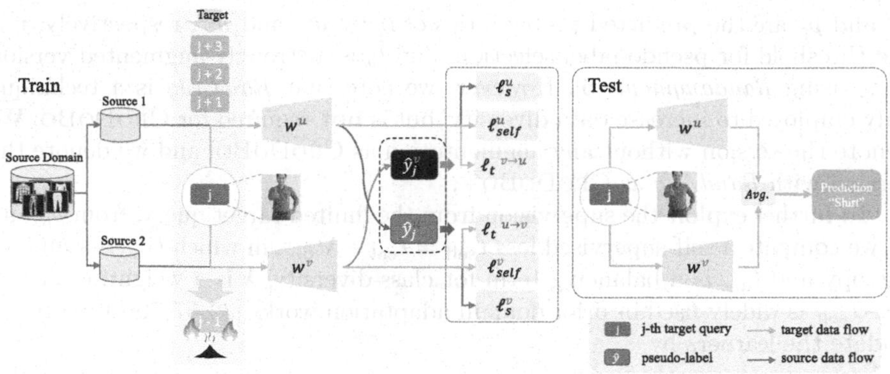

Fig. 3. The full pipeline of the proposed CroDoBo $K = 2$ method at j-th iteration. Only one target query j is currently available from target domain in this iteration. We bootstrap the source domain and combine with the current j-th query. The learners w^u (k = 1) and w^v (k = 2) exchange the generated pseudo-labels $\hat{y}_j^u$ and $\hat{y}_j^v$ as co-supervision. Each learner is updated by a supervised loss ℓ_s on source data, a self-supervised loss ℓ_{self} on the target data and a co-supervised loss ℓ_t. The test result is recorded by averaging the predictions of both learners. Once tested, query j is immediately deleted.

Exploit the Discrepancies via Co-supervision. After the independent learners have preserved the valuable discrepancies of cross-domain pairs, the question now is how to fully exploit the discrepancies to improve the online predictions on the target queries. On one hand, we want to integrate the learners' expertise into one better prediction on the current target query, on the other we hope to maintain their differences. Inspired by [81], we train the K learners jointly by exchanging their knowledge on the target domain as a form of co-supervision. Specifically, the K learners are trained independently with bootstrapped source supervision, but they exchange the pseudo-labels generated for target queries. We followed the *FixMatch* [63] to compute pseudo-labels on the target domain. We first consider $K = 2$ for simplicity, we denote the learners as $\boldsymbol{w}^u$ for $k = 1$ and $\boldsymbol{w}^v$ for $k = 2$, respectively.

Given the current target query T_j, the loss function $\mathcal{L}$ consists a supervised loss term ℓ_s from the source domain with the bootstrapped samples, and a self-supervised loss term ℓ_t from the target domain with pseudo-labels $\hat{y}_b$ from the peer learner, as illustrated in Fig. 3. We denote the cross-entropy between two probability distributions as $\mathcal{H}(;)$. Thus, the co-supervision objective ℓ_t is obtained via:

$$\ell_t^{v\to u} = B^{-1} \sum_{b=1}^{B} \mathbb{1}\left(p_b^v \geq \tau\right) \mathcal{H}\left(\hat{y}_b^v; p(c|\tilde{t}_b; \boldsymbol{w}^u)\right),$$

$$\ell_t^{u\to v} = B^{-1} \sum_{b=1}^{B} \mathbb{1}\left(p_b^u \geq \tau\right) \mathcal{H}\left(\hat{y}_b^u; p(c|\tilde{t}_b; \boldsymbol{w}^v)\right), \tag{2}$$

p_b^u and p_b^v are the predicted probabilities of t_b by $\boldsymbol{w}^u$ and $\boldsymbol{w}^v$, respectively. τ is the threshold for pseudo-label selection, and $\tilde{t}_b$ is a strongly-augmented version of t_b using *Randaugment* [5]. However, we note that *RandAug* is a technique only employed to increase data diversity, but is **not** required for CroDoBo. We denote the version without any augmentation as CroDoBo, and we denote the version with *RandAug* as CroDoBo+.

To further exploit the supervision from the limited target query, from p_b^u and p_b^v we compute a self-supervised loss $\ell_{\text{self}} = \ell_{\text{ent}} + \lambda \ell_{\text{div}}$, in which ℓ_{ent} is standard entropy and ℓ_{div} is a balancing term for class-diversity, λ is a weighting factor. The ℓ_{self} is widely used in prior domain adaptation works [32,57,70]. Finally, we update the learners by

$$\begin{aligned} \boldsymbol{w}^u &\leftarrow \boldsymbol{w}^u - \eta(\ \nabla \ell_s(\boldsymbol{w}^u, S_j^u) + \nabla \ell_t^{v\to u} + \nabla \ell_{\text{self}}(\boldsymbol{w}^u, T_j)), \\ \boldsymbol{w}^v &\leftarrow \boldsymbol{w}^v - \eta(\ \nabla \ell_s(\boldsymbol{w}^v, S_j^v) + \nabla \ell_t^{u\to v} + \nabla \ell_{\text{self}}(\boldsymbol{w}^v, T_j)). \end{aligned} \tag{3}$$

For $K > 2$, each learner $\boldsymbol{w}^k$ is updated with the co-supervision from the other $K-1$ learners (Fig. 2), weighted by $1/(K-1)$ for each $\ell_t^{z\to k}$ (z is the learner's index other than k). We update $\boldsymbol{w}^k$ by

$$\boldsymbol{w}^k \leftarrow \boldsymbol{w}^k - \eta(\nabla \ell_s(\boldsymbol{w}^k, S_j^u) + \frac{1}{K-1}\sum_{z=1}^{K-1} \nabla \ell_t^{z\to k} + \nabla \ell_{\text{self}}(\boldsymbol{w}^k, T_j)). \tag{4}$$

4 Experiments

We consider two metrics for evaluating online domain adaptation methods: *online average accuracy* and *one-pass accuracy*. We provide formulations for our metrics. Given a target sequence $D_T = \{T_0, T_1, ..., T_j, ..., T_{N_T}\}$, the online model at time j is $\boldsymbol{w}_j$. The test accuracy on the current T_j is acc_j, then the *online accuracy* $\text{ACC}_{\text{online}} = \frac{1}{N_T}\sum_{j=1}^{N_T} \text{acc}_j(T_j; \boldsymbol{w}_j)$ is the average of the entire streaming accuracies. Once the model finishes online update, we freeze the weights of $\boldsymbol{w}_{N_T}$ and compute *one-pass accuracy* $\text{ACC}_{\text{one-pass}} = \frac{1}{N_T}\sum_{j=1}^{N_T} \text{acc}(T_j; \boldsymbol{w}_{N_T})$. *One-pass* measures the model's generalizability to the entire target domain. We keep track of this metric in case the model keeps overfitting to the new target data only to achieve high *online accuracy* [43]. A *one-pass accuracy* much lower than *online average* indicates that the model might have overfitted to the fresh queries, but compromised its generalization ability to the early queries.

Dataset. We use **VisDA-C** [49], a classic benchmark adapting from synthetic images to real. We followed the data split used in prior offline settings [32,49,59]. We also use **COVID-DA** [84], adapting the CT images diagnosis from common pneumonia to the novel disease. This is a typical scenario where online domain adaptation is valuable in practice. When a novel disease breaks out, without any prior knowledge, one has to exploit a different but correlated domain to assist the diagnosis of the new pandemic in a time-sensitive manner. We also evaluate on a large-scale medical dataset *Camelyon17* from the **WILDS** [26], a histopathology image datasets with patient population shift from source to the target. Camelyon17 has 455k samples of breast cancer patients from 5 hospitals. Another practical scenario is the online fashion where the user-generated content (UGC) might be time-sensitive and cannot be saved for training purposes. Due to the lack of cross-domain fashion prediction dataset, we propose to evaluate adapting from **Fashion-MNIST** [78]-to-**DeepFashion** [35] category prediction branch. We select 6 fashion categories shared between the two datasets, and design the task as adapting from 36,000 grayscale samples of Fashion-MNIST to 200,486 real-world commercial samples from DeepFashion.

Implementation Details. We implement using Pytorch [47]. We follow [32,33] to use ResNet-101 [18] on VisDA-C pretrained on ImageNet [7,55]. We follow [84] to use pretrained ResNet-18 [18] on COVID-DA. We follow the leader-board on WILDS challenge [26][2] to use DenseNet-121 [20] on Camelyon17 with random initialization, we use the official WILDS codebase (v1.1.0) for data split and evaluation. We use pretrained ResNet-101 [18] on Fashion-MNIST-to-DeepFashion. Our target query batch-size and bootstrapped source batch-size are both set as 64. The confidence threshold $\tau = 0.95$ and diversity weight $\lambda = 0.4$ are fixed throughout the experiments. Our method is not sensitive to hyperparameters, the results are reported in supplementary.

Baselines. We compare **CroDoBo** without data augmentation and **CroDoBo**$^+$ with *RandAug* with eight state-of-the-art domain adaptation approaches, including **DAN** [36], **CORAL** [64], **DANN** [12], **ENT** [14,57], **MDD** [85], **CDAN** [37], **SHOT** [32] and **ATDOC** [33]. ATDOC has multiple variants of the auxiliary regularizer, we compared with the *Neighborhood Aggregation* (ATDOC-NA) with the best performance in [33]. Among the compared approaches, SHOT and ATDOC-NA require a memory module that collects and stores information of all the target samples, thus only apply the offline setting. For the other six approaches, we compare both offline and online results. Each offline model is trained for 10 epochs. Each online model is trained batch-by-batch for 1 epoch, during which the online test results are recorded after each model update. All the online baselines take the same randomly-perturbed target queries to make a fair comparison. The results of CroDoBo and CroDoBo+ reported in Table 1, 2, 3 and 4 have 2 learners (*i.e.* $K = 2$), the results with $K \geq 3$ are reported in Table 7.

Main Results. We summarize the results on VisDA-C [49] in Table 1, and plot the online results in Fig. 4 We follow [25,32,33,49] to provide the VisDA-C one-pass accuracy in class average. In Table 1: Online, the proposed CroDoBo largely outperforms other baselines. Without augmentation, our method outperforms the second by 11.5%. Our online result is on par with the state-of-the-art offline performance ATDOC-NA [32], outperforming many other offline baselines.

Comparing across the offline and online setting, the Source-Only baseline drops 2.4% in the online average and 7.2% in the one-pass accuracy, which indicates that the data diversity is also important in domain generalization. We observe that

[2] https://wilds.stanford.edu/leaderboard/.

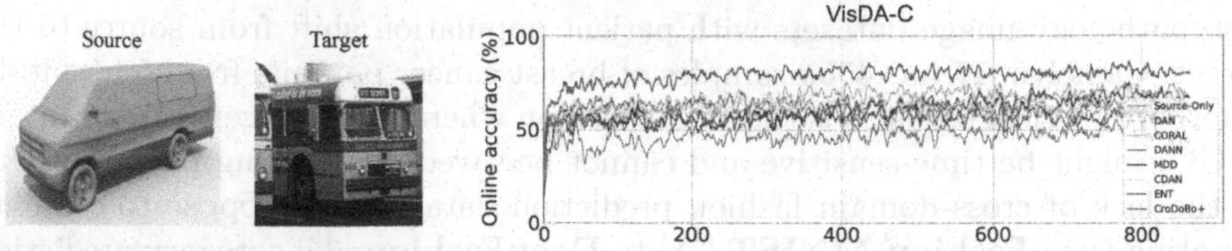

Fig. 4. Results of online adaptation from synthetic source domain to real target domain on VisDA-C [49] with "Burn After Reading". The x-axis is the online streaming timestep. Each query contains 64 samples. Each approach takes the same randomly perturbed sequence of target queries. Source-Only is in green, the proposed CroDoBo is in blue. Smoothed with 1-D uniform filter with length = 5. *Best viewed in color.*

ENT [57], which is an entropy regularizer on the posterior probabilities of the unlabeled target samples, has a noticeable performance drop in the online setting, and illustrates more obvious imbalanced results over the categories (superior at class "knife" but poor at "person" and "truck"). We consider it a typical example of bad objective choice for the online setting when the dataset is imbalanced. Without sufficient rounds to provide data diversity, entropy minimization might easily overfit the current target query. The 2.5% drop in one-pass from online further confirmed the model has deviated from the beginning.

Results on Two Medical Imaging Datasets. COVID-DA [84] and *WILDS*-Camelyon17 [26] are respectively summarized in Table 2 and Table 3. The online streaming accuracy is presented in Fig. 5. COVID-DA* is the method proposed along with the dataset in [84], which is a domain adversarial-based multi-classifier approach with focal loss regularization. Our method outperforms the other approaches on COVID-DA regarding the online and one-pass metric, and

Table 1. Accuracy on VisDA-C (%) using ResNet-101. In the online setting, individual class reports accuracy after one-pass, *one-pass* is the class average. Best offline (***italic bold***), best online (**bold**).

Methods (Syn → Real)		Plane	Bike	Bus	Car	Horse	Knife	Motor	Person	Plant	Skate	Train	Truck	Online	One-pass	Per-Class Acc.
Offline	Source-Only	67.7	27.4	50.0	61.7	69.5	13.7	85.9	11.5	64.4	34.4	84.2	19.2	–	–	49.1
	DAN [36]	84.4	50.9	68.4	66.8	82.0	17.0	82.3	22.0	73.3	47.4	81.2	18.3	–	–	57.8
	CORAL [64]	94.7	46.8	78.0	62.4	86.5	70.1	90.4	73.5	84.2	34.9	87.7	24.9	–	–	69.5
	DANN [12]	81.9	77.7	***82.8***	44.3	81.2	29.5	65.1	28.6	51.9	54.6	82.8	7.8	–	–	57.4
	ENT [57]	88.6	29.5	82.5	***75.8***	88.7	16.0	***93.2***	63.4	***94.2***	40.1	87.3	12.1	–	–	64.3
	MDD [85]	89.2	58.9	70.5	54.5	71.1	42.9	78.8	22.5	68.6	54.7	88.6	15.4	–	–	59.6
	CDAN [37]	89.4	40.3	74.6	65.2	81.5	62.2	90.1	69.3	73.3	58.6	84.8	19.1	–	–	67.4
	SHOT [32]	94.3	***88.5***	80.1	57.3	93.1	94.9	80.7	***80.3***	91.5	89.1	86.3	58.2	–	–	82.9
	ATDOC-NA [33]	***95.3***	84.7	82.4	75.6	***95.8***	***97.7***	88.7	76.6	94.0	***91.7***	***91.5***	***61.9***	–	–	***86.3***
Online	Source-Only	73.3	6.5	44.9	67.8	58.6	5.7	67.2	18.3	47.7	19.2	84.1	9.3	46.7	41.9	–
	DAN [36]	87.7	45.9	69.9	70.9	77.4	17.7	80.7	18.6	79.9	29.9	82.7	16.6	57.8	56.5	–
	CORAL [64]	94.7	51.0	79.6	63.2	88.2	69.4	**91.1**	73.1	87.7	41.8	88.4	24.2	66.7	71.0	–
	DANN [12]	84.5	39.2	70.2	60.4	77.1	28.6	90.9	20.5	67.7	39.9	**89.8**	10.5	49.0	56.6	–
	ENT [57]	87.1	14.8	87.9	71.9	87.8	**98.9**	90.3	0.0	5.2	15.0	80.4	0.2	55.8	53.3	–
	MDD [85]	**95.1**	52.2	87.9	57.9	90.3	94.8	88.4	45.7	76.2	50.5	77.7	25.7	60.4	70.1	–
	CDAN [37]	88.5	44.3	74.3	68.4	80.3	60.2	89.9	69.9	74.3	57.1	84.8	13.9	62.3	67.1	–
	CroDoBo (ours)	93.7	76.4	86.3	77.4	92.5	94.0	90.8	77.6	90.1	88.4	85.4	**37.7**	77.9	82.5	–
	CroDoBo^{+}(ours)	94.8	**87.5**	**90.5**	**76.0**	**94.9**	93.7	88.7	**80.1**	**94.8**	**89.4**	84.6	30.7	**79.4**	**84.0**	–

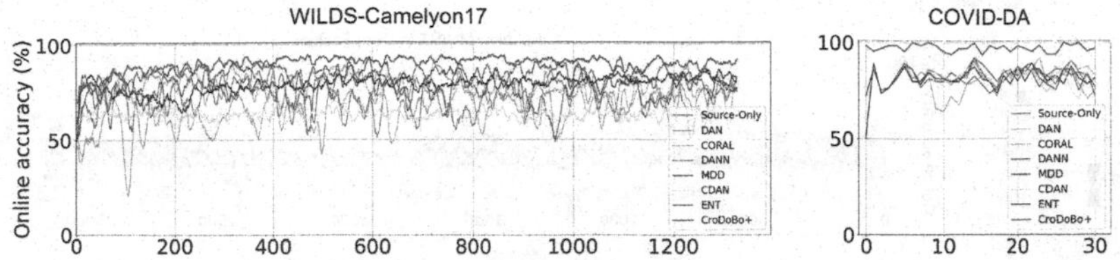

Fig. 5. Results of online accuracy on *WILDS*-Camelyon17 [26] with hospital patient population shift, and COVID-DA [84] adapting from common pneumonia to COVID-19 medical images with "Burn After Reading". Source-Only is in green, the proposed CroDoBo is the solid blue line. Smoothed with 1-D uniform filter with length = 5 for *WILDS*-Camelyon17. (Color figure online)

achieves competitive performance against the best offline accuracy. On the large-scale benchmark *WILDS*-Camelyon17, our CroDoBo is on par the best offline result, and CroDoBo+ outperforms the offline results by 1.7%, which validates the effectiveness of the approach. The good performance on larger number of target queries indicates that CroDoBo can well exploit the underlying information from the target domain. Similar observations are made on the large-scale Fashion benchmark [35,78]. Meanwhile, we reprint *Domain Generalization* results from the *WILDS* leaderboard for reference.

Results on Large-Scale Fashion Dataset, from Fashion-MNIST [78] to DeepFashion [35] category prediction branch, is summarized in Table 4. We provide the online results in Fig. 6. To the best of our knowledge, we are the first to report results on this meaningful adaptation scenario. The offline Source-Only merely achieves 23.1% accuracy, only 6.5% gain on the basis of the probability of

Table 2. Offline and online accuracy (%) on COVID-DA [84], adaptation from pneumonia to Covid. All the baselines use ResNet-18 as the backbone. COVID-DA* is the method proposed in [84] along with dataset.

Methods (Pneumonia → Covid)		Online	One-pass	Offline
Offline & Online	Source-Only	83.6	82.0	88.9
	DAN [36]	84.4	85.7	87.7
	CORAL [64]	67.6	45.4	65.4
	DANN [12]	83.0	87.1	87.7
	ENT [57]	84.3	87.3	89.8
	MDD [85]	83.2	86.2	81.0
	CDAN [37]	83.0	86.4	86.3
	SHOT [32]	–	–	93.2
	ATDOC-NA [33]	–	–	***98.1***
	COVID-DA* [84]	–	–	***98.1***
	CroDoBo (ours)	95.0	**97.1**	–
	CroDoBo$^+$ (ours)	**96.5**	**97.1**	–

Table 3. Accuracy on *WILDS*-Camelyon17 [26] (%) using DenseNet-121. *Domain Generalization* results are reprinted from *WILDS* leaderboard (see footnote 2).

Methods (Hospital 1, 2, 3 → Hospital 5)		Online	One-pass	Offline
Domain Generalization	ERM [26]	–	–	70.3
	Group DRO [26]	–	–	68.4
	IRM [26]	–	–	64.2
	FISH [61]	–	–	74.7
Offline & Online	Source-Only	71.7	60.1	63.6
	DAN [36]	76.3	78.0	69.0
	CORAL [64]	66.0	87.1	85.0
	DANN [12]	76.4	81.4	86.7
	ENT [57]	83.1	82.3	***87.5***
	MDD [85]	77.8	52.5	63.7
	CDAN [37]	62.7	60.1	58.5
	SHOT [32]	–	–	73.8
	ATDOC-NA [33]	–	–	86.3
	CroDoBo (ours)	87.5	89.2	–
	CroDoBo$^+$ (ours)	**89.2**	**91.9**	–

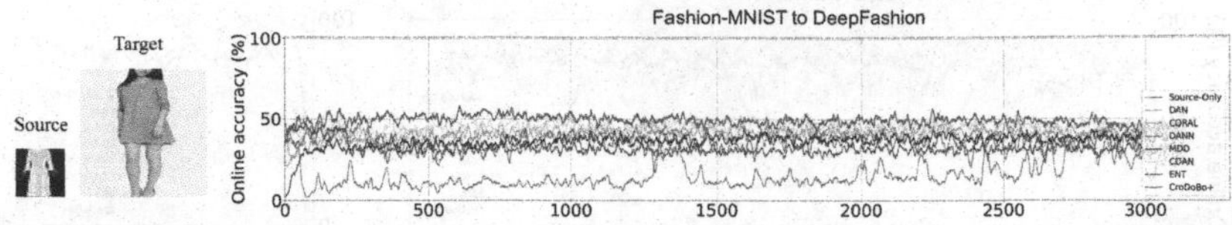

Fig. 6. Results of online adaptation from Fashion-MNIST [78]to DeepFashion [35] with "Burn After Reading". Smoothed with 1-D uniform filter with length = 10.

Table 4. Results on Fashion-MNIST [78] to DeepFashion [35] (%) using ResNet-101.

Methods (F-MNIST → DeepFashion)		Online	One-pass	Offline
Offline & Online	Source-Only	22.7	15.8	23.1
	DAN [36]	40.7	42.0	32.7
	CORAL [64]	40.4	40.7	39.6
	DANN [12]	35.6	26.5	40.5
	ENT [57]	31.9	31.2	31.1
	MDD [85]	36.5	38.0	39.0
	CDAN [37]	45.4	**47.6**	47.2
	SHOT [32]	–	–	42.3
	ATDOC-NA [33]	–	–	*47.4*
	CroDoBo (ours)	47.6	**47.6**	–
	CroDoBo$^+$ (ours)	**49.1**	46.3	–

Table 5. Ablation study of cross-domain bootstrapping on four datasets (%). VisDA-C one-pass accuracy is in per-class. Number of learners $K = 2$ in both w/ CRODOBO and w/o CRODOBO.

Method/Dataset		VisDA-C	COVID-DA	Camelyon17	Fashion
Online	w/o CroDoBo	78.5	94.4	86.2	42.3
	w/ CroDoBo	79.4	96.5	89.2	49.1
One-pass	w/o CroDoBo	84.0	97.1	89.4	39.9
	w/ CroDoBo	84.0	97.1	91.9	46.3

Table 6. Ablation study on the objectives on target domain on VisDA-C (%). T is the sharpening temperature in the MixMatch [2].

Method	Online	One-pass
default (w/o CroDoBo, $\tau = 0.95$, $\lambda = 0.4$)	78.5 (-)	84.0 (-)
w/o ℓ_{ent}	63.7 (↓)	53.1 (↓)
w/o ℓ_{div}	72.6 (↓)	73.0 (↓)
replace $\ell_{ent} + \ell_{div}$ w/ Pseudo-labeling [28] ($\tau = 0.95$)	70.2 (↓)	70.0 (↓)
replace $\ell_{ent} + \ell_{div}$ w/ MixMatch [2] ($T = 0.5$)	73.0 (↓)	75.3(↓)
replace ℓ_t w/ MixMatch [2] ($T = 0.5$)	76.3 (↓)	81.5 (↓)
use *Randaug* [5] on ℓ_{ent}, ℓ_{div}	77.6 (↓)	83.7 (↓)

Table 7. Accuracy on VisDA-C (%) using ResNet-101 with different number of learners K, and comparing the computation speed reported using 2 NVIDIA-P6000 GPUs.

CroDoBo$^+$	Plane	Bike	Bus	Car	Horse	Knife	Motor	Person	Plant	Skate	Train	Truck	Online	One-pass	Samples/sec
$K = 2$	94.8	87.5	90.5	76.0	94.9	93.7	88.7	80.1	94.8	89.4	84.6	30.7	79.4	84.0	25
$K = 3$	95.0	85.6	84.2	73.3	94.4	95.7	88.5	82.2	94.4	83.4	89.3	36.6	79.2	83.5	16
$K = 4$	95.5	85.0	85.0	76.1	95.3	96.0	92.7	81.8	92.7	88.9	86.8	37.3	81.3	84.4	12
$K = 5$	96.3	82.3	86.7	83.0	93.7	95.6	91.6	83.2	96.3	87.0	85.2	43.0	82.0	85.3	10

guessing, which indicates the benchmark is challenging. The sharp drop of performance from Source-Only online accuracy to one-pass accuracy (−6.8%) indicates the large domain gap, and how easy the model is dominated by the source domain supervision. Similar observation is made on *WILDS*-Camelyon17 Source-Only results (−11.6% from online to one-pass), this usually happens when the source domain is less challenging than the target domain, and the distribution of the two domains are far from each other. Faced with this challenging benchmark, CroDoBo improves the online performance to a remarkable 49.1%, outperforming the best result in the offline setting. Our one-pass accuracy is slightly shy compared to CDAN [37], but is better in online metric.

Ablation Study. We conduct ablation study on the impact of cross-domain bootstrapping in Table 5. Following Table 1, we provide the VisDA-C one-pass accuracy in class average. This study is to evaluate whether the improvement is introduced by cross-domain bootstrapping or simply the strong baseline with the objectives on the target domain (see Sect. 3.2). Thus, we devise a baseline by removing only the cross-domain bootstrapping, called w/o CroDoBo. The baseline model has one learner that is optimized by minimizing the objective $\ell_s + \ell_t + \ell_{\text{ent}} + \lambda \ell_{\text{div}}$, where $\ell_t = B^{-1} \sum_{b=1}^{B} \mathbb{1}(p_b \geq \tau) \mathcal{H}(\hat{y}_b; p(c|\tilde{t}_b; \boldsymbol{w}))$, which is Eq. (2) without exchanging the pseudo-labels. In Table 5, we observe that w/ CroDoBo is consistently better than w/o in the online average accuracy on all the datasets. Regarding one-pass accuracy, the effectiveness of cross-domain bootstrapping is unapparent on smaller datasets VisDA-C and COVID-DA, yet clearly outperforms w/o on large-scale *WILDS*-Camelyon17 and Fashion-MNIST-to-DeepFashion.

We further conduct ablation study on the objective terms (see Sect. 3.2) and report the results in Table 6. To eliminate the benefit of cross-domain boosting, our default setting is the model w/o CRODOBO. We leave out ℓ_{ent} and observe significant performance drop. Without ℓ_{div}, the performance decrease slight in the online metric, but far more sharply on the one-pass metric (which is calculated per-class). We analyze that the diversity term is important for imbalanced dataset like VisDA-C to achieve high class-average accuracy. We also report the results by replacing ℓ_{ent} and ℓ_{div} with Pseudo-labeling [28]. We replace either $\{\ell_{\text{ent}}, \ell_{\text{div}}\}$ or ℓ_t with MixMatch, and observe decent performance when employed together with $\{\ell_{\text{ent}}, \ell_{\text{div}}\}$ (see Table 6 row6). The RandAugment [5] on the entropy and diversity terms does not enhance the performance.

Number of Learners $K \geq 3$. We report the results of CroDoBo with varying number of learners $K \in \{2, 3, 4, 5\}$ on VisDA-C in Table 7. We observe that when $K = 3$ the performance is consistent with $K = 2$. However, from $K = 4$ the performance is improved with more learners with discrepancies. This observation reflects the effectiveness to exploit the discrepant learners via bootstrapping and co-supervision. The choice of K is a trade-off between computation cost and performance. We find that K=2 is sufficient to yield state-of-the-art performance in most times, thus is a better choice considering its computation efficiency.

5 Conclusion

In the context of the *the right to be forgotten*, we propose an online domain adaptation framework in which the target data is erased immediately after prediction. A novel online UDA algorithm is proposed to tackle the lack of data diversity, which is a fundamental drawback of the online setting. The proposed method achieves state-of-the-art online results and comparable results to the offline domain adaptation approaches. We would like to extend CroDoBo to more tasks like semantic segmentation [31,86].

References

1. de Barros, R.S.M., de Carvalho Santos, S.G.T., Júnior, P.M.G.: A boosting-like online learning ensemble. In: 2016 International Joint Conference on Neural Networks (IJCNN), pp. 1871–1878. IEEE (2016)
2. Berthelot, D., Carlini, N., Goodfellow, I., Papernot, N., Oliver, A., Raffel, C.: Mixmatch: a holistic approach to semi-supervised learning. arXiv preprint arXiv:1905.02249 (2019)
3. Chen, J., Wu, X., Duan, L., Gao, S.: Domain adversarial reinforcement learning for partial domain adaptation. IEEE Trans. Neural Netw. Learn. Syst. (2020)
4. Chen, Y., Luo, H., Ma, T., Zhang, C.: Active online learning with hidden shifting domains. In: International Conference on Artificial Intelligence and Statistics, pp. 2053–2061. PMLR (2021)
5. Cubuk, E.D., Zoph, B., Shlens, J., Le, Q.V.: RandAugment: practical automated data augmentation with a reduced search space. In: Proceedings of the IEEE/CVF Conference on Computer Vision and Pattern Recognition Workshops, pp. 702–703 (2020)
6. Delussu, R., Putzu, L., Fumera, G., Roli, F.: Online domain adaptation for person re-identification with a human in the loop. In: 2020 25th International Conference on Pattern Recognition (ICPR), pp. 3829–3836. IEEE (2021)
7. Deng, J., Dong, W., Socher, R., Li, L.J., Li, K., Fei-Fei, L.: Imagenet: a large-scale hierarchical image database. In: 2009 IEEE Conference on Computer Vision and Pattern Recognition, pp. 248–255. IEEE (2009)
8. Dredze, M., Crammer, K.: Online methods for multi-domain learning and adaptation. In: Proceedings of the 2008 Conference on Empirical Methods in Natural Language Processing, pp. 689–697 (2008)
9. Elliott, S.J., Rafaely, B.: Frequency-domain adaptation of causal digital filters. IEEE Trans. Sig. Process. **48**(5), 1354–1364 (2000)
10. Gal, Y., Ghahramani, Z.: Dropout as a Bayesian approximation: representing model uncertainty in deep learning. In: International Conference on Machine Learning, pp. 1050–1059. PMLR (2016)
11. Gal, Y., Hron, J., Kendall, A.: Concrete dropout. arXiv preprint arXiv:1705.07832 (2017)
12. Ganin, Y., Ustinova, E., Ajakan, H., Germain, P., Larochelle, H., Laviolette, F., Marchand, M., Lempitsky, V.: Domain-adversarial training of neural networks. JMLR **17**(1), 2096–2030 (2016)
13. Garg, S., Goldwasser, S., Vasudevan, P.N.: Formalizing data deletion in the context of the right to be forgotten. In: Canteaut, A., Ishai, Y. (eds.) EUROCRYPT 2020. LNCS, vol. 12106, pp. 373–402. Springer, Cham (2020). https://doi.org/10.1007/978-3-030-45724-2_13

14. Grandvalet, Y., Bengio, Y., et al.: Semi-supervised learning by entropy minimization. CAP **367**, 281–296 (2005)
15. Graves, L., Nagisetty, V., Ganesh, V.: Does AI remember? Neural Networks and the Right to be Forgotten (2020)
16. Guo, H., Chen, B., Tang, R., Zhang, W., Li, Z., He, X.: An embedding learning framework for numerical features in CTR prediction. In: Proceedings of the 27th ACM SIGKDD Conference on Knowledge Discovery and Data Mining, pp. 2910–2918 (2021)
17. Han, B., Sim, J., Adam, H.: Branchout: regularization for online ensemble tracking with convolutional neural networks. In: Proceedings of the IEEE Conference on Computer Vision and Pattern Recognition, pp. 3356–3365 (2017)
18. He, K., Zhang, X., Ren, S., Sun, J.: Deep residual learning for image recognition. In: Proceedings of the IEEE Conference on Computer Vision and Pattern Recognition, pp. 770–778 (2016)
19. Hu, J., et al.: Discriminative partial domain adversarial network. In: Vedaldi, A., Bischof, H., Brox, T., Frahm, J.-M. (eds.) ECCV 2020. LNCS, vol. 12372, pp. 632–648. Springer, Cham (2020). https://doi.org/10.1007/978-3-030-58583-9_38
20. Huang, G., Liu, Z., Van Der Maaten, L., Weinberger, K.Q.: Densely connected convolutional networks. In: Proceedings of the IEEE Conference on Computer Vision and Pattern Recognition, pp. 4700–4708 (2017)
21. Jaber, G., Cornuéjols, A., Tarroux, P.: Online learning: searching for the best forgetting strategy under concept drift. In: Lee, M., Hirose, A., Hou, Z.-G., Kil, R.M. (eds.) ICONIP 2013. LNCS, vol. 8227, pp. 400–408. Springer, Heidelberg (2013). https://doi.org/10.1007/978-3-642-42042-9_50
22. Jain, V., Learned-Miller, E.: Online domain adaptation of a pre-trained cascade of classifiers. In: CVPR 2011, pp. 577–584. IEEE (2011)
23. Jin, X., Chen, P.Y., Hsu, C.Y., Yu, C.M., Chen, T.: Cafe: catastrophic data leakage in vertical federated learning. arXiv preprint arXiv:2110.15122 (2021)
24. Kaissis, G.A., Makowski, M.R., Rückert, D., Braren, R.F.: Secure, privacy-preserving and federated machine learning in medical imaging. Nat. Mach. Intell. **2**(6), 305–311 (2020)
25. Kang, G., Jiang, L., Yang, Y., Hauptmann, A.G.: Contrastive adaptation network for unsupervised domain adaptation. In: Proceedings of the IEEE/CVF Conference on Computer Vision and Pattern Recognition, pp. 4893–4902 (2019)
26. Koh, P.W., et al.: Wilds: a benchmark of in-the-wild distribution shifts. In: International Conference on Machine Learning, pp. 5637–5664. PMLR (2021)
27. Lafarge, M.W., Pluim, J.P.W., Eppenhof, K.A.J., Moeskops, P., Veta, M.: Domain-adversarial neural networks to address the appearance variability of histopathology images. In: Cardoso, M.J., et al. (eds.) DLMIA/ML-CDS -2017. LNCS, vol. 10553, pp. 83–91. Springer, Cham (2017). https://doi.org/10.1007/978-3-319-67558-9_10
28. Lee, D.H., et al.: Pseudo-label: the simple and efficient semi-supervised learning method for deep neural networks. In: Workshop on Challenges in Representation Learning, ICML, vol. 3, p. 896 (2013)
29. Lee, S., Kim, D., Kim, N., Jeong, S.G.: Drop to adapt: learning discriminative features for unsupervised domain adaptation. In: ICCV (2019)
30. Li, Y., Liang, Y.: Learning overparameterized neural networks via stochastic gradient descent on structured data. arXiv preprint arXiv:1808.01204 (2018)
31. Li, Y., Yuan, L., Vasconcelos, N.: Bidirectional learning for domain adaptation of semantic segmentation. In: Proceedings of the IEEE/CVF Conference on Computer Vision and Pattern Recognition, pp. 6936–6945 (2019)

32. Liang, J., Hu, D., Feng, J.: Do we really need to access the source data? Source hypothesis transfer for unsupervised domain adaptation. In: International Conference on Machine Learning, pp. 6028–6039. PMLR (2020)
33. Liang, J., Hu, D., Feng, J.: Domain adaptation with auxiliary target domain-oriented classifier. In: Proceedings of the IEEE/CVF Conference on Computer Vision and Pattern Recognition, pp. 16632–16642 (2021)
34. Liu, W., Wang, Z., Liu, X., Zeng, N., Liu, Y., Alsaadi, F.E.: A survey of deep neural network architectures and their applications. Neurocomputing **234**, 11–26 (2017)
35. Liu, Z., Luo, P., Qiu, S., Wang, X., Tang, X.: DeepFashion: powering robust clothes recognition and retrieval with rich annotations. In: Proceedings of the IEEE Conference on Computer Vision and Pattern Recognition, pp. 1096–1104 (2016)
36. Long, M., Cao, Y., Wang, J., Jordan, M.: Learning transferable features with deep adaptation networks. In: International Conference on Machine Learning, pp. 97–105. PMLR (2015)
37. Long, M., Cao, Z., Wang, J., Jordan, M.I.: Conditional adversarial domain adaptation. arXiv preprint arXiv:1705.10667 (2017)
38. Lu, J., Liu, A., Dong, F., Gu, F., Gama, J., Zhang, G.: Learning under concept drift: a review. IEEE Trans. Knowl. Data Eng. **31**(12), 2346–2363 (2018)
39. Ma, X., Gao, J., Xu, C.: Active universal domain adaptation. In: Proceedings of the IEEE/CVF International Conference on Computer Vision, pp. 8968–8977 (2021)
40. Mancini, M., Karaoguz, H., Ricci, E., Jensfelt, P., Caputo, B.: Kitting in the wild through online domain adaptation. In: 2018 IEEE/RSJ International Conference on Intelligent Robots and Systems (IROS), pp. 1103–1109. IEEE (2018)
41. Minku, L.L., White, A.P., Yao, X.: The impact of diversity on online ensemble learning in the presence of concept drift. IEEE Trans. Knowl. Data Eng. **22**(5), 730–742 (2009)
42. Moon, J., Das, D., Lee, C.G.: Multi-step online unsupervised domain adaptation. In: ICASSP 2020–2020 IEEE International Conference on Acoustics, Speech and Signal Processing (ICASSP), pp. 41172–41576. IEEE (2020)
43. Nakkiran, P., Neyshabur, B., Sedghi, H.: The deep bootstrap framework: good online learners are good offline generalizers. arXiv preprint arXiv:2010.08127 (2020)
44. Nanni, L., Ghidoni, S., Brahnam, S.: Handcrafted vs. non-handcrafted features for computer vision classification. Pattern Recogn. **71**, 158–172 (2017)
45. Osband, I.: Risk versus uncertainty in deep learning: Bayes, bootstrap and the dangers of dropout. In: NIPS Workshop on Bayesian Deep Learning, vol. 192 (2016)
46. Pagallo, U., Durante, M.: Human rights and the right to be forgotten. In: Human Rights, Digital Society and the Law, pp. 197–208. Routledge (2019)
47. Paszke, A., et al.: Automatic differentiation in PyTorch (2017)
48. Peng, X., Bai, Q., Xia, X., Huang, Z., Saenko, K., Wang, B.: Moment matching for multi-source domain adaptation. In: Proceedings of the IEEE International Conference on Computer Vision, pp. 1406–1415 (2019)
49. Peng, X., Usman, B., Kaushik, N., Wang, D., Hoffman, J., Saenko, K.: Visda: a synthetic-to-real benchmark for visual domain adaptation. In: Proceedings of the IEEE Conference on Computer Vision and Pattern Recognition Workshops, pp. 2021–2026 (2018)
50. Politou, E., Alepis, E., Virvou, M., Patsakis, C.: The "right to be forgotten" in the GDPR: implementation challenges and potential solutions. In: Politou, E., Alepis, E., Virvou, M., Patsakis, C. (eds.) Privacy and Data Protection Challenges in the Distributed Era. earning and Analytics in Intelligent Systems, vol. 26, pp. 41–68. Springer, Cham (2022). https://doi.org/10.1007/978-3-030-85443-0_4

51. Prabhu, V., Chandrasekaran, A., Saenko, K., Hoffman, J.: Active domain adaptation via clustering uncertainty-weighted embeddings. In: Proceedings of the IEEE/CVF International Conference on Computer Vision, pp. 8505–8514 (2021)
52. Qi, G.J., Hua, X.S., Rui, Y., Tang, J., Zhang, H.J.: Two-dimensional multilabel active learning with an efficient online adaptation model for image classification. IEEE Trans. Pattern Anal. Mach. Intell. **31**(10), 1880–1897 (2008)
53. Rai, P., Saha, A., Daumé III, H., Venkatasubramanian, S.: Domain adaptation meets active learning. In: Proceedings of the NAACL HLT 2010 Workshop on Active Learning for Natural Language Processing, pp. 27–32 (2010)
54. Rosen, J.: The right to be forgotten. Stan. L. Rev. Online **64**, 88 (2011)
55. Russakovsky, O., et al.: Imagenet large scale visual recognition challenge. Int. J. Comput. Vision **115**(3), 211–252 (2015)
56. Sahoo, D., Pham, Q., Lu, J., Hoi, S.C.: Online deep learning: learning deep neural networks on the fly. arXiv preprint arXiv:1711.03705 (2017)
57. Saito, K., Kim, D., Sclaroff, S., Darrell, T., Saenko, K.: Semi-supervised domain adaptation via minimax entropy. In: Proceedings of the IEEE/CVF International Conference on Computer Vision, pp. 8050–8058 (2019)
58. Saito, K., Ushiku, Y., Harada, T., Saenko, K.: Adversarial dropout regularization. arXiv preprint arXiv:1711.01575 (2017)
59. Saito, K., Watanabe, K., Ushiku, Y., Harada, T.: Maximum classifier discrepancy for unsupervised domain adaptation. In: CVPR (2018)
60. Schmitz, A., Bansho, Y., Noda, K., Iwata, H., Ogata, T., Sugano, S.: Tactile object recognition using deep learning and dropout. In: 2014 IEEE-RAS International Conference on Humanoid Robots, pp. 1044–1050. IEEE (2014)
61. Shi, Y., et al.: Gradient matching for domain generalization. arXiv preprint arXiv:2104.09937 (2021)
62. Shu, R., Bui, H.H., Narui, H., Ermon, S.: A dirt-t approach to unsupervised domain adaptation. In: ICLR (2018)
63. Sohn, K., et al.: FixMatch: simplifying semi-supervised learning with consistency and confidence. arXiv preprint arXiv:2001.07685 (2020)
64. Sun, B., Feng, J., Saenko, K.: Return of frustratingly easy domain adaptation. In: AAAI (2016)
65. Sun, Y., Wang, X., Liu, Z., Miller, J., Efros, A., Hardt, M.: Test-time training with self-supervision for generalization under distribution shifts. In: International Conference on Machine Learning, pp. 9229–9248. PMLR (2020)
66. Taufique, A.M.N., Jahan, C.S., Savakis, A.: CONDA: continual unsupervised domain adaptation. arXiv preprint arXiv:2103.11056 (2021)
67. Tzeng, E., Hoffman, J., Saenko, K., Darrell, T.: Adversarial discriminative domain adaptation. In: CVPR (2017)
68. Varsavsky, T., Orbes-Arteaga, M., Sudre, C.H., Graham, M.S., Nachev, P., Cardoso, M.J.: Test-time unsupervised domain adaptation. In: Martel, A.L., et al. (eds.) MICCAI 2020. LNCS, vol. 12261, pp. 428–436. Springer, Cham (2020). https://doi.org/10.1007/978-3-030-59710-8_42
69. Villaronga, E.F., Kieseberg, P., Li, T.: Humans forget, machines remember: artificial intelligence and the right to be forgotten. Comput. Law Secur. Rev. **34**(2), 304–313 (2018)
70. Vu, T.H., Jain, H., Bucher, M., Cord, M., Pérez, P.: Advent: adversarial entropy minimization for domain adaptation in semantic segmentation. In: Proceedings of the IEEE/CVF Conference on Computer Vision and Pattern Recognition, pp. 2517–2526 (2019)

71. Wang, D., Shelhamer, E., Liu, S., Olshausen, B., Darrell, T.: Tent: fully test-time adaptation by entropy minimization. In: International Conference on Learning Representations (2020)
72. Wang, Q., Rao, W., Sun, S., Xie, L., Chng, E.S., Li, H.: Unsupervised domain adaptation via domain adversarial training for speaker recognition. In: 2018 IEEE International Conference on Acoustics, Speech and Signal Processing (ICASSP), pp. 4889–4893. IEEE (2018)
73. Wang, R., Wu, Z., Weng, Z., Chen, J., Qi, G.J., Jiang, Y.G.: Cross-domain contrastive learning for unsupervised domain adaptation. IEEE Trans. Multimedia (2022)
74. Warde-Farley, D., Goodfellow, I.J., Courville, A., Bengio, Y.: An empirical analysis of dropout in piecewise linear networks. arXiv preprint arXiv:1312.6197 (2013)
75. Wei, K., et al.: Federated learning with differential privacy: algorithms and performance analysis. IEEE Trans. Inf. Forensics Secur. **15**, 3454–3469 (2020)
76. Wei, Z., Chen, J., Goldblum, M., Wu, Z., Goldstein, T., Jiang, Y.G.: Towards transferable adversarial attacks on vision transformers. In: Proceedings of the AAAI Conference on Artificial Intelligence, vol. 36, pp. 2668–2676 (2022)
77. Wu, Z., et al.: DCAN: dual channel-wise alignment networks for unsupervised scene adaptation. In: Ferrari, V., Hebert, M., Sminchisescu, C., Weiss, Y. (eds.) ECCV 2018. LNCS, vol. 11209, pp. 535–552. Springer, Cham (2018). https://doi.org/10.1007/978-3-030-01228-1_32
78. Xiao, H., Rasul, K., Vollgraf, R.: Fashion-MNIST: a novel image dataset for benchmarking machine learning algorithms. arXiv preprint arXiv:1708.07747 (2017)
79. Xu, X., et al.: Information leakage by model weights on federated learning. In: Proceedings of the 2020 Workshop on Privacy-Preserving Machine Learning in Practice, pp. 31–36 (2020)
80. Yang, L., Balaji, Y., Lim, S.-N., Shrivastava, A.: Curriculum manager for source selection in multi-source domain adaptation. In: Vedaldi, A., Bischof, H., Brox, T., Frahm, J.-M. (eds.) ECCV 2020. LNCS, vol. 12359, pp. 608–624. Springer, Cham (2020). https://doi.org/10.1007/978-3-030-58568-6_36
81. Yang, L., et al.: Deep co-training with task decomposition for semi-supervised domain adaptation. arXiv preprint arXiv:2007.12684 (2020)
82. Zhang, N., et al.: AliCG: fine-grained and evolvable conceptual graph construction for semantic search at Alibaba. arXiv preprint arXiv:2106.01686 (2021)
83. Zhang, X., Chen, X., Liu, J.K., Xiang, Y.: DeepPAR and DeepDPA: privacy preserving and asynchronous deep learning for industrial IoT. IEEE Trans. Industr. Inf. **16**(3), 2081–2090 (2019)
84. Zhang, Y., et al.: Covid-DA: deep domain adaptation from typical pneumonia to Covid-19. arXiv preprint arXiv:2005.01577 (2020)
85. Zhang, Y., Liu, T., Long, M., Jordan, M.: Bridging theory and algorithm for domain adaptation. In: International Conference on Machine Learning, pp. 7404–7413. PMLR (2019)
86. Zhao, S., et al.: Multi-source domain adaptation for semantic segmentation. arXiv preprint arXiv:1910.12181 (2019)
87. Zhu, L., Han, S.: Deep leakage from gradients. In: Yang, Q., Fan, L., Yu, H. (eds.) Federated Learning. LNCS (LNAI), vol. 12500, pp. 17–31. Springer, Cham (2020). https://doi.org/10.1007/978-3-030-63076-8_2
88. Ziller, A., Usynin, D., Braren, R., Makowski, M., Rueckert, D., Kaissis, G.: Medical imaging deep learning with differential privacy. Sci. Rep. **11**(1), 1–8 (2021)

Mind the Gap in Distilling StyleGANs

Guodong Xu[1], Yuenan Hou[2], Ziwei Liu[3], and Chen Change Loy[3(✉)]

[1] The Chinese University of Hong Kong, Hong Kong, China
xg018@ie.cuhk.edu.hk

[2] Shanghai AI Laboratory, Shanghai, China
houyuenan@pjlab.org.cn

[3] S-Lab, Nanyang Technological University, Nanyang, China
{ziwei.liu,ccloy}@ntu.edu.sg

Abstract. StyleGAN family is one of the most popular Generative Adversarial Networks (GANs) for unconditional generation. Despite its impressive performance, its high demand on storage and computation impedes their deployment on resource-constrained devices. This paper provides a comprehensive study of distilling from the popular StyleGAN-like architecture. Our key insight is that the main challenge of StyleGAN distillation lies in the output discrepancy issue, where the teacher and student model yield different outputs given the same input latent code. Standard knowledge distillation losses typically fail under this heterogeneous distillation scenario. We conduct thorough analysis about the reasons and effects of this discrepancy issue, and identify that the mapping network plays a vital role in determining semantic information of generated images. Based on this finding, we propose a novel initialization strategy for the student model, which can ensure the output consistency to the maximum extent. To further enhance the semantic consistency between the teacher and student model, we present a latent-direction-based distillation loss that preserves the semantic relations in latent space. Extensive experiments demonstrate the effectiveness of our approach in distilling StyleGAN2 and StyleGAN3, outperforming existing GAN distillation methods by a large margin. Code is available at: https://github.com/xuguodong03/StyleKD.

1 Introduction

GAN compression [22,23,32] has been actively studied to enable the practical deployment of powerful GAN models [16,18,19] on mobile applications and edge devices. Among these techniques, knowledge distillation (KD) [9] is a widely adopted training strategy for GAN compression. The objective of GAN distillation is to transfer the rich dark knowledge from the original model (teacher) to the compressed model (student) so as to mitigate the performance gap between

Supplementary Information The online version contains supplementary material available at https://doi.org/10.1007/978-3-031-19827-4_25.

S. Avidan et al. (Eds.): ECCV 2022, LNCS 13693, pp. 423–439, 2022.
https://doi.org/10.1007/978-3-031-19827-4_25

these two models. There are two distillation strategies, i.e., pixel-level and distribution-level. The former minimizes the distance between generated images of two models, while the latter minimizes the distance between distributions. In this work, we focus on the first setting considering its prevalence in the GAN compression literature [6,22,23,32].

The majority of contemporary GAN distillation methods [6,22,23,32] focus on conditional GANs (cGANs), especially image-to-image translation [15,40], while the distillation of unconditional GANs (uncGANs) is relatively under-explored. Since there is a large difference between the learning dynamics of these two types of GANs, distillation methods tailored for cGANs cannot be directly applied to the unconditional setting.

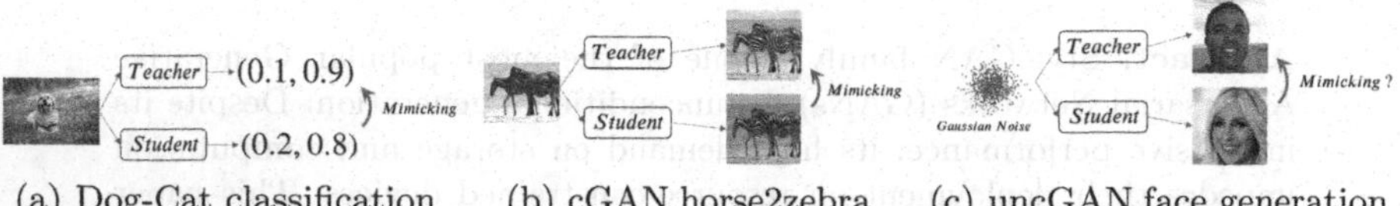

Fig. 1. Output discrepancy issue. For the classification task in (a), teacher and student naturally have similar output due to the label supervision. For the conditional GAN such as image-to-image translation in (b), teacher and student also have similar outputs because the input image imposes strong constraints on the output. However, for unconditional generation in (c), teacher and student may produce two images with totally different semantic features. In this condition, distillation is no longer meaningful and cannot bring gains to the student.

We find that the main difficulty of uncGAN distillation lies in the *output discrepancy* between the teacher and student model. An example is shown in Fig. 1. In fact, the implicit prerequisite of KD is that teacher and student should have similar outputs for the same input, otherwise the mimicking supervision is no longer meaningful. This prerequisite is easier to be satisfied in most of cGANs, because the output space of cGANs can be narrowed down by the given conditional input, especially when the condition is strong [15,40]. Take the horse→zebra task as an example. An input horse image determines which region should be added with zebra stripes and which region is background that should not be changed. Two generated images in cGAN may differ in some low-level details such as the shape of zebra stripes, but would largely resemble in their structure. Unlike cGANs, as shown in our experiments, it is impossible for an uncGAN student with random initialization to learn similar mapping function to the teacher, even though we leverage distillation loss to enforce the agreement between the outputs of two models.

To study the aforementioned output discrepancy problem, we focus our attention on the StyleGAN family, e.g., StyleGAN2 [19] and StyleGAN3 [17], which is one of the most applied unconditional GANs in various downstream tasks [2,20,33]. We carefully examine each component of the StyleGAN-like student model through comparative experiments. We identify that the mapping network plays a crucial role in deciding the semantic information of the generated images. Based on this finding, we propose a simple yet effective initialization strategy for the student model, i.e., inheriting the weights from the teacher mapping network and keeping the remaining convolutional layers randomly initialized. Such initialization strategy can work well even in heterogeneous distillation where the student architecture is obtained by neural architecture search (NAS) or manual design, and is totally different from the teacher model.

After resolving the output discrepancy problem, we further design an effective mimicking objective tailored for uncGAN distillation. As opposed to most of existing GAN distillation approaches that merely transfer the knowledge within a single image, we propose a novel latent-direction-based relational loss to fully exploit the rich relational knowledge between different images. Specifically, we exploit the good linear separability property of StyleGAN-like models in latent space and augment each latent code w by moving it along certain direction such that the resulting image only differs in a *single* semantic factor. Then, we compute the similarity matrix between original images and augmented images and take it as the dark knowledge to be mimicked by the student. The latent-direction-based augmentation disentangles various semantic factors and makes the learning of each factor easier, thus yielding better distillation performance.

Our **contributions** are summarized as follows: **1)** To the best of our knowledge, this is the first work that uncovers the *output discrepancy* issue in StyleGAN distillation. Through carefully designed comparative experiments, we identify that the mapping network is the determining factor to ensure output consistency. **2)** We propose a concise yet effective initialization strategy for the student to resolve the output discrepancy problem, demonstrating significant gains upon conventional uncGAN distillation. **3)** We further propose a latent-direction-based distillation loss to learn the rich relational knowledge between different images, and achieve state-of-the-art results in StyleGAN2/3 distillation, outperforming the existing state-of-the-art CAGAN [23] by a large margin.

2 Related Work

GAN Compression. We highlight a few recent methods among many GAN compression methods [5,6,10,22,28,32]. GAN Slimming [32] integrates model distillation, channel pruning and quantization into a unified framework. GAN Compression [22] searches a compact student architecture via NAS, and then forces the student to mimic the intermediate outputs and synthesized results of the teacher simultaneously. A common characteristic shared by these works is that they all focus on the cGANs such as pix2pixGAN [15] and CycleGAN [40].

Aguinaldo's work [1] focuses on the uncGANs (DCGAN) distillation on low-resolution (32×32) datasets, where the easy setting makes it possible to solve the output discrepancy by adding L1 loss. Our work explores the distillation of StyleGAN-like models on high resolution (256/1024) images. In this case, output discrepancy issue becomes much more challenging. The more recent MobileStyleGAN [3] and Content-Aware GAN compression (CAGAN) [23] shift the attention to styleGANs. MobileStyleGAN compresses the model by mimicking the wavelet transformation of generated images. CAGAN estimates the contribution of each channel to the generated faces and eliminates channels with little contribution. Subsequently, the pruned model inherits the parameters from the original network for both mapping network and convolutional layers, and are finetuned with adversarial loss and distillation loss afterwards. Though CAGAN involves the compression of uncGAN, it bypasses the issues of model heterogeneity between the teacher and student model by allowing the student to inherit the parameters. Such an requirement assumes the student to inherit the main structure of the teachers too despite pruning. As will be shown in the experiments, the performance of CAGAN greatly degrades in heterogeneous distillation. The proposed mimicking loss cannot guarantee the student to learn a similar mapping as the teacher. Moreover, we find that the content-aware pruning strategy in CAGAN is not an optimal solution for student initialization. With our proposed initialization strategy, the student model does not need to inherit any weights from convolutional layers of the teacher but achieves better results.

Knowledge Distillation. KD [9] is originally proposed to achieve model compression [4] for image classification, whose target is to transfer the dark knowledge from one or multiple cumbersome networks (teacher) to a small compact network (student). Vanilla KD [9] proposes to match the outputs of two classifiers by minimizing the KL-divergence of the softened output logits. Besides the output logits, other intermediate outputs such as feature maps [26], attention maps [11,38], Gram matrices [36], pre-activations [8], relation [25,30] and self-supervision signals [29,35] can also serve as the dark knowledge. However, it should be careful when adapting KD from classification tasks to generation tasks. The output consistency prerequisite is naturally satisfied in image classification since the supervision of labels guarantees different models to converge to similar mappings. As discussed in Sect. 1, the consistency prerequisite does not naturally hold for uncGANs. Therefore, a special distillation technique tailored for uncGANs is required to cope with the output discrepancy problem.

StyleGAN Linear Property. As shown in StyleGAN [18], for a well-trained model, the w latent space consists of linear subspaces. It should be possible to find direction vectors that consistently correspond to individual factors of variation. Recently, some works [14,24,27,31] have been conducted to find these meaningful directions. Among them, SeFa [27] finds the latent directions by computing the eigenvalues of the transformation matrix in the ModConv [13] layer. We adopt it in our latent-direction-based loss due to its fast computation and high performance. A recent work StyleAlign [34] provides a thorough analysis about the property of StyleGAN latent space. It finds that the latent directions control similar semantic factors for two aligned models even they work on very different domains. This finding aligns with our observation that the mapping network plays a vital roles in determining the semantics of generated images.

3 Methodology

3.1 Preliminaries

StyleGAN. There are two modules in StyleGAN-like models [17–19], i.e., a mapping network $S(\cdot)$ that maps Gaussian noise z to the style vector w and a convolution backbone $C(\cdot)$ that takes w as input and generates images. The style vector w is fed into the backbone $C(\cdot)$ through the modulated convolution (ModConv) layer [13,19]. StyleGAN allows the use of different w vectors in different ModConv layers. The image generation process can be formulated as:

$$G(z_1, z_2, \cdots, z_L) = C(w_1, w_2, \cdots, w_L) = C(S(z_1), S(z_2), \cdots, S(z_L)), \quad (1)$$

where L is the number of ModConv layers in the backbone, and the i-th ModConv layer uses w_i that comes from z_i. We define the output consistency condition as:

$$G_s(z_1, z_2, \cdots, z_L) = G_t(z_1, z_2, \cdots, z_L), \quad (2)$$

where the s and t represent student and teacher, respectively. Equation 2 suggests that the generated images of two models should be the same if they use the same z at corresponding layers.

StyleGAN Compression. A typical StyleGAN compression approach [23] contains two steps, i.e., pruning and finetuning. In the pruning stage, unimportant/unnecessary channels will be removed according to some heuristics [7,12, 21,23]. Note that pruning is only applied to the convolution backbone $C(\cdot)$ and the mapping network $S(\cdot)$ is kept *unchanged*. The pruned model will inherit the well-trained weights from the original model for both the mapping network and the convolution backbone [23]. In the finetuning stage, besides the normal adversarial loss, the pruned model is also required to mimic the original model's output to compensate the performance degradation brought by channel reduction. A typical mimicking loss includes RGB loss and LPIPS loss [39]:

$$\mathcal{L}_{\text{rgb}} = ||G_s(z) - G_t(z)||_1, \mathcal{L}_{\text{lpips}} = ||F(G_s(z)) - F(G_t(z))||_1, \quad (3)$$

where F is a well-trained frozen network that computes the perceptual distance between two images. L_{rgb} and L_{lpips} require that the generated image of student should be close to that of teacher in RGB space and perceptual space, respectively. The final loss function in the finetuning stage is:

$$\mathcal{L} = \lambda_{\text{GAN}}\mathcal{L}_{\text{GAN}} + \lambda_{\text{rgb}}\mathcal{L}_{\text{rgb}} + \lambda_{\text{lpips}}\mathcal{L}_{\text{lpips}}, \quad (4)$$

where λ_* is the loss weight of each item.

3.2 Framework Overview of Unconditional GAN Distillation

Knowledge distillation is a common strategy that can bring improvements in classification tasks. However, in generation tasks, its prerequisite, namely the student and teacher having consistent outputs for the same input, is rarely mentioned. In the absence of this prerequisite, the influence of mimicking losses on the training of student remains largely unknown. Here, we hypothesize that RGB or LPIPS loss is not compatible with GAN loss when the output discrepancy occurs and distillation will also bring no benefit to the student. We examine this hypothesis both qualitatively and quantitatively.

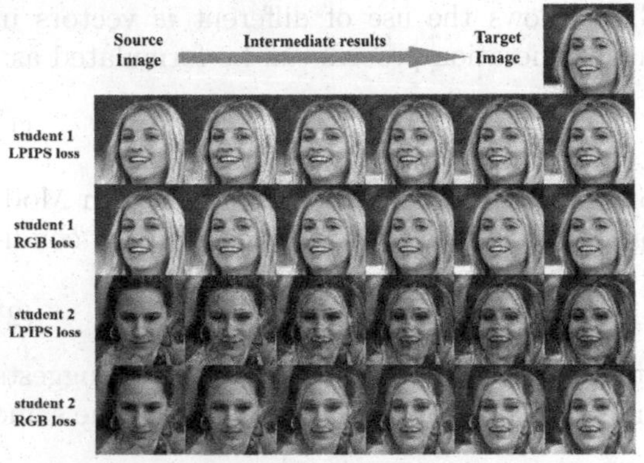

(a) Qualitative effects of RGB/LPIPS losses.

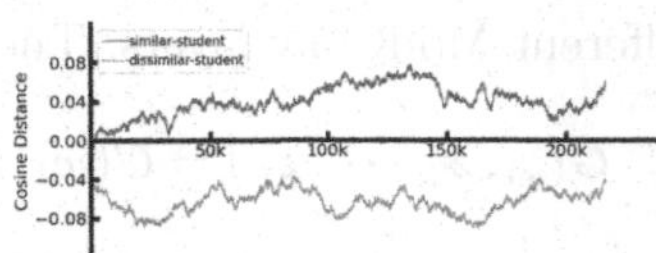

(b) Grad cosine between GAN and RGB loss.

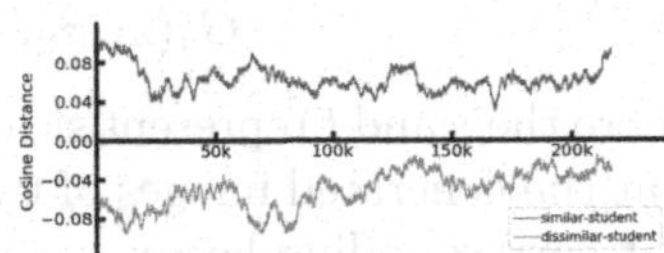

(c) Grad cosine between GAN and LPIPS loss

Fig. 2. (a) Student-1 has similar outputs with teacher and Student-2 has different outputs. The image in the top right corner is the teacher output. We demonstrate the intermediate results to show how RGB/LPIPS loss influences the image generation of student. (b)(c) Cosine distance between the gradient of GAN loss and RGB/LPIPS loss. The $x-$axis denotes training steps. For similar student, RGB/LPIPS loss is cooperating with GAN loss. For dissimilar student, RGB/LPIPS loss is competing with GAN loss.

Note that the three losses in Eq. 4 serve different roles. $\mathcal{L}_{\text{GAN}}$ requires the student to generate realistic images while $\mathcal{L}_{\text{rgb}}$ and $\mathcal{L}_{\text{lpips}}$ encourage similarity between the generated images by student and those of the teacher. Intuitively, if the generated image of the student is totally different from that of teacher for the same input, $\mathcal{L}_{\text{rgb}}$ and $\mathcal{L}_{\text{lpips}}$ will result in images that are slightly closer to teacher but with much less realism. To examine this hypothesis, we remove the GAN loss in Eq. 4 and keep only RGB or LPIPS loss. We also cut off the gradient backward path between the student generator and generated images. In this condition, the gradient of RGB/LPIPS loss directly works on the images. The change of synthesized images reflects how RGB/LPIPS loss influences the generation process. We select two student models, i.e., student-1 that has similar output with teacher for the same input and student-2 that has totally different outputs from teacher. Two students have identical architectures. The mapping network of student-1 inherits from teacher and the mapping network of student-2 is randomly initialized. The effects of RGB/LPIPS loss are shown in Fig. 2a. We can find that the intermediate results are a mixup of source and target images to some extent. If the source image is in the neighbourhood of the target image (1st and 2nd rows), the intermediate results are still perceptually realistic. However, if the source image is totally different from the target image (3rd and 4th rows), the intermediate results are no longer realistic. Though RGB and LPIPS losses are reducing the distance between source and target images, they cannot guarantee a smooth and face-like interpolation in the dissimilar setting. And this unrealistic intermediate results naturally contradict with GAN loss.

From quantitative perspective, we wish to prove that RGB/LPIPS loss is not compatible with GAN loss in the heterogeneous setting by gradient analysis. In the training process, for each batch, we perform backward propagation for GAN loss, RGB loss and LPIPS loss, respectively, and obtain three gradients of these losses. We then compute the cosine distance between GAN gradient and RGB/LPIPS gradients. As shown in Fig. 2b and Fig. 2c, the cosine distance between GAN gradient and RGB/LPIPS gradients of dissimilar student is always negative, suggesting that RGB/LPIPS gradients are competing with GAN gradients. On the contrary, the cosine distance of similar student is positive, indicating that the distillation loss is driving the model in the same direction as the adversarial loss. Our analysis above suggests that distillation is not beneficial in heterogeneous setting. Having similar outputs for the same input z is the prerequisite for uncGAN distillation.

3.3 Effect of the Mapping Network

As we will show in the experiments, if the student is randomly initialized, it cannot learn consistent outputs as teacher even though we leverage RGB/LPIPS loss to force the agreement between the outputs of two models. We hypothesize that the mapping network $S(z)$ plays a key role in determining whether two models can have consistent outputs. If the gap between mapping networks of student and teacher is too large, it is hard for the student to learn outputs consistent with the teacher. This hypothesis comes from the following motivation.

Suppose the student has a different mapping network from the teacher and the consistency condition (Eq. 2) is still satisfied. Our goal is to derive a contradiction. For the convenience of the following discussion, we define:

$$G(z_1, z_2; k) = C(w_1, w_2; k) = C(w_1, \cdots, w_1, w_2, w_1, \cdots, w_1), \tag{5}$$

where all the ModConv layers use w_1 except that the k-th layer uses w_2. The consistency condition of Eq. 2 requires that:

$$G_s(z_1, z_2; k) = G_t(z_1, z_2; k), 1 \leq k \leq L. \tag{6}$$

As shown in StyleGAN [18], for a well-trained model, it should be possible to find direction vectors that consistently correspond to individual factors of variation. An example is shown in supplementary material. Some individual semantic factors such as pose, glasses and hair color can be controlled by moving the style vector w of certain layer along a certain direction. Suppose the direction p at k-th layer controls the hair color of the generated face. The only difference between $C_t(w_0, w_1 + p; k)$ and $C_t(w_0, w_1; k)$ is that they are the same faces with different hair colors. The movement of w from w_1 to $w_1 + p$ corresponds to a consecutive change of hair color of the generated face. If we map the w back to the noise space:

$$z_1 = S_t^{-1}(w_1), \quad z_2 = S_t^{-1}(w_1 + p), \tag{7}$$

obviously, the line segment in w space corresponds to a curve in z space with two end points z_1 and z_2 due to the nonlinearity of $S_t(z)$. We denote this curve as $\widehat{z_1 z_2}$. Then $\{G_t(z_0, z; k) | z \in \widehat{z_1 z_2}\}$ represents a cluster of faces with different hair colors. According to the consistency constraint, $\{G_s(z_0, z; k) | z \in \widehat{z_1 z_2}\}$ should be the same cluster as $\{G_t(z_0, z; k) | z \in \widehat{z_1 z_2}\}$. We feed $z_0, z \in \widehat{z_1 z_2}$ into the student mapping network $S_s(\cdot)$:

$$w_0' = S_s(z_0), \quad \widehat{w_1' w_2'} = S_s(\widehat{z_1 z_2}). \tag{8}$$

Since $S_s(\cdot)$ is different from and independent of $S_t(\cdot)$, the result $\widehat{w_1' w_2'}$ is still a curve. Thus, the semantic factor of hair color in student model is controlled by a complex curve in w space, which contradicts the property of StyleGAN that various semantic factors are decoupled well in w space. Hence, having different mapping networks and consistency condition cannot hold simultaneously.

Fig. 3. The mapping network $S(\cdot)$ determines whether student can learn from the teacher's output.

We further conduct experiments to examine our hypothesis. Specifically, we select four students according to whether the mapping network is from teacher or not and whether the convolution is from teacher or not. We use GAN loss, RGB loss and LPIPS loss to train these models. The mapping network and convolution are updated together. The results are shown in Fig. 3. The student that inherits weights from the teacher's mapping network can learn a mapping that aligns well with the teacher's output, no matter how the convolution $C(\cdot)$ is initialized.

However, for the student whose mapping network is randomly initialized, there are no meaningful connections between student's and teacher's outputs. The analysis above clearly shows that the output consistency between student and teacher is determined by the mapping network.

3.4 Mapping Network Consistency in GAN Distillation

We have shown that the consistency between student and teacher outputs is the prerequisite of the distillation, and the mapping network determines whether two generators can have consistent outputs. Hence, to make distillation meaningful, it is necessary to impose extra constraints to guarantee the consistency between two mapping networks.

The simplest way is to keep the architecture of the mapping network unchanged and inherit teacher's parameters directly. In fact, the parameters and FLOPs of the mapping network account for only 7.5% and 0.005% of the convolution backbone. Preserving the mapping network is thus feasible in practice.

If there is a strong demand on the compression of the mapping network, one can perform a two-stage training to ensure a small gap between student and teacher mapping networks. In the first stage, the student mapping network is forced to mimic outputs of the teacher mapping network:

$$\mathcal{L} = \mathbb{E}_{z\sim\mathcal{N}(0,1)} D(S_s(z), S_t(z)), \tag{9}$$

where $D(\cdot,\cdot)$ is a distance metric. Considering $S_t(\cdot)$ and $S_s(\cdot)$ are both shallow MLPs, the training cost of this stage is negligible (0.59% of the normal GAN training in the second stage). In the second stage, the mapping network and generator backbone are finetuned together using the loss in Eq. 4. We will explore the effects of compressing the mapping network in Sect. 4.1.

3.5 Latent-Direction-Based Relation Distillation

Under the premise that consistency condition is satisfied, we further propose to incorporate relation mimicking into GAN distillation. Conventional relation-based distillation [30] in classification tasks computes feature similarity matrices using the samples in a minibatch. Here, we tailor it to better cater to StyleGAN.

Specifically, for a given teacher model, we compute its meaningful latent directions (LD) that control a single semantic factor and store them in a dictionary $\{d_1, d_2, \cdots, d_m\}$. Note that the latent direction is related to a specific layer. For example, if d_i is computed in k-layer, then only $C_t(w, w + d_i; k)$ has single semantic factor difference with $C_t(w)$. $C_t(w, w+d_i; j)_{j\neq k}$ does not has this property. In the training stage, we feed a batch of noise $\{z_i\}_{i=1:N}$ into the mapping network and obtain $\{w_i\}_{i=1:N}$. For each w_i we randomly sample a latent direction d from the dictionary. Thus, $C_t(w_i)$ and $C_t(w_i, w_i + \alpha d; k)$ (k is the layer related to d) are two images with single semantic factor difference with α controls the moving distance. We denote the intermediate features of $C_t(w_i)$

and $C_t(w_i, w_i + \alpha d; k)$ as f_i and f'_i, respectively. Then the similarity matrix M between original view and augmentation view can be computed as $A_{i,j} = f_i \cdot f'_j$. We then convert the similarity into probability via the softmax operation and minimize the distance using KL-divergence loss:

$$M_{i,j} = \frac{\exp(A_{i,j})}{\sum_{k=1}^{N} \exp(A_{i,k})}, \quad \mathcal{L}_{\mathrm{LD}} = -\sum_{i,j} M^t_{i,j} \log M^s_{i,j}. \tag{10}$$

The final learning objective is the combination of Eq. 4 and $\mathcal{L}_{\mathrm{LD}}$.

4 Experiments

We conduct experiments mainly on StyleGAN2/3 since they are the most powerful unconditional GANs so far. We use the FFHQ [18] and LSUN church [37] datasets. We adopt Fréchet Inception Distance (FID), Perceptual Path Length (PPL) [18] and PSNR [23] between real and projected images as evaluation metrics. More qualitative results are shown in the supplementary material.

Table 1. Effect of initialization. Surprisingly, we find that inheriting only mapping network is the best solution.

Mapping network initialization	Convolution initialization	Mimicking Loss	Student FID
Random	Random	No Mimic	10.92
		RGB	10.78
		RGB + LPIPS	11.27
Random	Inherit	RGB	10.81
		RGB+LPIPS	10.88
Inherit	Inherit	No Mimic	10.54
		RGB	9.41
		RGB + LPIPS	8.61
		RGB + LPIPS + LD	8.45
Inherit	Random	RGB	9.42
		RGB + LPIPS	8.23
		RGB + LPIPS + LD	**7.94**

For the ablation study in Sect. 4.1, we train the models on resolution 256×256 and use a smaller batch size of 8 to save the computation cost. For the comparison with state-of-the-art methods in Sect. 4.2, we train the models on both resolutions of 256×256 and 1024×1024. We also use a batch size of 16 that is the same as CAGAN [23] to ensure a fair comparison.

4.1 Ablation Study

The Initialization of the Student Model. Previous works usually treat StyleGAN2 as an integral module and initialize the mapping network and convolution backbone in the same way (from scratch or inherits teacher parameters). Based on our analysis in Sect. 3.3 that the mapping network plays a key role in determining the semantics of generated images, here we separate the mapping network $S(z)$ from the convolution backbone $C(w)$ and test three initialization strategies: 1) both $S(z)$ and $C(w)$ are randomly initialized, 2) both $S(z)$ and $C(w)$ are initialized with teacher weights, 3) only $S(z)$ inherits teacher weights and $C(w)$ is randomly initialized.

The results are shown in Table 1. For the setting where $S(z)$ and $C(w)$ are both randomly initialized, RGB loss can only bring marginal improvement. RGB+LPIPS even performs worse than No-Mimic, indicating that distillation cannot work well when output discrepancy occurs. If $S(z)$ and $C(w)$ both inherit teacher weights, the mimicking loss can achieve 1–2 FID improvement. To explore the effect of the mapping network, we also try inheriting only $S(z)$ and surprisingly find that this initialization obtains the best result. And loading $C(w)$ hampers the performance of distillation. This result contradicts with the conclusion in CAGAN. It shows that the general pruning strategy, i.e., determining which channels should be removed, is not important. Randomly initialization of convolution layers is the optimal solution if the mapping network is kept.

The Effects of Mapping Network Compression. We conduct experiments to investigate how to deal with the mapping network in StyleGAN-like models

Table 2. How to deal with the mapping network in StyleGAN2 distillation. The mapping network is comprised of MLPs. The numbers inside and outside the "[]" is the number of channels in each layer and the number of layers, respectively. The mapping network of the teacher is [512]*8. The FLOPs saving is computed with regard to the total FLOPs (the mapping network and convolution layers).

Setting	mapping network architecture	FLOPsSaving	$D(\cdot,\cdot)$	$\|\|S_s(z) - S_t(z)\|\|_1$	Student FID
Random initialization	[512] * 8	0%	N/A	1.027	11.78
Two-Stage	[512] * 8	0%	L1	0.156	9.69
	[512] * 8	0%	L2	0.260	10.80
	[512] * 5	0.0019%	L1	0.197	10.38
	[390] * 7+[512]	0.0019%	L1	0.210	10.55
	[256] * 7+[512]	0.0034%	L1	0.245	10.86
Inheriting	[512] * 8	0%	N/A	0	**8.30**

compression. Specifically, we consider three settings: 1) student has the same mapping network architecture as teacher but with random initialization, 2) student mapping network has a different architecture and uses the two-stage training strategy, 3) student has the same architecture and inherits weights from the teacher. For all the settings, the convolution backbones are randomly initialized. For the two-stage setting, we also explore how the architecture of the mapping network and mimicking loss in Eq. 9 affect the final performance. To emphasize the importance of the mapping network, we also list the average L1 distance between $S_s(z)$ and $S_t(z)$ before entering the normal GAN training stage.

The results are shown in Table 2. 'Random Initialization' obtains the worst FID because the output discrepancy makes the distillation ineffective. The 'Two-Stage' strategy improves the results by narrowing the gap between $S_s(z)$ and $S_t(z)$. From several two-stage settings, we can find that L1 is a better mimicking loss than L2 and reducing the number of layers is better than reducing the number of channels in each layer. It is also worth noting that there is a strong positive correlation between $|S_s(z) - S_t(z)|$ and FID, indicating that the gap between $S_s(z)$ and $S_t(z)$ determines the output consistency and further determines the

Table 3. Comparison with SOTA methods. "↓" ("↑") denotes the lower (higher) the better. "†" denotes that the numbers come from CAGAN [23]. **Bold** font denotes the results that outperform CAGAN. "heter" denotes the heterogeneous setting where the student is not a subnet of the teacher. Since StyleGAN3 removes the PPL loss in the training stage, we also do not measure the PPL for StyleGAN3. The PSNR (proposed by CAGAN) is a special-designed metric to measure the face projection ability. Thus, we do not measure it for the LSUN church dataset. We compute PSNR using our own implementation and leave the result of GAN slim blank due to the lack of the corresponding checkpoint.

Model	Dataset	Reso	Methods	RAM	FLOPs	FID (↓)	PPL (↓)	PSNR (↑)
StyleGAN2	FFHQ	256	Teacher	30.0M	45.1B	4.5	0.162	34.26
			Baseline	5.6M	4.1B	9.79	0.156	33.17
			GAN slim	–	5.0B	12.4†	0.313†	–
			CAGAN	5.6M	4.1B	7.9†	0.143†	33.34
			Ours	5.6M	4.1B	**7.25**	**0.135**	**33.49**
			CAGAN-heter	3.4M	2.7B	13.75	0.158	33.19
			Ours-heter	3.4M	2.7B	**9.96**	**0.141**	**33.54**
		1024	Teacher	49.1M	74.3B	2.7	0.162	33.52
			GAN slim	–	23.9B	10.1†	0.211†	–
			CAGAN	9.2M	7.0B	7.6†	0.157†	32.63
			Ours	9.2M	7.0B	**7.19**	**0.128**	**32.70**
	LSUNChurch	256	Teacher	30.0M	45.1B	4.92	0.168	N/A
			CAGAN	5.6M	4.1B	8.57	0.146	N/A
			Ours	5.6M	4.1B	**7.96**	**0.136**	N/A
StyleGAN3	FFHQ	256	Teacher	30.0M	45.1B	4.41	N/A	34.30
			CAGAN	5.6M	4.1B	7.75	N/A	33.39
			Ours	5.6M	4.1B	**7.14**	N/A	**33.58**

influence of distillation. Though the two-stage strategy brings performance gains, there is still a large gap between it and the 'Inheriting' variant. Thus, we conclude that the modification to the mapping network will greatly harm the final performance and the two-stage strategy can only mitigate the degradation to a certain degree. Considering that the scale of the original $S_t(z)$ is negligible compared to the convolution backbone, the best practice in StyleGAN2 compression is to preserve the mapping network architecture and inherit the weights from the teacher mapping network.

4.2 Comparison with State-of-the-Art Methods

Quantitative Results. We compare our method with the GAN Slimming [32] and CAGAN [23] methods. Since our method does not focus on the pruning, we directly adopt the student architecture used in CAGAN, i.e., a network that is the same as teacher but with fewer channels. We also compare with CAGAN in the heterogeneous setting where the student is not a subnet of the teacher. Specifically, we modify the kernel size of the second convolution layer in each residual block from 3 to 1, thus inheriting teacher convolution parameters is infeasible. Since CAGAN did not notice the output discrepancy issue and always initialize the mapping network and convolution backbone in the same way, we assume it does not inherit weights from teacher in the heterogeneous setting.

Fig. 4. StyleGAN2 synthesized results on FFHQ 256×256.

The results are shown in Table 3. For the distillation of StyleGAN2 on FFHQ dataset, our method outperforms CAGAN on FID by 0.65 and 0.41 on resolution 256×256 and 1024×1024, respectively, showing that our method can generate more realistic images. Note that these improvements are not marginal considering the images generated by CAGAN are already of high quality. For the PPL metric that measures the smoothness of latent space, we outperform CAGAN by 6% (relative improvement) on resolution 256×256. The gap is even larger (18.5%) on resolution 1024×1024. For PSNR that is related to the image projection ability, our method also surpasses CAGAN, demonstrating that our method can model the face distribution in real world better. Our superiority is much more significant in the heterogeneous setting, showing that our method can be applied in a more general situation where the student is not necessary to be a subnet of the teacher. On LSUN Church dataset, our method still achieves better results than CAGAN on both FID and PPL, showing that our method not only handles those well-aligned settings, but also works well in complex outdoor scenes. On StyleGAN3, our method also brings more gains, indicating that the proposed method has good generalization ability in various StyleGAN-like models.

Qualitative Results. We show StyleGAN2 generation results of FFHQ on resolution 256×256 in Fig. 4. For Two-Stage, we compress the original 8-layer mapping network into 5 layers. The images of each row are generated using the same input noise z. Note that all the students are trained with mimicking loss. Random $S_s(z)$ cannot make the student model generate images consistent with the teacher due to the different mapping networks. The Two-Stage method mitigates output discrepancy issue by directly mimicking the mapping network, but there still exist semantic differences from the teacher. Compared to CAGAN, our generated images have fewer artifacts and are more similar to the teacher in various semantic features such as the face color, haircut and expression.

Image Editing. We demonstrate an image editing case in Fig. 5. Specifically, we apply style mixing and interpolation to the image. The implementation details and more results are shown in the supplementary material.

Fig. 5. In coarse style mixing, our result corresponds better with source B on the mouth and face shape. In fine style mixing, our result corresponds better with source B on skin color. CAGAN also generates artifacts on hair in middle and fine style cases.

5 Conclusion

In this paper, we uncover the output discrepancy issue in uncGAN distillation. Through comparative experiments, we find that the mapping network is the key to the output discrepancy and propose a novel initialization strategy of student, which can help resolve the output discrepancy issue. The proposed latent-direction-based distillation loss further improves the distillation efficacy and we achieve state-of-the-art results in StyleGAN2/3 distillation, outperforming the rival method by a large margin on image realism, latent space smoothness and image projection fidelity.

Limitations. The computation and memory footprint of our method are larger than previous methods because it needs to compute the similarity between the original batch and transformed batch. Besides, we only consider the output discrepancy issue in unconditional GANs. In fact, this problem also exists in conditional setting when the condition is not strong enough (e.g., the conditional input is the class label). How to analyze the output discrepancy issues of uncGANs and cGANs in a more general form is also a direction worth exploring.

Acknowledgement. This study is supported under the RIE2020 Industry Alignment Fund Industry Collaboration Projects (IAF-ICP) Funding Initiative, as well as cash and in-kind contribution from the industry partner(s). It is also supported by Singapore MOE AcRF Tier 2 (MOE-T2EP20120-0001).

References

1. Aguinaldo, A., Chiang, P.Y., Gain, A., Patil, A., Pearson, K., Feizi, S.: Compressing GANS using knowledge distillation. arxiv:1902.00159 (2019)
2. Alaluf, Y., Patashnik, O., Cohen-Or, D.: Restyle: a residual-based stylegan encoder via iterative refinement. In: ICCV, pp. 6711–6720 (2021)
3. Belousov, S.: Mobilestylegan: a lightweight convolutional neural network for high-fidelity image synthesis (2021)
4. Buciluundefined, C., Caruana, R., Niculescu-Mizil, A.: Model compression. In: Proceedings of the 12th ACM SIGKDD International Conference on Knowledge Discovery and Data Mining (2006)
5. Chang, T.Y., Lu, C.J.: Tinygan: distilling biggan for conditional image generation. In: The Asian Conference on Computer Vision (ACCV) (2020)
6. Chen, H., et al.: Distilling portable generative adversarial networks for image translation. arXiv:2003.03519 (2020)
7. He, Y., Kang, G., Dong, X., Fu, Y., Yang, Y.: Soft filter pruning for accelerating deep convolutional neural networks. arXiv:1808.06866 (2018)
8. Heo, B., Kim, J., Yun, S., Park, H., Kwak, N., Choi, J.Y.: A comprehensive overhaul of feature distillation. In: The IEEE International Conference on Computer Vision (ICCV), pp. 1921–1930 (2019)
9. Hinton, G., Vinyals, O., Dean, J.: Distilling the knowledge in a neural network. In: NIPS Deep Learning and Representation Learning Workshop (2015)
10. Hou, L., Yuan, Z., Huang, L., Shen, H., Cheng, X., Wang, C.: Slimmable generative adversarial networks. In: Proceedings of the AAAI Conference on Artificial Intelligence, vol. 35, pp. 7746–7753 (2021)

11. Hou, Y., Ma, Z., Liu, C., Loy, C.C.: Learning lightweight lane detection CNNS by self attention distillation. In: The IEEE International Conference on Computer Vision (ICCV), pp. 1013–1021 (2019)
12. Hu, H., Peng, R., Tai, Y.W., Tang, C.K.: Network trimming: a data-driven neuron pruning approach towards efficient deep architectures. arXiv:1607.03250 (2016)
13. Huang, X., Belongie, S.: Arbitrary style transfer in real-time with adaptive instance normalization. In: The IEEE International Conference on Computer Vision (ICCV), pp. 1501–1510 (2017)
14. Härkönen, E., Hertzmann, A., Lehtinen, J., Paris, S.: Ganspace: discovering interpretable GAN controls. Proc. NeurIPS, **33**, 9841–9850 (2020)
15. Isola, P., Zhu, J.Y., Zhou, T., Efros, A.A.: Image-to-image translation with conditional adversarial networks. In: IEEE Conference on Computer Vision and Pattern Recognition (CVPR), pp. 1125–1134 (2017)
16. Karras, T., Aila, T., Laine, S., Lehtinen, J.: Progressive growing of gans for improved quality, stability, and variation. arXiv:1710.10196 (2018)
17. Karras, T., et al.: Alias-free generative adversarial networks. In: Proc. NeurIPS (2021)
18. Karras, T., Laine, S., Aila, T.: A style-based generator architecture for generative adversarial networks. In: IEEE Conference on Computer Vision and Pattern Recognition (CVPR), pp. 4401–4410 (2019)
19. Karras, T., Laine, S., Aittala, M., Hellsten, J., Lehtinen, J., Aila, T.: Analyzing and improving the image quality of StyleGAN. In: IEEE Conference on Computer Vision and Pattern Recognition (CVPR), pp. pp. 8110–8119 (2020)
20. Lang, Oet al.: Explaining in style: training a gan to explain a classifier in stylespace. arXiv:2104.13369 (2021)
21. Li, H., Kadav, A., Durdanovic, I., Samet, H., Graf, H.P.: Pruning filters for efficient convnets. arXiv:1608.08710 (2017)
22. Li, M., Lin, J., Ding, Y., Liu, Z., Zhu, J.Y., Han, S.: Gan compression: efficient architectures for interactive conditional Gans. In: IEEE Conference on Computer Vision and Pattern Recognition (CVPR), pp. 5284–5294 (2020)
23. Liu, Y., Shu, Z., Li, Y., Lin, Z., Perazzi, F., Kung, S.Y.: Content-aware gan compression. In: IEEE Conference on Computer Vision and Pattern Recognition (CVPR) , pp. 12156–12166 (2021)
24. Peebles, W., Peebles, J., Zhu, J.-Y., Efros, A., Torralba, A.: The hessian penalty: a weak prior for unsupervised disentanglement. In: Vedaldi, A., Bischof, H., Brox, T., Frahm, J.-M. (eds.) ECCV 2020. LNCS, vol. 12351, pp. 581–597. Springer, Cham (2020). https://doi.org/10.1007/978-3-030-58539-6_35
25. Peng, B., et al.: Correlation congruence for knowledge distillation. In: The IEEE International Conference on Computer Vision (ICCV), pp. 5007–5016 (2019)
26. Romero, A., Ballas, N., Kahou, S.E., Chassang, A., Gatta, C., Bengio, Y.: Fitnets: Hints for thin deep nets. arXiv:1412.6550 (2014)
27. Shen, Y., Zhou, B.: Closed-form factorization of latent semantics in gans. In: CVPR, pp. 1532–1540 (2021)
28. Shu, H., et al.: Co-evolutionary compression for unpaired image translation. In: The IEEE International Conference on Computer Vision (ICCV), pp. 3235–3244 (2019)
29. Tian, Y., Krishnan, D., Isola, P.: Contrastive representation distillation. In: International Conference on Learning Representations (ICLR) (2020)
30. Tung, F., Mori, G.: Similarity-preserving knowledge distillation. In: The IEEE International Conference on Computer Vision (ICCV), pp. 1365–1374 (2019)

31. Voynov, A., Babenko, A.: Unsupervised discovery of interpretable directions in the gan latent space. arxiv:2002.03754 (2020)
32. Wang, H., Gui, S., Yang, H., Liu, J., Wang, Z.: GAN slimming: all-in-one GAN compression by a unified optimization framework. In: Vedaldi, A., Bischof, H., Brox, T., Frahm, J.-M. (eds.) ECCV 2020. LNCS, vol. 12349, pp. 54–73. Springer, Cham (2020). https://doi.org/10.1007/978-3-030-58548-8_4
33. Wang, T., Zhang, Y., Fan, Y., Wang, J., Chen, Q.: High-fidelity Gan inversion for image attribute editing. arxiv:2109.06590 (2021)
34. Wu, Z., Nitzan, Y., Shechtman, E., Lischinski, D.: Stylealign: analysis and applications of aligned stylegan models. arxiv:2110.11323 (2021)
35. Xu, G., Liu, Z., Li, X., Loy, C.C.: Knowledge distillation meets self-supervision. In: Vedaldi, A., Bischof, H., Brox, T., Frahm, J.-M. (eds.) ECCV 2020. LNCS, vol. 12354, pp. 588–604. Springer, Cham (2020). https://doi.org/10.1007/978-3-030-58545-7_34
36. Yim, J., Joo, D., Bae, J., Kim, J.: A gift from knowledge distillation: fast optimization, network minimization and transfer learning. In: IEEE Conference on Computer Vision and Pattern Recognition (CVPR), pp. 4133–4141 (2017)
37. Yu, F., Seff, A., Zhang, Y., Song, S., Funkhouser, T., Xiao, J.: LSUN: construction of a large-scale image dataset using deep learning with humans in the loop. arXiv:1506.03365 (2016)
38. Zagoruyko, S., Komodakis, N.: Paying more attention to attention: improving the performance of convolutional neural networks via attention transfer. In: International Conference on Learning Representations (ICLR) (2017)
39. Zhang, R., Isola, P., Efros, A.A., Shechtman, E., Wang, O.: The unreasonable effectiveness of deep features as a perceptual metric. In: IEEE Conference on Computer Vision and Pattern Recognition (CVPR), pp. pp. 586–595 (2018)
40. Zhu, J.Y., Park, T., Isola, P., Efros, A.A.: Unpaired image-to-image translation using cycle-consistent adversarial networkss. In: The IEEE International Conference on Computer Vision (ICCV), pp. 2223–2232 (2017)

Improving Test-Time Adaptation Via Shift-Agnostic Weight Regularization and Nearest Source Prototypes

Sungha Choi(✉), Seunghan Yang, Seokeon Choi, and Sungrack Yun

Qualcomm AI Research, Seoul, South Korea
{sunghac,seunghan,seokchoi,sungrack}@qti.qualcomm.com

Abstract. This paper proposes a novel test-time adaptation strategy that adjusts the model pre-trained on the source domain using only unlabeled online data from the target domain to alleviate the performance degradation due to the distribution shift between the source and target domains. Adapting the entire model parameters using the unlabeled online data may be detrimental due to the erroneous signals from an unsupervised objective. To mitigate this problem, we propose a shift-agnostic weight regularization that encourages largely updating the model parameters sensitive to distribution shift while slightly updating those insensitive to the shift, during test-time adaptation. This regularization enables the model to quickly adapt to the target domain without performance degradation by utilizing the benefit of a high learning rate. In addition, we present an auxiliary task based on nearest source prototypes to align the source and target features, which helps reduce the distribution shift and leads to further performance improvement. We show that our method exhibits state-of-the-art performance on various standard benchmarks and even outperforms its supervised counterpart.

Keywords: Test-Time adaptation · Domain generalization · Source-free domain adaptation · On-Device AI

1 Introduction

After deep neural networks (DNNs) trained on a given dataset (*i.e.,* source domain) are deployed to a new environment (*i.e.,* target domain), the DNNs make predictions from the data in the target domain. However, in most cases, the distribution of the source and target domains varies significantly, which degrades the model's performance in the target domain. If the deployed model does not remain stationary during test time but adapts to the new environment using clues about unlabeled target data, its performance can be improved [25,38,39,42,52,59,63,66].

Qualcomm AI Research is an initiative of Qualcomm Technologies, Inc.

Supplementary Information The online version contains supplementary material available at https://doi.org/10.1007/978-3-031-19827-4_26.

S. Avidan et al. (Eds.): ECCV 2022, LNCS 13693, pp. 440–458, 2022.
https://doi.org/10.1007/978-3-031-19827-4_26

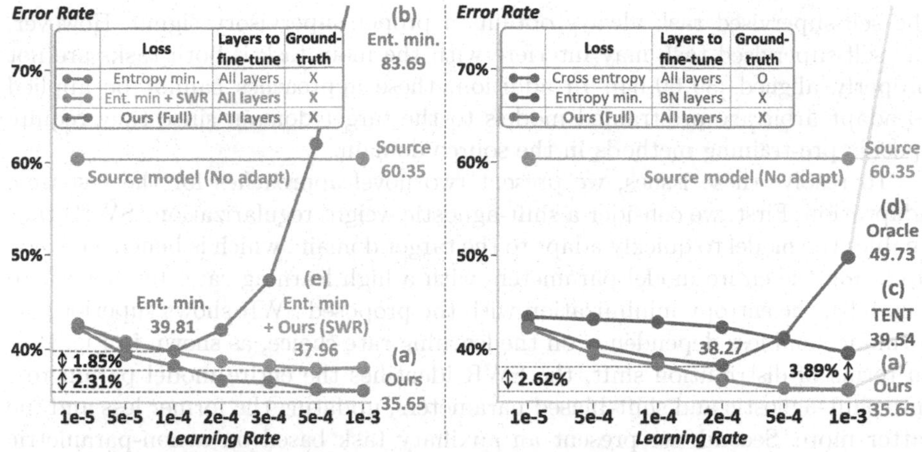

Fig. 1. Comparison of average error (%) between our approach and other methods with varying learning rates on CIFAR-100-C [20]. The x- and y-axes are the learning rate and average error rate, respectively. (a) Our method significantly outperforms the other three methods: (b) updating the entire parameters with only entropy minimization, (c) the state-of-the-art method, TENT [59], and (d) a supervised method. (e) Our proposed SWR keeps the performance stable with the combining of entropy minimization even at higher learning rates: [1e-3, 1e-4].

Recently, several studies [25,42,59,63] have proposed test-time adaptation to update the model during test time after model deployment. However, it is extremely challenging to adapt the model to the target domain with only unlabeled online data. As shown in Fig. 1(b), the adaptation of the entire model parameters may be detrimental due to the erroneous signals from the unsupervised objective such as entropy minimization [15,26,40,57,59], and the performance may be highly dependent on the learning rate. In addition, since the test-time adaptation can access unlabeled target data only once, and the adaptation proceeds simultaneously with the evaluation, updating all network parameters may result in overfitting [17,62]. Thus, several approaches present the methods to update only some part of the network architecture [25,42,59,63] such as batch normalization [24] or classifier layers. Especially, T3A [25] proposes an optimization-free method to adapt only the classifier layers using unlabeled target data, and TENT [59] updates batch statistics and affine parameters in the batch normalization layers by entropy minimization on unlabeled target data. However, updating only partial parameters or layers of the model may only result in marginal performance improvement, as shown in Fig. 1(c). Furthermore, such methods cannot be applied to the model architecture without a specific layer such as batch normalization or classifier layers.

Other approaches [39,52] propose to jointly optimize a main task[1] and a self-supervised task, such as rotation prediction [13] or instance discrimination [6,18], during pre-training in the source domain, and then update the model using only the self-supervised task during test time. In contrast to the unsupervised objective for the main task that highly depends on the model's prediction accuracy,

[1] refers to the ultimate objective of the model (*e.g.,* classification).

the self-supervised task always obtains a proper supervisory signal. However, the self-supervised task may interfere with the main task if both tasks are not properly aligned [39,50,64]. In addition, these approaches cannot be applied to adapt arbitrary pre-trained models to the target domain since they require specific pre-training methods in the source domain.

To resolve these issues, we present two novel approaches for the test-time adaptation. First, we consider a shift-agnostic weight regularization (SWR) that enables the model to quickly adapt to the target domain, which is beneficial when updating the entire model parameters with a high learning rate. In contrast to Fig. 1(b), the entropy minimization with the proposed SWR shows superior performance and less dependency on the learning rate choice, as shown in Fig. 1(e). In terms of distribution shift, the SWR identifies the entire model parameters into shift-agnostic and shift-biased parameters, updating the former less and the latter more. Second, we present an auxiliary task based on a non-parametric nearest source prototype (NSP) classifier, which pulls the target representation closer to its nearest source prototype. With the NSP classifier, both source and target representations can be well aligned, which significantly improves the performance of the main task. Our proposed method (Fig. 1(a)) outperforms the state-of-the-art method [59] (Fig. 1(c)) and even the supervised method using ground-truth labels (Fig. 1(d)).

Our method requires access to the source data to identify shift-agnostic and biased parameters and generate source prototypes before the model deployment, but it is applicable to any model regardless of its architecture or pre-training procedure. If a given model is pre-trained on open datasets, or if the source data owner deploys the model, source data is accessible before model deployment. In this case, our method significantly enhances the test-time adaptation capability by leveraging the source data without modifying the pre-trained model. Unlike TTT [52] and TTT++ [39], we do not change the pre-training method of a given model, so our method can take benefit from any pre-trained strong models, such as AugMix [21] (Table 1) or CORAL [51] (Table 6), as a good starting point for test-time adaptation. In these respects, we believe our method is practical.

The major contributions of this paper can be summarized as follows

- Two novel approaches for test-time adaptation are presented in this paper. The proposed SWR enables the model to quickly and reliably adapt to the target domain, and the NSP classifier aligns the source and target features to reduce the distribution shift, leading to further performance improvement.
- Our test-time adaptation method is model-agnostic and not dependent on the pre-training method in the source domain, and thus it can be applied to any pre-trained model. Therefore, our method can also complement other domain generalization approaches that mainly focus on the pre-training method in the source domain before model deployment.
- We show that our method achieves state-of-the-art performance through extensive experiments on CIFAR-10-C, CIFAR-100-C, ImageNet-C [20] and domain generalization benchmarks including PACS [31], OfficeHome [55], VLCS [10], and TerraIncognita [5]. Especially, our method even outperforms its supervised counterpart on CIFAR-100-C dataset.

2 Related Work

2.1 Source-Free Domain Adaptation

Unsupervised domain adaptation (UDA) [11,12,22,46,51,53,57] assumes simultaneous access to both the source and target domains. Data is often distributed across multiple devices. In such cases, UDA requires data sharing for simultaneous access to all data. However, it is often impossible due to data privacy concerns, limited bandwidth, and computational cost. Source-free domain adaptation [1,30,36,38, 58,60,61] overcomes this challenge by adapting a source pre-trained model to the target domain using only unlabeled target data. These approaches focus on offline adaptation in which the same target sample is fed to the model multiple times during target adaptation, whereas our method concentrates on online adaptation.

2.2 Test-Time Adaptation and Training

Test-time adaptation focuses on online adaptation in which all target data can be accessed only once at test time, and adaptation is performed simultaneously with evaluation. More specifically, it forward propagates target samples through the model for evaluation and then backpropagates the error signal from the model's output in an unsupervised manner for training [59]. Several studies adopt self-supervised learning, such as rotation prediction [52] or instance discrimination [39], to jointly optimize the main and self-supervised tasks on the source domain and then optimize only the self-supervised task on the target domain. However, these methods are not universally applicable to arbitrary pre-trained models as they require specific pre-training methods in the source domain. Recently, model-agnostic test-time adaptation methods independent of the pre-training method in the source domain have been proposed [25,42,59,63]. TENT [59] uses the batch statistics of the target domain and optimizes channel-wise affine parameters using entropy minimization loss. T3A [25] proposes an optimization-free method that adjusts a pre-trained linear classifier by updating the prototype for each class during test time. However, since these methods update only partial parameters or layers of the model, such as the batch normalization [42,59,63] or classifier layer [25], they may be suboptimal for target adaptation.

2.3 Domain Generalization

Since UDA aims to adapt the model to the predefined target domain before model deployment, it is not suitable to guarantee generalization performance to other arbitrary target domains. On the other hand, domain generalization (DG) differs from UDA in that it assumes that the model accesses only the source domain during training time before model deployment and aims to improve the generalization capability in arbitrary unseen target domains. Numerous DG approaches using meta-learning [3,32,33], normalization [7,8,44,47], adversarial training [34,37,45], and data augmentation [14,35,56,67] have been proposed to learn domain-agnostic feature representations for the target domain. However, these studies only focus on methods at training time before model deployment, whereas our method focuses on a test-time adaptation after model deployment.

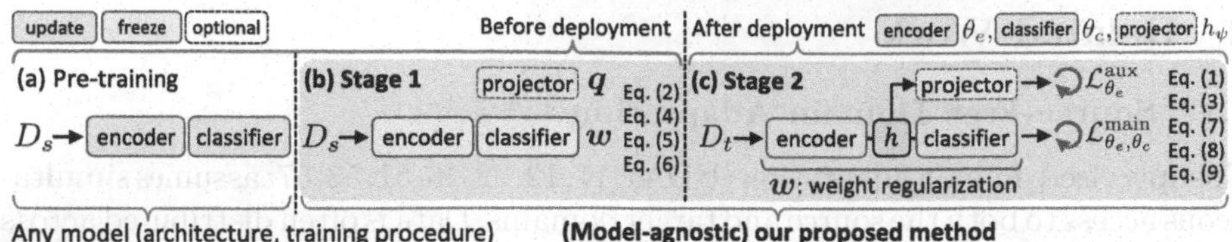

Fig. 2. Our method consists of two stages: (b) and (c). (a) our method takes the pre-trained model in an off-the-shelf manner and (b) generates penalty vector $\boldsymbol{w}$ and source prototypes $\boldsymbol{q}$ while keeping the model *frozen* before model deployment. After model deployment, (c) our method does not access labeled source data D_s other than unlabeled online target data D_t during test-time adaptation.

3 Proposed Method

Assume that the model parameters θ trained on the source domain consist of an encoder part θ_e and a classifier part θ_c, as shown in Fig. 2(c). After being deployed to the target domain, the model infers the class probability distribution of the target sample and then optimizes our proposed test-time adaptation loss $\mathcal{L}^{\text{target}}_{\theta_e,\theta_c}$. The overall loss of our proposed method is defined as

$$\mathcal{L}^{\text{target}}_{\theta_e,\theta_c} = \mathcal{L}^{\text{main}}_{\theta_e,\theta_c} + \mathcal{L}^{\text{aux}}_{\theta_e} + \lambda_r \sum_l w_l \|\boldsymbol{\theta}_l - \boldsymbol{\theta}^*_l\|_2^2, \tag{1}$$

where w_l denotes the l-th element of the penalty vector $\boldsymbol{w}$ used to control the update of the model parameters, $\boldsymbol{\theta}_l$ is the parameter vector of the l-th layer[2] of the model, $\boldsymbol{\theta}^*$ is the parameters from the previous update step, λ_r is the importance of the regularization term, and $\mathcal{L}^{\text{main}}_{\theta_e,\theta_c}$ and $\mathcal{L}^{\text{aux}}_{\theta_e}$ denote the main and auxiliary task losses, respectively. Optimizing the main task loss updates the entire model parameters θ_e and θ_c, whereas optimizing the auxiliary task loss updates only the encoder part θ_e. We first present a shift-agnostic weight regularization (SWR) and then describe an entropy objective of the main task. Finally, we propose an auxiliary task based on a nearest source prototype (NSP) classifier, which directly benefits the main task.

3.1 Shift-Agnostic Weight Regularization

The main idea of the SWR is to impose different penalties for each parameter update during test-time adaptation, depending on the sensitivity of each model parameter to the distribution shift. Assuming that the distribution shift is mainly caused by color and blur shifts, we mimic the distribution shift using transformation techniques such as color distortion and Gaussian blur. Experiments on variations of the SWR, including the use of other transform functions, can be found in the supplementary Section B.

[2] denotes a part divided into torch.nn.Module units defined in Pytorch. The gradient vector of each layer can be easily obtained using torch.nn.module.parameters().

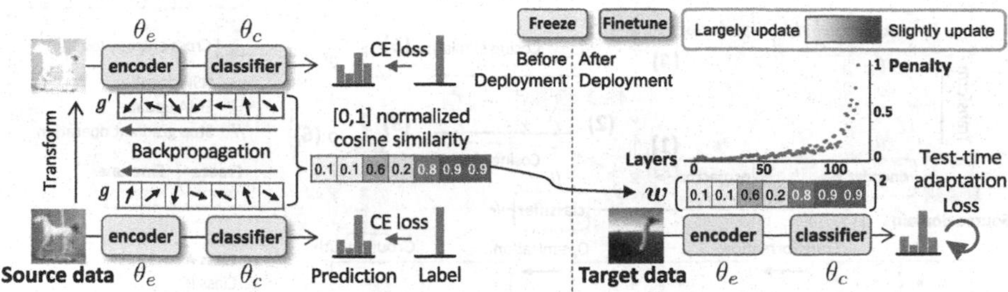

Fig. 3. Overall process of our proposed SWR. We first obtain the penalty vector $\boldsymbol{w}$ before model deployment and then use it as layer-wise penalties to control the update of the model parameters at test-time adaptation after model deployment.

To obtain the penalty vector $\boldsymbol{w}$ specified in Eq. (1), we first forward-propagate two input images (i.e., an original and its transformed image) through the pre-trained source model and then back-propagate the task loss (*i.e.*, cross entropy) using the source labels to produce two sets $\boldsymbol{g}$ and $\boldsymbol{g}'$ of L gradient vectors, respectively. Note that L is the total number of layers in the model. Then the l-th element w_l of the penalty vector $\boldsymbol{w}$ is calculated by employing the average cosine similarity s_l between two gradient vectors, $\boldsymbol{g}_l$ and $\boldsymbol{g}'_l$ from N source samples as

$$\begin{aligned} s_l &= \frac{1}{N}\sum_{i=1}^{N}\frac{\boldsymbol{g}_l^i \cdot \boldsymbol{g}_l'^i}{\|\boldsymbol{g}_l^i\|\|\boldsymbol{g}_l'^i\|} \in \mathbb{R}, \\ \boldsymbol{w} &= \left(\nu\left[s_1,\ldots,s_l,\ldots,s_L\right]\right)^2 \in \mathbb{R}^L, \end{aligned} \tag{2}$$

where $\nu[\cdot]$ denotes min-max normalization with the range of [0,1], $\boldsymbol{g}_l^i$ and $\boldsymbol{g}_l'^i$ denote the l-th gradient vectors for i-th source sample and its transformed sample, respectively. N denotes the total number of samples. Note that the penalty vector $\boldsymbol{w}$ is obtained from a frozen pre-trained source model before model deployment. Therefore, this process is independent of the source model's pre-training method and does not require source data after model deployment, as shown in Fig. 2.

As shown in Eq. (1) and Fig. 3, during test-time adaptation, we apply the layer-wise penalty value w_l to the difference between previous and current model parameters for each layer, and this controls the update of model parameters differently for each layer. Therefore, the model parameters belonging to the layers with high cosine similarity between the two gradient vectors are considered shift-agnostic, and we less update them by imposing high penalties. Section 4.6 experimentally shows that SWR takes advantage of using high learning rates to adapt the model to the target domain quickly.

3.2 Entropy Objective for the Main Task

The main task of the model f_θ is defined as the task performed by the parameters θ_e and θ_c. The loss function for the main task during test time is built using the entropy of model predictions $\tilde{y}$ on test samples from the target distribution. We adopt information maximization loss [23,27,48], validated in several test-time adaptation and source-free domain adaptation methods [38,42,58], as an

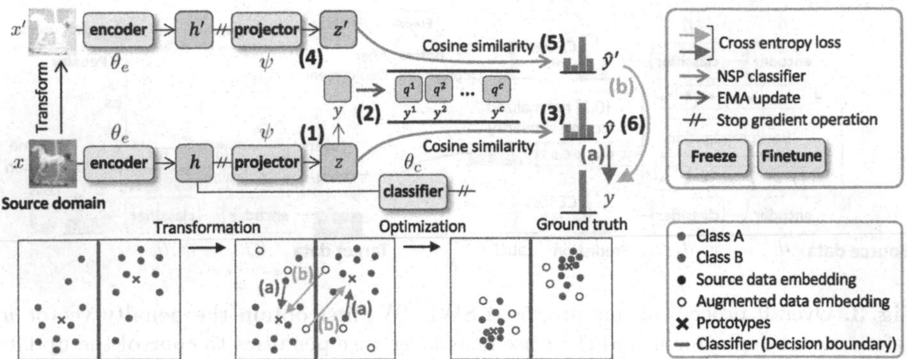

Fig. 4. Source prototype generation phase before model deployment. First, we repeat steps (1) and (2) until prototypes of all classes are generated, then train the projector and update the source prototype at the same time through an iterative process from (1) to (6) on the source data. (a) and (b) pull the original source projection and its transformed source projection, respectively, such that they become closer to the nearest source prototype from the original one.

unsupervised learning objective for the main task. This loss consists of entropy minimization [38,49,57,59] and mean entropy maximization [2,28,38,58] as

$$\mathcal{L}^{\text{main}}_{\theta_e,\theta_c} = \lambda_{m_1}\frac{1}{N}\sum_{i=1}^{N} H(\tilde{y}_i) - \lambda_{m_2}H(\bar{y}), \tag{3}$$

where $H(p) = -\sum_{k=1}^{C} p^k \log p^k$, $\bar{y} = \frac{1}{N}\sum_i \tilde{y}_i$, λ_{m_1} and λ_{m_2} indicate the importance of each term. The number of classes and the batch size are denoted by C and N. Intuitively, entropy minimization makes individual predictions confident, and mean entropy maximization encourages average prediction within a batch to be close to the uniform distribution.

3.3 Auxiliary Task Based on the Nearest Source Prototype

Due to the distribution shift between the source and target domains, the target features deviate from the source features at test time. To resolve this issue, we propose an auxiliary task based on the nearest source prototype (NSP) classifier, which pulls the target embeddings closer to their nearest source prototypes in the embedding space. Eventually, optimizing the auxiliary task improves performance significantly since it directly supports the main task by aligning the source and target representations. We first explain how to generate source prototypes and define the NSP classifier based on them.

Source Prototype Generation. The source prototypes are defined as the averages over source embeddings for each class. As shown in Fig. 4, we freeze the model f_θ trained on the source data and attach an additional projection layer h_ψ behind the encoder f_{θ_e}. The encoder f_{θ_e} infers the representation $\boldsymbol{h}$ from the source sample x, and the projector h_ψ maps $\boldsymbol{h}$ to the projection $\boldsymbol{z}$ in another

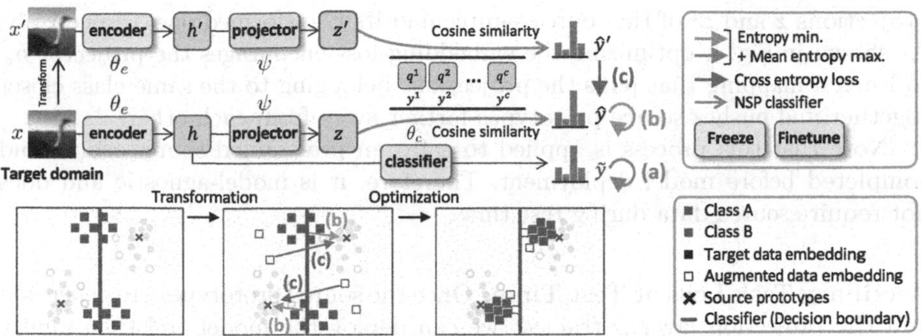

Fig. 5. Test-time adaptation phase after model deployment. (a) main task loss. (b),(c) auxiliary task loss. (b) and (c) pull the original target projection and its transformed target projection, respectively, such that they become closer to the nearest source prototype from the original one.

embedding space where the loss $\mathcal{L}_{\psi}^{\text{emb}}$ is applied as $\boldsymbol{z} = h_{\psi}(f_{\theta_e}(x))$. The source prototype $\boldsymbol{q}_t^k$ for class k is updated through exponential moving average (EMA) with the projection $\boldsymbol{z}_t^k$ of the source sample $(x, y^k)_{k\in[1,\text{C}]}$ at time t during the optimization trajectory as

$$\boldsymbol{q}_t^k = \alpha \cdot \boldsymbol{q}_{t-1}^k + (1-\alpha) \cdot \boldsymbol{z}_t^k, \tag{4}$$

where α=0.99 and $\boldsymbol{q}_0^k = \boldsymbol{z}_0^k$.

We define the NSP classifier as a non-parametric classifier. It measures the cosine similarity of a given target embedding to the source prototypes for all classes and then generates a class probability distribution $\hat{y}$ as

$$\hat{y} = \sum_{k=1}^{C} \left(\frac{\exp\left(S(\boldsymbol{z}, \boldsymbol{q}^k)/\tau\right)}{\sum_{j=1}^{C} \exp\left(S(\boldsymbol{z}, \boldsymbol{q}^j)/\tau\right)} \right) y^k, \tag{5}$$

where $S(\cdot,\cdot)$ is a cosine similarity function, $S(\boldsymbol{a}, \boldsymbol{b}) = (\boldsymbol{a} \cdot \boldsymbol{b})/\|\boldsymbol{a}\|\|\boldsymbol{b}\|$, τ denotes a temperature that controls the sharpness of the distribution, and y^k is the one-hot ground-truth label vector of k-th class.

In addition, inspired by recent self-supervised contrastive learning methods [4,6,18], we enable the projector h_{ψ} to learn transformation-invariant mapping. We obtain projection $\boldsymbol{z}'$ of the transformed source sample by $\boldsymbol{z}' = h_{\psi}(f_{\theta_e}(\mathcal{T}(x)))$, where $\mathcal{T}(\cdot)$ denotes an image transform function. The embedding loss $\mathcal{L}_{\psi}^{\text{emb}}$ consisting of two cross entropy loss terms is applied to the embedding space to train the projector h_{ψ} as

$$\mathcal{L}_{\psi}^{\text{emb}} = \frac{1}{N} \sum_{i=1}^{N} \left(\text{CE}\left(y_i, \hat{y}_i\right) + \text{CE}\left(y_i, \hat{y}_i'\right)\right), \tag{6}$$

where $\text{CE}(p, q) = -\sum_{k=1}^{C} p^k \log q^k$, and y_i is the ground-truth label of i-th source sample. Here, $\hat{y}$ and $\hat{y}'$ denote the outputs of the NSP classifier for the projections $\boldsymbol{z}$ and $\boldsymbol{z}'$ of the source sample and its transformed one, respectively. As shown in Fig. 4, optimizing the embedding loss encourages the projector h_ψ to learn a mapping that pulls the projections belonging to the same class closer together and pushes source prototypes farther away from each other.

Note that this process is applied to a frozen pre-trained source model and completed before model deployment. Therefore, it is model-agnostic and does not require source data during test time.

Auxiliary Task Loss at Test Time. Once the source prototypes are generated and the projection layer is trained, we can deploy the model and then jointly optimize both main and auxiliary tasks on unlabeled online data. The auxiliary task loss $\mathcal{L}_{\theta_e}^{\text{aux}}$ consists of two objective functions: the entropy objective $\mathcal{L}_{\theta_e}^{\text{aux\_ent}}$ using the entropy of the NSP classifier's prediction $\hat{y}$, and the self-supervised loss $\mathcal{L}_{\theta_e}^{\text{aux\_sel}}$ that encourages the model's encoder f_{θ_e} to learn transformation-invariant mappings as

$$\mathcal{L}_{\theta_e}^{\text{aux}} = \mathcal{L}_{\theta_e}^{\text{aux\_ent}} + \lambda_s \mathcal{L}_{\theta_e}^{\text{aux\_sel}}, \tag{7}$$

where λ_s denotes the importance of the self-supervised loss term. Similarly to Eq. (3), the entropy objective is built by using the entropy of the prediction $\hat{y}$ of the NSP classifier on the target sample as

$$\mathcal{L}_{\theta_e}^{\text{aux\_ent}} = \lambda_{a_1} \frac{1}{N} \sum_{i=1}^{N} H(\hat{y}_i) - \lambda_{a_2} H(\bar{y}), \tag{8}$$

where N is batch size, λ_{a_1} and λ_{a_2} indicate the importance of each term, $H(p) = -\sum_{k=1}^{C} p^k \log p^k$, and $\bar{y} = \frac{1}{N}\sum_{i=1}^{N} \hat{y}_i$. The self-supervised loss is applied to the prediction $\hat{y}'$ of the NSP classifier on the transformed target sample as

$$\mathcal{L}_{\theta_e}^{\text{aux\_sel}} = -\frac{1}{N} \sum_{i=1}^{N} \sum_{k=1}^{C} \hat{y}_i^k \log \hat{y}_i'^k. \tag{9}$$

As shown in Fig. 5, the entropy objective function (Fig. 5(b)) pulls the projection $\boldsymbol{z}$ of the target sample to move closer to its nearest source prototype, and the self-supervised objective (Fig. 5(c)) encourages the projection $\boldsymbol{z}'$ of the transformed target sample to get closer to the same target as $\boldsymbol{z}$.

4 Experiments

This section describes the experimental setup, implementation details, and the experimental results of the comparisons with other state-of-the-art methods in test-time adaptation. We also show that generalization performance can be further improved by combining our proposed method with an existing domain generalization strategy that mainly focuses on training time in the source domain.

4.1 Experimental Setup

Following TENT [59] and T3A [25], all experiments in this paper are conducted on the online adaptation setting, where adaptation is performed concurrently with evaluation at test time without seeing the same data twice or more. After a prediction is obtained, the model is updated via back-propagation. We evaluate our proposed method on **CIFAR-10-C**, **CIFAR-100-C**, **ImageNet-C**[3] [20] and four domain generalization benchmarks such as **PACS** [31], **Office-Home** [55], **VLCS** [10], and **TerraIncognita** [5]. Since our method can be used independently of the backbone networks and its pre-training method, we apply our method to publicly available pre-trained models for evaluation. We perform experiments on CIFAR datasets using WideResNet-28-10 [65] and WideResNet-40-2 [65] as backbone networks, based on RobustBench [9]. In the domain generalization setup, we use ResNet-50 [19] without the batch normalization layer, which is the default setting of DomainBed [16], DG benchmark framework. CIFAR-10/100 dataset [29] contains 50k images for training and 10k images for testing. Corruptions such as noise, blur, weather, and digital are applied to 10k images from CIFAR-10/100 test set to create CIFAR-10/100-C test images. For test-time adaptation, 50k images for CIFAR training set are defined as the source domain, and 10k images for CIFAR-C test set are defined as the target domain.

4.2 Implementation Details

We integrate our proposed method within the frameworks officially provided by other state-of-the-art methods [25,39,59] for fair comparisons. Specifically, different frameworks are used for each experiment as follows: TENT framework [59] for all experiments with WRN-40-2 and WRN-28-10 backbone networks on CIFAR-10/100-C, TTT++ framework [39] for all experiments with ResNet-50 on CIFAR-10/100-C, and T3A framework [25] for all domain generalization benchmarks. For experiments on CIFAR, we follow the default values provided by each framework for experimental settings such as batch size and optimizer.

Color distortion, random grayscale and Gaussian blurring are used as the image transformations specified in Fig. 3 and Fig. 5, and random cropping and random horizontal flipping are additionally applied for the image transformations in Fig. 4. We use batch statistics on test data instead of using running estimates. The hyper-parameters are empirically set as λ_{m_1}=0.2, λ_{a_1}=0.8 λ_{m_2}=0.25, λ_{a_2}=0.25, λ_s=0.1, λ_r=250, and softmax temperature τ=0.1. The epoch for training the projector is 20, and N=1024 in Eq. (2). Since these hyper-parameters are not sensitive to the backbone and datasets, they are fixed without individual tuning in most experiments in this paper unless noted otherwise. The projector as described in Sect. 3.3 can be configured as a single- or multi-layer perceptron (MLP). The MLP consists of a linear layer followed by batch normalization [24], ReLU [43], and a final linear layer with output dimension 512. The performance change according to the projector configuration is shown in Table 3, and the detailed architecture is described in the supplementary Section C.

[3] Experiments on ImageNet-C are in the supplementary Section B.

4.3 Robustness Against Image Corruptions

Table 1(a) shows a comparison of the robustness between our method and recent test-time adaptation methods for the most severe corruptions on CIFAR-100-C. TFA [39] and TTT++ [39] were originally implemented as offline adaptation methods that train a model by observing the same data multiple times across numerous epochs, so we change these methods to the online adaptation setting to reproduce the results. Our proposed method significantly outperforms other state-of-the-art methods with large margins of 3.89% for ResNet-50 and 2.59% for WRN-40-2. Table 1(b) shows the results on the most severe corruptions of CIFAR-10-C. Our method consistently outperforms other methods on CIFAR-10/100-C datasets across various backbone networks. In particular, WRN-40-2,

Table 1. Comparison with other methods. * denotes the reported results from the original paper, and the others are reproduced values in our environment based on the official framework provided by TENT [59] and TTT++ [39]. Source denotes the source pre-trained model without test-time adaptation.

(a) Comparison of error rate (%) on CIFAR-100-C with severity level 5

Backbone	Methods	Avg. err	Gaus.	Shot	Impu.	Defo.	Glas.	Moti.	Zoom	Snow	Fros.	Fog	Brig.	Cont.	Elas.	Pixe.	Jpeg
WRN-40-2 (AugMix) [21,65]	Source	46.75	65.7	60.1	59.1	32.0	51.0	33.6	32.3	41.4	45.2	51.4	31.6	55.5	40.3	59.7	42.4
	TENT [59]	35.53	40.1	39.5	42.0	29.6	41.9	30.7	29.7	34.5	34.8	39.1	27.5	32.9	37.6	32.8	40.3
	Core* [63]	35.30	39.8	39.3	41.5	29.5	41.7	30.6	29.8	34.2	34.9	38.6	27.5	32.6	37.1	32.7	40.1
	Ours	**32.71**	**37.6**	**36.6**	**35.1**	**28.0**	**39.5**	**28.7**	**28.5**	**31.3**	**32.6**	**34.4**	**26.3**	**29.0**	**35.5**	**30.1**	**37.7**
ResNet-50 [19]	Source	60.35	80.8	77.8	87.8	39.6	82.3	54.2	38.4	54.6	60.2	68.1	28.9	50.9	59.5	72.3	50.0
	SHOT [38]	43.53	49.0	47.1	61.2	33.8	58.3	41.0	31.3	45.0	42.0	52.0	29.7	33.4	47.9	41.8	39.4
	TFA [39]	44.13	49.0	47.0	61.4	34.2	58.9	41.5	32.1	46.8	43.0	54.6	31.2	33.7	48.9	39.8	39.7
	TTT++ [39]	44.38	50.2	47.7	66.1	35.8	61.0	38.7	35.0	44.6	43.8	48.6	28.8	30.8	49.9	39.2	45.5
	TENT [59]	39.54	43.8	42.0	54.1	31.2	51.7	37.0	29.9	42.3	39.6	45.6	30.1	30.9	44.5	34.2	36.4
	Ours	**35.65**	**40.0**	**38.4**	**46.3**	**29.3**	**46.0**	**32.5**	**27.9**	**37.3**	**36.6**	**37.3**	**27.5**	**28.8**	**41.0**	**31.4**	**34.7**

(b) Comparison of error rate (%) on CIFAR-10-C with severity level 5

Backbone	Methods	Avg. err	Gaus.	Shot	Impu.	Defo.	Glas.	Moti.	Zoom	Snow	Fros.	Fog	Brig.	Cont.	Elas.	Pixe.	Jpeg
WRN-40-2 (AugMix) [21,65]	Source	18.27	28.8	23.0	26.2	9.5	20.6	10.6	9.3	14.2	15.3	17.5	7.6	20.9	14.7	41.3	14.7
	TENT [59]	12.08	15.6	13.2	18.8	7.9	18.2	9.0	8.0	10.4	10.9	12.4	6.7	10.0	14.0	11.4	14.8
	Ours	**10.37**	**13.1**	**11.4**	**14.7**	**7.4**	**15.8**	**8.3**	**7.4**	**9.2**	**9.4**	**9.5**	**6.3**	**7.8**	**13.1**	**9.4**	**12.9**
WRN-28-10 [65]	Source	43.51	72.3	65.7	72.9	49.9	54.3	34.8	42.0	25.1	41.3	26.0	9.3	46.7	26.6	58.5	30.3
	TENT [59]	18.58	24.8	23.5	33.1	11.9	31.8	13.7	10.8	15.9	16.2	13.7	7.9	12.0	22.0	17.3	24.2
	Core* [63]	16.80	22.5	20.3	29.8	11.0	29.2	12.3	**10.2**	14.4	14.8	12.4	7.7	10.6	20.4	15.3	21.4
	Ours	**15.70**	**20.1**	**18.4**	**26.2**	**10.8**	**28.9**	**12.1**	**10.2**	**13.7**	**13.9**	**11.1**	**7.6**	**8.8**	**20.2**	**14.2**	**19.4**
ResNet-50 [19]	Source	29.14	48.7	44.0	57.0	11.8	50.8	23.4	10.8	21.9	28.2	29.4	**7.0**	13.13	23.4	47.9	19.5
	SHOT [38]	16.19	20.0	18.8	29.6	9.9	27.1	15.0	8.5	15.4	14.5	19.8	7.3	8.5	18.7	15.8	14.0
	TFA [39]	15.97	18.8	17.9	29.2	9.8	27.3	14.6	8.0	16.0	14.0	20.3	7.8	8.6	19.4	14.1	13.9
	TTT++ [39]	15.82	18.0	17.1	30.8	10.4	29.9	13.0	9.9	14.8	14.1	15.8	**7.0**	7.8	19.3	12.7	16.4
	TENT [59]	14.02	16.0	14.5	24.7	9.1	23.5	12.6	7.6	14.3	13.1	16.8	8.2	8.0	18.1	10.8	13.3
	Ours	**12.52**	**14.1**	**13.4**	**20.9**	**8.3**	**20.7**	**11.2**	**7.3**	**12.4**	**11.7**	**14.4**	7.3	**7.4**	**16.5**	**9.7**	**12.4**

(c) Comparison of average error (%) on CIFAR-100-C with all severity levels

Methods	Backbone	Lv.5		Lv.4		Lv.3		Lv.2		Lv.1	
TENT [59]	ResNet-50	39.54	3.89 ↓	36.09	3.27 ↓	33.35	2.81 ↓	31.30	2.38 ↓	29.62	2.11 ↓
Ours		**35.65**		**32.82**		**30.54**		**28.92**		**27.51**	
TENT [59]	WRN-40-2	35.53	2.82 ↓	32.89	2.40 ↓	30.72	1.87 ↓	29.06	1.53 ↓	27.67	1.29 ↓
Ours		**32.71**		**30.49**		**28.85**		**27.53**		**26.38**	

Table 2. Ablation study on CIFAR-100-C. ResNet-50 is used.

Methods	Learning rate	Average err (%)
Main	1e-3	75.70
Main (optimal learning rate)	1e-4	39.44
Main + **NSP** ($\mathcal{L}_{\theta_e}^{\text{aux\_ent}} + \mathcal{L}_{\theta_e}^{\text{aux\_sel}}$)	1e-4	37.55
Main + **SWR**	1e-3	37.76
Main + **SWR** + **NSP** ($\mathcal{L}_{\theta_e}^{\text{aux\_ent}}$)	1e-3	35.80
Main + **SWR** + **NSP** ($\mathcal{L}_{\theta_e}^{\text{aux\_ent}} + \mathcal{L}_{\theta_e}^{\text{aux\_sel}}$)	1e-3	**35.65**

Table 3. Comparison of error rate (%) according to changes in projector depth.

Datasets	Backbone	Projector depth			
		None	1	2	3
CIFAR-100-C	WRN-40-2	33.04	32.79	**32.71**	32.89
	ResNet-50	36.34	**35.43**	35.65	36.81
CIFAR-10-C	WRN-40-2	**10.37**	10.52	10.42	10.46
	WRN-28-10	**15.70**	16.45	16.09	16.39
	ResNet-50	**12.52**	12.91	12.95	12.87

which is trained with AugMix [21] for a data processing to increase the robustness of the model, outperforms the other backbone networks, and our method further enhances the performance by complementing it. Table 1(c) shows the results on CIFAR-100-C with all severity levels. Because severity denotes the strength of the corruption, it shows how much the distribution shift presents, and our method outperforms TENT [59] at all levels with a large margin.

4.4 Ablation Studies

Table 2 shows the effectiveness of our proposed shift-agnostic weight regularization (SWR) and nearest source prototype (NSP) classifier through ablation studies. At a high learning rate, optimizing only the main task loss based on the entropy of the model prediction results in poor performance, but adjusting the learning rate reduces the error rate to 39.44%. Adding the NSP to the main task loss leads to the performance improvement of 1.89%, and including the SWR improves the performance by 1.68% even at a high learning rate. Our method with both SWR and NSP achieves 35.65% error rate with 3.79% performance enhancement compared to using only the main task loss.

Table 4. Hyper-parameter impacts on CIFAR-100-C. ResNet-50 is used.

(a)

Width	Error (%)
128	36.34
256	35.85
512	**35.65**
1024	36.09

(b)

Transformation	Error (%)
No transform	37.88
Color distortion	35.79
+Crop. & Blur.	**35.65**

(c)

Backbone	Error (%)	
	WRN-40-2	ResNet-50
Freeze.	**32.71**	**35.65**
Finetune.	32.85	35.96

4.5 Projector Design and Hyper-parameter Impacts

Table 3 shows the performance impact of changing the projector depth (*i.e.*, number of projection layer). In addition, we conduct experiments to apply the auxiliary task loss $\mathcal{L}_{\theta_e}^{\text{aux}}$ directly to the feature representation $\boldsymbol{h}$, the encoder's output without using the projector. The model with the projector outperforms the one without the projector on CIFAR-100-C, and opposite results are obtained on CIFAR-10-C. Since the auxiliary task loss is applied to the embedding space based on the cosine similarity between the source prototypes and the target embeddings, its effect may be minimal if they are severely misaligned. To compensate for this issue, we attach and train the projector that minimizes the misalignment between the source and target embeddings by enabling transformation-invariant mapping and bringing the projections belonging to the same class closer together in the new embedding space. However, if the number of classes is small (*e.g.*, CIFAR-10-C), the source and target may already be relatively well aligned compared to the case with a large number of classes (*e.g.*, CIFAR-100-C). In this case, we conjecture that applying the auxiliary task loss directly to the encoder's output $\boldsymbol{h}$ rather than the new embedding space $\boldsymbol{z}$, the projector's output, generates a better-aligned representation $\boldsymbol{h}$ between the source and target, which can be more helpful to the classifier.

Table 4 shows the experimental results according to (a) the projector width (*i.e.*, output dimension of the last layer), (b) the transformation used for training the projector, and (c) whether to fine-tune or freeze the projector during test-time adaptation. Our default settings are marked with gray-colored cells, and these settings are also applied to the domain generalization benchmarks in the following section without additional tuning.

4.6 Quick Adaptation

As shown in Table 5, it is natural that the supervised method performs perfectly when learning and evaluating the same test samples iteratively. However, interestingly our method outperforms the supervised one in an online setting where the test sample is seen only once. Unlike the other methods that require a low learning rate to train (Fig. 1(b),(d)), our method updates the entire parameters

Table 5. Comparison of error rate (%) on CIFAR-100-C. Our method outperforms the supervised method in an online setting. LR denotes a learning rate.

Methods	**GT Label**	**Optimal LR**	**Epoch**		
			1 (online)	**2** (offline)	**3** (offline)
Entropy Minimization	No	1e-4	39.81	38.84	39.08
Cross Entropy (Supervised)	Yes	2e-4	38.27	**7.41**	**0.86**
Ours	No	1e-3	**35.65**	33.34	33.25

at a high learning rate. We conjecture that SWR enables quick convergence without performance degradation because only parameters sensitive to distribution shift (*i.e.*, parameters that need to quickly adapt to a new domain) are largely updated with a high learning rate.

4.7 Domain Generalization Benchmarks

To evaluate our method on the DG benchmarks, we follow the protocol proposed by DomainBed [16] and T3A [25]. Our method is model-agnostic, so we apply it to the pre-trained models using empirical risk minimization (ERM) [54] or CORAL [51] on the source domain in order to adapt the models to the target domain at test time. We use the leave-one-domain-out validation [16] for model selection in all experiments in Table 6. Our methods show state-of-the-art performance on average over four datasets and especially outperform T3A [25] and the source pre-trained models with a large margin on PACS, OfficeHome, and TerraIncognita datasets. The detailed experimental setup can be found in the supplementary Section C.

4.8 Qualitative Results

Figure 6 visualizes the features on CIFAR-10-C using t-SNE [41]. The results in the first row are from WRN-40-2 as a source pre-trained model, and the results in the second row are from ResNet-50. Even without test-time adaptation, WRN-40-2 (AugMix) [21] is more robust against corruptions than ResNet-50, so better results can be obtained. Our method significantly improves the performance in terms of intra-class cohesion and inter-class separation in both backbones.

Table 6. Comparison of accuracy (%) on four DG benchmarks. † denotes the reported results from DomainBed [16], and the others are reproduced values.

Methods	VLCS	PACS	OfficeHome	Terra	Average
ERM†	76.8±1.0	83.3±0.6	67.3±0.3	46.2±0.2	68.4
CORAL†	**77.0**±0.5	**83.6**±0.6	**68.6**±0.2	**48.1**±1.3	69.3
ERM	77.4±0.9	83.5±0.7	65.6±0.4	47.1±1.1	68.4
+T3A	**79.4**±0.4	86.5±0.3	67.8±0.5	45.6±0.7	69.8
+Ours	77.0±0.5	**88.9**±0.1	**69.2**±0.1	**49.5**±0.8	**71.2**
CORAL	77.9±0.9	85.3±0.1	67.8±0.3	44.1±0.4	68.8
+T3A	**79.3**±0.3	86.3±0.2	69.5±0.2	45.4±1.2	70.1
+Ours	78.7±0.4	**89.9**±0.1	**71.0**±0.0	**47.5**±0.6	**71.8**

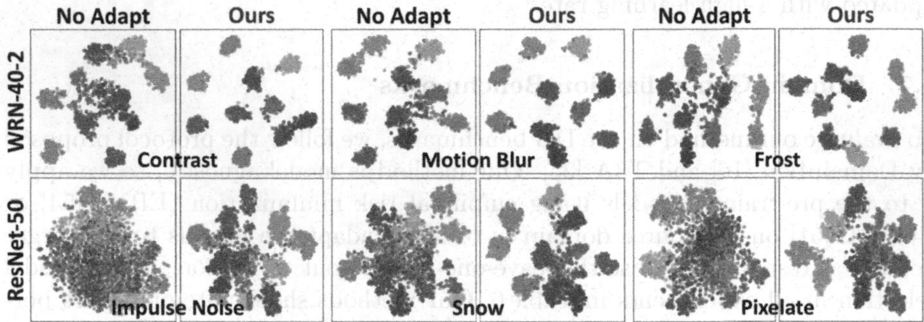

Fig. 6. t-SNE visualization of features from the target domain (CIFAR-10-C).

5 Conclusions

This paper proposed two novel approaches for model-agnostic test-time adaptation. Our proposed shift-agnostic weight regularization enables the model to reliably and quickly adapt to unlabeled online data from the target domain by controlling the update of the model parameters according to their sensitivity to the distribution shift. In addition, our proposed auxiliary task based on the nearest source prototype classifier boosts the performance by aligning the source and target representations. Test-time adaptation is a challenging but promising area in terms of allowing the model to evolve itself while adapting to a new environment without human intervention. In this regard, our efforts aim to promote the importance of this field and stimulate new research directions.

Acknowledgement. We would like to thank Kyuwoong Hwang, Simyung Chang, Hyunsin Park, Juntae Lee, Janghoon Cho, Hyoungwoo Park, Byeonggeun Kim, and Hyesu Lim of the Qualcomm AI Research team for their valuable discussions.

References

1. Agarwal, P., Paudel, D.P., Zaech, J.N., Van Gool, L.: Unsupervised robust domain adaptation without source data. In: IEEE/CVF Winter Conference on Applications of Computer Vision (WACV) (2022)
2. Assran, M., Caron, M., Misra, I., Bojanowski, P., Joulin, A., Ballas, N., Rabbat, M.: Semi-supervised learning of visual features by non-parametrically predicting view assignments with support samples. In: International Conference on Computer Vision (ICCV) (2021)
3. Balaji, Y., Sankaranarayanan, S., Chellappa, R.: Metareg: towards domain generalization using meta-regularization. In: Advances in Neural Information Processing Systems (NeurIPS) (2018)
4. Bardes, A., Ponce, J., LeCun, Y.: VICreg: variance-invariance-covariance regularization for self-supervised learning. arXiv preprint arXiv:2105.04906 (2021)
5. Beery, S., Van Horn, G., Perona, P.: Recognition in terra incognita. In: European Conference on Computer Vision (ECCV) (2018)
6. Chen, T., Kornblith, S., Norouzi, M., Hinton, G.: A simple framework for contrastive learning of visual representations. In: International Conference on Machine Learning (ICML) (2020)
7. Choi, S., Kim, T., Jeong, M., Park, H., Kim, C.: Meta batch-instance normalization for generalizable person re-identification. In: IEEE Conference on Computer Vision and Pattern Recognition (CVPR) (2021)
8. Choi, S., Jung, S., Yun, H., Kim, J.T., Kim, S., Choo, J.: RobustNet: improving domain generalization in urban-scene segmentation via instance selective whitening. In: IEEE Conference on Computer Vision and Pattern Recognition (CVPR) (2021)
9. Croce, F., et al.: RobustBench: a standardized adversarial robustness benchmark. arXiv preprint arXiv:2010.09670 (2020)
10. Fang, C., Xu, Y., Rockmore, D.N.: Unbiased metric learning: on the utilization of multiple datasets and web images for softening bias. In: International Conference on Computer Vision (ICCV) (2013)
11. Ganin, Y., Lempitsky, V.: Unsupervised domain adaptation by backpropagation. In: International Conference on Machine Learning (ICML) (2015)
12. Ganin, Y., et al.: Domain-adversarial training of neural networks. J. Mach. Learn. Res. (2016)
13. Gidaris, S., Singh, P., Komodakis, N.: Unsupervised representation learning by predicting image rotations. In: International Conference on Learning Representations (ICLR) (2018)
14. Gong, R., Li, W., Chen, Y., Gool, L.V.: DLOW: domain flow for adaptation and generalization. In: IEEE Conference on Computer Vision and Pattern Recognition (CVPR) (2019)
15. Grandvalet, Y., Bengio, Y.: Semi-supervised learning by entropy minimization. In: Advances in Neural Information Processing Systems (NeurIPS) (2004)
16. Gulrajani, I., Lopez-Paz, D.: In search of lost domain generalization. In: International Conference on Learning Representations (ICLR) (2020)
17. Guo, Y., Shi, H., Kumar, A., Grauman, K., Rosing, T., Feris, R.: SpotTune: transfer learning through adaptive fine-tuning. In: IEEE Conference on Computer Vision and Pattern Recognition (CVPR) (2019)
18. He, K., Fan, H., Wu, Y., Xie, S., Girshick, R.: Momentum contrast for unsupervised visual representation learning. In: IEEE Conference on Computer Vision and Pattern Recognition (CVPR) (2020)

19. He, K., Zhang, X., Ren, S., Sun, J.: Deep residual learning for image recognition. In: IEEE Conference on Computer Vision and Pattern Recognition (CVPR) (2016)
20. Hendrycks, D., Dietterich, T.: Benchmarking neural network robustness to common corruptions and perturbations. In: International Conference on Learning Representations (ICLR) (2018)
21. Hendrycks, D., Mu, N., Cubuk, E.D., Zoph, B., Gilmer, J., Lakshminarayanan, B.: Augmix: A simple data processing method to improve robustness and uncertainty. In: International Conference on Learning Representations (ICLR) (2019)
22. Hoffman, J., et al.: CYCADA: cycle-consistent adversarial domain adaptation. In: International Conference on Machine Learning (ICML) (2018)
23. Hu, W., Miyato, T., Tokui, S., Matsumoto, E., Sugiyama, M.: Learning discrete representations via information maximizing self-augmented training. In: International Conference on Machine Learning (ICML) (2017)
24. Ioffe, S., Szegedy, C.: Batch normalization: accelerating deep network training by reducing internal covariate shift. In: International Conference on Machine Learning (ICML) (2015)
25. Iwasawa, Y., Matsuo, Y.: Test-time classifier adjustment module for model-agnostic domain generalization. In: Advances in Neural Information Processing Systems (NeurIPS) (2021)
26. Jain, H., Zepeda, J., Pérez, P., Gribonval, R.: Learning a complete image indexing pipeline. In: IEEE Conference on Computer Vision and Pattern Recognition (CVPR) (2018)
27. Krause, A., Perona, P., Gomes, R.: Discriminative clustering by regularized information maximization. In: Advances in Neural Information Processing Systems (NeurIPS) (2010)
28. Krause, A., Perona, P., Gomes, R.: Discriminative clustering by regularized information maximization. In: Lafferty, J., Williams, C., Shawe-Taylor, J., Zemel, R., Culotta, A. (eds.) Advances in Neural Information Processing Systems (NeurIPS) (2010)
29. Krizhevsky, A., Hinton, G., et al.: Learning multiple layers of features from tiny images (2009)
30. Kundu, J.N., Venkat, N., Babu, R.V., et al.: Universal source-free domain adaptation. In: IEEE Conference on Computer Vision and Pattern Recognition (CVPR) (2020)
31. Li, D., Yang, Y., Song, Y.Z., Hospedales, T.M.: Deeper, broader and artier domain generalization. In: International Conference on Computer Vision (ICCV) (2017)
32. Li, D., Yang, Y., Song, Y.Z., Hospedales, T.M.: Learning to generalize: meta-learning for domain generalization. arXiv preprint arXiv:1710.03463 (2017)
33. Li, D., Zhang, J., Yang, Y., Liu, C., Song, Y.Z., Hospedales, T.M.: Episodic training for domain generalization. In: International Conference on Computer Vision (ICCV) (2019)
34. Li, H., Jialin Pan, S., Wang, S., Kot, A.C.: Domain generalization with adversarial feature learning. In: IEEE Conference on Computer Vision and Pattern Recognition (CVPR) (2018)
35. Li, L., et al.: Progressive domain expansion network for single domain generalization. In: IEEE Conference on Computer Vision and Pattern Recognition (CVPR) (2021)
36. Li, R., Jiao, Q., Cao, W., Wong, H.S., Wu, S.: Model adaptation: unsupervised domain adaptation without source data. In: IEEE Conference on Computer Vision and Pattern Recognition (CVPR) (2020)

37. Li, Y., et al.: Deep domain generalization via conditional invariant adversarial networks. In: European Conference on Computer Vision (ECCV) (2018)
38. Liang, J., Hu, D., Feng, J.: Do we really need to access the source data? source hypothesis transfer for unsupervised domain adaptation. In: International Conference on Machine Learning (ICML) (2020)
39. Liu, Y., Kothari, P., van Delft, B., Bellot-Gurlet, B., Mordan, T., Alahi, A.: TTT++: when does self-supervised test-time training fail or thrive? In: Advances in Neural Information Processing Systems (NeurIPS) (2021)
40. Long, M., Zhu, H., Wang, J., Jordan, M.I.: Unsupervised domain adaptation with residual transfer networks. In: Advances in Neural Information Processing Systems (NeurIPS) (2016)
41. Van der Maaten, L., Hinton, G.: Visualizing data using t-SNE. J. Mach. Learn. Res. (2008)
42. Mummadi, C.K., Hutmacher, R., Rambach, K., Levinkov, E., Brox, T., Metzen, J.H.: Test-time adaptation to distribution shift by confidence maximization and input transformation. arXiv preprint arXiv:2106.14999 (2021)
43. Nair, V., Hinton, G.E.: Rectified linear units improve restricted boltzmann machines. In: International Conference on Machine Learning (ICML) (2010)
44. Pan, X., Luo, P., Shi, J., Tang, X.: Two at once: enhancing learning and generalization capacities via IBN-Net. In: European Conference on Computer Vision (ECCV) (2018)
45. Rahman, M.M., Fookes, C., Baktashmotlagh, M., Sridharan, S.: Correlation-aware adversarial domain adaptation and generalization. Pattern Recogn. (2020)
46. Saito, K., Watanabe, K., Ushiku, Y., Harada, T.: Maximum classifier discrepancy for unsupervised domain adaptation. In: IEEE Conference on Computer Vision and Pattern Recognition (CVPR) (2018)
47. Seo, S., Suh, Y., Kim, D., Han, J., Han, B.: Learning to optimize domain specific normalization for domain generalization. arXiv preprint arXiv:1907.04275 (2019)
48. Shi, Y., Sha, F.: Information-theoretical learning of discriminative clusters for unsupervised domain adaptation. In: International Conference on Machine Learning (ICML) (2012)
49. Springenberg, J.T.: Unsupervised and semi-supervised learning with categorical generative adversarial networks. International Conference on Learning Representations (ICLR) (2016)
50. Su, J.C., Maji, S., Hariharan, B.: When does self-supervision improve few-shot learning? In: European Conference on Computer Vision (ECCV) (2020)
51. Sun, B., Saenko, K.: Deep coral: Correlation alignment for deep domain adaptation. In: European Conference on Computer Vision (ECCV) (2016)
52. Sun, Y., Wang, X., Liu, Z., Miller, J., Efros, A., Hardt, M.: Test-time training with self-supervision for generalization under distribution shifts. In: International Conference on Machine Learning (ICML) (2020)
53. Tzeng, E., Hoffman, J., Saenko, K., Darrell, T.: Adversarial discriminative domain adaptation. In: IEEE Conference on Computer Vision and Pattern Recognition (CVPR) (2017)
54. Vapnik, V.N.: An overview of statistical learning theory. IEEE Trans. Neural Netw. (1999)
55. Venkateswara, H., Eusebio, J., Chakraborty, S., Panchanathan, S.: Deep hashing network for unsupervised domain adaptation. In: IEEE Conference on Computer Vision and Pattern Recognition (CVPR) (2017)

56. Volpi, R., Namkoong, H., Sener, O., Duchi, J.C., Murino, V., Savarese, S.: Generalizing to unseen domains via adversarial data augmentation. In: Advances in Neural Information Processing systems 31 (2018)
57. Vu, T.H., Jain, H., Bucher, M., Cord, M., Pérez, P.: ADVENT: adversarial entropy minimization for domain adaptation in semantic segmentation. In: IEEE Conference on Computer Vision and Pattern Recognition (CVPR) (2019)
58. Wang, D., Liu, S., Ebrahimi, S., Shelhamer, E., Darrell, T.: On-target adaptation. arXiv preprint arXiv:2109.01087 (2021)
59. Wang, D., Shelhamer, E., Liu, S., Olshausen, B., Darrell, T.: Tent: fully test-time adaptation by entropy minimization. In: International Conference on Learning Representations (ICLR) (2020)
60. Yang, S., Wang, Y., van de Weijer, J., Herranz, L., Jui, S.: Generalized source-free domain adaptation. In: International Conference on Computer Vision (ICCV) (2021)
61. Yeh, H.W., Yang, B., Yuen, P.C., Harada, T.: SoFA: source-data-free feature alignment for unsupervised domain adaptation. In: IEEE/CVF Winter Conference on Applications of Computer Vision (WACV) (2021)
62. Yosinski, J., Clune, J., Bengio, Y., Lipson, H.: How transferable are features in deep neural networks? In: Advances in Neural Information Processing Systems (NeurIPS) (2014)
63. You, F., Li, J., Zhao, Z.: Test-time batch statistics calibration for covariate shift. arXiv preprint arXiv:2110.04065 (2021)
64. Yu, T., Kumar, S., Gupta, A., Levine, S., Hausman, K., Finn, C.: Gradient surgery for multi-task learning. In: Advances in Neural Information Processing Systems (NeurIPS) (2020)
65. Zagoruyko, S., Komodakis, N.: Wide residual networks. In: British Machine Vision Conference (BMVC) (2016)
66. Zhang, Y., Borse, S., Cai, H., Porikli, F.: AuxAdapt: stable and efficient test-time adaptation for temporally consistent video semantic segmentation. In: IEEE/CVF Winter Conference on Applications of Computer Vision (WACV) (2022)
67. Zhou, K., Yang, Y., Hospedales, T., Xiang, T.: Learning to generate novel domains for domain generalization. In: European Conference on Computer Vision (ECCV) (2020)

Learning Instance-Specific Adaptation for Cross-Domain Segmentation

Yuliang Zou[1(✉)], Zizhao Zhang[2], Chun-Liang Li[2], Han Zhang[3], Tomas Pfister[2], and Jia-Bin Huang[4]

[1] Virginia Tech, Blacksburg, USA
ylzou@vt.edu
[2] Google Cloud AI, California, USA
[3] Google Brain, California, USA
[4] University of Maryland, College Park, Maryland, USA

Abstract. We propose a test-time adaptation method for cross-domain image segmentation. Our method is simple: Given a new unseen instance at test time, we adapt a pre-trained model by conducting instance-specific BatchNorm (statistics) calibration. Our approach has two core components. First, we replace the manually designed BatchNorm calibration rule with a learnable module. Second, we leverage strong data augmentation to simulate random domain shifts for learning the calibration rule. In contrast to existing domain adaptation methods, our method does not require accessing the target domain data at training time or conducting computationally expensive test-time model training/optimization. Equipping our method with models trained by standard recipes achieves significant improvement, comparing favorably with several state-of-the-art domain generalization and one-shot unsupervised domain adaptation approaches. Combining our method with the domain generalization methods further improves performance, reaching a new state of the art. Our project page is https://yuliang.vision/InstCal/.

1 Introduction

Deep neural networks have shown impressive results in many computer vision applications. However, these models suffer from inevitable performance drops when deployed in out-of-distribution environments due to domain shift [3]. For example, segmentation models trained on sunny images may perform poorly on foggy or rainy scenes [9]. Improving the cross-domain performance of deep vision models has thus received considerable attention in recent years.

Domain Adaptation. One straightforward approach for reducing the domain shift is to collect diverse labeled data in the target domain of interest for supervised fine-tuning. However, collecting sufficient annotated data in the target

Supplementary Information The online version contains supplementary material available at https://doi.org/10.1007/978-3-031-19827-4_27.

S. Avidan et al. (Eds.): ECCV 2022, LNCS 13693, pp. 459–476, 2022.
https://doi.org/10.1007/978-3-031-19827-4_27

domain could be expensive or infeasible (e.g., in continuously changing environments). This is particularly challenging for many dense prediction tasks such as image segmentation as it requires *dense* (pixel-wise) labels. Unsupervised domain adaptation (UDA) [17,32,50,53] is an alternative route for reducing the domain gap by using *unlabeled* target data. However, UDA methods require accessing target domain data for model training *before* deployment. Such assumptions may not hold as we are not able to anticipate what scenarios the model would encounter (e.g., different weather conditions) and therefore cannot collect the unlabeled data accordingly. One-shot UDA [4,31] relaxes the constraint by requiring only one target example for model training. The model can thus use the first example encountered in the unseen target domain as the training example. However, the adaptation procedure often requires thousands of training steps [31], hindering its applicability as a plug-and-play module when deployed on new target domains. These UDA methods also require access to source data *during* the adaptation process, which may be unrealistic at test time.

Domain Generalization (DG). [1,27,34,60] overcomes the above limitations by learning invariant representations using multiple source domains to improve model robustness on unseen or continuously changing environments. Recent approaches [40,59] relax the constraint by requiring one single source domain only. However, as Dubey et al. [14] points out, the optimal model learned from training domains may be far from being optimal for an unseen target domain.

Test-Time Adaptation approaches have been proposed to tackle exactly the same problem. These methods can be roughly categorized into two groups: 1) optimizing model parameters at test time with a proxy task [2,49], prediction pseudo-label [29], or entropy regularizations [54], and 2) BatchNorm calibration [22,36,46]. These approaches can be applied to update models along with observing each target test data, thus observing the entire test distribution. Alternatively, they can be used to create an *instance-specific* model for each test example individually. Despite the flexibility, the optimization-based methods all require time-consuming backprop computation to update model parameters.

Our Work. In this paper, we present a simple test-time adaptation method for cross-domain segmentation (Fig. 1). Building upon BatchNorm calibration methods [36,46], we propose to learn *instance-specific* calibration rules using strong data augmentations to simulate various pseudo source domains. Our approach offers several advantages. First, compared with existing work [36,46] with *manually determined* calibration rules that require time-consuming grid searches and may not transfer to different models, our approach is *data-driven* and *instance-specific*. Second, unlike other test-time adaptation methods [2,29,49,54], our work does not involve expensive gradient-based optimization for updating model parameters at test time. Third, our method learns to calibrate BatchNorm statistics with *one* single instance (i.e., without accessing to a batch of samples). We validate our proposed methods on cross-domain semantic and panoptic segmentation tasks on several benchmarks. Our experiments show a sizable boost over existing adaptation methods.

Contributions. In summary, we make the following contributions:

- We propose a simple instance-specific test-time adaptation method and show its applicability to off-the-shelf segmentation models containing BatchNorm.
- We conduct a detailed ablation study and analysis to validate our design choices in semantic segmentation. Applying the optimal configuration to the more complex panoptic segmentation task leads to promising performance.
- When combined with the models pre-trained by standard recipes, our method compares favorably with state-of-the-art one-shot UDA methods and domain generalizing semantic segmentation methods. Our approach can also be combined with existing DG methods to improve the performance further.

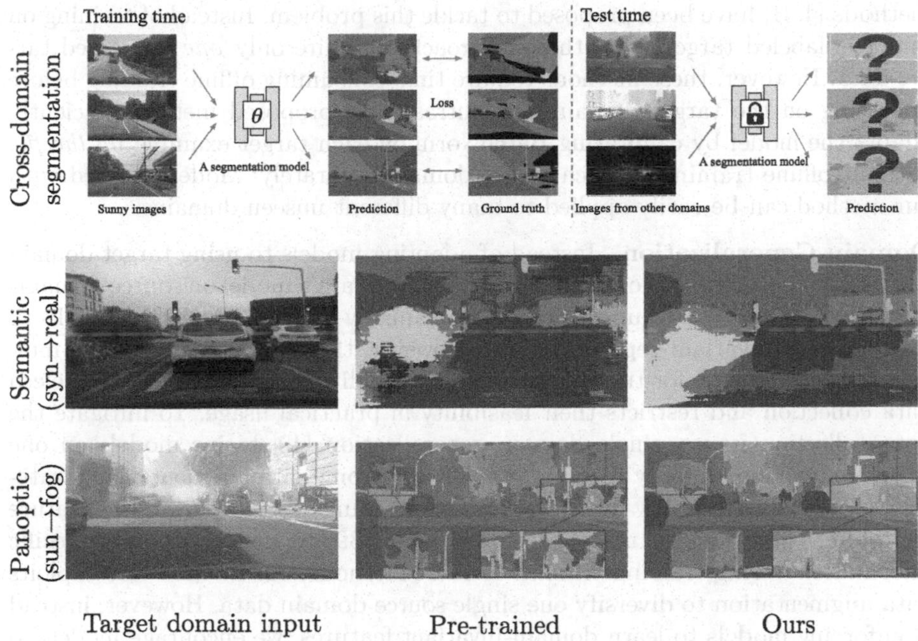

Fig. 1. Cross-domain segmentation. Models trained with the standard recipe on source domain data perform poorly on unseen target domains. On the contrary, the proposed method significantly improves upon off-the-shelf pre-trained models, without accessing the target domain at training time or parameter optimization at test-time.

2 Related Work

Domain Adaptation. Models trained on one (source) domain often suffers from a severe performance drop when processing samples from unseen (target) domains. Domain adaptation methods aim to mitigate this issue by adapting a pre-trained model using samples from target domains. Unsupervised domain adaptation (UDA) methods show promising results by leveraging *unlabeled* target data. These UDA techniques include 1) domain invariant learning, 2) generative models, and 3) self-training. Domain invariant learning methods learn invariant features for the source and target domains by imposing an adversarial loss [17,32,50,53], minimizing the domain distribution distance (e.g., MMD) [30,51] or correlation distance [48]. Applying data augmentation with generative models can also reduce domain gap using image-to-image translation [5,47,61], style transfer [15], or hybrid methods that integrate with domain invariance learning methods [7,21]. Self-training methods [62,63] select confident/reliable target data predictions and convert them into pseudo labels. These methods then iterate the fine-tuning and pseudo-labeling procedures until convergence. While we have observed remarkable progress in UDA, pre-collected target domain data requirement makes it less practical. Recently, one-shot UDA methods [4,31] have been proposed to tackle this problem. Instead of training on *many* unlabeled target data, these approaches require only *one* unlabeled target data. However, these methods require time-consuming offline training before deploying on the target domain. In contrast, our proposed method efficiently adapts the model by calibrating BatchNorm on each target example *on the fly*, without offline training on each target domain separately. Models trained with our method can be easily applied to many different unseen domains.

Domain Generalization. Instead of adapting models to using target domain data, domain generalization [1,27,34,60] aims to train a model on source domains that are *generalizable* to unseen target domains by encouraging the networks to learn domain-invariant representations. However, these approaches require multiple source domains for training, which poses additional challenges in (labeled) data collection and restricts their feasibility in practical usage. To mitigate the data collection issues, single domain generalization [40] trains models on one single source domain only by either exploiting strong data augmentation strategies [40,52,59] to diversify the source domain training data, or performing feature whitening operations or normalization [9,16,23,39] to remove domain-specific information during training. Similar to these methods, our method also exploits data augmentation to diversify one single source domain data. However, instead of enforcing models to learn domain-invariant features, we encourage models to calibrate BatchNorm on *each* unseen target data at test time, by training them on diverse pseudo domains generated with strong data augmentation strategies in training time. Our proposed method can also complement (single) domain generalization approaches to improve the performance further.

Test-Time Adaptation. Depending on the use of online training/optimization, test-time adaptation methods can be divided into two groups. First, *optimization-free* test-time adaptation methods mostly focus on calibrating the running statistics inside BatchNorm layers [22,25,35,36,46] because these feature statistics carry domain-specific information [28]. However, these methods either directly replace the running statistics with current input batch statistics or mix the running statistics and current input batch statistics with a *pre-defined* calibration rule. In contrast, we propose to learn the instance-specific Batch-

Norm calibration rule from source domain data. Second, *test-time optimization* methods adapt the model parameters using a training objective such as entropy minimization [54], pseudo-labeling [29], or self-supervised proxy tasks [10,49]. Our experiments show that integrating our method with test-time optimization boosts performance.

3 Learning Instance-Specific BatchNorm Calibration

Our method applies to off-the-shelf pre-trained segmentation models containing BatchNorm layers [24], a reasonable assumption in most modern CNN models. In Sect. 3.1, we first review BatchNorm and recent test-time calibration techniques. We then introduce our method (unconditional and conditional BatchNorm calibration) in Sect. 3.2.

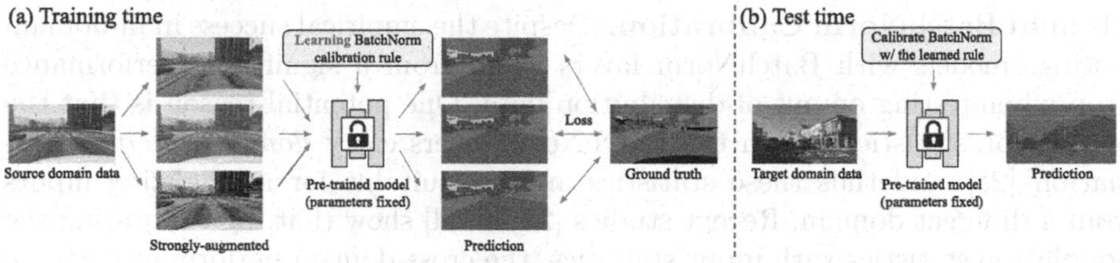

Fig. 2. Overview. (a) At training time, we learn the BatchNorm calibration rule (Eq. 8) by training only the newly initialized parameters on the strongly-augmented source domain data; (b) At test time, we conduct instance-specific BatchNorm calibration using the learned calibration rule. Note that our method does not perform test-time training or optimization, and thus the model parameters are fixed after training.

3.1 Background

A Brief Review of BatchNorm. BatchNorm has been empirically shown to stabilize model training and improve model convergence speed [55], making it an essential component in most modern CNN models. The inputs to each BatchNorm layer are CNN features $x \in \mathbb{R}^{B\times C\times H\times W}$, where B denotes the batch size, C denotes the number of feature channels, $H \times W$ denotes the spatial size. BatchNorm conducts normalization followed by an affine transformation on the inputs x to get outputs $y \in \mathbb{R}^{B\times C\times H\times W}$

$$y = \frac{x-\mu}{\sqrt{\sigma^2+\epsilon}} \times \gamma + \beta, \tag{1}$$

where ϵ is a small constant for numerical stability, $\gamma \in \mathbb{R}^C$ and $\beta \in \mathbb{R}^C$ are learnable parameters. We generalize the tensor operations by assuming broadcasting when the dimensions are not exactly the same. Note that the definition of μ and

σ^2 differs in training and test time. In training time, μ and σ^2 are set as the *input batch statistics*.[1]

$$\mu_B = \text{mean}(x, \text{axis} = (B, H, W)) \tag{2}$$

$$\sigma_B^2 = \text{var}(x, \text{axis} = (B, H, W)) \tag{3}$$

At test time, μ and σ^2 are set to *population statistics* $\mu_{pop}, \sigma^2_{pop}$, accumulated in training time using exponential moving averaging

$$\mu_{pop,t} = (1 - \alpha) \times \mu_{pop,t-1} + \alpha \times \mu_B \tag{4}$$

$$\sigma^2_{pop,t} = (1 - \alpha) \times \sigma^2_{pop,t-1} + \alpha \times \sigma^2_B \tag{5}$$

where α is a scalar called momentum, and the default value is 0.1 (in PyTorch convention). Note that the population statistics update happens during training in every feed-forward step.

Manual BatchNorm Calibration. Despite the empirical success in in-domain testing, models with BatchNorm layers suffer from a significant performance drop when testing on out-of-distribution data. One potential reason is that the population statistics within the BatchNorm layers carry *domain-specific* information [28], and thus these statistics are not suitable for normalizing inputs from a different domain. Recent studies [28,46,54] show that, by calibrating the population statistics with input statistics, the cross-domain performance can be significantly improved:

$$y = \frac{x - ((1 - m) \times \mu_{pop} + m \times \mu_{ins})}{\sqrt{((1 - m) \times \sigma^2_{pop} + m \times \sigma^2_{ins}) + \epsilon}} \times \gamma + \beta, \tag{6}$$

where m indicates *calibration strength*, each method has a different empirically specified value, $\mu_{ins} \in \mathbb{R}^{B \times C}$ and $\sigma^2_{ins} \in \mathbb{R}^{B \times C}$ indicate instance mean and variance. Note that the above calibration step happens in every BatchNorm layer, and thus the input features in later BatchNorm layers will be increasingly more calibrated.

In our study (Table 1(a)), we show that simply setting calibration strength m as the default momentum value 0.1 can improve overall cross-domain performance. However, we find several potential issues. First, the calibration strength m is specified *empirically*, requiring a grid search to obtain the optimal value. Nevertheless, the optimal value for one setting might not well transfer to other settings with different pre-trained models or target domains of interest. Second, the calibration strength m is a scalar. However, different feature channels may encode different semantic information [56]. Therefore, we may use different calibration strengths for different feature channels. Third, calibrating the mean and variance with the same strength leads to sub-optimal results.

[1] Following the "NamedTensor" practice [43], this computes the statistics over the B, H, W dimensions and return vectors with dimension C.

3.2 The Proposed Method

Learning to Calibrate BatchNorm (InstCal-U). To address the aforementioned issues, we propose to learn the calibration strengths *during training* instead of manually specifying them at test time. For simplicity, we define the following function

$$f_c(a, b, \mathbf{m}) = (\vec{1} - \mathbf{m}) \times a + \mathbf{m} \times b \tag{7}$$

The proposed calibration and normalization process can thus be written as

$$y = \frac{x - f_c\left(\mu_{pop}, \mu_{ins}, \mathbf{m}_\mu\right)}{\sqrt{f_c\left(\sigma^2_{pop}, \sigma^2_{ins}, \mathbf{m}_\sigma\right) + \epsilon}} \times \gamma + \beta, \tag{8}$$

where $\mathbf{m}_\mu \in \mathbb{R}^C$ and $\mathbf{m}_\sigma \in \mathbb{R}^C$ are two learnable parameters. More specifically, we initialize two learnable parameters $\mathbf{m}_\mu$ and $\mathbf{m}_\sigma$ with the default momentum value 0.1.

Given an off-the-shelf model, we convert all BatchNorm layers into the instance-specific calibrated format in Eq. 8. Note that we only train the newly initialized calibration parameters $\mathbf{m}_\mu$ and $\mathbf{m}_\sigma$, and we keep the other learnable parameters (including γ and β) fixed.

Using training data in the source domain, we train parameters $\mathbf{m}_\mu$ and $\mathbf{m}_\sigma$ on a diverse set of domains. Our intuition is that, by exposing the model to diverse (simulated) domains, we implicitly constrain the learnable calibration parameters $\mathbf{m}_\mu$ and $\mathbf{m}_\sigma$ to be robust and invariant to unseen target domains. However, since we only have one single source domain, we need to generate multiple pseudo domains based on the source domain. Instead of adopting complex generative models to generate pseudo domains, we find that applying appropriate strong data augmentation during training leads to promising results. We explore three different augmentation strategies: RandAugment [12], AugMix [20], and DeepAugment [19], and empirically find that DeepAugment performs the best (Table 1(b)). The details of augmentations are in supplementary materials.

Learning to Conditionally Calibrate BatchNorm (InstCal-C). While the goal is to learn the BatchNorm calibration parameters so that the models can adapt to unseen domains at test time, the learnable parameters $\mathbf{m}_\mu$ and $\mathbf{m}_\sigma$ are *fixed* after training. We propose an optional module to enable *conditional* calibration to increase the flexibility.

Instead of directly learning the parameters $\mathbf{m}_\mu$ and $\mathbf{m}_\sigma$, we propose to learn a set of parameters $\mathbf{m}_{\mu,i}$ and $\mathbf{m}_{\sigma,i}$ for mean and variance, respectively. These parameters can be viewed as the *basis* of calibration rules. We will use two lightweight MLPs (one for each statistic) to predict the coefficients to combine the basis to get the actual calibration strength for each test example, given the concatenation of instance and population statistics. Take $\mathbf{m}_\mu$ as an example, the computation step can be written as follows

$$\{c_{\mu,i}\}_1^K = \mathbf{Softmax}\left(g_\mu\left(\mathbf{Concat}(\mu_{pop}, \mu_{ins})\right)\right) \tag{9}$$

$$\mathbf{m}_\mu = \sum_i^K c_{\mu,i}\mathbf{m}_{\mu,i} \tag{10}$$

where $c_{\mu,i}$ is a scalar, $\mathbf{Concat}(\cdot)$ is the channel-wise concatenation operation, and $g_\mu(\cdot)$ is a small 2-layer MLP. The computation of $\mathbf{m}_\sigma$ is similar.

Thanks to the redesign, we further increase the learnable instance-specific BatchNorm calibration flexibility by setting the calibration rule to be conditional on the input features. As a result, the calibration rule is now *dynamically changing* according to different test target samples, while the inference process is still done within one forward pass. As shown in Sect. 4, in general, the performance of instance-specific calibration (InstCal-C) improves upon the unconditional calibration (InstCal-U) on synthetic-to-real settings where significant domain shifts exist.

4 Experimental Results

We mainly validate and analyze our method using the semantic segmentation tasks. In Sect. 4.8, we also apply the proposed method to panoptic segmentation and observe promising results.

4.1 Experimental Setup

We conduct experiments on the public semantic segmentation benchmarks: GTA5 [41], SYNTHIA [42], Cityscapes [11], BDD100k [57], Mapillary [37], and WildDash2 [58] datasets. The GTA5 and SYNTHIA datasets are synthetic, while the others are real-world datasets. For both synthetic datasets, we split the data following Chen et al. [6]. For the WildDash2 dataset, we only evaluate the 19 classes overlapping with Cityscapes and ignore the remaining classes. We evaluate model performance using the standard mean intersection-over-union (mIoU) metric. We provide the implementation details in the supplementary material.

4.2 Ablation Study

We use GTA5 as the source domain for ablation experiments and Cityscapes as the unseen target domain. We use the DeepLabv2 model with a ResNet-101 backbone.

Table 1. Ablation study. We show results from a DeepLabv2 model with a ResNet-101 backbone. We train models on the GTA5 dataset and treat the Cityscapes dataset as the unseen target domain for evaluation.

(a) Calibration parameters to learn

Strategy	mIoU (%)
Pre-trained	35.7
$m = 0.1$, fixed	40.1
$\mathbf{m} \in \mathbb{R}$ (scalar)	39.8
$\mathbf{m} \in \mathbb{R}^C$ (vector)	41.1
$\mathbf{m}_\mu \in \mathbb{R}^C$, $\mathbf{m}_\sigma \in \mathbb{R}^C$	**41.5**

(b) Different augmentations

Augmentation	InstCal-U	InstCal-C
Default	39.7	40.9
AugMix [20]	40.6	41.3
RandAugment [12]	41.1	40.0
DeepAugment [19]	**41.5**	**42.2**

(l) Not enough to pre-train with strong aug.

Augmentation	mIoU (%)
Default	35.7
AugMix [20]	35.9
RandAugment [12]	**37.9**
DeepAugment [19]	31.7

(d) Number of basis for InstCal-C

#basis	mIoU (%)
2	40.9
4	41.6
8	**42.2**
16	40.7

What Calibration Parameters Should we Learn? We first conduct experiments to study what calibration parameters should be learned. As shown in Table 1(a), suppose we directly learn a scalar parameter shared by the mean and variance. The performance is worse than using a default value of calibration strength (0.1) to calibrate BatchNorm. Learning a *vector* parameter works much better than a single *scalar* and outperforms the baseline calibration. Separating the learned vector for mean and variance leads to further improved performance.

Which Data Augmentation Strategy Should we Use? As we mentioned in Sect. 3.2, since we only require one source domain for model training, we need to use strong data augmentation to simulate a diverse set of training domains. In this experiment, we study the impact of data augmentation methods.

Table 1(b) shows that using the default weak augmentation, e.g., random scaling, cropping, the performance is even worse than the default baseline. While RandAugment [12] and AugMix [20] work well for InstCal-U or InstCal-C separately, these two augmentation strategies do not work well in both variants. Our results show that DeepAugment [19] achieves the best overall performance. We thus adopt DeepAugment as our default strong data augmentation strategy.

Pre-training with Strong Data Augmentation is not Sufficient. In the previous study, we show that the selection of strong data augmentation is critical. One may wonder if pre-training with strong data augmentation *without the proposed adaptation (InstCal-U and InstCal-C)* is sufficient for performance improvement. Table 1(c) shows that pre-training models using strong data augmentations do not achieve the models trained with our proposed adaptation methods. AugMix [20] and RandAugment [12] can improve the performance over the baseline with standard weak augmentation, but not as significant as using them in InstCal-U or InstCal-C. If we directly use DeepAugment [19] for model pre-training, the performance even drops significantly. The results suggest that it is necessary to apply strong data augmentation, but we need to use them in the InstCal-U/InstCal-C training stage instead of simply using them during pre-training.

Number of Basis for Conditional Calibration. In Table 1(d), we study the impact of number of basis (K in Eq. 9) for InstCal-C. Using eight basis leads to the best results among several options.

4.3 Comparison With Other Test-Time Adaptation Methods

We conduct experiments using the DeepLabv2 model with a ResNet-101 backbone. We first construct a baseline using a default value ($m = 0.1$) to calibrate BatchNorm statistics. We compare with one optimization-based approach (TENT [54]) and two BatchNorm calibration based methods (AdaptiveBN [46] and PT-BN [36]). We use the same protocols to separately conduct test-time adaptation on multiple unseen target domains. (i.e., setting test batch size to 1 and adapting to each test example individually).

Note that AdaptiveBN [46], PT-BN [36], and our baseline share the same formulation (equation 8) but using different m values. As shown in Table 2, while both the simple baseline and AdaptiveBN [46] show improved results, PT-BN [36] even hurts the pre-trained performance in many cases. TENT [54] also shows strong results in some of the test settings, but with the price of significantly increased computation time. In contrast, the proposed InstCal-U and InstCal-C outperform these test-time adaptation methods in most settings. We also note that InstCal-U performs better in real-world cross-domain settings, while InstCal-C achieves more promising results in synthetic-to-real settings.

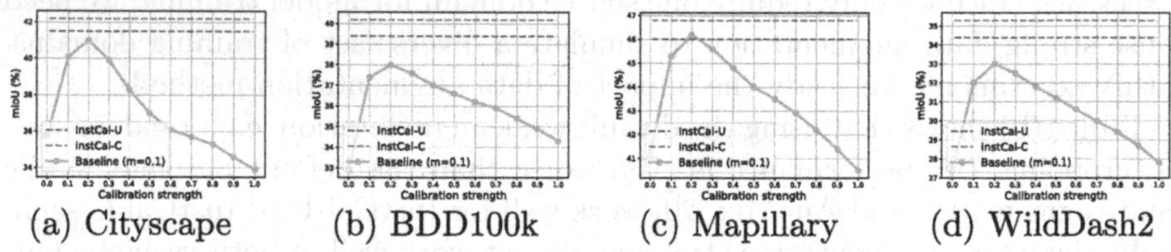

(a) Cityscape (b) BDD100k (c) Mapillary (d) WildDash2

Fig. 3. Manually set calibration strength m We show results from a DeepLabv2 model with a ResNet-101 backbone. The source domain is the GTA5 dataset.

In addition to setting the calibration strength to the default value (0.1), we also experiment with different values. We try from 0.0 to 1.0 with a step size of 0.1, and visualize the results in Fig. 3. As we can see, using scalar as strength to calibrate BatchNorm is highly sensitive to selecting the values. On the contrary, the proposed InstCal-U and InstCal-C consistently perform well across unseen target domains.

Table 2. Generalizing across multiple domains. We show results from DeepLabv2 models with a ResNet-101 backbone. The baseline uses calibration strength $m = 0.1$. "C" indicates Cityscapes, "B" indicates BDD100k, "M" indicates Mapillary, and "W" indicates WildDash2. The best performance is in **bold** and the second best is underlined.

Method	Source: GTA5					Source: Cityscapes			
	C	B	M	W	Avg.	B	M	W	Avg.
Pre-trained	35.7	32.9	41.1	27.4	34.3	41.2	49.5	33.9	41.5
Baseline ($m = 0.1$)	40.1	37.4	45.3	32.0	38.7	42.8	51.9	37.6	44.1
AdaptiveBN [46]	39.0	36.3	44.3	30.8	37.6	43.0	**52.4**	37.2	44.2
PT-BN [36]	33.9	34.3	40.5	27.8	34.1	34.4	39.1	28.8	34.1
TENT [54]	38.1	37.8	44.7	32.5	38.3	44.2	52.3	36.8	44.4
InstCal-U (Ours)	41.5	39.4	46.0	34.4	40.3	**45.1**	52.2	**40.3**	**45.9**
InstCal-C (Ours)	**42.2**	**40.2**	**46.8**	**35.3**	**41.1**	44.3	51.5	39.3	45.0

4.4 Analysis

For the following studies, we use DeepLabv2 models with a ResNet-101 backbone.

Improvement on In-Domain Performance. We test if our models can improve the performance for *source domain.* We do so by evaluating the trained model on the *test split* of the source data. We report in Table 3(a) that our learned BatchNorm calibration (both unconditional and conditional) still acheive sizable performance gain.

Table 3. Analysis. Results are from DeepLabv2 models with a ResNet-101 backbone.

(a) In-domain performance

Method	GTA5	Cityscapes
Pre-trained	69.1	66.1
InstCal-U	70.3	66.6
InstCal-C	**70.5**	**66.8**

(b) Input batch statistics

Batch size	1	2	4	8	16
Baseline ($m = 1$)	**40.1**	39.8	39.7	39.7	39.6
InstCal-U	**41.5**	41.2	40.9	40.8	40.7
InstCal-C	**42.2**	41.8	41.5	41.5	41.4

(c) Model calibration

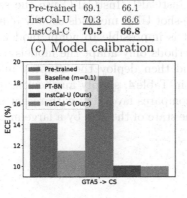

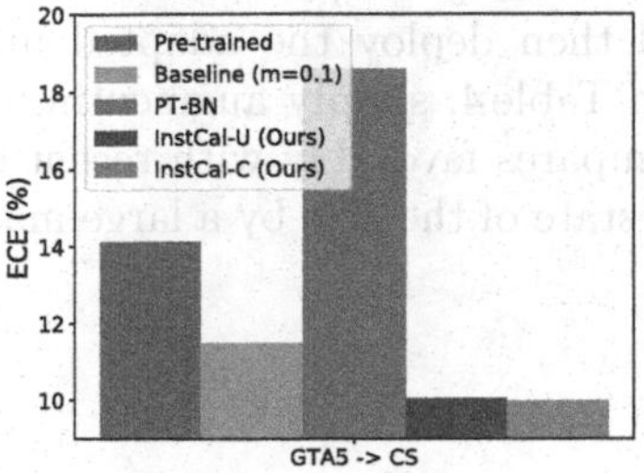

(d) Test-time optimization

Method	mIoU (%)
Pre-trained	35.7
TENT [54]	38.1
InstCal-U	41.5
InstCal-U + entropy min. [54]	44.1
InstCal-C	42.2
InstCal-C + entropy min. [54]	**44.2**

Input Batch Statistics v.s. Instance Statistics. As mentioned in Sect. 3.2, we compute input instance statistics for *each* test example, instead of computing the batch statistics for mixing statistics across different examples within a mini-batch. We validate this design choice by replacing instance statistics with batch statics using different batch sizes during test time. Table 3(b) shows that the performance drops as we increase the batch size, even though the test examples come from the same target distribution. We conjecture the performance will worsen if the mini-batch contains test examples from multiple target domains. Thus, we stick to using the input instance statistics.

Improvement on Model Calibration. We compute the expected calibration error (ECE) [18] for the pre-trained model, baseline update ($m = 0.1$), PT-BN [36], and the proposed InstCal-U/InstCal-C. As shown in Table 3(c), calibrating BatchNorm statistics indeed reduces model calibration error.

Compatible with Test-Time Optimization. We incorporate the optimization-based method, TENT [54], into our methods, by optimizing the prediction entropy at test-time. Following TENT [54], we only optimize the weight γ and bias β in BatchNorm layers. Moreover, we conduct instance-specific adaptation. Table 3(d) shows the complementary nature of these two strategies.

Running Time. We test the inference speed on Cityscapes on a single V100 GPU. The pre-trained model takes 39 ms to process each testing sample (1024×512 resolution). The BatchNorm calibration method [36] induce a 60 ms overhead. Our method increases the inference time by 58 ms (for InstCal-U) and 149 ms (InstCal-C).

4.5 Comparison With One-Shot Unsupervised Domain Adaptation

This section compares the proposed method with recent state-of-the-art one-shot UDA methods. One-shot UDA methods adapt source domain pre-trained models on one single unlabeled target example offline. In contrast, InstCal-U and InstCal-C adapt pre-trained models on the fly on each test example individually. Conceptually, one-shot UDA methods and InstCal-U/InstCal-C use the same amount of data for adaptation. However, one-shot UDA methods usually require time-consuming offline training, and thus it is impossible to adapt models on each target example separately. So these methods only adapt the models using one single unlabeled (training) example and then deploy the adapted model at test-time without adaptation. As shown in Table 4, simply augmenting pre-trained models with InstCal-U/InstCal-C, compares favorably with recent one-shot UDA methods and even outperforms the state of the arts by a large margin in Synthia→Cityscapes setting.

Table 4. Comparison with one-shot unsupervised domain adaptation. All results are from modified DeepLabv2 models (specific for domain adaptation). The best performance is in **bold** and the second best is underlined.

Method	GTA5→Cityscapes mIoU	Synthia→Cityscapes mIoU (13-class)	Synthia→Cityscapes mIoU (16-class)
CLAN [32]	37.7	40.4	–
AdvEnt [53]	36.1	39.9	–
CBST [62]	37.1	38.5	–
OST [4]	42.3	42.8	–
ASM [31]	**43.2**	40.7	34.6
Source-only pre-trained	36.2	36.2	31.6
+ InstCal-U (Ours)	<u>42.4</u>	<u>43.5</u>	<u>37.7</u>
+ InstCal-C (Ours)	42.2	**44.1**	**38.1**

4.6 Comparison With Domain Generalizing Segmentation

This section compares our InstCal-U/InstCal-C with recent domain generalizing (DG) semantic segmentation approaches. We use the DeepLabv3+ model with a ResNet-50 backbone. As shown in Table 5, upgrading non-DG pre-trained *weak* models with InstCal-U/InstCal-C compares favorably with these *strong* domain generalizing segmentation methods across different testing settings. Our method even outperforms all the methods except ISW [9] by a large margin.

Note that our method and these domain generalizing methods complement each other. Thus, we can also incorporate our methods on top of these domain generalizing segmentation methods. As shown in Fig. 4, the proposed method consistently improves the performance of these methods. Our method can even improve the strong ISW [9] approach and achieve a new state of the art.

4.7 Backbone Network Agnostic

In previous sections, we have shown the proposed method can improve pre-trained model performance on multiple unseen target domains. However, we only conduct experiments using the ResNet backbones. In this section, we use the DeepLabv3+ model with ShuffleNetV2 [33] and MobileNetV2 [45] as backbones, to demonstrate our methods is network-agnostic. As shown in Table 6, the proposed methods can also improve pre-trained models with these backbones by a large margin, outperforming the recent state of the arts.

Table 5. Comparison with state-of-the-art domain generalizing semantic segmentation methods. We show results from a DeepLabv3+ model with a ResNet-50 backbone. "C" indicates Cityscapes, "B" indicates BDD100k, and "M" indicates Mapillary. The best performance is in **bold** and the second best is <u>underlined</u>.

Method	Source: GTA5				Source: Cityscapes		
	C	B	M	Avg.	B	M	Avg.
SW [39]	29.9	27.5	29.7	29.0	48.5	55.8	52.2
IBN-Net [38]	33.9	32.3	37.8	34.7	48.6	57.0	52.8
IterNorm [23]	31.8	32.7	33.9	32.8	49.2	56.3	52.8
ISW [9]	36.6	**35.2**	**40.3**	**37.4**	<u>50.7</u>	**58.6**	<u>54.7</u>
Non-DG pre-trained	29.6	25.7	28.5	27.9	46.1	52.5	49.3
+ InstCal-U (Ours)	<u>39.8</u>	<u>32.9</u>	38.6	37.1	**51.1**	<u>58.5</u>	**54.8**
+ InstCal-C (Ours)	**40.3**	<u>32.9</u>	<u>38.7</u>	<u>37.3</u>	50.5	57.7	54.1

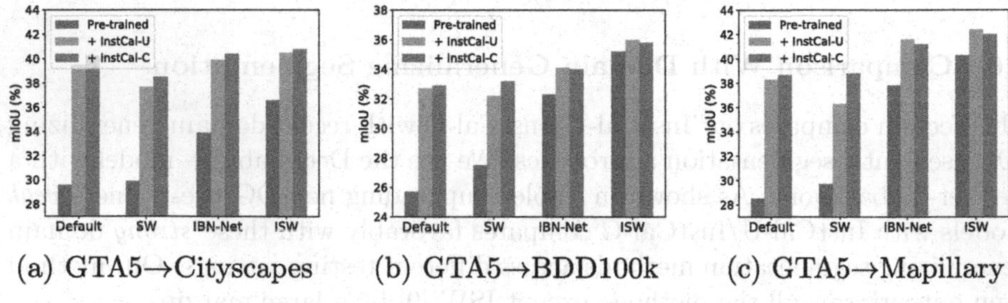

(a) GTA5→Cityscapes (b) GTA5→BDD100k (c) GTA5→Mapillary

Fig. 4. Combining domain generalization with our method. In addition to the model pre-trained with the standard recipe (non-DG, labeled as "Default"), we choose three DG methods: SW [39], IBN-Net [38], and ISW [9]. All methods use DeepLabv3+ models with a ResNet-50 backbone, trained on the GTA5 dataset.

4.8 Panoptic Segmentation Results

In this section, we directly apply InstCal-U/InstCal-C to an even more challenging task, panoptic segmentation [26]. We start with the off-the-shelf models from Panoptic-DeepLab [8] and train these models on the Cityscapes dataset. We test the models on Foggy Cityscapes [44], which inserts synthetic fog into the original Cityscapes clear images with three strength levels (0.005, 0.01, and 0.02). We adopt panoptic quality (PQ), mean intersection-over-union (mIoU), and mean average precision (mAP) as the evaluation metrics. As shown in Table 7, InstCal-U/InstCal-C greatly improves off-the-shelf Panoptic-DeepLab performance on out-of-distribution foggy scenes by a large margin, validating the proposed method is universally applicable to different image segmentation tasks without further tuning. We also provide visual results in Fig. 1 and supplementary material.

Table 6. The proposed module is backbone network agnostic. We show results from a DeepLabv3+ model with ShuffleNetV2 and MobileNetV2 as backbones. These models are trained on the GTA5 dataset. "C" indicates Cityscapes, "B" indicates BDD100k, and "M" indicates Mapillary. The best performance is in bold and the second best is underlined.

	ShuffleNetV2				MobileNetV2			
Method	C	B	M	Avg.	C	B	M	Avg.
IBN-Net [38]	27.1	31.8	34.9	31.3	30.1	27.7	27.1	28.3
ISW [9]	31.0	**32.1**	35.3	32.8	30.9	<u>30.1</u>	30.7	30.6
Non-DG pre-trained	25.7	22.1	28.3	25.4	27.1	27.5	27.3	27.3
+ InstCal-U (Ours)	<u>35.8</u>	<u>31.1</u>	**36.4**	**34.4**	<u>37.2</u>	**31.2**	**34.5**	**34.3**
+ InstCal-C (Ours)	**35.9**	30.8	<u>35.4</u>	<u>34.0</u>	**37.8**	30.0	<u>33.9</u>	<u>33.9</u>

Table 7. Panoptic segmentation results. We show results on two Panoptic-DeepLab model variants (w/ and w/o depthwise separable convolution). The best performance is in bold and the second best is underlined.

	Synthetic fog strength									
		0.005			0.01			0.02		
Method	w/ DSConv	PQ	mIoU	mAP	PQ	mIoU	mAP	PQ	mIoU	mAP
Pre-trained	×	53.3	72.2	25.3	45.0	64.9	18.8	32.6	52.8	11.6
+ InstCal-U	×	**56.6**	**75.7**	**28.9**	<u>51.1</u>	**71.9**	<u>24.3</u>	**42.8**	<u>64.5</u>	**18.5**
+ InstCal-C	×	**56.6**	**75.7**	<u>28.5</u>	**51.2**	**71.9**	**24.4**	<u>42.4</u>	**64.8**	<u>18.0</u>
Pre-trained	✓	53.0	73.2	24.5	45.3	66.5	18.3	33.1	54.8	11.5
+ InstCal-U	✓	<u>55.5</u>	<u>76.0</u>	<u>27.2</u>	**49.1**	<u>71.3</u>	<u>21.8</u>	<u>40.4</u>	<u>63.2</u>	<u>16.2</u>
+ InstCal-C	✓	**55.6**	**76.3**	**27.6**	<u>48.9</u>	**71.6**	**22.4**	**40.9**	**64.1**	**16.8**

5 Discussions

This paper proposes a simple learning-based test-time adaptation method for cross-domain segmentation. The proposed method is learned to perform *instance-specific* BatchNorm calibration during training, without time-consuming test-time parameter optimization. As a result, our method is efficient and effective, demonstrating competitive performance across multiple cross-domain image segmentation settings.

Limitations. Currently, we conduct calibration for every BatchNorm layers. It will be interesting to study which layer is more important and thus only calibrate specific layers to increase inference speed. And it will be interesting to extend our method to other normalization layers (e.g., LayerNorm for Vision Transformers [13]) and other challenging tasks. We leave these as future work.

References

1. Balaji, Y., Sankaranarayanan, S., Chellappa, R.: Metareg: towards domain generalization using meta-regularization. In: NeurIPS (2018)
2. Bartler, A., Bühler, A., Wiewel, F., Döbler, M., Yang, B.: Mt3: meta test-time training for self-supervised test-time adaption. arXiv preprint arXiv:2103.16201 (2021)
3. Ben-David, S., Blitzer, J., Crammer, K., Kulesza, A., Pereira, F., Vaughan, J.W.: A theory of learning from different domains. Mach. Learn. **79**(1), 151–175 (2010)
4. Benaim, S., Wolf, L.: One-shot unsupervised cross domain translation. In: NeurIPS (2018)
5. Bousmalis, K., Silberman, N., Dohan, D., Erhan, D., Krishnan, D.: Unsupervised pixel-level domain adaptation with generative adversarial networks. In: CVPR, pp. 3722–3731 (2017)
6. Chen, M., Xue, H., Cai, D.: Domain adaptation for semantic segmentation with maximum squares loss. In: ICCV, pp. 2090–2099 (2019)
7. Chen, Y.C., Lin, Y.Y., Yang, M.H., Huang, J.B.: Crdoco: pixel-level domain transfer with cross-domain consistency. In: CVPR, pp. 1791–1800 (2019)
8. Cheng, B., et al.: Panoptic-deeplab: a simple, strong, and fast baseline for bottom-up panoptic segmentation. In: CVPR, pp. 12475–12485 (2020)
9. Choi, S., Jung, S., Yun, H., Kim, J.T., Kim, S., Choo, J.: Robustnet: improving domain generalization in urban-scene segmentation via instance selective whitening. In: CVPR, pp. 11580–11590 (2021)
10. Cohen, T., Shulman, N., Morgenstern, H., Mechrez, R., Farhan, E.: Self-supervised dynamic networks for covariate shift robustness. arXiv preprint arXiv:2006.03952 (2020)
11. Cordts, M., et al.: The cityscapes dataset for semantic urban scene understanding. In: CVPR, pp. 3213–3223 (2016)
12. Cubuk, E.D., Zoph, B., Shlens, J., Le, Q.V.: Randaugment: practical automated data augmentation with a reduced search space. In: CVPR Workshop, pp. 702–703 (2020)
13. Dosovitskiy, A., et al.: An image is worth 16 × 16 words: transformers for image recognition at scale. In: ICLR (2021)
14. Dubey, A., Ramanathan, V., Pentland, A., Mahajan, D.: Adaptive methods for real-world domain generalization. In: CVPR, pp. 14340–14349 (2021)
15. Dundar, A., Liu, M.Y., Wang, T.C., Zedlewski, J., Kautz, J.: Domain stylization: a strong, simple baseline for synthetic to real image domain adaptation. arXiv preprint arXiv:1807.09384 (2018)
16. Fan, X., Wang, Q., Ke, J., Yang, F., Gong, B., Zhou, M.: Adversarially adaptive normalization for single domain generalization. In: CVPR, pp. 8208–8217 (2021)
17. Ganin, Y., Ustinova, E., Ajakan, H., Germain, P., Larochelle, H., Laviolette, F., Marchand, M., Lempitsky, V.: Domain-adversarial training of neural networks. JMLR **17**(1), 2030–2096 (2016)
18. Guo, C., Pleiss, G., Sun, Y., Weinberger, K.Q.: On calibration of modern neural networks. In: ICML, pp. 1321–1330 (2017)
19. Hendrycks, D., et al.: The many faces of robustness: a critical analysis of out-of-distribution generalization. In: ICCV, pp. 8340–8349 (2021)
20. Hendrycks, D., Mu, N., Cubuk, E.D., Zoph, B., Gilmer, J., Lakshminarayanan, B.: Augmix: a simple data processing method to improve robustness and uncertainty. In: ICLR (2020)

21. Hoffman, J., et al.: Cycada: cycle-consistent adversarial domain adaptation. In: ICML, pp. 1989–1998 (2018)
22. Hu, X., et al.: Mixnorm: Test-time adaptation through online normalization estimation. arXiv preprint arXiv:2110.11478 (2021)
23. Huang, L., Zhou, Y., Zhu, F., Liu, L., Shao, L.: Iterative normalization: beyond standardization towards efficient whitening. In: CVPR, pp. 4874–4883 (2019)
24. Ioffe, S., Szegedy, C.: Batch normalization: accelerating deep network training by reducing internal covariate shift. In: ICML, pp. 448–456 (2015)
25. Khurana, A., Paul, S., Rai, P., Biswas, S., Aggarwal, G.: Sita: single image test-time adaptation. arXiv preprint arXiv:2112.02355 (2021)
26. Kirillov, A., He, K., Girshick, R., Rother, C., Dollár, P.: Panoptic segmentation. In: CVPR, pp. 9404–9413 (2019)
27. Li, D., Zhang, J., Yang, Y., Liu, C., Song, Y.Z., Hospedales, T.M.: Episodic training for domain generalization. In: ICCV, pp. 1446–1455 (2019)
28. Li, Y., Wang, N., Shi, J., Liu, J., Hou, X.: Revisiting batch normalization for practical domain adaptation. In: ICLR Workshop (2017)
29. Liang, J., Hu, D., Feng, J.: Do we really need to access the source data? source hypothesis transfer for unsupervised domain adaptation. In: ICML, pp. 6028–6039 (2020)
30. Long, M., Cao, Y., Wang, J., Jordan, M.: Learning transferable features with deep adaptation networks. In: ICML, pp. 97–105 (2015)
31. Luo, Y., Liu, P., Guan, T., Yu, J., Yang, Y.: Adversarial style mining for one-shot unsupervised domain adaptation. In: NeurIPS (2020)
32. Luo, Y., Zheng, L., Guan, T., Yu, J., Yang, Y.: Taking a closer look at domain shift: category-level adversaries for semantics consistent domain adaptation. In: CVPR, pp. 2507–2516 (2019)
33. Ma, N., Zhang, X., Zheng, H.T., Sun, J.: Shufflenet v2: practical guidelines for efficient cnn architecture design. In: ECCV, pp. 116–131 (2018)
34. Matsuura, T., Harada, T.: Domain generalization using a mixture of multiple latent domains. In: AAAI, vol. 34, no. 07, pp. 11749–11756 (2020)
35. Mirza, M.J., Micorek, J., Possegger, H., Bischof, H.: The norm must go on: dynamic unsupervised domain adaptation by normalization. arXiv preprint arXiv:2112.00463 (2021)
36. Nado, Z., Padhy, S., Sculley, D., D'Amour, A., Lakshminarayanan, B., Snoek, J.: Evaluating prediction-time batch normalization for robustness under covariate shift. arXiv preprint arXiv:2006.10963 (2020)
37. Neuhold, G., Ollmann, T., Rota Bulo, S., Kontschieder, P.: The mapillary vistas dataset for semantic understanding of street scenes. In: ICCV, pp. 4990–4999 (2017)
38. Pan, X., Luo, P., Shi, J., Tang, X.: Two at once: enhancing learning and generalization capacities via ibn-net. In: ECCV, pp. 464–479 (2018)
39. Pan, X., Zhan, X., Shi, J., Tang, X., Luo, P.: Switchable whitening for deep representation learning. In: ICCV, pp. 1863–1871 (2019)
40. Qiao, F., Zhao, L., Peng, X.: Learning to learn single domain generalization. In: CVPR, pp. 12556–12565 (2020)
41. Richter, S.R., Vineet, V., Roth, S., Koltun, V.: Playing for data: ground truth from computer games. In: Leibe, B., Matas, J., Sebe, N., Welling, M. (eds.) ECCV 2016. LNCS, vol. 9906, pp. 102–118. Springer, Cham (2016). https://doi.org/10.1007/978-3-319-46475-6_7

42. Ros, G., Sellart, L., Materzynska, J., Vazquez, D., Lopez, A.M.: The synthia dataset: a large collection of synthetic images for semantic segmentation of urban scenes. In: CVPR, pp. 3234–3243 (2016)
43. Rush, A.: Tensor considered harmful. http://nlp.seas.harvard.edu/NamedTensor
44. Sakaridis, C., Dai, D., Van Gool, L.: Semantic foggy scene understanding with synthetic data. IJCV **126**(9), 973–992 (2018). Sep
45. Sandler, M., Howard, A., Zhu, M., Zhmoginov, A., Chen, L.C.: Mobilenetv 2: inverted residuals and linear bottlenecks. In: CVPR, pp. 4510–4520 (2018)
46. Schneider, S., Rusak, E., Eck, L., Bringmann, O., Brendel, W., Bethge, M.: Improving robustness against common corruptions by covariate shift adaptation. NeurIPS **33**, 11539–11551 (2020)
47. Shrivastava, A., Pfister, T., Tuzel, O., Susskind, J., Wang, W., Webb, R.: Learning from simulated and unsupervised images through adversarial training. In: CVPR, pp. 2107–2116 (2017)
48. Sun, B., Saenko, K.: Deep CORAL: correlation alignment for deep domain adaptation. In: Hua, G., Jégou, H. (eds.) ECCV 2016. LNCS, vol. 9915, pp. 443–450. Springer, Cham (2016). https://doi.org/10.1007/978-3-319-49409-8_35
49. Sun, Y., Wang, X., Liu, Z., Miller, J., Efros, A., Hardt, M.: Test-time training with self-supervision for generalization under distribution shifts. In: ICML, pp. 9229–9248 (2020)
50. Tzeng, E., Hoffman, J., Saenko, K., Darrell, T.: Adversarial discriminative domain adaptation. In: CVPR, pp. 7167–7176 (2017)
51. Tzeng, E., Hoffman, J., Zhang, N., Saenko, K., Darrell, T.: Deep domain confusion: maximizing for domain invariance. arXiv preprint arXiv:1412.3474 (2014)
52. Volpi, R., Namkoong, H., Sener, O., Duchi, J.C., Murino, V., Savarese, S.: Generalizing to unseen domains via adversarial data augmentation. In: NeurIPS (2018)
53. Vu, T.H., Jain, H., Bucher, M., Cord, M., Pérez, P.: Advent: adversarial entropy minimization for domain adaptation in semantic segmentation. In: CVPR, pp. 2517–2526 (2019)
54. Wang, D., Shelhamer, E., Liu, S., Olshausen, B., Darrell, T.: Tent: fully test-time adaptation by entropy minimization. In: ICLR (2021)
55. Wu, Y., Johnson, J.: Rethinking batch in batchnorm. arXiv preprint arXiv:2105.07576 (2021)
56. Yosinski, J., Clune, J., Nguyen, A., Fuchs, T., Lipson, H.: Understanding neural networks through deep visualization. In: ICML Workshop (2014)
57. Yu, F., et al.: Bdd100k: a diverse driving dataset for heterogeneous multitask learning. In: CVPR, pp. 2636–2645 (2020)
58. Zendel, O., Honauer, K., Murschitz, M., Steininger, D., Dominguez, G.F.: Wilddash - creating hazard-aware benchmarks. In: ECCV, pp. 402–416 (2018)
59. Zhao, L., Liu, T., Peng, X., Metaxas, D.: Maximum-entropy adversarial data augmentation for improved generalization and robustness. In: NeurIPS (2020)
60. Zhao, S., Gong, M., Liu, T., Fu, H., Tao, D.: Domain generalization via entropy regularization. NeurIPS **33**, 16096–16107 (2020)
61. Zhu, J.Y., Park, T., Isola, P., Efros, A.A.: Unpaired image-to-image translation using cycle-consistent adversarial networks. In: ICCV, pp. 2223–2232 (2017)
62. Zou, Y., Yu, Z., Kumar, B., Wang, J.: Unsupervised domain adaptation for semantic segmentation via class-balanced self-training. In: ECCV, pp. 289–305 (2018)
63. Zou, Y., Yu, Z., Liu, X., Kumar, B., Wang, J.: Confidence regularized self-training. In: ICCV, pp. 5982–5991 (2019)

RegionCL: Exploring Contrastive Region Pairs for Self-supervised Representation Learning

Yufei Xu[1], Qiming Zhang[1], Jing Zhang[1], and Dacheng Tao[1,2](✉)

[1] University of Sydney, Camperdown, Australia
{yuxu7116,qzha2506}@uni.sydney.edu.au, jing.zhang1@sydney.edu.au
[2] JD Explore Academy, Beijing, China
dacheng.tao@gmail.com

Abstract. Self-supervised learning methods (SSL) have achieved significant success via maximizing the mutual information between two augmented views, where cropping is a popular augmentation technique. Cropped regions are widely used to construct positive pairs, while the remained regions after cropping have rarely been explored in existing methods, although they together constitute the same image instance and both contribute to the description of the category. In this paper, we make the first attempt to demonstrate the importance of both regions in cropping from a complete perspective and the effectiveness of using both regions via designing a simple yet effective pretext task called Region Contrastive Learning (RegionCL). Technically, to construct the two kinds of regions, we randomly crop a region (called the paste view) from each input image with the same size and swap them between different images to compose new images together with the remained regions (called the canvas view). Then, instead of taking the new images as a whole for positive or negative samples, contrastive pairs are efficiently constructed from the regional perspective based on the following simple criteria, i.e., each view is (1) positive with views augmented from the same original image and (2) negative with views augmented from other images. With minor modifications to popular SSL methods, RegionCL exploits those abundant pairs and helps the model distinguish the regions features from both canvas and paste views, therefore learning better visual representations. Experiments on ImageNet, MS COCO, and Cityscapes demonstrate that RegionCL improves MoCov2, DenseCL, and SimSiam by large margins and achieves state-of-the-art performance on classification, detection, and segmentation tasks. The code is publicly available at https://github.com/Annbless/RegionCL.

Y. Xu and Q. Zhang—Equal contribution.

Supplementary Information The online version contains supplementary material available at https://doi.org/10.1007/978-3-031-19827-4_28.

S. Avidan et al. (Eds.): ECCV 2022, LNCS 13693, pp. 477–494, 2022.
https://doi.org/10.1007/978-3-031-19827-4_28

1 Introduction

Self-supervised learning (SSL) has become an active research topic in computer vision because of its ability to learn generalizable representations from large-scale unlabeled data and offer good performance in downstream tasks [6,28,44,59,60]. Contrastive learning, one of the popular directions in SSL, has attracted a lot of attention due to its ease of use in pretext designing and capacity to generalize across various visual tasks.

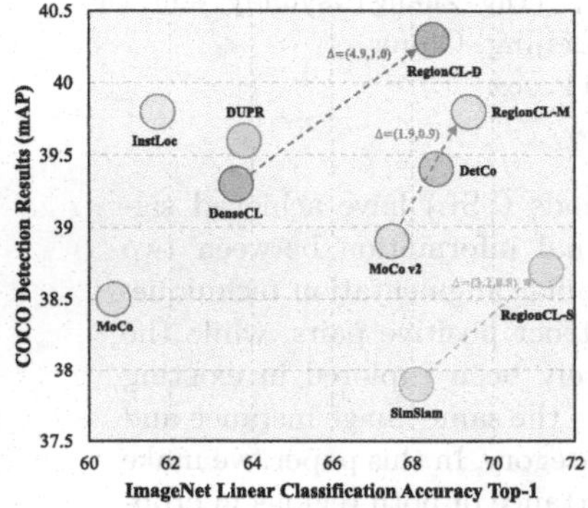

Fig. 1. Transfer results on the ImageNet [15] (classification) and MS COCO [10] (detection) datasets. Involving region-level contrastive pairs during pretraining, RegionCL helps DenseCL [47], MoCov2 [9], and SimSiam [11] achieve a better performance trade-off between image classification and object detection tasks.

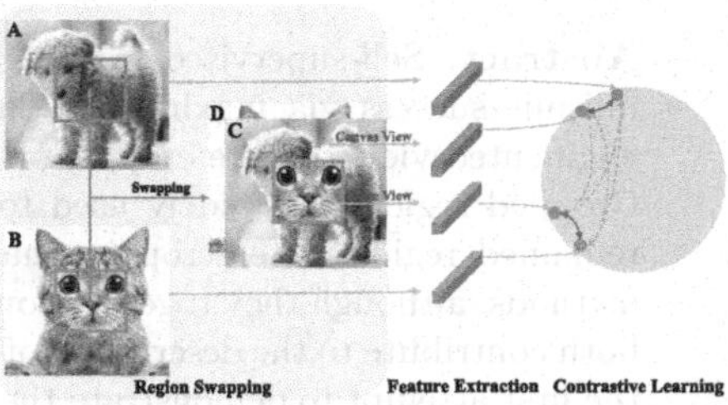

Fig. 2. Illustration of the region swapping strategy. Taking two images A and B as input, it randomly crops and swaps the paste views and generates the composite images C and D. As a result, the canvas and paste views in image C form a negative pair, while the canvas view and A (the paste view and B) are positive pairs.

Current contrastive learning methods typically use augmented views of the same image as positive pairs and maximize their mutual information. Cropping is by far the most popular augmentation technique. By randomly cropping regions from the same images and treating the cropped regions as positive pairs, the methods in [7–9,11,19,21] have shown promising results in image classification. Multi-crop [3,4] has been investigated as a way to improve performance even further by generating more diverse candidates and facilitating the model learning a better feature representation. Constrained cropping strategies [37,50,52,56,62] have recently been developed to ensure that two cropped views contain shared regions of a specific size and to improve models' performance on dense prediction tasks by constructing contrastive pairs within the shared regions. These methods have achieved superior performance on a variety of visual tasks by leveraging various cropping strategies to construct contrastive pairs during pretraining.

However, the remained regions after cropping have received little attention, despite the fact that the cropped and remained regions together make up the same image instance and both contribute to the category's description. We argue that using both regions during pretraining would help the model learn better complete visual representations of object instances, which will improve the model's performance on downstream classification and dense prediction tasks.

Based on this motivation, we propose a simple yet effective pretext task called Region Contrastive Learning (RegionCL) to demonstrate the effectiveness of using both regions for contrastive learning. Technically, given two different images, RegionCL randomly crops a region (called the **paste view**) from each image with the same size and swaps them to compose two new images together with the remained regions (called the **canvas view**), respectively. It is worth noting that the two views that compose the new images are from different source images. Then, contrastive pairs can be constructed from the regional perspective following the simple criteria, *i.e.*, each view is (1) positive with views augmented from the same original image and (2) negative with views augmented from other images. In this way, RegionCL generates abundant pairs that contain not only the instance-level pairs as other methods [7,9] but also the region-level pairs, *e.g.*, the paste and canvas views in the composite images. By exploiting these pairs in popular SSL frameworks, RegionCL helps the models learn better feature representations of object instances owing to the abundant contrastive supervisory signals at both instance and region levels, delivering better performance on various downstream tasks. As shown in Fig. 1, RegionCL helps MoCov2 [9], DenseCL [47], and SimSiam [11] improve their linear classification accuracy by 2%–5% on the ImageNet [15] dataset and object detection performance by 0.8–1.0 mAP on the MS COCO [10] dataset, simultaneously.

In summary, the contribution of the paper is threefold:

1. We make the first attempt to demonstrate the importance of both regions, *i.e.*, the cropped and remained regions in cropping, from a complete perspective for self-supervised learning.
2. We propose a simple yet effective pretext task, *i.e.*, RegionCL, to demonstrate the effectiveness of using both regions for learning. It is compatible with various popular SSL methods with minor modifications and improves their performance on many downstream visual tasks.
3. Extensive experimental results with MoCov2, SimSiam, and DenseCL on the ImageNet, MS COCO, and Cityscapes datasets demonstrate the effectiveness of the proposed RegionCL on classification, detection, and instance and semantic segmentation tasks.

2 Related Work

Self-supervised learning has shown great potential in learning visual representations that can generalize to a series of downstream visual tasks. Early works generate pseudo labels using specific tasks [25,33,35,61] such as image corruption and restoration, reordering, re-colorization. However, the models pretrained in these tasks may be too coupled with the designed tasks and the transfer results on other visual tasks may not be competitive.

Recently, contrastive learning [7–9,11,19,21,42] has made rapid progress and shown promising transfer performance. Typically, they take augmented views from the same (different) images as positive (negative) pairs and learn to pull the features from positive pairs while pushing away those from the negative pairs via a contrastive loss. Among the augmentation techniques, cropping plays an important role in improving the performance, as shown in [7]. Taking the cropped augmented views as input, SimCLR [7] obtains superior results on image classification. MoCo [9,21] utilizes a momentum encoder to better utilize the cropped views during pretraining, as it provides consistent optimization direction. However, as cropping at a single resolution may not provide enough descriptions of the target object, a multi-crop strategy is explored in [3,4] by fusing several cropped views at different resolutions. Such a strategy helps the models learn a better feature representation at different scales and boost their performance on the image classification task.

On the other hand, [36,37,47,52] focus on advancing the performance on dense prediction tasks by establishing dense correspondences between the augmented cropped views. Some methods [5,30,37,62] further design contrained cropping strategies during pretraining to improve the transfer results on detection, *e.g.*, they require the two cropped views have some shared regions and attract the dense positive features within the shared regions based on explicit spatial correspondences. By exploring different properties of cropping-based augmented views, these methods obtain superior performance. However, the remained regions after cropping have rarely been explored. Different from them, we make the first attempt to investigate the importance of both regions in this study via adopting a simple region swapping strategy to generate abundant contrastive pairs at both instance and region levels for contrastive learning (RegionCL), from which the model can learn better visual representations of object instances.

Although several methods also explore region-level contrastive learning, they have not yet explored the complementary remained regions after cropping, *i.e.*, the canvas view in our paper. For example, SCRL [37], DUPR [16], and MaskCo [62] incorporate bounding boxes generation and alignment between the shared area of two cropped views during pretraining. InstLoc [56] further introduces anchors with bounding boxes augmentations to boost the transfer results on dense prediction tasks at the cost of decreased image classification accuracy. DetCo [50] designs delicate cropping strategies to generate separate patches at different resolutions and uses extra memory banks to capture patch features. Without the requirement of extra information such as bounding boxes alignment, RegionCL adopts the most simple strategy to demonstrate that using both regions for contrastive learning isolated helps to boost the SSL methods performance without bells and whistles. The simple task is compatible with popular SSL frameworks, *e.g.*, we validate the effectiveness of using both regions for training with MoCov2 [9], SimSiam [11], and DenseCL [47], with only minor modifications to them. The theoretical analysis of these works have been well studied in [40,43,45,46] and is beyond this paper's scope. It is also noteworthy that although the adopted swapping strategy is similar to co-current methods like UnMix [38]/HEXA [26]/InsCon [57], they do not explore region-level pairs, *i.e.*, they still treat the composite images as a whole from the global perspective. RegionCL explores both region- and global-level pairs from the composite images, which is more efficient and obtains better performance on various vision tasks.

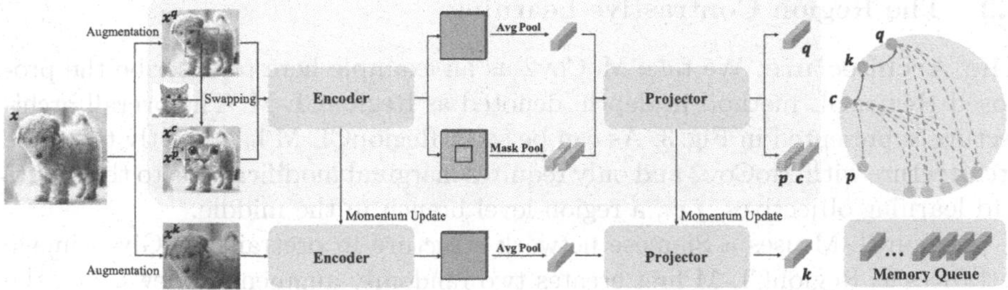

Fig. 3. Illustration of the proposed RegionCL with the MoCov2 framework, *i.e.*, RegionCL-M. Taking the two augmented views x^q, x^k as inputs, RegionCL employs region swapping among the batch of x^q to generate the composite images with paste views x^p and canvas views x^c. Then, mask pooling is used to extract the features belonging to the paste and canvas views, respectively. The resultant region-level features (with stripes in the figure) are batched with the instance-level features and processed by the projector.

3 Method

3.1 The Region Swapping Strategy

Different from current methods that only use the cropped regions, we take both the cropped and remained regions into consideration for self-supervised learning. Given two different images, we randomly crop a region with the same size from each image and swap them to compose two new images. As shown in Fig. 2-C, the composite image after region swapping contains two views: one is the paste view (the cropped region), *i.e.*, the cat's face, and the other is called the canvas view (the remained region), *i.e.*, the dog's body. Specifically, we first sample a size of the paste view, *i.e.*, the height and width, and then determine the coordinates of the origin point from which the cropping starts. We make sure the size and location of the cropped region match the network's downsampling ratio $\mathcal{R}$ during region swapping so that the region's feature can be directly extracted from the feature map by a simple operation of mask pooling. The height and width are determined by $\mathcal{R}$ and a discrete uniform distribution $\mathcal{C} \sim U(\mathcal{C}_L, \mathcal{C}_U)$, where the ratio $\mathcal{R}$ is typically 32 for ResNet [23] and $\mathcal{C}_L, \mathcal{C}_U$ are two predefined hyper-parameters shared for both spatial dimensions for simplicity. They are set to 3 and 5 in the paper unless specified. We sample twice from the distribution $\mathcal{C}$ and get two observations c_h and c_w. Then, we calculate the width and height as $r_h = c_h \times \mathcal{R}, r_w = c_w \times \mathcal{R}$, respectively. Then we uniformly sample the origin point coordinates (r_x, r_y) from a valid range that guarantees there is enough remaining area to crop a patch of size $r_w \times r_h$. In this way, the candidate region is determined by (r_x, r_y, r_w, r_h). It is noteworthy that within a mini-batch of the training images, we use the same coordinates (r_x, r_y, r_w, r_h) for efficient batch-wise implementation during training.

3.2 The Region Contrastive Learning

The Architecture. We take MoCov2 as an example here to describe the proposed RegionCL method in depth, denoted as RegionCL-M. The overall architecture is presented in Fig. 3. As can be seen, RegionCL-M has exactly the same architecture with MoCov2 and only requires marginal modifications to the inputs and learning objectives, *i.e.*, a region-level branch in the middle.

RegionCL-M uses a Siamese network structure in pretraining. Given image instances x, RegionCL-M first creates two randomly augmented views, *i.e.*, the query view x^q and the key view x^k following the same augmentation strategy as in MoCov2. The online network processes the query view, and the other branch, *i.e.*, the momentum updated network, processes the key view. Unlike other methods that also utilize region-level contrastive learning [16,37,62], we follow the same cropping strategies as in MoCov2 and do not need the two views x^q, x^k to have a sufficiently large overlap, which keeps the diversity of the contrastive pair candidates. We construct the region-level contrastive pairs using the region-swapping strategy. Specifically, given two image instances from the query view x^q, we randomly crop a region with the same size in each image instance and swap them to compose two new images x^{pc}, where the cropped region after swapping and the remained region in the new images are the paste view x^p and canvas view x^c, respectively.

The Region - and Instance-Level Contrastive Loss. In this way, we have a total of four different views, *i.e.*, the query view, the paste view, the canvas view, and the key view, denoted as x^q, x^p, x^c, x^k, respectively. RegionCL-M projects these views into the corresponding feature representations q, p, c, k, among which the features q, k are instance-level feature representations while the features p, c are region-level feature representations. Note that features of the paste view and canvas view are extracted from the feature maps of x^{pc} via mask pooling, where the mask is obtained according to the coordinates (r_x, r_y, r_w, r_h) as described in Sect. 3.1. The other views' features are from the global average pooling upon the corresponding feature maps. Then we can efficiently construct the contrastive pairs for these views according to the simple criteria, *i.e.*, each view is (1) positive with views augmented from the same original image and (2) negative with views augmented from other images. We follow the practice of MoCov2 in our implementation and ignore the positive pairs whose features are both generated by the online network to stabilize the training.

We use contrastive loss [20,21] as the learning objectives, which can be thought of as training an encoder for a dictionary lookup task at both instance and region levels. We first introduce the instance-level contrastive loss and then present the region-level one. Assume that we have a set of encoded samples $\{k_i|i = 1, 2, ..., K\}$ as keys of a dictionary. For each query feature q, if there is a single key (k^+) that matches the query q, the contrastive loss aims to increase the similarity between q and k^+ meanwhile reducing the similarity between q and all other keys (considered as the negative counterparts for q). We use L2-normalized dot product to measure the similarity between the queries and keys, and the contrastive loss, *i.e.*, the InfoNCE [34] loss, is therefore formulated as:

$$\mathcal{L}_{ins} = -\log \frac{\exp(q \cdot k^+/\tau)}{\sum_{i=0}^{K} \exp(q \cdot k_i/\tau)}, \tag{1}$$

where τ is a temperature hyper-parameter (set to 0.2 by default) [21,48]. Following MoCov2, the dictionary keys $\{k_i | i = 1, 2, ..., K\}$ in RegionCL-M are maintained using a first-in-first-out queue with a predefined maximum number of samples (K), which is set to 65,536. The features from the key view k is treated as the positive sample and used to progressively update the memory queue, which serves as the negative samples. This form of contrastive loss is the exact one that appeared in MoCov2 [21], while it can have other forms for different SSL methods [11,34]. Apart from the instance-level pairs, the features of other views formulate the region-level pairs with the modified contrastive loss:

$$\begin{aligned} \mathcal{L}_{reg} = &-\frac{1}{2}\log \frac{\exp(p \cdot k_p^+/\tau)}{\sum_{i=0}^{K} \exp(p \cdot k_i/\tau) + \exp(p \cdot sg(c)/\tau)} \\ &-\frac{1}{2}\log \frac{\exp(c \cdot k_c^+/\tau)}{\sum_{i=0}^{K} \exp(c \cdot k_i/\tau) + \exp(c \cdot sg(p)/\tau)}, \end{aligned} \tag{2}$$

where the features p, c are obtained from the identical composite image x^{pc} (thus the term is divided by $\frac{1}{2}$ for normalization). $sg(\cdot)$ represents 'stop gradient', which helps stabilize the training. p and c are indeed hard negative pairs since they involve some context information from each other due to convolution and pooling operations, thereby helping the model to learn robust and discriminative feature representations. Thus the total contrastive loss is formulated as:

$$\mathcal{L}_{total} = \mathcal{L}_{ins} + \mathcal{L}_{reg}. \tag{3}$$

Since the query, canvas, and paste views share the online network, we believe that the features of these views should be in the same feature space. Thus, RegionCL-M only needs a single queue to provide negative samples for features of all the three views, in contrast to the usage of multiple queues as in [50,56].

Extension to Other SSL Methods. As RegionCL defines a model-agnostic pretext task and requires minor modifications to the SSL methods, we also choose two other representative approaches, *i.e.*, DenseCL [47] and SimSiam [11], to further validate its effectiveness, denoted as RegionCL-D and RegionCL-S, respectively. Specifically, DenseCL [47] focuses on dense prediction tasks and has two learning objectives, *i.e.*, the instance-level contrastive loss as in MoCov2 and the pixel-level dense loss. Therefore, RegionCL-D includes the proposed region-level loss seamlessly as in RegionCL-M and keeps the pixel-level loss unchanged. For SimSiam [11], it only adopts instance-level positive pairs $\{p, k^+\}$ for training. Thus, we only enrich the positive pairs by collecting those abundant instance- and region-level positive pairs provided by RegionCL-S while retaining the other components. Similar strategy is adopted for vision transformer backbones [17,31,55] with MoBy [51]. Please refer to the supplementary for details.

4 Experiments

To thoroughly validate the improvements brought by introducing both regions into pretraining, we incorporate the RegionCL in representative state-of-the-art SSL methods, *i.e.*, MoCov2 [9], DenseCL [47], and SimSiam [11], and propose the RegionCL compatible models, *i.e.*, RegionCL-M, RegionCL-D, and RegionCL-S. The models are pretrained following the same settings as their own base methods, *i.e.*, we train RegionCL-M and RegionCL-D for 200 epochs, and RegionCL-S for 100 epochs, with an SGD [39] optimizer and corresponding augmentations, respectively. All the methods are based on ResNet-50 [23] backbone. Please refer to the supplementary material for more details. Vision transformer-based methods [51] are also explored to further evaluate RegionCL's effectiveness.

4.1 Image Classification on ImageNet

Settings. To evaluate the effectiveness of regional contrastive learning for image classification, we benchmark the RegionCL on ImageNet [15], which contains 1.28M images in the training set and 50K images in the validation set from 1,000 classes, respectively. The pretrained models of other SSL methods are either obtained from their authors or reproduced using their official codes. The performance of Top-1 and Top-5 accuracy on a single crop is reported. We have two experimental settings regards evaluation: linear classification and few-shot finetuning. The former setting follows the default setting of MoCov2 [9,21] and SimSiam [11] with SGD [39] and LARS [58] optimizer. The latter one using randomly sampled data per class from the training set.

Results with Linear Classification. We report the linear classification results of different methods in Table 1 and 2. 'Real' indicates that the labels used for evaluation are provided by [2]. From the table, we can see that RegionCL improves the aforementioned SSL baseline methods significantly by a large margin: +1.9% for RegionCL-M, +4.8% for RegionCL-D, and +3.2% for RegionCL-S. This proves RegionCL helps various SSL methods learn better feature representations owing to the abundant contrastive supervisory signals with contrastive pairs from both regional and global perspective. Comparing with methods that also exploring mixing two images for contrastive learning but from the global perspective only, *i.e.*, UnMix [38] and HEXA [26], RegionCL-M obtains better performance no matter using 200/800 epochs for training, demonstrating the benefits of leveraging regional contrastive pairs. Besides, RegionCL-S reaches 71.3% Top-1 accuracy using only 100 epochs, while the vanilla SimSiam requires a significantly longer training schedule of 800 epochs, proving the effectiveness of RegionCL in accelerating the model convergence and improving the performance. It is noteworthy that DenseCL focuses on dense prediction tasks and does not perform that well on classification. In contrast, RegionCL brings a large improvement on DenseCL for image classification, indicating that introducing remained regions to promote pretraining is not only compatible with classification-favored SSL methods but also generalizes well on dense prediction-favored approaches.

Results with Linear Few-Shot Finetuning. Table 3 presents the results of different methods at the linear few-shot finetuning setting. Thanks to the abundant contrastive pairs brought by RegionCL, the models pretrained by RegionCL have learned better feature representations from a complete perspective and can generalize well on classification tasks, thus delivering much more significant improvements over their baselines when only a limited number of data are available for finetuning, *i.e.*, a gain of +2.5%, +8.9%, +9.5% for 1% data and 1.8%, 6.4%, 8.1% for 10% data achieved by RegionCL-M, RegionCL-D, RegionCL-S.

Table 1. Linear classification results comparison on ImageNet [15].

	Epochs	ImageNet		Real
		Top-1	Top-5	Top-1
MoCo [21]	200	60.6	–	69.1
SimCLR [7]	1000	69.3	89.0	77.6
PIRL [32]	800	64.3	–	71.7
CPC-v2 [24]	200	63.8	85.3	–
InstLoc [56]	200	61.7	–	–
MaskCo [62]	200	65.1	–	–
ISD [41]	200	69.8	–	–
PCLv1 [27]	200	61.5	–	–
PCLv2 [27]	200	67.6	–	–
DUPR [16]	200	63.8	85.6	–
DetCo [50]	200	68.6	88.5	–
UnMix [38]	200	68.6	–	–
HEXA [26]	200	68.9	–	–
MoCov3 [12]	100	68.9	–	–
SimSiam [11]	800	71.3	–	–
MoCov2 [9]	200	67.5	88.2	77.8
RegionCL-M	**200**	**69.4**	**89.6**	**78.7**
DenseCL [47]	200	63.6	85.5	72.3
RegionCL-D	**200**	**68.5**	**89.0**	**78.4**
SimSiam [11]	100	68.1	88.2	77.8
RegionCL-S	**100**	**71.3**	**90.4**	**80.8**

Table 2. Linear classification results with more pretraining epochs. * means using symmetric loss.

	Epochs	ImageNet	
		Top-1	Top-5
MoCov2 [9]	800	71.1	90.2
UnMix [38]	800	71.8	–
HEXA [26]	800	71,7	–
RegionCL-M	**800**	**73.1**	**91.5**
MoCov2* [11]	800	72.3	–
RegionCL-M*	**800**	**73.9**	**92.0**
MoCov3 [12]	1000	74.6	–
RegionCL-M3	**1000**	**75.4**	**92.6**

Table 3. Linear classification results on ImageNet [15] using 1% and 10% data.

	1% Data		10% Data	
	Top-1	Top-5	Top-1	Top-5
MoCov2 [9]	43.6	70.9	58.8	82.4
RegionCL-M	**46.1**	**72.9**	**60.4**	**83.5**
DenseCL [47]	38.9	66.2	54.0	79.3
RegionCL-D	**47.8**	**74.0**	**60.4**	**83.1**
SimSiam [11]	32.8	61.5	51.8	77.7
RegionCL-S	**42.3**	**70.6**	**59.9**	**83.8**

4.2 Detection and Segmentation on MS COCO

Settings. We show the detection performance of the models pretrained with the RegionCL pretext task. The experiments are conducted on the MS COCO dataset [10], which contains about 118K images with bounding boxes and instance segmentation annotations and covers 80 object categories in total. We choose two representative detectors: the two-stage detector Mask-RCNN [22] and the one-stage detector RetinaNet [29], following the same settings as in [50,62].

Table 4. Object detection results on the MS COCO [10] dataset with Mask-RCNN [22] C4 and FPN (1x).

	Mask-RCNN-C4-1x						Mask-RCNN-FPN-1x					
	AP^{bb}	AP^{bb}_{50}	AP^{bb}_{75}	AP^{mk}	AP^{mk}_{50}	AP^{mk}_{75}	AP^{bb}	AP^{bb}_{50}	AP^{bb}_{75}	AP^{mk}	AP^{mk}_{50}	AP^{mk}_{75}
Rand Init	26.4	44.0	6.9	7.6	14.8	7.2	31.0	49.5	33.2	28.5	46.8	30.4
Supervised	38.2	58.2	41.2	33.3	54.7	35.2	38.9	59.6	42.7	35.4	56.5	38.1
InsDis [48]	37.7	57.0	40.9	33.0	54.1	35.2	37.4	57.6	40.6	34.1	54.6	36.4
PIRL [32]	37.4	56.5	40.2	32.7	53.4	34.7	37.5	57.6	41.0	34.0	54.6	36.2
SwAV [3]	32.9	54.3	34.5	29.5	50.4	30.4	38.5	60.4	41.4	35.4	57.0	37.7
MoCo [21]	38.5	58.3	41.6	33.6	54.8	35.6	38.5	58.9	42.0	35.1	55.9	37.7
DetCo [50]	39.4	59.2	42.3	34.4	55.7	36.6	39.5	60.3	43.1	35.9	56.9	38.6
DetCo-AA [50]	39.8	59.7	43.0	34.7	56.3	36.7	40.1	61.0	43.9	36.4	58.0	38.9
MoCo v2 [9]	38.9	58.4	42.0	34.2	55.2	36.5	38.9	59.4	42.4	35.5	56.5	38.1
RegionCL-M	**39.8**	**59.8**	**43.0**	**34.8**	**56.4**	**36.9**	**40.1**	**60.7**	**43.9**	**36.3**	**57.7**	**39.0**
DenseCL [47]	39.3	59.1	42.2	34.5	55.6	36.8	39.1	59.4	42.5	35.5	56.4	38.0
RegionCL-D	**40.3**	**60.3**	**43.9**	**35.2**	**57.0**	**37.3**	**40.4**	**61.3**	**44.2**	**36.7**	**58.2**	**39.4**
SimSiam [11]	37.9	57.5	40.9	33.2	54.2	35.2	37.3	57.2	40.5	33.9	54.2	36.1
RegionCL-S	**38.7**	**58.2**	**41.3**	**33.7**	**55.0**	**35.6**	**38.8**	**58.8**	**42.4**	**35.2**	**56.0**	**37.6**

Results of Mask-RCNN on MS COCO. Table 4 and 5 summarize the Mask-RCNN results on 1x and 2x schedules respectively, where the RegionCL variants are highlighted in bold. We can see that RegionCL has significantly improved all approaches with ResNet50-C4 and ResNet50-FPN backbones, confirming the benefits of region-level contrastive learning on various SSL methods. According to the tables, incorporating RegionCL into MoCov2 (RegionCL-M) can further improve the performance over the MoCov2 baseline with both backbones. It is also noticeable that RegionCL-M has already surpassed the previous representative SSL methods designed for dense prediction, *e.g.*, DetCo [50] and DenseCL [47]. More importantly, when incorporating RegionCL into DenseCL, RegionCL-D achieves the best scores for all metrics in both the 1x and 2x settings. It suggests that RegionCL can still help the dense prediction-favored methods to learn more discriminative features from a complete perspective.

Results of RetinaNet on MS COCO. The results of RetinaNet on MS COCO using different SSL methods are presented in Table 6. From the table, we can see that the improvement brought by RegionCL still holds in all metrics and at all the training settings. Similarly, RegionCL-D achieves the best results at 38.8 AP and 40.6 AP for the two training schedules respectively, significantly surpassing the supervised baseline by 1.4 AP and 1.7 AP. It is also noted that the improvement in the more stringent metric AP^{bb}_{75} is more significant than that in the AP^{bb} metric, demonstrating that leveraging both cropped and remained regions for contrastive learning contributes to learning better feature representations for object detection and thus improving the detection accuracy. These results show that the simple strategy RegionCL can help existing SSL methods achieve a better trade-off between the classification and detection tasks (see Fig. 1), further validating the benefits of using both regions for pretraining.

Table 5. Object detection results on the MS COCO [10] dataset with Mask-RCNN [22] C4 and FPN (2x).

	Mask-RCNN-C4-2x						Mask-RCNN-FPN-2x					
	AP^{bb}	AP^{bb}_{50}	AP^{bb}_{75}	AP^{mk}	AP^{mk}_{50}	AP^{mk}_{75}	AP^{bb}	AP^{bb}_{50}	AP^{bb}_{75}	AP^{mk}	AP^{mk}_{50}	AP^{mk}_{75}
Rand Init	35.6	54.6	38.2	31.4	51.5	33.5	36.7	56.7	40.0	33.7	53.8	35.9
Supervised	40.0	59.9	43.1	34.7	56.5	36.9	40.6	61.3	44.4	36.8	58.1	39.5
MoCo [21]	40.7	60.5	44.1	35.4	57.3	37.6	40.8	61.6	44.7	36.9	58.4	39.7
MaskCo [62]	40.8	60.5	44.2	35.5	57.1	38.0	–	–	–	–	–	–
UnMix [38]	–	–	–	–	–	–	41.2	60.9	44.7	–	–	–
DetCo [50]	41.4	61.2	44.7	35.8	57.8	38.3	41.5	62.1	45.6	37.6	59.2	40.5
DetCo-AA [50]	41.3	61.2	45.0	35.8	57.9	38.2	41.5	62.5	45.6	37.7	59.5	40.5
MoCo v2 [9]	41.0	60.6	44.5	35.6	57.2	38.0	40.9	61.5	44.7	37.0	58.7	39.8
RegionCL-M	**41.5**	**61.4**	**44.9**	**35.9**	**57.7**	**38.6**	**41.6**	**62.5**	**45.6**	**37.7**	**59.3**	**40.4**
DenseCL [47]	39.7	59.1	43.0	34.5	55.9	37.3	41.4	62.1	45.1	37.5	58.8	40.3
RegionCL-D	**41.8**	**61.6**	**45.4**	**36.4**	**58.5**	**39.2**	**42.1**	**62.9**	**45.9**	**38.0**	**60.0**	**40.7**
SimSiam [11]	38.8	58.0	41.9	34.0	55.1	36.2	40.1	60.6	43.8	36.4	57.7	39.1
RegionCL-S	**40.7**	**60.4**	**44.4**	**35.4**	**57.0**	**37.7**	**41.0**	**61.6**	**44.7**	**37.1**	**58.6**	**39.8**

4.3 Segmentation on Cityscapes

Settings. Further, we evaluate the models' transfer performance for both instance and semantic segmentation on the Cityscapes [14] dataset, which contains over 5K well-annotated images of street scenes from 50 different cities. We follow the same setting as in MoCov2 [21] for instance segmentation, with Mask-RCNN and trained for 24K iterations. UPerNet [49] in mmseg [13] is employed for semantic segmentation evaluation.

Results on Cityscapes. Table 7 presents the performance of different SSL methods and their variants with RegionCL. The second and third columns show the performance for instance and semantic segmentation, respectively. According to the table, RegionCL consistently improves the three representative SSL methods by large margins. For example, RegionCL-M reaches the best on instance segmentation at 34.9 AP and 62.5 AP_{75}, while RegionCL-D outperforms the others on semantic segmentation at 78.7 mIoU and 79.5 mIoU with different training schedules, confirming the generalization and the effectiveness of region-level contrastive learning with remained regions on segmentation tasks.

4.4 Generalization on Vision Transformer

To further evaluate the benefits of using both regions for pretraining, we apply RegionCL on vision transformer-based methods and train them following the design in MoBy [51]. As shown in Table 8, RegionCL improves MoBy by over 3.0 accuracy on both ImageNet and ImageNet Real with 100 epochs pretraining and over 1.5 accuracy with 300 epochs pretraining. It can be concluded that RegionCL can successfully improve the vision transformer's performance, validating its effectiveness for advanced neural architectures like vision transformers.

Table 6. Detection results on MS COCO [10] with RetinaNet [29].

	RetinaNet-1x			RetinaNet-2x		
	AP^{bb}	AP^{bb}_{50}	AP^{bb}_{75}	AP^{bb}	AP^{bb}_{50}	AP^{bb}_{75}
Rand Init	24.5	39.0	25.7	32.2	49.4	34.2
Supervised	37.4	56.5	39.7	38.9	58.5	41.5
InsDis [48]	35.5	54.1	38.2	38.0	57.4	40.5
PIRL [32]	35.7	54.2	38.4	38.5	57.6	41.2
SwAV [3]	35.2	54.9	37.5	38.6	58.8	41.1
MoCo [21]	36.3	55.0	39.0	38.7	57.9	41.5
DUPR [16]	38.0	57.2	40.7	40.0	59.6	43.0
DetCo [50]	38.0	57.4	40.7	39.8	59.5	42.4
DetCo-AA [50]	38.4	57.8	41.2	39.7	59.3	42.6
MoCov2 [9]	37.2	56.2	39.6	39.3	58.9	42.1
RegionCL-M	**38.4**	**58.1**	**41.2**	**40.1**	**59.9**	**43.2**
DenseCL [47]	37.7	56.4	40.2	39.8	59.2	42.8
RegionCL-D	**38.8**	**58.6**	**41.6**	**40.6**	**60.4**	**43.6**
SimSiam [11]	35.5	53.7	38.1	38.1	57.4	40.8
RegionCL-S	**36.8**	**55.9**	**39.5**	**39.1**	**58.5**	**41.8**

Table 7. Instance (Inst.) and semantic (Sem.) segmentation results (mIoU) on Cityscapes [14].

	Inst. Seg		Sem. Seg	
	AP	AP_{75}	40K	80K
Supervised	32.9	59.6	77.1	78.2
MoCov2 [9]	33.9	60.8	77.8	78.6
RegionCL-M	**34.9**	**62.5**	**78.1**	**79.0**
DenseCL [47]	34.5	61.9	78.3	79.1
RegionCL-D	**34.8**	**62.3**	**78.7**	**79.5**
SimSiam [11]	33.6	61.0	76.2	78.1
RegionCL-S	**34.9**	**61.6**	**77.8**	**78.7**

4.5 Ablation Study

We conduct the ablation studies with RegionCL-M. All models are trained for 100 epochs due to the limitation of computation resources and follow the practice of previous works [50,62]. We adopt a k-NN classifier to evaluate their classification accuracy on ImageNet [15] and train these models for 12K iterations on MS COCO [10] to evaluate their dense prediction performance.

Table 8. Linear classification results comparsion on ImageNet with vision transformer-based method MoBy [51].

	Backbone	Epochs	ImageNet		Real
			Top-1	Top-5	Top-1
MoBy [51]	Swin-T	100	70.9	89.7	77.5
RegionCL+MoBy	Swin-T	100	73.9	91.8	81.2
MoBy [51]	Swin-T	300	75.3	92.2	82.4
RegionCL+MoBy	Swin-T	300	77.0	93.1	83.9

The Size of the Paste View. We investigate the influence of the size of the paste view by varying the lower and upper bounds $\mathcal{C}_L$ and $\mathcal{C}_U$. Note that the image size is set as 224 during the training and the downsampling ratio for the backbone network ResNet-50 [23] is 32, thus $\mathcal{C}_L, \mathcal{C}_U$ are valid in the range [1, 7]. The optimal hyper-parameters are determined through two steps. **(1)** We first fix the upper bound $\mathcal{C}_U$ to 5 and search different configurations for the lower bound $\mathcal{C}_L$. As shown in Table 9, the performance on both classification and detection peaks with $\mathcal{C}_L = 3$. **(2)** Then we fix $\mathcal{C}_L$ to 3 and search for $\mathcal{C}_U$.

Table 9. The influence of paste view's size. $\mathcal{C}_L$ and $\mathcal{C}_U$ denote the lower and upper bound of the size for the paste view generation. '-' denotes no paste view is used during the training, *i.e.*, downgrading to the original MoCov2.

Configuration		ImageNet		MS COCO	
$\mathcal{C}_L$	$\mathcal{C}_U$	20-NN	100-NN	AP^{bb}	AP^{mk}
–	–	49.3	47.3	26.3	24.0
1	5	51.8	49.8	27.3	24.9
2	5	53.0	51.2	27.9	25.5
3	**5**	**54.7**	**52.7**	**28.0**	**25.6**
4	5	53.9	51.8	27.9	25.5
3	4	**55.1**	**52.8**	27.8	25.5
3	6	54.3	52.5	27.8	25.5

Table 10. The influence of paste and canvas views. 'Paste'/'Canvas' denote using paste/canvas views as positive pairs. 'Neg' means using the canvas and paste counterpart views in the composited images as negative pairs.

Configuration			ImageNet		MS COCO	
Paste	Canvas	Neg	20-NN	100-NN	AP^{bb}	AP^{mk}
×	×	×	49.3	47.3	26.3	24.0
×	✓	×	51.8	50.0	26.9	24.7
✓	×	×	50.0	50.2	27.0	24.7
✓	✓	×	54.6	52.4	27.8	25.5
✓	✓	✓	54.7	52.7	28.0	25.6

It is interesting to see that decreasing $\mathcal{C}_U$ from 5 to 4 slightly improves the performance on classification but degrades that on detection. This suggests that the optimal configurations of $\mathcal{C}_L, \mathcal{C}_U$ for classification and dense prediction tasks may be slightly different, and we select $\mathcal{C}_L = 3, \mathcal{C}_U = 5$ as default values to achieve a trade-off on both classification and dense prediction tasks.

The Influence of Using Paste and Canvas Views. We further investigate the importance of using both paste and canvas views during pretraining. The results are concluded in Table 10, where ✓ under Paste or Canvas denotes whether to use the former or latter term in Eq. (2). The 'Negative' option means whether to treat the canvas and paste counterpart views from the same composite image x^{pc} as negative pairs, *i.e.*, $\exp(c \cdot sg(p)/\tau)$ or $\exp(p \cdot sg(c)/\tau)$ in the denominator in Eq. (2). With all columns marked ×, the method becomes standard MoCov2. From the first three rows in the table, we can see that using either the paste or canvas views can bring performance gains, and the performance will be further boosted when considering both regions. For example, in the 4th row, the model gains more than 5% accuracy improvement over MoCov2 in both ImageNet 20- and 100-NN classification. We attribute it to that leveraging both regions during pretraining can help models learn better category features from a complete perspective. Comparing the 4th row with the last row, where intra-image negative pairs are utilized, the performance on both tasks is slightly improved. It demonstrates that using negative pairs within images can help models learn more discriminative features between different regions, again validating the importance of introducing region-level contrastive pairs in self-supervised learning.

4.6 Analysis of RegionCL

To better analyze the performance gains brought by RegionCL, we monitor the KNN accuracy and gradients of the target regions during training. We use

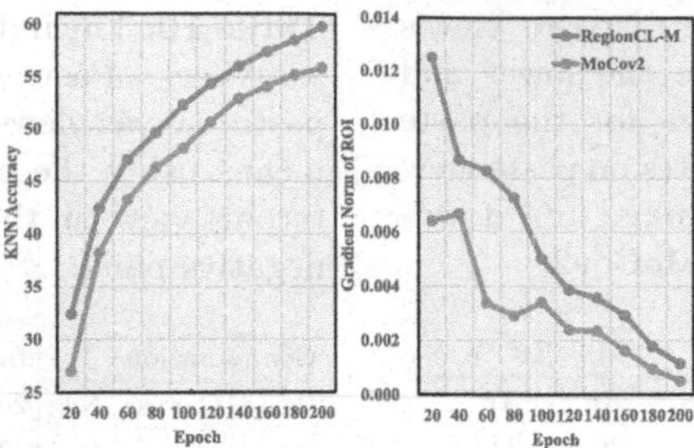

Fig. 4. The KNN accuracy and average gradient magnitude of MoCov2 [9] and RegionCL-M with different training epochs.

YOLOX [18] to detect the objects in the images and record the average magnitude of gradients back-propagated from the loss of MoCov2 and RegionCL-M in the object bounding boxes on the training set. As shown in Fig. 4, the KNN accuracy of RegionCL-M consistently outperforms MoCov2 while the gradients inside the object regions of RegionCL-M are larger than those of MoCov2, implying that using both regions for training can help models pay more attention on the targets and learn better object representation from a complete perspective.

5 Limitation and Discussion

We make the first attempt to demonstrate the importance of considering both cropped and remained regions in SSL via a simple yet effective RegionCL pretext task. The simple task makes minor modifications to representative SSL methods to show the benefits brought by leveraging regional contrastive pairs. Although RegionCL effectively improve these methods, there is still much to be explored in utilizing the remained regions for more tasks [1,28,53,54], *e.g.*, introducing additional bounding box selection and alignment modules or adopting multi-level supervision for learning. Besides, RegionCL temporally costs more computations per iteration (about 50% for RegionCL-M). Although it demonstrates better results with fewer computation resources as discussed in the supplementary, it will be beneficial to reduce the training costs, which we leave as our future work.

6 Conclusion

This paper demonstrates the importance of using both cropped and remained regions after cropping for self-supervised learning. A simple yet effective pretext task RegionCL is proposed to validate the models can learn better category feature representation from a complete perspective. Experimental results on image classification, object detection, and instance and semantic segmentation benchmarks demonstrate the effectiveness of leveraging remained regions in pretraining and its compatibility to representative self-supervised learning methods. We hope that this study will provide valuable insights into the subsequent studies of self-supervised learning in exploring region-based contrast methodology.

Acknowledgement. Mr. Yufei Xu, Mr. Qiming Zhang, and Dr. Jing Zhang are supported by ARC FL-170100117.

References

1. Bao, H., Dong, L., Piao, S., Wei, F.: BEiT: BERT pre-training of image transformers. In: International Conference on Learning Representations (2021)
2. Beyer, L., Hénaff, O.J., Kolesnikov, A., Zhai, X., van den Oord, A.: Are we done with ImageNet? arXiv preprint arXiv:2006.07159 (2020)
3. Caron, M., Misra, I., Mairal, J., Goyal, P., Bojanowski, P., Joulin, A.: Unsupervised learning of visual features by contrasting cluster assignments. arXiv preprint arXiv:2006.09882 (2020)
4. Caron, M., et al.: Emerging properties in self-supervised vision transformers. arXiv preprint arXiv:2104.14294 (2021)
5. Chen, K., Hong, L., Xu, H., Li, Z., Yeung, D.Y.: MultiSiam: self-supervised multi-instance siamese representation learning for autonomous driving. In: Proceedings of the IEEE/CVF International Conference on Computer Vision, pp. 7546–7554 (2021)
6. Chen, L.C., Papandreou, G., Kokkinos, I., Murphy, K., Yuille, A.L.: DeepLab: semantic image segmentation with deep convolutional nets, atrous convolution, and fully connected CRFs. IEEE Trans. Pattern Anal. Mach. Intell. **40**(4), 834–848 (2017)
7. Chen, T., Kornblith, S., Norouzi, M., Hinton, G.: A simple framework for contrastive learning of visual representations. In: International Conference on Machine Learning, vol. 1, pp. 1597–1607. PMLR (2020)
8. Chen, T., Kornblith, S., Swersky, K., Norouzi, M., Hinton, G.E.: Big self-supervised models are strong semi-supervised learners. In: Advances in Neural Information Processing Systems, vol. 33, pp. 22243–22255 (2020)
9. Chen, X., Fan, H., Girshick, R.B., He, K.: Improved baselines with momentum contrastive learning. arXiv preprint arXiv:2003.04297 (2020)
10. Chen, X., et al.: Microsoft coco captions: data collection and evaluation server. arXiv preprint arXiv:1504.00325(2015)
11. Chen, X., He, K.: Exploring simple siamese representation learning. In: Proceedings of the IEEE Conference on Computer Vision and Pattern Recognition (CVPR), pp. 15750–15758 (2021)
12. Chen, X., Xie, S., He, K.: An empirical study of training self-supervised vision transformers. In: Proceedings of the IEEE/CVF International Conference on Computer Vision, pp. 9640–9649 (2021)
13. Contributors, M.: MMSegmentation: openmmlab semantic segmentation toolbox and benchmark (2020). https://github.com/open-mmlab/mmsegmentation
14. Cordts, M., et al.: The cityscapes dataset for semantic urban scene understanding. In: Proceedings of the IEEE Conference on Computer Vision and Pattern Recognition (CVPR) (2016)
15. Deng, J., et al.: ImageNet: a large-scale hierarchical image database. In: Proceedings of the IEEE Conference on Computer Vision and Pattern Recognition (CVPR), pp. 248–255. IEEE (2009)
16. Ding, J., et al.: Unsupervised pretraining for object detection by patch reidentification. arXiv preprint arXiv:2103.04814 (2021)

17. Dosovitskiy, A., et al.: An image is worth 16x16 words: transformers for image recognition at scale. In: International Conference on Learning Representations (2020)
18. Ge, Z., Liu, S., Wang, F., Li, Z., Sun, J.: YOLOX: exceeding yolo series in 2021. arXiv preprint arXiv:2107.08430 (2021)
19. Grill, J.B., et al.: Bootstrap your own latent: a new approach to self-supervised learning. arXiv preprint arXiv:2006.07733 (2020)
20. Hadsell, R., Chopra, S., LeCun, Y.: Dimensionality reduction by learning an invariant mapping. In: Proceedings of the IEEE Conference on Computer Vision and Pattern Recognition (CVPR), vol. 2, pp. 1735–1742. IEEE (2006)
21. He, K., Fan, H., Wu, Y., Xie, S., Girshick, R.: Momentum contrast for unsupervised visual representation learning. In: Proceedings of the IEEE Conference on Computer Vision and Pattern Recognition (CVPR), pp. 9729–9738 (2020)
22. He, K., Gkioxari, G., Dollár, P., Girshick, R.: Mask R-CNN. In: Proceedings of the IEEE/CVF International Conference on Computer Vision (ICCV), pp. 2961–2969 (2017)
23. He, K., Zhang, X., Ren, S., Sun, J.: Deep residual learning for image recognition. In: Proceedings of the IEEE Conference on Computer Vision and Pattern Recognition (CVPR), pp. 770–778 (2016)
24. Henaff, O.: Data-efficient image recognition with contrastive predictive coding. In: International Conference on Machine Learning, pp. 4182–4192. PMLR (2020)
25. Larsson, G., Maire, M., Shakhnarovich, G.: Learning representations for automatic colorization. In: Leibe, B., Matas, J., Sebe, N., Welling, M. (eds.) ECCV 2016. LNCS, vol. 9908, pp. 577–593. Springer, Cham (2016). https://doi.org/10.1007/978-3-319-46493-0_35
26. Li, C., Li, X., Zhang, L., Peng, B., Zhou, M., Gao, J.: Self-supervised pretraining with hard examples improves visual representations. arXiv preprint arXiv:2012.13493 (2020)
27. Li, J., Zhou, P., Xiong, C., Hoi, S.: Prototypical contrastive learning of unsupervised representations. In: International Conference on Learning Representations (2020)
28. Li, Y., Mao, H., Girshick, R., He, K.: Exploring plain vision transformer backbones for object detection. arXiv preprint arXiv:2203.16527 (2022)
29. Lin, T.Y., Goyal, P., Girshick, R., He, K., Dollár, P.: Focal loss for dense object detection. In: Proceedings of the IEEE/CVF International Conference on Computer Vision (ICCV), pp. 2980–2988 (2017)
30. Liu, S., Li, Z., Sun, J.: Self-EMD: self-supervised object detection without ImageNet. arXiv preprint arXiv:2011.13677 (2020)
31. Liu, Z., et al.: Swin transformer: hierarchical vision transformer using shifted windows. In: Proceedings of the IEEE/CVF International Conference on Computer Vision, pp. 10012–10022 (2021)
32. Misra, I., van der Maaten, L.: Self-supervised learning of pretext-invariant representations. In: Proceedings of the IEEE Conference on Computer Vision and Pattern Recognition (CVPR), pp. 6707–6717 (2020)
33. Noroozi, M., Favaro, P.: Unsupervised learning of visual representations by solving Jigsaw puzzles. In: Leibe, B., Matas, J., Sebe, N., Welling, M. (eds.) ECCV 2016. LNCS, vol. 9910, pp. 69–84. Springer, Cham (2016). https://doi.org/10.1007/978-3-319-46466-4_5
34. van den Oord, A., Li, Y., Vinyals, O.: Representation learning with contrastive predictive coding. arXiv preprint arXiv:1807.03748 (2018)

35. Pathak, D., Krahenbuhl, P., Donahue, J., Darrell, T., Efros, A.A.: Context encoders: feature learning by inpainting. In: Proceedings of the IEEE Conference on Computer Vision and Pattern Recognition (CVPR), pp. 2536–2544 (2016)
36. Pinheiro, P.O., Almahairi, A., Benmalek, R.Y., Golemo, F., Courville, A.: Unsupervised learning of dense visual representations. arXiv preprint arXiv:2011.05499 (2020)
37. Roh, B., Shin, W., Kim, I., Kim, S.: Spatially consistent representation learning. In: Proceedings of the IEEE Conference on Computer Vision and Pattern Recognition (CVPR), pp. 1144–1153 (2021)
38. Shen, Z., Liu, Z., Liu, Z., Savvides, M., Darrell, T., Xing, E.: Un-mix: rethinking image mixtures for unsupervised visual representation learning. arXiv preprint arXiv:2003.05438 (2020)
39. Sutskever, I., Martens, J., Dahl, G., Hinton, G.: On the importance of initialization and momentum in deep learning. In: International Conference on Machine Learning, pp. 1139–1147. PMLR (2013)
40. Tao, C., et al.: Exploring the equivalence of siamese self-supervised learning via a unified gradient framework. arXiv preprint arXiv:2112.05141 (2021)
41. Tejankar, A., Koohpayegani, S.A., Pillai, V., Favaro, P., Pirsiavash, H.: ISD: self-supervised learning by iterative similarity distillation. In: Proceedings of the IEEE/CVF International Conference on Computer Vision, pp. 9609–9618 (2021)
42. Tian, Y., Krishnan, D., Isola, P.: Contrastive multiview coding. In: Vedaldi, A., Bischof, H., Brox, T., Frahm, J.-M. (eds.) ECCV 2020. LNCS, vol. 12356, pp. 776–794. Springer, Cham (2020). https://doi.org/10.1007/978-3-030-58621-8_45
43. Tian, Y.: Deep contrastive learning is provably (almost) principal component analysis. arXiv preprint arXiv:2201.12680 (2022)
44. Wang, G., Xu, C., Tao, D.: Self-supervised pose adaptation for cross-domain image animation. IEEE Trans. Artif. Intell. **1**(1), 34–46 (2020)
45. Wang, F., Liu, H.: Understanding the behaviour of contrastive loss. In: Proceedings of the IEEE/CVF Conference on Computer Vision and Pattern Recognition, pp. 2495–2504 (2021)
46. Wang, T., Isola, P.: Understanding contrastive representation learning through alignment and uniformity on the hypersphere. In: International Conference on Machine Learning, pp. 9929–9939. PMLR (2020)
47. Wang, X., Zhang, R., Shen, C., Kong, T., Li, L.: Dense contrastive learning for self-supervised visual pre-training. In: Proceedings of the IEEE Conference on Computer Vision and Pattern Recognition (CVPR), pp. 3024–3033 (2021)
48. Wu, Z., Xiong, Y., Yu, S.X., Lin, D.: Unsupervised feature learning via non-parametric instance discrimination. In: Proceedings of the IEEE Conference on Computer Vision and Pattern Recognition (CVPR), pp. 3733–3742 (2018)
49. Xiao, T., Liu, Y., Zhou, B., Jiang, Y., Sun, J.: Unified perceptual parsing for scene understanding. In: Ferrari, V., Hebert, M., Sminchisescu, C., Weiss, Y. (eds.) ECCV 2018. LNCS, vol. 11209, pp. 432–448. Springer, Cham (2018). https://doi.org/10.1007/978-3-030-01228-1_26
50. Xie, E., et al.: DetCo: unsupervised contrastive learning for object detection. In: Proceedings of the IEEE/CVF International Conference on Computer Vision (ICCV), pp. 8392–8401 (2021)
51. Xie, Z., et al.: Self-supervised learning with swin transformers. arXiv preprint arXiv:2105.04553 (2021)

52. Xie, Z., Lin, Y., Zhang, Z., Cao, Y., Lin, S., Hu, H.: Propagate yourself: Exploring pixel-level consistency for unsupervised visual representation learning. In: Proceedings of the IEEE Conference on Computer Vision and Pattern Recognition (CVPR), pp. 16684–16693 (2021)
53. Xu, Y., Zhang, J., Maybank, S.J., Tao, D.: DUT: learning video stabilization by simply watching unstable videos. IEEE Trans. Image Process. **31**, 4306–4320 (2022)
54. Xu, Y., Zhang, J., Zhang, Q., Tao, D.: Vitpose: simple vision transformer baselines for human pose estimation. arXiv preprint arXiv:2204.12484 (2022)
55. Xu, Y., Zhang, Q., Zhang, J., Tao, D.: Vitae: vision transformer advanced by exploring intrinsic inductive bias. In: Advances in Neural Information Processing Systems, vol. 34, pp. 28522–28535 (2021)
56. Yang, C., Wu, Z., Zhou, B., Lin, S.: Instance localization for self-supervised detection pretraining. In: Proceedings of the IEEE Conference on Computer Vision and Pattern Recognition (CVPR), pp. 3987–3996 (2021)
57. Yang, J., Zhang, K., Cui, Z., Su, J., Luo, J., Wei, X.: InsCon: instance consistency feature representation via self-supervised learning. arXiv preprint arXiv:2203.07688 (2022)
58. You, Y., Gitman, I., Ginsburg, B.: Large batch training of convolutional networks. arXiv preprint arXiv:1708.03888 (2017)
59. Zhang, J., Tao, D.: Empowering things with intelligence: a survey of the progress, challenges, and opportunities in artificial intelligence of things. IEEE Internet Things J. **8**(10), 7789–7817 (2020)
60. Zhang, Q., Xu, Y., Zhang, J., Tao, D.: ViTAEV2: vision transformer advanced by exploring inductive bias for image recognition and beyond. arXiv preprint arXiv:2202.10108 (2022)
61. Zhang, R., Isola, P., Efros, A.A.: Colorful image colorization. In: Leibe, B., Matas, J., Sebe, N., Welling, M. (eds.) ECCV 2016. LNCS, vol. 9907, pp. 649–666. Springer, Cham (2016). https://doi.org/10.1007/978-3-319-46487-9_40
62. Zhao, Y., Wang, G., Luo, C., Zeng, W., Zha, Z.J.: Self-supervised visual representations learning by contrastive mask prediction. In: Proceedings of the IEEE/CVF International Conference on Computer Vision (ICCV), pp. 10160–10169 (2021)

Long-Tailed Class Incremental Learning

Xialei Liu[1(✉)], Yu-Song Hu[1], Xu-Sheng Cao[1], Andrew D. Bagdanov[2], Ke Li[3], and Ming-Ming Cheng[1]

[1] TMCC, CS, Nankai University, Tianjin, China
xialei@nankai.edu.cn
[2] MICC, University of Florence, Florence, Italy
[3] Tencent Youtu Lab, Shanghai, China

Abstract. In class incremental learning (CIL) a model must learn new classes in a sequential manner without forgetting old ones. However, conventional CIL methods consider a balanced distribution for each new task, which ignores the prevalence of long-tailed distributions in the real world. In this work we propose two long-tailed CIL scenarios, which we term *ordered* and *shuffled* LT-CIL. *Ordered* LT-CIL considers the scenario where we learn from head classes collected with more samples than tail classes which have few. *Shuffled* LT-CIL, on the other hand, assumes a completely random long-tailed distribution for each task. We systematically evaluate existing methods in both LT-CIL scenarios and demonstrate very different behaviors compared to conventional CIL scenarios. Additionally, we propose a two-stage learning baseline with a learnable weight scaling layer for reducing the bias caused by long-tailed distribution in LT-CIL and which in turn also improves the performance of conventional CIL due to the limited exemplars. Our results demonstrate the superior performance (up to 6.44 points in average incremental accuracy) of our approach on CIFAR-100 and ImageNet-Subset. The code is available at https://github.com/xialeiliu/Long-Tailed-CIL.

1 Introduction

Deep neural networks have achieved spectacular success in many computer vision tasks. In general, most tasks assume a static world in which all data is available for training in a single learning session. The world is ever-changing, however, and future intelligent systems will have to master new tasks and adapt to new environments without forgetting previously acquired knowledge. Incremental learning, also known as continual or lifelong learning, is the paradigm of continually learning a sequence of tasks as new data becomes available [5,9,27,29]. The biggest challenge in incremental learning is avoiding *catastrophic forgetting* [28]

X. Liu and Y-S. Hu—The first two authors contribute equally.

Supplementary Information The online version contains supplementary material available at https://doi.org/10.1007/978-3-031-19827-4_29.

S. Avidan et al. (Eds.): ECCV 2022, LNCS 13693, pp. 495–512, 2022.
https://doi.org/10.1007/978-3-031-19827-4_29

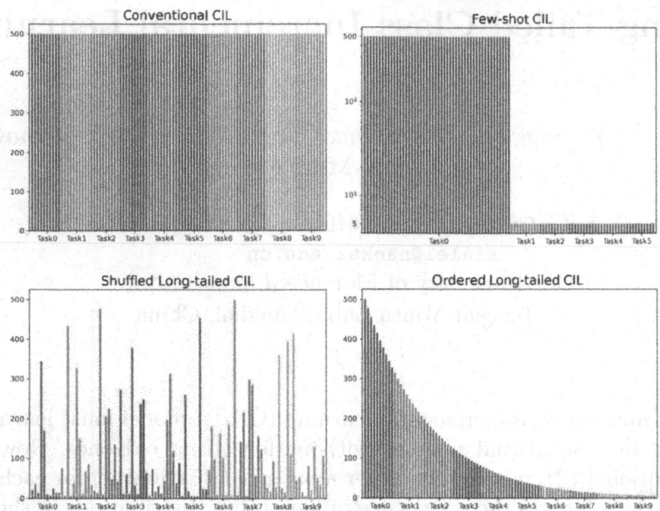

Fig. 1. An illustration of our proposed long-tailed CIL (LT-CIL) scenarios compared to conventional CIL [27] with balanced distribution and few-shot CIL [37].

when learning with only current task data and possibly a small memory of data from previous tasks.

Class incremental learning (CIL) considers a scenario in which no task boundary is provided during inference, which is significantly more challenging than task incremental learning with a known task boundary [38].

Although conventional CIL has seen significant progress, it assumes that the data is sampled from a balanced distribution. However, data sampled from the real world often follows a long-tailed distribution [14,24,40,49] in which some classes have many more samples than others. Learning from long-tailed distributions has been approach by re-sampling [11,15] or re-weighting [21,36,48] head classes and tail classes to learn a balanced classifier. Recently, transfer learning [24,44] between head and tail classes, two-stage learning [16,50] to decouple representation and classifier learning, and ensemble learning [39,42] of different experts have achieved superior performance. However, all these works consider a static world in which all data is immediately available for training. It is not straightforward to extend these methods with new classes without suffering catastrophic forgetting.

Due to the long-tailed and incremental nature of real-world learning problems, it is crucial to investigate the class incremental learning in the more realistic scenario with long-tailed distribution for different tasks. In this work, we propose two new scenarios based on long-tailed distributions: *Ordered* Long-tailed CIL (LT-CIL) and *Shuffled* Long-tailed CIL. As shown in Fig. 1, *Ordered* LT-CIL considers a scenario in which all classes are ordered according to the number of samples per class and then they are divided into different tasks. In contrast, *Shuffled* LT-CIL assumes that classes appearing in different tasks are random and each task may have varying degrees of imbalance to their distributions. Compared to current common CIL and few-shot CIL scenarios, LT-CIL considers more natural data distributions from the real-world.

We compare existing state-of-the-art CIL algorithms on these new LT-CIL scenarios, and our results show that they all perform much worse under long-tailed distributions. They are also less robust to different datasets and less consistent with increasing number of exemplars compared to conventional CIL. Therefore, we propose a two-stage strategy with a learnable weight scaling layer for LT-CIL to boost the performance of existing methods. As an extra bonus, we find that the two-stage strategy can also help on the conventional CIL scenario, where a limited memory for previous data and the large amount of current data can cause unbalanced data distribution as well. Importantly, our two-stage approach can be integrated into any CIL method.

The main contributions of this paper are:

- we propose two new CIL scenarios (Ordered and Shuffled LT-CIL) that consider long-tailed class distributions more common in the real world;
- we evaluate conventional CIL algorithms comprehensively and report several findings in these two new long-tailed scenarios; and
- we design a two-stage training strategy with a learnable weight scaling layer for LT-CIL scenarios which is complementary to existing CIL methods and show that it improves conventional CIL and both LT-CIL scenarios on CIFAR-100 and ImageNet.

2 Related Work

Here we review recent work from the literature on class incremental and long-tailed learning most relevant to our proposed approach.

2.1 Class Incremental Learning

Class incremental learning (CIL) is one of the primary scenarios for continual learning [38]. There are three main approaches to tackling this problem: regularization-based methods, parameter-isolation methods, and replay-based methods. Elastic Weight Consolidation (EWC) is a popular regularization-based method which identifies which parameters are more important for previous tasks and updating these less during learning of new tasks [18]. R-EWC [22], Synaptic Intelligence (SI) [45], and Memory Aware Synapses (MAS) [3] adopt the same strategy but with different techniques to identify important weights. Learning without Forgetting (LwF) is a widely-used baseline that uses knowledge distillation technique to constrain the output probabilities of new tasks [20].

Parameter-isolation methods increase model plasticity by adding more neurons, modules [31,33], branches [23] or masks [25,26,34]. Dynamically Expandable Networks (DEN) [19] performs selective retraining and dynamically expands network capacity, while Dark Experience Replay (DER) [43] dynamically expands the representation by freezing the previously-learned representation and augmenting it with additional feature dimensions from a new learnable feature extractor.

Replay-based methods are very effective and recall knowledge from previous tasks by maintaining a small memory of samples [2,4,7,13,32,41], representations [12], or synthetic data [35]. Incremental Classifier and Representation Learning (iCaRL) stores a fixed budget of exemplars to train and construct class means for classification [32]. Pooled Output Distillation (PODNET) applies various pooling operations to intermediate features to distill knowledge from past tasks [10].

These conventional CIL approaches all implicitly assume a balanced label distribution for each task. Recently, Kim et al. [17] proposed a multi-label classification problem with long-tailed distribution. Abdelsalam et al. [1] proposed another realistic CIL setting in which each class can have two granularity levels: each sample could have a high-level (coarse) label and a low-level (fine) label, but only one label is available for each task. In contrast to these works, we are interested in more realistic scenarios for CIL with long-tailed class distributions. We provide a comprehensive experimental evaluation of state-of-the-art CIL methods on such settings. Additionally, we propose a two-stage framework with a learnable weight scaling layer to further reduce the bias problem caused long-tailed distribution.

2.2 Long-Tailed Learning

The long-tailed learning problem has been comprehensively studied given the prevalence of the data imbalance problem in the real world [14,24,40,49]. Most previous works address this problem by re-sampling [11,15], re-weighting [21, 36,48] or transfer learning [24,44]. Re-sampling methods can over-sample the tail classes or under-sample the head classes. Re-weighting methods assign different weights to different classes or instances. Transfer learning aims to fuse knowledge between head and tail classes. Data augmentation is another way to increase the tail distribution [30]. Bi-lateral Branch Networks (BBNs) [51] use two network branches, a conventional learning branch and a re-balancing branch, to address the long-tailed recognition problem [51]. Learning from Multiple Experts (LFME) [42] and Routing Diverse Experts (RIDE) [39] adopt the same idea of ensemble learning to aggregate knowledge from multiple experts.

Recently, a two-step training method decoupled the representation learning and classifier learning, achieving superior performance compared to previous methods [16]. Mixup Shifted Label-Aware Smoothing (MiSLAS) [50] uses a regularization technique mixup [46] to further improve in a two-stage framework. Different from these works addressing the long-tailed learning problem in a static world, we propose class incremental learning scenarios with long-tailed distributions. This requires continually learning different long-tailed classes in a dynamic world without catastrophic forgetting.

3 A Two-Stage Approach to LT-CIL

In this section we first formulate two long-tailed CIL scenarios and then we adapt several existing state-of-the-art methods for conventional CIL to long-tailed CIL scenarios. Finally, we propose a two-stage training method with a learnable weight scaling layer for long-tailed CIL.

3.1 Long-Tailed CIL

In conventional CIL the model must sequentially learn different tasks where each new task consists of a set of new classes. Formally, for each training task t, the data is denoted as $\mathcal{D}_t$, where $\mathcal{D}_t = (\mathbf{x}_t^{(i)}, y_t^{(i)})_{i=1}^{n_t}$, and $\mathbf{x}_t^{(i)}$ is an input image, $y_t^{(i)}$ is the corresponding label and there are n_t samples in total at task t. Normally the number of samples per class is equally distributed and it can be calculated as $\frac{n_t}{C_t}$, in which C_t is the number of classes at task t. Therefore, the total number of classes learned up to current tasks is $C_{1:t}$. For replay-based methods, at each training task a memory of $\mathcal{M}$ (known as the memory of exemplars)is stored for previous classes up to task $t-1$, normally $\left\lfloor \frac{|\mathcal{M}|}{C_{1:t-1}} \right\rfloor$ samples stored for each class.

While class-incremental learning has many practical applications, the assumption of equally distributed samples is not always realistic. Most real-world class distributions are in face *long-tailed*. The long-tailed distribution follows an exponential decay in sample sizes across classes as described in [6]. This decay is parameterized by ρ which is the ratio between the most and least frequent classes. An example of different ratios can be found in Fig. 2, the larger the ratio, the more balanced the distribution. $\rho = 1$ is the conventional CIL case and ρ in (0,1) indicates different degrees of long-tailed distribution.

Given a sampled long-tailed class distribution, we propose two long-tailed CIL scenarios constructed from it:

- **Ordered LT-CIL** which starts learning from the most frequent classes as first task and ends with the last task containing the least frequent classes; and
- **Shuffled LT-CIL** which first shuffles the long-tailed distribution randomly, and then constructs different tasks based on the Shuffled class order. It thus has varying degrees of imbalance in each task.

In both conventional and long-tailed CIL the test set contains uniformly distributed samples for each class. Ordered LT-CIL is representative of real world applications where we are able to learn from easy-to-sample classes first, and then gradually increase the difficulty of learning with less frequent samples. Shuffled LT-CIL, on the other hand, considers a more general scenario without any assumptions of the arriving data distribution.

3.2 Conventional CIL Methods Applied to LT-CIL

A classification model can be roughly divided into two parts: a feature extractor f_θ, usually a convolutional neural network with parameters θ, and a classification

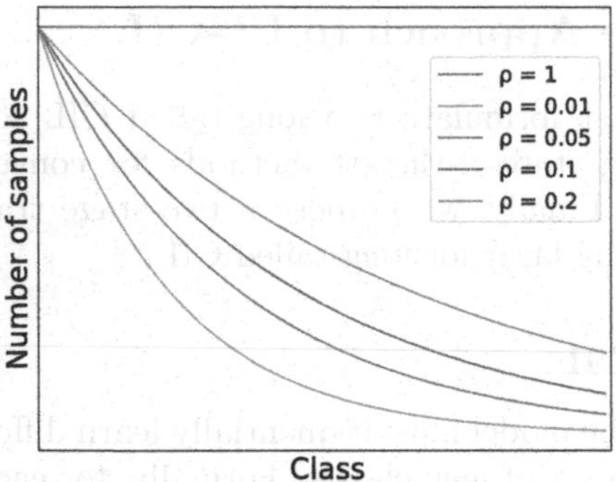

Fig. 2. An illustration imbalance ratios ρ for long-tailed distribution generation. $\rho = 1$ is the balanced distribution and corresponds to conventional CIL.

head h_ϕ with parameters ϕ. The cross entropy loss $\mathcal{L}_{CE}$ at task t is defined as:

$$\mathcal{L}_{\text{CE},t}(\mathbf{x}, y; \theta_t, \phi_t) = -\frac{1}{|\mathcal{D}_t| + |\mathcal{M}|} \sum_{(\mathbf{x},y) \in \mathcal{D}_t \cup \mathcal{M}} \mathbf{y} \cdot \log(\mathbf{p}_{1:t}(\mathbf{x})), \tag{1}$$

where $\mathbf{y}$ is a one-hot vector with 1 at the position of the correct class, and $\mathbf{p}_{1:t}(\mathbf{x})$ is a vector containing the probability predictions for image $\mathbf{x}$ over all classes up to task t.

Directly minimizing Eq. 1, even if replaying past-task exemplars sampled from $\mathcal{M}$, can result in catastrophic forgetting. Normally, a method-specific auxiliary loss L_{aux} is added to mitigate forgetting using regularization or by replaying past-task exemplars from $\mathcal{M}$. Examples of such an auxiliary loss include the many techniques based on knowledge distillation distillation [10,13,20].The total loss L_t for task t is thus:

$$L_t = L_{\text{CE},t} + L_{\text{aux},t} \tag{2}$$

where L_{aux} is the method-specific loss. In Sect. 4 we evaluate the LwF [20], EEIL [7], LUCIR [13] and PODNET [10] methods on our Ordered and Shuffled LT-CIL scenarios. These methods can be directly applied to both Ordered LT-CIL and Shuffled LT-CIL scenarios, but since they are not specifically designed for LT-CIL we are interested in how they perform in these more challenging scenarios.

3.3 A Two-Stage Method with a Learnable Weight Scaling Layer

Two-stage methods have shown state-of-the-art performance in long-tailed recognition [8,16,47,50]. In general, two-stage learning decouples representation learning from classifier learning:

- In the **first stage**, it aims to learn a better feature extractor f_θ using an instance-balanced sampler (also known as random sampler where each data point has the *same probability* of being sampled) that generalizes well;

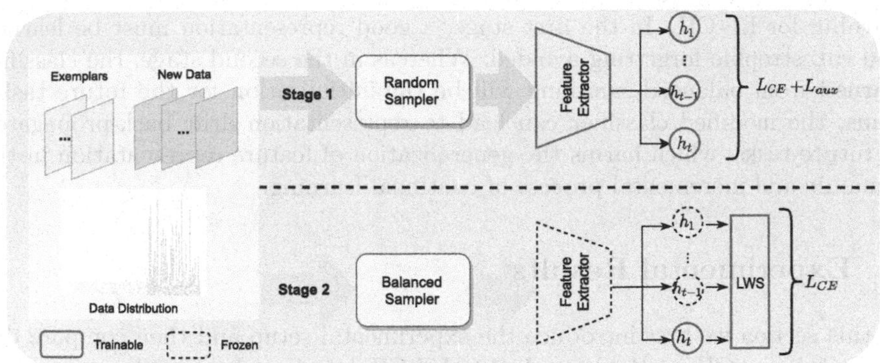

Fig. 3. An overview of our two-stage method with a learnable weight scaling layer for LT-CIL. Note that new data for the current task follows a long-tailed distribution and the memory contains a few samples from previous tasks. In the first stage, random sampling is used to learn a better feature extractor together with L_{CE} and method-specific loss L_{aux} to reduce forgetting.In the second stage, a balanced sampler is used to learn a balanced classifier together with a layer of learnable scaling weights (LWS). To reduce representation drift for future tasks, we fix the previous classifiers $h_{1:t-1}$ and only train the current head and LWS with cross entropy loss L_{CE}.

- In the **second stage**, a class-balanced sampler in which *each class* is sampled uniformly first and then each instance is sampled uniformly within it (also known as **balanced sampler**) is used to retrain the classifier h_ϕ to obtain better classification accuracy.

In LT-CIL, for task t we first learn a model from the first stage (seen in the top part of Fig. 3) using Eq. 2 with both cross entropy loss $L_{CE,t}$ and method-specific loss $L_{aux,t}$. In the second stage, we attach a single trainable layer, which we call a Learnable Weight Scaling (LWS) layer, $\mathbf{W} \in \mathrm{R}^{C_{1:t} \times 1}$ with dimension equal to the number of classes $C_{1:t}$ in the output of classifier $h_{1:t}$ at task t (as shown in the bottom part of Fig. 3).

The LWS is used to balance between classes with different numbers of samples in the long-tailed distribution. The final output of the model $\hat{\mathbf{z}}$ is calculated using an element-wise product of the classifier output with the LWS:

$$\hat{\mathbf{z}} = \mathbf{W} \odot h_{\phi_{1:t}}(f_{\theta_t}(\mathbf{x})) \tag{3}$$

We found it to be essential to fix previous head $h_{\phi_{1:t-1}}$ at the second stage when learning together with LWS layer, otherwise the modified $h_{\phi_{1:t-1}}$ can backpropagate in the future tasks and damage representation learning in the first stage. Note that only L_{CE} loss is used in the second stage no matter which loss is chosen for L_{aux}, and that the LWS layer $\mathbf{W}$ is applied only in the second stage for training and evaluation. The scaling layer for task t is discarded in the first stage training for the next task $t+1$.

Discussion. Conventional long-tailed learning considers a fixed set of classes, therefore it is challenging to apply two-stage methods directly to incremental learning for LT-CIL. In the first stage, a good representation must be learned and catastrophic forgetting avoided. Whereas in the second stage, the classifier learned from balanced sampling will be the initialization for the future tasks. Thus, the modified classifier can lead to representation drift back-propagated to future tasks, which harms the generalization of feature representation in the dynamic and incremental process of continual learning.

4 Experimental Results

In this section we first introduce the experimental setup and then compare different existing CIL methods applied to LT-CIL benchmarks. Finally we evaluate our two-stage method and conduct ablation study of key elements.

4.1 Experimental Setup

Implementation Details. We experiment on two datasets: CIFAR-100 and ImageNet-Subset with 100 classes. We use the publicly available implementations of existing CIL methods in the framework FACIL [27] and implement our two-stage algorithm with long-tailed data loader in the same framework for fair comparison. We follow LUCIR and PODNET by starting with a large first task with half of the classes in each dataset and equally dividing the remaining classes in subsequent tasks.

We use ResNet-32 for CIFAR-100 ResNet-18 for ImageNet-Subset. We use an initial learning rate of 0.1, and divide it by 10 after 80 and 120 epochs (160 epochs in total) for CIFAR-100. ImageNet-Subset, the learning rate starts from 0.1 and is divided by 10 after 30 and 60 epochs (90 epochs in total). The batch size is 128 for all experiments. For stage two training, the learning rate is set to 0.1 and we train it for 30 epochs.

Evaluation Protocols. We use average accuracy over all classes and average incremental accuracy over all tasks as evaluation metrics. We first evaluate different methods on LT-CIL scenarios with an imbalance ratio $\rho = 0.01$ and 20 exemplars per class, and report varying imbalance ratios and number of exemplars in Sect. 4.4.

4.2 Conventional Methods on LT-CIL Scenarios

In this section we analyze the performance of four popular CIL methods: LwF [20] with exempalrs, EEIL [7], LUCIR [13], and PODNET [10]). In Fig. 4(a) we first evaluate on conventional CIL as a reference. We then evaluate on the Ordered LT-CIL setting in Fig. 4(b). It is clear that LT-CIL is a more challenging scenario given that joint training drops from 68.64 to 36.94. Interestingly, LUCIR with nearest class mean (NCM) classifier obtains the best performance in average incremental accuracy. LUCIR is much better than PODNET for the tail classes with few samples in the end of training, except for the last task.

Similarly, as seen in Fig. 4(c), the overall performance on Shuffled LT-CIL scenario for all methods is much worse than in the conventional CIL scenario. LUCIR with NCM classifier again achieves the best performance.

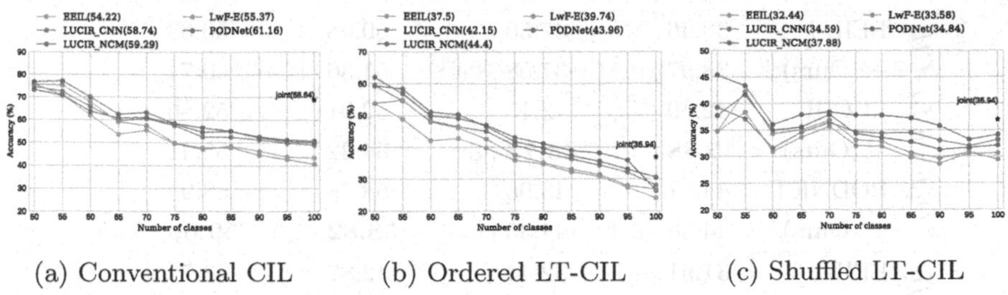

(a) Conventional CIL (b) Ordered LT-CIL (c) Shuffled LT-CIL

Fig. 4. Average accuracy for different scenarios on CIFAR-100. Average incremental accuracy is in the parentheses.

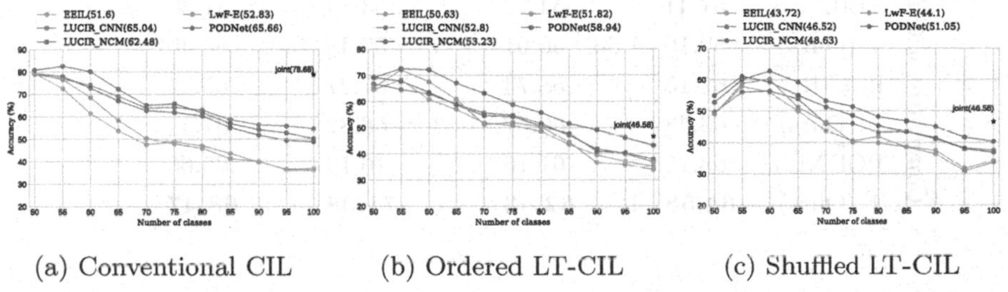

(a) Conventional CIL (b) Ordered LT-CIL (c) Shuffled LT-CIL

Fig. 5. Average accuracy for different scenarios on ImageNet-Subset. Average incremental accuracy is in parentheses.

In Fig. 5 we report on the same experiment performed on ImageNet-Subset. When we apply these methods to LT scenarios, PODNET achieves significantly better accuracy compared to other methods with average incremental accuracy of 58.94 and 51.05 for Ordered LT-CIL and Shuffled LT-CIL, respectively. For conventional CIL, methods often has similar rankings in terms of performance for different datasets as shown in Fig. 4 (a) and 5 (a). While for LT-CIL, we can see that LUCIR outperforms PODNET on CIFAR-100 but achieves worse results than PODNET on ImageNet-Subset. It suggests that these methods are not as robust as in the conventional CIL scenario.

4.3 Results for Our Two-Stage Method

Our Method for LT-CIL. In Table 1 we integrate our proposed two-stage strategy into three existing methods: EEIL, LUCIR (with CNN classifier), and

Table 1. Comparison of average incremental accuracy on CIFAR-100 and ImageNet-Subset in the LT-CIL and conventional CIL scenarios.

	Methods	CIFAR-100		ImageNet-Subset	
		5 tasks	*10 tasks*	*5 tasks*	*10 tasks*
Ordered LT-CIL	EEIL	38.46	37.50	50.68	50.63
	+ (Ours)	38.97+0.51	37.58+0.08	51.36+0.68	50.74+0.11
	LUCIR	42.69	42.15	52.91	52.80
	+ (Ours)	**45.88**+3.19	**45.73**+3.58	54.22+1.31	55.41+2.61
	PODNET	44.07	43.96	58.78	58.94
	+ (Ours)	44.38+0.31	44.35+0.39	**58.82**+0.04	**59.09**+0.15
Shuffled LT-CIL	EEIL	31.91	32.44	42.87	43.72
	+ (Ours)	34.19+2.28	33.70+1.26	49.31+6.44	48.26+4.54
	LUCIR	35.09	34.59	45.80	46.52
	+ (Ours)	**39.40**+4.31	**39.00**+4.41	**52.08**+6.28	51.91+5.39
	PODNET	34.64	34.84	49.69	51.05
	+ (Ours)	36.37+1.73	37.03+2.19	51.55+1.86	**52.60**+1.55
Conventional CIL	EEIL	57.41	54.22	53.84	47.30
	+ (Ours)	59.10+1.69	56.91+2.69	57.45+3.61	53.40+6.10
	LUCIR	61.15	58.74	67.21	65.04
	+ (Ours)	63.48+2.33	60.57+1.83	68.82+1.61	67.44+2.40
	PODNET	63.15	61.16	70.13	65.66
	+ (Ours)	**64.58**+1.43	**62.63**+1.47	**71.08**+0.95	**68.47**+2.81

PODNET. In general, the two-stage strategy helps on all three methods in both 5- and 10-task settings. The improvement is especially noticeable in the Shuffled LT-CIL scenario. Specifically, for EEIL, our method only improves by a small margin on Ordered LT-CIL scenario but boosts significantly on Shuffled LT-CIL. It outperforms EEIL by 2.28 and 1.26 on CIFAR-100 when $T = 5$ and $T = 10$, respectively for Shuffled LT-CIL. The improvement is even larger on ImageNet-Subset with 6.44 and 4.54 improvement in absolute accuracy. For LUCIR, we see a consistent boost by adding our method, improving from 1.31 to 6.28 for CIFAR-100 and ImageNet-Subset, respectively. PODNET is the best baseline in most scenarios where we observe a smaller gain with our proposed method compared to LUCIR. Overall, PODNET and LUCIR with our method can achieve very competitive results, which improves the consistency for both Ordered LT-CIL and Shuffled LT-CIL.

Our Method for Conventional CIL. Surprisingly, as seen in Table 1, when we combine ours with existing methods the performance is improved not only in LT-CIL scenarios but also for conventional CIL. We believe this is due to the imbalance caused by limited memory for storing exemplars from previous tasks.

Results on Real-World Long-Tailed Dataset. We experiment with 100 classes chosen from the iNaturalist dataset. We randomly chose 100 classes from the pantae super category and tested LUCIR and LUCIR+ with the data separated into 5 tasks with a base task of 50 classes. Results show that LUCIR can achieve an accuracy of 32.34%, and LUCIR+ with two stage training about 1.46% higher. iNaturalist is a real-world dataset with long-tailed distribution, and thus the value of ρ is undefined. We estimate it to be about 0.01. It shows how our method perform in real-world dataset under long-tailed distribution.

Further Results on AANets [23] and DER [43]. We report results for AANets (based on LUCIR) on Shuffle LT-CIL scenario (CIFAR-100 with 10-task setting). AANets outperforms LUCIR by a large margin achieving 38.53 in average incremental accuracy, and adding our method still improves over it by about 1%. We found that DER does not work well on long-tail scenarios (with only 29.54 in average accuracy), but our method improves it by about 4%.

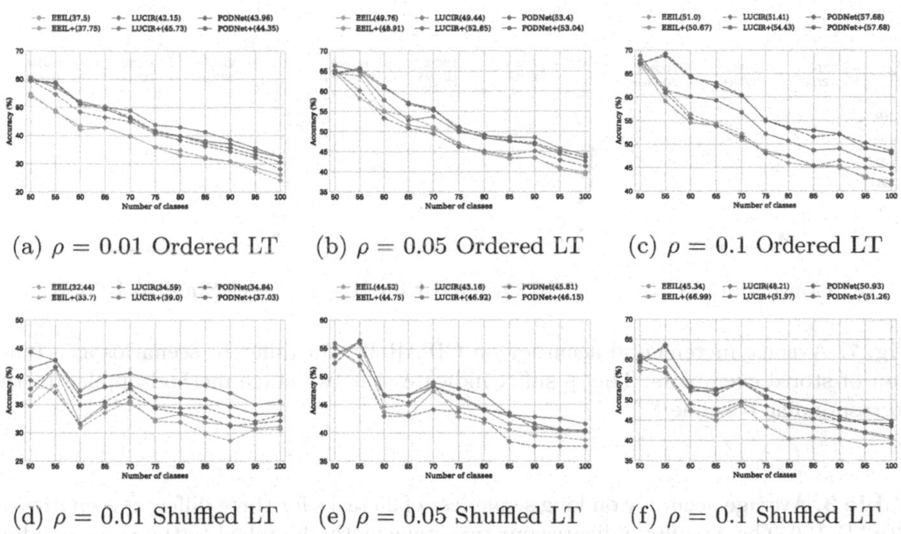

(a) $\rho = 0.01$ Ordered LT (b) $\rho = 0.05$ Ordered LT (c) $\rho = 0.1$ Ordered LT

(d) $\rho = 0.01$ Shuffled LT (e) $\rho = 0.05$ Shuffled LT (f) $\rho = 0.1$ Shuffled LT

Fig. 6. Average accuracy on CIFAR-100 dataset for different imbalance ratios. The top row is for Ordered LT-CIL and the bottom row for Shuffled LT-CIL. The + suffix indicates our two-stage method applied to the corresponding baseline.

Table 2. Ablation study on effectiveness of different components. $h_{1:t-1}$ denotes the classification heads up to task $t-1$.

Fix $h_{1:t-1}$	LWS	Conventional	Ordered	Shuffled
		26.28	33.54	23.41
✓		60.00	43.52	37.38
	✓	60.28	44.45	38.13
✓	✓	**60.57**	**45.73**	**39.01**

4.4 Ablation Study

Ablation on Imbalance Ratio. In this section we analyze three different imbalance ratios: $\rho = 0.01$, $\rho = 0.05$ and $\rho = 0.1$. The smaller the ratio, the more skewed the distribution. In Fig. 6 we give results for three different baselines (EEIL, LUCIR and PODNET) and our two-stage approach applied to them (EEIL+, LUCIR+ and PODNET+). As seen in Fig. 6(a–c), for the Ordered LT-CIL scenario PODNET surpasses LUCIR by a larger margin as imbalance ratio ρ increases. However, LUCIR obtains the best performance when $\rho = 0.01$ but is worse than PODNET by a large margin when $\rho = 0.1$. Overall, our two-stage method consistently boosts accuracy of most methods, especially for LUCIR+. For the Shuffled LT-CIL scenario in Fig. 6 (d–f), we see that PODNET outperforms LUCIR for all three ρ. The proposed two-stage method further improves performance, especially for LUCIR, resulting in LUCIR+ with the best overall performance. More results on ImageNet-Subset can be found in the supplementary material.

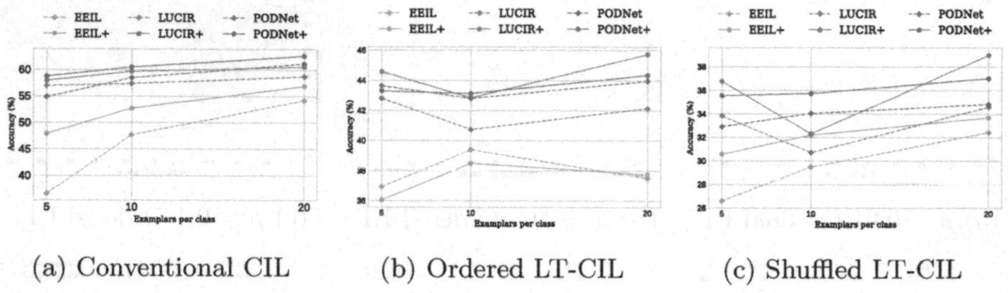

(a) Conventional CIL (b) Ordered LT-CIL (c) Shuffled LT-CIL

Fig. 7. Average incremental accuracy on CIFAR-100 for different scenarios as a function of stored exemplars. The + suffix indicates our two-stage method applied to the corresponding baseline.

Table 3. Average accuracy on long sequences of 25 tasks for three different scenarios on CIFAR-100. The + suffix indicates our two-stage method applied to the corresponding baseline.

	EEIL	EEIL+	LUCIR	LUCIR+	PODNet	PODNet+
Conventional	51.07	53.24	52.02	56.25	58.42	**60.47**
Ordered	39.47	40.03	38.31	**43.65**	41.47	40.78
Shuffled	32.20	34.68	30.68	**37.38**	35.75	37.09

Ablation on Exemplar Memory Size. We evaluate different methods with 5, 10, and 20 exemplars per class. As expected, we see in Fig. 7(a) that in the conventional CIL setting increasing exemplars results in better performance. However, for Ordered LT-CIL in Fig. 7(b) we see that LUCIR and our two-stage method LUCIR+ both drop when increasing from 5 to 10 exemplars, but recover with 20 exemplars. For both EEIL and EEIL+, the best performance is obtained with 10 exemplars, which may be due to the long-tailed distribution of the final tasks. Both PODNET and PODNET+ obtains better performance with more exemplars. Similarly, for Shuffled LT-CIL in Fig. 7(c) performance of both EEIL and PODNET increases with more exemplars, but LUCIR drops at 10 exemplars.

Effectiveness of Different Components. We ablate the two main components of fixing previous head $h_{1:t-1}$ until $t-1$ task and using LWS in the second stage. As seen from Table 2, without using either component the performance is very poor in all three scenarios. Both fixing the previous head $h_{1:t-1}$ and using LWS significantly boost accuracy, in particular for the conventional scenario which is up to 2.5 times higher. Using both components results in the best overall performance.

Long Task Sequences. In this experiment we evaluate on a longer sequence of 25 tasks in CIFAR-100 for all three scenarios. As we see in Table 3, our method improves over all baselines in this more challenging setting.LUCIR gains the most from our two-stage approach, with performance increasing by up to 6.7. More results on ImageNet-Subset can be found in the supplementary material.

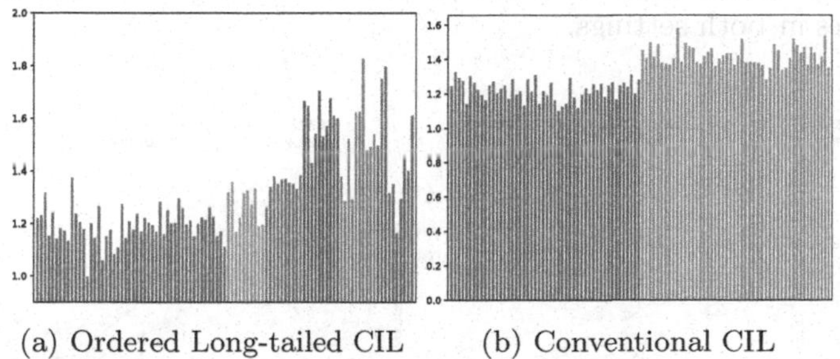

(a) Ordered Long-tailed CIL (b) Conventional CIL

Fig. 8. LWS weights for Ordered LT-CIL (6 tasks) and conventional CIL scenarios (2 tasks) on ImageNet-Subset. Different colors indicate the weights for different tasks. (Color figure online)

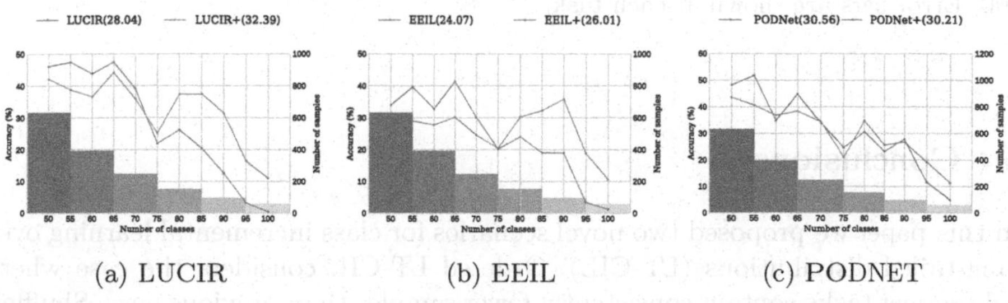

(a) LUCIR (b) EEIL (c) PODNET

Fig. 9. The average accuracy curves with data distribution bars at the last task for Ordered LT-CIL on CIFAR100.

Analysis of LWS Layer. In Fig. 8 we plot the weights of the LWS layer for LUCIR+ after learning the last task. Since the classes in the end of training consist of fewer and fewer samples, the LWS is capable of learning larger weights for them to balance with previous classes. In the conventional CIL scenario, the LWS weight for the current task is significantly larger than the older one, which can help predict correct labels for current classifier without modifying the feature representations too much in a two-stage framework, and thus reducing the forgetting of previous knowledge.

Visualization of Effectiveness of Our Method. As seen in Fig. 9, different methods and their corresponding two-stage versions are evaluated after learning the last task (5-tasks). It is clear that LUCIR+ and EEIL+ can significantly boost the performance of tail classes by losing relatively less for the head classes. PODNET+ improves over PODNET by a small margin for the tail classes with less drops for head classes.

Ablation on Class Order. To verify the robustness of our approach, we ran experiments with four different random seeds in the Shuffled LT-CIL scenario on CIFAR-100.As shown in Fig. 10, the compared methods behave differently but the overall trend for all methods are clear. LUCIR remains on the top in the last several tasks. All methods with the proposed two-stage strategy improve over the baselines in both settings.

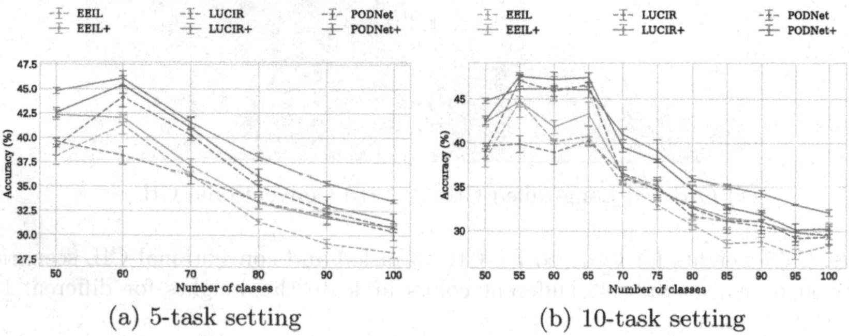

Fig. 10. Average accuracy for Shuffled LT-CIL with multiple random seeds on CIFAR-100. Error bars are shown at each task.

5 Conclusions

In this paper we proposed two novel scenarios for class incremental learning over long-tailed distributions (LT-CIL). Ordered LT-CIL considers the case where subsequent tasks contain consistently fewer samples than previous ones. Shuffled LT-CIL, on the other hand, refers to the case in which the degree of imbalance for each task is different and randomly distributed. Our experiments demonstrate that the existing state-of-the-art in CIL is significantly less robust when applied to long-tailed class distribution. To address the problem of LT-CIL, we propose a two-stage method with a learnable weight scaling layer that compensates for class imbalance. Our approach significantly outperforms the state-of-the-art on CIFAR-100 and ImageNet100 with long-tailed class imbalance. Our two-stage approach is complimentary to existing methods for CIL and can be easily and profitably integrated into them. We believe that our work can serve as a test bed for future development of long-tailed class incremental learning.

Acknowledgments. This work is funded by National Key Research and the Development Program of China (No. 2018AAA0100400), NSFC (No. 61922046), the S&T innovation project from the Chinese Ministry of Education, and by the European Commission under the Horizon 2020 Programme, grant number 951911 – AI4Media.

References

1. Abdelsalam, M., Faramarzi, M., Sodhani, S., Chandar, S.: IIRC: incremental implicitly-refined classification. In: Proceedings of the IEEE/CVF Conference on Computer Vision and Pattern Recognition, pp. 11038–11047 (2021)
2. Ahn, H., Kwak, J., Lim, S., Bang, H., Kim, H., Moon, T.: SS-IL: separated softmax for incremental learning. In: Proceedings of the IEEE/CVF International Conference on Computer Vision, pp. 844–853 (2021)
3. Aljundi, R., Babiloni, F., Elhoseiny, M., Rohrbach, M., Tuytelaars, T.: Memory aware synapses: learning what (not) to forget. In: Ferrari, V., Hebert, M., Sminchisescu, C., Weiss, Y. (eds.) ECCV 2018. LNCS, vol. 11207, pp. 144–161. Springer, Cham (2018). https://doi.org/10.1007/978-3-030-01219-9_9
4. Belouadah, E., Popescu, A.: IL2M: class incremental learning with dual memory. In: ICCV, pp. 583–592 (2019)
5. Belouadah, E., Popescu, A., Kanellos, I.: A comprehensive study of class incremental learning algorithms for visual tasks. Neural Netw. **135**, 38–54 (2020)
6. Cao, K., Wei, C., Gaidon, A., Arechiga, N., Ma, T.: Learning imbalanced datasets with label-distribution-aware margin loss. In: Advances in Neural Information Processing Systems (2019)
7. Castro, F.M., Marín-Jiménez, M.J., Guil, N., Schmid, C., Alahari, K.: End-to-end incremental learning. In: Ferrari, V., Hebert, M., Sminchisescu, C., Weiss, Y. (eds.) ECCV 2018. LNCS, vol. 11216, pp. 241–257. Springer, Cham (2018). https://doi.org/10.1007/978-3-030-01258-8_15
8. Chu, P., Bian, X., Liu, S., Ling, H.: Feature space augmentation for long-tailed data. In: Vedaldi, A., Bischof, H., Brox, T., Frahm, J.-M. (eds.) ECCV 2020, Part XXIX. LNCS, vol. 12374, pp. 694–710. Springer, Cham (2020). https://doi.org/10.1007/978-3-030-58526-6_41
9. Delange, M., et al.: A continual learning survey: defying forgetting in classification tasks. IEEE Trans. Pattern Anal. Mach. Intell. **44**, 3366–3385 (2021)
10. Douillard, A., Cord, M., Ollion, C., Robert, T., Valle, E.: PODNet: pooled outputs distillation for small-tasks incremental learning. In: Vedaldi, A., Bischof, H., Brox, T., Frahm, J.-M. (eds.) ECCV 2020. LNCS, vol. 12365, pp. 86–102. Springer, Cham (2020). https://doi.org/10.1007/978-3-030-58565-5_6

11. Han, H., Wang, W.-Y., Mao, B.-H.: Borderline-SMOTE: a new over-sampling method in imbalanced data sets learning. In: Huang, D.-S., Zhang, X.-P., Huang, G.-B. (eds.) ICIC 2005. LNCS, vol. 3644, pp. 878–887. Springer, Heidelberg (2005). https://doi.org/10.1007/11538059_91
12. Hayes, T.L., Kafle, K., Shrestha, R., Acharya, M., Kanan, C.: REMIND your neural network to prevent catastrophic forgetting. In: Vedaldi, A., Bischof, H., Brox, T., Frahm, J.-M. (eds.) ECCV 2020. LNCS, vol. 12353, pp. 466–483. Springer, Cham (2020). https://doi.org/10.1007/978-3-030-58598-3_28
13. Hou, S., Pan, X., Loy, C.C., Wang, Z., Lin, D.: Learning a unified classifier incrementally via rebalancing. In: International Conference on Computer Vision (2019)
14. Huang, C., Li, Y., Loy, C.C., Tang, X.: Deep imbalanced learning for face recognition and attribute prediction. IEEE Trans. Pattern Anal. Mach. Intell. **42**(11), 2781–2794 (2019)
15. Japkowicz, N., Stephen, S.: The class imbalance problem: a systematic study. Intell. Data Anal. **6**(5), 429–449 (2002)
16. Kang, B., et al.: Decoupling representation and classifier for long-tailed recognition. In: International Conference on Learning Representations (2020)
17. Kim, C.D., Jeong, J., Kim, G.: Imbalanced continual learning with partitioning reservoir sampling. In: Vedaldi, A., Bischof, H., Brox, T., Frahm, J.-M. (eds.) ECCV 2020. LNCS, vol. 12358, pp. 411–428. Springer, Cham (2020). https://doi.org/10.1007/978-3-030-58601-0_25
18. Kirkpatrick, J., et al.: Overcoming catastrophic forgetting in neural networks. PNAS, 201611835 (2017)
19. Lee, J., Yun, J., Hwang, S., Yang, E.: Lifelong learning with dynamically expandable networks. In: ICLR (2018)
20. Li, Z., Hoiem, D.: Learning without forgetting. PAMI **40**(12), 2935–2947 (2018)
21. Lin, T.Y., Goyal, P., Girshick, R., He, K., Dollár, P.: Focal loss for dense object detection. In: Proceedings of the IEEE International Conference on Computer Vision, pp. 2980–2988 (2017)
22. Liu, X., et al.: Rotate your networks: better weight consolidation and less catastrophic forgetting. In: ICPR (2018)
23. Liu, Y., Schiele, B., Sun, Q.: Adaptive aggregation networks for class-incremental learning. In: Proceedings of the IEEE/CVF Conference on Computer Vision and Pattern Recognition, pp. 2544–2553 (2021)
24. Liu, Z., Miao, Z., Zhan, X., Wang, J., Gong, B., Yu, S.X.: Large-scale long-tailed recognition in an open world. In: Proceedings of the IEEE/CVF Conference on Computer Vision and Pattern Recognition, pp. 2537–2546 (2019)
25. Mallya, A., Davis, D., Lazebnik, S.: Piggyback: adapting a single network to multiple tasks by learning to mask weights. In: Ferrari, V., Hebert, M., Sminchisescu, C., Weiss, Y. (eds.) ECCV 2018. LNCS, vol. 11208, pp. 72–88. Springer, Cham (2018). https://doi.org/10.1007/978-3-030-01225-0_5
26. Mallya, A., Lazebnik, S.: PackNet: adding multiple tasks to a single network by iterative pruning. In: CVPR, pp. 7765–7773 (2018)
27. Masana, M., Liu, X., Twardowski, B., Menta, M., Bagdanov, A.D., van de Weijer, J.: Class-incremental learning: survey and performance evaluation. arXiv preprint arXiv:2010.15277 (2020)
28. McCloskey, M., Cohen, N.J.: Catastrophic interference in connectionist networks: the sequential learning problem. Psychol. Learn. Motiv. **24**, 109–165 (1989)
29. Parisi, G.I., Kemker, R., Part, J.L., Kanan, C., Wermter, S.: Continual lifelong learning with neural networks: a review. Neural Netw. **113**, 54–71 (2019)

30. Perez, L., Wang, J.: The effectiveness of data augmentation in image classification using deep learning. arXiv preprint arXiv:1712.04621 (2017)
31. Rajasegaran, J., Hayat, M., Khan, S., Khan, F.S., Shao, L.: Random path selection for incremental learning. In: Advances in Neural Information Processing Systems (2019)
32. Rebuffi, S.A., Kolesnikov, A., Sperl, G., Lampert, C.H.: iCaRL: incremental classifier and representation learning. In: Proceedings of the IEEE conference on Computer Vision and Pattern Recognition, pp. 2001–2010 (2017)
33. Schwarz, J., et al.: Progress & compress: a scalable framework for continual learning. In: Proceedings of International Conference on Machine Learning, vol. 80, pp. 4528–4537 (2018)
34. Serra, J., Suris, D., Miron, M., Karatzoglou, A.: Overcoming catastrophic forgetting with hard attention to the task. In: ICML, pp. 4555–4564 (2018)
35. Shin, H., Lee, J.K., Kim, J., Kim, J.: Continual learning with deep generative replay. In: NIPS (2017)
36. Shu, J., et al.: Meta-weight-net: learning an explicit mapping for sample weighting. arXiv preprint arXiv:1902.07379 (2019)
37. Tao, X., Hong, X., Chang, X., Dong, S., Wei, X., Gong, Y.: Few-shot class-incremental learning. In: Proceedings of the IEEE/CVF Conference on Computer Vision and Pattern Recognition, pp. 12183–12192 (2020)
38. Van de Ven, G.M., Tolias, A.S.: Three scenarios for continual learning. arXiv preprint arXiv:1904.07734 (2019)
39. Wang, X., Lian, L., Miao, Z., Liu, Z., Yu, S.X.: Long-tailed recognition by routing diverse distribution-aware experts. In: International Conference on Learning Representations (2021)
40. Wang, Y.X., Ramanan, D., Hebert, M.: Learning to model the tail. In: Proceedings of the 31st International Conference on Neural Information Processing Systems, pp. 7032–7042 (2017)
41. Wu, Y., et al.: Large scale incremental learning. In: International Conference on Computer Vision (2019)
42. Xiang, L., Ding, G., Han, J.: Learning from multiple experts: self-paced knowledge distillation for long-tailed classification. In: Vedaldi, A., Bischof, H., Brox, T., Frahm, J.-M. (eds.) ECCV 2020. LNCS, vol. 12350, pp. 247–263. Springer, Cham (2020). https://doi.org/10.1007/978-3-030-58558-7_15
43. Yan, S., Xie, J., He, X.: DER: dynamically expandable representation for class incremental learning. In: Proceedings of the IEEE/CVF Conference on Computer Vision and Pattern Recognition, pp. 3014–3023 (2021)
44. Yin, X., Yu, X., Sohn, K., Liu, X., Chandraker, M.: Feature transfer learning for face recognition with under-represented data. In: Proceedings of the IEEE/CVF Conference on Computer Vision and Pattern Recognition, pp. 5704–5713 (2019)
45. Zenke, F., Poole, B., Ganguli, S.: Continual learning through synaptic intelligence. In: ICML, pp. 3987–3995. JMLR. org (2017)
46. Zhang, H., Cisse, M., Dauphin, Y.N., Lopez-Paz, D.: mixup: Beyond empirical risk minimization. In: International Conference on Learning Representations (2018)
47. Zhang, S., Li, Z., Yan, S., He, X., Sun, J.: Distribution alignment: a unified framework for long-tail visual recognition. In: Proceedings of the IEEE/CVF Conference on Computer Vision and Pattern Recognition, pp. 2361–2370 (2021)
48. Zhang, X., Fang, Z., Wen, Y., Li, Z., Qiao, Y.: Range loss for deep face recognition with long-tailed training data. In: Proceedings of the IEEE International Conference on Computer Vision, pp. 5409–5418 (2017)

49. Zhong, Y., et al.: Unequal-training for deep face recognition with long-tailed noisy data. In: Proceedings of the IEEE/CVF Conference on Computer Vision and Pattern Recognition, pp. 7812–7821 (2019)
50. Zhong, Z., Cui, J., Liu, S., Jia, J.: Improving calibration for long-tailed recognition. In: Proceedings of the IEEE/CVF Conference on Computer Vision and Pattern Recognition, pp. 16489–16498 (2021)
51. Zhou, B., Cui, Q., Wei, X.S., Chen, Z.M.: BBN: bilateral-branch network with cumulative learning for long-tailed visual recognition. In: Proceedings of the IEEE/CVF Conference on Computer Vision and Pattern Recognition, pp. 9719–9728 (2020)

DLCFT: Deep Linear Continual Fine-Tuning for General Incremental Learning

Hyounguk Shon[1], Janghyeon Lee[2], Seung Hwan Kim[2], and Junmo Kim[1(✉)]

[1] Korea Advanced Institute of Science and Technology, Daejeon, South Korea
{hyounguk.shon,junmo.kim}@kaist.ac.kr
[2] LG AI Research, Seoul, South Korea
{janghyeon.lee,sh.kim}@lgresearch.ai

Abstract. Pre-trained representation is one of the key elements in the success of modern deep learning. However, existing works on continual learning methods have mostly focused on learning models incrementally from scratch. In this paper, we explore an alternative framework to incremental learning where we *continually fine-tune* the model from a pre-trained representation. Our method takes advantage of linearization technique of a pre-trained neural network for simple and effective continual learning. We show that this allows us to design a linear model where quadratic parameter regularization method is placed as the optimal continual learning policy, and at the same time enjoying the high performance of neural networks. We also show that the proposed algorithm enables parameter regularization methods to be applied to class-incremental problems. Additionally, we provide a theoretical reason why the existing parameter-space regularization algorithms such as EWC underperform on neural networks trained with cross-entropy loss. We show that the proposed method can prevent forgetting while achieving high continual fine-tuning performance on image classification tasks. To show that our method can be applied to general continual learning settings, we evaluate our method in data-incremental, task-incremental, and class-incremental learning problems.

Keywords: Continual learning · Incremental learning

1 Introduction

The ability to incrementally accumulate knowledge from a sequence of datasets is a crucial functionality that modern AI systems require. It is well known that

H. Shon—Work done during an internship at LG AI Research.

Supplementary Information The online version contains supplementary material available at https://doi.org/10.1007/978-3-031-19827-4_30.

S. Avidan et al. (Eds.): ECCV 2022, LNCS 13693, pp. 513–529, 2022.
https://doi.org/10.1007/978-3-031-19827-4_30

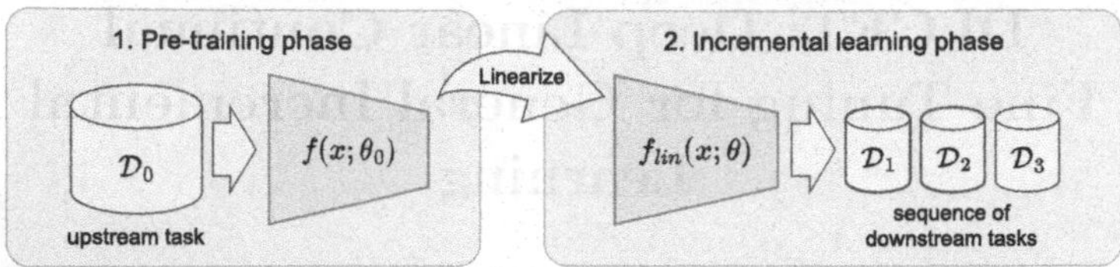

Fig. 1. Proposed continual fine-tuning framework. The model is first trained on a large dataset (e.g., ImageNet) to obtain general representation. At incremental learning phase, the model is continually fine-tuned and accumulates knowledge by learning from the sequentially arriving batches of dataset.

deep neural networks suffer from significant performance degradation when the learning is done sequentially. Such phenomena is referred as catastrophic forgetting (CF), which continual learning aims to address.

Transfer learning is one of the key contributing elements in the recent success of deep learning across various applications from visual to linguistic tasks. When dealing with visual signals, neural nets are often pre-trained on large datasets such as ImageNet [39] before training on the target task, which often brings significant performance boost. Although fine-tuning from a pre-trained representation is a standard practice adopted in a lot of modern deep learning applications, many of the existing approaches to continual learning assume a scenario where one needs to begin training from a randomly initialized model. In this work, we explore a practical alternative continual learning framework based on pre-training of neural network, coined *continual fine-tuning*.

Existing works on continual learning can be largely categorized into three groups: model regularization, data rehearsal, and parameter isolation [7]. Regularization-based methods aim to penalize the update either in function space [8,24] or in parameter space [2,9,18,20,22,23,32,38,45]. Parameter isolation methods [29,44] update the architecture in order to isolate the knowledge learned from each task in order to prevent forgetting. Rehearsal-based approaches [5,26,34,36] replay examples from previous tasks either by storing samples to an external memory buffer or learning a generative model. The rehearsal method has shown to be effective at regularization with a small extra cost.

Parameter regularization methods based on Fisher information matrix aim to represent the source task objective by second-order Taylor approximation, which is typically too expensive due to the quadratic memory cost of the Hessian matrix. Naturally, existing works have focused on efficient representation of the matrix via diagonal approximation [18,25] or Kronecker factorization [22,38]. Our work is motivated by a question that has been relatively overlooked in prior works: "Does better Hessian approximation improve continual learning?"

Although parameter regularization approaches are founded on a principled framework that computes the importance of the weights for each task, they have shown relatively underwhelming performance compared to rehearsal-based approaches. One of the main roadblocks of the regularization methods is to address the problems coming from their high parameter dimension and nonlinearity, which has left continual learning a particularly challenging problem to tackle. In this work, we show that it is possible to bring a significant boost to regularization methods by a simple modification on the loss function and reparametrization of the model.

The remaining portion of the paper is organized as follows: In Sect. 2, we provide background on continual learning methods, second-order derivative of neural networks, and linearization of neural networks. In Sect. 3.1, we provide reasoning on why existing parameter regularization methods underperform in mitigating catastrophic forgetting. In Sect. 3.2, we describe the proposed method, Deep Linear Continual Fine-tuning (DLCFT). In Sect. 3.3, we elaborate on how the proposed regularization method can be applied to the class-incremental problem where existing parameter regularization methods have been unable to be applied. In Sect. 4, we show the evaluation and analysis of the proposed method on data-/task-/class-incremental learning problems. Finally, in Sect. 5, we conclude the paper.

The main contributions of this work are summarized as follows:

- Instead of incrementally training a neural network from scratch, we propose an alternative approach to continual learning that leverages pre-trained representations, coined *continual fine-tuning.* We show that our approach introduces a novel method for simple and practical continual learning in deep learning.
- To continually adapt to a sequence of downstream tasks, we utilize pre-trained neural network through decomposing the model into nonlinear and linear components by linearization. We propose a learning algorithm that combines linearization and mean squared error loss that significantly boosts the effectiveness of quadratic weight regularization methods. Further, we provide justification on why linearization is the key component for a principled approach to optimal continual learning.
- Our method can be universally applied to various continual learning scenarios where new batches of data, task, or class are observed sequentially. Although data-incremental learning is an important open challenge to practical deep learning, relatively little attention has been given from the community. Notably, we show that our method can effectively learn in data-incremental scenario where batches of new data samples are observed sequentially. Additionally, we demonstrate our method in task-incremental and class-incremental learning scenarios with a small memory buffer.

2 Preliminaries

2.1 Continual Learning

Existing approaches to continual learning can be largely grouped into three families: regularization-based, rehearsal-based, and parameter isolation methods. Regularization method incorporates additional training objectives to prevent model from changing too much during training. One can regularize the outputs of the model to mitigate forgetting. Learning without forgetting (LwF) [24] is one of the early works that utilizes target task data as a surrogate for the source task samples. This method shows reasonably good performance when the source task domains and target task domains are similar, however is less effective when the task domains are dissimilar.

Parameter regularization methods aim to estimate the importance of parameters and use that as the prior for the parameters during training of the subsequent tasks. This was first adopted by elastic weight consolidation (EWC) [18] where the authors proposed to use the diagonal entries of Fisher information matrix. Online-structured Laplace approximation (OSLA) [38] used Kronecker-factored approximate curvature (K-FAC) [30] to incorporate off-diagonals of the Fisher information matrix. With neural networks having intra-batch dependency due to batch normalization, Extended K-FAC (XK-FAC) [22] generalized the method to take intra-batch dependency into account.

Rehearsal-based methods maintain a buffer that stores a small number of samples, and replay the examples in the training of the subsequent tasks. One of the pioneering methods is iCaRL [36] which keeps track of per-class samples for class-incremental learning problems. Some other line of works such as GEM [26] and A-GEM [5] performs constrained optimization by projecting the gradients so that they do not interfere with the previous tasks. DER [4] proposed to distill from the logits that are sampled and stored throughout the training. Parameter isolation methods [3,29,40,42] are based on dynamically allocating a set of parameters for each task so that the training does not interfere with each other.

2.2 Second-Order Derivatives of Neural Network

Computing and storing the Hessian matrix of neural networks is a difficult challenge due to their high parameter dimension. Hessian matrix of a probabilistic model can be approximated using Fisher information matrix (FIM) [33]. FIM can be interpreted as the second derivative of the KL-divergence between the model and target distribution, and can be efficiently estimated through Monte Carlo method.

Because the memory cost of the full Hessian matrix is quadratic to the size of the parameters, approximation or factorization technique is necessary to handle the matrix. One popular method is diagonal approximation of the Hessian, which neglects the influences of the off-digonal components. Another approach that can consider off-diagonal influences is block-diagonal approximation, which considers the correlations among intra-layer parameters. K-FAC [12,30] proposed to approximately factorize the block diagonals of a neural network's Fisher information matrix into a Kronecker product of covariance matrices:

$$\begin{aligned} F^{ll} &= \mathbb{E}_{y\sim p(y|x)}\left[\nabla_\theta \log p(y|x) \nabla_\theta \log p(y|x)^\top\right] \\ &= \mathbb{E}[(g\otimes a)(g\otimes a)^\top] = \mathbb{E}[(gg^\top)\otimes(aa^\top)] \\ &\approx \mathbb{E}[gg^\top]\otimes\mathbb{E}[aa^\top], \end{aligned} \tag{1}$$

where F^{ll} is the FIM diagonal block of the l-th layer, g is the pre-activation gradient, a is the input activation, and $\otimes$ indicates Kronecker product. K-FAC represents the curvature matrix in the form of a product between two factors, thereby reducing the memory cost from $\mathcal{O}(M^2 \times N^2)$ to $\mathcal{O}(M^2 + N^2)$, where M and N are the sizes of the input and output units of the layer, respectively.

Eigenvalue-corrected K-FAC [11] proposed to re-compute the diagonals in the eigenbasis obtained from K-FAC, thereby correcting the eigenvalues of the factorized FIM. Trace-restricted K-FAC (TK-FAC) [10] is a trace-exact variant which corrects the norm of the factorized FIM by further tracking the trace of FIM.

2.3 Linearization of Deep Neural Networks

Linear approximation in deep learning is a widely used concept as a means of estimating the proximal behavior of a neural network. Popular explanation methods such as Guided Backprop [43] and Grad-CAM [41] use the gradient with respect to the activations in order to estimate the network's the sensitivity against the input. Such techniques are based on the first-order derivatives of neural networks with respect to the input.

The first-order derivatives with respect to the parameters, on the other hand, have lead to interesting insights about the training of neural networks. Recent works regarding the training dynamics of deep neural networks [16,21] have found that randomly initialized neural networks behave linearly throughout gradient descent training in the infinite-width regime. In [16], it is shown that such model can be described by a specific kernel function, coined neural tangent kernel, defined by the first-order derivatives of the neural network. Moreover, recent works [1,31] have empirically shown that the observation also apply to finite-sized neural networks when they are pre-trained, and showed the linearized network can be fine-tuned to achieve comparable performance to the nonlinear network.

3 Continual Fine-Tuning

The goal of continual learning is to achieve the highest performance jointly on all tasks when the tasks arrive sequentially. Due to the sequential nature, the model is only allowed to observe a batch of data $\mathcal{D}_t$ at each task t. The performance of continual learning can be seen as upper bounded by multi-task learning, where the model trains jointly on all tasks,

$$\min_\theta \frac{1}{T}\sum_{t=1}^{T} \mathop{\mathbb{E}}_{(x,y)\in\mathcal{D}_t} \left[\lambda_t \mathcal{L}(f(x;\theta,t),y)\right], \tag{2}$$

where θ is the vectorized parameter of the linearized model, and λ_t controls the stability–plasticity between the tasks. To learn all tasks from sequentially arriving batches, parameter regularization methods aim to capture the source task objective as a quadratic function of parameters, *i.e.*,

$$\begin{aligned} \frac{1}{t}\sum_{i=1}^{t} \mathop{\mathbb{E}}_{(x,y)\in\mathcal{D}_i} [\lambda_i \mathcal{L}(f(x;\theta,i),y)] &= C + \frac{1}{2}(\theta-\theta_t)^\top A(\theta-\theta_t) + \mathcal{O}(\theta^3) \\ &\simeq C + \frac{1}{2}(\theta-\theta_t)^\top A(\theta-\theta_t), \end{aligned} \tag{3}$$

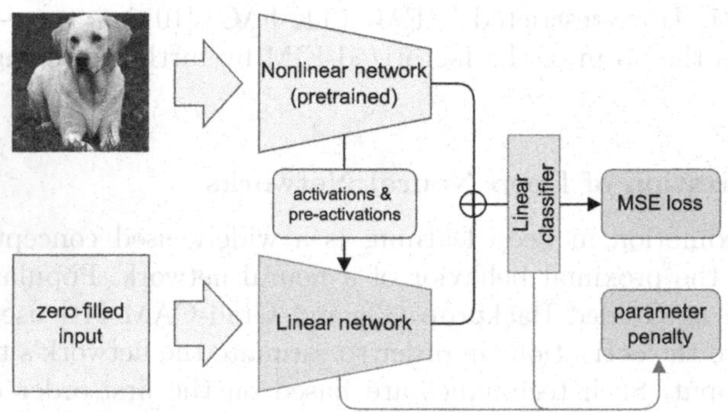

Fig. 2. Architecture of our deep linear continual fine-tuning model. Learnable modules are colored in blue. On forward pass, the image and a zero-filled tensor are passed into the nonlinear network (fixed) and linear network (learnable), respectively. The nonlinear feature and the linear residual feature are computed concurrently, which are then summed and passed to the linear classification layer. Notice that the output logits are strictly linear with respect to all learnable parameters. At training, MSE loss is used instead of cross-entropy. During continual learning, model is regularized by quadratic parameter penalty loss to prevent forgetting.

where A is the matrix whose each entry represents the importance of the corresponding parameter pair, C is a constant, and θ_t is the model parameters after learning the t-th task.

Parameter-based continual learning methods aim to accurately estimate the importance matrix A in order to closely approximate the multi-task learning objective. One popular approach is to use second-order Taylor approximation, where A becomes the Hessian matrix of the source task objective function.

3.1 Understanding the Problems of Quadratic Parameter Regularization

In this section, we provide why existing parameter regularizations show underwhelming performance in continual training of neural networks. We particularly look into two sources of problems which we call *vanishing curvature* and *higher-order error*. First, we show that softmax cross-entropy loss causes curvature to vanish to zero, thereby losing ability to represent parameter importance. Then, we show why this problem is amplified by nonlinearity of neural network.

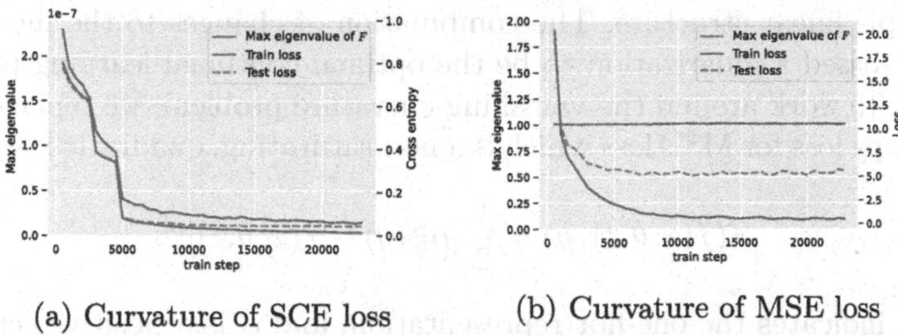

(a) Curvature of SCE loss (b) Curvature of MSE loss

Fig. 3. An MLP is trained on MNIST using softmax cross-entropy (SCE) and mean squared error (MSE) losses, and the maximum eigenvalue of the Fisher information matrix of each loss function is traced and plotted in red. The eigenvalues of SCE loss diminish to zero as the model fits the data, whereas that of MSE loss remains constant.

First, we investigate the behavior of FIM of a model that predicts categorical distribution and trained using cross-entropy loss. The second order derivatives of a probabilistic model is often estimated through FIM, which is the covariance matrix of the gradient with respect to the log-likelihood.

$$F_\theta = \mathbb{E}_{y\sim p_\theta(y|x)}\left[\nabla_\theta \log p_\theta(y|x) \nabla_\theta \log p_\theta(y|x)^\top\right] \tag{4}$$

It can be seen from Eq. (4) that as the model $p_\theta(y|x)$ perfectly fits the target label, the sampled y becomes the target label with probability$\rightarrow$1 and $\nabla_\theta \log p_\theta(y|x) \rightarrow 0$, therefore $F_\theta \rightarrow 0$. This indicates that FIM loses its ability to represent parameter importance at near zero-loss optima. See Sec. A in the supplementary for detailed proof. We name this *vanishing curvature problem*. Additionally, notice that this behavior is caused by choosing to fit a categorical distribution, e.g., softmax layer. Figure 3a shows that the maximum eigenvalue of FIM continues to vanish to zero as the negative log-likelihood approaches to zero loss, even after the test loss has converged. As a result, the parameters are under-regularized.

Secondly, quadratic approximation assumes that the objective function is a quadratic function with respect to the parameters. However, the true loss function is non-quadratic due to the cross-entropy loss and the non-linearity of neural networks. This introduces higher-order error terms to dominate in the second-order approximation. Combined with the vanishing curvature behavior, this amplifies the error of the loss approximation as the parameters are under-damped and the model can drift off the trust region of the local loss approximation which causes catastrophic forgetting.

3.2 Deep Linear Continual Fine-Tuning (DLCFT)

To this end, we propose an alternative approach based on continual fine-tuning framework. Our change to the model is two-fold; To tackle the vanishing curvature problem, we replace the cross-entropy loss with MSE loss function. To resolve the non-convexity problem, we choose to *approximate the model* such that it has simple linear structure. The combination of changes to the model allows parameter-based regularization to be the optimal continual learning policy.

Firstly, to work around the vanishing curvature problem, we replace softmax cross-entropy loss for MSE loss which is a non-saturating, quadratic loss function.

$$\ell(f(x;\theta,t),y) = \frac{1}{2}||\alpha\phi(y) - f(x;\theta,t)||^2 \tag{5}$$

Here, $\phi(\cdot)$ indicates the one-hot representation, and α is a positive scaling constant which is fixed throughout all tasks. We followed [1,14] and set $\alpha = 15$.

Secondly, to tackle the higher-order error problem, we linearize the neural network. We apply first-order Taylor approximation of a pre-trained neural network [1,31] which decomposes the feature extractor into a frozen non-linear network and a trainable linear network. Instead of fine-tuning the full non-linear neural network, we train the linearized neural network, *i.e.*,

$$g_{lin}(x;\psi) = g(x;\psi_0) + D_\psi g(x;\psi_0)\cdot\psi, \tag{6}$$

where $D_\psi g(x;\psi_0)$ is the Jacobian of the network evaluated at the pre-trained point ψ_0. Then we learn a linear classification layer using the linearized feature,

$$f(x;\theta,t) = w_t \cdot g_{lin}(x;\psi) + b_t, \tag{7}$$

where $g(x;\psi_0)$ is the pretrained nonlinear feature extraction network and $\theta = \{\psi, w_t, b_t\}$ corresponds to the parameters of the linearized model. For data-incremental learning setup, we train the linearized feature extraction network and a single linear classifier. We regularize both the feature extractor and the linear classifier $\{\psi, w_t, b_t\}$. For task-incremental learning setup, we use a shared linearized feature extraction network $g_{lin}(x;\psi)$ along with a linear classifier assigned to each task. We regularize only the feature extractor ψ as each task-specific classifier does not interfere with each other. For class-incremental learning, we train the feature extractor and append output units to the classifier at the beginning of each task.

Finally, notice that when combined with linear model, this change makes the objective function fully quadratic with respect to the parameters. This enables us to accurately represent the objective function while allowing the model to be highly accurate and expressive. The difference that these changes bring is that because the model is linear with respect to its parameters and the loss function is mean-squared error, the objective becomes quadratic with respect to the parameters. Most notably, it follows that the quadratic parameter penalty is the optimal strategy to represent the source task objective for continual learning, *i.e.*,

$$\begin{aligned} \ell(f(x;\theta,t),y) &= \frac{1}{2}||\alpha\phi(y) - f(x;\theta,t)||^2 \\ &= \frac{1}{2}(\theta-\theta_t)^\top H_\theta(\theta-\theta_t) + C, \end{aligned} \tag{8}$$

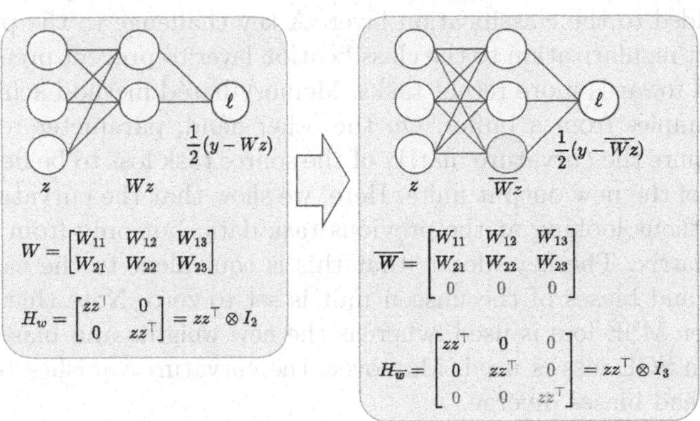

Fig. 4. Curvature for classifier in class-incremental learning. An example of a linear classification layer with two original output units and an appended unit. The appended output unit and its zero-initialized weights are outlined in red. Bias is omitted for simplicity. The corresponding updates to the weight matrix and the block diagonal of the Hessian matrix are marked in red (Color figure online).

where θ_t is the trained parameters after the t-th task. We can apply any curvature approximation algorithm to efficiently store H_θ in memory. *e.g.*, TK-FAC [10]. The final objective function for continual learning is,

$$\mathcal{L}_{data} = \mathbb{E}_{(x,y)\sim\mathcal{D}_t}[\ell(f(x;\theta,t),y)] \tag{9}$$

$$\mathcal{L}_{reg} = \frac{1}{2}(\theta-\theta_{t-1})^\top H(\theta-\theta_{t-1}) \tag{10}$$

$$\mathcal{L} = \frac{1}{t}\mathcal{L}_{data} + \frac{t-1}{t}\mathcal{L}_{reg}, \tag{11}$$

where the target task objective and source task objective are weighted by $1 : (t-1)$ for balancing, and H corresponds to the Hessian of the source task objectives.

3.3 Classifier Regularization for Class-Incremental Problem

In this section, we describe how the proposed method is extended to class-incremental learning problem. To the best of our knowledge, this is the first work that shows how parameter regularization can be reasonably applied to class-incremental learning problem.

In class-incremental learning, each task requires the model to learn a set of novel classes while the evaluation is done jointly over the current and previous tasks. Unlike task-incremental setup, task oracle is not provided at test time. At the beginning of each task, a set of output units that corresponds to the new classes is added to the classification layer. A key challenge to the problem is to apply correct regularization to the classification layer to prevent predictions from being biased towards more recent tasks. Memory-based method achieves this by replaying samples from a buffer. On the other hand, parameter regularization methods require the curvature matrix of the source task loss to be defined for the parameters of the new output units. Here, we show that the curvature matrix is obtained without looking at the previous task data, but only from the existing curvature matrix. The key idea is that this is equivalent to the case where all the weights and biases of the unseen unit is set to zero. Note that this is only possible when MSE loss is used, whereas the new weights and biases diverge to infinity when SCE loss is used. Moreover, the curvature vanishes to zero when the weights and biases diverge.

Let us consider a linear classification layer with increasing output units for class-incremental setup. Adding a set of classes amounts to adding a set of corresponding output units to the weight matrix W. Let $\overline{W}$ be the augmented weight matrix with the added output units, and y be the target. Then, for the loss function

$$\mathcal{L}\left(\overline{W}\right) = \mathbb{E}\left[\frac{1}{2}||y - \overline{W}z||^2\right], \tag{12}$$

the second derivative with respect to $\overline{w} := \text{Vec}\left(\overline{W}\right)$ is

$$\frac{\partial^2 \mathcal{L}}{\partial \overline{w} \partial \overline{w}^\top} = \frac{\partial}{\partial \overline{w}} \mathbb{E}[(y - \overline{W}z)z^\top] = \mathbb{E}[zz^\top \otimes I] = \mathbb{E}[zz^\top] \otimes I. \tag{13}$$

Because $\mathbb{E}[zz^\top]$ has been already obtained through K-FAC regularization, we do not need additional computation or data to compute the second derivative of the appended weight.

We additionally employ a small buffer memory $\mathcal{M}$ to replay samples of previous tasks. In previous works, combining replay with parameter regularization has not been a common practice due to underwhelming performance of curvature-based regularization. However in the proposed method, the only source of error is the approximation of the curvature matrix. Whereas in replay methods, the source of error is the subsampling of source task dataset. Therefore, we can combine the proposed parameter regularization with an additional replay loss to complement for the approximation error. The final regularization objective is,

$$\mathcal{L}_{reg} = \frac{\lambda}{2} \cdot (\theta - \theta_{t-1})^\top H(\theta - \theta_{t-1}) + (1 - \lambda) \cdot \mathbb{E}_{\mathcal{M}}[\ell(f(x; \theta, t), y)]. \tag{14}$$

4 Experiments

4.1 Evaluation Methods and Implementation Details

Evaluation Settings. We evaluate our method on three types of incremental learning (IL) problems: data-IL, task-IL, and class-IL.

Models. We use ResNet-18 [13] architecture for all benchmarks. For the linearized ResNet-18, we followed [1] and replace all ReLU nonlinearities with LeakyReLU [28]. We also followed [31] and folded the batch norm parameters into the convolution layers.

Pre-training. For the experiments using CIFAR-100 dataset [19], we use ImageNet32 [6] which consists of 32×32 downsampled images of ImageNet-1k dataset [6,39]. At pre-training phase, we train the model for 100 epochs using SGD optimizer with learning rate $\eta = 10^{-1}$, batch size $= 256$, weight decay $= 10^{-5}$. We use the cosine annealing [27] learning rate schedule. For the experiments using MIT-67 dataset [35], we use the pretrained ResNet-18 model downloaded using TorchVision[1], which trained on ImageNet-1k. To obtain the model with LeakyReLU nonlinearties, we replicate the scheme from [1] and fine-tune the downloaded model on ImageNet-1k for an additional epoch using SGD with learning rate $\eta = 10^{-4}$.

Datasets. For data-IL setting, we used Seq-CIFAR-100 dataset [19,36] split into 10 and 100 tasks, each task having 5000 and 500 samples, respectively. Additionally, we used Seq-MIT-67 for large-resolution dataset, which is MIT-67 dataset [35] split into 4 tasks. For task-IL and class-IL settings, we used Seq-CIFAR-100 with 10 tasks each containing a disjoint set of classes.

Curvature Approximation. For approximation of the Hessian matrix, we use K-FAC [12,30] and TK-FAC [10].

Data Augmentation. For Seq-CIFAR-100, we apply random crop with 4 pixels of zero padding, followed by random horizontal flip. For Seq-MIT-67, we first apply resizing to 256×256 then apply random crop to 224×224. At test time, we resize to 256×256 and apply center crop to 224×224.

Training Scheme and Hyperparameters. For training nonlinear models, we used softmax cross-entropy loss and SGD optimizer with initial learning rate 10^{-3} and momentum 0.9. For training linearized models, we used MSE loss and Adam optimizer [17] with initial learning rate 10^{-4} and $(\beta_1, \beta_2) = (0.9, 0.999)$. In data-IL and task-IL experiments, we enable batch normalization [15] at the first task only. For the loss used in class-IL, we set $\lambda = 1/2$.

Other Implementation Details. We used Nvidia RTX 3090 GPUs and PyTorch to conduct experiments. To add a pair of Kronecker-factored curvature matrices that each correspond to the source task and the target task, we take the weighted sum the factorized matrices by $(t-1) : t$ for each factors.

[1] https://github.com/pytorch/vision.

For all experiments, we used weight decay rate of 10^{-5}. For methods that uses buffer memory, we set the size of the buffer to 500 samples. We used reservoir sampling strategy to update the buffer.

4.2 Incremental Learning Benchmarks

Data-Incremental Learning We benchmark our method on data-IL setup in three different settings. Firstly, we tested on ten splits of Seq-CIFAR-100 training set to simulate a short sequence of data streams. Secondly, we tested on a hundred splits of Seq-CIFAR-100 training set to evaluate how the proposed method scales to a very long sequence. Finally, we tested on four splits of Seq-MIT-67 training to evaluate the methods on a high-resolution images.

Table 1. Experiment results for data-incremental learning. 'None' indicates no regularization applied during incremental learning. The experiments are averaged over three runs. † denotes that K-FAC [12,30] is used for curvature approximation and ‡ denotes TK-FAC [10] is used.

Dataset	Seq-CIFAR-100		Seq-MIT-67
Sequence length	10	100	4
None	78.74	71.83	63.48
LwF [24]	80.25	70.95	67.21
EWC [18]	78.88	72.61	63.68
MAS [2]	75.24	52.50	62.49
OSLA [38]	79.23	73.10	64.08
DLCFT† (Ours)	**81.95**	**75.92**	**70.55**
DLCFT‡ (Ours)	**82.70**	**80.07**	**70.52**
Joint	83.57		74.40

Table 1 shows performance in data-IL measured by final accuracy. We observed that Memory Aware Synapses (MAS) [2] fails to learn incrementally as it does not estimate accurate weight importance. On the other hand, our method performs much better than the baselines and achieves comparable performance to the joint training as it captures the curvature of the loss of the previous tasks accurately. Additionally, in Fig. 5, we show the performance trends plotted against increasing data-IL tasks. Notably, we observed that the proposed method significantly outperforms the baselines on the long sequence length setup.

Task-/Class-Incremental Learning Table 2 shows performance comparison on task-incremental setup. The benchmark consists of 10 tasks with disjoint class categories obtained from CIFAR-100, each consisting of 10 classes. We observe that our method performs better than the baselines.

4.3 Evaluation of Incrementally Learned Representations

Because we use pre-trained networks that has already learned transferable representation from a large labeled dataset, it is possible that the performance of the method is more attributed to the linear classification layer, rather than adjusting the features through the sequential tasks. To verify that our continual fine-tuning method does learn better representations through incremental learning, we use K-NN classifier to evaluate the quality of the representations learned through the continual fine-tuning process. The results are show in Fig. 6. The plot shows the discriminative performance of the fine-tuned feature by decoupling the linear classifier from the evaluation. We observed that the K-NN accuracy consistently and monotonically increases as the model observes more tasks.

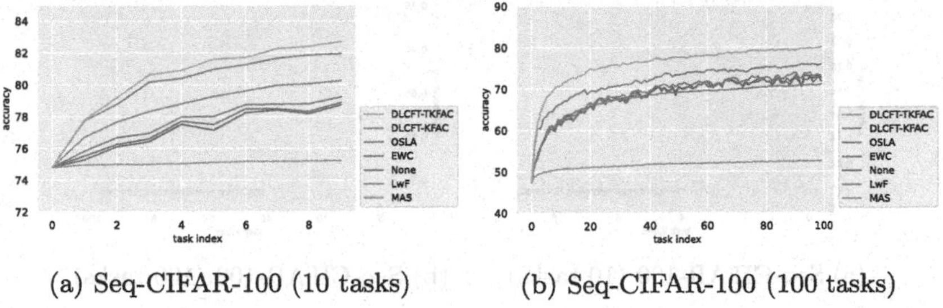

(a) Seq-CIFAR-100 (10 tasks) (b) Seq-CIFAR-100 (100 tasks)

Fig. 5. Data-IL evaluated after each task. Data-incremental learning using Seq-CIFAR-100. Here, we show the progress of the performance increase by evaluating after each task. Accuracy is evaluated on CIFAR-100 test set.

Table 2. Experiment results for task-/class-incremental learning. Experiments are conducted using Seq-CIFAR-100 with 10 tasks. TK-FAC [10] is used for our method.

Buffer size	Method	Task-IL	Class-IL
0	LwF [24]	92.16	–
	EWC [18]	77.44	–
	OSLA [38]	81.03	–
	DLCFT (Ours)	**95.79**	–
500	ER [37]	79.14	43.52
	DER [4]	91.47	58.07
	DER++ [4]	91.56	53.29
	DLCFT (Ours)	–	**59.98**

4.4 Ablations

Table 3 shows the ablation study of the components of the proposed method performed on the data-incremental and class-incremental setting. The result shows that jointly applying the linearization and MSE loss can significantly increase performance and mitigate forgetting. Note that between nonlinear networks trained with softmax cross-entropy, employing more accurate curvature approximation brings marginal performance difference. However, between linearized networks trained with MSE loss, adopting better curvature approximation brings significant performance gain. This is because in the former case, the effectiveness of better curvature is minimal due to the vanishing curvature and higher-order error problems.

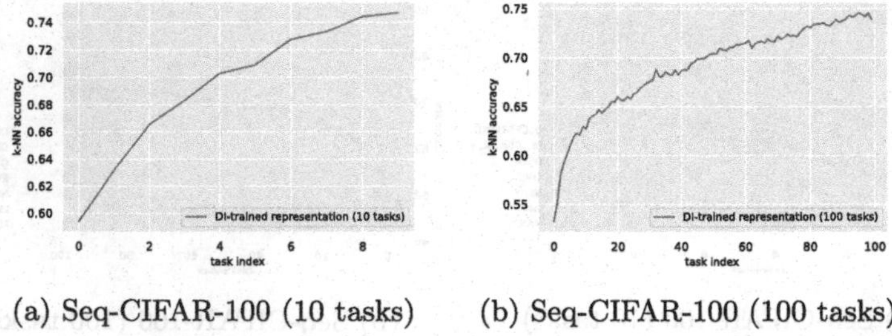

(a) Seq-CIFAR-100 (10 tasks) (b) Seq-CIFAR-100 (100 tasks)

Fig. 6. K-NN probing of the incrementally fine-tuned models. The quality of the representation is evaluated using K-NN classification accuracy on test set. Evaluation is performed after training each task in data-IL. At each evaluation, all training samples were used to perform inference.

Table 3. Ablations. Experiments are conducted on data- and class-IL benchmarks using Seq-CIFAR-100 dataset. 'Linear' indicates linearized model, and 'SCE' indicates softmax cross-entropy loss.

Curvature	Linear	Loss	Data-IL		Class-IL
			10 tasks	100 tasks	10 tasks
K-FAC [30]	✗	SCE	79.23	73.51	44.93
	✓	MSE	**81.95**	**75.92**	**59.86**
TK-FAC [10]	✗	SCE	79.58	73.18	44.66
	✓	MSE	**82.70**	**80.07**	**59.98**

5 Conclusion

In this paper, we have explored *continual fine-tuning*, which is a practical framework for incremental learning of deep neural networks. For this, we propose Deep Linear Continual Fine-tuning, which is a simple and effective continual learning algorithm using a pre-trained neural network. We provided theoretical reasons on why existing Hessian-based parameter regularization performs poorly with neural networks trained using softmax cross-entropy loss. We showed that a combination of model linearization technique and mean-squared error loss function allows the parameter regularization methods to closely match the optimal continual learning policy. We provided a principled approach to applying parameter regularization in class-incremental learning scenario, and showed that our method outperforms other baselines on data-/task-/class-incremental settings. Moreover, we show that our method can effectively accumulate knowledge over very long data-incremental tasks sequences.

Acknowledgements. This work was supported by Institute of Information & communications Technology Planning & Evaluation (IITP) grant funded by the Korea government(MSIT) (No. 2022-0-00951, Development of Uncertainty-Aware Agents Learning by Asking Questions).

References

1. Achille, A., Golatkar, A., Ravichandran, A., Polito, M., Soatto, S.: LQF: linear quadratic fine-tuning. In: Proceedings of the IEEE/CVF Conference on Computer Vision and Pattern Recognition (CVPR), pp. 15729–15739, June 2021
2. Aljundi, R., Babiloni, F., Elhoseiny, M., Rohrbach, M., Tuytelaars, T.: Memory aware synapses: learning what (not) to forget. In: Ferrari, V., Hebert, M., Sminchisescu, C., Weiss, Y. (eds.) ECCV 2018. LNCS, vol. 11207, pp. 144–161. Springer, Cham (2018). https://doi.org/10.1007/978-3-030-01219-9_9
3. Aljundi, R., Chakravarty, P., Tuytelaars, T.: Expert gate: lifelong learning with a network of experts. In: The IEEE Conference on Computer Vision and Pattern Recognition (CVPR), July 2017
4. Buzzega, P., Boschini, M., Porrello, A., Abati, D., Calderara, S.: Dark experience for general continual learning: a strong, simple baseline. In: Advances in Neural Information Processing Systems, vol. 33, pp. 15920–15930 (2020)
5. Chaudhry, A., Ranzato, M., Rohrbach, M., Elhoseiny, M.: Efficient lifelong learning with A-GEM. In: ICLR (2019)
6. Chrabaszcz, P., Loshchilov, I., Hutter, F.: A downsampled variant of ImageNet as an alternative to the cifar datasets. arXiv preprint arXiv:1707.08819 (2017)
7. Delange, M., et al.: A continual learning survey: defying forgetting in classification tasks. IEEE Trans. Pattern Anal. Mach. Intell. **44**, 3366–3385 (2021)
8. Dhar, P., Singh, R.V., Peng, K.C., Wu, Z., Chellappa, R.: Learning without memorizing. In: Proceedings of the IEEE/CVF Conference on Computer Vision and Pattern Recognition, pp. 5138–5146 (2019)
9. Ebrahimi, S., Elhoseiny, M., Darrell, T., Rohrbach, M.: Uncertainty-guided continual learning with Bayesian neural networks. In: International Conference on Learning Representations (2020). https://openreview.net/forum?id=HklUCCVKDB
10. Gao, K., et al.: A trace-restricted Kronecker-factored approximation to natural gradient. In: Proceedings of the AAAI Conference on Artificial Intelligence, vol. 35, no. 9, pp. 7519–7527, May 2021. https://ojs.aaai.org/index.php/AAAI/article/view/16921

11. George, T., Laurent, C., Bouthillier, X., Ballas, N., Vincent, P.: Fast approximate natural gradient descent in a kronecker factored eigenbasis. In: Bengio, S., Wallach, H., Larochelle, H., Grauman, K., Cesa-Bianchi, N., Garnett, R. (eds.) Advances in Neural Information Processing Systems, vol. 31. Curran Associates, Inc. (2018). https://proceedings.neurips.cc/paper/2018/file/48000647b315f6f00f913caa757a70b3-Paper.pdf
12. Grosse, R., Martens, J.: A Kronecker-factored approximate Fisher matrix for convolution layers. In: International Conference on Machine Learning, pp. 573–582 (2016)
13. He, K., Zhang, X., Ren, S., Sun, J.: Deep residual learning for image recognition. In: Proceedings of the IEEE Conference on Computer Vision and Pattern Recognition, pp. 770–778 (2016)
14. Hui, L., Belkin, M.: Evaluation of neural architectures trained with square loss vs cross-entropy in classification tasks. arXiv preprint arXiv:2006.07322 (2020)
15. Ioffe, S., Szegedy, C.: Batch normalization: accelerating deep network training by reducing internal covariate shift. In: International Conference on Machine Learning, pp. 448–456. PMLR (2015)
16. Jacot, A., Gabriel, F., Hongler, C.: Neural tangent kernel: convergence and generalization in neural networks. In: Bengio, S., Wallach, H., Larochelle, H., Grauman, K., Cesa-Bianchi, N., Garnett, R. (eds.) Advances in Neural Information Processing Systems, vol. 31. Curran Associates, Inc. (2018). https://proceedings.neurips.cc/paper/2018/file/5a4be1fa34e62bb8a6ec6b91d2462f5a-Paper.pdf
17. Kingma, D.P., Ba, J.: Adam: a method for stochastic optimization. arXiv preprint arXiv:1412.6980 (2014)
18. Kirkpatrick, J., et al.: Overcoming catastrophic forgetting in neural networks. Proc. Natl. Acad. Sci. **114**(13), 3521–3526 (2017)
19. Krizhevsky, A., Hinton, G., et al.: Learning multiple layers of features from tiny images (2009)
20. Kurle, R., Cseke, B., Klushyn, A., van der Smagt, P., Günnemann, S.: Continual learning with Bayesian neural networks for non-stationary data. In: International Conference on Learning Representations (2019)
21. Lee, J., et al.: Wide neural networks of any depth evolve as linear models under gradient descent. In: Advances in Neural Information Processing Systems, vol. 32, pp. 8572–8583 (2019)
22. Lee, J., Hong, H.G., Joo, D., Kim, J.: Continual learning with extended kronecker-factored approximate curvature. In: Proceedings of the IEEE/CVF Conference on Computer Vision and Pattern Recognition, pp. 9001–9010 (2020)
23. Lee, S.W.L., Kim, J.H., Jun, J., Ha, J.W., Zhang, B.T.: Overcoming catastrophic forgetting by incremental moment matching (IMM). In: Advances In Neural Information Processing Systems 30 (2017)
24. Li, Z., Hoiem, D.: Learning without forgetting. IEEE Trans. Pattern Anal. Mach. Intell. **40**(12), 2935–2947 (2018)
25. Liu, X., Masana, M., Herranz, L., Van de Weijer, J., Lopez, A.M., Bagdanov, A.D.: Rotate your networks: better weight consolidation and less catastrophic forgetting. In: 2018 24th International Conference on Pattern Recognition (ICPR), pp. 2262–2268. IEEE (2018)
26. Lopez-Paz, D., Ranzato, M.: Gradient episodic memory for continual learning. In: NIPS (2017)
27. Loshchilov, I., Hutter, F.: SGDR: stochastic gradient descent with warm restarts. arXiv preprint arXiv:1608.03983 (2016)

28. Maas, A., Hannun, A., Ng, A.: Rectifier nonlinearities improve neural network acoustic models. In: Proceedings of the International Conference on Machine Learning, vol. 30 (2013)
29. Mallya, A., Lazebnik, S.: PackNet: adding multiple tasks to a single network by iterative pruning. In: Proceedings of the IEEE conference on Computer Vision and Pattern Recognition, pp. 7765–7773 (2018)
30. Martens, J., Grosse, R.: Optimizing neural networks with Kronecker-factored approximate curvature. In: International Conference on Machine Learning, pp. 2408–2417 (2015)
31. Mu, F., Liang, Y., Li, Y.: Gradients as features for deep representation learning. In: International Conference on Learning Representations (2020). https://openreview.net/forum?id=BkeoaeHKDS
32. Nguyen, C.V., Li, Y., Bui, T.D., Turner, R.E.: Variational continual learning. In: International Conference on Learning Representations (2018)
33. Pascanu, R., Bengio, Y.: Revisiting natural gradient for deep networks. arXiv preprint arXiv:1301.3584 (2013)
34. Prabhu, A., Torr, P.H.S., Dokania, P.K.: GDumb: a simple approach that questions our progress in continual learning. In: Vedaldi, A., Bischof, H., Brox, T., Frahm, J.-M. (eds.) ECCV 2020. LNCS, vol. 12347, pp. 524–540. Springer, Cham (2020). https://doi.org/10.1007/978-3-030-58536-5_31
35. Quattoni, A., Torralba, A.: Recognizing indoor scenes. In: 2009 IEEE Conference on Computer Vision and Pattern Recognition, pp. 413–420 (2009). https://doi.org/10.1109/CVPR.2009.5206537
36. Rebuffi, S.A., Kolesnikov, A., Sperl, G., Lampert, C.H.: iCaRL: incremental classifier and representation learning. In: 2017 IEEE Conference on Computer Vision and Pattern Recognition (CVPR), pp. 5533–5542 (2017)
37. Riemer, M., Cases, I., Ajemian, R., Liu, M., Rish, I., Tu, Y., Tesauro, G.: Learning to learn without forgetting by maximizing transfer and minimizing interference. In: International Conference on Learning Representations (2019). https://openreview.net/forum?id=B1gTShAct7
38. Ritter, H., Botev, A., Barber, D.: Online structured laplace approximations for overcoming catastrophic forgetting. In: Advances in Neural Information Processing Systems, pp. 3738–3748 (2018)
39. Russakovsky, O., et al.: ImageNet large scale visual recognition challenge. Int. J. Comput. Vis. **115**(3), 211–252 (2015). https://doi.org/10.1007/s11263-015-0816-y
40. Rusu, A.A., et al.: Progressive neural networks. arXiv preprint arXiv:1606.04671 (2016)
41. Selvaraju, R.R., et al.: Grad-CAM: visual explanations from deep networks via gradient-based localization. In: ICCV (2016)
42. Serra, J., Suris, D., Miron, M., Karatzoglou, A.: Overcoming catastrophic forgetting with hard attention to the task. In: International Conference on Machine Learning, pp. 4548–4557. PMLR (2018)
43. Springenberg, J.T., Dosovitskiy, A., Brox, T., Riedmiller, M.: Striving for simplicity: the all convolutional net. arXiv preprint arXiv:1412.6806 (2014)
44. Yoon, J., Kim, S., Yang, E., Hwang, S.J.: Scalable and order-robust continual learning with additive parameter decomposition. In: International Conference on Learning Representations (2020). https://openreview.net/forum?id=r1gdj2EKPB
45. Zenke, F., Poole, B., Ganguli, S.: Continual learning through synaptic intelligence. In: International Conference on Machine Learning, pp. 3987–3995. PMLR (2017)

Adversarial Partial Domain Adaptation by Cycle Inconsistency

Kun-Yu Lin[1], Jiaming Zhou[1], Yukun Qiu[1], and Wei-Shi Zheng[1,2,3,4](✉)

[1] School of Computer Science and Engineering, Sun Yat-sen University, Guangzhou, China
{linky5,zhoujm55,qiuyk}@mail2.sysu.edu.cn, wszheng@ieee.org
[2] Peng Cheng Laboratory, Shenzhen, China
[3] Key Laboratory of Machine Intelligence and Advanced Computing, Ministry of Education, Guangzhou, China
[4] Guangdong Province Key Laboratory of Information Security Technology, Sun Yat-sen University, Guangzhou, China

Abstract. Unsupervised partial domain adaptation (PDA) is a unsupervised domain adaptation problem which assumes that the source label space subsumes the target label space. A critical challenge of PDA is the negative transfer problem, which is triggered by learning to match the whole source and target domains. To mitigate negative transfer, we note a fact that, it is impossible for a source sample of outlier classes to find a target sample of the same category due to the absence of outlier classes in the target domain, while it is possible for a source sample of shared classes. Inspired by this fact, we exploit the cycle inconsistency, *i.e.*, category discrepancy between the original features and features after cycle transformations, to distinguish outlier classes apart from shared classes in the source domain. Accordingly, we propose to filter out source samples of outlier classes by weight suppression and align the distributions of shared classes between the source and target domains by adversarial learning. To learn accurate weight assignment for filtering out outlier classes, we design cycle transformations based on domain prototypes and soft nearest neighbor, where center losses are introduced in individual domains to reduce the intra-class variation. Experiment results on three benchmark datasets demonstrate the effectiveness of our proposed method.

Keywords: Unsupervised partial domain adaptation · Negative transfer · Cycle inconsistency

1 Introduction

Deep neural networks have achieved remarkable success in various machine learning problems and applications [17,22,31,41,50]. Usually, training a deep neural

K. Lin and J. Zhou—Equal contributions.

Supplementary Information The online version contains supplementary material available at https://doi.org/10.1007/978-3-031-19827-4_31.

S. Avidan et al. (Eds.): ECCV 2022, LNCS 13693, pp. 530–548, 2022.
https://doi.org/10.1007/978-3-031-19827-4_31

network requires large amounts of labeled data and assumes that the training data follow identical distribution as the test ones. Therefore, networks may degrade drastically when applied in new scenarios, where the training and test data follow very different distributions [59,69]. By utilizing both labeled data from the source domain and unlabeled data from the target domain, *unsupervised domain adaptation (UDA)* [15,42] attempts to safely transfer knowledge from the label-sufficient source domain to the label-free target domain, such that networks can generalize to the target domain. Existing UDA methods typically mitigate the distribution shift by minimizing the discrepancy between the source and target domains [15,43,59,60].

UDA always assumes that the source and target domains share identical label space. Such an assumption would not be held in real-world applications since the labels of target data are unknown. In this paper, we focus on a variant of UDA, namely *unsupervised partial domain adaptation (PDA)*, which is challenging but realistic in real-world applications [4,5,72]. Compared with UDA, PDA does not assume that the source domain has identical label space as the target domain, but assumes that the target label space is a subset of the source label space. In this case, we term the classes absent in the target domain as *outlier classes* and the other classes as *shared classes*. A critical challenge of PDA is how to mitigate *negative transfer*, which causes that a transfer model performs even worse than a source-only model which is trained solely in the source domain.

We demonstrate an example about the negative transfer problem in PDA. Consider applying an adversarial learning method for standard UDA (*e.g.*, DANN [15]) in PDA scenarios. By confusing a domain discriminator, the adversarial learning method makes the distribution of the source domain (consisting of both shared and outlier classes) similar to the distribution of the target domain (consisting of only shared classes). However, in ideal cases, the distribution of source outlier classes should be dissimilar to the target distribution, since the outlier classes in the source domains are absent in the target domain. As a result, the adversarial learning method makes some target samples of the shared classes indistinguishable from the source samples of outlier classes, which hinders transferable discriminative feature learning and triggers negative transfer.

To mitigate the negative transfer problem, we attempt to match only the shared classes between the source and target domains. To this end, we should filter out source samples of outlier classes when applying adversarial learning. However, since no label information is available in the target domain, it is challenging to identify which classes are outlier for the target domain. To tackle the challenge, we explore the differences between outlier and shared classes. We note a fact that, it is *impossible* for a source sample of outlier classes to find a target sample of the same category due to *the absence of outlier classes in the target domain* while it is *possible* for a source sample of shared classes to find one, and it is also *possible* for a target sample to find a source sample of the same category since all target classes are shared across domains. Inspired by this fact, we develop a solution to distinguish outlier classes apart from shared classes based on *cycle inconsistency* modeling.

Specifically, we design a cycle transformation for source samples. The proposed cycle transformation first transforms a source sample feature into the

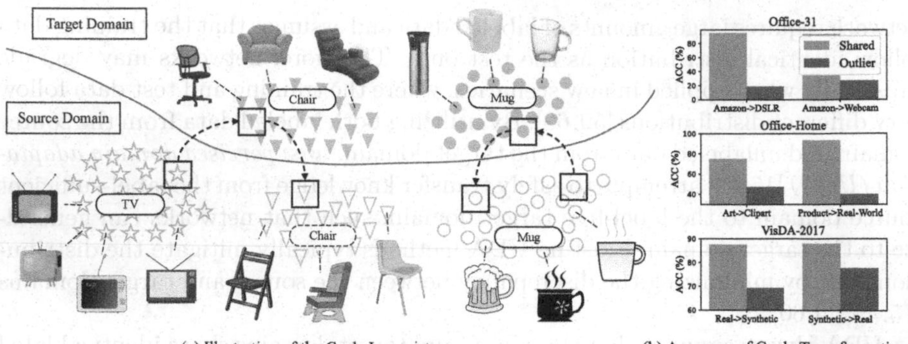

(a) Illustration of the Cycle Inconsistency (b) Accuracy of Cycle Transformations

Fig. 1. (a) A PDA example with two shared classes and one outlier class. In PDA, due to the absence of outlier classes in the target domain, a source sample of outlier classes *cannot* find a target sample of the same category, while it is *possible* for a source sample of shared classes to find one. Inspired by this fact, we design a cycle transformation to distinguish outlier classes from shared classes. Our assumption is that, source samples of outlier classes are *more likely* to alter their category after cycle transformations compared with source samples of shared classes, with appropriate transformation functions. (b) Assumption verification using source-only models on three real-world datasets. We conduct cycle transformations on source samples by two cross-domain feature transformations, which is implemented by searching the most similar samples across domains in feature space. Then we calculate the accuracy of cycle transformations, *i.e.*, the proportion of samples to keep their categories after cycle transformations. The empirical results show that the accuracy of samples in shared classes is much higher than samples in outlier classes, which verifies our assumption. Best viewed in color (Color figure online)

target domain and then transforms it back into the source domain. We hold an assumption that, source samples of outlier classes are *more likely* to alter their category after cycle transformations compared with source samples of shared classes, with appropriate transformation functions (see empirical verification in Fig. 1). Accordingly, we propose a weighted adversarial learning method with a novel weight assignment scheme based on *cycle inconsistency*, *i.e.*, the category discrepancy between the original features and features after cycle transformations. Our method filters out source samples in outlier classes by sample weight suppression and aligns the distributions of shared classes between the source and target domains iteratively. With such a filter-and-align manner, our method gradually learns accurate transformation functions based on feature similarity for exploiting cycle inconsistency. For accurate sample weight assignment, we design cross-domain feature transformation functions based on domain prototypes and soft nearest neighbor to alleviate unexpected category alteration under large intra-class variation. For further improving the accuracy of cross-domain feature transformations, we adopt center losses within individual domains to reduce the intra-class variation. We conduct quantitative and qualitative experiments on three benchmark datasets, which demonstrates the effectiveness of our method.

2 Related Work

2.1 Unsupervised Domain Adaptation

Unsupervised domain adaptation (UDA) is one of the most classical transfer learning tasks [48]. UDA aims to transfer knowledge from the label-sufficient source domain to the label-free target domain, such that the transfer model can generalize to the target domain. A critical challenge of the UDA problem is how to diminish the distribution discrepancy between the source and target domains.

Typically, existing UDA methods explore domain invariance based on feature alignment. A mainstream type of feature alignment methods explicitly minimizes well-defined statistical distances (*e.g.*, Maximum Mean Discrepancy) between the source and target domains [10,42,58,60,71]. Inspired by GANs [17], another mainstream type introduces an auxiliary domain discriminator and makes the feature extractor confuse the domain discriminator in an adversarial learning manner. Usually, these methods design different criteria for training domain discriminators [9,15,59,66,74]. Moreover, some works focus on specific differences between domains for implicit alignment [28,65]. Häusser et al. propose to reinforce associations between domains directly in feature space [7,21,30].

In addition to methods based on feature alignment, generative methods introduce GANs for synthesizing labeled target data and align the two domains in both pixel and feature levels [1,23,27,47,55]. Among them, Hoffman et al. [23] propose to utilize the cycle consistency constraint for better synthesis without cross-domain pairs, inspired by CycleGAN [75]. Furthermore, some methods attempt to explore domain-specific information [13,37,44,52,53,56]. For example, Saito et al. [52] and Liang et al. [37] assign pseudo labels to selected samples in the target domains, and Long et al. [44] and Shu et al. [56] apply the entropy minimization principle from the semi-supervised learning literature [18,73].

Although UDA makes generalization in label-free domains possible, it is not realistic in real-world applications. UDA always assumes that the source and target domains share identical label space, which is too rigorous as label information of the target domain is unknown. Therefore, recent works make attempts to relax the assumption. For example, *open-set domain adaptation* assumes there are private classes in the target domain, which requires models to recognize both known and unknown classes in the target domain [3,32,40,54]. *Universal domain adaptation* further assumes that both the source and target domains have private classes, leading to a large category gap between domains [14,34,70]. In addition, UDA usually assumes that both the source and target data are accessible, which violates the data privacy policy in some cases. Therefore, some works explore source-free settings with the source data unavailable [33,36,38,67,68].

2.2 Partial Domain Adaptation

Unsupervised partial domain adaptation (PDA) is an extreme case of imbalanced unsupervised domain adaptation [24]. PDA assumes that the source label space subsumes the target label space, which is more realistic than the standard

UDA. A critical challenge of PDA is the negative transfer problem triggered by learning to match the whole source and target domains. Typically, to mitigate negative transfer, existing methods introduce weighting schemes to filter out source samples of outlier classes and then apply adversarial learning methods for domain alignment. SAN [4] and PADA [5] propose class-wise weighting schemes according to the statistics of label predictors. IWAN [72] and ETN [6] assign sample-wise weights by introducing extra domain discriminators and label predictors, respectively. TWINs [46] proposes to estimate the label distribution using two classifiers. Apart from methods based on weighting schemes, there are PDA methods of other types. For example, Chen et al. [8] propose a reinforced data selector based on reinforcement learning, Liang et al. [39] propose a balanced and uncertainty-aware method which augments the small target domain to match the large source domain, Hu et al. [26] propose to maximize the distribution divergence between outlier and shared classes beyond aligning shared classes across domains, and Xiao et al. [63] propose to promote positive transfer by aligning the distributions of implicit semantic topics across domains.

In this paper, we propose a novel weighted adversarial learning method which filters out the source samples of outlier classes by cycle inconsistency. Existing weighted adversarial learning methods also make attempts to filter out the source samples of outlier classes. However, these methods usually calculate the weights of source samples *in indirect ways*, which apply extra auxiliary networks on top of features to infer the category gap between domains (*e.g.*, domain discriminator in IWAN [72], label predictor in ETN [6]). The quality of sample weights significantly depends on the performance of the auxiliary networks, as there are representation gaps between the feature extractor and auxiliary networks. By contrast, the proposed method exploits the category discrepancy between original and cycle-transformed features, which *directly* exploits the property of feature space without auxiliary networks and is more straightforward.

3 Methodology

In *unsupervised partial domain adaptation (PDA)*, the source domain $\mathcal{D}_s = \{(\mathbf{x}_i^s, y_i^s)\}_{i=1}^{n_s}$ consists of n_s labeled samples from $|\mathcal{C}_s|$ classes and the target domain $\mathcal{D}_t = \{\mathbf{x}_i^t\}_{i=1}^{n_t}$ consists of n_t unlabeled samples from $|\mathcal{C}_t|$ classes. The two domains follow *different but related* input distributions, *i.e.*, $p_s(\mathbf{x}_i^s) \neq p_t(\mathbf{x}_i^t)$, which is termed *domain gap*. Different from the standard *unsupervised domain adaptation (UDA)* problem, PDA further assumes a specific *category gap* between domains. In PDA, the label space of the target domain $\mathcal{C}_t$ is a subset of the label space of the source domain $\mathcal{C}_s$, *i.e.*, $\mathcal{C}_t \subset \mathcal{C}_s$. We term the classes absent in the target domain as outlier classes and the other classes as shared classes. The goal of PDA is to learn a generalizable model in the small target domain by transferring knowledge from the large source domain. In this paper, we aim to learn a transferable classification model, which is composed of a feature extractor $F : \mathcal{X} \to \mathcal{Z}$ and a label predictor $G : \mathcal{Z} \to \mathcal{Y}$.

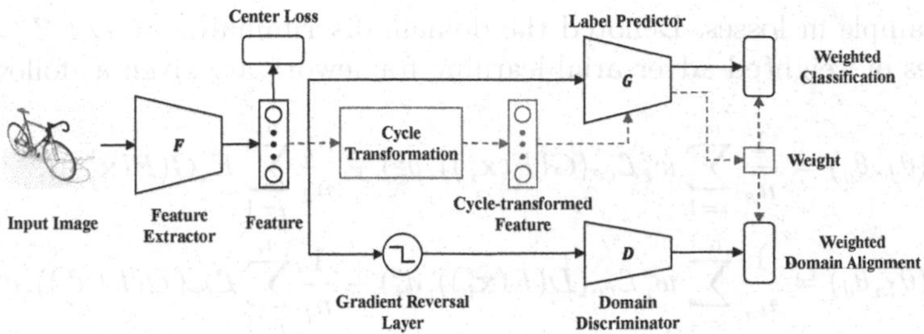

Fig. 2. An overview of the proposed weighted adversarial learning method based on cycle inconsistency. The blue components indicate the calculation process of sample weight, which is based on the category discrepancy between the original and cycle-transformed features. Three losses are involved during training, namely weighted classification, weighted domain alignment and center loss. Best viewed in color (Color figure online)

A critical challenge in PDA is the negative transfer problem, which is triggered by learning to match the whole source and target domains. To mitigate negative transfer, we design a cycle transformation consisting of two cross-domain feature transformations to distinguish outlier classes from shared classes. Our basic assumption is that, source samples of outlier classes are *more likely* to alter their category after cycle transformations compared with source samples of shared classes, with appropriate transformation functions. According to the assumption, we propose a weighted adversarial learning method with a cycle-inconsistency-based weighting scheme, which filters out source samples of outlier classes and aligns shared classes between the two domains iteratively. Next, we elaborate the proposed method, whose overview is given in Fig. 2.

3.1 Weighted Adversarial Learning for PDA

In this subsection, we illustrate the weighted adversarial learning framework. The framework is based on Domain Adversarial Neural Network (DANN) [15], which is one of the most widely used adversarial learning methods for the standard UDA problem. DANN introduces a domain discriminator and develops a two-player game for exploring domain invariance. Two losses are involved in DANN, namely classification losses for discriminating categories and domains, respectively. By confusing the domain discriminator, the feature extractor extracts domain-invariant features.

Although DANN is effective in UDA, it triggers the negative transfer problem in PDA. In principle, DANN implicitly learns to align the whole source and target domains. However, since there are outlier classes in the source domain in PDA, aligning the whole domains confuses some target samples with the source samples in outlier classes, leading to a loss of discriminative power in the target domain. Therefore, we should distinguish source samples of outlier classes apart from shared classes in adversarial learning. To this end, we assign a weight to each source sample in losses. Denoted the domain discriminator by $D : \mathcal{Z} \rightarrow \{0, 1\}$, the losses of weighted adversarial learning framework are given as follows:

$$\begin{aligned} \mathcal{L}^w_{cls}(\theta_f, \theta_g) &= \frac{1}{n_s} \sum_{i=1}^{n_s} w^s_i \mathcal{L}_{ce}(G(F(\mathbf{x}^s_i)), y^s_i) + \frac{\lambda_e}{n_t} \sum_{j=1}^{n_t} E(G(F(\mathbf{x}^t_j))), \\ \mathcal{L}^w_{adv}(\theta_f, \theta_d) &= \frac{1}{n_s} \sum_{i=1}^{n_s} w^s_i \mathcal{L}_{ce}(D(F(\mathbf{x}^s_i)), d^s_i) + \frac{1}{n_t} \sum_{j=1}^{n_t} \mathcal{L}_{ce}(D(F(\mathbf{x}^t_j)), d^t_j), \end{aligned} \quad (1)$$

where θ_f, θ_g and θ_d are parameters of the feature extractor F, label predictor G and domain discriminator D, respectively. $\mathcal{L}_{ce}(\cdot)$ is the cross-entropy loss, and $d^s_i = 0$ and $d^t_j = 1$ are domain labels. $E(\cdot)$ is the entropy function (entropy minimization encourages the low-density separation between classes [18]), and λ_e is a trade-off hyperparameter. w^s_i is the weight of the i-th source sample. Ideally, samples in shared classes have large weights and samples in outlier classes have zero weights. In this case, the adversarial learning ignores the source samples of outlier classes and aligns the distributions of shared classes between the two domains. Also, the weights are introduced in the classification loss for concentrating on classifying the shared classes. Next, we illustrate how to quantify the sample weights by *cycle inconsistency.*

3.2 Exploring Outlier Classes by Cycle Inconsistency

To quantify the sample weights, we exploit a key difference between source samples in shared and outlier classes by designing a cycle transformation. The cycle transformation consists of two cross-domain feature transformations by searching the most similar samples across domains in feature space. Specifically, given a source sample feature, we first transform it into the target domain and then transform it back into the source domain (*i.e.*, use the most similar feature cross domains as the transformed feature). We assume that, source samples of outlier classes are *more likely* to alter their category after cycle transformations compared with source samples of shared classes, if an appropriate similarity metric is learned. Empirically, we verify the assumption using source-only models as feature extractors on three real-world datasets, as shown in Fig. 1b. The assumption is inspired by a fact, *i.e.*, if a source sample belongs to outlier classes, applying the source-to-target transformation always alters its category. Since no label information is available in the target domain during training, we cannot verify the category alternation for filtering out outlier classes, thus we consider transforming the feature after source-to-target transformation back into the source domain.

According to the above assumption, we propose to exploit the *cycle inconsistency*, namely category discrepancy between the original and cycle-transformed features, to filter out source samples of outlier classes. Specifically, in each iteration, we assign weights to source samples based on the cycle inconsistency:

$$w^s_i = G(T_{t\rightarrow s}(T_{s\rightarrow t}(F(\mathbf{x}^s_i))))[y^s_i], \quad (2)$$

where $T_{s\to t} : \mathcal{Z} \to \mathcal{Z}$ and $T_{t\to s} : \mathcal{Z} \to \mathcal{Z}$ are functions for source-to-target and target-to-source feature transformations, respectively. $G(\mathbf{z})[c] : \mathcal{Z} \to [0, 1]$ denotes the c-th element of the classification probability vector given feature $\mathbf{z}$. In Eq. (2), we first extract the feature of $\mathbf{x}_i^s$ using the feature extractor F, then apply cycle transformation by $T_{s\to t}$ and $T_{t\to s}$, and finally get the cycle-transformed feature. We use the classifier G to predict the probability of category alternation after the cycle transformation as it is trained with labeled source samples. If the cycle-transformed feature has lower probability at its original category (*i.e.*, y_i^s), the sample $\mathbf{x}_i^s$ is more likely from the outlier classes (and vice versa).

Remark. The prerequisite of the proposed method is an appropriate feature similarity metric, based on which our method can find similar samples of the same categories across domains with acceptable accuracy for cross-domain feature transformations. In our method, the feature similarity metric is gradually learned by network training, and the cross-domain feature transformations gradually become more accurate as a result. The accuracy of cross-domain feature transformations is guaranteed by two factors. First, we use a source-only model as the initialization, since the model trained solely with source samples can distinguish target samples of different classes to some extent. Such an initialization scheme guarantees the accuracy of cross-domain similar sample search at the beginning of training (as shown in Fig. 1b). Second, our method uses a filter-and-align manner, which alternates between filtering out source samples of outlier classes by weight suppression and aligning the distributions of shared classes between the two domains by adversarial learning. As the training goes, our method gradually aligns shared classes across domains and thus the cross-domain similar sample search is gradually more accurate. In Sect. 3.3, we introduce prototype-based cross-domain feature transformation functions, which improve the accuracy of cross-domain similar sample search.

As the shared classes in the source and target domains gradually align during training, the classifier G gradually obtains classification power in the target domain. Therefore, if the classifier is confident in the prediction for the transformed feature $T_{s\to t}(F(\mathbf{x}_i^s))$, we can use the classifier to estimate the probability of category alternation after the source-to-target feature transformation $T_{s\to t}$, which contributes to filtering out source samples of outlier classes. Accordingly, by exploiting the category discrepancy between original features and features after source-to-target transformations, we propose a mixed strategy beyond cycle-inconsistency-based sample weighting, which is given as follows:

$$w_i^s = G(T_{t\to s}(T_{s\to t}(F(\mathbf{x}_i^s))))[y_i^s] + \lambda_w e_i^s G(T_{s\to t}(F(\mathbf{x}_i^s)))[y_i^s], \tag{3}$$

where λ_w is a trade-off hyperparameter and the entropy-aware weight $e_i^s = 1 + \exp\{-E(G(T_{s\to t}(F(\mathbf{x}_i^s))))\}$ indicates the classification confidence of the transformed feature $T_{s\to t}(F(\mathbf{x}_i^s))$. By using Eq. (3), our method considers the inconsistency in both cycle transformations and source-to-target transformations when the classifier is confident in its predictions, which contributes to more accurate sample weight assignment.

3.3 Prototype-Based Cross-Domain Feature Transformation

In previous sections, we have introduced the cycle transformation consisting of two cross-domain feature transformations, which are implemented by searching the most similar sample across domains in the whole feature space. However, such an exhaustive searching process is too time-consuming and not practical for training. In addition, the exhaustive searching process will introduce noise into cross-domain feature transformations, especially when classes have large intra-class variation in feature space. For example, if a sample belongs to a class with large intra-class variation in feature space, its feature may fall close to the classification boundary (or even be misclassified). Therefore, for a sample of shared classes, the large variation improves the probability of finding a sample of another category in the cross-domain similar sample search. In ideal cases, the adopted transformation functions keep the categories of samples in shared classes. Besides, for samples of shared classes, variation between the original and cycle-transformed features is permitted if the category is not altered.

To this end, we propose an efficient and accurate cross-domain feature transformation method based on domain prototypes (dynamically updated) [37,62,64]. Specifically, to abstract the dataset, we obtain $|\mathcal{C}_s|$ and K domain prototypes in the source and target domains by class-wise feature mean and K-means clustering, respectively. Considering hyperparameter tuning in practice, we set $K = |\mathcal{C}_s|$ as the number of target classes is unknown. The sets of prototypes in the source and target domains are denoted by $\{\mathbf{c}_k^s\}_{k=1}^{|\mathcal{C}_s|}$ and $\{\mathbf{c}_k^t\}_{k=1}^{K}$, respectively. Given the domain prototypes, we conduct cross-domain feature transformations by using the most similar prototypes across domains, which fall away from the classification boundaries. And, the cost of one feature transformation comes from calculating sample similarity at the feature level for only $|\mathcal{C}_s|/K$ times. Therefore, we reduce the computation cost of the exhaustive search and the noise induced by the large intra-class variation. Furthermore, to improve the representation power of transformed features, we propose cross-domain feature transformation functions based on soft nearest neighbor [12,16,57] as follows:

$$T_{s\to t}(\mathbf{z}^s) = \sum_{k=1}^{K} \frac{e^{\text{sim}(\mathbf{z}^s,\mathbf{c}_k^t)}}{\sum_{l=1}^{K} e^{\text{sim}(\mathbf{z}^s,\mathbf{c}_l^t)}}\mathbf{c}_k^t,\ T_{t\to s}(\mathbf{z}^t) = \sum_{k=1}^{|\mathcal{C}_s|} \frac{e^{\text{sim}(\mathbf{z}^t,\mathbf{c}_k^s)}}{\sum_{l=1}^{|\mathcal{C}_s|} e^{\text{sim}(\mathbf{z}^t,\mathbf{c}_l^s)}}\mathbf{c}_k^s, \quad (4)$$

where $\mathbf{z}^s/\mathbf{z}^t$ denotes a feature vector in the source/target domain, and $\text{sim}(\cdot,\cdot)$ is a function measuring the similarity between features. In our experiments, we adopt the negative square Euclidean distance as the similarity function for cross-domain feature transformations, *i.e.*, $\text{sim}(\mathbf{z}^s, \mathbf{c}_k^t) = -\|\mathbf{z}^s - \mathbf{c}_k^t\|_2^2$.

In each training iteration, domain prototypes are updated using on-the-fly features in the current batch. Specifically, the updating rules are given as follows:

$$\mathbf{c}_k^s \leftarrow \lambda_m \mathbf{c}_k^s + \bar{\lambda}_m \frac{\sum_{i=1}^{B} \delta(y_i^s = k)\mathbf{x}_i^s}{\sum_{i=1}^{B} \delta(y_i^s = k)},\ \mathbf{c}_k^t \leftarrow \lambda_m \mathbf{c}_k^t + \bar{\lambda}_m \frac{\sum_{j=1}^{B} \delta(\hat{y}_j^t = k)\mathbf{x}_j^t}{\sum_{j=1}^{B} \delta(\hat{y}_j^t = k)}, \quad (5)$$

where $\bar{\lambda}_m = 1-\lambda_m$, y_i^s is the ground-truth label, $\hat{y}_j^t = \arg\max_{k=1}^{K} \text{sim}(F(\mathbf{x}_j^t), \mathbf{c}_k^t)$ indicates the cluster assignment, B is the batch size, and λ_m is the momentum hyperparameter controlling the update rate. $\delta(\text{condition})$ is the indicator function, *i.e.*, $\delta(\text{condition}) = 1$ if the condition is satisfied and $\delta(\text{condition}) = 0$ otherwise. We do not update the prototypes absent in the current batch.

As discussed in previous works [62], classes will distribute in radial pattern in feature space, as the model is trained with a linear layer on top of the feature extractor and cross-entropy losses. Accordingly, the large intra-class variation in feature space negatively affects the source-to-target feature transformations and clustering in the target domain. Therefore, we adopt center losses within individual domains to reduce the intra-class variation, which are given as follows:

$$\mathcal{L}_{ctr}(\theta_f) = \frac{1}{2n_s}\sum_{i=1}^{n_s} \|F(\mathbf{x}_i^s) - \mathbf{c}_{y_i^s}^s\|_2^2 + \frac{1}{2n_t}\sum_{j=1}^{n_t} \|F(\mathbf{x}_j^t) - \mathbf{c}_{\hat{y}_j^t}^t\|_2^2. \tag{6}$$

By applying Eq. (6), each sample will be pushed closer to the corresponding prototype (*i.e.*, the ground-truth one in the source domain or the nearest one in the target domain) and classes will tend to distribute in sphere pattern in feature space. As a result, the center losses improve the compactness of classes and thus improve the accuracy of cross-domain feature transformations.

By cooperating the cycle-inconsistency-based weighting scheme with center losses, the overall objective of the proposed weighted adversarial learning method is given as follows:

$$\min_{\theta_f,\theta_g} \max_{\theta_d} \; \mathcal{L}_{cls}^w(\theta_f, \theta_g) - \lambda_{adv}\mathcal{L}_{adv}^w(\theta_f, \theta_d) + \lambda_{ctr}\mathcal{L}_{ctr}(\theta_f), \tag{7}$$

where λ_{adv} and λ_{ctr} are trade off hyperparameters. The above minimax game is implemented by Gradient Reversal Layer [15], and the network parameters and domain prototypes are optimized in an alternating manner.

4 Experiment

4.1 Setups

- Datasets. We use three benchmark datasets in our experiments, namely Office-31, Office-Home and VisDA-2017. Office-31 [51] is a small-sized standard domain adaptation benchmark which consists of three domains, namely Amazon (A), DSLR (D) and Webcam (W). It contains 31 categories of objects in office setting, and the 10 categories shared with Caltech-256 [19] are taken as the target categories. Office-Home [61] is a medium-sized benchmark which consists of four domains, namely Artistic images (A), Clip Art (C), Product images (P), and Real-World images (R). It contains 65 categories of objects in office and home settings, and the first 25 categories (in alphabetical order) are taken as the target categories. VisDA-2017 [49] is a challenging large-scale dataset consisting of real (Re.) and synthetic (Sy.) images of 12 object categories, where the first 6 categories (in alphabetical order) are taken as the target categories. On VisDA-2017, we use center crop (rather than random crop) for training following previous works. There are 6, 12 and 2 transfer settings in these datasets, respectively. Classification accuracy (ACC) is used for evaluation.

Table 1. Comparison with the state-of-the-art methods on Office-31 and VisDA-2017 in terms of ACC (%). † indicates existing weighted adversarial learning methods for PDA. * indicates that the source-only model is used as initialization. The best result is marked as bold red, and the second best result is marked as *italic blue*

Method	Office-31							VisDa-2017		
	A → D	A → W	D → A	D → W	W → A	W → D	Avg.	Re. → Sy	Sy. → Re	Avg
ResNet-50 [22]	83.44	75.59	83.92	96.27	84.97	98.09	87.05	64.30	45.30	54.80
ADDA [59]	83.41	75.67	83.62	95.38	84.25	99.85	87.03	–	–	–
CDAN+E [43]	77.07	80.51	93.58	98.98	91.65	98.09	89.98	–	–	–
RTN [44]	66.90	75.30	85.60	97.10	85.70	98.30	84.80	72.90	50.00	61.45
†PADA [5]	89.17	88.70	94.61	99.77	95.79	100.00	94.67	69.46	62.76	66.11
†SAN [4]	94.27	93.90	94.15	99.32	88.73	99.36	94.96	69.70	49.90	59.80
†IWAN [72]	88.54	89.94	93.84	99.77	94.75	99.36	94.37	*78.18*	63.87	*71.02*
†ETN [6]	95.03	94.52	*96.21*	100.00	94.64	100.00	96.73	69.69	63.99	66.84
†MWPDA [25]	95.12	96.61	95.02	100.00	95.51	100.00	97.05	–	–	–
SSPDA [2]	90.87	91.52	90.61	92.88	94.36	98.94	93.20	–	–	–
DRCN [35]	86.00	88.05	95.60	100.00	95.80	100.00	94.30	73.20	58.20	65.70
RTNet [8]	*97.60*	96.20	92.30	100.00	95.40	100.00	96.90	–	–	–
BA3US [39]	99.36	*98.98*	94.82	100.00	94.99	98.73	*97.81*	–	–	–
DPDAN [26]	96.82	96.27	96.35	100.00	95.62	100.00	97.51	–	*65.26*	-
A2KT [29]	96.79	97.28	96.13	100.00	*96.14*	100.00	97.72	–	–	–
AdvRew [20]	91.72	97.63	95.62	100.00	95.30	100.00	96.71	–	–	–
Source-only	76.86	74.46	86.60	97.97	86.71	98.94	86.92	63.13	51.90	57.51
*DANN (baseline) [15]	59.24	56.84	70.22	82.60	86.19	90.45	74.25	50.09	44.02	47.05
†*PADA [5]	89.17	95.03	94.82	99.77	95.69	99.79	95.71	65.84	58.12	61.98
†*IWAN [72]	86.84	91.30	94.02	100.00	94.82	99.79	94.46	73.47	57.79	65.63
†*ETN [6]	84.71	87.23	94.08	98.76	94.57	98.73	93.01	67.42	60.87	64.15
Ours	96.82	99.66	96.14	100.00	96.56	100.00	98.19	86.50	69.75	78.13

- **Existing Methods.** In our experiments, we compare the proposed method with both standard UDA and state-of-the-art PDA methods. Among existing PDA methods, we pay close attention to the methods based on weighted adversarial learning, which adopt different weighting schemes (*e.g.*, PADA [5] based on label predictor, IWAN [72] based on auxiliary domain discriminator). Apart from weighted adversarial learning methods, we also compare with PDA methods of other types, *e.g.*, RTNet [8], BA3US [39], DPDAN [26].

- **Implementation Details.** We adopt ResNet-50 [22] pre-trained on ImageNet [11] as the backbone and add a bottleneck layer of dimension 256 between the backbone and classification layer. All network parameters are optimized using mini-batch SGD with batch size of 36, momentum of 0.9 and weight decay of 0.001. The learning rates of the bottleneck layer, classification layer and domain discriminator are 10 times that of the backbone, which are set as 0.001 initially and adjusted following the rules in previous works [15,43]. By default, the hyper-parameters are set as $\lambda_e = 0.1$, $\lambda_{adv} = 1$, $\lambda_{ctr} = 0.2$ and $\lambda_m = 0.99$. For the mixed strategy, $\lambda_w = 1$ and e_i^s is normalized within each batch. We initialize our model by the source-only model. On Office-Home, we adopt the source center loss after the source-only pre-training for one epoch. We normalize the sample weights in a batch of size B by $w_i^s \leftarrow Bw_i^s / \sum_{i=1}^{B} w_i^s$ following the previous works [6,72].

4.2 Results

- Comparison with the State-of-the-Arts. Tables 1 and 2 summarize the results on Office-31, Office-Home and VisDA-2017. Overall, the proposed method outperforms the state-of-the-art methods on all the three datasets, and Ours obtains the best or second best performance on most transfer settings. On VisDA-2017, our method obtains significant improvement over the state-of-the-arts, *i.e.*, 8.32% on Re. → Sy. and 4.49% on Sy. → Re., respectively. In addition, Ours outperforms all existing weighted adversarial learning methods (marked by †, *e.g.*, PADA [5], IWAN [72], etc.), which demonstrates the superiority of the proposed cycle-inconsistency-based sample weighting scheme. We also make a comparison with weighted adversarial learning methods using the source-only model as initialization (*i.e.*, *PADA, *IWAN and *ETN). Although such an initialization brings performance improvement in some cases (*e.g.*, *IWAN vs. IWAN on Office-Home), our method still outperforms them, which demonstrates that our performance improvement does not come from the initialization.

Table 2. Comparison with the state-of-the-art methods and ablation study on Office-Home in terms of ACC (%). † indicates existing weighted adversarial learning methods for PDA. * indicates that the source-only model is used as initialization. The best result is marked as bold red, and the second best result is marked as *italic blue*

Method	A → C	A → P	A → R	C → A	C → P	C → R	P → A	P → C	P → R	R → A	R → C	R → P	Avg
ResNet-50 [22]	46.33	67.51	75.87	59.14	59.94	62.73	58.22	41.79	74.88	67.40	48.18	74.17	61.35
ADDA [59]	45.23	68.79	79.21	64.56	60.01	68.29	57.56	38.89	77.45	70.28	45.23	78.32	62.82
CDAN+E [43]	47.52	65.91	75.65	57.07	54.12	63.42	59.60	44.30	72.39	66.02	49.91	72.80	60.73
SAFN [65]	58.93	76.25	81.42	70.43	72.97	77.78	72.36	55.34	80.40	75.81	60.42	79.92	71.83
†PADA [5]	49.31	71.95	82.09	57.73	58.86	65.03	67.03	41.87	83.60	79.55	52.12	84.37	66.13
†SAN [4]	44.42	68.68	74.60	67.49	64.99	77.80	59.78	44.72	80.07	72.18	50.21	78.66	65.30
†IWAN [72]	59.28	74.49	82.99	61.40	64.43	70.96	68.93	53.49	83.78	78.30	59.60	80.73	69.87
†ETN [6]	59.24	77.03	79.54	62.92	65.73	75.01	68.29	55.37	84.37	75.72	57.66	84.54	70.45
†MWPDA [25]	55.39	77.53	81.27	57.08	61.03	62.33	68.74	56.42	86.67	76.70	57.67	80.06	68.41
SSPDA [2]	51.95	67.00	78.74	52.16	53.78	59.03	52.61	43.22	78.79	73.73	56.60	77.09	62.06
DRCN [35]	54.00	76.40	83.00	62.10	64.50	71.00	70.80	49.80	80.50	77.50	59.10	79.90	69.00
RTNet [8]	*63.20*	80.10	80.70	66.70	69.30	77.20	71.60	53.90	84.60	77.40	57.90	85.50	72.30
BA3US [39]	60.62	83.16	88.39	71.75	72.79	83.40	75.45	61.59	86.53	79.25	62.80	86.05	75.98
DPDAN [26]	59.40	–	79.04	–	–	–	–	–	81.79	76.77	58.67	82.18	–
A2KT [29]	62.54	83.92	86.69	65.44	74.96	75.04	67.40	55.14	84.37	73.25	60.51	84.09	72.78
AdvRew [20]	62.13	79.22	89.12	73.92	75.57	84.37	78.42	61.91	87.85	82.19	*65.37*	85.27	77.11
Source-only	46.45	69.04	79.79	57.45	58.04	65.54	59.35	38.23	76.31	69.76	45.27	76.06	61.77
*DANN (baseline) [15]	47.22	58.71	71.67	48.45	44.50	54.74	53.38	40.48	69.57	63.09	47.74	71.02	55.88
†*PADA [5]	49.97	70.78	82.18	59.44	59.35	66.91	68.84	44.78	83.42	78.70	55.02	84.33	66.98
†*IWAN [72]	59.34	81.49	85.64	68.07	71.75	74.51	71.84	57.15	83.86	77.32	62.37	83.16	73.04
†*ETN [6]	52.78	70.84	78.29	69.54	69.76	73.37	63.12	50.10	74.47	75.18	55.07	79.23	67.65
Ours-Cycle w/o $\mathcal{L}_{ctr}$	62.45	84.71	89.18	*76.40*	75.57	77.75	77.04	59.70	86.86	82.37	62.87	*85.77*	76.72
Ours-Cycle	62.51	*85.71*	90.17	74.75	75.57	82.66	77.96	62.87	86.36	*84.76*	63.76	85.60	*77.72*
Ours-Cycle-Hard	64.84	84.99	90.72	75.30	*75.69*	82.83	77.23	*63.10*	85.42	80.62	63.64	84.87	77.44
Ours-Src2Trg	60.48	85.66	89.23	73.92	72.89	79.85	80.72	56.72	88.57	80.26	62.75	84.99	76.33
Ours (Full)	61.73	86.89	*90.50*	77.23	76.86	*83.77*	*79.61*	63.82	*88.46*	85.03	65.79	86.22	78.83
Oracle	69.19	82.75	88.99	75.94	76.88	83.99	77.29	66.19	90.06	84.14	74.33	91.04	80.07

- Ablation Study. On Office-Home, we conduct an in-depth analysis of our model components. We first compare the source-only model with DANN [15], a classical UDA method based on adversarial learning. Although using source-only

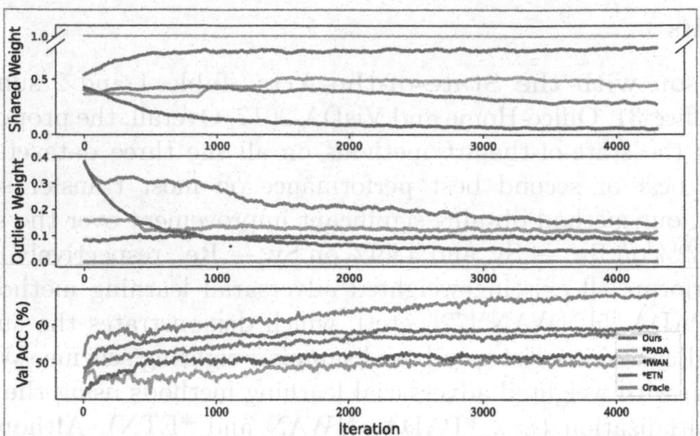

Fig. 3. Quantitative analysis of our method and existing weighted adversarial learning methods based on mean sample weights and validation ACCs during training on the A → C setting of Office-Home. Best viewed in color (Color figure online)

models as initialization, DANN obtains worse performance, which is caused by negative transfer. By introducing the proposed cycle-inconsistency-based weighting scheme, our method (Ours-Cycle w/o $\mathcal{L}_{ctr}$) obtains significant performance improvement over the source-only model. The result demonstrates the effectiveness of the proposed cycle-inconsistency-based weighting scheme, which mitigates negative transfer. By further introducing center losses, Ours-Cycle obtains higher performance, which attributes to the reduction of intra-class variation. By using the vanilla nearest neighbor (prototype) search for cross-domain feature transformations, Ours-Cycle-Hard obtains slightly lower performance compared with that using the soft nearest neighbor (Ours-Cycle), which is because that the soft-nearest-neighbor-based transformations improve the representation power of transformed features. If we cancel the cycle-back operation in the cycle-inconsistency-based weighting scheme (Ours-Src2Trg), the performance drops (*e.g.*, A → C, P → C), which demonstrates the effectiveness of cycle inconsistency modeling. This is because the model has weak classification power in the target domain at the early stages of training, resulting in inaccurate weight assignment. Furthermore, by adopting the mixed strategy, Ours (Full) obtains further improvement since it considers the inconsistency in both cycle transformations and source-to-target transformations. Also, we report the results of the oracle method (Oracle) as the upper bound, *i.e.*, *an ideal weighted adversarial learning method which assigns sample weights according to the ground-truth.* Compared with all existing methods, our performance is the closest to that of Oracle.

- Analysis of Sample Weights. Figure 3 shows variation curves of the mean sample weight of our method during training on the A → C setting of Office-Home (the **blue** curves). Overall, our method assigns large weights to samples of shared classes and small weights to samples of outlier classes. At the beginning of training, the sample weights of shared classes are moderate (about 0.5) and the sample weights of outlier classes are small (about 0.1). As the training goes, the sample weights of shared classes gradually increase (from 0.5 to 0.8) while the sample weights of outlier classes keep stably low, and the validation ACC gradually increases as the shared classes across domains gradually align. Also, we compare our method with existing weighted adversarial learning methods, and we report the results of the oracle method (Oracle) as the upper bound. From the figure, we find that our method assigns much more accurate weights to samples compared with existing methods (*i.e.*, *PADA, *IWAN, *ETN). Specifically, our method assigns much higher weights to samples in shared classes and assigns relatively lower weights (with respect to shared weights) to samples in outlier classes. As a result, our method obtains higher validation ACC. Besides, our method performs closely with Oracle in terms of mean sample weights and obtains the closest performance to the upper bound compared with others.

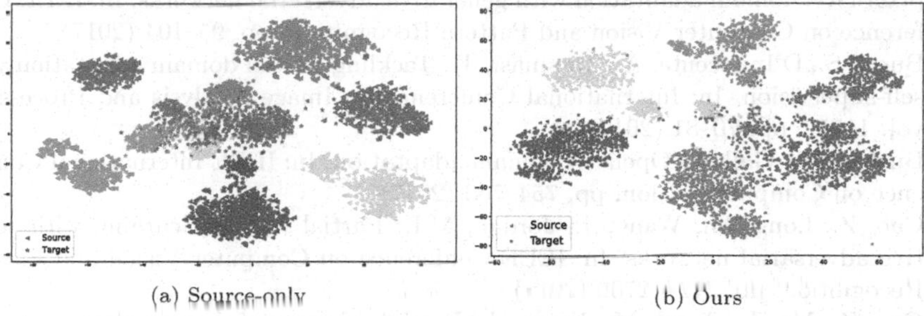

Fig. 4. Feature distribution by t-SNE of the (a) source-only model and (b) our model on VisDA-2017. The triangle and star markers denote the source and target samples, and different colors denote different categories. For better visualization, we only show the shared classes. Best viewed in color (Color figure online)

- Feature Distribution Visualization. Figure 4 shows the feature distribution by t-SNE [45]. From Fig. 4a, we find that the source-only model can discriminate target samples of different classes to some extent. However, the source-only model does not align the shared classes in the source and target domains and confuse the target samples from different classes at the central area. By contrast, as shown in Fig. 4b, our model aligns the two domains well and the classification boundaries are much clearer in the target domain.

5 Conclusion

To address unsupervised partial domain adaptation, in this work, we propose a weighted adversarial learning method with a novel sample weighting scheme. Our method exploits the cycle inconsistency, i.e., category discrepancy between original and cycle-transformed features, to distinguish outlier classes from shared classes in the source domain. Accordingly, our method filters out the source samples of outlier classes and aligns shared classes across domains iteratively. With such a filter-and-align manner, our method gradually learns accurate cycle transformation functions based on feature similarity. Extensive experiments demonstrate the effectiveness of our method. In the future, we will explore properties of the feature space in more practical settings, *e.g.*, universal domain adaptation.

Acknowledgments. This work was supported partially by the NSFC (U21A2-0471, U1911401, U1811461), Guangdong NSF Project (No. 2020B1515120085, 2018B030312002), Guangzhou Research Project (201902010037), and the Key-Area Research and Development Program of Guangzhou (202007030004).

References

1. Bousmalis, K., Silberman, N., Dohan, D., Erhan, D., Krishnan, D.: Unsupervised pixel-level domain adaptation with generative adversarial networks. In: IEEE Conference on Computer Vision and Pattern Recognition, pp. 95–104 (2017)
2. Bucci, S., D'Innocente, A., Tommasi, T.: Tackling partial domain adaptation with self-supervision. In: International Conference on Image Analysis and Processing, vol. 11752, pp. 70–81 (2019)
3. Busto, P.P., Gall, J.: Open set domain adaptation. In: IEEE International Conference on Computer Vision, pp. 754–763 (2017)
4. Cao, Z., Long, M., Wang, J., Jordan, M.I.: Partial transfer learning with selective adversarial networks. In: IEEE Conference on Computer Vision and Pattern Recognition, pp. 2724–2732 (2018)
5. Cao, Z., Ma, L., Long, M., Wang, J.: Partial adversarial domain adaptation. In: Proceedings of the European Conference on Computer Vision, pp. 139–155 (2018)
6. Cao, Z., You, K., Long, M., Wang, J., Yang, Q.: Learning to transfer examples for partial domain adaptation. In: IEEE Conference on Computer Vision and Pattern Recognition, pp. 2985–2994 (2019)
7. Chen, C., Li, J., Zheng, Z., Huang, Y., Ding, X., Yu, Y.: Dual bipartite graph learning: a general approach for domain adaptive object detection. In: IEEE/CVF International Conference on Computer Vision, pp. 2683–2692 (2021)
8. Chen, Z., Chen, C., Cheng, Z., Jiang, B., Fang, K., Jin, X.: Selective transfer with reinforced transfer network for partial domain adaptation. In: IEEE/CVF Conference on Computer Vision and Pattern Recognition, pp. 12703–12711 (2020)
9. Cui, S., Wang, S., Zhuo, J., Su, C., Huang, Q., Tian, Q.: Gradually vanishing bridge for adversarial domain adaptation. In: IEEE/CVF Conference on Computer Vision and Pattern Recognition, pp. 12452–12461 (2020)
10. Damodaran, B.B., Kellenberger, B., Flamary, R., Tuia, D., Courty, N.: DeepJDOT: deep joint distribution optimal transport for unsupervised domain adaptation. In: Proceedings of the European Conference on Computer Vision, pp. 467–483 (2018)
11. Deng, J., Dong, W., Socher, R., Li, L., Li, K., Fei-Fei, L.: ImageNet: a large-scale hierarchical image database. In: IEEE Computer Society Conference on Computer Vision and Pattern Recognition, pp. 248–255 (2009)
12. Dwibedi, D., Aytar, Y., Tompson, J., Sermanet, P., Zisserman, A.: Temporal cycle-consistency learning. In: IEEE Conference on Computer Vision and Pattern Recognition, pp. 1801–1810 (2019)

13. French, G., Mackiewicz, M., Fisher, M.H.: Self-ensembling for visual domain adaptation. In: International Conference on Learning Representations (2018)
14. Fu, B., Cao, Z., Long, M., Wang, J.: Learning to detect open classes for universal domain adaptation. In: Vedaldi, A., Bischof, H., Brox, T., Frahm, J.-M. (eds.) ECCV 2020. LNCS, vol. 12360, pp. 567–583. Springer, Cham (2020). https://doi.org/10.1007/978-3-030-58555-6_34
15. Ganin, Y., et al.: Domain-adversarial training of neural networks. J. Mach. Learn. Res. **17**, 59:1–59:35 (2016)
16. Goldberger, J., Roweis, S.T., Hinton, G.E., Salakhutdinov, R.: Neighbourhood components analysis. In: Advances in Neural Information Processing Systems, pp. 513–520 (2004)
17. Goodfellow, I.J., et al.: Generative adversarial nets. In: Advances in Neural Information Processing Systems, pp. 2672–2680 (2014)
18. Grandvalet, Y., Bengio, Y.: Semi-supervised learning by entropy minimization. In: Advances in Neural Information Processing Systems, pp. 529–536 (2004)
19. Griffin, G., Holub, A., Perona, P.: Caltech-256 object category dataset (2007)
20. Gu, X., Yu, X., Yang, Y., Sun, J., Xu, Z.: Adversarial reweighting for partial domain adaptation. In: Advances in Neural Information Processing Systems (2021)
21. Häusser, P., Frerix, T., Mordvintsev, A., Cremers, D.: Associative domain adaptation. In: IEEE International Conference on Computer Vision, pp. 2784–2792 (2017)
22. He, K., Zhang, X., Ren, S., Sun, J.: Deep residual learning for image recognition. In: IEEE Conference on Computer Vision and Pattern Recognition, pp. 770–778 (2016)
23. Hoffman, J., et al.: CyCADA: cycle-consistent adversarial domain adaptation. In: Proceedings of the 35th International Conference on Machine Learning, vol. 80, pp. 1994–2003 (2018)
24. Hsu, T.H., Chen, W., Hou, C., Tsai, Y.H., Yeh, Y., Wang, Y.F.: Unsupervised domain adaptation with imbalanced cross-domain data. In: IEEE International Conference on Computer Vision, pp. 4121–4129 (2015)
25. Hu, J., Tuo, H., Wang, C., Qiao, L., Zhong, H., Jing, Z.: Multi-weight partial domain adaptation. In: 30th British Machine Vision Conference, p. 5 (2019)
26. Hu, J., et al.: Discriminative partial domain adversarial network. In: Vedaldi, A., Bischof, H., Brox, T., Frahm, J.-M. (eds.) ECCV 2020. LNCS, vol. 12372, pp. 632–648. Springer, Cham (2020). https://doi.org/10.1007/978-3-030-58583-9_38
27. Hu, L., Kan, M., Shan, S., Chen, X.: Duplex generative adversarial network for unsupervised domain adaptation. In: IEEE Conference on Computer Vision and Pattern Recognition, pp. 1498–1507 (2018)
28. Jin, Y., Wang, X., Long, M., Wang, J.: Minimum class confusion for versatile domain adaptation. In: Vedaldi, A., Bischof, H., Brox, T., Frahm, J.-M. (eds.) ECCV 2020. LNCS, vol. 12366, pp. 464–480. Springer, Cham (2020). https://doi.org/10.1007/978-3-030-58589-1_28
29. Jing, T., Xia, H., Ding, Z.: Adaptively-accumulated knowledge transfer for partial domain adaptation. In: ACM International Conference on Multimedia, pp. 1606–1614 (2020)
30. Kang, G., Wei, Y., Yang, Y., Zhuang, Y., Hauptmann, A.G.: Pixel-level cycle association: a new perspective for domain adaptive semantic segmentation. In: Larochelle, H., Ranzato, M., Hadsell, R., Balcan, M., Lin, H. (eds.) Advances in Neural Information Processing Systems (2020)

31. Krizhevsky, A., Sutskever, I., Hinton, G.E.: ImageNet classification with deep convolutional neural networks. In: Advances in Neural Information Processing Systems, pp. 1106–1114 (2012)
32. Kundu, J.N., Venkat, N., Revanur, A., V., R.M., Babu, R.V.: Towards inheritable models for open-set domain adaptation. In: IEEE/CVF Conference on Computer Vision and Pattern Recognition, pp. 12373–12382 (2020)
33. Kundu, J.N., Venkat, N., V., R.M., Babu, R.V.: Universal source-free domain adaptation. In: IEEE/CVF Conference on Computer Vision and Pattern Recognition, pp. 4543–4552 (2020)
34. Li, G., Kang, G., Zhu, Y., Wei, Y., Yang, Y.: Domain consensus clustering for universal domain adaptation. In: IEEE Conference on Computer Vision and Pattern Recognition, pp. 9757–9766 (2021)
35. Li, S., Liu, C.H., Lin, Q., Wen, Q., Su, L., Huang, G., Ding, Z.: Deep residual correction network for partial domain adaptation. IEEE Trans. Pattern Anal. Mach. Intell. **43**(7), 2329–2344 (2021)
36. Liang, J., Hu, D., Feng, J.: Do we really need to access the source data? Source hypothesis transfer for unsupervised domain adaptation. In: Proceedings of the 37th International Conference on Machine Learning, vol. 119, pp. 6028–6039 (2020)
37. Liang, J., Hu, D., Feng, J.: Domain adaptation with auxiliary target domain-oriented classifier. In: IEEE Conference on Computer Vision and Pattern Recognition, pp. 16632–16642 (2021)
38. Liang, J., Hu, D., Wang, Y., He, R., Feng, J.: Source data-absent unsupervised domain adaptation through hypothesis transfer and labeling transfer. IEEE Trans. Pattern Anal. Mach. Intell. (2021)
39. Liang, J., Wang, Y., Hu, D., He, R., Feng, J.: A balanced and uncertainty-aware approach for partial domain adaptation. In: Vedaldi, A., Bischof, H., Brox, T., Frahm, J.-M. (eds.) ECCV 2020. LNCS, vol. 12356, pp. 123–140. Springer, Cham (2020). https://doi.org/10.1007/978-3-030-58621-8_8
40. Liu, H., Cao, Z., Long, M., Wang, J., Yang, Q.: Separate to adapt: open set domain adaptation via progressive separation. In: IEEE Conference on Computer Vision and Pattern Recognition, pp. 2927–2936 (2019)
41. Long, J., Shelhamer, E., Darrell, T.: Fully convolutional networks for semantic segmentation. In: IEEE Conference on Computer Vision and Pattern Recognition, pp. 3431–3440 (2015)
42. Long, M., Cao, Y., Wang, J., Jordan, M.I.: Learning transferable features with deep adaptation networks. In: Proceedings of the 32nd International Conference on Machine Learning, vol. 37, pp. 97–105 (2015)
43. Long, M., Cao, Z., Wang, J., Jordan, M.I.: Conditional adversarial domain adaptation. In: Advances in Neural Information Processing Systems, pp. 1647–1657 (2018)
44. Long, M., Zhu, H., Wang, J., Jordan, M.I.: Unsupervised domain adaptation with residual transfer networks. In: Advances in Neural Information Processing Systems, pp. 136–144 (2016)
45. Van der Maaten, L., Hinton, G.: Visualizing data using t-SNE. J. Mach. Learn. Res. **9**(11) (2008)
46. Matsuura, T., Saito, K., Harada, T.: TWINs: two weighted inconsistency-reduced networks for partial domain adaptation. CoRR abs/1812.07405 (2018)
47. Murez, Z., Kolouri, S., Kriegman, D.J., Ramamoorthi, R., Kim, K.: Image to image translation for domain adaptation. In: IEEE Conference on Computer Vision and Pattern Recognition, pp. 4500–4509 (2018)

48. Pan, S.J., Yang, Q.: A survey on transfer learning. IEEE Trans. Knowl. Data Eng. **22**(10), 1345–1359 (2010)
49. Peng, X., Usman, B., Kaushik, N., Hoffman, J., Wang, D., Saenko, K.: VisDA: the visual domain adaptation challenge. CoRR abs/1710.06924 (2017)
50. Ren, S., He, K., Girshick, R.B., Sun, J.: Faster R-CNN: towards real-time object detection with region proposal networks. In: Advances in Neural Information Processing Systems, pp. 91–99 (2015)
51. Saenko, K., Kulis, B., Fritz, M., Darrell, T.: Adapting visual category models to new domains. In: Daniilidis, K., Maragos, P., Paragios, N. (eds.) ECCV 2010. LNCS, vol. 6314, pp. 213–226. Springer, Heidelberg (2010). https://doi.org/10.1007/978-3-642-15561-1_16
52. Saito, K., Ushiku, Y., Harada, T.: Asymmetric tri-training for unsupervised domain adaptation. In: Proceedings of the 34th International Conference on Machine Learning, vol. 70, pp. 2988–2997 (2017)
53. Saito, K., Watanabe, K., Ushiku, Y., Harada, T.: Maximum classifier discrepancy for unsupervised domain adaptation. In: IEEE Conference on Computer Vision and Pattern Recognition, pp. 3723–3732 (2018)
54. Saito, K., Yamamoto, S., Ushiku, Y., Harada, T.: Open set domain adaptation by backpropagation. In: Ferrari, V., Hebert, M., Sminchisescu, C., Weiss, Y. (eds.) ECCV 2018. LNCS, vol. 11209, pp. 156–171. Springer, Cham (2018). https://doi.org/10.1007/978-3-030-01228-1_10
55. Sankaranarayanan, S., Balaji, Y., Castillo, C.D., Chellappa, R.: Generate to Adapt: aligning domains using generative adversarial networks. In: IEEE Conference on Computer Vision and Pattern Recognition, pp. 8503–8512 (2018)
56. Shu, R., Bui, H.H., Narui, H., Ermon, S.: A DIRT-T approach to unsupervised domain adaptation. In: International Conference on Learning Representations (2018)
57. Snell, J., Swersky, K., Zemel, R.S.: Prototypical networks for few-shot learning. In: Advances in Neural Information Processing Systems, pp. 4077–4087 (2017)
58. Sun, B., Saenko, K.: Deep CORAL: correlation alignment for deep domain adaptation. In: Hua, G., Jégou, H. (eds.) ECCV 2016. LNCS, vol. 9915, pp. 443–450. Springer, Cham (2016). https://doi.org/10.1007/978-3-319-49409-8_35
59. Tzeng, E., Hoffman, J., Saenko, K., Darrell, T.: Adversarial discriminative domain adaptation. In: IEEE Conference on Computer Vision and Pattern Recognition, pp. 2962–2971 (2017)
60. Tzeng, E., Hoffman, J., Zhang, N., Saenko, K., Darrell, T.: Deep domain confusion: maximizing for domain invariance. CoRR abs/1412.3474 (2014)
61. Venkateswara, H., Eusebio, J., Chakraborty, S., Panchanathan, S.: Deep hashing network for unsupervised domain adaptation. In: IEEE Conference on Computer Vision and Pattern Recognition, pp. 5385–5394 (2017)
62. Wen, Y., Zhang, K., Li, Z., Qiao, Yu.: A discriminative feature learning approach for deep face recognition. In: Leibe, B., Matas, J., Sebe, N., Welling, M. (eds.) ECCV 2016. LNCS, vol. 9911, pp. 499–515. Springer, Cham (2016). https://doi.org/10.1007/978-3-319-46478-7_31
63. Xiao, W., Ding, Z., Liu, H.: Implicit semantic response alignment for partial domain adaptation. In: Advances in Neural Information Processing Systems (2021)
64. Xie, S., Zheng, Z., Chen, L., Chen, C.: Learning semantic representations for unsupervised domain adaptation. In: Proceedings of the 35th International Conference on Machine Learning, pp. 5419–5428 (2018)

65. Xu, R., Li, G., Yang, J., Lin, L.: Larger norm more transferable: an adaptive feature norm approach for unsupervised domain adaptation. In: IEEE/CVF International Conference on Computer Vision, pp. 1426–1435 (2019)
66. Yang, J., Zou, H., Zhou, Y., Zeng, Z., Xie, L.: Mind the Discriminability: Asymmetric adversarial domain adaptation. In: Proceedings of the European Conference on Computer Vision. pp. 589–606 (2020)
67. Yang, S., Wang, Y., van de Weijer, J., Herranz, L., Jui, S.: Exploiting the intrinsic neighborhood structure for source-free domain adaptation. CoRR abs/2110.04202 (2021)
68. Yang, S., Wang, Y., van de Weijer, J., Herranz, L., Jui, S.: Generalized source-free domain adaptation. In: IEEE/CVF International Conference on Computer Vision, pp. 8978–8987 (2021)
69. Yosinski, J., Clune, J., Bengio, Y., Lipson, H.: How transferable are features in deep neural networks? In: Advances in Neural Information Processing Systems, pp. 3320–3328 (2014)
70. You, K., Long, M., Cao, Z., Wang, J., Jordan, M.I.: Universal domain adaptation. In: IEEE Conference on Computer Vision and Pattern Recognition, pp. 2720–2729 (2019)
71. Zellinger, W., Grubinger, T., Lughofer, E., Natschläger, T., Saminger-Platz, S.: Central moment discrepancy (CMD) for domain-invariant representation learning. In: International Conference on Learning Representations (2017)
72. Zhang, J., Ding, Z., Li, W., Ogunbona, P.: Importance weighted adversarial nets for partial domain adaptation. In: IEEE Conference on Computer Vision and Pattern Recognition, pp. 8156–8164 (2018)
73. Zhang, Y., Zhang, H., Deng, B., Li, S., Jia, K., Zhang, L.: Semi-supervised models are strong unsupervised domain adaptation learners. CoRR abs/2106.00417 (2021)
74. Zhang, Y., Liu, T., Long, M., Jordan, M.I.: Bridging theory and algorithm for domain adaptation. In: Proceedings of the 36th International Conference on Machine Learning, vol. 97, pp. 7404–7413 (2019)
75. Zhu, J., Park, T., Isola, P., Efros, A.A.: Unpaired image-to-image translation using cycle-consistent adversarial networks. In: IEEE International Conference on Computer Vision, pp. 2242–2251 (2017)

Combating Label Distribution Shift for Active Domain Adaptation

Sehyun Hwang[1], Sohyun Lee[2], Sungyeon Kim[1], Jungseul Ok[1,2], and Suha Kwak[1,2](✉)

[1] Department of Computer Science and Engineering, POSTECH, Pohang, Korea
suha.kwak@posetch.ac.kr
[2] Graduate School of Artificial Intelligence, Pohang, Korea
http://cvlab.postech.ac.kr/research/LAMDA/

Abstract. We consider the problem of active domain adaptation (ADA) to unlabeled target data, of which subset is actively selected and labeled given a budget constraint. Inspired by recent analysis on a critical issue from label distribution mismatch between source and target in domain adaptation, we devise a method that addresses the issue for the first time in ADA. At its heart lies a novel sampling strategy, which seeks target data that best approximate the entire target distribution as well as being representative, diverse, and uncertain. The sampled target data are then used not only for supervised learning but also for matching label distributions of source and target domains, leading to remarkable performance improvement. On four public benchmarks, our method substantially outperforms existing methods in every adaptation scenario.

Keywords: Active domain adaptation · Active learning · Domain adaptation · Label distribution shift

1 Introduction

Domain adaptation is the task of adapting a model trained on a label-sufficient source domain to a label-scarce target domain when their input distributions are different. It has played crucial roles in applications that involve significant input distribution shifts such as recognition under adverse conditions (*e.g.*, climate changes [10,25,45,46] and nighttime [44]) and synthetic-to-real adaptation [35]. The most popular direction in this field is unsupervised domain adaptation [4,15] which assumes a totally unlabeled target domain. However, in practice, labeling a small part of target data is usually feasible. Hence, label-efficient domain adaptation tasks such as semi-supervised domain adaptation [26,27,43,61,62] and active domain adaptation [14,36,40,52] have attracted increasing attention.

J. Ok and S. Kwak—Co-corresponding authors.

Supplementary Information The online version contains supplementary material available at https://doi.org/10.1007/978-3-031-19827-4_32.

S. Avidan et al. (Eds.): ECCV 2022, LNCS 13693, pp. 549–566, 2022.
https://doi.org/10.1007/978-3-031-19827-4_32

In this paper, we consider active domain adaptation (ADA) [14,36,40,52], where we can interact with an oracle to obtain annotations on a subset of target data given budget constraint, while utilizing the annotations for domain adaptation. The key to the success of ADA is to co-design sampling mechanism selecting a subset of target data to be annotated and utilization of the annotations. Existing ADA methods utilize the obtained annotations only for supervised learning, similar to existing Active Learning (AL) methods [3,47,51,56]. Accordingly, they count diversity, representativeness, and uncertainty of the data to boost the effect of supervised learning.

We argue that for domain adaptation, there is another use of the sampled data, which deserves attention but is missing in the previous work: matching label distributions of source and target domains. In practice, domain adaptation often encounters label distribution shift, i.e., the frequencies of classes significantly differ between source and target domains. It has been proven in [6,63] that matching label distributions of source and target domains is a necessary condition for successful domain adaptation [6,63]. Also, it has been empirically verified in [6] that mismatched label distributions restrict or even deteriorate performance of existing domain adaptation methods [15,29,30].

Motivated by this, we present a new method that addresses the label distribution shift for the first time in ADA. At the heart of our method lies LAbel distribution Matching through Density-aware Active sampling, and thus it is dubbed LAMDA. Its key idea is to use sampled data for label distribution matching as well as supervised learning. During training, it estimates the label distribution of the target domain through the annotated labels of sampled target data, and builds each source data mini-batch in a way that the label frequencies of the batch follow the estimated target label distribution. To this end, we design a new sampling strategy useful for label distribution estimation as well as supervised learning. For supervised learning, sampled data are encouraged to be representative, diverse, and uncertain. For label distribution estimation, on the other hand, sampled data should well approximate the entire data distribution of the target domain. As will be demonstrated empirically, existing ADA methods often fail to satisfy the second condition since they blindly select uncertain instances or do not take the overall target distribution into account.

Our sampling method satisfies both of the above conditions. Specifically, it selects a subset of target data whose statistical distance from the entire target data is minimized. Since the distribution of the sampled data well approximates that of the entire target data, their labels are expected to follow the latent target label distribution. They also spontaneously become diverse and representative in order to cover the entire target data distribution. In addition, LAMDA asks the oracle for labeling only uncertain instances in the sampled subset; it in turn utilizes the manually labeled samples for both supervised learning and label distribution estimation, while the rest are assigned pseudo labels by the model's prediction and used only for label distribution estimation. This strategy lets LAMDA annotate and exploit only uncertain data in the subset for supervised learning, and estimate the target label distribution accurately by using the entire subset. The advantage of our sampling method is illustrated in Fig. 1.

In addition, we propose to use the cosine classifier [16,38], instead of the conventional linear classifier, in order to further alleviate the adverse effect of label distribution shift. The cosine classifier is known to be less biased to dominant classes since its classification weights are ℓ_2-normalized, and thus has been used for long-tailed recognition [21] and few-shot learning [5,16,38]. We find that such a property is also useful to combat label distribution shift; it is empirically verified that the cosine classifier significantly improves ADA performance when combined with a domain alignment method.

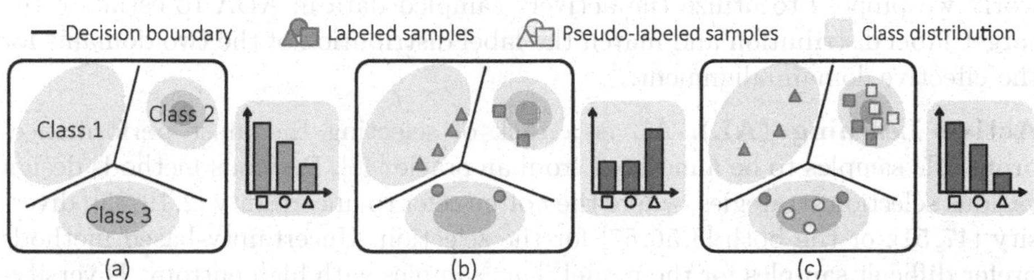

Fig. 1. Comparison between sampling methods. (a) Data distribution and label distribution of target data. (b) Uncertainty preferred sampling of conventional ADA and the label distribution of corresponding sampled data. (c) Density-aware sampling of LAMDA and the label distribution of corresponding sampled data.

To evaluate and compare LAMDA with existing ADA methods thoroughly, we present a unified evaluation protocol for ADA. Extensive experiments based on the evaluation protocol demonstrate impressive performance of LAMDA, which largely surpasses records of existing ADA methods [14,36,40], on four public benchmarks for domain adaptation [34,35,53,55]. The main contribution of this paper is four-fold:

- LAMDA is the first attempt to tackle the label distribution shift for ADA. The importance of this research direction is demonstrated by the outstanding performance of LAMDA.
- We propose a new sampling strategy for choosing target data best preserving the entire target data distribution as well as being representative, diverse, and uncertain. Data selected by our strategy are useful for both label distribution matching and supervised learning.
- For the first time, we benchmark existing ADA methods [14,36,40] on four public datasets for domain adaptation [34,35,53,55] through a unified evaluation protocol.
- In our experiment with each of the four domain adaptation datasets, LAMDA substantially outperforms all the existing ADA models.

2 Related Work

Unsupervised Domain Adaptation (UDA). Major approaches in UDA aim at learning domain invariant features so that a classifier trained on the labeled source domain data can be transferred to the unlabeled target domain data [4]. To do so, previous methods align feature distribution between the two domains using various domain discrepancy measures such as MMD [28,30], Wasserstein discrepancy [7,8,11,24], and $\mathcal{H}$-divergence [1,9,15,29,37,54]. On the other hand, recent studies [6,63] found that such domain alignment is only effective when the label distributions of the two domains are matched. This condition is difficult to be satisfied due to the limited access to the target class distribution. In this work, we propose to utilize the actively sampled data in ADA to estimate the target label distribution and match the label distribution of the two domains for the effective domain alignment.

Active Learning (AL). AL is a task of selecting the most performance-profitable samples to be annotated from an oracle [48]. Previous methods design various selection strategies, where they often refer to uncertainty [2,19,33], diversity [47,51], or the both [3,56,57] for the selection. Uncertainty-based methods prefer difficult samples for the model, *e.g.*, samples with high entropy. Diversity-based methods prefer samples that are different from the selected ones. Our method shares a similar idea with Wang [56,57] in that we use MMD [17], but we additionally select the easy-but-representative samples as a pseudo-labeled set to precisely estimate the target label distribution, which can be used to help domain adaptation process.

Active Domain Adaptation (ADA). ADA is a variant of active learning that selects samples to maximize the domain adaptation performance. ADA is first introduced by Rai *et al.* [39] and first adapted to image classification by AADA [52]. Existing methods mainly refer to the difficulty of samples (*i.e.*, uncertainty) for selection. TQS [14] selects uncertain samples by combining three sampling criteria: disagreement among ensemble models [49], top-2 margin of predictive probabilities [42], and confidence of domain discriminator [52]. CLUE [36] additionally considers the diversity among the selected samples along with the uncertainty by using entropy-weighted k-means clustering [20]. S^3VAADA [40] designs a set-based scoring function that favors three properties: vulnerability to adversarial perturbation, diversity within the sampled set, and representativeness to avoid outliers. More recent methods utilize a free energy biases [23] of the two domains [58], K-medoids algorithm [12,41], and the distance to different class centers [59] for the selection. To newly tackle the critical issue of label distribution shift in ADA, we propose a sampling strategy that considers the data distribution of the target domain. The main technical difference between the sampling of conventional ADA and ours is illustrated in Fig. 1.

3 Problem Formulation

Given a labeled source dataset $\mathcal{D}_\mathrm{S} = \{(\mathbf{x}_i, y_i)\}_{i=1}^{n_\mathrm{S}}$ of size n_S and an unlabeled target dataset $\mathcal{D}_\mathrm{T} = \{\mathbf{x}_i\}_{i=1}^{n_\mathrm{T}}$ of size n_T, we study a standard ADA scenario of R rounds, in each of which B samples of target data are newly labeled and utilized for model update, *i.e.*, the per-round budget is B and the total budget is $RB \leq n_\mathrm{T}$. Let $\mathcal{D}_\mathrm{L}$ be the labeled target dataset actively collected, which grows up to size RB. We consider image classification such that $\mathbf{x}_i$ is an image and $y_i \in \mathcal{Y} = \{1, 2, \ldots, C\}$ is a categorical variable, where a model, parameterized by $\boldsymbol{\theta}$, predicts $\mathrm{argmax}_{y \in \mathcal{Y}}\, p_{\boldsymbol{\theta}}(y|\mathbf{x})$ for input image $\mathbf{x}$. The goal of ADA is to maximize the test accuracy of $\boldsymbol{\theta}$ in the target domain, where $\boldsymbol{\theta}$ is trained on $\mathcal{D}_\mathrm{S}$, $\mathcal{D}_\mathrm{T}$ and $\mathcal{D}_\mathrm{L}$ in the iterative manner.

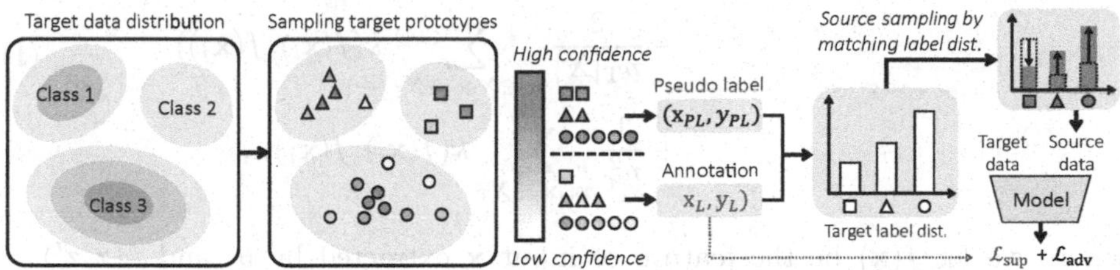

Fig. 2. LAMDA first samples a set of target prototypes that well represent the entire target data distribution. The prototypes are annotated by an oracle if their predictions are uncertain or assigned pseudo labels otherwise. It then estimates the target label distribution using the prototypes, and builds source data mini-batches whose label distributions follow the estimated target label distribution. Finally, our model is trained by the cross-entropy loss $\mathcal{L}_{\mathrm{sup}}$ and the domain adversarial loss $\mathcal{L}_{\mathrm{adv}}$

4 Proposed Method

4.1 Overview of LAMDA

We present a novel ADA method, named LAMDA, that addresses *label distribution shift* between source and target domains. Our core idea is to select and utilize target samples useful for both label distribution matching and supervised learning. This idea is implemented in LAMDA by three components: prototype sampling, label distribution matching, and model training. First, LAMDA selects a set of prototypes, *i.e.*, target data that best approximate the entire target data distribution. Uncertain prototypes in the set are then identified by the model and annotated by oracle, while the rest are assigned pseudo-labels (Sect. 4.2). Next, LAMDA estimates the target label distribution using the assigned labels of the prototypes and adjusts the label distribution of source data being drawn within each mini-batch according to the estimated target label distribution (Sect. 4.3). Under the matched label distribution, the model is trained by both cross-entropy loss and domain adversarial loss (Sect. 4.4). The overall framework of LAMDA is illustrated in Fig. 2. In what follows, we describe each component at a round.

4.2 Prototype Set Sampling in Target Data

We begin with a model $\boldsymbol{\theta}$ which is from the previous round, or pretrained on source dataset $\mathcal{D}_{\mathrm{S}}$ for the first round. Let $X_{(\cdot)}$ denote the set of images in dataset $\mathcal{D}_{(\cdot)}$ for notational simplicity. To select the prototype set that represents the target data distribution, we first seek subset $X \subset X_{\mathrm{T}}$ which minimizes a statistical distance between X and the entire target data X_{T}. Inspired by the sampling technique for example-based model explanation [22], we employ the squared Maximum Mean Discrepancy (MMD) [17] between X and X_{T} on the feature space, which is formally given by

$$\begin{aligned}\mathrm{MMD}^2(X, X_{\mathrm{T}}) := & \frac{1}{|X|^2} \sum_{\mathbf{x}_i, \mathbf{x}_j \in X} k(f(\mathbf{x}_i), f(\mathbf{x}_j)) \\ & - \frac{2}{n_{\mathrm{T}}|X|} \sum_{\mathbf{x}_i \in X, \mathbf{x}_j \in X_{\mathrm{T}}} k(f(\mathbf{x}_i), f(\mathbf{x}_j)) \\ & + \frac{1}{n_{\mathrm{T}}^2} \sum_{\mathbf{x}_i, \mathbf{x}_j \in X_{\mathrm{T}}} k(f(\mathbf{x}_i), f(\mathbf{x}_j)) ,\end{aligned} \tag{1}$$

where we let $f(\mathbf{x})$ be the feature of input $\mathbf{x}$ extracted by $\boldsymbol{\theta}$, and $k(\mathbf{z}, \mathbf{z}') = \exp(-\gamma||\mathbf{z} - \mathbf{z}'||^2)$ be the Radial Basis Function (RBF) kernel. Noting that the last term in Eq. (1) is constant with respect to X, we define $J(X)$ as follows:

$$\begin{aligned}J(X) := & \mathrm{MMD}^2(\emptyset, X_{\mathrm{T}}) - \mathrm{MMD}^2(X, X_{\mathrm{T}}) \\ = & \frac{2}{n_{\mathrm{T}}|X|} \sum_{\mathbf{x}_i \in X, \mathbf{x}_j \in X_{\mathrm{T}}} k(f(\mathbf{x}_i), f(\mathbf{x}_j)) - \frac{1}{|X|^2} \sum_{\mathbf{x}_i, \mathbf{x}_j \in X} k(f(\mathbf{x}_i), f(\mathbf{x}_j)) .\end{aligned} \tag{2}$$

where a constant $\mathrm{MMD}^2(\emptyset, X_{\mathrm{T}})$ is added to make $J(\emptyset) = 0$, and the first and second terms measure representativeness and diversity of X, respectively.

The prototypes can be then identified by a constrained combinatorial optimization to maximize $J(X)$ given a certain size limit n_{P}, *i.e.*,

$$\max_{X \in 2^{X_{\mathrm{T}}} : |X| \leq n_{\mathrm{P}}} J(X) . \tag{3}$$

This is generally intractable due to the exponentially many candidates. However, a greedy process selecting samples one after one to locally maximize J can efficiently find a near-optimal solution in polynomial time since $J(X)$ is monotone submodular when k is RBF kernel [22]. To be specific, the greedy process is proven to achieve at least $1 - [(n_{\mathrm{P}} - 1)/n_{\mathrm{P}}]^{n_{\mathrm{P}}}$ of the optimum [32]. We hence adopt the greedy process to select subset X_{P} from the unlabeled target data.

We note that setting $n_{\mathrm{P}} = B$ and spending all the budget for X_{P} would be a waste of budget when X_{P} includes easy prototypes, whose labels are accurately predicted by $\boldsymbol{\theta}$. We hence set n_{P} in an adaptive way so that we spend budget B only for hard prototypes. To be specific, starting from $X_{\mathrm{PL}} = \emptyset$ and X_{L} from the previous round (or $X_{\mathrm{PL}} = X_{\mathrm{L}} = \emptyset$ for the first round), each greedy selection

Algorithm 1 Prototype sampling at a round

Require: Model parameter $\boldsymbol{\theta}$ from the previous round, labeled source dataset $\mathcal{D}_\mathrm{S}$, unlabeled target image set X_T, per-round budget B, threshold Δ.

Retrieve X_L from the previous round or set it as empty set for the first round.
Set $X_\mathrm{PL} \leftarrow \emptyset$ and $X_\mathrm{P} \leftarrow X_\mathrm{L} \cup X_\mathrm{PL}$.
repeat
  $\mathbf{x}^* \leftarrow \mathrm{argmax}_{\mathbf{x}_i \in X_\mathrm{T} \setminus X_\mathrm{P}} (J(X_\mathrm{P} \cup \{\mathbf{x}_i\}) - J(X_\mathrm{P}))$ ▷ Prototype selection w.r.t. $J(X)$ in Eq. (2)
  $\hat{y}_1 \leftarrow \mathrm{argmax}_{y \in \mathcal{Y}} p_{\boldsymbol{\theta}}(y|\mathbf{x}^*)$, $\hat{y}_2 \leftarrow \mathrm{argmax}_{y \in \mathcal{Y} \setminus \{\hat{y}_1\}} p_{\boldsymbol{\theta}}(y|\mathbf{x}^*)$ ▷ Get top-1 and top-2 prediction
  if $p_{\boldsymbol{\theta}}(\hat{y}_1|\mathbf{x}^*) - p_{\boldsymbol{\theta}}(\hat{y}_2|\mathbf{x}^*) > \Delta$ **then** ▷ Identify easy/hard prototype by margin
    $X_\mathrm{PL} \leftarrow X_\mathrm{PL} \cup \{\mathbf{x}^*\}$ ▷ Pseudo-labeling for easy prototype
  else
    $X_\mathrm{L} \leftarrow X_\mathrm{L} \cup \{\mathbf{x}^*\}$ ▷ Oracle-labeling for hard prototype
  end if
  $X_\mathrm{P} \leftarrow X_\mathrm{P} \cup \{\mathbf{x}^*\}$ ▷ $X_\mathrm{P} = X_\mathrm{L} \cup X_\mathrm{PL}$
until B samples are newly added to X_L (and labeled by oracle)
return $X_\mathrm{P}, X_\mathrm{PL}, X_\mathrm{L}$

is added to either X_PL or X_L. X_PL includes only easy prototypes of X_P whose margin between top-1 and top-2 predictions is larger than threshold Δ, and only hard prototypes in $X_\mathrm{L} = X_\mathrm{P} \setminus X_\mathrm{PL}$ are labeled by oracle. For X_PL, we use top-1 prediction as the pseudo label which is given by

$$\hat{y}_{i,1} := \operatorname*{argmax}_{y \in \mathcal{Y}} p_{\boldsymbol{\theta}}(y|\mathbf{x}_i) . \tag{4}$$

In each round, we continue the sampling process until B hard samples are newly annotated by oracle. Thus, $n_\mathrm{P} = |X_\mathrm{P}| \geq B$ is determined by the adaptation scenario and the model in hand. This is possible because the greedy selection can return a near-optimal solution at any iteration. The sampling process is illustrated in Fig. 2, and described formally in Algorithm 1.

We denote the set of labeled prototypes by $\mathcal{D}_\mathrm{L} = \{(\mathbf{x}_i, y_i)\}_{i=1}^{B}$ and that of pseudo-labeled prototypes by $\mathcal{D}_\mathrm{PL} = \{(\mathbf{x}_i, \hat{y}_{i,1})\}_{i=1}^{n_\mathrm{PL}}$. $\mathcal{D}_\mathrm{L}$ is used for both supervised learning and label distribution estimation, while $\mathcal{D}_\mathrm{PL}$ is used only for label distribution estimation; details will be described in the following section.

4.3 Label Distribution Matching

We use the prototype set to estimate the target data distribution $p_\mathrm{T}(y)$, which is in turn used for label distribution matching. To estimate $p_\mathrm{T}(y)$, we investigate the frequency of each class within $\mathcal{D}_\mathrm{L}$ and $\mathcal{D}_\mathrm{PL}$. The frequency of class c in $\mathcal{D}_\mathrm{L}$ is computed by

$$n_{\mathrm{L},c} := \sum_{(\mathbf{x}_i, y_i) \in \mathcal{D}_\mathrm{L}} \mathbb{1}[y_i = c] , \tag{5}$$

where $\mathbb{1}$ is an indicator function. On the other hand, the class frequency in $\mathcal{D}_\mathrm{PL}$ is weighted by the corresponding predictive probability, which is given by

$$\hat{n}_{\mathrm{PL},c} := \sum_{(\mathbf{x}_i, \hat{y}_{i,1}) \in \mathcal{D}_\mathrm{PL}} \mathbb{1}[\hat{y}_{i,1} = c] p_{\boldsymbol{\theta}}(\hat{y}_{i,1}|\mathbf{x}_i) , \tag{6}$$

Then, the target label distribution $p_{\mathrm{T}}(y)$ is estimated by

$$\hat{p}_{\mathrm{T}}(y) := \frac{n_{\mathrm{L},y} + \hat{n}_{\mathrm{PL},y} + 1}{n_{\mathrm{L}} + \hat{n}_{\mathrm{PL}} + C}\,, \tag{7}$$

where $\hat{n}_{\mathrm{PL}} = \sum_c \hat{n}_{\mathrm{PL},c}$ and C is the number of classes. Note that we add an offset 1 to each category frequency of Eq. (7) to ensure at least a single instance is considered to be present in the target domain. This is consistent with the assumption of UDA, where both domains have the same label space $\mathcal{Y}$. To make the observed source label distribution follow $\hat{p}_{\mathrm{T}}(y)$, we apply class-weighted sampling when building source mini-batches. The ratio between the source label distribution $p_{\mathrm{S}}(y)$ and the estimated target label distribution $\hat{p}_{\mathrm{T}}(y)$ is denoted by $w(y) := \frac{\hat{p}_{\mathrm{T}}(y)}{p_{\mathrm{S}}(y)}$. Then, the probability of sampling $(\mathbf{x}_i, y_i)$ from $\mathcal{D}_{\mathrm{S}}$ for source mini-batch construction is defined by

$$\rho_i := \frac{w(y_i)}{\sum_{(\mathbf{x}_j, y_j)\in\mathcal{D}_{\mathrm{S}}} w(y_j)}\,, \tag{8}$$

where i indicates the sample index.

4.4 Model Training

Loss Functions. As the label frequencies of a source mini-batch match those of the target domain by Eq. (8), we can now apply a domain alignment loss while alleviating the label distribution shift. We choose the domain adversarial loss [15], but any other losses [15,29,30] for domain alignment can be employed. For domain adversarial training, a domain discriminator, parameterized by ϕ, is trained to classify the domain of input feature by probability $p_{\boldsymbol{\theta}_f,\phi}(d|\mathbf{x})$, where $d \in \{0, 1\}$ is domain label. In the meantime, the feature extractor parameterized by $\boldsymbol{\theta}_f$ is adversarially trained to confuse the discriminator. The domain adversarial loss with the matched label distributions is given by

$$\mathcal{L}_{\mathrm{adv}} := \mathbb{E}_{\mathbf{x}_i \overset{\rho_i}{\sim} X_{\mathrm{S}}}[-\log p_{\boldsymbol{\theta}_f,\phi}(d|\mathbf{x}_i)] + \mathbb{E}_{\mathbf{x}_j \overset{\mathrm{iid}}{\sim} X_{\mathrm{T}}}[-\log(1 - p_{\boldsymbol{\theta}_f,\phi}(d|\mathbf{x}_j))]\,, \tag{9}$$

where the first expectation is taken over ρ_i of X_{S} and the second one is taken over uniform distribution of X_{T}. The $\boldsymbol{\theta}_f$ is updated to maximize $\mathcal{L}_{\mathrm{adv}}$, while ϕ is updated to minimize $\mathcal{L}_{\mathrm{adv}}$. Meanwhile, the cross-entropy loss for labeled data $\mathcal{D}_{\mathrm{S}}$ and $\mathcal{D}_{\mathrm{L}}$ is given by

$$\mathcal{L}_{\mathrm{sup}} := \mathbb{E}_{(\mathbf{x}_i, y_i)\overset{\rho_i}{\sim}\mathcal{D}_{\mathrm{S}}}[-\log p_{\boldsymbol{\theta}}(y_i|\mathbf{x}_i)] + \mathbb{E}_{(\mathbf{x}_j, y_j)\overset{\mathrm{iid}}{\sim}\mathcal{D}_{\mathrm{L}}}[-\log p_{\boldsymbol{\theta}}(y_j|\mathbf{x}_j)]\,. \tag{10}$$

In summary, the total training loss for the proposed framework is given by

$$\mathcal{L} := \mathcal{L}_{\mathrm{sup}} + \mathcal{L}_{\mathrm{adv}}\,. \tag{11}$$

Cosine Classifier. To further alleviate the negative effect of label distribution shift, LAMDA employs a cosine classifier [16,38], which measures cosine similarities between the classifier weights and an embedding vector as classification scores. The norm of classifier weight is known to be greatly affected by the label distribution [16,21,60]. Since the norm does not interfere with the classification score in the cosine classifier, it can alleviate the label distribution shift. Specifically, let $\mathbf{W} := \{\mathbf{w}_c\} \in \mathbb{R}^{d \times C}$, where $\mathbf{w}_c \in \mathbb{R}^d$ indicates a weight of classifier for class c with embedding dimension d. Then, the class probability predicted by the cosine classifier is given by

$$p_\theta(y = c|\mathbf{x}_i) := \text{softmax}\left(\frac{h \circ f(\mathbf{x}_i)^\top \mathbf{w}_c}{\tau \, ||h \circ f(\mathbf{x}_i)|| \, ||\mathbf{w}_c||}\right), \tag{12}$$

where h is a single hidden layer that projects feature vector $f(\mathbf{x})$ into d-dimensional embedding space, and τ is a temperature term that adjusts sharpness of the predicted probability.

5 Experiments

We first describe datasets, experiment setup, and implementation details in Sect. 5.1. Then LAMDA is evaluated and compared with previous work in Sect. 5.2, and contributions of its components are scrupulously analyzed in Sect. 5.3.

5.1 Setup

Datasets. We use four domain adaptation datasets with different characteristics: OfficeHome [55], OfficeHome-RSUT [53], VisDA-2017 [35], and DomainNet [34]. OfficeHome contains 16k images from four domains {Art, Clipart, Product, Real}, where we conduct a diverse set of domain adaptation for each of 12 source-target permutations. OfficeHome-RSUT is a dataset sub-sampled from three domains {Clipart, Product, Real} of OfficeHome, where the subsampling protocol, called reversely-unbalanced source and unbalanced target (RSUT), is employed to make a large label shift between source and target domains. VisDA-2017 is a large-scale dataset consisting of 207k images from two domains {Synthetic, Real} in a realistic scenario of synthetic-to-real domain adaptation. DomainNet is also a large-scale dataset but has a prevalent labeling noise. In DomainNet, we use five domains {Real, Clipart, Painting, Sketch, Quickdraw}[1] consisting of 362k images. We use 10% of the datasets for validation and the rest are kept for training. While DomainNet includes an independent test set, the other datasets do not provide an explicit test set. Hence, for OfficeHome, OfficeHome-RSUT, and VisDA-2017, we use the whole dataset (*i.e.*, trainval set) as the test set following the conventional protocol of UDA and previous work on ADA [14,36].

Experimental Setup. We compare LAMDA to the state-of-the-art ADA methods: TQS [14], CLUE [36], and S^{3}VAADA [40]. We note that the existing ADA

[1] The domains are chosen considering their consistency with existing benchmarks [36].

works have evaluated their methods with different evaluation protocols (e.g., budget size, sampling interval, and dataset). For fair comparison, we first benchmark them on four public datasets for domain adaptation through a unified evaluation protocol. We conduct 5 rounds of data sampling, each of which updates the model from the previous round after newly acquiring labels of 2%-budget, *i.e.*, 10%-budget in total, where we let *n%-budget* denote $n\%$ of the target train set size. For both of our method and the previous methods, the model is selected based on the validation accuracy. For each of the methods, we use the original authors' official implementation. The detailed descriptions are provided in the supplementary material (Sect. C).

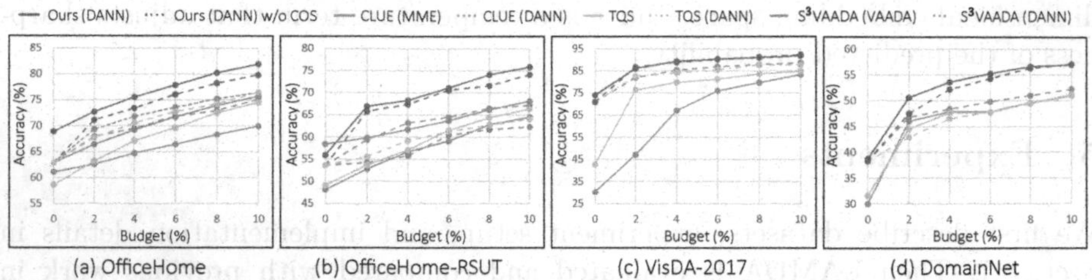

Fig. 3. Accuracy versus the percent of labeled target instances as budget. The accuracies are averaged on *all* scenarios of the OfficeHome, OfficeHome-RSUT, VisDA-2017, and DomainNet. The solid lines represent the results of using the specialized adaptation technique of each method, and the dotted lines represent the results of using the same adaptation technique (*i.e.*, DANN [15]). w/o COS: Ours without cosine classifier

Implementation Details. We use ResNet-50 [18] backbone initialized with pre-trained weights from ImageNet [13] classification for both our and the previous methods. Our classifier consists of 2 fully connected layers where the embedding dimension d is 512. For all experiments, we use an identical set of hyper-parameters. Our model is trained using SGD optimizer with a learning rate of 0.1, and a weight decay of 5^{-4} for 100 epochs. We set the margin threshold Δ to 0.8, the temperature τ in Eq. (12) to 0.1 and the γ of RBF kernel in Eq. (1) to an inverse of the feature dimension, which in our case is $\frac{1}{2048}$.

5.2 Results

Overall Superiority of LAMDA with Varying Budget. In Fig. 3, we compare the performance of LAMDA and the existing approaches[2] varying budget for each of OfficeHome, OfficeHome-RSUT, VisDa-2017, and DomainNet datasets. Note that each method is equipped with its own domain adaptation technique (*e.g.*, VAADA [50] for S^{3}VAADA, and MME [43] for CLUE) and classifier (*i.e.*, cosine classifier for LAMDA). We evaluate these methods while varying their adaptation techniques or classifier to examine the contribution of their

[2] Unfortunately, S^{3}VAADA [40] for DomainNet and VisDA-2017 requires infeasible memory consumption, in the supplementary material, we report its performance on a part of scenarios of DomainNet which our resource allows.

components thoroughly. The results show that LAMDA clearly outperforms the previous arts in every setting on all the datasets. In particular, LAMDA with only 2%-budget is often as competitive as or even outperforms the methods with 10%-budget. The performance gap between LAMDA and other methods increases as the budget increases. This suggests that LAMDA utilizes the budget effectively by both ways: label distribution matching and supervised learning.

Advantages of LAMDA Across Diverse Source-Target Domain Pairs. In Table 1, 2, we compare LAMDA and the existing ADA methods in every domain adaptation scenario of the four datasets given 10%-budget, where LAMDA always outperforms the others. Regarding that OfficeHome-RSUT has a significant class distribution shift compared to OfficeHome, the advantage of LAMDA equipped with the label distribution matching becomes clearer in OfficeHome-RSUT (Table 2a) than OfficeHome (Table 1). Table 2b demonstrates the scalability of LAMDA, where it clearly outperforms the previous work by about 4% or more in all scenarios of the large-scale datasets, VisDA 2017 and DomainNet. In the supplementary material (Sect. B.1), we also show that LAMDA surpasses state-of-the-art SSDA methods [26,27].

Table 1. Accuracy (%) on OfficeHome using 10%-budget for each source-target pair of four domains: **A**rt, **C**lipart, **P**roduct, and **R**eal. w/o COS: Ours without cosine classifier

DA method	AL method	OfficeHome												
		A $\rightarrow$ C	A $\rightarrow$ P	A $\rightarrow$ R	C $\rightarrow$ A	C $\rightarrow$ P	C $\rightarrow$ R	P $\rightarrow$ A	P $\rightarrow$ C	P $\rightarrow$ R	R $\rightarrow$ A	R $\rightarrow$ C	R $\rightarrow$ P	Avg
–	TQS [14]	64.3	84.8	83.5	66.1	81.0	76.7	66.5	61.4	82.0	73.7	65.9	88.5	74.5
MME	CLUE [36]	62.1	80.6	73.9	55.2	76.4	75.4	53.9	62.1	80.7	67.5	63.0	88.1	69.9
VAADA	S^{3}VAADA [40]	67.8	83.9	82.9	67.0	81.5	79.5	65.8	65.9	82.4	74.8	68.6	87.8	75.7
DANN	TQS [14]	68.7	80.1	83.1	64.0	83.1	76.9	67.7	71.0	84.4	76.4	72.7	90.0	76.5
	CLUE [36]	70.3	81.9	80.4	65.6	83.8	75.8	64.7	73.9	82.7	76.1	74.3	87.0	76.4
	S^{3}VAADA [40]	65.5	79.6	80.0	65.4	82.2	75.5	68.4	68.1	84.0	73.5	70.7	88.6	75.1
	Ours w/o COS	73.0	87.6	84.2	69.5	85.9	81.0	71.9	74.6	85.3	77.3	75.9	91.6	79.8
	Ours	**74.8**	**88.5**	**86.9**	**73.8**	**88.2**	**83.3**	**74.6**	**75.5**	**86.9**	**80.8**	**77.8**	**91.7**	**81.9**

Table 2. (a) Accuracy (%) on OfficeHome-RSUT using 10%-budget for each source-target pair of three domains: **C**lipart, **P**roduct, and **R**eal. (b) Accuracy (%) on VisDA-2017 and DomainNet using 10%-budget where VisDA-2017 consists of two domains: **R**eal and **S**ynthetic, and DomainNet consists of five domains: **R**eal, **C**lipart, **S**ketch, **P**ainting, and **Q**uickdraw. w/o COS: Ours without cosine classifier

DA method	AL method	OfficeHome-RSUT						
		C $\rightarrow$ P	C $\rightarrow$ R	P $\rightarrow$ C	P $\rightarrow$ R	R $\rightarrow$ C	R $\rightarrow$ P	Avg
-	TQS [14]	69.4	65.7	53.0	76.3	53.1	81.1	66.4
MME	CLUE [36]	69.7	65.9	57.1	73.4	59.5	82.7	68.1
VAADA	S^{3}VAADA [40]	73.0	63.0	50.7	69.6	52.6	78.3	64.5
	TQS [14]	67.6	61.4	54.8	74.7	53.6	77.6	64.9
	CLUE [36]	71.5	64.3	56.3	76.5	54.6	79.9	67.2
DANN	S^{3}VAADA [40]	66.9	61.4	53.0	75.4	52.4	76.4	64.2
	Ours w/o COS	78.1	72.1	61.5	**82.3**	64.2	86.5	74.1
	Ours	**81.2**	**75.7**	**64.1**	81.6	**65.1**	**87.2**	**75.8**

(a)

DA method	AL method	VisDa-2017	DomainNet				
		S $\rightarrow$ R	R $\rightarrow$ C	C $\rightarrow$ S	S $\rightarrow$ P	C $\rightarrow$ Q	Avg
-	TQS [14]	84.8	54.2	51.7	51.4	47.4	51.2
MME	CLUE [36]	83.3	60.7	50.4	53.5	39.4	51.0
	TQS [14]	87.7	59.3	50.9	52.4	41.5	51.0
DANN	CLUE [36]	88.6	60.9	52.2	52.4	43.7	52.3
	Ours w/o COS	**92.3**	64.6	**56.4**	**58.7**	**48.5**	**57.1**
	Ours	91.8	**65.3**	56.1	58.1	48.3	57.0

(b)

5.3 Analysis

Contribution of Each Component of LAMDA. Table 3 quantifies the contribution of each components of LAMDA: (i) prototype set sampling in Sect. 4.2; (ii) label distribution matching in Sect. 4.3; and (iii) cosine classifier in Sect. 4.4. Every component in LAMDA improves the performance in both OfficeHome and OfficeHome-RSUT. The performance gap between the last (random sampling with DANN [15]) and the second last rows verifies that our prototype sampling method boost the effect of supervised learning. Comparing the second and the third rows, one can see the remarkable performance gain by our label distribution matching strategy, in particular on OfficeHome-RSUT with significant label distribution shift. Finally, the use of cosine classifier further improves

Table 3. Accuracy (%) averaged over *all* scenarios when using 10%-budget, where we conduct an ablation study from ablation baseline at the last row to LAMDA at the first row by sequentially adding three components: (i) Prototype: sampling described in Sect. 4.2 (o/w, sampling uniformly at random); (ii) Matching: label distribution matching in Sect. 4.3 (o/w, replacing p_i in Eq. (8) with uniform distribution); and (iii) Cosine: cosine classifier described in Sect. 4.4 (o/w, linear classifier). (·): accuracy gain by adding each component

Prototype	Matching	Cosine	OfficeHome	OfficeHome-RSUT
✓	✓	✓	81.9 (+2.1)	75.8 (+1.7)
✓	✓	✗	79.8 (+2.7)	74.1 (+6.8)
✓	✗	✗	77.1 (+3.8)	67.3 (+3.7)
✗	✗	✗	73.3	63.6

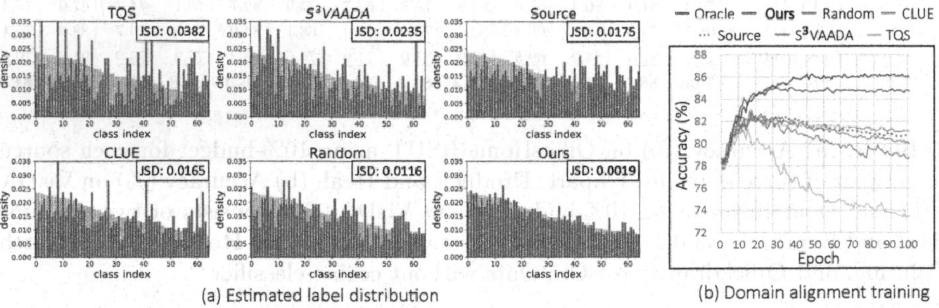

Fig. 4. (a) The true (red) and the estimated (green) label distribution of target domain, where each sampling methods estimates the distribution using 10%-budget. The methods are sorted by the estimation quality. JSD: Jensen-Shannon Divergence between the estimated and the true label distribution (lower is better). Source: Label distribution of source data. (b) Training curve of domain alignment learning (Eq. (9)) combined with label distribution matching using the estimations in (a). Source: naive domain alignment. Oracle: using true target label distribution (Color figure online)

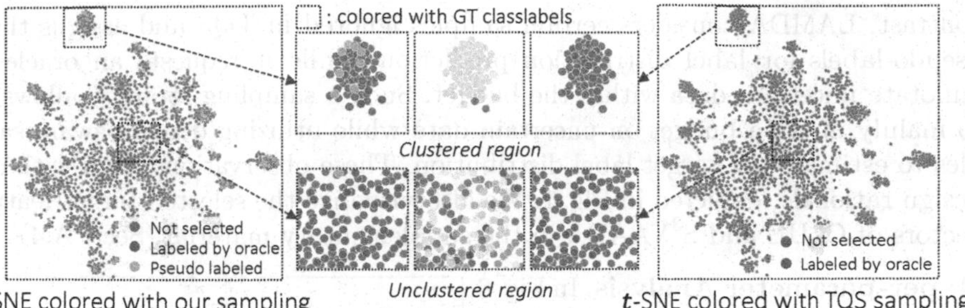

Fig. 5. *t*-SNE [31] visualization of target feature vectors from source pre-trained model on OfficeHome real to art scenario

performance by 1.9% in average. The results for every individual adaptation scenarios are reported in the supplementary material (Sect. A.1).

Quality of Estimated Label Distribution. As described in Sect. 4.3, estimating target label distribution plays a prominent role in LAMDA. In Fig. 4a, we visualize label distributions of sampled data of LAMDA and those of the previous work, and compute Jensen-Shannon divergence (JSD) between the estimated distributions and the true one. The results demonstrate that LAMDA enables to estimate target label distribution most accurately compared to the previous work and the random sampling, which is a naive but intuitive sampling strategy for the estimation. Note that the previous work is even worse than the random sampling in terms of the estimation accuracy, which empirically reconfirm that the sampling strategies of the previous work are not aware of the target data distribution. When solely utilizes all of the pseudo-labels from source pretrained model for the estimation, it gives JSD of 0.025 which is worse than 'Source' baseline. This is mainly due to the bias of the pseudo-labeled data; they are highly confident samples. Our sampling method avoids this bias by combining labeled and pseudo-labeled data.

Benefit of Label Distribution Matching. In Fig. 4b, we plot training curves of domain alignment combined with label distribution matching, where each methods utilizes identical source classification loss and domain alignment loss as in Eq. (9), but with different label distribution estimated from each sampling methods in Fig. 4a. Training without label distribution matching (*e.g.*, *Source*) or matching with inaccurate target label distribution degrade accuracy, while ours does not, thanks to the accurate estimation of target label distribution. It is worth noting that our model using 10%-budget shows comparable accuracy with *Oracle*, which has access to the true target label distribution.

Visualization of Sampled Data by *t*-SNE. Fig. 5 visualizes distributions of target features and those selected by LAMDA and TQS, to show the difference of their sampling strategies. Since TQS prefers to select uncertain data, mostly located in unclustered regions, its samples do not reflect the target data distribution, *e.g.*, the certain instances in the clustered region are undersampled. In contrast, LAMDA considers certain samples ignored in TQS and assigns them pseudo-labels for label distribution prediction, while it requests an oracle to annotate uncertain data within the budget. Such a sampling strategy allows us to mainly invest a budget on uncertain data while utilizing density-aware samples to estimate the target label distribution. These observations align with our design rationale, depicted in Fig. 1. We also visualize the selected target feature vectors of CLUE and S^3VAADA in the supplementary material (Sect. A.4).

Hyper-parameter Analysis. In Fig. 6, we evaluate the sensitivity of LAMDA to the choice of the threshold Δ in Algorithm 1. LAMDA is surprisingly robust to the change of Δ, where the change of accuracy is less than 1% for both OfficeHome and OfficeHome-RSUT when the Δ is between 0.7 and 0.9. We note that while the optimal value of Δ varies among the datasets, we use the same value for all of our experiments. When we do not utilize the pseudo label in LAMDA (*i.e.*, $\Delta = 1$), the accuracy drops 4% and 1.1% in OfficeHome and OfficeHome-RSUT, respectively. This shows the effectiveness of our prototype sampling strategy.

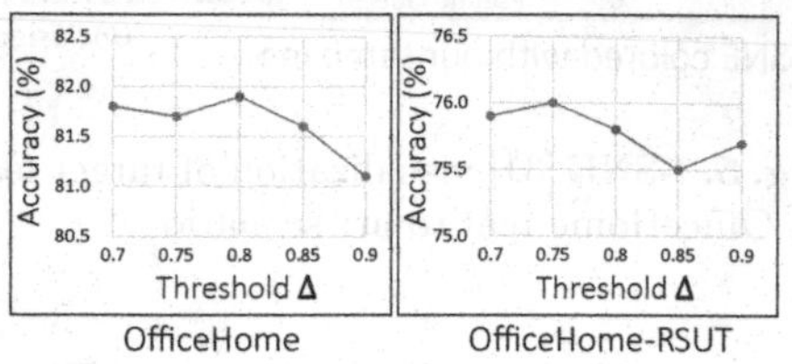

Fig. 6. Accuracy of LAMDA versus hyper-parameter Δ. The blue dot indicates the value used in the main paper (Color figur online)

Analysis of Cosine Classifier. To inspect the cosine classifier, we compare in Fig. 7 the frequencies and the weight norm of the linear classifier for each class. The norm of the linear classifier is positively correlated to the frequencies of each class within the source domain (blue and green lines). Since a large norm of classifier weights has been known to result in predictions biased to major classes [21], the mismatch between the classifier norm and the target domain class frequencies (red and blue lines) is undesirable. The cosine classifier alleviates this issue by normalizing its weight scale. In the supplementary material (Sect. B.2), we also provide an evaluation of existing ADA methods combined with cosine classifier.

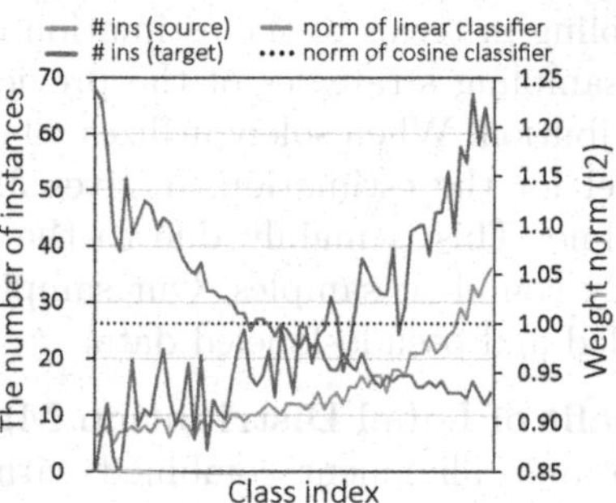

Fig. 7. The frequencies (# ins) of each class in source and target domain (OfficeHome-RSUT Clipart to Product scenario) and the l2-norm of the corresponding classifier weight trained with the source data

6 Conclusion

We proposed LAMDA, a new method to address the issue of label distribution shift in ADA. It selects target data best preserving the target data distribution as well as being representative, diverse, and uncertain. During training, LAMDA estimates the label distribution of the target domain, and builds each source data mini-batch in a way that the label frequencies of the batch follow the estimated target label distribution. On the four different domain adaptation datasets, the proposed method substantially outperforms all the existing ADA models.

Acknowledgments. This work was supported by the NRF grant and the IITP grant funded by Ministry of Science and ICT, Korea (NRF-2018R1A5-A1060031, NRF-2021R1A2C3012728, IITP-2019-0-01906, IITP-2020-0-00842, IITP-2021-0-02068, IITP-2022-0-00290).

References

1. Ajakan, H., Germain, P., Larochelle, H., Laviolette, F., Marchand, M.: Domain-adversarial neural networks. arXiv preprint arXiv:1412.4446 (2014)
2. Asghar, N., Poupart, P., Jiang, X., Li, H.: Deep active learning for dialogue generation. In: Proceedings of the 6th Joint Conference on Lexical and Computational Semantics (*SEM 2017) (2017)
3. Ash, J.T., Zhang, C., Krishnamurthy, A., Langford, J., Agarwal, A.: Deep batch active learning by diverse, uncertain gradient lower bounds. In: Proceedings of the International Conference on Learning Representations (ICLR) (2020)
4. Ben-David, S., Blitzer, J., Crammer, K., Kulesza, A., Pereira, F., Vaughan, J.W.: A theory of learning from different domains. Mach. Learn. **79**(1), 151–175 (2010)
5. Chen, W.Y., Liu, Y.C., Kira, Z., Wang, Y.C.F., Huang, J.B.: A closer look at few-shot classification. In: Proceedings of the International Conference on Learning Representations (ICLR) (2019)
6. Tachet des Combes, R., Zhao, H., Wang, Y.X., Gordon, G.J.: Domain adaptation with conditional distribution matching and generalized label shift. In: Proceedings of the Neural Information Processing Systems (NeurIPS) (2020)
7. Courty, N., Flamary, R., Habrard, A., Rakotomamonjy, A.: Joint distribution optimal transportation for domain adaptation. In: Proceedings of the Neural Information Processing Systems (NeurIPS) (2017)
8. Courty, N., Flamary, R., Tuia, D., Rakotomamonjy, A.: Optimal transport for domain adaptation. IEEE Trans. Pattern Anal. Mach. Intell. (TPAMI) **39**(9), 1853–1865 (2016)
9. Cui, S., Wang, S., Zhuo, J., Su, C., Huang, Q., Tian, Q.: Gradually vanishing bridge for adversarial domain adaptation. In: Proceedings of the Neural Information Processing Systems (NeurIPS) (2020)
10. Dai, D., Sakaridis, C., Hecker, S., Van Gool, L.: Curriculum model adaptation with synthetic and real data for semantic foggy scene understanding. Int. J. Comput. Vis. (IJCV) **128**, 1182–1204 (2020). https://doi.org/10.1007/s11263-019-01182-4
11. Damodaran, B.B., Kellenberger, B., Flamary, R., Tuia, D., Courty, N.: DeepJDOT: deep joint distribution optimal transport for unsupervised domain adaptation. In: Ferrari, V., Hebert, M., Sminchisescu, C., Weiss, Y. (eds.) ECCV 2018. LNCS, vol. 11208, pp. 467–483. Springer, Cham (2018). https://doi.org/10.1007/978-3-030-01225-0_28

12. Deheeger, F., MOUGEOT, M., Vayatis, N., et al.: Discrepancy-based active learning for domain adaptation. In: Proceedings of the International Conference on Learning Representations (ICLR) (2021)
13. Deng, J., Dong, W., Socher, R., Li, L.J., Li, K., Fei-Fei, L.: ImageNet: a large-scale hierarchical image database. In: Proceedings of the IEEE/CVF Conference on Computer Vision and Pattern Recognition (CVPR) (2009)
14. Fu, B., Cao, Z., Wang, J., Long, M.: Transferable query selection for active domain adaptation. In: Proceedings of the IEEE/CVF Conference on Computer Vision and Pattern Recognition (CVPR) (2021)
15. Ganin, Y., et al.: Domain-adversarial training of neural networks. J. Mach. Learn. Res. (JMLR) **17**(1), 2096–2030 (2016)
16. Gidaris, S., Komodakis, N.: Dynamic few-shot visual learning without forgetting. In: Proceedings of the IEEE/CVF Conference on Computer Vision and Pattern Recognition (CVPR) (2018)
17. Gretton, A., Borgwardt, K.M., Rasch, M.J., Schölkopf, B., Smola, A.: A kernel two-sample test. J. Mach. Learn. Res. (JMLR) **13**(1), 723–773 (2012)
18. He, K., Zhang, X., Ren, S., Sun, J.: Deep residual learning for image recognition. In: Proceedings of the IEEE/CVF Conference on Computer Vision and Pattern Recognition (CVPR) (2016)
19. He, T., Jin, X., Ding, G., Yi, L., Yan, C.: Towards better uncertainty sampling: active learning with multiple views for deep convolutional neural network. In: 2019 IEEE International Conference on Multimedia and Expo (ICME) (2019)
20. Huang, J.Z., Ng, M.K., Rong, H., Li, Z.: Automated variable weighting in k-means type clustering. IEEE Trans. Pattern Anal. Mach. Intell. (TPAMI) **27**(5), 657–668 (2005)
21. Kang, B., et al.: Decoupling representation and classifier for long-tailed recognition. In: Proceedings of the International Conference on Learning Representations (ICLR) (2020)
22. Kim, B., Khanna, R., Koyejo, O.O.: Examples are not enough, learn to criticize! Criticism for interpretability. In: Proceedings of the Neural Information Processing Systems (NeurIPS) (2016)
23. LeCun, Y., Chopra, S., Hadsell, R., Ranzato, M., Huang, F.: A tutorial on energy-based learning. Predict. Struct. Data **1**(0) (2006)
24. Lee, C.Y., Batra, T., Baig, M.H., Ulbricht, D.: Sliced Wasserstein discrepancy for unsupervised domain adaptation. In: Proceedings of the IEEE/CVF Conference on Computer Vision and Pattern Recognition (CVPR) (2019)
25. Lee, S., Son, T., Kwak, S.: FIFO: learning fog-invariant features for foggy scene segmentation. In: Proceedings of the IEEE/CVF Conference on Computer Vision and Pattern Recognition (CVPR) (2022)
26. Li, J., Li, G., Shi, Y., Yu, Y.: Cross-domain adaptive clustering for semi-supervised domain adaptation. In: Proceedings of the IEEE/CVF Conference on Computer Vision and Pattern Recognition (CVPR) (2021)
27. Li, K., Liu, C., Zhao, H., Zhang, Y., Fu, Y.: ECACL: a holistic framework for semi-supervised domain adaptation. In: Proceedings of the IEEE/CVF International Conference on Computer Vision (ICCV) (2021)
28. Long, M., Cao, Y., Wang, J., Jordan, M.: Learning transferable features with deep adaptation networks. In: Proceedings of the International Conference on Machine Learning (ICML). PMLR (2015)
29. Long, M., Cao, Z., Wang, J., Jordan, M.I.: Conditional adversarial domain adaptation. In: Proceedings of the Neural Information Processing Systems (NeurIPS) (2018)

30. Long, M., Zhu, H., Wang, J., Jordan, M.I.: Deep transfer learning with joint adaptation networks. In: Proceedings of the International Conference on Machine Learning (ICML). PMLR (2017)
31. Van der Maaten, L., Hinton, G.: Visualizing data using t-SNE. J. Mach. Learn. Res. (JMLR) **9**(11) (2008)
32. Nemhauser, G.L., Wolsey, L.A., Fisher, M.L.: An analysis of approximations for maximizing submodular set functions-I. Math. Program. **14**(1), 265–294 (1978)
33. Ostapuk, N., Yang, J., Cudré-Mauroux, P.: Activelink: deep active learning for link prediction in knowledge graphs. In: The World Wide Web Conference (WWW) (2019)
34. Peng, X., Bai, Q., Xia, X., Huang, Z., Saenko, K., Wang, B.: Moment matching for multi-source domain adaptation. In: Proceedings of the IEEE/CVF International Conference on Computer Vision (ICCV) (2019)
35. Peng, X., et al.: VisDA: a synthetic-to-real benchmark for visual domain adaptation. In: Proceedings of the IEEE Conference on Computer Vision and Pattern Recognition Workshops, pp. 2021–2026 (2018)
36. Prabhu, V., Chandrasekaran, A., Saenko, K., Hoffman, J.: Active domain adaptation via clustering uncertainty-weighted embeddings. In: Proceedings of the IEEE/CVF International Conference on Computer Vision (ICCV) (2021)
37. Purushotham, S., Carvalho, W., Nilanon, T., Liu, Y.: Variational recurrent adversarial deep domain adaptation. In: Proceedings of the International Conference on Learning Representations (ICLR) (2016)
38. Qi, H., Brown, M., Lowe, D.G.: Low-shot learning with imprinted weights. In: Proceedings of the IEEE/CVF Conference on Computer Vision and Pattern Recognition (CVPR) (2018)
39. Rai, P., Saha, A., Daumé III, H., Venkatasubramanian, S.: Domain adaptation meets active learning. In: Proceedings of the NAACL HLT 2010 Workshop on Active Learning for Natural Language Processing (2010)
40. Rangwani, H., Jain, A., Aithal, S.K., Babu, R.V.: S3VAADA: submodular subset selection for virtual adversarial active domain adaptation. In: Proceedings of the IEEE/CVF International Conference on Computer Vision (ICCV) (2021)
41. Rdusseeun, L., Kaufman, P.: Clustering by means of medoids. In: Proceedings of the Statistical Data Analysis Based on the L1 Norm Conference, Neuchatel, Switzerland, vol. 31 (1987)
42. Roth, D., Small, K.: Margin-based active learning for structured output spaces. In: Fürnkranz, J., Scheffer, T., Spiliopoulou, M. (eds.) ECML 2006. LNCS (LNAI), vol. 4212, pp. 413–424. Springer, Heidelberg (2006). https://doi.org/10.1007/11871842_40
43. Saito, K., Kim, D., Sclaroff, S., Darrell, T., Saenko, K.: Semi-supervised domain adaptation via minimax entropy. In: Proceedings of the IEEE/CVF International Conference on Computer Vision (ICCV) (2019)
44. Sakaridis, C., Dai, D., Gool, L.V.: Guided curriculum model adaptation and uncertainty-aware evaluation for semantic nighttime image segmentation. In: Proceedings of the IEEE/CVF International Conference on Computer Vision (ICCV) (2019)
45. Sakaridis, C., Dai, D., Hecker, S., Van Gool, L.: Model adaptation with synthetic and real data for semantic dense foggy scene understanding. In: Ferrari, V., Hebert, M., Sminchisescu, C., Weiss, Y. (eds.) ECCV 2018. LNCS, vol. 11217, pp. 707–724. Springer, Cham (2018). https://doi.org/10.1007/978-3-030-01261-8_42

46. Sakaridis, C., Dai, D., Van Gool, L.: Semantic foggy scene understanding with synthetic data. Int. J. Comput. Vis. **126**(9), 973–992 (2018). https://doi.org/10.1007/s11263-018-1072-8
47. Sener, O., Savarese, S.: Active learning for convolutional neural networks: a core-set approach. In: Proceedings of the International Conference on Learning Representations (ICLR) (2018)
48. Settles, B.: Active learning literature survey (2009)
49. Seung, H.S., Opper, M., Sompolinsky, H.: Query by committee. In: Proceedings of the Fifth Annual Workshop on Computational Learning Theory, pp. 287–294 (1992)
50. Shu, R., Bui, H.H., Narui, H., Ermon, S.: A DIRT-T approach to unsupervised domain adaptation. In: Proceedings of the International Conference on Learning Representations (ICLR) (2018)
51. Sinha, S., Ebrahimi, S., Darrell, T.: Variational adversarial active learning. In: Proceedings of the IEEE/CVF International Conference on Computer Vision (ICCV) (2019)
52. Su, J.C., Tsai, Y.H., Sohn, K., Liu, B., Maji, S., Chandraker, M.: Active adversarial domain adaptation. In: Proceedings of the IEEE/CVF Winter Conference on Applications of Computer Vision (WACV) (2020)
53. Tan, S., Peng, X., Saenko, K.: Class-imbalanced domain adaptation: an empirical Odyssey. In: Bartoli, A., Fusiello, A. (eds.) ECCV 2020. LNCS, vol. 12535, pp. 585–602. Springer, Cham (2020). https://doi.org/10.1007/978-3-030-66415-2_38
54. Tzeng, E., Hoffman, J., Darrell, T., Saenko, K.: Simultaneous deep transfer across domains and tasks. In: Proceedings of the IEEE/CVF International Conference on Computer Vision (ICCV) (2015)
55. Venkateswara, H., Eusebio, J., Chakraborty, S., Panchanathan, S.: Deep hashing network for unsupervised domain adaptation. In: Proceedings of the IEEE/CVF Conference on Computer Vision and Pattern Recognition (CVPR) (2017)
56. Wang, Z., Du, B., Tu, W., Zhang, L., Tao, D.: Incorporating distribution matching into uncertainty for multiple kernel active learning. IEEE Trans. Knowl. Data Eng. **33**(1), 128–142 (2019)
57. Wang, Z., Ye, J.: Querying discriminative and representative samples for batch mode active learning. ACM Trans. Knowl. Discov. Data (TKDD) **9**(3), 1–23 (2015)
58. Xie, B., Yuan, L., Li, S., Liu, C.H., Cheng, X., Wang, G.: Active learning for domain adaptation: An energy-based approach. In: Proceedings of the AAAI Conference on Artificial Intelligence (AAAI) (2022)
59. Xie, M., et al.: Learning distinctive margin toward active domain adaptation. In: Proceedings of the IEEE/CVF Conference on Computer Vision and Pattern Recognition (CVPR) (2022)
60. Xu, R., Li, G., Yang, J., Lin, L.: Larger norm more transferable: an adaptive feature norm approach for unsupervised domain adaptation. In: Proceedings of the IEEE/CVF International Conference on Computer Vision (ICCV) (2019)
61. Yang, L., et al.: Deep co-training with task decomposition for semi-supervised domain adaptation. In: Proceedings of the IEEE/CVF International Conference on Computer Vision (ICCV) (2021)
62. Yoon, J., Kang, D., Cho, M.: Semi-supervised domain adaptation via sample-to-sample self-distillation. In: Proceedings of the IEEE/CVF Winter Conference on Applications of Computer Vision, pp. 1978–1987 (2022)
63. Zhao, H., Des Combes, R.T., Zhang, K., Gordon, G.: On learning invariant representations for domain adaptation. In: Proceedings of the International Conference on Machine Learning (ICML). PMLR (2019)

GIPSO: Geometrically Informed Propagation for Online Adaptation in 3D LiDAR Segmentation

Cristiano Saltori[1(✉)], Evgeny Krivosheev[1], Stéphane Lathuiliére[2], Nicu Sebe[1], Fabio Galasso[3], Giuseppe Fiameni[4], Elisa Ricci[1,5], and Fabio Poiesi[5]

[1] University of Trento, Trento, Italy
cristiano.saltori@unitn.it
[2] LTCI, Télécom-Paris, Intitute Polytechnique de Paris, Palaiseau, France
[3] Sapienza University of Rome, Rome, Italy
[4] NVIDIA AI Technology Center, Rome, Italy
[5] Fondazione Bruno Kessler, Trento, Italy

Abstract. 3D point cloud semantic segmentation is fundamental for autonomous driving. Most approaches in the literature neglect an important aspect, i.e., how to deal with domain shift when handling dynamic scenes. This can significantly hinder the navigation capabilities of self-driving vehicles. This paper advances the state of the art in this research field. Our first contribution consists in analysing a new unexplored scenario in point cloud segmentation, namely Source-Free Online Unsupervised Domain Adaptation (SF-OUDA). We experimentally show that state-of-the-art methods have a rather limited ability to adapt pre-trained deep network models to unseen domains in an online manner. Our second contribution is an approach that relies on adaptive self-training and geometric-feature propagation to adapt a pre-trained source model online without requiring either source data or target labels. Our third contribution is to study SF-OUDA in a challenging setup where source data is synthetic and target data is point clouds captured in the real world. We use the recent SynLiDAR dataset as a synthetic source and introduce two new synthetic (source) datasets, which can stimulate future synthetic-to-real autonomous driving research. Our experiments show the effectiveness of our segmentation approach on thousands of real-world point clouds (Code and synthetic datasets are available at https://github.com/saltoricristiano/gipso-sfouda).

Keywords: Online domain adaptation · Source-free unsupervised domain adaptation · Point cloud segmentation · Geometric propagation

Supplementary Information The online version contains supplementary material available at https://doi.org/10.1007/978-3-031-19827-4_33.

S. Avidan et al. (Eds.): ECCV 2022, LNCS 13693, pp. 567–585, 2022.
https://doi.org/10.1007/978-3-031-19827-4_33

1 Introduction

Autonomous driving requires accurate and efficient 3D visual scene perception algorithms. Low-level visual tasks such as detection and segmentation are crucial to enable higher-level tasks such as path planning [11,35] and obstacle avoidance [46]. Deep learning-based methods have proven to be the most suitable option to meet these requirements so far, but at the cost of requiring large-scale annotated dataset for training [29]. Relying only on annotated data is not always a viable solution. This problem can be mitigated by considering synthetic data, as it can be generated at low cost with potentially unlimited annotations and under different environmental conditions [12,23]. However, when a model trained on synthetic data is deployed in the real world, typically it will underperform due to domain shift, *e.g.*, caused by varying lighting conditions, clutter, occlusions and materials with different reflective properties [56]. We argue that a 3D semantic segmentation algorithm running on an autonomous vehicle should be capable of adapting online – handling scenarios that are visited for the first time while driving – and it should do so by only using the newly captured data. A variety of research works have addressed the adaptation problem in the context of 3D semantic segmentation. However, most approaches operate offline and assume to have access to training (source) data [28,61,63,69,72,73]. In this paper, we argue that these two assumptions are too restrictive in an autonomous driving scenario (Fig. 1). On the one hand, offline adaptation would be equivalent to performing model adaptation on the data a vehicle has captured when the navigation has terminated, which is clearly a sub-optimal solution for autonomous driving [30]. On the other hand, having to rely on source data may not be a viable option, as it requires the method to store and query potentially large amount of data, thus hindering scalability [33,36].

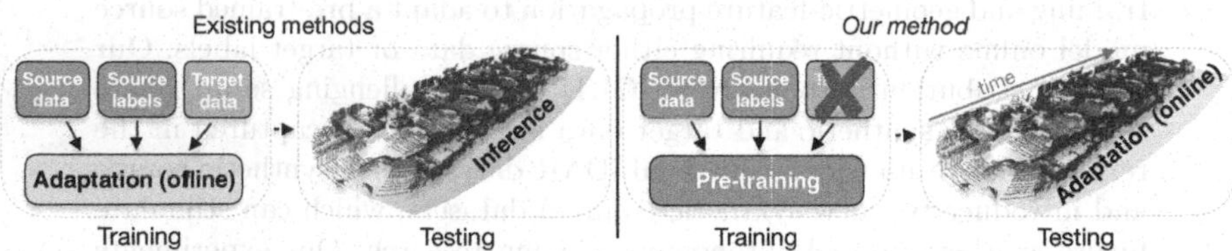

Fig. 1. Existing methods adapt 3D semantic segmentation networks *offline*, requiring both source and target data. Differently, real-world applications urge solutions capable of adapting to unseen scenes online having access only to a pre-trained model.

To overcome these limitations, in this paper we explore the new problem of Source-Free Online Unsupervised Domain Adaptation (SF-OUDA) for semantic segmentation, *i.e.*, that of adapting a deep semantic segmentation model while a vehicle navigates in an unseen environment without relying on human supervision. Specifically, in this work we first implement, adapt and thoroughly analyze existing adaptation methods for the 3D semantic segmentation problem in a SF-OUDA setup. We experimentally observe that none of these methods provides consistent and satisfactory performance when employed in a SF-OUDA setting. However, there are elements of interest that, when carefully combined and extended, can be generally applicable. This leads us to move toward and design GIPSO (Geometrically Informed Propagation for Source-free Online adaptation), the first SF-OUDA method for 3D point cloud segmentation that builds upon recent advances in the literature, and exploits geometry information and temporal consistency to support the domain adaptation process. We also introduce two new synthetic datasets to benchmark SF-OUDA in two different real-world datasets, *i.e.* SemanticKITTI [3,13,14] and nuScenes [4]. We validate our approach on these new synthetic-to-real benchmarks. Our motivation for creating these datasets is to make evaluation more comprehensive and to assess the generalization ability of different techniques to different experimental setups. In summary, our contributions are:

- A thorough experimental analysis of existing domain adaptation methods for 3D semantic segmentation in a SF-OUDA setting;
- A novel method for SF-OUDA that exploits low-level geometric properties and temporal information to continuously adapt a 3D segmentation model;
- The introduction of two new LiDAR synthetic datasets that are compatible with the SemanticKITTI and nuScenes datasets.

2 Related Work

Point Cloud Semantic Segmentation. Point cloud segmentation methods can be classified into quantization-free and quantization-based architectures. The former processes the input point clouds in their original 3D format. Examples include PointNet [43] that is based on a series of multi layer perceptrons. PointNet++ [44] builds upon PointNet by using multi-scale sampling and neighbourhood aggregation to encode both global and local features. RandLA-Net [21] extends PoinNet++ [44] by embedding local spatial encoding, random sampling and attentive pooling. These methods are computationally inefficient when large-scale point clouds are used. The latter provides a computationally efficient alternative as input point clouds can be mapped into efficient representations, namely range maps [39,60,61], polar maps [67], 3D voxel grids [8,16,17,70] or 3D cylindrical voxels [71]. Quantization-based approaches can be based on sparse convolutions [16,17] or Minkowski convolutions [8]. We use the Minkowski Engine [8] as it provides a suitable trade off between accuracy and efficiency.

Unsupervised Domain Adaptation. Offline UDA can be performed either using source data [20,37,48,72] or without using source data (source-free UDA) [33,36,49,62]. Online UDA can be used to adapt a model to an unlabelled continuous target data stream through source domain supervision [58]. It can be employed for classification [40], image semantic segmentation [58], depth estimation [55,68], robot manipulation [38], human mesh reconstruction [19] and occupancy mapping [54]. The assumption of unsupervised target input data can be relaxed and applied for online adaptation in classification [31], video-object segmentation [57] and motion planning [53]. Recently, test-time adaptation methods have been applied to online UDA in classification by using supervision from source data [50,52,59]. We tackle source-free online UDA for point cloud segmentation for the first time.

Domain Adaptation for Point Cloud Segmentation. Domain shift in point cloud segmentation occurs due to differences in (i) sampling noise, (ii) structure of the environment and (iii) class distributions [26,61,63,69]. The domain adaptation problem can be formulated as a 3D surface completion task [63] or addressed with ray casting system capable of transferring the target sensor sampling pattern to the source data [28]. Other approaches tackle the domain adaptation problem in the synthetic-to-real setting (*i.e.,* point cloud in the source domain are synthetic, while target ones are collected with LiDAR sensors) [60,61,69]. Attention models can be used to aggregate contextual information with large receptive fields at early layers of the model [60,61]. Geodesic correlation alignment and progressive domain calibration can be also used to further improve domain adaptation effectiveness [61]. Authors in [69] argue that the method in [61] cannot be trained end-to-end as it employs a multi-stage pipeline. Therefore, they propose an end-to-end approach to simulate the dropout noise of real sensors on synthetic data through a generative adversarial network. Unlike these methods, we focus on SF-OUDA and propose a novel adaptation method which invokes geometry for propagating reliable pseudo-labels on target data.

Table 1. Comparison between public synthetic datasets and Synth4D in terms of sensor specifications, acquisition areas, number of scans, number of points, presence of odometry data, and whether the semantic classes are all or partially shared.

Name	Specifications		Areas	Scans	Points	Odometry	Shared semantic classes	
	Sensor	FOV					S-KITTI [3]	nuScenes [4]
SynthCity [18]	MLS	360°	City	1	367M		No	No
GTA-LiDAR [61]	HDL64E	90°	Town	121087	–		Partial	No
PreSIL [23]	HDL64E	90°	Town	51074	3135M		Partial	No
SynLiDAR [2]	HDL64E	360°	City, town Harbor, rural	198396	19482M		All	No
Synth4D (ours)	HDL64E HDL32E	360°	City, town Rural, highway	20000 20000	2000M 2000M	✓	All	All

3 Datasets for Synthetic-to-Real Adaptation

Autonomous driving simulators enable users to create ad-hoc synthetic datasets that can resemble real-world scenarios. Examples of popular simulators are GTA-V [64] and CARLA [12]. In principle, synthetic datasets should be compatible with their real-world counterpart [3,4,14], *i.e.*, they should share the same semantic classes and the same sensor specifications, such as the resolution (32 vs. 64 channels) and the horizontal field of view (e.g., 90° vs. 360°). However, this is not the case for most of the synthetic datasets in literature. The SynthCity [18] dataset contains large-scale point clouds that are generated from collections of several LiDAR scans, making it unsuitable for online domain adaptation as no odometry data is provided. PreSIL [23] and GTA-LiDAR's [61] point clouds are captured from a moving vehicle using a simulated Velodyne HDL64E [34], as that of SemanticKITTI, however they are rendered with a different field of view, *i.e.*, 90° as opposed to 360° of SemantiKITTI. SynLIDAR's [2] point clouds are obtained using a simulated Velodyne HDL64E with 360° field of view, as in SemantiKITTI. However, the odometry data is not provided, *i.e.*, point clouds are all configured in their local reference frame. Therefore, domain adaptation algorithms that are based on ray-casting like [28] cannot be used.

To enable full compatibility with SemanticKITTI [3] and nuScenes [4], we present a new synthetic dataset, namely Synth4D, which we created using the CARLA simulator [12]. Table 1 compares Synth4D to the other synthetic datasets. Synth4D is composed of two sets of point cloud sequences, one compatible with SemanticKITTI and one compatible with nuScenes. Each set is composed of 20K labelled point clouds. Synth4D is captured using a vehicle navigating in four scenarios, *i.e.*, town, highway, rural area and city. Because UDA requires consistent labels between source and target, we mapped the labels of Synth4D with those of SemanticKITTI/nuScenes using the original instructions given to annotators [3,4], thus producing eight macro classes: *vehicle*, *pedestrian*, *road*, *sidewalk*, *terrain*, *manmade*, *vegetation* and *unlabelled*. Figure 2 shows examples of annotated point clouds from Synth4D. See Supp. Mat. for more details.

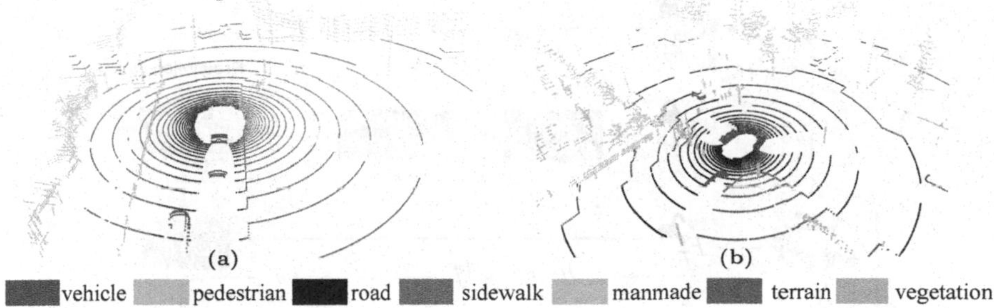

Fig. 2. Example of point clouds from Synth4D using the simulated Velodyne (a) HDL32E and (b) HDL64E.

4 SF-OUDA

We formulate the problem of SF-OUDA for 3D point cloud segmentation as follows. Given a deep network model $F_{\mathcal{S}}$ that is pre-trained with supervision on the source domain $\mathcal{S}$, we aim to adapt $F_{\mathcal{S}}$ on the target domain $\mathcal{T}$ given an unlabelled point cloud stream as input. $F_{\mathcal{S}}$ is pre-trained using the source data

$\Gamma_{\mathcal{S}} = \{(X^i_{\mathcal{S}}, Y^i_{\mathcal{S}})\}_{i=1}^{M_{\mathcal{S}}}$, where $X^i_{\mathcal{S}}$ is a synthetic point cloud, $Y^i_{\mathcal{S}}$ is the segmentation mask of $X^i_{\mathcal{S}}$ and $M_{\mathcal{S}}$ is the number of available synthetic point clouds. Let $X^t_{\mathcal{T}}$ be a point cloud of our stream at time t and $F^t_{\mathcal{T}}$ be the target model adapted using $X^t_{\mathcal{T}}$ and $X^{t-w}_{\mathcal{T}}$, with $w > 0$. $Y_{\mathcal{T}}$ is the set of unknown target labels and C is the number of classes contained in $Y_{\mathcal{T}}$. The source classes and the target classes are coincident.

4.1 Our Approach

The input to GIPSO is the point cloud $X^t_{\mathcal{T}}$ and an already processed point cloud $X^{t-w}_{\mathcal{T}}$. These point clouds are used to adapt $F_{\mathcal{S}}$ to $\mathcal{T}$ through self-supervision (Fig. 3). The input is processed by two modules. The first module aims to create labels for self-supervision by segmenting $X^t_{\mathcal{T}}$ with the source model $F_{\mathcal{S}}$. Because these labels are produced by an unsupervised deep network, we refer to them as *pseudo-labels*. We select a subset of segmented points that have reliable pseudo-labels through an adaptive selection criteria, and propagate them to less reliable points. The propagation uses geometric similarity in the feature space to increase the number of pseudo-labels available for self-supervision. To this end, we use an auxiliary deep network (F_{aux}) that is specialized in extracting geometrically-informed representations from 3D points. The second module aims to encourage temporal regularization of semantic information between $X^t_{\mathcal{T}}$ and $X^{t-w}_{\mathcal{T}}$. Unlike recent works [22], where a global point cloud descriptor of the scene is learnt, we exploit a self-supervised framework based on stop gradient [6]

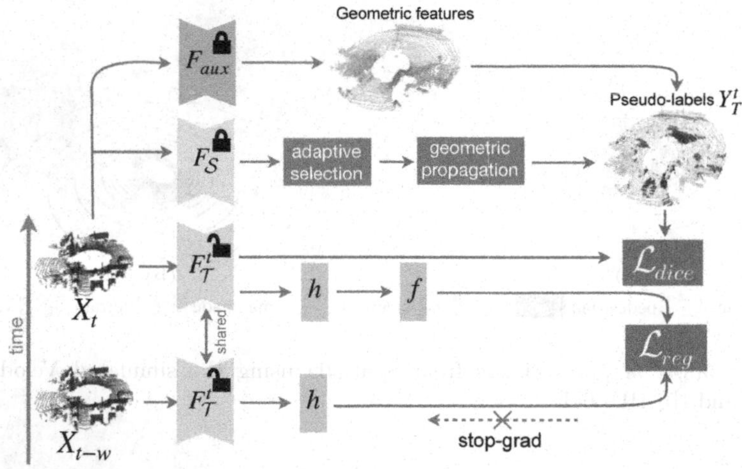

Fig. 3. Overview of GIPSO. A source pre-trained model $F_{\mathcal{S}}$ selects *seed pseudo-labels* through our adaptive-selection approach. An auxiliary model F_{aux} extracts geometric features to guide pseudo-label propagation. $\mathcal{L}_{dice}$ is minimised over the pseudo-labels $Y^t_{\mathcal{T}}$. In parallel, semantic smoothness is enforced with $\mathcal{L}_{reg}$ over time. (🔒) frozen parameters. (🔓) learnable parameters.

to ensure smoothness over time. Self-supervision through pseudo-label geometric propagation and temporal regularization are concurrently optimized to achieve the desired domain adaptation objective (Sect. 4.2).

Adaptive Pseudo-label Selection. An accurate selection of pseudo-labels is key to reliably adapt a model. In dynamic real-world scenarios, where new structures appear/disappear in/from the LiDAR field of view, traditional pseudo-labeling techniques [7,51] can suffer from unexpected variations of class distributions, producing overconfident incorrect pseudo-labels and making more populated classes prevail on others [72,73]. We overcome this problem by designing a class-balanced adaptive-thresholding strategy to choose reliable pseudo-labels. First, we compute an uncertainty index to filter out likely unreliable pseudo-labels. Second, we apply a different threshold for each class based on the uncertainty index distribution. This uncertainty index is directly related to the robustness of the output class distribution for each point. Robust pseudo-labels can be extracted from those points that consistently provide similar output distributions under different dropout perturbations [27]. We found that this approach works better than alternative confidence based approaches [72,73].

Given the point cloud $X^t_{\mathcal{T}}$, we perform J iterations of inference with $F_{\mathcal{S}}$ by using dropout and obtain

$$p^t_{\mathcal{T}} = \frac{1}{J}\sum_{j=1}^{J} p\left(F_{\mathcal{S}}|X^t_{\mathcal{T}}, d_j\right), \tag{1}$$

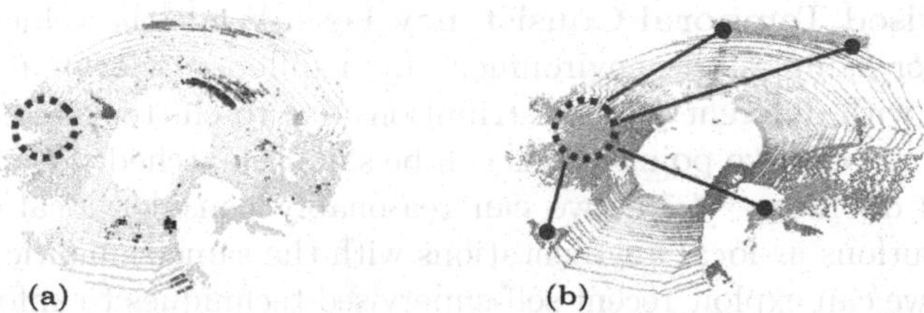

Fig. 4. Example of geometric propagation: a) starting from *seed pseudo-labels*, b) geometric features are used to expand labels toward geometrically consistent regions.

where $p^t_{\mathcal{T}}$ is the averaged output distribution of $F_{\mathcal{S}}$ given $X^t_{\mathcal{T}}$ and d_j, *i.e.* the dropout at j-th iteration. We compute the uncertainty index $\nu^t_{\mathcal{T}}$ as the variance over the C classes of $p^t_{\mathcal{T}}$ as

$$\nu^t_{\mathcal{T}} = E\left[\left(p^t_{\mathcal{T}} - \mu^t_{\mathcal{T}}\right)^2\right], \tag{2}$$

where $\mu^t_{\mathcal{T}} = E[p^t_{\mathcal{T}}]$ is the expected value of $p^t_{\mathcal{T}}$. Then, we select the least uncertain points by using a different uncertainty threshold for each class. Let λ^t_c be the uncertainty threshold of class c at time t. Since $\nu^t_{\mathcal{T}}$ defines the uncertainty for each point, we group $\nu^t_{\mathcal{T}}$ values per class and compute λ^t_c as the a-th percentile of

ν_T^t for class c. Therefore, at time t and for class c, we select only those pseudo-labels having the corresponding uncertainty index lower than λ_c^t and use the corresponding pseudo-labels as *seed pseudo-labels.*

Geometric Pseudo-label Propagation. Typically, seed pseudo-labels are few and uninformative for the adaptation of the target model – the deep network is already confident about them. Therefore, we aim to propagate these pseudo-labels to potentially informative points. This is challenging because the model may drift during adaptation. We propose to use the features produced by an auxiliary geometrically-informed encoder F_{aux} to propagate seed pseudo-labels to geometrically-similar points. Geometric features can be extracted using deep networks that compute 3D local descriptors [1,15,41]. 3D local descriptors are compact representations of local geometries with great generalization abilities across domains. Our intuition is that, while the propagation in the metric space may propagate only in the spatial neighborhood of seed pseudo-labels, the use of geometric features would allow us to propagate to geometrically similar points, which can be distant from their seeds in the metric space (Fig. 4).

Given a seed pseudo-labeled point $\tilde{\mathbf{x}}^t \in X_T^t$, we compute a set of geometric similarities as

$$\mathcal{G}_{\tilde{\mathbf{x}}}^t = \|F_{aux}(\tilde{\mathbf{x}}^t) - F_{aux}(X_T^t)\|_2, \tag{3}$$

where $\|\cdot\|_2$ is the l_2-norm and $\mathcal{G}_{\tilde{\mathbf{x}}}^t$ is the set that contains the similarity values between $\tilde{\mathbf{x}}^t$ and all the other points of X_T^t (except $\tilde{\mathbf{x}}^t$). Then, we select the points that correspond to top K values in $\mathcal{G}_{\tilde{\mathbf{x}}}^t$ and assign the pseudo-label of $\tilde{\mathbf{x}}^t$ to them. Let Y_T^t be the final set of pseudo-labels that we use for fine-tuning our model.

Self-supervised Temporal Consistency Loss. While the vehicle moves, the LiDAR sensor samples the environment from different viewpoints generating point clouds with different point distributions due to clutter and/or occlusions. As points of consecutive point clouds can be simply matched over time by using the vehicle's odometry [4,14], we can reasonably consider local variations of point distributions as local augmentations with the same semantic information. As a result, we can exploit recent self-supervised techniques to enforce temporal smoothness of our semantic features.

We begin by computing the set of corresponding points between X_T^{t-w} and X_T^t by using the vehicle's odometry. Let $T_{t-w\to t} \in \mathbb{R}^{4\times 4}$ be the rigid transformation (from odometry) that maps X_T^{t-w} in the reference frame of X_T^t. We define the set of corresponding point $\Omega^{t,t-w}$ as

$$\begin{aligned}\Omega^{t,t-w} = \{&\{\mathbf{x}^t \in X_T^t, \mathbf{x}^{t-w} \in X_T^{t-w}\}:\\ &\mathbf{x}^t = \mathtt{NN}\left(T_{t-w\to t} \circ \mathbf{x}^{t-w}, X_T^t\right),\\ &\|\mathbf{x}^t - \mathbf{x}^{t-w}\|_2 < \tau\},\end{aligned} \tag{4}$$

where $\mathtt{NN}(n, m)$ is the nearest-neighbour search given the set m and the query n, $\circ$ is the operator that applies $T_{t-w\to t}$ to a 3D point and τ is a distance threshold.

We adapt the self-supervised learning framework proposed in SimSiam [6] to semantically smooth point clouds over time. We add an encoder network $h(\cdot)$

and a predictor head $f(\cdot)$ to the target model $F_{\mathcal{T}}$ and minimize the negative cosine similarity between consecutive semantic representations of corresponding points. Let $z^t \triangleq h(x^t)$ be the encoder features over the target backbone for x^t and let $q^t \triangleq f(h(x^t))$ be the respective predictor features. We minimize the negative cosine similarity as

$$\mathcal{D}_{t \to t-w}(q^t, z^{t-w}) = -\frac{q^t}{\|q^t\|_2} \cdot \frac{z^{t-w}}{\|z^{t-w}\|_2} \tag{5}$$

Time consistency is symmetric in the backward direction, hence we use the corresponding point of x^t from $\Omega^{t,t-w}$ and define our self-supervised temporal consistency loss as

$$\mathcal{L}_{reg} = \frac{1}{2}\mathcal{D}_{t \to t-w}(q^t, z^{t-w}) + \frac{1}{2}\mathcal{D}_{t-w \to t}(q^{t-w}, z^t) \tag{6}$$

where stop-grad is applied on z^t and z^{t-w}.

4.2 Online Model Update

Classes are typically highly unbalanced in each point cloud, *e.g.*, a pedestrian class may be 1% the number of points of the *vegetation* class. To this end, we use the soft Dice loss [25] as we found it works well when classes are unbalanced. Let $\mathcal{L}_{dice}$ be our soft Dice loss that uses the pseudo-labels selected though Eq. 3 as supervision. We define the overall adaptation objective as $\mathcal{L}_{tot} = \mathcal{L}_{dice} + \mathcal{L}_{reg}$, where $\mathcal{L}_{reg}$ is our regularization loss defined in Eq. 6.

Table 2. Synth4D → SemanticKITTI online adaptation. Source: pre-trained source model (lower bound). We report absolute mIoU for Source and mIoU relative to Source for the other methods. Key. SF: Source-Free. UDA: Unsupervised DA. O: Online.

Model	SF	UDA	O	Vehicle	Pedestrian	Road	Sidewalk	Terrain	Manmade	Vegetation	Avg
Source				63.90	12.60	38.10	47.30	20.20	26.10	43.30	35.93
Target	✓		✓	+16.84	+5.49	+8.48	+34.44	+51.92	+45.68	+39.09	+28.85
ADABN [32]	✓	✓		−7.80	−2.00	−10.20	−18.60	−7.70	+5.80	−0.70	−5.89
RayCast [28]		✓		+3.80	−2.60	−3.10	−0.50	+7.30	+4.50	+0.20	+1.37
ProDA*	✓	✓	✓	−57.77	−12.34	−37.36	−46.95	−19.97	−25.62	−42.48	−34.64
SHOT*	✓	✓	✓	−62.44	−12.00	−28.27	−40.20	−20.00	−25.47	−42.55	−32.99
ONDA [38]	✓	✓	✓	−13.60	−1.70	−10.60	−20.00	−7.10	+3.90	−5.10	−7.74
CBST*	✓	✓	✓	−0.13	**+0.58**	−1.00	−1.12	+0.88	+1.69	+1.03	+0.28
TPLD*	✓	✓	✓	+0.36	+1.18	−0.76	−0.71	+0.95	+1.74	+1.15	+0.56
GIPSO (ours)	✓	✓	✓	**+13.12**	−0.54	**+1.19**	**+2.45**	**+2.78**	**+5.64**	**+5.54**	**+4.31**

5 Experiments

5.1 Experimental Setup

Source and Target Datasets. We pre-train our source models on Synth4D and SynLiDAR [2], and validate our approach on the official validation sets of

SemanticKITTI [3] and nuScenes [4] (target domains). In SemanticKITTI, we use the sequence 08 that is composed of 4071 point clouds 10 Hz. In nuScenes, we use 150 sequences, each composed of 40 point clouds 2 Hz.

Implementation Details. We use MinkowskiNet as deep network for point cloud segmentation [8]. We use ADAM: initial learning rate of 0.01 with exponential decay, batch-size 16 and weight decay 10^{-5}. As auxiliary network F_{aux}, we use the PointNet-based architecture proposed in [41] trained on Synth4D that outputs a geometric features (descriptor) for a given 3D point. For online adaptation, we fix the learning rate to 10^{-3} and do not use schedulers as they would require prior knowledge about the stream length. Because we adapt our model on each new incoming point cloud, we use batch-size equal to 1. We set $J = 5$, $a = 1$, $\tau = 0.3$ cm and use 0.5 dropout probability. We set $K = 10$, $w = 5$ on SemanticKITTI, and $K = 5$, $w = 1$ on nuScenes. Parameters are the same in all the experiments.

Evaluation Protocol. We follow the traditional evaluation procedure for online learning methods [5,65], *i.e.*, we evaluate the model performance on a new incoming frame using the model adapted up to the previous frame. We compute the Intersection over Union (IoU) [45] and report the average IoU (mIoU) improvement over the source (averaged over all the target sequences). We also evaluate the online version of our source model by fine-tuning it with ground-truth labels for all the points in the scene (target). We also evaluate the target upper bound (target) of our method obtained from the online finetuning of our source models over labelled target point clouds.

5.2 Benchmarking Existing Methods for SF-OUDA

Because our approach is the first that specifically tackles SF-OUDA in the context of 3D point cloud segmentation, we perform an in-depth analysis of the literature to identify previous adaptation methods that can be re-purposed for SF-OUDA. Additionally, we experimentally evaluate their effectiveness on the considered datasets. We identify three categories of methods, as detailed below.

Batch normalization-based methods perform domain adaptation by considering different statistics for source and target samples within Batch Normalization (BN) layers. Here, we consider ADABN [32] and ONDA [38]. ADABN [32] is a source-free adaptation method which operates by updating the BN statistics assuming that all target data are available (offline adaptation). ONDA [38] is the online version of ADABN [32], where the target BN statistics are updated online based on the target data within a mini-batch. This can be regarded as a SF-OUDA method. However, these approaches are general-purpose methods and have not been previously evaluated for 3D point cloud segmentation.

Prototype-based adaptation methods use class centroids, *i.e.* prototypes, to generate target pseudo-labels that can be transferred to other samples via clustering. We implement SHOT [33] and ProDA [66]. SHOT [33] exploits Information Maximization (IM) to promote cluster compactness during offline adaptation.

We implement SHOT by adapting the pre-trained model with the proposed IM loss online on each incoming target point cloud. ProDA [66] adopts a centroid-based weighting strategy to denoise target pseudo-labels, while also considering supervision from source data. We adapt ProDA to SF-OUDA by applying the same weighting strategy but removing source data supervision. We update target centroids at each incremental learning step. We refer to our SF-OUDA version of SHOT and PRODA as SHOT* and ProDA*, respectively.

Self-training-based methods exploit source model predictions to adapt on the target domain by re-training the model. We implement CBST [72] and TPLD [51]. CBST [72] relies on a prediction confidence to select the most reliable pseudo labels. A confidence threshold is computed offline for each target class to avoid class unbalance. Our implementation of CBST, which we denote as CBST*, uses the same class balance selection strategy but updates the thresholds online on each incoming frame. Moreover, no source data are considered as we are in a SF-OUDA setting. TPLD [51], originally designed for 2D semantic segmentation, uses the pseudo-label selection mechanism in [72] but introduces a pixel pseudo label densification process. We implement TPLD by removing source supervision and replace the densification procedure with a 3D spatial nearest-neighbor propagation. Our version of TPLD is denoted as TPLD*.

Besides re-purposing existing approaches for SF-OUDA, we also evaluate an additional baseline, *i.e.* the rendering-based method RayCast [28]. This approach is based on the idea that target-like data can be obtained with photorealistic rendering applied to the source point clouds. Thus, adaptation is performed by simply training on target-like data. While RayCast can be regarded as an offline adaptation approach, we select it as it only requires the parameters of the real sensor to obtain target-like data from source point clouds.

5.3 Results

Evaluating GIPSO. Tables 2, 3 and 4 report the results of our quantitative evaluation in the cases of Synth4D → SemanticKITTI, Synlidar → SemanticKITTI and Synth4D → nuScenes, respectively. The numbers in the

Table 3. SynLiDAR → SemanticKITTI online adaptation. Source: pre-trained source model (lower bound). We report absolute mIoU for Source and mIoU relative to Source for the other methods. Key. SF: Source-Free. UDA: Unsupervised DA. O: Online.

Model	SF	UDA	O	Vehicle	Pedestrian	Road	Sidewalk	Terrain	Manmade	Vegetation	Avg
Source				59.80	14.20	34.90	53.50	31.00	37.40	50.50	40.19
Target	✓		✓	+21.32	+8.09	+11.51	+28.13	+40.46	+33.67	+30.63	+24.83
ADABN [32]	✓	✓		+3.90	−6.40	−0.20	−3.70	−5.70	+1.40	+0.30	−1.49
RayCast [28]		✓		–	–	–	–	–	–	–	–
ProDA*	✓	✓	✓	−53.30	−13.79	−33.83	−52.78	−30.52	−36.68	−49.29	−38.60
SHOT*	✓	✓	✓	−57.83	−12.64	−24.80	−46.02	−30.80	−36.83	−49.32	36.89
ONDA [38]	✓	✓	✓	−2.90	−6.40	−2.20	−8.80	−7.60	−1.20	−6.70	−5.11
CBST*	✓	✓	✓	+0.99	−0.83	+0.55	+0.20	+0.74	−0.07	+0.38	+0.28
TPLD*	✓	✓	✓	+0.90	−0.48	+0.59	+0.33	+0.84	+0.07	+0.37	+0.37
GIPSO (ours)	✓	✓	✓	**+13.95**	−6.76	**+3.26**	**+5.01**	**+3.00**	**+3.34**	**+4.08**	**+3.70**

Table 4. Synth4D → nuScenes online adaptation. Source: pre-trained source model (lower bound). We report absolute mIoU for Source and mIoU relative to Source for the other methods. Key. SF: Source-Free. UDA: Unsupervised DA. O: Online.

Model	SF	UDA	O	Vehicle	Pedestrian	Road	Sidewalk	Terrain	Manmade	Vegetation	Avg
Source				22.54	14.38	42.03	28.39	15.58	38.18	54.14	30.75
Target	✓		✓	+3.76	+0.92	+9.41	+16.95	+19.79	+10.92	+10.71	+10.35
ADABN [32]	✓	✓		+1.23	−2.74	−1.24	+0.14	+0.53	+0.70	+4.03	+0.38
RayCast [28]		✓		−1.36	−9.69	−3.53	−3.42	−2.77	−2.54	−0.91	−3.46
ProDA*	✓	✓	✓	+0.57	**−1.40**	+0.73	+0.09	+0.71	+0.40	+0.91	+0.29
SHOT*	✓	✓	✓	**+0.82**	−1.77	+0.68	−0.05	−0.70	−0.54	+1.09	−0.07
ONDA [38]	✓	✓	✓	+0.34	−1.90	−1.19	−0.62	+0.18	−0.40	+0.58	−0.43
CBST*	✓	✓	✓	+0.37	−2.61	−1.35	−0.79	+0.19	−0.36	−0.45	−0.71
TPLD*	✓	✓	✓	+0.65	−1.90	−0.96	−0.39	+0.43	+0.07	+0.86	−0.18
GIPSO (ours)	✓	✓	✓	+0.55	−3.76	**+1.64**	**+1.72**	**+2.28**	**+1.18**	**+2.36**	**+0.85**

tables indicate the improvement over the source model. GIPSO achieves an average IoU improvement of +4.31 on Synth4D → SemanticKITTI, +3.70 on Synlidar → SemanticKITTI and +0.85 on Synth4D → nuScenes. GIPSO outperforms both offline and online methods by a large margin on Synth4D → SemanticKITTI and Synlidar → SemanticKITTI, while it achieves a lower improvement over Synth4D → nuScenes. On SemanticKITTI, GIPSO can effectively improve *road*, *sidewalk*, *terrain*, *manmade* and *vegetation*. *vehicle* is the best performing class, which can achieve a mIoU above +13. *pedestrian* is the worst performing class on all the datasets. *pedestrian* is a challenging class because it is significantly unbalanced compared to the others, also in the source domain. Although we attempted to mitigate the problem of unbalanced classes using adaptive thresholding and soft Dice loss, there are still situations that are difficult to address (see Sect. 6 for details). On nuScenes, the improvement is minor because at its lower resolutions makes patterns less distinguishable and more difficult to segment.

Evaluating State-of-the-Art Methods. We also analyze the performance of the existing methods discussed in Sect. 5.2. Batch-normalisation based methods perform poorly on all the datasets, with only ADABN [32] showing a minor improvement on nuScenes. We argue that non-i.i.d. batch samples arising in the online setting are playing an important role in this degradation, as they can have detrimental effects on models with BN layers [24]. SHOT* and ProDA* perform poorly in almost all the experiments, except on Synth4D → nuScenes where ProDA* achieves +0.29. This minor improvement may be due to the short sequences of nuScenes (40 frames) making centroids less likely to drift. This does not occur in SemanticKITTI where the long sequence causes a rapid drift (see detailed in Sect. 5.4). CBST* and TPLD* improve on SemanticKITTI and perform poorly on nuScenes. This can be ascribed to the noisy pseudo-labels that are selected using their confidence-based filtering approach. Lastly, RayCast [28] achieves +1.37 on Synth4D → SemanticKITTI, but underperform on Synth4D → nuScenes with a degradation of −3.46. RayCast was originally proposed for

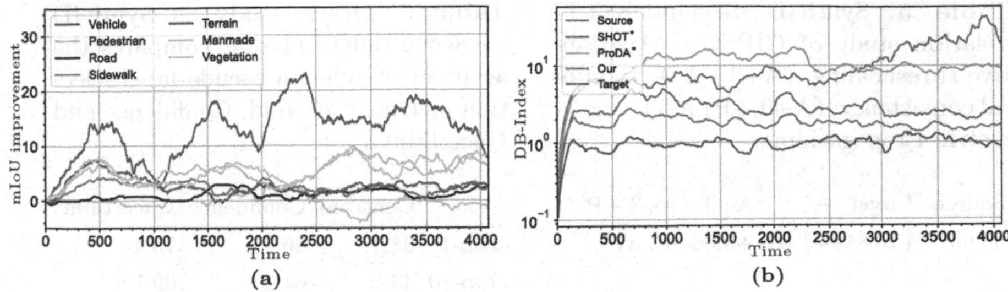

Fig. 5. (a) Per-class improvement of GIPSO over time on Synth4D→SemanticKITTI. (b) DB-Index over time on Synth4D→SemanticKITTI. The lower the DB-Index, the better the class separation of the features.

real-to-real adaptation, therefore we believe that its performance may be affected by the large difference in point cloud resolution between Synth4D and nuScenes. RayCast underperforms GIPSO in the online setup, thus showing how offline solutions can fail in dynamic domains. Note that RayCast cannot be evaluated using Synlidar, because Synlidar does not provide odometry information.

5.4 In-Depth Analyses

Ablation Study. Table 5 shows the results of our ablation study on Synth4D → SemanticKITTI. When we use only the adaptive pseudo-label selection (A) we can achieve +1.07 compared to the source. When we combine A with the temporal regularization (T) we can further improve by +3.65. Then we can achieve our best performance through the geometric propagation (P) of the pseudo labels.

Oracle Study. We analyze the importance of using a reliable pseudo-label selection metric. Table 6 shows the pseudo-label accuracy as a function of the points that are selected as the K-th best candidates based on the distance from their centroids (as proposed in [66]), confidence (as proposed in [72]) and uncertainty (ours). Centroid-based selection shows a low accuracy even at $K = 1$, which tends to worsen as K increases. Confidence-based selection is more reliable than the centroid-based selection. We found uncertainty-based selection to be more reliable at smaller values of K, which we deem to be more important than having more pseudo-labels but less reliable.

Per-Class Temporal Behavior. Figure 5a shows the mIoU over time for each class on Synth4D → SemanticKITTI. We can observe that six out of seven classes have a steady improvement: *vehicle* is the best performing class, followed by *vegetation* and *manmade.* Drops in mIoU are typically due to sudden geometric variations of the point cloud, *e.g.*, a road junction after a straight road, or a jammed road after a empty road. *pedestrian* confirms to be the most challenging class.

Table 5. Synth4D→SemanticKITTI ablation study of GIPSO: (A) Adaptive thresholding; (A+T) A + Temporal consistency; (A+T+P) A+T + geometric Propagation.

Source	Target	A	A+T	A+T+P
35.95	+28.85	+1.07	+3.65	+4.31

Table 6. Oracle study on Synth4D → SemanticKITTI that compares the accuracy of different pseudo-label selection metrics: Centroid, Confidence and Uncertainty.

	Centroid	Confidence	Uncertainty
Top-1	38.1	66.7	76.1
Top-10	43.8	61.4	69.7

Temporal Compactness of Features. We assess how well points are organized in the feature space over time. We use the DB Index (DBI) that is typically used in clustering to measures the feature intra- and inter-class distances [10]. The lower the DBI, the better the quality of the features. We use SHOT* and ProDA* as comparisons with our method, and the source and target models as references. Figure 5b shows the DBI variations over time. SHOT* behavior is typical of a drift, as features of different classes become interwoven. ProDA* does not drift, but it produces features that are worse than the source model. Our approach is between source and target models, with a tendency to get closer to target.

Different 3D Local Descriptors. We assess the effectiveness of different 3D local descriptors. We test FPFH [47] (handcrafted) and FCGF [9] (deep learning) descriptors. GIPSO achieves +3.56 mIoU with FPFH, +4.12 mIoU with FCGF and +4.31 mIoU with DIP. This is inline with the experiments shown in [42], where DIP shows a superior generalization capability across domains than FCGF.

Performance with Global Features. We assess the GIPSO performance on Synth4D→SemanticKITTI when the global temporal consistency loss proposed in STRL [22] is used instead of our per-point loss (Eq. 5). This variation achieves +1.74 mIoU, showing that per-point temporal consistency is key.

Qualitative Results. Figure 6 shows the comparison between GIPSO and the source model on Synth4D→SemanticKITTI. The first row shows frame 178 of SemanticKITTI with an improvement of +27.14 mIoU (large). The classes *vehicle*, *sidewalk* and *terrain* are incorrectly segmented by the source model, we can see a significant improvement in segmentation on these classes after adaptation. The second and third rows show frame 1193 and frame 2625 with an improvement of +10.00 mIoU (medium) and +4.99 mIoU (small). Improvements are visible after adaptation in the classes *vehicle*, *sidewalk* and *road*. The last row shows a segmentation drift for *road* that is caused by incorrect pseudo-labels.

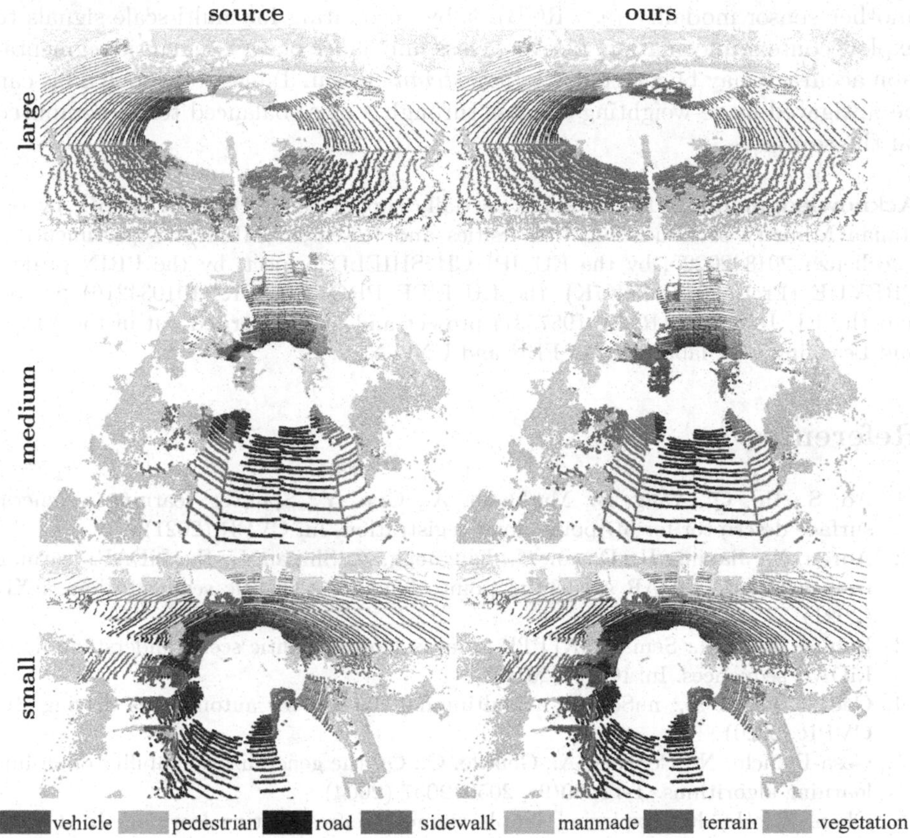

Fig. 6. Results on Synth4D→SemanticKITTI with three different ranges of mIoU improvements, i.e., large (+27.2), medium (+10.0) and small (+5.1).

6 Discussions

Conclusions. We studied for the first time the problem of SF-OUDA for 3D point cloud segmentation in a synthetic-to-real setting. We experimentally showed that existing approaches do not suffice in coping with domain shift in this scenario. We presented GIPSO that relies on adaptive self-training and geometric-features propagation to address SF-OUDA. We also introduced a novel synthetic dataset, namely Synth4D composed of two splits and matching the sensor setup of SemanticKITTI and nuScenes, respectively. Experiments on three different benchmarks showed that GIPSO outperforms state-of-the-art approaches.

Limitations. GIPSO limitations are related to geometric propagation and long-tailed classes. If objects of different classes share similar geometric structures, the geometric propagation may be deleterious. This can be mitigated by using another sensor modality (e.g. RGB) or by accounting for multi-scale signals to exploit context information. If severe class unbalance occurs, semantic segmentation accuracy may be affected, e.g. *pedestrian* class in Tables 2, 3 and 4. This can be mitigated by re-weighting the loss through a class-balanced term (computed on the source).

Acknowledgments. This work was partially supported by OSRAM GmbH, by the Italian Ministry of Education, Universities and Research (MIUR) "Dipartimenti di Eccellenza 2018–2022", by the EU JPI/CH SHIELD project, by the PRIN project PREVUE (Prot. 2017N2RK7K), the EU ISFP PROTECTOR (101034216) project and the EU H2020 MARVEL (957337) project and, it was carried out in the Vision and Learning joint laboratory of FBK and UNITN.

References

1. Ao, S., Hu, Q., Yang, B., Markham, A., Guo, Y.: SpinNet: learning a general surface descriptor for 3D point cloud registration. In: CVPR (2021)
2. Aoran, X., Jiaxing, H., Dayan, G., Fangneng, Z., Shijian, L.: SynLiDAR: learning from synthetic LiDAR sequential point cloud for semantic segmentation. arXiv (2021)
3. Behley, J., et al.: SemanticKITTI: a dataset for semantic scene understanding of LiDAR sequences. In: ICCV (2019)
4. Caesar, H., et al.: nuScenes: a multimodal dataset for autonomous driving. In: CVPR (2020)
5. Cesa-Bianchi, N., Conconi, A., Gentile, C.: On the generalization ability of on-line learning algorithms. T-IT **50**(9), 2050–2057 (2004)
6. Chen, X., He, K.: Exploring simple siamese representation learning. In: CVPR (2021)
7. Chen, Y., Li, W., Sakaridis, C., Dai, D., van Gool, L.: Domain adaptive faster R-CNN for object detection in the wild. In: CVPR (2018)
8. Choy, C., Gwak, J., Savarese, S.: 4D spatio-temporal ConvNets: Minkowski convolutional neural networks. In: CVPR (2019)
9. Choy, C., Park, J., Koltun, V.: Fully convolutional geometric features. In: ICCV (2019)
10. Davies, D., Bouldin, D.: A cluster separation measure. T-PAMI **PAMI-1**(2) , 224–227 (1979)
11. Dolgov, D., Thrun, S., Montemerlo, M., Diebel, J.: Path planning for autonomous vehicles in unknown semi-structured environments. IJRR **29**(5), 485–501 (2010)
12. Dosovitskiy, A., Ros, G., Codevilla, F., Lopez, A., Koltun, V.: CARLA: an open urban driving simulator. In: ACRL (2017)
13. Geiger, A., Lenz, P., Stiller, C., Urtasun, R.: Vision meets robotics: the KITTI dataset. IJRR **32**(11), 1231–1237 (2013)
14. Geiger, A., Lenz, P., Urtasun, R.: Are we ready for autonomous driving? The KITTI vision benchmark suite. In: CVPR (2012)
15. Gojcic, Z., Zhou, C., Wegner, J., Andreas, W.: The perfect match: 3D point cloud matching with smoothed densities. In: CVPR (2019)
16. Graham, B., Engelcke, M., van der Maaten, L.: 3D semantic segmentation with submanifold sparse convolutional networks. In: CVPR (2018)

17. Graham, B., van der Maaten, L.: Submanifold sparse convolutional networks. arXiv (2017)
18. Griffiths, D., Boehm, J.: SynthCity: a large scale synthetic point cloud. arXiv (2019)
19. Guan, S., Xu, J., Wang, Y., Ni, B., Yang, X.: Bilevel online adaptation for out-of-domain human mesh reconstruction. In: CVPR (2021)
20. Hoffman, J., et al.: CyCADA: cycle-consistent adversarial domain adaptation. In: ICML (2018)
21. Hu, Q., et al.: RandLA-Net: efficient semantic segmentation of large-scale point clouds. In: CVPR (2020)
22. Huang, S., Xie, Y., Zhu, S., Zhu, Y.: Spatio-temporal self-supervised representation learning for 3D point clouds. In: ICCV (2021)
23. Hurl, B., Czarnecki, K., Waslander, S.: Precise synthetic image and LiDAR (PreSIL) dataset for autonomous vehicle perception. In: IVS (2019)
24. Ioffe, S.: Batch renormalization: towards reducing minibatch dependence in batch-normalized models. arXiv (2017)
25. Jadon, S.: A survey of loss functions for semantic segmentation. In: CIBCB (2020)
26. Jaritz, M., Vu, T.H., de Charette, R., Wirbel, E., Pérez, P.: xMUDA: cross-modal unsupervised domain adaptation for 3D semantic segmentation. In: CVPR (2020)
27. Kendall, A., Badrinarayanan, V., Cipolla, R.: Bayesian SegNet: model uncertainty in deep convolutional encoder-decoder architectures for scene understanding. In: BMVC (2017)
28. Langer, F., Milioto, A., Haag, A., Behley, J., Stachniss, C.: Domain transfer for semantic segmentation of LiDAR data using deep neural networks. In: IROS (2021)
29. LeCun, Y., Bengio, Y., Hinton, G.: Deep learning. Nature **521**(7553), 436–444 (2015)
30. Levinson, J., et al.: Towards fully autonomous driving: systems and algorithms. In: IV (2011)
31. Li, D., Hospedales, T.: Online meta-learning for multi-source and semi-supervised domain adaptation. In: Vedaldi, A., Bischof, H., Brox, T., Frahm, J.-M. (eds.) ECCV 2020. LNCS, vol. 12361, pp. 382–403. Springer, Cham (2020). https://doi.org/10.1007/978-3-030-58517-4_23
32. Li, Y., Wang, N., Shi, J., Liu, J., Hou, X.: Revisiting batch normalization for practical domain adaptation. arXiv (2016)
33. Liang, J., Hu, D., Feng, J.: Do we really need to access the source data? Source hypothesis transfer for unsupervised domain adaptation. In: ICML (2020)
34. Velodyne Lidar: VelodyneLidar (2021). www.velodynelidar.com
35. Liu, C., Lee, S., Varnhagen, S., Tseng, H.: Path planning for autonomous vehicles using model predictive control. In: IV (2017)
36. Liu, Y., Zhang, W., Wang, J.: Source-free domain adaptation for semantic segmentation. In: CVPR (2021)
37. Long, M., Cao, Z., Wang, J., Jordan, M.: Conditional adversarial domain adaptation. In: NeurIPS (2018)
38. Mancini, M., Karaoguz, H., Ricci, E., Jensfelt, P., Caputo, B.: Kitting in the wild through online domain adaptation. In: IROS (2018)
39. Milioto, A., Vizzo, I., Behley, J., Stachniss, C.: RangeNet++: fast and accurate LiDAR semantic segmentation. In: IROS (2019)
40. Moon, J., Das, D., Lee, C.: Multi-step online unsupervised domain adaptation. In: ICASSP (2020)
41. Poiesi, F., Boscaini, D.: Distinctive 3D local deep descriptors. In: ICPR (2021)

42. Poiesi, F., Boscaini, D.: Learning general and distinctive 3D local deep descriptors for point cloud registration. T-PAMI (2022)
43. Qi, C., Su, H., Mo, K., Guibas, L.: PointNet: deep learning on point sets for 3D classification and segmentation. In: CVPR (2017)
44. Qi, C., Yi, L., Su, H., Guibas, L.: PointNet++: deep hierarchical feature learning on point sets in a metric space. arXiv (2017)
45. Rahman, M.A., Wang, Y.: Optimizing intersection-over-union in deep neural networks for image segmentation. In: Bebis, G., et al. (eds.) ISVC 2016. LNCS, vol. 10072, pp. 234–244. Springer, Cham (2016). https://doi.org/10.1007/978-3-319-50835-1_22
46. Rosolia, U., Bruyne, S.D., Alleyne, A.: Autonomous vehicle control: a nonconvex approach for obstacle avoidance. T-CST **25**(2), 469–484 (2016)
47. Rusu, R., Blodow, N., Beetz, M.: Fast point feature histograms (FPFH) for 3D registration. In: ICRA (2009)
48. Saito, K., Watanabe, K., Ushiku, Y., Harada, T.: Maximum classifier discrepancy for unsupervised domain adaptation. In: CVPR (2018)
49. Saltori, C., Lathuiliére, S., Sebe, N., Ricci, E., Galasso, F.: SF-UDA^{3}D: source-free unsupervised domain adaptation for LiDAR-based 3D object detection. arXiv (2020)
50. Schneider, S., Rusak, E., Eck, L., Bringmann, O., Brendel, W., Bethge, M.: Improving robustness against common corruptions by covariate shift adaptation. In: NeurIPS (2020)
51. Shin, I., Woo, S., Pan, F., Kweon, I.S.: Two-phase pseudo label densification for self-training based domain adaptation. In: Vedaldi, A., Bischof, H., Brox, T., Frahm, J.-M. (eds.) ECCV 2020. LNCS, vol. 12358, pp. 532–548. Springer, Cham (2020). https://doi.org/10.1007/978-3-030-58601-0_32
52. Sun, Y., Wang, X., Liu, Z., Miller, J., Efros, A., Hardt, M.: Test-time training with self-supervision for generalization under distribution shifts. In: ICML (2020)
53. Tanneberg, D., Peters, J., Rueckert, E.: Efficient online adaptation with stochastic recurrent neural networks. In: Humanoids (2017)
54. Tompkins, A., Senanayake, R., Ramos, F.: Online domain adaptation for occupancy mapping. arXiv (2020)
55. Tonioni, A., Tosi, F., Poggi, M., Mattoccia, S., Stefano, L.D.: Real-time self-adaptive deep stereo. In: CVPR (2019)
56. Torralba, A., Efros, A.: Unbiased look at dataset bias. In: CVPR (2011)
57. Voigtlaender, P., Leibe, B.: Online adaptation of convolutional neural networks for video object segmentation. arXiv (2017)
58. Volpi, R., Jorge, P.D., Larlus, D., Csurka, G.: On the road to online adaptation for semantic image segmentation. In: CVPR (2022)
59. Wang, D., Shelhamer, E., Liu, S., Olshausen, B., Darrell, T.: Tent: fully test-time adaptation by entropy minimization. In: ICLR (2021)
60. Wu, B., Wan, A., Yue, X., Keutzer, K.: SqueezeSeg: convolutional neural nets with recurrent CRF for real-time road-object segmentation from 3D LiDAR point cloud. In: ICRA (2018)
61. Wu, B., Zhou, X., Zhao, S., Yue, X., Keutzer, K.: SqueezeSegV2: improved model structure and unsupervised domain adaptation for road-object segmentation from a LiDAR point cloud. In: ICRA (2019)
62. Yang, S., van de Weijer, J., Herranz, L., Jui, S., et al.: Exploiting the intrinsic neighborhood structure for source-free domain adaptation. In: NeurIPS (2021)
63. Yi, L., Gong, B., Funkhouser, T.: Complete & label: a domain adaptation approach to semantic segmentation of LiDAR point clouds. arXiv (2021)

64. Yue, X., Wu, B., Seshia, S., Keutzer, K., Sangiovanni-Vincentelli, A.: A LiDAR point cloud generator: from a virtual world to autonomous driving. In: ICMR (2018)
65. Zhan, X., Xie, J., Liu, Z., Ong, Y., Loy, C.: Online deep clustering for unsupervised representation learning. In: CVPR (2020)
66. Zhang, P., Zhang, B., Zhang, T., Chen, D., Wang, Y., Wen, F.: Prototypical pseudo label denoising and target structure learning for domain adaptive semantic segmentation. In: CVPR (2021)
67. Zhang, Y., et al.: PolarNet: an improved grid representation for online LiDAR point clouds semantic segmentation. In: CVPR (2020)
68. Zhang, Z., Lathuilière, S., Pilzer, A., Sebe, N., Ricci, E., Yang, J.: Online adaptation through meta-learning for stereo depth estimation. arXiv (2019)
69. Zhao, S., et al.: ePointDA: an end-to-end simulation-to-real domain adaptation framework for LiDAR point cloud segmentation. arXiv (2020)
70. Zhou, Y., Tuzel, O.: VoxelNet: end-to-end learning for point cloud based 3D object detection. In: CVPR (2018)
71. Zhu, X., et al.: Cylindrical and asymmetrical 3D convolution networks for LiDAR segmentation. In: CVPR (2021)
72. Zou, Y., Yu, Z., Vijaya Kumar, B.V.K., Wang, J.: Unsupervised domain adaptation for semantic segmentation via class-balanced self-training. In: Ferrari, V., Hebert, M., Sminchisescu, C., Weiss, Y. (eds.) ECCV 2018. LNCS, vol. 11207, pp. 297–313. Springer, Cham (2018). https://doi.org/10.1007/978-3-030-01219-9_18
73. Zou, Y., Yu, Z., Liu, X., Kumar, B., Wang, J.: Confidence regularized self-training. In: ICCV (2019)

CoSMix: Compositional Semantic Mix for Domain Adaptation in 3D LiDAR Segmentation

Cristiano Saltori[1(✉)], Fabio Galasso[2], Giuseppe Fiameni[3], Nicu Sebe[1], Elisa Ricci[1,4], and Fabio Poiesi[4]

[1] University of Trento, Trento, Italy
cristiano.saltori@unitn.it
[2] Sapienza University of Rome, Rome, Italy
[3] NVIDIA AI Technology Center, Rome, Italy
[4] Fondazione Bruno Kessler, Trento, Italy

Abstract. 3D LiDAR semantic segmentation is fundamental for autonomous driving. Several Unsupervised Domain Adaptation (UDA) methods for point cloud data have been recently proposed to improve model generalization for different sensors and environments. Researchers working on UDA problems in the image domain have shown that sample mixing can mitigate domain shift. We propose a new approach of sample mixing for point cloud UDA, namely Compositional Semantic Mix (CoSMix), the first UDA approach for point cloud segmentation based on sample mixing. CoSMix consists of a two-branch symmetric network that can process labelled synthetic data (source) and real-world unlabelled point clouds (target) concurrently. Each branch operates on one domain by mixing selected pieces of data from the other one, and by using the semantic information derived from source labels and target pseudo-labels. We evaluate CoSMix on two large-scale datasets, showing that it outperforms state-of-the-art methods by a large margin (Our code is available at https://github.com/saltoricristiano/cosmix-uda).

Keywords: Unsupervised domain adaptation · Point clouds · Semantic segmentation · LiDAR

1 Introduction

Point cloud semantic segmentation is the problem of assigning a finite set of semantic labels to a set of 3D points [6,42]. When deep learning-based approaches are employed to perform this task, large-scale datasets with point-level annotations are required to learn accurate models [3,4,20]. This implies a costly and cumbersome data collection procedure, as point clouds need to be captured in

Supplementary Information The online version contains supplementary material available at https://doi.org/10.1007/978-3-031-19827-4_34.

S. Avidan et al. (Eds.): ECCV 2022, LNCS 13693, pp. 586–602, 2022.
https://doi.org/10.1007/978-3-031-19827-4_34

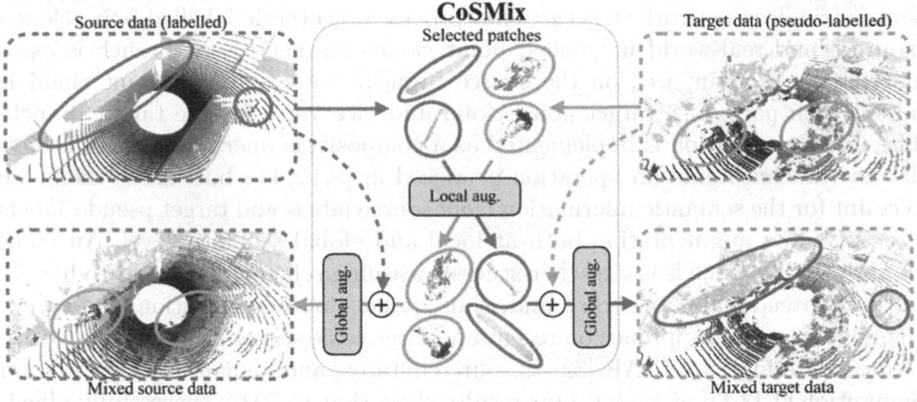

Fig. 1. CoSMix applied to source and target data. Given (labelled) source and (pseudo-labelled) target data, we select domain-specific patches with semantic information to be mixed across domains. The resulting mixed data are a compositional semantic mix between the two domains, mixing source supervision in the target domain and target self-supervision (object and scene structure) in the source domain. Augmentations are applied at both local and global levels.

the real world and manually annotated. An alternative is to use synthetic data, which can be conveniently generated with simulators [8]. However, deep neural networks are known to underperform when trained and tested on data from different domains, due to *domain shift* [7]. Although significant effort has been invested to design simulators that can reproduce the acquisition sensor with high fidelity, further research is still needed to neutralize the domain shift between real and synthetic domains [32].

Unsupervised Domain Adaptation (UDA) for semantic segmentation has been widely studied for image data [9,25,28,44,45], however less attention has been paid to adaptation techniques for point clouds. Approaches to address synthetic-to-real UDA for point clouds can operate in the input space [32,41] by using dropout rendering [41], or in the feature space through feature alignment [30], or can use adversarial networks [32]. In the last few years, data augmentation approaches based on mixing of training samples and their labels, such as Mixup [38] or CutMix [36], have been proposed to promote generalization. These techniques can be used for image classification [36,38], image recognition [17,33], and 2D semantic segmentation [9,25]. A few works proposed to exploit sample mixing for point cloud data [5,19,39,43], but they are formulated for supervised applications. We argue that the major challenge in extending 2D mix-based UDA approaches to point clouds lies in the application of these to geometric signals rather than photometric signals, e.g., the weighted alpha blending performed of labels in 2D [36,38] is still unclear how to extend it to 3D.

In this paper, we propose a novel UDA framework for 3D LiDAR segmentation, named CoSMix, which can mitigate the domain shift by creating two new intermediate domains of composite point clouds obtained by applying a novel mixing strategy at input level (Fig. 1). Our framework is based on a two-branch symmetric deep network structure that processes synthetic labelled point clouds (source) and real-world unlabelled point clouds (target). Each branch is associated to a domain, *i.e.*, on the source branch, a given source point cloud is mixed with parts of a target point cloud and vice versa for the target branch. The mixing operation is implemented as a composition operation, which is similar to the concatenation operation proposed in [5,19,43], but unlike them, we account for the semantic information from source labels and target pseudo-labels to apply data augmentation both at local and global semantic level. An additional key difference is the teacher-student learning scheme that we introduce to improve pseudo-label accuracy and, thus, point cloud composition. We extensively evaluate our approach on recent and large scale segmentation benchmarks, *i.e.*, considering SynLiDAR [32] as source dataset, and SemanticPOSS [20] and SemanticKITTI [3] as target. Our results show that CoSMix successfully alleviates the domain shift and outperforms state-of-the-art methods. We also perform an in-depth analysis of CoSMix and an ablation study on each component, highlighting its strengths and discussing its main limitations. To the best of our knowledge, this is the first work to have proposed a sample mixing scheme for adaptation in the context of 3D point cloud segmentation.

Our main contributions can be summarised as follows:

- We introduce a novel scheme for mixing point clouds by leveraging semantic information and data augmentation.
- We show that the proposed mixing strategy can be used for reducing the domain shift and design CoSMix, the first UDA method for 3D LiDAR semantic segmentation based on point cloud mixing.
- We conduct extensive experiments on two challenging synthetic-to-real 3D LiDAR semantic segmentation benchmarks demonstrating the effectiveness of CoSMix, which outperforms state-of-the-art methods.

2 Related Works

Point Cloud Semantic Segmentation. Point cloud segmentation can be performed by using PointNet [21] that is based on a series of multilayer perceptrons. PointNet++ [22] improves PointNet by leveraging point aggregations performed at neighbourhood level and multi-scale sampling to encode both local features and global features. RandLA-Net [13] extends PoinNet++ [22] by embedding local spatial encoding, random sampling and attentive pooling. These methods are computationally inefficient when large-scale point clouds are processed. Recent segmentation methods have improved the computational efficiency by projecting 3D points on 2D representations or by using 3D quantization approaches. The former includes 2D projection based approaches that use 2D range maps and exploit standard 2D architectures [24] to segment these maps prior to a re-projection in the 3D space. RangeNet++ [18], SqueezeSeg networks [29,30], 3D-MiniNet [2] and PolarNet [40] are examples of these approaches. Although these approaches are efficient, they tend to loose information when the input data are projected in 2D and re-projected in 3D. The latter includes 3D quantization-based approaches that discretize the input point cloud into a 3D discrete representations and that employ

3D convolutions [37] or 3D sparse convolutions [6,12] to predict per-point classes. In this category, we find methods such as VoxelNet [37], SparseConv [11,12], MinkowskiNet [6] and, Cylinder3D [42]. In our work, we use the MinkowskiNet [6] which provides a trade off between accuracy and efficiency.

Unsupervised Domain Adaptation for Point Cloud Segmentation. Unsupervised Domain Adaptation (UDA) for point cloud segmentation can be used in the case of real-to-real [15,16,35] and synthetic to real scenarios [29,30,41]. Real-to-real adaptation can be used when a deep network is trained with data of real-world scenes captured with a LiDAR sensors and then tested on unseen scenes captured with a different LiDAR sensor [16,35]. Therein, domain adaptation can be formulated as a 3D surface completion task [35] or by transferring the sensor pattern of the target domain to the source domain through ray casting [16]. Synthetic-to-real domain adaptation can be used when the source data are acquired with a simulated LiDAR sensor [8] and the target data are obtained with a real LiDAR sensor. In this case, domain shift occurs due to differences in (i) sampling noise, (ii) structure of the environment and (iii) class distributions [30,41]. Attention models can be used to aggregate contextual information [29,30] and geodesic correlation alignment with progressive domain calibration can be adopted to improve domain adaptation [30]. In [41], real dropout noise is simulated on synthetic data through a generative adversarial network. Similarly, in [32] domain shift is disentangled into appearance difference and sparsity difference and a generative network is applied to mitigate each difference. In our work, we do not use a learning-based approach to perturb the input data, but we formulate a novel compositional semantic point cloud mixing approach that enables the deep network to improve its performance on the unlabelled target domain self-supervisedly.

Sample Mixing for UDA. Deep neural networks often exhibit undesired behaviours such as memorization and overfitting. To alleviate this problem, mixing strategies [36,38] train a network on additional data derived from the convex combination of paired samples and labels, which are obtained either mixing the whole samples [38] or cutting and pasting their patches [36]. Mixing strategies showed their effectiveness also in reducing domain shift in UDA for image classification [31,33] and semantic segmentation [9,25,34]. In DACS [25], mixed samples are created by mixing pairs of images from different domains by using source ground-truth annotations pasted on pseudo-labelled target images. In DSP [9], authors adopt a strategy that prioritize the selection of long-tail classes from the source domain images, and to paste their corresponding image patches on other source images and on target images. The first point cloud mixing strategies [5,19,39] showed that point cloud pairs and their point-level annotations can be mixed for improving accuracy in semantic segmentation [19] and classification [5,39]. Zou *et al.* [43] propose to use Mix3D [19] as a pretext task for classification by predicting the rotation angle of mixed pairs. Apply mixing strategy to address UDA in 3D semantic segmentation has not been previously investigated. We fill this gap by introducing a novel compositional semantic mixing strategy that goes beyond the standard concatenation of two point clouds [19,39] or of randomly selected crops [39].

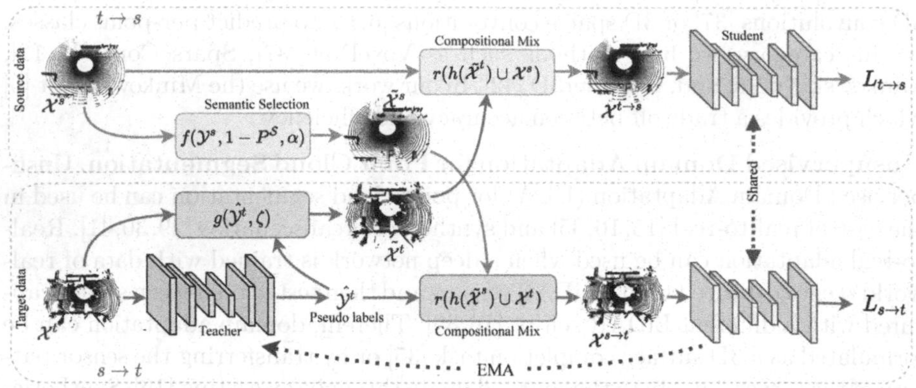

Fig. 2. Block diagram of CoSMix. In the top branch, the input source point cloud $\mathcal{X}^s$ is mixed with the target point cloud $\mathcal{X}^t$ obtaining $\mathcal{X}^{t\to s}$. In the bottom branch, the input target point cloud $\mathcal{X}^t$ is mixed with the source point cloud $\mathcal{X}^s$ obtaining $\mathcal{X}^{s\to t}$. A teacher-student learning architecture is used to improve pseudo-label accuracy while adapting over target domain. Semantic Selection (f and g) selects subsets of points (patches) to be mixed based on the source labels $\mathcal{Y}^s$ and target pseudo-labels $\hat{\mathcal{Y}}^t$ information. Compositional Mix applies local h and global r augmentations and mixes the selected patches among domains.

3 Our Approach

CoSMix implements a teacher-student learning scheme that exploits the supervision from the source domain and the self-supervision from the target domain to improve the semantic segmentation on the target domain. Our method is trained on two different mixed point cloud sets. The first is the composition of the source point cloud with pseudo-labelled pieces, or *patches*, of the target point cloud. Target patches bring the target modality in the source domain pulling the source domain closer to the target domain. The second is the composition of the target point cloud with randomly selected patches of the source point cloud. Source patches pull the target domain closer to the source domain, preventing overfitting from noisy pseudo-labels. The teacher-student network enables the iterative improvement of pseudo labels, progressively reducing the domain gap.

Figure 2 shows the block diagram of CoSMix. Let $\mathcal{S} = \{(\mathcal{X}^s, \mathcal{Y}^s)\}$ be the source dataset that is composed of $N^s = |\mathcal{S}|$ labelled point clouds, where $\mathcal{X}^s$ is a point cloud and $\mathcal{Y}^s$ is its point-level labels, and $|.|$ is the cardinality of a set. Labels take values from a set of semantic classes $\mathcal{C} = \{c\}$, where c is a semantic class. Let $\mathcal{T} = \{\mathcal{X}^t\}$ be the target dataset composed of $N^t = |\mathcal{T}|$ unlabelled point clouds. On the top branch, the source point cloud $\mathcal{X}^s$ is mixed with selected patches of the target point cloud $\mathcal{X}^t$. The target patches are subsets of points that correspond to the most confident pseudo-labels $\hat{\mathcal{Y}}^t$ that the teacher network produces during training. On the bottom branch, the target point cloud $\mathcal{X}^t$ is mixed with the selected patches of the source point cloud $\mathcal{X}^s$. The source patches are subsets of points that are randomly selected based on their class frequency distribution in the training set. Let $\mathcal{X}^{t\rightarrow s}$ be the mixed point cloud obtained from the top branch, and $\mathcal{X}^{s\rightarrow t}$ be the mixed point cloud obtained from the bottom branch. We define the branch that mixes target point cloud patches to the source point cloud as $t \rightarrow s$ and the branch that does the vice versa as $s \rightarrow t$. Lastly, let Φ_θ and $\Phi_{\theta'}$ be the student and teacher deep networks with learnable parameters θ and θ', respectively.

We explain how the semantic selection operates on the source and target point clouds in Sect. 3.1. We detail the modules in charge of mixing the point clouds coming from the different domains in Sect. 3.2. Then, we describe how the teacher network is updated during training and the loss functions that we use to train the student networks in Sect. 3.3.

3.1 Semantic Selection

In order to train the student networks with balanced data, we select reliable and informative point cloud patches prior to mixing points and labels across domains. A point cloud patch corresponds to a subset of points of the same semantic class. To select patches from the source point cloud, we rely on the class frequency distribution by counting the number of points for each semantic class within $\mathcal{S}$. Unlike DSP [9], we do not select long-tail classes in advance, but we instead exploit the source distribution and the semantic classes available to dynamically sample classes at each iteration.

We define the class frequency distribution of $\mathcal{S}$ as $P^s_{\mathcal{Y}}$ and create a function f that randomly selects a subset of classes based on the labels $\tilde{\mathcal{Y}}^o \subset \mathcal{Y}^o$ for supervision at each iteration. The likelihood that f selects a class c is inversely proportional to its class frequency in $\mathcal{S}$. Specifically,

$$\tilde{\mathcal{Y}}^s = f(\mathcal{Y}^s, 1 - P^s_{\mathcal{Y}}, \alpha), \tag{1}$$

where α is an hyperparameter that regulates the ratio of selected classes for each point cloud. For example, by setting $\alpha = 0.5$, the algorithm will select a number of patches corresponding to the 50% of the classes available by sampling them based on their class frequency distribution, i.e., long-tailed classes will have a higher likelihood to be selected. We define the set of points that correspond to $\tilde{\mathcal{Y}}^s$ as $\tilde{\mathcal{X}}^s$, and a patch as the set of points $\tilde{\mathcal{X}}^s_c \subset \tilde{\mathcal{X}}^s$ that belong to class $c \in \mathcal{C}$.

To select patches from the target point clouds, we apply the same set of operations but using the pseudo-labels produced by the teacher network based on their prediction confidence. Specifically, we define a function g that selects reliable pseudo-labels based on their confidence value. The selected pseudo-labels are defined as

$$\tilde{\mathcal{Y}}^t = g(\Phi_{\theta'}(\mathcal{X}^t), \zeta), \tag{2}$$

where $\Phi_{\theta'}$ is the teacher network, ζ is the confidence threshold used by the function g and $\tilde{\mathcal{Y}}^t \subset \hat{\mathcal{Y}}^t$. We define the set of points that correspond to $\tilde{\mathcal{Y}}^t$ as $\tilde{\mathcal{X}}^t$.

3.2 Compositional Mix

The goal of our compositional mixing module is to create mixed point clouds based on the selected semantic patches. The compositional mix involves three consecutive operations: *local random augmentation*, patches are augmented randomly and independently from each other; *concatenation*, the augmented patches are concatenated to the point cloud of the other domain to create the mixed point cloud; *global random augmentation*, the mixed point cloud is randomly augmented. This module is applied twice, once for the $t \rightarrow s$ branch (top of Fig. 2), where target patches are mixed within the source point cloud, and once for the $s \rightarrow t$ branch (bottom of Fig. 2), where source patches are mixed within the target point cloud. Unlike Mix3D [19], our mixing strategy embeds data augmentation at local and global level.

In the $s \rightarrow t$ branch, we apply the local random augmentation h to all the points $\tilde{\mathcal{X}}^s_c \subset \tilde{\mathcal{X}}^s$. We repeat this operation for all $c \in \tilde{\mathcal{Y}}^s$. Note that h is a random augmentation that produces a different result each time it is applied to a set of points. Therefore, we define the result of this operation as

$$h(\tilde{\mathcal{X}}^s) = \left\{ h(\tilde{\mathcal{X}}^s_c), \forall c \in \tilde{\mathcal{Y}}^s \right\}. \tag{3}$$

Then, we concatenate $h(\tilde{\mathcal{X}}^s)$ with the source point cloud and apply the global random augmentation. Their respective labels are concatenated accordingly, such as

$$\mathcal{X}^{s \rightarrow t} = r(h(\tilde{\mathcal{X}}^s) \cup \mathcal{X}^t), \qquad \mathcal{Y}^{s \rightarrow t} = \tilde{\mathcal{Y}}^s \cup \mathcal{Y}^t, \tag{4}$$

where r is the global augmentation function. The same operations are also performed in the $t \rightarrow s$ branch by mixing target patches within the source point cloud. Instead of using source labels, we use the teacher network's pseudo-labels obtained from the target data and concatenate them with the labels of the source data. This results in $\mathcal{X}^{t \rightarrow s}$ and $\mathcal{Y}^{t \rightarrow s}$.

3.3 Network Update

We leverage the teacher-student learning scheme to facilitate the transfer of knowledge acquired during the course of the training with mixed domains. We use the teacher network $\Phi_{\theta'}$ to produce target pseudo-labels $\hat{\mathcal{Y}}^t$ for the student network Φ_θ, and train Φ_θ to segment target point clouds by using the mixed point clouds $\mathcal{X}^{s \rightarrow t}$ and $\mathcal{X}^{t \rightarrow s}$ based on their mixed labels and pseudo-labels (Sect. 3.2).

At each batch iteration, we update the student parameters Φ_θ to minimize a total objective loss $\mathcal{L}_{tot}$ defined as

$$\mathcal{L}_{tot} = \mathcal{L}_{s \rightarrow t} + \mathcal{L}_{t \rightarrow s}, \tag{5}$$

where $\mathcal{L}_{s \rightarrow t}$ and $\mathcal{L}_{t \rightarrow s}$ are the $s \rightarrow t$ and $t \rightarrow s$ branch losses, respectively. Given $\mathcal{X}^{s \rightarrow t}$ and $\mathcal{Y}^{s \rightarrow t}$, we define the segmentation loss for the $s \rightarrow t$ branch as

$$\mathcal{L}_{s \rightarrow t} = \mathcal{L}_{seg}(\Phi_\theta(\mathcal{X}^{s \rightarrow t}), \mathcal{Y}^{s \rightarrow t}), \tag{6}$$

the objective of which is to minimize the segmentation error over $\mathcal{X}^{s \to t}$, thus learning to segment source patches in the target domain. Similarly, given $\mathcal{X}^{t \to s}$ and $\mathcal{Y}^{t \to s}$, we define the segmentation loss for the $t \to s$ branch as

$$\mathcal{L}_{t \to s} = \mathcal{L}_{seg}(\Phi_\theta(\mathcal{X}^{t \to s}), \mathcal{Y}^{t \to s}), \tag{7}$$

whose objective is to minimize the segmentation error over $\mathcal{X}^{t \to s}$ where target patches are composed with source data. We implement $\mathcal{L}_{seg}$ as the Dice segmentation loss [14], which we found effective for the segmentation of large-scale point clouds as it can cope with long-tail classes well.

Lastly, we update the teacher parameters θ' every γ iterations following the exponential moving average (EMA) [9] approach

$$\theta'_i = \beta\theta'_{i-1} + (1 - \beta)\theta, \tag{8}$$

where i indicates the training iteration and β is a smoothing coefficient hyperparameter.

4 Experiments

We evaluate our method in the synthetic-to-real UDA scenario for LiDAR segmentation. We use the SynLiDAR dataset [32] as (synthetic) source domain, and the SemanticKITTI [1,3,10] and SemanticPOSS [20] datasets as (real) target domains (more details in Sect. 4.1). We describe CoSMix implementation in Sect. 4.2. We compare CoSMix with five state-of-the-art UDA methods: two general purpose adaptation methods (ADDA [26], Ent-Min [27]), one image segmentation method (ST [45]) and, two point cloud segmentation methods (PCT [32], ST-PCT [32]) (Sect. 4.3). Like [32], we compare CoSMix against methods working on 3D point clouds for synthetic to real, such as PCT [32] and ST-PCT [32]. These are the only two state-of-the-art methods for synthetic-to-real UDA that use 360° LiDAR point clouds. Results of baselines are taken from [32].

4.1 Datasets and Metrics

SynLiDAR [32] is a large-scale synthetic dataset that is captured with the Unreal Engine [8]. It is composed of 198,396 LiDAR scans with point-level segmentation annotations over 32 semantic classes. We follow the authors' instructions [32], and use 19,840 point clouds for training and 1,976 point clouds for validation.

SemanticPOSS [20] consists of 2,988 real-world scans with point-level annotations over 14 semantic classes. Based on the official benchmark guidelines [20], we use the sequence 03 for validation and the remaining sequences for training.

SemanticKITTI [3] is a large-scale segmentation dataset consisting of LiDAR acquisitions of the popular KITTI dataset [1,10]. It is composed of 43,552 scans captured in Karlsruhe (Germany) and point-level annotations over 19 semantic classes. Based on the official protocol [3], we use sequence 08 for validation and the remaining sequences for training.

Class Mapping. Like [32], we make source and target labels compatible across our datasets, i.e., SynLiDAR → SemanticPOSS and SynLiDAR → SemanticKITTI. We map SynLiDAR labels into 14 segmentation classes for SynLiDAR → SemanticPOSS and 19 segmentation classes for SynLiDAR → SemanticKITTI [32].

Metrics. We follow the typical evaluation protocol for UDA in 3D semantic segmentation [32] and evaluate the segmentation performance before and after adaptation. We compute the Intersection over the Union (IoU) [23] for each segmentation class and report the per-class IoU. Then, we average the IoU over all the segmented classes and report the mean Intersection over the Union (mIoU).

4.2 Implementation Details

We implemented CoSMix in PyTorch and run our experiments on 4×NVIDIA A100 (40 GB SXM4). We use MinkowskiNet as our point cloud segmentation network [6]. For a fair comparison, we use MinkUNet32 as in [32]. We use warm-up, i.e., our network is pre-trained on the source domain for 10 epochs with Dice loss [14] starting from randomly initialized weights. During the adaptation step, we initialize student and teacher networks with the parameters obtained after warm-up. The warm-up and adaptation stage share the same hyperparameters. In both the warm-up and adaptation steps, we use Stochastic Gradient Descent (SGD) with a learning rate of 0.001. We set α by analyzing the long-tailed classes in the source domain during adaptation. We experimentally found $\alpha = 50\%$ to be a good value in each task. In the target semantic selection function g, we set ζ such that about 80% of pseudo-labelled points per scene can be selected. On SynLiDAR→SemanticPOSS, we use a batch size of 12 and perform adaptation for 10 epochs. We set source semantic selection f with $\alpha = 0.5$ while target semantic selection g with a confidence threshold $\zeta = 0.85$ (Sect. 3.1). On SynLiDAR→SemanticKITTI, we use a batch size of 16, adapting for 3 epochs. During source semantic selection f we set $\alpha = 0.5$ while in target semantic selection g we use a confidence threshold of $\zeta = 0.90$. We use the same compositional mix (Sect. 3.2) parameters for both the adaptation directions. We implement the local augmentation h as rigid rotation around the z-axis, scaling along all the axes and random point downsampling. We bound rotations between $[-\pi/2, \pi/2]$ and scaling between $[0.95, 1.05]$, and perform random downsampling for 50% of the patch points. For global augmentation r, we use a rigid rotation, translation and scaling along all the three axes. We set r parameters to the same used in [6]. During the network update step (Sect. 3.3), we obtain the teacher parameters θ'_i with $\beta = 0.99$ every $\gamma = 1$ steps on SynLiDAR→SemanticPOSS and every $\gamma = 500$ steps on SynLiDAR→SemanticKITTI.

4.3 Quantitative Comparisons

Table 1 and Table 2 reports the adaptation results on SynLiDAR→Semantic POSS, and on SynLiDAR→SemanticKITTI, respectively. The Source model is the lower bound of each scenario with 20.7 mIoU on SynLiDAR→SemanticPOSS

Table 1. Adaptation results on SynLiDAR → SemanticPOSS. Source corresponds to the model trained on the source synthetic dataset (lower bound in gray). Results are reported in terms of mean Intersection over the Union (mIoU).

Model	pers.	rider	car	trunk	plants	traf.	pole	garb.	buil.	cone.	fence	bike	grou.	mIoU
Source	3.7	25.1	12.0	10.8	53.4	0.0	19.4	12.9	49.1	3.1	20.3	0.0	59.6	20.7
ADDA [26]	27.5	35.1	18.8	12.4	53.4	2.8	27.0	12.2	64.7	1.3	6.3	6.8	55.3	24.9
Ent-Min [27]	24.2	32.2	21.4	18.9	61.0	2.5	36.3	8.3	56.7	3.1	5.3	4.8	57.1	25.5
ST [45]	23.5	31.8	22.0	18.9	63.2	1.9	**41.6**	13.5	58.2	1.0	9.1	6.8	60.3	27.1
PCT [32]	13.0	35.4	13.7	10.2	53.1	1.4	23.8	12.7	52.9	0.8	13.7	1.1	66.2	22.9
ST-PCT [32]	28.9	34.8	27.8	18.6	63.7	4.9	41.0	16.6	64.1	1.6	12.1	6.6	63.9	29.6
CoSMix (ours)	**55.8**	**51.4**	**36.2**	**23.5**	**71.3**	**22.5**	34.2	**28.9**	**66.2**	**20.4**	**24.9**	**10.6**	**78.7**	**40.4**

Table 2. Adaptation results on SynLiDAR → SemanticKITTI. Source corresponds to the model trained on the source synthetic dataset (lower bound in gray). Results are reported in terms of mean Intersection over the Union (mIoU).

Model	car	bi.cle	mt.cle	truck	oth-v.	pers.	b.clst	m.clst	road	park.	sidew.	oth-g.	build.	fence	veget.	trunk	terra.	pole	traff.	mIoU
Source	42.0	5.0	4.8	0.4	2.5	12.4	43.3	1.8	48.7	4.5	31.0	0.0	18.6	11.5	60.2	30.0	48.3	19.3	3.0	20.4
ADDA [26]	52.5	4.5	11.9	0.3	3.9	9.4	27.9	0.5	52.8	4.9	27.4	0.0	61.0	17.0	57.4	34.5	42.9	23.2	4.5	23.0
Ent-Min [27]	58.3	5.1	14.3	0.3	1.8	14.3	**44.5**	0.5	50.4	4.3	34.8	0.0	48.3	19.7	67.5	34.8	**52.0**	33.0	6.1	25.8
ST [45]	62.0	5.0	12.4	1.3	9.2	16.7	44.2	0.4	53.0	2.5	28.4	0.0	57.1	18.7	69.8	**35.0**	48.7	32.5	6.9	26.5
PCT [32]	53.4	5.4	7.4	0.8	10.9	12.0	43.2	0.3	50.8	3.7	29.4	0.0	48.0	10.4	68.2	33.1	40.0	29.5	6.9	23.9
ST-PCT [32]	70.8	**7.3**	13.1	1.9	8.4	12.6	44.0	0.6	56.4	4.5	31.8	0.0	**66.7**	**23.7**	**73.3**	34.6	48.4	**39.4**	11.7	28.9
CoSMix (ours)	**75.1**	6.8	**29.4**	**27.1**	**11.1**	**22.1**	25.0	**24.7**	**79.3**	**14.9**	**46.7**	**0.1**	53.4	13.0	67.7	31.4	32.1	37.9	**13.4**	**32.2**

and 22.2 mIoU on SynLiDAR→SemanticKITTI. We highlight in gray the associated results in both tables. In SynLiDAR→SemanticPOSS (Table 1), CoSMix outperforms the baselines on all the classes, with the exception of *pole* where ST achieves better results. On average, we achieve 40.4 mIoU surpassing ST-PCT by +10.8 mIoU and improving over the Source of +19.7 mIoU. Interestingly, CoSMix improves also on difficult classes as in the case of *person*, *traffic-sign*, *cone* and, *bike*, whose performance were low before adaptation. SemanticKITTI is a more challenging domain as the validation sequence includes a wide range of different scenarios with a large number of semantic classes. In SynLiDAR→SemanticKITTI (Table 2), CoSMix improves on all the classes when compared to Source, with the exception of *bicyclist* and *terrain*. We relate this behaviour to the additional noise introduced by pseudo labels on these classes and in related classes such as *sidewalk*. Compared to the other baselines, CoSMix improves on 11 out of 19 classes, with a large margin in the classes *car*, *motorcycle*, *truck*, *person*, *road*, *parking* and *sidewalk*. On average, also in this more challenging scenario, we achieve the new state-of-the-art performance of 32.2 mIoU, outperforming ST-PCT by +3.3 mIoU and improving over Source of about +11.8 mIoU.

4.4 Qualitative Results

We report qualitative examples of the adaptation performance before (source) and after CoSMix adaptation (ours), and compare them to ground-truth annotations (gt). Figure 3 shows the adaptation results on SynLiDAR→SemanticPOSS,

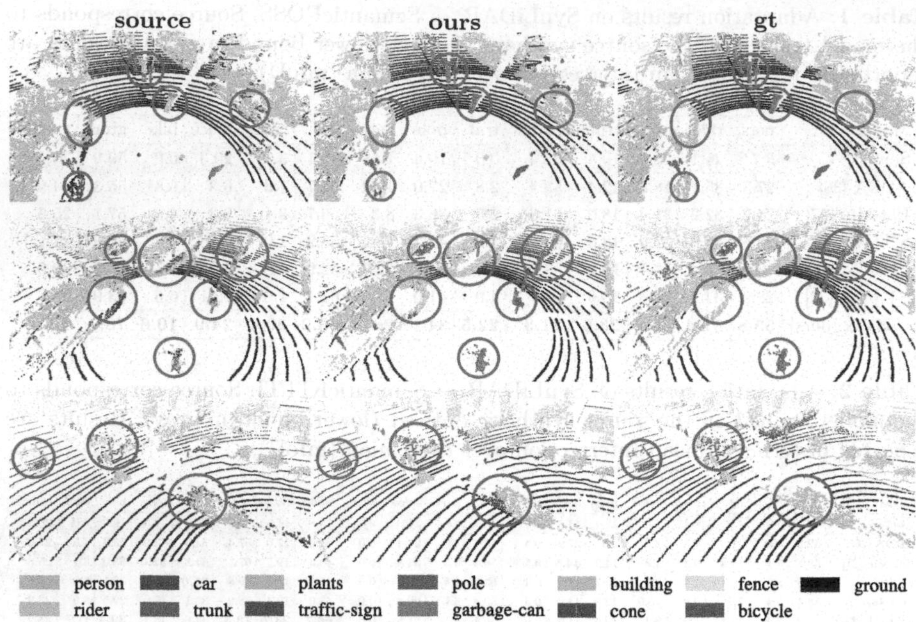

Fig. 3. Results on SynLiDAR→SemanticPOSS. Source predictions are often wrong and mingled in the same region. After adaptation, CoSMix improves segmentation with homogeneous predictions and correctly assigned classes. The red circles highlight regions with interesting results. (Color figure online)

while Fig. 4 show the results on SynLiDAR→SemanticKITTI. Red circles highlight regions with interesting results. In Fig. 3, improvements are visible in multiple regions of the examples. Source predictions are often not homogeneous with completely wrong regions. After adaptation, CoSMix improves segmentation with more homogeneous regions and correctly assigned classes. In Fig. 4, source predictions are less sparse but wrong for several spatial regions. After adaptation, CoSMix allows better and correct predictions. Additional examples can be found in the Supplementary Material.

5 Ablation Study

We perform an ablation study of CoSMix by using the SynLiDAR → SemanticPOSS setup. We compare our mixing approach with a recent point cloud mixing strategy [19] by applying it to the synthetic-to-real setting (Sect. 5.2). In Sect. 5.3, we investigate the importance of confidence threshold in CoSMix.

5.1 Method Components

We analyze CoSMix by organizing its components into three groups: mixing strategies (*mix*), augmentations (*augs*) and other components (*others*). In the

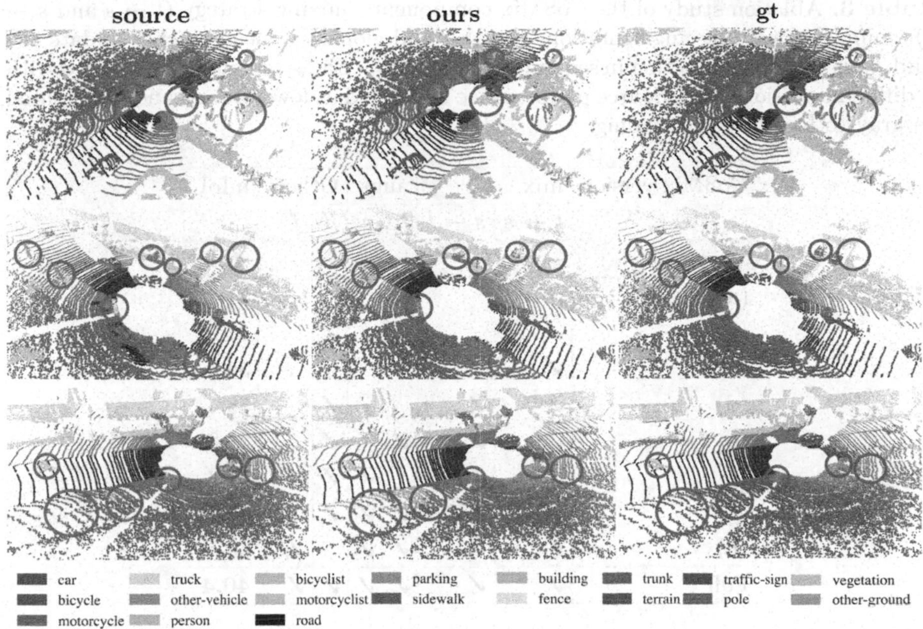

Fig. 4. Results on SynLiDAR→SemanticKITTI. Source predictions are often wrong and mingled in the same region. After adaptation, CoSMix improves segmentation with homogeneous predictions and correctly assigned classes. The red circles highlight regions with interesting results. (Color figure online)

mix group, we assess the importance of the mixing strategies ($t \rightarrow s$ and $s \rightarrow t$) used in our compositional mix (Sect. 3.2) after semantic selection. In the *augs* group, we assess the importance of the local h and global r augmentations that are used in the compositional mix (Sect. 3.2). In the *others* group, we assess the importance of the mean teacher update (β) (Sect. 3.3) and of the long-tail weighted sampling f (Sect. 3.1). When the $t \rightarrow s$ branch is active, also the pseudo-label filtering g is utilized, while when f is not active, $\alpha = 0.5$ source classes are selected randomly. With different combinations of components, we obtain different versions of CoSMix which we name CoSMix (a–h). The complete version of our method is named *Full*, where all the components are activated. The Source performance (Source) is also added as a reference for the lower bound. See Table 3 for the definition of these different versions.

When the $t \rightarrow s$ branch is used, CoSMix (a) achieves an initial 31.6 mIoU showing that the $t \rightarrow s$ branch provides a significant adaptation contribution over the Source. When we also use the $s \rightarrow t$ branch and the mean teacher β, CoSMix (b–d) further improve performance achieving a 35.4 mIoU. By introducing local and global augmentations in CoSMix (e–h), we can improve performance up to 39.1 mIoU. The best performance of 40.4 mIoU is achieved with CoSMix Full where all the components are activated.

Table 3. Ablation study of the CoSMix components: mixing strategy ($t \rightarrow s$ and $s \rightarrow t$), compositional mix augmentations (local h and global r), mean teacher update (β) and, weighted class selection in semantic selection (f). Each combination is named with a different version (a-h). Source performance are added as lower bound and highlighted in gray to facilitate the reading.

CoSMix version	mix		augs		Others		mIoU
	$t \rightarrow s$	$s \rightarrow t$	h	r	β	f	
Source	–	–	–	–	–	–	20.7
(a)	✓						31.6
(b)	✓				✓		31.9
(c)	✓	✓					35.0
(d)	✓	✓			✓		35.4
(e)	✓	✓	✓		✓		36.8
(f)	✓	✓		✓	✓		37.3
(g)	✓	✓	✓	✓	✓		39.0
(h)	✓	✓	✓	✓		✓	39.1
Full	✓	✓	✓	✓	✓	✓	**40.4**

5.2 Point Cloud Mix

We compare CoSMix with Mix3D [19] and PointCutMix [39] to show the effectiveness of the different mixing designs. As per our knowledge, Mix3D [19] is the only mixup strategy designed for 3D semantic segmentation, while PointCutMix is the only strategy for mixing portions of different point clouds. We implement Mix3D [19] and PointCutMix [39] based on authors descriptions: we concatenate point clouds (random crops for PointCutMix) of the two domains, i.e., $\mathcal{X}^s$ and $\mathcal{X}^t$, as well as their labels and pseudo-labels, i.e., $\mathcal{Y}^s$ and $\hat{\mathcal{Y}}^t$, respectively. CoSMix double is our two-branch network with sample mixing. For a fair comparison, we deactivate the weighted sampling and the mean teacher update. We keep local and global augmentations (h and r) activated.

Figure 5 shows that Mix3D [19] outperforms the Source model, achieving 28.5 mIoU, while PointCutMix [5] achieves 31.6 mIoU. When we use the $t \rightarrow s$ branch alone we can achieve 32.9 mIoU and when we use the $s \rightarrow t$ branch alone, CoSMix can further improve the results, achieving 34.8 mIoU. This shows that the supervision from the source to target is effective for adaptation on the target domain. When we use the contribution from both branches simultaneously, CoSMix achieves the best result with 38.9 mIoU.

5.3 Pseudo Label Filtering

We investigate the robustness of CoSMix to increasingly noisier pseudo-labels and study the importance of setting the correct confidence threshold ζ for

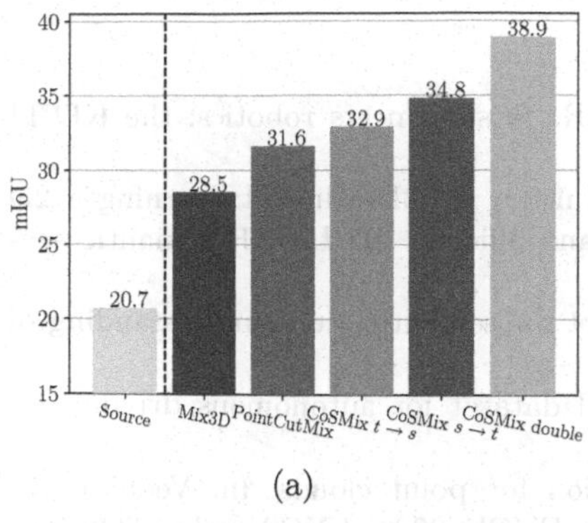

(a)

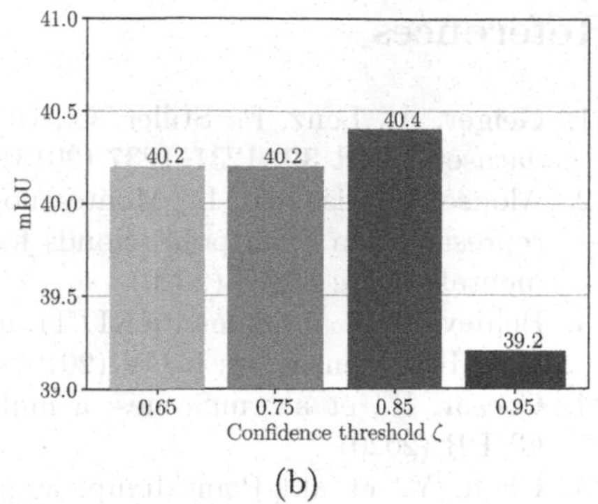

(b)

Fig. 5. Comparison of the adaptation performance with (a) different point cloud mix up strategies and (b) on confidence threshold values. (a) Compared to the recent mixing strategy Mix3D [19], our mixing strategy and its variations achieve superior performance. (b) Adaptation results show that ζ should be set such that to achieve a trade-off between pseudo-label correctness and object completeness.

pseudo-label distillation in g (Sect. 3.1). We repeat the experiments with a confidence threshold from 0.65 to 0.95 and report the obtained adaptation performance in Fig. 5. CoSMix is robust to noisy pseudo-labels reaching a 40.2 mIoU with the low threshold of 0.65. The best adaptation performance of 40.4 mIoU is achieved with a confidence threshold of 0.85. By using a high confidence threshold of 0.95 performance is affected reaching 39.2 mIoU. With this configuration, too few pseudo-labels are selected to provide an effective contribution for the adaptation.

6 Conclusions

In this paper, we proposed the first UDA method for 3D semantic segmentation based on a novel 3D point cloud mixing strategy that exploits semantic and structural information concurrently. We performed an extensive evaluation in the synthetic-to-real UDA scenario by using large-scale publicly available LiDAR datasets. Experiments showed that our method outperforms all the compared state-of-the-art methods by a large margin. Furthermore, in-depth studies highlighted the importance of each CoSMix component and that our mixing strategy is beneficial for solving domain shift in 3D LiDAR segmentation. Future research directions may include the introduction of self-supervised learning tasks and the extension of CoSMix to source-free adaptation tasks.

Acknowledgements. This work was partially supported by OSRAM GmbH, by the Italian Ministry of Education, Universities and Research (MIUR) "Dipartimenti di Eccellenza 2018–2022", by the EU JPI/CH SHIELD project, by the PRIN project PREVUE (Prot. 2017N2RK7K), the EU ISFP PROTECTOR (101034216) project and the EU H2020 MARVEL (957337) project and, it was carried out in the Vision and Learning joint laboratory of FBK and UNITN.

References

1. Geiger, A., Lenz, P., Stiller, C., Urtasun, R.: Vision meets robotics: the KITTI dataset. IJRR **32**, 1231–1237 (2013)
2. Alonso, I., Riazuelo, L., Montesano, L., Murillo, A.: 3D-MiniNet: learning a 2D representation from point clouds for fast and efficient 3D LiDAR semantic segmentation. In: IROS (2020)
3. Behley, J., et al.: SemanticKITTI: a dataset for semantic scene understanding of LiDAR sequences. In: ICCV (2019)
4. Caesar, H., et al.: nuScenes: a multimodal dataset for autonomous driving. In: CVPR (2020)
5. Chen, Y., et al.: PointMixup: augmentation for point clouds. In: Vedaldi, A., Bischof, H., Brox, T., Frahm, J.-M. (eds.) ECCV 2020. LNCS, vol. 12348, pp. 330–345. Springer, Cham (2020). https://doi.org/10.1007/978-3-030-58580-8_20
6. Choy, C., Gwak, J., Savarese, S.: 4D Spatio-temporal ConvNets: Minkowski convolutional neural networks. In: CVPR (2019)
7. Csurka, G.: Domain adaptation for visual applications: a comprehensive survey. arXiv (2017)
8. Dosovitskiy, A., Ros, G., Codevilla, F., Lopez, A., Koltun, V.: CARLA: an open urban driving simulator. In: ACRL (2017)
9. Gao, L., Zhang, J., Zhang, L., Tao, D.: DSP: dual soft-paste for unsupervised domain adaptive semantic segmentation. In: ACMM (2021)
10. Geiger, A., Lenz, P., Urtasun, R.: Are we ready for autonomous driving? The KITTI vision benchmark suite. In: CVPR (2012)
11. Graham, B., Engelcke, M., van der Maaten, L.: 3D semantic segmentation with submanifold sparse convolutional networks. In: CVPR (2018)
12. Graham, B., van der Maaten, L.: Submanifold sparse convolutional networks. arXiv (2017)
13. Hu, Q., et al.: RandLA-Net: efficient semantic segmentation of large-scale point clouds. In: CVPR (2020)
14. Jadon, S.: A survey of loss functions for semantic segmentation. In: CIBCB (2020)
15. Jaritz, M., Vu, T.H., de Charette, R., Wirbel, E., Pérez, P.: xMUDA: cross-modal unsupervised domain adaptation for 3D semantic segmentation. In: CVPR (2020)
16. Langer, F., Milioto, A., Haag, A., Behley, J., Stachniss, C.: Domain transfer for semantic segmentation of LiDAR data using deep neural networks. In: IROS (2021)
17. Mancini, M., Akata, Z., Ricci, E., Caputo, B.: Towards recognizing unseen categories in unseen domains. In: Vedaldi, A., Bischof, H., Brox, T., Frahm, J.-M. (eds.) ECCV 2020. LNCS, vol. 12368, pp. 466–483. Springer, Cham (2020). https://doi.org/10.1007/978-3-030-58592-1_28
18. Milioto, A., Vizzo, I., Behley, J., Stachniss, C.: RangeNet++: fast and accurate LiDAR semantic segmentation. In: IROS (2019)
19. Nekrasov, A., Schult, J., Litany, O., Leibe, B., Engelmann, F.: Mix3D: out-of-context data augmentation for 3D scenes. In: 3DV (2021)
20. Pan, Y., Gao, B., Mei, J., Geng, S., Li, C., Zhao, H.: SemanticPOSS: a point cloud dataset with large quantity of dynamic instances. arXiv (2020)
21. Qi, C., Su, H., Mo, K., Guibas, L.: PointNet: deep learning on point sets for 3D classification and segmentation. In: CVPR (2017)
22. Qi, C., Yi, L., Su, H., Guibas, L.: PointNet++: deep hierarchical feature learning on point sets in a metric space. arXiv (2017)

23. Rahman, M.A., Wang, Y.: Optimizing intersection-over-union in deep neural networks for image segmentation. In: Bebis, G., et al. (eds.) ISVC 2016. LNCS, vol. 10072, pp. 234–244. Springer, Cham (2016). https://doi.org/10.1007/978-3-319-50835-1_22
24. Ronneberger, O., Fischer, P., Brox, T.: U-Net: convolutional networks for biomedical image segmentation. In: Navab, N., Hornegger, J., Wells, W.M., Frangi, A.F. (eds.) MICCAI 2015. LNCS, vol. 9351, pp. 234–241. Springer, Cham (2015). https://doi.org/10.1007/978-3-319-24574-4_28
25. Tranheden, W., Olsson, V., Pinto, J., Svensson, L.: DACS: domain adaptation via cross-domain mixed sampling. In: WACV (2021)
26. Tzeng, E., Hoffman, J., Saenko, K., Darrell, T.: Adversarial discriminative domain adaptation. In: CVPR (2017)
27. Vu, T., Jain, H., Bucher, M., Cord, M., Pérez, P.: ADVENT: adversarial entropy minimization for domain adaptation in semantic segmentation. In: CVPR (2019)
28. Wang, Q., Dai, D., Hoyer, L., Gool, L.V., Fink, O.: Domain adaptive semantic segmentation with self-supervised depth estimation. In: ICCV (2021)
29. Wu, B., Wan, A., Yue, X., Keutzer, K.: SqueezeSeg: convolutional neural nets with recurrent CRF for real-time road-object segmentation from 3D LiDAR point cloud. In: ICRA (2018)
30. Wu, B., Zhou, X., Zhao, S., Yue, X., Keutzer, K.: SqueezeSegV2: improved model structure and unsupervised domain adaptation for road-object segmentation from a LiDAR point cloud. In: ICRA (2019)
31. Wu, Y., Inkpen, D., El-Roby, A.: Dual mixup regularized learning for adversarial domain adaptation. In: Vedaldi, A., Bischof, H., Brox, T., Frahm, J.-M. (eds.) ECCV 2020. LNCS, vol. 12374, pp. 540–555. Springer, Cham (2020). https://doi.org/10.1007/978-3-030-58526-6_32
32. Xiao, A., Huang, J., Guan, D., Zhan, F., Lu, S.: SynLiDAR: learning from synthetic LiDAR sequential point cloud for semantic segmentation. In: AAAI (2022)
33. Xu, M., et al.: Adversarial domain adaptation with domain mixup. In: AAAI (2020)
34. Yang, Y., Soatto, S.: FDA: Fourier domain adaptation for semantic segmentation. In: CVPR (2020)
35. Yi, L., Gong, B., Funkhouser, T.: Complete and label: a domain adaptation approach to semantic segmentation of LiDAR point clouds. arXiv (2021)
36. Yun, S., Han, D., Oh, S.J., Chun, S., Choe, J., Yoo, Y.: CutMix: regularization strategy to train strong classifiers with localizable features. In: ICCV (2019)
37. Zhou, Y., Tuzel, O.: VoxelNet: end-to-end learning for point cloud based 3D object detection. In: CVPR (2018)
38. Zhang, H., Cisse, M., Dauphin, Y., Lopez-Paz, D.: Mixup: beyond empirical risk minimization. In: ICLR (2018)
39. Zhang, J., et al.: PointCutMix: regularization strategy for point cloud classification. arXiv (2021)
40. Zhang, Y., et al.: PolarNet: an improved grid representation for online LiDAR point clouds semantic segmentation. In: CVPR (2020)
41. Zhao, S., et al.: ePointDA: an end-to-end simulation-to-real domain adaptation framework for LiDAR point cloud segmentation. arXiv (2020)
42. Zhu, X., et al.: Cylindrical and asymmetrical 3D convolution networks for LiDAR segmentation. In: CVPR (2021)
43. Zou, L., Tang, H., Chen, K., Jia, K.: Geometry-aware self-training for unsupervised domain adaptation on object point clouds. In: CVPR (2021)

44. Zou, Y., Yu, Z., Vijaya Kumar, B.V.K., Wang, J.: Unsupervised domain adaptation for semantic segmentation via class-balanced self-training. In: Ferrari, V., Hebert, M., Sminchisescu, C., Weiss, Y. (eds.) ECCV 2018. LNCS, vol. 11207, pp. 297–313. Springer, Cham (2018). https://doi.org/10.1007/978-3-030-01219-9_18
45. Zou, Y., Yu, Z., Liu, X., Kumar, B., Wang, J.: Confidence regularized self-training. In: ICCV (2019)

A Unified Framework for Domain Adaptive Pose Estimation

Donghyun Kim[2(✉)], Kaihong Wang[1], Kate Saenko[1,2], Margrit Betke[1], and Stan Sclaroff[1]

[1] Image and Video Computing, Department of Computer Science, Boston University, Boston, USA
{kaiwkh,saenko,betke,sclaroff}@bu.edu
[2] MIT-IBM Watson AI Lab, Cambridge, USA
donhk@bu.edu

Abstract. While pose estimation is an important computer vision task, it requires expensive annotation and suffers from domain shift. In this paper, we investigate the problem of domain adaptive 2D pose estimation that transfers knowledge learned on a synthetic source domain to a target domain without supervision. While several domain adaptive pose estimation models have been proposed recently, they are not generic but only focus on either human pose or animal pose estimation, and thus their effectiveness is somewhat limited to specific scenarios. In this work, we propose a unified framework that generalizes well on various domain adaptive pose estimation problems. We propose to align representations using both input-level and output-level cues (pixels and pose labels, respectively), which facilitates the knowledge transfer from the source domain to the unlabeled target domain. Our experiments show that our method achieves state-of-the-art performance under various domain shifts. Our method outperforms existing baselines on human pose estimation by up to 4.5 percent points (pp), hand pose estimation by up to 7.4 pp, and animal pose estimation by up to 4.8 pp for dogs and 3.3 pp for sheep. These results suggest that our method is able to mitigate domain shift on diverse tasks and even unseen domains and objects (*e.g.*, trained on horse and tested on dog). Our code will be publicly available at: https://github.com/VisionLearningGroup/UDA_PoseEstimation.

Keywords: Unsupervised domain adaptation · Pose estimation · Semi-supervised learning · Transfer learning

1 Introduction

Recent developments in dense prediction tasks, *e.g.*, semantic segmentation [1,4,26,33] or pose estimation [30,36,42], are limited by the difficulty in the

D. Kim and K. Wang—Equal Contribution.

Supplementary Information The online version contains supplementary material available at https://doi.org/10.1007/978-3-031-19827-4_35.

S. Avidan et al. (Eds.): ECCV 2022, LNCS 13693, pp. 603–620, 2022.
https://doi.org/10.1007/978-3-031-19827-4_35

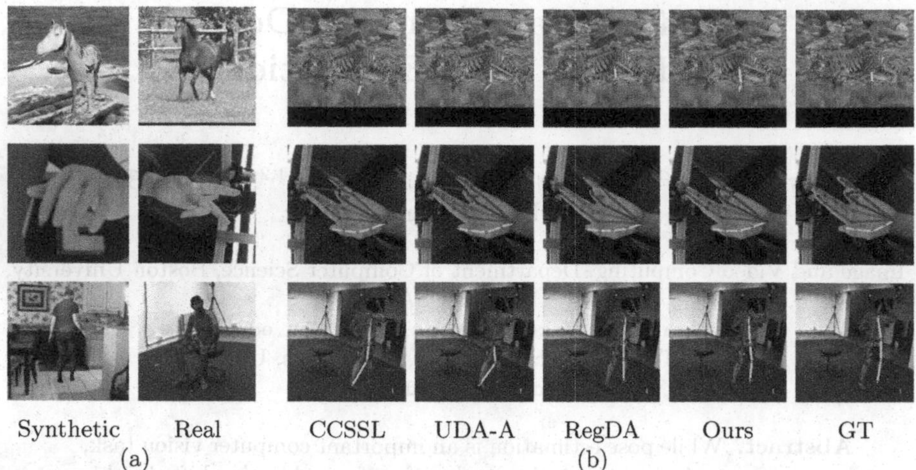

Fig. 1. (a) Top row: An example of high input-level variance in animal pose estimation benchmarks (large color and textual differences). Middle and bottom row: An example of high output-level variance in human and hand pose estimation benchmarks (large pose differences). (b) Visualization of pose estimation results from baselines, our method and ground-truth (GT). Note that both CCSSL and UDA-Animal (UDA-A) are proposed for animal pose estimation, while RegDA is only validated on hand and human pose estimation tasks. Most baseline methods suffer from performance degradation when applied to the other task. In comparison, our unified framework can more accurately estimate poses of hand, human and animal under various scenarios

acquisition of massive datasets [5,6,10,16] due to the expensiveness as well as the unreliability that originates from the annotation phase. In addition, these models often perform poorly under domain shift. In this work, we address the problem of 2D pose estimation in the unsupervised domain adaptation (UDA) setting. The UDA setting allows us to train a pose estimation model with supervision from synthetic (source) domains, where data and accurate annotations are much cheaper to acquire, and optimize the model's performance on an unlabeled real (target) domain. Nevertheless, the domain gap between source and target domains due to distributional shift greatly undermines the ability of the model to transfer learned knowledge across different domains. This is a challenge that has been addressed previously for UDA for classificational tasks [14,25,27,34].

Less attention has been paid to using UDA for regression tasks such as 2D pose estimation. Existing works are not generic but specifically target human pose estimation (RegDA [17]) or animal pose estimation (CCSSL [29], UDA-Animal [23]). A reason for this specialization may be the nature of the particular datasets used in those benchmarks. Animal datasets typically show large input-level variance (Fig. 1(a) top) while human and hand datasets show large output-level variance (Fig. 1(a) middle and bottom). Therefore, existing UDA methods do not generalize well to different objects of interest, for example, training and testing a human pose estimation model on an animal species or vice versa.

To address the aforementioned problems and keep the framework model-agnostic, we propose to bridge the domain gap via both input-level and output-level adaptations, *i.e.*, alignments across domains in both the input and the output space of a pose estimation model. In input-level adaptation, we first translate images through a pre-trained style transfer model [15] that can extract similar visual features and bridge the gap between domains. In output-level adaptation, we borrow the architecture of Mean Teacher [8,37] that enforces consistency in the output space of a student and a teacher model to generate reliable pseudo labels and learn from the unlabeled target domain.

As a typical approach for pose estimation, heatmap regression [38] predicts probabilities of the presence of keypoints in 2D space. However, unlike the output probabilities from other classification models that represent relative significance in the output space and sum to 1, the output heatmaps from a pose estimation model, which learns the task as predicting absolute value, are not normalized. The learning objectives of the student model, guided by the non-normalized output from the teacher model, will then be diverted from learning relative significance in the heatmap to learning absolute values, which is a more challenging task as the output space is no longer constrained. Therefore, the stability of the consistency learning is greatly undermined, and the lack of constraints leads to a problem we identify as a drift effect. Meanwhile, the drifted output heatmap also poses challenges while selecting confident guidance from the teacher model via the confidence thresholding method in Mean Teacher, as it potentially brings in noise that further deteriorates unsupervised learning. Therefore, we propose to normalize the output of the teacher model to make the guidance more stable. Our empirical results demonstrate the importance of this simple yet crucial step to deploy the Mean Teacher model for regression tasks.

In addition to revising consistency learning for the regression task, we design differing self-guiding strategies for student and teacher, developed especially for domain adaptive pose estimation. With style transfer, we generate target-like images from the source images and train a model to minimize the supervised loss with source labels. For the target domain, we generate source-like images from the target images to generate high-quality pseudo-labels from the teacher and give better guidance to the student model. In addition, in the student branch, we adaptively apply an occlusion mechanism, which has shown promising effectiveness especially in pose estimation tasks [7,19,43], based on the feedback of the teacher model. This strengthens the robustness of the pose estimation model.

In experiments we validate the effectiveness and generalization ability of our method under various scenarios including hand and human pose estimation as well as animal pose estimation. Our results show significant improvements over the existing domain adaptive pose estimation baselines by up to 4.5 percent point (pp) on hand pose, 7.4 pp on human pose estimation, and 4.8 pp for dog as well as 3.3 pp for sheep on animal pose estimation. Additionally, we present generalization experiments where we test models on unseen datasets or categories (*i.e.*, different animals), and verify the generalization capability. Further sensitivity analysis and ablation studies reveal the relation and interaction between modules and explain the effectiveness of each component of our unified framework. To summarize, our contributions in this work include:

- Unlike prior works, we propose a unified framework for general pose estimation that generalizes well on diverse objects in the pose estimation task.
- We propose a multi-level (*i.e.*, input-level and output-level) alignment method for domain adaptive pose estimation that can effectively address domain gap problems in different levels under different scenarios (*e.g.*, Fig. 1(a)).
- We address the drifting problem in the Mean Teacher paradigm and facilitate its learning from unlabeled data especially for pose estimation tasks.
- We unified benchmarks from human pose estimation and animal pose estimation in this work and present state-of-the-art performance in general pose estimation, providing a stronger baseline in this line of research.

2 Related Works

2.1 Pose Estimation

Pose estimation has become an active research topic for years. In this paper, we focus on 2D pose estimation. Hourglass [30] is one of the dominant approaches for human pose estimation which applies an encoder-decoder style network with residual modules and finally generate heatmaps. A mean-squared error loss is applied between the predicted heatmap and ground-truth heatmap consisting of a 2D Gaussian centered on the annotated joint location [38]. Xiao *et al.* [42] propose a simple baseline model that combines upsampling and deconvolutional layers without using residual modules. HRNet [36] is proposed to maintain high-resolution in the model and achieves promising results. In this paper, we adopt the architecture of the Simple baseline model [42] following [17] to fairly compare our method with prior domain adaptation algorithms.

2.2 Unsupervised Domain Adaptation

Unsupervised Domain Adaptation (UDA) aims to bridge the domain gap between a labeled source domain and unlabeled target domain. Existing domain adaptation methods utilize adversarial learning [9,28], minimize feature distances using MMD [11], optimal transport [2], pixel-level adaptation [13], or maximum classifier discrepancy [34] for classification. In addition several other UDA methods have been proposed for dense prediction tasks including semantic segmentation [14,25,39,44] and depth estimation [21,22,32]. Compared to other visual tasks, domain adaptation for regression tasks are still not well explored.

2.3 Domain Adaptive Pose Estimation

There are two categories in domain adaptation pose estimation: (1) For human pose estimation, RegDA [17] made changes in MDD [45] for human and hand pose estimation tasks, which measures discrepancy by estimating false predictions on the target domain. (2) For animal pose estimation, pseudo-labeling based approaches have been proposed in [23,29]. Mu *et al.* [29] proposed invariance and equivariance consistency learning with respect to transformations as

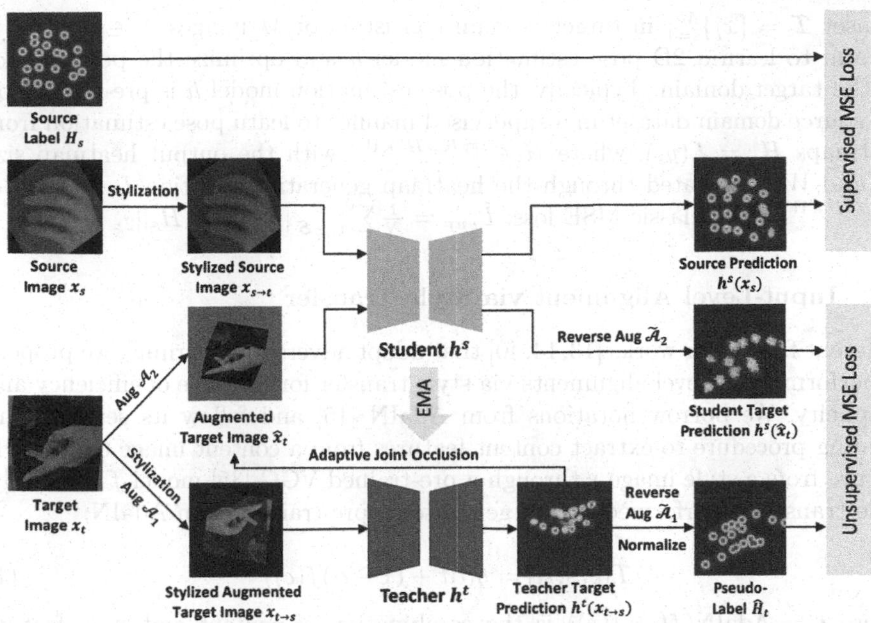

Fig. 2. An overview of our unified framework comprising a supervised branch that learns from source domain data with corresponding annotation, as well as an unsupervised branch that learns from unlabeled target domain data. We perform domain alignment both in the input-level via style-transfer with style references from the opposite domain, and the output-level of the model that guides the training on the target domain with more reliable pseudo-labels. The student model is trained by the combination of two losses, while the teacher model is updated with the exponential moving average weights of the student

well as temporal consistency learning with a video. Li *et al.* [23] proposed a refinement module and a self-feedback loop to obtain reliable pseudo labels. Besides, WS-CDA [3] leverages human pose data and a partially annotated animal pose dataset to perform semi-supervised domain adaptation. In our experiments, we observed that (1) and (2) do not work well on the other tasks. A likely cause could be that each estimation task has different types of domain shifts, as shown in Fig. 1(a). To address this, we propose a unified framework that generalizes well on diverse tasks by utilizing both input-level and out-level cues.

3 Method

3.1 Preliminaries

Given a labeled pose dataset $\mathcal{S} = \{(x_s^i, y_s^i)\}_{i=1}^N$ in source domain consisting of N pairs of images $x_s \in \mathbb{R}^{H\times W\times 3}$ and corresponding annotation heatmap $y_s \in \mathbb{R}^{K\times 2}$ representing the coordinates of K keypoints, as well as an unlabeled pose dataset $\mathcal{T} = \{x_t^i\}_{i=1}^M$ in target domain consisting of M images $x_t \in \mathbb{R}^{H \times W \times 3}$, we aim to learn a 2D pose estimation model h and optimize the performance on the target domain. Typically, the pose estimation model h is pre-trained on the source domain dataset in a supervised manner to learn pose estimation from heatmaps $H_s = L(y_s)$, where $H \in \mathbb{R}^{K \times H' \times W'}$ with the output heatmap size H' and W', generated through the heatmap generating function $L : \mathbb{R}^{K \times 2} \rightarrow \mathbb{R}^{K \times H' \times W'}$, with classic MSE loss: $L_{sup} = \frac{1}{N} \sum_{x_s \in \mathcal{S}} ||h(x_s) - H_s||_2$.

3.2 Input-Level Alignment via Style Transfer

Different from prior works [13,14,40] that adopt adversarial learning, we propose to perform input-level alignments via style transfer for the sake of efficiency and simplicity. We borrow notations from AdaIN [15] and follow its settings and training procedure to extract content features from a content image c and style feature from a style image s through a pre-trained VGG [35] model f. Formally, style transfer is performed with a generator g pre-trained as in AdaIN:

$$T(c, s, \alpha) = g(\alpha t + (1 - \alpha) f(c)) \tag{1}$$

where $t = \text{AdaIN}(f(c), f(s))$ is the combination of content and style feature through adaptive instance normalization and α is the content-style trade-off parameter. Exemplar results are illustrated in the appendix. With a fixed AdaIN model, we transform source domain images with styles from target domain $x_{s \rightarrow t} = T(x_s, x_t, \alpha)$ and revise the supervised loss above:

$$L_{sup} = \frac{1}{N} \sum_{x_s \in \mathcal{S}} ||h(x_{s \rightarrow t}) - H_s||_2 \tag{2}$$

3.3 Output-Level Alignment via Mean Teacher

To better exploit information from the unlabeled target domain, we adopt the paradigm of Mean Teacher that trains a student pose estimation model h^s by the guidance produced by its self-ensemble, i.e., the teacher pose estimation model h^t in an unsupervised learning branch. The input image for each model is augmented by $\mathcal{A}_1$ and $\mathcal{A}_2$ stochastically sampled from data augmentation $\mathcal{A}$. While the student h^s is updated according to the supervised loss in Eq. 2 and self-guidance from the teacher h^t, the weights of the latter are updated as the estimated moving average of the former.

On the opposite direction to the supervised learning branch that transforms the source image to the target domain, we also propose to transform the target domain image back to the direction of the source domain where supervised learning happens and bridge the domain gap when generating guidance from the teacher model. Formally, we take a source domain image as the style reference and generate $x_{t \rightarrow s} = T(\mathcal{A}_1(x_t), x_s, \alpha)$. After that, we pass the transformed image through the teacher model and get corresponding heatmap $H_t = h^t(x_{t \rightarrow s})$.

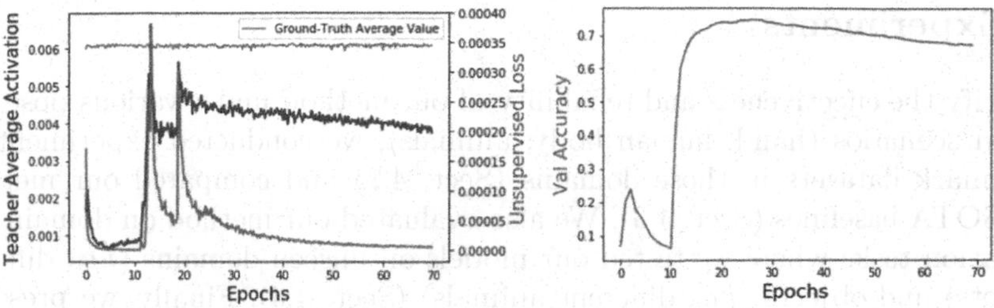

Fig. 3. Drift effect and its influence to the consistency learning. In the left plot, the gray curve represents the averaged value of the ground-truth heatmap. We observe that the averaged activation of teacher's output (blue curve) gradually decreases and drift away from the gray curve while minimizing the unsupervised loss (red curve). This leads to a degradation in accuracy as shown in the right plot (Color figure online)

With the generated guidance heatmap from the teacher model, we still need to address the drifting effect that brings in instability in the unsupervised learning, as illustrated in Fig. 3. Technically, we generate pseudo-labels $\hat{H}_t = L(\hat{y}_t)$ with the positions that produce maximum activation $\hat{y}_t = \arg\max_p H_t^{:,p}$ from each keypoints of the guidance heatmap to normalize the heatmap. We also revise the typical thresholding mechanism using a fixed value in Mean Teacher and determine the confidence threshold τ_{conf} with the top $p\%$-th values among maximum activation from each keypoint to exclude noises and further improve the quality of the self-guidance.

In addition to improving the quality of the teacher's prediction, we also seek to challenge the student model by adaptively occluding the input to the student model according to feedback from the teacher. To be more specific, we mask the regions where the teacher model makes confident prediction of a keypoint with activation greater than τ_{occ} via an occlusion operation: $\hat{x}_t = O(\mathcal{A}_2(x_t), \tau_{occ})$, and let the student to learn robust prediction based on its contextual correlation with other keypoints from teacher's pseudo-label after reversing augmentations $\tilde{\mathcal{A}}_1$ and $\tilde{\mathcal{A}}_2$. Overall, the student model h^s will be guided by the normalized heatmap $\hat{H}_t$ via an unsupervised learning loss on keypoints k producing maximum activation $H_t^{k,\hat{y}_t}$ greater than or equal to threshold τ_{conf}:

$$L_{unsup} = \frac{1}{M} \sum_{x_t \in \mathcal{T}} \sum_{k=0}^{K} \mathbb{1}(H_t^{k,\hat{y}_t} \geq \tau_{conf}) || \tilde{\mathcal{A}}_1(\hat{H}_t{}^k) - \tilde{\mathcal{A}}_2(h^s(\hat{x}_t)^k) ||_2 \quad (3)$$

Combining our supervised learning loss from Eq. 2 and unsupervised learning loss from Eq. 3, we present the illustration for the overall pipeline in Fig. 2 and the final learning objectives:

$$L = L_{sup} + \lambda L_{unsup} \quad (4)$$

4 Experiments

To verify the effectiveness and reliability of our method under various pose estimation scenarios (hand, human body, animals), we conducted experiments on benchmark datasets in those domains (Sect. 4.2) and compared our methods with SOTA baselines (Sect. 4.3). We also evaluated our method on domain generalization tasks where we tested our models on unseen domains (*i.e.*, different datasets) and objects (*i.e.*, different animals) (Sect. 4.4). Finally, we present a sensitivity analysis on hyper-parameters and ablation studies to analyze the contribution and interaction between each component in our paradigm (Sects. 4.5 and 4.6).

4.1 Experiment Protocols

We adopted the architecture of Simple Baseline [42] as our pose estimation model for both h^s and h^t, with backbone of pre-trained ResNet101 [12]. Following Simple Baseline and RegDA, we adopted Adam [20] as the optimizer and set the base learning rate as 1e−4. It decreased to 1e−5 at 45 epochs and 1e−6 at 60 epochs, while the whole training procedure consisted of 70 epochs. The batch size was set to 32 and there are in total 500 iterations for each epoch. The confidence thresholding ratio p is 0.5, while the occlusion thresholding value τ_{occ} is 0.9. The momentum η for the update of the teacher model is 0.999 and the unsupervised learning weight was set to 1 to balance the supervised and unsupervised loss to a similar level. Also, the model was only trained by the supervised loss on the source domain for the first 40 epochs. On the basis of augmentation in RegDA, we added rotation (−30°, 30°) and random 2D translation (−5%, 5%) for the input source and target domain images. Finally, it should be noted that we used the same hyper-parameters for all experiments, did not tune the number of training epochs on test sets, and always report the accuracy of models from the last epoch. As for the architecture and optimization procedure of the style transfer model, we follow settings in AdaIN, except that we pre-train the model bidirectionally, i.e., both source and target domain image can be a content or a style image. Additional details can be found in the appendix.

4.2 Dataset

Rendered Hand Pose Dataset [47] (RHD) provides $44k$ synthetic hand images including $41.2k$ training images and $2.7k$ test images along with corresponding 21 hand keypoints annotations. **Hand-3D-Studio** [46] (H3D) is a real-world multi-view indoor hand pose images dataset with $22k$ frames. We follow RegDA's policy to split $3.2k$ frames as the test set. **FreiHAND** [48] includes $44k$ frames of real-world multi-view hand pose images with more varied pose and view points. It contains $130k$ training image, and we still follow settings in RegDA to select $32k$ test images. **SURREAL** [41] provides more than 6 million synthetic human body pose images with annotations. **Human3.6M** [16] contains 3.6 million frames of real-world indoor human body pose images captured

Table 1. Prediction accuracy PCK@0.05 on *RHD→H3D*, i.e., source dataset is RHD, target dataset H3D, for four hand parts and the full hand. Higher values are better

Method	MCP	PIP	DIP	Fin	All
Source only	67.4	64.2	63.3	54.8	61.8
Oracle	97.7	97.2	95.7	92.5	95.8
CCSSL [29]	81.5	79.9	74.4	64.0	75.1
UDA-Animal [23]	82.3	79.6	72.3	61.5	74.1
RegDA [17]	79.6	74.4	71.2	62.9	72.5
Ours	**86.7**	**84.6**	**78.9**	**68.1**	**79.6**

from videos. We follow protocols in [24] and split 5 subjects (S1, S5, S6, S7, S8) as the training set and 2 subjects (S9, S11) as test set. **Leeds Sports Pose** [18] (LSP) is a real-world outdoor human body pose dataset containing $2k$ images. **Synthetic Animal Dataset** [29] is a synthetic animal pose dataset rendered from CAD models. The dataset contains 5 animal classes, horse, tiger, sheep, hound, and elephant, each with $10k$ images. **TigDog Dataset** [31] includes $30k$ frames from real-world videos of horses and tigers. **Animal-Pose Dataset** [3] provides $6.1k$ real-world images from 5 animals including dog, cat, cow, sheep, and horse.

4.3 Experimental Results

Baselines. We consider the following SOTA baselines: semi-supervised learning based CCSSL [29], UDA-Animal [23], and RegDA [17] under various adaptation tasks. For the sake of fair comparison, we re-train CCSSL and UDA-Animal with the backbone of ResNet-101 as ours, and train CCSSL jointly among all categories in animal pose estimation tasks. Oracle is the performance of a model trained jointly with target 2D annotations following previous works
Metrics. We adopt the evaluation metric of Percentage of Correct Keypoint (PCK) for all experiments and report PCK@0.05 that measures the ratio of correct prediction within the range of 5% with respect to the image size.

Results on Hand Pose Estimation. First, we present the adaption results on the hand pose estimation task *RHD→H3D* on 21 keypoints. We report different anatomical parts of a hand including metacarpophalangeal (MCP), proximal interphalangeal (PIP), distal interphalangeal (DIP), and fingertip (Fin). Our baselines can greatly improve the performance of their pose estimation model on the target domain (Table 1), while UDA-Animal, which is originally proposed for animal pose estimation tasks, achieves a performance of 75.1%. In comparison, our method outperforms all the baseline methods by a noticeable margin of 4.5% and reaches 79.6%.

Results on Human Body Pose Estimation. As for the adaptation in human body pose estimation, we measure the performance of all baselines and ours in the

Table 2. PCK@0.05 on *SURREAL→Human3.6M* and *SURREAL→LSP*. Sld: Shoulder, Elb: Elbow

Method	*SURREAL→Human3.6M*							*SURREAL→LSP*						
	Sld	Elb	Wrist	Hip	Knee	Ankle	All	Sld	Elb	Wrist	Hip	Knee	Ankle	All
Source only	69.4	75.4	66.4	37.9	77.3	77.7	67.3	51.5	65.0	62.9	68.0	68.7	67.4	63.9
Oracle	95.3	91.8	86.9	95.6	94.1	93.6	92.9	–	–	–	–	–	–	–
CCSSL [29]	44.3	68.5	55.2	22.2	62.3	57.8	51.7	36.8	66.3	63.9	59.6	67.3	70.4	60.7
UDA-Animal [23]	51.7	83.1	68.9	17.7	79.4	76.6	62.9	61.4	77.7	75.5	65.8	76.7	78.3	69.2
RegDA [17]	73.3	86.4	72.8	**54.8**	82.0	84.4	75.6	62.7	76.7	71.1	81.0	80.3	75.3	74.6
Ours	**78.1**	**89.6**	**81.1**	52.6	**85.3**	**87.1**	**79.0**	**69.2**	**84.9**	**83.3**	**85.5**	**84.7**	**84.3**	**82.0**

task of *SURREAL→Human3.6M* and *SURREAL→LSP* on 16 keypoints on the human body grouped with different parts, *i.e.*, shoulders, elbow, wrist, hip, knee, and ankle. RegDA can successfully adapt its model closer to the target domain, while CCSSL and UDA-Animal, designed for animal pose estimation, fail to adapt under such scenarios (Table 2). This could probably be because their self-guidance paradigm is more hyper-parameter sensitive and cannot guarantee to generalize to other scenarios, including the high out-level variance (*i.e.*, high pose variance) in human pose estimation. Our method, in contrast, enables effective and robust unsupervised learning via the heatmap normalization which addresses the drift effect and therefore ensures the high quality of the self-guidance.

Results on Animal Pose Estimation. We finally compare our method with the baselines in domain adaptive animal pose estimation under *SynAnimal→TigDog* and *SynAnimal→AnimalPose* as shown in Tables 3 and 4. In *SynAnimal→TigDog*, we follow settings in UDA-Animal and estimate 18 keypoints from different parts including eye, chin, shoulder, hip, elbow, knee, and hoof of horse and tiger shared in the Synthetic Animal and the TigDog datasets. In *SynAnimal→AnimalPose*, we also perform adaptation on the hound and sheep categories for 14 keypoint estimation of eye, hoof, knee, and elbow. For a fair comparison, we run all experiments with the same data augmentation as in CCSSL and UDA-Animal for all tasks, as these augmentations provide crucial improvement (see first and second rows in Table 3). The first row in Table 3 represents the reported [23] source-only performance without augmentations; the second row with augmentation, which, e.g., increases the performance from 32.8% to 71.4% in the horse keypoint estimation (column All).

Among the baseline methods, UDA-Animal achieves the best performance in estimating a horse's pose and approaches the oracle performance from a model trained jointly by the annotated source and target domains. Our method achieves slightly lower performance in the horse set that is close to the oracle level but slightly outperforms UDA-Animal in the tiger set.

In despite of the promising results in *SynAnimal→TigDog*, we observe that UDA-Animal significantly underperforms than RegDA and ours in the Animal-Pose dataset from Table 4. This is because *SynAnimal→AnimalPose* is more challenging than *SynAnimal→TigDog* by comparing the accuracy of source only models (32.2% vs. 71.4%). Even though we can still see improvements from the source only with augmentations, CCSSL and UDA-Animal face more noisy pseudo-labels during self-training possibly due to their hyper-parameter sensitivity, so that improvements are marginal. On the contrary, RegDA shows noticeable improvement compared to source only. Our method can handle these challenging settings via heatmap normalization in pseudo-labeling and obtain the best performance in these experiments in both categories.

Table 3. PCK@0.05 on *SynAnimal→TigDog*. Sld: shoulder, Elb: Elbow. Source only* indicates training on only source domain data with strong augmentation

Method	Horse								Tiger							
	Eye	Chin	Sld	Hip	Elb	Knee	Hoof	All	Eye	Chin	Sld	Hip	Elb	Knee	Hoof	All
Source only	49.3	53.5	31.3	53.5	38.7	28.7	18.3	32.8	42.8	32.1	24.2	51.1	32.6	28.1	32.7	33.2
Source only*	87.1	91.4	69.4	76.3	70.1	71.3	61.9	71.4	91.1	86.5	46.5	67.9	44.3	53.1	63.2	60.7
Oracle	92.0	95.8	73.6	90.9	84.4	84.2	79.1	84.1	98.5	97.4	75.1	94.7	74.1	76.0	81.6	82.1
CCSSL [29]	89.3	**92.6**	69.5	78.1	70.0	73.1	65.0	73.1	94.3	91.3	49.5	70.2	53.9	59.1	70.2	66.7
UDA-Animal [23]	86.9	93.7	**76.4**	**81.9**	70.6	**79.1**	**72.6**	**77.5**	98.4	87.2	49.4	**74.9**	49.8	62.0	73.4	67.7
RegDA [17]	89.2	92.3	70.5	77.5	71.5	72.7	63.2	73.2	93.3	92.8	50.3	67.8	50.2	55.4	60.7	61.8
Ours	**91.3**	92.5	74.0	74.2	**75.8**	77.0	66.6	76.4	**98.5**	**96.9**	**56.2**	63.7	**52.3**	**62.8**	**72.8**	**67.9**

Table 4. PCK@0.05 on *SynAnimal→AnimalPose*. Source only* indicates training on only source domain data with strong augmentation

Method	Dog					Sheep				
	Eye	Hoof	Knee	Elb	All	Eye	Hoof	Knee	Elb	All
Source only	39.8	22.8	16.5	17.4	22.0	42.6	31.0	28.2	21.4	29.3
Source only*	26.6	44.0	30.8	25.1	32.2	53.3	63.0	51.5	32.1	49.6
Oracle	88.8	74.9	57.1	51.1	65.1	88.2	84.9	79.9	59.6	76.9
CCSSL [29]	24.7	37.4	25.4	19.6	27.0	44.3	55.4	43.5	28.5	42.8
UDA-Animal [23]	26.2	39.8	31.6	24.7	31.1	48.2	52.9	49.9	29.7	44.9
RegDA [17]	46.8	54.6	32.9	31.2	40.6	**62.8**	68.5	57.0	42.4	56.9
Ours	**56.1**	**59.2**	**38.9**	**32.7**	**45.4**	61.6	**77.4**	**57.7**	**44.6**	**60.2**

4.4 Generalization to Unseen Domains and Objects

So far, we have focused on accuracy in a given target domain, but we may face other types of unseen domains during training in real-world applications. Thus, we compare the generalization capacity of our method with baselines in a domain generalization setting where we test models on unseen domains and objects.

Domain Generalization on FreiHAND. For hand pose estimation, we test models adapted on the RHD→H3D setting with the other real-world hand dataset FreiHAND (FHD). We compare the accuracy on FHD and measure how well each method generalizes on the unseen domain FHD. As presented in Table 5, the test performance on FHD is generally poor compared to the source only and oracle performance, presumably because of the larger domain gap between H3D and FHD. It is worth noticing the performance of CCSSL is lower than the source-only, even if it outperforms that in the *RHD→H3D* setting by a large margin, revealing its lack of generalization capacity to the unseen domain, probably because of the lack of input-level alignment. On the other hand, RegDA and our method show better ability to generalize while ours achieves the best performance under most circumstances.

Domain Generalization on Human3.6M. We test the generalization ability of a model adapted from *SURREAL→LSP* on Human3.6M. It should be noted that LSP contains only 2K images which are very small compared to Human3.6M. Thus, this task is challenging since we use small number of real data for domain generalization. In Table 5, we show that our method can generalize better than the baselines and achieves 74.3% of accuracy. Our accuracy on the generalization task (74.3%) is also comparable to the baselines performances of *SURREAL→Human3.6M* (*e.g.*, RegDA: 75.6), by using only $2k$ images.

Table 5. Domain generalization experiments on FreiHand (FHD) and Human3.6M. We report PCK@0.05. Fin: Fingertip. Sld: shoulder, Elb: Elbow. Source only indicates training only on RHD or SURREAL while Oracle indicates training only on FHD or Human3.6M

Method	*FreiHand*					*Human3.6M*						
	MCP	PIP	DIP	Fin	All	Sld	Elb	Wrist	Hip	Knee	Ankle	All
Source only	34.9	48.7	52.4	48.5	45.8	51.5	65.0	62.9	68.0	68.7	67.4	63.9
Oracle	92.8	90.3	87.7	78.5	87.2	95.3	91.8	86.9	95.6	94.1	93.6	92.9
CCSSL [29]	34.3	46.3	48.4	44.4	42.6	52.7	76.9	63.1	31.6	75.7	72.9	62.2
UDA-Animal [23]	29.6	46.6	50.0	45.3	42.2	54.4	75.3	62.1	21.6	70.4	69.2	58.8
RegDA [17]	**37.8**	51.8	53.2	47.5	46.9	76.9	80.2	69.7	**52.0**	80.3	80.0	73.2
Ours	35.6	**52.3**	**55.4**	**50.6**	**47.1**	**77.0**	**85.9**	**73.8**	47.6	**80.7**	**80.6**	**74.3**

Table 6. Domain generalization experiments on AnimalPose. We report PCK@0.05. Source only indicates training only on Synthetic Animal

Method	Horse	Dog	Cat	Sheep	Cow	All
Source only	52.2	31.0	14.7	37.5	41.8	33.4
CCSSL [29]	59.8	31.1	16.6	46.4	48.9	37.7
UDA-Animal [23]	**63.2**	32.4	17.6	48.3	53.0	39.8
RegDA [17]	58.4	34.9	17.4	45.1	46.3	39.0
Ours	61.6	**40.7**	**21.6**	**50.1**	**53.5**	**44.0**

Domain Generalization on AnimalPose. Finally, we evaluate the generalization capacity of models adapted from *SynAnimal→TigDog* and test it on

Animal Pose Dataset. It should be noted that models are only trained on horse and tiger images from the Synthetic Animal Dataset and tested on unseen animals (*e.g.*, dog) in Animal Pose Dataset. Based on the results in Table 6, we can also witness an obvious improvement of our method above all the baselines and generalize better on unseen animals from unseen domains.

Qualitative Results. We provide additional qualitative results on generalization in Figs. 4. In Fig. 4, it is clear that the baselines proposed for animal pose estimation do not work well. Our method produces more accurate keypoints compared to baselines. More qualitative results on animal are available in the appendix.

4.5 Sensitivity Analysis

To further validate the robustness and generalization capacity of our method, we conducted sensitivity analysis regarding three major hyper-parameters in our framework, including the confidence thresholding ratio p, occlusion thresholding value τ_{occ}, the momentum η in Mean Teacher on *RHD→H3D*. Additionally, we randomly split a separate validation set with the same size as the test set

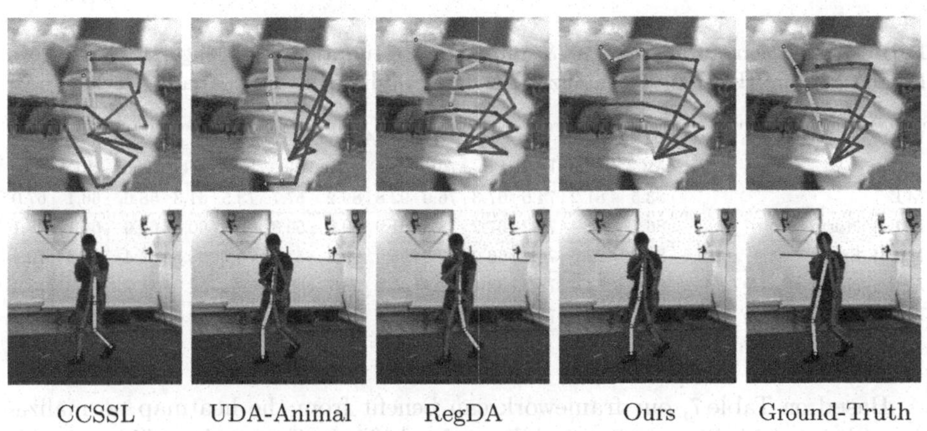

Fig. 4. Qualitative results of generalization to unseen domains

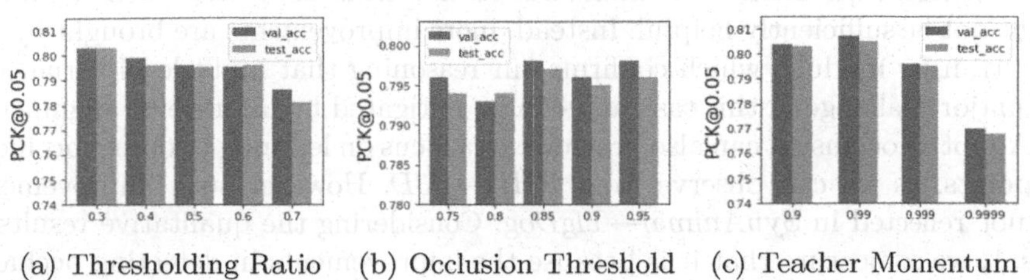

(a) Thresholding Ratio (b) Occlusion Threshold (c) Teacher Momentum

Fig. 5. Sensitivity analysis on the thresholding, occlusion ratio, and momentum. Our method shows stable performance over hyper-parameters

from the target domain training data to simulate the hyper-parameter tuning process and avoid directly tuning the test accuracy. Based on the results presented in Fig. 5, we find that our framework works stably under various settings. Meanwhile, we also find that the performance gradually decreases when we have a higher thresholding ratio for pseudo-labels, presumably because it brings in lower confident predictions as pseudo-labels and that deteriorates the unsupervised learning process. Also, we find that a greater teacher momentum is more likely to limit the framework to learn actively and harm the performance. More importantly, we can also learn that the validation accuracy in all experiments is highly correlated with that on the test sets, which also indicates the generalization capacity of our method and the reliability to give indicative clues when tuning hyper-parameters on a separate validation set.

4.6 Ablation Studies

We perform ablation studies in our framework to test their effectiveness and interaction with the rest of the framework. This also justify our other motivations regarding the task and the framework. Experiments are conducted under our major benchmarks including *RHD→H3D* and *SynAnimal→TigDog*. Additional ablation studies can be found in the appendix.

Table 7. Ablation studies on hand & animal pose estimation. Fin: Fingertip. MT: Mean Teacher, Norm: Heatmap Normalization, Style: Stylization, Occ: Adapt. Occlusion

Method	*RHD→H3D*					*SynAnimal→TigDog*							
	MCP	PIP	DIP	Fin	All	Eye	Chin	Sld	Hip	Elb	Knee	Hoof	All
MT	83.5	81.2	74.6	67.3	76.9	92.8	89.2	57.7	73.5	61.3	58.6	66.1	67.0
MT + Norm	86.1	84.4	77.2	67.2	78.8	91.9	89.9	59.3	62.7	60.8	67.6	64.1	68.1
MT + Style	84.6	82.5	76.6	66.9	77.6	95.0	93.8	57.8	74.7	63.5	67.4	67.4	70.4
MT + Norm + Style	86.6	84.4	78.3	68.1	79.1	95.9	94.7	65.7	68.2	64.9	71.7	72.3	73.4
MT + Norm + Style + Occ	86.7	84.6	78.9	68.1	79.6	95.7	94.7	64.1	69.0	64.5	70.7	69.8	72.4

Based on Table 7, our framework can benefit from the heatmap normalization (denoted by Norm) that stabilizes the drifting effect and enables effective unsupervised learning from pseudo-labels via output-level domain alignment. Nevertheless, experiments on animal adaptation tasks show that such alignment might not be sufficiently helpful. Instead, more improvements are brought by the style transfer module, which confirms our reasoning that input-level variance is the major challenge in this task and can be mitigated by input-level alignments.

Adaptive occlusion can also provide extra focus on learning to detect occluded keypoints, as we can observe from *RHD→H3D*. However such improvements are not reflected in *SynAnimal→TigDog*. Considering the qualitative results in Figs. 1, we conjecture that it is because the improvements in detecting occluded keypoints are not verifiable as their annotations are not available in the real animal dataset and therefore these predictions are not included in the PCK@0.05 evaluation protocol. More ablation studies are available in the appendix.

5 Conclusion

While existing baselines focus on specific scenarios, we propose a unified framework that can be applied to diverse problems of domain adaptive pose estimation including hand pose, human body, and animal pose estimation. Considering the challenges from different types of domain shifts, our method addresses both input and output-level discrepancies across domains and enables a more generic adaptation paradigm. Extensive experiments demonstrate that our method not only achieves state-of-the-art performance under various domain adaptation scenarios but also exhibits excellent generalization capacity to unseen domains and objects. We hope our work can unify branches from different directions and provide a solid baseline for following works in this line of research.

Acknowledgements. This work has been partially supported by NSF Award, DARPA, DARPA LwLL, ONR MURI grant N00014-19-1-2571 associated with AUSMURIB000001 (to M.B.) and by NSF grant 1535797, 1551572, (to. M.B.).

References

1. Badrinarayanan, V., Kendall, A., Cipolla, R.: SegNet: a deep convolutional encoder-decoder architecture for image segmentation. IEEE Trans. Pattern Anal. Mach. Intell. (TPAMI) **39**(12), 2481–2495 (2017)
2. Damodaran, B.B., Kellenberger, B., Flamary, R., Tuia, D., Courty, N.: DeepJDOT: deep joint distribution optimal transport for unsupervised domain adaptation. In: Ferrari, V., Hebert, M., Sminchisescu, C., Weiss, Y. (eds.) ECCV 2018. LNCS, vol. 11208, pp. 467–483. Springer, Cham (2018). https://doi.org/10.1007/978-3-030-01225-0_28
3. Cao, J., Tang, H., Fang, H., Shen, X., Tai, Y., Lu, C.: Cross-domain adaptation for animal pose estimation. In: IEEE International Conference on Computer Vision (ICCV), pp. 9497–9506 (2019)
4. Chen, L., Papandreou, G., Kokkinos, I., Murphy, K., Yuille, A.L.: DeepLab: semantic image segmentation with deep convolutional nets, atrous convolution, and fully connected CRFs. IEEE Trans. Pattern Anal. Mach. Intell. (TPAMI) **40**, 834–848 (2018)
5. Cordts, M., et al.: The cityscapes dataset for semantic urban scene understanding. In: IEEE Conference on Computer Vision and Pattern Recognition (CVPR), pp. 3213–3223 (2016)
6. Deng, J., Dong, W., Socher, R., Li, L., Li, K., Fei-Fei, L.: ImageNet: a large-scale hierarchical image database. In: IEEE Conference on Computer Vision and Pattern Recognition (CVPR), pp. 248–255 (2009)
7. Devries, T., Taylor, G.W.: Improved regularization of convolutional neural networks with cutout. arXiv preprint arXiv:1708.04552 (2017)
8. French, G., Mackiewicz, M., Fisher, M.H.: Self-ensembling for visual domain adaptation. In: International Conference on Learning Representations (ICLR) (2018)
9. Ganin, Y., et al.: Domain-adversarial training of neural networks. J. Mach. Learn. Res. (JMLR) **17**, 2030–2096 (2016)
10. Geiger, A., Lenz, P., Stiller, C., Urtasun, R.: Vision meets robotics: the KITTI dataset. Int. J. Robot. Res. **32**, 1231–1237 (2013)

11. Gretton, A., et al.: Optimal kernel choice for large-scale two-sample tests. In: Advances in Neural Information Processing Systems (NeurIPS) (2012)
12. He, K., Zhang, X., Ren, S., Sun, J.: Deep residual learning for image recognition. In: IEEE Conference on Computer Vision and Pattern Recognition (CVPR), pp. 770–778 (2016)
13. Hoffman, J., et al.: CyCADA: cycle-consistent adversarial domain adaptation. In: International Conference on Machine Learning (ICML), pp. 1994–2003 (2018)
14. Hoffman, J., Wang, D., Yu, F., Darrell, T.: FCNs in the wild: pixel-level adversarial and constraint-based adaptation. arXiv preprint arXiv:1612.02649 (2016)
15. Huang, X., Belongie, S.J.: Arbitrary style transfer in real-time with adaptive instance normalization. In: IEEE International Conference on Computer Vision (ICCV), pp. 1510–1519 (2017)
16. Ionescu, C., Papava, D., Olaru, V., Sminchisescu, C.: Human3.6M: large scale datasets and predictive methods for 3D human sensing in natural environments. IEEE Trans. Pattern Anal. Mach. Intell. (TPAMI) **36**, 1325–1339 (2014)
17. Jiang, J., Ji, Y., Wang, X., Liu, Y., Wang, J., Long, M.: Regressive domain adaptation for unsupervised keypoint detection. In: IEEE Conference on Computer Vision and Pattern Recognition (CVPR), pp. 6780–6789 (2021)
18. Johnson, S., Everingham, M.: Clustered pose and nonlinear appearance models for human pose estimation. In: British Machine Vision Conference (BMVC), pp. 1–11 (2010)
19. Ke, L., Chang, M.-C., Qi, H., Lyu, S.: Multi-scale structure-aware network for human pose estimation. In: Ferrari, V., Hebert, M., Sminchisescu, C., Weiss, Y. (eds.) ECCV 2018. LNCS, vol. 11206, pp. 731–746. Springer, Cham (2018). https://doi.org/10.1007/978-3-030-01216-8_44
20. Kingma, D.P., Ba, J.: Adam: a method for stochastic optimization. In: International Conference on Learning Representations (ICLR) (2015)
21. Kundu, J.N., Lakkakula, N., Radhakrishnan, V.B.: UM-Adapt: unsupervised multi-task adaptation using adversarial cross-task distillation. In: IEEE International Conference on Computer Vision (ICCV), pp. 1436–1445 (2019)
22. Kundu, J.N., Uppala, P.K., Pahuja, A., Babu, R.V.: AdaDepth: unsupervised content congruent adaptation for depth estimation. In: IEEE Conference on Computer Vision and Pattern Recognition (CVPR), pp. 2656–2665 (2018)
23. Li, C., Lee, G.H.: From synthetic to real: unsupervised domain adaptation for animal pose estimation. In: IEEE Conference on Computer Vision and Pattern Recognition (CVPR), pp. 1482–1491 (2021)
24. Li, S., Chan, A.B.: 3D human pose estimation from monocular images with deep convolutional neural network. In: Cremers, D., Reid, I., Saito, H., Yang, M.-H. (eds.) ACCV 2014. LNCS, vol. 9004, pp. 332–347. Springer, Cham (2015). https://doi.org/10.1007/978-3-319-16808-1_23
25. Li, Y., Yuan, L., Vasconcelos, N.: Bidirectional learning for domain adaptation of semantic segmentation. In: IEEE Conference on Computer Vision and Pattern Recognition (CVPR), pp. 6936–6945 (2019)
26. Long, J., Shelhamer, E., Darrell, T.: Fully convolutional networks for semantic segmentation. In: IEEE Conference on Computer Vision and Pattern Recognition, CVPR 2015, Boston, MA, USA, 7–12 June 2015, pp. 3431–3440 (2015)
27. Long, M., Cao, Y., Wang, J., Jordan, M.I.: Learning transferable features with deep adaptation networks. In: International Conference on Machine Learning (ICML), pp. 97–105 (2015)

28. Long, M., Cao, Z., Wang, J., Jordan, M.I.: Conditional adversarial domain adaptation. In: Advances in Neural Information Processing Systems (NeurIPS), pp. 1640–1650 (2018)
29. Mu, J., Qiu, W., Hager, G.D., Yuille, A.L.: Learning from synthetic animals. In: IEEE Conference on Computer Vision and Pattern Recognition (CVPR), pp. 12383–12392 (2020)
30. Newell, A., Yang, K., Deng, J.: Stacked hourglass networks for human pose estimation. In: Leibe, B., Matas, J., Sebe, N., Welling, M. (eds.) ECCV 2016. LNCS, vol. 9912, pp. 483–499. Springer, Cham (2016). https://doi.org/10.1007/978-3-319-46484-8_29
31. Pero, L.D., Ricco, S., Sukthankar, R., Ferrari, V.: Articulated motion discovery using pairs of trajectories. In: IEEE Conference on Computer Vision and Pattern Recognition (CVPR), pp. 2151–2160 (2015)
32. Rodriguez, A.L., Mikolajczyk, K.: DESC: domain adaptation for depth estimation via semantic consistency. In: British Machine Vision Conference 2020 (BMVC) (2020)
33. Ronneberger, O., Fischer, P., Brox, T.: U-Net: convolutional networks for biomedical image segmentation. In: Navab, N., Hornegger, J., Wells, W.M., Frangi, A.F. (eds.) MICCAI 2015. LNCS, vol. 9351, pp. 234–241. Springer, Cham (2015). https://doi.org/10.1007/978-3-319-24574-4_28
34. Saito, K., Watanabe, K., Ushiku, Y., Harada, T.: Maximum classifier discrepancy for unsupervised domain adaptation. In: IEEE Conference on Computer Vision and Pattern Recognition (CVPR), pp. 3723–3732 (2018)
35. Simonyan, K., Zisserman, A.: Very deep convolutional networks for large-scale image recognition. In: International Conference on Learning Representations (ICLR) (2015)
36. Sun, K., Xiao, B., Liu, D., Wang, J.: Deep high-resolution representation learning for human pose estimation. In: IEEE Conference on Computer Vision and Pattern Recognition (CVPR), pp. 5693–5703 (2019)
37. Tarvainen, A., Valpola, H.: Mean teachers are better role models: weight-averaged consistency targets improve semi-supervised deep learning results. In: International Conference on Learning Representations (ICLR) (2017)
38. Tompson, J.J., Jain, A., LeCun, Y., Bregler, C.: Joint training of a convolutional network and a graphical model for human pose estimation. In: Advances in Neural Information Processing Systems (NeurIPS) (2014)
39. Tsai, Y., Hung, W., Schulter, S., Sohn, K., Yang, M., Chandraker, M.: Learning to adapt structured output space for semantic segmentation. In: IEEE Conference on Computer Vision and Pattern Recognition (CVPR), pp. 7472–7481 (2018)
40. Tzeng, E., Hoffman, J., Saenko, K., Darrell, T.: Adversarial discriminative domain adaptation. In: IEEE Conference on Computer Vision and Pattern Recognition (CVPR), pp. 2962–2971 (2017)
41. Varol, G., et al.: Learning from synthetic humans. In: IEEE Conference on Computer Vision and Pattern Recognition (CVPR), pp. 4627–4635 (2017)
42. Xiao, B., Wu, H., Wei, Y.: Simple baselines for human pose estimation and tracking. In: Ferrari, V., Hebert, M., Sminchisescu, C., Weiss, Y. (eds.) ECCV 2018. LNCS, vol. 11210, pp. 472–487. Springer, Cham (2018). https://doi.org/10.1007/978-3-030-01231-1_29
43. Xie, R., Wang, C., Zeng, W., Wang, Y.: An empirical study of the collapsing problem in semi-supervised 2D human pose estimation. In: IEEE International Conference on Computer Vision (ICCV), pp. 11240–11249 (2021)

44. Yang, Y., Soatto, S.: FDA: Fourier domain adaptation for semantic segmentation. In: IEEE Conference on Computer Vision and Pattern Recognition (CVPR), pp. 4084–4094 (2020)
45. Zhang, Y., Liu, T., Long, M., Jordan, M.: Bridging theory and algorithm for domain adaptation. In: International Conference on Machine Learning (ICML), pp. 7404–7413. PMLR (2019)
46. Zhao, Z., Wang, T., Xia, S., Wang, Y.: Hand-3D-Studio: a new multi-view system for 3D hand reconstruction. In: IEEE International Conference on Acoustics, Speech and Signal Processing ICASSP, pp. 2478–2482 (2020)
47. Zimmermann, C., Brox, T.: Learning to estimate 3D hand pose from single RGB images. In: IEEE International Conference on Computer Vision (ICCV), pp. 4913–4921 (2017)
48. Zimmermann, C., Ceylan, D., Yang, J., Russell, B.C., Argus, M.J., Brox, T.: FreiHAND: a dataset for markerless capture of hand pose and shape from single RGB images. In: IEEE International Conference on Computer Vision (ICCV), pp. 813–822 (2019)

A Broad Study of Pre-training for Domain Generalization and Adaptation

Donghyun Kim[2(✉)], Kaihong Wang[1], Stan Sclaroff[1], and Kate Saenko[1,2]

[1] Department of Computer Science, Boston University, Boston, USA
{kaiwkh,sclaroff,saenko}@bu.edu
[2] MIT-IBM Watson AI Lab, Cambridge, USA
donhk@bu.edu

Abstract. Deep models must learn robust and transferable representations in order to perform well on new domains. While domain transfer methods (*e.g.*, domain adaptation, domain generalization) have been proposed to learn transferable representations across domains, they are typically applied to ResNet backbones pre-trained on ImageNet. Thus, existing works pay little attention to the effects of pre-training on domain transfer tasks. In this paper, we provide a broad study and in-depth analysis of pre-training for domain adaptation and generalization, namely: network architectures, size, pre-training loss, and datasets. We observe that simply using a state-of-the-art backbone outperforms existing state-of-the-art domain adaptation baselines and set new baselines on Office-Home and DomainNet improving by 10.7% and 5.5%. We hope that this work can provide more insights for future domain transfer research.

Keywords: Transfer learning · Pre-training · Domain generalization · Domain adaptation

1 Introduction

It is well-known that deep models often perform poorly on out-of-distribution test data [20]. Domain transfer has been an active research topic for years, aiming to learn more robust feature representations that generalize from training data (source domains) to novel data distributions (target domains). There has been significant progress in domain transfer for visual recognition tasks, such as image classification [12], semantic segmentation [55] and object detection [47].

Domain transfer consists of two steps: 1) *pre-training*, where a model is first pre-trained on an upstream task with a massive supervised dataset, *e.g.*, ImageNet, and 2) *transfer (adaptation)*, where the model is fine-tuned on downstream multi-domain data, see Fig. 1(a). In the latter step, *Domain Adaptation (DA)* tunes on both a labeled source and an unlabeled target domain, while

Supplementary Information The online version contains supplementary material available at https://doi.org/10.1007/978-3-031-19827-4_36.

S. Avidan et al. (Eds.): ECCV 2022, LNCS 13693, pp. 621–638, 2022.
https://doi.org/10.1007/978-3-031-19827-4_36

Domain Generalization (DG) tunes only on labeled source data. While many DA and DG methods (*e.g.*, adversarial learning [12,34,56], entropy optimization [34,44] or clustering [22]) have been proposed and studied extensively in prior work, little attention has been paid to pre-training for domain transfer. In this paper, we provide comprehensive experiments and an in-depth analysis of pre-training.

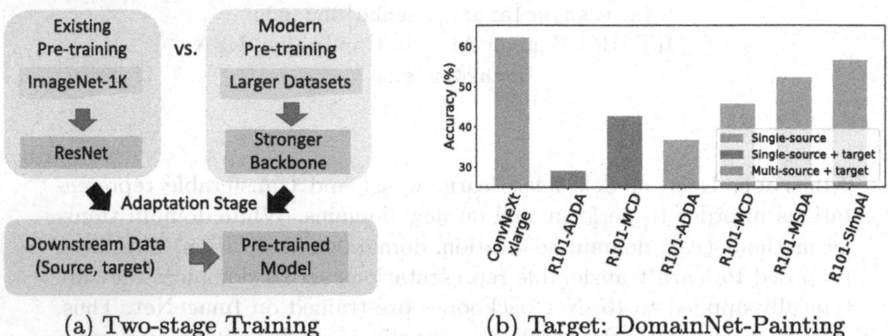

Fig. 1. (a) Existing domain transfer approaches use a ResNet pre-trained on ImageNet-1K and focus on the adaptation stage. We analyze the effect of pre-training on the adaptation stage. (b) Simply using strong pre-training outperforms all domain adaptation (DA) baselines. We compare accuracy on the target domain (*Painting*) with a SOTA architecture, *ConvNeXt-XL*, pre-trained on ImageNet 22k vs. the standard *ResNet backbones* pre-trained on ImageNet-1K. *Red* bars represent the accuracy of model trained only on a single source (*Real* domain). *Blue* bars represent DA models trained on the single source and the unlabeled target domain. *Green* bars represent DA models trained on multiple source domains and the unlabeled target domain. ConNeXt-XL fine-tuned only on a single source domain outperforms all the existing DA baselines (Color figure online)

Pre-training is a very successful transfer learning technique for many visual tasks, including domain transfer tasks, as it provides a strong initial representation [9,27]. Pre-training is especially useful when annotations are limited. We decompose pre-training into three parts: (a) network architecture (backbone), (b) dataset, and (c) loss function. It is a common practice of most domain transfer methods to use a ResNet backbone pre-trained on ImageNet-1K with a supervised loss function (*i.e.*, cross-entropy loss). We argue that this evaluation standard is outdated and ignores the effect of modern large-scale pre-training on domain transfer. To illustrate the potential impact of pre-training, Fig. 1(b) shows an experiment that compares the performance of different backbones to SOTA results on the DomainNet [39] DA benchmark. Simply using a recent backbone [33] pre-trained with ImageNet-22K with no adaptation outperforms existing domain transfer methods. This raises the question, will SOTA DA methods still provide similar gains if applied to the stronger backbones?

To fully explore these issues, in this paper we pose the following questions:

1. **What is the effect of network architecture?** ResNet-based backbones [17] are commonly used in domain generalization [15], single source [12, 34, 45] and multi-source DA [39, 59]. Since larger and more powerful backbones such as Swin-Transformer [32] or ConvNext [33] have been recently proposed, we ask whether they may be more robust to domain shift. Transformers were recently shown to be more robust than CNNs to image corruptions and adversarial examples [1]. We thus conduct an extensive analysis of the impact of network size and architectures, including state-of-the-art Transformers and CNNs on domain transfer tasks.
2. **What is the effect of pre-training dataset?** Several datasets that are larger than the standard ImageNet-1K could potentially improve transfer: ImageNet-22K [41], JFT-300M [19] and Conceptual Captions [8, 49]. These datasets have been very effective for diverse downstream visual tasks (*e.g.*, [10, 30]), but not well explored for domain transfer tasks. We therefore study the effect of a wider range of pre-training datasets, including ImageNet-21K, JFT-300M, and language-vision datasets, on domain transfer.
3. **Supervised vs. Self-supervised Pre-training.** In terms of loss functions, self-supervised learning (*e.g.*, [7, 9, 63]) has obtained powerful performance on diverse visual tasks and often outperforms its supervised counterparts on downstream problems [3, 7, 9]. We therefore compare self-supervised and supervised pre-training for domain transfer.
4. **Domain Adaptation with SOTA Pre-training.** Finally, we investigate a fundamental research question in domain transfer: With the help of the state-of-the-art pre-trained models, do we still need sophisticated domain adaptation methods? We explore the applicability of several existing DA methods to our more advanced pre-training setting.

We conduct the study on four standard multi-domain benchmarks. While we find that with better pre-training, DA methods still improve performance compared to a source-only trained model, an outdated DA method outperforms state-of-the-art DA methods. This raises serious fundamental research questions about the current evaluation protocol.

In summary, our work's main contribution is to provide the field with a broad comparison of modern pre-training approaches for domain transfer tasks. To our knowledge, this is the first work to do such an in-depth analysis. One of our key findings is that SOTA pre-training outperforms SOTA domain transfer methods by a large margin even without access to a target domain, as shown in Fig. 1(b). We also observe network architectures, sizes, and pre-training datasets play a big role but in a domain-dependent way. Finally, we show that SOTA DA methods work less than older DA methods under modern pre-training. We hope our work will modernize current domain transfer benchmarks and provide helpful and practical insights for future domain adaptation research.

2 Related Work

Domain Transfer. Domain transfer tasks aim to improve generalization and mitigate domain shift between source and target domains. We study generalization to *natural* data shifts caused by the changes in visual styles, background, lighting, etc. [18,26,42] as opposed to artificial corruptions [14]. In this problem setup, we are given a single source domain or multi-source labeled domains. The key is how to learn transferable features that will be useful for the unlabeled target domain. Depending on the specific setup, this task can be categorized into two: (1) domain adaptation (DA) where we can access the target domain and (2) domain generalization (DG) where we do not have access to a target domain. Depending on the number of labeled source domains, each category can be further divided into single-source or multi-source DA (or DG). Typically, there are two stages: (1) pre-training and (2) adaptation. Most of these methods focus on the second adaptation stage for domain alignment with adversarial domain classifier [12,34], entropy optimization [25,34,44], minimizing maximum discrepancy across domain distributions [48,69], maximum mean discrepancy [35], or optimal transport [5]. While domain alignment methods have been proposed actively in recent years for the adaptation stage, the importance of the pre-training stage has not been well explored. Pre-training can provide strong weight initialization by learning a general transferable representation that can be useful for diverse downstream tasks [27]. While typical DA or DG methods use ResNet backbones pre-trained on ImageNet-1K, we focus on the pre-training stage and provide an in-depth analysis of its effects on domain transfer tasks.

Network Architectures and Datasets for Pre-training. Since the transferability of the model is closely correlated with the performance on downstream tasks as shown in [27], having a strong pre-trained model is important. In terms of architectures, convolutional neural networks (CNN) has been standard and state-of-the-art models in many visual tasks for years. After the introduction of AlexNet [29] with ImageNet-1K [41], new CNN-based architectures have been proposed with deeper, wider, and more effective convolutional layers, *e.g.*, VGGNet [50], ResNe(X)t [17,65], SENet [21], EfficientNet [52], and ConvNeXt [33]. A newer line of work uses self-attention layers or Transformers for vision. Inspired by the Transformers for NLP [58], transformers for vision have been introduced in Vision Transformers (ViT) [10] and shows encouraging results by training with larger training sets than ImageNet-1K such as JFT-300M [51] or ImageNet-22K. DeiT [54] propose an efficient training strategy to train ViT. Swin Transformers employ a hierarchical transformer with a sliding window strategy where self-attention is performed within a local window. Swin Transformers achieve state-of-the-art performance in a range of computer vision tasks including object detection and segmentation. Bai *et al.* [1] show that Transformers can improve the generalization capability on out-of-distribution samples compared to CNNs. However, Liu *et al.* [33] propose ConvNeXt, which modernizes the ResNet architecture and show that a CNN can still outperform Transformers in vision and more robust to distribution shift. In addition to network architectures, it is shown that larger pre-training datasets such as ImageNet-22K, JFT-300M, or image-text pairs can further improve the transferability [10,23,30,33,40,64]. Inspired by these observations, we further study the effect of backbones and pre-training datasets on domain transfer evaluation benchmarks.

Self-supervised Learning. Self-supervised learning [11,13,37,63] devises pretext tasks with self-supervisory signals without requiring human annotations. These pretext tasks allow a model to learn discriminative and transferable representations with only unlabeled data for later use in downstream tasks. Representative methods include: solving a jigsaw puzzle [37], rotation prediction [13], Instance Discrimination (ID) [9,16,63], contrasting cluster assignments [6], self knowledge distillation [7], and masked image modeling [2]. Instance Discrimination [63] learns an embedding that maps visually similar images closer to each other and far from dissimilar images by classifying an image as its unique class. Some of these self-supervised methods outperform the supervised pre-training on several downstream tasks. For example, SwAV outperforms its supervised pre-training on object detection and image classification tasks on VOC [57] and INaturalist [57]. It is notable that in the VisDA-2021 competition for universal domain adaptation [3], the self-supervised masked image modeling approach with a transformer backbone [2] is the first place solution. We further investigate the effect of self-supervised pre-training approaches for domain transfer tasks.

3 Analysis Setup

Our goal is to analyze the effect of pre-training on domain transfer tasks. We assume a single source domain $\mathcal{D}_s = \{(\mathbf{x}_i^s, y_i^s)\}_{i=1}^{N_s}$ with N_s images x and labels y and an unlabeled target domain $\mathcal{D}_t = \{\mathbf{x}_i^t\}_{i=1}^{N_t}$. Given a pre-trained model f, we evaluate two types of domain transfer tasks: 1) domain generalization, *i.e.* fine-tune f on $\mathcal{D}_s$ and test on $\mathcal{D}_t$, and 2) domain adaptation, *i.e.* fine-tune f on $\mathcal{D}_s, \mathcal{D}_t$ and test on $\mathcal{D}_t$.

Pre-training Datasets. Typically, ImageNet-1K is widely used for pre-training. ImageNet-1K contains 1.2M images of mutually exclusive 1000 classes. ImageNet-22K (the superset of ImageNet-1K) is also used for pre-training (*e.g.*, [32,33]), which contains 14.1M images of 22K classes. In addition, Xie *et al.* [64] use a larger dataset JFT-300M to further improve the accuracy. Recently, language-vision models [23,30,40] can be used in image classification using image and text description pairs. We choose ALBEF [30], which achieves the-state-of-the-art performance and uses publicly available language-vision datasets. In total, ALBEF is pre-trained on ImageNet-1K, web crawled datasets (Conceptual Captions [8,49], SBU Captions [38]) and two human annotated datasets (COCO [31] and Visual Genome [28]). We explore models pre-trained on these datasets.

Downstream Datasets. We choose Office-Home (OH) [60], DomainNet (DN) [39], CUB [61,62], and iWildCAM2020 (WILD) [4,26,43]. Office-Home contains 15K images from 4 domains (Real (Rw), Painting (Pa), Clipart (Cl), Art (Ar)) on 65 classes. DomainNet contains 586K images from 6 domains (Clipart (Cl), Infograph (In), Painting (Pa), Quickdraw (Qu), Real (Rw), Sketch(Sk)) on 345 classes. Office-Home and DomainNet contain many common classes with ImageNet such as a chair, clock, and table. CUB contains 15K images from two domains (Real and Painting) on 200 fine-grained bird classes. For WILD, the source domain and target domain contains 182 different animal species from camera traps in different locations spread across multiple countries in the world. The source domain contains 129K images from 243 camera traps and the target domain contains 14K from 32 camera traps. Then we use the test set with 42K images from 48 different camera traps. The sets of camera traps in source and target domains are disjoint. The images of WILD are all realistic images from camera traps. ImageNet contains many animal classes, but the annotations are more fine-grained in CUB and WILD. While the main cause of domain-shift is visual styles in Office-Home, DomainNet, CUB, the domain-shift of WILD is mainly caused by location differences between camera traps in the world.

Backbone. For CNNs, we investigate the variants of ResNet [17], EfficientNet [52], and ConvNeXt [33]. For Transformers, we explore the variants of ViT [10], DeiT [54] and Swin [32]. Variants include different depths and sizes (*e.g.*, Swin-{S,B,L}).

Self-supervised Learning for Pre-training. In addition to the supervised pre-training, we also explore recent self-supervised learning approaches for pre-training. We study SwAV [6], MoCo [16], DINO [7], and BEiT [2].

Challenges of Evaluating Models. We use pre-trained models, which are publicly available. One of the big challenges is that it is not possible to fairly compare all possible combinations of pre-training datasets, backbones, and self-supervised learning. For example, SwAV (self-supervised method) only provides pre-trained models on one architecture (*e.g.*, ResNet-50) and ImageNet-1K. Therefore, it is not possible to fairly compare these with self-supervised pre-training and supervised pre-training, which use the state-of-the-art architecture (*e.g.*, ConvNeXt) and larger datasets (*e.g.*, ImageNet-22K).

Fine-Tuning Details. From each pre-trained model, we fine-tune the model with a downstream dataset. We use source domain data to train a model and keep 20% of the source data as a validation set. We choose the learning rate and optimizer by tuning on the validation set. We test different learning rates (lr = 1e−1, 1e−2, 1e−3) of SGD and learning rates (lr = 1e−3, 1e−4, 1e−5) of the Adam optimizer. We add a new FC layer for downstream tasks and train it from scratch with a learning rate 10 times that of the pre-trained layers. We use the image size of 224×224 with random resized cropping. We also use random color jittering, gray-scaling, and horizontal flipping for augmentation for all models. Additional training details can be found in appendix.

4 Experiments

In this section, our goal is to explore the effects of pre-training for domain transfer. We reiterate that most of the prior domain adaptation (DA) or generalization (DG) work use a ResNet backbone pre-trained on ImageNet-1K. A model is denoted by *X-Y* where X represents the name of architecture and Y represents the size of the backbone. For example, Swin-T, Swin-S, and Swin-B represent the tiny, small, and base model of Swin Transformer. Unless specified otherwise, pre-trained models are trained with a supervised loss (*i.e.*, cross-entropy loss). We now evaluate different pre-trained models in domain transfer tasks. In Sect. 4.1, we investigate single source DG and analyze the architecture, pre-training datasets, and loss functions. We also compare these models with the existing DA works. In Sect. 4.2, we explore the existing DA with new architectures. Lastly, we provide feature analysis in Sect. 4.3. Our code is available at: https://github.com/VisionLearningGroup/Benchmark_Domain_Transfer.

Table 1. Accuracy comparison on architectures in single source domain generalization. Each backbone pre-trained on ImageNet1-K is fine-tuned on a single domain (*Real*) and tested on the remaining domains in each benchmark. Recent architectures achieve higher accuracy than ResNet

Backbone	Pre-train. Data	Params	Office-Home			CUB	WILD	DomainNet					AVG
			Ar	Cl	Pr	Pa	–	Cl	In	Pa	Qu	Sk	
ResNet-50	ImageNet-1K	23 M	66.1	49.0	77.2	42.3	70.7	46.6	17.3	45.2	6.5	35.3	45.6
ConvNeXt-T	ImageNet-1K	27 M	67.4	48.7	77.9	42.5	74.0	**52.8**	**20.6**	**50.8**	**7.8**	**41.2**	48.4
DeiT-S	ImageNet-1K	21 M	70.0	**51.3**	**81.2**	**58.0**	73.4	49.5	19.4	49.2	6.9	36.1	**49.5**
Swin-T	ImageNet-1K	27 M	**71.3**	49.4	81.1	52.0	**74.2**	51.8	19.8	49.3	7.3	37.3	49.3
ResNet-101	ImageNet-1K	42 M	68.5	52.4	79.9	46.1	74.0	49.3	19.2	48.6	**8.7**	38.5	48.5
ConvNeXt-S	ImageNet-1K	49 M	72.2	52.7	80.9	43.7	76.2	54.9	22.2	**52.8**	8.1	**43.0**	50.7
Swin-S	ImageNet-1K	48 M	**73.8**	**54.5**	**84.2**	**56.5**	**78.6**	**55.9**	**22.5**	51.8	8.6	41.4	**52.8**

4.1 Single Source Domain Generalization

For this experiment, we fine-tune different pre-trained models with only a single source domain. We take the *Real* domain as the source domain on Office-Home, DomainNet, and CUB and treat the remaining domains as target domains. For WILD, we follow the split in [26]. We do not use the target domain data.

Analysis of Network Architectures. We first compare generalization performance of architectures in Table 1. All models are pre-trained on ImageNet-1K. ConvNeXt and Transformers (DeiT, Swin) outperform their ResNet counterparts. In this experiment, Transformer models achieve the highest accuracy on average. Swin-T outperforms ResNet-50 by 3.7%. This improvement becomes larger in the deeper model. Swin-S outperforms ResNet-101 by 4.3%. We further analyze the effect of depth in a later section. The big difference between ConvNeXt and Transformers is in the CUB experiment. While DeiT-S significantly improves the accuracy by 15.7%, ConvNeXt-T could not improve much compared to ResNet. However, ConvNeXt attains slightly higher accuracy on DomainNet compared to Swin. This suggests that CNN and Transformers may be robust to different types of domain shift. We put additional results of larger networks (*e.g.*, DeiT-B) in the appendix.

Analysis of Pre-training Datasets. We now analyze the effect of additional datasets during pre-training as shown in Fig. 2. Due to the availability of pre-trained models (see *Challenges of Evaluating Models* in the above section), we use different backbones to compare the effect of pre-training datasets. In Fig. 2(a), we compare the accuracy between ImageNet-1K and ImageNet-22K on Swin-B and ConvNeXt-B for Office-Home and DomainNet. We report the accuracy averaged over all settings in each benchmark. In both architectures, pre-training with ImageNet-22K boosts the accuracy for all benchmarks. Especially, there are significant boosts in accuracy on Office-Home and CUB. To be specific, the accuracy of ConvNeXt-B on CUB increases by 19.8%. In Fig. 2(b), we study the effect of JFT-300M. Since a supervised pre-trained model on JFT-300M is not released publicly, we use the publicly available self-trained EfficientNet-B7 [64] on ImageNet-1K and JFT-300M. While it shows similar accuracy improvements on Office-Home, the accuracy improvements on CUB are smaller than ImageNet-22K. This could be because self-training uses pseudo-labeling and the number of classes is still limited to 1K. In Fig. 2(c), we study the effect of vision-language datasets containing image-text pairs. We study ALBEF, which uses ViT-B as an image encoder and BERT_{base} as a text encoder. We made one modification for ALBEF. We first extract the sentence representation from the text encoder with the prompt template "A photo of a {label}" following [40]. Then we initialize the weights of the last FC layer with the sentence representations. While it shows similar behavior on Office-Home, it seriously hurts the performance of CUB. In contrast, ALBEF obtains the highest accuracy on DomainNet compared to all the other models. This indicates that improvement depends on both the pre-training dataset and the downstream task at the same time.

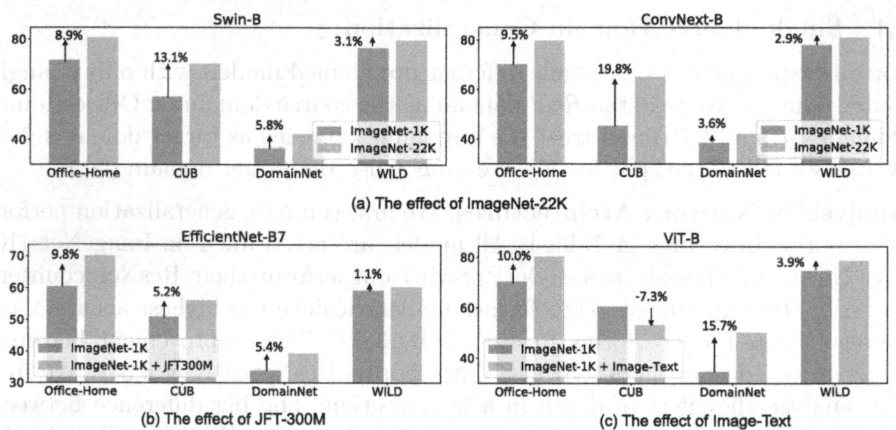

Fig. 2. The effect of additional datasets in pre-training on single source domain generalization. We investigate the following pre-training datasets, (a) ImageNet-22K, (b) JFT-300M, and (c) Image-Text pairs

Analysis of Network Depth. We investigate the accuracy gained from the deeper layers. In Fig. 3, we report the accuracy of ConvNeXt-{B,L,XL}, Swin-{B,L}, and ViT-{S,B,L} pre-trained on ImageNet-22K. In general, ViT shows bigger changes in accuracy according to its depth. The accuracy of Swin and ConvNeXt increases slightly on the benchmarks except for CUB. In WILD, all the architectures show minimal changes according to their depth. When comparing the adaptation methods, we often choose a shallow and light model to reduce computational costs. For example, most of the domain generalization methods [15] employ ResNet-18 rather than ResNet-101. However, the results suggest that we should be careful when choosing a backbone. If we compare adaptation methods and want to use a shallow model for efficiency, it is more desirable to use Swin or ConvNeXt than ViT.

Supervised vs. Self-supervised Learning. Recently, several self-supervised learning (*e.g.*, [7,9,63]) methods outperformed their supervised counterparts on various downstream tasks [2,3,6,7,9]. In Table 2, we investigate the effect of self-supervised learning approaches in pre-training for domain transfer. In Table 2(a), we observe that supervised learning (denoted as Sup.) performs better than self-supervised learning in most cases. Especially on Office-Home and CUB, self-supervised learning significantly hurts performance compared to supervised learning. In Table 2(b), we explore the BEiT, the winner of the VisDA 2021 DA competition [3]. BEiT uses both self-supervised and supervised learning. When self-supervised learning is combined with supervised learning and improves the performance on CUB, DomainNet (denoted as DN), and WILD. While most of the self-supervised approaches focus on only unlabeled data, combining it with labels should be considered to improve further in future research.

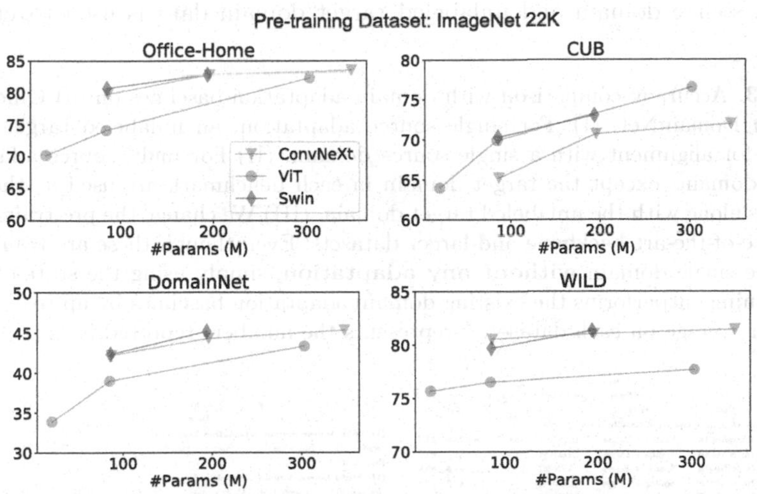

Fig. 3. The effect of architecture depth (number of layers) on single source domain generalization. While ConvNeXt and Swin tend to have slight improvements in accuracy, but the accuracy of ViT is more sensitive to its depth

Table 2. Accuracy comparison between supervised and self-supervised learning in pre-training. (a) In this domain generalization task, supervised pre-trainining outperforms the self-supervised pre-training in most cases. (b) When self-supervised learning is combined with supervised learning, the performance can be improved

Backbone	Training	Dataset			
		OH	CUB	WILD	DN
(a) Pre-training Data: ImageNet-1K					
ResNet-50	Sup	**64.1**	**42.3**	**70.7**	30.2
ResNet-50	MoCo	53.7	37.1	67.9	28.0
ResNet-50	SwAV	56.5	39.2	68.4	**30.7**
ResNet-50	DINO	56.6	37.2	67.6	23.1
DeiT-S	Sup	**58.0**	**58.0**	73.4	**32.2**
ViT-S	DINO	56.3	57.9	**75.1**	29.8
(b) Pre-training Data: ImageNet-22K					
ViT-L	Sup	**82.3**	76.5	77.7	43.3
ViT-L	Sup.+BEiT	80.9	**78.4**	**79.7**	**45.1**

Comparison with Domain Adaptation Baselines. We provide a performance comparison with the existing DA baselines in Table 3. In this comparison we use Office-Home and DomainNet, which are most extensively explored in prior work. In each table, (I) reports the performance of single source DA, where a labeled source domain and unlabeled target domain data is used together for

Table 3. Accuracy comparison with domain adaptation baselines on (a) Office-Home and (b) DomainNet. (I): For single source adaptation, an unlabeled target domain is used for alignment with a single source domain. (II) For multi source adaptation, all the domains except the target domain in each benchmark are used as the source domains along with the unlabeled target domain. (III) We change the pre-training with the state-of-the-art backbone and larger datasets. Even though these are trained with only one single domain **without any adaptation**, simply using the state-of-the-art pre-training outperforms the existing domain adaptation baselines by up to 10.7% and 5.5% on average on each dataset. * represents the numbers reported in [24,39,53,59]

(a) Office-Home

Backbone	Pre-training Data	Downstream Data	Adaptation	Target Domain			AVG
				Ar	Cl	Pr	
(I) Single source domain adaptation baselines							
ResNet-50*	ImageNet-1K	Source + Target	DANN [12]	63.2	51.8	76.8	63.9
ResNet-50*	ImageNet-1K	Source + Target	CDAN [34]	70.9	56.7	81.6	69.7
ResNet-50*	ImageNet-1K	Source + Target	AFN [67]	70.9	57.1	81.5	69.8
ResNet-50*	ImageNet-1K	Source + Target	MDD [69]	72.5	60.2	82.3	71.7
ResNet-50*	ImageNet-1K	Source + Target	SRDC [53]	76.3	57.1	85.0	72.8
(II) Multi source domain adaptation baselines							
ResNet-50*	ImageNet-1K	Multi source + Target	MFSAN [70]	72.1	62	80.3	71.5
ResNet-50*	ImageNet-1K	Multi source + Target	SImpAl [59]	70.8	56.3	80.2	69.1
ResNet-101*	ImageNet-1K	Multi source + Target	SImpAl [59]	73.4	62.4	81.0	72.3
(III) Single source only baselines without adaptation							
ResNet-50*	ImageNet-1K	Source	✗	53.9	41.2	59.9	46.1
ConvNeXt-XL	ImageNet-22K	Source	✗	**85.1**	74.0	**91.4**	**83.5**
ViT-L	ImageNet-22K	Source	✗	84.0	73.0	89.9	82.3
Swin-L	ImageNet-22K	Source	✗	83.4	**74.3**	90.9	82.8
ViT-B	ALBEF [30]	Source	✗	81.7	72.5	87.2	80.4

(b) DomainNet

Backbone	Pre-training Data	Downstream Data	Adaptation	Target Domain					AVG
				Cl	In	Pa	Qu	Sk	
(I) Single source domain adaptation baselines									
ResNet-101*	ImageNet-1K	Source + target	ADDA [56]	39.5	14.5	29.1	14.9	30.7	25.7
ResNet-101*	ImageNet-1K	Source + target	MCD [48]	42.6	19.6	42.6	3.8	30.8	27.9
(II) Multi source domain adaptation baselines									
ResNet-101*	ImageNet-1K	Multi source + target	ADDA [56]	47.5	11.4	36.7	14.7	33.5	28.8
ResNet-101*	ImageNet-1K	Multi source + target	MCD [48]	54.3	22.1	45.7	7.6	43.5	34.6
ResNet-101*	ImageNet-1K	Multi source + target	DCTN [66]	48.6	23.5	48.8	7.2	47.3	35.1
ResNet-101*	ImageNet-1K	Multi source + target	MSDA [39]	58.6	26.0	52.3	6.3	49.5	38.5
ResNet-101*	ImageNet-1K	Multi source + target	SImpAl [59]	66.4	26.5	56.6	18.9	55.5	44.8
(III) Single source only baselines without adaptation									
ResNet-101*	ImageNet-1K	Source	✗	48.4	22.2	49.4	6.4	38.8	33.0
ConvNext-XL	ImageNet-22K	Source	✗	67.7	29.7	62.2	11.4	55.5	45.3
ViT-L	ImageNet-22K	Source	✗	65.5	27.3	61.3	10.2	52.1	43.3
Swin-L	ImageNet-22K	Source	✗	67.2	30.6	62.5	11.2	54.1	45.1
ViT-B	ALBEF [30]	Source	✗	**73.6**	**37.3**	**65.3**	**12.8**	**62.2**	**50.3**

Table 4. Single source domain adaptation with the state-of-the-art pre-training. We report the target accuracy on each bencmark. For Office-Home, CUB, and DomainNet, we use the *Real* domain as a source domain. Surprisingly, more recent adaptation methods (AFN, MDD, MCC) underperform CDAN on average

Backbone	Adaptation	Office-Home				CUB	WILD	DomainNet					
		Ar	Cl	Pr	AVG	Pa	–	Cl	In	Pa	Qu	Sk	AVG
Swin-L	Source-only	74.3	83.4	90.9	82.8	73.0	81.4	67.2	30.6	62.5	11.2	54.1	45.1
ConvNeXt-XL	Source-only	74.0	**85.1**	91.4	83.5	71.9	81.5	67.7	29.7	62.2	11.4	55.5	45.3
Swin-L	DANN [12]	87.3	79.5	93.0	86.6	82.0	68.4	70.4	36.7	66.6	13.0	60.5	49.4
ConvNext-XL	DANN [12]	87.2	79.8	93.1	86.7	80.4	66.2	70.2	36.7	66.6	8.6	62.1	48.8
Swin-L	CDAN [35]	90.1	81.9	93.1	88.4	**84.3**	81.5	72.0	**39.7**	**67.5**	10.8	61.8	50.4
ConvNext-XL	CDAN [35]	**90.2**	84.6	93.8	**89.5**	83.7	**82.5**	**72.1**	39.5	67.3	**13.9**	**63.4**	**51.2**
Swin-L	AFN [67]	87.4	77.6	92.0	85.7	79.9	78.9	68.0	34.5	64.7	6.9	58.1	46.4
ConvNext-XL	AFN [67]	86.0	77.7	92.8	85.5	77.7	79.7	68.0	33.4	65.0	7.8	59.2	46.7
Swin-L	MDD [69]	87.8	78.0	93.6	86.5	83.6	81.1	62.8	34.5	60.7	2.8	46.6	41.5
ConvNext-XL	MDD [69]	88.0	77.6	93.6	86.4	78.8	**82.5**	58.9	29.6	62.8	11.4	51.4	42.8
Swin-L	MCC [24]	89.6	81.1	94.1	88.3	66.7	79.5	71.5	36.4	66.3	3.0	58.2	47.1
ConvNext-XL	MCC [24]	89.5	82.9	**94.4**	88.9	78.8	79.8	71.3	27.7	66.8	1.9	60.2	45.6

adaptation. In (II), multiple labeled source domains are used in addition to the unlabeled target domain. (I, II) use ResNet backbones pre-trained on ImageNet-1K. (III) only uses one single source (*Real*) domain with the recent backbones and larger pre-training datasets. It is surprising that (III), the state-of-art backbones pre-trained on a larger dataset, significantly outperform DA baselines (I, II) despite being trained only on a single source and *not using any adaptation on the target domain.* While ConvNext-XL obtains the best results and outperforms adaptation baselines by up to 10.7% on Office-Home, ViT-B with ALBEF gains more improvements and outperforms adaptation baselines by up to 5.5% on DomainNet. This observation raises a question, is it still fair and reasonable to use ResNet backbones pre-trained on ImageNet-1K as a standard backbone for the comparison of adaptation methods? From the results, it is clear that the standard backbone in the existing domain adaptation benchmarks are outdated. The pre-training stage for DA needs to be updated to reflect recent advances in pre-training.

4.2 Domain Adaptation with Modern Pre-training

The observation in Sect. 4.1 leads us to the next question, will SOTA DA methods still provide gains when these are applied to the recent stronger architectures and pre-training? We study the transferability of prior adaptation methods with new architectures pre-trained on larger datasets.

Transferability of Domain Adaptation. We employ DANN (JMLR'16), CDAN (NeurIPS'18), AFN (ICCV'19), MDD (ICML'19), and MCC(ECCV'20). Table 4 provides the performance of domain adaptation between Swin-L and ConvNeXt-XL pre-trained on ImageNet-22K. First, DA methods still improve the accuracy on average compared to source only (SO) models. However, we observe negative transfer in some settings where DA hurts the performances compared SO. To be specific, all the adaptation methods badly affect the performance on *Real* → *Clipart*(*Cl*) in Office-Home. Second, the relative ranking among adaptation methods on new architectures is different from the ranking on ResNet-based backboes. While MCC obtains SOTA accuracy on ResNet, but CDAN outperforms AFN, MDD, and MCC with these new architectures, which was proposed earlier than the others. This behavior raises another practical question, which adaptation method should we consider the state-of-the-art? We certainly want to have a model with strong performance, but the existing adaptation benchmark with outdated pre-training can not choose the strongest model. We argue that adaptation methods should have transferability on various backbones in order to avoid the potential risk of overfitting to a specific backbone, so that it is able to successfully transfer to new architectures in future.

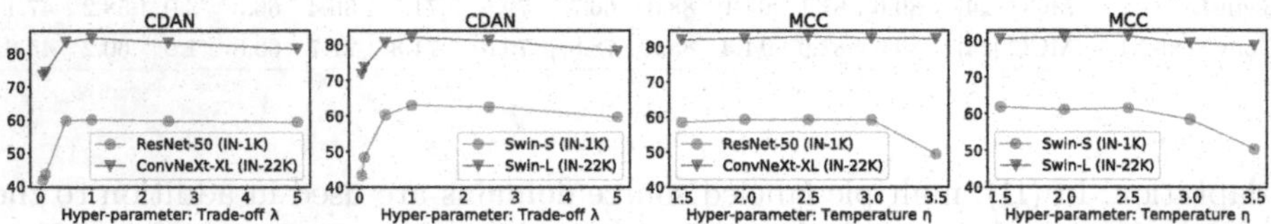

Fig. 4. Analysis on the transferability of hyper-parameters in adaptation methods between a shallow and deep network. We report the accuracy of CNN and Transformers on the *Real* → *Clipart* setting in Office-Home. We observe that the shallow and deep network achieve the highest accuracy on the same value of hyper-parameters in both CDAN and MCC

Analysis on Hyper-parameter. In this experiment, we analyze the transferability of hyper-parameters to new architectures in each adaptation method. The question is whether the optimal hyper-parameters in a shallow network (*e.g.*, ResNet-50) are still optimal in a deep network (*e.g.*, ConvNeXt-XL). We believe this is a practically important question as training a big network is computationally expensive. Hyper-parameter search in a big network can be prohibitively expensive in terms of computational cost. Therefore, the desired property is that hyper-parameters in adaptation methods are transferable between different architectures and their depth. Fig. 4 shows the analysis of performance depending on the hyper-parameters between a shallow and deep network. We investigate two adaptation methods CDAN and MCC. Following [46], we vary the trade-off ($\lambda = 0.05, 0.1, 0.5, 1.0, 2.5, 5.0$) hyper-parameter in CDAN, which controls the trade-off between domain confusion loss and classification loss on the source domain. The default λ in ResNet is 1.0. For MCC, we vary the temperature hyper-parameter ($\eta = 1.5, 2.0, 2.5, 3.0, 3.5$), which affects of classifier's confusion loss. The default η in ResNet is 2.5. We employ ResNet-50 as a shallow network and ConvNeXt-XL as a deep network for CNN, and Swin-S as a shallow network and Swin-L as a deep network. The shallow networks are pre-trained on

ImageNet-1K and deep networks are pre-trained on ImageNet-22K. The accuracy across the depth (shallow vs. deep) and architectures (CNN vs. Transformers) show similar tendency and obtain the highest accuracy with the same hyper-parameter values. Therefore, we observe that the default hyper-parameters of λ and η in shallow networks are transferable to deep networks. Additionally, the sensitivity of deep networks is small compared to that of shallow networks. We measure the standard deviation of accuracy. Swin-L obtains a standard deviation of 4.2%, but Swin-S obtains a much higher standard deviation of 8.3%.

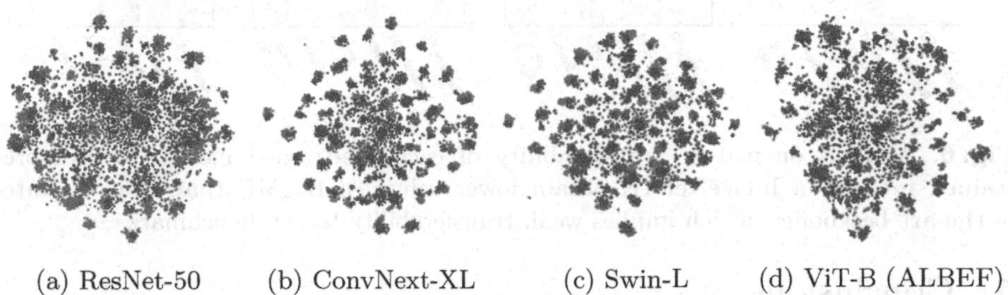

(a) ResNet-50 (b) ConvNext-XL (c) Swin-L (d) ViT-B (ALBEF)

Fig. 5. t-SNE visualization of pre-trained models. We use the Real (red) and Clipart (**blue**) domains in Office-Home. We directly utilize features from each pre-trained model without fine-tuning. Compared to (a) the ResNet-50 pre-trained on ImageNet-1K, (b) ConvNext-XL and (c) Swin-L pre-trained on ImageNet-22K produce more discriminative as well as domain-aligned representations (Color figure online)

4.3 Feature Analysis

We provide feature analysis in this section. We use features directly obtained from each pre-training without fine-tuning on domain adaptation benchmarks.

Feature Visualization. First, we show the t-SNE [36] feature visualization of each pre-trained models in Fig. 5. We compare (a) ResNet-50 pre-trained on ImageNet-1K with (b) ConvNeXt-XL, (c) Swin-L pre-trained on ImageNet-22K, and (d) ViT-B from ALBEF [30]. We directly extract features from the pre-trained models on the Real (colored by red) and Clipart (colored by **blue**) domains in Office-Home. While the red and blue dots are highly separated in ResNet-50, these are aligned with each other in ConvNeXt-XL and Swin-L. It is also clear that ConvNeXt-XL and Swin-L obtain better clustered and discriminative representations. (d) ViT-B pre-trained (ALBEF) on image-text pairs shows different patterns, where the blue dots are red dots are somewhat aligned but it does not provide clustered representations. This could be probably due to that the pretext task of ALBEF is to align image and text, but not classification.

Analysis on Feature Transferability. We employ LogME [68] to evaluate the transferability of features for downstream tasks. LogME is used to assess pre-trained models, which estimates the maximum value of label evidence from the extracted features of downstream data. A higher value LogME implies better transferability to downstream tasks. We measure LogME of each pre-training for all domains in the benchmarks as shown in Fig. 6. As expected, ResNet backbones pre-trained on ImageNet-1K obtain very low values of LogME compared to the state-of-the-art backbones. We reiterate that the pre-training stage should be modernized according to the recent advances in computer vision.

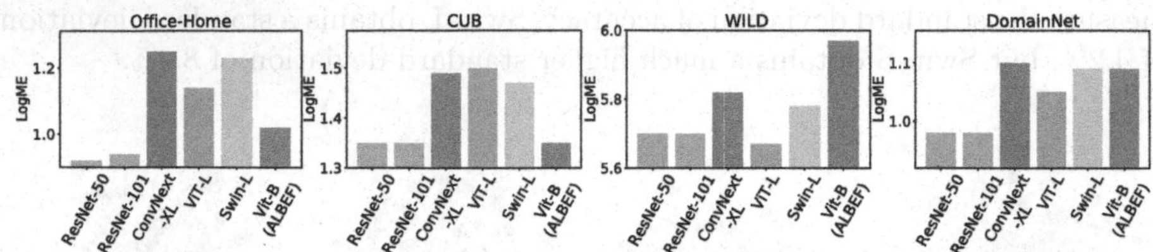

Fig. 6. Analysis on feature transferability of each pre-trained model. ResNet pre-trained models on ImageNet-1K obtain lower values of LogME than that of state-of-the-art backbones, which implies weak transferability to DA benchmarks

5 Conclusions

Most domain transfer works pay little attention to the importance of the pre-training stage. In this work, we provide an in-depth analysis of the effect of modern pre-training on domain transfer. We summarize some of our key findings:

1. **What makes strong pre-training for domain transfer?** In Sect. 4.1, we observe that many factors, including network architecture, pre-training dataset, and network size contribute to the improvements in domain transfer tasks. However, there is no single winner across all benchmark datasets. The transferability of pre-training depends on the target benchmark, adaptation method, and network depth. Most importantly, we observe that simply using the SOTA pre-training outperforms all the domain adaptation baselines.
2. **Do we still need domain adaptation with modern pre-training?** In Sect. 4.2, while we find that adaptation methods still improve the accuracy with modern pre-training, the relative ranking of domain adaptation methods is not preserved. With modern pre-training, an outdated DA method performs better than more recent DA methods in our experiments.

Limitations. Due to the availability of pre-trained models, we could not analyze full ablations (*e.g.*, SOTA backbones pre-trained on JFT-300M). In this work, we use a very simple fine-tuning strategy by adding a single FC layer, but there could be other simple better ways to fine-tune pre-trained models for downstream tasks. In addition to image classification tasks, other computer vision tasks including domain adaptive object detection, segmentation, or video domain adaptation should be explored with modern pre-training in future research. We hope future work should use these results as a new baseline.

Acknowledgments. This work was supported by DARPA LwLL and NSF Award No. 1535797.

References

1. Bai, Y., Mei, J., Yuille, A.L., Xie, C.: Are transformers more robust than CNNs? In: Advances in Neural Information Processing Systems (NeurIPS), vol. 34 (2021)
2. Bao, H., Dong, L., Piao, S., Wei, F.: BEit: BERT pre-training of image transformers. In: International Conference on Learning Representations (2022). www.openreview.net/forum?id=p-BhZSz59o4
3. Bashkirova, D., et al.: Visda-2021 competition universal domain adaptation to improve performance on out-of-distribution data. arXiv preprint arXiv:2107.11011 (2021)
4. Beery, S., Cole, E., Gjoka, A.: The iwildcam 2020 competition dataset. arXiv preprint arXiv:2004.10340 (2020)
5. Bhushan Damodaran, B., Kellenberger, B., Flamary, R., Tuia, D., Courty, N.: Deepjdot: deep joint distribution optimal transport for unsupervised domain adaptation. In: European Conference on Computer Vision (ECCV), pp. 447–463 (2018)
6. Caron, M., Misra, I., Mairal, J., Goyal, P., Bojanowski, P., Joulin, A.: Unsupervised learning of visual features by contrasting cluster assignments. In: Advances in Neural Information Processing Systems (NeurIPS), vol. 33, pp. 9912–9924 (2020)
7. Caron, M., et al.: Emerging properties in self-supervised vision transformers. In: IEEE International Conference on Computer Vision (ICCV), pp. 9650–9660 (2021)
8. Changpinyo, S., Sharma, P., Ding, N., Soricut, R.: Conceptual 12m: pushing web-scale image-text pre-training to recognize long-tail visual concepts. In: IEEE Conference on Computer Vision and Pattern Recognition (CVPR), pp. 3558–3568 (2021)
9. Chen, T., Kornblith, S., Norouzi, M., Hinton, G.: A simple framework for contrastive learning of visual representations. In: International Conference on Machine Learning (ICML), pp. 1597–1607. PMLR (2020)
10. Dosovitskiy, A., et al.: An image is worth 16x16 words: transformers for image recognition at scale. In: International Conference on Learning Representations (ICLR) (2021). www.openreview.net/forum?id=YicbFdNTTy
11. Dosovitskiy, A., Fischer, P., Springenberg, J.T., Riedmiller, M., Brox, T.: Discriminative unsupervised feature learning with exemplar convolutional neural networks. IEEE Trans. Pattern Anal. Mach. Intell. **38**(9), 1734–1747 (2015)
12. Ganin, Y., et al.: Domain-adversarial training of neural networks. J. Mach. Learn. Res. **17**(1), 2030–2096 (2016)
13. Gidaris, S., Singh, P., Komodakis, N.: Unsupervised representation learning by predicting image rotations. arXiv preprint arXiv:1803.07728 (2018)
14. Goodfellow, I.J., Shlens, J., Szegedy, C.: Explaining and harnessing adversarial examples. arXiv preprint arXiv:1412.6572 (2014)
15. Gulrajani, I., Lopez-Paz, D.: In search of lost domain generalization. In: International Conference on Learning Representations (2021). www.openreview.net/forum?id=lQdXeXDoWtI
16. He, K., Fan, H., Wu, Y., Xie, S., Girshick, R.: Momentum contrast for unsupervised visual representation learning. In: IEEE Conference on Computer Vision and Pattern Recognition (CVPR), pp. 9729–9738 (2020)
17. He, K., Zhang, X., Ren, S., Sun, J.: Deep residual learning for image recognition. In: IEEE Conference on Computer Vision and Pattern Recognition (CVPR), pp. 770–778 (2016)

18. Hendrycks, D., Dietterich, T.: Benchmarking neural network robustness to common corruptions and perturbations. In: International Conference on Learning Representations (2019). www.openreview.net/forum?id=HJz6tiCqYm
19. Hinton, G., Vinyals, O., Dean, J.: Distilling the knowledge in a neural network. arXiv preprint arXiv:1503.02531 (2015)
20. Hoffman, J., Tzeng, E., Donahue, J., Jia, Y., Saenko, K., Darrell, T.: One-shot adaptation of supervised deep convolutional models. In: International Conference on Learning Representations (ICLR) (2014)
21. Hu, J., Shen, L., Sun, G.: Squeeze-and-excitation networks. In: IEEE Conference on Computer Vision and Pattern Recognition (CVPR), pp. 7132–7141 (2018)
22. Huang, J., Dong, Q., Gong, S., Zhu, X.: Unsupervised deep learning by neighbourhood discovery. arXiv preprint arXiv:1904.11567 (2019)
23. Jia, C., et al.: Scaling up visual and vision-language representation learning with noisy text supervision. In: International Conference on Machine Learning (ICML), pp. 4904–4916. PMLR (2021)
24. Jin, Y., Wang, X., Long, M., Wang, J.: Minimum class confusion for versatile domain adaptation. In: Vedaldi, A., Bischof, H., Brox, T., Frahm, J.-M. (eds.) ECCV 2020. LNCS, vol. 12366, pp. 464–480. Springer, Cham (2020). https://doi.org/10.1007/978-3-030-58589-1_28
25. Kim, D., Saito, K., Oh, T.H., Plummer, B.A., Sclaroff, S., Saenko, K.: CDS: Cross-domain self-supervised pre-training. In: IEEE International Conference on Computer Vision (ICCV), pp. 9123–9132 (2021)
26. Koh, P.W., et al.: Wilds: A benchmark of in-the-wild distribution shifts. In: International Conference on Machine Learning (ICML), pp. 5637–5664. PMLR (2021)
27. Kornblith, S., Shlens, J., Le, Q.V.: Do better ImageNet models transfer better? In: IEEE Conference on Computer Vision and Pattern Recognition (CVPR), pp. 2661–2671 (2019)
28. Krishna, R., et al.: Visual genome: connecting language and vision using crowdsourced dense image annotations. Int. J. Comput. Vis. **123**(1), 32–73 (2017)
29. Krizhevsky, A., Sutskever, I., Hinton, G.E.: ImageNet classification with deep convolutional neural networks. In: Advances in Neural Information Processing Systems (NIPS), vol. 25 (2012)
30. Li, J., Selvaraju, R., Gotmare, A., Joty, S., Xiong, C., Hoi, S.C.H.: Align before fuse: vision and language representation learning with momentum distillation. In: Advances in Neural Information Processing Systems (NeurIPS), vol. 34 (2021)
31. Lin, T.-Y., et al.: Microsoft COCO: Common Objects in Context. In: Fleet, D., Pajdla, T., Schiele, B., Tuytelaars, T. (eds.) ECCV 2014. LNCS, vol. 8693, pp. 740–755. Springer, Cham (2014). https://doi.org/10.1007/978-3-319-10602-1_48
32. Liu, Z., et al.: Swin transformer: Hierarchical vision transformer using shifted windows. In: IEEE International Conference on Computer Vision (ICCV), pp. 10012–10022 (2021)
33. Liu, Z., Mao, H., Wu, C.Y., Feichtenhofer, C., Darrell, T., Xie, S.: A ConvNet for the 2020s. arXiv preprint arXiv:2201.03545 (2022)
34. Long, M., Cao, Z., Wang, J., Jordan, M.I.: Conditional adversarial domain adaptation. In: Advances in Neural Information Processing Systems (NeurIPS), pp. 1640–1650 (2018)
35. Long, M., Zhu, H., Wang, J., Jordan, M.I.: Unsupervised domain adaptation with residual transfer networks. In: Advances in Neural Information Processing Systems (NeurIPS), pp. 136–144 (2016)
36. Van der Maaten, L., Hinton, G.: Visualizing data using t-SNE. J. Mach. Learn. Res. **9**(11) (2008)

37. Noroozi, M., Favaro, P.: Unsupervised learning of visual representations by solving jigsaw puzzles. In: Leibe, B., Matas, J., Sebe, N., Welling, M. (eds.) ECCV 2016. LNCS, vol. 9910, pp. 69–84. Springer, Cham (2016). https://doi.org/10.1007/978-3-319-46466-4_5
38. Ordonez, V., Kulkarni, G., Berg, T.: Im2text: describing images using 1 million captioned photographs. In: Advances in Neural Information Processing Systems (NeurIPS), vol. 24 (2011)
39. Peng, X., Bai, Q., Xia, X., Huang, Z., Saenko, K., Wang, B.: Moment matching for multi-source domain adaptation. In: IEEE International Conference on Computer Vision (ICCV), pp. 1406–1415 (2019)
40. Radford, A., et al.: Learning transferable visual models from natural language supervision. In: International Conference on Machine Learning (ICML), pp. 8748–8763. PMLR (2021)
41. Russakovsky, O., et al.: Imagenet large scale visual recognition challenge. Int. J. Comput. Vis. **115**(3), 211–252 (2015)
42. Saenko, K., Kulis, B., Fritz, M., Darrell, T.: Adapting visual category models to new domains. In: Daniilidis, K., Maragos, P., Paragios, N. (eds.) ECCV 2010. LNCS, vol. 6314, pp. 213–226. Springer, Heidelberg (2010). https://doi.org/10.1007/978-3-642-15561-1_16
43. Sagawa, S., et al.: Extending the WILDS benchmark for unsupervised adaptation. In: International Conference on Learning Representations (2022). www.openreview.net/forum?id=z7p2V6KROOV
44. Saito, K., Kim, D., Sclaroff, S., Darrell, T., Saenko, K.: Semi-supervised domain adaptation via minimax entropy. In: IEEE International Conference on Computer Vision (ICCV) (2019)
45. Saito, K., Kim, D., Sclaroff, S., Saenko, K.: Universal domain adaptation through self supervision. arXiv preprint arXiv:2002.07953 (2020)
46. Saito, K., Kim, D., Teterwak, P., Sclaroff, S., Darrell, T., Saenko, K.: Tune it the right way: unsupervised validation of domain adaptation via soft neighborhood density. In: IEEE International Conference on Computer Vision (ICCV), pp. 9184–9193 (2021)
47. Saito, K., Ushiku, Y., Harada, T., Saenko, K.: Strong-weak distribution alignment for adaptive object detection. In: IEEE Conference on Computer Vision and Pattern Recognition (CVPR), pp. 6956–6965 (2019)
48. Saito, K., Watanabe, K., Ushiku, Y., Harada, T.: Maximum classifier discrepancy for unsupervised domain adaptation. In: IEEE Conference on Computer Vision and Pattern Recognition (CVPR), pp. 3723–3732 (2018)
49. Sharma, P., Ding, N., Goodman, S., Soricut, R.: Conceptual captions: a cleaned, hypernymed, image alt-text dataset for automatic image captioning. In: Proceedings of the 56th Annual Meeting of the Association for Computational Linguistics (Volume 1: Long Papers), pp. 2556–2565 (2018)
50. Simonyan, K., Zisserman, A.: Very deep convolutional networks for large-scale image recognition. arXiv preprint arXiv:1409.1556 (2014)
51. Sun, C., Shrivastava, A., Singh, S., Gupta, A.: Revisiting unreasonable effectiveness of data in deep learning era. In: IEEE International Conference on Computer Vision (ICCV), pp. 843–852 (2017)
52. Tan, M., Le, Q.: Efficientnet: rethinking model scaling for convolutional neural networks. In: International Conference on Machine Learning (ICML), pp. 6105–6114. PMLR (2019)

53. Tang, H., Chen, K., Jia, K.: Unsupervised domain adaptation via structurally regularized deep clustering. In: IEEE Conference on Computer Vision and Pattern Recognition (CVPR), pp. 8725–8735 (2020)
54. Touvron, H., Cord, M., Douze, M., Massa, F., Sablayrolles, A., Jégou, H.: Training data-efficient image transformers & distillation through attention. In: International Conference on Machine Learning (ICML), pp. 10347–10357. PMLR (2021)
55. Tsai, Y.H., Sohn, K., Schulter, S., Chandraker, M.: Domain adaptation for structured output via discriminative patch representations. In: IEEE International Conference on Computer Vision (ICCV), pp. 1456–1465 (2019)
56. Tzeng, E., Hoffman, J., Zhang, N., Saenko, K., Darrell, T.: Deep domain confusion: maximizing for domain invariance. arXiv preprint arXiv:1412.3474 (2014)
57. Van Horn, G., et al.: The inaturalist species classification and detection dataset. In: IEEE Conference on Computer Vision and Pattern Recognition (CVPR), pp. 8769–8778 (2018)
58. Vaswani, A., et al.: Attention is all you need 30 (2017)
59. Venkat, N., Kundu, J.N., Singh, D., Revanur, A., et al.: Your classifier can secretly suffice multi-source domain adaptation. In: Advances in Neural Information Processing Systems (NeurIPS), vol. 33, pp. 4647–4659 (2020)
60. Venkateswara, H., Eusebio, J., Chakraborty, S., Panchanathan, S.: Deep hashing network for unsupervised domain adaptation. In: IEEE Conference on Computer Vision and Pattern Recognition (CVPR), pp. 5018–5027 (2017)
61. Wah, C., Branson, S., Welinder, P., Perona, P., Belongie, S.: The Caltech-UCSD birds-200-2011 dataset (2011)
62. Wang, S., Chen, X., Wang, Y., Long, M., Wang, J.: Progressive adversarial networks for fine-grained domain adaptation. In: IEEE Conference on Computer Vision and Pattern Recognition (CVPR), pp. 9213–9222 (2020)
63. Wu, Z., Xiong, Y., Yu, S.X., Lin, D.: Unsupervised feature learning via nonparametric instance discrimination. In: IEEE Conference on Computer Vision and Pattern Recognition (CVPR), pp. 3733–3742 (2018)
64. Xie, Q., Luong, M.T., Hovy, E., Le, Q.V.: Self-training with noisy student improves imagenet classification. In: IEEE Conference on Computer Vision and Pattern Recognition (CVPR), pp. 10687–10698 (2020)
65. Xie, S., Girshick, R., Dollár, P., Tu, Z., He, K.: Aggregated residual transformations for deep neural networks. In: IEEE Conference on Computer Vision and Pattern Recognition (CVPR), pp. 1492–1500 (2017)
66. Xu, R., Chen, Z., Zuo, W., Yan, J., Lin, L.: Deep cocktail network: multi-source unsupervised domain adaptation with category shift. In: IEEE Conference on Computer Vision and Pattern Recognition (CVPR), pp. 3964–3973 (2018)
67. Xu, R., Li, G., Yang, J., Lin, L.: Larger norm more transferable: An adaptive feature norm approach for unsupervised domain adaptation. In: IEEE International Conference on Computer Vision (ICCV), pp. 1426–1435 (2019)
68. You, K., Liu, Y., Wang, J., Long, M.: Logme: practical assessment of pre-trained models for transfer learning. In: International Conference on Machine Learning (ICML), pp. 12133–12143. PMLR (2021)
69. Zhang, Y., Liu, T., Long, M., Jordan, M.: Bridging theory and algorithm for domain adaptation. In: International Conference on Machine Learning (ICML), pp. 7404–7413. PMLR (2019)
70. Zhu, Y., Zhuang, F., Wang, D.: Aligning domain-specific distribution and classifier for cross-domain classification from multiple sources. In: Proceedings of the AAAI Conference on Artificial Intelligence, vol. 33, pp. 5989–5996 (2019)

Prior Knowledge Guided Unsupervised Domain Adaptation

Tao Sun[1(✉)], Cheng Lu[2], and Haibin Ling[1]

[1] Stony Brook University, Stony Brook, USA
{tao,hling}@cs.stonybrook.edu
[2] XPeng Motors, Guangzhou, China
luc@xiaopeng.com

Abstract. The waive of labels in the target domain makes Unsupervised Domain Adaptation (UDA) an attractive technique in many real-world applications, though it also brings great challenges as model adaptation becomes harder without labeled target data. In this paper, we address this issue by seeking compensation from target domain prior knowledge, which is often (partially) available in practice, *e.g.*, from human expertise. This leads to a novel yet practical setting where in addition to the training data, some prior knowledge about the target class distribution are available. We term the setting as Knowledge-guided Unsupervised Domain Adaptation (KUDA). In particular, we consider two specific types of prior knowledge about the class distribution in the target domain: *Unary Bound* that describes the lower and upper bounds of individual class probabilities, and *Binary Relationship* that describes the relations between two class probabilities. We propose a general rectification module that uses such prior knowledge to refine model generated pseudo labels. The module is formulated as a Zero-One Programming problem derived from the prior knowledge and a smooth regularizer. It can be easily plugged into self-training based UDA methods, and we combine it with two state-of-the-art methods, SHOT and DINE. Empirical results on four benchmarks confirm that the rectification module clearly improves the quality of pseudo labels, which in turn benefits the self-training stage. With the guidance from prior knowledge, the performances of both methods are substantially boosted. We expect our work to inspire further investigations in integrating prior knowledge in UDA. Code is available at https://github.com/tsun/KUDA.

Keywords: Unsupervised Domain Adaptation · Class prior

1 Introduction

Deep neural networks have shown significant performance improvement in a variety of vision tasks [8,12,23,30]. However, such performance highly relies on massive annotated data, which is often expensive to obtain. Unsupervised Domain

Supplementary Information The online version contains supplementary material available at https://doi.org/10.1007/978-3-031-19827-4_37.

S. Avidan et al. (Eds.): ECCV 2022, LNCS 13693, pp. 639–655, 2022.
https://doi.org/10.1007/978-3-031-19827-4_37

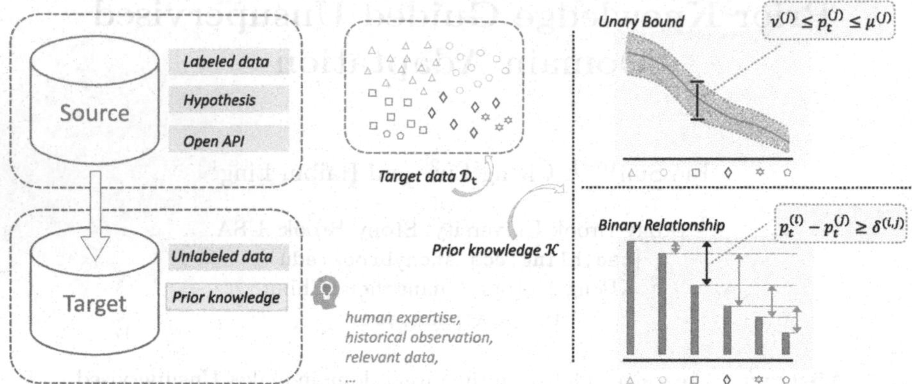

Fig. 1. (Left) Knowledge-guided Unsupervised Domain Adaptation (KUDA). In addition to target data, some prior knowledge about target class distribution is available. (Right) two types of prior knowledge considered in the paper.

Adaptation (UDA) addresses this issue by transferring a predictive model learned from a labeled source domain to an unlabeled target domain [25,38,40]. Despite the advancement made in recent years, UDA remains a challenging task due to the absence of labels in the target domain. On the other hand, in many real-world applications, prior knowledge about the target domain is often readily available. In particular, some information about class distribution is often available without bothering labeling specific target samples. For example, botanists can estimate the proportion of wild species within a reserve using historical information; economists can tell whether vans are more possessed than other vehicles based on the local industrial structure; *etc.* Such prior knowledge may provide valuable clues that are complementary to the unlabeled training data, and can be especially beneficial when there exists a large distribution shift between source and target domains. In fact, prior knowledge has been used to compensate the deficiency of labeled data [14,33], but its systematical integration into UDA solutions remains under-explored.

Inspired by the above observation, in this paper we study a novel setting of UDA, named *Knowledge-guided Unsupervised Domain Adaptation* (KUDA), as illustrated in Fig. 1. Specifically, in addition to target training samples $\mathcal{D}_t$, a collection of prior knowledge $\mathcal{K}$ on target class distribution $p_t(y)$ is accessible. In particular, we consider two types of prior knowledge: *Unary Bound* that describes the lower and upper bounds of individual class probability $p_t^{(c)}$ (*e.g.*, the probability of "square" is between 0.1 and 0.3), and *Binary Relationship* that describes the relations between probabilities of two classes, $p_t^{(c_1)}$ and $p_t^{(c_2)}$ (*e.g.*, there are more "triangles" than "squares"). The task of KUDA is to adapt a predictive model learned from a source domain to a target domain under the guidance from such prior knowledge. It is worth mentioning that there can be many other types of prior knowledge which may help to improve UDA performance, and we choose unary and binary statistics over the class distribution for their generality and accessibility in practice.

To incorporate the prior knowledge into domain adaptation, we propose a novel *rectification module* to refine model generated pseudo labels. We formulate the rectification procedure using prior knowledge as a *Zero-One Programming* (ZOP) [41] problem, where its optimal solution returns the updated pseudo labels. Moreover, smooth regularization is applied to maintain consistency of pseudo labels in neighboring samples. This module can be easily integrated into self-training-based UDA methods. To validate its effectiveness, we choose two recent state-of-the-art UDA methods, SHOT [18] and DINE [19], and improve them with the rectification module.

The experimental validation is conducted on four commonly used UDA benchmarks, two of which have a large label distribution shift by design. The results confirm that the rectification module improves the quality of pseudo labels and hence benefits the self-training stage. Consequently, the performances of two methods under the guidance of prior knowledge, named respectively kSHOT and kDINE, are substantially boosted compared with the vanilla versions. Our work demonstrates that it is important to consider target class prior knowledge, especially when the domain gap is large.

In summary, we make the following contributions:

- We study a novel and practical setting of Knowledge-guided Unsupervised Domain Adaptation (KUDA), where prior knowledge about target class distribution available in addition to unlabeled training samples.
- We introduce a general rectification module that refines pseudo labels with the guidance from prior knowledge. It can be easily plugged into self-training based UDA methods.
- Extensive experiments on both standard and label-shifted benchmarks validate that incorporating prior knowledge can significantly boost the performance of adapted models, reducing the reliance on target training data.

2 Related Work

Incorporating Prior Knowledge. There has been a long history of incorporating prior knowledge into machine learning tasks. Using prior knowledge removes or reduces the reliance on training data. The knowledge can be expressed in various forms, such as statistical descriptions from other data or human expertise, inductive biases, physical models, *etc.* The most related one to our work is *target prior*, where the distribution of target variable $p(y)$ is known [14,33]. In [24], the class distribution prior conditioned on certain inputs is captured by generalized expectation. Zhu *et al.* [46] employ class priors to set thresholds on the propagation of labels. Wang *et al.* [39] assume that a parametric target prior model $p_\eta(y)$ can be obtained from relevant subjects yet having no correspondence with training data. Inductive biases have been widely used in deep neural networks. A canonical one is translation equivariance through convolutions [10,13,37]. Lin *et al.* [20] add geometric priors based on Hough transform in line detection. Physical models of image formation have been integrated into the tasks of image decomposition [1], rain image restoration [17], day-night adaptation [15], *etc.*

Domain Adaptation Settings. Domain Adaptation (DA) presents under many different settings. In the vanilla Unsupervised Domain Adaptation (UDA) [3,29,35,45], only labeled data from a source domain and unlabeled data from a target domain are available. Since no labeled target data is available, UDA can be a challenging task when the domain gap is large. Semi-supervised DA (SSDA) [11,16,32] assumes a few labeled target data is available, which often greatly boosts performance compared with UDA. Active DA [5,28,42] further selects the most informative samples to query their labels from the oracle. Then human-defined criteria like uncertainty and diversity can be injected to measure the informativeness of samples. SSDA and Active DA can be viewed as incorporating additional instance-level label information compared with UDA. Another line is to reduce the information released by source domain, usually due to some privacy issues. Source-data free UDA [2,4,9,18] assumes only a trained model is offered by the source domain while source data are inaccessible. To conceal model details, the black-box source model [19,21,43] is further studied.

Our Study. Our proposed KUDA methods incorporate class distribution-level information and is complementary to all of the above-mentioned settings. It is the first work along this direction, and we expect to see further studies to explore richer prior knowledge for UDA or to extend the idea to general DA scenarios.

3 Knowledge-Guided UDA

Preliminaries. In this paper, we focus on C-way classification problem for UDA tasks. We use $\mathcal{X}$ and $\mathcal{C} = \{0, 1, \ldots, C-1\}$ to denote the input space and the label space respectively. In a vanilla UDA task, we are given labeled samples $\mathcal{D}_s = \{(\boldsymbol{x}_i^s, y_i^s)\}_{i=0}^{n_s-1}$ from a source domain $\mathcal{P}_S(\mathcal{X}, \mathcal{C})$, and unlabeled samples $\mathcal{D}_t = \{(\boldsymbol{x}_i^t)\}_{i=0}^{n_t-1}$ from a target domain $\mathcal{P}_T(\mathcal{X}, \mathcal{C})$. The goal of UDA is to learn a labeling function $f_t = h_t \circ g_t : \mathcal{X} \rightarrow \mathcal{C}$ for target domain, where g_t is the feature extractor and h_t is the label predictor.

Prior Knowledge of Target Class Distribution. The class distribution of target domain, $p_t(y)$, is an important quantity while inaccessible in UDA. One way is to estimate it from model predictions on unlabeled target data [22]. However, this can often be unreliable when the domain gap is large. The deficiency of labeled target samples can be compensated with prior knowledge, *e.g.*, from human expertise. In fact, it is often possible to obtain some information about class distribution without bothering labeling specific target samples in real-world applications. Table 1 lists two types of prior knowledge considered in this paper. *Unary Bound* describes the lower and upper bounds of individual class probability $p_t^{(c)}$, and *Binary Relationship* describes the relations between probabilities of two classes, $p_t^{(c_1)}$ and $p_t^{(c_2)}$. Both statistics over the class distribution are general and easy to obtain in practice. Other types of prior knowledge beyond these can be similarly defined in terms of three or more probabilities.

Setting of KUDA. We study a novel and realistic setting termed **Knowledge-guided Unsupervised Domain Adaptation (KUDA)**. In KUDA, in addition to $\mathcal{D}_s$ and $\mathcal{D}_t$, we have access to some prior knowledge $\mathcal{K}$ about the target

Table 1. Two types of prior knowledge considered in the paper.

Knowledge type	Formulation
Unary Bound (UB)	$\mathcal{K} = \left\{\left(\nu^{(c)} \le p_t^{(c)} \le \mu^{(c)}\right) \middle| c \in \mathcal{C}\right\}$
Binary Relationship (BR)	$\mathcal{K} = \left\{\left(p_t^{(c_1)} - p_t^{(c_2)} \ge \delta^{(c_1,c_2)}\right) \middle| c_1, c_2 \in \mathcal{C}\right\}$

class distribution p_t^c. Such prior knowledge may provide valuable clues that are complementary to the unlabeled training data, and can be especially beneficial when there exists a large distribution shift between source and target domains. In particular, we assume that $\mathcal{K}$ can be expressed in a collection of inequality constraints as listed in Table 1. The goal is to learn an optimal target labeling function f_t under the guidance from the prior knowledge $\mathcal{K}$.

4 Method

4.1 Rectify Pseudo Labels with Prior Knowledge

Let us consider a general situation. Suppose we have a model predicted class probability matrix $P \in \mathbb{R}^{n_t \times C}$ of target data. The pseudo label of the i-th sample can be obtained via $\hat{y}_i^t = \arg\max \boldsymbol{p}_i$, where $\boldsymbol{p}_i$ is the i-th row of P. This procedure can be equivalently expressed in a more compact form using one-hot label representation $\boldsymbol{l}_i$ and its matrix form L (*i.e.*, $\boldsymbol{l}_i$ is the i-th row of L)

$$\hat{L} = \arg\max_{L} \langle L, P \rangle, \quad \text{s.t.} \begin{cases} \sum_c L_{i,c} = 1, \forall i \in [n_t] \\ L_{i,c} \in \{0,1\}, \forall c \in \mathcal{C}, i \in [n_t] \end{cases} \tag{1}$$

where $\langle \cdot, \cdot \rangle$ is the inner product of two matrices, and $[n_t] \triangleq \{0, 1, \dots, n_t - 1\}$. For the optimal solution $\hat{L}$ of Eq. 1, $\hat{L}_{i,\hat{y}_i^t} = 1$ and $\hat{L}_{i,c} = 0\ \forall c \neq \hat{y}_i^t$.

Without any prior knowledge, the optimal $\boldsymbol{l}_i$ is assigned independently for each target sample. The empirical class probability $\hat{p}_t^{(c)} = \sum_i L_{i,c}/n_t$ is expected to be close to $p_t^{(c)}$. However, this is often violated when the model predictions are noisy. When the prior knowledge $\mathcal{K}$ about p_t is available, we can use it to rectify pseudo labels so that $\hat{p}_t$ is more compliant with p_t.

Hard Constraint Form. Given the inequalities listed in Table 1, we plug in $\hat{p}_t$ and add the constraints to the optimization problem in Eq. 1. Then the optimization problem in hard constraint form can be formulated as:

- **Unary Bound.**

$$\hat{L} = \arg\max_{L} \langle L, P \rangle, \quad \text{s.t.} \begin{cases} \sum_c L_{i,c} = 1 \quad \forall i \in [n_t] \\ L_{i,c} \in \{0,1\}, \quad \forall c \in \mathcal{C}, i \in [n_t] \\ \sum_i L_{i,c} \ge n_t \nu^{(c)}, \quad \forall c \in \mathcal{C} \\ -\sum_i L_{i,c} \ge -n_t \mu^{(c)}, \quad \forall c \in \mathcal{C} \end{cases} \tag{2}$$

– **Binary Relationship**.

$$\hat{L} = \arg\max_{L} \langle L, P \rangle, \text{ s.t. } \begin{cases} \sum_c L_{i,c} = 1 \quad \forall i \in [n_t] \\ L_{i,c} \in \{0,1\}, \quad \forall c \in \mathcal{C}, i \in [n_t] \\ \sum_i (L_{i,c_1} - L_{i,c_2}) \geq n_t \delta^{(c_1,c_2)}, \quad \forall c_1, c_2 \in \mathcal{C} \end{cases} \tag{3}$$

Equation 2 and Eq. 3 are *Zero-One Programming* problems [41], and can be solved with standard solvers [7]. However, using hard constraint form is not favored. When these constraints are inconsistent, the optimization problem becomes infeasible.

Soft Constraint Form. To overcome the drawbacks of hard constraint form, we convert prior knowledge into soft constraints by introducing slack variables:

- **Unary Bound.**

$$\hat{L} = \arg\max_{L} \langle L, P \rangle - M \sum_c (\xi_c^{(\nu)} + \xi_c^{(\mu)})$$
$$\text{s.t.} \begin{cases} \sum_c L_{i,c} = 1 \quad \forall i \in [n_t] \\ L_{i,c} \in \{0,1\}, \quad \forall c \in \mathcal{C}, i \in [n_t] \\ \xi_c^{(\nu)} = \max\left(0, -\sum_i L_{i,c} + n_t \nu^{(c)}\right), \quad \forall c \in \mathcal{C} \\ \xi_c^{(\mu)} = \max\left(0, \sum_i L_{i,c} - n_t \mu^{(c)}\right), \quad \forall c \in \mathcal{C} \end{cases} \tag{4}$$

- **Binary Relationship.**

$$\hat{L} = \arg\max_{L} \langle L, P \rangle - M \sum_{c_1, c_2} \xi_{c_1,c_2}$$
$$\text{s.t.} \begin{cases} \sum_c L_{i,c} = 1 \quad \forall i \in [n_t] \\ L_{i,c} \in \{0,1\}, \quad \forall c \in \mathcal{C}, i \in [n_t] \\ \xi_{c_1,c_2} = \max\left(0, -\sum_i (L_{i,c_1} - L_{i,c_2}) + n_t \delta^{(c_1,c_2)}\right), \quad \forall c_1, c_2 \in \mathcal{C} \end{cases} \tag{5}$$

In both Eq. 4 and Eq. 5, M is a pre-defined non-negative constant. When M is large enough, their solutions will be the same as those of Eq. 2 and Eq. 3 respectively, providing the hard constraints from prior knowledge are satisfiable. When $M = 0$, Eq. 4 and Eq. 5 will degenerate to the vanilla problem in Eq. 1.

Smooth Regularization. Previous optimization problems utilize prior knowledge about class distribution to refine pseudo labels. However, this solely relies on the model predicted probability matrix P without considering the data distribution in the feature space. In classification tasks, it is expected that the label prediction is locally smoothed. Hence, we add a smooth regularization that enforces the pseudo label of neighboring samples to be consistent.

We select a subset of target samples $\mathcal{S}_t \subseteq \mathcal{D}_t$ whose model predictions are uncertain. For each $\boldsymbol{x}_i^t \in \mathcal{S}_t$, let its nearest neighbor in $\mathcal{D}_t \backslash \mathcal{S}_t$ be $\boldsymbol{x}_{ki}^t$. The smooth regularization is a collection of equality constraints, $\mathcal{R} = \{(\boldsymbol{l}_i = \boldsymbol{l}_{ki}) | \boldsymbol{x}_i^t \in \mathcal{S}_t\}$. Converting these equalities into soft constraints is non-trivial as it will bring second-order terms in the objective. Instead, we directly add them as hard constraints to the optimization problem in Eq. 4 and Eq. 5.

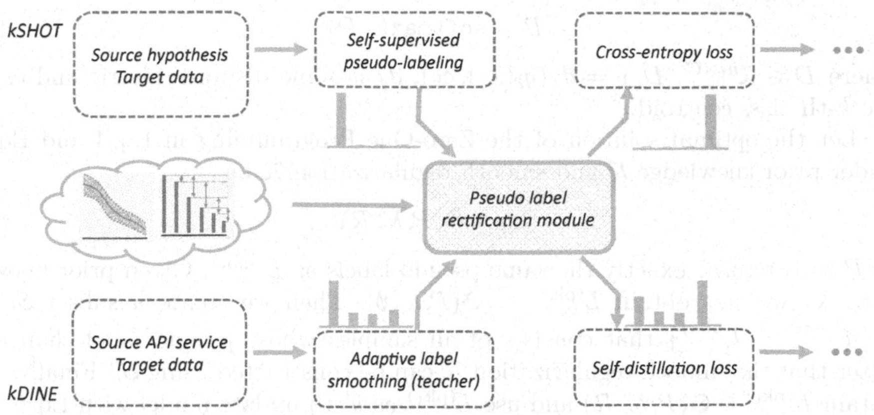

Fig. 2. Illustration of how our proposed rectification module is integrated into SHOT and DINE to get knowledge-guided SHOT and DINE. This can be easily extended to other self-training based UDA methods in a similar manner.

4.2 Knowledge-Guided UDA Methods

Our proposed rectification module is general, and can be easily plugged into self-training based UDA methods. To validate its effectiveness, we choose two recent UDA algorithms, SHOT [18] and DINE [19]. This leads to knowledge-guided SHOT and DINE, dubbed as kSHOT and kDINE, respectively. The frameworks are illustrated in Fig. 2. It should be noted that the main purpose of this part is to demonstrate the benefits of considering class prior knowledge through our rectification module, rather than simply extending the two algorithms.

Knowledge-Guide SHOT. SHOT [18] is a state-of-the-art self-training based UDA method. It assumes a source-data free setting, *i.e.*, only the source hypothesis is available during adaptation. Then both self-supervised pseudo-labeling and mutual information maximization are exploited to fine-tune the feature extractor module of the source hypothesis. Since only target samples are involved, it provides us a convenient platform to observe how prior knowledge affects the performance of adapted models. The full objective is

$$\mathcal{L}_{\text{shot}} = \mathbb{E}_{(\boldsymbol{x}_i^t, \hat{y}_i^t)} \ell_{\text{ce}}(h_t \circ g_t(\boldsymbol{x}_i^t), \hat{y}_i^t) - \alpha \mathcal{L}_{\text{im}} \tag{6}$$

where ℓ_{ce} is the cross entropy loss, $\mathcal{L}_{\text{im}}$ is the Information Maximization loss [6, 34], and α is a hyper-parameter. A critical step is to obtain the pseudo label $\hat{y}_i^t$. SHOT uses the distances between samples and class centroids in the feature space to refine model predictions. While this improves the quality of pseudo labels to some extent, their empirical distribution could still be very different from the ground-truth, as shown in Fig. 5. We show how prior knowledge can be incorporated to alleviate this issue.

We plug the rectification module into SHOT. After obtaining pseudo labels $L^{(\text{shot})}$ (*i.e.*, the one-hot representation of $\hat{y}^t$) and feature-to-centroid distances from SHOT, we convert the distances into class probabilities using `softmax` as

$$P = \texttt{softmax}(-D) \tag{7}$$

where $D \in \mathbb{R}^{n_t \times C}$, $D_{i,k} = d_f(g_t(\boldsymbol{x}_i^t), c_k)$, d_f is some distance metric and c_k is the k-th class centroid.

Let the optimal solution of the Zero-One Programming in Eq. 4 and Eq. 5 under prior knowledge $\mathcal{K}$ and smooth regularization $\mathcal{R}$ be

$$L^* = \mathfrak{S}(P, \mathcal{K}, \mathcal{R}) \tag{8}$$

$\mathfrak{S}(P, \emptyset, \emptyset)$ returns exactly the same pseudo labels as $L^{(\text{shot})}$. Given prior knowledge $\mathcal{K}$, we first obtain $L^{(\text{pk}_0)} = \mathfrak{S}(P, \mathcal{K}, \emptyset)$. Then we create a subset $\mathcal{S}_t = \{x_i^t | \boldsymbol{l}_i^{(\text{shot})} \neq \boldsymbol{l}_i^{(\text{pk}_0)}\}$ that consists of all samples whose pseudo label changed. After that the smooth regularization $\mathcal{R}$ can be constructed using $\mathcal{S}_t$. Finally, we obtain $L^{(\text{pk}_1)} = \mathfrak{S}(P, \mathcal{K}, \mathcal{R})$ and use $L^{(\text{pk}_1)}$ as $\hat{y}^t$ to update model with Eq. 6.

Knowledge-Guide DINE. DINE [19] is a very recent algorithm that assumes only black-box source models (*e.g.*, source API service) are available during adaptation. It first distills knowledge from the source predictor to a target model, and then fine-tunes the distilled model with target data. Two kinds of structural regularization, including interpolation consistency training [44] and mutual information maximization [34], are applied. The objective is

$$\mathcal{L}_{\text{dine}} = \mathbb{E}_{\boldsymbol{x}_i^t} \mathcal{D}_{\text{kl}} \left(P^{\text{tch}}(\boldsymbol{x}_i^t) \| f_t(\boldsymbol{x}_i^t) \right) + \beta \mathcal{L}_{\text{mix}} - \mathcal{L}_{\text{im}} \tag{9}$$

where $\mathcal{D}_{\text{kl}}$ denotes the Kullback-Leibler divergence, $\mathcal{L}_{\text{mix}}$ and $\mathcal{L}_{\text{im}}$ are two regularizers, and β is a trade-off parameter. To obtain the teacher prediction $P^{\text{tch}}(\boldsymbol{x}_i^t)$, the authors propose to revise the predictions of source model with adaptive label smoothing, and maintain an exponential moving average (EMA) prediction.

Given prior knowledge $\mathcal{K}$, we aim to rectify the teacher prediction $P^{\text{tch}}(\boldsymbol{x}_i^t)$ to be more compliant with the ground-truth. We adopt a similar strategy as in kSHOT. The pseudo labels of DINE are obtained by $\hat{y}_i^{(\text{dine})} = \arg\max P^{\text{tch}}(\boldsymbol{x}_i^t)$. Let the corresponding one-hot representation be $\boldsymbol{l}_i^{(\text{dine})}$. We take $P^{\text{tch}}(\boldsymbol{x}_i^t)$ as the i-th row of P, and obtain $L^{(\text{pk}_0)} = \mathfrak{S}(P, \mathcal{K}, \emptyset)$. Then we create a subset $\mathcal{S}^t = \{\boldsymbol{x}_i^t | \boldsymbol{l}_i^{(\text{dine})} \neq \boldsymbol{l}_i^{(\text{pk}_0)}\}$ to construct the smooth regularization $\mathcal{R}$. Finally, we obtain $L^{(\text{pk}_1)} = \mathfrak{S}(P, \mathcal{K}, \mathcal{R})$. The new objective function is

$$\mathcal{L}_{\text{kdine}} = \mathbb{E}_{\boldsymbol{x}_i^t} \mathcal{D}_{\text{kl}} \left(\frac{P^{\text{tch}}(\boldsymbol{x}_i^t) + \tilde{\boldsymbol{l}}_i^{(\text{pk}_1)}}{2} \middle\| f_t(\boldsymbol{x}_i^t) \right) + \beta \mathcal{L}_{\text{mix}} - \mathcal{L}_{\text{im}} \tag{10}$$

where $\tilde{\boldsymbol{l}}_i^{(\text{pk}_1)} = 0.9 \cdot \boldsymbol{l}_i^{(\text{pk}_1)} + 0.1/C$ is the smoothed label.

5 Experiments

5.1 Experimental Setup

Datasets. We report our results on both standard UDA benchmarks and benchmarks designed with label distribution shift. **Office-Home** is an image classification dataset with 65 classes from four environments: Artistic (A), Clip

Table 2. Classification accuracies (%) on **Office-Home RS-UT** and **Office**.

Method	$\mathcal{K}$	σ	Office-Home RS-UT							Office						
			R→P	R→C	P→R	P→C	C→R	C→P	Avg.	A→D	A→W	D→A	D→W	W→A	W→D	Avg.
SHOT	–	–	77.0	50.3	75.9	47.0	64.3	64.6	63.2	94.0	90.1	74.7	98.4	74.3	**99.9**	88.6
kSHOT	UB	0.0	**78.8**	51.3	**79.1**	**49.8**	71.3	**69.7**	**66.6**	**97.6**	**98.5**	75.0	**99.0**	76.2	99.8	**91.0**
	UB	0.1	78.3	**51.7**	79.0	48.6	**71.6**	69.4	66.4	96.7	97.2	75.5	98.7	**76.5**	99.8	90.7
	UB	0.5	76.7	50.6	77.3	48.4	68.4	67.3	64.8	93.9	92.8	**75.7**	97.7	75.2	99.7	89.2
	UB	1.0	76.3	50.0	76.9	48.4	66.7	65.8	64.0	93.7	92.4	75.5	97.7	75.5	99.7	89.1
	UB	2.0	76.4	50.0	76.0	47.9	65.3	64.1	63.3	93.7	92.4	75.0	97.7	75.2	99.7	89.0
	BR	–	78.6	51.6	78.7	49.3	70.1	68.8	66.2	96.9	97.1	74.0	98.8	76.1	99.8	90.5

Art (C), Product (P), and Real-world (R). **Office** [31] contains 31 classes of office objects from three domains: Amazon (A), DSLR (D) and Webcam (W). **VisDA-2017** [27] is a large-scale Synthetic-to-Real dataset with 12 categories of objects. **Office-Home RS-UT** [36] is a subset of Office-Home created with Reverse-unbalanced Source and Unbalanced Target manner. Both source and target label distributions are long-tailed. The majority classes in source domain are minority ones in target domain. Hence, it has a big label distribution shift. **DomainNet** [26] is a large UDA benchmark. We use the subset [36] of 40-commonly seen classes from four domains: Clipart (C), Painting (P), Real (R), Sketch (S). It has a natural label distribution shift.

Creating Prior Knowledge. We create prior knowledge from ground-truth labels of target training data, $\{y_i^t\}_{i=0}^{n_t-1}$, for experimental purposes only. The noisiness and completeness of the prior knowledge are discussed in Sect. 5.3. Let $q_c = \sum_i \mathbb{I}[y_i^t = c]/n_t$ be the empirical probability of the c-th class.

- **Unary Bound**. We create UB as $\{(q_c \cdot (1-\sigma) \leq p_t^{(c)} \leq q_c \cdot (1+\sigma))|c \in \mathcal{C}\}$, where σ is hyper-parameter controlling the tightness of the bounds. In the experiments, we choose $\sigma \in \{0.0, 0.1, 0.5, 1.0, 2.0\}$.
- **Binary Relationship**. We first sort all classes based on q_c in descending order. Assuming the corresponding indexes are $[c_0^q, c_1^q, \cdots, c_{C-1}^q]$. Then we create BR as $\{(p_t^{(c_i^q)} - p_t^{(c_{i+1}^q)} \geq 0)|i \in \{0, 1, \cdots, C-2\}\}$. We simply take the right hand to be 0, which makes them relatively loose constraints and more easily available in practice.

Implementation Details. We solve the optimization problem of the rectification module with Gurobi Optimizer [7]. Both kSHOT and kDINE are based on the official Pytorch implementations by the authors. We use a pretrained ResNet-101 [8] backbone for VisDA-2017, and ResNet-50 [8] for others. To fairly compare with SHOT and DINE, we adopt the same hyper-parameters as used in the original papers. We run every task for 3 times and report the mean evaluation values. For standard UDA benchmarks, we report the accuracy. For benchmarks with label distribution shift (*i.e.*, Office-Home RS-UT and DomainNet), we report per-class average accuracy, in consistent with previous works [29,36].

Table 3. Classification accuracies (%) on **Office-Home** and **VisDA-2017**.

Method	$\mathcal{K}$	σ	Office-Home													VisDA
			A→C	A→P	A→R	C→A	C→P	C→R	P→A	P→C	P→R	R→A	R→C	R→P	Avg.	
SHOT	–	–	57.1	78.1	81.5	68.0	78.2	78.1	67.4	54.9	82.2	73.3	58.8	84.3	71.8	82.9
kSHOT	UB	0.0	58.2	80.0	82.9	71.1	80.3	80.7	71.3	56.8	83.2	75.5	60.3	86.6	73.9	86.1
	UB	0.1	58.1	79.2	83.2	70.4	80.0	80.7	71.4	56.5	83.0	75.6	60.8	86.0	73.7	85.8
	UB	0.5	57.4	79.1	82.1	69.4	78.1	79.5	69.3	55.2	81.8	74.0	60.2	85.1	72.6	83.9
	UB	1.0	57.0	79.0	82.1	68.6	77.8	79.3	68.4	55.1	81.7	73.5	59.3	84.8	72.2	83.0
	UB	2.0	56.4	78.7	82.1	68.3	77.8	79.3	67.9	54.2	81.7	73.3	58.7	84.8	71.9	82.6
	BR	–	57.4	78.8	82.9	70.7	80.0	80.5	70.8	55.0	82.8	74.6	59.9	86.0	73.3	83.6

Table 4. Classification accuracies (%) on **DomainNet**.

Method	$\mathcal{K}$	σ	R→C	R→P	R→S	C→R	C→P	C→S	P→R	P→C	P→S	S→R	S→C	S→P	Avg.
SHOT	–	–	79.4	75.4	72.8	88.4	74.0	75.5	89.8	77.7	76.2	88.3	80.5	70.8	79.1
kSHOT	UB	0	83.6	77.5	75.3	91.5	76.4	77.0	91.7	82.3	76.3	89.7	80.2	70.3	81.0
	UB	0.1	82.2	77.6	75.2	89.5	76.8	76.9	91.2	81.7	76.9	88.5	79.4	70.1	80.5
	UB	0.5	80.3	77.2	73.5	88.8	75.4	75.6	89.0	78.4	76.6	88.3	78.9	70.4	79.4
	UB	1.0	79.9	76.8	72.9	88.8	73.7	75.3	88.6	77.6	76.4	88.0	80.0	69.9	79.0
	UB	2.0	79.2	76.3	73.1	88.8	75.4	75.5	88.6	77.8	76.2	87.9	80.1	71.1	79.2
	BR	–	82.1	76.8	74.3	89.1	73.7	76.4	91.7	80.6	75.9	88.8	79.1	70.2	79.9

5.2 Results

Results of kSHOT. Tables 2, 4 list results of kSHOT on two benchmarks with label distribution shift. In UB($\sigma = 0$), it improves the accuracy by +3.4% on Office-Home RS-UT and +1.9% on DomainNet. As σ grows, the prior knowledge becomes less informative, and consequently the improvements reduce. Interestingly in BR where only the relative order of class probabilities is known, it still improves +3.0% on Office-Home RS-UT. Since this dataset is manually created to be long-tailed, and class distributions of two domains are reversed version of each other, having prior knowledge about target class distribution would be very helpful. This conforms to our experimental results. Results on three standard benchmarks are listed in Tables 2, 3. Using prior knowledge consistently improves on them. Similar trends on σ can be observed. Compared with previous benchmarks, the phenomenon of label distribution shift is less severe. Still prior knowledge can be helpful to correct mistaken pseudo labels during training.

Results of kDINE. Since using vanilla label smoothing is sub-optimal to the adaptive label smoothing used in DINE [19], the true performance gain from prior knowledge could be reduced. To make a fair comparison, we also provide results when replacing $\boldsymbol{l}_i^{(\mathrm{pk}_1)}$ with the $\boldsymbol{l}_i^{(\mathrm{dine})}$ in Eq. 10, and term it as DINE*. As can be seen in Tables 6, 7, DINE* indeed performs worse than DINE. Nevertheless, incorporated with prior knowledge, kDINE achieves much higher accuracy, and even better performance than DINE.

Table 5. Classification accuracies (%) on **Office-Home** for PDA.

Method	$\mathcal{K}$	σ	:A	:C	:P	:R	Avg.
SHOT	–	–	78.9	65.2	82.9	90.3	79.3
kSHOT	UB	0.0	85.4	74.1	94.2	93.6	86.8
	BR	–	84.9	72.3	90.2	92.2	84.9
DINE	–	–	77.6	59.2	82.7	85.2	76.2
DINE*	–	–	73.1	54.8	80.0	83.9	73.0
kDINE	UB	0.0	82.1	66.4	91.3	91.7	82.9
	BR	–	79.7	63.3	88.2	89.5	80.2

Table 6. Classification accuracies (%) on **Office**.

Method	$\mathcal{K}$	σ	A→D	A→W	D→A	D→W	W→A	W→D	Avg.
DINE	–	–	91.6	86.8	72.2	96.2	73.3	98.6	86.4
DINE*	–	–	90.6	86.5	70.6	95.2	72.0	99.3	85.7
kDINE	UB	0.0	94.7	92.2	71.0	96.8	72.6	99.8	87.9
	UB	0.1	93.6	91.2	71.0	96.5	72.1	99.5	87.3
	UB	0.5	91.7	88.3	70.4	95.2	71.6	99.3	86.1
	UB	1.0	90.6	86.4	70.6	95.2	72.3	99.3	85.8
	UB	2.0	90.6	86.5	70.7	95.2	72.0	99.3	85.7
	BR	–	93.4	91.1	70.5	96.4	72.1	99.5	87.2

Table 7. Classification accuracies (%) on **Office-Home**.

Method	$\mathcal{K}$	σ	A→C	A→P	A→R	C→A	C→P	C→R	P→A	P→C	P→R	R→A	R→C	R→P	Avg.
DINE	–	–	52.2	78.4	81.3	65.3	76.6	78.7	62.7	49.6	82.2	69.8	55.8	84.2	69.7
DINE*	–	–	51.8	76.0	79.6	63.1	75.1	76.5	60.4	48.5	80.7	69.4	55.9	83.5	68.4
kDINE	UB	0.0	54.8	78.6	81.7	67.1	78.3	79.6	66.8	52.3	82.5	72.0	58.1	85.4	71.4
	UB	0.1	55.0	78.8	81.1	66.4	77.7	79.2	66.4	51.8	82.3	71.5	58.0	84.9	71.1
	UB	0.5	52.9	76.7	79.9	64.5	76.3	77.8	63.8	51.0	80.9	70.5	57.1	84.2	69.6
	UB	1.0	52.3	76.0	79.6	63.5	75.2	76.5	62.1	49.0	80.7	69.9	56.4	83.4	68.7
	UB	2.0	51.8	76.0	79.6	63.0	75.1	76.5	60.8	49.2	80.7	69.6	55.5	83.5	68.4
	BR	–	54.2	79.4	81.5	66.8	78.6	79.2	65.6	50.9	82.6	71.4	58.1	85.3	71.1

Results for PDA. We further evaluate on Office-Home for Partial-set DA (PDA), where there are totally 25 classes (the first 25 classes in alphabetical order) in the target domain and 65 classes in the source domain. This thus can be viewed as an extreme situation where class probabilities of the rest 40 classes are all zero. Table 5 lists the results averaged over tasks with the same target domain (*e.g.*, the :A column averages over C→A, P→A and R→A). As can be seen, using prior knowledge significantly improves in this situation.

5.3 Analysis

How prior knowledge guides UDA? To see why prior knowledge is helpful, we consider the following two aspects:

- **Ambiguous samples**. As illustrated Fig. 3 (left), our rectification module updates pseudo labels globally to match prior knowledge. This in effect moves decision boundaries in the feature space. The pseudo labels of ambiguous samples lying near the boundaries could be corrected during this process. Figure 3 (center) plots the accuracies of three set of pseudo labels, $L^{(\text{shot})}$, $L^{(\text{pk}_0)}$ and $L^{(\text{pk}_1)}$, during the training process of kSHOT with UB($\sigma = 0.0$) on Office A→W. Clearly using prior knowledge obtains more accurate pseudo labels. This in turn benefits the subsequent self-training stage.

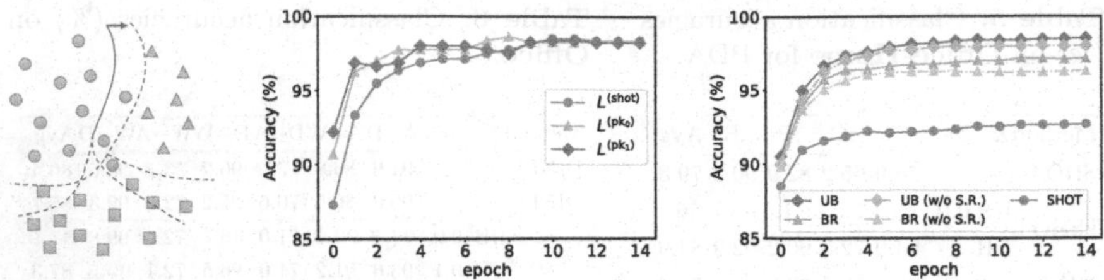

Fig. 3. (Left) Prior knowledge rectifies the pseudo label of ambiguous samples; (center) accuracies of pseudo labels before and after rectification using prior knowledge during the training of kSHOT on Office A→W; (right) convergence curves on Office A→W for comparison methods (S.R. is short for Smooth Regularization).

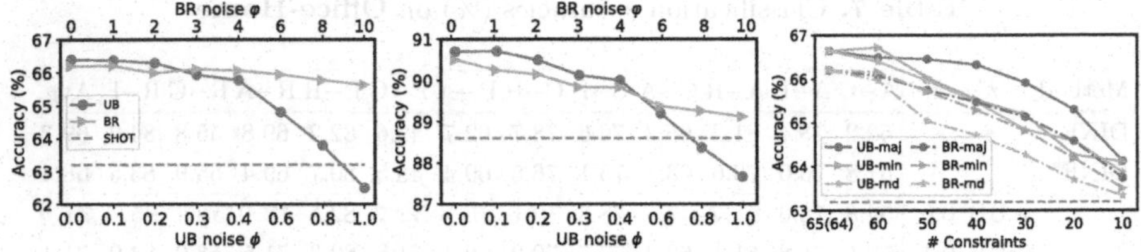

Fig. 4. Using noisy prior knowledge in kSHOT on (left) Office-Home RS-UT and (center) Office; (right) using partial prior knowledge in kSHOT on Office-Home RS-UT.

- **Label distribution.** Figure 5 plots distributions of ground-truth labels and pseudo labels on Office-Home RS-UT P→C in one seudo-labeling step. The accuracy of pseudo labels is $\sim 55\%$. As can be seen, the distribution of $L^{(\text{shot})}$ severely deviates from the ground-truth. In contrast, distributions of pseudo labels after rectification with prior knowledge are better compliant with the ground-truth. Figure 6 plots distributions of network predictions throughout the training process. The vanilla SHOT method hardly improves the label distribution after adaptation, whereas using prior knowledge drives it to be more similar to the ground-truth distribution in kSHOT.

Noisiness of the Prior Knowledge. In practice, the prior knowledge might contain some level of noises. To study its effects, we manually add noises to the estimated class prior q_c. For UB, uniform noises are added through $\tilde{q}_c = q_c + \mathcal{U}(-q_c\phi, q_c\phi)$, where $\phi \in [0, 1]$ controls the noise level. The noises have been centered to ensure that $\tilde{q}_c$ is a valid probability. Then $\tilde{q}_c$ is used to create the unary bound discussed in Sect. 5.1. For BR, after sorting all classes based on q_c, we randomly swap neighboring classes. Suppose the index of class c_k in the sorted order is I_{c_k}, uniform noises are added through $\tilde{I}_{c_k} = I_{c_k} + \mathcal{U}(-\varphi, \varphi)$, where φ controls the neighborhood size. Then we sort all classes based on the noisy indexes $\tilde{I}_{c_k}$, and use the resorted order to create binary relationship. Figure 4 (left and center) shows that under moderate noises, incorporating prior knowledge is still helpful and improves over the SHOT baseline.

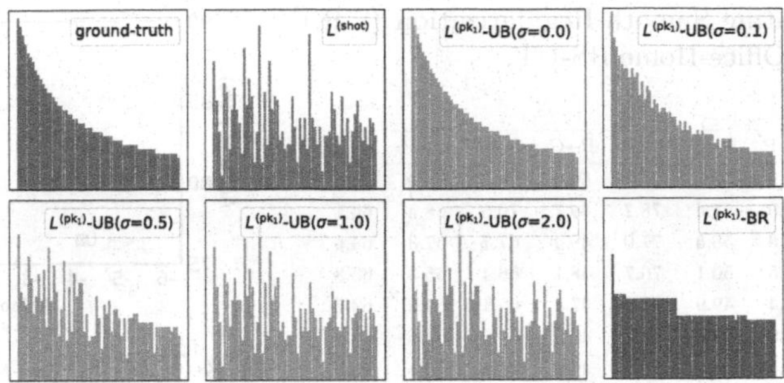

Fig. 5. Prior knowledge rectifies distribution of pseudo labels in one pseudo-labeling step of kSHOT (Office-Home RS-UT P→C).

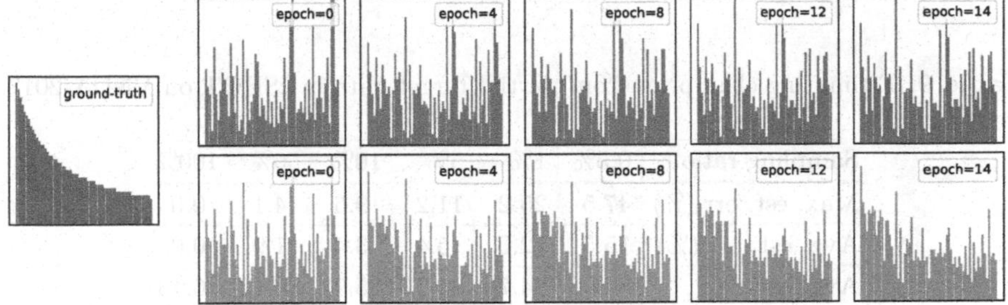

Fig. 6. Label distributions of network (f_t) predictions in SHOT (upper) and kSHOT (lower) (Office-Home RS-UT P→C).

Completeness of the Prior Knowledge. Until then, the prior constraints are assumed to cover every class. It is straightforward to generalize to partial constraints. We randomly select a portion of constraints that corresponds to the major (maj.), minor (min) or random (rnd) classes. Figure 4 (right) present the results under different number of selected constraints. Partial constrains imply less prior information, but still can benefit UDA training. Note that BR-rnd reduces the performance most, partially because the randomly selected binary relationship constraints hardly form the complete order of a subset of classes.

Estimating Class Prior from Partial Data. Table 9 presents the experimental results when estimating q_c from partial target data in kSHOT with UB(σ = 0.0) on VisDA-2017. As sampling ratio reduces, the estimation error (relative deviations from using full data) increases. Nevertheless, even when the average estimation error is about 15.5% at a sampling ratio of 0.5%, using prior knowledge still improves over SHOT by +1.16% (82.9% → 84.06%).

Effects of Smooth Regularization. Table 8 presents the ablation study on smooth regularization. Generally, using smooth regularization achieves comparable or better performance. The penalty depends on $|\mathcal{S}_t| = \sum_i \mathbb{I}[\boldsymbol{l}_i^{(\text{shot})} \neq \boldsymbol{l}_i^{(\text{pk}_0)}]$, and varies across different tasks. In UB with large σ, the prior knowledge is not

Table 8. Ablating Smooth Regularization (S.R.) in kSHOT on Office-Home RS-UT.

	$\mathcal{K}$	σ	R→P	R→C	P→R	P→C	C→R	C→P	Avg.
wo/ S.R.	UB	0.0	77.9	52.0	78.8	50.0	70.3	68.9	66.3
	UB	0.1	77.9	51.4	78.7	49.7	70.5	68.4	66.1
	UB	0.5	76.6	50.5	77.0	48.4	67.7	67.3	64.6
	UB	1.0	76.5	50.1	76.7	48.1	66.4	65.3	63.8
	UB	2.0	76.4	49.9	75.8	47.8	65.1	64.2	63.2
	BR	–	77.9	51.2	78.1	49.2	69.0	67.6	65.5
w/ S.R.	UB	0.0	78.8	51.3	79.1	49.8	71.3	69.7	66.6
	UB	0.1	78.3	51.7	79.0	48.6	71.6	69.4	66.4
	UB	0.5	76.7	50.6	77.3	48.4	68.4	67.3	64.8
	UB	1.0	76.3	50.0	76.9	48.4	66.7	65.8	64.0
	UB	2.0	76.4	50.0	76.0	47.9	65.3	64.1	63.3
	BR	–	78.6	51.6	78.7	49.3	70.1	68.8	66.2

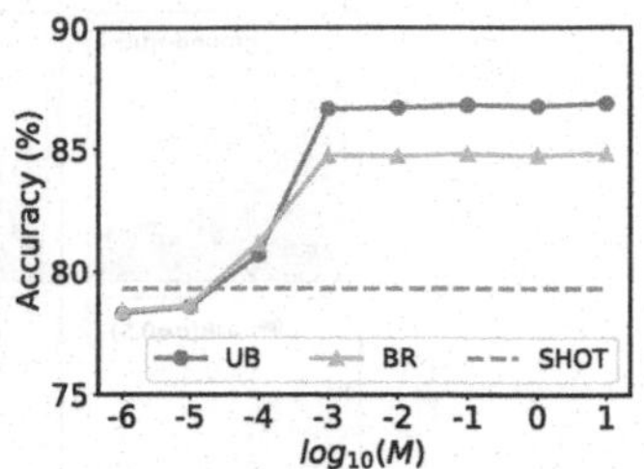

Fig. 7. Effects of constant M (by a scalar n_t) in kSHOT on Office-Home for PDA (averaged over 12 tasks).

Table 9. Estimating class prior from partial target data in kSHOT on VisDA-2017.

Sampling ratio	0.5%	1%	5%	10%	50%	100%
Max. est. err (%)	47.5	25.2	11.2	9.6	4.1	0.0
Avg. est. err (%)	15.5	12.0	5.4	3.4	1.9	0.0
Avg. acc (%)	84.06	84.76	85.77	85.93	86.12	86.13

informative, hence $|\mathcal{S}_t|$ is small. We underline cases where using smooth regularization increases the accuracy significantly. The amount of improvement is most significant on tasks like R→P, C→R, C→P. Comparing two types of prior knowledge, it is more helpful in BR. Since BR only tells the order of class probabilities, adding smooth regularization provides complementary information.

Choice of Constant M. The prior knowledge is considered to be reliable, hence we expect the prior constraints to be satisfied in the rectified pseudo labels. To achieve this, M need to be some large constant in Eq. 4, 5. Figure 7 shows how M affects the performance on Office-Home under PDA setting in kSHOT. When M is very small, the method degenerates to SHOT. When M is larger than some threshold (*e.g.*, $10^{-3} \cdot n_t$), all soft constraints will in fact be satisfied. In our experiments, we use $M = 10 \cdot n_t$ for all tasks in both kSHOT and kDINE.

6 Conclusions

We present a new yet realistic setting termed Knowledge-guided Unsupervised Domain Adaptation (KUDA). In KUDA, in addition to labeled source data and unlabeled target data, we have access to some prior knowledge about target label distribution. We present a novel rectification module that refines pseudo labels using prior knowledge through solving a constrained optimization problem. Then we integrate it into two representative self-training based methods, SHOT and

DINE. Extensive experiments show that using prior knowledge can significantly improve the performance. We expect our work to inspire further investigations along the direction.

References

1. Baslamisli, A.S., Le, H.A., Gevers, T.: CNN based learning using reflection and retinex models for intrinsic image decomposition. In: CVPR, pp. 6674–6683 (2018)
2. Chen, D., Wang, D., Darrell, T., Ebrahimi, S.: Contrastive test-time adaptation. In: CVPR, pp. 295–305 (2022)
3. Chen, L., et al.: Reusing the task-specific classifier as a discriminator: discriminator-free adversarial domain adaptation. In: CVPR, pp. 7181–7190 (2022)
4. Ding, N., Xu, Y., Tang, Y., Xu, C., Wang, Y., Tao, D.: Source-free domain adaptation via distribution estimation. In: CVPR, pp. 7212–7222 (2022)
5. Fu, B., Cao, Z., Wang, J., Long, M.: Transferable query selection for active domain adaptation. In: CVPR, pp. 7272–7281 (2021)
6. Gomes, R., Krause, A., Perona, P.: Discriminative clustering by regularized information maximization. In: NeurIPS (2010)
7. Gurobi Optimization, LLC: Gurobi Optimizer Reference Manual (2022). https://www.gurobi.com
8. He, K., Zhang, X., Ren, S., Sun, J.: Deep residual learning for image recognition. In: CVPR, pp. 770–778 (2016)
9. Huang, J., Guan, D., Xiao, A., Lu, S.: Model adaptation: historical contrastive learning for unsupervised domain adaptation without source data. In: NeurIPS (2021)
10. Kayhan, O.S., Gemert, J.C.V.: On translation invariance in CNNs: convolutional layers can exploit absolute spatial location. In: CVPR, pp. 14274–14285 (2020)
11. Kim, T., Kim, C.: Attract, perturb, and explore: learning a feature alignment network for semi-supervised domain adaptation. In: Vedaldi, A., Bischof, H., Brox, T., Frahm, J.-M. (eds.) ECCV 2020. LNCS, vol. 12359, pp. 591–607. Springer, Cham (2020). https://doi.org/10.1007/978-3-030-58568-6_35
12. LeCun, Y., Bengio, Y., Hinton, G.: Deep learning. Nature **521**(7553), 436–444 (2015)
13. LeCun, Y., et al.: Backpropagation applied to handwritten zip code recognition. Neural Comput. **1**(4), 541–551 (1989)
14. Lefort, R., Fablet, R., Boucher, J.-M.: Weakly supervised classification of objects in images using soft random forests. In: Daniilidis, K., Maragos, P., Paragios, N. (eds.) ECCV 2010. LNCS, vol. 6314, pp. 185–198. Springer, Heidelberg (2010). https://doi.org/10.1007/978-3-642-15561-1_14
15. Lengyel, A., Garg, S., Milford, M., van Gemert, J.C.: Zero-shot day-night domain adaptation with a physics prior. In: ICCV, pp. 4399–4409 (2021)
16. Li, B., Wang, Y., Zhang, S., Li, D., Keutzer, K., Darrell, T., Zhao, H.: Learning invariant representations and risks for semi-supervised domain adaptation. In: CVPR, pp. 1104–1113 (2021)
17. Li, R., Cheong, L.F., Tan, R.T.: Heavy rain image restoration: Integrating physics model and conditional adversarial learning. In: CVPR, pp. 1633–1642 (2019)
18. Liang, J., Hu, D., Feng, J.: Do we really need to access the source data? source hypothesis transfer for unsupervised domain adaptation. In: ICML, pp. 6028–6039 (2020)

19. Liang, J., Hu, D., Feng, J., He, R.: Dine: domain adaptation from single and multiple black-box predictors. In: CVPR, pp. 8003–8013 (2022)
20. Lin, Y., Pintea, S.L., van Gemert, J.C.: Deep Hough-transform line priors. In: Vedaldi, A., Bischof, H., Brox, T., Frahm, J.-M. (eds.) ECCV 2020. LNCS, vol. 12367, pp. 323–340. Springer, Cham (2020). https://doi.org/10.1007/978-3-030-58542-6_20
21. Lipton, Z., Wang, Y.X., Smola, A.: Detecting and correcting for label shift with black box predictors. In: ICML, pp. 3122–3130 (2018)
22. Liu, X., et al.: Adversarial unsupervised domain adaptation with conditional and label shift: infer, align and iterate. In: ICCV, pp. 10367–10376 (2021)
23. Long, J., Shelhamer, E., Darrell, T.: Fully convolutional networks for semantic segmentation. In: CVPR, pp. 3431–3440 (2015)
24. Mann, G.S., McCallum, A.: Simple, robust, scalable semi-supervised learning via expectation regularization. In: ICML, pp. 593–600 (2007)
25. Pan, S.J., Yang, Q.: A survey on transfer learning. TKDE **22**(10), 1345–1359 (2009)
26. Peng, X., Bai, Q., Xia, X., Huang, Z., Saenko, K., Wang, B.: Moment matching for multi-source domain adaptation. In: ICCV, pp. 1406–1415 (2019)
27. Peng, X., Usman, B., Kaushik, N., Hoffman, J., Wang, D., Saenko, K.: Visda: the visual domain adaptation challenge. arXiv preprint arXiv:1710.06924 (2017)
28. Prabhu, V., Chandrasekaran, A., Saenko, K., Hoffman, J.: Active domain adaptation via clustering uncertainty-weighted embeddings. In: ICCV, pp. 8505–8514 (2021)
29. Prabhu, V., Khare, S., Kartik, D., Hoffman, J.: Sentry: Selective entropy optimization via committee consistency for unsupervised domain adaptation. In: CVPR. pp. 8558–8567 (2021)
30. Ren, S., He, K., Girshick, R., Sun, J.: Faster R-CNN: towards real-time object detection with region proposal networks. In: NeurIPS (2015)
31. Saenko, K., Kulis, B., Fritz, M., Darrell, T.: Adapting visual category models to new domains. In: Daniilidis, K., Maragos, P., Paragios, N. (eds.) ECCV 2010. LNCS, vol. 6314, pp. 213–226. Springer, Heidelberg (2010). https://doi.org/10.1007/978-3-642-15561-1_16
32. Saito, K., Kim, D., Sclaroff, S., Darrell, T., Saenko, K.: Semi-supervised domain adaptation via minimax entropy. In: ICCV, pp. 8050–8058 (2019)
33. Schapire, R.E., Rochery, M., Rahim, M., Gupta, N.: Incorporating prior knowledge into boosting. In: ICML, pp. 538–545 (2002)
34. Shi, Y., Sha, F.: Information-theoretical learning of discriminative clusters for unsupervised domain adaptation. In: ICML (2012)
35. Sun, T., Lu, C., Zhang, T., Ling, H.: Safe self-refinement for transformer-based domain adaptation. In: CVPR, pp. 7191–7200 (2022)
36. Tan, S., Peng, X., Saenko, K.: Class-imbalanced domain adaptation: an empirical odyssey. In: Bartoli, A., Fusiello, A. (eds.) ECCV 2020. LNCS, vol. 12535, pp. 585–602. Springer, Cham (2020). https://doi.org/10.1007/978-3-030-66415-2_38
37. Urban, G., et al.: Do deep convolutional nets really need to be deep and convolutional? In: ICLR (2017)
38. Wang, M., Deng, W.: Deep visual domain adaptation: a survey. Neurocomputing **312**, 135–153 (2018)
39. Wang, Z., Lyu, S., Schalk, G., Ji, Q.: Learning with target prior. In: NeurIPS (2012)
40. Wilson, G., Cook, D.J.: A survey of unsupervised deep domain adaptation. ACM TIST **11**(5), 1–46 (2020)

41. Wolsey, L.A.: Integer Programming. Wiley, New York (2020)
42. Xie, B., Yuan, L., Li, S., Liu, C.H., Cheng, X., Wang, G.: Active learning for domain adaptation: an energy-based approach. In: AAAI, pp. 8708–8716 (2022)
43. Zhang, H., Zhang, Y., Jia, K., Zhang, L.: Unsupervised domain adaptation of black-box source models. arXiv preprint arXiv:2101.02839 (2021)
44. Zhang, H., Cisse, M., Dauphin, Y.N., Lopez-Paz, D.: mixup: beyond empirical risk minimization. In: ICLR (2018)
45. Zhang, Y., Liu, T., Long, M., Jordan, M.: Bridging theory and algorithm for domain adaptation. In: ICML, pp. 7404–7413 (2019)
46. Zhu, X., Ghahramani, Z., Lafferty, J.D.: Semi-supervised learning using gaussian fields and harmonic functions. In: ICML, pp. 912–919 (2003)

GCISG: Guided Causal Invariant Learning for Improved Syn-to-Real Generalization

Gilhyun Nam[1(✉)], Gyeongjae Choi[1], and Kyungmin Lee[2]

[1] Agency for Defense Development (ADD), Daejeon, Korea
ngh707@gmail.com, def6488@gmail.com

[2] Korea Advanced Institute of Science and Technology (KAIST), Daejeon, Korea
kyungmnlee@kaist.ac.kr

Abstract. Training a deep learning model with artificially generated data can be an alternative when training data are scarce, yet it suffers from poor generalization performance due to a large domain gap. In this paper, we characterize the domain gap by using a causal framework for data generation. We assume that the real and synthetic data have common content variables but different style variables. Thus, a model trained on synthetic dataset might have poor generalization as the model learns the nuisance style variables. To that end, we propose causal invariance learning which encourages the model to learn a style-invariant representation that enhances the syn-to-real generalization. Furthermore, we propose a simple yet effective feature distillation method that prevents catastrophic forgetting of semantic knowledge of the real domain. In sum, we refer to our method as Guided Causal Invariant Syn-to-real Generalization that effectively improves the performance of syn-to-real generalization. We empirically verify the validity of proposed methods, and especially, our method achieves state-of-the-art on visual syn-to-real domain generalization tasks such as image classification and semantic segmentation.

1 Introduction

While deep neural networks have shown their great capability on various computer vision tasks, the majority of them count on a sufficient amount of training data with qualified labels. However, obtaining data or labels is expensive or difficult. Thus, a manually generated training dataset can be an alternative to the shortage or absence of training data. Also, by using the computer graphics engine [18,30,32], one can obtain labels without any cost of human labor [16,39].

However, training with synthetic data cannot fully replace the real training data as they suffer from poor generalization performance in the real domain. Many previous works explain the reason for inferior performance by the existence of a large domain gap [29,42] which makes the model overfits to the synthetic domain. In this paper, we break down the domain gap between the synthetic and

Supplementary Information The online version contains supplementary material available at https://doi.org/10.1007/978-3-031-19827-4_38.

S. Avidan et al. (Eds.): ECCV 2022, LNCS 13693, pp. 656–672, 2022.
https://doi.org/10.1007/978-3-031-19827-4_38

real data by using the causal model. We build a causal model that an image is generated from two latent variables: style variables such as texture and content variables such as shape. We assume that the synthetic and real data differ in style variables while having common content variables that are relevant to the downstream tasks. Furthermore, we also assume that the model learns the task-irrelevant style variables, therefore exhibiting poor generalization on the real domain. The recent studies [1,17] show that convolutional neural networks tend to rely on texture rather than shape which supports our claim.

To that end, we propose causal invariant learning for syn-to-real generalization by promoting causal invariance loss to learn style-invariant representation. Our method is related to the contrastive learning method, which learns representation by aligning positive pairs. We apply data augmentation to generate a pair of images with the same content but different style variables, then align their distributions of representations to achieve style-invariance. Our loss function is similar to that of [15,34,46,50], where those methods are for other than syn-to-real generalization such as self-supervised learning or knowledge distillation.

Furthermore, many methods show that using real-domain guidance with ImageNet pre-trained model for regularization is effective for syn-to-real generalization [5,6]. Chen et al. [6] utilized the knowledge distillation loss by re-using the pre-trained ImageNet classifier and Chen et al. [5] used intermediate features of the ImageNet pre-trained network to compute negative samples in contrastive learning. Those methods posit that the ImageNet classification is strongly correlated to the syn-to-real generalization performance. Instead, we propose to directly guide the model by simply regularizing the feature distance with the ImageNet pre-trained model, yet the key is to extract the semantic knowledge by using self-attention pooling. We empirically show that the simple guidance loss with self-attention pooling successfully guides the model to localize the object in the image, and helps the syn-to-real generalization.

In summary, we propose *Guided Causal Invariant Syn-to-real Generalization* (GCISG), where we propose causal invariance loss that helps to learn style-invariant features and guidance loss with self-attention pooling that helps extract semantic information from ImageNet pre-trained neural network. Our contributions are listed below:

- By adopting the causal framework for a syn-to-real setup, we propose causal invariance loss which regularizes the model to learn a style-invariant representation that is relevant to syn-to-real generalization.
- We present a simple and effective guidance loss that guides the model with real-domain guidance from ImageNet pre-trained model by utilizing self-attention pooling.
- We empirically show that our method significantly outperforms competing syn-to-real generalization methods on various vision tasks such as image classification, semantic segmentation, and object detection.

2 Related Work

Domain Generalization. The domain generalization problem aims to train on the source domain and generalize to an unseen target domain. The biggest

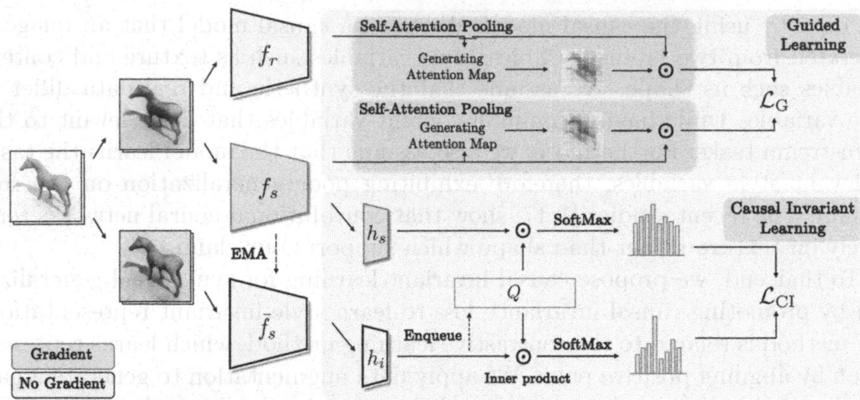

Fig. 1. Overall demonstration of proposed GCISG. There are two branches: 1) the guidance loss that preserves semantic information from ImageNet pre-trained model by using self-attention pooling, and 2) the causal invariance loss that learns style-invariant representation using contrastive learning framework.

concern of domain generalization is that there is a large domain gap between source and target domains, which deteriorates the performance. Therefore, many methods proposed an adversarial learning framework to match the feature distributions with a prior distribution [24] or diversify the style of the source domain to enhance the generalization [44,47]. Others focused on the effect of batch normalization on domain generalization. Pan et al. [33] showed that using instance normalization can boost the generalization, and RobustNet [10] used instance selective whitening to improve the robustness. Recent studies showed that using the knowledge from the real domain is effective for syn-to-real domain generalization problems [5,6,9], and our work is concurrent to those approaches.

Contrastive Learning and Style Invariance. Recently, contrastive learning with multi-view data augmentation has shown their efficacy in self-supervised representation learning [4,19,31,45] and domain generalization [28]. Our contrastive learning objective is similar to that of SEED [15], ReSSL [50], and RELIC [31], while SEED uses the contrastive objective to distill the representational knowledge on smaller networks, and ReSSL and RELIC are for self-supervised representation learning. Remark that CSG [5] also uses contrastive learning for syn-to-real generalization, while it is different from ours as they compute contrastive loss across ImageNet pre-trained networks, while ours aim to learn style-invariant representation on the synthetic data.

Learning with Guidance. Training a model by guidance with a pre-trained model's knowledge is not only effective for syn-to-real generalization but also for various machine learning tasks such as knowledge distillation [21,43] and incremental learning [2,25]. In syn-to-real generalization or adaptation, models are enforced to retain the knowledge from the ImageNet pre-trained networks by minimizing the feature distance [9], matching the outputs of ImageNet classification [6], or using the contrastive learning objective [5]. Similarly, the knowledge distillation methods use similar tactics to compress the knowledge from bigger networks to smaller ones [41,46]. And for incremental learning, similar methods were used to prevent catastrophic forgetting [36].

Our method uses self-attention pooled feature minimization to guide the model to enhance the generalization on a real domain. Transferring the knowledge by using attention has been also studied for knowledge distillation [48], and incremental learning [13]. While Chen et al. [5] used attention pooling for syn-to-real generalization, there are differences in that they pool features for contrastive learning, while our objective directly minimizes the distance between them.

3 Proposed Method

3.1 Causal Invariance for Syn-to-Real Generalization

We consider a causal model for synthetic and real data generation. In Fig. 2, we assume that the synthetic data X_{syn} is generated from the content variable C and style variable S_{syn}, and a real data X_{real} is generated from the content variable C and style variable S_{real}. Thus, we claim that the domain gap occurs because of the difference between the latent style variables of the two domains. We also assume that the task label Y is only dependent on the content variable. Those assumptions give us insight into why the model shows inferior generalization when solely trained with synthetic data: the model learns nuisance style variables irrelevant to the task. Also, a previous study [17] corroborates our hypothesis that the convolutional neural networks are biased toward texture (i.e. the style variable).

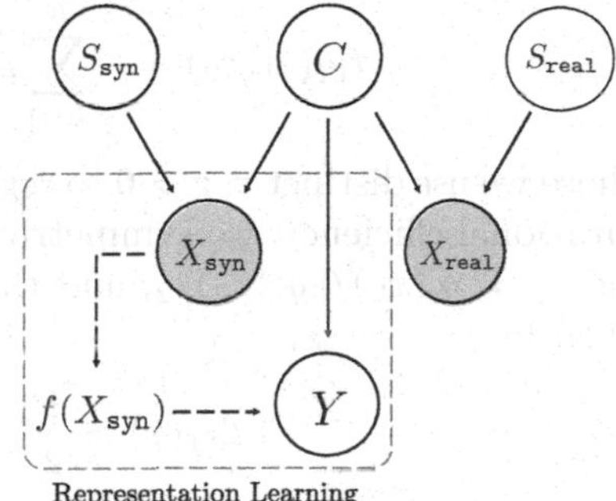

Fig. 2. Causal graph for synthetic and real data.

If one can extract style-invariant or content-preserving representation from the synthetic data, the model can enhance its generalization capability in the real domain. Thus, our goal is to extract style-invariant representation which is useful in the generalization on the real domain. To that end, we propose causal invariant syn-to-real generalization which is composed of two folds: first, we further diversify the style variable by using a strong data augmentation module such as RandAugment [12], and second, we use a contrastive learning framework to learn style-invariant representations.

In Fig. 1, for the synthetic training model f_s, we attach projector h_s to project onto a smaller dimension. For projector, we use two-layer multi-layer perceptron (MLP) as used in many contrastive representation learning frameworks [4,7]. Let us denote the encoder by $g_s = h_s \circ f_s$ and we build target encoder $\bar{g}_s = h_i \circ \bar{f}_s$, while h_i is the initial state of projector h_s. The weights of $\bar{f}_s$ are updated by the exponential moving average of the weight of the encoder f_s. Given a synthetic data x, let x_1 and x_2 be the two augmented views of x. Denote $z_1 = g_s(x_1)/\|g_s(x_1)\|_2 \in \mathbb{R}^d$ and $\bar{z}_2 = \bar{g}_s(x_2)/\|\bar{g}_s(x_2)\|_2 \in \mathbb{R}^d$ be the outputs of each encoder and target encoder with ℓ_2 normalization. To achieve stable causal invariance, we aim to match the distributions of z_1 and $\bar{z}_2$ with enough amount of support samples, which is a similar approach to prior works in other tasks [15,31,50]. We pertain support samples $Q \in \mathbb{R}^{K \times d}$, and aim to minimize the probabilistic discrepancy between the relational distributions $p(z_1; Q)$ and $p(\bar{z}_2; Q)$.

$$p_\tau(z; Q)[k] := \frac{\exp\left(z^\top q_k/\tau\right)}{\sum_{k'=1}^{K} \exp\left(z^\top q_{k'}/\tau\right)}, \tag{1}$$

where q_k is the k-th component of support samples Q and $\tau > 0$ is a temperature hyperparameter. Then we define the causal invariance loss between z_1 and $\bar{z}_2$ by the cross-entropy loss between the relation similarities as following:

$$\ell_{\text{CI}}(z_1, \bar{z}_2) = -\sum_{k=1}^{K} p_{\bar{\tau}}(\bar{z}_2; Q)[k] \log\left(p_\tau(z_1; Q)[k]\right), \tag{2}$$

where we use distinct $\tau, \bar{\tau} > 0$ to regulate the sharpness of distributions. For computational efficiency, we symmetrically compute between $\bar{z}_1 = \bar{g}_s(x_1)/\|\bar{g}_s(x_1)\|_2$ and $z_2 = g_s(x_2)/\|g_s(x_2)\|_2$, and the total causal invariance loss for a data x is given by

$$\mathcal{L}_{\text{CI}}(x) = \frac{1}{2}\ell_{\text{CI}}(z_1, \bar{z}_2) + \frac{1}{2}\ell_{\text{CI}}(z_2, \bar{z}_1). \tag{3}$$

The support samples Q are managed by a queue, where we enqueue the outputs of the target encoder at each iteration, and dequeue the oldest ones. We set K to 65536 to ensure the relational distribution contains sufficient information to learn style-invariant representations. Remark that the temperature parameter greatly affects the stability of the learning with causal invariance loss. Generally, we choose $\bar{\tau}$ to be smaller than τ, so that the target distribution is sharper.

Dense Causal Invariant Learning for Semantic Segmentation. For the semantic segmentation task, an image contains various objects and semantic features. Therefore, we use dense causal invariance loss where we compute the loss over the patches of the representations. Following the method in [5], we crop the feature maps into N_l patches and pass them forward to the projector to compute causal invariance loss on each cropped representation:

$$\mathcal{L}_{\text{CI-Dense}}(x) = \frac{1}{N_l}\sum_{n=1}^{N_l} \frac{1}{2}\ell_{\text{CI}}\left(z_{1,n}, \bar{z}_{2,n}\right) + \frac{1}{2}\ell_{\text{CI}}\left(z_{2,n}, \bar{z}_{1,n}\right), \tag{4}$$

where each $z_{i,n}, \bar{z}_{i,n}$ is the encoder output of n-th feature map. In our experiments, we use $N_l = 8 \times 8$.

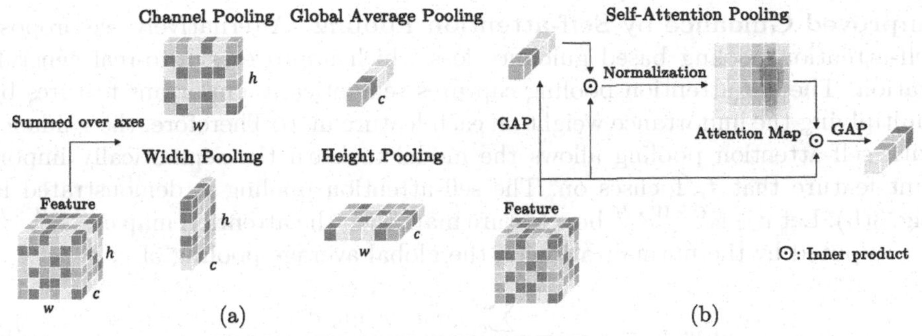

Fig. 3. (a) Example images of channel, global average, width and height pooled feature map. (b) Mechanism of self-attention pooling for guidance loss.

3.2 Guided Learning for Syn-to-Real Generalization

In this section, we present a simple, yet effective method to guide a model with real-domain guidance from the ImageNet-pretrained model by using feature distillation. In contrast to previous approaches such as ASG [6] and CSG [5], our method does not require any task-specific information or complicated loss function.

Pooled Feature Distillation. For a data x, let $f_s(x), f_r(x) \in \mathbb{R}^{C\times H\times W}$ be the feature map of an intermediate convolutional layer of ImageNet pre-trained network f_r and training network f_s. Then it is straightforward to minimize the squared distance between the feature maps $f_s(x)$ and $f_r(x)$ for guidance loss to retain the knowledge of f_r as much as possible while learning task-related knowledge from the synthetic data. To design the guidance loss, there are two opposite concepts that must be considered: rigidity and plasticity. The rigidity is on how much the model can retain the knowledge of f_r, and the plasticity accounts for the flexibility of the model to learn from the synthetic domain.

While the direct minimization with the feature maps has high rigidity, it has low plasticity that the model cannot sufficiently learn task-related knowledge with synthetic data. Douillard et al. [14] showed that by using an appropriate pooling operator, the model can balance the rigidity and plasticity to conduct incremental learning. Similarly, we use the pooling operator to extract sufficient information from the feature maps and balance the rigidity and plasticity to improve syn-to-real generalization.

In Fig. 3(a), we list various pooling methods that we consider in this paper. Let P be such pooling operators in Fig. 3(a), then the guidance loss is given by the ℓ_2 distance between the normalized pooled feature maps of $f_s(x)$ and $f_r(x)$:

$$\mathcal{L}_{\mathtt{G}}(x; P) = \left\| \frac{P(f_s(x))}{\|P(f_s(x))\|_2} - \frac{P(f_r(x))}{\|P(f_r(x)\|_2} \right\|_2^2 \tag{5}$$

Improved Guidance by Self-attention Pooling. Alternatively, we propose self-attention pooling based guidance loss which improves syn-to-real generalization. The self-attention pooling captures semantically important features by multiplying the importance weight on each feature map. Therefore, the guidance with self-attention pooling allows the model to learn the semantically important feature that f_r focuses on. The self-attention pooling is demonstrated in Fig. 3(b). Let $v \in \mathbb{R}^{C\times W\times H}$ be a feature map, then the attention map $a \in \mathbb{R}^{W\times H}$ is computed by the normalization on the global average pooling of v:

$$a[w,h] = \frac{\sum_{c=1}^{C} v[c,w,h]g[c]}{\sum_{w'=1}^{W}\sum_{h'=1}^{H}\sum_{c=1}^{C} v[c,w',h']g[c]}, \tag{6}$$

where $g[c] = \frac{1}{HW}\sum_{w=1}^{W}\sum_{h=1}^{H} v[c,w,h]$ is global average pooling of v. Then the self-attention pooling operator P_a outputs an importance-weighted feature map with weights given by the attention map:

$$P_a(v)[c] = \sum_{w=1}^{W}\sum_{h=1}^{H} v[c,w,h]a[w,h]. \tag{7}$$

Then our final guidance loss with self-attention pooling operator P_a is given by

$$\mathcal{L}_{\mathtt{G}}(x;P_a) = \left\| \frac{P_a(f_s(x))}{\|P_a(f_s(x))\|_2} - \frac{P_a(f_r(x))}{\|P_a(f_r(x)\|_2} \right\|_2^2 \tag{8}$$

The empirical analysis on the effect of pooling on the guidance loss is explored in Sect. 4.2.

3.3 Guided Causal Invariant Syn-to-Real Generalization

In this section, we present the overall description of our method for syn-to-real generalization, which we refer to *Guided Causal Invariant Syn-to-real generalization* (GCISG). Given a task loss $\mathcal{L}_{\mathtt{task}}$ that takes synthetic data x with corresponding label y, the GCISG adds guidance loss $\mathcal{L}_G$ that regularizes the model to retain the semantic knowledge of ImageNet pre-trained model and causal invariance loss $\mathcal{L}_{\mathtt{CI}}$ to achieve style-invariant representation that promotes generalization on a real domain. Thus, the overall loss is computed by following:

$$\mathcal{L}(x) = \mathcal{L}_{\mathtt{Task}}(x,y) + \lambda_{\mathtt{G}}\mathcal{L}_{\mathtt{G}}(x) + \lambda_{\mathtt{CI}}\mathcal{L}_{\mathtt{CI}}(x). \tag{9}$$

Remark that our GCISG framework is agnostic to tasks, as guidance loss and causal invariance loss are computed in an unsupervised manner.

Stage-Wise Loss Computation. The causal invariance loss $\mathcal{L}_{\texttt{CI}}$ and the guidance loss $\mathcal{L}_{\texttt{G}}$ can be computed for each intermediate layer. Denote $f^{(l)}$ to be l-th layer of the neural network, (e.g. the block layers of ResNet [20]), then the GCISG is computed for each layer by following:

$$\mathcal{L}(x) = \mathcal{L}_{\texttt{Task}}(x, y) + \sum_{l} \lambda_{\texttt{G}}^{(l)} \mathcal{L}_{\texttt{G}}^{(l)}(x) + \sum_{l} \lambda_{\texttt{CI}}^{(l)} \mathcal{L}_{\texttt{CI}}^{(l)}(x). \tag{10}$$

In Sect. 4.2, we conduct an ablation study on the effect of choosing layer.

4 Experiments

In this section, we empirically validate the effectiveness of our method on various syn-to-real generalization tasks. We report the performance of a synthetic-trained model in the unseen real domain for evaluation. Furthermore, we analyze the model with various auxiliary evaluation metrics to support our claims.

Evaluation Metrics for Causal Invariance. To quantify the style-invariance of a representation, we introduce *match rate* ($\mathcal{M}$), which evaluates the consistency of a model on images that have the same semantics but different styles. For each image, we generate another stylized image and check if it produces the same output as the original one. Formally, we report the match rate by the number of consistent samples out of the number of the entire validation set. To generate stylized images, we use photometric transforms such as Gaussian blurring and color jittering as done in [10].

Evaluation Metrics for Guidance. We present two different measures to quantify the quality of guidance from the ImageNet pre-trained model. First, we bring the linear classification layer of the pre-trained ImageNet model and attach it to the synthetic-trained model. Then we report the ImageNet validation accuracy ($\text{Acc}_{\texttt{IN}}$) by inferring on the ImageNet validation dataset. Second, we evaluate the similarity between ImageNet pre-trained model and the synthetic-trained model by using *centered kernel alignment* (CKA) similarity [23]. Here, the high ImageNet validation accuracy demonstrates that our model avoids the catastrophic forgetting of the task information, and the high CKA similarity proves the preservation of representational knowledge of a real pre-trained model. For the computation of CKA similarity, we collect the features of the penultimate layers of the ImageNet pre-trained model and synthetic-trained model on the validation dataset. The detailed implementations are in the supplementary material.

4.1 Image Classification

Datasets. We demonstrate the effectiveness of GCISG on VisDA-17 [35] image classification benchmark. The synthetic training set consists of the images rendered from 3D models with various angles and illuminations. The real validation set is a subset of MS-COCO [27]. Each dataset contains the same 12 object categories.

Table 1. Top-1 accuracy (%) on VisDA-17 (VisDA) and ImageNet (IN) validation datasets of various syn-to-real generalization methods. All methods used ResNet-101 as a base architecture.

Method	Acc_{VisDA}	Acc_{IN}
Oracle on ImageNet	53.3	**77.4**
Vanilla L2 distance	56.4	49.1
ROAD [49]	57.1	**77.4**
SI [9]	57.6	53.9
ASG [6]	61.1	76.7
CSG [5]	64.1	73.8
GCISG	**67.5**	75.4

Table 2. Top: Comparison with CSG and oracle on ImageNet by evaluation metrics for invariance ($\mathcal{M}$) and guidance (Acc_{IN}, CKA). The oracle freezes the backbone and fine-tune the classification head. Bottom: Effects of $\mathcal{L}_G$ and $\mathcal{L}_{CI}$ in GCISG.

Method	$\mathcal{L}_G$	$\mathcal{L}_{CI}$	Acc_{VisDA}	$\mathcal{M}$	Acc_{IN}	CKA
Oracle	✗	✗	53.3	69.5	77.4	1.0
CSG [5]	✓	✗	64.1	77.0	73.8	0.89
GCISG	✗	✗	55.9	73.3	52.7	0.72
	✗	✓	58.6	74.4	51.9	0.73
	✓	✗	64.3	76.6	**75.9**	**0.95**
	✓	✓	**67.5**	**78.6**	75.4	0.93

Implementation Details. We adopt ImageNet pre-trained ResNet-101 as the backbone. We use an SGD optimizer with a learning rate of 0.001, a batch size of 64 for 30 epochs. For data augmentations, we use the RandAugment [12] following the protocol of CSG [5]. The momentum rate is 0.996 and the number of the support sample is 65536 throughout the training.

Results. In Table 1, we report the top-1 validation accuracy on VisDA-17 (Acc_{VisDA}) of synthetic-trained model with various syn-to-real generalization methods. We also report the ImageNet validation accuracy (Acc_{IN}) of the same synthetic-trained model as a guidance metric. We observe that GCISG outperforms the competing methods on VisDA-17 on a large margin. As shown in Table 1, there is a correlation between the ImageNet classification accuracy and syn-to-real generalization performance. However, the correlation is not strong that the methods with higher ImageNet accuracy such as ASG [6] and ROAD [9], do not necessarily have higher validation accuracy on VisDA-17. Thus, sufficiently high ImageNet validation accuracy might be useful for syn-to-real generalization, but it may hamper the generalization if it is too much as it transfers knowledge that is overfitted to the ImageNet classification task.

Table 2 shows that our method not only achieves a higher VisDA-17 validation accuracy but also has a higher match rate ($\mathcal{M}$) and CKA similarity than CSG. The higher match rate indicates that the learned representation is invariant to the style change, and the higher CKA similarity indicates the conformation of learned representation to the ImageNet pre-trained network. Therefore, one can observe that both factors have positive impacts on syn-to-real generalization.

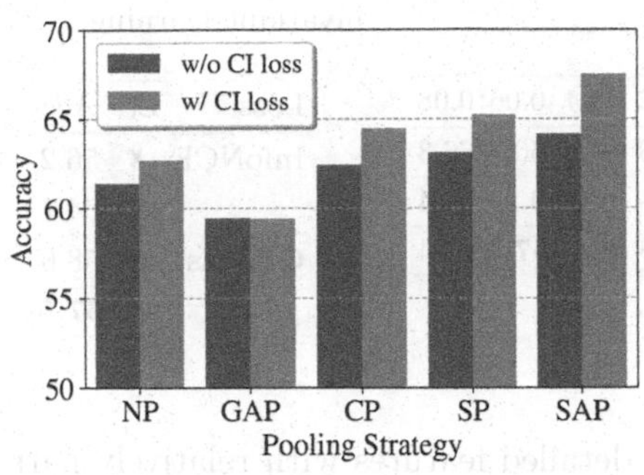

Fig. 4. Ablation of feature pooling strategies for $\mathcal{L}_G$. NP, GAP, CP, SP, and SAP denote no pooling, global average pooling, channel pooling, spatial pooling, and self-attention pooling respectively.

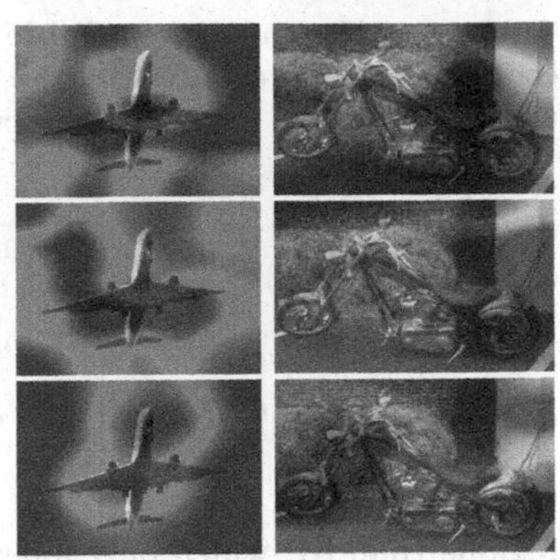

Fig. 5. Visualized attention of feature pooling methods. From top to bottom, rows correspond to NP, GAP, SAP. The red area corresponds to high score for class.

Table 2 reports the effect of using causal invariance loss and guidance loss on VisDA-17 validation accuracy and auxiliary evaluation metrics. Remark that CSG [5] applied guidance loss in contrastive learning with ImageNet pre-trained features. We observe that the guidance loss generally boosts ImageNet validation accuracy and CKA similarity. This clearly demonstrates that the transferring knowledge from the ImageNet pre-trained model which holds useful knowledge of real domain helps the syn-to-real generalization. Moreover, using the causal invariance loss generally boosts both match rate and VisDA-17 validation accuracy. This also demonstrates that the style-invariance of the model enhances the syn-to-real generalization.

4.2 Ablation Study

Ablation on Pooling Operators for Guidance Loss. As explained in Sect. 3.2, the choice of pooling operator for guidance loss affects the learning. We conduct an ablation study on the effect of the pooling operator on VisDA-17 syn-to-real generalization. We compare 5 different pooling strategies: no pooling (NP), global average pooling (GAP), channel pooling (CP), spatial pooling (SP), and self-attention pooling (SAP), where spatial pooling takes both height pooling and width pooling. In Fig. 4, we show the generalization performance in VisDA-17 for various pooling strategies. We also conduct the ablation study on removing causal invariance loss to identify the effect of the pooling operator on the generalization. In both situations, we observe that self-attention pooling outperforms other pooling strategies.

We also investigate the attention map using Grad-CAM [40] to qualitatively analyze the effect of pooling operators for guidance loss. In Fig. 5, we observe a tendency that SAP comprehensively includes more semantically meaningful

Table 3. Ablation on the choice of feature stages S_{G} and S_{CI}.

S_{G}	S_{CI}	Acc
{0,1,2}	{0,1,2}	59.8
{0,1,2}	{3,4}	55.9
{3,4}	{0,1,2}	66.2
{3,4}	{3,4}	**67.5**

Table 4. Ablation on the choice of temperatures $\tau, \bar{\tau}$ for $\mathcal{L}_{\mathrm{CI}}$.

$\bar{\tau}$	0.02	0.04	0.06	0.08
$\tau = 0.12$	66.6	**67.5**	66.5	66.3
τ	0.08	0.1	0.12	0.14
$\bar{\tau} = 0.04$	66.8	67.1	**67.5**	67.4

Table 5. Ablation on the loss functions for style-invariant learning.

Loss	$\mathcal{L}_{\mathrm{G}}$	Acc
InfoNCE	✗	56.2
	✓	64.7
CI loss	✗	58.6
	✓	**67.5**

regions than NP which only focuses on detailed features with relatively narrow receptive fields. Also, one can observe that SAP focuses less on meaningless parts compared to GAP, which does not sufficiently encode informative features with a relatively wide receptive field.

Ablation on Feature Stages. We conduct an ablation study on generalization performance with different feature stage for $\mathcal{L}_{\mathrm{CI}}$ and $\mathcal{L}_{\mathrm{G}}$. Let us denote S_{G} and S_{CI} to be the set of layers that we used for computation of guidance loss and causal invariance loss. In ResNet-101, there is one convolutional layer and 4 Res-Blocks. We grouped the first three layers and last two layers and experimented on 4 combinations of guidance loss and causal invariance loss with different layer groups. As shown in Table 3, the computation of guidance loss and causal invariance loss with deeper feature stages is more effective in generalization than the shallower one, as the deeper stage of features holds richer semantic information. This result is consistent with the tendency of deep layers to encode content discriminative information as Pan et al. pointed out in IBN-Net [33].

Ablation on Temperature Scale. We conduct an ablation study on the effect of different temperature scales for causal invariance loss. In Table 4, when $\tau = 0.12$ we observe that small value of $\bar{\tau}$ is beneficial for the performance. Conversely, when $\bar{\tau}$ is fixed to 0.04, relatively high value of τ has better performance. Thus, we choose $\tau = 0.12$ and $\bar{\tau} = 0.04$ for our experiments.

Ablation on Causal Invariance Loss. We conduct an ablation study on the effect of different contrastive losses for causal invariance loss. We compare proposed $\mathcal{L}_{\mathrm{CI}}$ and InfoNCE loss [7] on VisDA-17 image classification. To see the effect of causal invariance loss solely, we further removed the guidance loss. In Table 5, we observe that $\mathcal{L}_{\mathrm{CI}}$ is more effective in syn-to-real-generalization that InfoNCE loss regardless of the guidance loss.

4.3 Semantic Segmentation

Datasets. For semantic segmentation, the source domain is GTAV [38] and the target domain is Cityscapes [11]. GTAV is a large-scale dataset containing 24,996 synthetic driving-scene images with resolution 1914×1052, taken from the Grand Theft Auto V game engine. Cityscapes street scene dataset contains 2,975

Table 6. Comparison of mIoU (%) with existing synthetic-to-real generalization and domain generalization methods on GTAV-Cityscapes datasets. All methods used ResNet-50 as a base architecture.

Method	IBN-Net [33]	DRPC [47]	RobustNet [10]	ASG [6]	CSG [5]	**GCISG**
No adapt	22.17	32.45	28.95	23.29	25.43	26.67
Adapt	29.64	37.42	36.58	29.65	35.27	**39.01**
mIoU ↑(%)	7.47	4.97	7.63	6.36	9.84	**12.34**

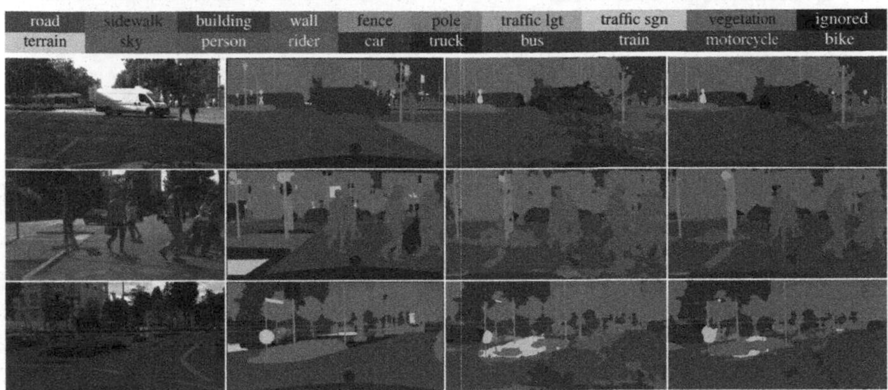

Fig. 6. Segmentation results on GTAV to Cityscapes. From left to right, columns correspond to original images, ground truth, prediction results of CSG, and GCISG.

train images and 500 validation images with resolution 2048×1024, taken from European cities. All the images in the source and target dataset have pixel-level annotations with 19 semantic categories. For evaluation, we report the mean intersection over union (mIoU) on the Cityscapes validation set.

Implementation Details. We adopt DeepLab-V3 [3] with ImageNet pretrained ResNet-50 backbone for our semantic segmentation network. We employ an SGD optimizer with a learning rate of 0.001 and a batch size of 8 for 40 epochs. We crop an image with the size of 512×512 and apply color jittering and multi-scale resizing.

Results. In Table 6, we report the mIoU (%) of the semantic segmentation models trained with various syn-to-real generalization methods. We observe that the model trained with GCISG achieves the best performance gain. It is worth noting that IBN-Net [33] and RobustNet [10] modifies the normalization blocks, and DRPC [47] requires preparation steps of stylizing images before training. In contrast, our method can be applied to any general architecture with no additional preparation steps. In Fig. 6, we qualitatively compare with CSG [5] by visualizing the results of segmentation on validation images.

Table 7. The average precision (AP) of Sim10k to Cityscapes object detection with various methods. All experiments are run by us.

Method	AP	AP_{50}	AP_{75}
Baseline	24.8	45.1	24.0
CSG	28.5	50.4	28.1
GCISG	**30.6**	**54.6**	**29.5**

Table 8. Top-1 accuracy (%) of unsupervised domain adaptation on VisDA-17 by using CBST initialized with different methods.

Method	Acc_{VisDA}
Source only + CBST [52]	76.4
ASG + CBST [6]	82.5
GCISG + CBST	**83.6**

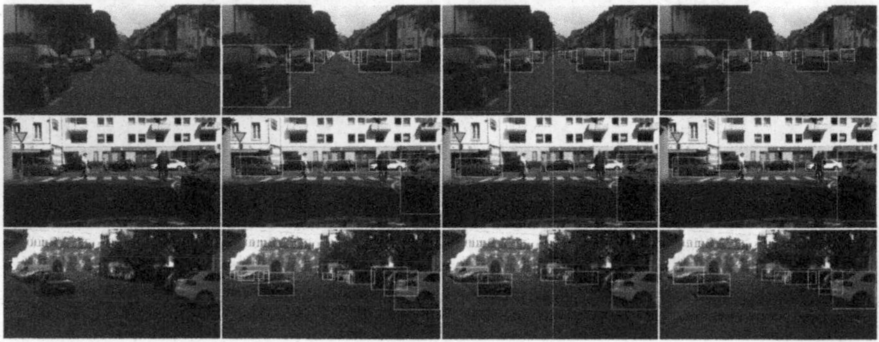

Fig. 7. Object detection results on Sim10k to Cityscapes. From left to right, columns correspond to original images, ground truth, prediction results of CSG, and GCISG.

4.4 Object Detection

Datasets. We conduct object detection experiments on the source domain of Sim10k [22] to the target domain of Cityscapes. Sim10k dataset consists of 10,000 images with bounding box annotations on the car object. Images in Sim10k are rendered by the Grand Theft Auto V game engine, where the resolution of the images are 1914×1052. Since Cityscapes does not contain bounding box labels, we generate bounding box labels from polygon labels, following the method of [8].

Implementation Details. We experiment on Faster R-CNN [37] as the base detector and ImageNet pre-trained ResNet-101 with FPN [26] as the backbone. We use an SGD optimizer with a learning rate of 0.001, and a batch size of 4 for 30 epochs. We use the same hyperparameter settings for the original Faster R-CNN except that we add color jittering for data augmentation. Since CSG [5] does not contain experiments on object detection, we implement the CSG framework for our experiments for a fair comparison.

Results. We evaluate the average precision of bounding boxes on each generalization method following the COCO [27] evaluation protocol. The results are shown in Table 7. Compared to the previous state-of-the-art syn-to-real generalization method [5], GCISG achieves around 2.1% points improvement in AP and 4.2% points improvement in AP50. In Fig. 7, we qualitatively compare with the CSG [5] by visualizing the results of the object detection on validation images.

4.5 Unsupervised Domain Adaptation

In this section, we demonstrate the effectiveness of GCISG for the unsupervised domain adaptation (UDA) task. We conduct experiments on class-balanced self-training (CBST) [51] framework, where we use the model trained with GCISG as a starting point for the adaptation.

We perform UDA experiments on the VisDA-17 image classification dataset. We follow the setting of [52], where we set the starting portion of the pseudo label p to 20%, and empirically add 5% to p for each epoch until it reaches 50%. Remark that, unlike previous syn-to-real generalization tasks, we freeze the normalization layers when training the source model, where we empirically found it better for the UDA task.

In Table 8, we present an accuracy on VisDA-17 validation dataset under various initialization methods for CBST framework. Compared to the baseline, our method remarkably boosts the performance by 7%, achieving 83.6%. Also, the model trained from GCISG outperforms that from ASG by 1%.

5 Conclusion

In this work, we present GCISG, which enhances the syn-to-real generalization by learning style-invariant representation and retaining the semantic knowledge of the ImageNet pre-trained model simultaneously. Through extensive experiments on VisDA-17 image classification, GTAV-Cityscapes semantic segmentation, and object detection, we demonstrate the effectiveness of our method.

Our work shows that we can extract useful information over the style changes that are useful for generalization. For future works, we aim to design style transformation methods that can better disentangle the style and content which suits our causal model. We believe that those style transformations can lead to better syn-to-real generalization under our method as they seek better causal invariance. We leave them for future work.

Acknowledgements. Kyungmin Lee is supported by Institute of Information & communications Technology Planning & Evaluation (IITP) grant funded by the Korea government (MSIT) (No. 2019-0-00075, Artificial Intelligence Graduate School Program (KAIST)).

References

1. Baker, N., Lu, H., Erlikhman, G., Kellman, P.J.: Deep convolutional networks do not classify based on global object shape. PLoS Ccomput. Biol. **14**(12), e1006613 (2018)
2. Castro, F.M., Marín-Jiménez, M.J., Guil, N., Schmid, C., Alahari, K.: End-to-end incremental learning. In: Ferrari, V., Hebert, M., Sminchisescu, C., Weiss, Y. (eds.) ECCV 2018. LNCS, vol. 11216, pp. 241–257. Springer, Cham (2018). https://doi.org/10.1007/978-3-030-01258-8_15
3. Chen, L., Papandreou, G., Schroff, F., Adam, H.: Rethinking atrous convolution for semantic image segmentation. arXiv:1706.05587 (2017)
4. Chen, T., Kornblith, S., Norouzi, M., Hinton, G.: A simple framework for contrastive learning of visual representations. In: ICML (2020)
5. Chen, W., Yu, Z., Mello, S., Liu, S., Alvarez, J.M., Wang, Z., Anandkumar, A.: Contrastive Syn-to-real generalization. In: ICLR (2021)
6. Chen, W., Yu, Z., Wang, Z., Anandkumar, A.: Automated synthetic-to-real generalization. In: ICML (2020)
7. Chen, X., Fan, H., Girshick, R., He, K.: Improved baselines with momentum contrastive learning. arXiv:2003.04297 (2020)
8. Chen, Y., Li, W., Sakaridis, C., Dai, D., Van Gool, L.: Domain adaptive faster r-CNN for object detection in the wild. In: CVPR (2018)
9. Chen, Y., Li, W., Van Gool, L.: Road: Reality oriented adaptation for semantic segmentation of urban scenes. In: CVPR (2018)
10. Choi, S., Jung, S., Yun, H., Kim, J.T., Kim, S., Choo, J.: RobustNet: improving domain generalization in urban-scene segmentation via instance selective whitening. In: CVPR (2021)
11. Cordts, M., Omran, M., Ramos, S., Rehfeld, T., Enzweiler, M., Benenson, R., Franke, U., Roth, S., Schiele, B.: The cityscapes dataset for semantic urban scene understanding. In: CVPR (2016)
12. Cubuk, E.D., Zoph, B., Shlens, J., Le, Q.V.: RandAugment: practical automated data augmentation with a reduced search space. In: CVPR Workshops (2020)
13. Dhar, P., Singh, R.V., Peng, K.C., Wu, Z., Chellappa, R.: Learning without memorizing. In: CVPR (2019)
14. Douillard, A., Cord, M., Ollion, C., Robert, T., Valle, E.: PODNet: pooled outputs distillation for small-tasks incremental learning. In: Vedaldi, A., Bischof, H., Brox, T., Frahm, J.-M. (eds.) ECCV 2020. LNCS, vol. 12365, pp. 86–102. Springer, Cham (2020). https://doi.org/10.1007/978-3-030-58565-5_6
15. Fang, Z., Wang, J., Wang, L., Zhang, L., Yang, Y., Liu, Z.: Seed: self-supervised distillation for visual representation. arXiv:2101.04731 (2021)
16. Gaidon, A., Wang, Q., Cabon, Y., Vig, E.: Virtual worlds as proxy for multi-object tracking analysis. In: CVPR (2016)
17. Geirhos, R., Rubisch, P., Michaelis, C., Bethge, M., Wichmann, F.A., Brendel, W.: ImageNet-trained CNNs are biased towards texture; increasing shape bias improves accuracy and robustness. arXiv:1811.12231 (2018)
18. Handa, A., Pătrăucean, V., Stent, S., Cipolla, R.: SceneNet: an annotated model generator for indoor scene understanding. In: ICRA (2016)
19. He, K., Fan, H., Wu, Y., Xie, S., Girshick, R.: Momentum contrast for unsupervised visual representation learning. In: CVPR (2020)
20. He, K., Zhang, X., Ren, S., Sun, J.: Deep residual learning for image recognition. In: CVPR (2016)

21. Hinton, G., et al.: Distilling the knowledge in a neural network. arXiv:1503.02531 (2015)
22. Johnson-Roberson, M., Barto, C., Mehta, R., Sridhar, S.N., Rosaen, K., Vasudevan, R.: Driving in the matrix: can virtual worlds replace human-generated annotations for real world tasks? In: ICRA (2017)
23. Kornblith, S., Norouzi, M., Lee, H., Hinton, G.: Similarity of neural network representations revisited. In: ICML (2019)
24. Li, H., Pan, S.J., Wang, S., Kot, A.C.: Domain generalization with adversarial feature learning. In: CVPR (2018)
25. Li, Z., Hoiem, D.: Learning without forgetting. In: Li, Z., Hoiem, D.: Learning without forgetting. Trans. Pattern Anal. Mach. Intell. (2017)
26. Lin, T., Dollár, P., Girshick, R.B., He, K., Hariharan, B., Belongie, S.J.: Feature pyramid networks for object detection. arXiv:1612.03144 (2016)
27. Lin, T.-Y., Maire, M., Belongie, S., Hays, J., Perona, P., Ramanan, D., Dollár, P., Zitnick, C.L.: Microsoft COCO: common objects in context. In: Fleet, D., Pajdla, T., Schiele, B., Tuytelaars, T. (eds.) ECCV 2014. LNCS, vol. 8693, pp. 740–755. Springer, Cham (2014). https://doi.org/10.1007/978-3-319-10602-1_48
28. Mahajan, D., Tople, S., Sharma, A.: Domain generalization using causal matching. In: ICML (2021)
29. Maximov, M., Galim, K., Leal-Taixe, L.: Focus on defocus: bridging the synthetic to real domain gap for depth estimation. In: CVPR (2020)
30. McCormac, J., Handa, A., Leutenegger, S., Davison, A.J.: SceneNet RGB-D: 5M photorealistic images of synthetic indoor trajectories with ground truth. arXiv:1612.05079 (2016)
31. Mitrovic, J., McWilliams, B., Walker, J., Buesing, L., Blundell, C.: Representation learning via invariant causal mechanisms. arXiv:2010.07922 (2020)
32. Müller, M., Casser, V., Lahoud, J., Smith, N., Ghanem, B.: Sim4Cv: a photo-realistic simulator for computer vision applications. Int. J. Comput. Vis. **126**, 902–919 (2018)
33. Pan, X., Luo, P., Shi, J., Tang, X.: Two at once: enhancing learning and generalization capacities via IBN-Net. In: Ferrari, V., Hebert, M., Sminchisescu, C., Weiss, Y. (eds.) ECCV 2018. LNCS, vol. 11208, pp. 484–500. Springer, Cham (2018). https://doi.org/10.1007/978-3-030-01225-0_29
34. Park, W., Kim, D., Lu, Y., Cho, M.: Relational knowledge distillation. In: CVPR (2019)
35. Peng, X., Usman, B., Kaushik, N., Hoffman, J., Wang, D., Saenko, K.: Visda: the visual domain adaptation challenge. arXiv:1710.06924 (2017)
36. Rebuffi, S.A., Kolesnikov, A., Sperl, G., Lampert, C.H.: iCaRL:Incremental classifier and representation learning. In: CVPR (2017)
37. Ren, S., He, K., Girshick, R., Sun, J.: Faster R-CNN: towards real-time object detection with region proposal networks. In: TPAMI (2017)
38. Richter, S.R., Vineet, V., Roth, S., Koltun, V.: Playing for data: ground truth from computer games. In: Leibe, B., Matas, J., Sebe, N., Welling, M. (eds.) ECCV 2016. LNCS, vol. 9906, pp. 102–118. Springer, Cham (2016). https://doi.org/10.1007/978-3-319-46475-6_7
39. Ros, G., Sellart, L., Materzynska, J., Vazquez, D., Lopez, A.: The SYNTHIA Dataset: a large collection of synthetic images for semantic segmentation of urban scenes. In: CVPR (2016)
40. Selvaraju, R.R., Cogswell, M., Das, A., Vedantam, R., Parikh, D., Batra, D.: Grad-CAM: visual explanations from deep networks via gradient-based localization. In: ICCV (2017)

41. Tian, Y., Krishnan, D., Isola, P.: Contrastive representation distillation. arXiv:1910.10699 (2019)
42. Tremblay, J., et al.: Training deep networks with synthetic data: Bridging the reality gap by domain randomization. In: CVPR Workshops (2018)
43. Tung, F., Mori, G.: Similarity-preserving knowledge distillation. In: ICCV (2019)
44. Wang, Z., Luo, Y., Qiu, R., Huang, Z., Baktashmotlagh, M.: Learning to diversify for single domain generalization. In: ICCV (2021)
45. Wu, Z., Xiong, Y., Yu, S.X., Lin, D.: Unsupervised feature learning via non-parametric instance discrimination. In: CVPR (2018)
46. Xu, G., Liu, Z., Li, X., Loy, C.C.: Knowledge distillation meets self-supervision. In: Vedaldi, A., Bischof, H., Brox, T., Frahm, J.-M. (eds.) ECCV 2020. LNCS, vol. 12354, pp. 588–604. Springer, Cham (2020). https://doi.org/10.1007/978-3-030-58545-7_34
47. Yue, X., Zhang, Y., Zhao, S., Sangiovanni-Vincentelli, A.L., Keutzer, K., Gong, B.: Domain randomization and pyramid consistency: simulation-to-real generalization without accessing target domain data. In: ICCV (2019)
48. Zagoruyko, S., Komodakis, N.: Paying more attention to attention: Improving the performance of convolutional neural networks via attention transfer. arXiv:1612.03928 (2016)
49. Zenke, F., Poole, B., Ganguli, S.: Continual learning through synaptic intelligence. In: ICML (2017)
50. Zheng, M., You, S., Wang, F., Qian, C., Zhang, C., Wang, X., Xu, C.: ReSSL: relational self-supervised learning with weak augmentation. In: NIPS (2021)
51. Zou, Y., Yu, Z., Vijaya Kumar, B.V.K., Wang, J.: Unsupervised Domain adaptation for semantic segmentation via class-balanced self-training. In: Ferrari, V., Hebert, M., Sminchisescu, C., Weiss, Y. (eds.) ECCV 2018. LNCS, vol. 11207, pp. 297–313. Springer, Cham (2018). https://doi.org/10.1007/978-3-030-01219-9_18
52. Zou, Y., Yu, Z., Liu, X., Kumar, B.V., Wang, J.: Confidence regularized self-training. In: ICCV (2019)

AcroFOD: An Adaptive Method for Cross-Domain Few-Shot Object Detection

Yipeng Gao[1,3], Lingxiao Yang[1], Yunmu Huang[2], Song Xie[2], Shiyong Li[2], and Wei-Shi Zheng[1,3,4](✉)

[1] School of Computer Science and Engineering, Sun Yat-sen University, Guangzhou, China
gaoyp23@mail2.sysu.edu.cn, yanglx9@mail.sysu.edu.cn, wszheng@ieee.org
[2] Huawei Technologies Co., Ltd., Shenzhen, China
{huangyunmu,xiesong5,lishiyong}@huawei.com
[3] Key Laboratory of Machine Intelligence and Advanced Computing, Ministry of Education, Guangzhou, China
[4] Guangdong Province Key Laboratory of Information Security Technology, Sun Yat-sen University, Guangzhou, China

Abstract. Under the domain shift, cross-domain few-shot object detection aims to adapt object detectors in the target domain with a few annotated target data. There exists two significant challenges: (1) Highly insufficient target domain data; (2) Potential over-adaptation and misleading caused by inappropriately amplified target samples without any restriction. To address these challenges, we propose an adaptive method consisting of two parts. First, we propose an adaptive optimization strategy to select augmented data similar to target samples rather than blindly increasing the amount. Specifically, we filter the augmented candidates which significantly deviate from the target feature distribution in the very beginning. Second, to further relieve the data limitation, we propose the multi-level domain-aware data augmentation to increase the diversity and rationality of augmented data, which exploits the cross-image foreground-background mixture. Experiments show that the proposed method achieves state-of-the-art performance on multiple benchmarks. The code is available at https://github.com/Hlings/AcroFOD.

Keywords: Domain adaptation · Few-shot learning · Object detection

1 Introduction

Due to the domain discrepancy, apparent performance drop is common when applying a trained detector in an unseen domain. Recently, many researchers try to address it as a domain adaption task. As one of the domain adaption adaptation sub-tasks, cross-domain few-shot object detection is proposed with the

Supplementary Information The online version contains supplementary material available at https://doi.org/10.1007/978-3-031-19827-4_39.

S. Avidan et al. (Eds.): ECCV 2022, LNCS 13693, pp. 673–690, 2022.
https://doi.org/10.1007/978-3-031-19827-4_39

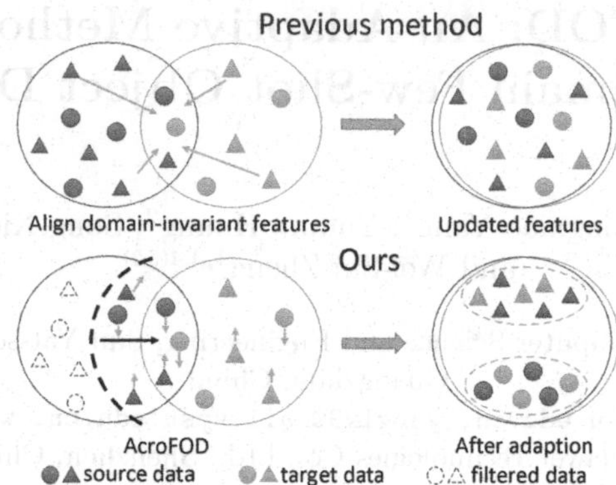

Fig. 1. We address the task of cross-domain few-shot object detection. Top: Existing feature-aligning based methods fail to extract discriminative features within limited labeled data in the target domain. Bottom: Our method filters (thick black dotted line) source data that is far away from the target domain.

observation that a few samples can still reflect the major characteristics changes of domain shifts [40], such as view variations [10,17], weather diversification [38] and lighting difference [1,28,31]. Different from unsupervised domain adaptation (UDA), few labeled target samples are available in few-show domain adaptation (FDA) setting, as well as a large amount samples from source domain.

Existing methods [41,51] in the FDA setting are feature-aligning based methods that first pre-train the model in source domain and then align to the target domain. Besides, some methods mainly overcome domain gaps under UDA setting [19,34,35,43]. However, UDA methods depend on labeled data from the source domain and sufficient unlabeled data from the target domain to fully describe the distribution for both domains, before any explicit or implicit feature alignment operation.

However, a large amount of unlabeled data may not available in the target domain [40]. Without sufficient data, most UDA methods performs disappointingly under the FDA setting [5–7,25,33,45,48,52]. An intuitive way to overcome such a problem is to incorporate limited target data with source data and augment them. However, we argue that not all the augmented data are useful. Blind augmentation may even exacerbate the domain discrepancy due the samples that plays as outliers of target data distribution. To overcome this problem, the adaptive optimization of directive augmentation towards target data distribution should be considered very carefully.

In this work, we present an **A**daptive method for **Cro**ss-domain **F**ew-shot **O**bject **D**etection (AcroFOD), which is architecture-agnostic and generic. The AcroFOD mainly consists of two parts: an adaptive and iterative distribution optimization for augmented data filtering and multi-level domain-aware augmentation. With a large amount of data available in the source domain, it could be intuitive to train the detector using the whole set of images from source and target domains. However, we argue that such an ungrounded training method is likely to introduce much unsuitable and low-quality data relative to the target domain, which will mislead the model during the training process. To deal with this issue, we design an adaptive distribution optimization strategy to eliminate unsuitable introduced images as shown in Fig. 1. Such a strategy allows the detector to fit the feature distribution of target domain faster and more accurately. Moreover, as both background and foreground information can reflect the characteristic of the target domain, we propose multi-level domain-aware augmentation to make a fusion of source and target domain images more diverse and rational.

There are several advantages of the proposed AcroFOD for cross-domain few-shot object detection: 1) **Wide application scenarios.** In contrast to most of the previous methods [14,14,35,41,43], our method requires neither complicated architecture changes nor generative models for creating additional synthetic data; 2) **Fast convergence.** The AcroFOD is almost 2× faster than existing methods [34] to reach better performance in some established scenarios because no pre-training phase is required; 3) **Less cost of collecting data.** Compared with UDA methods [19,34,35,43], we greatly reduce the cost of collecting massive amounts of data in the target domain but introduce the cost of annotation.

We conduct a comprehensive and fair benchmark to demonstrate the effectiveness of AcroFOD to mitigate different kinds of domain shifts. Our method can achieve new state-of-the-art results on these benchmarks in the FDA setting. The main contributions of this work are summarized as follows:

- The proposed adaptive optimization strategy attaches importance to the quality of augmentation. It also prevents the model from over-adaptation which is similar to over-fitting because of lacking data.
- To enhance the diversity of merging images from source and target domain, we construct generalized formulations of multi-level domain-aware augmentation. Then, we provide several instances and discuss them.

2 Related Work

Existing UDA methods leverage a large number of unlabeled images from the target domain to explicitly mitigate the domain shift. They can be divided into domain-alignment [4,22,37,50], domain-mapping [8,16,29] and self-labeling techniques [34]. Zheng et al. [49], propose a hybrid framework to minimize L2 distance between single-class specific prototypes across domains at instance-level and use adversarial training at image-level. ViSGA [35] uses a similarity-based grouping scheme to aggregate information into multiple groups in a class agnostic manner. To overcome pseudo-label noise in self-labeling, [34] proposed a three-step training method with domain-mixed data augmentation, gradual self-adaptation and teacher-guided finetuning.

In the FDA scenario, we expect the model to overcome the domain discrepancy and performance drop due to domain shift in the target domain with only a few target domain data available. In [40], adversarial learning is used to learn an embedded subspace that simultaneously maximizes the confusion between two domains while semantically aligning their embedding. In cross-domain few-shot object detection, Wang et al. [41] first adopted a pairing alignment mechanism to overcome the issue of insufficient data. Different from the perspective of modifying the model structure that fails to transfer on other ones, we focus on optimizing the enlarged target data distribution with source data distribution adaptively.

Data augmentation is an effective technique for improving the performance of deep learning models. Such techniques are mainly divided into two aspects: image-level [2,46,47] and box-level [13] with pixel-level label [12,15,18]. Some other methods consider the combination of multiple geometric and color transformations [23,24], while search strategy can find appropriate collocation of them [11,30]. Recent works [34,36,39] apply the mixing images technique in cross-domain scenarios. We further propose formulations of both image-level and box-level domain-aware augmentation and conduct them as a cost-free way to generate data between domains diversely.

Our FDA setting follows the prior work [41], which prompts model to have stronger generalization ability with only a few samples of target domain.

3 Approach

In this section, we present the details of the proposed adaptive method for cross-domain few-shot object detection (AcroFOD). First, we adaptively and iteratively optimize the distribution of candidates towards the target domain for training a robust detector. Then, we generate a lot of candidates to address the problem of insufficiency and sameness of target augmented samples with the proposed multi-level domain-aware augmentation.

The proposed method is motivated by the observation that limited data can still reflect the major characteristics of the target domain [41]. To deal with the lack of data in the target domain, the AcroFOD comprises an adaptive optimization strategy with cross-domain augmentation for reasonable data expansion to overcome domain shifts. Section 3.2 presents our adaptive optimization strategy to promise that augmented target data with source data approximately follow the distribution of target domain. Section 3.3 introduces the formulation of multi-level domain-aware augmentation. Finally, Sect. 3.4 summarizes the whole iterative training process of the AcroFOD.

3.1 Problem Statement

Suppose we have a large data set $D_s = \{(x_i^s, y_i^s)\}_{i=1}^{n_s}$ from the source domain and a few examples $D_t = \{(x_j^t, y_j^t)\}_{j=1}^{n_t}$ from the target domain, where $x_i^s, x_i^t \in \mathcal{X}$ are input images, $y_i^s, y_j^t \in \mathcal{Y}$ consist of bounding box coordinates and object categories for x_i^s and x_j^t. We consider scenarios in which there exists the discrepancy between the input source distribution $\mathcal{P}_s : \mathcal{X} \times \mathcal{Y} \rightarrow \mathbb{R}^+$ of D_s and target distribution $\mathcal{P}_t : \mathcal{X} \times \mathcal{Y} \rightarrow \mathbb{R}^+$ of D_t.

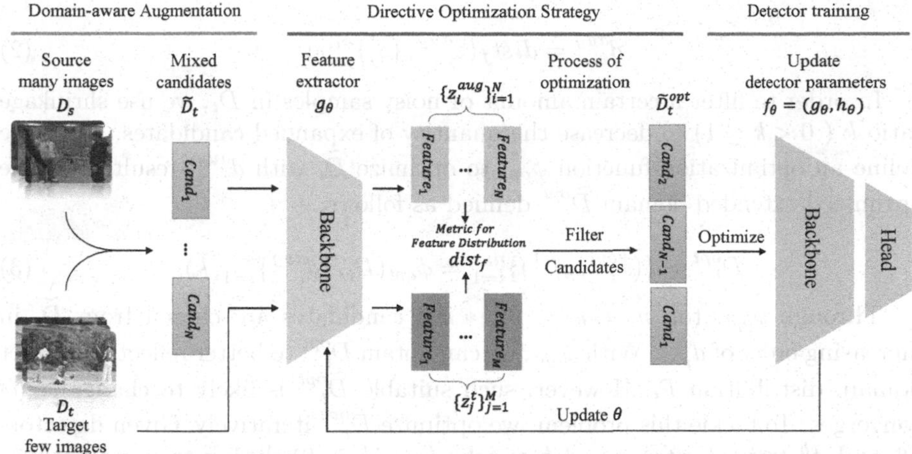

Fig. 2. The AcroFOD includes the following three steps. (1) Using the proposed multi-level domain-aware augmentation, we can expand the data distribution of the target domain. (2) Then, the augmented and target domain data is fed into the backbone of the detector to obtain the extracted feature vector. Through the directive optimization strategy, the samples which are unsuitable for mitigating domain shifts can be filtered. (3) Finally, optimized samples will help the detector mitigate domain shifts.

Our goal is to train an adaptive detector $f : \mathcal{X} \rightarrow \mathcal{Y}$ which can alleviate performance drop due to domain gap. However, it is difficult for f to capture domain invariant representation with only a few data D_t. To effectively exploit the limited information of annotations, we extend $D_t \sim \mathcal{P}_t$ with $D_s \sim \mathcal{P}_s$ to $\widetilde{D}_t$. Supposing $\widetilde{D}_t$ is sampled discretely in assumption distribution $\mathcal{P}_{aug} : \mathcal{X} \times \mathcal{Y} \rightarrow \mathbb{R}^+$, we are able to approximate $\mathcal{P}_t(y|x)$ with $\mathcal{P}_{aug}(y|x)$. In fact, we assume $\mathcal{P}_s(y|x) = \mathcal{P}_t(y|x) = \mathcal{P}_{aug}(y|x)$ but $\mathcal{P}_s(x) \neq \mathcal{P}_t(x) \neq \mathcal{P}_{aug}(x)$. It's obvious that some noisy data in $\widetilde{D}_t$ which are dissimilar to D_t may weaken the generalization ability of f. In the following subsections, we present the details of AcroFOD.

3.2 Adaptive Optimization for Directive Data Augmentation

As shown in Fig. 2, we are able to generate a bunch of data $\widetilde{D}_t = Aug(D_s, D_t)$ with the introduced domain-aware augmentation which we will discuss later. We expect $\widetilde{D}_t = \{(x_i^{aug}, y_i^{aug})\}_{i=1}^{n_a} \sim \mathcal{P}_{aug}$ to approximate distribution $\mathcal{P}_t$ as close as possible. We assume that the detector $f_\theta = (g_\theta, h_\theta)$ is defined by a set of parameters θ and consists of backbone g_θ and head h_θ. The AcroFOD uses g_θ as feature extractor to output representations of x_j^t in D_t, x_i^{aug} in $\widetilde{D}_t$ as follows:

$$z_i^{aug} = g_\theta(x_i^{aug}), z_j^t = g_\theta(x_j^t). \tag{1}$$

Then, the AcroFOD sorts augmented candidates x_i^{aug} according to the distance of representations between x_i^{aug} and $\{x_j^t\}_{j=1}^{n_t}$ measured by metric function $dist_f$:

$$d_i^{aug} = dist_f(z_i^{aug}, \{z_j^t\}_{j=1}^{n_t}). \tag{2}$$

In order to filter a certain amount of noisy samples in $\widetilde{D}_t$, we use shrinkage ratio k ($0 < k \leq 1$) to decrease the quantity of expanded candidates. Then, we define an optimization function ϕ_{opt} to optimize $\widetilde{D}_t$ with d_i^{aug}, resulting in the optimized extended domain $\widetilde{D}_t^{opt}$ defined as follows:

$$\widetilde{D}_t^{opt} = \{(x_i^{opt}, y_i^{opt})\}_{i=1}^{n_b} = \phi_{opt}(\widetilde{D}_t, \{d_i^{aug}\}_{i=1}^{n_a}, k). \tag{3}$$

Through ϕ_{opt}, top n_b ($n_b = \lfloor n_a * k \rfloor$) candidates are chosen from $\widetilde{D}_t$ in increasing order of d_i^{aug}. With ϕ_{opt}, we can obtain $\widetilde{D}_t^{opt}$ to better reflect the target domain distribution $\mathcal{P}_t$. However, such suitable $\widetilde{D}_t^{opt}$ is likely to change as f_θ converges. To tackle this problem, we optimize $\widetilde{D}_t^{opt}$ iteratively. Given detectors f_θ^a and f_θ^b trained after a and b epochs ($a > b \geq 0$) during training process. The error of f_θ in source and target domain $\epsilon_{D_s}(f_\theta^a), \epsilon_{D_t}(f_\theta^a)$ are expected to be smaller than $\epsilon_{D_s}(f_\theta^b), \epsilon_{D_t}(f_\theta^b)$ due to g_θ, h_θ updating. So, g_θ^a is able to represent x_i^{aug} and x_i^t more accurately than g_θ^b. Then, we can iteratively optimize $\widetilde{D}_t^{opt}$ by $dist_f$ with updating feature representation z_i^{aug} and z_i^t.

At the nth ($n \geq 1$) epoch, $\widetilde{D}_{t^n}^{opt}$ can be obtained by filtering $\widetilde{D}_t$ as follows:

$$\widetilde{D}_{t^n}^{opt} = \phi_{opt}(\widetilde{D}_t, \{dist_f(g_\theta^n(x_i^{aug}), \{g_\theta^n(x_j^t)\}_{j=1}^{n_t})\}_{i=1}^{n_a}, k). \tag{4}$$

Finally, the adaptive detector $f_\theta^n = (g_\theta^n, h_\theta^n)$ can also be optimized iteratively by $(x_i^{opt}, y_i^{opt}) \in \widetilde{D}_{t^n}^{opt}$ as follows:

$$g_\theta^{n+1}, h_\theta^{n+1} \leftarrow optimizer((g_\theta^n, h_\theta^n), \nabla_\theta \mathcal{L}_\theta(f_\theta^n(x_i^{opt}), y_i^{opt}), \eta), \tag{5}$$

where the *optimizer* is an optimizer, η is the learning rate for g_θ, h_θ and $\mathcal{L}$ is the loss function.

We intend to measure the correlation between z_i^{aug} and $\{z_j^t\}_{j=1}^{n_t}$. Therefore, we utilize two widely-used metric functions MMD, CS as $dist_f$.

First: Maximum Mean Discrepancy. The Maximum Mean Discrepancy (MMD) [20] distance is used to measure the distance of these two distributions in the Reproducing Keral Hilbert Space (RKHS). For z_i^{aug}, $\{z_i^t\}_{i=1}^{n_t}$ defined in Eq. 1, $dist_f$ is instantiated to MMD^2 as:

$$MMD^2(z_i^{aug}, \{z_j^t\}_{j=1}^{n_t}) = ||\frac{1}{n_t}\sum_{j=1}^{n_t} z_j^t - z_i^{aug}||_2^2. \tag{6}$$

Second: Cosine Distance. Cosine distance is an effective metric to measure the similarity of samples in the embedding space [3,21,32]. Equation 2 can be rewritten as CS in the following expression:

$$CS(z_i^{aug}, \{z_j^t\}_{j=1}^{n_t}) = \sum_{j=1}^{n_t}(1 - \frac{z_j^t \cdot z_i^{aug}}{||z_j^t||_2 \cdot ||z_i^{aug}||_2}). \tag{7}$$

3.3 Multi-level Domain-Aware Augmentation

From Sect. 3.2, the convergence of f_θ relies on the D_t^{opt} optimized by $D_t^{aug} = Aug(D_s, D_t)$. The simple combination of D_s and D_t limits the variety of D_t^{aug}. To generate more adequate samples while controlling the overhead of training computation, we propose domain-aware augmentation as Aug at **image-level** and **box-level**. Here, we give uniform formulations for each level of Aug and then provide several specific instantiations of them.

Image-Level Domain-Aware Augmentation. Given a batch of data in source domain $B_s = \{(x_i^s, y_i^s)\}_i^{n_{bs}}$ and target domain $B_t = \{(x_i^t, y_i^t)\}_i^{n_{bt}}$. We sample $m \leq n_{bs}$ and $n \leq n_{bt}$ data from B_s and B_t from these two domains respectively. Then, we randomly mix them to a single image x^{aug} as follows:

$$x^{aug} = x_0^{aug} + \sum_{i=1}^{m}\sum_{j=1}^{n} A_{(i,j)}(\lambda_i x_i^s + \lambda_j x_j^t), \tag{8}$$

where x_0^{aug} is an initialized empty image whose size is different from both x_i^s and x_i^t, $A_{(i,j)}$ is the hand-crafted transformation matrix for image pair$\{x_i^s, x_j^t\}$. λ_i and λ_j $(1 \geq \lambda_i + \lambda_j \geq 0)$ are the corresponding weights of x_i^s and x_j^t, respectively. Then, we can recompute the label set $y^{aug} = \{(y_{box}^{aug}, y_{cls}^{aug})\}$ of x^{aug} as follows:

$$\begin{aligned} y_{box}^{aug} &= \underset{i=1...m, j=1...n}{Concat}(A_{(i,j)}^T y_{i(box)}^s, A_{(i,j)}^T y_{j(box)}^t), \\ y_{cls}^{aug} &= \underset{i=1...m, j=1...n}{Concat}(\lambda_i^{cls} y_{i(cls)}^s + \lambda_j^{cls} y_{j(cls)}^t), \end{aligned} \tag{9}$$

where $y_{i(box)}^s$ and $y_{j(box)}^t$ denote the bounding box coordinates of interest instances from source and target domains. $y_{i(cls)}^s$ and $y_{j(cls)}^t$ represent corresponding confidences of categories. λ_i^{cls} and λ_j^{cls} are weights of the corresponding confidence scores.

With Eq. 8 and Eq. 9, we describe two versions of image-level domain-aware augmentation. First, we define $m+n = 4 (m, n \in \mathbb{N}^+)$, $\lambda_i = \lambda_i^{cls}$ and $\lambda_i | \lambda_j = 1$ as $\underline{domain - splice}$. Second, to increase the degree of interaction at the image-level, we choose $m + n = 2 (m, n \in \mathbb{N}^+)$ and then weight two images with $\lambda_i + \lambda_j = 1, 1 \geq \lambda_i, \lambda_j \geq 0$, $\lambda \sim Beta(\alpha, \alpha)$ and $\lambda_i \& \lambda_j = 1$ as $\underline{domain - reallocation}$. The above two methods can also be combined to generate more diverse images.

Box-Level Domain-Aware Augmentation. To effectively utilize limited instance annotation, we can separate them from the background and then put them on the other regions. In order to improve the generality of proposed augmentations, we focus on utilizing domain-aware box-level labels rather than pixel-level labels which are often used in previous works [12,15,18]. Here, we propose the formulation of box-level domain-aware augmentation with bounding box labels.

For bounding box b^s and b^t from source and target domain with the resized width w and height h, we exchange them to combine the characteristic of each other. The formulation is presented as follows:

$$b_{(p,q)}^{aug} = \beta_{(p,q)} b_{(p,q)}^s + (1 - \beta_{(p,q)}) b_{(p,q)}^t, \tag{10}$$

where $(p, q), p = 1, 2...w, q = 1, 2...h$ represents the index of pixels in box b^s and b^t. $\beta(p, q) \in [0, 1]$ is the corresponding weight for each index. From Eq. 10, we denote $\beta(p, q) = 0(\forall p, q)$ as <u>*direct*</u> exchange and define $\beta(p, q) = \beta_{mix}, \beta_{mix} \sim Beta(\alpha_m, \alpha_m)$ as <u>*mixture*</u> exchange, where α_m is a hyper-parameter.

Instances under different scales have different degrees of dependence on context information [9]. In order to obtain scale-aware weights for each pixels, we propose <u>*Gaussian*</u> exchange which adopts the Gaussian map defined as follows:

$$\beta(p, q) = exp(-(\frac{(p - \mu_x)^2}{\sigma_x^2} + \frac{(q - \mu_y)^2}{\sigma_y^2})), \quad \sigma_x = \frac{w}{W}\sqrt{\frac{hw}{2\pi}} \quad \sigma_y = \frac{h}{H}\sqrt{\frac{hw}{2\pi}}, \tag{11}$$

where H, W are height and weight of the image, σ_x, σ_y are the variance of x and y axes in box b^s and b^t. μ_x, μ_y are the corresponding mean in box b^s and b^t. The comparison of three box-level augmentations is shown in Fig. 3.

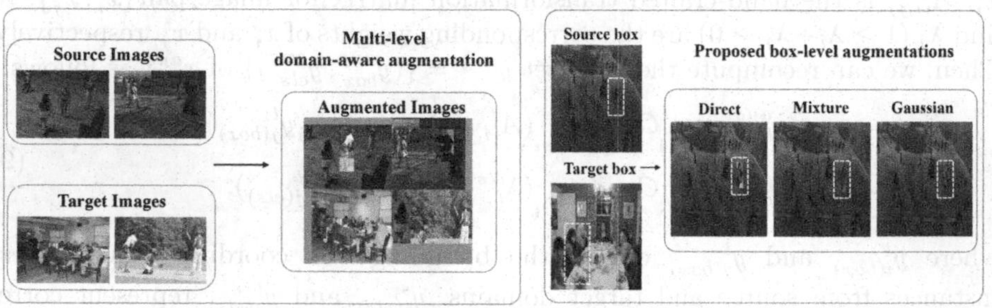

Fig. 3. Left: visualization of multi-level domain-aware augmentation. Right: three types of proposed box-level cross-domain augmentations.

3.4 Cross-Domain Training Framework

We expect that the augmented samples are still closer to the distribution of the target domain. Therefore, these data will be fed into the backbone network of the target detector to calculate features, and then suitable data will be selected according to the distance from the target domain. The feature extractor used for obtaining $\widetilde{D}_t^{opt}$ will update after every epoch. Note that our model, including the backbone and the detector module, is trained from scratch. Details of our AcroFOD are presented in Algorithm 1.

4 Experiments

We present the results of proposed adaptive method for cross-domain few-shot object detection (AcroFOD) in various scenarios like adverse weather, synthetic-to-real and cross-camera domain shifts in Sect. 4.2. Then, we provide qualitative

Algorithm 1. Adaptive Method AcroFOD

Input: Initialized detector θ^{ini}, the source domain $D_s = \{(x_i^s, y_i^s)\}_{i=1}^{n_s}$, few data target domain $D_t = \{(x_j^t, y_j^t)\}_{j=1}^{n_t}$, total epochs T, distance function $dist_f$, amount of steps for every epoch N, domain-aware augmentation function Aug, shrinkage ratio k, loss function $\mathcal{L}$.

Output: Adaptive Detector $f_\theta = (g_\theta, h_\theta)$

Initialize $\theta \leftarrow \theta^{ini}$

Initialize feature extractor g_θ

for $epoch \leftarrow 1, ..., T$ **do**

  $\widetilde{D}_t = \{(x_i^{aug}, y_i^{aug})\}_{i=1}^{n_a} = Aug(D_s, D_t)$

  $\widetilde{D}_t^{opt} = \phi_{opt}(\widetilde{D}_t, \{dist_f(g_\theta(x_i^{aug}), \{g_\theta(x_j^t)\}_{j=1}^{n_t})\}_{i=1}^{n_a}, k)$

  for $step \leftarrow 1, ..., N$ **do**

    sample batch $B = \{(x_i^{opt}, y_i^{opt})\}_{i=1}^{bs}$ from $\widetilde{D}_t^{opt}$

    $pred = f_\theta(\{x_1^{opt}, ..., x_{bs}^{opt}\})$

    $loss = \mathcal{L}(pred, \{y_1^{opt}, ..., y_{bs}^{opt}\})$

    Update θ to minimize $loss$

  $g_\theta, h_\theta \leftarrow \theta$

$f_\theta \leftarrow \theta$

results of adverse weather benchmark in Sect. 4.3. Furthermore, we analyze effect of multiple parts of the AcroFOD in Sect. 4.4. Finally, we explore the performance of our method on different data magnitudes in Sect. 4.5.

4.1 Experimental Setup

- **Adverse Weather Benchmark (C → F).** In this scenario, we use Cityscapes [10] as the source dataset. It contains 3,475 real urban images, with 2,975 images used for training and 500 for validating. Foggy version of Cityscapes [38] is used as the target dataset. Highest fog intensity (least visibility) images of 8 different categories are used in our experiments, matching prior work [44]. Following [41], we used the tightest bounding box of an instance segmentation mask as ground truth box. This scenario is referred to C → F.
- **Synthetic-to-real Benchmark (S → C, V → O).** SIM10k [28] is a simulated dataset that contains 10k synthetic images. In this dataset, we use all 58,701 car bounding boxes available as the source data during training. For the target data and evaluation, we use Cityscapes [10] and only consider the car instances. This scenario is referred to S → C. ViPeD [1] contains 200K frames collected from the video game with bounding box annotations for person class. We select one frame per 10 frames and a total of 20K frames as the source dataset. We select COCO [31] as the target dataset and only consider the person class. We denote this scenario as V → O.
- **Cross-camera Benchmark (K → C).** In this scenario, we use the KITTI [17] as our source data. KITTI contains 7,481 images and we use all of them for training. Similar to the previous scenarios, we use Cityscapes [10] as the

Table 1. Results in C → F scenario. "V" and "R" stand for VGG16 and ResNet50 backbone respectively. "X" stands for a type of yolov5 model. In FDA setting, only 8 fully annotated images are used for domain adaption per round. * and † represent only using optimization and augmentation respectively. The last row combines both of them.

Setting	Method	Arch.	Person	Rider	Car	Truck	Bus	Train	Mcycle	Bicycle	mAP50	Gain
	Source	V	24.1	29.9	32.7	10.9	13.8	5.0	14.6	27.9	19.9	–
	Source	R	27.2	31.8	32.5	16.0	25.5	5.6	19.9	27.0	22.8	–
	Source	X	30.8	27.8	43.7	8.2	24.3	4.8	11.0	24.6	21.9	–
	Pre+FT	X	31.2 ± 0.3	28.1 ± 0.2	44.1 ± 0.5	8.3 ± 0.2	24.3 ± 0.1	5.9 ± 0.6	11.1 ± 0.3	24.6 ± 0.2	22.2 ± 0.2	0.3
	Proportion	X	30.0 ± 0.4	28.7 ± 0.7	41.8 ± 1.2	13.1 ± 0.5	22.3 ± 0.7	9.6 ± 1.5	19.3 ± 1.8	24.7 ± 0.7	23.7 ± 0.5	1.8
UDA	DA-Faster [8]	V	25.0	31.0	40.5	22.1	35.3	20.2	20.0	27.1	27.6	7.7
	FAFRCNN [41]	V	29.1	39.7	42.9	20.8	37.4	24.1	26.5	29.9	31.3	11.4
	SWDA [37]	R	31.8	44.3	48.9	21.0	43.8	28.0	28.9	35.8	35.3	12.5
	ViSGA [35]	R	38.8	45.9	57.2	29.9	50.2	51.9	31.9	40.9	**43.3**	**20.5**
FDA	ADDA [40]	V	24.4 ± 0.3	29.1 ± 0.9	33.7 ± 0.5	11.9 ± 0.5	13.3 ± 0.8	7.0 ± 1.5	13.6 ± 0.6	27.6 ± 0.2	20.1 ± 0.8	0.2
	DT_f+FT [27]	V	23.5 ± 0.5	28.5 ± 0.6	30.1 ± 0.8	11.4 ± 0.6	26.1 ± 0.9	9.6 ± 2.1	17.7 ± 1.0	26.2 ± 0.6	21.7 ± 0.6	1.8
	DA-Faster [8]	V	24.0 ± 0.8	28.8 ± 0.7	27.1 ± 0.7	10.3 ± 0.7	24.3 ± 0.8	9.6 ± 2.8	14.3 ± 0.8	26.3 ± 0.8	20.6 ± 0.8	0.7
	SimRoD [34]	X	34.3 ± 1.3	35.8 ± 0.3	55.9 ± 0.8	9.6 ± 1.8	18.0 ± 0.6	5.9 ± 0.3	10.6 ± 0.2	29.2 ± 0.8	24.9 ± 0.2	4.7
	FsDet [42]	X	32.3 ± 1.2	29.8 ± 1.2	44.0 ± 1.7	14.1 ± 2.2	24.2 ± 1.4	8.4 ± 1.2	22.9 ± 1.6	26.2 ± 2.2	25.2 ± 1.1	3.3
	AcroFOD*	X	31.8 ± 0.9	30.9 ± 1.2	43.9 ± 2.3	15.3 ± 2.1	27.8 ± 1.8	8.8 ± 1.3	26.2 ± 1.9	26.3 ± 0.8	26.4 ± 1.0	4.5
	AcroFOD†	X	36.5 ± 1.4	37.4 ± 1.3	51.6 ± 0.9	17.9 ± 1.1	33.0 ± 0.7	26.4 ± 1.2	27.5 ± 1.1	31.5 ± 1.5	32.7 ± 0.6	10.8
	AcroFOD	X	**46.2** ± 0.5	**47.3** ± 0.6	**63.5** ± 0.4	**20.1** ± 1.6	**41.5** ± 0.8	**34.2** ± 1.8	**36.1** ± 0.7	**39.6** ± 0.9	**41.1** ± 0.8	**19.2**

target data. Following prior works [34,35], only the car class is used. This scenario is abbreviated as K → C.

- **Implementation Details.** We adopt the single-stage detector YOLOv5 [26] as the baseline and compare with unsupervised domain adaptation (UDA) and few-shot domain adaptation (FDA) methods at the same time. For UDA setting [35], we report their results based on the full amount of target domain data. For FDA setting [41], we report mean and deviation for 5 rounds using the same number of images. Meanwhile, we also compare our method with proportional sampling (denote as "proportion") which samples data from source and target domains uniformly for training and few-shot object detection method FsDet [42] in the FDA setting. In all experiments, we adopt adaptive optimization strategy from scratch and set shrinkage ratio $k = 0.8$. The effect of k will analyze in Sect. 4.4. For a fair comparison, we resize input images to 640×640 in all experiments without any extra dataset (such as COCO [31]) for model pre-training. For evaluation metrics, We denote average precision with IoU threshold of 0.5 as AP50 for a single class or mAP50 for multi classes, and AP or mAP for 10 averaged IoU thresholds of 0.5:0.05:0.95 [31].

4.2 Main Results

In this section, we evaluate the proposed method by conducting extensive experiments on the established scenarios.

- **Results for Scenarios C → F.** As summarized in Table 1, our proposed AcroFOD performs significantly better than other compared FDA methods in all categories. Besides, the AcroFOD achieves mAP50 at 41.1%, which is

19.2% higher than the baseline method, solely trained on source data. It is observable that other baseline methods only obtain less improvement for both mAP50 and gain. The compared SimRoD [34] also employees domain-mix augmentation and improves the generation ability of the used detector. Our AcroFOD also achieves significantly better performance than SimRoD, which indicates that a simple augmentation is not sufficient to train a robust object detector to mitigate the domain gap.

- **Results for Other Three Scenarios.** As presented in Table 2a and Table 2b, results show similar trends with previous evaluation C → F. In FDA setting, our AcroFOD performs better than previous methods in single class domain adaptation, such as car and person. Meanwhile, we obtain comparable performance to many UDA methods. Other methods in UDA setting sometimes perform better than AcroFOD which only uses 8 target images in FDA setting. As shown in Table 3, our AcroFOD outperforms pre-training + fine-tuning paradigm (denoted as Pre+FT) about 1.7%AP50 and 0.3%AP in V → O scenario, which suggests our framework can still handle complex domain shift in person class.

Table 2. Results of AP50 for the S → C and K → C adaptation scenarios. In FDA setting, we randomly choice 8 images in target domain. "Source" refers to the model trained using source data only. "Adaptation" means the model adapted by target data. * and † represent only using optimization and augmentation respectively. The last row combines both of them.

(a) S → C

Setting	Method	Source	Adaptation	Gain
UDA	FAFRCNN [41]	33.5	41.2	7.7
	DA-Faster [8]	31.9	41.9	10.0
	SWDA [37]	31.9	44.6	12.7
	ViSGA [35]	31.9	49.3	**17.4**
FDA	Pre+FT	49.0	49.4 ± 0.3	0.4
	proportion	49.0	50.2 ± 0.6	1.2
	FsDet [42]	49.0	52.9 ± 1.2	3.9
	SimRoD [34]	49.0	54.2 ± 0.5	5.2
	AcroFOD*	49.0	55.6 ± 2.6	6.6
	AcroFOD†	49.0	57.4 ± 2.1	8.4
	AcroFOD	49.0	**62.5** ± 1.6	**13.5**

(b) K → C

Setting	Method	Source	Adaptation	Gain
UDA	DA-Faster [8]	32.5	41.8	9.3
	SWDA [37]	32.5	43.2	10.7
	ViSGA [35]	32.5	47.6	15.1
	GPA [44]	32.5	47.9	**15.3**
FDA	Pre+FT	47.4	47.7 ± 0.3	0.3
	proportion	47.4	47.6 ± 0.2	0.2
	FsDet [42]	47.4	52.9 ± 1.2	5.5
	SimRoD [34]	47.4	55.8 ± 0.6	8.4
	AcrFOD*	47.4	51.9 ± 2.9	4.5
	AcrFOD†	47.4	53.9 ± 1.6	6.5
	AcrFOD	47.4	62.6 ± 2.1	**15.2**

4.3 Qualitative Results

Figure 4 shows some qualitative results of C → F. It can be clearly observed that 1) the AcroFOD motivates the detector to place higher confidence on detected objects, especially for occluded objects; 2) the model after adaptation detects more targets than the one trained with only source data.

Table 3. Results of V → O adaptation scenario. We randomly select 60 fully annotated images from coco person for each round. * and † represent only using optimization and augmentation respectively. The last row combines both of them.

Method	AP50	AP	Gain-AP50	Gain-AP
Source	30.4	13.0	–	–
Proportion	31.8 ± 1.5	13.5 ± 0.3	1.4	0.5
Pre+FT	43.2 ± 0.8	21.0 ± 0.5	13.2	8.0
FsDet [42]	36.7 ± 1.9	15.9 ± 0.8	6.3	2.9
SimRoD [34]	42.8 ± 1.0	19.5 ± 0.7	12.4	6.5
AcroFOD*	42.0 ± 1.2	19.2 ± 1.3	11.6	6.2
AcorFOD†	41.4 ± 0.7	18.7 ± 0.6	11.0	5.7
AcroFOD	$\mathbf{45.8 \pm 0.6}$	$\mathbf{22.5 \pm 0.4}$	**15.4**	**9.5**

Fig. 4. Qualitative result. The results are sampled from C → F scenario, we set the bounding box visualization threshold of 0.3. The first/second rows are output results from unadapted/adapted training models respectively.

4.4 Ablation Study

To evaluate the impact of various components of the AcroFOD on detection performance, we use all four scenarios for evaluation. Following prior settings [41], in C → F, S → C and K → C adaptation scenarios, we randomly sample 8 images in the target domain for domain adaptation in each round. For V → O scenarios, we choose 60 images from target domain randomly.

Instantiations of Domain-Aware Augmentation. Table 4 shows the effects of different types of domain-aware augmentation in our AcroFOD. For a fair comparison, we choose Eq. 6 as distance function in the optimization strategy for all the experiments. From the results, we can notice that either the introduced image-level or the box-level augmentations can both bring significant performance improvements. Meanwhile, combining different types of multi-level domain-aware augmentation can further improve the detection results.

Table 4. Instantiations of different types of multi-level domain-aware augmentation. "Source" and "Target" represent that model is only trained in the source and target dataset respectively. "Oracle" means pre-training in the source domain and fine-tuning with the full amount of target domain data. "Spl" and "Rea" denote the image-level domain-splice and domain-reallocation. "Dir", "Gau" and "Mix" represent the direct, Gaussian and mixture box-level exchange methods.

	Img-level		Box-level			S → C		K → C		V → O		C → F	
	Spl	Rea	Dir	Gau	Mix	AP50	AP	AP50	AP	AP50	AP	mAP50	mAP
Source	✓	✓		✓		49.0	26.5	47.4	22.4	30.4	13.0	21.9	12.0
Target	✓	✓		✓		75.1	49.2	75.1	49.2	81.9	56.6	45.1	21.3
Oracle	✓	✓		✓		76.9	51.8	76.1	50.1	82.2	56.9	46.3	26.4
AcroFOD						55.6 ± 2.6	33.2 ± 2.4	51.9 ± 2.9	27.7 ± 2.4	42.0 ± 1.2	19.2 ± 1.3	26.4 ± 1.0	15.8 ± 0.9
	✓					60.2 ± 1.8	36.4 ± 1.9	58.3 ± 1.9	32.1 ± 1.3	44.9 ± 0.7	22.1 ± 1.2	27.5 ± 1.5	15.5 ± 1.3
	✓		✓			61.4 ± 3.0	37.1 ± 2.3	58.6 ± 1.7	33.6 ± 2.1	44.8 ± 0.6	21.3 ± 0.6	25.6 ± 1.3	14.9 ± 1.1
	✓			✓		60.3 ± 2.4	36.3 ± 2.2	58.4 ± 2.2	33.1 ± 2.2	44.5 ± 1.4	21.1 ± 1.2	25.1 ± 1.2	14.3 ± 0.8
	✓				✓	61.2 ± 1.9	36.8 ± 1.4	57.5 ± 2.3	32.9 ± 1.8	43.6 ± 1.2	20.2 ± 0.8	28.2 ± 1.0	16.1 ± 0.9
	✓	✓				62.3 ± 2.7	38.0 ± 2.3	61.4 ± 3.1	36.2 ± 2.3	44.8 ± 1.3	21.7 ± 0.6	**41.1** ± 0.8	**23.2** ± 0.7
	✓	✓	✓			62.2 ± 3.2	37.7 ± 2.5	61.6 ± 2.1	35.5 ± 2.2	44.7 ± 0.6	21.5 ± 0.6	38.6 ± 0.5	21.9 ± 0.4
	✓	✓		✓		**62.5** ± 1.6	**38.1** ± 1.8	**62.6** ± 2.1	**36.5** ± 2.4	43.9 ± 1.1	20.4 ± 0.7	38.3 ± 0.6	21.4 ± 0.5
	✓	✓			✓	62.3 ± 2.1	38.0 ± 1.0	62.1 ± 1.9	35.8 ± 2.3	**45.8** ± 0.6	**22.5** ± 0.4	36.9 ± 1.0	20.8 ± 0.7

Table 5. Influence of different strategies for sample selection in S → C and K → C adaptation scenario.

Method	S → C		K → C	
	AP50	AP	AP50	AP
Source	49.0	26.5	47.4	22.4
Cosine distance	55.2 ± 2.7	32.7 ± 2.6	51.4 ± 2.1	27.3 ± 2.3
MMD distance	**55.6** ± 2.6	**33.2** ± 2.4	**51.9** ± 2.9	**27.7** ± 1.8

Different Choices of $dist_f$. Table 5 compares different types of distance metric function $dist_f$. The simple proportional sampling strategy achieves better performance than the baseline method trained with source-only data. Optimizing augmented data with MMD distance obtains the best results among all choices. In summary, MMD can better reflect the sample distance between source and target domains than others.

Analysis of Shrinkage Ratio k. Figure 5 shows the effect of k on S → C and C → F scenarios. $k = 1$ means training without any process of optimization. All experiments use Eq. 6 as $dist_f$. The above two figures show that our proposed adaptive optimization strategy helps model transfer better. Meanwhile, within a certain range of k, the performance of the model is relatively stable.

4.5 Experiment with More Data

We conduct a series of experiments to verify the effect of different numbers of data in target domain and choose the challenging V → O scenario for verification. We choose 0.1%, 1% and 10% data from COCO person for model training, corresponding to 60, 600 and 6000 images respectively, and test on the validation set of COCO person. The evaluations are conducted on person category and test time on 4 Nvidia V100 GPUs. As shown in Table 6, we notice that the AcroFOD can outperform the general Pre+FT by a large margin in all cases. Meanwhile, our method is faster than both previous work [34] and Pre+FT paradigm.

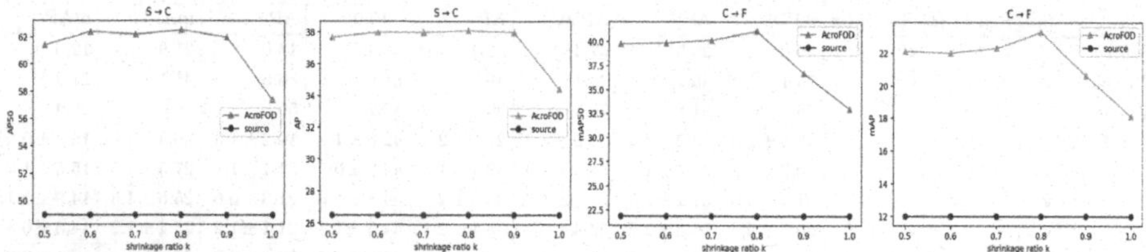

Fig. 5. Experiments on different values of k on S → C and C → F scenarios.

Table 6. Results of more data in V → O adaptation scenario. "Source" and "Target" represent that the model is only trained in source and target datasets respectively. "Epochs" means the total number of epochs. "Times" corresponds to the time required to achieve optimum performance.

Proportion	Method	AP50	AP	Epochs	Times
–	Source	30.4	13.0	300	48 h
0.1%	Target	–	–	–	–
	Pre+FT	43.2 ± 1.3	21.0 ± 0.9	500	56 h
	AcroFOD	**45.8** ± 0.6	**22.5** ± 0.4	300	**32 h**
1%	Target	43.9 ± 1.7	20.7 ± 1.1	300	24 h
	Pre+FT	50.9 ± 0.3	28.2 ± 0.5	600	72 h
	AcroFOD	**61.1** ± 0.9	**34.1** ± 0.6	300	**34 h**
10%	Target	71.5 ± 0.5	44.3 ± 0.4	300	42 h
	Pre+FT	69.7 ± 0.3	44.5 ± 0.3	600	90 h
	AcroFOD	**75.1** ± 0.6	**50.2** ± 0.4	300	**38 h**

5 Conclusion

We present AcroFOD for adapting detector under domain shift with only a few data in the target domain. Our adaptive optimization for directive data augmentation helps expand limited target data to cover the data distribution of the target domain. Our method achieves significant gains in terms of model robustness compared to existing baselines in few-shot domain adaptation setting. The results indicate that the AcroFOD can mitigate the effect of domain shifts due to various changes. Through the ablation study, we find some insights on how adaptive optimization and data augmentation from a cross-domain perspective can help model perform better. We hope this adaptive method will benefit future progress of robust object detection in cross-domain few-shot object detection research.

Acknowledgment. This work was supported partially by the NSFC (U21A20471, U1911401, U1811461), Guangdong NSF Project (No. 2022A1515011254, 2020B1515120085, 2018B030312002), Guangzhou Research Project (201902010037), and the Key-Area Research and Development Program of Guangzhou (20200703-0004).

References

1. Amato, G., Ciampi, L., Falchi, F., Gennaro, C., Messina, N.: Learning pedestrian detection from virtual worlds. In: Ricci, E., Rota Bulò, S., Snoek, C., Lanz, O., Messelodi, S., Sebe, N. (eds.) ICIAP 2019. LNCS, vol. 11751, pp. 302–312. Springer, Cham (2019). https://doi.org/10.1007/978-3-030-30642-7_27
2. Bochkovskiy, A., Wang, C.Y., Liao, H.Y.M.: YOLOv4: optimal speed and accuracy of object detection. arXiv preprint arXiv:2004.10934 (2020)
3. Chen, C., et al.: Progressive feature alignment for unsupervised domain adaptation. In: Proceedings of the IEEE/CVF Conference on Computer Vision and Pattern Recognition, pp. 627–636 (2019)
4. Chen, C., Zheng, Z., Ding, X., Huang, Y., Dou, Q.: Harmonizing transferability and discriminability for adapting object detectors. In: Proceedings of the IEEE/CVF Conference on Computer Vision and Pattern Recognition, pp. 8869–8878 (2020)
5. Chen, H., Wang, Y., Wang, G., Qiao, Y.: LSTD: a low-shot transfer detector for object detection. In: Proceedings of the AAAI Conference on Artificial Intelligence, vol. 32 (2018)
6. Chen, T.I., et al.: Dual-awareness attention for few-shot object detection. arXiv preprint arXiv:2102.12152 (2021)
7. Chen, W.Y., Liu, Y.C., Kira, Z., Wang, Y.C.F., Huang, J.B.: A closer look at few-shot classification. In: International Conference on Learning Representations (2018)
8. Chen, Y., Li, W., Sakaridis, C., Dai, D., Van Gool, L.: Domain adaptive faster R-CNN for object detection in the wild. In: Proceedings of the IEEE/CVF Conference on Computer Vision and Pattern Recognition, pp. 3339–3348 (2018)
9. Chen, Y., et al.: Scale-aware automatic augmentation for object detection. In: Proceedings of the IEEE/CVF Conference on Computer Vision and Pattern Recognition, pp. 9563–9572 (2021)
10. Cordts, M., et al.: The cityscapes dataset for semantic urban scene understanding. In: Proceedings of the IEEE/CVF Conference on Computer Vision and Pattern Recognition, pp. 3213–3223 (2016)
11. Cubuk, E.D., Zoph, B., Mane, D., Vasudevan, V., Le, Q.V.: AutoAugment: learning augmentation strategies from data. In: Proceedings of the IEEE/CVF Conference on Computer Vision and Pattern Recognition, pp. 113–123 (2019)

12. Dvornik, N., Mairal, J., Schmid, C.: Modeling visual context is key to augmenting object detection datasets. In: Ferrari, V., Hebert, M., Sminchisescu, C., Weiss, Y. (eds.) ECCV 2018. LNCS, vol. 11216, pp. 375–391. Springer, Cham (2018). https://doi.org/10.1007/978-3-030-01258-8_23
13. Dwibedi, D., Misra, I., Hebert, M.: Cut, paste and learn: surprisingly easy synthesis for instance detection. In: Proceedings of the IEEE/CVF International Conference on Computer Vision, pp. 1301–1310 (2017)
14. Fan, Q., Zhuo, W., Tang, C.K., Tai, Y.W.: Few-shot object detection with attention-RPN and multi-relation detector. In: Proceedings of the IEEE/CVF Conference on Computer Vision and Pattern Recognition, pp. 4013–4022 (2020)
15. Fang, H.S., Sun, J., Wang, R., Gou, M., Li, Y.L., Lu, C.: InstaBoost: boosting instance segmentation via probability map guided copy-pasting. In: Proceedings of the IEEE/CVF International Conference on Computer Vision, pp. 682–691 (2019)
16. Ganin, Y., Lempitsky, V.: Unsupervised domain adaptation by backpropagation. In: International Conference on Machine Learning, pp. 1180–1189. PMLR (2015)
17. Geiger, A., Lenz, P., Urtasun, R.: Are we ready for autonomous driving? The KITTI vision benchmark suite. In: Proceedings of the IEEE/CVF Conference on Computer Vision and Pattern Recognition, pp. 3354–3361. IEEE (2012)
18. Ghiasi, G., et al.: Simple copy-paste is a strong data augmentation method for instance segmentation. In: Proceedings of the IEEE/CVF Conference on Computer Vision and Pattern Recognition, pp. 2918–2928 (2021)
19. Gopalan, R., Li, R., Chellappa, R.: Domain adaptation for object recognition: an unsupervised approach. In: Proceedings of the IEEE/CVF International Conference on Computer Vision, pp. 999–1006. IEEE (2011)
20. Gretton, A., Borgwardt, K.M., Rasch, M.J., Schölkopf, B., Smola, A.: A kernel two-sample test. J. Mach. Learn. Res. **13**, 723–773 (2012)
21. Guo, H., Pasunuru, R., Bansal, M.: Multi-source domain adaptation for text classification via distancenet-bandits. In: Proceedings of the AAAI Conference on Artificial Intelligence, vol. 34, pp. 7830–7838 (2020)
22. He, Z., Zhang, L.: Multi-adversarial faster-RCNN for unrestricted object detection. In: Proceedings of the IEEE/CVF International Conference on Computer Vision, pp. 6668–6677 (2019)
23. Hendrycks, D., et al.: The many faces of robustness: a critical analysis of out-of-distribution generalization. In: Proceedings of the IEEE/CVF International Conference on Computer Vision, pp. 8340–8349 (2021)
24. Hendrycks, D., Mu, N., Cubuk, E.D., Zoph, B., Gilmer, J., Lakshminarayanan, B.: AugMix: a simple data processing method to improve robustness and uncertainty. arXiv preprint arXiv:1912.02781 (2019)
25. Hu, T., Yang, P., Zhang, C., Yu, G., Mu, Y., Snoek, C.G.: Attention-based multi-context guiding for few-shot semantic segmentation. In: Proceedings of the AAAI Conference on Artificial Intelligence. vol. 33, pp. 8441–8448 (2019)
26. Jocher., G.: Ultralytics/YOLOv5: v3.0 - third release. In: Zenodo, December 2020
27. Johnson, J., Alahi, A., Fei-Fei, L.: Perceptual losses for real-time style transfer and super-resolution. In: Leibe, B., Matas, J., Sebe, N., Welling, M. (eds.) ECCV 2016. LNCS, vol. 9906, pp. 694–711. Springer, Cham (2016). https://doi.org/10.1007/978-3-319-46475-6_43
28. Johnson-Roberson, M., Barto, C., Mehta, R., Sridhar, S.N., Rosaen, K., Vasudevan, R.: Driving in the matrix: can virtual worlds replace human-generated annotations for real world tasks? In: 2017 IEEE International Conference on Robotics and Automation (ICRA), pp. 746–753. IEEE (2017)

29. Kim, T., Jeong, M., Kim, S., Choi, S., Kim, C.: Diversify and match: a domain adaptive representation learning paradigm for object detection. In: Proceedings of the IEEE/CVF Conference on Computer Vision and Pattern Recognition, pp. 12456–12465 (2019)
30. Lim, S., Kim, I., Kim, T., Kim, C., Kim, S.: Fast AutoAugment. In: Advances in Neural Information Processing Systems 32, pp. 6665–6675 (2019)
31. Lin, T.-Y., Maire, M., Belongie, S., Hays, J., Perona, P., Ramanan, D., Dollár, P., Zitnick, C.L.: Microsoft COCO: common objects in context. In: Fleet, D., Pajdla, T., Schiele, B., Tuytelaars, T. (eds.) ECCV 2014. LNCS, vol. 8693, pp. 740–755. Springer, Cham (2014). https://doi.org/10.1007/978-3-319-10602-1_48
32. Luo, Y., Zheng, L., Guan, T., Yu, J., Yang, Y.: Taking a closer look at domain shift: category-level adversaries for semantics consistent domain adaptation. In: Proceedings of the IEEE/CVF Conference on Computer Vision and Pattern Recognition, pp. 2507–2516 (2019)
33. Michaelis, C., Bethge, M., Ecker, A.: One-shot segmentation in clutter. In: International Conference on Machine Learning, pp. 3549–3558. PMLR (2018)
34. Ramamonjison, R., Banitalebi-Dehkordi, A., Kang, X., Bai, X., Zhang, Y.: SimROD: a simple adaptation method for robust object detection. In: Proceedings of the IEEE/CVF International Conference on Computer Vision, pp. 3570–3579 (2021)
35. Rezaeianaran, F., Shetty, R., Aljundi, R., Reino, D.O., Zhang, S., Schiele, B.: Seeking similarities over differences: Similarity-based domain alignment for adaptive object detection. In: Proceedings of the IEEE/CVF International Conference on Computer Vision, pp. 9204–9213 (2021)
36. Sahoo, A., Shah, R., Panda, R., Saenko, K., Das, A.: Contrast and mix: temporal contrastive video domain adaptation with background mixing. In: Advances in Neural Information Processing Systems 34, pp. 23386–23400 (2021)
37. Saito, K., Ushiku, Y., Harada, T., Saenko, K.: Strong-weak distribution alignment for adaptive object detection. In: Proceedings of the IEEE/CVF Conference on Computer Vision and Pattern Recognition, pp. 6956–6965 (2019)
38. Sakaridis, C., Dai, D., Van Gool, L.: Semantic foggy scene understanding with synthetic data. Int. J. Comput. Vis. **126**(9), 973–992 (2018)
39. Tranheden, W., Olsson, V., Pinto, J., Svensson, L.: DACS: domain adaptation via cross-domain mixed sampling. In: Proceedings of the IEEE/CVF Winter Conference on Applications of Computer Vision, pp. 1379–1389 (2021)
40. Tzeng, E., Hoffman, J., Saenko, K., Darrell, T.: Adversarial discriminative domain adaptation. In: Proceedings of the IEEE/CVF Conference on Computer Vision and Pattern Recognition, pp. 7167–7176 (2017)
41. Wang, T., Zhang, X., Yuan, L., Feng, J.: Few-shot adaptive faster R-CNN. In: Proceedings of the IEEE/CVF Conference on Computer Vision and Pattern Recognition, pp. 7173–7182 (2019)
42. Wang, X., Huang, T.E., Darrell, T., Gonzalez, J.E., Yu, F.: Frustratingly simple few-shot object detection. arXiv preprint arXiv:2003.06957 (2020)
43. Xu, C.D., Zhao, X.R., Jin, X., Wei, X.S.: Exploring categorical regularization for domain adaptive object detection. In: Proceedings of the IEEE/CVF Conference on Computer Vision and Pattern Recognition, pp. 11724–11733 (2020)
44. Xu, M., Wang, H., Ni, B., Tian, Q., Zhang, W.: Cross-domain detection via graph-induced prototype alignment. In: Proceedings of the IEEE/CVF Conference on Computer Vision and Pattern Recognition, pp. 12355–12364 (2020)

45. Yue, X., et al.: Prototypical cross-domain self-supervised learning for few-shot unsupervised domain adaptation. In: Proceedings of the IEEE/CVF Conference on Computer Vision and Pattern Recognition, pp. 13834–13844 (2021)
46. Yun, S., Han, D., Oh, S.J., Chun, S., Choe, J., Yoo, Y.: CutMix: regularization strategy to train strong classifiers with localizable features. In: Proceedings of the IEEE/CVF International Conference on Computer Vision, pp. 6023–6032 (2019)
47. Zhang, H., Cisse, M., Dauphin, Y.N., Lopez-Paz, D.: mixup: beyond empirical risk minimization. arXiv preprint arXiv:1710.09412 (2017)
48. Zhang, J., Chen, Z., Huang, J., Lin, L., Zhang, D.: Few-shot structured domain adaptation for virtual-to-real scene parsing. In: Proceedings of the IEEE/CVF International Conference on Computer Vision Workshops (2019)
49. Zheng, Y., Huang, D., Liu, S., Wang, Y.: Cross-domain object detection through coarse-to-fine feature adaptation. In: Proceedings of the IEEE/CVF Conference on Computer Vision and Pattern Recognition, pp. 13766–13775 (2020)
50. Zhu, X., Pang, J., Yang, C., Shi, J., Lin, D.: Adapting object detectors via selective cross-domain alignment. In: Proceedings of the IEEE/CVF Conference on Computer Vision and Pattern Recognition, pp. 687–696 (2019)
51. Zhuang, C., Han, X., Huang, W., Scott, M.: iFAN: image-instance full alignment networks for adaptive object detection. In: Proceedings of the AAAI Conference on Artificial Intelligence, vol. 34, pp. 13122–13129 (2020)
52. Zou, H., Zhou, Y., Yang, J., Liu, H., Das, H.P., Spanos, C.J.: Consensus adversarial domain adaptation. In: Proceedings of the AAAI Conference on Artificial Intelligence, vol. 33, pp. 5997–6004 (2019)

Unsupervised Domain Adaptation for One-Stage Object Detector Using Offsets to Bounding Box

Jayeon Yoo, Inseop Chung, and Nojun Kwak(✉)

Seoul National University, Seoul, South Korea
{jayeon.yoo,jis3613,nojunk}@snu.ac.kr

Abstract. Most existing domain adaptive object detection methods exploit adversarial feature alignment to adapt the model to a new domain. Recent advances in adversarial feature alignment strives to reduce the negative effect of alignment, or negative transfer, that occurs because the distribution of features varies depending on the category of objects. However, by analyzing the features of the anchor-free one-stage detector, in this paper, we find that negative transfer may occur because the feature distribution varies depending on the regression value for the offset to the bounding box as well as the category. To obtain domain invariance by addressing this issue, we align the feature conditioned on the offset value, considering the modality of the feature distribution. With a very simple and effective conditioning method, we propose OADA (Offset-Aware Domain Adaptive object detector) that achieves state-of the-art performances in various experimental settings. In addition, by analyzing through singular value decomposition, we find that our model enhances both discriminability and transferability.

Keywords: Unsupervised domain adaptation · Object detection · Offset-aware

1 Introduction

Deep-learning-based object detection has shown successful results by learning from a large amount of labeled data. However, if the distribution of test data is significantly different from that of training data, the model performance is severely impaired. In practice, this performance degradation can be very fatal because the domains in which the object detection model should operate can be very diverse. To address this problem, the most effective way is to re-train the model with a lot of data from the new environment whenever the environment changes. However, obtaining a large amount of labeled data is a very expensive process, especially in object detection task which requires annotating the

Supplementary Information The online version contains supplementary material available at https://doi.org/10.1007/978-3-031-19827-4_40.

S. Avidan et al. (Eds.): ECCV 2022, LNCS 13693, pp. 691–708, 2022.
https://doi.org/10.1007/978-3-031-19827-4_40

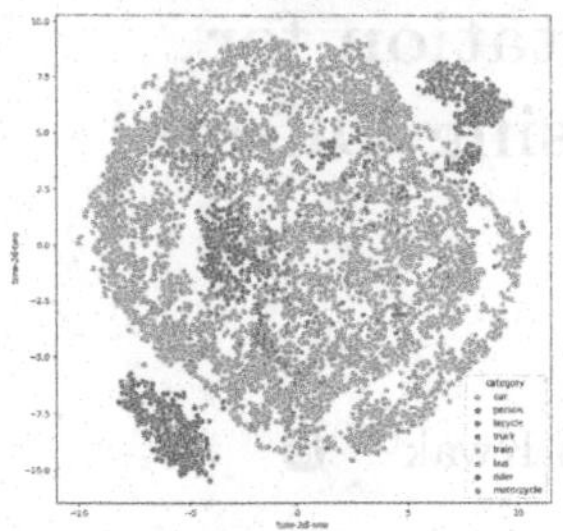

(a) According to the classes. Orange and blue indicate *car* and *person* respectively.

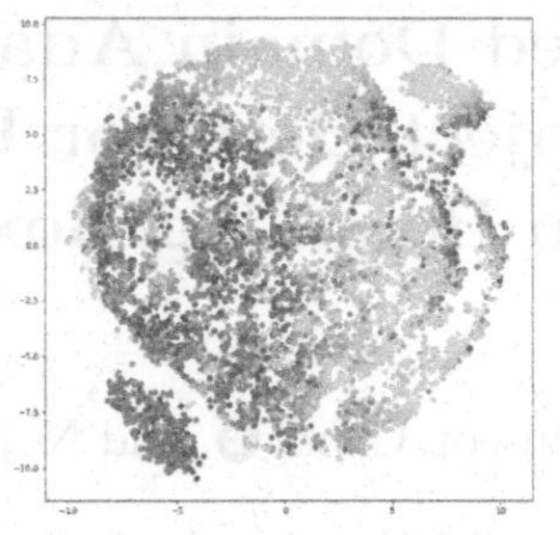

(b) According to the offset to the top side of the GT bounding box (t).

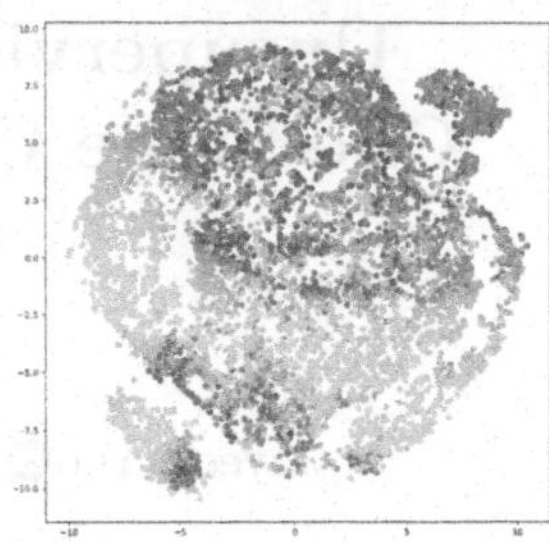

(c) According to the offset to the bottom side of the GT bounding box (b).

Fig. 1. TSNE visualization of the source domain backbone features of a detector that is trained only on the source domain. Different colors in (a) refer to different classes while in (b) and (c), the colors represent the distance from a location of a feature with high classification confidence to the top and bottom of the ground-truth bounding box respectively. The redder the color, the greater the distance. (Color figure online)

bounding boxes and the classes of objects in an image. Unsupervised Domain Adaptation (UDA) provides an efficient solution to this domain-shift problem in a way that it adapts the model to a new environment by training with unlabeled datasets from the new environment (target domain) as well as rich datasets from the original environment (source domain). Based on the theoretical analysis of [11], aligning the feature distribution of the source and the target domain in an adversarial manner is one of the most effective ways in various tasks such as classification [1,11,26,40] and segmentation [6,7,27,42]. A seminal work [5] is the first to deal with *Domain Adaptive Object Detection* (DAOD) aligning backbone features via an adversarial method, and many follow-up studies have continued in this line of research. Unlike classification and segmentation tasks classifying an image and each pixel as one category, object detection is a task of classifying the categories and regressing the bounding box of each foreground object. Focusing on this difference, many studies further align local features [32] or instance-level features corresponding to the foreground rather than the background [14,38].

While one-stage detectors such as FCOS [36] and YOLO [28] are more advantageous for real-world environments because of its efficient structures and high inference speed, most DAOD studies [2,5,9,15,32,37,43] have been conducted on two-stage detectors, such as Faster R-CNN [29]. They use proposals generated by Region Proposal Network (RPN) to obtain instance-level features corresponding to the objects, making it difficult to extend straightforwardly to one-stage detectors that do not rely on RPN. Recently, several DAOD methods specialized in one-stage detector have been proposed [14,25]. They prevent negative transfer that can occur when a feature is indiscriminately aligned by focusing on a foreground object or further aligning a feature according to the category of the object. However, for FCOS, an one-stage detector that estimates offsets from each point of the feature map to the four sides of a bounding box, the features differ in distribution not only by categories but also by offsets. Accordingly, existing feature alignment may not be sufficient to prevent negative transfer.

Figure 1 shows the TSNE of features corresponding to foreground objects obtained from the backbone of FCOS trained on the Cityscape dataset [8] consisting of 8 classes. In Fig. 1a, different colors refer to different classes. Since instances of *Car* (orange) and *Person* (blue) are dominant, the difference in feature distribution between the *Car* and the *Person* is clearly visible. This phenomenon fits well with the intention of [3, 37, 39, 43, 44] which align the feature distribution of the source and the target domain in a class-wise manner. Figure 1b and 1c show the feature distribution in another perspective, the distance to the boundary of the GT bounding box. In Fig. 1b, color codes are used to measure the offset, the distance from the feature point to the top side of the bounding box, in the log scale: the redder, the larger the offset is, while the bluer, the smaller. It shows that the distribution of the backbone features varies markedly with offsets. Comparing Fig. 1a and 1b, even features in the same category have varying distribution depending on their offset. Since object detection requires bounding box regression as well as classification, especially in case of FCOS which predicts the offsets of *(left, top, right, bottom)* to the four sides of bounding boxes, the backbone features are not only clustered by categories but also distributed according to the offsets. Paying attention to this analysis, we conditionally align features of the source and the target domains according to their offsets.

Therefore, in this paper, we propose an Offset-Aware Domain Adaptive object detection method (OADA) that aligns the features of the source and the target domain conditional to the offset values to suppress the negative transfer in an anchor-free one-stage detector such as FCOS. Specifically, to align instance-level features and obtain reliable offset values, we use label information for the source domain and classification confidence for the target domain. And then, we convert continuous offsets into categorical probability vectors and get offset-aware features by outer-producting that probability vectors and backbone features. We prevent negative transfer that may occur while aligning the features to have the same marginal distribution by making the offset-aware features domain-invariant using a domain discriminator. Essentially, this is equivalent to intentionally forming a discriminator embedding space that is roughly partitioned by the offset. As a result, we can efficiently align features with a single strong discriminator, opening up new possibilities for offset-aware feature alignment in a very simple yet effective manner. Our contributions can be summarized as follows:

- We present a domain adaptation method which is specialized for anchor-free one-stage detector by analyzing the characteristics of it.
- We prevent negative transfer when aligning instance-level features in domain adaptive object detection by making domain-invariant offset-aware features in a highly efficient manner.
- We find that our proposed method enhances both discriminability and transferability by analyzing through singular value decomposition.

- We show the effectiveness of our proposed method (OADA) through extensive experiments on three widely used domain adaptation benchmarks, Cityscapes → Foggy Cityscapes and Sim10k, KITTI → Cityscapes and it achieves state-of-the-art performance in all benchmarks.

2 Related Works

2.1 Object Detection

Deep-learning-based object detection can be categorized into anchor-based and anchor-free methods. Anchor-based detectors define various sizes and ratios of anchors in advance and utilize them to match the output of the detector with the ground-truth. On the other hand, anchor-free detectors do not utilize any anchors but rather directly localize objects employing fully convolutional layers. Moreover, depending on whether region proposal network (RPN) is used or not, object detectors can also be classified into two-stage and one-stage detectors. Faster R-CNN [29] is a representative anchor-based two-stage detector while SSD [22] and YOLO [28] are anchor-based one-stage detectors. There are some renowned anchor-free one-stage detectors as well. Cornernet [20] and Centernet [10] localize objects by predicting the keypoints or the center of an object while FCOS [36] directly computes the offset from each location on the feature map to the ground-truth bounding box. Most works of DAOD have been conducted on Faster R-CNN, a two-stage detector and relatively few works have been done using an anchor-free one-stage detector. There are several works [3,18,30] that have been conducted on SSD, a representative one-stage anchor-based detector and only [14,25] carried out domain adaptation using FCOS, an anchor-free one-stage detector. Our work focuses on boosting the domain adaptation performance on FCOS [36] leveraging its anchor-free architecture and fast speed.

2.2 UDA for Object Detection

There are three main approaches of UDA for object detection tasks: adversarial alignment, image translation, and self-training. Image-translation-based methods translate the source domain images into another domain using a generative model [2,9,15,19,30,34] to adapt to the target domain. Self-training-based methods [9,17,18,25,31] generate pseudo-labels for the target domain images with the model pre-trained on the source domain and re-train the model with the pseudo labels. For adversarial alignment methods, [5] is a seminal work that aligns the feature distribution of the source and the target domain using a domain discriminator based on the Faster R-CNN [29]. Since then, there have been studies to align feature distribution at multiple levels [13,32], studies focusing on the importance of local features in detection, and studies to align instance-level features that may correspond to objects [14,38,43]. Recently, there have been attempts [3,37,39,43,44] to align the instance-level features in a class-wise manner, focusing on the fact that the distribution of instance-level features is clustered by class. Based on our observation that the feature distribution varies depending on the offset values in FCOS [36] and the detection task requires not only classification but also regression, we propose an adversarial alignment scheme with state-of-the-art performances in various experimental settings by aligning the features in an offset-aware manner.

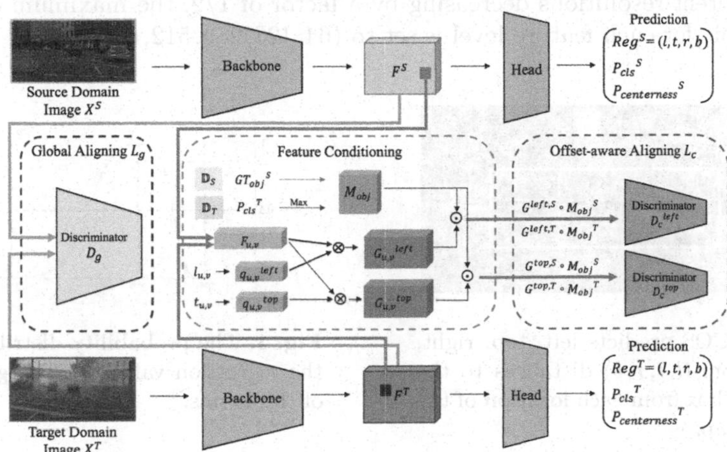

Fig. 2. The overall structure of our framework. F^S and F^T are the lv-th level features ($lv \in \{3, .., 7\}$, lv is omitted for simple notation) of the source image X^S and the target image X^T, respectively. The overall feature maps F^S and F^T are aligned by the global domain discriminator, D_g. To generate a mask M_{obj} corresponding to the objects, the GT labels are used for the source domain and maximum values of class confidence higher than threshold is used for the target domain. The GT offsets of the source domain and the predicted offsets of the target domain are converted into probability vector $q_{u,v}$, and they produce $G_{u,v}$ via the outer-product with $F_{u,v}$. We use D_c^{left} and D_c^{top} to align the conditioned features $G_{u,v}^l$ and $G_{u,v}^t$ according to the left and top offsets, respectively.

3 Method

In this section, we describe our method shown in Fig. 2, which aligns instance-level features between the two domains in an offset-aware manner in detail. Since our method investigates domain adaptation of a representative anchor-free one-stage detector, FCOS [36], a brief introduction about it is given in Sect. 3.1.

3.1 Preliminary: FCOS

FCOS [36] is a representative one-stage detector that predicts object categories and bounding boxes densely in feature maps without a RPN. FCOS uses five levels of feature maps (F_3–F_7) produced from the backbone network following FPN [21] to detect various sizes of objects. At each location of the feature map, it predicts the corresponding object category, the centerness indicating how central the current location is to the object, and the distances from the current location to the left, top, right, and bottom (l, t, r, b) of the nearest ground-truth bounding box as shown in Fig. 3. With a design that five levels of feature maps have different resolutions decreasing by a factor of 1/2, the maximum distance responsible for each feature level is set to $(64, 128, 256, 512, \infty)$.

Fig. 3. FCOS predicts left, top, right, and bottom (l, t, r, b) distances to the bounding box from each location of the feature map.

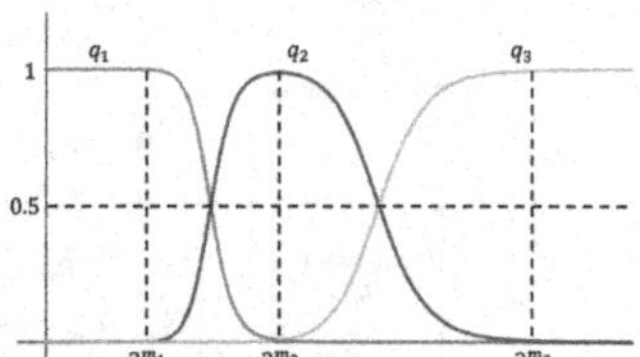

Fig. 4. The probability distribution of the regression value belonging to each of three bins.

FCOS differs from conventional anchor-based or RPN-based object detectors which regress four values to correct anchors or proposals. We observe that the features are distributed according not only to object categories but also to offsets, the distances to the nearest bounding boxes, and it is more pronounced in FCOS due to its characteristics of predicting (l, t, r, b) directly using the features. Focusing on this observation, our proposed method tries to align the features of the source and the target domains by conditioning the features with the offsets.

3.2 Problem Formulation

Consider the setting where we adapt the object detector to the target domain using labeled source domain data $\mathbb{D}_S$ and unlabeled target domain data $\mathbb{D}_T$ which share the same label space consisting of C classes. When training a detector, we only have access to $\mathbb{D}_S = (x_i^S, y_i^S, b_i^S)_{i=1}^{N_S}$ and $\mathbb{D}_T = (x_i^T)_{i=1}^{N_T}$, where x_i is the input image, and $y_i \in [C]^{k\times 1}$ and $b_i \in \mathbb{R}^{k\times 4}$ are the object categories and the bounding box coordinates of all the k objects existing in x_i. N_S and N_T are the numbers of samples in $\mathbb{D}_S$ and $\mathbb{D}_T$.

3.3 Global Alignment

To ensure that the object detector works well on the target domain, we align the features of both the source and the target domain to have a marginally similar distribution through an adversarial aligning method using a global domain discriminator D_g. Let F^S and F^T be the feature maps obtained by feeding the source domain image x^S and the target domain image x^T to the backbone, respectively. When the spatial size of a feature map F is $H \times W$, D_g is trained to classify the domain of the feature map F pixel-wisely by the binary cross entropy loss as in (1). The label of the source domain is 1, while that of the target is 0.

$$\mathcal{L}_g(x^S, x^T) = -\sum_{u=1}^{H}\sum_{v=1}^{W} \log(D_g(F^S_{u,v})) + \log(1 - D_g(F^T_{u,v})). \quad (1)$$

Using the gradient reversal layer (GRL) proposed in [11], the backbone is adversarially trained to prevent the domain discriminator from correctly distinguishing the source and the target domains, thereby generating domain-invariant features.

3.4 Generating Conditional Features to Offset Values

In order to align features in an offset-aware manner, the features and the corresponding offsets can be concatenated and inputted to the domain discriminator. However, simply concatenating them is not enough to fully utilize the correlation between features and offset values. Inspired by [24], which considers the correlation between features and categorical predictions, our method does not simply concatenate but outer-product features and offset values. Unlike classification which uses a categorical vector, an offset value is a continuous real value. Hence, the product of the feature and the offset value only has the effect of scaling the feature. To effectively condition the feature according to the corresponding offset values, each offset value of (l, t, r, b) is converted into a probability vector corresponding to N_{bin} bins using (2). In the equation, $z^n_{u,v}$ refers to the offset value for $n \in \{l, t, r, b\}$ at the location (u, v) in the feature map. To convert the offset $z_{u,v}$ to an N_{bin}-dimensional probability vector, we calculate the probability using the distance of the log of the offset value to a predefined value m_i for the i-th bin. Note that we have N_{bin} bins and $m_1 < m_2 < \cdots < m_{N_{bin}}$. Assuming that the probability of $z_{u,v}$ belonging to the i-th bin is proportional to a normal distribution with its mean m_i and a shared variance σ^2, it becomes as follows:

$$q_i(z^n_{u,v}) = \frac{\exp(-\frac{(\log_2(z^n_{u,v}) - m^n_i)^2}{2\sigma^2/\tau})}{\sum_{j=1}^{N_{bin}} \exp(-\frac{(\log_2(z^n_{u,v}) - m^n_j)^2}{2\sigma^2/\tau})}, i \in [N_{bin}], n \in \{l, t, r, b\}. \quad (2)$$

Here, τ is a temperature value to make the distribution smooth, and in all of our experiments, both σ and τ are set to 0.1. In all of our main experiments, N_{bin} is set to 3 for each feature level, and m_i for each bin is set to $(m_1, m_2, m_3) = (lv - \frac{1}{2}, lv + \frac{1}{2}, lv + \frac{3}{2})$ for lv-th level ($lv \in \{3, ..., 7\}$) to satisfy $\frac{m_1 + m_2}{2} = lv$ and $\frac{m_2 + m_3}{2} = lv + 1$ because each feature level is responsible for a different object scale. Figure 4 shows the probability of $z_{u,v}$ belonging to each bin when there are three bins. The obtained probability vector $q \triangleq [q_1, \cdots, q_{N_{bin}}]^T \in \mathbb{R}^{N_{bin}}_{+}$ still maintains the relative distance relationship of the real offset value as $D_{KL}(q(a)||q(b)) < D_{KL}(q(a)||q(c))$ if $a < b < c$.

However, the probability vector is uniformly initialized for all N_{bin} bins since the regressed offsets may not be accurate at the beginning of training. During the first I warm-up iterations, we gradually increase the rate of using the probability vector $q_{u,v}$ as iteration ($iter$) progresses utilizing the alpha-blending as follows:

$$\tilde{q}_{u,v} = ((1-\alpha)q_{u,v} + \alpha\frac{1}{N_{bin}}\mathbb{1}), \quad \text{where} \quad \alpha = \max(1-\frac{iter}{I}, \alpha_0). \tag{3}$$

Here, α_0 is the constant value between 0 and 1 that smoothes the probability vector $\tilde{q}$, and the closer it is to 1, the more uniform $\tilde{q}$ becomes. We show the effects of α_0 in Sect. 4.5. In all the experiments, I is set to 6k, the half of the first learning rate decay point. $\mathbb{1}$ is a vector consisting of only ones.

Using $\tilde{q}_{u,v}$, we can obtain the features which are conditional to the offset values by outer-producting them as follows:

$$g_{u,v} = f_{u,v} \otimes \tilde{q}_{u,v}. \tag{4}$$

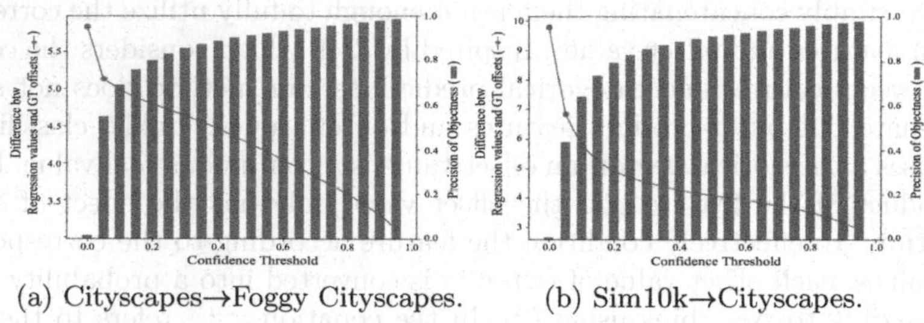

(a) Cityscapes→Foggy Cityscapes. (b) Sim10k→Cityscapes.

Fig. 5. The difference between the predicted regression value and the GT value (Red line) and the precision (Blue bar) according to the confidence threshold ρ. (Color figure online)

Here, $f_{u,v} \in \mathbb{R}^D$ is a feature vector located at location (u, v) in the feature map $F \in \mathbb{R}^{D\times HW}$ and $\tilde{q}_{u,v} \in \mathbb{R}_+^{N_{bin}}$ is the probability vector of the corresponding offset value obtained from (3). By outer-producting $f_{u,v}$ and $\tilde{q}_{u,v}$, we can get a new feature, $g_{u,v} \in \mathbb{R}^{D\times N_{bin}}$ conditioned on the offsets. By flattening $g_{u,v}$, the conditioned feature map $G \in \mathbb{R}^{(D\times N_{bin})\times HW}$ with the same spatial resolution as F is obtained, which is fed into the domain discriminator D_c.

Outer product is effective in conditioning because it considers the correlation between features and offsets without loss of information, hence it enables features to have different characteristics depending on offset values. Consider a case where $N_{bin} = 3$ and $(m_1, m_2, m_3) = (3.5, 4.5, 5.5)$ for F_4, and conditionally align to t, the top offsets. Suppose that feature vector $f_{u_1,v_1} \in \mathbb{R}^D$ located at (u_1, v_1) have a small top offset prediction, i.e. $t = 13$ and $\log_2 t = 3.7$, resulting in the probability vector $q_{u_1,v_1} = (0.98, 0.02, 0.0)$ via (2). Conditioned feature g_{u_1,v_1} obtained by outer-producting f_{u_1,v_1} and q_{u_1,v_1} is a $3 \times D$ matrix. The first row of g_{u_1,v_1} would be similar to the original feature f_{u_1,v_1}, but the elements in the other rows would be almost zero. On the other hand, g_{u_2,v_2} obtained by e.g. $q_{u_2,v_2} = (0, 0.01, 0.99)$ with a large top offset would have the original feature f_{u_2,v_2} in the third row but have almost zero elements in another rows. Therefore, a domain discriminator is trained to classify the domain of the features in different subspaces according to the offsets. As a result, the backbone will generate features that are domain invariant conditioned on offsets to fool the discriminator.

3.5 How to Get a Confident Offset Value?

To generate a feature conditioned on the offsets, we need to know which location in the feature map corresponds to the object and the accurate offset value at that location. For the labeled source domain, we can easily obtain the ground-truth value of which location corresponds to the object in each feature map and the offsets. Since FCOS calculates the object mask corresponding to each category in the feature map and the distance from each location to the GT bounding box, we can utilize this mask and the ground-truth offset values, (l^*, t^*, r^*, b^*). On the other hand, in the unlabeled target domain, we should inevitably use predicted values. Although classification confidence is the probability of predicting the category of an object rather than a regression, by using it, we can simply and effectively select instance-level features with high objectness and obtain reliable regression values for those features. Figure 5 is the analysis of features obtained by feeding a target domain image into the globally aligned model of Sect. 3.3. The blue bar represents the ratio corresponding to the actual objects among the features having a confidence value higher than the threshold value of the x-axis, and the red line represents the average of the difference between the regression values and the GT offsets of the features. The higher the confidence threshold, the higher the probability of the feature's location belonging to an actual object, and the closer the regression value is to the GT offset value. In $p_{cls}^{u,v} \in \mathbb{R}_+^C$, which is the category classification probability at the (u, v)-th location of the feature map, $\max_{c\in[C]}(p_{cls}^{u,v})$ (the maximum probability among all classes) can be viewed as objectness which is the probability that the location corresponds to an object. Therefore, we generate a mask where $\max_{c\in[C]}(p_{cls}^{u,v})$ is higher than a threshold ρ, and we weight the activated part with that max probability value as follows:

$$M_{obj}^T = \mathbb{I}_{\max_c(p_{cls})>\rho} \odot \max_c(p_{cls}). \tag{5}$$

Finally, we align the distribution of features G of the source and the target which is conditioned on the offset by minimizing the following adversarial loss:

$$\begin{aligned} \mathcal{L}_c^n(x^S, x^T) &= -\sum_{u,v}^{H,W} \log(D_c^n(\hat{G}_{u,v}^{n,S})) + \log(1 - D_c^n(\hat{G}_{u,v}^{n,T})) \\ \hat{G}^{n,d} &= G^{n,d} \odot M_{obj}^d, \quad d \in \{S, T\}. \end{aligned} \tag{6}$$

Here, $\mathcal{L}_c^n$ is the adversarial loss conditional to the offset value $n \in \{l, t\}$ using the discriminator D_c^n. Since the correlation between the regression values for the left

l and the right r and between the top t and the bottom b are strong, conditioning is performed only for the left and the top. d represents whether the domain is the source or the target. $\mathbb{I}$ is the indicator function and $\odot$ is the elementwise multiplication. Through this, the instance-level features of both domains can be aligned to have the same distribution conditional to the offset.

3.6 Overall Loss

Using labeled source domain data, the backbone and heads of FCOS are trained by minimizing object detection loss $\mathcal{L}_{det}$ consisting of object classification loss $\mathcal{L}_{det\text{-}cls}$ and bounding box regression loss $\mathcal{L}_{det\text{-}reg}$, as in [36]:

$$\mathcal{L}_{det}(x^S) = \mathcal{L}_{det\text{-}cls} + \mathcal{L}_{det\text{-}reg}. \tag{7}$$

In addition, we introduce $\mathcal{L}_g$ in (1) to ensure that the overall features of both domains have the similar marginal distribution and $\mathcal{L}_c$ in (6) to allow the instance-level features to have the same conditional distribution to offsets, as follows:

$$\mathcal{L}_{total} = \mathcal{L}_{det}(x^S) + \lambda_g \mathcal{L}_g(x^S, x^T) + \lambda_c(\mathcal{L}_c^{left}(x^S, x^T) + \mathcal{L}_c^{top}(x^S, x^T)). \tag{8}$$

where λ_g and λ_c are parameters balancing the loss components.

Table 1. Results of Cityscapes → Foggy Cityscapes. EPM* denotes our re-implementation and GA† is the result of the global alignment of Sect. 3.3. *Source Only* is trained with only source domain without adaptation and *Oracle* is trained with labeled target domain, providing the upper bound of UDA.

Method	Detector	person	rider	car	truck	bus	train	mbike	bicycle	$mAP^r_{0.5}$
Source Only	Faster-RCNN	17.8	23.6	27.1	11.9	23.8	9.1	14.4	22.8	18.8
DAFaster [5]		25.0	31.0	40.5	22.1	35.3	20.2	20.0	27.1	27.6
Selective DA [45]		33.5	38.0	48.5	26.5	39.0	23.3	28.0	33.6	33.8
MAF [13]		28.2	39.5	43.9	23.8	39.9	33.3	29.2	33.9	34.0
SWDA [32]		29.9	42.3	43.5	24.5	36.2	32.6	30.0	35.3	34.3
HTCN [2]		33.2	47.5	47.9	31.6	47.4	40.9	32.3	37.1	39.8
UMT [9]		34.2	48.8	51.1	30.8	51.9	42.5	33.9	38.2	41.2
MeGA-CDA [37]		37.7	49.0	52.4	25.4	49.2	46.9	34.5	39.0	41.8
Oracle		37.2	48.2	52.7	35.2	52.2	48.5	35.3	38.8	43.5
Source Only	FCOS	30.2	27.4	34.2	6.8	18.0	2.7	14.4	29.3	20.4
EPM [14]		41.9	38.7	56.7	22.6	41.5	26.8	24.6	35.5	36.0
EPM* [14]		44.9	44.4	60.6	26.5	45.5	28.9	30.6	37.5	39.9
SSAL [25]		45.1	**47.4**	59.4	24.5	**50.0**	25.7	26.0	38.7	39.6
GA†		43.2	40.5	58.2	28.2	43.6	24.2	27.1	35.3	37.5
OADA (Offset-Left)		46.2	45.0	62.2	26.8	49.0	39.2	33.1	39.1	42.6
OADA (Offset-Top)		45.9	46.3	61.8	30.0	48.2	36.0	34.2	39.0	42.7
OADA (Offset-Left & Top)		**47.3**	45.6	**62.8**	**30.7**	48.0	**49.4**	**34.6**	**39.5**	**44.8**
OADA (Offset-Left & Top + Self-Training)		47.8	46.5	62.9	32.1	48.5	50.9	34.3	39.8	45.4
Oracle		49.6	47.5	67.2	31.3	52.2	42.1	32.9	41.7	45.6

4 Experiments

4.1 Datasets

We conduct experiments on three scenarios: adaptation to adverse weather driving (Cityscapes to Foggy Cityscapes, i.e. CS → FoggyCS), adaptation from synthetic data to real data (Sim10k to Cityscapes, i.e. Sim10k → CS), and adaptation to a different camera modality (KITTI to Cityscapes, i.e. KITTI → CS).

- **Cityscapes** [8] consists of clear city images under driving scenarios, summing to 2,975 and 500 images for training and validation, respectively. There are 8 categories, *i.e.,* person, rider, car, truck, bus, train, motorcycle and bicycle.
- **Foggy Cityscapes** [33] is a synthetic dataset that is rendered by adding fog to the Cityscapes images. We use Cityscapes as the source, and Foggy Cityscapes as the target to simulate domain shift caused by the weather condition.
- **Sim10k** [16] consists of 10,000 synthesized city images. For the adaptation scenario from synthetic data to real data, we set Sim10k as the source domain and Cityscapes as the target domain. Only *car* class is considered.
- **KITTI** [12] consisting of 7,481 images is a driving scenario dataset similar to Cityscapes, but there is a difference in camera modality. For adaptive scenarios to other camera modalities, we use KITTI as the source and Cityscapes as the target. Similar to Sim10k to Cityscapes, only *car* category is used.

4.2 Implementation Details

We use VGG-16 [35] backbone and fully-convolutional head consisting of three branches of classification, regression and centerness following [36]. For the domain discriminators, D_g and D_c, fully-convolutional layers with the same structure as the head are used. We initialize the backbone with the Image-Net pretrained model and reduce the overall domain gap using only object detection loss $\mathcal{L}_{det}$ and global alignment $\mathcal{L}_g$ at the beginning of training. Then, we train the model for 20k iterations with weight decay of 1e-4, initial learning rate of 0.02 for CS → FoggyCS, 0.01 for Sim10k → CS and 0.005 for KITTI → CS, respectively. We decay the learning rate at 12k and 18k iteration by the rate of one-tenth. During training, λ_g and λ_c are fixed as 0.01 and 0.1, respectively. We set the weight for the Gradient Reversal Layer (GRL) to 0.02 for global alignment and 0.2 for our conditional alignment. Also, we set the confidence threshold in (5) as $\rho = 0.3$ for CS → FoggyCS and $\rho = 0.5$ for Sim10k, KITTI → Cityscapes to reduce the effects of incorrect predictions. We set I to 6k which is the half of the first learning rate decay point and α_0 in (3) to 0.2. Input image is resized to 800 for shorter side, and 1333 or less for longer side following [14,25,36].

Table 2. Results of Sim10k, KITTI → Cityscapes. EPM* denotes the results of our re-implementations. GA† is the result of the global alignment of Sect. 3.3.

Method	Detector	Sim10k	KITTI
		$mAP^r_{0.5}$	$mAP^r_{0.5}$
Source Only	Faster-RCNN	34.3	30.2
DAFaster [45]		38.9	38.5
SWDA [32]		40.1	37.9
MAF [13]		41.1	41.0
HTCN [2]		42.5	–
Selective DA [45]		43.0	42.5
UMT [9]		43.1	–
MeGA-CDA [37]		44.8	43.0
Oracle		69.7	69.7
Source Only	FCOS	40.4	44.2
EPM [14]		49.0	45.0
EPM* [14]		51.1	43.7
SSAL [25]		51.8	45.6
GA†		49.7	43.1
OADA (Offset-Left)		55.4	45.6
OADA (Offset-Top)		55.7	45.8
OADA (Offset-Left & Top)		**56.6**	**46.3**
OADA (Offset-Left & Top + Self-Training)		59.2	47.8
Oracle		72.7	72.7

4.3 Overall Performance

In Table 1, we compare the performance of our method (*OADA*) with other existing methods in CS → FoggyCS setting. When *EPM* [14] based on FCOS is trained in the exact same setting as ours, the performance is 3.9%p higher than what was reported. Conditional alignment on the offsets to the left and the top side of the bounding box improves performance by 22.2%p and 22.3%p respectively compared to *Source Only*, by 5.7%p and 6.0%p compared to GA† which is only globally aligned and by 2.7%p and 2.8%p compared to *EPM** that we reimplemented. Since Foggy Cityscapes has 8 categories of objects and has various aspect ratios, when conditioning is performed on both the left and the top offsets, the additional performance gain is very larger by 2.1%p or more, achieving the state-of-the-art regardless of the detector architecture. By initializing with the *OADA (Offset-Left & Top)* pre-trained model and training once more with self-training [23], we get a model almost similar to *Oracle* lagging only by 0.2%p. Detailed implementation of self-training is explained in the supplementary.

Table 2 shows the adaptation results of Sim10k and KITTI → CS. In Sim10k → CS, conditional alignment using left and top offsets improves mAP by 15.0%p and 15.3%p, respectively, compared to *Source-Only* and 4.3%p and 4.6%p over re-implemented *EPM**. Likewise, in KITTI → CS, our methods using left and top offsets improve the performance by 1.4%p and 1.6%p, respectively, over *Source-Only* and 1.9%p and 2.1%p over *EPM**. In these two benchmarks, only the *car* class is considered, so the gain of OADA (Offset-Left & Top) is not as large as the multi-category setting, but there are still additional gain of 0.9%p and 0.5%p for Sim10k and KITTI. Our conditional aligning alone already achieves the state-of-the-art performance but greater performance can be obtained by employing the self-training as in OADA (Offset-Left & Top + Self-Training).

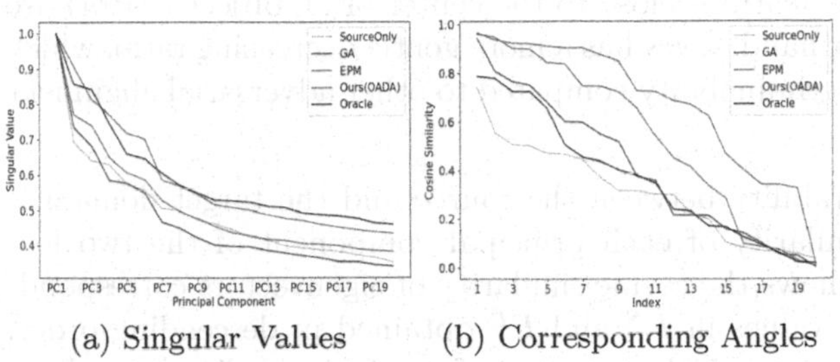

(a) Singular Values (b) Corresponding Angles

Fig. 6. Measures of discriminability and transferability (Color figure online)

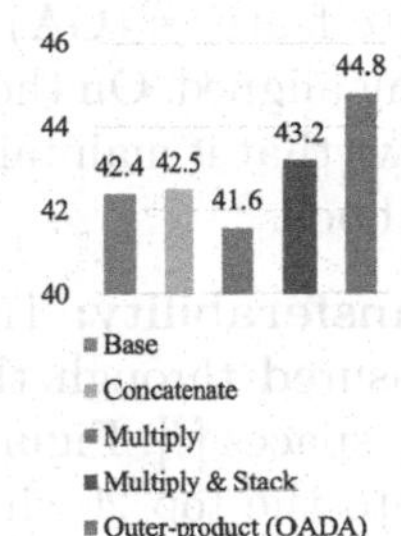

Fig. 7. Conditioning

4.4 Analysis on Discriminability and Transferability

Chen et al. [4] argued that aligning the feature distribution through adversarial alignment increases the transferability of features, but they did not take the discriminability into account, the ability to perform tasks well. They measure the discriminability via singular value decomposition (SVD) of the target domain feature maps and measure the transferability by estimating the corresponding angle between the feature spaces of the source and the target domain. Using their proposed metrics [4,41], we compare the discriminability and transferability of *Ours (OADA)* with *Source Only*, *GA* of Sect. 3.3, *EPM* [14] and *Oracle* models in CS → Foggy CS. When $F^S = [f_1^S ... f_{N_S}^S]$ and $F^T = [f_1^T ... f_{N_T}^T]$ are feature matrix of the source and the target domain respectively, we apply SVD as follows:

$$F^S = U_S \Sigma_S V_S^\top, \quad F^T = U_T \Sigma_T V_T^\top. \tag{9}$$

Discriminability: Figure 6a plots the top-20 greatest singular values of F^T obtained from the five models. The singular values are sorted in descending order from left to right on the x-axis. These values are normalized so that the maximum singular value is 1. It can be seen that *Ours* (red) has a similar

Table 3. mAP$^r_{0.5}$ according to α_0 of (3) and number of bins in CS → Foggy CS.

Model	α_0					N_{bin}				
	0.0	0.1	0.2	0.5	1.0	1	2	3	4	5
OADA (Offset-Left & Top)	42.6	43.4	**44.8**	43.3	42.6	42.4	44.2	**44.8**	44.3	41.4

decreasing ratio to the *Oracle* model (black), while *GA* and *EPM* models have significantly larger one singular value and relatively much smaller other singular values than the largest one. This means that informative signals corresponding to small singular values are greatly compromised in *GA* and *EPM*, where the entire features (GA) or the features close to the center of an object (EPM) are being aligned. On the other hand, *Ours* has a more gentle decreasing ratio, which shows that it maintains discriminability compared to other adversarial alignment methods.

Transferability: Transferability between the source and the target domain is measured through the similarity of each principal component of the two feature spaces [4]. Figure 6b shows the cosine similarity of eigenvectors corresponding to the top 20 singular values in F^S and F^T obtained in descending order. While *SourceOnly* and *Oracle*, which do not perform feature alignment, have low corresponding angles of principal components between F^S and F^T, overall correspondences increase in models that align feature spaces in an adversarial manner. Particularly, *Ours* shows higher similarity between the source and the target domain feature space than *GA* and *EPM*. From this observation, it can be seen that aligning the features in an offset-aware manner is effective in increasing the transferability without harming the discriminability for object detection.

4.5 Ablation Studies

α_0 in (3): Table 3 shows the effect of α_0 that smoothes $\tilde{q}$ used for feature conditioning. When $\alpha_0 = 0$, conditioning is done using only q, which is the probability vector of an offset, without smoothing after the warm-up period. Since the softmax in (2) makes q almost one-hot vector in most cases, the values of certain rows of conditioned feature g are almost zero. This strongly constrains the dimension of the conditioned features. On the other hand, when $\alpha_0 = 1$, we outer-product the feature with an uniform vector $\frac{1}{N_{bin}}\mathbb{1}$ without offeset-aware conditioning throughout training. In this case, the feature dimension given to the discriminator is the same, but performance is greatly degraded because there is no conditioning according to the offset. $\alpha_0 = 0.2$, in which relatively strongly constrained features are used in the discriminator, is most appropriate.

Number of Bins: Table 3 also shows ablations results of the number of bins, N_{bin}. The reference value m_i for the i-th bin is set according to the size of objects for which the feature of each level is responsible. The detailed values are in the supplementary. When $N_{bin} = 1$, there is no conditioning on offsets and only the mask M_{obj} is used, nevertheless it is more effective than *GA* and *EPM*. $N_{bin} = 3$ is sufficiently effective in offset conditioning, improving $\mathrm{mAP}^r_{0.5}$ by 2.4%p. When the number of bins is increased excessively, the constraint on the subspace of the conditioned feature becomes too strong, resulting in performance deterioration.

Table 4. Comparison of $\mathrm{mAP}^r_{0.5}$ according to the confidence threshold (ρ)

Model	Datasets	Confidence threshold (ρ)			
		0.0	0.3	0.5	0.7
OADA (Offset-Top)	Cityscapes → Foggy Cityscapes	37.0	**42.7**	41.7	37.3
	Sim10k → Cityscapes	48.5	53.6	**55.7**	53.6
	KITTI → Cityscapes	43.8	44.8	**45.8**	44.0

Conditioning Strategies: We compare various conditioning strategies in Fig. 7. When the feature and offset values are simply concatenated (*Concatenate*) and the feature is multiplied by offset values (*Multiply*), there is a very slight performance improvement of 0.1%p or performance degradation of −0.8%p compared to the case when only the unconditioned feature is used (*Base*). In order to compare the method of conditioning while increasing the dimension of features to the same as *OADA*, we also experiment with the case, *Multiply&Stack*, where original features, features multiplied by top (left) offsets and features multiplied by bottom (right) offsets are stacked. In this case, there is a significant performance improvement, but it is still far behind our *OADA*, which means that it is much more effective to convert the offset value into a probability vector and outer-product it with the feature for conditioning.

Confidence Thresholds: In (5), the confidence threshold, ρ, is used to generate a mask which activates spatial locations with high objectness and accurate regression values for the target domain. Table 4 shows ablation results for ρ when conditioning is performed only on the top offsets. In CS → Foggy CS, the performance is best when $\rho = 0.3$ and in Sim10k, KITTI → CS when $\rho = 0.5$. We conjecture that it is due to the difference of the domain gap between the source and the target domain in each scenario. Referring to Fig. 5a, in the case of CS → Foggy CS, when the confidence is more than 0.3, the precision is already more than 0.9 and the difference between GT and regression value is less than 5. However, in the case of Sim10k → CS, the confidence must be at least 0.5 to obtain a similar level of precision and difference as shown in Fig. 5b. This shows that ρ must be adjusted with respect to the domain gap.

5 Conclusions

In this paper, we propose an Offset-Aware Domain Adaptive object detection method which conditionally aligns the feature distribution according to the offsets. Our method improves both discriminability and transferability by addressing negative transfer considering the modality of the feature distribution of an anchor-free one-stage detector. On various benchmarks, ours also achieves the state-of-the-art performance by significantly outperforming existing methods.

Acknowledgments. This work was supported by the National Research Foundation of Korea (NRF) grant (2021R1A2C3006659) and IITP grant (NO. 2021-0-01343, Artificial Intelligence Graduate School Program - Seoul National University), both funded by the Korea government (MSIT). It was also supported by SNUAILAB.

References

1. Caron, M., Bojanowski, P., Joulin, A., Douze, M.: Deep clustering for unsupervised learning of visual features. In: Ferrari, V., Hebert, M., Sminchisescu, C., Weiss, Y. (eds.) Computer Vision – ECCV 2018. LNCS, vol. 11218, pp. 139–156. Springer, Cham (2018). https://doi.org/10.1007/978-3-030-01264-9_9
2. Chen, C., Zheng, Z., Ding, X., Huang, Y., Dou, Q.: Harmonizing transferability and discriminability for adapting object detectors (2020)
3. Chen, C., Zheng, Z., Huang, Y., Ding, X., Yu, Y.: I3Net: implicit instance-invariant network for adapting one-stage object detectors. In: Proceedings of the IEEE/CVF Conference on Computer Vision and Pattern Recognition (CVPR) (2021)
4. Chen, X., Wang, S., Long, M., Wang, J.: Transferability vs. discriminability: batch spectral penalization for adversarial domain adaptation. In: Proceedings of the 36th International Conference on Machine Learning (ICML) (2019)
5. Chen, Y., Li, W., Sakaridis, C., Dai, D., Gool, L.V.: Domain adaptive faster R-CNN for object detection in the wild. In: Proceedings of the IEEE/CVF Conference on Computer Vision and Pattern Recognition (CVPR) (2018)
6. Chung, I., Kim, D., Kwak, N.: Maximizing cosine similarity between spatial features for unsupervised domain adaptation in semantic segmentation. In: Proceedings of the Winter Conference on Applications of Computer Vision (WACV) (2022)
7. Chung, I., Yoo, J., Kwak, N.: Exploiting inter-pixel correlations in unsupervised domain adaptation for semantic segmentation (2022)
8. Cordts, M., et al.: The cityscapes dataset for semantic urban scene understanding. In: Proceedings of the IEEE Conference on Computer Vision and Pattern Recognition (2016)
9. Deng, J., Li, W., Chen, Y., Duan, L.: Unbiased mean teacher for cross-domain object detection (2021)
10. Duan, K., Bai, S., Xie, L., Qi, H., Huang, Q., Tian, Q.: CenterNet: keypoint triplets for object detection. In: Proceedings of the IEEE/CVF International Conference on Computer Vision (ICCV) (2019)
11. Ganin, Y., Lempitsky, V.: Unsupervised domain adaptation by backpropagation. In: Proceedings of the 32nd International Conference on Machine Learning (2015)
12. Geiger, A., Lenz, P., Urtasun, R.: Are we ready for autonomous driving? The KITTI vision benchmark suite. In: Proceedings of the IEEE/CVF Conference on Computer Vision and Pattern Recognition (CVPR) (2012)
13. He, Z., Zhang, L.: Multi-adversarial faster-RCNN for unrestricted object detection. In: Proceedings of the IEEE/CVF International Conference on Computer Vision (2019)
14. Hsu, C.-C., Tsai, Y.-H., Lin, Y.-Y., Yang, M.-H.: Every pixel matters: center-aware feature alignment for domain adaptive object detector. In: Vedaldi, A., Bischof, H., Brox, T., Frahm, J.-M. (eds.) ECCV 2020. LNCS, vol. 12354, pp. 733–748. Springer, Cham (2020). https://doi.org/10.1007/978-3-030-58545-7_42

15. Hsu, H.K., et al.: Progressive domain adaptation for object detection. In: Proceedings of the Winter Conference on Applications of Computer Vision (WACV) (2020)
16. Johnson-Roberson, M., Barto, C., Mehta, R., Sridhar, S.N., Rosaen, K., Vasudevan, R.: Driving in the matrix: Can virtual worlds replace human-generated annotations for real world tasks? arXiv preprint arXiv:1610.01983 (2016)
17. Khodabandeh, M., Vahdat, A., Ranjbar, M., Macready, W.G.: A robust learning approach to domain adaptive object detection. In: Proceedings of the IEEE/CVF International Conference on Computer Vision (ICCV) (2019)
18. Kim, S., Choi, J., Kim, T., Kim, C.: Self-training and adversarial background regularization for unsupervised domain adaptive one-stage object detection (2019)
19. Kim, T., Jeong, M., Kim, S., Choi, S., Kim, C.: Diversify and match: a domain adaptive representation learning paradigm for object detection. In: Proceedings of the IEEE/CVF Conference on Computer Vision and Pattern Recognition (CVPR) (2019)
20. Law, H., Deng, J.: CornerNet: detecting objects as paired keypoints. In: Ferrari, V., Hebert, M., Sminchisescu, C., Weiss, Y. (eds.) Computer Vision – ECCV 2018. LNCS, vol. 11218, pp. 765–781. Springer, Cham (2018). https://doi.org/10.1007/978-3-030-01264-9_45
21. Lin, T.Y., Dollár, P., Girshick, R., He, K., Hariharan, B., Belongie, S.: Feature pyramid networks for object detection. In: Proceedings of the IEEE/CVF Conference on Computer Vision and Pattern Recognition (CVPR) (2017)
22. Liu, W., et al.: SSD: single shot multibox detector. In: Leibe, B., Matas, J., Sebe, N., Welling, M. (eds.) ECCV 2016. LNCS, vol. 9905, pp. 21–37. Springer, Cham (2016). https://doi.org/10.1007/978-3-319-46448-0_2
23. Liu, Y.C., et al.: Unbiased teacher for semi-supervised object detection. In: Proceedings of the International Conference on Learning Representations (ICLR) (2021)
24. Long, M., Cao, Z., Wang, J., Jordan, M.I.: Conditional adversarial domain adaptation (2018)
25. Munir, M.A., Khan, M.H., Sarfraz, M.S., Ali, M.: Synergizing between self-training and adversarial learning for domain adaptive object detection. In: Conference on Neural Information Processing Systems (NIPS) (2021)
26. Na, J., Jung, H., Chang, H.J., Hwang, W.: FixBi: bridging domain spaces for unsupervised domain adaptation. In: Proceedings of the IEEE/CVF Conference on Computer Vision and Pattern Recognition (CVPR) (2021)
27. Pan, F., Shin, I., Rameau, F., Lee, S., Kweon, I.S.: Unsupervised intra-domain adaptation for semantic segmentation through self-supervision. In: Proceedings of the IEEE/CVF Conference on Computer Vision and Pattern Recognition (CVPR) (2020)
28. Redmon, J., Divvala, S., Girshick, R., Farhadi, A.: You only look once: unified, real-time object detection. In: Proceedings of the IEEE/CVF Conference on Computer Vision and Pattern Recognition (CVPR) (2016)
29. Ren, S., He, K., Girshick, R., Sun, J.: Faster R-CNN: towards real-time object detection with region proposal networks (2016)
30. Rodriguez, A.L., Mikolajczyk, K.: Domain adaptation for object detection via style consistency. In: Proceedings of the British Machine Vision Conference (BMVC) (2019)
31. RoyChowdhury, A., et al.: Automatic adaptation of object detectors to new domains using self-training. In: Proceedings of the IEEE/CVF Conference on Computer Vision and Pattern Recognition (CVPR) (2019)

32. Saito, K., Ushiku, Y., Harada, T., Saenko, K.: Strong-weak distribution alignment for adaptive object detection. In: Proceedings of the IEEE/CVF Conference on Computer Vision and Pattern Recognition (2019)
33. Sakaridis, C., Dai, D., Van Gool, L.: Semantic foggy scene understanding with synthetic data. Int. J. Comput. Vis. (IJCV) **126**, 973–992 (2018). https://doi.org/10.1007/s11263-018-1072-8
34. Shan, Y., Lu, W.F., Chew, C.M.: Pixel and feature level based domain adaption for object detection in autonomous driving (2018)
35. Simonyan, K., Zisserman, A.: Very deep convolutional networks for large-scale image recognition. In: Proceedings of the International Conference on Learning Representations (ICLR) (2015)
36. Tian, Z., Shen, C., Chen, H., He, T.: FCOS: fully convolutional one-stage object detection. In: Proceedings of the IEEE/CVF international conference on computer vision (2019)
37. VS, V., Gupta, V., Oza, P., Sindagi, V.A., Patel, V.M.: Mega-CDA: memory guided attention for category-aware unsupervised domain adaptive object detection. In: Proceedings of the IEEE/CVF Conference on Computer Vision and Pattern Recognition (2021)
38. Xu, C.D., Zhao, X.R., Jin, X., Wei, X.S.: Exploring categorical regularization for domain adaptive object detection. In: Proceedings of the IEEE/CVF Conference on Computer Vision and Pattern Recognition (CVPR) (2020)
39. Xu, M., Wang, H., Ni, B., Tian, Q., Zhang, W.: Cross-domain detection via graph-induced prototype alignment. In: Proceedings of the IEEE/CVF Conference on Computer Vision and Pattern Recognition (CVPR) (2020)
40. Xu, M., Zhang, J., Ni, B., Li, T., Wang, C., Tian, Q., Zhang, W.: Adversarial domain adaptation with domain mixup. In: Thirty-Fourth AAAI Conference on Artificial Intelligence (AAAI) (2020)
41. Yang, J., Zou, H., Zhou, Y., Zeng, Z., Xie, L.: Mind the discriminability: asymmetric adversarial domain adaptation. In: Vedaldi, A., Bischof, H., Brox, T., Frahm, J.-M. (eds.) ECCV 2020. LNCS, vol. 12369, pp. 589–606. Springer, Cham (2020). https://doi.org/10.1007/978-3-030-58586-0_35
42. Yang, Y., Soatto, S.: FDA: Fourier domain adaptation for semantic segmentation. In: Proceedings of the IEEE/CVF Conference on Computer Vision and Pattern Recognition (CVPR) (2020)
43. Zhao, Z., Guo, Y., Shen, H., Ye, J.: Adaptive object detection with dual multi-label prediction. In: Vedaldi, A., Bischof, H., Brox, T., Frahm, J.-M. (eds.) ECCV 2020. LNCS, vol. 12373, pp. 54–69. Springer, Cham (2020). https://doi.org/10.1007/978-3-030-58604-1_4
44. Zheng, Y., Huang, D., Liu, S., Wang, Y.: Cross-domain object detection through coarse-to-fine feature adaptation. In: Proceedings of the IEEE/CVF Conference on Computer Vision and Pattern Recognition (CVPR) (2020)
45. Zhu, X., Pang, J., Yang, C., Shi, J., Lin, D.: Adapting object detectors via selective cross-domain alignment. In: Proceedings of the IEEE/CVF Conference on Computer Vision and Pattern Recognition (CVPR) (2019)

Visual Prompt Tuning

Menglin Jia[1,2(✉)], Luming Tang[1], Bor-Chun Chen[2], Claire Cardie[1], Serge Belongie[3], Bharath Hariharan[1], and Ser-Nam Lim[2]

[1] Cornell University, Ithaca, USA
mj493@cornell.edu
[2] Meta AI, New York, USA
[3] University of Copenhagen, Copenhagen, Denmark

Abstract. The current *modus operandi* in adapting pre-trained models involves updating all the backbone parameters, *i.e.*, full fine-tuning. This paper introduces Visual Prompt Tuning (VPT) as an efficient and effective alternative to full fine-tuning for large-scale Transformer models in vision. Taking inspiration from recent advances in efficiently tuning large language models, VPT introduces only a small amount (less than 1% of model parameters) of trainable parameters in the input space while keeping the model backbone frozen. Via extensive experiments on a wide variety of downstream recognition tasks, we show that VPT achieves significant performance gains compared to other parameter efficient tuning protocols. Most importantly, VPT even outperforms full fine-tuning in many cases across model capacities and training data scales, while reducing per-task storage cost. Code is available at `github.com/kmnp/vpt`.

1 Introduction

For a variety of recognition applications, the most accurate results are now obtained by adapting large *foundation models* pre-trained on massive curated or raw data, a finding that mirrors developments in natural language processing (NLP) [5].[1] At first glance, this is a success story: one can make rapid progress on multiple recognition problems simply by leveraging the latest and greatest foundation model. In practice, however, *adapting* these large models to downstream tasks presents its own challenges. The most obvious (and often the most effective) adaptation strategy is *full fine-tuning* of the pre-trained model on the task at hand, end-to-end. However, this strategy requires one to store and deploy a separate copy of the backbone parameters for every single task. This is an

[1] As pointed out in [5], all state-of-the-art models in contemporary NLP are now powered by a few Transformer-based models (*e.g.*, BERT [13], T5 [49], BART [34], GPT-3 [6]) This also applies to vision-language field recently, *i.e.*, CLIP [48].

M. Jia and L. Tang—Equal contribution.

Supplementary Information The online version contains supplementary material available at https://doi.org/10.1007/978-3-031-19827-4_41.

S. Avidan et al. (Eds.): ECCV 2022, LNCS 13693, pp. 709–727, 2022.
https://doi.org/10.1007/978-3-031-19827-4_41

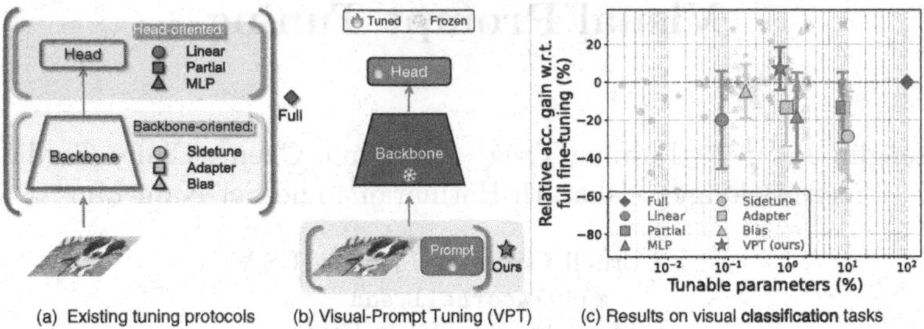

(a) Existing tuning protocols (b) Visual-Prompt Tuning (VPT) (c) Results on visual classification tasks

Fig. 1. Visual-Prompt Tuning (VPT) *vs.* other transfer learning methods. (a) Current transfer learning protocols are grouped based on the tuning scope: Full fine-tuning, Head-oriented, and Backbone-oriented approaches. (b) VPT instead adds extra parameters in the input space. (c) Performance of different methods on a wide range of downstream classification tasks adapting a pre-trained ViT-B backbone, with mean and standard deviation annotated. VPT outperforms Full fine-tuning 20 out of 24 cases while using less than 1% of all model parameters

expensive and often infeasible proposition, especially for modern *Transformer*-based architectures, which are significantly larger than their convolutional neural networks (ConvNet) counterparts, *e.g.*, ViT-Huge [15] (632M parameters) *vs.* ResNet-50 [24] (25M parameters). We therefore ask, **what is the best way to adapt large pre-trained Transformers to downstream tasks in terms of effectiveness and efficiency**?

One straightforward approach is to turn to other strategies that we have perfected for adapting ConvNets to new tasks, as in Fig. 1(a). A popular approach is to fine-tune only a subset of the parameters, such as the classifier head [10,28,42] or the bias terms [7]. Prior research has also looked at adding additional residual blocks (or *adapters*) to the backbone [51,66]. One could implement similar strategies for Transformers. However, in general these strategies *under-perform* full fine-tuning in accuracy.

We explore a different route in this paper. Instead of altering or fine-tuning the pre-trained Transformer itself, we modify the *input* to the Transformer. Drawing inspiration from the recent advances on Prompting in NLP [33,35,37,38], we propose a new simple and efficient method to adapt transformer models for downstream vision tasks (Fig. 1(b)), namely **Visual-Prompt Tuning** (VPT). Our method only introduces a small amount of task-specific learnable parameters into the input space while freezing the entire pre-trained Transformer backbone during downstream training. In practice, these additional parameters are simply prepended into the input sequence of each Transformer layer and learned together with a linear head during fine-tuning.

On 24 downstream recognition tasks spanning different domains using a pre-trained ViT backbone, VPT beats all other transfer learning baselines, even surpassing full fine-tuning in 20 cases, while maintaining the advantage of storing remarkably fewer parameters (less than 1% of backbone parameters) for each individual task (Fig. 1(c)). This result demonstrates the distinctive strength of *visual* prompting: whereas in NLP, prompt tuning is only able to *match* full fine-tuning performance under certain circumstances [33]. VPT is especially effective in the low-data regime, and maintains its advantage across data scales. Finally, VPT is competitive for a range of Transformer scales and designs (ViT-Base/Large/Huge, Swin). Put together, our results suggest that VPT is one of the most effective ways of adapting ever-growing vision backbones.

2 Related Work

Transformer models [56] have gained huge success in NLP [6,13,49]. The triumph of the Transformer architecture also extends to various computer vision tasks, including image classification [15,39], object detection [8,36], semantic and panoptic segmentation [54,60,68], video understanding [17,20,61] and few-shot learning [14], surpassing previous state-of-the-art approaches. Transformers are also being widely used in recent self-supervised pre-training methods [3,10,23]. Given their superior performance and much larger scale compared to ConvNets, how to efficiently adapt Transformers to different vision tasks remains an important open problem. Our proposed VPT provides a promising path forward.

Transfer learning has been extensively studied for vision tasks in the context of ConvNets [71] and many techniques have been introduced including side tuning [66], residual adapter [50], bias tuning [7], *etc.* Relatively little attention has been paid to vision Transformers adaptation and how well these aforementioned methods perform on this brand new type of architecture remains unknown. On the other hand, given the dominance of large-scale pre-trained Transformer-based Language Models (LM) [6,13,49], many approaches [21,22,27] have been proposed to efficiently fine-tune LM for different downstream NLP tasks [58,59]. Among them, we focus on the following two representative methods in our experiments for benchmarking purposes: Adapters [47] and BitFit [4].

Adapters [26] insert extra lightweight modules inside each Transformer layer. One adapter module generally consists of a linear down-projection, followed by a nonlinear activation function, and a linear up-projection, together with a residual connection [46,47]. Instead of inserting new modules, [7] proposed to update the bias term and freeze the rest of backbone parameters when fine-tuning ConvNets. BitFit [3] applied this technique to Transformers and verified its effectiveness on LM tuning. Our study demonstrates that VPT, in general, provides improved performance in adapting Transformer models for vision tasks, relative to the aforementioned two well-established methods in NLP.

Prompting [37] originally refers to prepending language instruction to the input text so that a pre-trained LM can "understand" the task. With manually chosen prompts, GPT-3 shows strong generalization to downstream transfer learning tasks even in the few-shot or zero-shot settings [6]. In addition to the follow-up works on how to construct better prompting texts [29,53], recent works propose to treat the prompts as task-specific continuous vectors and directly optimize them via gradients during fine-tuning, namely Prompt Tuning [33,35,38]. Compared to full fine-tuning, it achieves comparable performance but with 1000× less parameter storage. Although prompting has also

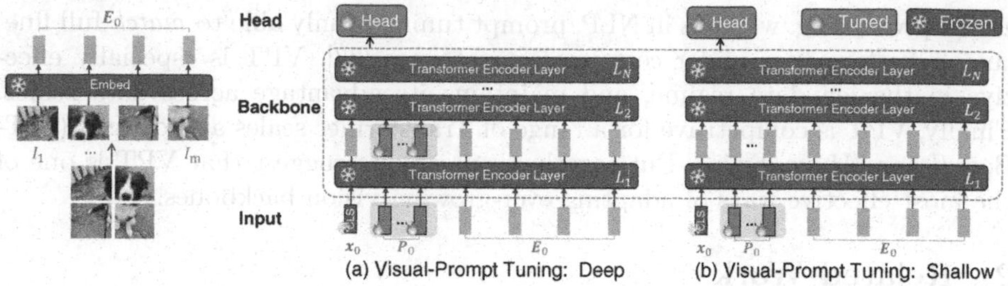

Fig. 2. Overview of our proposed Visual-Prompt Tuning. We explore two variants: (a) prepend a set of learnable parameters to each Transformer encoder layer's input (VPT-DEEP); (b) only insert the prompt parameters to the first layer's input (VPT-SHALLOW). During training on downstream tasks, only the parameters of prompts and linear head are updated while the whole Transformer encoder is frozen.

been applied to vision-language models recently [18,31,48,63,70], prompting is still limited to the input of *text* encoders. Due to the disparity between vision and language modalities, in this paper we ask: can the same method can be applied successfully to image encoders? We are the first work (see related concurrent works [2,11,52,62]) to tackle this question and investigate the generality and feasibility of visual prompting via *extensive* experiments spanning multiple kinds of recognition tasks across multiple domains and backbone architectures.

3 Approach

We propose Visual-Prompt Tuning (VPT) for adapting large pre-trained vision Transformer models. VPT injects a small number of learnable parameters into Transformer's input space and keeps the backbone frozen during the downstream training stage. The overall framework is presented in Fig. 2. We first define the notations in Sec. 3.1, then describe VPT formally in Sec. 3.2.

3.1 Preliminaries

For a plain Vision Transformer (ViT) [15] with N layers, an input image is divided into m fixed-sized patches $\{I_j \in \mathbb{R}^{3\times h\times w} \mid j \in \mathbb{N}, 1 \leq j \leq m\}$. h, w are the height and width of the image patches. Each patch is then first embedded into d-dimensional latent space with positional encoding:

$$\mathbf{e}_0^j = \texttt{Embed}(I_j) \qquad \mathbf{e}_0^j \in \mathbb{R}^d, j = 1, 2, \ldots m \ . \tag{1}$$

We denote the collection of image patch embeddings, $\mathbf{E}_i = \{\mathbf{e}_i^j \in \mathbb{R}^d \mid j \in \mathbb{N}, 1 \leq j \leq m\}$, as inputs to the ($i$+1)-th Transformer layer (L_{i+1}). Together with an extra learnable classification token (`[CLS]`), the whole ViT is formulated as:

$$[\mathbf{x}_i, \mathbf{E}_i] = L_i([\mathbf{x}_{i-1}, \mathbf{E}_{i-1}]) \qquad i = 1, 2, \ldots, N \tag{2}$$

$$\mathbf{y} = \texttt{Head}(\mathbf{x}_N) \ , \tag{3}$$

where $\mathbf{x}_i \in \mathbb{R}^d$ denote [CLS]'s embedding at L_{i+1}'s input space. $[\cdot,\cdot]$ indicates stacking and concatenation on the sequence length dimension, *i.e.*, $[\mathbf{x}_i, \mathbf{E}_i] \in \mathbb{R}^{(1+m)\times d}$. Each layer L_i consists of Multiheaded Self-Attention (MSA) and Feed-Forward Networks (FFN) together with LayerNorm [1] and residual connections [24]. A neural classification head is used to map the final layer's [CLS] embedding, $\mathbf{x}_N$, into a predicted class probability distribution $\mathbf{y}$.[2]

3.2 Visual-Prompt Tuning (VPT)

Given a pre-trained Transformer model, we introduce a set of p continuous embeddings of dimension d, *i.e.*, *prompts*, in the input space after the Embed layer. Only the task-specific prompts are being updated during fine-tuning, while the Transformer backbone is kept frozen. Depending on the number of Transformer layers involved, our approach has two variants, VPT-SHALLOW and VPT-DEEP, as shown in Fig. 2.

VPT-Shallow. Prompts are inserted into the first Transformer layer L_1 only. Each prompt token is a learnable d-dimensional vector. A collection of p prompts is denoted as $\mathbf{P} = \{\mathbf{p}^k \in \mathbb{R}^d \mid k \in \mathbb{N}, 1 \le k \le p\}$, the shallow-prompted ViT is:

$$[\mathbf{x}_1, \mathbf{Z}_1, \mathbf{E}_1] = L_1([\mathbf{x}_0, \mathbf{P}, \mathbf{E}_0]) \tag{4}$$

$$[\mathbf{x}_i, \mathbf{Z}_i, \mathbf{E}_i] = L_i([\mathbf{x}_{i-1}, \mathbf{Z}_{i-1}, \mathbf{E}_{i-1}]) \qquad i = 2, 3, \ldots, N \tag{5}$$

$$\mathbf{y} = \texttt{Head}(\mathbf{x}_N) \ , \tag{6}$$

where $\mathbf{Z}_i \in \mathbb{R}^{p\times d}$ represents the features computed by the i-th Transformer layer, and $[\mathbf{x}_i, \mathbf{Z}_i, \mathbf{E}_i] \in \mathbb{R}^{(1+p+m)\times d}$. The colors • and • indicate learnable and frozen parameters, respectively. Notably for ViT, $\mathbf{x}_N$ is invariant to the location of prompts since they are inserted after positional encoding, *e.g.*, $[\mathbf{x}_0, \mathbf{P}, \mathbf{E}_0]$ and $[\mathbf{x}_0, \mathbf{E}_0, \mathbf{P}]$ are mathematically equivalent. This also applies to VPT-Deep.

VPT-Deep. Prompts are introduced at *every* Transformer layer's input space. For $(i+1)$-th Layer L_{i+1}, we denote the collection of input learnable prompts as $\mathbf{P}_i = \{\mathbf{p}_i^k \in \mathbb{R}^d \mid k \in \mathbb{N}, 1 \le k \le m\}$. The deep-prompted ViT is formulated as:

$$[\mathbf{x}_i, \_\_, \mathbf{E}_i] = L_i([\mathbf{x}_{i-1}, \mathbf{P}_{i-1}, \mathbf{E}_{i-1}]) \qquad i = 1, 2, \ldots, N \tag{7}$$

$$\mathbf{y} = \texttt{Head}(\mathbf{x}_N) \ . \tag{8}$$

Storing Visual Prompts. VPT is beneficial in presence of multiple downstream tasks. We only need to store the learned prompts and classification head

[2] Some Transformer architectures in Vision such as Swin [39] do not use [CLS] and treat global pooled $\mathbf{E}_N$ as input for Head. We follow their designs when adapting VPT to these Transformer variants. See the Appendix for more details.

for each task and re-use the original copy of the pre-trained Transformer model, significantly reducing the storage cost. For instance, given a ViT-Base with 86 million (M) parameters and $d = 768$, 50 shallow prompts and deep prompts yield additional $p \times d = 50 \times 768 = 0.038$M, and $N \times p \times d = 0.46$M parameters, amounting to only 0.04% and 0.53% of all ViT-Base parameters, respectively.

4 Experiments

We evaluate VPT for a wide range of downstream recognition tasks with pre-trained Transformer backbones across scales. We first describe our experimental setup in Sec. 4.1, including the pre-trained backbone and downstream tasks, and a brief introduction of alternative transfer learning methods. Then we demonstrate the effectiveness and practical utility of our method in Sec. 4.2. We also systematically study how different design choices would affect performance (Sec. 4.3), which leads to an improved understanding of our approach.

4.1 Experiment Setup

Pre-trained Backbones. We experiment with two Transformer architectures in vision, Vision Transformers (ViT) [15] and Swin Transformers (Swin [39]). All backbones in this section are pre-trained on ImageNet-21k [12]. We follow the original configurations, *e.g.*, number of image patches divided, existence of [CLS], *etc.* More details are included in the Appendix.

Baselines. We compare both variants of VPT with other commonly used fine-tuning protocols:
(a) FULL: fully update *all* backbone and classification head parameters.
(b) Methods that focus on the classification head. They treat the pre-trained backbone as a feature extractor, whose weights are fixed during tuning:

- LINEAR: only use a linear layer as the classification head.
- PARTIAL-k: fine-tune the last k layers of backbone while freezing the others, as adopted in [23,45,64,67]. It redefines the boundary of backbone and classification head.
- MLP-k: utilize a multilayer perceptron (MLP) with k layers, instead of a linear layer, as classification head.

(c) Methods that update a subset backbone parameters or add new trainable parameters to backbone during fine-tuning:

- SIDETUNE [66]: train a "side" network and linear interpolate between pre-trained features and side-tuned features before being fed into the head.
- BIAS [4,7]: fine-tune only the bias terms of a pre-trained backbone.
- ADAPTER [26,46,47]: insert new MLP modules with residual connection inside Transformer layers.

Table 1. ViT-B/16 pre-trained on supervised ImageNet-21k. For each method and each downstream task group, we report the average test accuracy score and `number of wins in` (·) compared to FULL. "Total params" denotes total parameters needed for all 24 downstream tasks. "Scope" denotes the tuning scope of each method. "Extra params" denotes the presence of additional parameters besides the pre-trained backbone and linear head. Best results among all methods except FULL are **bolded**. VPT outshines the full fine-tuning 20 out of 24 cases with significantly less trainable parameters

	ViT-B/16 (85.8M)	Total params	Scope Input	Scope Backbone	Extra params	FGVC	VTAB-1k Natural	VTAB-1k Specialized	VTAB-1k Structured
	Total # of tasks					5	7	4	8
(a)	FULL	24.02×		✓		88.54	75.88	83.36	47.64
(b)	LINEAR	1.02×				79.32 (0)	68.93 (1)	77.16 (1)	26.84 (0)
	PARTIAL-1	3.00×				82.63 (0)	69.44 (2)	78.53 (0)	34.17 (0)
	MLP-3	1.35×			✓	79.80 (0)	67.80 (2)	72.83 (0)	30.62 (0)
(1)	SIDETUNE	3.69×		✓	✓	78.35 (0)	58.21 (0)	68.12 (0)	23.41 (0)
	BIAS	1.05×		✓		88.41 (3)	73.30 (3)	78.25 (0)	44.09 (2)
	ADAPTER	1.23×		✓	✓	85.66 (2)	70.39 (4)	77.11 (0)	33.43 (0)
(ours)	VPT-SHALLOW	1.04×	✓		✓	84.62 (1)	76.81 (4)	79.66 (0)	46.98 (4)
	VPT-DEEP	1.18×				**89.11 (4)**	**78.48 (6)**	**82.43 (2)**	**54.98 (8)**

Downstream Tasks. We experiment on the following two collections of datasets:

FGVC consists of 5 benchmarked Fine-Grained Visual Classification tasks including CUB-200-2011 [57], NABirds [55], Oxford Flowers [44], Stanford Dogs [32] and Stanford Cars [19]. If a certain dataset only has `train` and `test` sets publicly available, we randomly split the training set into `train` (90%) and `val` (10%), and rely on `val` to select hyperparameters.

VTAB-1k [65] is a collection of 19 diverse visual classification tasks, which are organized into three groups: *Natural* - tasks that contain natural images captured using standard cameras; *Specialized* - tasks that contain images captured via specialized equipment, such as medical and satellite imagery; and *Structured* - tasks that require geometric comprehension like object counting. Each task of VTAB contains 1000 training examples. Following [65], we use the provided 800-200 split of the `train` set to determine hyperparameters and run the final evaluation using the full training data. We report the average accuracy score on `test` set within three runs.

We report the average accuracy on the FGVC datasets, and the average accuracy on each of the three groups in VTAB. The individual results on each task are in the Appendix, as are image examples of these aforementioned tasks.

4.2 Main Results

Table 1 presents the results of fine-tuning a pre-trained ViT-B/16 on averaged across 4 diverse downstream task groups, comparing VPT to the other 7 tuning protocols. We can see that:

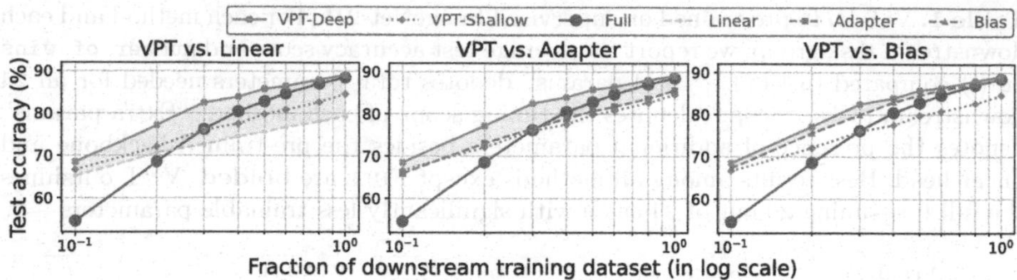

Fig. 3. Performance comparison on different downstream data scales, averaged across 5 FGVC tasks. VPT-DEEP is compared with LINEAR (left), ADAPTER (middle) and BIAS (right). Highlighted region shows the accuracy difference between VPT-DEEP and the compared method. Results of VPT-SHALLOW are FULL presented in all plots for easy reference. The size of markers are proportional to the percentage of tunable parameters in log scale

1. **VPT-Deep outperforms Full (Table 1 (a)) on 3 out of the 4 problem classes** (20 out of 24 tasks), while using significantly fewer total model parameters (1.18× *vs*. 24.02×). Thus, *even if storage is not a concern*, VPT is a promising approach for adapting larger Transformers in vision. Note that this result is in contrast to comparable studies in NLP, where prompt tuning matches, but *does not exceed* full fine-tuning [33].
2. **VPT-Deep outperforms all the other parameter-efficient tuning protocols (Table 1 (b,c)) across all task groups**, indicating that VPT-DEEP is the best fine-tuning strategy in storage-constrained environments.
3. Although sub-optimal than VPT-DEEP, VPT-SHALLOW still offers non-trivial performance gain than head-oriented tuning methods in Table 1(b), indicating that VPT-SHALLOW is a worthwhile choice in deploying multi-task fine-tuned models if the storage constraint is severe.

VPT on Different Downstream Data Size. We look at the impact of training data size on accuracy in the FGVC tasks (VTAB has only 1k training examples). We vary the training data between 10% and 80% and compare all methods. The same pre-trained ViT-B is used for downstream training. Task-averaged results for each method on different training data scales are presented in Fig. 3.

Figure 3 shows that VPT-DEEP outperforms all the other baselines across data scales. Digging deeper, methods that use less trainable parameters, *i.e.*, VPT, LINEAR, ADAPTER, BIAS, dominate over FULL in the low-data regimes. This trend, however, is *reversed* when more training data is available for LINEAR and ADAPTER. In contrast, VPT-DEEP still consistently outperforms FULLacross training data sizes. Although BIAS offers similar advantages, it still marginally under-performs VPT-DEEP across the board (Fig. 3 right).

VPT on Different Backbone Scales. Figure 4 shows VTAB-1k performance under 3 different backbone scales: ViT-**B**ase/**L**arge/**H**uge. VPT-DEEP is significantly better than LINEAR and VPT-SHALLOW across all 3 backbone choices

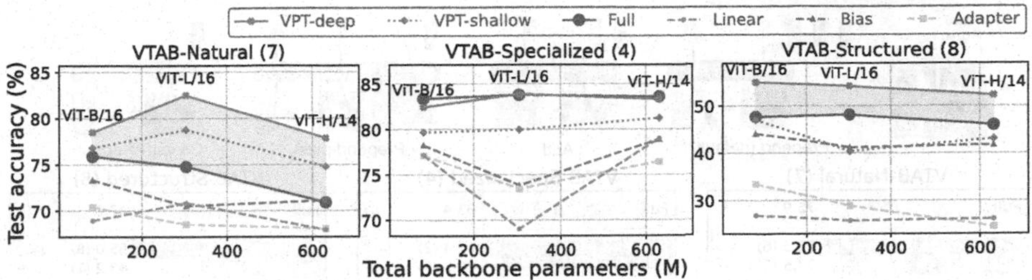

Fig. 4. VPT *vs.* FULL across model scales (ViT-B, ViT-L and ViT-H), for 3 VTAB task groups. Highlighted region shows the accuracy difference between VPT-DEEP and the full fine-tuning (FULL). The size of markers are proportional to the percentage of trainable parameters in log scale

Table 2. Different Transformer architecture: Swin-B pre-trained on supervised ImageNet-21k as backbone. For each method and each downstream task group, we report the average test accuracy score and `number of wins in` (·) compared to FULL. The column "Total params" denotes total parameters needed for all 19 downstream tasks. Best results among all methods except FULL are **bolded**

	Swin-B (86.7M)	Total params	VTAB-1k Natural	Specialized	Structured
	Total # of tasks		7	4	8
(a)	FULL	19.01×	79.10	86.21	59.65
(b)	LINEAR	1.01×	73.52 (5)	80.77 (0)	33.52 (0)
	MLP-3	1.47×	73.56 (5)	75.21 (0)	35.69 (0)
	PARTIAL	3.77×	73.11 (4)	81.70 (0)	34.96 (0)
(1)	BIAS	1.06×	74.19 (2)	80.14 (0)	42.42 (0)
(ours)	VPT-SHALLOW	1.01×	**79.85** **(6)**	82.45 (0)	37.75 (0)
	VPT-DEEP	1.05×	76.78 **(6)**	**84.53** (0)	**53.35** (0)

and 3 subgroups of VTAB-1k. More importantly, the advantages of VPT-DEEP over FULL indeed still hold as the model scale increases, *i.e.*, VPT-DEEP significantly outperforms FULL on *Natural* and *Structured* groups, while offering nearly equivalent performance on *Specialized.*

VPT on Hierarchical Transformers. We extend VPT to Swin [39], which employs MSA within local shifted windows and merges patch embeddings at deeper layers. For simplicity and without loss of generality, we implement VPT in the most straightforward manner: the prompts are attended within the local windows, but are ignored during patch merging stages. The experiments are conducted on the ImageNet-21k supervised pre-trained Swin-Base. VPT continues to outperform other parameter-efficient fine-tuning methods (b, c) for all three subgroups of VTAB Table 2, though in this case FULL yields the highest accuracy scores overall (at a heavy cost in total parameters).

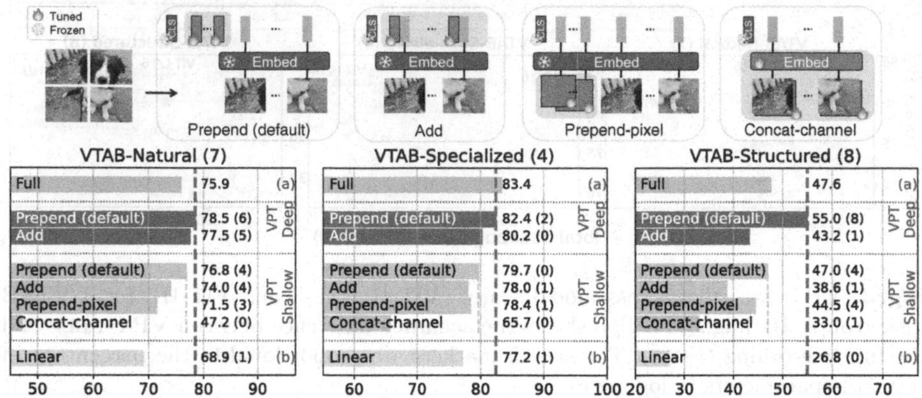

Fig. 5. Ablation on prompt location. We illustrate different location choices at top, and present the results at bottom. For easy comparison, two blue dashed lines represent the performance of the default VPT-DEEP and VPT-SHALLOW respectively (Color figure online)

It is surprising that the advantage of VPT-DEEP over VPT-SHALLOW diminishes for *Natural*: VPT-SHALLOW yields slightly better accuracy scores than full fine-tuning.

4.3 Ablation on Model Design Variants

We ablate different model design choices on the supervised ImageNet-21k pre-trained ViT-Base and evaluate them on VTAB, with same setup in Table 1. See more in the Appendix.

Prompt Location. An important distinction between VPT and other methods is the extra learnable parameters introduced as *inputs* for the Transformer layers. Figure 5 ablates different choices on how and where to insert prompts in the input space, and how they would affect the final performance.

Prepend or Add? Instead of prepending prompts to the sequence of the image patches embeddings $\mathbf{E}_i$ as described in Sect. 3.2, another option is to directly *add* prompts element-wise to those embeddings, keeping the Transformer's input sequence length the same as before. Though this variant is competitive to FULL in some cases (*e.g.*, VTAB-*Natural*), its performance generally falls behind with the default `Prepend` in both deep and shallow settings. More discussion on this phenomenon is in the Appendix.

Latent or pixel space? Instead of inserting the prompts as latent vectors for the first Transformer layer, one could introduce prompts in the *pixel* level before the `Embed` layer in Eq. (1), *i.e.*, `Prepend-pixel` and `Concat-channel`. Figure 5 shows that the adaption performance *decreases* for these two variants. For example, the accuracy score of prepending shallow prompts before the projection

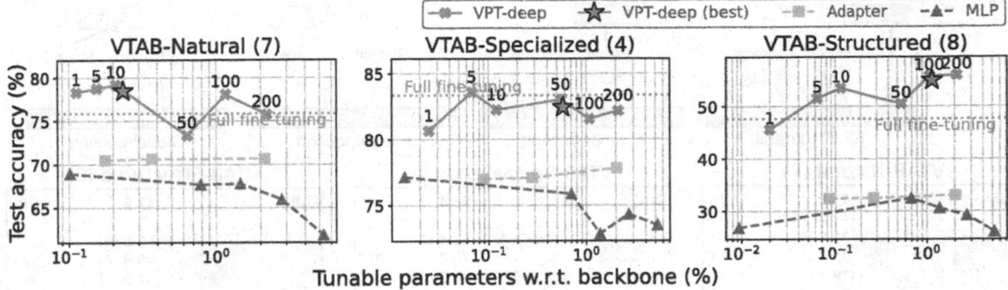

Fig. 6. Ablation on prompt length. We vary the number of prompts for VPT-DEEP and show the averaged results for each VTAB subgroup. The averaged best VPT-DEEP results for each task is also shown for easy reference

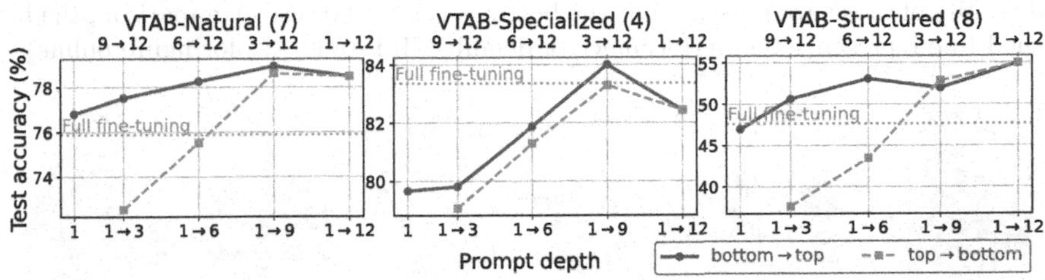

Fig. 7. Ablation on prompt depth. We select the best prompt length for each variant with `val` sets. $i \rightarrow j$ indicates the Transformer layer indices that prompts are inserted into. The 1-st layer refers to the one closest to input. ViT-B has 12 layers in total

layer (`Prepend-pixel`) drops 6.9%, compared to the default prepending in the embedding space (`Prepend`) on VTAB-*Natural*. The performance further deteriorates (even as large as 30 accuracy scores drop on VTAB-*Natural*) if we instead concatenate a new channel to the input image (`Concat-channel`). These observations suggest that it's easier for prompts to learn condensed task-dependent signals in the latent input space of Transformers.

Prompt Length. This is the only additional hyper-parameter needed to tune for VPT compared to full fine-tuning. For easy reference, we also ablate two other baselines on their individual additional hyper-parameters, *i.e.*, number of layers for MLP and reduction rate for ADAPTER. As shown in Fig. 6, the optimal prompt length varies across tasks. Notably, even with as few as only *one* prompt, VPT-DEEP still significantly outperforms the other 2 baselines, and remains competitive or even better compared to full fine-tuning on VTAB-*Structured* and *Natural*.

Prompt Depth. Figure 7 ablates which and how many layers to insert prompts. Each variant reports the best prompt length selected with `val` set. VPT's performance is positively correlated with the prompt depth in general. Yet the accuracy drops if we insert prompts from top to bottom, suggesting that prompts at earlier Transformer layers matter more than those at later layers.

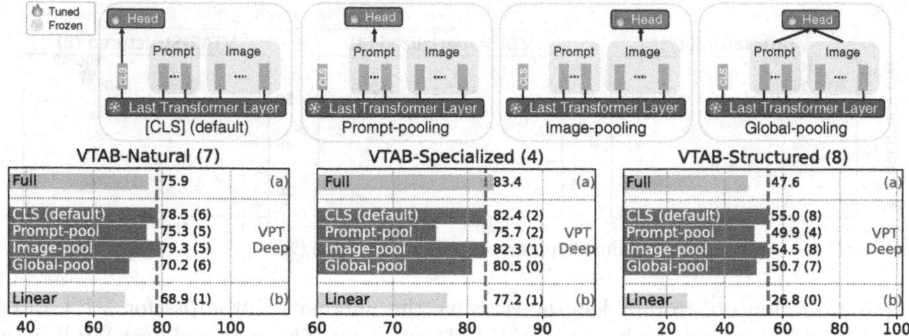

Fig. 8. Ablation on final output. Illustration of different strategies is included at top, and results of those are presented at the bottom section. For easy comparison, the blue dashed line represents the performance of default VPT-DEEP (Color figure online)

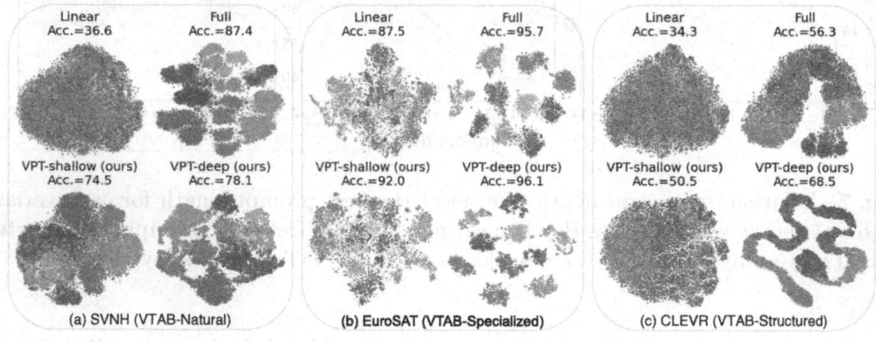

Fig. 9. t-SNE visualizations of the final `[CLS]` embedding $\mathbf{x}_N$ of 3 VTAB tasks from the `test` set, from Table 1. VPT could produce linearly separable features without updating backbone parameters

Final Output. Following the original configuration of ViT, we use the final embedding of `[CLS]`, *i.e.*, $\mathbf{x}_N$, as the classification head input, which is also the default setting in our ViT experiments. As shown in Fig. 8, if we use the average pooling on image patch output embeddings $\mathbf{E}_N$ as final output (`Image-pool`), the results essentially remain the same (*e.g.*, 82.4 *vs.* 82.3 for VTAB-*Specialized*). However, if the pooling involves final prompt outputs $\mathbf{Z}_N$ (`Prompt-pool` and `Global-pool`), the accuracy could drop as large as 8 points.

5 Analysis and Discussion

Visualization. Figure 9 shows t-SNE [41] visualizations of $\mathbf{x_N}$, *i.e.*, embeddings of `[CLS]` after the last Transformer layer and before the classification head, for 3 tasks in VTAB (SVNH [43], EuroSAT [25], Clevr/count [30]), one for each subgroup. All plots show that VPT-DEEP enables linearly separable representations while using less parameters than FULL. We also observe that extra tunable

Table 3. Semantic Segmentation: ADE20k [69] validation results with SETR [68] on ViT-L. The best mIoU scores among all methods but FULL are **bolded**. Results of fully fine-tuning a ResNet-101 [9] are included. SS/MS: single/multi-scale inference

Backbone	ViT-L/16					ResNet-101
Method	FULL [68]	HEAD ONLY	BIAS	VPT-DEEP	VPT+BIAS	FULL [9]
mIoU-SS	48.31	35.12	43.40	42.11	**44.04**	45.47
mIoU-MS	50.07	37.46	45.33	44.06	**45.63**	46.27
Tunable params (M)	318.31	13.18	13.46	13.43	15.79	63.0

Table 4. Different pre-trained objectives: MAE [23] and MoCo v3 [10] with a ViT-B backbone. For each method and each downstream task group, we report the average test accuracy score and `number of wins in` $(\cdot)$ compared to FULL. "Total params" denotes total parameters needed for all 24 downstream tasks. Best results among all methods except FULL are **bolded**

	ViT-B/16 (85.8M)	MAE Total params	MAE VTAB-1k Natural	MAE VTAB-1k Specialized	MAE VTAB-1k Structured	MoCo v3 Total params	MoCo v3 VTAB-1k Natural	MoCo v3 VTAB-1k Specialized	MoCo v3 VTAB-1k Structured
	Total # of tasks		7	4	8		7	4	8
(a)	FULL	19.01×	59.29	79.68	53.82	19.01×	71.95	84.72	51.98
(b)	LINEAR	1.01×	18.87 (0)	53.72 (0)	23.70 (0)	1.01×	67.46 (4)	81.08 (0)	30.33 (0)
	PARTIAL-1	2.58×	**58.44 (5)**	**78.28** (1)	47.64 (**1**)	2.58×	72.31 (5)	**84.58 (2)**	47.89 (1)
(c)	BIAS	1.03×	54.55 (1)	75.68 (1)	**47.70** (0)	1.03×	72.89 (3)	81.14 (0)	**53.43 (4)**
	ADAPTER	1.17×	54.90 (3)	75.19 (1)	38.98 (0)	1.22×	**74.19** (4)	82.66 (1)	47.69 (2)
(ours)	VPT-SHALLOW	1.01×	39.96 (1)	69.65 (0)	27.50 (0)	1.01×	67.34 (3)	82.26 (0)	37.55 (0)
	VPT-DEEP	1.04×	36.02 (0)	60.61 (1)	26.57 (0)	1.01×	70.27 (4)	83.04 (0)	42.38 (0)

parameters for every Transformer layer (VPT-DEEP) improve the performance, compared to VPT-SHALLOW, which only inserts prompts for the first layer's input. Interestingly on Clevr/count (Fig. 9(c)), VPT-DEEP and FULL recover the underlying manifold structure of the task (counting objects in images *vs.* street number or landscape recognition), unlike VPT-SHALLOW and LINEAR.

Apply VPT to More Vision Tasks. We explore the feasibility of VPT beyond visual classification, by evaluating ADE20K [69] semantic segmentation task with a Transformer model, SETR-PUP [68]. It adds a standard ConvNet head to the ViT backbone to perform segmentation. The de-facto approach is still fully fine-tuning the pre-trained backbone together with the ConvNet head (FULL). We include two more protocols for comparison: only update the head layers (HEAD ONLY), update head layers and bias vectors in the backbone (BIAS). In Table 3, we report `val` mIoU results with and without multi-scale inference. Though parameter-efficient protocols could not compete with FULL, VPT is still comparable with BIAS. Notably, VPT offers competitive results to a fully fine-tuned state-of-the-art ConvNet model (DeepLab v3+ [9]), while tuning significantly less parameters (15M *vs.* 64M, respectively).

Apply VPT to More Pre-training Methods. In addition to the backbones pre-trained with labeled data, we experiment with two self-supervised objectives: MAE [23] and MoCo v3 [10]. Table 4 reports the results on VTAB-1k with ViT-

Table 5. Apply VPT to ConvNets: ResNet-50 and ConvNeXt-Base. For each method and each downstream task group, we report the average test accuracy score and **number of wins in** (·) compared to FULL. "Total params" denotes total parameters needed for all 19 downstream tasks. Best results among all methods except FULL are **bolded**

		ConvNeXt-Base (87.6M)				ResNet-50 (23.5M)			
		Total	VTAB-1k			Total	VTAB-1k		
		params	Natural	Specialized	Structured	params	Natural	Specialized	Structured
	Total # of tasks		7	4	8		7	4	8
(a)	FULL	19.01×	77.97	83.71	60.41	19.08×	59.72	76.66	54.08
(b)	LINEAR	1.01×	74.48 (5)	81.50 (0)	34.76 (**1**)	1.08×	63.75 (**6**)	77.60 (**3**)	30.96 (0)
	PARTIAL-1	2.84×	73.76 (4)	81.64 (0)	39.55 (0)	4.69×	64.34 (**6**)	**78.64** (2)	**45.78** (**1**)
	MLP-3	1.47×	73.78 (5)	81.36 (**1**)	35.68 (**1**)	7.87×	61.79 (**6**)	70.77 (1)	33.97 (0)
(c)	BIAS	1.04×	69.07 (2)	72.81 (0)	25.29 (0)	1.10×	63.51 (**6**)	77.22 (2)	33.39 (0)
(ours)	Visual-Prompt Tuning	1.02×	**78.48** (**6**)	**83.00** (**1**)	**44.64** (**1**)	1.09×	**66.25** (**6**)	77.32 (2)	37.52 (0)

B. We observe that both variants of VPT surpass LINEAR, yet the comparisons among other techniques are less conclusive. For MAE, other parameter-efficient methods, *e.g.*, PARTIAL-1, outperform both VPT and LINEAR. In the case of MoCo v3, VPT no longer holds the best performance, though it is still competitive with the others. This suggests that these two self-supervised ViTs are fundamentally different from the supervised ones in previous sections. Exactly why and how these differences arise remain open questions.

Apply VPT to ConvNets. We examine the idea of adding trainable parameters in the input space of ConvNets: padding both height and width by p learnable prompt pixels for the input image. Though this operation seems unconventional, we implement VPT this way given there is no obvious solution to add location-invariant prompts similar to the Transformer counterparts. In fact this approach has been explored before in the adversarial attack literature [16]. The value of p in our experiment is 2 orders of magnitude smaller than previous work: *e.g.*, 5 *vs.* 263. Most importantly, we cast this idea in the lens of transfer learning. See the Appendix for more discussion.

Table 5 presents the results for ConvNeXt-B [40] (pre-trained on ImageNet-21k) and ResNet-50 [24] (pre-trained on ImageNet-1k), respectively. VPT works well in a larger ConvNet backbone, ConvNeXt-B, offering accuracy gains over other sparse tuning protocols (b, c), and outperforming FULL on 8 out of 19 cases. The advantages of VPT, however, diminish with smaller ConvNet (ResNet-50), as there is no clear winner for all 19 VTAB-1k tasks.

6 Conclusion

We present Visual Prompt Tuning, a new parameter-efficient approach to leverage large vision Transformer models for a wide range of downstream tasks. VPT introduces task-specific learnable prompts in the input space, keeping the pre-trained backbone fixed. We show that VPT can surpass other fine-tuning protocols (often including full fine-tuning) while dramatically reducing the storage cost. Our experiments also raise intriguing questions on fine-tuning dynamics of vision Transformers with different pre-training objectives, and how to transfer to broader vision recognition tasks in an efficient manner. We therefore hope our work will inspire future research on how best to tap the potential of large foundation models in vision.

Acknowledgement. Menglin is supported by a Meta AI research grant awarded to Cornell University, Luming and Bharath is supported by NSF IIS-2144117, Serge is supported in part by the Pioneer Centre for AI, DNRF grant number P1. We would like to thank Alexander Rush, Yin Cui for valuable suggestions and discussion.

References

1. Ba, J.L., Kiros, J.R., Hinton, G.E.: Layer normalization. arXiv preprint. arXiv:1607.06450 (2016)
2. Bahng, H., Jahanian, A., Sankaranarayanan, S., Isola, P.: Visual prompting: modifying pixel space to adapt pre-trained models. arXiv preprint. arXiv:2203.17274 (2022)
3. Bao, H., Dong, L., Piao, S., Wei, F.: BEit: BERT pre-training of image transformers. In: ICLR (2022)
4. Ben Zaken, E., Goldberg, Y., Ravfogel, S.: BitFit: simple parameter-efficient fine-tuning for transformer-based masked language-models. In: Proceedings of the 60th Annual Meeting of the Association for Computational Linguistics (Volume 2: Short Papers), pp. 1–9. Association for Computational Linguistics, Dublin, Ireland (2022). https://aclanthology.org/2022.acl-short.1/, https://doi.org/10.18653/v1/2022.acl-short.1
5. Bommasani, R., et al.: On the opportunities and risks of foundation models. arXiv preprint. arXiv:2108.07258 (2021)
6. Brown, T., et al.: Language models are few-shot learners. In: Larochelle, H., Ranzato, M., Hadsell, R., Balcan, M.F., Lin, H. (eds.) NeurIPS, vol. 33, pp. 1877–1901. Curran Associates, Inc. (2020)
7. Cai, H., Gan, C., Zhu, L., Han, S.: Tinytl: reduce memory, not parameters for efficient on-device learning. In: NeurIPS, vol. 33, pp. 1285–11297 (2020)
8. Carion, N., Massa, F., Synnaeve, G., Usunier, N., Kirillov, A., Zagoruyko, S.: End-to-End object detection with transformers. In: Vedaldi, A., Bischof, H., Brox, T., Frahm, J.-M. (eds.) ECCV 2020. LNCS, vol. 12346, pp. 213–229. Springer, Cham (2020). https://doi.org/10.1007/978-3-030-58452-8_13
9. Chen, L.-C., Zhu, Y., Papandreou, G., Schroff, F., Adam, H.: Encoder-decoder with atrous separable convolution for semantic image segmentation. In: Ferrari, V., Hebert, M., Sminchisescu, C., Weiss, Y. (eds.) ECCV 2018. LNCS, vol. 11211, pp. 833–851. Springer, Cham (2018). https://doi.org/10.1007/978-3-030-01234-2_49
10. Chen, X., Xie, S., He, K.: An empirical study of training self-supervised vision transformers. In: ICCV (2021)
11. Conder, J., Jefferson, J., Jawed, K., Nejati, A., Sagar, M., et al.: Efficient transfer learning for visual tasks via continuous optimization of prompts. In: Sclaroff, S., Distante, C., Leo, M., Farinella, G.M., Tombari, F. (eds.) ICIAP 2022. LNCS, vol. 13231. Springer, Cham (2022). https://doi.org/10.1007/978-3-031-06427-2_25
12. Deng, J., et al.: Imagenet: a large-scale hierarchical image database. In: CVPR (2009)

13. Devlin, J., Chang, M.W., Lee, K., Toutanova, K.: BERT: Pre-training of deep bidirectional transformers for language understanding. In: Proceedings of the 2019 Conference of the North American Chapter of the Association for Computational Linguistics: Human Language Technologies, Vol. 1 (Long and Short Papers), pp. 4171–4186. Association for Computational Linguistics, Minneapolis, Minnesota (2019)
14. Doersch, C., Gupta, A., Zisserman, A.: Crosstransformers: spatially-aware few-shot transfer. In: NeurIPS, vol. 33, pp. 21981–21993 (2020)
15. Dosovitskiy, A., et al.: An image is worth 16x16 words: transformers for image recognition at scale. In: ICLR (2020)
16. Elsayed, G.F., Goodfellow, I., Sohl-Dickstein, J.: Adversarial reprogramming of neural networks. In: ICLR (2019)
17. Feichtenhofer, C., Fan, H., Li, Y., He, K.: Masked autoencoders as spatiotemporal learners. arXiv preprint. arXiv:2205.09113 (2022)
18. Ge, C., et al.: Domain adaptation via prompt learning. arXiv preprint. arXiv:2202.06687 (2022)
19. Gebru, T., Krause, J., Wang, Y., Chen, D., Deng, J., Fei-Fei, L.: Fine-grained car detection for visual census estimation. In: AAAI (2017)
20. Girdhar, R., Carreira, J., Doersch, C., Zisserman, A.: Video action transformer network. In: CVPR, pp. 244–253 (2019)
21. Guo, D., Rush, A., Kim, Y.: Parameter-efficient transfer learning with diff pruning. In: Proceedings of the 59th Annual Meeting of the Association for Computational Linguistics and the 11th International Joint Conference on Natural Language Processing (Vol. 1: Long Papers), pp. 4884–4896. Association for Computational Linguistics, Online (2021)
22. He, J., Zhou, C., Ma, X., Berg-Kirkpatrick, T., Neubig, G.: Towards a unified view of parameter-efficient transfer learning. In: ICLR (2022)
23. He, K., Chen, X., Xie, S., Li, Y., Dollár, P., Girshick, R.: Masked autoencoders are scalable vision learners. In: CVPR, pp. 16000–16009 (2022)
24. He, K., Zhang, X., Ren, S., Sun, J.: Deep residual learning for image recognition. In: CVPR, pp. 770–778 (2016)
25. Helber, P., Bischke, B., Dengel, A., Borth, D.: Eurosat: a novel dataset and deep learning benchmark for land use and land cover classification. IEEE Journal of Selected Topics in Applied Earth Observations and Remote Sensing, vol. 12, no. 7, pp. 2217–2226 (2019)
26. Houlsby, N., et al.: Parameter-efficient transfer learning for NLP. In: ICML, pp. 2790–2799. PMLR (2019)
27. Hu, E.J., et al.: Lora: low-rank adaptation of large language models. arXiv preprint. arXiv:2106.09685 (2021)
28. Jia, M., Wu, Z., Reiter, A., Cardie, C., Belongie, S., Lim, S.N.: Exploring visual engagement signals for representation learning. In: ICCV (2021)
29. Jiang, Z., Xu, F.F., Araki, J., Neubig, G.: How can we know what language models know? Trans. Assoc. Comput. Linguist. **8**, 423–438 (2020)
30. Johnson, J., Hariharan, B., van der Maaten, L., Fei-Fei, L., Lawrence Zitnick, C., Girshick, R.: Clevr: a diagnostic dataset for compositional language and elementary visual reasoning. In: CVPR (2017)
31. Ju, C., Han, T., Zheng, K., Zhang, Y., Xie, W.: Prompting visual-language models for efficient video understanding. arXiv preprint. arXiv:2112.04478 (2021)
32. Khosla, A., Jayadevaprakash, N., Yao, B., Fei-Fei, L.: Novel dataset for fine-grained image categorization. In: First Workshop on Fine-Grained Visual Categorization,

IEEE Conference on Computer Vision and Pattern Recognition. Colorado Springs, CO (2011)
33. Lester, B., Al-Rfou, R., Constant, N.: The power of scale for parameter-efficient prompt tuning. In: Proceedings of the 2021 Conference on Empirical Methods in Natural Language Processing, pp. 3045–3059. Association for Computational Linguistics, Online and Punta Cana, Dominican Republic (2021)
34. Lewis, M. et al.: Bart: Denoising sequence-to-sequence pre-training for natural language generation, translation, and comprehension. In: Proceedings of the 58th Annual Meeting of the Association for Computational Linguistics, pp. 7871–7880 (2020)
35. Li, X.L., Liang, P.: Prefix-tuning: Optimizing continuous prompts for generation. In: Proceedings of the 59th Annual Meeting of the Association for Computational Linguistics and the 11th International Joint Conference on Natural Language Processing (Vol. 1: Long Papers), pp. 4582–4597. Association for Computational Linguistics, Online (2021)
36. Li, Y., Xie, S., Chen, X., Dollar, P., He, K., Girshick, R.: Benchmarking detection transfer learning with vision transformers. arXiv preprint. arXiv:2111.11429 (2021)
37. Liu, P., Yuan, W., Fu, J., Jiang, Z., Hayashi, H., Neubig, G.: Pre-train, prompt, and predict: a systematic survey of prompting methods in natural language processing. arXiv preprint. arXiv:2107.13586 (2021)
38. Liu, X., Ji, K., Fu, Y., Du, Z., Yang, Z., Tang, J.: P-tuning v2: prompt tuning can be comparable to fine-tuning universally across scales and tasks. arXiv preprint. arXiv:2110.07602 (2021)
39. Liu, Z., et al.: Swin transformer: hierarchical vision transformer using shifted windows. In: ICCV (2021)
40. Liu, Z., Mao, H., Wu, C.Y., Feichtenhofer, C., Darrell, T., Xie, S.: A convnet for the 2020. In: CVPR (2022)
41. Van der Maaten, L., Hinton, G.: Visualizing data using t-SNE. J. Mach. Learn. Res. **9**(11), 2579–2605 (2008)
42. Mahajan, D., et al.: Exploring the limits of weakly supervised pretraining. In: Ferrari, V., Hebert, M., Sminchisescu, C., Weiss, Y. (eds.) ECCV 2018. LNCS, vol. 11206, pp. 185–201. Springer, Cham (2018). https://doi.org/10.1007/978-3-030-01216-8_12
43. Netzer, Y., Wang, T., Coates, A., Bissacco, A., Wu, B., Ng, A.Y.: Reading digits in natural images with unsupervised feature learning. In: NIPS Workshop on Deep Learning and Unsupervised Feature Learning (2011)
44. Nilsback, M.E., Zisserman, A.: Automated flower classification over a large number of classes. In: 2008 6th Indian Conference on Computer Vision, Graphics & Image Processing, pp. 722–729. IEEE (2008)
45. Noroozi, M., Favaro, P.: Unsupervised learning of visual representations by solving jigsaw puzzles. In: Leibe, B., Matas, J., Sebe, N., Welling, M. (eds.) ECCV 2016. LNCS, vol. 9910, pp. 69–84. Springer, Cham (2016). https://doi.org/10.1007/978-3-319-46466-4_5
46. Pfeiffer, J., Kamath, A., Rücklé, A., Cho, K., Gurevych, I.: Adapterfusion: non-destructive task composition for transfer learning. arXiv preprint. arXiv:2005.00247 (2020)
47. Pfeiffer, J., et al.: Adapterhub: a framework for adapting transformers. In: Proceedings of the 2020 Conference on Empirical Methods in Natural Language Processing (EMNLP 2020): Systems Demonstrations, pp. 46–54. Association for Computational Linguistics, Online (2020)

48. Radford, A., et al.: Learning transferable visual models from natural language supervision. In: International Conference on Machine Learning, pp. 8748–8763. PMLR (2021)
49. Raffel, C., et al.: Exploring the limits of transfer learning with a unified text-to-text transformer. J. Mach. Learn. Res. **21**(140), 1–67 (2020)
50. Rebuffi, S.A., Bilen, H., Vedaldi, A.: Learning multiple visual domains with residual adapters. In: NeurIPS, vol. 30 (2017)
51. Rebuffi, S.A., Bilen, H., Vedaldi, A.: Efficient parametrization of multi-domain deep neural networks. In: CVPR, pp. 8119–8127 (2018)
52. Sandler, M., Zhmoginov, A., Vladymyrov, M., Jackson, A.: Fine-tuning image transformers using learnable memory. In: CVPR, pp. 12155–12164 (2022)
53. Shin, T., Razeghi, Y., Logan IV, R.L., Wallace, E., Singh, S.: Autoprompt: eliciting knowledge from language models with automatically generated prompts. arXiv preprint. arXiv:2010.15980 (2020)
54. Strudel, R., Garcia, R., Laptev, I., Schmid, C.: Segmenter: transformer for semantic segmentation. In: CVPR, pp. 7262–7272 (2021)
55. Van Horn, G., et al.: Building a bird recognition app and large scale dataset with citizen scientists: the fine print in fine-grained dataset collection. In: CVPR, pp. 595–604 (2015)
56. Vaswani, A., et al.: Attention is all you need. In: NeurIPS, vol. 30 (2017)
57. Wah, C., Branson, S., Welinder, P., Perona, P., Belongie, S.: The caltech-ucsd birds-200-2011 dataset. Technical report CNS-TR-2011-001, California Institute of Technology (2011)
58. Wang, A., et al.: Superglue: a stickier benchmark for general-purpose language understanding systems. In: NeurIPS, vol. 32 (2019)
59. Wang, A., Singh, A., Michael, J., Hill, F., Levy, O., Bowman, S.: GLUE: a multi-task benchmark and analysis platform for natural language understanding. In: Proceedings of the 2018 EMNLP Workshop BlackboxNLP: Analyzing and Interpreting Neural Networks for NLP, pp. 353–355. Association for Computational Linguistics, Brussels, Belgium (2018). https://aclanthology.org/W18-5446/, https://doi.org/10.18653/v1/W18-5446
60. Wang, H., Zhu, Y., Adam, H., Yuille, A., Chen, L.C.: Max-deeplab: end-to-end panoptic segmentation with mask transformers. In: CVPR, pp. 5463–5474 (2021)
61. Wang, R., et al.: Bevt: bert pretraining of video transformers. In: CVPR, pp. 14733–14743 (2022)
62. Wang, Z., et al.: Learning to prompt for continual learning. In: CVPR, pp. 139–149 (2022)
63. Yao, Y., Zhang, A., Zhang, Z., Liu, Z., Chua, T.S., Sun, M.: Cpt: colorful prompt tuning for pre-trained vision-language models. arXiv preprint. arXiv:2109.11797 (2021)
64. Yosinski, J., Clune, J., Bengio, Y., Lipson, H.: How transferable are features in deep neural networks? NeurIPS, vol. 27 (2014)
65. Zhai, X., et al.: A large-scale study of representation learning with the visual task adaptation benchmark. arXiv preprint. arXiv:1910.04867 (2019)
66. Zhang, J.O., Sax, A., Zamir, A., Guibas, L., Malik, J.: Side-Tuning: a baseline for network adaptation via additive side networks. In: Vedaldi, A., Bischof, H., Brox, T., Frahm, J.-M. (eds.) ECCV 2020. LNCS, vol. 12348, pp. 698–714. Springer, Cham (2020). https://doi.org/10.1007/978-3-030-58580-8_41
67. Zhang, R., Isola, P., Efros, A.A.: Colorful image colorization. In: Leibe, B., Matas, J., Sebe, N., Welling, M. (eds.) ECCV 2016. LNCS, vol. 9907, pp. 649–666. Springer, Cham (2016). https://doi.org/10.1007/978-3-319-46487-9_40

68. Zheng, S., et al.: Rethinking semantic segmentation from a sequence-to-sequence perspective with transformers. In: CVPR, pp. 6881–6890 (2021)
69. Zhou, B., et al.: Semantic understanding of scenes through the ADE20K dataset. Int. J. Comput. Vis. **127**(3), 302–321 (2018). https://doi.org/10.1007/s11263-018-1140-0
70. Zhou, K., Yang, J., Loy, C.C., Liu, Z.: Learning to prompt for vision-language models. arXiv preprint. arXiv:2109.01134 (2021)
71. Zhuang, F., et al.: A comprehensive survey on transfer learning. Proc. IEEE **109**(1), 43–76 (2020)

Quasi-Balanced Self-Training on Noise-Aware Synthesis of Object Point Clouds for Closing Domain Gap

Yongwei Chen[1,2], Zihao Wang[1], Longkun Zou[1], Ke Chen[1,3(✉)], and Kui Jia[1,3(✉)]

[1] South China University of Technology, Guangzhou, China
{eecyw,eezihaowang,eelongkunzou}@mail.scut.edu.cn,
{chenk,kuijia}@scut.edu.cn

[2] DexForce Co. Ltd., Shenzhen, China

[3] Peng Cheng Laboratory, Shenzhen, China

Abstract. Semantic analyses of object point clouds are largely driven by releasing of benchmarking datasets, including synthetic ones whose instances are sampled from object CAD models. However, learning from synthetic data may not generalize to practical scenarios, where point clouds are typically incomplete, non-uniformly distributed, and noisy. Such a challenge of Simulation-to-Reality (Sim2Real) domain gap could be mitigated via learning algorithms of domain adaptation; however, we argue that generation of synthetic point clouds via more physically realistic rendering is a powerful alternative, as systematic non-uniform noise patterns can be captured. To this end, we propose an integrated scheme consisting of physically realistic synthesis of object point clouds via rendering stereo images via projection of speckle patterns onto CAD models and a novel quasi-balanced self-training designed for more balanced data distribution by sparsity-driven selection of pseudo labeled samples for long tailed classes. Experiment results can verify the effectiveness of our method as well as both of its modules for unsupervised domain adaptation on point cloud classification, achieving the state-of-the-art performance. Source codes and the SpeckleNet synthetic dataset are available at https://github.com/Gorilla-Lab-SCUT/QS3.

1 Introduction

As raw observations of 3D sensors, object point clouds are popularly used for a variety of 3D semantic analysis tasks, including shape classification [15,32,39, 40,51], part segmentation of object surface [28,39,40], estimation of object poses in indoor scenes [8,14,30], and 3D detection in autonomous driving [11,26,55].

Y. Chen and Z. Wang—Equal Contribution.

Supplementary Information The online version contains supplementary material available at https://doi.org/10.1007/978-3-031-19827-4_42.

S. Avidan et al. (Eds.): ECCV 2022, LNCS 13693, pp. 728–745, 2022.
https://doi.org/10.1007/978-3-031-19827-4_42

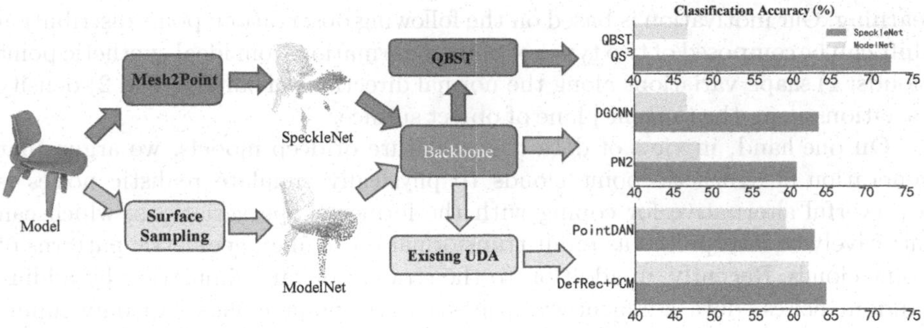

Fig. 1. We propose an integrated scheme of Quasi-balanced Self-training on Speckle-projected Synthesis (QS^3) to cope with shape and density shift between synthetic and real point clouds. Given identical CAD models, we generate a point cloud SpeckleNet dataset simulating realistic noises in stereo imaging and matching; while point clouds in existing ModelNet dataset [53] are sampled from object surface of those models. Moreover, we design a novel quasi-balanced self-training (QBST) strategy to further boost the UDA performance. In comparison with two representative UDA methods (DefRec+PCM [1], PointDAN [41]) and two representative point cloud classification networks (PointNet++ [40], DGCNN [51]), our integrated QS^3 can perform consistently better, when evaluating on real world data – an adapted DepthScanNet dataset.

The current progress along this line has largely been driven by the publicly released synthetic benchmarks (*e.g.*, the ModelNet [53] and the ShapeNet [7]). Object point cloud instances in those datasets are sampled from object CAD models, which are ideally noise-free and uniformly distributed on the complete object surface. Very high accuracies (*e.g.*, 96.2% on classification accuracy of the DGCNN [51] with the ModelNet10 dataset [41]) can be gained by a large number of recent point classifiers [15,31,32,39,40,51]. However, point clouds collected in real-world applications are typically incomplete, non-uniformly distributed and noisy, due to unavoidable sensor noises and interaction with contextual objects. In this way, classification of real-world object point clouds can be difficult, as pointed out in recent works [50,54] (*e.g.*, 78.4% on classification accuracy by the DGCNN with the realistic ScanNet10 [41]).

Classification of object point clouds is made more challenging when considering Sim2Real domain discrepancy of semantic patterns (*i.e.*, training point classifiers on synthetic data and testing on real data), which has been investigated in recent works [1,2,41,57,58]. Such a problem can be formulated into a practical unsupervised domain adaptation (UDA) problem, where supervision signals are only available for source synthetic data. Existing methods either adapt effective UDA algorithms on 2D images to point clouds directly as one application [2] or capture domain-invariant geometry patterns in self-supervised learning style [1,58]. Although these methods have gained remarkable success on alleviating the suffering of Sim2Real domain gap in the style of point distribution shift, our paper attempts to address the challenge in a new perspective – an integrated scheme of physically realistic synthesis of object point clouds for domain-adapted feature learning. Our motivation is based on the following observation: point distribution shift can be composed of two types of point deformation from ideal synthetic point clouds: 1) shape variations along the normal directions of surface; and 2) density variations along the tangent plane of object surface.

On one hand, in view of data-driven nature of deep models, we argue that generation of synthetic point clouds to physically simulate realistic noises is a powerful alternative for coping with the former shape variations, which can intuitively be interpreted as input transformation to align geometric patterns of point clouds. Recently, in addition to the straightforward simulation by adding random noises, data augmentation on synthetic point clouds can only mimic partiality and non-uniformness of real point clouds by deformation on a (sub)set of points, whose output is termed as augmented point clouds in this paper. However, only a few works [17,37,38] focus on simulating realistic non-uniform systematic sensor noises in photorealistic rendering and depth image generation, whose output is utilized to convert point clouds. In view of this, we introduce a Mesh-to-Point (Mesh2Point) pipeline to generate synthetic point clouds based on a photorealistic rendering of a stereo camera. Specifically speaking, by using physically based rendering to simulate the workflow of a real-world depth scanner, our Mesh2Point can approach non-uniform systematic noises of depth sensors affected by projection patterns and the method of depth computation.

On the other hand, physically realistic synthesis of object point clouds via a virtual depth sensor cannot ensure that similar point densities to those of realistic target data, which encourages us to use UDA techniques to further bridge Sim2Real domain gap. Inspired by positive effects of balanced data distribution to suppress negative transfer [21,49,52], we design a novel quasi-balanced self-training (QBST) with updating the sample selector with pseudo labeled target samples only, which can effectively model geometric patterns of real point clouds in target domain. Note that, the class balanced sampling strategy to ease the long-tailed data distribution has been widely adopted in different fields, but we argue that it remains non-trivial in the context of UDA. Its main challenge lies in learning to construct a class-balanced self-training set with diverse samples via selection and pseudo annotation on unlabeled target samples, whose data distribution is unknown. Our QBST method is simple yet effective, owing to 1) sparsity-sensitive weight sampling filtered by a confidence threshold; and 2) self-training only with pseudo labeled target samples, thus resulting in robust performance against long tailed distributions. Experiments on a raw benchmark – DepthScanNet10 of the ScanNet, without any pre-processing on object samples except resizing, can confirm that our integrated scheme of Quasi-balanced Self-training on Speckle-projected Synthesis (QS^3) can significantly improve performance on the challenging Sim2Real UDA task, as shown in Fig. 1.

Main contributions of this paper are as follows.

- We propose a unique QS^3 scheme of integrating a physically realistic synthesis of object point clouds and a UDA point classifier, to jointly cope with shape and density shift between synthetic and real point clouds.
- A new synthetic dataset – the SpeckleNet is constructed via the Mesh2Point generation, which can be readily scaled given sufficient CAD models.

- A novel quasi-balanced self-training method is proposed to inhibit negative transfer, owing to balanced data distribution via sparsity-driven selection of pseudo-labeled target samples.
- Experiment results of the proposed QS^3 can achieve the state-of-the-art performance on the challenging Sim2Real domain adaptation task.

2 Related Work

UDA on Point Cloud Classification – Recently, a few works [1,41,58] propose the problem of UDA on an irregular point-based representation, which inherits the challenge of semantic gap as other UDA problems on images and also has its specific challenge of domain-agnostic feature encoding from local geometries of point clouds. Qin *et al.* [41] explore the first attempt of UDA on point cloud classification by explicitly aligning local features across domains. Achituve *et al.* [1] propose to incorporate domain-insensitive local geometric patterns, in a self-supervised reconstruction from partially distorted point clouds, into a global representation, with a simple yet effective data augmentation of point cloud mixup to inherently alleviate imbalanced data distribution. Zou *et al.* [58] combine self-paced self-training for preserving intrinsic target discrimination and self-supervised learning for domain invariant geometric features, which can capture both global and local geometric patterns invariant across domains. Different from existing methods concerning superior cross-domain generalization via feature alignment, in our paper, we propose an integrated scheme consisting of the synthesis of realistic point clouds and a quasi-balanced self-training, which can be interpreted as alignment in both input and feature space, to reduce negative effects of domain gap.

Generation of Synthetic Data – Different from benchmarking image classifiers on real images, recent progress of geometric deep learning on point clouds has been largely driven by synthetic datasets [7,12,18–20,46,53,56], in view of difficulties in acquiring and annotating real-world 3D data. Recent works [12,27,56] mainly focus on utilizing Physically Based Rendering (PBR) for the synthesis of photorealistic RGB images, while depth images as a byproduct are typically noise-free or simply perturbed by Gaussian noises, which are evidently different from non-uniform systematic noises in practice. Such an observation encourages a number of works to explore physical simulation of 3D sensors to approach realistic noises. Early attempts [4,6,19,35] in a theoretical style fail to cover all kinds of realistic noises. Recently, a number of works including ours prefer the Physically Based Rendering owing to its capability of replicating realistic systematic noises. Specifically, based on PBR, Blensor [17] as well as [13,34,42,48] are able to simulate time-of-flight based 3D sensors while other works [16,24,37,38] mainly focus on simulation of structured light based ones. The most relevant works to ours are DepthSynth [38] and DDS [37], as all of these methods employ speckle pattern projection in PBR for realistic depth acquisition during simulation. However, both of DepthSynth [38] and DDS [37] concern about realistic simulation of depth sensors only, while the goal of our synthesis in the context of UDA is to mitigate domain gap, coupled with a new quasi-balanced self-training in a unified QS^3 scheme.

Self-training – Self-training utilizes pseudo labels generated from predictions of a model learned on labeled data, as supervision signals for unlabeled data, which is widely used in semi-supervised learning [3,25,45] and UDA [43,44]. Sohn *et al.* [45] use pseudo labels predicted from a weakly-augmented input image as supervision of its strongly-augmented counterpart; for semantic segmentation on 2D images, while Zou *et al.* [59] propose a self-paced learning based self-training framework (SPST), which is formulated as a self-paced learning with latent variable objective optimization [23]. However, these methods directly choose pseudo-labels with high prediction confidence, which will result in model bias towards easy classes and thus ruin the transforming performance for the hard classes. To solve this problem, a class-balanced self-training (CBST) scheme is proposed in [59] for semantic segmentation, which shows comparable domain adaptation performance to the best adversarial training based methods. The method in [29] proposes a self-motivated pyramid curriculum domain adaptation method using self-training. More recently, CRST [60] further integrates a variety of confidence regularizers to CBST [59], producing better domain adaption results. Our QBST method shares similar spirit with CBST [59] to neglect negative transfer caused by imbalanced data distribution, but can encourage a more balanced self-training dataset of high confident samples, regardless of source data distribution.

3 Methodology

For unsupervised domain adaptation on point cloud classification, given a labeled source domain $\mathcal{S} = \{\mathcal{P}_i^s\}_{i=1}^{n_s}$ with their corresponding class labels $\{y^s\}_{i=1}^{n_s} \in \mathcal{Y}$ and an unlabeled target domain $\mathcal{T} = \{\mathcal{P}_i^t\}_{i=1}^{n_t}$, where n_s and n_t denote the size of samples in source and target domains respectively and point cloud $\mathcal{P} \in \mathcal{X}$ consists of a set of 3d coordinates covering object surface, the semantic label space $\mathcal{Y}$ is shared between both domains. The objective of UDA on point sets is to learn a domain-adapted mapping function $\Phi : \mathcal{X} \rightarrow \mathcal{Y}$ that classifies any testing sample $\mathcal{P}$ from target domain $\mathcal{T}$ correctly into one of $K = |\mathcal{Y}|$ object categories. In the context of deep learning, the mapping function Φ can be decomposed into a cascade of a feature encoder $\Phi_{\text{fea}} : \mathcal{X} \rightarrow \mathcal{F}$ for any input $\mathcal{P}$ and a classifier $\Phi_{\text{cls}} : \mathcal{F} \rightarrow \mathcal{Y}$ as follows: $\Phi(\mathcal{P}) = \Phi_{\text{cls}}(\boldsymbol{F}) \circ \Phi_{\text{fea}}(\mathcal{P})$, where the feature output $\boldsymbol{F} \in \mathcal{F}$ of $\Phi_{\text{fea}}(\mathcal{P})$ and $\mathcal{F}$ denotes feature space.

Existing UDA classifiers on point sets [1,41,58] concern on reducing domain discrepancy of feature encoding Φ_{fea}, while our paper starts from the origin of Sim2Real domain gap, which is caused by point distribution shift of the shape representations of CAD models. In other words, given an identical CAD model, the procedure of generating synthetic point clouds determines Sim2Real domain gap. As a result, the problem of this paper can be reformulated as the following: given a set of labeled CAD models $\mathcal{M} = \{M_i, y_i\}_{i=1}^{n_s}$ as source domain $\mathcal{S}$ and an unlabeled set of real point clouds $\{\mathcal{P}_i^t\}_{i=1}^{n_t}$ as target domain $\mathcal{T}$, the point cloud of source domain $\{\mathcal{P}_i^s\}$ are generated from each CAD model M. The goal is to learn a feature mapping from point clouds $\mathcal{P} \in \mathcal{X}$ to the labels $y \in \mathcal{Y}$. Most of existing synthetic point clouds are directly sampled from CAD models' surface and optionally with moderate pre-defined noises, while the remaining ones can be obtained via physically realistic simulation of rendering of depth images.

In a geometric perspective, we argue that point distribution shift can be decomposed into 1) shape changes of each point along the normal direction of surface due to all kinds of noises and 2) points' density changes along their tangent plane (*i.e.*, approximately equivalent to the object surface). Such a geometric interpretation of Sim2Real domain gap encourages us to propose an integrated scheme for domain-adapted feature learning – Quasi-balanced Self-training on Speckle-projected Synthesis (QS^3), which consists of physically realistic 3D synthesis of realistically systematic noises causing shape changes and feature encoding with domain-invariant patterns on density variations. Specifically, we introduce 1) a Mesh-to-Point data generation based on photorealistic rendering of stereo images with projection of speckle patterns, which generates a new synthetic point cloud dataset – SpeckleNet (see Sect. 3.1), and 2) a novel self-training method on our SpeckleNet data to mitigate the suffering from unknown data distribution of target domain (see Sect. 3.2).

3.1 Synthesis of Realistic Point Clouds via Physical Simulation

Previous works [4,6,19,35] have shown neither theoretical noisy models nor data augment strategies can cover a diversity of noises appearing in real-world depth sensor scanning, *e.g.*, axial noise, shadow noise and structural noise, which are induced by scene illumination, object material, hardware of sensors and composition of the scanned scene (see the survey [33] for more details). Different from existing UDA methods on point cloud classification only enforcing feature alignment across domains, we argue that the synthesis of object point clouds sharing similar statistical distribution with target data is a powerful alternative, via simulating realistic non-uniform noises, which can be viewed as a special alignment in the input space. Inspired by recent works [17,37,38] utilizing Physical Based Rendering (PBR) for depth sensor simulation, we leverage photorealistic rendering to reproduce realistic noises via a virtual depth sensor. As consuming RGB-D sensors (*e.g.*, Microsoft Kinect V1, Intel RealSense) actively projecting speckle patterns are widely used for indoor scene scanning, we build a virtual active stereo based depth scanner based on PBR. Note that, physical simulation of the depth sensor is not limited to projection of speckle patterns adopted in our paper, which can be replaced by other styles of depth sensors such as time-of-flight depth sensors or structured light based depth sensors via fringe pattern projection.

For replicating a typical active stereo based depth sensor, we organize a stereo camera and a projector, as an active illuminant to project pre-defined speckle pattern, in a simulation platform, *e.g.*, Blender [9] adopted in this paper. The whole pipeline of the Mesh-to-Point synthesis is shown in Fig. 2. In details, we set two identical optical imaging sensors (*i.e.*, left camera O_L and right camera O_R in Fig. 2) for a stereo camera, where the image planes of two cameras are coplanar and translation between two cameras only along the x-axis of the left camera.

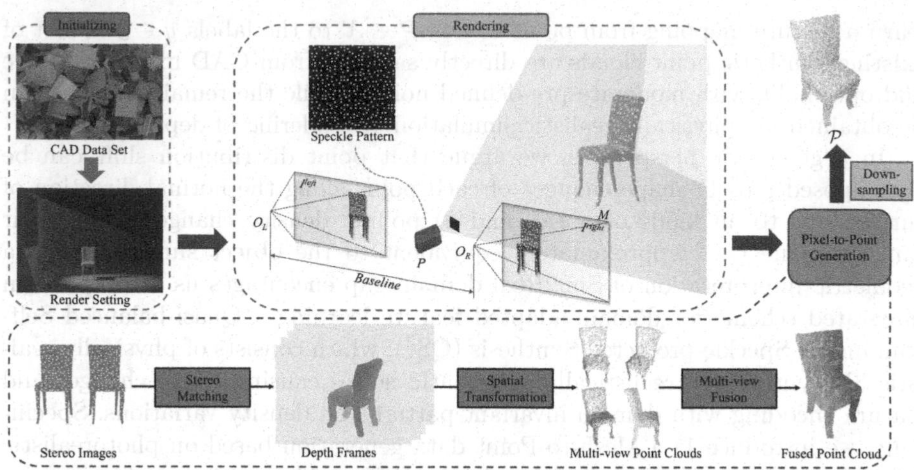

Fig. 2. Pipeline of the Mesh-to-Point method. During data pre-processing, we first scale the mesh-based model $\mathcal{M}$ to a unit-cube with an arbitrary rotation along the z-axis, which are fed into the Rendering module together with the settings of scene illumination and object reflection. In the Rendering module, we virtually organize a stereo camera and a projector. Given the model M, the projector P actively projects a speckle pattern to M, then the stereo camera (O_L, O_R) outputs stereo images I^{left} and I^{right} to the next Pixel-to-Point Generation module. Depth images are converted via stereo matching on stereo images I^{left} and I^{right}, which are further projected into 3D space using intrinsic parameters and extrinsic poses of the camera. Synthetic point clouds under multiple views are fused to produce a dense one carrying richer geometric information, which is then down-sampled to a sparse point set $\mathcal{P}$ as the final output.

The intrinsic and extrinsic parameters of the stereo camera are defined as prior knowledge in our virtual depth sensor. A projector P is positioned in the middle of stereo cameras, actively projecting pre-defined speckle patterns on object surface to provide visual appearance, which thus benefits for discovering pixel correspondence in stereo matching. Given the CAD set $\mathcal{M}$ together with their labels $y \in \mathcal{Y}$ as input, the bidirectional scattering distribution function (BSDF) material [5] is adopted to model the scattered pattern of light by a surface, by following the default setting of BSDF function in [9] to initialize object models' material. We further place one area light source on top of the object model to be rendered, which can thus provide a uniform scene illumination. Note that, our paper concerns on simulating systematic noises due to modules' precision, with an empirically simplified rendering condition.

With the aforementioned settings, pairs of RGB images $\{I_i^{\text{left}}, I_i^{\text{right}}, y_i\}_{i=1}^{n_s}$ for each CAD model M can be generated via photorealistic rendering. For generating a point cloud $\mathcal{P}$, we firstly perform stereo matching [47] on the stereo RGB images I^{left} and I^{right} to gain disparity maps, each element d of which can be used to compute its depth distance as follows [47]: $(f \cdot b)/d$, where f and b are the focal length and the baseline of the camera. We further project depth images into 3D space to generate point clouds using intrinsic parameters and extrinsic poses of the camera. To mimic generation of realistic point clouds from RGB-D videos scanning object in multiple poses in practice, synthetic point clouds under multiple camera poses are fused together to produce dense sets, which are then down-sampled to the final point set $\mathcal{P}$.

SpeckleNet10 – For a comparative evaluation, we use the same 10 categories of the ModelNet object models as PointDAN [41], and a new synthetic dataset, namely SpeckleNet10, can be generated via simulation of the above virtual active stereo based depth sensor. Given the same size of CAD models as the ModelNet10, the only difference between ModelNet10 and our SpeckleNet10 lies in the procedure of the synthesis of object point clouds, *i.e.*, reality of simulated noises. Parameter settings of our virtual depth sensor are empirically selected for typical real-world indoor scenarios instead of fitting a specific type depth sensor, based on the fact that practical noises of depth sensors are mainly affected by the types of projection patterns and the corresponding methods to compute depth, rather than extrinsic settings. In our implementation, given an object model located in the scene, a stereo camera is randomly placed 3 to 5 m away from the model, with an arbitrary elevation angle within $[20^{\circ}, 50^{\circ}]$ in the simulator, where the baseline distance b between two imaging sensors in the stereo camera is set to 10 cm. For multi-view fusing under different viewing angles, one camera pose is randomly selected as an anchor to satisfy the aforementioned constraints, while the remaining as the variants of the anchored pose, lying in $(-10\,\text{cm}, 10\,\text{cm})$ in translation and $(-0.1, 0.1)$ in the Euler rotation. With the setting of rendering, we can obtain stereo images with 1080×1080 resolution and utilize the block matching algorithm provided by the OpenCV to compute disparity from stereo images, which are then converted to depth images with a down-sampling operation to $270 * 270$. As point clouds transformed from depth images remain rather dense, sparse point sets of 2048 points are down-sampled via the Farthest Point Sample (FPS), as the input of UDA on point classification.

3.2 Quasi-Balanced Self-Training

Given the generated synthetic point clouds $X_s = \{\mathcal{P}^s\} \in \mathcal{S}$ with their corresponding class labels $Y_s = \{y^s\} \in \mathcal{Y}$ and real point clouds $X_t = \{\mathcal{P}^t\} \in \mathcal{T}$ respectively, the remaining part of domain-adapted feature learning shares the same setting as existing 3D UDA methods. In this section, we propose a simple yet effective quasi-balanced self-training (QBST) method to dynamically select target instances for data balanceness when assigning pseudo labels in self-training. An overview of our QBST is shown in Fig. 3, which consists of three steps below, with iteratively updating by the latter two.

(a) In the *warm-up*, a supervised classification uses labeled source data (i.e., $\{X_s, Y_s\}$) to train a model $\boldsymbol{\Phi_o}$ as an initialized pseudo-label generator $\boldsymbol{G_o}$.
(b) In the *target instance selection with pseudo labels*, $\boldsymbol{G}$ is used to obtain class prediction of unlabeled target data, and confident prediction will be assigned as pseudo labels for selected target samples.

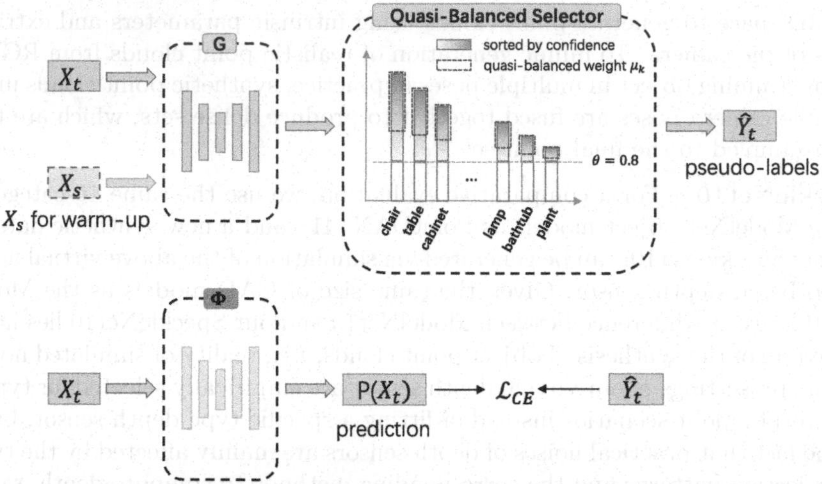

Fig. 3. Overview of our proposed *Quasi-Balanced Self-Training.* **Top:** illustration of a data sparsity-driven strategy for pseudo label generation – a quasi-balanced selector. During self-training, labeled source data is only used for training a model as an initialized pseudo-label generator and does not participate in self-training. In the legend, the blue box indicates predicated confidence (the darker, the higher); the red dashed box denotes selection range by the quasi-balanced weight μ_k, *i.e.*, selecting a μ_k proportion of samples from the target samples classified as class k with predicted confidence greater than θ (*e.g.*, $\theta = 0.8$) as pseudo-label samples. **Bottom:** Training with selected pseudo-labels, where $\mathcal{L}_{CE}$ refers to the cross-entropy loss function. (Color figure online)

(c) In the *self-training*, instead of fine-tuning the Φ_o as [58], an initial model Φ_{init} is trained from scratch by selected target point clouds with pseudo-labels.

Pseudo-label Generation – The generic pseudo-label generation strategy can be simplified to the following form when the model parameter w is fixed:

$$\min_{\widehat{Y}_t} \mathcal{L}_{CE}(w, \widehat{Y}_t) = -\frac{1}{|X_t|} \sum_{\mathcal{P}_t \in X_t} \sum_{k=1}^{K} \hat{y}_t^{(k)} \log \frac{p(k|\mathcal{P}_t, w)}{\theta}$$

$$\text{s.t.} \quad \hat{y}_t \in \{[\text{onehot}]^K\} \cup 0, \forall \hat{y}_t \in \widehat{Y}_t$$

where θ indicates the confidence threshold, and $\hat{y}_t = [\hat{y}_t^{(1)}, \hat{y}_t^{(2)}, ..., \hat{y}_t^{(K)}]$ is required to be a one-hot vector or all-zero vector. Therefore, $\hat{y}_t^{(K)}$ can be solved:

$$\hat{y}_t^k = \begin{cases} 1, & \text{if } k = \arg\max_k p(k|\mathcal{P}_t, w) \text{ and } p(k|\mathcal{P}_t, w) > \theta \\ 0, & \text{otherwise.} \end{cases}$$

Inspired by self-paced self-training (SPST) [59], we adopt a threshold θ that gradually increases with self-training iterations evolve (*i.e.*, each iteration increases by a constant ϵ, with more details in Alg. 1 of supplementary material). Target instances to be assigned with pseudo-labels are selected by following a class-balanced rule [59]: the more sparsity of data in a class k is, the higher weight. To this end, we generate target data distribution from the pseudo-labeled samples selected according to data sparsity. In other words, unlabeled target samples that are predicted as class k are sorted by confidence and selected in descending order of confidence according to the weight of $\mu_k = (1 - \frac{L_k}{L})$, where L_k denotes the number of unlabeled target samples classified into class k, and L is the total number of all unlabeled target samples whose predicted confidence greater than θ. In contrast, CBST [59] selects samples with the same proportion for all object classes, which cannot avoid label noises caused by low-confident mis-classified samples of long-tailed classes. To avoid negative effects of imbalanced data distribution of source data, only selected target samples with pseudo labels are self-trained in our QBST, which is again different from the CBST.

4 Experiments

4.1 Data and Settings

Benchmarking Data in the Sim2Real UDA Setting – We construct a new and challenging benchmark for evaluating point cloud classification on Sim2Real domain adaptation, where a synthetic point cloud data is generated as source domain while a real-world one is set as target domain. Inspired by PointDA-10 [41], a pioneering Sim2Real benchmark, we directly use the CAD models of ModelNet10 from the PointDA-10 to generate synthetic data as source domain. Different from point clouds uniformly sampled from the CAD models of object classes as the ModelNet10, realistically-simulated point clouds generated by our Mesh-to-Point are collected as the SpeckleNet presented in Sec. 3.1. The PointDA-10 builds a real ScanNet10 as target domain via extracting the same 10 classes instances from ScanNet [10], where point clouds are directly generated from mesh vertices of the reconstructed surface. As meshing in shape reconstruction can alleviate realistic sensor noises, the point clouds in original ScanNet10 cannot reflect the true challenge of severe noises in practical classification of object point clouds. Moreover, meshing of partial and noisy point clouds is challenging and demands extra processing, which is typically unsuitable for real-time perception. To this end, we follow the setting in the PointDA-10 and choose the same scenes from the ScanNet to generate a more challenging real-world dataset – DepthScanNet10, directly from the raw outputs of depth sensors. Specifically, to gain the point cloud of a single object instance, 2D instance segmentation is first applied to crop a depth image patch of the instance from the whole frame, which can then be converted to a point cloud. Multi-view fusion is employed to gather point clouds from several different viewpoints, followed by down-sampling to produce a fixed size of 2048 points. Note that, only those more than 1000 points will be kept for multi-view fusion whose size of viewpoints is set to 10.

Settings – On the Sim2Real benchmarking data, our proposed pipeline is compared with recent methods. ModelNet10 (**M**) and SpeckleNet10 (**S**) are employed

Table 1. Effects of simulation of realistic noises with real data DepthScanNet (**D**) on classification accuracy (%).

Method	M→D	S→D
Pointnet++ [40]	48.4 ± 1.3	**60.9 ± 0.8**
DGCNN [51]	46.7 ± 1.4	**64.0 ± 1.0**
RSCNN [32]	49.7 ± 1.1	**53.9 ± 0.2**
SimpleView [15]	54.6 ± 0.7	**62.3 ± 1.3**

as source domain, while we choose testing split of DepthScanNet10 (**D**)) as target domain, following the setting of the PointDA-10. Specifically, all object point clouds are normalized within a unit ball and down-sampled to 1024 points using the FPS algorithm. Random rotation along the z-axis and jittering as [39] is employed for data augmentation during training. Moreover, the same data split of the ScanNet10 is used in the DepthScanNet10.

Comparative Methods – We evaluate several UDA classification methods, including Point Domain Adaptation Network (**PointDAN**) [41], Deformation Reconstruction Network with Point Cloud Mixup (**DefRec+PCM**) [1] and Geometry-Aware Self-Training (**GAST**) [58], by following the settings of the best performance in their paper, for simulation-to-reality domain adaptation.

Implementation Details – All the networks are implemented based on PyTorch [36]. Beyond the SpeckleNet10 generated by our Mesh2Point simulator, we utilize DGCNN [51] with Point Cloud Mixup (PCM) [1] as our network baseline, followed by our proposed QBST as the self-training strategy to perform feature alignment on the SpeckleNet10. To implement recent UDA methods on point classification, except for PointDAN [41] using official released source codes, other UDA methods are implemented based on DGCNN [51] as the backbone network. We choose the ADAM [22] as our optimizer with an initial learning rate of 0.001 and weight decay of 0.00005 and an epoch-wise cosine annealing learning rate scheduler for the UDA methods as [58]. With the cross-entropy loss, we train all the methods for 200 epochs with a batch size 16 on an NVIDIA GTX-1080 Ti GPU. In each iteration of self-training, we adopt the ADAM with learning rate 1×10^{-3} and batch size 32 for 10 epochs. The initial threshold θ_0 is set to 0.8, and the constant ϵ is set to 5×10^{-3}. The mean accuracy and standard error of the mean (SEM) is reported on three trials of random seeds.

4.2 Results

Effects of the Synthesis of Realistic Noises with Ordinary Point Cloud Classifiers – We report comparative evaluation on real data **D** of ordinary point cloud classification with four popular classifiers in columns of M→D and S→D of Table 1. Following recent SimpleView [15], the following four classification networks, *i.e.*, PointNet++ [40], DGCNN [51], RSCNN [32] and SimpleView [15], are evaluated and compared. It is evident that all the methods training

Table 2. Comparative evaluation in classification accuracy (%) averaged over 3 seeds (± SEM) on the Sim2Real data with recent UDA methods.

Method	M→D	S→D
Supervised	90.4 ± 0.4	90.4 ± 0.4
DGCNN [51] (w/o Adapt)	46.7 ± 1.4	64.0 ± 1.0
PointDAN [41]	58.9 ± 0.9	62.9 ± 1.6
DefRec [1]	57.8 ± 1.1	60.8 ± 0.6
DefRec+PCM [1]	62.1 ± 0.8	64.4 ± 0.7
GAST w/o SPST [58]	62.4 ± 1.1	61.8 ± 1.0
GAST [58]	64.8 ± 1.4	64.4 ± 0.2
QBST (ours)	**66.4** ± 1.1	–
QS^3 (ours)	–	**72.4** ± 0.8

on synthetic point clouds (from the **S**) of the Mesh2Point method can perform better than those on simply-augmented synthetic data (from the **M**), *i.e.*, results in the column of **S→D** are significantly superior to those in the column of **M→D** in Table 1, which demonstrate our motivation of using physical simulation to alleviate Sim2Real domain gap, owing to capturing realistic noises underlying in real data.

Rationale of Balanced Data Distribution for UDA Point Cloud Classification – In Table 2, a number of recent UDA methods are evaluated and compared on simulation-to-reality tasks. The **Supervised** method trains DGCNN [51] backbone with labeled target data only, and the **DGCNN w/o Adapt** method trains the identical net with only labeled source samples, treated as a reference of the upper and lower performance bound respectively. On one hand, models training on the physically simulated instances (from the **S**) cannot be consistently superior to those on augmented ones (from the **M**). Specifically, superior performance of DefRec, GAST and its degenerated GAST w/o SPST with the **M** to the proposed **S** when evaluation on real data **D**, where domain gap of **M→D** is verified to be larger than those of **S→D** as shown in Table 1. Such a phenomena can be explained by that these self-supervised methods (*i.e.*, DefRec and GAST) rely on capturing domain-invariant geometric patterns from local regions, where synthetic data in the **S** are generated from partially visible surfaces and thus suffers more than those complete ones in the **M** to learn cross-domain local geometric patterns. DefRec+PCM can significantly improve performance on **S→D** over DefRec, which can be credited to the extra PCM data augmentation to enrich data diversity and inherently balance data distribution by increasing samples shared with long-tailed classes. On the other hand, it is observed that all the UDA methods on **M→D** can outperform the backbone DGCNN, while very marginal improvement or even negative transfer performance of most of methods can be gained on the remaining task. With the PCM and SPST modules respectively, negative transfer on DefRec and GAST can be alleviated, which can confirm their effectiveness. As [58], the SPST cannot

Table 3. Effects of our QBST with classification accuracy (%) averaged over 3 seeds (± SEM) on the sim2real data.

Method	M→D	S→D
Supervised	90.4 ± 0.4	90.4 ± 0.4
DGCNN [51] (w/o Adapt)	46.7 ± 1.4	64.0 ± 1.0
DGCNN+CBST	41.8 ± 2.0	58.6 ± 1.7
DGCNN+SPST	45.2 ± 0.5	63.3 ± 0.5
DGCNN+QBST	45.6 ± 0.4	63.8 ± 0.1
DGCNN+PCM	61.2 ± 0.6	68.5 ± 1.1
DGCNN+PCM+CBST	62.5 ± 3.0	62.9 ± 0.9
DGCNN+PCM+SPST	65.4 ± 0.6	71.9 ± 0.7
DGCNN+PCM+QBST	**66.4 ± 1.1**	**72.4 ± 0.8**

guarantee the correctness of pseudo labels assigned to target instances but under the assumption that they are mostly correct, which are largely affected by performance of instance selector. Inspired by the success of PCM, it is encouraged to propose a self-training method to achieve balanced data distribution.

Effects of Quasi-Balanced Self-Training – With the DGCNN as the identical backbone, we compare our QBST with its direct competitors – SPST and CBST as well as PCM, whose results are reported in Table 3. As aforementioned, the PCM and SPST can effectively inhibit negative transfer, it is observed that both SPST and CBST can work better together with the PCM owing to improvement on selection of confident target samples gained by the PCM. In light of this, based on the backbone DGCNN and the PCM, superior performance of the proposed QBST can confirm its effectiveness by consistently beating its direct competitor SPST and CBST as well as the state-of-the-art DefRec+PCM and GAST (refer to Table 2) for both Sim2Real tasks. Superior performance of our QBST to SPST and CBST can be credited to using data sparsity-sensitive weight sampling on high-confident target samples, while comparative methods (i.e., SPST and CBST) cannot alleviate negative effects from mis-classified samples of long-tailed classes with low confidence.

Comparison with the State-of-the-Art Methods – Our QS^3 scheme and the degenerated QBST are compared with recent UDA methods, whose results are shown in Table 2. It is evident that classification accuracy of our QS^3 scheme can reach 72.4%, a large marginal improvement over other UDA methods, when testing on the DepthScanNet. Using our QBST on the ideal synthetic point clouds from the ModelNet (*i.e.*, M→D), superior performance to the state-of-the-art UDA methods can still be achieved, which can again verify the effectiveness of the proposed QBST.

Ablation Studies about Simulation of Realistic Data with Ordinary Point Cloud Classifiers – Motivation of our physically rendering is to simulate non-neglected systematic noises, which is considered as the key factor to

Table 4. Ablation studies about simulation of realistic noises of stereo rendering and matching with real dataset **D** on classification accuracy (%).

Method	S_c→D	B→D	M_d→D	S→D
Pointnet++ [40]	50.2 ± 2.0	52.4 ± 1.3	57.9 ± 1.2	**60.9 ± 0.8**
DGCNN [51]	53.2 ± 1.6	56.6 ± 2.1	50.4 ± 1.0	**64.0 ± 1.0**
RSCNN [32]	48.8 ± 0.1	51.7 ± 2.0	**56.5 ± 1.0**	53.9 ± 0.2
SimpleView [15]	56.2 ± 1.2	**65.1 ± 0.2**	57.4 ± 0.7	62.3 ± 1.3

reduction of shape shift in Sim2Real domain gap. To verify it, we generate a clean depth image, whose pixels' depth value are directly measured according to distance between the corresponding point on object surface and the camera along its optical axis, to avoid depth computation via stereo imaging and matching. Synthetic data from these ideally clean depth frames are termed as a SpeckleNet10-Clean ($\mathbf{S}_c$). Some works [9,37,38] on sensor simulation can be adopted in our scheme to replace the Mesh2Point method. Therefore, we compare one of the representative simulators – Blensor [17], an open-source depth sensor simulator based on Blender [9], which output a set of point clouds (namely Blensor10, **B**) using the same setting as our Specklenet10. Moreover, we also provide a better baseline for the ModelNet10 where we perform random region dropout on point clouds to simulate missing parts typically encountered in real data as further data augmentation. Such an augmented dataset is named as ModelNet10-Dropout ($\mathbf{M}_d$). Results in Table 4 can demonstrate superior performance of most of models training on the SpeckleNet10 (**S**), which can be credited to simulation of realistic noises. Good performance of the RSCNN on M_d →D and the SimpleView on B→D can verify our claim that density shift should not be omitted beyond systemic noises of the depth sensor.

5 Conclusion

This paper investigates an effective pipeline to mitigate Sim2Real domain gap in a novel perspective of physically realistic synthesis of object point clouds. The synthesis of realistic data can inherently be robust against imbalanced data distribution, as we can observe negative transfer of existing UDA methods in our experiments, which encourages us to propose the quasi-balanced self-training for further suppression. Experiment results can verify the effectiveness of the unified QS^3 scheme as well as both physical simulation of realistic noises and also our quasi-balanced self-training, achieving the state-of-the-art performance on the challenging Sim2Real domain adaptation tasks. Moreover, the proposed Mesh2Point method is not differentiable and parameter settings of the synthesis pipeline are empirically selected, which could cause sub-optimal generation for specific tasks. Inspired by DDS [37], incorporating differentiable physics-based rendering into our QS^3 scheme in an end-to-end learning manner can be a promising direction in future.

Acknowledgements. This work is supported in part by the National Natural Science Foundation of China (Grant No.: 61902131), the Program for Guangdong Introducing Innovative and Enterpreneurial Teams (Grant No.: 2017ZT07X183), the Guangdong Provincial Key Laboratory of Human Digital Twin (Grant No.: 2022B1212010004).

References

1. Achituve, I., Maron, H., Chechik, G.: Self-supervised learning for domain adaptation on point clouds. In: Proceedings of the IEEE/CVF Winter Conference on Applications of Computer Vision (WACV), pp. 123–133 (2021)
2. Ajakan, H., Germain, P., Larochelle, H., Laviolette, F., Marchand, M.: Domain-adversarial neural networks. Stat **1050**, 15 (2014)
3. Arazo, E., Ortego, D., Albert, P., O'Connor, N.E., McGuinness, K.: Pseudo-labeling and confirmation bias in deep semi-supervised learning. In: International Joint Conference on Neural Networks (IJCNN), pp. 1–8. IEEE (2020)
4. Barron, J.T., Malik, J.: Intrinsic scene properties from a single RGB-D image. In: Proceedings of the IEEE/CVF Conference on Computer Vision and Pattern Recognition (CVPR), pp. 17–24 (2013)
5. Bartell, F.O., Dereniak, E.L., Wolfe, W.L.: The theory and measurement of bidirectional reflectance distribution function (BRDF) and bidirectional transmittance distribution function (BTDF). In: Radiation Scattering in Optical Systems (RSOS), vol. 257, pp. 154–160. SPIE (1981)
6. Bohg, J., Romero, J., Herzog, A., Schaal, S.: Robot arm pose estimation through pixel-wise part classification. In: IEEE International Conference on Robotics and Automation (ICRA), pp. 3143–3150. IEEE (2014)
7. Chang, A.X., et al.: ShapeNet: an information-rich 3d model repository. arXiv preprint arXiv:1512.03012 (2015)
8. Chen, W., Jia, X., Chang, H.J., Duan, J., Shen, L., Leonardis, A.: FS-Net: fast shape-based network for category-level 6d object pose estimation with decoupled rotation mechanism. In: Proceedings of the IEEE/CVF Conference on Computer Vision and Pattern Recognition (CVPR), pp. 1581–1590 (2021)
9. Blender Online Community: Blender - a 3D modelling and rendering package. Blender Foundation, Stichting Blender Foundation, Amsterdam (2018). www.blender.org
10. Dai, A., Chang, A.X., Savva, M., Halber, M., Funkhouser, T., Nießner, M.: ScanNet: richly-annotated 3d reconstructions of indoor scenes. In: Proceedings of the IEEE/CVF Conference on Computer Vision and Pattern Recognition (CVPR), pp. 5828–5839 (2017)
11. Deng, S., Liang, Z., Sun, L., Jia, K.: VISTA: boosting 3d object detection via dual cross-view spatial attention. In: Proceedings of the IEEE/CVF Conference on Computer Vision and Pattern Recognition (CVPR), pp. 8448–8457 (2022)
12. Denninger, M., et al.: BlenderProc: reducing the reality gap with photorealistic rendering. In: Robotics: Science and Systems (RSS) (2020)
13. Fang, J., et al.: Augmented lidar simulator for autonomous driving. IEEE Robot. Autom. Lett. (RA-L) **5**(2), 1931–1938 (2020)
14. Gao, G., Lauri, M., Wang, Y., Hu, X., Zhang, J., Frintrop, S.: 6d object pose regression via supervised learning on point clouds. In: IEEE International Conference on Robotics and Automation (ICRA), pp. 3643–3649 (2020)

15. Goyal, A., Law, H., Liu, B., Newell, A., Deng, J.: Revisiting point cloud shape classification with a simple and effective baseline. In: International Conference on Machine Learning (ICML), pp. 3809–3820. PMLR (2021)
16. Grans, S., Tingelstad, L.: Blazer: laser scanning simulation using physically based rendering. arXiv preprint arXiv:2104.05430 (2021)
17. Gschwandtner, M., Kwitt, R., Uhl, A., Pree, W.: BlenSor: blender sensor simulation toolbox. In: Bebis, G., et al. (eds.) Blensor: Blender sensor simulation toolbox. LNCS, vol. 6939, pp. 199–208. Springer, Heidelberg (2011). https://doi.org/10.1007/978-3-642-24031-7_20
18. Handa, A., Patraucean, V., Badrinarayanan, V., Stent, S., Cipolla, R.: Understanding real world indoor scenes with synthetic data. In: Proceedings of the IEEE/CVF Conference on Computer Vision and Pattern Recognition (CVPR), pp. 4077–4085 (2016)
19. Handa, A., Whelan, T., McDonald, J., Davison, A.J.: A benchmark for RGB-D visual odometry, 3d reconstruction and slam. In: IEEE International Conference on Robotics and Automation (ICRA), pp. 1524–1531. IEEE (2014)
20. Heindl, C., Brunner, L., Zambal, S., Scharinger, J.: BlendTorch: a real-time, adaptive domain randomization library. In: Del Bimbo, A., et al. (eds.) ICPR 2021. LNCS, vol. 12664, pp. 538–551. Springer, Cham (2021). https://doi.org/10.1007/978-3-030-68799-1_39
21. Kim, J., Hur, Y., Park, S., Yang, E., Hwang, S.J., Shin, J.: Distribution aligning refinery of pseudo-label for imbalanced semi-supervised learning. In: Advances in Neural Information Processing Systems (NeurIPS), vol. 33 (2020)
22. Kingma, D.P., Ba, J.: Adam: a method for stochastic optimization. In: International Conference on Learning Representations (ICLR) (2015)
23. Kumar, M.P., Packer, B., Koller, D.: Self-paced learning for latent variable models. In: Advances in Neural Information Processing Systems (NeurIPS), pp. 1189–1197 (2010)
24. Landau, M.J., Choo, B.Y., Beling, P.A.: Simulating kinect infrared and depth images. IEEE Trans. Cybernet. **46**(12), 3018–3031 (2015)
25. Lee, D.H.: Pseudo-label: the simple and efficient semi-supervised learning method for deep neural networks. In: ICML Workshop on Challenges in Representation Learning (WREPL) (2013)
26. Li, B., Zhang, T., Xia, T.: Vehicle detection from 3d lidar using fully convolutional network. In: Robotics: Science and Systems (RSS) (2016)
27. Li, Wet al.: InteriorNet: mega-scale multi-sensor photo-realistic indoor scenes dataset. In: British Machine Vision Conference (BMVC) (2018)
28. Li, Y., Bu, R., Sun, M., Wu, W., Di, X., Chen, B.: PointCNN: convolution on x-transformed points. In: Advances in Neural Information Processing Systems (NeurIPS), vol. 31, pp. 820–830 (2018)
29. Lian, Q., Lv, F., Duan, L., Gong, B.: Constructing self-motivated pyramid curriculums for cross-domain semantic segmentation: a non-adversarial approach. In: Proceedings of the IEEE/CVF Conference on Computer Vision and Pattern Recognition (CVPR), pp. 6758–6767 (2019)
30. Lin, J., Wei, Z., Li, Z., Xu, S., Jia, K., Li, Y.: DualposeNet: category-level 6d object pose and size estimation using dual pose network with refined learning of pose consistency. In: Proceedings of the IEEE/CVF International Conference on Computer Vision (ICCV), pp. 3560–3569 (2021)
31. Lin, X., Chen, K., Jia, K.: Object point cloud classification via poly-convolutional architecture search. In: Proceedings of the ACM International Conference on Multimedia (MM), pp. 807–815 (2021)

32. Liu, Y., Fan, B., Xiang, S., Pan, C.: Relation-shape convolutional neural network for point cloud analysis. In: Proceedings of the IEEE/CVF Conference on Computer Vision and Pattern Recognition (CVPR), pp. 8895–8904 (2019)
33. Mallick, T., Das, P.P., Majumdar, A.K.: Characterizations of noise in kinect depth images: a review. IEEE Sens. J. **14**(6), 1731–1740 (2014)
34. Manivasagam, S., et al.: LiDARsim: realistic lidar simulation by leveraging the real world. In: Proceedings of the IEEE/CVF Conference on Computer Vision and Pattern Recognition (CVPR), pp. 11167–11176 (2020)
35. Nguyen, C.V., Izadi, S., Lovell, D.: Modeling kinect sensor noise for improved 3d reconstruction and tracking. In: International Conference on 3D Imaging, Modeling, Processing, Visualization & Transmission (3DIMPVT), pp. 524–530. IEEE (2012)
36. Paszke, A., et al.: PyTorch: an imperative style, high-performance deep learning library. In: Advances in Neural Information Processing Systems (NeurIPS), vol. 32, pp. 8026–8037 (2019)
37. Planche, B., Singh, R.V.: Physics-based differentiable depth sensor simulation. In: Proceedings of the IEEE/CVF International Conference on Computer Vision (ICCV), pp. 14387–14397 (2021)
38. Planche, B., et al.: DepthSynth: real-time realistic synthetic data generation from cad models for 2.5 d recognition. In: International Conference on 3D Vision (3DV), pp. 1–10. IEEE (2017)
39. Qi, C.R., Su, H., Mo, K., Guibas, L.J.: PointNet: deep learning on point sets for 3d classification and segmentation. In: Proceedings of the IEEE/CVF Conference on Computer Vision and Pattern Recognition (CVPR), pp. 652–660 (2017)
40. Qi, C.R., Yi, L., Su, H., Guibas, L.J.: PointNet++: deep hierarchical feature learning on point sets in a metric space. In: Advances in Neural Information Processing Systems (NeurIPS), vol. 30 (2017)
41. Qin, C., You, H., Wang, L., Kuo, C.C.J., Fu, Y.: PointDAN: a multi-scale 3d domain adaption network for point cloud representation. In: Advances in Neural Information Processing Systems (NeurIPS), vol. 32 (2019)
42. Reitmann, S., Neumann, L., Jung, B.: Blainder-a blender AI add-on for generation of semantically labeled depth-sensing data. Sensors **21**(6), 2144 (2021)
43. Roy, S., Siarohin, A., Sangineto, E., Bulò, S.R., Sebe, N., Ricci, E.: Unsupervised domain adaptation using feature-whitening and consensus loss. In: Proceedings of the IEEE/CVF Conference on Computer Vision and Pattern Recognition (CVPR), pp. 9463–9472 (2019)
44. Saito, K., Ushiku, Y., Harada, T.: Asymmetric tri-training for unsupervised domain adaptation. In: International Conference on Machine Learning (ICML), vol. 70, pp. 2988–2997 (2017)
45. Sohn, K., et al.: FixMatch: simplifying semi-supervised learning with consistency and confidence. In: Advances in Neural Information Processing Systems (NeurIPS), vol. 33, pp. 596–608 (2020)
46. Straub, J., et al.: The replica dataset: a digital replica of indoor spaces. arXiv preprint arXiv:1906.05797 (2019)
47. Szeliski, R.: Computer Vision: Algorithms and Applications. Springer, London (2010). https://doi.org/10.1007/978-1-84882-935-0
48. Tallavajhula, A., Meriçli, Ç., Kelly, A.: Off-road lidar simulation with data-driven terrain primitives. In: IEEE International Conference on Robotics and Automation (ICRA), pp. 7470–7477. IEEE (2018)

49. Tang, H., Chen, K., Jia, K.: Unsupervised domain adaptation via structurally regularized deep clustering. In: Proceedings of the IEEE/CVF Conference on Computer Vision and Pattern Recognition (CVPR) (2020)
50. Uy, M.A., Pham, Q., Hua, B., Nguyen, T., Yeung, S.: Revisiting point cloud classification: a new benchmark dataset and classification model on real-world data. In: Proceedings of the IEEE/CVF International Conference on Computer Vision (ICCV), pp. 1588–1597 (2019)
51. Wang, Y., Sun, Y., Liu, Z., Sarma, S.E., Bronstein, M.M., Solomon, J.M.: Dynamic graph CNN for learning on point clouds. ACM Trans. Graph. (TOG) **38**(5), 1–12 (2019)
52. Wei, C., Sohn, K., Mellina, C., Yuille, A., Yang, F.: CReST: a class-rebalancing self-training framework for imbalanced semi-supervised learning. In: Proceedings of the IEEE/CVF Conference on Computer Vision and Pattern Recognition (CVPR), pp. 10857–10866 (2021)
53. Wu, Z., et al.: 3d shapenets: a deep representation for volumetric shapes. In: Proceedings of the IEEE/CVF Conference on Computer Vision and Pattern Recognition (CVPR), pp. 1912–1920 (2015)
54. Xu, Z., Chen, K., Liu, K., Ding, C., Wang, Y., Jia, K.: Classification of single-view object point clouds. arXiv preprint arXiv:2012.10042 (2020)
55. Yang, B., Luo, W., Urtasun, R.: PIXOR: real-time 3d object detection from point clouds. In: Proceedings of the IEEE/CVF Conference on Computer Vision and Pattern Recognition (CVPR), pp. 7652–7660 (2018)
56. Zhang, Y., et al.: Physically-based rendering for indoor scene understanding using convolutional neural networks. In: Proceedings of the IEEE/CVF Conference on Computer Vision and Pattern Recognition (CVPR) (2017)
57. Zhang, Y., Lin, J., He, C., Chen, Y., Jia, K., Zhang, L.: Masked surfel prediction for self-supervised point cloud learning. arXiv preprint arXiv:2207.03111 (2022)
58. Zou, L., Tang, H., Chen, K., Jia, K.: Geometry-aware self-training for unsupervised domain adaptation on object point clouds. In: Proceedings of the IEEE/CVF International Conference on Computer Vision (ICCV), pp. 6403–6412 (2021)
59. Zou, Y., Yu, Z., Vijaya Kumar, B.V.K., Wang, J.: Unsupervised domain adaptation for semantic segmentation via class-balanced self-training. In: Ferrari, V., Hebert, M., Sminchisescu, C., Weiss, Y. (eds.) ECCV 2018. LNCS, vol. 11207, pp. 297–313. Springer, Cham (2018). https://doi.org/10.1007/978-3-030-01219-9_18
60. Zou, Y., Yu, Z., Liu, X., Kumar, B.V., Wang, J.: Confidence regularized self-training. In: Proceedings of the IEEE/CVF International Conference on Computer Vision (ICCV) (2019)

Author Index

Adam, Aikaterini 108
Azov, Guy 176

Bagdanov, Andrew D. 495
Behnke, Sven 73
Belongie, Serge 709
Betke, Margrit 603

Cao, Xu-Sheng 495
Cardie, Claire 709
Chen, Bor-Chun 709
Chen, Ke 728
Chen, Yingcong 369
Chen, Yongwei 728
Chen, Zeyuan 404
Cheng, Ming-Ming 495
Chng, Shin-Fang 264
Choi, Gyeongjae 656
Choi, Seokeon 440
Choi, Sungha 440
Chung, Inseop 691
Cohen-Or, Daniel 176
Cole, Forrester 20

Dai, Angela 125
Dai, Dengxin 388
Dai, Jingzhao 197
Del Bue, Alessio 247
Du, Sidan 197

Fiameni, Giuseppe 567, 586
Firman, Michael 1
Freeman, William T. 20

Galasso, Fabio 567, 586
Gan, Chuang 351
Gao, Mingfei 404
Gao, Yipeng 673
Gibson, John 1
Giryes, Raja 176
Godard, Clément 1
Gong, Shenjian 388
Gordon, Brian 176
Govindu, Venu Madhav 56
Guo, Xiaoqing 334

Harada, Tatsuya 159
Hariharan, Bharath 709
Hou, Yuenan 423
Hu, Xuejiao 197
Hu, Yunzhe 38
Hu, Yu-Song 495
Huang, Gao 230
Huang, Jia-Bin 459
Huang, Yunmu 673
Hwang, Sehyun 549

James, Stuart 247
Jia, Jiaya 369
Jia, Kui 728
Jia, Menglin 709
Jin, Xueqian 197

Karantzalos, Konstantinos 108
Kim, Donghyun 603, 621
Kim, Junmo 513
Kim, Seung Hwan 513
Kim, Sungyeon 549
Klein, Reinhard 281
Klinghoffer, Tzofi 300
Krivosheev, Evgeny 567
Kwak, Nojun 691
Kwak, Suha 549

Lai, Xin 369
Lai, Zihang 230
Lathuiliére, Stéphane 567
Lee, Janghyeon 513
Lee, Kyungmin 656
Lee, Sohyun 549
Li, Chun-Liang 459
Li, Ke 495
Li, Ming 197
Li, Shiyong 673
Li, Yali 90
Li, Yang 197

Li, Zhengqi 20
Lim, Ser-Nam 709
Lin, Hongbin 351
Lin, Kun-Yu 530
Ling, Haibin 639
Litany, Or 125
Liu, Jie 334
Liu, Mingxuan 317
Liu, Shu 369
Liu, Xialei 495
Liu, Xin 90
Liu, Yanxia 351
Liu, Zhe 38
Liu, Ziwei 423
Loy, Chen Change 423
Lu, Cheng 639
Lucey, Simon 142, 264

Manam, Lalit 56
Müller, Jan U. 281

Nam, Gilhyun 656
Nam, Giljoo 73
Niu, Shuaicheng 351

Ok, Jungseul 549

Pajdla, Tomas 108
Pan, Xuran 230
Patten, Timothy 214
Pfister, Tomas 459
Poiesi, Fabio 567, 586
Prisacariu, Victor 1

Qiu, Yukun 530
Qiu, Zhen 351

Raab, Sigal 176
Ramaiah, Chetan 404
Ramasinghe, Sameera 142, 264
Raskar, Ramesh 300
Ricci, Elisa 317, 567, 586
Rosu, Radu Alexandru 73
Roy, Subhankar 317
Rozenberszki, David 125
Rubinstein, Michael 20

Saenko, Kate 603, 621
Saito, Shunsuke 73
Saltori, Cristiano 567, 586
Sattler, Torsten 108
Sayed, Mohamed 1
Schiele, Bernt 388
Schreiberhuber, Simon 214
Sclaroff, Stan 603, 621
Sebe, Nicu 317, 567, 586
Shao, Xiaofei 90
Sherrah, Jamie 264
Shon, Hyounguk 513
Shrivastava, Abhinav 404
Snavely, Noah 20
Song, Shiji 230
Sun, Tao 639

Taiana, Matteo 247
Tan, Mingkui 351
Tang, Luming 709
Tao, Dacheng 477
Tian, Zhuotao 369
Tiwary, Kushagra 300
Tomizuka, Masayoshi 38
Toso, Matteo 247

Vincze, Markus 214

Wang, Bo 90
Wang, Guangming 38
Wang, Hesheng 38
Wang, Kaihong 603, 621
Wang, Liwei 369
Wang, Shengjin 90
Wang, Zihao 728
Wang, Ziyan 73
Watson, Jamie 1
Weibel, Jean-Baptiste 214
Weinmann, Michael 281
Wu, Chenglei 73

Xie, Song 673
Xu, Guodong 423
Xu, Ran 404
Xu, Tianhan 159
Xu, Xiaogang 369
Xu, Yufei 477

Yang, Jian 388
Yang, Lingxiao 673
Yang, Luyu 404
Yang, Seunghan 440
Yoo, Jayeon 691

Yuan, Yixuan 334
Yun, Sungrack 440

Zhan, Wei 38
Zhang, Han 459
Zhang, Jing 477
Zhang, Qiming 477
Zhang, Shanshan 388
Zhang, Yifan 351
Zhang, Zhoutong 20
Zhang, Zizhao 459
Zhao, Hengshuang 369
Zheng, Wei-Shi 530, 673
Zhong, Zhun 317
Zhou, Jiaming 530
Zhou, Yiyang 38
Zou, Longkun 728
Zou, Yuliang 459

Printed in the United States
by Baker & Taylor Publisher Services

Printed in the United States
by Baker & Taylor Publisher Services